Lecture Notes in Computer Science   11959

Editors
Kenneth G. Paterson
ETH Zürich
Zurich, Switzerland

Douglas Stebila
Department of Combinatorics
and Optimization
University of Waterloo
Waterloo, ON, Canada

ISSN 0302-9743   ISSN 1611-3349   (electronic)
Lecture Notes in Computer Science
ISBN 978-3-030-38470-8   ISBN 978-3-030-38471-5   (eBook)
https://doi.org/10.1007/978-3-030-38471-5

LNCS Sublibrary: SL4 – Security and Cryptology

This Springer imprint is published by the registered company Springer Nature Switzerland AG
The registered company address is: Gewerbestrasse 11, 6330 Cham, Switzerland

Lecture Notes in Computer Science 11959

More information about this series at http://www.springer.com/series/7410

Kenneth G. Paterson · Douglas Stebila (Eds.)

Selected Areas
in Cryptography –
SAC 2019

26th International Conference
Waterloo, ON, Canada, August 12–16, 2019
Revised Selected Papers

 Springer

Editors
Kenneth G. Paterson
ETH Zürich
Zurich, Switzerland

Douglas Stebila
Department of Combinatorics
and Optimization
University of Waterloo
Waterloo, ON, Canada

ISSN 0302-9743   ISSN 1611-3349   (electronic)
Lecture Notes in Computer Science
ISBN 978-3-030-38470-8   ISBN 978-3-030-38471-5   (eBook)
https://doi.org/10.1007/978-3-030-38471-5

LNCS Sublibrary: SL4 – Security and Cryptology

This Springer imprint is published by the registered company Springer Nature Switzerland AG
The registered company address is: Gewerbestrasse 11, 6330 Cham, Switzerland

Preface

Selected Areas in Cryptography (SAC) is Canada's research conference on cryptography, held annually since 1994. We were very pleased to host the 26th edition of SAC, back for its 4th time at the University of Waterloo.

There are four areas covered at each SAC conference. Three of the areas are permanent:

1. Design and analysis of symmetric key primitives and cryptosystems, including block and stream ciphers, hash function, MAC algorithms, cryptographic permutations, and authenticated encryption schemes
2. Efficient implementations of symmetric and public key algorithms
3. Mathematical and algorithmic aspects of applied cryptology

The special selected topic for SAC 2019 was:

4. Real-world cryptography/cryptographic protocols in practice

Given the current interest in post-quantum cryptography, we made a special note in the call for papers welcoming papers in any of the above areas with a focus on post-quantum cryptography.

SAC 2019 received 74 submissions. We thank all the researchers who submitted their work for consideration at SAC 2019. Although we had a relatively short review period, our Program Committee of 45 members had a vigorous review and discussion period; each paper was assigned at least 4 reviews, and there were extensive discussions on many of the papers. In the end, we were able to accept 28 papers for publication at SAC 2019.

There were three invited talks at SAC 2019. Since 2003, one of the invited lectures has been denoted the Stafford Tavares Invited Lecture, honouring Stafford Tavares' vision and many years of service to the SAC workshops; we are very pleased that Tetsu Iwata from Nagoya University agreed to give this year's Stafford Tavares Invited Lecture, on "Block cipher modes of operation and provable security." Douglas R. Stinson from the University of Waterloo gave a reflective talk on his long involvement with SAC and his career in cryptography, entitled "Looking back—my life as a mathematician and cryptographer." Craig Costello from Microsoft Research gave the final invited talk on "The state-of-the-art in supersingular isogenies: the SIKE protocol and its cryptanalysis."

Immediately preceding the conference, SAC hosted the 5th iteration of the SAC Summer School (S3). Targeting graduate students, post-docs, early career researchers, and industry researchers, the purpose of the SAC Summer School is to provide participants with an opportunity to gain in-depth knowledge of specific areas of cryptography related to the current SAC topics. For the 2019 edition of the SAC Summer School, we were pleased to have four speakers:

- Craig Costello, Microsoft Research: "A gentle introduction to elliptic curve cryptography and post-quantum ECC"
- Tetsu Iwata, Nagoya University: "Provably security in symmetric key cryptography"
- Seny Kamara, Brown University: "Encrypted search"
- Nele Mentens, KU Leuven: "Hands-on hardware design for cryptography"

Many people contributed to the scientific and logistical organization of SAC 2019. We would like to thank the SAC Board, our Program Committee, the student volunteers assisting during the event, and the communications team at the University of Waterloo, Faculty of Mathematics. A special thank you is due to the staff from the Department of Combinatorics and Optimization at the University of Waterloo, who worked for many months to make so much of this conference happen: Carol Seely-Morrison, Chloe Potovszky, Dana Hociung, and Melissa Cambridge.

We would like to highlight the financial support of our sponsors, which has allowed us to keep registration fees low and provide stipends for some students and early career researchers to attend: Communications Security Establishment Canada; the Fields Institute; ISARA; the University of Waterloo CryptoWorks21 program; the University of Waterloo Cybersecurity and Privacy Institute; and the University of Waterloo Faculty of Mathematics.

Thank you to all who helped make SAC 2019 a success!

October 2019

Kenneth G. Paterson
Douglas Stebila

Organization

SAC 2019 was held in cooperation with the International Association for Cryptologic Research (IACR).

Chairs

Kenneth G. Paterson　　　ETH Zurich, Switzerland
Douglas Stebila　　　　　University of Waterloo, Canada

SAC Board

Carlisle Adams　　　　　University of Ottawa, Canada
Roberto Avanzi　　　　　Qualcomm, USA
Jan Camenisch　　　　　Dfinity, Switzerland
Carlos Cid　　　　　　　Royal Holloway, University of London, UK
Howard Heys　　　　　　Memorial University of Newfoundland, Canada
Michael J. Jacobson, Jr.　University of Calgary, Canada
　(Chair)
Tanja Lange　　　　　　Technische Universiteit Eindhoven, The Netherlands
Petr Lisonek　　　　　　Simon Fraser University, Canada
Amr M. Youssef　　　　　Concordia University, Canada

Program Committee

Andreas Hülsing　　　　　Eindhoven University of Technology, The Netherlands
Atefeh Mashatan　　　　　Ryerson University, Canada
Atul Luykx　　　　　　　Visa Research, USA
Bart Mennink　　　　　　Radboud University, The Netherlands
Benjamin Dowling　　　　Royal Holloway, University of London, UK
Bertram Poettering　　　　IBM Zurich, Switzerland
Chris Peikert　　　　　　University of Michigan, USA
Christophe Petit　　　　　University of Birmingham, UK
Craig Costello　　　　　　Microsoft Research, USA
Diego Aranha　　　　　　Aarhus University, Denmark, and University
　　　　　　　　　　　　of Campinas, Brazil
Fabrice Benhamouda　　　IBM Research, USA
Fang Song　　　　　　　Texas A&M University, USA
Gareth T. Davies　　　　　University of Paderborn, Germany
Giorgia Azzurra Marson　　NEC Laboratories Europe, Germany
Guang Gong　　　　　　University of Waterloo, Canada
Javad Doliskani　　　　　University of Waterloo, Canada

Jean Paul Degabriele	TU Darmstadt, Germany
Joppe W. Bos	NXP Semiconductors, Belgium
Juraj Somorovsky	Ruhr-Universität Bochum, Germany
Kan Yasuda	NTT, Japan
Leonie Simpson	Queensland University of Technology, Australia
Máire O'Neill	CSIT, Queen's University Belfast, UK
Marc Joye	OneSpan, Belgium
Marcel Keller	Data61, Australia
Mridul Nandi	Indian Statistical Institute Kolkata, India
Nele Mentens	KU Leuven, Belgium
Orr Dunkelman	University of Haifa, Israel
Patrick Longa	Microsoft Research, USA
Paul Grubbs	Cornell Tech, USA
Paulo Barreto	University of Washington Tacoma, USA
Reihaneh Safavi-Naini	University of Calgary, Canada
Renate Scheidler	University of Calgary, Canada
Somitra Kumar Sanadhya	Indian Institute of Technology Ropar, India
Takanori Isobe	University of Hyogo, Japan
Tarik Moataz	Brown University, USA
Tibor Jager	Universität Paderborn, Germany
Tim Güneysu	Ruhr-Universität Bochum and DFKI, Germany
Tomer Ashur	KU Leuven, Belgium
Vadim Lyubashevsky	IBM Research, Switzerland
Willi Meier	FHNW, Switzerland
Yosuke Todo	NTT Secure Platform Laboratories, Japan
Yuval Yarom	University of Adelaide and Data61, Australia
Zhenfeng Zhang	Institute of Software, Chinese Academy of Sciences, China

Additional Reviewers

Aaram Yun
Alex May
Alexander Ushakov
Benjamin Pring
Brian Goncalves
Christian Majenz
Christine van Vredendaal
Cyprien Delpech de Saint Guilhem
Daniel Kales
David Niehues
Dominik Leichtle
Dung Duong
Ekin Ozman

Elena Kirshanova
Falk Schellenberg
Frederik Vercauteren
Frederik Armknecht
Fukang Liu
Geoffroy Couteau
Geovandro Pereira
Greg Zaverucha
Gregor Seiler
Gustavo Banegas
Hao Chen
Harry Bartlett
Itai Dinur

Jan Richter-Brockmann
Javier Silva
Jinhui Liu
Jintai Ding
Jo Vliegen
John Schanck
Jonathan Bootle
Joost Renes
Jovan Golic
Kalikinkar Mandal
Kazuhiko Minematsu
Keita Xagawa
Kenneth Wong
Koichiro Akiyama
Leo Ducas
Lisa Kohl
Lorenz Panny
Lorenzo Grassi
Luke Mather
Mathias Herrmann
Matthias Gierlings
Michael Naehrig
Olivier Blazy
Pedro Alves
Pedro Massolino
Philippe Gaborit
Pierre-Louis Cayrel

Péter Kutas
Qingju Wang
Rafaël del Pino
Raghvendra Rohit
Răzvan Roşie
Reinhard Lueftenegger
Riham AlTawy
Saqib Kakvi
Satrajit Ghosh
Sebastian Lauer
Shi Bai
Simon-Philipp Merz
Steven Galbraith
Subhadeep Banik
Tobias Oder
Travis Morrison
Weiqiang Wen
Wouter Castryck
Yann Rotella
Yasufumi Hahimoto
Yasuhiko Ikematsu
Youming Qiao
Yu Sasaki
Zhengzhong Jin
Zhenzhen Bao
Zhiniang Peng

Sponsors

Communications Security Establishment Canada
Fields Institute
ISARA
University of Waterloo CryptoWorks21
University of Waterloo Cybersecurity and Privacy Institute
University of Waterloo Faculty of Mathematics

Block Cipher Modes of Operation and Provable Security (Abstract of Invited Talk)

Tetsu Iwata

Nagoya University, Japan
tetsu.iwata@nagoya-u.jp

Block ciphers have wide applications, including encryption modes, MACs (message authentication codes), authenticated encryption schemes, and hash functions. To obtain these functionalities, a block cipher is used in a mode of operation. Following the analyses of CBC MAC [2] and basic encryption modes [1], provable security (or reduction-based security) is the main security goal for block cipher modes of operation.

A provable security result gives strong confidence about the security of block cipher modes, since it guarantees for *any* adversary with given resources the mode cannot be broken as long as the underlying block cipher remains secure. This in turn implies that to assess the overall security of the mode, one can focus on the analysis of the underlying block cipher.

A significant number of block cipher modes were developed with a proof of security. In fact, many modes of operation used in practice or standardized in standardization bodies are supported by proofs. However, it is non-trivial to write a correct security proof of a complex scheme like an authenticated encryption scheme, and we have witnessed several cases where security proofs of standardized modes have been found to be wrong or contain a gap. In some cases, the proof can be repaired without changing the scheme, or sometimes a tiny gap in the proof triggers various attacks on the scheme.

In this talk, we review the cases of GCM [4, 9] and OCB2 [11]. For GCM, the gap in the proof could be repaired [8], while the security bound is weaker than the original one in the general case of variable length nonces. The bound was later improved [10], and the security bound of GCM is close to the original bound in [9]. For OCB2, a gap in the security proof resulted in various efficient attacks both in authenticity and confidentiality [6].

A gap in a proof should be found before wide-spread use or standardization, and we discuss ways to improve the situation. We illustrate the case of OMAC/CMAC [3, 7] to see multiple security proofs with different proof strategies, slightly different settings, or improved security bounds help to gain confidence in the security. We cover the direction of automated security proofs [5], and discuss its potential and limitations. We also discuss the importance of third-party verification of published proofs. The term "provable security" may discourage cryptanalysts to look into the scheme. However, we emphasize that the correctness of proofs and the overall security of the scheme need to be verified through public scrutiny.

References

1. Bellare, M., Desai, A., Jokipii, E., Rogaway, P.: A concrete security treatment of symmetric encryption. In: FOCS 1997, pp. 394–403. IEEE Computer Society (1997). https://doi.org/10.1109/SFCS.1997.646128
2. Bellare, M., Kilian, J., Rogaway, P.: The security of the cipher block chaining message authentication code. J. Comput. Syst. Sci. **61**(3), 362–399 (2000). https://doi.org/10.1006/jcss.1999.1694
3. Dworkin, M.: Recommendation for block cipher modes of operation: The CMAC mode for authentication. NIST Special Publication 800-38B (2005). https://doi.org/10.6028/NIST.SP.800-38B
4. Dworkin, M.: Recommendation for block cipher modes of operation: Galois/Counter mode (GCM) and GMAC. NIST Special Publication 800-38D (2007). https://doi.org/10.6028/NIST.SP.800-38D
5. Hoang, V.T., Katz, J., Malozemoff, A.J.: Automated analysis and synthesis of authenticated encryption schemes. In: Ray, I., Li, N., Kruegel, C. (eds.) ACM CCS 2015, pp. 84–95. ACM (2015). https://doi.org/10.1145/2810103.2813636
6. Inoue, A., Iwata, T., Minematsu, K., Poettering, B.: Cryptanalysis of OCB2: attacks on authenticity and confidentiality. In: Boldyreva, A., Micciancio, D. (eds.) CRYPTO 2019, Part I. LNCS, vol. 11692, pp. 3–31. Springer, Cham (2019). https://doi.org/10.1007/978-3-030-26948-7_1
7. Iwata, T., Kurosawa, K.: OMAC: One-key CBC MAC. In: Johansson, T. (ed.) FSE 2003. LNCS, vol. 2887, pp. 129–153. Springer, Heidelberg (2003). https://doi.org/10.1007/978-3-540-39887-5_11
8. Iwata, T., Ohashi, K., Minematsu, K.: Breaking and repairing GCM security proofs. In: Safavi-Naini, R., Canetti, R. (eds.) CRYPTO 2012. LNCS, vol. 7417, pp. 31–49. Springer, Heidelberg (2012). https://doi.org/10.1007/978-3-642-32009-5_3
9. McGrew, D.A., Viega, J.: The security and performance of the Galois/Counter Mode (GCM) of operation. In: Canteaut, A., Viswanathan, K. (eds.) INDOCRYPT 2004. LNCS, vol. 3348, pp. 343–355. Springer, Heidelberg (2004). https://doi.org/10.1007/978-3-540-30556-9_27
10. Niwa, Y., Ohashi, K., Minematsu, K., Iwata, T.: GCM security bounds reconsidered. In: Leander, G. (ed.) FSE 2015. LNCS, vol. 9054, pp. 385–407. Springer, Heidelberg (2015). https://doi.org/10.1007/978-3-662-48116-5_19
11. Rogaway, P.: Efficient instantiations of tweakable blockciphers and refinements to modes OCB and PMAC. In: Lee, P.J. (ed.) ASIACRYPT 2004. LNCS, vol. 3329, pp. 16–31. Springer, Heidelberg (2004). https://doi.org/10.1007/978-3-540-30539-2_2

Contents

Real-World Cryptography

Stream Ciphers and Lightweight Cryptography

Post-quantum Analysis

Post-quantum Implementations

Symmetric Cryptography

Post-quantum Constructions

Invited Talks

Looking Back—My Life as a Mathematician and Cryptographer

Douglas R. Stinson$^{(\boxtimes)}$

David R. Cheriton School of Computer Science,
University of Waterloo, Waterloo, ON N2L 3G1, Canada
dstinson@uwaterloo.ca

Abstract. In this paper, I look back at my career as a mathematician and mathematical cryptographer, mainly concentrating on my student days and the early parts of my career. I also discuss my research philosophy and what I mean by the term "combinatorial cryptography." Along the way, I recall some influential people, books and papers.

1 Overview

I would like to thank the SAC 2019 organizers for inviting me to give an invited talk at SAC 2019, which was held at the University of Waterloo. This talk was also happening in conjunction with my retirement from the University of Waterloo, which took place on September 1, 2019. I suggested that I might give a (mostly) non-technical talk of a somewhat autobiographical nature, and they agreed. Thus, I used the talk to look back at my career as a mathematician and mathematical cryptographer, mainly concentrating on my student days and the early parts of my career. This paper will serve as a summary of the material in my talk.

The following are the main topics I discussed.

- My involvement with SAC
- Transitions: math contests → mathematical research → computer science → mathematical cryptography
- Combinatorial cryptography: what is it?
- Influences: people, books, papers
- Research philosophy and mathematical exposition.

2 SAC and Me

I have been involved with SAC from the beginning. I attended and spoke at the first SAC Workshop, which was held at Queen's University in 1994. My talk there was entitled "Recent results on resilient functions." I was an invited speaker at SAC 1995, SAC 2013, and SAC 2019. I was Co-chair of SAC in 2000 and 2010.

D. R. Stinson's research is supported by NSERC Discovery grant RGPIN-03882.

K. G. Paterson and D. Stebila (Eds.): SAC 2019, LNCS 11959, pp. 3–20, 2020.
https://doi.org/10.1007/978-3-030-38471-5_1

I was Chair of the SAC organizing board from 2000–2007 and a Member of the SAC organizing board from 2000–2014. I created the first SAC web pages in 2003.

The first six editions of SAC were held at Queen's University and Carleton University. In 2000, SAC was held at the University of Waterloo for the first time and there was discussion there about the future direction of SAC. I was an early voice calling for SAC to be held exclusively in Canada. The following quote is from the minutes of the SAC 2000 Board Meeting:

> "It was suggested by D. Stinson that SAC be officially designated as a 'Canadian workshop series in cryptography' in the Draft Guidelines."

Given my long participation with SAC, it was a pleasure and an honour to be invited to speak at SAC 2019.

3   Cribbage

One of my first "mathematical" memories was watching my parents and grandparents play cribbage. I do not recall my age exactly, but I was perhaps 6 or 7 years old at the time. I was very interested in scoring the hands, where points are given for pairs, combinations of cards that sum to 15, runs of three or more, etc. The details aren't important, but the scoring system is rather complex. Two facts that I found fascinating were that

– a count of 19 is impossible and
– 29 is the maximum possible count.

I suppose this was my first experience with the concept of mathematical impossibility.

One example of a 29-count hand in cribbage would consist of the five of clubs, diamonds and hearts and the jack of spades. If the five of spades is then "cut" (this is a card that is common to all the players' hands), then the result is a 29-count hand:

– $\binom{4}{2} = 6$ pairs $\rightarrow$ 12 points
– $4 + \binom{4}{3} = 8$ fifteens $\rightarrow$ 16 points
– 1 point for the "Jack of nobs" (i.e, the player's hand contains the jack of the same suit as the card that is cut)
– total: $12 + 16 + 1 = 29$ points.

Note that three of a kind $= \binom{3}{2} =$ three pairs and four of a kind $= \binom{4}{2} = 6$ pairs. This is combinatorics in action! Perhaps this inspired me to become a combinatorial mathematician.

4   Math Contests

I always enjoyed math classes in school, in part because I could do tests without having to memorize boring facts![1] However, my serious involvement in mathematics really started with high school math contests. I began high school in 1970 (grade 9) at John F. Ross Collegiate and Vocational Institute in Guelph, which is just a few minutes down the highway from Waterloo. The University of Waterloo ran the *Junior Math Contest*, which was a multiple choice contest for students in grades 9–11.

That year, a grade 10 student (Bob Saul) finished first in our school and I finished second. The next year, when I was in grade 10, I finished in the top 15 in Ontario and I was invited to the Junior Math Contest Seminar held at the University of Waterloo in June 1972. I attended the JMC seminar again in June 1973 after finishing in the top 10 in Ontario.

5   Ross Honsberger

I first heard Ross Honsberger speak at the JMC seminars. Ross (1929–2016) was a masterful mathematical expositor and an entertaining speaker who was a long-time faculty member at UW. For many years, Ross taught a popular course on problem solving, consisting of 100 problems.

Ross was the author of numerous books such as "Ingenuity in Mathematics" [9]. One particularly memorable lecture I recall from the 1973 JMC seminar was on the topic of a checker-jumping problem known as "Conway's Soldiers".

As it is explained in Wikipedia:[2]

> *"Conway's Soldiers* or the *checker-jumping problem* is a one-person mathematical game or puzzle devised and analyzed by mathematician John Horton Conway in 1961. A variant of peg solitaire, it takes place on an infinite checkerboard. The board is divided by a horizontal line that extends indefinitely. Above the line are empty cells and below the line are an arbitrary number of game pieces, or "soldiers". As in peg solitaire, a move consists of one soldier jumping over an adjacent soldier into an empty cell, vertically or horizontally (but not diagonally), and removing the soldier which was jumped over. The goal of the puzzle is to place a soldier as far above the horizontal line as possible. Conway proved that, regardless of the strategy used, there is *no finite series of moves that will allow a soldier to advance more than four rows above the horizontal line.* His argument uses a carefully chosen weighting of cells (involving the golden ratio), and he proved that the total weight can only decrease or remain constant. This argument has been reproduced in a number of popular math books."

---

[1] I did have to memorize the multiplication table, but this did not bother me.

[2] This quote is from the Wikipedia article "Conway's Soldiers" (https://en.wikipedia. org/wiki/Conway's_Soldiers), which is released under the Creative Commons Attribution-Share-Alike License 3.0.

The weight of the destination cell four rows above the x-axis is $>$ the weights of all the cells (an infinite number of them) below the x-axis. Since the total weight never decreases with any move, the destination cell cannot be reached. I did not understand all the intricacies of the proof at the time, but I was convinced I had seen something remarkable!

6 From High School to University

Ontario used to have a fifth year of high school, which was designated as grade 13. A diploma would be awarded after grade 12, but students who intended to go to university would take grade 13. I took grade 11 and grade 12 math while I was enrolled in grade 11. While I was in grade 12 (1973–1974), I took the three grade 13 math courses and I applied for early admission to UW. My parents took me to UW to meet with the Dean of Mathematics, Ken Fryer, who indicated that Waterloo would be happy to accept me even though I would not have a grade 13 diploma. I continued to be involved in various math contests—that year I won the *UW Descartes Math Contest* with a score of 99/100 and I finished second in the *Canadian Math Olympiad*.

7 The 1974 "Special K" Math Contest

Murray Klamkin (1921–2004) joined UW as a visiting professor in 1974. At the time he was the principal research scientist at Ford Motor Company. Later Murray was chair of the Mathematics Department at the University of Alberta, from 1976–1981.

Murray was well-known as a *"prolific proposer and editor of professionally challenging mathematical problems"*.[3] In 1974, he instituted the *Special K* and *Euler* math contests for undergraduates. I won the Special K contest (for first-year students) that year.

One of the problems in the Special K contest that year was written up by Ross Honsberger in his book "Mathematical Morsels" [10], which was published in 1978. Here is the description of the problem, which Ross termed the "Chauffeur problem":

"Mr. Smith, a commuter, is picked up each day at the train station at exactly 5 o'clock. One day he arrived unannounced on the 4 o'clock train and began to walk home. Eventually he met the chauffeur driving to the station to get him. The chauffeur drove the rest of the way home, getting him there 20 min earlier than usual.

On another day, Mr. Smith arrived unexpectedly on the 4:30 train, and again began walking home. Again he met the chauffeur and rode the rest of

---

[3] This quote is from the Wikipedia article "Murray S. Klamkin" (https://en.wikipedia.org/wiki/Murray_S._Klamkin), which is released under the Creative Commons Attribution-Share-Alike License 3.0.

the way with him. How much ahead of time were they this time? (Assume constant speeds of walking and driving and that no time is lost in turning the car around and picking up Mr. Smith.)

The answer to the problem (namely, 10 min) is intuitively obvious, but a bit of work is required to give a convincing mathematical proof. I provided an algebraic solution to this question. My solution was correct but not very illuminating. Another student who wrote the contest, Rick Cameron, provided a much more satisfying solution, which was related by Ross Honsberger in [10]. The basic idea is to plot "distance from the station" on one axis and "time" on the other axis.[4] See Fig. 1.

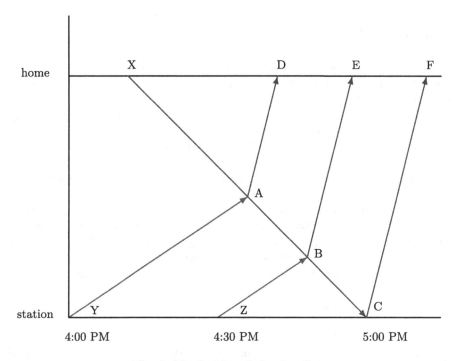

Fig. 1. Mr. Smith and the chauffeur

- On a normal day, the chauffeur proceeds from X to C where he meets Mr. Smith. They then drive to F.
- When Mr. Smith arrives on the 4:00 train, the chauffeur proceeds from X to A. There he meets Mr. Smith, who has walked from Y to A. They then drive to D.

---

[4] This is sometimes called a *Minkowski diagram*.

– When Mr. Smith arrives on the 4:30 train, the chauffeur proceeds from X to B. There he meets Mr. Smith, who has walked from Z to B. They then drive to E.

We observe that XAD, XBE and XCF are similar triangles, as are YAC and ZBC. The length of the line segment YZ is the same as the length of the line segment ZC, so the line segments AB and BC have the same lengths. Hence, the line segments DE and EF have the same lengths. Since we are told that DF has length 20 (minutes), it follows that EF has length 10 (minutes).

I can honestly say that I do not remember the details of the solution I gave, and I cannot remember any of the other problems in this contest. What sticks in my mind 45 years later is Rick's solution.

8   Ron Mullin

After my second year of undergraduate studies, Ron Mullin hired me as a undergraduate research assistant in 1976. Ron of course is well-known as a leading researcher in combinatorics (especially design theory) and cryptography. Ron eventually became my PhD supervisor; he was clearly the main influence in my mathematical career. Among many other things, I credit Ron with helping me make the transition from problem solver to researcher. Ron was the first graduate of the University of Waterloo—he received the very first degree (an MA in mathematics) awarded at the very first convocation in June, 1960. Another bit of trivia is that Ron and I are both natives of Guelph, Ontario.

At Ron's suggestion, I attended the ManiWat Workshop in the summer of 1976. The ManiWat workshops took place from 1975–1985 at a former convent in St. Pierre, Manitoba that was owned by Ralph Stanton (1923–2010). These workshops were modelled after Oberwolfach. This was my first "up-close" exposure to mathematicians "in the wild" doing research, with a bottle of beer in one hand and a piece of chalk in the other hand!

That year, the workshop consisted of one week of computational number theory followed by a week of design theory. I recall hearing lectures from Dan Shanks about the SQUFOF (*SQU*are *FO*rm *F*actorization) factoring algorithm. In the design theory week, Ron Mullin gave a series of talks on the problem of packing pairs into quadruples. This problem requires the determination of the maximum number of four-subsets of a v-set such that no pair is contained in more than one four-subset; I was working at the time on some special cases of that problem for Ron.

Ron Mullin hired me as a URA for three consecutive years. I worked on various problems including packings, mutually orthogonal latin squares and skew Room squares. Mostly I was doing computational work as I found the theory very complicated.

I was especially mystified by recursive constructions for block designs, which I felt was the most complicated mathematics I had ever seen. I tried to read various papers by Hanani, Mills, Wilson, etc., but the methods and notation were daunting. In retrospect, it took a considerable amount of time for me to become comfortable with the theoretical underpinnings of recursive constructions for designs. However, finally there was an epiphany. I vividly recall in 1978 when Ron showed me a new PBD (pairwise balanced design) construction on the blackboard in his office. For the first time, I really understood how a recursive PBD construction worked. This construction, which appeared in [11], was of fundamental importance in attacking the skew Room square problem since it could provide PBDs of odd orders whose block sizes were orders of skew Room squares (i.e., odd integers ≥ 7).

Here is a brief summary of the construction. First, it requires the construction of two small designs:

1. Deleting a point from a transversal design TD(7,9), we obtain a group-divisible design (GDD) with group type $8^1 6^9$ and having blocks of size 7 and 9.
2. Start with a TD(7,8). Adjoint a new point to each group and then delete some other point. The result is a GDD with group type $8^1 6^8$ and having blocks of size 7 and 9.

We use these two GDDs as "building blocks" in a recursive construction. Start with a TD(10, m) and then delete $m-t$ points from one group (where $0 \leq t \leq m$). This produces a GDD with group type $m^9 t^1$ and having blocks of size 9 and 10.

Next, give the points in one group of size m weight 8, give all other points weight 6 and apply Wilson's Fundamental GDD Construction (see [20]). Each block B of the GDD is replaced by a copy of one of our two "building blocks," in such a way that the groups of the GDD align with the copies of the points in B: a block of size 10 is replaced by the blocks of the GDD #1, and a block of size 9 is replaced by the blocks of the GDD #2.

This yields a GDD of group type $(6m)^8 (8m)^1 (6t)^1$, having blocks of size 7 and 9. If we now add one new point to each of the groups, we obtain a pairwise balanced design (PBD) on $56m+6t+1$ points, having block sizes $7, 9, 6m+1, 6t+1$ and $8m+1$.

9 Graduate Studies

I completed my Bachelor of Mathematics degree at the University of Waterloo in 1978, majoring in C&O (Combinatorics and Optimization) and Pure Mathematics. Then I started graduate school at Ohio State, but I already had a "head start" of two years on learning how to do research. Ohio State was a hotbed of combinatorics in the 1970s. Furthermore, a number of now well-known combinatorial researchers were grad students at OSU at the time, including Jeff Dinitz, Dan Archdeacon, KT Arasu, Jeff Kahn, and Ernie Brickell. Ohio State was where I met my long-time friend and frequent collaborator Jeff Dinitz.

I obtained a Masters Degree at Ohio State in 1980 and then I returned to Waterloo to complete my PhD. I received my PhD in Combinatorics and

Optimization from UW in 1981. The title of my thesis was "Some classes of frames, and the spectra of skew Room squares and Howell designs."

Various people have asked me how I managed to complete a PhD in three years. I firmly believe that the reason I was able to do this was due to the two years of "apprenticeship" under Ron's guidance while I was still an undergrad: the hard work of learning how to do research was already in place before I began my graduate studies.

10   Easing into the World of Computer Science

The academic job market in math was very challenging in 1981, but there seemed to be substantially more opportunities in computer science than there were in mathematics at that time. I applied for and was awarded an NSERC PDF (post-doctoral fellowship), which I decided to hold at the Computer Science department at the University of Manitoba. This was in spite of the fact that I had essentially no computer science training as a student. However, at that time, there were several people in the Computer Science Department at the University of Manitoba who had research interests in combinatorics, including Ralph Stanton, John van Rees, John Bate and Bill Kocay, so it was actually quite a good academic fit for me.

A year later, in 1982, I was awarded an NSERC University Research Fellowship which I held at the University of Manitoba from 1982–1989. Being in a computer science department, I expanded my research to pursue more algorithmic aspects of combinatorial designs, such as isomorphism testing, enumeration of designs and hill-climbing algorithms. Actually, I had previously worked on hill-climbing algorithms with Jeff Dinitz while we were grad students. Jeff and I devised the first successful hill-climbing algorithm to construct a nontrivial combinatorial structure, namely, strong starters in cyclic groups. However, when we published our paper [7] in 1981, we were not even aware of the term "hill-climbing algorithm."

11   Cryptography

After obtaining my PhD, I was interested in broadening my research expertise, but this was a slow process. In the early 1980s, I started to become aware of cryptography through the work by Blake, Fuji-Hara, Mullin and Vanstone [3] on the discrete logarithm problem in finite fields of characteristic 2. This Waterloo research group solved the discrete logarithm problem in $\mathbb{F}_{2^{127}}$ using some new extensions of index calculus methods. There was a commercial implementation of key exchange in $\mathbb{F}_{2^{127}}$ at the time, which was rendered insecure by this algorithm.

I also heard research talks by Gus Simmons on the topic of unconditionally secure authentication codes.[5] Ernie Brickell, who was working for Gus Simmons at Sandia Labs, was also investigating authentication codes, but from a more

---

[5] Gus was another important influence on my career.

combinatorial point of view. (Ernie was a grad student at OSU at the same time I was there. We later collaborated on several cryptography papers starting in the late 1980s.)

Ernie presented a paper [5] on authentication codes entitled "A few results in message authentication" at the Southeastern Conference on Combinatorics, Graph Theory and Computing held in Baton Rouge in 1984. This paper includes a (three-dimensional) $6 \times 6 \times 6$ Howell cube on 12 points. The Howell cube could be used to construct a certain type of "optimal" authentication code that was termed "doubly perfect" by Ernie.

The Howell cube can be described as three orthogonal one-factorizations of a certain 6-regular graph on 12 vertices. The construction of two-dimensional Howell designs was one of the main problems I addressed (and solved) in my PhD thesis. Ernie's paper was the first time I saw a cryptographic application of combinatorial designs.

Ernie's Howell cube can be presented as a list of quadruples. Each quadruple has the form (row, column, level, pair). The row, column and level specify a cell in a cube, and the cell contains an unordered pair of elements. The quadruples in Brickell's cube are as follows:

$1, 1, 1, \{1, 2\}$	$3, 1, 3, \{7, 12\}$	$5, 1, 5, \{4, 8\}$
$1, 2, 2, \{3, 4\}$	$3, 2, 6, \{2, 8\}$	$5, 2, 3, \{10, 11\}$
$1, 3, 3, \{5, 6\}$	$3, 3, 1, \{4, 9\}$	$5, 3, 4, \{2, 3\}$
$1, 4, 4, \{7, 8\}$	$3, 4, 2, \{6, 10\}$	$5, 4, 6, \{5, 9\}$
$1, 5, 5, \{9, 10\}$	$3, 5, 4, \{1, 11\}$	$5, 5, 1, \{6, 12\}$
$1, 6, 6, \{11, 12\}$	$3, 6, 5, \{3, 5\}$	$5, 6, 2, \{1, 7\}$
$2, 1, 2, \{9, 11\}$	$4, 1, 4, \{5, 10\}$	$6, 1, 6, \{3, 6\}$
$2, 2, 1, \{5, 7\}$	$4, 2, 5, \{1, 6\}$	$6, 2, 4, \{9, 12\}$
$2, 3, 6, \{1, 10\}$	$4, 3, 2, \{8, 12\}$	$6, 3, 5, \{7, 11\}$
$2, 4, 5, \{2, 12\}$	$4, 4, 1, \{3, 11\}$	$6, 4, 3, \{1, 4\}$
$2, 5, 3, \{3, 8\}$	$4, 5, 6, \{4, 7\}$	$6, 5, 2, \{2, 5\}$
$2, 6, 4, \{4, 6\}$	$4, 6, 3, \{2, 9\}$	$6, 6, 1, \{8, 10\}$

Each two dimensional projection of the Howell cube is a 6×6 array such that every symbol occurs once in each row and once in each column, and no pair of symbols occurs in more than one cell of the array.

It took me a couple more years, but by 1986 I started to work on combinatorial aspects of authentication codes and I presented my first cryptography paper [15] at CRYPTO'86. The CRYPTO conferences have been held annually in Santa Barbara since 1981.

At the CRYPTO'86 conference, I heard a number of fascinating talks on various aspects of cryptography. I was particularly intrigued by the notion of a threshold scheme and I published my first paper on that topic ([18], joint with Scott Vanstone) at CRYPTO'87. Our paper used combinatorial designs to construct threshold schemes.

Over the next few years, I wrote a number of papers on these two topics. Obviously this was a natural way for me to leverage my expertise in combinatorics in a new research area. Combinatorial cryptography began to establish itself as a distinct subarea of cryptography by the early 1990s as more examples of combinatorial cryptography were studied.

Here are a few topics in combinatorial cryptography, along with the year that I first studied them, over the following 17 years. (There are numerous additional topics in combinatorial cryptography that I have studied since then.)

- authentication codes (1986)
- threshold schemes (1987)
- resilient and correlation-immune functions (1992)
- visual cryptography (1996)
- broadcast encryption (1996)
- combinatorial key predistribution (1997)
- frameproof codes and traceability codes (1998)
- all-or-nothing transforms (2001)
- unconditionally secure commitment schemes (2002)
- generic algorithms for the discrete logarithm problem (2003)

12   What Is Combinatorial Cryptography?

I like to conceptualize combinatorial cryptography as a process:

starting point: define an unconditionally secure[6] cryptographic primitive or protocol;

security definitions are phrased in terms of probability distributions;

optimal and/or "uniform" cases lead to the consideration of combinatorial objects;

cryptographic requirements motivate the mathematics that is used;

solutions might use "off-the-shelf" designs, codes, and extremal set systems, for example, but they might also motivate the study of new mathematical problems;

combinatorial characterizations, which establish the equivalence of cryptographic primitives and combinatorial structures, can sometimes be proven.

13   Shannon and the One-Time Pad

Claude Shannon (1916–2001) was one of the giants of 20th-century science. He invented information theory and did seminal work in coding theory, cryptography, and digital circuit design. One of Shannon's many contributions in cryptography was to give the first proof of security (in 1949) of the *Vernam One-time Pad*, provided the key is only used once (see [13]). I consider Shannon's security proof as being the birth of combinatorial cryptography.

---

[6] Unconditional security is basically the same thing as being secure against an infinitely powerful adversary.

An interesting historical fact is that the *One-time Pad* was invented in 1882 by Frank Miller, a Sacramento banker (see [1]). (Gilbert Vernam rediscovered the *One-time Pad* in 1917.)

The *One-time Pad* encrypts an n-bit plaintext $\mathbf{x}$ with an n-bit key $\mathbf{K}$, obtaining an n-bit ciphertext

$$\mathbf{y} = \mathbf{x} \oplus \mathbf{K}.$$

The ciphertext is decrypted by computing

$$\mathbf{x} = \mathbf{y} \oplus \mathbf{K}.$$

Shannon defined the concept of *perfect secrecy* to describe the situation where

$$\Pr[\mathbf{X} = \mathbf{x} | \mathbf{Y} = \mathbf{y}] = \Pr[\mathbf{X} = \mathbf{x}]$$

for all plaintexts $\mathbf{x}$ and all ciphertexts $\mathbf{Y}$. "Perfect secrecy" means that an observer does not gain any information about the plaintext after seeing a ciphertext.

It is not hard to prove that

$$|\mathcal{K}| \geq |\mathcal{Y}| \geq |\mathcal{X}|$$

if perfect secrecy is achieved. Furthermore, in the "boundary case" where

$$|\mathcal{K}| = |\mathcal{Y}| = |\mathcal{X}|,$$

perfect secrecy is achieved if and only if the encryption matrix is a latin square of order $|\mathcal{X}|$. That is, this optimal solution has a combinatorial characterization.

Here is an example of the *One-time Pad* with $n = 3$:

	K							
$\mathbf{x}$	000	001	010	011	100	101	110	111
000	000	001	010	011	100	101	110	111
001	001	000	011	010	101	100	111	110
010	010	011	000	001	110	111	100	101
011	011	010	001	000	111	110	101	100
100	100	101	110	111	000	001	010	011
101	101	100	111	110	001	000	011	010
110	110	111	100	101	010	011	000	001
111	111	110	101	100	011	010	001	000

The encryption matrix of the *One-time Pad* is a latin square of order 2^n, so it achieves perfect secrecy. The proof makes clear the underlying combinatorial structure of the optimal solution, as opposed to the algebraic description of the *One-time Pad*. Any latin square yields an encryption scheme that provides perfect secrecy. Thus, the security is based on the combinatorial structure, not the fact that encryption is done using XOR (exclusive-or) operations.

14   My Paper with Jim Massey

My most famous co-author was Paul Erdös, but in cryptography, I would point to my paper with Jim Massey (1934–2013). Jim is well-known for his work in decoding algorithms (e.g., the Berlekamp-Massey algorithm), block cipher design, convolutional codes, etc.

Jim and I co-authored a 1995 paper on resilient functions [17], entitled "An infinite class of counterexamples to a conjecture concerning nonlinear resilient functions," that was published in the *Journal of Cryptology*. This paper provides a nice example of how coding theory was used to disprove a conjecture, based on an appropriate combinatorial characterization.

An (n, k, t)-*resilient function* (or *RF*) is a function $f : (\mathbb{Z}_2)^n \to (\mathbb{Z}_2)^k$ such that, if any t inputs are fixed and the remaining $n-t$ inputs are chosen uniformly and independently at random, then every output k-tuple is equally likely. Given n and k, the fundamental problem is to maximize t.

A resilient function f is *linear* if $f(\mathbf{x}) = \mathbf{x}M$ for some n by k binary matrix M. It was known that the existence of an $[n, k, d]$-binary code is equivalent to the existence of a linear $(n, k, d-1)$-RF. Thus, studying linear resilient functions is equivalent to studying linear codes. Perhaps based on this equivalence, it was conjectured in 1988 by Bennett, Brassard and Robert [2] that, if an (n, k, t)-RF exists, then a linear (n, k, t)-RF exists.

I proved the following combinatorial characterization of (n, k, t)-RF in 1993 in [16]: An (n, k, t)-RF is equivalent to a large set of orthogonal arrays $OA_\lambda(t, n, 2)$, where $\lambda = 2^{n-k-t}$. In a bit more detail, if f is an (n, k, t)-RF, then, for any binary k-tuple $\mathbf{y}$, the inverse image $f^{-1}(\mathbf{y})$ is an orthogonal array and the 2^k orthogonal arrays thus obtained comprise a large set (i.e., they partition the entire space $\{0,1\}^n$).

The above-mentioned characterization allows coding-theoretic methods to be used to study arbitrary (linear or nonlinear) resilient functions. Using the (nonlinear) Kerdock codes, it is possible to construct a $(2^{r+1}, 2^{r+1}-2r-2, 5)$-RF. The Kerdock code has dual distance $d' = 6$ and hence it is an orthogonal array with strength $t = 5$. In the original version of the paper, which was submitted to the *Journal of Cryptology*, I provided a complicated method of extending this OA to a large set of OAs. The nonexistence of a linear RF with the same parameters followed from known results in coding theory. A referee of the paper pointed out that my construction was not needed because the Kerdock code is systematic and hence a large set of orthogonal arrays (consisting of translates of the code) exist trivially. The editor-in-chief of the *Journal of Cryptology* at the time, Gilles Brassard, suggested that I include the referee as a co-author (if the referee was willing). The referee turned out to be Jim Massey.

It is interesting to note that most of the disproof of the conjecture used "off-the-shelf" coding theory, ultimately based on Delsarte's seminal work [6]. The tricky part was extending a nonlinear orthogonal array to a large set of orthogonal arrays. However, as described above, this turned out to be not so tricky after all!

15   Research Philosophy

Up to the present day, I have continued my research in combinatorial mathematics, applications of combinatorics and various aspects of cryptography, including, of course, combinatorial cryptography. I have never been so interested in developing theory for its own sake—I like to see some kind of motivation for the problems I study. I also try to be cognizant of the danger of researching ever more specialized problems which may not be of interest to anyone but the author, such as "hemi-demi-flippoids that vanish under close inspection."[7]

I choose my research topics based on various criteria:

- intrinsic interest of the problem (aesthetics)
- my ability to make a contribution based on my knowledge and skill set, and
- potential applications of the problem in any area of computer science.

I have often sought out "practically motivated" problems raised by others when I think that combinatorial techniques will prove fruitful in their solution. At the same time, I also work on any mathematical problems (usually combinatorial) that happen to appeal to me.

16   Some Influential Books

I thought it might be of interest to mention a few examples of extremely well-written books from which I have learned a great deal.

H. J. Ryser, *Combinatorial Mathematics*, 1963 [12]. From the preface: "But effort and ingenuity lead to mastery, and our subject holds rich rewards for those who learn its secrets." This book is a very short but well written classic treatment of combinatorial theory up to the year 1963. It still makes excellent reading today.

M. Garey and D. S. Johnson, *Computers and Intractability: A Guide to the Theory of NP-Completeness*, 1979 [8]. Wikipedia states: "In a 2006 study, the CiteSeer search engine listed the book as the most cited reference in computer science literature."[8] This is, in my opinion, the best example of a clearly written book on a very technical subject. It is how I (as a complete novice) learned about this theory in the early 1980s.

G. J. Simmons (Editor), *Contemporary Cryptology: The Science of Information Integrity*, 1992 [14]. This book is an edited collection of extremely useful survey articles, which is now (unavoidably) somewhat out of date. The field of cryptography needs more survey papers! These are invaluable to keep track of research trends and to summarize the most important developments in the field.

---

[7] I attribute this amusing term to Curt Lindner.

[8] This quote is from the Wikipedia article "Computers and Intractability" (https://en.wikipedia.org/wiki/Computers_and_Intractability), which is released under the Creative Commons Attribution-Share-Alike License 3.0.

J. H. van Lint and R. M. Wilson, *A Course in Combinatorics, 2nd Edition*, 2001 [19]. This is my favourite combinatorics book. It is extremely well written and it contains a wealth of information on many areas of combinatorics. A reader can just pick it up and start reading any random page, and there will be interesting, beautiful mathematics to be found.

17 Mathematical Exposition

I would like to stress the importance of clear mathematical exposition. The following quote is sometimes attributed (perhaps erroneously[9]) to Albert Einstein:

"If you can't explain it simply, you don't understand it well enough."

I saw this quote last winter on a poster on the door of an engineering faculty member's office door that I passed each day when I walked indoors from my car to the Davis Centre.

My goal is always to explain things clearly and precisely. Here are a few guiding principles for my mathematical writing and research talks:

- Use mathematics and English to reinforce each other. For example, give precise mathematical definitions but also explain what the definitions mean in plain language.
- Do not overburden the reader (or listener) with cumbersome notation, unnecessary jargon, etc.
- Whenever possible, provide examples to illustrate concepts, definitions, proofs, etc. An example is worth a hundred proofs!
- If something is complicated, try to simplify it! Simplification benefits the reader, of course, but it can also lead to a deeper understanding by the writer, which may suggest generalizations, extensions, etc. There have been many times when my understanding of a research paper has been accomplished by simplifying the ideas, notation, etc., and this has led to me doing additional research on the same problem.

The following definition is from a recent preprint on the IACR eprint server. It is a typical example of the kind of notation that is commonly encountered in cryptographic definitions.[10]

---

[9] There is apparently no source to substantiate the claim that Einstein actually said this, but it is still a good quote.

[10] I should emphasize that I am not specifically criticizing the wording and notation in this definition. I am just using it to illustrate how complicated cryptographic definitions have become in recent years.

Intuitively, a secure secret sharing scheme must be such that all qualified subsets of players can efficiently reconstruct the secret, whereas all unqualified subset have no information (possibly in a computational sense) about the secret.

Definition 2 (Secret sharing scheme). Let $n \in \mathbb{N}$, and $\mathcal{A}$ be an access structure for n parties. We say that $\Sigma = (\mathsf{Init}, \mathsf{Share}, \mathsf{Rec})$ is a secret sharing scheme realizing access structure $\mathcal{A}$ in the CRS model, with message space $\mathcal{M}$ and share space $\mathcal{S} = \mathcal{S}_1 \times \cdots \times \mathcal{S}_n$, if it is an n-party secret sharing in the CRS model with the following properties.

(i) **Correctness:** For all $\lambda \in \mathbb{N}$, all $\omega \in \mathsf{Init}(1^\lambda)$, all messages $m \in \mathcal{M}$, and for all subsets $\mathcal{I} \in \mathcal{A}$, we have that $\mathsf{Rec}(\omega, (\mathsf{Share}(\omega, m))_\mathcal{I}) = m$, with overwhelming probability over the randomness of the sharing algorithm.

(ii) **Privacy:** For all PPT adversaries $\mathsf{A} = (\mathsf{A}_1, \mathsf{A}_2)$, we have

$$\{\mathbf{Privacy}_{\Sigma,\mathsf{A}}(\lambda, 0)\}_{\lambda \in \mathbb{N}} \approx_c \{\mathbf{Privacy}_{\Sigma,\mathsf{A}}(\lambda, 1)\}_{\lambda \in \mathbb{N}},$$

where the experiment $\mathbf{Privacy}_{\Sigma,\mathsf{A}}(\lambda, b)$ is defined by

$$\mathbf{Privacy}_{\Sigma,\mathsf{A}}(\lambda, b) := \left\{ \begin{array}{c} \omega \leftarrow_{\$} \mathsf{Init}(1^\lambda); (m_0, m_1, \mathcal{U} \notin \mathcal{A}, \alpha_1) \leftarrow_{\$} \mathsf{A}_1(\omega) \\ s \leftarrow_{\$} \mathsf{Share}(\omega, m_b); b' \leftarrow_{\$} \mathsf{A}_2(\alpha_1, s_\mathcal{U}) \end{array} \right\}.$$

The above mathematical definition is very hard to decipher for anyone who is not already an expert. There is nothing unusual about this example, as cryptography papers are frequently burdened by extremely complicated notation, definitions, proofs, etc. However, it should be noted that the paragraph preceding the formal definition conveys the essential idea in a concise and understandable way, which is a definite positive.

18 How to Turn a Complex Mystery into a Simple Truth

The eminent combinatorial mathematician Curt Lindner gave a memorable after-dinner speech at the 1984 Southeastern Conference on Combinatorics, Graph Theory and Computing, having the above-mentioned title. I emailed Curt recently to fill in a few details about this talk. Curt said this:

> "I showed how to get an embedding for a partial idempotent quasigroup of order n into a complete idempotent quasigroup of order $4n$ with a simple picture ... then I gave a proof that the containing quasigroup was finite using universal algebra. The universal algebra proof was 50 pages and used reduction chains to canonical forms.
>
> I conjectured that if I gave the universal algebra proof at a famous university it would be considered beautiful mathematics ... whereas if I gave the $4n$ proof most of the people in the audience would say 'who the hell invited this idiot to give a talk.'
>
> I was illustrating the fact for many people it's the machinery that matters, not the result."

Of course the first result is much stronger than the second one. The question Curt is raising is whether complicated "deep" mathematics is really to be preferred over simple, direct arguments. Personally, I have always been most inspired by clarity, creativity, and originality.

19   Photo

The following photo was taken at a reception at SAC 2019 immediately following my talk. From left to right, there is Ron Mullin (my PhD supervisor), me, and Atefeh Mashatan. Atefeh introduced my talk; she is a former PhD student of mine who is now a faculty member at Ryerson University in Toronto.

20   Dedications

Research is much easier and enjoyable with the contributions of collaborators. I would like to dedicate this talk to all my co-authors over the years:

B. Alspach, B. Anderson, D. Archdeacon, A. Assaf, G. Ateniese, M. Atici, T. Berson, J. Bierbrauer, E. Billington, S. Blackburn, C. Blundo, E. Brickell, H. Cao, J. Carter, M. Carter, M. Chateauneuf, D. Chen, K. Chen, C. Colbourn, M. Colbourn, P. D'Arco, A. De Bonis, A. De Santis, D. Deng, J. Dinitz, P. Dukes, P. Eisen, P. Erdös, T. Etzion, H. Ferch, L. Frota-Mattos, A. Giorgio Gaggia, I. Goldberg, G. Gong, K. Gopalakrishnan, D. Gordon, M. Grainger, C. Guo, A. Hamel, A. Hartman, K. Henry, D. Hoffman, J. Horton, E. Ihrig, T. Johansson, S. Judah, B. Kacsmar, M. Kendall, K. Khoo, W. Kishimoto, W. Kocay, E. Kramer, D. Kreher, K. Kurosawa, T. Laing, K. Lauinger, J. Lee, P.-C. Li, C. Lindner, A. Ling, X. Ma, S. Magliveras, K. Martin, W. Martin, A. Mashatan, J. Massey, B. Masucci, A. Mattern, J. McSorley, E. Mendelsohn, W. Mills, J. Muir, R. Mullin, M. Nandi, N. Nasr Esfahani, S.-L. Ng, M. Nojoumian, W. Ogata, K. Okada, P. Ostergard, K. Ouafi, A. Panoui, M. Paterson, R. Phan,

K. Phelps, M. Qu, R. Rees, C. Rodger, A. Rosa, B. Roy, H. Saido, P. Sarkar, P. Schellenberg, E. Seah, V. Sós, J. Staddon, R. Stanton, R. Strobl, J. Sui, B. Sunar, C. Swanson, L. Teirlinck, T. Tillson, T. V. Tran, J. Upadhyay, U. Vaccaro, J. Van Rees, S. Vanstone, S. Veitch, D. Wagner, W. Wallis, Y. Wang, R. Wei, W. Wei, Y.-J. Wei, J. Wu, J. Yates, J. Yin, G. Zaverucha, S. Zhang, and L. Zhu.

As well, I would like to dedicate this paper to my family: my wife, Janet; my children, Michela and Aiden; and my brothers, Murray and Tom.

References

1. Bellovin, S.M.: Frank Miller: inventor of the one-time pad. Cryptologia **35**, 203–222 (2011)
2. Bennett, C.H., Brassard, G., Robert, J.-M.: Privacy amplification by public discussion. SIAM J. Comput. **17**, 210–229 (1988)
3. Blake, I.F., Fuji-Hara, R., Mullin, R.C., Vanstone, S.A.: Computing logarithms in finite fields of characteristic two. SIAM J. Algebraic Discrete Methods **5**, 276–285 (1984)
4. Brian, G., Faonio, A., Venturi, D.: Continuously non-malleable secret sharing for general access structures. Cryptology ePrint Archive: Report 2019/602
5. Brickell, E.F.: A few results in message authentication. Congressus Numerantium **43**, 141–154 (1984)
6. Delsarte, P.: The association schemes of coding theory. Ph.D. thesis, Université Catholique de Louvain, June 1973
7. Dinitz, J.H., Stinson, D.R.: A fast algorithm for finding strong starters. SIAM J. Algebraic Discrete Methods **2**, 50–56 (1981)
8. Garey, M.R., Johnson, D.: Computers and Intractability: A Guide to the Theory of NP-Completeness. W. H. Freeman and Company, New York (1979)
9. Honsberger, R.: Ingenuity in Mathematics. Mathematical Association of America, Washington, DC (1975)
10. Honsberger, R.: Mathematical Morsels. Mathematical Association of America, New York (1979)
11. Mullin, R.C., Stinson, D.R., Wallis, W.D.: Concerning the spectrum of skew room squares. Ars Combinatoria **6**, 277–291 (1978)
12. Ryser, H.: Combinatorial Mathematics. Mathematical Association of America, New York (1963)
13. Shannon, C.E.: Communication theory of secrecy systems. Bell Syst. Tech. J. **28**, 656–715 (1949)
14. Simmons, G.J. (ed.): Contemporary Cryptology: The Science of Information Integrity. IEEE Press, Piscataway (1992)
15. Stinson, D.R.: Some constructions and bounds for authentication codes. In: Odlyzko, A.M. (ed.) CRYPTO 1986. LNCS, vol. 263, pp. 418–425. Springer, Heidelberg (1987). https://doi.org/10.1007/3-540-47721-7_30
16. Stinson, D.R.: Resilient functions and large sets of orthogonal arrays. Congressus Numerantium **92**, 105–110 (1993)
17. Stinson, D.R., Massey, J.L.: An infinite class of counterexamples to a conjecture concerning non-linear resilient functions. J. Cryptol. **8**, 167–173 (1995)

18. Stinson, D.R., Vanstone, S.A.: A combinatorial approach to threshold schemes. In: Pomerance, C. (ed.) CRYPTO 1987. LNCS, vol. 293, pp. 330–339. Springer, Heidelberg (1988). https://doi.org/10.1007/3-540-48184-2_28
19. van Lint, J.H., Wilson, R.M.: A Course in Combinatorics, 2nd edn. Cambridge University Press, Cambridge (2001)
20. Wilson, R.M.: Constructions and uses of pairwise balanced designs. In: Hall, M., van Lint, J.H. (eds.) Combinatorics. ASIC, vol. 16, pp. 19–42. (1975). https://doi.org/10.1007/978-94-010-1826-5_2

Supersingular Isogeny Key Exchange for Beginners

Craig Costello[(✉)]

Microsoft Research, Redmond, USA
craigco@microsoft.com

Abstract. This is an informal tutorial on the supersingular isogeny Diffie-Hellman protocol aimed at non-isogenists.

1 Introduction

A non-specialist seeking a basic understanding of the schemes remaining in the NIST post-quantum standardisation effort [15] would likely find that the SIKE protocol [8] has one of the highest barriers of entry. Indeed, it is occasionally an experience of the author that the sheer amount of background and jargon needed to get an isogeny-based talk off the ground is enough to overwhelm audience members into their laptops or underwhelm them to sleep. The purpose of this tutorial is to try and give a beginner's guide to Jao and De Feo's supersingular isogeny Diffie-Hellman (SIDH) protocol [9] by way of an illustrated toy example. Any reader that can grasp the toy example will find it trivial to extrapolate their understanding to the parameters of cryptographic size, e.g. those in the SIKE[1] proposal.

The aim is that this be a starting point for non-isogenists seeking a gentle introduction to the topic. As such, it is not intended to act as any kind of survey of the field of isogeny-based cryptography. The last few years have seen an avalanche of new constructions and protocols based on isogenies, and this tutorial will solely focus on the original Jao-De Feo SIDH protocol – the paper that triggered this avalanche. Furthermore, excellent surveys of the now broad field of isogeny-based cryptography already exist: the lecture notes of De Feo [4] and the Galbraith-Vercauteren [7] and Smith [13] surveys all give much more in-depth expositions. The hope is that potential newcomers to the field may dip their toes in here first, find (via an explicit toy example) that the isogeny waters are much less daunting than they seem, and then feel more comfortable diving into [4], [7], [13], or into the fast-expanding literature on the field. A recommended alternative starting point is Urbanik's friendly introduction [16].

---

[1] SIKE stands for supersingular isogeny key encapsulation, a variant of SIDH whose differences are mostly unimportant in this tutorial (further details are in Sect. 7).

© Springer Nature Switzerland AG 2020
K. G. Paterson and D. Stebila (Eds.): SAC 2019, LNCS 11959, pp. 21–50, 2020.
https://doi.org/10.1007/978-3-030-38471-5_2

2 The Set of Supersingular j-invariants

SIDH works in the quadratic extensions of large prime fields $\mathbb{F}_p$ with $p \equiv 3 \bmod 4$, for which we typically choose the most convenient representation as $\mathbb{F}_{p^2} = \mathbb{F}_p(i)$ with $i^2 + 1 = 0$; elements are then of the form $u + vi$ where $u, v \in \mathbb{F}_p$.

Of the p^2 elements in $\mathbb{F}_{p^2}$, we are interested in a subset of size $\lfloor p/12 \rfloor + z$, where $z \in \{0, 1, 2\}$. The value of z depends on $p \bmod 12$ [12, Theorem V.4.1(c)], but it is unimportant; what is important to note is that as p grows exponentially large, so does the size of the subset we are interested in. This subset is precisely the set of supersingular j-invariants in $\mathbb{F}_{p^2}$ (we will describe what this terminology means in a moment).

For the purpose of being able to write this full set down, and in order to be able to carry out and visualise a mini SIDH protocol in full, herein we will focus on the toy example with

$$p := 431.$$

In this case there are $\lfloor p/12 \rfloor + 2 = 37$ supersingular j-invariants in $\mathbb{F}_{p^2}$, and they are depicted in Fig. 1.

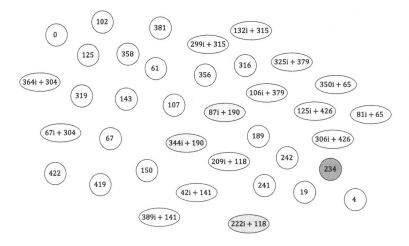

Fig. 1. The set of 37 supersingular j-invariants in $\mathbb{F}_{431^2}$. (Color figure online)

Every elliptic curve has a unique j-invariant, and two elliptic curves are isomorphic to each other if and only if they have the same j-invariant. Each of the j-invariants in Fig. 1 should therefore be thought of as representing any (and all) elliptic curve(s) with that j-invariant. For example, elliptic curves in Montgomery form [11]

$$E_a : y^2 = x^3 + ax^2 + x$$

have j-invariant

$$j(E_a) = \frac{256(a^2 - 3)^3}{(a^2 - 4)}.$$

Taking $a_1 = 208i + 161$ and $a_2 = 172i + 162$ gives

$$j(E_{a_1}) = j(E_{a_2}) = 364i + 304,$$

so

$$E_{a_1} : y^2 = x^3 + (208i + 161)x^2 + x$$

and

$$E_{a_2} : y^2 = x^3 + (172i + 162)x^2 + x$$

are isomorphic, and both correspond to the leftmost j-invariant depicted in Fig. 1. The isomorphisms are

$$\psi: \quad E_{a_1} \to E_{a_2},$$
$$(x, y) \mapsto \big((66i + 182)x + (300i + 109), (122i + 159)y\big),$$

and

$$\psi^{-1}: \quad E_{a_2} \to E_{a_1},$$
$$(x, y) \mapsto \big((156i + 40)x + (304i + 202), (419i + 270)y\big).$$

Write $\mathcal{O}_1$ and $\mathcal{O}_2$ for the identity elements (i.e. points at infinity) on E_{a_1} and E_{a_2}. Note that[2] $\psi(\mathcal{O}_1) = \mathcal{O}_2$ and $\psi^{-1}(\mathcal{O}_2) = \mathcal{O}_1$, and since the maps above do not have denominators, they are well-defined for all of the other (affine) points in $E_{a_1}(\mathbb{F}_{p^2})$ and $E_{a_2}(\mathbb{F}_{p^2})$. The composition of these two maps is the identity map on E_{a_1} or E_{a_2} (depending on the ordering).

An elliptic curve in characteristic p is either *supersingular*, or it is *ordinary*. In practice the supersingular case offers a number of advantages; instantiating efficient constructions is much easier, and the best known classical and quantum attacks against the related computational problems have exponential complexity[3].

The 37 j-invariants in Fig. 1 are *all* of the supersingular j-invariants in characteristic p; supersingular curves always have j-invariants in $\mathbb{F}_{p^2}$ [12, Theorem V.3.1], so there are no more supersingular j-invariants to be found in higher extension fields.

---

[2] Those unfamiliar with projective space can take this at face value, while those in the know can substitute $x = X/Z$ and $y = y/Z$ to cast these equations into $\mathbb{P}^2$ and observe that $\psi((0\colon 1\colon 0)) = (0\colon 1\colon 0)$, and vice versa.

[3] Note that this is the opposite of the situation for discrete logarithm-based ECC, where supersingular curves are avoided for security reasons. Discrete logarithms are no longer useful as hard underlying problems in the post-quantum setting, and they have no relevance to the security of SIDH.

SIDH in a Nutshell. At this point it helps to see the high-level analogue between SIDH and the traditional Diffie-Hellman protocol in a generic, cyclic group G. Let g be the public generator with $\langle g \rangle = G$, and let Alice and Bob's respective public keys be g^a and g^b, so that g^{ab} is their shared secret. Referring back to Fig. 1, the (blue) j-invariant $87i + 190$ is where Alice and Bob both begin; this is analogous to the generator g. In our example, Alice will choose a secret integer that, in turn, moves her around a subset of the 37 values until she arrives at the (green) j-invariant $222i + 118$; this will be the public key she sends to Bob, analogous to g^a. Bob will also choose a secret integer that moves him around some of the values in Fig. 1, and he will eventually arrive at the yellow j-invariant $344i + 190$; he sends this as his public key to Alice, analogous to g^b. Together with Bob's public key and her secret integer, Alice then performs another sequence of moves to land at the (red) j-invariant 234; this acts as the analogue of g^{ab}, and it is the same j-invariant Bob will arrive at when he starts at Alice's public j-invariant and walks according to his secret integer.

The public keys contain additional information that is used to ensure that Alice and Bob can arrive at the same shared secret, but these details will come later. The purpose of the next section is to describe how both parties move between j-invariants: these moves are made with *isogenies*.

3   Isogenies

Just like the isomorphisms ψ and ψ^{-1} above, maps on a given elliptic curve, or between two elliptic curves, are written as $(x, y) \mapsto (f(x, y), g(x, y))$ for some functions f and g. The main reason Montgomery-form elliptic curves are often the preferred choice in both old-school ECC and in isogeny-based cryptography is that they facilitate very efficient x-only arithmetic, i.e. maps that ignore the y-coordinates entirely. In what follows we will also ignore the y-coordinates and simply write maps as

$$x \mapsto f(x),$$

but any reader wanting to complete the picture can recover the full maps by taking

$$(x, y) \mapsto (f(x), c \cdot y f'(x)),$$

where f' is the derivative of f and c is a fixed constant.

Consider the *multiplication-by-2* or *point doubling* map on a fixed Montgomery curve $E_a \colon y^2 = x^3 + ax^2 + x$, written as

$$[2]: \qquad E_a \to E_a, \qquad x \mapsto \frac{(x^2 - 1)^2}{4x(x^2 + ax + 1)}. \tag{1}$$

Observe that, unlike the isomorphisms in the previous section, the doubling map has a denominator that will create exceptional points. Viewing the curve equation, we see that these are the three points with $y = 0$, namely $(0, 0)$, $(\alpha, 0)$ and $(1/\alpha, 0)$, where $\alpha^2 + a\alpha + 1 = 0$. Indeed, these are the three points of order 2 on E_a, and together with the neutral element, $\mathcal{O}$, they are the entire kernel of the doubling map. This kernel forms a subgroup of the points in E_a, with group structure

$$\ker([2]) \cong \mathbb{Z}_2 \times \mathbb{Z}_2,$$

i.e. the *2-torsion* is precisely three cyclic subgroups of order 2. Each subgroup has one of the three points of exact order 2, together with the identity element $\mathcal{O}$. This is depicted in Fig. 2.

Now consider the *multiplication-by-3* or *point tripling* map on $E_a : y^2 = x^3 + ax^2 + x$, written as

$$[3]: \qquad E_a \to E_a, \qquad x \mapsto \frac{x(x^4 - 6x^2 - 4ax^3 - 3)^2}{(3x^4 + 4ax^3 + 6x^2 - 1)^2} \qquad (2)$$

Again, the denominator will give rise to exceptional points to the tripling map. Suppose its four roots are $\beta, \delta, \zeta, \theta$; each of these correspond to x-coordinates of points of order 3 in E_a, and this time there are two (non-zero) y-coordinates for each such x. Together with $\mathcal{O}$, there are then 9 points that are sent to $\mathcal{O}$ under [3], and this time we have

$$\ker([3]) \cong \mathbb{Z}_3 \times \mathbb{Z}_3,$$

i.e. the *3-torsion* is precisely four cyclic subgroups of order 3. This is depicted in Fig. 3.

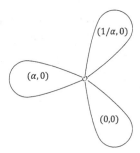

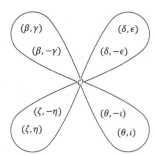

Fig. 2. The kernel $\ker([2]) \cong \mathbb{Z}_2 \times \mathbb{Z}_2$ of the doubling map; three cyclic subgroups of order 2.

Fig. 3. The kernel $\ker([3]) \cong \mathbb{Z}_3 \times \mathbb{Z}_3$ of the tripling map; four cyclic subgroups of order 3.

It turns out that this pattern holds true for any ℓ where $p \nmid \ell$. The set of points in the ℓ-torsion, i.e. the set of points sent to $\mathcal{O}$ under the multiplication-by-ℓ map, is such that

$$\ker([\ell]) \cong \mathbb{Z}_\ell \times \mathbb{Z}_\ell,$$

forming $\ell + 1$ cyclic subgroups of order ℓ.

Both the doubling and tripling maps above are rather special cases of more general maps between elliptic curves that we call *isogenies*. In both of these instances, it just so happens that their domain and codomain are the same elliptic curve. In general, an isogeny is a map

$$\phi\colon E \to E'$$

from one elliptic curve to another. Isogenies are said to be either *separable* or *inseparable*; these definitions are not important here, but it should be said that we will only be interested in the former case.

A key fact to digest is that separable isogenies are in one-to-one correspondence with finite subgroups: every subgroup G of points on an elliptic curve E gives rise to a unique isogeny $\phi\colon E \to E'$ whose kernel is G, and vice versa. In this case we often see the codomain being written as E/G. Vélu's formulas [18] make this explicit: on input of (the curve constants defining) E and the points in G, these formulas output the constants defining $E' = E/G$ and the explicit maps for ϕ, i.e. the maps that move any points on E (except those in the kernel G) to their corresponding image on E'. Writing the general form of Vélu's formulas down is unnecessary here, as we will only require two instances. Nevertheless, it is worth noting that these formulas are simply rational functions of the inputs mentioned above, and the degrees of these functions are the same size as the size of the subgroup G.

Referring back to Fig. 2, suppose we set $G = \{\mathcal{O}, (\alpha, 0), (1/\alpha, 0), (0, 0)\}$ and input it into Vélu's formulas, together with the curve E_a. The output would then be the unique map with kernel G, i.e. the doubling map in (1), together with E_a itself.

Suppose we instead choose our kernel to be one of the cyclic subgroups of order 2, e.g. set $G = \{\mathcal{O}, (\alpha, 0)\}$, and input this and E_a into Vélu's formulas. In this case the map we get is

$$\phi\colon \qquad E_a \to E_{a'}, \qquad x \mapsto \frac{x(\alpha x - 1)}{x - \alpha},$$

with

$$a' = 2(1 - 2\alpha^2). \tag{3}$$

This map can be used to compute 2-isogenies on any Montgomery curve. For example, recall one of the curves from Sect. 2 as

$$E_a\colon y^2 = x^3 + (208i + 161)x^2 + x, \qquad \text{with} \qquad j(E_a) = 364i + 304.$$

The point $(\alpha, 0) \in E_a$ with $\alpha = 350i + 68$ has order 2. Applying (3) yields the image curve

$$E_{a'}\colon y^2 = x^3 + (102i + 423)x^2 + x, \qquad \text{with} \qquad j(E_{a'}) = 344i + 190,$$

and the map

$$\phi\colon x \mapsto \frac{x((350i + 68)x - 1)}{x - (350i + 68)} \tag{4}$$

that will take (the x-coordinate of) any point not in $\{\mathcal{O}, (\alpha, 0)\}$ to the (x-coordinate of the) corresponding point on $E_{a'}$.

Now suppose we set the kernel as one of the subgroups of order 3 in Fig. 3, e.g. $G = \{\mathcal{O}, (\beta, \gamma), (\beta, -\gamma)\}$. Vélu's formulas output

$$\phi: \qquad E_a \to E_{a'}, \qquad x \mapsto \frac{x(\beta x - 1)^2}{(x - \beta)^2},$$

with

$$a' = (a\beta - 6\beta^2 + 6)\beta \tag{5}$$

The point $(\beta, \gamma) = (321i + 56, 303i + 174)$ has order 3 on $E_a : y^2 = x^3 + (208i + 161)x^2 + x$. Applying (5) yields the image curve

$$E_{a'} : y^2 = x^3 + 415x^2 + x, \qquad \text{with} \qquad j(E_{a'}) = 189,$$

and the map

$$\phi: x \mapsto \frac{x((321i + 56)x - 1)^2}{(x - (321i + 56))^2}$$

that will move points from E_a to $E_{a'}$.

Unlike the isomorphisms in Sect. 2 which preserve the j-invariant, the isogenies in this section give image curves with different j-invariants; in this case the curves are no longer isomorphic, but are instead said to be *isogenous*.

The *degree* of a non-zero separable isogeny is the number of elements in its kernel [12, Theorem III.4.10], and it is also the degree of the isogeny as a rational map (in the sense of [12, p. 21]). For our purposes, one can see from eyeballing any of the examples above that the number of kernel elements match the degree of the corresponding map.

Isomorphisms are actually a special case of an isogeny where the kernel is trivial, i.e. the kernel is just $\{\mathcal{O}\}$ (as we saw in Sect. 2), so they are isogenies of degree 1. By definition, composing an isomorphism with its inverse gives the identity map. In general, however, isogenies do not have an inverse that behaves like this; instead, every isogeny has a unique *dual isogeny* [12, Theorem III.6.1], that almost behaves like an inverse. If $\phi : E \to E'$ is an isogeny of degree d, then the dual isogeny $\hat{\phi}$ is such that the composition $(\hat{\phi} \circ \phi) = [d]$, i.e. the multiplication-by-d map on E, and the composition $(\phi \circ \hat{\phi})$ is the multiplication-by-d map on E'. Just like inverse isomorphisms, the composition of dual isogenies lands us back on the same curve; the difference is that the kernel of this composition becomes the d-torsion in general (which is non-trivial when $d > 1$). As an example, composing the degree-2 isogeny $\phi : E_a \to E_{a'}$ in (3) with its degree-2 dual $\hat{\phi} : E_{a'} \to E_a$ gives the degree-4 doubling map in (1) (whose kernel is in Fig. 2).

It is important to note that isogenies are well-behaved maps (the fancy word is morphisms [12, p. 12]) in both the geometric *and* algebraic sense. Our focus above has mostly been on the former side, where we have seen them map points between two geometric curves. But isogenies are also algebraic in that they are *group homomorphisms*: an isogeny $\phi\colon E \to E'$ satisfies

$$\phi(P + Q) = \phi(P) + \phi(Q)$$

for all $P, Q \in E$ [12, Theorem III.4.8]; the sum on the left corresponds to the elliptic curve group law on E, while the sum on the right is the group law on E'.

In terms of SIDH, it is helpful to see what this homomorphic behaviour means with some examples. Returning to the 2-isogeny in (4) from

$$E_a\colon y^2 = x^3 + (208i + 161)x^2 + x \qquad \text{to} \qquad E_{a'}\colon y^2 = x^3 + (102i + 423)x^2 + x,$$

recall that the kernel of ϕ was $\{\mathcal{O}, (\alpha, 0)\}$ with $\alpha = 350i + 68$.

We will now observe what becomes of various points on E as they move through ϕ, momentarily returning to both coordinates under the map $\phi\colon (x, y) \mapsto (f(x), c \cdot y f'(x))$, with $f(x)$ as above and with the constant c satisfying $c^2 = \alpha$. The points

$$P = (390i + 23, 104i + 7) \qquad \text{and} \qquad Q = (151i + 140, 110i + 136)$$

both have order 8 on E_a, but when ϕ is the 2-isogeny above, the points

$$\phi(P) = (23i + 231, 309i + 61) \qquad \text{and} \qquad \phi(Q) = (80i + 261, 192i + 259)$$

have orders 4 and 8 on $E_{a'}$, respectively. The reason the order of P decreased is because it *lies above* a non-trivial element in the kernel: $[4]P = (\alpha, 0) \in \ker(\phi)$, thus $\phi([4]P) = \mathcal{O}$ on $E_{a'}$, and since ϕ is a homomorphism, $\phi([4]P) = [4]\phi(P)$; given that $[2]P \notin \ker(\phi)$, it must therefore be that $\phi(P)$ has order 4. The same reasoning shows that, in general, a degree-d isogeny will decrease the order of any point lying above the kernel by a factor of d. On the other hand, other points preserve their orders when moving through isogenies, as we saw above for the point Q. As another example, the image of the point $R = (\beta, \gamma) = (321i+56, 303i+174)$ of order 3 on E_a is the point $\phi(R) = (102i+238, 346i+193)$ of order 3 on $E_{a'}$. In general, evaluating a degree-d isogeny at a point of order ℓ will preserve this order if d and ℓ are coprime; it is useful to keep this property in mind in the sections that follow.

A theorem of Tate [14] says that two elliptic curves $E/\mathbb{F}_q$ and $E'/\mathbb{F}_q$ are isogenous over $\mathbb{F}_q$ if and only if they have the same number of points over $\mathbb{F}_q$. Returning to our running example, all of the j-invariants in Fig. 1 correspond to elliptic curves $E/\mathbb{F}_{431^2}$ with group orders $\#E(\mathbb{F}_{431^2}) = 432^2$. Moreover, they all have the same group structure $\mathbb{Z}_{432} \times \mathbb{Z}_{432}$. This is an instance of the general case in which supersingular curves $E/\mathbb{F}_{p^2}$ always have their full rational $(p-1)$- or $(p+1)$-torsion defined over $\mathbb{F}_{p^2}$. Moreover, in our case the elliptic curve group is precisely the $(p+1)$-torsion and, as we saw at the beginning of the section, we have $\ker([p+1]) \cong \mathbb{Z}_{p+1} \times \mathbb{Z}_{p+1}$, from which it follows that

$$E(\mathbb{F}_{p^2}) \cong \mathbb{Z}_{p+1} \times \mathbb{Z}_{p+1}.$$

Suppose $\phi\colon E \to E'$ is an $\mathbb{F}_q$-rational isogeny of degree $d > 1$, i.e. $\#\ker(\phi) = d$. One point of confusion that can sometimes arise for isogeny newcomers is how $E/\mathbb{F}_q$ and $E'/\mathbb{F}_q$ can have the same number of points. There are d elements mapped to $\mathcal{O}$ under ϕ, meaning there are $\#E(\mathbb{F}_q) - d$ elements in $E(\mathbb{F}_q)$ which are carried through to non-zero points in $E'(\mathbb{F}_q)$. If $d > 1$, then at first sight it can appear that the group orders should not match. However, the unbalance that seems to arise is resolved by points in higher extension fields that map down to $E'(\mathbb{F}_q)$ under ϕ, and the same thing happens in the reverse direction when considering the dual isogeny from E' back to E.

The *composition* of isogenies is as we might expect. Composing the two isogenies

$$\phi\colon E \to E' \qquad \text{and} \qquad \psi\colon E' \to E''$$

gives the isogeny

$$(\psi \circ \phi)\colon E \to E'',$$

whose degree is the product of the two individual degrees. We have already seen a special example of this above: when ϕ is the degree-2 isogeny in (3), then composing with the degree-2 dual isogeny $\hat{\phi}$ gave the degree-4 doubling map in (1).

As we will get a glimpse of in Sect. 5, this notion of composition is crucial to the practicality of SIDH. In real-world instantiations, we compute isogenies whose degrees are exponentially large, e.g. isogenies of degree 2^e for $e > 200$. Given that algorithms for general isogeny computation are linear in the degree of the isogeny, this would be out of the question if it was not for our being able to instead compute it as the composition of e individual 2-isogenies.

Finally, when speaking of isogenies, we are often implicitly speaking *up to isomorphism*. For example, in the fact we stated above whereby every subgroup of points gives rise to a unique isogeny, it would be more precise to state that this isogeny is unique up to isomorphism. We could always compose an isogeny with an isomorphism to get a different looking map, but for all intents and purposes these isogenies will be considered equivalent.

4 Isogeny Graphs

Recall that, for each prime p, we are working with the set of all j-invariants in $\mathbb{F}_{p^2}$ that correspond to supersingular curves in characteristic p. We will continue with our example of $p = 431$, for which the 37 j-invariants are depicted back in Fig. 1. The important notion illustrated in this section is that, when we introduce any other prime $\ell \neq p$, this set becomes a *graph* with surprising properties. The vertices of each graph remain fixed as the j-invariants themselves, but the edges between them correspond to ℓ-isogenies, and therefore the edges change for each ℓ. In SIDH we only need two of the graphs: one for Alice, for which we usually take $\ell = 2$, and one for Bob, for which we usually take $\ell = 3$ (these choices of the two smallest primes currently give the most efficient instantiation of SIDH).

To draw the graphs for our example, we proceed as in the previous section. Recall that the 2-isogeny in (4) was from the curve $E_a \colon y^2 = x^3 + (208i + 161)x^2 + x$ with $j(E_a) = 364i + 304$ to the curve $E_{a'} \colon y^2 = x^3 + (102i + 423)x^2 + x$ with $j(E_{a'}) = 344i + 190$; the kernel was generated by $(\alpha, 0) \in E_a$ with $\alpha = 350i + 68$. Thus, we can draw an edge between these two j-invariants. Furthermore, recall (see Fig. 2) that there are two other kernels of 2-isogenies on E_a: one generated by $(1/\alpha, 0)$ and the other generated by $(0, 0)$. These produce two more edges, one connecting $j = 364i + 304$ to $j = 67$ and one connecting $j = 364i + 304$ to $j = 319$. Continuing in this fashion, we visit every j-invariant in the graph until all three 2-torsion points have been used to generate three outgoing edges, and eventually we produce the full 2-isogeny graph that is depicted in Fig. 4.

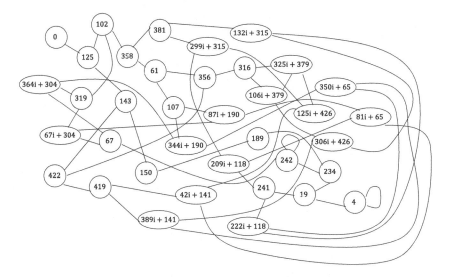

Fig. 4. The 2-isogeny graph for $p = 431$. The 37 nodes are the supersingular j-invariants and the edges between them correspond to 2-isogenies.

Observe that, for all $j \notin \{0, 4, 242\}$ (we will talk about these exceptions in Sect. 6), there are exactly 3 edges connecting a given node to other 2-isogenous j-invariants. Moreover, we have not written any directions on the arrows; the reasoning here is that, for any edge from $j(E)$ to $j(E')$ corresponding to an isogeny $\phi \colon E \to E'$, the dual isogeny gives an edge from $j(E')$ back to $j(E)$.

The 3-isogeny graph is drawn analogously, but recall (see Fig. 3) that there are now four outgoing edges corresponding to every j-invariant (we again have a small number of exceptions for $j \in \{0, 4, 125, 242\}$). We saw explicitly in Sect. 3 that the point $(\beta, \gamma) = (321i + 56, 303i + 174)$ of order 3 on E_a (as above) was the kernel of an isogeny to the curve $E_{a'} \colon y^2 = x^3 + 415x^2 + x$ with $j(E_{a'}) = 189$. Inputting the three other 3-torsion subgroups into Vélu's formulas gives three image curves with $j = 19$, $j = 42i + 141$, and $j = 106i + 379$. Again, working through each node gives rise to the graph depicted in Fig. 5.

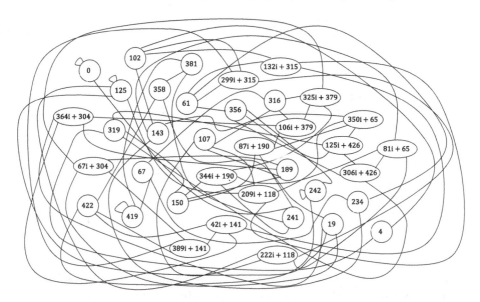

Fig. 5. The 3-isogeny graph for $p = 431$. The 37 nodes are the supersingular j-invariants and the edges between them correspond to 3-isogenies.

We are now in a position to discuss how SIDH primes are chosen. State-of-the-art instantiations of SIDH (including those in the SIKE specification [8]) always fix primes p of the form

$$p = 2^{e_A} 3^{e_B} - 1,$$

where e_A and e_B are such that $2^{e_A} \approx 3^{e_B}$. In fact, SIDH actually allows more flexibility by introducing a cofactor f and permitting primes of the form $p = f \cdot 2^{e_A} 3^{e_B} - 1$, but (as it currently stands) the case of $f = 1$ is flexible enough to find suitable primes at all of the interesting security levels.

The rationale behind choosing primes of this form ties back to the discussion in the previous section; we work with supersingular curves for which the elliptic curve group $E(\mathbb{F}_{p^2})$ is the full $(p+1)$-torsion, that which is isomorphic to $\mathbb{Z}_{p+1} \times \mathbb{Z}_{p+1}$. Thus, for our choice of primes, the elliptic curve group is

$$E(\mathbb{F}_{p^2}) \cong \mathbb{Z}_{(2^{e_A}3^{e_B})} \times \mathbb{Z}_{(2^{e_A}3^{e_B})}.$$

In other words, there are two points P and Q, both of order $2^{e_A}3^{e_B}$, that are a basis for the full elliptic curve group $E(\mathbb{F}_{p^2})$. Moreover, linear combinations $[\alpha]P + [\beta]Q$ with $\alpha, \beta \in \mathbb{Z}_{(2^{e_A}3^{e_B})}$ can be used to generate *all* of the points whose orders are *any* factor of $2^{e_A}3^{e_B}$. In particular, every point of order 2^{e_A} or of order 3^{e_B} lies in $E(\mathbb{F}_{p^2})$. We will see at the beginning of the next section that these are precisely the points that are used as secret generators of subgroups (i.e. isogenies) in the SIDH framework, so choosing primes in the above fashion ultimately means that Alice and Bob will only ever have to work with points inside $E(\mathbb{F}_{p^2})$.

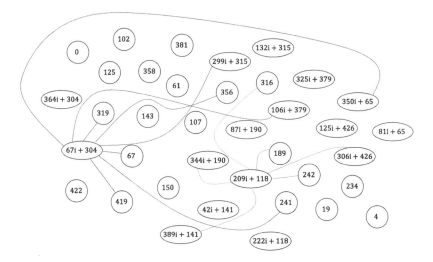

Fig. 6. The 6 edges at the node $j = 209i + 118$ corresponding to the 5-isogeny graph, and the 8 edges at the node $67i + 304$ corresponding to the 7-isogeny graph.

It is worth revisiting the fact that, although we only need to consider the graphs corresponding to $\ell = 2$ and $\ell = 3$, isogeny graphs exist for every prime ℓ for which $p \nmid \ell$. In Fig. 6 we give the 6 edges corresponding to $\ell = 5$ at $j = 209i + 118$, and the 8 edges corresponding to $\ell = 7$ at $j = 67i + 304$ (these could be done at every node, but Fig. 5 was already messy enough!). Although the j-invariants connected by these edges are always in $\mathbb{F}_{p^2}$, the isogenies corresponding to $\ell \notin \{2, 3\}$ would be computed using points that are not $\mathbb{F}_{p^2}$-rational. In other words, points of order ℓ^e for $\ell \notin \{2, 3\}$ are not found in $E(\mathbb{F}_{p^2})$ (with our prime p chosen as above), so to compute these isogenies we would have to perform computations in the larger extension fields of $\mathbb{F}_p$ where these points are found.

We will further discuss the properties of cryptographically sized supersingular isogeny graphs in Sect. 7.

5   Walking Through the Protocol

This section walks step by step through the entire toy example of the SIDH protocol. During both Alice and Bob's public key generation, every computation is provided explicitly so active readers (perhaps equipped with their favourite computer algebra package) can follow along; on the other hand, readers finding the repetition tedious can happily skip the details. The shared secret computations are analogous, so less details are given there. We start with a high-level and general description of the protocol, before returning to our concrete example.

A High-Level Overview. For the reasons detailed in Sect. 4, SIDH instantiations typically take $p = 2^{e_A} 3^{e_B} - 1$ with $2^{e_A} \approx 3^{e_B}$. The protocol begins on an initial curve E in the corresponding supersingular isogeny graph.

Alice's secrets will be isogenies of degree (or, equivalently, subgroups of order) 2^{e_A}, and Bob's will be of degree 3^{e_B}. Recall from Sect. 3 that the ℓ-torsion is 2-dimensional, so Alice will compute generators of her secret subgroups by computing secret linear combinations of two public basis points, where

$$\langle P_A, Q_A \rangle = E[2^{e_A}] \cong \mathbb{Z}_{2^{e_A}} \times \mathbb{Z}_{2^{e_A}}.$$

Similarly, Bob will compute his secret generators as secret linear combinations of two public points, P_B and Q_B, where

$$\langle P_B, Q_B \rangle = E[3^{e_B}] \cong \mathbb{Z}_{3^{e_B}} \times \mathbb{Z}_{3^{e_B}}.$$

This necessarily means P_A and Q_A both have order 2^{e_A} and P_B and Q_B both have order 3^{e_B}. In practice (e.g. in SIKE [8]), they will typically choose their secret generator points, S_A and S_B, by simply taking

$$S_A = P_A + [k_A]Q_A \quad \text{with} \quad k_A \in [0, 2^{e_A}),$$

and

$$S_B = P_B + [k_B]Q_B \quad \text{with} \quad k_B \in [0, 3^{e_B}).$$

To compute her public key, Alice chooses $k_A \in \{0, 1, \ldots 2^{e_A} - 1\}$, computes S_A as above, and then computes the secret isogeny $\phi_A \colon E \to E_A$, where $E_A = E/\langle S_A \rangle$. She does this by composing e_A isogenies of degree 2, i.e. taking e_A steps in the 2-isogeny graph, which are defined by S_A. Her public key is then

$$\mathrm{PK}_A = (E_A, P_B', Q_B') = (\phi_A(E), \phi_A(P_B), \phi_A(Q_B)),$$

where the first element is the image *curve* $E_A = \phi_A(E)$, while the second and third elements are the images of Bob's public basis *points* (we will discuss why these points are needed in a moment).

Bob chooses $k_B \in \{0, 1, \ldots 3^{e_B} - 1\}$, computes S_B as above, and then computes his secret isogeny $\phi_B \colon E \to E_B$, where $E_B = E/\langle S_B \rangle$. He does this by composing e_B isogenies of degree 3, i.e. taking e_B steps in the 3-isogeny graph, which are defined by S_B. His public key is then

$$\mathrm{PK}_B = (E_B, P_A', Q_A') = (\phi_B(E), \phi_B(P_A), \phi_B(Q_A)).$$

On input of her secret integer k_A and Bob's public key, Alice computes the secret subgroup $S_A' = P_A' + [k_A]Q_A'$ on E_B, and then computes another secret isogeny $\phi_A' \colon E_B \to E_{AB}$, where $E_{AB} = E_B/\langle S_A' \rangle$. She then computes the shared secret as $j_{AB} = j(E_{AB})$.

On Bob's side, he takes $S_B' = P_B' + [k_B]Q_B'$ on E_A, computes the secret isogeny $\phi_B' \colon E_A \to E_{BA}$, where $E_{BA} = E_A/\langle S_B' \rangle$. He then computes the shared secret as $j_{BA} = j(E_{BA})$.

Why the Image Points? Before proceeding, it is important to discuss why Alice and Bob must move each other's basis points through their secret isogenies and include these images in their public keys. Unlike traditional Diffie-Hellman (see the end of Sect. 2) where exponents commute to give $(g^a)^b = (g^b)^a$, in the SIDH setting we do not have this property. Indeed, it does not even make sense to consider a composition of the isogenies $\phi_A \colon E \to E_A$ and $\phi_B \colon E \to E_B$, given their domains/codomains. Instead, Alice needs a way to describe an isogeny whose domain is E_B, and Bob needs an analogous way to start from E_A. Moving each other's basis points through the secret isogeny during key generation solves this problem; it allows both parties to essentially redo the same computations on the curves transmitted in the public keys and to ultimately arrive at the same j-invariant[4].

Public Parameters. We now continue with our example of $p = 2^4 3^3 - 1$, and take the public starting curve as

$$E_{a_0} \colon y^2 = x^3 + a_0 x^2 + x, \quad \text{with} \quad a_0 = 329i + 423 \quad \text{and} \quad j(E_{a_0}) = 87i + 190.$$

We can take any four public basis points we like E_{a_0}, so long as $E[2^4] = \langle P_A, Q_A \rangle$ and $E[3^3] = \langle P_B, Q_B \rangle$. We fix

$$P_A := (100i + 248, 304i + 199) \quad \text{and} \quad Q_A := (426i + 394, 51i + 79),$$

together with

$$P_B := (358i + 275, 410i + 104) \quad \text{and} \quad Q_B := (20i + 185, 281i + 239).$$

Alice's Public Key Generation. Suppose Alice chooses the secret

$$k_A := 11$$

from $\{0, 1, \ldots 15\}$. Her first step is to compute the secret generator corresponding to k_A, as

$$\begin{aligned} S_A &= P_A + [k_A]Q_A \\ &= (100i + 248, 304i + 199) + [11](426i + 394, 51i + 79) \\ &= (271i + 79, 153i + 430), \end{aligned}$$

which is a point of order 16 on the starting curve E_{a_0}. Alice now proceeds to compute her public key using only a combination of the point doubling operation in (1) and the 2-isogeny operation in (3). Below we will use prime superscripts to denote values that are updated/overwritten throughout the procedure, and again, though we refer to the x-only maps in Sect. 3, we will still write the points in full under the extension from $x \mapsto f(x)$ to $(x, y) \mapsto (f(x), cyf'(x))$ (where $c^2 = \alpha$ and $(\alpha, 0)$ is the kernel of the 2-isogeny at hand).

---

[4] Astute readers wanting to prove that $j_{AB} = j_{BA}$ can argue that both j-invariants correspond to the isomorphism class of $E/\langle S_A, S_B \rangle$ by using the identity $E/\langle P, Q \rangle \cong (E/\langle P \rangle)/\langle \phi(Q) \rangle$ with $\phi \colon E \to E/\langle P \rangle$. Otherwise, see [9, §3].

- *Compute ϕ_0.* Initialise $S'_A = S_A = (271i + 79, 153i + 430)$. Three repeated applications of the doubling in (1) produces the point $R'_A = [8]S'_A = (18i + 37, 0)$, which has order 2 on E_{a_0}. Inputting R'_A into (3) gives $\phi_0 \colon E_{a_0} \to E_{a_1}$, with $a_1 = 275i + 132$ and $j(E_{a_1}) = 107$. It also gives the map $\phi_0 \colon x \mapsto \frac{x((18i+37)x-1)}{x-(18i+37)}$, which is used to update $P'_B = \phi(P'_B) = (118i+85, 274i+150)$, $Q'_B = (62i+124, 64i+269)$, and $S'_A = (36i+111, 175i+67)$; the orders of P'_B and Q'_B on E_{a_1} are unchanged, but the order of the new S'_A has decreased from 16 to 8. Figure 7 shows ϕ_0 as Alice's first step in the 2-isogeny graph.
- *Compute ϕ_1.* Two repeated applications of the doubling in (1) produces the point $R'_A = [4]S'_A = (7i + 49, 0)$, which has order 2 on E_{a_1}. Inputting R'_A into (3) gives $\phi_1 \colon E_{a_1} \to E_{a_2}$, with $a_2 = 273i + 76$ and $j(E_{a_2}) = 344i + 190$. It also gives the map $\phi_1 \colon x \mapsto \frac{x((7i+49)x-1)}{x-(7i+49)}$, which is used to update $P'_B = \phi(P'_B) = (274i + 251, 316i + 59)$, $Q'_B = (214i + 94, 354i + 193)$, and $S'_A = (274i + 374, 84i + 77)$; the order of the new S'_A has decreased from 8 to 4. Figure 7 shows ϕ_1 as Alice's second step in the 2-isogeny graph.
- *Compute ϕ_2.* One doubling via (1) produces the point $R'_A = [2]S'_A = (245i + 27, 0)$, which has order 2 on E_{a_2}. Inputting R'_A into (3) gives $\phi_2 \colon E_{a_2} \to E_{a_3}$, with $a_3 = 93i + 136$ and $j(E_{a_3}) = 350i + 65$. It also gives the map $\phi_2 \colon x \mapsto \frac{x((245i+27)x-1)}{x-(245i+27)}$, which is used to update $P'_B = \phi(P'_B) = (77i + 209, 75i + 79)$, $Q'_B = (339i + 356, 12i + 419)$, and $S'_A = (227i + 150, 0)$; the order of the new S'_A has decreased from 4 to 2. Figure 7 shows ϕ_2 as Alice's third step in the 2-isogeny graph.
- *Compute ϕ_3.* $S'_A = (227i + 150, 0)$ already has order 2 on E_{a_3}, so no scalar multiplication is necessary in the final stage. Inputting S'_A into (3) gives $\phi_3 \colon E_{a_3} \to E_{a_4}$, with $a_4 = 423i + 179$ and $j(E_{a_4}) = 222i + 118$. It also gives the map $\phi_3 \colon x \mapsto \frac{x((227i+150)x-1)}{x-(227i+150)}$, which is used to update $P'_B = \phi(P'_B) = (142i + 183, 119i + 360)$, $Q'_B = (220i + 314, 289i + 10)$; the point S'_A is in the kernel and is not carried through. Figure 7 shows ϕ_3 as Alice's fourth and final step in the 2-isogeny graph.

Alice's secret 2^4-isogeny is the composition of the four 2-isogenies detailed above, i.e. $\phi_A \colon E_{a_0} \to E_{a_4}$, $Q \mapsto \phi_A(Q)$, with $\phi_A = (\phi_3 \circ \phi_2 \circ \phi_1 \circ \phi_0)$ - see Fig. 7. Her public key, PK_A, is then

$$
\begin{aligned}
\mathrm{PK}_A &= (\phi_A(E_{a_0}), \phi_A(P_B), \phi_A(Q_B)) \\
&= (423i + 179, (142i + 183, 119i + 360), (220i + 314, 289i + 10)). \quad (6)
\end{aligned}
$$

Rather than send the j-invariant $j(E_{a_4}) \in \mathbb{F}_{p^2}$ as the value defining the curve, Alice can simply send $a_4 \in \mathbb{F}_{p^4}$, and Bob will do the same. The j-invariant function is only used during the shared secret computation to guarantee that Alice and Bob arrive at the same value.

Bob's Public Key Generation. Suppose Bob chooses the secret

$$
k_B := 2
$$

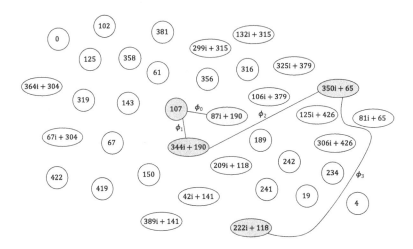

Fig. 7. Alice's key generation. She starts at the public curve corresponding to $j = 87i + 190$, her secret key is the isogeny $\phi_A = (\phi_3 \circ \phi_2 \circ \phi_1 \circ \phi_0)$, and the destination node $222i + 118$ becomes part of her public key.

from $\{0, 1, \ldots, 26\}$. His first step is to compute the secret generator corresponding to k_B, as

$$
\begin{aligned}
S_B &= P_B + [k_B]Q_B \\
&= (358i + 275, 410i + 104) + [2](20i + 185, 281i + 239) \\
&= (122i + 309, 291i + 374),
\end{aligned}
$$

which is a point of order 27 on E_{a_0}.

Bob proceeds to compute his public key using only a combination of the point tripling operation in (2) and the 3-isogeny operation in (5). Below we will use the same conventions as we did for Alice, overriding the notations for E_{a_i} and ϕ_i to save additional subscripts.

- *Compute ϕ_0.* Initialise $S'_B = S_B = (122i + 309, 291i + 374)$. Two repeated applications of the tripling in (2) produces the point $R'_B = [9]S'_B = (23i + 37, 4i + 302)$, which has order 3 on E_{a_0}. Inputting R'_B into (5) gives $\phi_0 \colon E_{a_0} \to E_{a_1}$, with $a_1 = 134i + 2$ and $j(E_{a_1}) = 106i + 379$. It also gives the map $\phi_0 \colon x \mapsto \frac{x((23i+37)x-1)^2}{(x-(23i+37))^2}$, which is used to update $P'_A = \phi(P'_A) = (418i + 155, 288i + 331)$, $Q'_A = (159i + 242 : 310i + 425)$, and $S'_B = (295i + 256, 253i + 64)$; the orders of P'_A and Q'_A on E_{a_1} are unchanged, but the order of the new S'_B has decreased from 27 to 9. Figure 8 shows ϕ_0 as Bob's first step in the 3-isogeny graph.
- *Compute ϕ_1.* One tripling via (2) produces the point $R'_B = [3]S'_B = ((98i + 36, 56i + 155)$, which has order 3 on E_{a_1}. Inputting R'_B into (5) gives $\phi_1 \colon E_{a_1} \to E_{a_2}$, with $a_2 = 117i + 54$ and $j(E_{a_2}) = 325i + 379$. It also gives the map $\phi_1 \colon x \mapsto \frac{x((98i+36)x-1)^2}{(x-(98i+36))^2}$, which is used to update $P'_A = \phi(P'_A) = (252i + 425, 315i + 19)$, $Q'_A = (412i + 81 : 111i + 172)$,

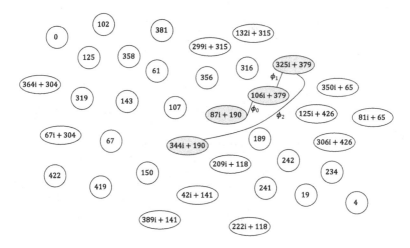

Fig. 8. Bob's key generation. He starts at the public curve corresponding to $j = 87i + 190$, his secret key is the isogeny $\phi_B = (\phi_2 \circ \phi_1 \circ \phi_0)$, and the destination node $344i + 190$ becomes part of his public key.

and $S'_B = (102i + 405, 375i + 313)$; the order of the new S'_B has decreased from 9 to 3. Figure 8 shows ϕ_1 as Bob's second step in the 3-isogeny graph.

- *Compute* ϕ_2. $S'_B = (102i + 405, 375i + 313)$ already has order 3 on E_{a_2}, so no scalar multiplication is needed. Inputting R'_B into (5) gives $\phi_2 \colon E_{a_2} \to E_{a_3}$, with $a_2 = 273i + 76$ and $j(E_{a_2}) = 344i + 190$. It also gives the map $\phi_1 \colon x \mapsto \frac{x((98i+36)x-1)^2}{(x-(98i+36))^2}$, which is used to update $P'_A = \phi(P'_A) = (187i+226, 43i+360)$, $Q'_A = (325i + 415, 322i + 254)$, and $S'_B = (102i + 405, 375i + 313)$; the point S'_B is in the kernel and is not carried through. Figure 8 shows ϕ_2 as Bob's third and final step in the 3-isogeny graph.

Bob's secret 3^3-isogeny is the composition of the three 3-isogenies detailed above, i.e. $\phi_B \colon E_{a_0} \to E_{a_3}$, $Q \mapsto \phi_B(Q)$, with $\phi_B = (\phi_2 \circ \phi_1 \circ \phi_0)$ - see Fig. 8. His public key, PK_B, is then

$$\begin{aligned}
\text{PK}_B &= (\phi_B(E_{a_0}), \phi_B(P_A), \phi_B(Q_A)) \\
&= (273i + 76, (187i + 226, 43i + 360), (325i + 415, 322i + 254)). \quad (7)
\end{aligned}$$

Alice's Shared Secret Computation. Alice starts from the curve output in Bob's public key in (7), taking her new starting curve E_{a_0} with $a_0 = 273i + 76$. Her first step is again to compute a secret generator on E_{a_0} corresponding to her secret k_A, as

$$\begin{aligned}
S_A &= \phi_B(P_A) + [k_A]\phi_B(Q_A) \\
&= (187i + 226, 43i + 360) + [11](325i + 415, 322i + 254) \\
&= (125i + 357, 415i + 249).
\end{aligned}$$

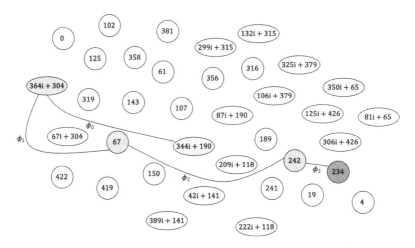

Fig. 9. Alice's shared secret computation. She starts at the curve from Bob's public key with $j = 344i + 190$, and uses her secret key to compute the walk to the node with $j = 234$, which is the shared secret.

She now proceeds exactly as before, performing the analogous sequence of operations as during key generation. The only difference is that she no longer needs to move any basis points through the isogeny, saving some computation because it is only the destination curve that she needs. The four 2-isogeny computations are summarised as

$$
\begin{aligned}
\phi_0 &: E_{a_0} \to E_{a_1}, & \text{with} \quad a_1 &= 289i + 341 & \text{and} \quad j(E_{a_1}) &= 364i + 304; \\
\phi_1 &: E_{a_1} \to E_{a_2}, & \text{with} \quad a_2 &= 414i + 428 & \text{and} \quad j(E_{a_2}) &= 67; \\
\phi_2 &: E_{a_2} \to E_{a_3}, & \text{with} \quad a_3 &= 246i & \text{and} \quad j(E_{a_3}) &= 242; \\
\phi_3 &: E_{a_3} \to E_{a_4}, & \text{with} \quad a_4 &= 230 & \text{and} \quad j(E_{a_4}) &= 234.
\end{aligned}
$$

Figure 9 depicts Alice's shared secret computation.

Bob's Shared Secret Computation. Bob starts from the curve output in Alice's public key in (6), taking his new starting curve E_{a_0} with $a_0 = 142i + 183$. His first step is again to compute a secret generator on E_{a_0} corresponding to her secret k_A, as

$$
\begin{aligned}
S_B &= \phi_A(P_B) + [k_B]\phi_A(Q_B) \\
&= (142i + 183, 119i + 360) + [2](220i + 314, 289i + 10) \\
&= (393i + 124, 187i + 380).
\end{aligned}
$$

Again, Bob proceeds exactly as he did during key generation, with the exception of moving Alice's basis points through the isogeny. His three 3-isogeny computations are summarised as

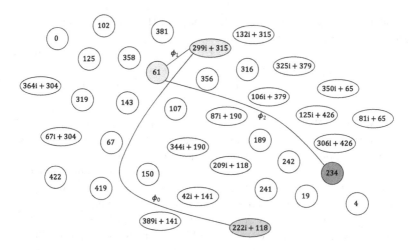

Fig. 10. Bob's shared secret computation. He starts at the curve from Alice's public key with $j = 222i + 118$, and uses his secret key to compute the walk to the node with $j = 234$, which is the shared secret.

$$\phi_0: E_{a_0} \to E_{a_1}, \quad \text{with} \quad a_1 = 183i + 177 \quad \text{and} \quad j(E_{a_1}) = 299i + 315;$$
$$\phi_1: E_{a_1} \to E_{a_2}, \quad \text{with} \quad a_2 = 31 \quad \text{and} \quad j(E_{a_2}) = 61;$$
$$\phi_2: E_{a_2} \to E_{a_3}, \quad \text{with} \quad a_3 = 230 \quad \text{and} \quad j(E_{a_3}) = 234.$$

Figure 10 depicts Bob's shared secret computation. Referring back to Fig. 9, we see that Alice and Bob have indeed arrived at the same shared value.

6 SIDH in Practice

As promised in Sect. 1, extending one's understanding from the running toy example to parameters of cryptographic size is rather straightforward. The four sets of primes in the SIKE proposal [8] are defined in exactly the same way as the toy prime $p = 2^4 3^3 - 1$. They are also of the form $p = 2^{e_A} 3^{e_B} - 1$, but instead have

$$
\begin{array}{llllll}
e_A = 216 & \text{and} & e_B = 137 & \text{in} & \text{SIKEp434;} \\
e_A = 250 & \text{and} & e_B = 159 & \text{in} & \text{SIKEp503;} \\
e_A = 305 & \text{and} & e_B = 192 & \text{in} & \text{SIKEp610;} \\
e_A = 372 & \text{and} & e_B = 239 & \text{in} & \text{SIKEp751.}
\end{array}
\tag{8}
$$

So, in SIKEp434 for example, Alice will be computing 216 steps in the 2-isogeny graph and Bob will be computing 137 steps in the 3-isogeny graph. The name SIKEp434 refers to the underlying prime p having 434 bits, and in this case the number of supersingular j-invariants (or nodes in the corresponding supersingular isogeny graphs) is between 2^{429} and 2^{430}.

The remainder of this section aims to highlight the more subtle differences that arise when ramping up from toy parameters to those of cryptographic size, and to bring the reader up to speed with the current state-of-the-art in SIDH.

Curse of the Toy Example. Of the 37 supersingular j-invariants over $\mathbb{F}_{431^2}$, 21 of them are defined over the ground field $\mathbb{F}_{431}$. This may seem to suggest that most (or at least a reasonable fraction) of the j-invariants will be defined over $\mathbb{F}_p$ in general, but it is important to stress that, as p grows large, this is not the case. As we saw in Sect. 2, the number of supersingular j-invariants in characteristic p is roughly $\lfloor p/12 \rfloor$, but it turns out that the number of supersingular j-invariants defined over $\mathbb{F}_p$ is in $\tilde{O}(\sqrt{p})$. In other words, for the types of supersingular isogeny graphs we work with in practice, the probability of a randomly chosen node (i.e. j-invariant) being defined over $\mathbb{F}_p$ is negligibly small. The reason that this is important is that the underlying problem of finding isogeny paths between two supersingular curves (more on this in Sect. 7) becomes much easier when both curves are defined over $\mathbb{F}_p$. For the problem to be as hard as possible, we need at least one of E and E' to have a j-invariant that is not in $\mathbb{F}_{p^2}$, and thus we want the chances of accidentally walking into such a j-invariant to be negligible.

Referring back to Figs. 4 and 5, recall that the nodes corresponding to $j \in \{0, 4, 125, 242\}$ appeared to have unusual edge behaviour in one or both of the 2- and 3-isogeny graphs. In all of these cases, there is either an edge from the given node back to itself, there is not the usual number of edges connecting to this node, or both. These correspond to exceptional cases where either (i) isogenies degenerate into isomorphisms (e.g. the 2-isogeny with kernel $(0,0)$ on E_0), or (ii) two or more kernel elements produce the same image j-invariant (e.g. the 3-isogenies emanating from the curve with $j = 4$). Again, with 4 out of 37 nodes being exceptional in our example, it may seem that the number of exceptional nodes is non-negligible as p grows large. However, the number of exceptional nodes stays this small as p grows larger, as can be seen by trying to force these exceptions in the isogeny formulas.

Finally, observe that Alice and Bob both walked to (or through) the node with $j = 344i + 190$ during key generation. This is another anomaly that occured because of the size of our example, which will be overwhelmingly unlikely for large parameter sets. Besides the exceptional j's mentioned above, the edges in Figs. 4 and 5 appear to be completely unrelated, and indeed this lack of any meaningful connection between Alice and Bob's graphs is at the heart of the security underlying SIDH.

Efficient Isogeny Computations. The isogeny computation routines we walked through in Sect. 5 give the general picture of how we compute ℓ^e-isogenies for $\ell \in \{2,3\}$. Namely, we start with a secret generator P of order ℓ^e, compute the point $[\ell^{e-1}]P$ of order ℓ by a scalar multiplication, and then use this point as the kernel of our first ℓ-isogeny $\phi_0 \colon E_0 \to E_1$. We then move the original point

P through ϕ_0 to compute $\phi_0(P)$ as the point of order ℓ^{e-1} on E_1, and start iterating this process by beginning with another scalar multiplication $[\ell^{e-2}]\phi_0(P)$. This was the method used in the original Jao and De Feo paper [9], but in the extended De Feo-Jao-Plût paper [5] it was shown that it is possible to do much better.

To sketch the idea, note that during the first scalar multiplication $P \mapsto [\ell^{e-1}]P$, we can store an intermediate multiple of P, say $Q = [\ell^d]P$ for $1 \leq d \leq e-2$. Then, rather than moving P through $\phi_0(P)$ and computing the scalar multiplication $\phi_0(P) \mapsto [\ell^{e-2}]\phi_0(P)$, we can move Q through, and use it to compute the scalar multiplication $\phi_0(Q) \mapsto [\ell^{e-d-2}]\phi_0(Q)$ instead. The larger we choose d, the more we save on this second scalar multiplication. However, the larger we choose d, the fewer the number of iterations the point $Q = [\ell^d]P$ is of use; each time we compute an isogeny, the orders of its successive images decrease by a factor of ℓ, until it is eventually moved to the point at infinity and is of no use thereafter. One fix that may spring to mind is to store all of the intermediate multiples of P for $1 \leq d \leq e-2$, which is certainly plausible, but this then means we would have to pull all $e-3$ of these points through the first isogeny, $e-4$ through the second isogeny, and so on, which becomes cumbersome. Determining exactly which multiples to store in the first step, and every consecutive step thereafter, becomes a rather complicated looking combinatorial problem whose optimisation factors in the value of e, and the cost ratios of scalar multiplication and isogeny operations. Fortunately, De Feo, Jao and Plût provide a fully optimised solution to this problem [5, §4.2.2] that becomes relatively simple to implement in practice. Interested readers can consult the SIKE specification [8] and the source codes that accompany it for further details.

Note that, while the explicit formulas for point and isogeny operations in this tutorial have been presented in affine space, i.e. with inversions, all of them have projective analogues that avoid inversions entirely. Just like in old school ECC, every secret operation in SIDH can be performed projectively and avoid all but the final inversion, which is used to normalise the result into its unique affine representation.

Compressed Public Keys. For ease of exposition, in Sect. 5 we conformed to the original specification of public keys, where Alice and Bob both produce public keys of the form

$$\mathrm{PK} = \big(\phi(E), \phi(P), \phi(Q)\big), \tag{9}$$

with ϕ being their secret isogeny, E is the starting curve, and with P and Q being the basis points of the other party. We wrote the curve E using one element of $\mathbb{F}_{p^2}$ (the Montgomery a parameter), and the points P and Q using two elements of $\mathbb{F}_{p^2}$ each. In practice, however, we actually specify the public keys inside the x-only Montgomery framework as $\mathrm{PK} = [x(\phi(P)), x(\phi(Q)), x(\phi(Q-P))]$, where $x(\phi(P))$ is the x-coordinate of $\phi(P)$, etc., and where these three elements can be used to recover the Montgomery a coordinate in a handful of field operations [8,

§1.1]. This requires only 3 elements of $\mathbb{F}_{p^2}$, is preferable to what we used in Sect. 5, and this is the state-of-the-art for "uncompressed" SIDH public keys.

It turns out that we can actually compress the public keys much further [2] by focussing on the second and third components of the public key in (9). The high level idea is that the $\mathbb{F}_{p^2}$ elements used to transmit the points $\phi(P)$ and $\phi(Q)$ are rather large compared to the size of the integer coefficients that are needed to represent them with respect to a given basis. We will return to our toy example to illustrate, recalling Alice's public key from (6) as

$$\begin{aligned}
\mathrm{PK}_A &= (\phi_A(E_{a_0}), \phi_A(P_B), \phi_A(Q_B)) \\
&= (423i + 179, (142i + 183, 119i + 360), (220i + 314, 289i + 10)),
\end{aligned}$$

where she had moved to the curve $E \colon y^2 = x^3 + (423i + 179)x^2 + x$, on which the points $\phi_A(P_B)$ and $\phi_A(Q_B)$ have order 3^3. For *any* basis of the 3^3-torsion on E, say the points R and S with $E[3^3] = \langle R, S \rangle$, we can write the points $\phi_A(P_B)$ and $\phi_A(Q_B)$ as

$$\phi_A(P_B) = [\alpha]R + [\beta]S \qquad \text{and} \qquad \phi_A(Q_B) = [\gamma]R + [\delta]S, \tag{10}$$

for some $\alpha, \beta, \gamma, \delta \in \{0, 1, 2, \ldots, 26\}$. If Alice can send $(\alpha, \beta, \gamma, \delta)$ instead of $\phi_A(P_B)$ and $\phi_A(Q_B)$, or even instead of $x(\phi_A(P_B))$ and $x(\phi_A(Q_B))$, this will be a significant decrease in bandwidth; 4 elements of $\mathbb{Z}_{27}$ is much smaller than the 4 elements of $\mathbb{F}_{431}$ that would be needed to send $x(\phi_A(P_B))$ and $x(\phi_A(Q_B))$. This whole idea hinges on Alice being able to indeed send $(\alpha, \beta, \gamma, \delta)$ to Bob without sending the basis points. This is achieved by Alice computing a basis $\{R, S\}$ deterministically from the curve $\phi_A(E_{a_0})$, in such a way that Bob will be able to start with her compressed public key

$$\big(\phi_A(E_{a_0}), (\alpha, \beta, \gamma, \delta)\big),$$

use $\phi_A(E_{a_0})$ to recover the same basis points R and S, and then recover $\phi_A(P_B)$ and $\phi_A(Q_B)$ exactly as in (10). Fortunately, it is relatively easy to devise methods to derive bases deterministically – see [8]. All that then remains is to show how Alice can decompose her points $\phi_A(P_B)$ and $\phi_A(Q_B)$ into $(\alpha, \beta, \gamma, \delta)$ with respect to this basis. This requires that Alice can solve two-dimensional discrete logarithm problems of the form in (10), which turns out to be possible in practice due to all of our supersingular elliptic curves having very smooth group orders[5], i.e. group orders whose largest prime factors are 3.

In general, both Alice and Bob can compress their public keys to be of the form $\big(\phi_A(E_{a_0}), (\alpha, \beta, \gamma, \delta)\big)$ and $\big(\phi_B(E_{a_0}), (\alpha', \beta', \gamma', \delta')\big)$, improving from three elements in $\mathbb{F}_{p^2}$ to one element of $\mathbb{F}_{p^2}$ and 4 elements of either $\mathbb{Z}_{2^{e_A}}$ or $\mathbb{Z}_{3^{e_B}}$. Furthermore, one of the integer components can be neglected in both cases by performing a normalisation across the bases. Assuming that $2^{e_A} \approx 3^{e_B} \approx p^{1/2}$, this shrinks both public keys to around 60% of their original size – see [8] for further details.

---

[5] We remind the reader that the security of SIDH/SIKE is unrelated to discrete logarithm problems!

7 Security and Cryptanalysis

We conclude the tutorial with a brief discussion on the security of SIDH. The first order of business is to address the difference between SIDH and SIKE.

SIDH Versus SIKE. The computational problems related to the SIDH protocol are usually stated by listing a tuple corresponding to all of the information that a passive adversary would see, and then asking the attacker to either find the underlying secret isogeny (the search problem – see [7, Definition 2]), or to decide whether or not the tuple is indeed a well-formed instance of the SIDH problem (the decisional problem – see [7, Definition 3]). Given the four basis points in the public parameters, and their image points that are included in the public keys, these tuples contain substantially more information than just the preimage and image curves of the secret isogeny. One of the main assumptions made in the SIDH landscape is that all of these preimage and image points do not help a *passive* adversary in solving the more general problem which is to *compute the degree-ℓ^e isogeny*

$$\phi \colon E \to E', \tag{11}$$

that connects the curves E and E' in the supersingular isogeny graph. This assumption has remained valid to date, and there have been no known passive attacks that can make use of the auxiliary image points for the types of SIDH parameters used in practice.

However, the need to transmit these image points becomes a significant drawback when considering the combination of active adversaries and the use of static keys. Galbraith, Petit, Shani and Ti [6] showed that, if Alice or Bob is reusing a secret key for many protocol instances, a malicious party can actively learn their entire secret by performing as many interactions as the bitlength of their key.

We will return to our running example in Sect. 5 to illustrate the basic idea. Recall from (6) that Alice's public key was

$$\begin{aligned}
\mathrm{PK}_A &= (\phi_A(E_{a_0}), \phi_A(P_B), \phi_A(Q_B)) \\
&= (423i + 179, (142i + 183, 119i + 360), (220i + 314, 289i + 10)),
\end{aligned}$$

which corresponded to her secret $k_A = 11$, and recall that Bob's public key was

$$\begin{aligned}
\mathrm{PK}_B &= (\phi_B(E_{a_0}), \phi_B(P_A), \phi_B(Q_A)) \\
&= (273i + 76, (187i + 226, 43i + 360), (325i + 415, 322i + 254)),
\end{aligned}$$

which corresponded to his secret $k_B = 2$. Furthemore, recall that the first step in Alice's shared secret computation was to use Bob's public key and her secret to compute the new kernel as

$$\begin{aligned}
S_A &= \phi_B(P_A) + [k_A]\phi_B(Q_A) \\
&= (187i + 226, 43i + 360) + [11](325i + 415, 322i + 254) \\
&= (125i + 357, 415i + 249).
\end{aligned}$$

Now suppose that Bob wants to learn Alice's static secret. Following [6, §3.1], rather than sending his second image point $\phi_B(Q_A) = (325i + 415, 322i + 254)$, he will add it to a point of order 2 on $E_{273i+76}$, say $T_2 = (245i + 27, 0)$, to get $(325i + 415, 322i + 254) + (245i + 27, 0) = (76i + 247, 114i + 208)$, and instead send the malicious public key

$$\mathrm{PK}'_B = (\phi_B(E_{a_0}), \phi_B(P_A), \phi_B(Q_A) + T_2)$$
$$= (273i + 76, (187i + 226, 43i + 360), (76i + 247, 114i + 208)),$$

where the first two components remain unchanged. Bob will proceed as usual, taking Alice's static key and his secret $k_B = 2$ to arrive at the shared secret $j_B = 234$ as in Fig. 10. However, Alice will now compute

$$S'_A = \phi_B(P_A) + [k_A](\phi_B(Q_A) + T_2)$$
$$= (187i + 226, 43i + 360) + [11](90i + 354, 21i + 317)$$
$$= (353i + 23, 152i + 277),$$

which is a point of order 16 that is different from S_A. Moreover, $\langle S'_A \rangle \neq \langle S_A \rangle$, so the two isogenies generated by these two kernels will be different. Indeed, Alice computes the 16-isogeny from $E_{273i+76}$ with kernel $\langle S'_A \rangle$ and arrives at the node with $j_A = 242$.

The SIDH protocol will fail because $j_B \neq j_A$, at which point Bob immediately knows the final bit of Alice's secret; if Alice's secret were even, then it is easy to see that Bob's adding the point T_2 to $\phi_B(Q_A)$ would have produced $S'_A = S_A$, and the protocol would have gone through smoothly. Thus, whether or not the protocol succeeds, Bob learns a bit of Alice's secret. In [6, §3.2] the attack is continued *bit by bit* until Bob reconstructs all but the last two bits of Alice's secret, which can be brute forced with no further interaction – see [6, Algorithm 1].

Unfortunately there is currently no known way for Alice to check that Bob's public key is well-formed and non-malicious, and this is the reason that SIDH must either (i) insist that both parties use purely ephemeral secret keys, i.e. use each secret key once, or (ii) use a generic passive-to-active transformation (see [8]) to allow one of the two parties to reuse a long-term secret.

SIKE stands for supersingular isogeny key encapsulation, which applies such a generic transformation to SIDH in order to allow Alice to safely use a long-term static secret. The basic idea is that Bob must use Alice's fixed public key and his secret key to compute the true shared secret j before sending any information to Alice. Moreover, the secret key k_B he uses is computed as the output of a cryptographic hash function whose input is Alice's public key and a randomly chosen value m, i.e. he uses $k_B = H(\mathrm{PK}_A, m)$. Along with his usual public key, he *encapsulates* the random value m by XOR-ing it with a hash of the shared secret, $H'(j)$, and sends

$$(\mathrm{PK}_B, H'(j) \oplus m)$$

to Alice, where PK_B is as usual. She can now use PK_B and her secret key to compute j and then $H'(j)$, and this allows her to recover Bob's initial random value m. Alice can then recompute Bob's secret $k_B = H(\text{PK}_A, m)$ and then check that PK_B is exactly as it should be, i.e. that Bob has not acted maliciously. If this check passes, Alice can carry on as usual, but if not, she can presume Bob is acting maliciously and can output garbage. This way, Bob will always get back garbage if he tampers with the protocol, and he will learn nothing about Alice's secret through doing so.

Basic Properties of Supersingular Isogeny Graphs. In discussing the security landscape of SIDH, it is important to understand some basic facts about supersingular isogeny graphs; these can be seen for our toy example by eyeballing Figs. 4 and 5, but they hold true in general. Supersingular ℓ-isogeny graphs are both *connected*, meaning there is always a path between any two nodes, and $(\ell + 1)$-*regular*, meaning every vertex has precisely $\ell + 1$ connected neighbouring vertices[6]. They are also instances of *expander graphs* which are said to have *rapid mixing*. Very roughly speaking, this means that when starting at any node in the graph, only a relatively small number of steps (i.e. logarithmic in the number of nodes) is needed for a random walk to converge to a uniform distribution. In other words, we can pick any node in the graph, and so long as our walks are of a requisite (but relatively small) length, they can take us to any other node in the graph. Another way to state this is in terms of the graph's *diameter*, which is the maximum number of steps needed to connect any two nodes in the graph; an expander graph with N nodes has a diameter in $O(\log N)$. Astute readers should consult [5, §2] and the references therein for more precise statements[7].

The van Oorschot-Wiener Collision Finding Algorithm. We now turn to describing the current state-of-the-art in cryptanalysis against SIDH. Assuming that both Alice and Bob use one-time ephemeral SIDH keys, or that SIKE is used to protect one side's static keys, we are now back in the situation where the best known attacks do not use any of the basis points, and where we are trying to solve the problem in (11): given two ℓ^e-isogenous curves E and E' in the supersingular isogeny graph, compute the corresponding isogeny.

For concreteness, consider the smallest set of SIKE parameters with $p = 2^{216}3^{137} - 1$, for which there are more than 2^{429} nodes in the corresponding supersingular isogeny graph, and suppose we are trying to find Alice's secret isogeny of degree 2^{216}.

$$\phi_A \colon E \to E_A$$

Since the degree of our isogeny is fixed and known, this problem is a rather special instance of the general isogeny problem, which asks to find an isogeny connecting *any* two nodes in the graph. Our job is a lot easier than solving

---

[6] Edges can have multiplicities greater than 1, which takes care of the tiny handful of anomalies we discussed in Sect. 6.

[7] An even less formal but more visual interpretation of this property (with respect to Figs. 4 and 5) would be to say that there is no way to position the nodes so that drawing the edges makes the pictures appreciably less messy.

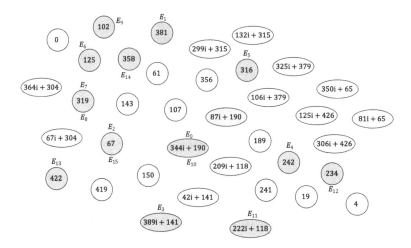

Fig. 11. Alice's possible destination nodes (in green) when starting at E with $j(E) = 87i + 190$, and computing 2^4-isogenies to the curves $E_k = E/\langle P_A + [k]Q_A \rangle$ with $k \in \{0, 1, \ldots, 15\}$. (Color figure online)

this general problem among the $\approx 2^{429}$ nodes, since the 216 steps taken by Alice falls significantly short of the diameter of the graph. To see this, we can count the number of possible destination nodes for Alice's 2^{216} by counting the number of distinct order-2^{216} subgroups on E; the number of order-ℓ^e subgroups is $\ell^{e-1}(\ell+1)$ in general, so in our case there are exactly $2^{216} + 2^{215}$ possibilities for E_A. We depict this property for our toy example in Fig. 11, but emphasise that as p grows large the destination (green) nodes become exponentially sparse among all nodes; the graphs have $O(p)$ nodes and only $O(\sqrt{p})$ of them are possible destination nodes.

It is for this reason that random walk algorithms for solving the general isogeny problem are not the best known algorithms against SIDH. The 216 steps is much smaller than the average number of steps connecting two given nodes (across all pairs of nodes), so it is overwhelmingly likely that the walk Alice took from E to E_A is the shortest walk between those two nodes. Thus, the best algorithms for computing ϕ_A are *meet-in-the-middle* algorithms, whereby we perform walks of 108 steps from both E and E_A until two of these walks reach *the* middle node; it is then overwhelmingly likely that these two walks connect to be exactly the walk that Alice took, and the problem is solved.

The generic version of meet in the middle builds a table of *all* of the curves that are 2^{108}-isogenous to E_A (of which there are $2^{108} + 2^{107}$), and then computes each 2^{108}-isogeny from E, one at a time, until a match is found in the table. Since $2^{108} \approx p^{1/4}$, this gives an attack that runs in $O(p^{1/4})$ time and requires $O(p^{1/4})$ memory (so long as SIDH instances are constructed with $2^{e_A} \approx 3^{e_B}$, then these complexities remain the same when targeting either party's secret isogeny). Indeed, these were the asymptotic complexities originally stated by

Jao and De Feo [9], and those that were used to analyse SIKE's security in the Round 1 submission.

A 2018 paper by Adj, Cervantes-Vázquez, Chi-Domínguez, Menezes and Rodríguez-Henríquez [1] analysed the security of SIDH and SIKE more concretely, and showed that the generic version of meet-in-the-middle is, overall, not the best algorithm for solving the underlying isogeny problems. More specifically, they argued that the exponential storage requirements (of more than 2^{108} bits in the smallest case of `SIKEp434`) essentially makes generic meet-in-the-middle irrelevant, particularly when comparing its runtime to the runtimes of attacks against other cryptographic primitives (as is required when positioning the security against NIST's target levels – see [15]). Adj *et al.* proposed that the correct way to analyse security is to fix an upper bound on the possible memory (they specified $w = 2^{80}$ as a possible yet still presently infeasible such bound), and to analyse the runtimes of the best known algorithms subject to this storage capacity. Their conclusion is that the van Oorschot-Wiener (vOW) parallel collision finding algorithm [17] is then the superior algorithm for finding ϕ.

We will briefly sketch the intuition behind the vOW algorithm in our context. Since all of the curves that are 2^{108}-isogenous to E_A can no longer fit in our table (of, say, size $w = 2^{80}$), we instead fill the table with curves from both sides, i.e. image curves that are either 2^{108}-isogenous to E or curves that are 2^{108}-isogenous to E_A. As before, we are still hoping for a collision in the table, when a walk from E produces the same image curve as a walk from E_A. However, given the storage capacity, even when we come across this middle curve from one side, the chances that it is already in the table are very small, and we have no way of knowing that this is the middle curve until we have run into it from the other side. Thus, we can either discard that image curve, or use it to replace an existing memory element. Either way, we could be discarding one side of the solution we seek, or the other side could have previously been overwritten.

Henceforth we will stop using the term (image) curves and instead refer to the elements of a set S, which we define to be the set of all j-invariants that are 2^{108}-isogenous to E or 2^{108}-isogenous to E_A. A better way to use the 2^{80} memory is to instead define a deterministic but pseudo-random walk on S, and to define a property that *distinguishes* certain elements of S; these elements are the only ones that we send to memory. In this case we have roughly 2^{109} elements in S, so we could define a property that distinguishes around 1 in every 2^{30} elements in order to fit all (if not close to all) of the distinguished elements in memory. Our pseudo-random function

$$f \colon S \to S$$

will take a j-invariant, feed it into a cryptographic hash function to produce a new string, use one bit of this string to decide whether we are to compute an isogeny from E or E_A, and then use the rest of the string to choose a subgroup/isogeny, which in turn produces a new j-invariant. To produce pseudo-random walks on S, we start with an initial element $x_0 \in S$ and use the function $f \colon x_i \mapsto x_{i+1}$ to iterate until we come across an element, x_n, that is distinguished[8]. When this happens, we store the distinguished element (together with the initial value x_0) in memory, otherwise we keep walking. We pick starting points at random, and perform many of these walks to collect pairs of initial and distinguished elements in memory; moreover, these walks are independent of each other so the process parallelises perfectly.

Let $x \in S$ and $y \in S$ be such that $x \neq y$, $f(x) = f(y) = z$, x gets mapped (via f) through a subgroup on E, and y gets mapped through a subgroup on E_A. It follows that z is the middle j-invariant that solves our problem. Now, it is very unlikely that z will be a distinguished element, but so long as we have a walk that finds x and another walk that finds y, f being deterministic guarantees that they will then walk on the same elements and thus into the same distinguished element. When the second of these two walks sends its distinguished element to memory, we will find that this distinguished element has already been found, and we will then be able to redo both walks and recover x and y.

Using such a function f and a distinguished element criterion solves our problem of not being able to store all of the elements corresponding to E_A in memory, but in doing so it introduces several new problems. Many of these are closely related to f behaving like a random function. For example, while we know that there is a unique subgroup on E and a unique subgroup on E_A that solves the problem, our particular choice of f (recall that it involves a cryptographic hash function) might be such that there is no x and/or y that pass through these subgroups under f, so that we will never terminate with the solution. Or, even if there are values of x and y that solve the problem under f, it could be that x and y themselves have no preimages under f. In this case our only chance of solving the problem is in the overwhelmingly unlikely case that we happen to pick both of them as starting points of our random walks. Furthermore, the solution we seek is no longer the only $x \neq y$ with $f(x) = f(y)$; in fact, we have introduced many, many more such collisions by virtue of f behaving like a random function.

What we would ultimately hope for is that we use a function f for which both x and y exist (ideally, several such x and y would exist), and for which there are many random walks that lead to x and y under f. The problem is, we have no way of knowing how good or bad a given random function f is for our particular problem instance. Thus, as is discussed by van Oorschot and Wiener [17], after filling and refilling/overwriting our entire memory under a given function f, the optimisation of this entire process forces us to abandon all of the prior computations and switch to an entirely new function, essentially restarting the attack.

Both the implementation and the concrete runtime analysis [17, §4.2] of this algorithm are non-trivial. In summary, a line of recent works studying and implementing the attack [1,3,10] all essentially confirm the original runtime analysis of van Oorschot and Wiener in the context of SIDH: if the available memory

---

[8] This distinguishing property can essentially be anything, so long as it yields the right fraction of elements; in our example, a good choice would be to hash the element and check for 30 leading zeros.

can hold w elements from the set of size S, and with m processors working in parallel, the runtime, T, of the algorithm is

$$T = \left(\frac{2.5}{m} \sqrt{\frac{|S|^3}{w}} \right) \cdot t,$$

where t is the time taken to compute one function iteration, which boils down to one $\ell^{e/2}$-isogeny computation. In SIDH we have $|S| \approx p^{1/4}$, so (with $w = 2^{80}$) we can see that the runtime of vOW becomes worse than the runtime of generic meet-in-the-middle for all of the SIKE parameters, and this gap widens as p grows larger. Nevertheless, this remains the best known concrete algorithm for solving the specialised isogeny problems underlying SIDH.

Finally, we remark that the vOW algorithm is entirely classical. An excellent recent paper by Jaques and Schanck [10] investigated a range of *quantum* attacks against SIDH, but ultimately showed that the concrete improvement across all relevant avenues of quantum attack is rather minimal, if at all.

References

1. Adj, G., Cervantes-Vázquez, D., Chi-Domínguez, J., Menezes, A., Rodríguez-Henríquez, F.: On the cost of computing isogenies between supersingular elliptic curves. In: Cid, C., Jacobson, M.J. (eds.) SAC 2018. LNCS, vol. 11349, pp. 322–343. Springer, Berlin (2018). https://doi.org/10.1007/978-3-030-10970-7_15
2. Azarderakhsh, R., Jao, D., Kalach, K., Koziel, B., Leonardi, C:. Key compression for isogeny-based cryptosystems. In: Emura, K., Hanaoka, G., Zhang, R. (eds.) Proceedings of the 3rd ACM International Workshop on ASIA Public-Key Cryptography, AsiaPKC@AsiaCCS, Xi'an, China, 30 May–03 June 2016, pp. 1–10. ACM (2016)
3. Costello, C., Longa, P., Naehrig, M., Renes, J., Virdia, F.: Improved classical cryptanalysis of the computational supersingular isogeny problem. IACR Cryptol. ePrint Archive **2019**, 298 (2019)
4. De Feo, L.: Mathematics of isogeny based cryptography. CoRR, abs/1711.04062 (2017). https://arxiv.org/pdf/1711.04062.pdf
5. De Feo, L., Jao, D., Plût, J.: Towards quantum-resistant cryptosystems from supersingular elliptic curve isogenies. J. Math. Cryptol. **8**(3), 209–247 (2014)
6. Galbraith, S.D., Petit, C., Shani, B., Ti, Y.B.: On the security of supersingular isogeny cryptosystems. In: Cheon, J.H., Takagi, T. (eds.) ASIACRYPT 2016. LNCS, vol. 10031, pp. 63–91. Springer, Heidelberg (2016). https://doi.org/10.1007/978-3-662-53887-6_3
7. Galbraith, S.D., Vercauteren, F.: Computational problems in supersingular elliptic curve isogenies. Quantum Inf. Process. **17**(10), 265 (2018)
8. Jao, D., et al.: SIKE: supersingular isogeny key encapsulation. Manuscript available at sike.org/ (2017)
9. Jao, D., De Feo, L.: Towards quantum-resistant cryptosystems from supersingular elliptic curve isogenies. In: Yang, B.-Y. (ed.) PQCrypto 2011. LNCS, vol. 7071, pp. 19–34. Springer, Heidelberg (2011). https://doi.org/10.1007/978-3-642-25405-5_2

10. Jaques, S., Schanck, J.M.: Quantum cryptanalysis in the RAM model: claw-finding attacks on SIKE. In: Boldyreva, A., Micciancio, D. (eds.) CRYPTO 2019. LNCS, vol. 11692, pp. 32–61. Springer, Cham (2019). https://doi.org/10.1007/978-3-030-26948-7_2

11. Montgomery, P.L.: Speeding the Pollard and elliptic curve methods of factorization. Math. Comput. **48**(177), 243–264 (1987)

12. Silverman, J.H.: The Arithmetic of Elliptic Curves. Graduate Texts in Mathematics, 2nd edn. Springer, Berlin (2009)

13. Smith, B.: Pre- and Post-quantum Diffie–Hellman from groups, actions, and isogenies. In: Budaghyan, L., Rodríguez-Henríquez, F. (eds.) WAIFI 2018. LNCS, vol. 11321, pp. 3–40. Springer, Cham (2018). https://doi.org/10.1007/978-3-030-05153-2_1

14. Tate, J.: Endomorphisms of abelian varieties over finite fields. Inventiones Math. **2**(2), 134–144 (1966)

15. The National Institute of Standards and Technology (NIST): Submission requirements and evaluation criteria for the post-quantum cryptography standardization process, December 2016. https://csrc.nist.gov/CSRC/media/Projects/Post-Quantum-Cryptography/documents/call-for-proposals-final-dec-2016.pdf

16. Urbanik, D.: A friendly introduction to supersingular isogeny Diffie-Hellman, May 2017. https://csclub.uwaterloo.ca/~dburbani/work/friendlysidh.pdf

17. van Oorschot, P.C., Wiener, M.J.: Parallel collision search with cryptanalytic applications. J. Cryptol. **12**(1), 1–28 (1999)

18. Vélu, J.: Isogénies entre courbes elliptiques. CR Acad. Sci. Paris Sér. AB **273**, A238–A241 (1971)

Differential Cryptanalysis

Probabilistic Mixture Differential Cryptanalysis on Round-Reduced AES

Lorenzo Grassi[1,2](✉)

[1] IAIK, Graz University of Technology, Graz, Austria
lorenzo.grassi@iaik.tugraz.at
[2] Know-Center GmbH, Graz, Austria

Abstract. At Eurocrypt 2017 the first secret-key distinguisher for 5-round AES has been presented. Although it allows to distinguish a random permutation from an AES-like one, it seems (rather) hard to exploit such a distinguisher in order to implement a key-recovery attack different than brute-force like. On the other hand, such result has been exploited to set up a new (competitive) secret-key distinguisher for 4-round AES, called "Mixture Differential Cryptanalysis".

In this paper, we combine this new 4-round distinguisher with a modified version of a truncated differential distinguisher in order to set up a new 5-round distinguisher, that exploits properties which are independent of the secret key, of the details of the S-Box and of the Mix-Columns matrix. As a result, while a "classical" truncated differential distinguisher exploits the probability that a pair of (two) texts satisfies or not a given differential trail independently of the others pairs, our distinguisher works with sets of $N \gg 2$ (related) pairs of texts. In particular, our new 5-round AES distinguisher exploits the fact that such sets of texts satisfy some properties with a different probability than for a random permutation.

Even if such 5-round distinguisher has a higher complexity than e.g. the "multiple-of-8" one present in the literature, it can be used as starting point to set up the *first* key-recovery attack on 6-round AES that exploits *directly* a 5-round secret-key distinguisher. The goal of this paper is indeed to present and explore new approaches, showing that even a distinguisher like the one presented at Eurocrypt – believed to be hard to exploit – can be the starting point for new secret-key distinguishers and/or key-recovery attacks.

Keywords: AES · Secret-key distinguisher · Key-recovery attack · Truncated differential · Mixture differential cryptanalysis

1 Introduction

One of the weakest attacks that can be launched against a secret-key cipher is a secret-key distinguisher. In this attack, there are two oracles: one that simulates the cipher for which the cryptographic key has been chosen at random and

© Springer Nature Switzerland AG 2020
K. G. Paterson and D. Stebila (Eds.): SAC 2019, LNCS 11959, pp. 53–84, 2020.
https://doi.org/10.1007/978-3-030-38471-5_3

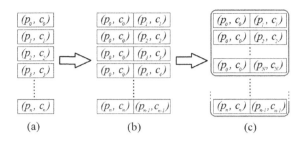

Fig. 1. *New Differential Secret-Key Distinguishers for up to 5-round AES.* Consider n (plaintexts, ciphertexts) (a). In a "classical" differential attack (b), one works independently on each pair of two texts, and exploits the probability that it satisfies a certain differential trail. In our attack (c), one divides the pairs of texts into *non-random* sets of cardinality (much) larger than 2, and exploits particular (differential) properties that hold among the texts that belong to the same set in order to set up a distinguisher.

one that simulates a truly random permutation. The adversary can query both oracles and her task is to decide which oracle is the cipher and which is the random permutation. The attack is considered to be successful if the number of queries required to make a correct decision is below a well defined level.

At Eurocrypt 2017, Grassi *et al.* [10] presented the first secret-key distinguisher for 5-round AES which exploits a property which is independent of the secret key and of the details of the S-Box. This distinguisher is based on a new structural property for up to 5 rounds of AES: by appropriate choices of a number of input pairs it is possible to make sure that the number of times that the difference of the resulting output pairs lie in a particular subspace is *always* a multiple of 8. This distinguisher allows to distinguish an AES permutation from a random one using 2^{32} chosen texts and a computational cost of $2^{35.6}$ look-ups.

Later, at FSE/ToSC 2019 "mixture-differential cryptanalysis" [8] has been proposed, a way to translate the (complex) "multiple-of-8" 5-round distinguisher into a simpler and more convenient one (though, on a smaller number of rounds). Given a pair of chosen plaintexts, the idea is to construct new pairs of plaintexts by mixing the generating variables of the original pair of plaintexts. It is possible to prove that for 4-round AES the corresponding ciphertexts of the original pair of plaintexts lie in a particular subspace if and only if the corresponding pairs of ciphertexts of the new pairs of plaintexts have the same property.

Such technique has then been used in [1], where authors showed how to attack 5-round AES in data, memory and time complexities of less than $2^{22.5}$, which is about 500 times faster than any previous attack on the same variant. Moreover, by extending this technique to larger versions of AES, authors also obtained new attacks on 7-round AES-192 (and AES-256) with practical data and memory complexities.

1.1 A New Secret-Key Distinguisher for up to 5-Round AES

In this paper, we present a new secret-key distinguisher for 5-round AES which exploits in a different way the multiple-of-8 property presented at Eurocrypt 2017 [10] and the property exhibited by mixture-differential cryptanalysis [8]. Such distinguishers – presented in detail in Sect. 5 – can be seen as a generalization of "classical" truncated differential attacks, as introduced by Knudsen in [12]. A comparison of all known secret-key distinguishers on 5-round AES and the ones proposed in this paper is given in Table 1.

Differential attacks exploit the fact that pairs of plaintexts with certain differences yield other differences in the corresponding ciphertexts with a non-uniform probability distribution[1]. Such a property can be used both to distinguish an AES permutation from a random one, and to recover the secret key. One possible variant is the truncated differential one [12], in which the attacker considers only part of the difference between pairs of texts, i.e. a differential attack where only part of the difference in the ciphertexts can be predicted. We emphasize that in these cases the attacker focuses on the probability that a single pair of plaintexts with certain difference yield other difference in the corresponding pair of ciphertexts, working *independently* on each pair of texts.

Our new distinguishers proposed in this paper are also differential in nature. However, instead of working on each pair of two texts independently of the others as in the previous case, in our case one divides the pairs of texts in set of cardinality larger than two and works on the relations that hold among the pairs of texts that belong to the same set. In other words, *given a single pair of two texts with a certain input/output difference, one studies how such pair influences other pairs of texts to satisfy particular input/output differences.* The

Table 1. *Secret-Key Distinguishers for 5-round AES – Independent of the Secret-Key.* The complexity is measured in minimum number of chosen plaintexts/ciphertexts (CP/CC) or/and adaptive chosen plaintexts/ciphertexts (ACP/ACC) which are needed to distinguish the AES permutation from a random one with probability higher than 95% (all distinguishers work both in the encryption and decryption mode). Time complexity is measured in equivalent encryptions (E), memory accesses (M) or XOR operations (XOR) – using the common approximation 20 M $\approx$ 1 Round of Encryption. Distinguisher of this paper is in bold.

Property	Data	Cost	Ref.
Yoyo	2^{12} CP + $2^{25.8}$ ACC	$2^{24.8}$ XOR	[13]
Multiple-of-8	2^{32} CP	$2^{35.6}$ M $\approx 2^{29}$ E	[10]
Variance Diff.	2^{34} CP	$2^{37.6}$ M $\approx 2^{31}$ E	[9]
Truncated Diff.	2^{49} CP	$2^{52.6}$ M $\approx 2^{46}$ E	[9]
Prob. Mixture Diff.	**2^{52} CP**	**$2^{71.5}$ M $\approx 2^{64.9}$ E**	**Sect. 5**

Prob. Mixture Diff.: Probabilistic Mixture Differential

---

[1] *A pair of texts has a certain difference if and only if the texts belong to the same coset of a particular subspace $\mathcal{X}$.*

Table 2. *Comparison of Key-Recovery Attacks on 6-round AES-128.* Data complexity is measured in number of required chosen plaintexts/ciphertexts (CP/CC). Time complexity is measured in round-reduced AES encryption equivalents (E) – the number in the brackets denotes the precomputation cost (if not negligible). Memory complexity is measured in texts (16 bytes). R_{Dist} denotes the number of rounds of the secret-key distinguisher exploited to set up the attack. Attack presented in this paper is in bold.

Attack	Data	Computation	Memory	R_{Dist}	Ref.
MitM	2^8 CP	$2^{106.2}$	$2^{106.2}$	-	[6]
Mixture Diff.	$2^{27.5}$ CP	2^{81}	$2^{27.5}$	4	[1]
Partial Sum	2^{32} CP	2^{42}	2^{40}	4	[15]
Integral	2^{35} CP	$2^{69.7}$	2^{32}	4	[5]
Prob. Mix Diff.	$\mathbf{2^{72.8}}$ **CP**	$\mathbf{2^{105}}$	$\mathbf{2^{33}}$	**5**	**Sect. 6**
Imp. Differential	$2^{91.5}$ CP	2^{122}	2^{89}	4	[3]

MitM: Meet-in-the-Middle, EE: Extension at End, EB: Extension at Beginning

sets are constructed in a such a way that pairs with similar properties belong to the same sets.

Referring to Fig. 1, given n chosen (plaintexts, ciphertexts), in a "classical" (differential) attack one works on each pair of two texts independently of the others – case (b). In our distinguishers/attacks, one first divides the pairs in (non-random) sets of cardinality $N \geq 2$ – case (c). These sets are defined such that particular relationships (that involve differential and linear relations) hold among the plaintexts that belong to the same set. In more details, such relations are the same ones proposed in *Mixture Differential Cryptanalysis* [8]. Exploiting particular (differential) properties that hold among the ciphertexts that are in the same set, it's possible to set up distinguishers/attacks on round-reduced AES.

Probabilistic Mixture Differential **5-Round Secret-Key Distinguisher.** Our 5-round secret-key "*Probabilistic Mixture Differential*" distinguisher exploits the following property. Given sets of $N \geq 2$ *non-independent* pairs of texts, it is possible to prove the following:

consider the number of sets for which two ciphertexts of at least one pair belong to the same coset of a particular subspace $\mathcal{M}$; if the sets are properly defined, then this number of sets is (a little) lower for 5-round AES than for a random permutation (details are given in Sect. 5).

As we are going to show, *this property is independent of the secret key, of the details of the S-Box and of the MixColumns matrix.*

Other Similar *Distinguishers* for 5-Round AES. Before going on, we mention that similar (but less competitive) distinguishers – namely, an "Impossible Mixture Differential" distinguisher and a "Threshold Mixture Differential" one – have been proposed in [7]. Such distinguishers are constructed using the same strategy just proposed for the "Probabilistic Mixture Differential" one, but they exploit different properties (e.g. an impossible differential property in the first case).

1.2 New Key-Recovery Attack on 6-Round AES-128

Even if our distinguisher has higher data and computational complexities than e.g. the one presented in [10], it allows to set up *the first 6 rounds key-recovery attack on AES-128 that exploits directly a 5-round secret-key distinguisher* (i.e. based on a property which is independent of the secret key) – see Table 2. The idea of this attack – proposed in detail in Sect. 6 – is to choose plaintexts in the same coset of a particular subspace $\mathcal{D}$ which is mapped after one round into a coset of another subspace $\mathcal{C}$. Using the distinguisher just introduced and the facts that

- the way in which the pairs are divided in sets depends on the (partially) guessed key,
- the behavior of a set for a wrongly guessed key is (approximately) the same as the case of a random permutation,

it is possible to deduce the right key.

2 Preliminary – Description of AES

The Advanced Encryption Standard [5] is a *Substitution-Permutation network* that supports a key size of 128, 192 and 256 bits. The 128-bit plaintext initializes the internal state represented by a 4×4 matrix of bytes seen as values in the finite field $\mathbb{F}_{256}$, defined using the irreducible polynomial $x^8 + x^4 + x^3 + x + 1$. Depending on the version of AES, N_r round are applied to the state: $N_r = 10$ for AES-128, $N_r = 12$ for AES-192 and $N_r = 14$ for AES-256. An AES round applies four operations to the state matrix:

- *SubBytes* (S-Box) – applying the same 8-bit to 8-bit invertible S-Box 16 times in parallel on each byte of the state (provides non-linearity in the cipher);
- *ShiftRows* (SR) – cyclic shift of each row (i-th row is shifted by i bytes to the left);
- *MixColumns* (MC) – multiplication of each column by a constant 4×4 invertible matrix over the field $GF(2^8)$ (together with the ShiftRows operation, it provides diffusion in the cipher);
- *AddRoundKey* (ARK) – XORing the state with a 128-bit subkey.

One round of AES can be described as $R(x) = K \oplus MC \circ SR \circ$ S-Box(x). In the first round an additional AddRoundKey operation (using a whitening key) is applied, and in the last round the MixColumns operation is omitted.

Notation Used in the Paper. Let x denote a plaintext, a ciphertext, an intermediate state or a key. Then $x_{i,j}$ with $i, j \in \{0, ..., 3\}$ denotes the byte in the row i and in the column j. We denote by k^r the key of the r-th round (k^0 is equivalent to the secret key for AES-128). If only one subkey is used (e.g. the first subkey k^0), then we denote it by k to simplify the notation. Finally, we denote by R one round[2] of AES, while we denote r rounds of AES by R^r. As a last thing, in the paper we often use the term "partial collision" (or "*collision*") when two texts belong to the same coset of a given subspace $\mathcal{X}$.

3 Subspace Trail Cryptanalysis

The concept of *trails of subspaces* [11] has been introduced at FSE/ToSC 2017 as a generalization of invariant subspace.

Definition 1. *Let F denote a round function in an iterative block cipher and let $(V_1, V_2, \ldots, V_{r+1})$ denote a set of $r+1$ subspaces with $\dim(V_i) \leq \dim(V_{i+1})$. If for each $i = 1, \ldots, r$ and for each a_i, there exists a_{i+1} s.t. $F(V_i \oplus a_i) \subseteq V_{i+1} \oplus a_{i+1}$, then $(V_1, V_2, \ldots, V_{r+1})$ is subspace trail of length r for the function F.*

This means that if F^t denotes the application of t rounds with fixed keys, then $F^t(V_1 \oplus a_1) = V_{t+1} \oplus a_{t+1}$. We refer to [11] for more details about the concept of subspace trails. Our treatment here is however meant to be self-contained.

3.1 Subspace Trails of AES

Here we briefly recall the subspace trails of AES presented in [11] – we refer to Appendix A for more details. In the following, we only work with vectors and vector spaces over $\mathbb{F}_{2^8}^{4 \times 4}$, and we denote by $\{e_{0,0}, \ldots, e_{3,3}\}$ the unit vectors of $\mathbb{F}_{2^8}^{4 \times 4}$ (e.g. $e_{i,j}$ has a single 1 in row i and column j).

Definition 2. *For each $i \in \{0, 1, 2, 3\}$:*

- *the column spaces $\mathcal{C}_i$ are defined as $\mathcal{C}_i = \langle e_{0,i}, e_{1,i}, e_{2,i}, e_{3,i} \rangle$;*
- *the diagonal spaces $\mathcal{D}_i$ are defined as $\mathcal{D}_i = SR^{-1}(\mathcal{C}_i)$; similarly, the inverse-diagonal spaces $\mathcal{ID}_i$ are defined as $\mathcal{ID}_i = SR(\mathcal{C}_i)$;*
- *the i-th mixed spaces $\mathcal{M}_i$ are defined as $\mathcal{M}_i = MC(\mathcal{ID}_i)$.*

Definition 3. *For $I \subseteq \{0, 1, 2, 3\}$, let $\mathcal{C}_I$, $\mathcal{D}_I$, $\mathcal{ID}_I$ and $\mathcal{M}_I$ be defined as*

$$\mathcal{C}_I = \bigoplus_{i \in I} \mathcal{C}_i, \qquad \mathcal{D}_I = \bigoplus_{i \in I} \mathcal{D}_i, \qquad \mathcal{ID}_I = \bigoplus_{i \in I} \mathcal{ID}_i, \qquad \mathcal{M}_I = \bigoplus_{i \in I} \mathcal{M}_i.$$

As shown in detail in [11]:

- for any coset $\mathcal{D}_I \oplus a$ there exists unique $b \in \mathcal{C}_I^\perp$ such that $R(\mathcal{D}_I \oplus a) = \mathcal{C}_I \oplus b$;
- for any coset $\mathcal{C}_I \oplus a$ there exists unique $b \in \mathcal{M}_I^\perp$ such that $R(\mathcal{C}_I \oplus a) = \mathcal{M}_I \oplus b$.

Theorem 1 ([11]). *For each $I \subseteq \{0, 1, 2, 3\}$ and for each $a \in \mathcal{D}_I^\perp$, there exists one and only one $b \in \mathcal{M}_I^\perp$ s.t. $R^2(\mathcal{D}_I \oplus a) = \mathcal{M}_I \oplus b$.*

---

[2] Sometimes we use the notation R_k instead of R to highlight the round key k.

Observe that if X is a subspace, $X \oplus a$ is a coset of X and x and y are two elements of the (same) coset $X \oplus a$, then $x \oplus y \in X$. It follows that:

Lemma 1. *For all x, y and for all $I \subseteq \{0, 1, 2, 3\}$:*

$$Prob(R^2(x) \oplus R^2(y) \in \mathcal{M}_I \,|\, x \oplus y \in \mathcal{D}_I) = 1. \tag{1}$$

Theorem 2. *For each $I, J \subseteq \{0, 1, 2, 3\}$:*

$$\mathcal{M}_I \cap \mathcal{D}_J = \{0\} \quad \text{if and only if} \quad |I| + |J| \leq 4.$$

It follows that for each $I, J \subseteq \{0, 1, 2, 3\}$ s.t. $|I| + |J| \leq 4$ and for all $x \neq y$:

$$Prob(R^4(x) \oplus R^4(y) \in \mathcal{M}_I \,|\, x \oplus y \in \mathcal{D}_J) = 0.$$

We remark that all these results can be re-described using a more "classical" truncated differential notation. E.g., if two texts t^1 and t^2 are equal except for the bytes in the i-th diagonal[3] for each $i \in I$, then they belong to the same coset of $\mathcal{D}_I$. A coset of $\mathcal{D}_I$ corresponds to a set of $2^{32 \cdot |I|}$ texts with $|I|$ active diagonals. Again, two texts t^1 and t^2 belong to the same coset of $\mathcal{ID}_I$ if the difference of the bytes that lie in the i-th anti-diagonal for each $i \notin I$ is equal to zero. Similar considerations hold for the column space $\mathcal{C}_I$ and the mixed space $\mathcal{M}_I$.

We finally introduce some notation that we largely use in the following.

Definition 4. *Given two different texts $t^1, t^2 \in \mathbb{F}_{2^8}^{4 \times 4}$, we say that $t^1 \leq t^2$ if $t^1 = t^2$ or if there exists $i, j \in \{0, 1, 2, 3\}$ such that (1) $t_{k,l}^1 = t_{k,l}^2$ for all $k, l \in \{0, 1, 2, 3\}$ with $k + 4 \cdot l < i + 4 \cdot j$ and (2) $t_{i,j}^1 < t_{i,j}^2$. Moreover, we say that $t^1 < t^2$ if $t^1 \leq t^2$ (with respect to the definition just given) and $t^1 \neq t^2$.*

Definition 5. *Let $\mathcal{X}$ be one of the previous subspaces, that is $\mathcal{C}_I, \mathcal{D}_I, \mathcal{ID}_I$ or $\mathcal{M}_I$. Let $x_0, ..., x_{n-1} \in \mathbb{F}_{2^8}^{4 \times 4}$ be a basis of $\mathcal{X}$ – i.e. $\mathcal{X} \equiv \langle x_0, x_1, ..., x_{n-1} \rangle$ where $n = 4 \cdot |I|$ – s.t. $x_i < x_{i+1}$ for each $i = 0, ..., n - 1$. Let t be an element of an arbitrary coset of $\mathcal{X}$, that is $t \in \mathcal{X} \oplus a$ for arbitrary a. We say that t is "generated" by the generating variables $(t^0, ..., t^{n-1})$ – in the following, $t \equiv (t^0, ..., t^{n-1})$ – if and only if*

$$t \equiv (t^0, ..., t^{n-1}) \quad \text{iff} \quad t = a \oplus \bigoplus_{i=0}^{n-1} t^i \cdot x_i.$$

As an example, let $\mathcal{X} = \mathcal{M}_0 \equiv \langle MC(e_{0,0}), MC(e_{3,1}), MC(e_{2,2}), MC(e_{1,3}) \rangle$, and let $p \in \mathcal{M}_0 \oplus a$. Then $p \equiv (p^0, p^1, p^2, p^3)$ if and only if

$$p \equiv p^0 \cdot MC(e_{0,0}) \oplus p^1 \cdot MC(e_{1,3}) \oplus p^2 \cdot MC(e_{2,2}) \oplus p^3 \cdot MC(e_{3,1}) \oplus a. \tag{2}$$

Similarly, let $\mathcal{X} = \mathcal{C}_0 \equiv \langle e_{0,0}, e_{1,0}, e_{2,0}, e_{3,0} \rangle$, and let $p \in \mathcal{C}_0 \oplus a$. Then $p \equiv (p^0, p^1, p^2, p^3)$ if and only if $p \equiv a \oplus p^0 \cdot e_{0,0} \oplus p^1 \cdot e_{1,0} \oplus p^2 \cdot e_{2,0} \oplus p^3 \cdot e_{3,0}$.

---

[3] The i-th diagonal of a 4×4 matrix A is defined as the elements that lie on row r and column c such that $r - c = i \bmod 4$. The i-th anti-diagonal of a 4×4 matrix A is defined as the elements that lie on row r and column c such that $r + c = i \bmod 4$.

3.2   Intersections of Subspaces and Useful Probabilities

Here we list some useful probabilities largely used in the following[4]. A *proof* of the following probabilities is provided in Appendix B. For our goal, we focus on the mixed space $\mathcal{M}$.

Let $I, J \subseteq \{0, 1, 2, 3\}$. We first recall that a random element x belongs to the subspace $\mathcal{M}_I$ with probability $Prob(x \in \mathcal{M}_I) \simeq 2^{-32 \cdot (4-|I|)}$. Moreover, as shown in detail in [11], given two random elements $x \neq y$ in the same coset of $\mathcal{M}_I$, they belong after one round to the same coset of $\mathcal{M}_J$ with probability:

$$Prob(R(x) \oplus R(y) \in \mathcal{M}_J \mid x \oplus y \in \mathcal{M}_I) \simeq (2^8)^{-4 \cdot |I| + |I| \cdot |J|}.$$

By definition, it's simple to observe that $\mathcal{M}_I \cap \mathcal{M}_J = \mathcal{M}_{I \cap J}$ (where $\mathcal{M}_I \cap \mathcal{M}_J = \{0\}$ if $I \cap J = \emptyset$). Thus, the probability $p_{|I|}$ that a random text x belongs to the subspace $\mathcal{M}_I$ for a certain $I \subseteq \{0, 1, 2, 3\}$ with $|I| = l$ fixed is well approximated by

$$p_{|I|} \equiv Prob(\exists I \; |I| = l \text{ s.t. } x \in \mathcal{M}_I) = (-1)^{|I|} \cdot \sum_{i=4-|I|}^{3} (-1)^i \cdot c_{|I|, i} \cdot \binom{4}{i} \cdot 2^{-32 \cdot i}. \tag{3}$$

where $c_{2,3} = 3$ and $c_{|I|, i} = 1$ for $\{|I|, i\} \neq \{2, 3\}$.

Let x, y be two random elements with $x \neq y$. Assume there exists $I \subseteq \{0, 1, 2, 3\}$ such that $x \oplus y \in \mathcal{M}_I$ ($x \oplus y \notin \mathcal{M}_L$ for each L s.t. $|L| < |I|$). The probability $p_{|J|, |I|}$ that there exists $J \subseteq \{0, 1, 2, 3\}$ – with $|J| = l$ fixed – such that $R(x) \oplus R(y) \in \mathcal{M}_J$ is well approximated by

$$p_{|J|, |I|} \equiv Prob(\exists J \; |J| = l \text{ s.t. } R(x) \oplus R(y) \in \mathcal{M}_J \mid x \oplus y \in \mathcal{M}_I) =$$
$$= (-1)^{|J|} \cdot \sum_{i=4-|J|}^{3} (-1)^i \cdot c_{|J|, i} \cdot \binom{4}{i} \cdot 2^{-8 \cdot i \cdot |I|}. \tag{4}$$

where $c_{2,3} = 3$ and $c_{|J|, i} = 1$ for $\{|J|, i\} \neq \{2, 3\}$.

Assume that $x \oplus y \notin \mathcal{M}_I$ for each $I \subseteq \{0, 1, 2, 3\}$. Then, the probability $\hat{p}_{|J|, 3}$ that $\exists J \subseteq \{0, 1, 2, 3\}$ with $|J| = l$ fixed such that $R(x) \oplus R(y) \in \mathcal{M}_J$ is well approximated by

$$\hat{p}_{|J|, 3} \equiv Prob(\exists J \text{ s.t. } R(x) \oplus R(y) \in \mathcal{M}_J \mid x \oplus y \notin \mathcal{M}_I \; \forall I) = \frac{p_{|J|} - p_{|J|, 3} \cdot p_3}{1 - p_3}. \tag{5}$$

To provide a numerical example, if $|I| = |J| = 3$ the previous probabilities are well approximated by

$$p_3 = 2^{-30} - 3 \cdot 2^{-63} + 2^{-94} \qquad p_{3,3} = 2^{-22} - 3 \cdot 2^{-47} + 2^{-70}$$
$$\hat{p}_{3,3} = 2^{-30} - 2\,043 \cdot 2^{-63} + 390\,661 \cdot 2^{-94} + \ldots$$

where p_3 and $\hat{p}_{3,3}$ are usually approximated by 2^{-30} and $p_{3,3}$ by 2^{-22}.

---

[4] We mention that the following probabilities are "sufficiently good" approximations for the target of the paper, i.e. *the errors of these approximations are so small that they do not affect the results of this paper*. We refer to [7, Appendix A.2] for a discussion about this point.

4   "Multiple-of-8" and Mixture Differential Cryptanalysis

The starting point of our secret-key distinguisher is the "*mixture differential cryptanalysis*" proposed in [8], based on the 5-round "multiple-of-8" secret-key distinguisher of AES (independent of the secret key) proposed in [10]. Here we limit ourselves to recall the main result useful for our work, and we refer to the corresponding papers for a complete discussion.

Theorem 3 ("Multiple-of-8" Property [10]). *Let $\mathcal{D}_I$ and $\mathcal{M}_J$ be the subspaces defined as before for certain fixed I and J with $1 \leq |I| \leq 3$. Given an arbitrary coset of $\mathcal{D}_I$ (i.e. $\mathcal{D}_I \oplus a$ for a fixed $a \in \mathcal{D}_I^\perp$), let (p^i, c^i) for $i = 0, ..., 2^{32 \cdot |I|} - 1$ the $2^{32 \cdot |I|}$ plaintexts and the corresponding ciphertexts after 5 rounds, where $p^i \in \mathcal{D}_I \oplus a$ and $c^i = R^5(p^i)$. The number n of different pairs of ciphertexts (c^i, c^j) for $i \neq j$ such that $c^i \oplus c^j \in \mathcal{M}_J$ (i.e. c^i and c^j belong to the same coset of $\mathcal{M}_J$) is always a multiple of 8 with prob. 1.*

The "multiple-of-8" property is related to the following result presented in [8]. Given two plaintexts in a coset of $\mathcal{C}_I$ with two equal generating variables, consider other pairs of plaintexts obtained e.g. by swapping the (different) generating variables. For 4-round AES, the corresponding ciphertexts of the first pair belong to the same coset of $\mathcal{M}_J$ *if and only if* the corresponding ciphertexts of the other pairs satisfy the same property. For the follow-up, we emphasize that the previous result is independent of the secret-key, of the details of the S-Box and of the MixColumns matrix.

Theorem 4 (Mixture Differential Cryptanalysis [8] – Special Case). *Given the subspace $\mathcal{C}_0 \cap \mathcal{D}_{0,3} \equiv \langle e_{0,0}, e_{1,0} \rangle \subseteq \mathcal{C}_0$, consider two plaintexts p^1 and p^2 in the same coset $(\mathcal{C}_0 \cap \mathcal{D}_{0,3}) \oplus a$ generated by $p^1 \equiv (z^1, w^1)$ and $p^2 \equiv (z^2, w^2)$. Let $\tilde{p}^1, \tilde{p}^2 \in \mathcal{C}_0 \oplus a$ be two other plaintexts generated by*

$$\tilde{p}^1 \equiv (z^1, w^1, \alpha, \beta), \ \tilde{p}^2 \equiv (z^2, w^2, \alpha, \beta) \quad or \quad \tilde{p}^1 \equiv (z^1, w^2, \alpha, \beta), \ \tilde{p}^2 \equiv (z^2, w^1, \alpha, \beta)$$

where α and β can take any possible value in $\mathbb{F}_{2^8}$. The following event

$$R^4(p^1) \oplus R^4(p^2) \in \mathcal{M}_J \quad if \ and \ only \ if \quad R^4(\tilde{p}^1) \oplus R^4(\tilde{p}^2) \in \mathcal{M}_J$$

holds with prob. 1 for 4-round AES, independently of the secret key, of the details of the S-Box and of the MixColumns matrix.

For completeness, we mention that a re-visitation of such result has been recently proposed in [2], where authors show that the above property is an immediate consequence of an equivalence relation on the input pairs, under which the difference at the output of the round function is invariant. Moreover, we remark that similar results can be obtained in the case in which the two plaintexts (p^1, p^2) share only one equal generating variable or in the case in which all generating variables are different.

Case $|I| = 2$ and $|I| = 3$. For the follow-up, we mention that similar considerations can be done for the cases $|I| \geq 2$. W.l.o.g consider $|I| = 2$ and assume $I = \{0, 1\}$ (the other cases are analogous). Given two texts p and q in the same coset of $\mathcal{M}_I$, that is $\mathcal{M}_I \oplus a$ for a given $a \in \mathcal{M}_I^\perp$, there exist $p_0', p_0'', p_1', p_1'', p_2', p_2'', p_3', p_3'' \in \mathbb{F}_{2^8}$ and $q_0', q_0'', q_1', q_1'', q_2', q_2'', q_3', q_3'' \in \mathbb{F}_{2^8}$ such that:

$$p = a \oplus \begin{bmatrix} p_0' & p_3'' & 0 & 0 \\ p_1' & p_0'' & 0 & 0 \\ p_2' & p_1'' & 0 & 0 \\ p_3' & p_2'' & 0 & 0 \end{bmatrix}, \qquad q = a \oplus \begin{bmatrix} q_0' & q_3'' & 0 & 0 \\ q_1' & q_0'' & 0 & 0 \\ q_2' & q_1'' & 0 & 0 \\ q_3' & q_2'' & 0 & 0 \end{bmatrix}.$$

As for the case $|I| = 1$, the idea is to consider all the possible combinations of the variables $p_0 \equiv (p_0', p_0''), p_1 \equiv (p_1', p_1''), p_2 \equiv (p_2', p_2''), p_3 \equiv (p_3', p_3'')$ and $q_0 \equiv (q_0', q_0''), q_1 \equiv (q_1', q_1''), q_2 \equiv (q_2', q_2''), q_3 \equiv (q_3', q_3'')$. In other words, the idea is to consider variables in $(\mathbb{F}_{2^8})^2 \equiv \mathbb{F}_{2^8} \times \mathbb{F}_{2^8}$ and not in $\mathbb{F}_{2^8}$. For $|I| = 3$, the idea is to work with variables in $(\mathbb{F}_{2^8})^3$.

Number of Pairs of Texts with n Equal Generating "Variable(s) in $(\mathbb{F}_{2^8})^{|I|}$". For the follow-up, we recall that, given texts in the same cosets of $\mathcal{C}_I$ or $\mathcal{M}_I$ for $I \subseteq \{0, 1, 2, 3\}$, the number of pairs of texts with v _equal_ generating "variable(s) in $(\mathbb{F}_{2^8})^{|I|}$" for $0 \le v \le 3$ is given by (see Appendix B.1 for details)

$$\binom{4}{v} \cdot 2^{32 \cdot |I| - 1} \cdot \left(2^{8 \cdot |I|} - 1\right)^{4-v}. \tag{6}$$

Why Is It (rather) _hard_ to set up Key-Recovery Attacks on AES-128 that Exploit the "Multiple-of-8" Distinguisher? Before going on, we briefly propose a possible answer to this question, which motivated the work presented in this paper. As already mentioned in [8, Section 3], a possible way to set up a key-recovery attack would be to extend such distinguisher by adding one round and guessing the corresponding subkey. However, since a coset of $\mathcal{M}_J$ (resp. of $\mathcal{D}_I$) is mapped into the full space after 1-round encryption (resp. decryption), it seems hard to check this property without guessing the entire key, or equivalently to set up a key-recovery attack different than a brute force one.

5   A New 5-Round Secret-Key Distinguisher for AES

Using the 4-round "mixture differential" distinguisher presented in [8] and recalled in Theorem 4 as starting point, we propose a way to extend it by 1 round at the end. As a result, we are able to set up a _new probabilistic 5-round secret-key distinguisher for AES which exploits a property which is independent of the secret key, of the details of the S-Box and of the MixColumns matrix._ Even if such a 5-round distinguisher has higher complexity than the deterministic one presented in [10], it can be used to set up a key-recovery attack on 6-round AES (better than a brute-force one) exploiting a distinguisher of the type [10] – believed to be hard to exploit. As a result, this is _the first key-recovery attack for 6-round AES set up by a 5-round secret-key distinguisher for AES._

5.1   5-Round *Probabilistic Mixture Differential* Distinguisher

Given n (plaintexts, ciphertexts) and the corresponding $\binom{n}{2}$ pairs, the idea is to divide them in sets such that particular relations hold among the variables that define the plaintexts that lie in the same set. The distinguisher that we are going to present exploits the following property:

> consider *the number of sets for which two ciphertexts of at least one pair lie in the same subspace* $\mathcal{M}_J$ *for* $|J| = 3$ (in other words, the number of sets for which two ciphertexts of at least one pair are equal in one anti-diagonal – if the final MixColumns operation is omitted). If the sets are properly defined, it is possible to prove that this number of sets *is a little lower for 5-round AES than for a random permutation, independently of the secret key*.

This property allows to set up a new distinguisher which is independent of the secret key, of the details of the S-Box and of the MixColumns matrix, and a new key-recovery attack on 6-round. In the following, we give all the details.

Details of the 5-Round "Probabilistic Mixture Diff." Distinguisher.
Consider 2^{32} chosen plaintexts with one active column (4 active bytes), e.g. a coset of $\mathcal{C}_0$, and the corresponding ciphertexts after 5-round. For each $(x_0, x_1), (y_0, y_1) \in \mathbb{F}_{2^8}^2$ such that $x_0 \neq y_0$ and $x_1 \neq y_1$, let $\mathcal{S}^{0,1}_{(x_0,x_1),(y_0,y_1)}$ be the set of pairs of plaintexts be defined as follows

$$\mathcal{S}^{0,1}_{(x_0,x_1),(y_0,y_1)} = \left\{ (p,q) \in \mathbb{F}_{2^8}^{4\times4} \times \mathbb{F}_{2^8}^{4\times4} \,\middle|\, p \equiv (x_0, x_1, A, B), q \equiv (y_0, y_1, A, B) \right.$$

$$\left. \text{or} \quad p \equiv (x_0, y_1, A, B), q \equiv (y_0, x_1, A, B) \quad \text{for each } A, B \in \mathbb{F}_{2^8} \right\}.$$

E.g., the pair of plaintexts $p, q \in \mathcal{C}_0 \oplus a$ in $\mathcal{S}^{0,1}_{(x_0,x_1),(y_0,y_1)}$ are of the form

$$p \equiv a \oplus \begin{bmatrix} x_0 & 0 & 0 & 0 \\ x_1 & 0 & 0 & 0 \\ A & 0 & 0 & 0 \\ B & 0 & 0 & 0 \end{bmatrix} \qquad q \equiv a \oplus \begin{bmatrix} y_0 & 0 & 0 & 0 \\ y_1 & 0 & 0 & 0 \\ A & 0 & 0 & 0 \\ B & 0 & 0 & 0 \end{bmatrix},$$

or

$$p \equiv a \oplus \begin{bmatrix} x_0 & 0 & 0 & 0 \\ y_1 & 0 & 0 & 0 \\ A & 0 & 0 & 0 \\ B & 0 & 0 & 0 \end{bmatrix} \qquad q \equiv a \oplus \begin{bmatrix} y_0 & 0 & 0 & 0 \\ x_1 & 0 & 0 & 0 \\ A & 0 & 0 & 0 \\ B & 0 & 0 & 0 \end{bmatrix}.$$

Similar definitions can be given for the set $\mathcal{S}^{i,j}_{(x_0,x_1),(y_0,y_1)}$ for $0 \leq i < j \leq 3$, where the active bytes are in row i and j. Given 2^{32} plaintexts as before, it is possible to construct $\frac{1}{2^{17}} \cdot 6 \cdot 2^{31} \cdot (2^8 - 1)^2 \simeq 2^{32.574}$ different sets $\mathcal{S}$ (the number of pairs of texts with 2 equal generating variables is given by formula (6), while 6 is the number of different combinations of i, j), where each set contains exactly 2^{17} different pairs of plaintexts (note that these pairs of plaintexts are not independent, since a relationship – among the generating variables – holds).

Given $n \gg 1$ sets $\mathcal{S}^{i,j}_{(x_0,x_1),(y_0,y_1)}$ – $\mathcal{S}$ for simplicity in the following –, consider the number of sets that contain *at least* one pair of plaintexts for which the corresponding ciphertexts (generated by 5-round AES or by a random permutation) belong to the same coset of a subspace $\mathcal{M}_J$ for $J \subseteq \{0,1,2,3\}$ and $|J| = 3$. As we are going to prove, this number is on average *smaller* for 5-round AES than for a random permutation, independently of the secret key, of the details of the S-Box and of the MixColumns matrix. In more details, the numbers of sets that satisfy the required property for 5-round AES – denoted by n_{AES} – and for a random permutation – denoted by n_{rand} – are well approximated by

$$n_{AES} \simeq n \cdot p_{AES} \qquad n_{rand} \simeq n \cdot p_{rand}$$

where $n \simeq 2^{32.574}$ is the number of sets $\mathcal{S}$ contained in each coset of $\mathcal{C}_0$ and where p_{AES} and p_{rand} are the probabilities[5] (resp. for AES and for a random permutation) that a given set $\mathcal{S}$ satisfies the required property

$$p_{AES} \simeq 2^{-13} - 2^{-27} \ -\mathbf{1.30213} \cdot \mathbf{2^{-43}} +...$$
$$p_{rand} \simeq 2^{-13} - 2^{-27} \ +\mathbf{2.66665} \cdot \mathbf{2^{-43}} +...$$

Even if the difference between the two probabilities is small, it is possible to distinguish the two cases with probability higher than 95% if the number n of sets $\mathcal{S}$ satisfies $n \geq 2^{71.243}$.

In the following, we prove this result (practically tested on a small scale AES) and we give all the details about the data and the computational costs.

Similarity with "classical" Truncated Differential Attack. Before going on, we emphasize the similarity with the 3-round distinguisher that exploits a truncated differential trail [12]. In that case, the idea is to count the number of pairs of texts that satisfy the truncated differential trail. In particular, given pairs of plaintexts in the same coset of a diagonal space $\mathcal{D}_i$, one counts the number of pairs for which the corresponding ciphertexts belong to the same coset of a mixed space $\mathcal{M}_J$ for $|J| = 3$. Since the probability of this event is higher for an AES permutation than for a random one[6], one can distinguish the two cases simply counting the number of pairs that satisfy the previous property. The idea of our distinguisher is similar. However, instead of working on single pairs, one works with particular sets $\mathcal{S}$ of pairs and counts the number of sets for which at least one pair satisfies the (given) differential trail.

---

[5] More precisely:

$$p_{AES} \simeq 2^{-13} - 524\,287 \cdot 2^{-46} - 22\,370\,411\,853 \cdot 2^{-77} + ...$$
$$p_{rand} \simeq 2^{-13} - 524\,287 \cdot 2^{-46} + 45\,812\,722\,347 \cdot 2^{-77} + ...$$

[6] As recalled in Sect. 3.2, this probability is approximately equal to 2^{-6} for the AES case and 2^{-30} for the random case.

Proof – 5-Round AES. As first thing, we prove the results just given, starting with the 5-round AES case.

Initial Considerations – 5-Round AES. Our 5-round distinguisher is based on Theorem 4. Given plaintexts in the same coset of $\mathcal{C}_0$ and for a fixed $J \subseteq \{0, 1, 2, 3\}$, each set $\mathcal{S}^{i,j}_{(x_0,x_1),(y_0,y_1)}$ just defined has the following property after 4 rounds:

1. the two texts (of each pair) belong to the same coset of $\mathcal{M}_I$ after 4-round;
2. the two texts (of each pair) do *not* belong to the same coset of $\mathcal{M}_I$ after 4-round.

In other words, for a given set $\mathcal{S}_{(x_0,x_1),(y_0,y_1)}$, it is not possible that the two texts of some – not all – pairs belong to the same coset of $\mathcal{M}_J$ after 4-round and others not, while this can happen for a random permutation.

What is the probability of the two previous events for an AES permutation? Given a set $\mathcal{S}^{i,j}_{(x_0,x_1),(y_0,y_1)}$, the probability that the two texts of each pair belong to the same coset of $\mathcal{M}_J$ after 4-round is approximately 2^{-30}.

To prove this fact, let the event $\mathcal{E}^r_i$ be defined as following.

Definition 6. *Let $J \subseteq \{0, 1, 2, 3\}$ be fixed. Given a set $\mathcal{S}_{(x_0,x_1),(y_0,y_1)}$, we define $\mathcal{E}^r_i$ as the event that the i-th pair of $\mathcal{S}_{(x_0,x_1),(y_0,y_1)}$ for $i = 1, 2, ..., 2^{17}$ belong to the same coset of $\mathcal{M}_J$ after r rounds.*

In the following, let $\overline{\mathcal{E}^r_i}$ be the complementary event of $\mathcal{E}^r_i$. It follows that

$$Prob(\mathcal{E}^4_1 \wedge \mathcal{E}^4_2 \wedge ... \wedge \mathcal{E}^4_{2^{17}}) = Prob(\mathcal{E}^4_1) \cdot Prob(\mathcal{E}^4_2 \wedge ... \wedge \mathcal{E}^4_{2^{17}} \,|\, \mathcal{E}^4_1) =$$
$$= Prob(\mathcal{E}^4_1) \equiv p_3 = 2^{-30} - 3 \cdot 2^{-63} + 2^{-94},$$

where p_3 is defined as in (3). Indeed, note that $Prob(\mathcal{E}^4_i \,|\, \mathcal{E}^4_1) = 1$ for each $i = 2, ..., 2^{17}$ since if two texts of one pair belong (or not) to the same coset of $\mathcal{M}_J$ after 4 rounds, then the texts of all the other pair have the same property. We remark again that this is due to the way in which the sets $\mathcal{S}$ are defined/constructed.

Using these initial considerations as starting point, we analyze in detail our proposed 5-round distinguisher.

1st Case. As we have just seen, the two texts of all the pairs of each set belong to the same coset of a subspace $\mathcal{M}_I$ for $|I| = 3$ *after 4-round* with probability $p_3 \simeq 2^{-30}$. In other words, on average there are $2^{-30} \cdot n$ sets $\mathcal{S}$ such that the two texts of all the pairs belong to the same coset of a subspace $\mathcal{M}_J$ for $|J| = 3$ *after 4-round*.

Let $|J| = 3$. Since $Prob(R(x) \oplus R(y) \in \mathcal{M}_J \,|\, x \oplus y \in \mathcal{M}_I) = p_{3,3} \simeq 2^{-22}$ (see (4) for details) and since each set is composed of 2^{17} different pairs, the probability that the two ciphertexts of at least one pair of $\mathcal{S}$ belong to the same coset of $\mathcal{M}_J$ for $|J| = 3$ *after 5 rounds* is well approximated by

$$1 - (1 - \hat{p}_{3,3})^{2^{17}} = 1 - \left(1 - \frac{p_3 \cdot (1 - p_{3,3})}{1 - p_3}\right)^{2^{17}} = 2^{-13} - 526\,327 \cdot 2^{-46} + ...$$

where $\hat{p}_{3,3}$ is defined in (5).

Remark. Before going on, we mention that a better approximation of the previous probability can be obtained by taking into account the fact that, for each $x, y \in \mathcal{C}_0 \oplus a$, then $R^3(x) \oplus R^3(y) \notin \mathcal{M}_J$ for each J with $|J| \leq 3$ (see Theorem 2). In other words, the previous probability $\hat{p}_{3,3}$ is independent of the condition $R^{-1}(x) \oplus R^{-1}(y)$, while we actually know that $R^{-1}(x) \oplus R^{-1}(y) \notin \mathcal{M}_J$ for each J with $|J| \leq 3$ due to the choice of the plaintexts in a coset of $\mathcal{C}_0$.

2nd Case. In the same way, the two texts of all the pairs of each set do not belong to the same coset of a subspace $\mathcal{M}_J$ for $|J| = 3$ *after 4-round* with probability $1 - p_3 \simeq 1 - 2^{-30}$. In other words, on average there are $(1 - 2^{-30}) \cdot n$ sets $\mathcal{S}$ such that the two ciphertexts of all the pairs of each set do not belong to the same coset of a subspace $\mathcal{M}_J$ for $|J| = 3$ *after 4-round*.

Let $|J| = 3$. Since $Prob(R(x) \oplus R(y) \in \mathcal{M}_J \,|\, x \oplus y \notin \mathcal{M}_I) = \hat{p}_{3,3} \simeq 2^{-30}$ (see (5) for details) and since each set is composed of 2^{17} different pairs, the probability that the two texts of at least one pair of $\mathcal{S}$ belong to the same coset of $\mathcal{M}_J$ for $|J| = 3$ *after 5 rounds* is well approximated by

$$1 - \left(1 - p_{3,3}\right)^{2^{17}} = 2^{-5} - 524\,287 \cdot 2^{-30} + 45\,812\,722\,347 \cdot 2^{-53} + \ldots$$

Final Result. The desired result is finally obtained using the *law* (or formula) *of total probability*

$$Prob(A) = \sum_i Prob(A \,|\, B_i) \cdot Prob(B_i)$$

which holds for each event A such that $\bigcup_i B_i$ is the *sample space*, i.e. the set of all the possible outcomes.

Given a set $\mathcal{S}$, the probability that two ciphertexts c^1 and c^2 of at least one pair satisfy the required property (i.e. $c^1 \oplus c^2 \in \mathcal{M}_J$ for $|J| = 3$) is given by

$$
\begin{aligned}
p_{AES} &= \left[1 - Prob(\overline{\mathcal{E}_1^5} \wedge \overline{\mathcal{E}_2^5} \wedge \ldots \wedge \overline{\mathcal{E}_{2^{17}}^5} \,|\, \mathcal{E}_i^4)\right] \cdot Prob(\mathcal{E}_i^4) + \\
&\quad + \left[1 - Prob(\overline{\mathcal{E}_1^5} \wedge \overline{\mathcal{E}_2^5} \wedge \ldots \wedge \overline{\mathcal{E}_{2^{17}}^5} \,|\, \overline{\mathcal{E}_i^4})\right] \cdot Prob(\overline{\mathcal{E}_i^4}) = \\
&= (1 - p_3) \cdot \left[1 - \left(1 - \frac{p_3 \cdot (1 - p_{3,3})}{1 - p_3}\right)^{2^{17}}\right] + p_3 \cdot \left[1 - \left(1 - p_{3,3}\right)^{2^{17}}\right] = \quad (7) \\
&= 2^{-13} - 524287 \cdot 2^{-46} - \underbrace{22\,370\,411\,853 \cdot 2^{-77}}_{\approx 2.604 \cdot 2^{-44}} + \ldots
\end{aligned}
$$

for a certain $i \in \{1, \ldots, 2^{17}\}$. Note that $Prob(\mathcal{E}_i^5 \wedge \mathcal{E}_j^5) = Prob(\mathcal{E}_i^5) \times Prob(\mathcal{E}_j^5)$ since the events $\mathcal{E}_i^5$ and $\mathcal{E}_j^5$ are independent for $i \neq j$.

Proof – *Random Permutation.* For a random permutation, given a set $\mathcal{S}$ defined as before, what is the probability that two ciphertexts – generated by a random permutation – of at least one pair satisfy the required property? By simple computation, such event occurs with (approximately) probability

$$p_{rand} = 1 - \left(1 - p_3\right)^{2^{17}} = 1 - \left[1 - \left(2^{-30} - 3 \cdot 2^{-63} + 2^{-94}\right)\right]^{2^{17}} =$$
$$= 2^{-13} - 524\,287 \cdot 2^{-46} + \underbrace{45\,812\,722\,347 \cdot 2^{-77}}_{\approx\, 5.333 \cdot 2^{-44}} + ... \tag{8}$$

Remark. Before going on, we emphasize again that while a "classical" truncated differential distinguisher counts the number of pairs of texts that satisfy a particular differential trail, in our case we consider the number of sets of texts for which at least one pair satisfies a particular differential trail. This implies *a difference between the probabilities* that the previous event occurs for a random permutation (namely, p_{rand}) and for 5-round AES (namely, p_{AES}).

5.2 Data and Computational Complexity

Data Complexity. Since the difference between the two probabilities is very small

$$\frac{|n_{AES} - n_{rand}|}{n_{AES}} \simeq \frac{|n_{AES} - n_{rand}|}{n_{rand}} \ll 1$$

where n_{AES} and n_{rand} denote respectively the number of sets that satisfy the required property for the AES case and for a random permutation, *what is the minimum number of sets S (or equivalently of cosets C_I) to guarantee that the distinguisher works with high probability?* Our goal here is to derive a good approximation for the number of initial cosets of C_I that is sufficient to detect this difference with probability *prob*.

To solve this problem, note that given n sets S of 2^{17} pairs defined as before, the probability distribution of our model is simply described by a *binomial distribution*. By definition, a binomial distribution with parameters n and p is the discrete probability distribution of the number of successes in a sequence of n independent yes/no experiments, each of which yields success with probability p. In our case, given n sets S, each of them satisfies or not the above property/requirement with a certain probability. Thus, this model can be described using a binomial distribution. We recall that for a random variable Z that follows the binomial distribution, that is $Z \sim \mathcal{B}(n, p)$, the mean μ and the variance σ^2 are respectively given by $\mu = n \cdot p$ and $\sigma^2 = n \cdot p \cdot (1 - p)$.

To derive concrete numbers for our distinguisher and based on De Moivre-Laplace theorem[7], we approximate the binomial distribution with a normal one. Moreover, we can simply consider the difference of the two distributions, which is again a normal distribution. That is, given $X \sim \mathcal{N}(\mu_1, \sigma_1^2)$ and $Y \sim \mathcal{N}(\mu_2, \sigma_2^2)$, then $X - Y \sim \mathcal{N}(\mu, \sigma^2) = N(\mu_1 - \mu_2, \sigma_1^2 + \sigma_2^2)$. Indeed, in order to distinguish the two cases, note that it is sufficient to guarantee that the number of sets that satisfy the required property in the random case is higher than for the 5-round

---

[7] A normal distribution is a valid approximation in the case in which the skewness (i.e. the asymmetry) of the binomial distribution is close to zero. The skewness γ of a binomial distribution $\mathcal{B}(n, p)$ – given by $\gamma = (1 - 2p)/\sqrt{np(1 - p)}$ – is close to zero when $p = 0.5$ and/or $n \cdot p \gg 1$.

AES case. As a result, the mean μ and the variance σ^2 of the difference between the AES distribution and the random one are given by:

$$\mu = n \cdot |p_{rand} - p_{AES}| \qquad \sigma^2 = n \cdot \left[p_{rand} \cdot (1 - p_{rand}) + p_{AES} \cdot (1 - p_{AES})\right]. \quad (9)$$

Since the probability density of the normal distribution is $f(x \mid \mu, \sigma^2) = \frac{1}{\sigma\sqrt{2\pi}} e^{-\frac{(x-\mu)^2}{2\sigma^2}}$, it follows that

$$prob = \int_{-\infty}^{0} \frac{1}{\sigma\sqrt{2\pi}} e^{-\frac{(x-\mu)^2}{2\sigma^2}} dx = \int_{-\infty}^{-\mu/\sigma} \frac{1}{\sqrt{2\pi}} e^{-\frac{x^2}{2}} dx = \frac{1}{2}\left[1 + \mathrm{erf}\left(\frac{-\mu}{\sigma\sqrt{2}}\right)\right],$$
(10)

where $\mathrm{erf}(x)$ is the error function, defined as the probability of a random variable with normal distribution of mean 0 and variance $1/2$ falling in the range $[-x, x]$. We emphasize that the integral is computed in the range $(-\infty, 0]$ since we work in the case in which the number of sets with the required property for AES is lower than for the random case.

To have a probability of success higher than $prob$, the number of sets n has to satisfy[8]:

$$n > \frac{4 \cdot \max(p_{rand}, p_{AES})}{(p_{rand} - p_{AES})^2} \cdot \left[\mathrm{erfinv}\left(2 \cdot prob - 1\right)\right]^2 \quad (11)$$

where $\mathrm{erfinv}(x)$ is the inverse error function. Before going on, we emphasize that *the data cost n just given depends both on the mean value μ and also on the variance σ^2 of the analyzed probabilistic distribution* (both given in (9)).

Data Cost. First of all, given a single coset of a column space $\mathcal{C}_I$ for $|I| = 1$, the number of different pairs with two equal generating variables is given by $6 \cdot 2^{16} \cdot 2^{15} \cdot (2^8 - 1)^2 \simeq 2^{49.574}$ (see Eq. (6)), while the number of sets $\mathcal{S}$ that one can construct is well approximated by $2^{49.574}/2^{17} \simeq 2^{32.574}$.

For a probability of success of approximately 95% and since $|p_{AES} - p_{rand}| \simeq 2^{-41.01}$ and $p_{AES} \simeq p_{rand} \simeq 2^{-13}$, it follows that n must satisfy $n > 2^{71.243}$. Since a single coset of $\mathcal{C}_I$ for $|I| = 1$ contains approximately $2^{32.574}$ different sets $\mathcal{S}$, one needs approximately $2^{71.243} \cdot 2^{-32.574} \simeq 2^{38.669}$ different initial cosets of $\mathcal{C}_I$, that is approximately $2^{38.669} \cdot 2^{32} \simeq 2^{70.67}$ chosen plaintexts.

We mention that it is possible to set up a modified version of this distinguisher that requires lower data (and computational) cost(s). In particular, in Appendix D we show that a similar distinguisher can be set up using only 2^{52} chosen plaintexts in the same initial coset of $\mathcal{C}_I$ with $|I| = 2$. Our choice to present a "less competitive" distinguisher is due to the fact that it will be the starting point for a key-recovery attack on 6-round, as shown in detail in the next section[9].

---

[8] For $p_{rand}, p_{AES} \ll 1$: $p_{rand} \cdot (1 - p_{rand}) + p_{AES} \cdot (1 - p_{AES}) < p_{rand} + p_{AES} < 2 \cdot \max(p_{rand}, p_{AES})$.

[9] In Appendix E, we briefly explain why it is *not* possible to set up the key-recovery attack using cosets of $\mathcal{D}_I$ with $|I| = 2$ instead of $|I| = 1$.

Computational Complexity. We propose a detailed analysis of the computational complexity necessary to set up the previous distinguisher in Appendix C. A complete pseudo-code is also given there – see Algorithm 1. As showed there, by re-ordering the texts w.r.t. a particular partial order, the distinguisher just described can be implemented using $2^{78.13}$ table look-ups, or approximately $2^{71.5}$ five-round encryptions (assuming[10] 20 table look-ups ≈ 1 round of encryption).

5.3   Practical Verification on Small Scale AES

In order to have a practical verification of the proposed distinguisher (and of the following key-recovery attack), we have practically verified[11] the probabilities p_{AES} and p_{rand} given above on a small scale AES, as proposed in [4]. We emphasize that our verification on the small scale variant of AES is strong evidence[12] for it to hold for the real AES, since the strategy used to theoretically compute such probabilities is independent of the fact that each word of AES is of 4 or 8 bits and of the details of the AES components.

Theoretical Background. To compare the practical values with the theoretical ones, we list the theoretical probabilities p_{AES} and p_{rand} for the small scale AES case. First of all, for small scale AES the probabilities p_3 and $p_{3,3}$ are respectively equal to $p_3 = 2^{-14} - 3 \cdot 2^{-31} + 2^{-46}$ and $p_{3,3} = 2^{-10} - 3 \cdot 2^{-23} + 2^{-34}$.

Using the previous procedure and formula, the (approximate) probabilities that a set S satisfies the required property for 5-round small scale AES and for the random case are respectively

$$p_{AES} = 2^{-5} - 2\,047 \cdot 2^{-22} - \underbrace{221\,773 \cdot 2^{-37}}_{\approx 3.384 \cdot 2^{-21}} + ...$$

$$p_{rand} = 2^{-5} - 2\,047 \cdot 2^{-22} + \underbrace{698\,027 \cdot 2^{-37}}_{\approx 10.651 \cdot 2^{-21}} + ...$$

---

[10] The approximation "20 table look-ups ≈ 1 round of encryption" – *largely used in the literature* – is due to the fact that the cost of each round of AES is well approximated by the cost of 20 S-Box look-ups (16 for the round + 4 for the key-schedule). Even if this approximation is not formally correct – the size of the table of an S-Box look-up (equal to 2^8) is smaller than the size of the table used for our distinguisher (approximately of 2^{32} – see Algorithm 1), it allows to give a comparison between our distinguishers and the others currently present in the literature.

[11] The source codes of the distinguishers/attacks are available at https://github.com/Krypto-iaik/Distinguisher_5RoundAES.

[12] To the best of our knowledge, the only case in which the behavior of small scale AES does not match the one of real AES is the case of zero-sum distinguishers – see e.g. [14, Table 6]. In such a case, due to the degree of S-Box$(x) = x^{-1}$ in $\mathbb{F}_2^n$ for $n = 4, 8$, it is possible to cover more rounds (with a smaller data cost) for small scale AES than for real AES using zero-sum distinguishers. Since our results are independent of the details of the S-Box, we claim that our verification on the small scale variant of AES is strong evidence for it to hold for the real AES.

As a result, using formula (11) for $p_{rand} \simeq p_{AES} \simeq 2^{-5}$ and $|p_{rand} - p_{AES}| \simeq 2^{-17.19}$, it follows that $n \geq 2^{31.6}$ different sets $\mathcal{S}$ are sufficient to set up the distinguisher with probability higher than 95%.

W.l.o.g. we worked with cosets of $\mathcal{C}_0$ to practically test the two probabilities. Note that for small scale AES, a single coset of $\mathcal{C}_0$ contains 2^{16} (plaintexts, ciphertexts), or approximately $2^{15} \cdot (2^{16} - 1) \simeq 2^{31}$ different pairs. Since the number of pairs with two equal generating variables is given by $6 \cdot 2^8 \cdot 2^7 \cdot (2^4-1)^2 \simeq 2^{25.4}$ (also verified by computer test), it is possible to construct $3 \cdot 2^7 \cdot (2^4 - 1)^2 = 86400 \simeq 2^{16.4}$ sets $\mathcal{S}$ of 2^9 pairs. It follows that $2^{31.6} \cdot 2^{-16.4} = 2^{15.2}$ different initial cosets of $\mathcal{C}_0$ should be used, for a cost of $2^{47.2}$ chosen plaintexts.

Practical Results: Number of Sets $\mathcal{S}$ that satisfy the Required Property. For our tests, we used 2^{16} different initial cosets of $\mathcal{C}_0$ (keys used to encrypt the plaintexts in the AES case are randomly chosen and different for each coset – the key is not fixed) – note that we used more initial cosets than the ones necessary in order to set up the distinguisher. For each coset, we have used Algorithm 1 to count the number of sets $\mathcal{S}$ that satisfy the required property (i.e. the number of sets for which two ciphertexts of at least one pair are in the same coset of $\mathcal{M}_J$ for certain J with $|J| = 3$). In all our practical experiments, the random permutation is defined as 30-round AES.

By practical experiments, we found that the *total* numbers of sets $\mathcal{S}$ – for all the 2^{16} different initial cosets of $\mathcal{C}_0$ – that satisfy the required property for 5-round small scale AES and for a random permutation are given by

$$N_{rand}^T = 174\,212\,383 \qquad\qquad N_{AES}^T = 174\,174\,372$$
$$N_{rand}^P = 174\,207\,861 \qquad\qquad N_{AES}^P = 174\,163\,427$$

where the superscripts T and P denote respectively the theoretical expectation and the practical results.

Equivalently, the average numbers of sets $\mathcal{S}$ – for each one of the 2^{16} different initial cosets of $\mathcal{C}_0$ – that satisfy the required property for 5-round small scale AES and for a random permutation are given by

$$\mu_{rand}^T = 86\,400 \cdot p_{rand} \simeq 2\,658.272 \qquad\qquad \mu_{AES}^T = 86\,400 \cdot p_{AES} \simeq 2\,657.694$$
$$\mu_{rand}^P \simeq 2\,658.20 \qquad\qquad\qquad \mu_{AES}^P \simeq 2\,657.52$$

Note that *the numbers of sets found in our experiments are close to the theoretical ones, and that the average number of sets for AES case is lower than the corresponding numbers for the random one, as predicted.* Hence 5-round AES can be distinguished from the case of a random permutation.

Practical Results: Probability Distribution of the Number of Sets $\mathcal{S}$ that Satisfy the Required Property. Last thing to verify is the probability distribution that, given a coset of $\mathcal{C}_0$, describes the number of different sets $\mathcal{S}$ for which two ciphertexts of at least one pair lie in the same subspace $\mathcal{M}_J$ for $|J| = 3$. As we have just seen in the previous section, the data complexity of the distinguisher depends (obviously) on the average number of sets $\mathcal{S}$ that satisfy

Table 3. *(Theoretical and Practical) Probability Distributions of 5-round small scale AES and of a Random Permutation.* Given a coset of $\mathcal{C}_0$ (which contains 86 400 different sets $\mathcal{S}$), the mean value and the variance of the Probability Distribution of the number of sets $\mathcal{S}$ for which two ciphertexts of (at least) one pair lie in the same coset of $\mathcal{M}_J$ (equivalently, are equal in one anti-diagonal before final MC operation) are given in the table. Practical results are obtained by considering 2^{16} different initial cosets.

	(small scale) 5-round AES	Random Permutation
Theoretical mean value μ_T	2 657.694	2 658.272
Practical mean value μ_P	2 657.52	2 658.20
Theoretical variance σ_T^2	2 575.942	2 576.485
Practical variance σ_P^2	2 575.83	2 576.38

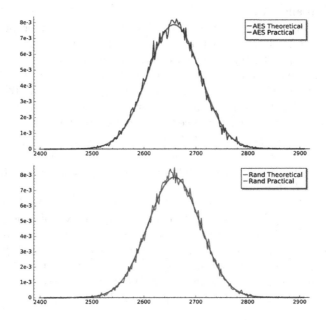

Fig. 2. *Probability distributions of the number of collisions (i.e. number of pairs of ciphertexts in $\mathcal{S}$ that belong to the same coset of $\mathcal{M}_I$) for 5-round small scale AES and for a random permutation - obtained using 20 000 initial cosets.*

the required property, but also on the variance of the probability distribution that describes such event – see e.g. Eq. (10) for details.

As already shown before, the probability distributions of the number of sets $\mathcal{S}$ that satisfy the required property both for AES and for the random case are well described by a binomial distribution $\mathcal{B}$. Mean values and variances (equivalent, standard deviations) of both these two distributions are given in Table 3, where a comparison is given between the practical and the theoretical expected results. For completeness, a comparison between the practical and the theoretical probability distributions of the number of collisions for the AES and the random cases are also proposed given in Fig. 2. These pictures are obtained using $20\,000 \equiv 2^{14.3}$ initial cosets. Both by the results proposed in Table 3 and by Fig. 2, it is possible to observe that e.g. the theoretical values of the statistical parameters – e.g. the mean, the variance or standard deviation, the skewness/asymmetry (close to zero) – match the practical ones in both cases.

6 Key-Recovery Attack on 6 Rounds of AES-128

Using the previous distinguisher on 5-round AES (based on a property which is independent of the secret key) as starting point, we propose the first key-recovery attack on 6 rounds of AES that exploits a 5-round secret-key distinguisher. The strategy of the attack is similar to the one largely exploited by linear and differential cryptanalysis.

For the distinguisher just presented, the idea is to consider plaintexts in cosets of $\mathcal{C}_I$ for $I \subseteq \{0, 1, 2, 3\}$ with $|I| = 1$, construct all the possible pairs of two (plaintexts, ciphertexts) with two equal generating variables, divide them into sets $\mathcal{S}$ of 2^{17} pairs and count the number of sets for which two ciphertexts of at least one pair belong to the same coset of $\mathcal{M}_J$ for $|J| = 3$. To set up the key-recovery attack, the idea is simply to start with cosets of $\mathcal{D}_I$, and to repeat the previous procedure for each guessed combination of the I-th diagonal of the secret key. *The crucial point is that the guessed 4-bytes of the key influence the way in which the pairs of texts are divided into the sets $\mathcal{S}$.* As a consequence, if the 4 guessed bytes are wrong (i.e. different from the right ones), the pairs are divided into sets $\mathcal{S}$ in a random way.

As we are going to prove, *for a wrongly guessed key the probability that a set $\mathcal{S}$ satisfies the required property* (that is, two ciphertexts of at least one pair belong to the same coset of $\mathcal{M}_J$) *is (approximately) equal to the probability of the random case p_{rand}, which is higher than the probability p_{AES} for the case of the right key.* As a result, the number of sets $\mathcal{S}$ for which two ciphertexts of at least one pair belong to the same coset of $\mathcal{M}_J$ for $|J| = 3$ is minimum for the right key. This allows to recover one diagonal of the secret key.

Key-Recovery Attack – Details. Consider texts in a coset of $\mathcal{C}_I$ which is obtained by 1-round encryption of a coset of $\mathcal{D}_I$ with respect to a (partially) guessed key. Here we theoretically compute the probability that a set $\mathcal{S}$ satisfies the required property (that is, two ciphertexts of at least one pair belong to the same coset of $\mathcal{M}_J$) when the guessed key is not the right one. In other words, we are going to show that the behavior in the case of a wrongly guessed key (in the following denoted by "AES with a wrong key") is similar to the one of a random permutation.

Observe that the main difference between "AES with a wrong key" and a random permutation is given by the possibility in the first case to study the distribution of the pairs after each round – note that for a random permutation it is meaningless to consider the distribution of the texts after (e.g.) one round. In particular, a coset of a diagonal space $\mathcal{D}_I$ is always mapped into a coset of a column space $\mathcal{C}_I$ after one round independently of the key. On the other hand, we stress that *the way in which the pairs are distributed in the sets $\mathcal{S}$ depends on the guessed key.*

Consider a key-recovery attack on 6-round AES

$$\mathcal{D}_I \oplus a \xrightarrow[KeyGuess]{R(\cdot)} \text{5-round Secret-Key Distinguisher of Sect. 5}$$

$$\bigcup_{(x,y)} \mathcal{S}_{x,y}^{i,j} \subseteq \mathcal{C}_I \oplus b \xrightarrow[\text{prob. 1}]{R(\cdot)} \mathcal{M}_I \oplus c \xrightarrow{R(\cdot)} \mathcal{D}_J \oplus a' \xrightarrow[\text{prob. 1}]{R^2(\cdot)} \mathcal{M}_J \oplus c' \xrightarrow{R(\cdot)} \mathcal{M}_K \oplus c''$$

and focus on the middle round $\mathcal{M}_I \oplus c \xrightarrow{R(\cdot)} \mathcal{D}_J \oplus a'$ for $|I| = 1$ and $|J| = 3$. Assume the guessed key is wrong, and consider one set $\mathcal{S}_{(x_0,x_1),(y_0,y_1)}^{i,j}$. For this set, the number of pairs that belong to the same coset of $\mathcal{M}_J$ after four rounds can take any possible value between 0 and 2^{17} (that is, 0, 1, 2, ... or 2^{17}). Indeed, since the pairs are divided in sets $\mathcal{S}_{(x_0,x_1),(y_0,y_1)}^{i,j}$ in a random way, it is not possible to guarantee that the number of pairs that belong to the same coset of $\mathcal{M}_J$ after 4 rounds is only 0 or 2^{17} (as for "AES with the right key").

Using the same calculation as before and for a wrongly guessed key, given a set $\mathcal{S}_{(x_0,x_1),(y_0,y_1)}^{i,j}$, the probability $p_{AES}^{WrongKey}$ that two texts of at least one pair belong to the same coset of $\mathcal{M}_K$ for a certain $|K| = 3$ after 6 rounds is given by

$$p_{AES}^{WrongKey} = \sum_{n=0}^{2^{17}} \binom{2^{17}}{n} \cdot p_3^n \cdot (1-p_3)^{2^{17}-n} \cdot \left[1 - \left(1 - p_{3,3}\right)^n \cdot \left(1 - \frac{p_3 \cdot (1 - p_{3,3})}{1 - p_3}\right)^{2^{17}-n} \right],$$

which is well approximated by

$$p_{AES}^{WrongKey} = 2^{-13} - 524\,287 \cdot 2^{-46} + 45\,812\,722\,347 \cdot 2^{-77} + \dots$$

Note that this probability is approximately equal to the one of the random case (given in (8)), while we remember that the probability for "AES with the right key" is

$$p_{AES} = 2^{-13} - 524\,287 \cdot 2^{-46} - 22\,370\,411\,853 \cdot 2^{-77} + \dots$$

where the difference between these two probabilities is approximately $|p_{AES}^{WrongKey} - p_{AES}| \simeq 2^{-41.011}$.

Data Cost. Assume the goal is to discover the I-th diagonal of the key with probability higher than 95%. Equivalently, the goal is to guarantee that the number of sets $\mathcal{S}_{(x_0,x_1),(y_0,y_1)}^{i,j}$ that satisfy the required property is the lowest one for the right key with probability higher than 95%.

To compute the data cost, the idea is to use the same analysis proposed for the 5-round distinguisher in Sect. 5.2. In particular, since there are 2^{32} candidates for each diagonal of the keys, one has to guarantee that the number of sets $\mathcal{S}_{(x_0,x_1),(y_0,y_1)}^{i,j}$ that satisfy the previous required property is the lowest one for the right key with probability higher than $(0.95)^{2^{-32}}$ (note that the 2^{32} tests – one for each candidate – are all independent).

Using formula (11), one needs approximately $2^{73.343}$ different sets $\mathcal{S}_{(x_0,x_1),(y_0,y_1)}^{i,j}$ for each candidate of the i-th diagonal of the key. Since it is possible to construct approximately $3 \cdot 2^{15} \cdot (2^8 - 1)^2 \approx 2^{32.574}$ different sets for each initial coset of $\mathcal{D}_I$, one needs approximately $2^{73.343} \cdot 2^{-32.573} = 2^{40.77}$ different initial cosets of $\mathcal{D}_I$ to discover the I-th diagonal of the key with probability higher than 95%, for a total cost of $2^{40.77} \cdot 2^{32} = 2^{72.77}$ chosen plaintexts.

When one diagonal of the key is found, due to the computational cost of this step we propose to find the entire key (i.e. the other three diagonals) using a brute force attack.

Computational Complexity. We propose a complete and detailed analysis of the computational complexity of the previous attack in Appendix E. A complete pseudo-code of is given there – see Algorithm 2. As we show there[13], the total cost of finding one diagonal of the key is well approximated by $2^{111.82}$ table look-ups, or equivalently $2^{104.92}$ six-round encryptions. The total cost of finding the entire key (using brute force on the last three diagonal) is of $2^{104.92} + 2^{96} = 2^{104.93}$ six-round encryptions.

Acknowledgements. The author thanks the anonymous reviewers for their valuable comments and suggestions, and Willi Meier for shepherding the paper. This work has been partially supported by IOV42.

A   Subspace Trails for AES

In this section, we give all the details about the subspace trails of AES presented in [11], and briefly recalled in Sect. 3.

Definition 7. *The column spaces $\mathcal{C}_i$ are defined as $\mathcal{C}_i = \langle e_{0,i}, e_{1,i}, e_{2,i}, e_{3,i} \rangle$.*

For instance, $\mathcal{C}_0$ corresponds to the symbolic matrix

$$\mathcal{C}_0 = \left\{ \begin{bmatrix} x_1 & 0 & 0 & 0 \\ x_2 & 0 & 0 & 0 \\ x_3 & 0 & 0 & 0 \\ x_4 & 0 & 0 & 0 \end{bmatrix} \middle| \forall x_1, x_2, x_3, x_4 \in \mathbb{F}_{2^8} \right\} \equiv \begin{bmatrix} x_1 & 0 & 0 & 0 \\ x_2 & 0 & 0 & 0 \\ x_3 & 0 & 0 & 0 \\ x_4 & 0 & 0 & 0 \end{bmatrix}.$$

Definition 8. *The diagonal spaces $\mathcal{D}_i$ are defined as $\mathcal{D}_i = SR^{-1}(\mathcal{C}_i)$. Similarly, the inverse-diagonal spaces $\mathcal{ID}_i$ are defined as $\mathcal{ID}_i = SR(\mathcal{C}_i)$.*

For instance, $\mathcal{D}_0$ and $\mathcal{ID}_0$ correspond to symbolic matrix

$$\mathcal{D}_0 \equiv \begin{bmatrix} x_1 & 0 & 0 & 0 \\ 0 & x_2 & 0 & 0 \\ 0 & 0 & x_3 & 0 \\ 0 & 0 & 0 & x_4 \end{bmatrix}, \qquad \mathcal{ID}_0 \equiv \begin{bmatrix} x_1 & 0 & 0 & 0 \\ 0 & 0 & 0 & x_2 \\ 0 & 0 & x_3 & 0 \\ 0 & x_4 & 0 & 0 \end{bmatrix}$$

for all $x_1, x_2, x_3, x_4 \in \mathbb{F}_{2^8}$.

---

[13] For completeness, we mention that *potentially* it is possible to (slightly) reduce the data cost by relaxing the property that the number of sets $\mathcal{S}$ that satisfy the required property is the lowest one for the right key. The right key is then found by a brute force attack on the candidates that pass the test.

Definition 9. *The i-th mixed spaces $\mathcal{M}_i$ are defined as $\mathcal{M}_i = MC(\mathcal{ID}_i)$.*

For instance, $\mathcal{M}_0$ corresponds to symbolic matrix

$$\mathcal{M}_0 \equiv \begin{bmatrix} 0x02 \cdot x_1 & x_4 & x_3 & 0x03 \cdot x_2 \\ x_1 & x_4 & 0x03 \cdot x_3 & 0x02 \cdot x_2 \\ x_1 & 0x03 \cdot x_4 & 0x02 \cdot x_3 & x_2 \\ 0x03 \cdot x_1 & 0x02 \cdot x_4 & x_3 & x_2 \end{bmatrix}$$

for all $x_1, x_2, x_3, x_4 \in \mathbb{F}_{2^8}$.

B   Proof – Probabilities of Sect. 3.2

In this section, we prove the probabilities given in Sect. 3.2. We remark that *all the following probabilities are not the exact ones, but "good enough" approximations useful for the target of the paper.* In particular, as discussed in detail in [7, Appendix A.2], the error in all the following probabilities is of magnitude 2^{-128}.

Let $I, J \subseteq \{0, 1, 2, 3\}$. We recall that

$$\mathcal{M}_I \cap \mathcal{M}_J = \mathcal{M}_{I \cap J}. \tag{12}$$

where $\mathcal{M}_I \cap \mathcal{M}_J = \{0\}$ if $I \cap J = \emptyset$. Moreover, referring to [11], we recall that the probability that a random text x belongs to $\mathcal{M}_I$ is well approximated by $Prob(x \in \mathcal{M}_I) = 2^{-32 \cdot (4 - |I|)}$, while given two random texts $x \neq y$

$$Prob(R(x) \oplus R(y) \in \mathcal{M}_J \mid x \oplus y \in \mathcal{M}_I) = (2^8)^{-4 \cdot |I| + |I| \cdot |J|}.$$

Proposition 1. *The probability $p_{|I|}$ that a random text x belongs to the subspace $\mathcal{M}_I$ for a certain $I \subseteq \{0, 1, 2, 3\}$ with $|I| = l$ fixed is well approximated by*

$$p_{|I|} = Prob(\exists I \subseteq \{0, 1, 2, 3\} \, |I| = l \text{ s.t. } x \in \mathcal{M}_I) = (-1)^{|I|} \cdot \sum_{i=4-|I|}^{3} (-1)^i \cdot c_{|I|, i} \cdot \binom{4}{i} \cdot 2^{-32 \cdot i}$$

where $c_{2,3} = 3$ and $c_{|I|, i} = 1$ for $\{|I|, i\} \neq \{2, 3\}$.

Proof. By definition, given the events $A_1, ..., A_n$ in a probability space $(\Omega, \mathcal{F}, \mathbb{P})$ then:

$$Prob\left(\bigcup_{i=1}^{n} A_i\right) = \sum_{k=1}^{n} \left((-1)^{k-1} \sum_{\substack{I \subset \{1,...,n\} \\ |I|=k}} Prob\left(\bigcap_{i \in I} A_i\right)\right),$$

where the last sum runs over all subsets I of the indexes $1, ..., n$ which contain exactly k elements[14]. Due to (12), it follows that for $|I| = 1$

$$Prob(\exists I \subseteq \{0, 1, 2, 3\} \, |I| = 1 \text{ s.t. } x \oplus y \in \mathcal{M}_I) =$$

$$= \sum_{I \subseteq \{0,1,2,3\}, |I|=1} Prob(x \oplus y \in \mathcal{M}_I) = 4 \cdot 2^{-96}.$$

---

[14] For example for $n = 2$, it follows that $Prob(A_1 \cup A_2) = Prob(A_1) + Prob(A_2) - \mathbb{P}(A_1 \cap A_2)$, while for $n = 3$ it follows that $Prob(A_1 \cup A_2 \cup A_3) = Prob(A_1) + Prob(A_2) + Prob(A_3) - Prob(A_1 \cap A_2) - Prob(A_1 \cap A_3) - Prob(A_2 \cap A_3) + Prob(A_1 \cap A_2 \cap A_3)$.

For $|I| = 3$, the probability is given by:

$$Prob(\exists I \subseteq \{0,1,2,3\} \,|I| = 3 \text{ s.t. } x \in \mathcal{M}_I) =$$

$$= \sum_{I \subseteq \{0,1,2,3\}, |I|=3} Prob(x \in \mathcal{M}_I) - \sum_{I \subseteq \{0,1,2,3\}, |I|=2} Prob(x \in \mathcal{M}_I) +$$

$$+ \sum_{I \subseteq \{0,1,2,3\}, |I|=1} Prob(x \in \mathcal{M}_I) = 4 \cdot 2^{-32} - 6 \cdot 2^{-64} + 4 \cdot 2^{-96},$$

since given 4 different sets $\mathcal{M}_I$ for $|I| = 3$ there are $\binom{4}{2} = 6$ possible intersections of 2 sets and $\binom{4}{3} = 4$ possible intersections of 3 sets (all intersections are not empty). Finally for $|I| = 2$

$$Prob(\exists I \subseteq \{0,1,2,3\} \,|I| = 2 \text{ s.t. } x \oplus y \in \mathcal{M}_I) =$$

$$= \sum_{I \subseteq \{0,1,2,3\}, |I|=2} Prob(x \oplus y \in \mathcal{M}_I) - \sum_{I \subseteq \{0,1,2,3\}, |I|=1} Prob(x \oplus y \in \mathcal{M}_I) =$$

$$= 6 \cdot 2^{-64} - 12 \cdot 2^{-96},$$

since given 6 different sets $\mathcal{M}_I$ for $|I| = 2$ there are $\binom{6}{2} = 15$ possible intersections of 2 sets. However, note that only 12 of them are not empty (since $\mathcal{M}_{0,1} \cap \mathcal{M}_{2,3} = \mathcal{M}_{0,2} \cap \mathcal{M}_{1,3} = \mathcal{M}_{0,3} \cap \mathcal{M}_{1,2} = \emptyset$). The result follows from $\binom{6}{1} = \binom{4}{2} = 6$ and $\binom{6}{2} - 3 = \binom{4}{3} \cdot 3 = 12$. □

Proposition 2. *Let x, y be two random elements. Assume that there exists $I \subseteq \{0,1,2,3\}$ such that $x \oplus y \in \mathcal{M}_I$ ($x \oplus y \notin \mathcal{M}_L$ for all $L \subseteq \{0,1,2,3\}$ with $|L| < |I|$). The probability that $\exists J \subseteq \{0,1,2,3\}$ with $|J| = l$ fixed such that $R(x) \oplus R(y) \in \mathcal{M}_J$ is well approximated by*

$$p_{|J|,|I|} \equiv Prob(\exists J \,|J| = l \text{ s.t. } R(x) \oplus R(y) \in \mathcal{M}_J \,|\, x \oplus y \in \mathcal{M}_I) =$$

$$= (-1)^{|J|} \cdot \sum_{i=4-|J|}^{3} (-1)^i \cdot c_{|J|,i} \cdot \binom{4}{i} \cdot 2^{-8 \cdot i \cdot |I|}.$$

where $c_{2,3} = 3$ and $c_{|J|,i} = 1$ for $\{|J|, i\} \neq \{2,3\}$.

Proof. As before, for $|J| = 3$:

$$Prob(\exists J \,|J| = 3 \text{ s.t. } R(x) \oplus R(y) \in \mathcal{M}_J \,|\, x \oplus y \in \mathcal{M}_I) =$$

$$= \sum_{z=1}^{3} \sum_{J \subseteq \{0,1,2,3\}, |J|=z} (-1)^{z+1} \cdot Prob(R(x) \oplus R(y) \in \mathcal{M}_J \,|\, x \oplus y \in \mathcal{M}_I) =$$

$$= 4 \cdot 2^{-8 \cdot |I|} - 6 \cdot 2^{-16 \cdot |I|} + 4 \cdot 2^{-24 \cdot |I|} = (-1)^3 \cdot \sum_{i=1}^{3} (-1)^i \cdot \binom{4}{i} \cdot 2^{-8 \cdot i \cdot |I|}.$$

Similar results for $|J| = 2$ and $|J| = 1$ can be computed in a similar way. □

Proposition 3. *Let x, y be two random elements such that $x \oplus y \notin \mathcal{M}_I$ for each $I \subseteq \{0, 1, 2, 3\}$. Then, the probability that $\exists J \subseteq \{0, 1, 2, 3\}$ for $|J| = l$ fixed such that $R(x) \oplus R(y) \in \mathcal{M}_J$ is well approximated by*

$$\hat{p}_{|J|,3} \equiv Prob(\exists J \ \text{s.t.} \ R(x) \oplus R(y) \in \mathcal{M}_J \,|\, x \oplus y \notin \mathcal{M}_I \,\forall I) = \frac{p_{|J|} - p_{|J|,3} \cdot p_3}{1 - p_3}.$$

Proof. Let A and B be two events, and let C be the event such that $A \cup C$ is equal to the sample space and such that $A \cap C = \emptyset$. By definition

$$Prob(B) = Prob(B \,|\, A) \cdot Prob(A) + Prob(B \,|\, C) \cdot Prob(C).$$

Thus

$$p_{|J|} \equiv Prob(\exists J \ \text{s.t.} \ R(x) \oplus R(y) \in \mathcal{M}_J) =$$
$$= Prob(\exists J \ \text{s.t.} \ R(x) \oplus R(y) \in \mathcal{M}_J \,|\, x \oplus y \notin \mathcal{M}_I \,\forall I) \cdot Prob(x \oplus y \notin \mathcal{M}_I \,\forall I) +$$
$$+ Prob(\exists J \ \text{s.t.} \ R(x) \oplus R(y) \in \mathcal{M}_J \,|\, \exists I \ \text{s.t.} \ x \oplus y \in \mathcal{M}_I) \cdot Prob(\exists I \ \text{s.t.} \ x \oplus y \in \mathcal{M}_I).$$

Note that[15]

$$Prob(\exists I \ \text{s.t.} \ x \oplus y \in \mathcal{M}_I) = Prob\left(x \oplus y \in \bigcup_{\forall I \subseteq \{0,1,2,3\}} \mathcal{M}_I \right) =$$

$$= Prob\left(x \oplus y \in \bigcup_{I \subseteq \{0,1,2,3\}, |I|=3} \mathcal{M}_I \right) \equiv p_3.$$

It follows that $p_{|J|} = p_{|J|,3} \cdot p_3 + \hat{p}_{|J|,3} \cdot (1 - p_3)$, that is the thesis.   □

B.1   Pairs with n Equal Generating "Variables in $(\mathbb{F}_{2^8})^{|I|}$"

Here we show that given texts in the same cosets of $\mathcal{C}_I$ (and similar for $\mathcal{M}_I$) for $I \subseteq \{0, 1, 2, 3\}$, the number of pairs of texts with v equal generating "variable(s) in $(\mathbb{F}_{2^8})^{|I|}$" for $0 \le v \le 3$ is given by

$$\binom{4}{v} \cdot 2^{32 \cdot |I| - 1} \cdot (2^{8 \cdot |I|} - 1)^{4-v}$$

First of all, what is a "variable(s) in $(\mathbb{F}_{2^8})^{|I|}$"? W.l.o.g consider $|I| = 2$ and assume $I = \{0, 1\}$ (the other cases are analogous). Given a text p in a coset of $\mathcal{M}_I$, that is $\mathcal{M}_I \oplus a$ for a given $a \in \mathcal{M}_I^\perp$, $\exists p_0', p_0'', p_1', p_1'', p_2', p_2'', p_3', p_3'' \in \mathbb{F}_{2^8}$ s.t.

$$p = a \oplus \begin{bmatrix} p_0' & p_3'' & 0 & 0 \\ p_1' & p_0'' & 0 & 0 \\ p_2' & p_1'' & 0 & 0 \\ p_3' & p_2'' & 0 & 0 \end{bmatrix}.$$

---

[15] If $x \oplus y \in \mathcal{M}_I$ for $|I| < 3$, then $\exists J$ with $|J| = 3$ and $I \subseteq J$ such that $x \oplus y \in \mathcal{M}_J$.

As for the case $|I| = 1$, the text p is defined by a (p_0, p_1, p_2, p_3) where $p_0 \equiv (p'_0, p''_0), p_1 \equiv (p'_1, p''_1), p_2 \equiv (p'_2, p''_2), p_3 \equiv (p'_3, p''_3)$. In other words, the idea is to consider variables in $(\mathbb{F}_{2^8})^2 \equiv \mathbb{F}_{2^8} \times \mathbb{F}_{2^8}$ and not in $\mathbb{F}_{2^8}$. For $|I| = 3$, the idea is to work with variables in $(\mathbb{F}_{2^8})^3$.

Note. Given $x = (x_0, x_1)$ and $y = (y_0, y_1)$ in $(\mathbb{F}_{2^8})^2$, we say that $x = y$ if and only if $x_0 = y_0$ and $x_1 = y_1$. E.g. if $x_0 = y_0$ and $x_1 \neq y_1$ (or viceversa), it follows that $x \neq y$ as variables in $(\mathbb{F}_{2^8})^2$. Analogous result holds in $(\mathbb{F}_{2^8})^3$.

Proof. W.l.o.g. consider for simplicity the case $|I| = 1$. First of all, note that there are $\binom{4}{v}$ different combinations of $v \leq 4$ variables. If $v \geq 1$, the v variables that must be equal for the two texts of the pair can take $(2^8)^v$ different values. For each one of the remaining $4 - v$ variables, the variables must be different for the two texts of each pair. Thus, these $4 - v$ variables can take exactly $\left[(2^8)^{4-v} \cdot (2^8 - 1)^{4-v}\right]/2$ different values. The result follows immediately.

The formula for the other cases is obtained in an analogous way.   □

C   Distinguisher on 5-Round AES – Cost

Here we discuss the computational cost of distinguisher on 5-round AES proposed in Sect. 5 for the case of cosets of $\mathcal{C}_I$ with $|I| = 1$.

A first possibility is to construct all the pairs, to divide them in sets $\mathcal{S}$ defined above, and to count the number of sets that satisfy the required property working on each set separately. Since just the cost to construct all the pairs given $2^{38.67}$ cosets is approximately of $2^{38.67} \cdot 2^{31} \cdot (2^{32} - 1) \simeq 2^{101.67}$ table look-ups, we present a more efficient way to implement the distinguisher.

To do this, we introduce a partial order $\preceq$.

Definition 10. *Let $I \subset \{0, 1, 2, 3\}$ with $|I| = 3$ and let $l \in \{0, 1, 2, 3\} \setminus I$. Let $t^1, t^2 \in \mathbb{F}_{2^8}^{4 \times 4}$ with $t^1 \neq t^2$. Texts t^1 and t^2 satisfy $t^1 \preceq t^2$ if and only if one of the two following conditions is satisfied (indexes are taken modulo 4):*

- *there exists $j \in \{0, 1, 2, 3\}$ s.t. $MC^{-1}(t^1)_{i,l-i} = MC^{-1}(t^2)_{i,l-i}$ for all $i < j$ and $MC^{-1}(t^1)_{j,l-j} < MC^{-1}(t^2)_{j,l-j}$;*
- *$MC^{-1}(t^1)_{i,l-i} = MC^{-1}(t^2)_{i,l-i}$ for all $i = 0, ..., 3$, and $MC^{-1}(t^1) < MC^{-1}(t^2)$ where $<$ is defined in Definition 4.*

Let $J \subseteq \{0, 1, 2, 3\}$ with $|J| = 3$. First of all, one has to re-order the ciphertexts with respect to a partial order $\preceq$ just defined. The cost to re-order a set of n texts w.r.t. a given partial order is $\mathcal{O}(n \cdot \log n)$ table look-ups.

For each coset of $\mathcal{C}_0$, *given ordered (plaintexts, ciphertexts) and working only on consecutive ciphertexts*, the idea is to count the number of collisions for each set $\mathcal{S}^{i,j}_{(x_0, x_1), (y_0, y_1)}$. In more details, for each coset of $\mathcal{C}_0$ it is possible to construct $N = 3 \cdot 2^{15} \cdot (2^8 - 1)^2$ different sets $\mathcal{S}^{i,j}_{(x_0, x_1), (y_0, y_1)}$ for each $i, j \in \{0, 1, 2, 3\}$ with $i \neq j$ and for each $x_0 \neq y_0$ and $x_1 \neq y_1$. The idea is to consider a vector $A[0, ..., N-1]$ such that

$$A[x] = \begin{cases} 1 & \text{if the } x\text{-th set } \mathcal{S} \text{ satisfies the required property;} \\ 0 & \text{otherwise} \end{cases}$$

Data: 2^{32} plaintexts in 1 coset of $\mathcal{C}_0$ (e.g. $\mathcal{C}_0 \oplus a$) and corresponding ciphertexts after 5 rounds

Result: Number of sets $\mathcal{S}$ such that two ciphertexts of at least one pair of plaintexts belong to the same coset of $\mathcal{M}_J$ for a certain J with $|J| = 3$

Let $A[0, ..., N-1]$ be an array initialized to zero, where $N = 3 \cdot 2^{15} \cdot (2^8 - 1)^2$

// $A[i]$ refers to the i-th set $\mathcal{S}$ (as defined in the main text)

for *each j from 0 to 3 let $J = \{0,1,2,3\} \setminus j$ ($|J| = 3$)* **do**

    let (p^i, c^i) for $i = 0, ..., 2^{32} - 1$ be the (plaintexts, ciphertexts) in $\mathcal{C}_0 \oplus a$;

    re-order this set of elements w.r.t. the partial order $\preceq$ defined in Def. 10;

    // $\preceq$ depends on J

    $i \leftarrow 0$;

    while $i < 2^{32} - 1$ **do**

        $j \leftarrow i$;

        while $c^j \oplus c^{j+1} \in \mathcal{M}_J$ **do**

         | $j \leftarrow j + 1$;

        end

        for *each k from i to j* **do**

            for *each l from $k+1$ to j* **do**

                if $p^k \oplus p^l \in \mathcal{D}_I$ *for a certain $|I| = 2$ (p^k and p^l have two equal generating variables)* // *necessary condition s.t. $p^k \oplus p^l \in \mathcal{S}^{x,y}$*

                for $x, y \in \{0, 1, 2, 3\}$ with $x \neq y$ **then**

                 | $A[\varphi(p^k, p^l)] \leftarrow 1$; // *$\varphi(p^k, p^l)$ defined in (13) returns the index of the set $\mathcal{S}^{x,y}$ s.t. $p^k \oplus p^l \in \mathcal{S}^{x,y}$*

                end

            end

        end

        | $i \leftarrow j + 1$;

    end

end

$n \leftarrow \sum_{i=0}^{N-1} A[i]$;

return n.

Algorithm 1. Given (plaintexts, ciphertexts) pairs in the same coset of $\mathcal{C}_0$, *this algorithm counts the number of sets $\mathcal{S}$ for which two ciphertext of at least one pair belong in the same coset of $\mathcal{M}_J$ for $|J| = 3$.*

All details are given in the following – pseudo-code is given in Algorithm 1.

To set up the distinguisher, it is sufficient to define a function φ that returns the index of a set $\mathcal{S}^{i,j}_{(x_0,x_1),(y_0,y_1)}$ (where $i < j$) in the vector $A[0, ..., N-1]$. Assuming $x_0 < y_0$ and $x_1 < y_1$ (note that a set $\mathcal{S}$ contains all plaintexts generated by different combinations of these four variables, so this condition is always fulfilled), the function $\varphi(\cdot) : (\mathbb{F}_{2^8})^4 \times (\{0,1,2,3\})^2 \rightarrow \mathbb{N}$ can be defined as

$$\varphi(x_0, x_1, y_0, y_1, i, j) = 1\,065\,369\,600 \times \phi(i,j) + \Phi(x_0, x_1, y_0, y_1) \qquad (13)$$

where $1\,065\,369\,600 = 32\,640^2$ (where $32\,640 = 2^{n-1} \cdot (2^n - 1)$ for $n = 8$), where $\phi(0,1) = 0$, $\phi(0,2) = 1$, $\phi(0,3) = 2$, $\phi(1,2) = 3$, $\phi(1,3) = 4$, $\phi(2,3) = 5$ and

$$\Phi(x_0, x_1, y_0, y_1) = \left[x_0 + \frac{y_0 \times (y_0 - 1)}{2} \right] + 32\,640 \times \left[x_1 + \frac{y_1 \times (y_1 - 1)}{2} \right]$$

where each value of $x_0, x_1, y_0, y_1 \in \mathbb{F}_{2^8}$ is replaced by its corresponding number in $\{0, 1, ..., 255\}$. The previous formula for Φ is obtained by observing that

1. for a fixed $y \geq 1$, there are exactly y different pairs (x, y) that satisfy $x \geq 0$ and $x < y$;
2. for a fixed $z \geq 1$, there are exactly $\sum_{i=1}^{z-1} i = \frac{z \cdot (z-1)}{2}$ different pairs (x, y) that satisfy $x, y \geq 0$ and $x < y \leq z$.
3. given a pair (w, z) (where $0 \leq w < z$), there are exactly

$$w + \frac{z \cdot (z-1)}{2}$$

different pairs (x, y) that satisfy (1) $y < z$ or (2) $y = z$ and $x \leq w$.

As a result, using Algorithm 1 to implement the distinguisher, the computational cost is well approximated by

$$4 \cdot \left[2^{32} \cdot \log(2^{32}) \text{ (re-ordering process)} + \left(2^{32} + 2 \cdot 2^{31}\right) \text{ (access to } (p^i, c^i) \text{ and to } A[\cdot] \text{ -} \right.$$

$$\left. \text{- increment number of collisions)} \right] + \frac{1}{2^{18}} \cdot 6 \cdot 2^{16} \cdot (2^8 - 1)^2 \text{ (final "for")} \simeq 2^{39.07}$$

table look-ups for each initial coset, where $\binom{2^{32}}{2} \cdot 2^{-32} \simeq 2^{31}$ is the average number of pairs such that the two ciphertexts belong to the same coset of $\mathcal{M}_J$ for J fixed with $|J| = 3$. Since the attacker must use $2^{38.66}$ different initial cosets to have a probability of success higher than 95%, the *total computational cost* is of $2^{39.07} \cdot 2^{38.66} = 2^{77.73}$ table look-ups, or $\approx 2^{71.1}$ five-round encryptions.

D   Variant of the 5-Round AES Distinguisher of Sect. 5

In this section, we propose two variants of the 5-round secret-key distinguisher proposed in Sect. 5. The second one is the most competitive distinguisher (from the point of view of the data and the computational costs), but it can not be used for a key-recovery attacks, as discuss in the following.

To set up the distinguisher, we must recall one result from [8,10]:

Theorem 5. *Given the subspace $\mathcal{C}_0 \cap \mathcal{D}_{0,2,3} \equiv \langle e_{0,0}, e_{1,0}, e_{2,0} \rangle \subseteq \mathcal{C}_0$, consider two plaintexts p^1 and p^2 in the same coset of $(\mathcal{C}_0 \cap \mathcal{D}_{0,2,3}) \oplus a$ generated by $p^1 \equiv (x^1, y^1, w^1)$ and $p^2 \equiv (x^2, y^2, w^2)$. Let $\hat{p}^1, \hat{p}^2 \in (\mathcal{D}_{0,2,3} \cap \mathcal{C}_0) \oplus a$ be other two plaintexts generated by*

1. (x^1, y^1, w^1, z) *and* (x^2, y^2, w^2, z);   2. (x^2, y^1, w^1, z) *and* (x^1, y^2, w^2, z);
3. (x^1, y^2, w^1, z) *and* (x^2, y^1, w^2, z);   4. (x^1, y^1, w^2, z) *and* (x^2, y^2, w^1, z).

where z can take any possible value in $\mathbb{F}_{2^8}$. The following event

$$R^4(p^1) \oplus R^4(p^2) \in \mathcal{M}_J \quad \text{if and only if} \quad R^4(\hat{p}^1) \oplus R^4(\hat{p}^2) \in \mathcal{M}_J$$

holds with prob. 1 for 4-round AES, independently of the secret key, of the details of the S-Box and of the MixColumns matrix.

Variant of the 5-Round Distinguisher of Sect. 5: Plaintexts in $\mathcal{C}_{0,1}$

Details of the Distinguisher. Consider 2^{64} chosen plaintexts with two active column (8 active bytes), e.g. a coset of $\mathcal{C}_{0,1}$, and the corresponding ciphertexts after 5-round. For each $(\mathbf{x}, \mathbf{y}) \in \mathbb{F}_{2^8}^6 \times \mathbb{F}_{2^8}^6$ where $\mathbf{x} = (x_0, x_1, x_2, ..., x_5)$ and $\mathbf{y} = (y_0, y_1, y_2, ..., y_5)$ such that $(x_0, x_1) \neq (y_0, y_1)$, $(x_2, x_3) \neq (y_2, y_3)$ and $(x_4, x_5) \neq (y_4, y_5)$, let $\mathcal{T}_{(\mathbf{x},\mathbf{y})}^3$ be the set of pairs of plaintexts be defined as follows

$$\mathcal{T}_{(\mathbf{x},\mathbf{y})}^3 = \{(p,q) \in \mathbb{F}_{2^8}^{4 \times 4} \times \mathbb{F}_{2^8}^{4 \times 4} \text{ s.t. for each } A, B \in \mathbb{F}_{2^8} :$$

$$p \equiv ((x_0, x_2, x_4, A), (B, x_1, x_3, x_5)), q \equiv ((y_0, y_2, y_4, A), (B, y_1, y_3, y_5)) \quad \text{or}$$
$$p \equiv ((y_0, x_2, x_4, A), (B, y_1, x_3, x_5)), q \equiv ((x_0, y_2, y_4, A), (B, x_1, y_3, y_5)) \quad \text{or}$$
$$p \equiv ((x_0, y_2, x_4, A), (B, x_1, y_3, x_5)), q \equiv ((y_0, x_2, y_4, A), (B, y_1, x_3, y_5)) \quad \text{or}$$
$$p \equiv ((x_0, x_2, y_4, A), (B, x_1, x_3, y_5)), q \equiv ((y_0, y_2, x_4, A), (B, y_1, y_3, x_5)) \quad \}.$$

In other words, the pair of plaintexts $p, q \in \mathcal{C}_0 \oplus a$ can be of the form

$$p \equiv \begin{bmatrix} x_0 & B & 0 & 0 \\ x_2 & x_1 & 0 & 0 \\ x_4 & x_3 & 0 & 0 \\ A & x_5 & 0 & 0 \end{bmatrix} \quad q \equiv \begin{bmatrix} y_0 & B & 0 & 0 \\ y_2 & y_1 & 0 & 0 \\ y_4 & y_3 & 0 & 0 \\ A & y_5 & 0 & 0 \end{bmatrix} \quad \text{or} \quad p \equiv \begin{bmatrix} y_0 & B & 0 & 0 \\ x_2 & y_1 & 0 & 0 \\ x_4 & x_3 & 0 & 0 \\ A & x_5 & 0 & 0 \end{bmatrix} \quad q \equiv \begin{bmatrix} x_0 & B & 0 & 0 \\ y_2 & x_1 & 0 & 0 \\ y_4 & y_3 & 0 & 0 \\ A & y_5 & 0 & 0 \end{bmatrix}$$

and so on. Similar definitions can be given for the set $\mathcal{T}_{(\mathbf{x},\mathbf{y})}^i$ for each $i \in \{0, 1, 2, 3\}$, where the constant bytes is in the i-th diagonal. Given 2^{64} plaintexts as before, it is possible to construct $\frac{1}{2^{18}} \cdot 4 \cdot 2^{63} \cdot (2^{16} - 1)^3 \simeq 2^{95}$ different sets, where each set contains exactly 2^{18} different pairs of plaintexts (we emphasize that these pairs of plaintexts are not independent, in the sense that a particular relationships among the generating variable holds).

Consider $n \gg 1$ random sets, and count the number of sets for which two ciphertexts (generated by 5-round AES or by a random permutation) of at least one pair of texts belong to the same coset of a subspace $\mathcal{M}_J$ for $J \subseteq \{0, 1, 2, 3\}$ and $|J| = 3$. As we are going to prove, this number is on average lower for AES than for a random permutation, independently of the secret key, of the details of the S-Box and of the MixColumns matrix. In more details, the numbers of sets for 5-round AES n_{AES} and for a random permutation n_{rand} are well approximated by $n_{AES} \simeq n \cdot p_{AES}$ and $n_{rand} \simeq n \cdot p_{rand}$ where

$$p_{AES} \simeq 2^{-12} - 1048575 \cdot 2^{-45} + \underbrace{46\,884\,625\,075 \cdot 2^{-76}}_{\approx 2.73 \cdot 2^{-42}} + ...$$

$$p_{rand} \simeq 2^{-12} - 1048575 \cdot 2^{-45} + \underbrace{183\,251\,413\,675 \cdot 2^{-76}}_{\approx 10.667 \cdot 2^{-42}} + ...$$

These numbers are derived using the same proof[16] proposed in Sect. 5.

Data Cost. In order to compute the data cost, we use the same argumentation of Sect. 5.2. Since $|p_{AES} - p_{rand}| \simeq 2^{-39.011}$ and $p_{AES} \simeq p_{rand} \simeq 2^{-12}$, it follows

---

[16] A complete proof will be provide in the extended-version of this paper.

that n must satisfy $n > 2^{68.243}$ for a probability of success of approximately 95%. Since a single coset of $\mathcal{C}_I$ for $|I| = 2$ contains approximately 2^{95} different sets $\mathcal{T}$, less than a single coset is sufficient to implement the distinguisher. In particular, a subset of the coset $\mathcal{C}_{0,1} \oplus a$ of the form

$$\left\{ a \oplus \begin{bmatrix} x_0 & y_1 & 0 & 0 \\ z_0 & x_1 & 0 & 0 \\ w_0 & z_1 & 0 & 0 \\ y_0 & w_1 & 0 & 0 \end{bmatrix} \; \middle| \; \forall x_0, x_1, y_0, y_1, z_0, z_1 \in \mathbb{F}_{2^8}^2, \; \forall w_0, w_1 \in \{0x00, 0x01, 0x02, 0x03\} \right\}$$

for a certain constant a is sufficient to set up the distinguisher. Indeed, for such a set it is possible to construct approximately $\frac{1}{2^{18}} \cdot 3 \cdot (2^{48} \cdot 4^2) \cdot [(2^{16} - 1)^2 \cdot (16 - 1)] \simeq 2^{71.5}$ different sets $\mathcal{T}$ (remember that we are working with variables in $\mathbb{F}_{2^8}^2$), for a total of $(2^8)^6 \cdot 4^2 \simeq 2^{52}$ chosen plaintexts.

Computational Cost. About the computational cost, the idea is to exploit Algorithm 1 opportunely modified and adapted to the sets $\mathcal{T}$ in order to implement the distinguisher. Using 2^{52} chosen plaintexts in the same coset of $\mathcal{C}_I$ for $|I| = 2$, the cost to count the number of sets $\mathcal{T}$ for which two ciphertexts of at least one pair of plaintexts belong to the same coset of $\mathcal{M}_J$ is

$$4 \cdot \left[2^{52} \cdot \log(2^{52}) \; \text{(re-ordering process)} \; + \left(2^{52} + 2 \cdot 2^{57} \right) \; \text{(access to } (p^i, c^i) \text{and to}\right.$$
$$\left. A[\cdot] - \text{increment number of collisions)} \; \right] + 2^{71.5} \; \text{(final "for")} \simeq 2^{71.5}$$

table look-ups, where $\binom{2^{52}}{2} \cdot 2^{-32} \cdot (4 \cdot 2^{-16}) \simeq 2^{57}$ is the average number of pairs such that the two ciphertexts belong to the same coset of $\mathcal{M}_J$ for a fixed J with $|J| = 3$ and the two plaintexts are in the same coset of $\mathcal{C}_{0,1} \cap \mathcal{D}_I$ for a certain I with $|I| = 3$ (by definition of $\mathcal{T}$). Equivalently, the total cost is well approximated by $2^{64.86}$ five-round encryptions.

E   Key-Recovery Attack on 6-Round AES – Cost

Here we analyze the computational cost of the key-recovery attack on 6-round AES proposed in Sect. 6. The attack is implemented by exploiting Algorithm 1 for each possible guessed key in order to count the number of sets $\mathcal{S}$ that satisfy the required property (i.e. two ciphertexts of at least one pair belong to the same coset of $\mathcal{M}_J$ for a certain J with $|J| = 3$). Since this number of sets is higher for a wrongly guessed key than for the right one, it is possible to recover the right candidate of the key.

An implementation of the attack is described by the pseudo-code given in Algorithm 2. To compute the computational cost, it is sufficient to re-consider the cost of the 5-round distinguisher. Given a coset of $\mathcal{C}_0$, the cost to count the number of sets $\mathcal{S}$ with the required property is $2^{39.1}$ table look-ups. This step is repeated for each one of the 2^{32} (partially) guessed key and for each one of the $2^{40.77}$ initial cosets of $\mathcal{D}_0$, for a cost of $2^{39.05} \cdot 2^{40.77} \cdot 2^{32} = 2^{111.82}$ table look-ups. Moreover, one needs to partially compute 1-round encryption for each

Data: $2^{40.77}$ cosets of $\mathcal{D}_0$ (e.g. $\mathcal{D}_0 \oplus a_i$ for $a_i \in \mathcal{D}_0^\perp$) and corresponding
ciphertexts after 6 rounds
Result: 4 bytes of the secret key - $(k_{0,0}, k_{1,1}, k_{2,2}, k_{3,3})$
Let $N[0, ..., 2^{32} - 1]$ be an array initialized to zero; // $N[k]$ denotes the number
of sets $\mathcal{S}$ that satisfy the required property for the key k
/* *1st Step*: for each guessed key, count the number of sets $\mathcal{S}$ with the required
property   */
for *each $\hat{k}$ from* (0x00, 0x00, 0x00, 0x00) *to* (0xff, 0xff, 0xff, 0xff) **do**
   for *each coset $\mathcal{D}_0 \oplus a_i$* **do**
      (partially) encrypt the 2^{32} plaintexts w.r.t. the guessed key $\hat{k}$;
      use Algorithm 1 to count the number n of sets $\mathcal{S}$ that satisfy the
      required property;
      $N[\psi(\hat{k})] \leftarrow N[\psi(\hat{k})] + n$; // where $\psi(\hat{k} \equiv (k_0, k_1, k_2, k_3)) = \sum_{i=0}^{3} k_i \cdot 2^{8 \cdot i}$
   end
end
/* *2nd Step*: look for the key for which number of sets $\mathcal{S}$ is minimum   */
$min \leftarrow N[0]$;   // minimum number of sets
$\delta \leftarrow$ (0x00, 0x00, 0x00, 0x00);
for *each $\hat{k}$ from* (0x00, 0x00, 0x00, 0x00) *to* (0xff, 0xff, 0xff, 0xff) **do**
   if $N[\varphi(\hat{k})] < min$ **then**
     $min \leftarrow N[\varphi(\hat{k})]$; $\delta \leftarrow \hat{k} \equiv (k_{0,0}, k_{1,1}, k_{2,2}, k_{3,3})$;
   end
end
return δ – *candidate of* $(k_{0,0}, k_{1,1}, k_{2,2}, k_{3,3})$

Algorithm 2. *6-round key-recovery attack on AES exploiting a 5-round secret-key distinguisher.* The goal of the attack is to find 4 bytes of the secret key. The remaining bytes (the entire key) are found by brute force.

possible guessed key and for each initial coset, for a cost of $4 \cdot 2^{32} \cdot 2^{40.77} \cdot 2^{32} = 2^{106.77}$ S-Box look-ups. As a result, the total cost of finding one diagonal of the key is well approximated by $2^{111.82}$ table look-ups, or equivalently $2^{104.92}$ six-round encryptions (under the assumption 20 table/S-Box look-ups $\approx$ 1-round encryption). The total cost to find the entire key (using brute force on the last three diagonal) is of $2^{104.92} + 2^{96} = 2^{104.93}$ six-round encryptions.

Why is it not possible to set up the key-recovery attack using cosets of $\mathcal{D}_I$ with $|I| = 2$ instead of $|I| = 1$ (that is, the one proposed in Appendix D)? Without going into details, one has to guess 64 bits of the key instead of 32 for the attack that exploits the distinguisher proposed in Appendix D. As a consequence, this attack requires approximately $2^{88.1}$ chosen plaintexts (in $2^{24.1}$ different initial cosets of $\mathcal{D}_I$ with $|I| = 2$) and it has a total computational cost of approximately $2^{176.2}$ six-round encryptions, (much) higher than the cost of a brute force attack.

References

1. Bar-On, A., Dunkelman, O., Keller, N., Ronen, E., Shamir, A.: Improved key recovery attacks on reduced-round AES with practical data and memory complexities. In: Shacham, H., Boldyreva, A. (eds.) CRYPTO 2018. LNCS, vol. 10992, pp. 185–212. Springer, Cham (2018). https://doi.org/10.1007/978-3-319-96881-0_7
2. Boura, C., Canteaut, A., Coggia, D.: A general proof framework for recent AES distinguishers. IACR Trans. Symmetric Cryptol. **2019**(1), 170–191 (2019)
3. Cheon, J.H., Kim, M.J., Kim, K., Jung-Yeun, L., Kang, S.W.: Improved impossible differential cryptanalysis of Rijndael and Crypton. In: Kim, K. (ed.) ICISC 2001. LNCS, vol. 2288, pp. 39–49. Springer, Heidelberg (2002). https://doi.org/10.1007/3-540-45861-1_4
4. Cid, C., Murphy, S., Robshaw, M.J.B.: Small scale variants of the AES. In: Gilbert, H., Handschuh, H. (eds.) FSE 2005. LNCS, vol. 3557, pp. 145–162. Springer, Heidelberg (2005). https://doi.org/10.1007/11502760_10
5. Daemen, J., Rijmen, V.: The Design of Rijndael: AES - The Advanced Encryption Standard. Information Security and Cryptography. Springer, Heidelberg (2002). https://doi.org/10.1007/978-3-662-04722-4
6. Derbez, P., Fouque, P.-A.: Exhausting Demirci-Selçuk meet-in-the-middle attacks against reduced-round AES. In: Moriai, S. (ed.) FSE 2013. LNCS, vol. 8424, pp. 541–560. Springer, Heidelberg (2014). https://doi.org/10.1007/978-3-662-43933-3_28
7. Grassi, L.: Mixture differential cryptanalysis and structural truncated differential attacks on round-reduced AES. Cryptology ePrint Archive, Report 2017/832 (2017). https://eprint.iacr.org/2017/832
8. Grassi, L.: Mixture differential cryptanalysis: a new approach to distinguishers and attacks on round-reduced AES. IACR Trans. Symmetric Cryptol. **2018**(2), 133–160 (2018)
9. Grassi, L., Rechberger, C.: New rigorous analysis of truncated differentials for 5-round AES. IACR Cryptol. ePrint Arch. **2018**, 182 (2018)
10. Grassi, L., Rechberger, C., Rønjom, S.: A new structural-differential property of 5-round AES. In: Coron, J.-S., Nielsen, J.B. (eds.) EUROCRYPT 2017. LNCS, vol. 10211, pp. 289–317. Springer, Cham (2017). https://doi.org/10.1007/978-3-319-56614-6_10
11. Grassi, L., Rechberger, C., Rønjom, S.: Subspace trail cryptanalysis and its applications to AES. IACR Trans. Symmetric Cryptol. **2016**(2), 192–225 (2017). http://ojs.ub.rub.de/index.php/ToSC/article/view/571
12. Knudsen, L.R.: Truncated and higher order differentials. In: Preneel, B. (ed.) FSE 1994. LNCS, vol. 1008, pp. 196–211. Springer, Heidelberg (1995). https://doi.org/10.1007/3-540-60590-8_16
13. Rønjom, S., Bardeh, N.G., Helleseth, T.: Yoyo tricks with AES. In: Takagi, T., Peyrin, T. (eds.) ASIACRYPT 2017. LNCS, vol. 10624, pp. 217–243. Springer, Cham (2017). https://doi.org/10.1007/978-3-319-70694-8_8
14. Todo, Y.: Structural evaluation by generalized integral property. In: Oswald, E., Fischlin, M. (eds.) EUROCRYPT 2015. LNCS, vol. 9056, pp. 287–314. Springer, Heidelberg (2015). https://doi.org/10.1007/978-3-662-46800-5_12
15. Tunstall, M.: Improved "Partial Sums"-based square attack on AES. In: International Conference on Security and Cryptography - SECRYPT 2012. LNCS, vol. 4817, pp. 25–34 (2012)

Iterative Differential Characteristic of TRIFLE-BC

Fukang Liu[1,3(✉)] and Takanori Isobe[2,3]

[1] Shanghai Key Laboratory of Trustworthy Computing,
East China Normal University, Shanghai, China
liufukangs@163.com
[2] National Institute of Information and Communications Technology,
Koganei, Japan
[3] University of Hyogo, Hyogo, Japan
takanori.isobe@ai.u-hyogo.ac.jp

Abstract. TRIFLE is a Round 1 candidate of the NIST Lightweight Cryptography Standardization process. In this paper, we present an interesting 1-round iterative differential characteristic of the underlying block cipher TRIFLE-BC used in TRIFLE, which holds with probability of 2^{-3}. Consequently, it allows to mount distinguishing attack on TRIFLE-BC for up to 43 (out of 50) rounds with data complexity 2^{124} and time complexity 2^{124}. Most importantly, with such an iterative differential characteristic, the forgery attack on TRIFLE can reach up to 21 (out of 50) rounds with data complexity 2^{63} and time complexity 2^{63}. Finally, to achieve key recovery attack on reduced TRIFLE, we construct a differential characteristic covering three blocks by carefully choosing the positions of the iterative differential characteristic. As a result, we can mount key-recovery attack on TRIFLE for up to 11 rounds with data complexity 2^{63} and time complexity 2^{104}. Although the result in this paper cannot threaten the security margin of TRIFLE, we hope it can help further understand the security of TRIFLE.

Keywords: AEAD · TRIFLE · Differential attack · Distinguisher · Forgery

1 Introduction

With the development of the emerging areas like sensor networks, healthcare, distributed control systems, the Internet of Things, and cyber physical systems, where highly-constrained devices are interconnected, typically communicating wirelessly with one another, and working in concert to accomplish some task, new requirements for cryptographic algorithms start to appear. The new requirements covers such aspects as energy, power, area and throughput. Consequently, recent years have witnessed many new designs of lightweight block ciphers, hash functions and stream ciphers like PRESENT [7], KATAN [8], PICOLO [20], PHOTON [12], SIMON/SPECK [4], Midori [2], SKINNY [5], Plantlet [16], and QARMA [1], just to name a few. The main reason why there is a

© Springer Nature Switzerland AG 2020
K. G. Paterson and D. Stebila (Eds.): SAC 2019, LNCS 11959, pp. 85–100, 2020.
https://doi.org/10.1007/978-3-030-38471-5_4

demand for lightweight designs lies in that conventional cryptographic algorithms designed for desktop/server environments cannot fit into constrained device. To standardize lightweight cryptographic algorithms that are suitable for use in constrained environments, the National Institute of Standards and Technology (NIST) started a public lightweight cryptography competition project in as early as 2013 and initiated the call for submissions in 2018, with the hope to select a lightweight cryptographic standard by combining the efforts of both academia and industry. The 56 Round 1 candidates of the NIST Lightweight Cryptography Standardization project became public on April 18, 2019. Since the publication, the cryptanalysis has started. For instance, a probability 1 iterative differential characteristic in the SNEIK permutation was identified in [18], which was quickly exploited to mount forgery attack on full SNEIKEN [13]. As a response for this attack, the designer of SNEIK has updated SNEIK accordingly. Very recently, Eichlseder et al. also showed a forgery attack on FlexAEAD [11].

Since there exist several advanced cryptanalysis techniques to evaluate the security of a primitive, the resistance against differential attack [6], linear attack [15], integral attack [14, 22, 23], cube attack [10] and many other attack methods have been well analyzed by the designers for most submitted primitives. The feasibility of efficient security evaluation against classical cryptanalysis is owing to the emerging automatical cryptanalysis techniques to model the corresponding attacks [17, 19, 21, 24, 25] and solve with existing state-of-the-art solvers.

TRIFLE is one of the Round 1 candidates [9]. It is an Authenticated Encryption with Associated Data (AEAD) algorithm, which is constructed based on the underlying block cipher TRIFLE-BC. TRIFLE employs a MAC-then-Encrypt type paradigm, where CBC style authentication is done on the nonce, associated data and the plaintext to generate the tag. This tag is then used as a random IV in an output feedback mode of encryption to generate the ciphertext. The authors make a security claim for TRIFLE under the IND-CPA and INT-CTXT security model, which requires that the data complexity cannot exceed 2^{64} and time complexity cannot exceed 2^{128}. In other words, the total number of blocks (among all messages and associated data) processed through the underlying block cipher for a fixed master key at the online phase cannot exceed 2^{64}. Moreover, the designers claim that the linear transform in TRIFLE-BC can provide the maximal diffusion. However, as will be shown, an iterative differential characteristic with hamming weight 1 is identified for TRIFLE-BC. Although such an iterative differential characteristic cannot be exploited to mount distinguishing attack on full TRIFLE-BC, we can attack 43 out of 50 rounds of TRIFLE-BC, revealing the powerful effect of such an iterative differential characteristic. In a word, when taking into account the combination of the S-box and linear transform in TRIFLE-BC, an interesting and surprising iterative differential characteristic with hamming weight 1 is identified, which holds with probability 2^{-3}. Some related analytical results are presented in Table 1.

Table 1. The analytical results of TRIFLE

Attack type	Target	Rounds	Data	Time	Ref
Distinguishing attack	TRIFLE-BC	43	2^{124}	2^{124}	Sect. 4.1
Forgery attack	TRIFLE	21	2^{63}	2^{63}	Sect. 4.2
Key-recovery attack	TRIFLE	11	2^{63}	2^{104}	Sect. 4.3
Key-recovery attack	TRIFLE-BC	44	2^{126}	2^{126}	Sect. 4.3

Organization. This paper is organized as follows. The notations and the description of TRIFLE are given in Sect. 2. Then, we reveal the iterative differential characteristic of TRIFLE-BC in Sect. 3. The application of this iterative differential characteristic on distinguishing attack, forgery attack and key-recovery attack is detailed in Sect. 4. Finally, we conclude the paper in Sect. 5.

2 Preliminaries

In this section, we give a description of the notations and the primitive TRIFLE.

2.1 Notation

For a better understanding of this paper, some notations are given below.

1. W represents the internal state of TRIFLE-BC.
2. W^i represents the input state of the i-th round of RIFLE-BC where ($0 \leq i \leq 49$).
3. W_s^i/W_p^i respectively represent the internal state after **SubNibbles/BitPermutaion** in the i-th round of TRIFLE-BC.
4. $\Delta W^i/\Delta W_s^i/\Delta W_p^i$ respectively represent the xor difference of W^i, W_s^i and W_p^i.
5. $Z[i]$ represents the i-th bit of Z (Z can be W^i, W_s^i, W_p^i $\cdots$). $Z[0]$ denotes the least significant bit of Z.
6. $Z[j \sim i]$ represents the j-th bit to the i-th bit of Z (Z can be W^i, W_s^i, W_p^i $\cdots$). For example, $Z[1 \sim 0]$ denotes the two bits $Z[1]$ and $Z[0]$.
7. $\ggg$ and $\oplus$ respectively represent the logic operation: rotate right and exclusive or.
8. $A||B$ represents the concatenation of A and B.

2.2 Specification of TRIFLE

TRIFLE is a block cipher based authenticated encryption mode with block size $n = 128$ that receives an encryption key $K \in \{0,1\}^{128}$, a nonce $N \in \{0,1\}^{128}$, an associated data $A \in \{0,1\}^*$ and a message $M \in \{0,1\}^*$ as inputs and returns a ciphertext $C \in \{0,1\}^{|M|}$ and a tag $T \in \{0,1\}^{128}$, where $|M|$ represents the length of M in number of bits. The underlying block cipher is denoted by TRIFLE-BC. TRIFLE employs a MAC-then-Encrypt type paradigm, where CBC style authentication is done on the nonce, associated data and the plaintext to generate the tag. This tag is then used as a random IV in an output feedback mode of encryption to generate the ciphertext. The construction of TRIFLE is depicted in Fig. 1, where **Prefix** is a constant to represent whether the associated data A and message M are empty. Besides, OZP is the function that applies optional 10^* padding on n bits, i.e., $OZP(X) = 0^{n-|X|-1}||1||X$ when $|X| < n$, and $OZP(X) = X$, if $|X| = n$. More details of TRIFILE can be found at [9].

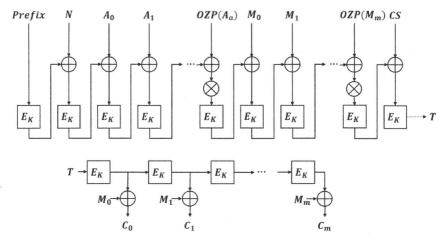

$$CS = Prefix \oplus N \oplus A_0 \oplus A_1 \oplus \cdots \oplus OZP(A_a) \oplus M_0 \oplus M_1 \oplus \cdots \oplus OZP(M_m)$$

Fig. 1. The construction of TRIFLE

The underlying block cipher TRIFLE-BC (E_K in Fig. 1) used in TRIFLE receives a 128-bit plaintext P and a 128-bit key $K = (K_7||K_6||...||K_0)$, where $K_i \in F_2^{16}$ ($0 \leq i \leq 7$). The internal state of TRIFLE-BC W can be viewed as 32 4-bit nibbles. The block cipher TRIFLE-BC is composed of 50 rounds and each round consists of four consecutive operations **SubNibbles**, **BitPermutation**, **AddRoundKey** and **AddRoundConst**, as specified in the following. More details can be found at [9].

SubNibbles. TRIFLE-BC uses an invertible 4-bit S-box and applies it to every nibble of the internal state. The specification of this S-box can be found at Table 4. The corresponding Differential Distribution Table (DDT) can be found at Table 2.

BitPermutation. TRIFLE-BC uses an optimal bit permutation to create maximal diffusion. This permutation maps bits from bit position i of the cipher state to bit position $P(i)$, where $P(i) = i/4 + (i \bmod 4) \times 32$. The bit mapping table can be seen at Table 3.

Table 2. DDT of S-box of TRIFLE-BC

Δ_{in}/Δ_{out}	0	1	2	3	4	5	6	7	8	9	a	b	c	d	e	f
0	16	0	0	0	0	0	0	0	0	0	0	0	0	0	0	0
1	0	0	0	0	0	0	2	2	2	0	2	0	4	2	2	0
2	0	2	0	0	0	2	0	0	0	4	0	2	2	2	2	0
3	0	2	2	0	2	2	0	4	0	2	0	2	0	0	0	0
4	0	0	2	4	0	0	0	2	0	2	2	2	0	2	0	0
5	0	0	0	0	4	2	2	0	2	2	0	0	2	0	2	0
6	0	0	2	2	2	0	0	2	2	0	2	0	0	0	4	0
7	0	0	2	2	4	0	0	0	0	2	0	2	2	0	0	2
8	0	0	0	2	2	2	4	2	0	0	0	2	0	0	2	0
9	0	2	2	0	0	0	0	0	2	0	2	4	2	2	0	0
a	0	0	0	2	0	2	0	0	0	0	4	2	2	0	2	2
b	0	2	4	0	0	0	2	0	0	2	0	0	2	2	0	2
c	0	2	0	0	2	2	2	0	2	0	0	0	0	4	2	0
d	0	4	0	2	0	0	2	0	2	0	0	0	2	0	2	2
e	0	0	0	2	2	0	2	2	4	2	0	0	0	0	0	2
f	0	2	2	0	2	2	0	0	2	0	2	0	0	0	0	4

Table 3. The TRIFLE-BC BitPermutation

i	0	1	2	3	4	5	6	7	8	9	10	11	12	13	14	15
$P(i)$	0	32	64	96	1	33	65	97	2	34	66	98	3	35	67	99
i	16	17	18	19	20	21	22	23	24	25	26	27	28	29	30	31
$P(i)$	4	36	68	100	5	37	69	101	6	38	70	102	7	39	71	103
i	32	33	34	35	36	37	38	39	40	41	42	43	44	45	46	47
$P(i)$	8	40	72	104	9	41	73	105	10	42	74	106	11	43	75	107
i	48	49	50	51	52	53	54	55	56	57	58	59	60	61	62	63
$P(i)$	12	44	76	108	13	45	77	109	14	46	78	110	15	47	79	111
i	64	65	66	67	68	69	70	71	72	73	74	75	76	77	78	79
$P(i)$	16	48	80	112	17	49	81	113	18	50	82	114	19	51	83	115
i	80	81	82	83	84	85	86	87	88	89	90	91	92	93	94	95
$P(i)$	20	52	84	116	21	53	85	117	22	54	86	118	23	55	87	119
i	96	97	98	99	100	101	102	103	104	105	106	107	108	109	110	111
$P(i)$	24	56	88	120	25	57	89	121	26	58	90	122	27	59	91	123
i	112	113	114	115	116	117	118	119	120	121	122	123	124	125	126	127
$P(i)$	28	60	92	124	29	61	93	125	30	62	94	126	31	63	95	127

AddRoundKey. The round key is xored with the internal state $(W[4i + 1], W[4i + 2])$ $(0 \leq i \leq 31)$. Specifically, suppose the 128-bit $K^i = (K_7^i \| K_6^i \| ... \| K_0^i)$ $(0 \leq i \leq 49)$ represents the key used in the i−th round. Then, at round i, the key addition is proceeded as follows.

$$U^i[31] \| ... \| U^i[0] \leftarrow K_4^i \| K_5^i,$$
$$V^i[31] \| ... \| V^i[0] \leftarrow K_1^i \| K_0^i,$$
$$W[4j + 2] \leftarrow W[4j + 2] \oplus U^i[j] \ (0 \leq j \leq 31),$$
$$W[4j + 1] \leftarrow W[4j + 1] \oplus V^i[j] \ (0 \leq j \leq 31).$$

As can be seen, we can also denote the i-th round key by (U^i, V^i), where $U^i \in F_2^{32}$ and $V^i \in F_2^{32}$. After key addition, the round key used for next round is generated as follows, which is similar to the one used in GIFT-128 [3].

$$K_7^{i+1} \| ... \| K_0^{i+1} \leftarrow K_1^i \ggg 2 \| K_0^i \ggg 12 \| K_7^i \| ... \| K_2^i.$$

AddRoundConst. The 6-bit round constant is xored with the following 6 internal state bits: $W[23]$, $W[19]$, $W[15]$, $W[11]$, $W[7]$ and $W[3]$. Besides, a constant bit 1 is added to in the most significant bit $W[127]$. The 6-bit round constant is generated with the same 6-bit affine LFSR used in SKINNY [5].

Table 4. The S-box of TRIFLE-BC

x	0	1	2	3	4	5	6	7	8	9	a	b	c	d	e	f
$S(x)$	0	c	9	7	3	5	e	4	6	b	a	2	d	1	8	f

2.3 Security Claim of TRIFLE

The designers of TRIFLE make a security claim for TRIFLE under IND-CPA and INT-CTXT security mode, as shown in Table 5. The data complexity of the attack quantifies the online resource requirements, and includes the total number of blocks (among all messages and associated data) processed through the underlying block cipher for a fixed master key. Therefore, the data complexity of our forgery attack and key-recovery attack are both below 2^{64}. Note that the security claims are valid in nonce-misuse scenario as well.

Table 5. Security claim of TRIFLE by the designers

Security mode	Data complexity	Time complexity
IND-CPA	2^{64}	2^{128}
INT-CTXT	2^{64}	2^{128}

3   1-Round Iterative Differential Characteristic of TRIFLE-BC

The 1-round iterative differential characteristic of TRIFLE-BC is found with an MILP method based on Sun et al.'s work [21]. Actually, even without such an MILP-based method, such a result can be obtained as well if taking a detailed look at the Differential Distribution Table (DDT) and the **BitPermutation**. The 1-round iterative differential characteristic $\Delta W^i \rightarrow \Delta W^{i+1}$ is

$$\Delta W^i = \text{0x0000 0000 0000 0000 0000 0400 0000 0000},$$
$$\Delta W^{i+1} = \text{0x0000 0000 0000 0000 0000 0400 0000 0000},$$

which holds with probability of 2^{-3}. An illustration can be seen in Fig. 2.

The correctness of this differential can be seen as follows. Based on DDT, the following difference propagation $\Delta W^i \rightarrow \Delta W^i_s$ will hold with probability of 2^{-3}.

$$\Delta W^i = \text{0x0000 0000 0000 0000 0000 0400 0000 0000},$$
$$\Delta W^i_s = \text{0x0000 0000 0000 0000 0000 0200 0000 0000}.$$

As can be observed, $\Delta W^i_s[41] = 1$ and $\Delta W^i_s[j] = 0$ $(0 \leq j \leq 127, j \neq 41)$. According to the definition of **BitPermutation** in Table 3, we have

$$\Delta W^i_p[42] = \Delta W^i_s[41] = 1,$$
$$\Delta W^i_p[j] = 0 \ (0 \leq j \leq 127, j \neq 42).$$

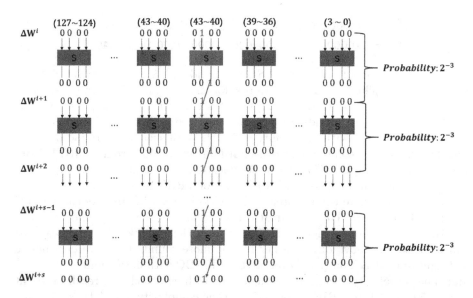

Fig. 2. The s-round iterative differential characteristic. The gray box represents the active s-box and the blue box represents the inactive s-box. (Color figure online)

Consequently,

$$\Delta W^{i+1} = \Delta W_p^i = \text{0x0000 0000 0000 0000 0000 0400 0000 0000}.$$

4   Application

With the 1-round iterative differential characteristic, we can mount distinguishing attack on reduced TRIFLE-BC, forgery attack on reduced TRIFLE and key-recovery attack on reduced TRIFLE. The details of the three attacks will be presented as follows.

4.1   Distinguishing Attack on Reduced TRIFLE-BC

Since there is a 1-round iterative differential characteristic holding with probability of 2^{-3}, an intuitive way is to construct an n-round distinguisher holding with probability of 3^{-3n}. Indeed, the distinguisher can be better. Instead of starting from the input difference Δ_{it} and ending at the output difference Δ_{it} for the n-round differential, where

$$\Delta_{it} = \text{0x0000 0000 0000 0000 0000 0400 0000 0000},$$

we can start from the input difference Δ_{st} and end at the output difference Δ_{en} so that the difference propagation in the first round ($\Delta_{st} \rightarrow \Delta_{it}$) and the last round ($\Delta_{it} \rightarrow \Delta_{end}$) can hold with the highest probability. According to DDT, the choice for Δ_{st} and Δ_{en} is

$$\Delta_{st} = \text{0x0000 0000 0000 0000 0000 0b00 0000 0000},$$
$$\Delta_{en} = \text{0x0000 0000 0000 0000 0000 0400 0000 0400}.$$

The reason is that both $S(b \oplus x) \oplus S(x) = 2$ and $S(4 \oplus x) \oplus S(x) = 3$ ($x \in F_2^4$) hold with probability 2^{-2}. In other words, for the n-round differential characteristic $\Delta_{st} \rightarrow \Delta_{en}$, the iterative differential characteristic $\Delta_{it} \rightarrow \Delta_{it}$ is located in the intermediate $n - 2$ rounds. As a result, the n-round differential characteristic $\Delta_{st} \rightarrow \Delta_{en}$ will hold with probability of 2^{2-3n}. With such an n-round differential characteristic, we can mount distinguishing attack on n-round TRIFLE-BC with data complexity 2^{3n-2} and time complexity 2^{3n-2}. Thus, the distinguishing attack can reach up to 42 (out of 50) rounds of TRIFLE-BC.

Indeed, since there is no whitening key used in TRIFLE-BC, we can peel off the **SubNibbles** and **BitPermutation** operations in the first round. In other words, we start the distinguishing attack from the state W_p^0. In this way, we can increase the above distinguisher by one more round. Thus, we can mount distinguishing attack on $(n+1)$-round TRIFLE-BC with data complexity 2^{3n-2} and time complexity 2^{3n-2}. Thus, the distinguishing attack can reach up to 43 (out of 50) rounds of TRIFLE-BC, whose time complexity and data complexity are both 2^{124}.

Remark. The designers of TRIFLE [9] have used the MILP method [21] to find the best differential characteristics for up to 10 rounds and list their corresponding probability. The best differential characteristics for r ($4 \leq r \leq 10$) rounds all hold with probability of 2^{2-3r}. In fact, according to the DDT, we can observe that all the difference transitions ($1 \rightarrow 8, 2 \rightarrow 1, 4 \rightarrow 2, 8 \rightarrow 4$) through an S-box hold with probability 2^{-3}. Since the linear transform is only a bit permutation, one can always construct 128 such differential characteristics, where only one bit is active in the input of each round, thus explaining why the solver returns such a result. Among all of them, the one-round iterative differential characteristic is unique and can be easily utilized to mount forgery attack, as will be detailed below.

4.2   Forgery Attack on Reduced TRIFLE

The overview of our forgery attack on n-round TRIFLE is illustrated in Fig. 3, where

$$\Delta_{it} = \text{0x0000 0000 0000 0000 0000 0400 0000 0000}.$$

Specifically, insert difference at the nonce N and the first associated data block A_0 so that $\Delta_N = \Delta_{it}$ and $\Delta_{A_0} = \Delta_{it}$. In this way, $\Delta_{CS} = \Delta_N \oplus \Delta_{A_0} = 0$. Then, if the output difference of the second block equals to Δ_{it}, a collision of the tag T is found. Therefore, the success probability to mount the forgery attack on n-round TRIFLE is equal to the probability of the n-round differential characteristic $\Delta_{it} \rightarrow \Delta_{it}$, which holds with probability 2^{-3n}. The procedure of our forgery attack is as follows. Since the data complexity cannot exceed 2^{64}, we set the message M empty.

Step 1: The attacker randomly choose a nonce N and a 128-bit associated data A. Then, he sends an encryption query (A, M, N) and receives (C, T).

Step 2: The attacker then sends an decryption query $(A \oplus \Delta_{it}, C, T, N \oplus \Delta_{it})$. If the decryption succeeds, a forgery is achieved. Otherwise, return Step 1 until the decryption succeeds.

Therefore, we can mount forgery attack on TRIFLE for up to 21 rounds. The corresponding data complexity and time complexity are both 2^{63}. Note that a generic forgery attack on full TRIFLE will require 2^{64} queries. Therefore, our forgery attack on 21 rounds of TRIFLE only slightly outperforms the generic attack. For forgery attack on smaller rounds r ($1 \leq r \leq 20$), the data and time complexity are both 2^{3r}. Since the designers claim that TRIFLE is a nonce misuse resistant primitive, the same nonce can be reused. Thus, we can efficiently construct a forgery under the same master key with only one query after the above forgery attack procedure succeeds. Specifically, once we know (A,M,N) and $(A \oplus \Delta_{it}, M, N \oplus \Delta_{it})$ can generate the same tag T, where M is empty, we can randomly choose another value for A' and send an encryption query (A', M, N) to receive (C', T'). Then, we can always know that $(A' \oplus \Delta_{it}, C', T', N \oplus \Delta_{it})$ is a valid forgery.

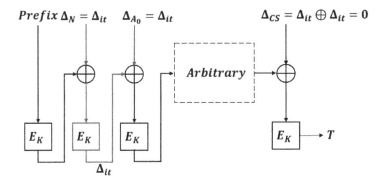

Fig. 3. Overview of forgery attack

4.3   Key-Recovery Attack on Reduced TRIFLE

In this section, we present a key-recovery attack on reduced TRIFLE under the classical differential attack framework. Similarly, we firstly give an overview of our attack in Fig. 4. Different from the forgery attack, we expect there is difference in the input to the last block to generate the tag. Therefore, we set $\Delta_N \neq \Delta_{it}$ so that $\Delta_{CS} \neq 0$ and $\Delta_T \neq 0$. However, to make the best use of the iterative differential characteristic, we have to ensure that the 1-round differential characteristic $\Delta_N \to \Delta_{it}$ and $\Delta_N \oplus \Delta_{it} = \Delta_{CS} \to \Delta_{it}$ is possible. Actually, similar case has been discussed in the distinguishing attack. According to DDT, we set the choice for Δ_N as

$$\Delta_N = \text{0x0000 0000 0000 0000 0000 0f00 0000 0000}.$$

Then, Δ_{CS} will be

$$\Delta_{CS} = \text{0x0000 0000 0000 0000 0000 0b00 0000 0000}.$$

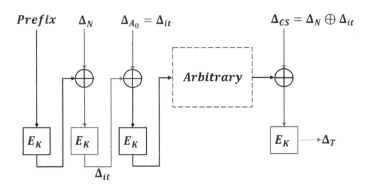

Fig. 4. Overview of key-recovery attack

In this way, the 1-round differential characteristic $\Delta_N \rightarrow \Delta_{it}$ and $\Delta_{CS} \rightarrow \Delta_{it}$ will hold with probability of 2^{-3} and 2^{-2} respectively.

Suppose the aim is to mount key-recovery attack on r rounds of TRIFLE. Then, at the last block to generate the tag, we guess the last two round keys $(U^{r-1}, V^{r-1}, U^{r-2}, V^{r-2})$ and compute backward to observe the input difference of the two active S-boxes in the $(r-2)$-th round. In this case, the differential used for the key-recovery attack is equivalent to a $(2r-2)$-round differential $(\Delta_N \rightarrow \Delta_{en})$, as depicted in Fig. 5. The value of Δ_{en} is the same as defined in Sect. 4.2, as shown below.

$$\Delta_{en} = \text{0x0000 0000 0000 0000 0000 0400 0000 0400}.$$

Consequently, the equivalent $(2r-2)$-round differential $(\Delta_N \rightarrow \Delta_{en})$ will hold with probability of $2^{2-3(2r-2)}$. Since the data complexity cannot exceed 2^{64}, r can be at most 11. In other words, to mount key-recovery attack on 11-round TRIFLE, we can use an equivalent 20-round iterative differential characteristic as a distinguisher, which holds with probability 2^{-58}.

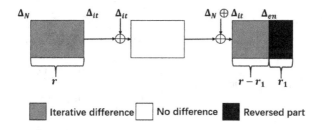

Fig. 5. Presentation of the differential used for key-recovery attack

Now, we give a detailed description of the phase to recover the key with the equivalent 20-round differential $(\Delta_N \rightarrow \Delta_{en})$. According to Δ_{en}, we need to observe the difference $\Delta W^9[43 \sim 40]$ and $\Delta W^9[11 \sim 8]$. Before stating the procedure to recover the key, we firstly explain which bits of the last two round key should be guessed. An illustration is given in Fig. 6 and a detailed description is given below.

- To compute $W^9[43 \sim 40]$, we need to know $(W_p^9[106], W_p^9[74], W_p^9[42], W_p^9[10])$, which requires the knowledge of $(U^9[26], U^9[18], U^9[10], U^9[2])$.
- To compute $(W^{10}[106], W^{10}[74], W^{10}[42], W^{10}[10])$, we need to know $W_p^{10}[i]$, where

$$i \in \{122, 90, 58, 26, 114, 82, 50, 18, 106, 74, 42, 10, 98, 66, 34, 2\}.$$

Thus, we need to guess $U^{10}[j]$, where

$$j \in \{30, 22, 14, 6, 28, 20, 12, 4, 26, 18, 10, 2, 24, 16, 8, 0\}.$$

– To compute $W^9[11 \sim 8]$, we need to know $(W_p^9[98], W_p^9[66], W_p^9[34], W_p^9[2])$, which requires the knowledge of $(U^9[24], U^9[16], U^9[8], U^9[0])$.

– To compute $(W^{10}[98], W^{10}[66], W^{10}[34], W^{10}[2])$, we need to know $W_p^{10}[i]$, where

$$i \in \{120, 88, 56, 24, 112, 80, 48, 16, 104, 72, 40, 8, 96, 64, 32, 0\}.$$

According to the definition of **AddRoundKey**, all the above 16 bits can be directly deduced from the value of tag. This is because that only partial bits of the internal states are xored with the round key.

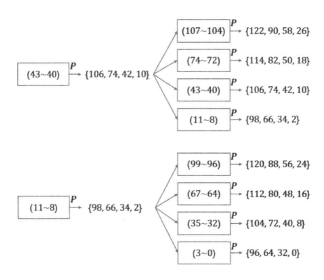

Fig. 6. To-be-guessed key bits in the last two rounds

As can be seen from the above explanation, we need to guess $16 + 8 = 24$ key bits in total in order to observe the difference $\Delta W^9[43 \sim 40]$ and $\Delta W^9[11 \sim 8]$. Now, we give the complete procedure to recover the key as follows.

Step 1: **Data Collection.** The attacker randomly chooses a nonce N and a 128-bit associated A and an empty message M. Then, he sends an encryption query (A, M, N) and receives (C, T). Then, he choose a new nonce $N' = N \oplus \Delta_N$ and a new 128-bit associated $A' = A \oplus \Delta_{it}$ and an empty message M. Then, he sends an encryption query (A', M, N') and receives (C', T'). He repeats this step 2^{t_0} times so as to obtain 2^{t_1} valid pairs (T, T') for key recovery phase. A valid pair (T, T') should satisfy that some bits of $\Delta_T = T \oplus T'$ are zero, i.e., $\Delta_T[j]$ should be zero, where

$$\begin{cases} 0 \leq j \leq 127 \\ j \notin \{122, 90, 58, 26, 114, 82, 50, 18, 106, 74, 42, 10, 98, 66, 34, 2\} \\ j \notin \{120, 88, 56, 24, 112, 80, 48, 16, 104, 72, 40, 8, 96, 64, 32, 0\} \end{cases}$$

Besides, since $W^{10}[i]$ are computable without knowing the key information, where

$$i \in \{120, 88, 56, 24, 112, 80, 48, 16, 104, 72, 40, 8, 96, 64, 32, 0\},$$

we need to check whether the difference ΔW^{10} is valid for the obtained (T, T'), i.e., among the above 16 bits, only $W^{10}[98], W^{10}[66], W^{10}[34]$ and $W^{10}[2]$ are allowed to have difference.

Step 2: **Key-Recovery.** The attacker initialize an array **CNT** of size 2^{24} with zero. Each row number of the array represents one possible value of the 24 to-be-guessed key bits. For the collected 2^{t_1} valid pairs (T, T'), the attacker guess the round key as follows.

Step 2.1: Independently guess the value of $(U^{10}[30], U^{10}[22], U^{10}[14],$ $U^{10}[6])$, $(U^{10}[28], U^{10}[20], U^{10}[12], U^{10}[4])$, $(U^{10}[26], U^{10}[18],$ $U^{10}[10], U^{2}[4])$ and $(U^{10}[24], U^{10}[16], U^{10}[8], U^{10}[0])$ and independently check whether the difference of $W^{10}[107 \sim 104]$, $W^{10}[74 \sim 72]$, $W^{10}[43 \sim 40]$ and $W^{10}[11 \sim 8]$ are valid difference, i.e., only $W^{10}[106], W^{10}[74], W^{10}[42]$ and $W^{10}[10]$ are allowed to have difference. If they are, record the corresponding guess. After this step, the attacker is expected to obtain about 2^4 possible values for the 16 guessed key bits of U^{10}. The time complexity of this step is $4 \times 2^4 = 2^6$. For each of the obtained possible values, the attacker carries out Step 2.2.

Step 2.2: The attacker independently guess the value of $U^9[i]$ ($i \in \{26, 18, 10, 2\}$) and $U^9[i]$ ($i \in \{24, 16, 8, 0\}$). Then, if the guessed value for $U^9[i]$ ($i \in \{26, 18, 10, 2\}$) and $U^9[i]$ ($i \in \{24, 16, 8, 0\}$) can make W^9 equal to Δ_{en}, the attacker accordingly increase the element by 1 in the row of **CNT** while represents the corresponding guessed value for the 24 to-be-guessed key bits.

Step 3: **Determine.** After all valid pairs (T, T') are used, check the array **CNT**. It is expected that the correct guess for the 24 to-be-guessed key bits will correspond to a row with maximum value.

Since the equivalent 20-round differential holds with probability 2^{-58} and the data complexity cannot exceed 2^{64}, we choose 2^{62} randomly values for (A, N) and expect to obtain 2^4 valid pairs (T, T') so that we can further confirm the correctness of the value for 24 to-be-guessed key bits. In this way, we can recover 24 bits of the key with time complexity and data complexity 2^{63}. The remaining 104 key bits can be guessed by brute force at the offline phase based on the key scheduling algorithm of TRIFLE-BC. Thus, the time complexity and data complexity of the key-recovery attack on 11-round TRIFLE are 2^{104} and 2^{63} respectively.

Key-Recovery Attack on TRIFLE-BC. It is also interesting to investigate the key-recovery attack on TRIFLE-BC to help further understand the security of TRIFLE-BC, even though such an attack cannot work for real TRIFLE. Indeed the above key-recovery strategy can be completely applied to TRIFLE-BC trivially. Thus, we are able to mount key-recovery attack on TRIFLE-BC for up to $42 + 2 = 44$ rounds by using the 42-round differential that holds with probability of 2^{-121}. We reduce the number of rounds of the distinguisher in Sect. 4.1 so that it can increase our confidence of the correctness of this attack. Similarly, we prepare $2^{121+4} = 2^{125}$ pairs of plaintext so that there are 2^4 valid ciphertext pairs for usage. Therefore, the total complexity of this key-recovery attack is dominated by the data collection phase, which requires 2^{126} plaintexts and 2^{126} time. We believe that such a key-recovery attack can be improved.

4.4   Experiments

To make the above theoretical results more convincing, we list a forgery (collision) for 10-round TRIFLE as following to demonstrate the correctness of the iterative differential characteristic. It is found with the reference implementation of TRIFLE [9]. To make the output in the implementation consistent with this paper, we changed the output format from the little-endian format to big-endian format.

$$K = \texttt{0x0a0a061117090f121b011a08030e0802},$$
$$N = \texttt{0x1b050b100d130a060919000415190e19},$$
$$A = \texttt{0x061e1a0c040104100202161a1b021a09},$$
$$M = \text{Empty string},$$
$$T = \texttt{0x28fa5821bf3278167acaa1b8f6de4603}.$$

$$N \oplus \Delta_{it} = \texttt{0x1b050b100d130a060919040415190e19},$$
$$A \oplus \Delta_{it} = \texttt{0x061e1a0c040104100202121a1b021a09},$$
$$M = \text{Empty string},$$
$$T = \texttt{0x28fa5821bf3278167acaa1b8f6de4603}.$$

5   Conclusion

Although the designers claim that linear transform in TRIFLE-BC can provide sufficient diffusion, we can still find an iterative differential characteristic with hamming weight 1 by taking into account the combination of S-box and linear transform. With such a low-hamming-weight iterative differential characteristic, we can mount distinguishing attack on TRIFLE-BC for up to 43 rounds, forgery attack on TRIFLE for up to 21 rounds and key-recovery attack on TRIFLE for up to 11 rounds. We hope our result can help further understand the security of TRIFLE.

Acknowledgement. We thank the anonymous reviewers of SAC 2019 and the TRI-FLE team for their comments. According to the discussion with TRIFLE team, they are aware of such 1-1 differential transition and therefore make such a transition through an S-box hold with probability 2^{-3} rather than 2^{-2}. Fukang Liu is supported by Invitation Programs for Foreigner-based Researchers of the National Institute of Information and Communications Technology (NICT). Takanori Isobe is supported by Grant-in-Aid for Scientific Research (B) (KAKENHI 19H02141) for Japan Society for the Promotion of Science.

References

1. Avanzi, R.: The QARMA block cipher family. Almost MDS matrices over rings with zero divisors, nearly symmetric even-mansour constructions with non-involutory central rounds, and search heuristics for low-latency s-boxes. IACR Trans. Symmetric Cryptol. **2017**(1), 4–44 (2017)

2. Banik, S., et al.: Midori: a block cipher for low energy. In: Iwata, T., Cheon, J.H. (eds.) ASIACRYPT 2015. LNCS, vol. 9453, pp. 411–436. Springer, Heidelberg (2015). https://doi.org/10.1007/978-3-662-48800-3_17

3. Banik, S., Pandey, S.K., Peyrin, T., Sasaki, Y., Sim, S.M., Todo, Y.: GIFT: a small present - towards reaching the limit of lightweight encryption. In: Fischer, W., Homma, N. (eds.) CHES 2017. LNCS, vol. 10529, pp. 321–345. Springer, Cham (2017). https://doi.org/10.1007/978-3-319-66787-4_16

4. Beaulieu, R., Shors, D., Smith, J., Treatman-Clark, S., Weeks, B., Wingers, L.: SIMON and SPECK: block ciphers for the internet of things. IACR Cryptol. ePrint Arch. **2015**, 585 (2015)

5. Beierle, C., et al.: The SKINNY family of block ciphers and its low-latency variant MANTIS. In: Robshaw, M., Katz, J. (eds.) CRYPTO 2016. LNCS, vol. 9815, pp. 123–153. Springer, Heidelberg (2016). https://doi.org/10.1007/978-3-662-53008-5_5

6. Biham, E., Shamir, A.: Differential cryptanalysis of DES-like cryptosystems. In: Menezes, A.J., Vanstone, S.A. (eds.) CRYPTO 1990. LNCS, vol. 537, pp. 2–21. Springer, Heidelberg (1991). https://doi.org/10.1007/3-540-38424-3_1

7. Bogdanov, A., et al.: PRESENT: an ultra-lightweight block cipher. In: Paillier, P., Verbauwhede, I. (eds.) CHES 2007. LNCS, vol. 4727, pp. 450–466. Springer, Heidelberg (2007). https://doi.org/10.1007/978-3-540-74735-2_31

8. De Cannière, C., Dunkelman, O., Knežević, M.: KATAN and KTANTAN — a family of small and efficient hardware-oriented block ciphers. In: Clavier, C., Gaj, K. (eds.) CHES 2009. LNCS, vol. 5747, pp. 272–288. Springer, Heidelberg (2009). https://doi.org/10.1007/978-3-642-04138-9_20

9. Datta, N., Ghoshal, A., Mukhopadhyay, D., Patranabis, S., Picek, P., Sadhukhan, R.: TRIFLE (2019). https://csrc.nist.gov/Projects/Lightweight-Cryptography/Round-1-Candidates

10. Dinur, I., Shamir, A.: Cube attacks on tweakable black box polynomials. In: Joux, A. (ed.) EUROCRYPT 2009. LNCS, vol. 5479, pp. 278–299. Springer, Heidelberg (2009). https://doi.org/10.1007/978-3-642-01001-9_16

11. Eichlseder, M., Kales, D., Schofnegger, M.: Forgery attacks on FlexAE and Flex-AEAD. Cryptology ePrint Archive, Report 2019/679 (2019). https://eprint.iacr.org/2019/679

12. Guo, J., Peyrin, T., Poschmann, A.: The PHOTON family of lightweight hash functions. In: Rogaway, P. (ed.) CRYPTO 2011. LNCS, vol. 6841, pp. 222–239. Springer, Heidelberg (2011). https://doi.org/10.1007/978-3-642-22792-9_13

13. Khairallah, M.: Forgery attack on SNEIKEN. Cryptology ePrint Archive, Report 2019/408 (2019). https://eprint.iacr.org/2019/408

14. Knudsen, L., Wagner, D.: Integral cryptanalysis. In: Daemen, J., Rijmen, V. (eds.) FSE 2002. LNCS, vol. 2365, pp. 112–127. Springer, Heidelberg (2002). https://doi.org/10.1007/3-540-45661-9_9

15. Matsui, M.: Linear cryptanalysis method for DES cipher. In: Helleseth, T. (ed.) EUROCRYPT 1993. LNCS, vol. 765, pp. 386–397. Springer, Heidelberg (1994). https://doi.org/10.1007/3-540-48285-7_33

16. Mikhalev, V., Armknecht, F., Müller, C.: On ciphers that continuously access the non-volatile key. IACR Trans. Symmetric Cryptol. **2016**(2), 52–79 (2016)

17. Mouha, N., Wang, Q., Gu, D., Preneel, B.: Differential and linear cryptanalysis using mixed-integer linear programming. In: Wu, C.-K., Yung, M., Lin, D. (eds.) Inscrypt 2011. LNCS, vol. 7537, pp. 57–76. Springer, Heidelberg (2012). https://doi.org/10.1007/978-3-642-34704-7_5

18. Perrin, L.: Probability 1 iterated differential in the SNEIK permutation. Cryptology ePrint Archive, Report 2019/374 (2019). https://eprint.iacr.org/2019/374

19. Sasaki, Y., Todo, Y.: New impossible differential search tool from design and cryptanalysis aspects. In: Coron, J.-S., Nielsen, J.B. (eds.) EUROCRYPT 2017. LNCS, vol. 10212, pp. 185–215. Springer, Cham (2017). https://doi.org/10.1007/978-3-319-56617-7_7

20. Shibutani, K., Isobe, T., Hiwatari, H., Mitsuda, A., Akishita, T., Shirai, T.: *Piccolo*: an ultra-lightweight blockcipher. In: Preneel, B., Takagi, T. (eds.) CHES 2011. LNCS, vol. 6917, pp. 342–357. Springer, Heidelberg (2011). https://doi.org/10.1007/978-3-642-23951-9_23

21. Sun, S., Hu, L., Wang, P., Qiao, K., Ma, X., Song, L.: Automatic security evaluation and (related-key) differential characteristic search: application to SIMON, PRESENT, LBlock, DES(L) and other bit-oriented block ciphers. In: Sarkar, P., Iwata, T. (eds.) ASIACRYPT 2014. LNCS, vol. 8873, pp. 158–178. Springer, Heidelberg (2014). https://doi.org/10.1007/978-3-662-45611-8_9

22. Todo, Y.: Structural evaluation by generalized integral property. In: Oswald, E., Fischlin, M. (eds.) EUROCRYPT 2015. LNCS, vol. 9056, pp. 287–314. Springer, Heidelberg (2015). https://doi.org/10.1007/978-3-662-46800-5_12

23. Todo, Y., Morii, M.: Bit-based division property and application to SIMON family. In: Peyrin, T. (ed.) FSE 2016. LNCS, vol. 9783, pp. 357–377. Springer, Heidelberg (2016). https://doi.org/10.1007/978-3-662-52993-5_18

24. Wang, Q., Hao, Y., Todo, Y., Li, C., Isobe, T., Meier, W.: Improved division property based cube attacks exploiting algebraic properties of superpoly. In: Shacham, H., Boldyreva, A. (eds.) CRYPTO 2018. LNCS, vol. 10991, pp. 275–305. Springer, Cham (2018). https://doi.org/10.1007/978-3-319-96884-1_10

25. Xiang, Z., Zhang, W., Bao, Z., Lin, D.: Applying MILP method to searching integral distinguishers based on division property for 6 lightweight block ciphers. In: Cheon, J.H., Takagi, T. (eds.) ASIACRYPT 2016. LNCS, vol. 10031, pp. 648–678. Springer, Heidelberg (2016). https://doi.org/10.1007/978-3-662-53887-6_24

Tweakable Block Ciphers

Plaintext Recovery Attacks Against XTS Beyond Collisions

Takanori Isobe[1,3]([⊠]) and Kazuhiko Minematsu[2]([⊠])

[1] University of Hyogo, Kobe, Japan
takanori.isobe@ai.u-hyogo.ac.jp
[2] NEC Corporation, Kawasaki, Japan
k-minematsu@nec.com
[3] National Institute of Information and Communications Technology, Tokyo, Japan

Abstract. XTS is a popular encryption scheme for storage devices standardized by IEEE and NIST. It is based on Rogaway's XEX tweakable block cipher and is known to be secure up to the collisions between the blocks, thus up to around $2^{n/2}$ blocks for n-bit blocks. However this only implies that the theoretical indistinguishability notion is broken with $O(2^{n/2})$ queries and does not tell the practical risk against the plaintext recovery if XTS is targeted. We show several plaintext recovery attacks against XTS beyond collisions, and evaluate their practical impacts.

Keywords: XTS · Storage encryption · Mode of operation · Even-Mansour cipher

1 Introduction

XTS is a symmetric-key encryption scheme for storage devices such as HDD or USB memory sticks. It has been developed by IEEE Storage in Security Workgroup (SISWG) in 2007, based on a block cipher mode called XEX proposed by Rogaway in 2004 [19]. It has been standardized as IEEE standard for storage encryption (IEEE P1619) [11]. In 2010, NIST specified XTS as one of the recommended schemes with the explicit use of AES as the underlying block cipher. This scheme is called XTS-AES and is described in NIST SP800-38E [5] with a parameter restriction not presented in the IEEE document. XTS is quite widely deployed, such as Bitlocker, dm-crypt, and Truecrypt and its successors.

Since XTS is built on XEX, the security of XTS is basically inherited from that of XEX. Assuming the underlying n-bit block cipher is secure, XEX is provably secure as long as the number of processed blocks is sufficiently smaller than $2^{n/2}$ [15,19]. This bound comes from a collision between two inputs to the block cipher, which is expected to happen with high probability for $2^{n/2}$ blocks due to the birthday paradox. Hence it is called "birthday bound". The security analysis of XTS largely follows this result, except the case that the last block in a sector

© Springer Nature Switzerland AG 2020
K. G. Paterson and D. Stebila (Eds.): SAC 2019, LNCS 11959, pp. 103–123, 2020.
https://doi.org/10.1007/978-3-030-38471-5_5

is partial (i.e. not n bits) for which a variant of the classical ciphertext stealing is applied.

Most popular block cipher modes are secure up to the birthday bound. This implies that if we take n large enough the scheme is secure in practice. However, it is also important to study what will happen if the attacker can perform $2^{n/2}$ encryptions, that is, security analysis beyond the birthday bound. This allows to learn the limit of key lifetime and the danger of small-block ciphers. Recently, the security of CBC and CTR modes beyond the birthday are explored [1,13].

Our Contributions. In this paper, we study the security of XTS beyond the birthday bound, in particular, the security against plaintext recovery. We note that it is not hard to derive a collision-based distinguishing attack against XEX thus XTS, however, this only implies the tightness of the security bound. The collision attack needs $O(2^{n/2})$ encrypted blocks for one sector, and only reveals the blockcipher mask used by this sector. Once the mask is known, XTS largely reduces to the basic ECB mode, hence the attack trivially reveals (a part of) plaintexts of the target sector when they are chosen or known with a low entropy. Unfortunately, this observation does not tell anything beyond, say how easy to recover the plaintext stored in sectors that was not the target of the collision attack. This is the problem we want to solve.

Under a reasonable adversary model for storage encryption (e.g. [6,12]), we derived several plaintext recovery attacks against XTS. Specifically, we classify the sectors of an XTS-encrypted storage into two categories, called reference sectors and target sectors. At the reference sectors, the adversary can encrypt a known plaintext and decrypt any ciphertext, that is, a combination of known-plaintext attack (KPA) and chosen-ciphertext attack. At the target sectors, the adversary can only perform a ciphertext-only attack or a partially-known-plaintext attack, where the definition of "partial" depends on the attack. The goal is to recover the plaintext at one of the target sectors for the corresponding ciphertext obtained by encryption queries to that sector.

Our attacks are not a trivial application of collision attack described above in that it does not need $O(2^{n/2})$ encrypted blocks of the sector for which the target plaintext is stored. The key observation of our attacks is a similarity between XTS and single-key Even-Mansour (SEM) ciphers: it allows us to convert attacks against SEM into XTS. Specifically, we show that once a mask is recovered by the collision attack at the reference sector, XTS at target sectors can be seen as a variant of SEM. Then, we propose plaintext-recovery attacks beyond collisions at target sectors in several practical settings. In a partially-known plaintext setting where a part of plaintext blocks at the target sector is known, e.g. fixed header files, we are able to recover the remaining unknown plaintext blocks by a variant of key recovery attacks on SEM [4]. For a 64-bit block cipher, our plaintext-recovery attack is feasible with only 2^8 known blocks in the target sectors, and 2^{56} local computations independently from the key size of the underlying block cipher. Besides, we show that this attack works with the almost same attack complexity even if there is no blocks that is completely known, e.g. only one

Table 1. Summary of our attacks in the several attack settings.

Attack setting	Attack type	$n = 64$			$n = 128$		
		Time	Data	Memory	Time	Data	Memory
pKPA 1 (Sect. 7.1)	Plaintext recovery	2^{56}	2^8	2^8	2^{96}	2^{32}	2^{32}
pKPA 2 (Sect. 7.2)	Plaintext recovery	2^{55}	2^{10}	2^{57}	2^{98}	2^{32}	2^{122}
pKPA 2 (Sect. 7.2)	Plaintext recovery	2^{57}	2^{10}	2^{10}	2^{120}	2^{32}	2^{32}
Ciphertext-only (Sect. 7.3)	Plaintext Recovery	2^{60}	2^{60}	2^{60}	2^{124}	2^{124}	2^{124}

pKPA 1: Partially-known plaintext setting where plaintext blocks of Data are known.
pKPA 2: Partially-known plaintext setting where only one byte of each block of Data is known.

byte in a block is known. Finally, we show that in the ciphertext-only setting where the adversary does not have any information of plaintext at target sectors, we are able to guess a target plaintext with higher than random guessing.

Table 1 shows the summary of our attacks. Time and Memory are adversary's local computations and memory cost, respectively. Data is the number of required known plaintext/ciphertext blocks at target sectors in pKPA 1, and in pKPA 2, only one byte in a corresponding plaintext block is known. In the ciphertext-only setting, Data is the number of required ciphertexts at target sectors and there is no any information of plaintexts. For example, in pKPA 2 for $n = 64$, given 2^{10} known plaintext blocks in which only 1 byte is known at a target sector, all other plaintext blocks and unknown 7 bytes of 2^{10} known plaintext blocks in the target sector can be recovered with local 2^{57} computations and 2^{10} memory. In the ciphertext-only setting for $n = 60$, given 2^{60} ciphertexts, we can correctly guess one of them with time complexity of 2^{60} and 2^{60} memory, while it ideally should require 2^{64} ciphertexts to successfully guess a 64-bit plaintext.

We stress that our plaintext recovery attacks at target sectors are feasible with less than $O(2^{n/2})$ data unlike a trivial application of the collision attack to the target sectors which requires $O(2^{n/2})$ data. Note that collecting known plaintext blocks in the target sectors is the most difficult task for real world applications. In this sense, our attack is more practical. Especially, for $n = 64$, our plaintext recovery attacks at target sectors are successful with a small number of known plaintext blocks (e.g. 2^8) and practical local computations, independently from the key size. Therefore, our results reveal that 64-bit block ciphers with XTS mode, which is commercially deployed in some products, are practically insecure as storage encryption schemes.

2 Preliminaries

2.1 Basic Notations

Let $\mathbb{N}$ be the set of positive integers. Let $[n]$ denote $\{1, \ldots, n\}$. The bit length of binary sequence X is written as $|X|$, and $|X|_n$ denotes $\lceil |X|/n \rceil$. Let $(M_1, \ldots, M_m) \xleftarrow{n} M$ denote the n-bit block parsing of M, where $m = |M|_n$, $|M_i| = n$ for $1 \le i \le m-1$ and $|M_m| \in [n]$. For a binary string X, its first s bits and last s bits are written as $\mathsf{msb}_s(X)$ and $\mathsf{lsb}_s(X)$.

Galois Field. Any n-bit value may be taken as an element of $\mathrm{GF}(2^n)$ by seeing it as the sequence of coefficients of the polynomial. In particular, for $X, Y \in \{0,1\}^n$, we write $X \otimes Y$ to denote $\mathrm{GF}(2^n)$-multiplication of X and Y. A division of X by $Y \neq 0$ is written as X/Y.

2.2   Tweakable Block Cipher

A tweakable blockcipher (TBC) is an extension of ordinary block cipher proposed by Liskov et al. [14]. A TBC is a keyed function $\widetilde{E} : \mathcal{K} \times \mathcal{T} \times \mathcal{M} \to \mathcal{M}$ such that for each $(K, T) \in \mathcal{K} \times \mathcal{T}$, $\widetilde{E}(K, T, \cdot)$ is a permutation over $\mathcal{M}$. Here, K is the key and T is a public value called tweak. A conventional block cipher is a TBC with $\mathcal{T}$ being a singleton, and specifically written as $E : \mathcal{K} \times \mathcal{M} \to \mathcal{M}$. The encryption of $X \in \mathcal{M}$ under key $K \in \mathcal{K}$ and tweak $T \in \mathcal{T}$ is $\widetilde{E}(K, T, X)$ and is also written as $\widetilde{E}_K(T, X)$ or $\widetilde{E}_K^T(X)$. For blockcipher we write as $E_K(X)$. The decryption is written as $\widetilde{E}_K^{-1,T}(Y)$ for TBCs and $E_K^{-1}(Y)$ for blockciphers. For any $T \in \mathcal{T}$ and $K \in \mathcal{K}$, when $Y = \widetilde{E}_K^T(X)$ we have $\widetilde{E}_K^{-1,T}(Y) = X$.

We say $f : \mathcal{T} \times \mathcal{M} \to \mathcal{M}$ is a tweakable permutation if $f(T, *)$ is a permutation for any $T \in \mathcal{T}$. Let $\widetilde{\mathsf{P}} : \mathcal{T} \times \mathcal{M} \to \mathcal{M}$ be the ideal tweakable random permutation distributed uniformly over the set of all tweakable permutations : $\mathcal{T} \times \mathcal{M} \to \mathcal{M}$. The security of a TBC $\widetilde{E} : \mathcal{K} \times \mathcal{T} \times \mathcal{M} \to \mathcal{M}$ is measured by the computational indistinguishability from $\widetilde{\mathsf{P}}$ using chosen encryption queries (T, X) and chosen decryption queries (T, Y) [14, 19].

3   Specification of XTS

XTS is a tweakable encryption over message space $\mathcal{M} = \{0,1\}^*$ with tweak space $\mathcal{T}_{\mathsf{XTS}} = \{0,1\}^n$.

Let $E : \mathcal{K} \times \{0,1\}^n \to \{0,1\}^n$ be an n-bit block cipher, and let $K = (K_1, K_2) \in \mathcal{K}^2$ be a pair of keys of E. The core component of XTS is a single-block tweakable blockcipher written as $\mathsf{XEX2} : \mathcal{K}^2 \times \{0,1\}^n \times \mathcal{T}_{\mathsf{XEX2}} \to \{0,1\}^n$, where $\mathcal{T}_{\mathsf{XEX2}} = \mathcal{T}_{\mathsf{XTS}} \times \mathbb{N}$ is a tweak space. It encrypts n-bit plaintext block X to create ciphertext block Y using tweak $\overline{T} = (T, j) \in \mathcal{T}_{\mathsf{XEX2}}$ as

$$Y = S \oplus E_{K_1}(M \oplus S), \tag{1}$$

where $S = E_{K_2}(T) \otimes \alpha^j$. Here, α denotes the generator of the field, i.e. the polynomial x, and α^j denotes the multiplication by α for j times.

XTS encrypts plaintext $M \in \{0,1\}^*$ with a tweak $T \in \mathcal{T}_{\mathsf{XTS}}$ by first (1) parsing M as $(M_1, \dots, M_m) \xleftarrow{n} M$ and (2) encrypting M_j for $j \in [m-1]$ by XEX2 taking tweak (T, j). The encryption of the last block M_m depends on whether $|M_m| = n$ or shorter, in a similar manner to Ciphertext Stealing in CBC mode. See Fig. 1.

Algorithm $\text{XTS}_K.\text{Enc}(M, T)$	**Algorithm** $\text{XTS}_K.\text{Dec}(C, T)$
1. $(M_1, \ldots, M_m) \xleftarrow{n} M$	1. $(C_1, \ldots, C_m) \xleftarrow{n} C$
2. **for** $i = 1$ **to** $m - 1$ **do**	2. **for** $i = 1$ **to** $m - 1$ **do**
3. $C_i \leftarrow \text{XEX2}_K.\text{Enc}(M_i, (T, i))$	3. $M_i \leftarrow \text{XEX2}_K.\text{Dec}(C_i, (T, i))$
4. **if** $\|M_m\| = n$ **then**	4. **if** $\|C_m\| = n$ **then**
5. $C_m \leftarrow \text{XEX2}_K.\text{Enc}(M_m, (T, m))$	5. $M_m \leftarrow \text{XEX2}_K.\text{Dec}(C_m, (T, m))$
6. **else**	6. **else**
7. $C_m \leftarrow \text{msb}_{\|M_m\|}(C_{m-1})$	7. $M_m \leftarrow \text{msb}_{\|C_m\|}(M_{m-1})$
8. $D \leftarrow \text{lsb}_{n-\|M_m\|}(C_{m-1})$	8. $D \leftarrow \text{lsb}_{n-\|M_m\|}(M_{m-1})$
9. $\widetilde{M}_m \leftarrow M_m \| D$	9. $\widetilde{C}_m \leftarrow C_m \| D$
10. $C_{m-1} \leftarrow \text{XEX2}_K.\text{Enc}(\widetilde{M}_m, (T, m))$	10. $M_{m-1} \leftarrow \text{XEX2}_K.\text{Dec}(\widetilde{C}_m, (T, m))$
11. $C \leftarrow (C_1 \| C_2 \| \ldots \| C_m)$	11. $M \leftarrow (M_1 \| M_2 \| \ldots \| M_m)$
12. **return** C	12. **return** M
Algorithm $\text{XEX2}_K.\text{Enc}(X, (T, j))$	**Algorithm** $\text{XEX2}_K.\text{Dec}(Y, (T, j))$
1. $(K_1, K_2) \xleftarrow{n} K$	1. $(K_1, K_2) \xleftarrow{n} K$
2. $S \leftarrow E_{K_2}(T) \otimes \alpha^j$	2. $S \leftarrow E_{K_2}(T) \otimes \alpha^j$
3. $Y \leftarrow S \oplus E_{K_1}(X \oplus S)$	3. $X \leftarrow S \oplus E_{K_1}^{-1}(Y \oplus S)$
4. **return** Y	4. **return** X

Fig. 1. XTS encryption mode.

3.1   LRW Mode

Before XTS, IEEE SISWG considered a mode called LRW [9] named after the paper by Liskov et al. [14]. It can be seen as a predecessor of XEX. An encryption of LRW is the same as Eq. (1), however

$$S = L \otimes \overline{T}$$

is used instead, where $L \in \{0, 1\}^n$ is the second key independent of K, and $\overline{T} \in \{0, 1\}^n$ identifies the target block in the storage, which is typically considered as a combination of sector number and block index. LRW may look much slower than XTS as it involves a full multiplication over $\text{GF}(2^n)$ for every update of tweak. However this is not the case if sector number and block index are properly encoded, e.g. when $\overline{T}$ is $(T \| j)$ with sector number $T \in \{0, 1\}^{n/2}$ and block index $j \in \{0, 1\}^{n/2}$, $L \otimes (T \| j + 1)$ is obtained by $L \otimes (T \| j) \otimes \alpha$, hence basically the same cost as XTS. LRW mode was consequently not adapted as a standard, however, some encryption software still use it, in particular with 64-bit block ciphers (see Sect. 8).

4   Attack Model

Motivation. We first need to clarify the adversary model, i.e. how the adversary accesses to a storage encrypted by XTS and what is the goal of the adversary, in a way that reflects practical use cases, at least to some extent. This must be done first, as it is known that, unlike encryption or authenticated encryption, there is no widely accepted security notion that captures XTS beyond single-block tweakable block cipher, i.e., XEX2 (see e.g. Rogaway [18]). It is rather straightforward to derive a birthday attack to break Tweakable Strong Pseudorandom Permutation (TSPRP) notion of XEX2, however this is not sufficient for our purpose.

Informally, we classify the sectors of an XTS-encrypted storage into two categories, called reference sectors and target sectors. At the reference sectors, the adversary can encrypt a known plaintext and decrypt any ciphertext, that is, a combination of known-plaintext attack (KPA) and chosen-ciphertext attack (CCA)[1]. This implies that the plaintext recovery is trivial at these sectors if we have ciphertext at a reference sector for unknown plaintext. However, at the target sectors, the adversary can only perform a ciphertext-only attack (COA) or a partially-known-plaintext attack (pKPA, the definition of "partial" depends on the attack) against the target sectors, and cannot perform decryption at all. The goal is to recover the plaintext at one of the target sectors for the corresponding ciphertext obtained by encryption queries to that sector.

The assumption of reference sector(s) follows the existing attack models for storage encryption, such as Ferguson [6, Section 2.7] and Khati et al. [12]. Intuitively, in many cases, there are encrypted sectors where we already know (some part of) the plaintext and can modify the ciphertext and somehow see the resulting plaintext. For example, Windows OS has a boot screen and the default value is known, and the result of a modification of the encrypted sectors that contains this boot screen image can be visible by just booting OS and see how the boot screen has been corrupted. There should be other types of sectors that work as reference sectors, depending on applications and OSs. Individual analysis of each case is beyond the scope of our paper.

For the target sectors it is reasonable to assume that we have few knowledge of the plaintext.

Simplified Model. Let $T^{(r)}$ be the single reference sector and $T^{(t)}$ be the target sector. We assume the sector size is always mn bits for some positive integer m; the size and whether the last block is partial or not is irrelevant to our attacks. To simplify the description of attacks while capturing the core of our ideas, we assume the adversary only queries to these two sectors, and each query is given directly to XEX2 rather than XTS. Thus an encryption query is $(M, \overline{T})$ and a decryption query is $(C, \overline{T})$, both are elements of $\{0,1\}^n \times \mathcal{T}_{\text{XEX2}}$.

As we described, the adversary can issue encryption queries $(M, (T^{(r)}, j))$ with some known (possibly random) M for any $j \in [m]$, and decryption queries $(C, (T^{(r)}, j))$ with any $C \in \{0,1\}^n$ and any $j \in [m]$. In fact, the condition for the adversary can be further reduced, so that we only require existence of two different blocks, $j, j' \in [m]$ in the reference sector that accept above queries.

---

[1] Here it means an attack with decryption queries of any chosen ciphertext and does not mean a combination with chosen-plaintext attack.

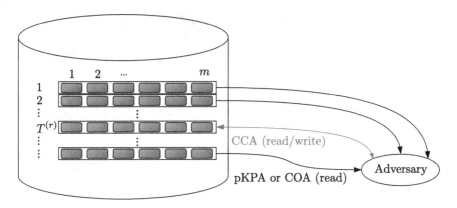

Fig. 2. Attack model.

Encryption queries to target sectors $(M, (T^{(t)}, j))$ can be done with unknown M (COA) or partially-known M (pKPA). When the adversary correctly guess M it means the win. Depending on the available queries at $T^{(t)}$, we derive different attacks.

All attacks are extended to the case where there are multiple target sectors. This captures the case that all sectors of HDD are target except the reference sector. The overview of our attack model is described in Fig. 2.

5   Overview of Our Attacks

Our attacks consist of two phases. In the first phase, we perform a *collision attack* at a reference sector $T^{(r)}$ to obtain a mask key $E_{K_2}(T^{(r)})$. This attack is a beyond-birthday attack in that it requires $2^n/2$ encryptions. Once $E_{K_2}(T^{(r)})$ is known, input/output pairs of the internal function E_{K_1} are available in the reference sector $T^{(r)}$. Note that the same internal function E_{K_1} is used in other sectors including the target sector $T^{(t)}$.

In the second phase, we mount *plaintext recovery attacks* at a target sector $T^{(t)}$. Due to a direct access to the internal function E_{K_1} via the reference sector $T^{(r)}$, XTS_K is regarded as a single-key Even-Mansour construction in the target sector $T^{(t)}$. Then, we are able to perform plaintext recovery attacks on the target sector $T^{(t)}$ in several practical attack settings.

Importantly, our plaintext recovery attack works independently from the key size of the internal function E_{K_1}. In other words, the key size of E_{K_1} does not affect the attack complexity.

6   Collision Attack at Reference Sector

We first describe a collision attack that obtains a mask key $E_{K_2}(T^{(r)})$ at a reference sector $T^{(r)}$.

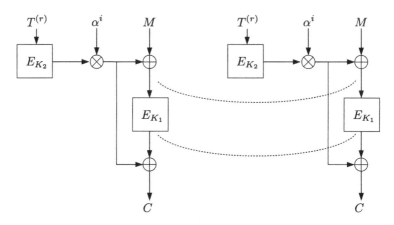

Fig. 3. Collision attack at the reference sector $T^{(r)}$.

Assumption and Goal. As mentioned in Sect. 4, the adversary can issue encryption queries $(M, (T^{(r)}, j))$ with some known M, and decryption queries $(C, (T^{(r)}, j))$ with any $C \in \{0,1\}^n$ for two distinct block j and j' in the reference sector $T^{(r)}$.

The purpose of this attack is to recover $E_{K_2}(T^{(r)})$ without knowing K_1 and K_2.

Idea for Collision Attack. We utilize an event where two inputs of E_{K_1} at two distinct blocks j and j' in the reference sector $T^{(r)}$ are the same as illustrated in Fig. 3. When this event happens, we get the following equation with respect to inputs of E_{K_1}.

$$M \oplus (E_{K_2}(T^{(r)}) \otimes \alpha^j) = M' \oplus (E_{K_2}(T^{(r)}) \otimes \alpha^{j'}) \tag{2}$$

Since E_{K_1} is a permutation, we also have the following equation with respect to outputs of E_{K_1}.

$$C \oplus (E_{K_2}(T^{(r)}) \otimes \alpha^j) = C' \oplus (E_{K_2}(T^{(r)}) \otimes \alpha^{j'}) \tag{3}$$

From Eqs. (2) and (3), we obtain the equation regarding plaintexts and ciphertexts.

$$M \oplus C = M' \oplus C'. \tag{4}$$

Given $2^{n/2}$ sets of (M, C) and (M', C'), respectively, there exists two pairs of (M, C) and (M', C') that satisfy Eq. (4) with a high probability, in which, Eqs. (2) and (3) hold with probability of $1 - 2^{-n}$. Once such two pairs of (M, C) and (M', C') are found, we can recover a mask key $E_{K_2}(T^{(r)})$ from ciphertexts without knowing K_1 and K_2 as

$$E_{K_2}(T^{(r)}) = (C \oplus C')/(\alpha^j + \alpha^{j'}).$$

To find the collision pairs such that $M \oplus C = M' \oplus C'$, in a straight forward way, we should evaluate $2^n (= 2^{n/2} \times 2^{n/2})$ combinations of each $2^{n/2}$ sets of (M, C) and (M', C'). Using the meet-in-the-middle technique, we can efficiently find collision pairs. Specifically, we first make a table of $2^{n/2}$ pairs of (M, C) indexed by $M \oplus C$, and then access the table with $2^{n/2}$ values of $(M' \oplus C')$ to find pairs such that $M \oplus C = M' \oplus C'$. Then, the time complexity for finding collision pairs is estimated as about $2^{n/2}$ operations.

Attack Procedure. Based on the above idea of the collision attack, the procedure of the mask recovery attack is given as follow.

1. Choose two distinct block indexes, j and j' at a reference sector $T^{(r)}$.
2. Obtain $2^{n/2}$ pairs of (M, C) at j, and store $2^{n/2}$ tuples of $(C, M \oplus C)$ in a table.
3. Obtain $2^{n/2}$ pairs of (M', C') at j', and find a pair of (C, C') such that $M \oplus C = M' \oplus C'$ by accessing the table of $(C, M \oplus C)$ with values of $M' \oplus C'$.
4. Output $(C \oplus C')/(\alpha^j + \alpha^{j'})$ as a candidate for $E_{K_2}(T^{(r)})$.

Complexity Evaluation. $2^{n/2}$ known plaintext/ciphertext pairs are required in Step 2 and 3, respectively, and $2^{n/2}$ memory is required for the table in Step 2. The time complexity to find a collision of $M \oplus C = M' \oplus C'$ in Step 2 and 3 is bounded by $2^{n/2}$ encryption calls, assuming the cost of the sum of a single memory access in Step 2 and Step 3 and computations of $(M \oplus C)$ and $(M' \oplus C')$ is less than a single encryption function call.

In summary, the attack complexity is estimated as follows.

- Time: $2^{n/2}$ encryptions
- Data: $2^{n/2+1}$ known plaintexts/ciphertexts
- Memory : $2^{n/2}$ blocks[2]

Example 1. For $n = 64$, our collision attack is feasible with 2^{33} known plaintext/ciphertexts, 2^{32} computations, and 2^{32} memory.

Example 2. For $n = 128$, our collision attack is feasible with 2^{65} known plaintext/ciphertexts, 2^{64} computations, and 2^{64} memory.

Especially, for $n = 64$, attack complexity is practical.

Reference Sector as Oracle. After the collision attack against the reference sector $T^{(r)}$ is succeeded, the adversary is able to obtain inputs X and outputs Y of E_{K_1} by knowledge of $E_{K_2}(T^{(r)})$ and a known pair of (M, C) as follows.

$$X = M \oplus (E_{K_2}(T^{(r)}) \otimes \alpha^j)$$
$$Y = C \oplus (E_{K_2}(T^{(r)}) \otimes \alpha^{j'})$$

---

[2] Using Floyd's cycle-finding algorithm [7], this attack is feasible with the same complexity and negligible memory.

In our plaintext recovery attack at the target sectors $T^{(t)}$, we will use this reference sector as encryption/decryption oracle that output a Y/X, given X/Y. Since E_{K_1} is regarded as a public permutation by queries to the reference sector $T^{(r)}$, XTS_K at any target sector $T^{(t)}$ can be treated as a single-key Even-Mansour (SEM) cipher.

7   Plaintext-Recovery Attacks at Target Sector

In this section, we propose plaintext-recovery attacks at a target sector $T^{(t)}$ in several attack settings such as a partially-known plaintext setting and a ciphertext only setting. All attacks are performed after the collision attack in the reference sector $T^{(r)}$ described at Sect. 6, and the adversary is assumed to has access to the encryption/decryption oracle of E_{K_1}.

7.1   Partially-Known Plaintext Attack 1

First, we describe a plaintext-recovery attack at a target sector $T^{(t)}$ in the partially-known-plaintext setting. Informally, we assume only some blocks in $T^{(t)}$ are known.

Assumption and Goal. The adversary is able to collect plaintext/ciphertext block pairs of indexes at some $j \in J^{kp}$ in a target sector $T^{(t)}$, where J^{kp} is a set of known plaintext blocks in $T^{(t)}$. Note that all ciphertexts at the target sector $T^{(t)}$ are available.

The purpose of this attack is to recover a set of unknown plaintext blocks $j \ni J^{kp}$ in the target sector $T^{(t)}$.

Attack Idea. The equation with respect to a mask key $E_{K_2}(T^{(t)})$ is given as follows.

$$E_{K_2}(T^{(t)}) = (\alpha^j)^{-1} \otimes (M \oplus X) = (\alpha^j)^{-1} \otimes (C \oplus Y)$$

This equation is rewritten as

$$(\alpha^j) \otimes E_{K_2}(T^{(t)}) = M \oplus X = C \oplus Y. \tag{5}$$

According to Eq. (5), a valid tuple of (M, C, X, Y) must satisfy the equation of $X \oplus Y = M \oplus C$. Given a valid tuple of (M, C, X, Y), $E_{K_2}(T^{(t)})$ is obtained as $E_{K_2}(T^{(t)}) = (\alpha^j)^{-1} \otimes (C \oplus Y)$ in the same manner to the key recovery attack against SEM by Dunkelman et al. [4].

Candidates of M and C are obtained at blocks of $j \in J^{kp}$ in the target sector $T^{(t)}$. As shown in Fig. 4, X and Y are obtained in the reference sector $T^{(r)}$ by querying $X \oplus E_{K_2}(T^{(r)}) \otimes (\alpha^j)$ as a plaintext to an encryption oracle, and obtaining the answer (ciphertext) of $Y \oplus E_{K_2}(T^{(r)}) \otimes (\alpha^j)$ where $E_{K_2}(T^{(r)})$ and (α^j) are known values. Let q^t and q^r be the number of available $M \oplus C$ and

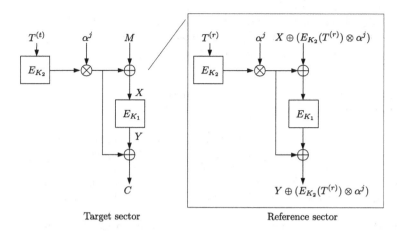

Fig. 4. Partially-known plaintext attack 1.

$X \oplus Y$, respectively. When $q^t \times q^r \geq 2^n$, there exists a valid tuple of (M, C, X, Y) with high probability.

After $E_{K_2}(T^{(t)})$ is found, with knowledge of $E_{K_2}(T^{(t)})$ and decryption oracle access to E_{K_1} in the reference sector $T^{(r)}$, all unknown plaintext blocks $J^t \notin J^{kp}$ can be recovered.

Attack Procedure. The attack procedure of the plaintext recovery attack in the partially-known plaintext setting is as follows.

1. Obtain q^r pairs of (X, Y) from the reference sector $T^{(r)}$, and store tuples of $(X, Y, X \oplus Y)$ to a table.
2. Obtain q^t known plaintext/ciphertext pairs (M, C) at the target sector $T^{(t)}$ such that $q^t \times q^r \approx 2^n$, and find a tuple of (M, C, X, Y) such that $X \oplus Y = M \oplus C$ by accessing the table of $(X, Y, X \oplus Y)$ with values of $(M \oplus C)$.
3. Output $(\alpha^j)^{-1} \otimes (C \oplus Y)$ as a candidate of $E_{K_2}(T)$.
4. Decrypt ciphertexts of block indexes in J^t by a decryption query to E_{K_1} at the reference sector $T^{(r)}$ and the knowledge of $E_{K_2}(T)$, and then obtain the corresponding plaintexts.

Complexity Evaluation. We estimate the number of queries to the reference sector $T^{(r)}$ as time complexity, as the adversary is able to locally compute input/output pairs of E_{K_1}, (X, Y), at the reference sector $T^{(r)}$ after the collision attack. We evaluate data complexity by the number of queries to the target sectors $T^{(r)}$, as partially-known plaintext/ciphertext blocks are given to the adversary in the target sectors. Thus, our attack is feasible by q^t known plaintext/ciphertext blocks at $T^{(t)}$ in Step 2 and q^r encryptions at $T^{(r)}$ in Step 1. The memory requirement is estimated as q^r blocks in Step 1. Note that in the case of $q^r > q^t$, by changing Step 1 and 2, the memory requirement is reduced while keeping the same time and data complexity, i.e. $(M, C, M \oplus C)$ is stored in a table instead of $(X, Y, X \oplus Y)$. Our attack is successful if $q^t \times q^r \geq 2^n$.

The attack complexity is estimated as follows.

- Time: q^r encryptions
- Data: $q^t (= 2^n / q^r)$ known plaintexts/ciphertexts blocks
- Memory: $\min(q^r, q^t)$ blocks

Example 1. For $n = 64$, this plaintext-recovery attack is feasible with 2^8 known plaintext/ciphertext blocks, 2^{56} encryptions, and 2^8 memory.

Example 2. For $n = 128$, this plaintext-recovery attack is feasible with 2^{32} known plaintext/ciphertext blocks, 2^{96} encryptions, and 2^{32} memory.

For $n = 64$, this attack is practically feasible by the standard commercial computer resource in this time. For $n = 128$, time complexity is not very practical but it is still feasible by cloud-based computations and dedicated hardware. Note that our attacks does not need $O(2^{n/2})$ encrypted blocks of the sector for which the target plaintext is stored unlike a trivial application of collision attack in the target sector. It makes our attack more practical in real world settings.

Multi-target Setting. Since the same key of K_1 is used at any sector, q^r pairs of (X, Y) of E_{K_1}, which are obtained in the reference sector $T^{(r)}$, can be used for plaintext recovery attacks at any sector. Thus, we are able to mount plaintext recovery attacks in multiple sectors at the same time. In the Multi-target setting where we try to compromise at least one of them [2,8,10,16], given $q^r \geq 2^n / q^t$ plaintexts/ciphertexts from multiple target sectors, $E_{K_2}(T^{(t)})$ is recovered at the one of target sectors $T^{(t)}$, and then all plaintexts in this target sector can be recovered. This setting makes our attack more practical because collecting known plaintexts/ciphertexts are most difficult task in the real world.

Example. For $n = 64$, our plaintext recovery attack is feasible with 2^{10} known plaintext/ciphertexts, and 2^{54} computations with 2^{10} memory. If the adversary knows the first eight blocks of plaintexts in target $2^7 (= 128)$ sectors, e.g. fixed header files, as shown in Fig. 5, our multi-target attack is successful, that is, unknown plaintext blocks of at least one sector out of 128 target sectors are recovered. This attack is more practical in the real world.

7.2   Partially-Known Plaintext Attack 2

In this section, we propose another variant of partially-known plaintext recovery attacks in which there is no block in $T^{(t)}$ that is completely known.

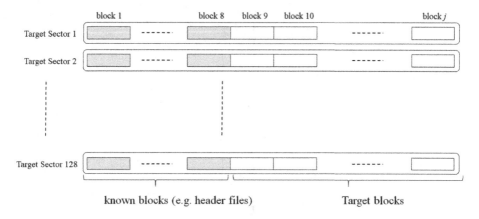

Fig. 5. Partially-known plaintext attack 1 in the multi-target setting.

Assumption and Goal. The adversary is able to collect plaintext/ciphertext pairs at blocks of index $j \in J^{kp} \subseteq [m]$ in a target sector $T^{(t)}$, however only b bits $(b < n)$ out of n bits of each plaintext block of index $j \in J^{kp}$ are known and the other $n - b$ bits are unknown. For simplicity, we assume that first b bits of n-bit plaintext block M, denoted by $M_A = \mathsf{msb}_b(M)$, is known, the last $(n - b)$-bit $M_B = \mathsf{lsb}_{n-b}(M)$ is unknown at blocks of index $j \in J^{kp}$, where $M = M_A \parallel M_B$, while our attack is applicable when any part of b bits of each plaintext block is known.

The purpose of this attack is to recover a set of unknown plaintext blocks $j \notin J^{kp}$ and unknown bits of blocks of $j \in J^{kp}$ at the target sector.

Attack Idea. Given q^t pairs of (M, C) and q^r pairs of (X, Y) such that $q^t \cdot q^r = 2^n$, there are $2^{n-b}(= 2^n/2^b)$ tuples of (M_A, C, X, Y) satisfying a corresponding b-bit relation of $X_A \oplus Y_A = M_A \oplus C_A$, where X_A, Y_A, and C_A are lower b bits of X, Y and C, respectively. In this case, 2^{n-b} candidates of $E_{K_2}(T^{(t)}) = (\alpha^j)^{-1} \otimes (C \oplus Y)$ are obtained. Among them, there exists a correct $E_{K_2}(T^{(t)})$ with high probability because of $q^t \cdot q^r = 2^n$.

To efficiently sieve candidates of $E_{K_2}(T^{(t)})$, we obtain N^s sets of 2^{n-b} candidates of $E_{K_2}(T^{(t)})$ by preparing N^s sets of q^r pairs of (X, Y), and then find the duplicated one in all different N^s sets, assuming that the correct one is included in each set. Since the probability that a wrong key in a set 1 is included in the other $N^s - 1$ sets is $(2^{n-b}/2^n)^{N^s-1}$, the expected number of surviving wrong pairs is estimated as

$$2^{n-b} \cdot \left(2^{n-b}/2^n\right)^{N^s-1} = 2^{n-N^s b}.$$

If $2^{n-N^s b}$ is sufficiently small, we exhaustively test surviving key candidates of $1 + 2^{n-N^s b}$ to find the correct one. The overview of this attack is illustrated in Fig. 6.

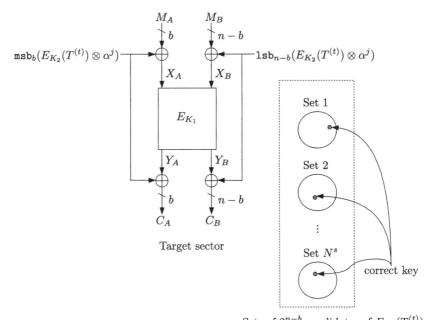

Fig. 6. Partially-known plaintext attack 2.

Attack Procedure. The attack procedure of the plaintext recovery attack in the partial known plaintext setting is as follows.

1. Obtain q^t known plaintext/ciphertext pairs (M, C) at the target sector $T^{(t)}$, and store tuples of $(M_A, C, M_A \oplus C_A)$ to a table.
2. Obtain N^s sets of q^r pairs of (X, Y) at $T^{(r)}$ such that $q^t \times q^r \approx 2^n$, and find N^s sets of 2^{n-b} tuples of (M_A, C, X, Y) satisfying the b-bit relation of $X_A \oplus Y_A = M_A \oplus C_A$ by accessing the table of $(M_A, C, M_A \oplus C_A)$ with the values of $(X_A \oplus Y_A)$.
3. Output N^s sets of 2^{n-b} candidates of mask keys $E_{K_2}(T) = (\alpha^j)^{-1} \otimes (C \oplus Y))$ from valid tuples of (M_A, C, X, Y), and find the duplicated ones in all N^s sets. The expected number of remaining keys are estimated as $(1 + 2^{n-N^s b})$.
4. Exhaustively search $(1 + 2^{n-N^s b})$ surviving key candidates, and find the correct $E_{K_2}(T)$.
5. Decrypt ciphertexts of index in J^t by a decryption query to E_{K_1} at the reference sector $T^{(r)}$ and the knowledge of $E_{K_2}(T)$, and then obtain the corresponding unknown plaintexts.

Complexity Evaluation. The required data is q^t known plaintexts/ciphertexts in Step 1 where only b bits of each block are known. The time complexity is estimated as the sum of $N^s \times q^r$ encryptions in Step 2 and $1 + 2^{n-N^s b}$ encryptions in Step 4. The memory requirement is the sum of $N^s \times q^t$ (Step 1) and $N^s \times 2^{n-b}$ (Step 3). The attack complexity is estimated as follows.

Table 2. Time and data complexity in each b (the number of known bits in n-bit block) with optimal values of Ns of partially-known plaintext attack 2.

	$b = 2$			$b = 4$			$b = 8$			$b = 16$			$b = 24$		
N^s	5	10	15	3	5	8	2	3	4	1	2	3	1	1	2
Data	2^{10}	2^{20}	2^{30}	2^{10}	2^{20}	2^{30}	2^{10}	2^{20}	2^{30}	2^{10}	2^{20}	2^{30}	2^{10}	2^{20}	2^{30}
Time	$2^{56.3}$	$2^{47.3}$	$2^{37.9}$	$2^{55.6}$	$2^{46.3}$	2^{37}	2^{55}	$2^{45.6}$	2^{36}	2^{54}	2^{45}	$2^{35.6}$	2^{54}	2^{44}	2^{35}
Data $\times$ Time	$2^{66.3}$	$2^{67.3}$	$2^{67.9}$	$2^{65.6}$	$2^{66.3}$	2^{67}	2^{65}	$2^{65.6}$	2^{66}	2^{64}	2^{65}	$2^{65.6}$	2^{64}	2^{64}	2^{65}

- Time: $N^s \times q^r$ (Step 1) $+ 1 + 2^{n-N^s b}$ (Step 4)
- Data: $q^t (= 2^n / q^r)$ partial known plaintexts/ciphertexts in which only b bits of each plaintext are known.
- Memory: $N^s \times q^t$ (Step 1) $+ N^s \times 2^{n-b}$ (Step 3)

Note that the value N^s such that $N^s \times q^r = 1 + 2^{n-N^s b}$ is optimal for time complexity.

Table 2 shows time and data complexity in each b with optimal values of Ns. Surprisingly, even when only b bits in q^t plaintexts are known, the key recovery attack is feasible with almost the same data and time complexity, that is, the product of time and data is around 2^n.

Example 1. For $n = 64$, $b = 8$ (1 byte) and $q^r = 2^{54}$, when $N^s = 2$ the expected number of surviving wrong pairs is $2^{48} (= 2^{64-8\cdot 2})$. The plaintext-recovery attack is feasible with 2^{10} known plaintext/ciphertexts, $2^{55} (= 2 \times 2^{54} + 1 + 2^{48})$ computations, and $2^{57} (= 2 \times 2^{10} + 2 \times 2^{56})$ memory.

Example 2. For $n = 128$, $b = 8$ (1 byte) and $q^r = 2^{96}$, when $N^s = 4$ the expected number of surviving wrong pairs is $2^{96} (= 2^{128-8\cdot 4})$. The plaintext-recovery attack is feasible with 2^{32} known plaintext/ciphertexts, $2^{98} (= 4 \times 2^{96} + 1 + 2^{96})$ computations, and $2^{122} (= 4 \times 2^{32} + 4 \times 2^{120})$ memory.

Multi-target Attack. This attack is naturally extended to a multi-target attack. It makes collecting (M, C) easier as discussed in the previous section. Figure 7 illustrates the case of only one byte is known ($b = 8$) in 1024 target sectors for $n = 64$. In this case, when $N^s = 2$, the expected number of surviving wrong pairs is $2^{48} (= 2^{64-8\cdot 2})$. The plaintext recovery attack in Multi-target setting is feasible with $2^{58} (= 2 \times 2^{57} + 1 + 2^{48})$ computations, and $2^{57} (= 2^7 + 2 \times 2^{57} + 1 + 2^{48})$ memory. The adversary recovers unknown plaintext blocks in one of 1024 target sectors.

Low-Memory Attack. When $N_s = 1$, we can mount low-memory attacks although time complexity increases. In this case, 2^{n-b} candidates in Step 3 are exhaustively searched without the duplication check. Thus, we do not need to store 2^{n-b} key candidates. Thus, the memory requirement of Step 3 to store key candidates are not necessary. The attack complexity is estimated as follows.

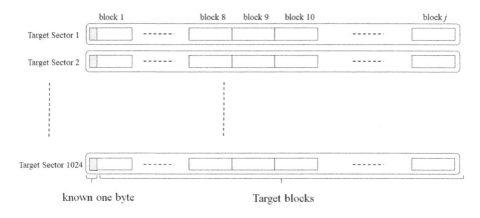

Fig. 7. Partial-known plaintext attack 2 in the multi-target setting.

- Time: q^r (Step 1) $+ 1 + 2^{n-b}$
- Data: $q^t (= 2^n/q^r)$ partial known plaintexts/ciphertexts in which only b bits of each plaintext are known.
- Memory : q^t blocks

When $q^r > 1 + 2^{n-b}$, the attack is feasible with the almost same complexity and data requirements, namely the product of time and data is around 2^n, otherwise it becomes less efficient.

Example 1. For $n = 64$, $b = 8$ (1 byte) and $q^r = 2^{54}$, the expected number of surviving wrong pairs is $2^{56} (= 2^{64-8})$ to be exhaustively searched. The plaintext recovery attack is feasible with 2^{10} known plaintext/ciphertexts, $2^{57} (= 2^{54} + 1 + 2^{56})$ computations, and 2^{10} memory.

Example 2. For $n = 128$, $b = 8$ (1 byte) and $q^r = 2^{96}$, the expected number of surviving wrong pairs is $2^{120} (= 2^{128-8})$ to be exhaustively searched. The plaintext recovery attack is feasible with 2^{32} known plaintext/ciphertexts, $2^{120} (= 2^{96} + 1 + 2^{120})$ computations, and 2^{32} memory.

7.3 Ciphertext-Only Attack

In this section, we propose a plaintext recovery attack in the weakest, ciphertext-only setting where the adversary does not have any information about plaintexts.

Assumption and Goal. The adversary is able to collect ciphertexts at a target sector $T^{(t)}$, and does not have any information about plaintexts.

The purpose of the attack is to guess plaintext at the target sector $T^{(t)}$ with higher probability than random guessing.

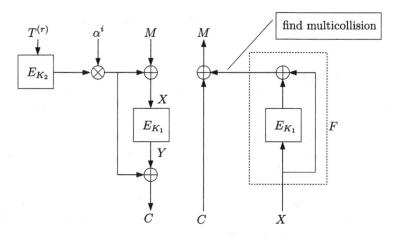

Fig. 8. Ciphertext-only attack.

Attack Idea. From Eq. 5, an n-bit equation with respect to a plaintext is given as

$$M = C \oplus (X \oplus Y(= E_{K_1}(X))).$$

Interestingly, a plaintext M is expressed as C, X and Y without including the value of E_{K_2} as shown in Fig. 8. These are obtained in the target sector $T^{(t)}$ and the reference sector $T^{(r)}$, respectively, even in the ciphertext-only setting,

We utilize a *multi collision technique* in $(X \oplus Y(= E_{K_1}(X)))$ to guess a plaintext M from only a corresponding ciphertext C with higher probability than random guessing, while this technique was originally used for key-recovery attacks on a 2-round single-key Even-Mansour cipher [3,17].

Specifically, we exploit t-way collisions of $F(X) = (X \oplus E_{K_1}(X))$ for a value of v such that

$$X^{(1)} \oplus E_{K_1}(X^{(1)}) = X^{(2)} \oplus E_{K_1}(X^{(2)}) = \cdots = X^{(t)} \oplus E_{K_1}(X^{(t)}) = v,$$

i.e., t input values of $X^{(1)}, \ldots X^{(t)}$ map to the same output value v through the function F. Assuming that there are t-way collisions with respect to v in $F(X)$, the probability of $M = C \oplus v$ is estimated as $\frac{t}{2^n}$, which is t times higher than the expected $1/2^n$.

Attack Procedure. Our plaintext recovery attack in the ciphertext-only setting consists of two phases. In the first phase, we find t-way collisions of $F(X) = (X \oplus E_{K_1}(X)) = v$ by accessing the reference sector $T^{(r)}$. In the second phase, we guess a plaintext as $M = P \oplus v$. The attack procedure using t-way collisions is given as follows.

1. Obtain q^r pairs of (X, Y) at the reference sector $T^{(r)}$ and evaluate $(X \oplus Y)$.
2. Find t-way collisions of $F(X) = (X \oplus Y(= E_{K_1}(X)))$, which map to the same value v.

3. Guess a values of a target plaintext M at $T^{(t)}$ from a corresponding ciphertext C as $M = C \oplus v$.

Complexity Evaluation. For the accurate estimation of the cost for finding t-way collisions of $F(X)$ in the Step 2, we assume that in-degree of an element in the range of $F(X)$ is distributed according to the Poisson distribution with an expectation λ, which is equal to the average in-degree, i.e., $\lambda = q^r/2^n$ is the ratio between the sizes of the domain and range as with Dinur et al. [3]. For a parameter t, the probability that an arbitrary element v will have an in-degree of t is $(\lambda^t \cdot e^{-\lambda})/t!$. Since there are 2^n elements in the range, it is expected that about $(2^n \cdot \lambda^t \cdot e^{-\lambda})/t!$ vertexes have an in-degree of t.

Assuming that a value of v in has t-way collisions, the success probability of our plaintext recovery attack is estimated as $t/2^n$. The time complexity is estimated as q^r for finding t-way collisions at the reference sector $T^{(r)}$.

Example 1. For $n = 64$ and $q^r = 2^{60}$, which implies $\lambda = 2^{60}/2^{64} = 2^{-4}$, and $t = 10$, the number of 10-way collisions is estimated as $num = (2^n \cdot \lambda^t \cdot e^{-\lambda})/t! = (2^{64} \cdot (2^{-4})^{10} \cdot e^{-2^{-4}}/10!) = 4$. With these parameters, the time complexity is estimated as 2^{60} encryptions and its memory complexity is 2^{60}. Then, the success probability in Step 3 is $10/2^{64} = 2^{-60.68}$ while ideally it should be 2^{-64}.

Example 2. For $n = 128$ and $q^r = 2^{124}$, which implies $\lambda = 2^{124}/2^{128} = 2^{-4}$, and $t = 25$, the number of 18-way collisions is estimated as $num = (2^n \cdot \lambda^t \cdot e^{-\lambda})/t! = (2^{128} \cdot (2^{-4})^{18} \cdot e^{-2^{-4}}/18!) = 4$. With these parameters, time complexity is estimated as 2^{124} encryptions and its memory complexity is 2^{124}. Then, the success probability in Step 3 is $18/2^{128} = 2^{-123.83}$ while ideally it should be 2^{-128}.

Multiple t-way Collision. For $n = 64$ and $q^r = 2^{60}$, we are able to find $2^{16.6}$ 8-way collisions. Given a ciphertext, the probability that the corresponding plaintext is included in a set of $P = C \oplus v$, $v \in V^s$, where V^s is a set of $2^{16.6}$ 8 vertexes, is estimated as $2^{44.4} (= 2^{16.6} \times 8/2^{64})$, while ideally it should be $2^{47.4} (= 2^{16.6}/2^{64})$. Table 3 shows the expected number of vertexes for each q^r, the success probability of our plaintext recovery attack which is estimated as the probability that a plaintext is included in a set of $P = C \oplus v'$, where v' is a set of corresponding vertexes.

Multi-target Setting. Once t-way collisions are found in Step 2, plaintext recovery attacks are applicable to any ciphertext at any target sector $T^{(t)}$ with the same success probability (namely multi-target attack). Thus, in the above case, there are $2^{44.4}$ ciphertexts in the whole target storage device, the attack is successful one of them with a high probability.

Table 3. The expected number of vertexes for each q^r computations and the success probability of our ciphertext-only plaintext recovery attacks using multiple t-way collision for $n = 64$.

q^r	Vertex	Expected number of vertexes	Success probability	Ideal probability
2^{62}	12	1787	$2^{-49.6}$	$2^{-53.2}$
	10	$2^{21.8}$	$2^{-38.9}$	$2^{-42.2}$
2^{60}	10	4	2^{-60}	2^{-62}
	8	$2^{16.6}$	$2^{-44.4}$	$2^{-47.4}$
	6	$2^{30.4}$	$2^{-31.0}$	$2^{-33.6}$
	4	$2^{43.3}$	$2^{-18.7}$	$2^{-20.7}$
2^{56}	6	90	$2^{-54.9}$	$2^{-57.5}$
	4	$2^{27.4}$	$2^{-32.0}$	$2^{-34.0}$
2^{52}	4	2739	$2^{-51.6}$	$2^{-53.6}$

8 Practical Impact

Since our attacks are based on collisions, the data complexity is at least $2^{n/2}$ for one key of XTS, which is not considered as an urgent risk when $n = 128$ including the case of XTS-AES. However, we stress that the storage encryption is crucially different from encryption of communication that allows re-keying for each session to thwart the attacks that need a large amount of data per key. Since a key in a storage encryption is hard to renew since this implies total re-encryption of storage devices. Hence it is likely to be used very long time (or forever), the risk of birthday attack is larger than the communication encryption. In case of 64-bit block ciphers however, as demonstrated by Sweet32 [1], a collision can occur around 2^{32} 8-byte blocks which is about 32 Gbyte. In this case, our attacks have a practical complexity.

We performed a survey on existing encryption software that employ 64-bit block ciphers with LRW or XTS. The survey is on specification documents and the product website, and we did not look into the source codes.

Fortunately, most of popular products with active developments, such as VeraCrypt[3], solely use XTS-AES or XTS with strong 128-bit block ciphers (e.g. AES finalists) in addition to AES. Nevertheless, we can find some examples of storage/file encryption software that use 64-bit block ciphers with LRW. We note that our attacks against XTS are also applicable to LRW with minor modifications, since our attacks are independent of the mechanism for deriving each masks. We list some examples:

- BestCrypt[4] is a popular encryption software and it employs 64-bit block ciphers such as Blowfish, CAST, and GOST 28147-89 with LRW. We have informed our findings to the developer of BestCrypt.

---

[3] https://www.veracrypt.fr/en/Home.html.
[4] https://www.jetico.com/data-encryption.

– Old version of TrueCrypt[5], specifically the version up to 4.2, supported Blowfish, CAST-128, and TDES with LRW.
– A successor of TrueCrypt called CipherShed[6] used Blowfish, Cast, and DES with LRW.
– Some popular encryption systems on linux such as dm-crypt[7] may support 64-bit ciphers and LRW. The supported ciphers will depend on the kernel.

9   Conclusion

In this paper, we have studied the security of XTS storage encryption scheme from the aspects of plaintext recovery. The provable security result of the core of XTS (XEX2) suggests that the attack is not feasible without data of $2^{n/2}$, and indeed it is rather easy to derive an attack based on collision, using that amount of data. However this attack only breaks the indistinguishability. Starting from this simple collision attack, we have shown several plaintext recovery attacks, based on the popular adversary model against storage encryption. Our main observation is that, once a collision attack was successful, XTS can be seen as a variant of Single-key Even-Mansour (SEM) cipher, therefore we can adapt the known attacks against SEM. To our knowledge, our work is the first to study the plaintext recovery security of XTS. Since all attacks have $2^{n/2}$ to even close to 2^n complexity, the attacks do not show a practical threat against the standard XTS-AES for its $n = 128$-bit block. However, as we observed, there still exist systems that use 64-bit block ciphers with XTS or LRW for storage encryption. For those systems, our attacks can be a practical threat.

Acknowledgments. The authors would like to thank the anonymous referees of SAC 2019 for their insightful comments and suggestions. Takanori Isobe is supported by Grant-in-Aid for Scientific Research (B) (KAKENHI 19H02141) for Japan Society for the Promotion of Science.

References

1. Bhargavan, K., Leurent, G.: On the practical (in-)security of 64-bit block ciphers: collision attacks on HTTP over TLS and OpenVPN. In: Weippl, E.R., Katzenbeisser, S., Kruegel, C., Myers, A.C., Halevi, S. (eds.) Proceedings of the 2016 ACM SIGSAC Conference on Computer and Communications Security, Vienna, Austria, 24–28 October 2016, pp. 456–467. ACM (2016)
2. Biham, E.: How to decrypt or even substitute des-encrypted messages in 2^{28} steps. Inf. Process. Lett. **84**(3), 117–124 (2002)
3. Dinur, I., Dunkelman, O., Keller, N., Shamir, A.: Key recovery attacks on iterated Even-Mansour encryption schemes. J. Cryptol. **29**(4), 697–728 (2016)

---

[5] http://truecrypt.sourceforge.net/.

[6] https://www.ciphershed.org/.

[7] https://wiki.archlinux.org/index.php/dm-crypt.

4. Dunkelman, O., Keller, N., Shamir, A.: Minimalism in cryptography: the Even-Mansour scheme revisited. In: Pointcheval, D., Johansson, T. (eds.) EUROCRYPT 2012. LNCS, vol. 7237, pp. 336–354. Springer, Heidelberg (2012). https://doi.org/10.1007/978-3-642-29011-4_21

5. Dworkin, M.: Recommendation for Block Cipher Modes of Operation: The XTS-AES Mode for Confidentiality on Storage Devices. Standard, National Institute of Standards and Technology (2010)

6. Ferguson, N.: AES-CBC + Elephant diffuser - A Disk Encryption Algorithm for Windows Vista (2006)

7. Floyd, R.W.: Nondeterministic algorithms. J. ACM **14**(4), 636–644 (1967)

8. Fouque, P.-A., Joux, A., Mavromati, C.: Multi-user collisions: applications to discrete logarithm, Even-Mansour and PRINCE. In: Sarkar, P., Iwata, T. (eds.) ASIACRYPT 2014. LNCS, vol. 8873, pp. 420–438. Springer, Heidelberg (2014). https://doi.org/10.1007/978-3-662-45611-8_22

9. Halevi, S.: Storage Encryption: A Cryptographer's View. Invited Talk at SCN 2008 (2008)

10. Hoang, V.T., Tessaro, S., Thiruvengadam, A.: The multi-user security of GCM, revisited: tight bounds for nonce randomization. In: Proceedings of the 2018 ACM SIGSAC Conference on Computer and Communications Security, CCS 2018, New York, NY, USA, pp. 1429–1440. ACM (2018)

11. Standard for Cryptographic Protection of Data on Block-Oriented Storage Devices. Standard, IEEE Security in Storage Working Group

12. Khati, L., Mouha, N., Vergnaud, D.: Full disk encryption: bridging theory and practice. In: Handschuh, H. (ed.) CT-RSA 2017. LNCS, vol. 10159, pp. 241–257. Springer, Cham (2017). https://doi.org/10.1007/978-3-319-52153-4_14

13. Leurent, G., Sibleyras, F.: The missing difference problem, and its applications to counter mode encryption. In: Nielsen, J.B., Rijmen, V. (eds.) EUROCRYPT 2018. LNCS, vol. 10821, pp. 745–770. Springer, Cham (2018). https://doi.org/10.1007/978-3-319-78375-8_24

14. Liskov, M., Rivest, R.L., Wagner, D.: Tweakable block ciphers. In: Yung, M. (ed.) CRYPTO 2002. LNCS, vol. 2442, pp. 31–46. Springer, Heidelberg (2002). https://doi.org/10.1007/3-540-45708-9_3

15. Minematsu, K.: Improved security analysis of XEX and LRW modes. In: Biham, E., Youssef, A.M. (eds.) SAC 2006. LNCS, vol. 4356, pp. 96–113. Springer, Heidelberg (2007). https://doi.org/10.1007/978-3-540-74462-7_8

16. Mouha, N., Luykx, A.: Multi-key security: the Even-Mansour construction revisited. In: Gennaro, R., Robshaw, M. (eds.) CRYPTO 2015. LNCS, vol. 9215, pp. 209–223. Springer, Heidelberg (2015). https://doi.org/10.1007/978-3-662-47989-6_10

17. Nikolić, I., Wang, L., Wu, S.: Cryptanalysis of round-reduced LED. In: Moriai, S. (ed.) FSE 2013. LNCS, vol. 8424, pp. 112–129. Springer, Heidelberg (2014). https://doi.org/10.1007/978-3-662-43933-3_7

18. Rogaway, P.: Evaluation of some blockcipher modes of operation. CRYPTREC Report (2011)

19. Rogaway, P.: Efficient instantiations of tweakable blockciphers and refinements to modes OCB and PMAC. In: Lee, P.J. (ed.) ASIACRYPT 2004. LNCS, vol. 3329, pp. 16–31. Springer, Heidelberg (2004). https://doi.org/10.1007/978-3-540-30539-2_2

Cryptanalysis of SKINNY in the Framework of the SKINNY 2018–2019 Cryptanalysis Competition

Patrick Derbez[1(✉)], Virginie Lallemand[2,3], and Aleksei Udovenko[4]

[1] Univ Rennes, CNRS, IRISA, Rennes, France
`patrick.derbez@irisa.fr`
[2] Université de Lorraine, CNRS, Inria, LORIA, Nancy, France
[3] Horst Görtz Institute for IT Security, Ruhr-Universität Bochum, Bochum, Germany
`virginie.lallemand@loria.fr`
[4] SnT and CSC, University of Luxembourg, Esch-sur-Alzette, Luxembourg
`aleksei.udovenko@uni.lu`

Abstract. In April 2018, Beierle et al. launched the 3rd SKINNY cryptanalysis competition, a contest that aimed at motivating the analysis of their recent tweakable block cipher SKINNY. In contrary to the previous editions, the focus was made on practical attacks: contestants were asked to recover a 128-bit secret key from a given set of 2^{20} plaintext blocks. The suggested SKINNY instances are 4- to 20-round reduced variants of SKINNY-64-128 and SKINNY-128-128. In this paper, we explain how to solve the challenges for 10-round SKINNY-128-128 and for 12-round SKINNY-64-128 in time equivalent to roughly 2^{52} simple operations. Both techniques benefit from the highly biased sets of messages that are provided and that actually correspond to the encryption of various books in ECB mode.

Keywords: Cryptanalysis · SKINNY · Low data attack · Truncated differential · Higher order differential · Integral cryptanalysis

1 Introduction

In order to motivate external cryptanalyses of their family of ciphers, SKINNY designers launched several one-year competitions. The first one started in 2016 and called for cryptanalyses of small-scaled variants of 18 up to 26 rounds of SKINNY-64-128, and of 22 up to 30 rounds of SKINNY-128-128. The two papers that won the competition are [1] for being the first submission that attacks

Patrick Derbez was supported by the French Agence Nationale de la Recherche through the CryptAudit project under Contract ANR-17-CE39-0003. This work was initiated while Virginie Lallemand was with the Horst Görtz Institute for IT Security at the Ruhr-Universität Bochum. The work of Aleksei Udovenko was partially supported by the Fonds National de la Recherche, Luxembourg (project reference 9037104).

K. G. Paterson and D. Stebila (Eds.): SAC 2019, LNCS 11959, pp. 124–145, 2020.
https://doi.org/10.1007/978-3-030-38471-5_6

up to 20 rounds of SKINNY-64-128 and [9] for being the first submitted work to successfully attack up to 23 rounds of SKINNY-64-128.

The challenges launched in 2017 were similar, except that the number of rounds one has to break were higher. Nobody won these contests.

The last competition started on the 1st of April 2018 and ended on February 28, 2019. This time, the goal was to mount a practical key recovery attack of small-scaled versions of SKINNY for which sets of only 2^{20} pairs (plaintext, ciphertext) were provided. The designers offered rewards for the teams that would break the maximum number of rounds for SKINNY-64-128 or SKINNY-128-128[1].

Contributions. In this paper, we describe our practical attacks on 12-round SKINNY-64-128 and on 10-round SKINNY-128-128 in the setting of the third SKINNY Cryptanalysis Competition. At the time of writing and as far as we know, these attacks are the ones that cover the largest number of rounds (Table 1).

Table 1. Complexities of our attacks: the data complexity corresponds to the number of messages that are actually exploited in the attack, while time complexity is expressed in number of basic operations.

Version	Rounds	Technique	Data	Time	Memory
SKINNY-64-128	12	Truncated diff.	64	$2^{51.95}$	256 GB
SKINNY-128-128	10	2nd-order truncated diff.	24	2^{52}	0.5 GB

Paper Organization. After briefly recalling the description of the SKINNY block cipher (Sect. 2), we study the structure of the provided set of 2^{20} messages in Sect. 3 and show that the observed bias comes from the fact that the plaintexts are sentences of various famous books encrypted in ECB mode. We then describe in Sect. 4 how we can benefit from this to find distinguishers that would not have been possible if the input messages were uniformly distributed. More into details, Sect. 5 reports a truncated differential attack that works with time close to 2^{52} operations. In this attack, a careful study of the tweakey schedule showed that a 4-bit guess can be saved, while the key recovery algorithm is optimised so that the required memory stays practical. In Sect. 6, we use second-order truncated differentials to break 10-round SKINNY-128-128 with 2^{52} basic operations.

The source codes of our attacks are available at

http://skinnysac19.gforge.inria.fr/

2 A Brief Description of SKINNY

SKINNY is a family of lightweight tweakable block ciphers that was designed by Beierle et al. and published at Crypto 2016 [3]. The objective pursued (and

---

[1] All the information on the competitions and on the cipher in general can be found on https://sites.google.com/site/skinnycipher/home.

achieved) by the designers was to propose a family of ciphers that would have similar performances to those of the NSA cipher Simon [2] but with strong security arguments on top.

The SKINNY ciphers follow the TWEAKEY framework from [6] so each instance takes as input a plaintext P and a tweakey TK to produce a ciphertext C. The different variants in the family are noted SKINNY-n-t, where n represents the block size (64 or 128 bits) and where t is the tweakey size (n, $2n$ or $3n$).

As for the AES and many other SPN, the internal state is organised in a matrix of 4×4 elements. Depending on the block size, each cell is either a nibble (4 bits, when $n = 64$) or a byte (8 bits, when $n = 128$). Similarly, the tweakey is arranged in $z = t/n$ such 4×4 matrices, noted TK1 up to TKz. Both the messages and the tweakey states are loaded row-wise, and we number the nibbles in this way (see Fig. 8).

In the following we only provide a high-level description of SKINNY and refer to the original specification [3] for further details.

Round Function. SKINNY round function is illustrated in Fig. 1. It can be noted that contrary to most ciphers, the (tweak)key is added after the non-linear operation (SubCells), and not before.

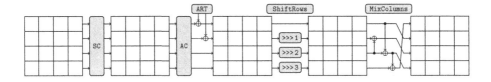

Fig. 1. SKINNY round function (figure credits: [5]).

Also, no whitening keys are used and the last MixColumns is not omitted, which means that all the rounds iterate exactly the same sequence of operations, that are:

- SubCells (SC): Each of the 16 cells of the internal state is modified by the 4×4 Sbox $\mathcal{S}_4$ described in Table 4 if each cell is a nibble, or by the 8×8 Sbox $\mathcal{S}_8$ described in Table 5 if each cell is a byte.
- AddConstants (AC): Constants generated by an LFSR are added in the first 3 cells of the first column.
- AddRoundTweakey (ART): The tweakey material is XORed to the first two lines of the state.
- ShiftRows (SR): The second, third and fourth rows of the internal state are respectively right-rotated by 1 cell, 2 cells, and 3 cells.
- MixColumns (MC): Each input column of the internal state is multiplied by the following binary matrix M:

$$M = \begin{pmatrix} 1 & 0 & 1 & 1 \\ 1 & 0 & 0 & 0 \\ 0 & 1 & 1 & 0 \\ 1 & 0 & 1 & 0 \end{pmatrix}$$

The number of times the round function is repeated for each version of SKINNY is detailed in Table 2.

Table 2. Number of iterated rounds for each version of the cipher, depending on the tweakey size $(t = z \times n)$ and on the block size n.

Block size	Tweakey size		
	$z = 1$	$z = 2$	$z = 3$
$n = 64$	32	36	40
$n = 128$	40	48	56

Tweakey Schedule. SKINNY follows the Tweakey framework defined in [6] that allows an user to add an additional parameter, the so-called tweak. In the setting of the third cryptanalysis competition, the 128 bits of tweakey of SKINNY-64-128 or SKINNY-128-128 are unknown, and consequently the 128 bits are considered as key only.

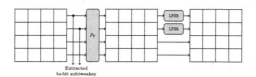

Fig. 2. Tweakey schedule of SKINNY (figure credits: [5])

The tweakey schedule is represented in Fig. 2. For SKINNY-128-128 there is only one tweakey block (TK1) organised in a square matrix of bytes. At each round, the first two lines of the matrix are extracted and used as round tweakey in the step ART of the round function. Then, the bytes are permuted by the permutation P_T, given by:

$$P_T = [9, 15, 8, 13, 10, 14, 12, 11, 0, 1, 2, 3, 4, 5, 6, 7].$$

This process is repeated for the following rounds.

In the case of SKINNY-64-128 we have $z = 2$, which means that we have two tweakey states (TK_1 and TK_2) organised as 4×4 matrices of nibbles. A round tweakey is made by extracting the first two rows of each tweakey state and XORing them together. To produce the next tweakey, TK_1 and TK_2 are first updated by applying the permutation P_T that reorder their 16 nibbles. The 8 nibbles of the first two rows of TK_2 are then further modified by the following linear operation:

$$L : (x_3||x_2||x_1||x_0) \mapsto (x_2||x_1||x_0||x_3 \oplus x_2)$$

where x_0 is the LSB of the cell.

3   Remark on the Provided Messages

While looking for messages with specific patterns, we realized that the plaintexts provided for the challenges were not uniformly distributed.

To illustrate this, we provide in Fig. 3 the distribution of the value of nibble 0 (top left corner in the Skinny internal state) and of nibble 15 (bottom right) in the set provided for the 12-round attack on SKINNY-64-128.

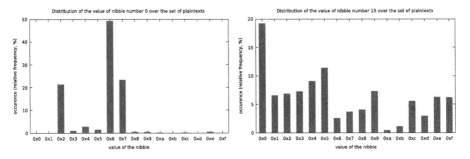

Fig. 3. Distribution of the value of nibble 0 (left) and of nibble 15 (right) of the 2^{20} plaintexts provided for the 12-round attack on SKINNY-64-128.

In fact, the bias observed in Fig. 3 is present on the other nibble positions too, and we made the following observations:

- All the nibbles positioned at even indices (when considering the numbering of Fig. 8) have a distribution similar to the one of the left bar chart of Fig. 3: the most frequent value is 0x6 (occurring roughly half of the time), followed by 0x7 and 0x2. The other values are very rare.
- The nibbles at odd positions don't have such a strong bias. Still, some values are more frequent than the others, like 0x0 that appears in one case out of 5.

It is rather direct to make the link between this distribution and the one of a text in UTF-8 code: indeed, the first hint comes from the fact that the UTF-8 code of the lower-case letters goes from 0x61 to 0x7a, which explains the overwhelming occurrence of the nibble 0x6 (followed by the nibble 0x7) in the distribution of nibbles at even positions. Also, a character that is ought to appear frequently is the space, encoded by 0x20. This one explains the third dominant higher nibble value (0x2) and the high number of occurrences of 0x0 in the lower nibbles.

This guess was confirmed once we printed the plaintexts. For instance, looking at the messages given for the challenge on 4 rounds SKINNY-64-128, we read:

> Project Gutenberg's Alice's Adventures in Wonderland, by Lewis Carroll
> This eBook is for the use of anyone anywhere at no cost and with almost no restrictions whatsoever.

And few lines later, confirming that this is the book, one can read:

> [...] when suddenly a White Rabbit with pink eyes ran close by her. There was nothing so VERY remarkable in that; nor did Alice think it so VERY much out of the way to hear the Rabbit say to itself, 'Oh dear! Oh dear! I shall be late!'

Other data sets correspond to other books (for instance Metamorphosis, by Franz Kafka or The Prince, by Nicolo Machiavelli).

This high bias in the messages implies that we have some collisions on the plaintext values. In the file provided for 12 rounds of SKINNY-64-128 we counted 925615 different pairs ($2^{19.82}$, so $2^{16.90}$ collisions) out of the 2^{20} provided. The plaintext that appears the most corresponds to $\boxed{.”\ “}$ (dot (0x2e), closed quote (0xe2809d), space (0x20), open quote (0xe2809c)) with 289 occurrences.

In the following, we detail how these biases work to our advantage by inducing a set of messages with low entropy, helping us pushing further our attacks.

4   Mining Truncated Differentials in the Provided Datasets

Any human-readable text has a low entropy and so does the book whose encryption was provided in the SKINNY 2018–2019 cryptanalysis competition. This fact can be exploited by a cryptanalyst, who can devise attacks that would be ineffective in the classic known-plaintext scenario with uniformly distributed plaintexts. In this section, we show that many pairs or even quadruples of plaintext blocks can be found in the provided datasets for which particular (differential) zero-sum properties hold with probability 1 after 6 rounds of SKINNY-64-128 and 7 rounds of SKINNY-128-128.

We restrict our search to truncated differentials holding with probability 1. Such distinguishers require only a few message pairs fitting them to provide a strong filtering procedure for the key recovery. In addition to this, we also consider second-order differentials [7,8]: instead of studying the propagation of differences between 2 messages as it is done with (first-order) differentials, we look at the differences between a set of 2^2 messages. Note that finding such sets of four distinct plaintext blocks that sum to zero has higher chances to happen when these blocks differ only in a few cells. In our case, the low entropy of the text facilitates such events.

4.1   Search Strategy

Our general search strategy is as follows. Instead of enumerating all possible truncated differentials in the structure, we search precisely for those differentials that fit the given set of plaintexts for any possible key. In order to find them, we encrypt the plaintexts under several randomly chosen keys and search for differential properties in the obtained ciphertexts. This empirical approach allows tailoring the search to the given dataset.

Let P denote the set of provided plaintexts. We fix a SKINNY instance, a number of rounds r in the target distinguisher, and a maximum number $m(1 \leq m \leq 15)$ of active cells after the first round.

First, we compute all subsets of plaintexts such that all plaintexts inside any such subset take the same value in at least $16 - m$ cells, i.e. at most m cells are active. In this step we exploit the fact that the first tweakey addition is done after the non-linear operation and thus differences after the first round do not depend on the key. In order to compute these subsets, we enumerate all possible patterns of active cells and for each pattern we simply group the plaintexts by the values of inactive cells.

We further process each such subset $S \subseteq P$ as follows. We choose t random keys $k_0, \ldots, k_{t-1}$ and encrypt each plaintext $p \in S$ using r-round SKINNY with those keys. For each cell i of the output state, we record the vector $v_{p,i}$ of values computed in that cell:

$$v_{p,i} = \Big((E_{k_0}(p))_i, (E_{k_1}(p))_i, \ldots, (E_{k_{t-1}}(p))_i \Big),$$

where E_k denotes r-round SKINNY encryption with the key k. Such vectors are $4t$ bits long in the case of SKINNY-64 and $8t$ bits long in the case of SKINNY-128.

Assume that we find a 2-vector collision, i.e. $v_{p,i} = v_{p',i'}$ for some $(p, i) \neq (p', i')$. It is easy to see that $i \neq i'$ is unlikely because of the use of random keys. Therefore, we obtain $p \neq p'$ and $i = i'$ and we conclude that the chosen SKINNY instance with overwhelming probability has zero difference in cell i after r rounds of encryption of plaintexts p and p'. By increasing t, the probability of error can be made negligible. Furthermore, any such concrete truncated differential is usually easy to verify.

If no 2-vector zero-sum occurred, we aim to find 4-vector zero-sums, which would possibly lead to distinguishers on more rounds. This can be done in time $O(|S|^2 t)$ for each subset $S \subseteq P$ by computing all pairwise vector differences and finding a collision. More precisely, for each pair of elements $v_{p,i}, v_{p',i'} \in S$ we add their difference $v_{p,i} \oplus v_{p',i'}$ to a hash table. A collision of such differences means that we have found four vectors $v_{p,i}, v_{p',i'}, v_{p'',i''}, v_{p''',i'''}$ such that

$$v_{p,i} \oplus v_{p',i'} \oplus v_{p'',i''} \oplus v_{p''',i'''} = 0.$$

The converse is also true, i.e., any 4-vector zero-sum implies a difference collision that this approach would find.

In practice, there are two cases that may happen:

1. the four vectors are $v_{p,i}, v_{p',i}, v_{p,i'}, v_{p',i'}$ with $p \neq p', i \neq i'$ (i.e. $p = p'', p' = p''', i = i''', i' = i''$);
2. the four vectors are $v_{p,i}, v_{p',i}, v_{p'',i}, v_{p''',i}$ with p, p', p'', p''' pairwise distinct (i.e. $i = i' = i'' = i'''$).

The first case corresponds to a truncated differential with input difference $\Delta p = p \oplus p'$ and the property that $\Delta c_i = \Delta c_{i'}$, where $\Delta c = c \oplus c'$, c and c' are ciphertexts corresponding to r-round SKINNY encryptions of plaintexts p and p'. Such event may occur when the input difference of MixColumns has inactive cells. For example,

$$\text{MixColumn}(\Delta, 0, 0, 0) = (0, \Delta, 0, \Delta)$$

for any cell difference Δ.

The second case corresponds to the zero-sum property

$$c_i \oplus c'_i \oplus c''_i \oplus c'''_i = 0,$$

where c, c', c'', c''' are ciphertexts corresponding to r-round SKINNY encryptions of plaintexts p, p', p'', p'''. This event usually requires that the plaintexts form a second-order difference, i.e. they also sum to zero.

4.2   Truncated Distinguishers of SKINNY Instances

We applied this search strategy for the challenge datasets of 12-round SKINNY-64-128 and 10-round SKINNY-128-128 with at most $m = 3$ active bytes after the first round. The results are summarized in Table 3.

For 12-round SKINNY-64-128, we found distinguishers for up to 7 rounds and only of the first type. For example, there are 57 pairs of plaintexts in the dataset for which $\Delta c_0 = \Delta c_{12}$ after 7 rounds. An example of such plaintext pair (p, p') is given by

$$p = \boxed{\texttt{a pouch,}} ,$$
$$p' = \boxed{\texttt{a pause,}} .$$

We use this distinguisher to attack 12-round SKINNY-64-128 and recover the secret key. The process is described in Sect. 5.

For the 10-round SKINNY-128-128, we found distinguishers for up to 6 rounds among which both distinguisher types are present. For example, there are 9 quadruples of plaintexts for which after 6 rounds of SKINNY-128-128 the cell number 9 sums to zero. An example of such quadruple is given by

$$p = \boxed{\texttt{for a moment an}} ,$$
$$p' = \boxed{\texttt{for a moment at}} ,$$
$$p'' = \boxed{\texttt{for a moment in}} ,$$
$$p''' = \boxed{\texttt{for a moment it}} .$$

Table 3. Truncated distinguishers with maximum number of rounds found using our approach in the datasets of 12-round SKINNY-64-128 and 10-round SKINNY-128-128. Bold font shows distinguishers used in our attacks.

Version	Rounds/ Dataset Rounds	Property	#Plaintexts in Structure	#Structures in Dataset
SKINNY-64-128	7/12	$\Delta c_2 = \Delta c_{14}$	2	76
		$\Delta c_5 = \Delta c_{13}$	2	76
		$\mathbf{\Delta c_0 = \Delta c_{12}}$	**2**	**57**
		$\Delta c_7 = \Delta c_{15}$	2	57
		$\Delta c_3 = \Delta c_{15}$	2	50
		$\Delta c_6 = \Delta c_{14}$	2	50
		$\Delta c_1 = \Delta c_{13}$	2	22
		$\Delta c_4 = \Delta c_{12}$	2	22
SKINNY-128-128	6/10	$\Delta c_3 = \Delta c_{15}$	2	12180
		$\Delta c_6 = \Delta c_{14}$	2	12093
		$\Delta c_5 = \Delta c_{13}$	2	2443
		$\Delta c_2 = \Delta c_{14}$	2	2412
		$\Delta c_4 = \Delta c_{12}$	2	600
		$\Delta c_1 = \Delta c_{13}$	2	598
		$\Delta c_7 = \Delta c_{15}$	2	430
		$\Delta c_0 = \Delta c_{12}$	2	413
		$\Delta c_3 = \Delta c_7$	2	16
		$\Delta c_1 = \Delta c_5$	2	11
		$\Delta c_0 = \Delta c_4$	2	8
		$\Delta c_2 = \Delta c_6$	2	1
		$\bigoplus \mathbf{c_9 = 0}$	**4**	**9**
		$\bigoplus c_{10} = 0$	4	7
		$\bigoplus c_8 = 0$	4	5
		$\bigoplus c_{11} = 0$	4	1

We use this distinguisher to recover the secret key of this SKINNY instance in Sect. 6.

Figure 4 depicts one representative of each of the properties given in Table 3. As can be seen in the table, each distinguisher has 3 other variants, corresponding to its column rotations.

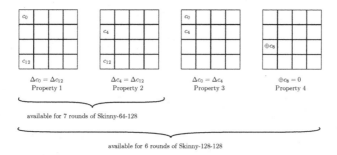

Fig. 4. Four properties found with our search strategy

5   Attacking 12-Round SKINNY-64-128

5.1   Our Truncated Differential Trail

To attack 12 rounds, we use the truncated differential distinguisher described in Sect. 4.2 which benefits from the not-so-uniform distribution of the provided messages. As depicted in Fig. 5, we consider a truncated differential path that starts at round 2 with a difference of only one nibble, in $X_1[12]$. After 6 rounds, the first and last nibbles of the first column, denoted by "U_1" and "U_2" in the figure, are always equal.

As already explained in Sect. 4, the fact that the first tweakey addition is made after the non-linear layer makes the search for conforming pairs straightforward. For any pair, an attacker can compute the difference at the end of round 1 to check if only $X_1[12]$ is active. If this condition is met, the rest of the characteristic (up to X_7) is fulfilled with probability 1.

Once the attacker has determined the conforming pairs, she can deduce information on the key by simply making guesses on the last round keys and checking if she obtains equality between the differences in the nibbles $X_7[0]$ and $X_7[12]$.

5.2   From the Truncated Differential Path to the Attack: The Key Recovery Part

The first step of our attack consists in exploring the set of 2^{20} messages to extract the pairs that comply with the start of the truncated differential path (that are pairs with a single active nibble at the beginning of round 1, at $X_1[12]$). There are 57 such pairs[2], which contrasts with what one would have obtain for a uniformly distributed set (since the occurrence probability would have been 2^{-60}).

---

[2] As seen previously, another possibility would have been to use the 76 pairs available for the same trail shifted by 2 columns, that are starting with only one nibble active at position 14 after 1 rounds and resulting into nibbles in position 2 and 14 that are equal at the end of round 7 (see Table 3).

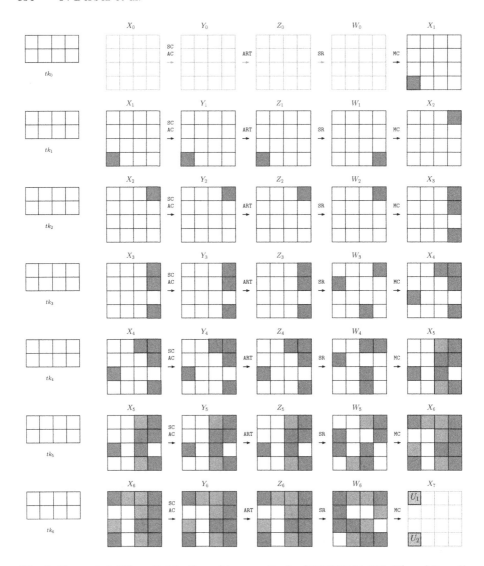

Fig. 5. Truncated differential trail used in our attack of SKINNY-64-128. The white cells are inactive, the green ones are active for sure, while the yellow ones might be active. If one pair of messages only differs on $X_1[12]$, the difference in the two nibbles $X_7[0]$ and $X_7[12]$ (denoted U_1 and U_2) are equal with probability one. (Color figure online)

Once this is done, an attacker makes key guesses to compute the differences in $X_7[0]$ and $X_7[12]$ to check if they are equal. If they are not, the guessed key is for sure incorrect, while if the equality is verified for all the considered pairs the key guess might be the right one.

The key and state nibbles that need to be guessed are represented in Fig. 7.

Out of the 19 tweakey nibbles that need to be guessed, 1 can be saved thanks to the tweakey schedule relations:

Saving a Nibble by Taking into Account the Tweakey Schedule. The definition of the tweakey schedule of SKINNY implies that the round tweakeys of all the even rounds (similarly of all the odd rounds) are related together by linear relations. In the case of SKINNY-64-128, this might lead to a reduction in the number of key guesses if we consider more than 4 consecutive rounds in the key recovery.

To see how we can benefit from this in our attack, let us denote by x_i ($0 \leq i \leq 15$) the nibbles of the first tweakey state (TK_1) of tk_7 and by y_i ($0 \leq i \leq 15$) the nibbles of its second tweakey state (TK_2) (see Fig. 6).

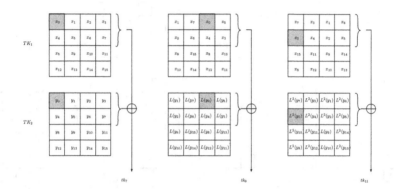

Fig. 6. Close up of the tweakey schedule in the final rounds.

With these notations, $tk_7[0]$, $tk_9[2]$ and $tk_{11}[4]$ can be written as follows:

$$tk_7[0] = x_0 \oplus y_0$$
$$tk_9[2] = x_0 \oplus L(y_0)$$
$$tk_{11}[4] = x_0 \oplus L(L(y_0))$$

where L denotes one application of the linear operation (that can be seen as a LFSR) defined in Sect. 2. If the attacker has already made a guess on the values of $tk_9[2]$ and $tk_{11}[4]$, the previous relations imply that she can deduce the value of $tk_7[0]$ by computing:

$$tk_7[0] = L^{-1}(tk_9[2] \oplus tk_{11}[4]) \oplus tk_9[2] \tag{1}$$

Which induces a save of a 4-bit guess in the key recovery process.

Algorithmic Description of the Key Recovery. In addition to Fig. 7, we give in Algorithm 2 in Appendix a step by step description of the naive way to implement the recovery of the round tweakeys involved in the computation of U_1 and U_2. Quite naturally, the key recovery is organised so that the key nibbles that are required to compute both U_1 and U_2 are guessed first. Then, one part of the algorithm is dedicated to the guess of the remaining key nibbles required

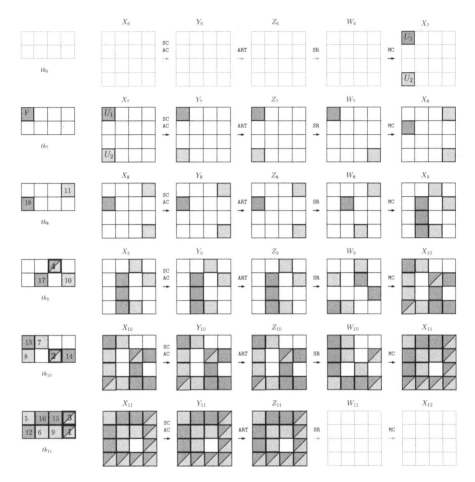

Fig. 7. Nibble dependencies in the key recovery process. We want to recover the difference U_1 and U_2. To compute U_1 from a pair of ciphertexts we need the value of the blue nibbles of the internal state and of the blue nibble of the round tweakeys. Similarly, the pink nibbles are required to recover the difference U_2. The numbers correspond to the order in which is done the key guessing: we start by the nibbles that are needed for both U_1 and U_2. The round tweakey nibble denoted by F comes for free if $tk_{11}[4]$ and $tk_9[2]$ are known, which is why we mark $tk_9[2]$ as required for both U_1 and U_2. (Color figure online)

to obtain U_1 and another one, independently, deals with U_2. Remember that the numbering of the state nibbles that is used is the one of Fig. 8.

Note that we don't give the tedious details of how the nibbles are computed, as we consider that this is rather obvious from the cipher description. Indeed, as per usual in key recovery algorithms, the operations consist in decrypting partially from the ciphertext, nibble after nibble, for the positions that are required to get U_1 and U_2. Just to give an example, $X_{11}[7]$ is obtained by computing $X_{11}[7] = \mathcal{S}_4^{-1}(Z_{11}[7] \oplus tk_{11}[7])$.

$$\begin{bmatrix} 0 & 1 & 2 & 3 \\ 4 & 5 & 6 & 7 \\ 8 & 9 & 10 & 11 \\ 12 & 13 & 14 & 15 \end{bmatrix}$$

Fig. 8. Numbering of the nibbles in the internal state.

In the naive version of Algorithm 2, T_1 (respectively T_2) contains 2^{44} lines composed of the 32 computed values of U_1 (resp. U_2) concatenated to the tweakey guess of 11 nibbles. To reduce this huge memory requirement we exploit further the fact that U_1 and U_2 both depend on $tk_{11}[7]$, $tk_{10}[6]$, $tk_{11}[3]$ and $tk_9[2]$.

The idea consists in going over all the possible values of the 4 common nibbles, and to repeat the building of the two tables once the values of these 4 are fixed (so without storing them in the tables). This optimisation (and others) are presented in Algorithm 1.

In this way, the two tables V_1 and V_2 contain 2^{28} rows. Each row is made of $4 \times 2^4 = 64$ bits (corresponding to the computed nibble of difference U_1 or U_2 for all the 2^4 input pairs). In this first step, we don't keep track of the value of the other tweakey nibbles in order to reduce memory as far as possible. The goal is only to get a reduced set of possibilities for the 4 nibbles $tk_{11}[7]$, $tk_{10}[6]$, $tk_{11}[3]$ and $tk_9[2]$. Once this is done, a second iteration gives the desired result. The second iteration takes as parameter the value of the previous match so that the filtering is quicker. Matching on these at the second iterations means we are considering the same value for the other nibbles of key guesses.

Similarly to the naive algorithm, building each table requires to guess 2^{44} bits. Once V_1 and V_2 are filled, they are sorted[3]. We then merge the two tables on the 2^4 4-bit values of U_1 and U_2: the probability of a match is equal to 2^{-64}, which implies that $2^{16} \times 2^{28+28-64} = 2^{16} \times 2^{-8}$ values of the 4 tweakey nibbles $tk_{11}[7]$, $tk_{10}[6]$, $tk_{11}[3]$ and $tk_9[2]$ survive this filter.

To decide on which of these is correct, we repeat the previous process for the same 2^4 pairs plus 2^4 new ones for the 2^8 surviving values (this time we keep track of all the guessed values in tk_{11}). Only one value of tk_{11} passes the test.

In this optimised version, we focus on recovering tk_{11} only. To recover the other round tweakeys, the attacker peels off the last round by using tk_{11} and launches a similar and faster attack on 11-round SKINNY, and so on until the master key can be recovered.

Total Complexity. The complexity of the key recovery is dominated by the cost of recovering tk_{11}, that can be decomposed as follows:

$$2^{16} \times (\underbrace{2 \times 32 \times 2^{28}}_{\text{filling } V_1 \text{ and } V_2} + \underbrace{2 \times 28 \times 2^{28}}_{\text{sorting } V_1 \text{ and } V_2} + \underbrace{2^{-8} \times 2 \times 64 \times 2^{28}}_{\text{filling for the 32 pairs}})$$

which is equal to $2^{51.95}$ operations.

---

[3] Sorting a table of n elements requires roughly $n \log n$ operation so we consider that the complexity of this step is equal to 28×2^{28}.

The memory complexity is dominated by the space required to store V_1 and V_2. Since each table contains 2^{28} rows of 64 bits, each core stores $2^{28} \times 64 \times 2 = 2^{35}$ bits. The 64 cores store a total of 2^{41} bits, which are 256 GB.

5.3 Details on the Practical Execution of the Attack

The program was written in C++ and it was executed on 64 cores clocked at 2,10 Ghz on an Intel Xeon CPU E5-2695. The result of Algorithm 1 was returned after less than 2 days (a total of 114 CPU days). As said previously 256 GB of memory were required.

Implementation Choices. The time complexity of the attack being around 2^{52} simple operations we needed to optimize the implementation. We made two main choices:

Algorithm 1. Improved recovery of tk_{11}

Input: 2^5 pairs of messages following the truncated differential path
Output: Last round tweakey tk_{11}.
for $tk_{11}[7] \leftarrow 0$ **to** f **do**
   for $tk_{10}[6] \leftarrow 0$ **to** f **do**
      for $tk_{11}[3] \leftarrow 0$ **to** f **do**
         for $tk_9[2] \leftarrow 0$ **to** f **do**
            Initialise a table V_2
            for *all possible values of* $tk_{11}[0]$, $tk_{11}[5]$, $tk_{10}[1]$, $tk_{10}[4]$, $tk_{11}[6]$, $tk_9[7]$ *and* $tk_8[3]$ **do**
               compute the difference in $X_7[12]$ for the first 2^4 pairs and store it in V_2
            end
            Initialise a table V_1
            for *all possible values of* $tk_{11}[4]$, $tk_{10}[0]$, $tk_{10}[7]$, $tk_{11}[2]$, $tk_{11}[1]$, $tk_9[5]$ *and* $tk_8[4]$ **do**
               compute the difference in $X_7[0]$ for the first 2^4 pairs and store it in V_1
            end
            Sort V_1 and V_2
            Merge V_1 and V_2 on the 2^4 values of $X_7[12]$ and $X_7[0]$
            if *the intersection is not empty* **then**
               repeat the algorithm for 2^5 pairs (the same 2^4 plus 2^4 new), passing the matching value as parameter
               only one guess of tk_{11} survives, return this one
            else
               the guess for $tk_{11}[7]$, $tk_{10}[6]$, $tk_{11}[3]$ and $tk_9[2]$ is incorrect
            end
         end
      end
   end
end

---

1. It is possible to decrease the memory requirement to only $2^{7 \times 4} \times 64 = 2^{34}$ bits by making the code parallel only once the 4 nibbles $tk_9[2]$, $tk_{10}[6]$, $tk_{11}[3]$ and $tk_{11}[7]$ are set. However, we found experimentally that this is much slower than making the whole code parallel. Indeed, filling V_i requires only $2 \times 32 \times 2^{28} = 2^{34}$ simple operations and using 64 cores for this is not worth.

2. It seems possible to save some time complexity by using an hash table instead of two sorted arrays. While this is true in theory, in practice we found the sorted arrays to be much faster. The main reason is the non-sequential accesses to the hash table, which are likely to lead to a cache miss at each access due to its size.

Once we have the full round tweakey tk_{11} we decrypt the last round and launch a similar attack on 11 rounds (with complexities that are negligible in comparison to the 12-round one) an so on until the master key is recovered.

5.4   On the Choice of the Distinguisher

As detailed in Sect. 3, another distinguisher is available over 7 rounds of SKINNY-64-128, corresponding to the equality of the difference in one nibble of the second row with the difference in the nibble in the last row and same column (see Property 2 in Fig. 4). However, this option would have lead to an heavier key-recovery step as more nibbles of the key need to be guessed to obtain the required differences at the end of the distinguisher. More generally, our attack scenario can be played with different parameters as one can change the active nibble of the truncated characteristic and/or nibbles involved in the distinguisher. Hence we used the tool devised in the Crypto 16 article *Automatic Search of Meet-in-the-Middle and Impossible Differential Attacks* by Patrick Derbez and Pierre-Alain Fouque [4] to exhaust all cases and keep the one leading to the smallest complexity.

6   Attacking 10-Round SKINNY-128-128

In Sect. 4, we found 9 structures of 4 plaintexts each such that the cell number 9 sums to zero over the 6-round SKINNY-128-128 encryptions of those plaintexts. These quadruples of plaintexts differ in two bytes and sum to zero. In other words, these quadruples form a second-order difference with two active bytes and the described distinguisher is a second-order truncated differential distinguisher[4] (see [7,8]). This distinguisher can be defined for arbitrary differences $\alpha, \beta \in \mathbb{F}_2^8$ as

$$
\begin{bmatrix} 0 & 0 & 0 & 0 \\ 0 & 0 & 0 & 0 \\ 0 & 0 & 0 & 0 \\ 0 & 0 & \alpha & 0 \end{bmatrix} \otimes \begin{bmatrix} 0 & 0 & 0 & 0 \\ 0 & 0 & 0 & 0 \\ 0 & 0 & 0 & 0 \\ 0 & 0 & 0 & \beta \end{bmatrix} \xrightarrow{\text{6 rounds}} \begin{bmatrix} ? & ? & ? & ? \\ ? & ? & ? & ? \\ ? & B & ? & ? \\ ? & ? & ? & ? \end{bmatrix},
$$

---

[4] Such distinguishers are also called *integral* distinguishers.

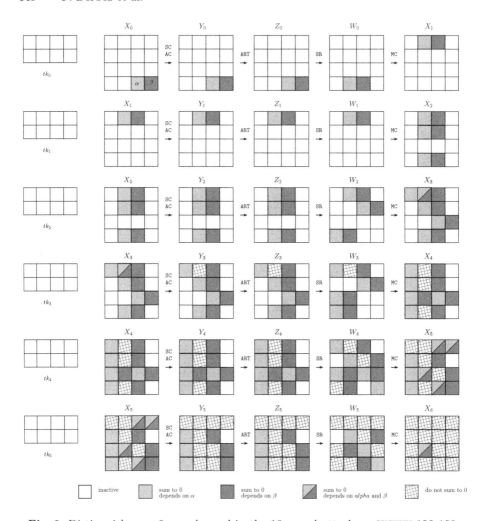

Fig. 9. Distinguisher on 6 rounds used in the 10-round attack on SKINNY-128-128.

where $\otimes$ means that the second-order differential is formed by the two operands as the basis, B means that the cell sums to zero and ? means that the sum is unspecified. That is, the last two bytes must have differences $(0,0), (\alpha, 0), (0, \beta), (\alpha, \beta)$ from one of the plaintexts in the quadruple, for any $\alpha, \beta \in \mathbb{F}_2^8$. A graphical representation of the truncated path of this distinguisher is given in Fig. 9.

6.1   Key-Recovery Using Truncated Differentials

The key recovery step is rather straightforward. The cell number 9 after 6 rounds of SKINNY-128-128, denoted $X_6[9]$, can be computed from the 10-round ciphertext using only 6 bytes of the key. Let I denote the inverse of the SKINNY-128

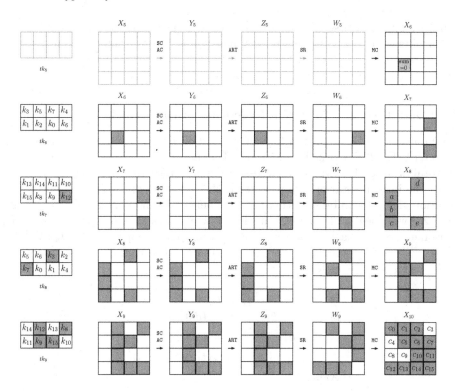

Fig. 10. Key recovery step used in the 10-round attack on SKINNY-128-128.

S-Box, $C \in (\mathbb{F}_2^8)^{16}$ denote the ciphertext and $k \in (\mathbb{F}_2^8)^{16}$ denote the master key. Then

$$X_6[9] = I(I(k_{12} \oplus a \oplus b \oplus c) \oplus I(d \oplus e)), \text{ where}$$
$$a = I(3 \oplus k_7 \oplus I(k_9 \oplus C_6 \oplus C_{10} \oplus C_{14}) \oplus I(C_7 \oplus C_{15}) \oplus I(C_0 \oplus C_{12})),$$
$$b = I(2 \oplus I(k_{15} \oplus C_7 \oplus C_{11} \oplus C_{15}) \oplus I(C_1 \oplus C_{13})),$$
$$c = I(I(k_8 \oplus C_7) \oplus I(C_2 \oplus C_{14})),$$
$$d = I(k_3 \oplus I(k_{15} \oplus C_7 \oplus C_{11} \oplus C_{15})),$$
$$e = I(I(k_{12} \oplus C_5) \oplus I(C_0 \oplus C_{12})).$$

It follows that $X_6[9]$ depends only on 6 key bytes:

$$k_3, k_7, k_8, k_9, k_{12}, k_{15}.$$

As can be seen in Fig. 10, we again benefit from the tweakey schedule as the tweakey byte required in tk_7 is equal to one of the 4 bytes guessed in tk_9, namely the byte k_{12} of the master key.

It is enough to consider 6 out of 9 quadruples following the trail in order to obtain a filter of probability 2^{-48}. Then, the 6 involved bytes of the key can be found by exhaustive search. The check consists in computation of $X_6[9]$ from ciphertexts using the equation above and verifying that the sum is equal to zero.

The rest of the key can be recovered in a similar way, but with complexity negligible compared to the main attack.

6.2   Details on the Practical Execution of the Attack

We implemented the attack in C language and executed it on 8 cores of an Intel Xeon CPU E5-2637 clocked at 3.50 GHz. It exhausted the search space in 4 days (at total of 32 CPU days) and successfully determined the right key.

In the implementation, we performed the following optimisation. The computation of $X_6[9]$ can be structured as a sequence of four table lookups of size at most 2^{24} with negligible precomputation time and less than $6 \times 4 \times 2^{24}$ bytes of extra memory. For each ciphertext C, we precompute mappings $t_1, t_2, t_4 : \mathbb{F}_2^{24} \to \mathbb{F}_2^8$, $t_3 : \mathbb{F}_2^{16} \to \mathbb{F}_2^8$ such that $X_6[9]$ can be computed from the master key bytes $k_7, k_8, k_9, k_3, k_{12}, k_{15}$ as follows:

$$
\begin{aligned}
t_1 &= t_1(k_7, k_8, k_9) = a \oplus c, \\
t_2 &= t_2(k_3, k_{12}, k_{15}) = I(d \oplus e), \\
t_3 &= t_3(k_{12}, k_{15}) = k_{12} \oplus b, \\
t_4 &= t_4(t_1, t_2, t_3) = I(I(t_1 \oplus t_3) \oplus t_2), \\
X_6[9] &= t_4.
\end{aligned}
$$

The final complexity of the attack is dominated by verifying the zero-sum property for one of the quadruples, which requires 4 computations of $X_6[9]$, i.e. 16 24-bit table lookups. The total complexity is thus 2^{52} table lookups. The memory complexity is equal to $(2 \times 6 + 1) \times 2^{24} + 6 \times 2^{16}$ bytes ≈ 208 MB (note that t_4 does not depend on the ciphertext) and can be further reduced if necessary.

6.3   On the Choice of the Distinguisher

We remark that choosing another distinguishers from Table 3 would lead to similar or higher complexities.

The properties $\bigoplus c_i$ for $8 \leq i \leq 11$ are equivalent in the sense that corresponding cells c_i can be computed from the ciphertext using only 6 key bytes. However, for the case $i = 9$ there are more structures in the provided data set.

All properties $\Delta c_i = \Delta c_j$ from Table 3 lead to similar or higher time complexity of the key recovery. Indeed, for each of these properties at least one of the two cells c_i, c_j requires at least 6 key bytes to be guessed to compute the corresponding difference. For example, consider the property $\Delta c_0 = \Delta c_{12}$ after 6 rounds (similar to the 7-round distinguisher used to attack SKINNY-64-128). The cell c_0 can be computed from the ciphertext using 5 key bytes $k_0, k_3, k_{10}, k_{14}, k_{15}$; the cell c_{12} can be computed from the ciphertext using 6 key bytes $k_3, k_4, k_{10}, k_{11}, k_{12}, k_{15}$. The attacker first guesses 3 common key bytes

k_3, k_{10}, k_{15}. Then she enumerates all values of k_0, k_{14}, computes the differences Δc_0 and puts them in a table. Finally, she enumerates all values of k_4, k_{11}, k_{12}, computes the differences Δc_{12} and checks if they are in the table. This approach requires $O(2^{48})$ time and $O(2^{16})$ memory.

7   Conclusion

In this cryptanalysis report we detailed practical key recovery attacks of 12-round SKINNY-64-128 and 10-round SKINNY-128-128 from given sets of 2^{20} messages. Our attacks consist in leveraging a distinguisher based on a probability-1 truncated first-order and second-order differential paths. The attacks are possible because the provided sets of messages give much more exploitable pairs than what one could have expected from a random set.

Appendix

Table 4. 4-bit Sbox used in SKINNY-64.

x	0	1	2	3	4	5	6	7	8	9	a	b	c	d	e	f
$S_4(x)$	c	6	9	0	1	a	2	b	3	8	5	d	4	e	7	f

Table 5. 8-bit Sbox used in SKINNY-128.

	00	01	02	03	04	05	06	07	08	09	0a	0b	0c	0d	0e	0f
00	65	4c	6a	42	4b	63	43	6b	55	75	5a	7a	53	73	5b	7b
10	35	8c	3a	81	89	33	80	3b	95	25	98	2a	90	23	99	2b
20	e5	cc	e8	c1	c9	e0	c0	e9	d5	f5	d8	f8	d0	f0	d9	f9
30	a5	1c	a8	12	1b	a0	13	a9	05	b5	0a	b8	03	b0	0b	b9
40	32	88	3c	85	8d	34	84	3d	91	22	9c	2c	94	24	9d	2d
50	62	4a	6c	45	4d	64	44	6d	52	72	5c	7c	54	74	5d	7d
60	a1	1a	ac	15	1d	a4	14	ad	02	b1	0c	bc	04	b4	0d	bd
70	e1	c8	ec	c5	cd	e4	c4	ed	d1	f1	dc	fc	d4	f4	dd	fd
80	36	8e	38	82	8b	30	83	39	96	26	9a	28	93	20	9b	29
90	66	4e	68	41	49	60	40	69	56	76	58	78	50	70	59	79
a0	a6	1e	aa	11	19	a3	10	ab	06	b6	08	ba	00	b3	09	bb
b0	e6	ce	ea	c2	cb	e3	c3	eb	d6	f6	da	fa	d3	f3	db	fb
c0	31	8a	3e	86	8f	37	87	3f	92	21	9e	2e	97	27	9f	2f
d0	61	48	6e	46	4f	67	47	6f	51	71	5e	7e	57	77	5f	7f
e0	a2	18	ae	16	1f	a7	17	af	01	b2	0e	be	07	b7	0f	bf
f0	e2	ca	ee	c6	cf	e7	c7	ef	d2	f2	de	fe	d7	f7	df	ff

Algorithm 2. Recovery of the tweakey nibbles involved in the computation of U_1 and U_2

Input: Pairs of messages following the truncated differential path
Output: Last round tweakey tk_{11}, nibbles 0, 1, 4, 6 and 7 of tk_{10}, nibbles 2, 5 and 7 of tk_9,
           nibbles 3 and 4 of tk_8 (and 0 of tk_7).
Initialise two tables T_1 and T_2 and compute $X_{11}[8-15]$ and $Z_{11}[0-7]$ from the ciphertexts
for $tk_{11}[7] \leftarrow 0$ **to** f **do**
    compute $X_{11}[7]$
    for $tk_{10}[6] \leftarrow 0$ **to** f **do**
        for $tk_{11}[3] \leftarrow 0$ **to** f **do**
            compute $X_{10}[6]$, $X_{11}[3]$ and $X_{10}[12]$
            for $tk_9[2] \leftarrow 0$ **to** f **do**
                compute $X_9[2]$
                for $tk_{11}[0] \leftarrow 0$ **to** f **do**
                    compute $X_{11}[0]$ and $X_{10}[13]$
                    for $tk_{11}[5] \leftarrow 0$ **to** f **do**
                        compute $X_{11}[5]$
                        for $tk_{10}[1] \leftarrow 0$ **to** f **do**
                            compute $X_{10}[1]$, $X_9[14]$ and $X_8[15]$
                          for $tk_{10}[4] \leftarrow 0$ **to** f **do**
                              compute $X_{10}[4]$
                            for $tk_{11}[6] \leftarrow 0$ **to** f **do**
                                compute $X_{11}[6]$ and $X_{10}[8]$
                              for $tk_9[7] \leftarrow 0$ **to** f **do**
                                  compute $X_9[7]$
                                  for $tk_8[3] \leftarrow 0$ **to** f **do**
                                    compute the difference in $X_7[12]$ for all the
                                    pairs and store it in T_2 next to the key
                                    guesses
                              end
                          end
                      end
                  end
                end
            end
        for $tk_{11}[4] \leftarrow 0$ **to** f **do**
            compute $tk_7[0]$ by using Equation (1)
            compute $X_{11}[4]$ and $X_{10}[10]$
            for $tk_{10}[0] \leftarrow 0$ **to** f **do**
                compute $X_{10}[0]$ and $X_9[13]$
                for $tk_{10}[7] \leftarrow 0$ **to** f **do**
                    compute $X_{10}[7]$
                    for $tk_{11}[2] \leftarrow 0$ **to** f **do**
                      compute $X_{11}[2]$, $X_{10}[15]$ and $X_9[9]$
                      for $tk_{11}[1] \leftarrow 0$ **to** f **do**
                        compute $X_{11}[1]$ and $X_{10}[14]$
                        for $tk_9[5] \leftarrow 0$ **to** f **do**
                          for $tk_8[4] \leftarrow 0$ **to** f **do**
                            compute the difference in $X_7[0]$ for all the
                            pairs and store it in T_1 next to the key
                            guesses
                        end
                    end
                  end
                end
                end
            end
        end
        Merge T_1 and T_2 and return the corresponding keys
        end
        end
        end
    end
end

References

1. Ankele, R., et al.: Related-key impossible-differential attack on reduced-round SKINNY. In: Gollmann, D., Miyaji, A., Kikuchi, H. (eds.) ACNS 2017. LNCS, vol. 10355, pp. 208–228. Springer, Cham (2017). https://doi.org/10.1007/978-3-319-61204-1_11

2. Beaulieu, R., Shors, D., Smith, J., Treatman-Clark, S., Weeks, B., Wingers, L.: SIMON and SPECK: block ciphers for the internet of things. Cryptology ePrint Archive, Report 2015/585 (2015). http://eprint.iacr.org/2015/585

3. Beierle, C., et al.: The SKINNY family of block ciphers and its low-latency variant MANTIS. In: Robshaw and Katz [10], pp. 123–153

4. Derbez, P., Fouque, P.A.: Automatic search of meet-in-the-middle and impossible differential attacks. In: Robshaw and Katz [10], pp. 157–184

5. Jean, J.: TikZ for Cryptographers (2016). https://www.iacr.org/authors/tikz/

6. Jean, J., Nikolić, I., Peyrin, T.: Tweaks and keys for block ciphers: the TWEAKEY framework. In: Sarkar, P., Iwata, T. (eds.) ASIACRYPT 2014. LNCS, vol. 8874, pp. 274–288. Springer, Heidelberg (2014). https://doi.org/10.1007/978-3-662-45608-8_15

7. Knudsen, L.R.: Truncated and higher order differentials. In: Preneel, B. (ed.) FSE 1994. LNCS, vol. 1008, pp. 196–211. Springer, Heidelberg (1995). https://doi.org/10.1007/3-540-60590-8_16

8. Lai, X.: Higher Order Derivatives and Differential Cryptanalysis. In: Blahut, R.E., Costello, D.J., Maurer, U., Mittelholzer, T. (eds.) Communications and Cryptography. The Springer International Series in Engineering and Computer Science (Communications and Information Theory), vol. 276, pp. 227–233. Springer, Boston (1994). https://doi.org/10.1007/978-1-4615-2694-0_23

9. Liu, G., Ghosh, M., Song, L.: Security analysis of SKINNY under related-tweakey settings (long paper). IACR Trans. Symm. Cryptol. **2017**(3), 37–72 (2017)

10. Robshaw, M., Katz, J. (eds.): CRYPTO 2016. LNCS, vol. 9815. Springer, Heidelberg (2016). https://doi.org/10.1007/978-3-662-53008-5

Block Ciphers and Permutations

Algebraic Cryptanalysis of Variants of FRIT

Christoph Dobraunig[1], Maria Eichlseder[1(✉)], Florian Mendel[2], and Markus Schofnegger[1]

[1] Graz University of Technology, Graz, Austria
maria.eichlseder@iaik.tugraz.at
[2] Infineon Technologies AG, Neubiberg, Germany

Abstract. FRIT is a cryptographic 384-bit permutation recently proposed by Simon et al. and follows a novel design approach for built-in countermeasures against fault attacks. We analyze the cryptanalytic security of FRIT in different use cases and propose attacks on the full-round primitive. We show that the inverse $FRIT^{-1}$ of FRIT is significantly weaker than FRIT from an algebraic perspective, despite the better diffusion of the inverse of the mixing functions σ: Its round function has an effective algebraic degree of only about 1.325. We show how to craft structured input spaces to linearize up to 4 (or, conditionally, 5) rounds and thus further reduce the degree. As a result, we propose very low-dimensional start-in-the-middle zero-sum partitioning distinguishers for unkeyed FRIT, as well as integral distinguishers for reduced-round FRIT and full-round $FRIT^{-1}$. We also consider keyed FRIT variants using Even-Mansour or arbitrary round keys. By using optimized interpolation attacks and symbolically evaluating up to 5 rounds of $FRIT^{-1}$, we obtain key-recovery attacks with a complexity of either 2^{59} chosen plaintexts and 2^{67} time, or 2^{18} chosen ciphertexts and time (about 5 seconds in practice).

Keywords: Cryptanalysis · FRIT · Higher-order differentials · Interpolation

1 Introduction

Attacks that target the implementation of a scheme, such as side-channel [32,33] and fault attacks [11,12], are a threat to cryptographic security in practice, especially in situations where an attacker has physical access to the device performing the cryptographic computations. In order to mitigate such attacks, a variety of countermeasures has been proposed, such as masking [15,27] and threshold implementations [39–41] to protect against side-channel attacks, or the integration of some form of error detection [44] to protect against fault attacks. The overhead cost of implementing these countermeasures typically depends on properties of the cryptographic primitive, such as its multiplicative complexity in the case of masking. This has motivated cryptographers to design primitives that

© Springer Nature Switzerland AG 2020
K. G. Paterson and D. Stebila (Eds.): SAC 2019, LNCS 11959, pp. 149–170, 2020.
https://doi.org/10.1007/978-3-030-38471-5_7

minimize these costs. For example, Noekeon [17], KECCAK [9], or ASCON [23] aim to reduce the cost of masking countermeasures by using low degree S-boxes, while other designs like Zorro [26] even use incomplete S-box layers in order to be easier to mask, i.e., only part of the state is updated by the S-box layer, the rest remains unchanged.

The recently proposed permutation FRIT [46] takes this approach further and does not only allow efficient masking, but has been designed to also provide low-cost built-in fault detection. FRIT is a 384-bit cryptographic permutation designed by Simon, Batina, Daemen, Grosso, Massolino, Papagiannopoulos, Regazzoni, and Samwel [46]. The round function uses 128 AND gates per round as its only source of non-linearity. Its operations are carefully chosen to minimize the cost of maintaining an additional 128-bit checksum of the current state to provide redundancy and detect faults. As a result, even protected implementations with both side-channel and fault countermeasures are still relatively lightweight. With its 384-bit blocksize, it is well-suited as a building block for the modes of permutation-based cryptography, such as sponge and duplex modes [7,8,10], but it can also be transformed into a big-state Even-Mansour block cipher [25].

Related Work. As a consequence of the design choices, FRIT shares some similarities with constructions like Zorro and LowMC [1] that have incomplete S-box layers. Clearly, such novel designs require third-party cryptanalysis in order to strengthen the trust in their security, or to learn how to improve for future designs. Zorro paved the way for interesting cryptanalytic results that exploit the existence of good differential or linear characteristics in such incomplete S-box layers [4,43,50], as well as invariant subspace attacks [35]. MORUS [51], like FRIT, divides its large state in branches and builds on the Toffoli gate for nonlinearity, but the construction permits good linear approximations due to relatively weak diffusion [2,45]. On the other hand, the analysis results [18,22] for LowMC exploit the low degree of its round function together with its partial S-box layer.

The increasing prominence of primitives with low-degree round functions, such as KECCAK-p [9], ASCON's permutation [23], Xoodoo [16], or GIMLI [6], as well as more experimental designs that aggressively minimize the number of AND gates, such as Flip [38], Kreyvium [13,14], LowMC [1], or Rasta [21], has led to many advances and insights in algebraic cryptanalysis. Examples include extensions of zero-sums [3] and cube attacks [20], such as cube-like attacks [19,24] and conditional cube attacks [29,36,37], but also variants that exploit the algebraic properties in other ways, like collisions [47] and preimage attacks [28] on reduced-round KECCAK that linearize parts of the permutation. Moreover, new techniques like the division property [48,49] as a generalization of the integral attack [31] have been recently proposed to construct integral distinguishers further exploiting low-degree round functions.

In very recent follow-up work, Qin et al. [42] extend the algebraic distinguisher and initial structures discussed in this paper to cube attacks on reduced-round FRIT in a duplex-based authenticated encryption mode.

Contributions. We analyze the security of FRIT and provide distinguishers for the unkeyed primitive as well as key-recovery attacks for keyed FRIT. Our analysis takes advantage of the relatively low algebraic degree of FRIT's round function, but even more so of the properties of its inverse FRIT^{-1}, including its algebraic degree and certain diffusion properties. As observed by the designers of FRIT, the algebraic degree of the FRIT round function is 2, but an upper bound on the algebraic degree of multi-round FRIT is given by the Fibonacci sequence. It can thus be argued that the effective degree of its round function, i.e., the growth rate of the degree over multiple rounds, is the golden ratio $\varphi \approx 1.618$, and at least 11 (out of 16) rounds of FRIT are necessary to reach a degree larger than 128, while 13 rounds are necessary to reach the maximum degree of 383. The same upper bound can be shown for FRIT^{-1}. However, we show that this bound is far from tight, and prove an upper bound corresponding to an effective degree of $\alpha_0 \approx 1.325$. This observation implies that the algebraic degree of 16-round FRIT^{-1} is only 114. We show how to craft initial structures that linearize up to 4 rounds of FRIT^{-1} (or 5 rounds under certain additional bit conditions on the input).

Furthermore, we analyze the use of FRIT as an Even-Mansour [25] block cipher. If we allow chosen-ciphertext queries, we can take advantage of the properties of FRIT^{-1} to recover the key using 2^{18} chosen ciphertexts in about 5 seconds. However, since FRIT^{-1} is generally more costly to evaluate than FRIT, it seems more likely that FRIT would in practice be used in a construction that allows only chosen-plaintext queries. For this potential use case, we propose an optimized interpolation attack [18]. We take advantage of the relatively low algebraic degree of FRIT to set up an integral distinguisher for 11 rounds and combine this with a 5-round key-recovery technique using interpolation. The complexity of the interpolation profits not only from the very low degree of FRIT^{-1}, but also from its limited diffusion that leads to a rather low monomial count when expressing intermediate state bits as a function of the ciphertext and key bits. With this approach, we can recover the Even-Mansour key for full-round FRIT using 2^{59} chosen plaintexts and about 2^{67} time.

In Sect. 2, we briefly describe the FRIT design. In Sect. 3, we analyze the algebraic degree of FRIT and FRIT^{-1} and propose initial structures to linearize several rounds. Based on these properties, we propose key-recovery attacks on keyed FRIT in Sect. 4.

2   Description of FRIT

FRIT is a cryptographic permutation designed by Simon et al. [46]. Its 384-bit state is divided into three 128-bit limbs a, b, c which are updated in 16 rounds using simple bitwise operations, as illustrated in Fig. 1 (left). The only nonlinear operation is one 128-bit bitwise AND ($\odot$) per round, used in a Toffoli gate. Diffusion is achieved by two rotation-invariant linear mixing functions using 128-bit bitwise XOR ($\oplus$) and bitwise circular left shifts ($\lll$), which we refer to as σ_a and σ_c. Both σ_a and σ_c compute each output bit as the XOR of 3 input bits and have a bitwise branch number of 4 bits. The 16 rounds are identical except for the value of the round constant RC_r.

FRIT (for "Fault-Resistant Iterative Transformation") was designed to support the implementation of countermeasures against physical attacks. The design follows a more general approach proposed by its designers to provide built-in protection against differential fault attacks (DFA). The core idea of this approach is to extend the state by an extra limb and to implement an extended round function that updates all limbs such that the XOR of all limbs remains constant. The operations in the FRIT round function were selected such that this extended round function is very efficient, and they are additionally well-suited for side-channel countermeasures such as threshold implementations (TI). Our attack is however independent of implementation details such as the extra limb, so we refer to the original design paper for the detailed specification [46].

In Fig. 1 (right), we also list FRIT's inverse, FRIT^{-1}. Inverting corresponds to executing the operations in reverse order, where the Feistel swap is reversed and the mixing functions σ_a, σ_c are replaced with their inverses $\sigma_a^{-1}, \sigma_c^{-1}$. These inverses are again rotation-invariant, but they require significantly more operations: while σ_a and σ_c XOR 3 rotated copies of the input, σ_a^{-1} requires 65 rotations and σ_c^{-1} requires 33 (since σ_c has only even rotation constants and can thus be partitioned into the parallel application of two 64-bit σ functions). FRIT is thus more likely to be used in modes and constructions that do not require the inverse. Its 384-bit size is well-suited for sponge and duplex modes [7,8,10], but it can also be transformed into a big-state Even-Mansour block cipher [25].

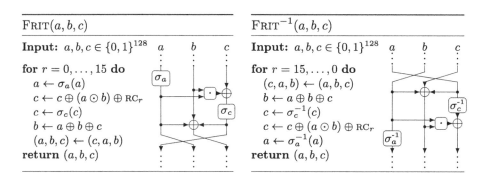

FRIT(a, b, c)

Input: $a, b, c \in \{0,1\}^{128}$

for $r = 0, \ldots, 15$ do
  $a \leftarrow \sigma_a(a)$
  $c \leftarrow c \oplus (a \odot b) \oplus \mathrm{RC}_r$
  $c \leftarrow \sigma_c(c)$
  $b \leftarrow a \oplus b \oplus c$
  $(a, b, c) \leftarrow (c, a, b)$
return (a, b, c)

FRIT$^{-1}(a, b, c)$

Input: $a, b, c \in \{0,1\}^{128}$

for $r = 15, \ldots, 0$ do
  $(c, a, b) \leftarrow (a, b, c)$
  $b \leftarrow a \oplus b \oplus c$
  $c \leftarrow \sigma_c^{-1}(c)$
  $c \leftarrow c \oplus (a \odot b) \oplus \mathrm{RC}_r$
  $a \leftarrow \sigma_a^{-1}(a)$
return (a, b, c)

Fig. 1. The permutation $\mathrm{FRIT}(a, b, c)$ [46] and its inverse $\mathrm{FRIT}^{-1}(a, b, c)$, where $\sigma_a(a) = a \oplus (a \lll 110) \oplus (a \lll 87)$ and $\sigma_c(c) = c \oplus (c \lll 118) \oplus (a \lll 88)$.

3   Algebraic Degree of FRIT and FRIT^{-1}

In this section, we analyze the algebraic degree of r-round FRIT and FRIT^{-1}. We show that the degree of FRIT^{-1} grows significantly slower than that of FRIT. We introduce the notion of the "effective degree" of the round function as the growth rate of the degree. We show that the effective degrees of FRIT and FRIT^{-1} are bounded by $\varphi \approx 1.618$ and $\alpha_0 \approx 1.325$, respectively, while the generic bound for degree-2 round functions is 2.

3.1 Designers' Analysis of FRIT

The FRIT design team analyze the algebraic degree of r-round FRIT, denoted FRIT$_r$, in the appendix [46] and observe the following. Let

$$(a_r, b_r, c_r) = \mathrm{FRIT}_1(a_{r-1}, b_{r-1}, c_{r-1}) = \mathrm{FRIT}_r(a_0, b_0, c_0).$$

Let $F_0 = 0, F_1 = 1$, and $F_i = F_{i-1} + F_{i-2}$ for $i \geq 2$ denote the Fibonacci sequence. Then, using the definition of FRIT$_1$ and the initial conditions $\deg a_0 = \deg b_0 = \deg c_0 = 1$, it is easy to see by induction that $\deg a_r \leq F_{r+2}$, $\deg c_r \leq F_{r+2}$, and $\deg b_r \leq F_{r+1}$:

$$
\begin{aligned}
\deg b_r &= \deg \sigma_a(a_{r-1}) \leq F_{r+1}, \\
\deg a_r &= \deg \sigma_c(c_{r-1} \oplus b_{r-1} \odot \sigma_a(a_{r-1})) \leq F_r + F_{r+1} = F_{r+2}, \qquad \text{(FRIT)} \\
\deg c_r &= \deg(b_{r-1} \oplus b_r \oplus a_r) \leq F_{r+2}.
\end{aligned}
$$

A similar bound applies for FRIT$_r^{-1}$, where we obtain with the same reasoning

$$\deg c_r \leq F_{r+2}, \qquad \deg b_r \leq F_{r+1}, \qquad \deg a_r \leq F_r, \qquad \text{(FRIT}^{-1}\text{)}$$

except for the initial condition $\deg a_0 = 1$. Thus, $d_r = F_{r+2}$ is an upper bound for the algebraic degree $\deg \mathrm{FRIT}_r \leq d_r$ and $\deg \mathrm{FRIT}_r^{-1} \leq d_r$.

Since $F_{15} = 610 \geq 383$, at least 13-round (14-round) FRIT or 13-round (15-round) FRIT^{-1} is necessary to achieve the maximum degree in some (all) limbs of the state.

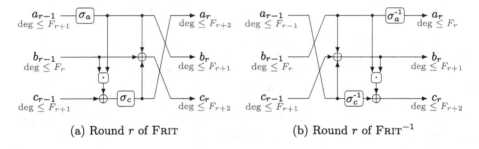

(a) Round r of FRIT   (b) Round r of FRIT^{-1}

Fig. 2. Fibonacci bound on the degree of FRIT$_r$ [46] and FRIT$_r^{-1}$.

3.2 Algebraic Degree of FRIT^{-1}

In the following, we have a closer look at FRIT^{-1} to derive a tighter recursive bound on the degree of FRIT^{-1} that looks quite similar to the case of FRIT and shares the same initial conditions, but grows significantly slower.

Recursive Bound for the Degree. To see that the previous bound is not tight for FRIT^{-1}, consider the first two rounds of the inverse. Note that the σ functions and their inverses do not change the degree, so we write $\bar{x}$ for any $\sigma(x)$ or $\sigma^{-1}(x)$. After one round, the algebraic degrees of limbs (a_1, b_1, c_1) are $(1, 1, 2)$ since $c_1 = b_1 \odot \bar{a}_1 \oplus \bar{a}_0$. Now consider c_2 after two rounds, which is essentially computed as $c_2 = b_1 \odot (c_1 \oplus \ldots) \oplus \ldots$ and thus has a degree of at most $1 + 2 = 3$. However, c_1 is itself the result of a multiplication by b_1, and since $b_1^2 = b_1$, the actual degree of the result is only 2, not 3.

More generally, using the bound d_r defined by the recursion $d_r = d_{r-2} + d_{r-3}$ and initial conditions $d_0 = d_{-1} = d_{-2} = 1$, the degree of FRIT^{-1} is bounded by

$$\deg c_r \leq d_r, \qquad \deg b_r \leq d_{r-1}, \qquad \deg a_r \leq d_{r-2}.$$

We can prove this inductively using the fact that by definition, $c_r = b_r \odot \bar{a}_r \oplus \bar{a}_{r-1}$:

$$\deg a_r = \deg \bar{b}_{r-1} \leq d_{r-2},$$
$$\deg b_r = \deg (c_{r-1} \oplus b_{r-1} \oplus a_{r-1}) \leq d_{r-1}, \qquad\qquad (\mathrm{FRIT}^{-1})$$
$$\deg c_r = \deg (\bar{a}_{r-1} \oplus b_{r-1} \odot (a_{r-1} \oplus b_{r-1} \oplus c_{r-1}))$$
$$= \deg (\bar{a}_{r-1} \oplus b_{r-1} \odot (a_{r-1} \oplus 1 \oplus \bar{a}_{r-1} \oplus \bar{a}_{r-2})) \leq d_{r-2} + d_{r-3} = d_r.$$

In summary, we obtain the recursion

$$\deg \mathrm{FRIT}_r^{-1} \leq d_r = d_{r-2} + d_{r-3}, \qquad\qquad d_0 = d_{-1} = d_{-2} = 1.$$

Using the method of differences to rewrite $d_r = d_{r-1} + (d_r - d_{r-1})$, we can also derive a different recursion for FRIT^{-1} very similar to that of FRIT:

$$\deg \mathrm{FRIT}_r \leq d_r = d_{r-1} + d_{r-2}, \qquad\qquad d_1 = 2, \quad d_0 = 1,$$
$$\deg \mathrm{FRIT}_r^{-1} \leq d_r = d_{r-1} + d_{r-2} - d_{r-4}, \qquad d_1 = 2, \quad d_0 = d_{-1} = d_{-2} = 1.$$

Despite the apparent similarity of the recursions, the tighter bound for FRIT^{-1} grows significantly slower, as we will discuss in the following (see Fig. 3). We practically verified the resulting degrees for up to 4 rounds of FRIT^{-1} by symbolically evaluating the cipher with Sage, and the bound of degree 4 is tight. We also verified up to 7 rounds (degree 9) symbolically with a simplified model of the cipher, as well as up to 11 rounds (degree 28) by testing the zero-sum property, and all results confirm these bounds.

Effective Degree. The recursive definition of the bound identified above can also be translated to a closed-form expression, in analogy to the bound of $d_r = 2^r$ for the degree after r rounds of degree $d = 2$. For the permutation FRIT, the designers' Fibonacci argument that we recalled in Subsect. 3.1 yields the following explicit exponential form using Binet's formula:

$$d_r = F_{r+2} = \frac{\varphi^{r+2} - (1 - \varphi)^{r+2}}{\sqrt{5}} = \left\lfloor \frac{\varphi^{r+2}}{\sqrt{5}} \right\rceil,$$

where $\varphi = \frac{1+\sqrt{5}}{2}$ is the golden ratio and $\lfloor \cdot \rceil$ denotes rounding to the nearest integer. We thus refer to $\varphi \approx 1.618$ as (an upper bound d for) the effective degree of FRIT.

We can obtain a similar exponential form for FRIT^{-1} by considering the generating function $D(z) \in \mathbb{C}[z]$ of the recursive form $d_r = d_{r-2} + d_{r-3}$:

$$D(z) = z^3 - z - 1.$$

The polynomial $D(z)$ has three roots $\alpha_0, \alpha_1, \alpha_2$ over the complex plane. Two roots α_1, α_2 are complex with absolute value less than 1, only one root $\alpha_0 \approx 1.325$ is real. It is well-known that d_r can be written as a linear combination of powers of these roots, where the coefficients t_0, t_1, t_2 depend on the initial conditions d_0, d_1, d_2. By solving the resulting system of three linear equations, we obtain that $|t_1 \alpha_1^r + t_2 \alpha_2^r| < 0.4$ for all $r \geq 0$ and thus the effective degree is (bounded by) $d = \alpha_0$:

$$d_r = t_0 \alpha_0^r + t_1 \alpha_1^r + t_2 \alpha_2^r = \lfloor t_0 \alpha_0^r \rceil, \qquad t_0 \approx 1.267, \quad \alpha_0 \approx 1.325.$$

Figure 3 compares the resulting degrees after r rounds for effective degrees 2, φ, and α_0.

		$r = 0$	1	2	3	4	5	6	7	8	9	$\ldots$
$d = 2$	$d_r = 2d_{r-1}$ $\qquad = 1$		2	4	8	16	32	64	128	256	512	$\ldots$
$d = \varphi \approx 1.618$	$d_r = d_{r-1} + d_{r-2} = 1$		2	3	5	8	13	21	34	55	89	$\ldots$
$d = \alpha_0 \approx 1.325$	$d_r = d_{r-2} + d_{r-3} = 1$		2	2	3	4	5	7	9	12	16	$\ldots$

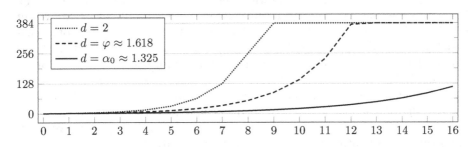

Fig. 3. Upper bounds d_r on deg FRIT$_r^{-1}$ based on different effective degrees d.

3.3   (Conditional) Initial Structures and Integral Distinguishers

So far, we analyzed the algebraic degrees of FRIT$_r$ and FRIT$_r^{-1}$ with respect to the 384 input variables representing the permutation input (or output). While the bound for the degree of any of the limbs is below the generic bound of 383 that holds for any bijective function, we can use this property to distinguish the permutation. More specifically, we can use the methods of higher-order differential cryptanalysis [34] to obtain an integral distinguisher: Say we have an upper bound d on the degree of the r-round permutation FRIT_r or FRIT_r^{-1} (or on at least one limb of the state). If we apply the r-round permutation to all elements of some $(d+1)$-dimensional (affine) subspace of $\mathbb{F}_2^{384}$ and compute the XOR of the resulting outputs, we will obtain 0 in all bit positions of the state (or limb).

In the following, we will extend these simple integral distinguishers by several rounds. We will craft structured $(d+1)$-dimensional affine input subspaces such that applying s rounds of the permutation will again produce a $(d+1)$-dimensional affine subspace as an intermediate result, thus extending the integral distinguisher to $s+r$ rounds. In other words, if we write the structured input space V as a linear combination $V = \left\{ \sum v_i \cdot e_i \right\} = \left\{ E \cdot v \mid v \in \mathbb{F}_2^{d+1} \right\}$ of some basis vectors e_i, $0 \le i < d+1$, then the s-round permutation is a linear function with respect to the coordinates v_i. We thus consider the Algebraic Normal Form (ANF) after s rounds when substituting the appropriate linear combination of v_i plus a symbolic constant for each input variable, and show that the resulting degree with respect to the variables v_i is 1. We also consider conditional initial structures where we require b bit conditions on the constants (the key) to ensure that the s-round permutation is linear. Finally, we propose low-dimensional inside-out zero-sum partitioning distinguishers for the permutation.

In the remainder of the section, we use the following notation. For simplicity, we will liberally refer to tuples of elements as "vectors" and to modules, affine vectorspaces, etc. as "spaces". We denote bitwise XOR by $\oplus$, bitwise AND by $\odot$, and the number of non-zero coordinates of a vector by $\text{wt}(\cdot)$. We consider the 384-bit state and each 128-bit limb as a vector of polynomials in the variables v_i, $0 \le i < d+1$, i.e., as an element of the 384-dimensional or 128-dimensional space over $\mathbb{F}_2[v_0, \dots, v_d]$. However, as we will later consider keyed FRIT variants in an Even-Mansour construction, the coefficients may depend on a constant 384-bit key $K = (k_0, \dots, k_{383})$ and thus be unknown to the attacker, so we sometimes variably use the base ring $(\mathbb{F}_2[k_0, \dots, k_{383}])[v_0, \dots, v_d]$. We refer to the graded part of degree j $(0 \le j \le d+1)$ of a polynomial with respect to the variables v_i as $\text{d}_j(\cdot)$; for example, $\text{d}_1(k_0 + k_1 v_1 + v_2 + v_1 v_2) = k_1 v_1 + v_2$. We want to find s-round initial structures such that $\text{d}_j(a_s, b_s, c_s) = 0$ for $j \ge 2$. We will identify the polynomial vector x with $\text{d}_j(x) = 0, j \ge 2$ with the affine vector space $\text{d}_0(x) + V$ spanned by $d+1$ basis vectors, where the i-th basis vector is obtained by substituting $v_i = 1$, $v_{i'} = 0$ for $i' \ne i$ in $\text{d}_1(x)$.

Initial Structures for FRIT. First consider s-round FRIT and assume we target some relatively small dimension $d+1 \le 128$, i.e., $r \le 10$. By keeping the two limbs a_0, b_0 constant and limiting the variables v_i to limb c_0, we can easily linearize $s = 2$ rounds of FRIT: After one round, $b_1 = \sigma_a(a_0)$ will be constant, while a_1 and c_1 will depend linearly on the variables v_i in c_0. Consequently, in the second round, again no variables are multiplied by the AND gate, so a_2, b_2, c_2 all depend linearly on the v_i. The structure is illustrated in Fig. 4a, where 1 denotes a constant limb and $v, \bar{v}, v', \dots$ denotes different linear limbs $(\text{d}_{\ge 2}(\cdot) = 0)$. Two limbs x, y denoted by the same symbol share the same linear part $(\text{d}_1(x) = \text{d}_1(y))$, and $\text{d}_1(\bar{x}) = \sigma(\text{d}_1(x))$. In other words, if we apply FRIT_2 to all elements of some $(d+1)$-dimensional affine subspace of $\mathbb{F}_2^{384}$ whose basis vectors e_i are all 0 in the first 256 bits, we will obtain another $(d+1)$-dimensional affine subspace as a result after 2 rounds. Note that the basis of this output space depends on the initial constants in a_0 and is thus not necessarily known; in particular, for keyed FRIT, the space depends on the key, so the sum over a space of dimension d is no longer a key-independent constant.

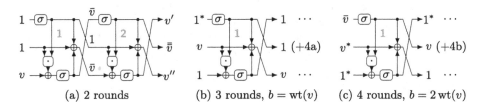

(a) 2 rounds   (b) 3 rounds, $b = \mathrm{wt}(v)$ (c) 4 rounds, $b = 2\,\mathrm{wt}(v)$

Fig. 4. Initial structures to (conditionally) linearize $s \leq 4$ rounds of FRIT.

There are several ways to extend this structure by one or more rounds at the expense of imposing some bit conditions on the constant part of the input. One of them is illustrated in Fig. 4b and c. To linearize 3 rounds, we prepend one round to the 2-round structure of Fig. 4a and start with variables only in b_0, see Fig. 4b. Additionally, we require that the constant in a_0, denoted by 1^*, is such that $\sigma_a(a_0)$ is zero in all b bit positions where b_0 is non-constant, that is, $\sigma_a(a_0) \odot \mathrm{d}_1(b_0) = 0$. Then, the output of the AND gate of the first round is constant, producing exactly the input structure of Fig. 4a at the input to the second round. The number of conditions is $b = \mathrm{wt}(\mathrm{d}_1(v)) \geq d+1$. An attacker can either satisfy these conditions directly in an unkeyed setting, or can guess the relevant linear function of the key and repeat the distinguisher 2^b times with suitable plaintexts in a keyed setting.

For a 4-round structure, we can prepend one more round by satisfying a total of $b = 2\,\mathrm{wt}(\mathrm{d}_1(v))$ conditions, as illustrated in Fig. 4c: Let $\bar{a}_0 = \sigma_a(a_0)$. First, we require that $\mathrm{d}_1(\bar{a}_0 \odot b_0) = 0$ to ensure that a_1 is constant. Since $\mathrm{d}_1(\bar{a}_0) = \mathrm{d}_1(b_0)$, this can be satisfied with $\mathrm{wt}(\mathrm{d}_1(v))$ bit conditions on $\mathrm{d}_0(b_0)$ using the fact that $(x+0) \cdot (x+1) = x + x = 0$: we simply require $\mathrm{d}_0(b_0) = 1 + \mathrm{d}_0(\bar{a}_0)$ in all relevant bit positions of b_0. Additionally, each of the previous $\mathrm{wt}(\mathrm{d}_1(v))$ conditions from Fig. 4b translates to a bit condition that depends nonlinearly on a_0, b_0, but can be satisfied like a linear condition by varying c_0.

Table 1 summarizes the resulting degree after $s + r \leq 16$ rounds of FRIT with different initial structures. With unconditional structures, we can distinguish up to 12 rounds (Fig. 4a, degree 89) or 13 rounds (degree 377) of FRIT. With conditional structures and degree 89, we can distinguish 13 rounds (90 conditions) or 14 rounds (179 conditions).

Table 1. Degree after $s + r \leq 16$ rounds of FRIT using the initial structures of Fig. 4. The last 3 rows list the degrees in $a_{s+r}, b_{s+r}, c_{s+r}$ based on an initial structure for the first s rounds, with $s \in \{0, 2, 3, 4\}$. Bold numbers indicate the maximum number $r + s$ with degree < 127 and < 383 for one limb.

FRIT	$s+r$	–	0	1	2	3	4	5	6	7	8	9	10	11	12	**13**	14	15	16
	0–1 (Fig. 4a)	2	3	4	5	6	7	8	9	10	11	**12**	13	14	15	16		
	0–2 (Fig. 4b)	3	4	5	6	7	8	9	10	11	12	**13**	14	15	16			
	0–3 (Fig. 4c)	4	5	6	7	8	9	10	11	12	13	**14**	15	16				
a_{s+r}	Init. Str.	1	2	3	5	8	13	21	34	55	89	144	233	377	*	*	*	*
b_{s+r}		1	1	2	3	5	8	13	21	34	55	89	144	233	377	*	*	*
c_{s+r}		1	2	3	5	8	13	21	34	55	89	144	233	377	*	*	*	*

Initial Structures for FRIT^{-1}. For FRIT^{-1}, we can use similar techniques and some additional observations to linearize up to 5 rounds. Figure 5a illustrates an unconditional 2-round structure for FRIT^{-1} starting from the same structure as Fig. 4a, but with different effects: In the first round, the AND gate multiplies a linear and a constant limb; the latter acts as a mask such that the non-zero elements of $d_1(v')$ are a subset of those in $d_1(v)$. In the second round, the first XOR just inverts this selected subset. Then, in each bit position, the AND gate either multiplies two linear terms with identical linear parts $d_1(b_1) = d_1(b_2)$, or at least one of the inputs is constant. In either case, the result is at most linear, and the non-zero linear part $d_1(v''')$ is another subset of $d_1(v)$. We can trivially prepend another round as illustrated in Fig. 5b.

Under certain conditions, we can also append a fourth round, as indicated in Fig. 5c: Say we are interested in a low dimension of $d + 1 \leq 36$. We start the construction by restricting the linear part $d_1(\bar{v})$ in limb a_3 (corresponds to a_2 in Fig. 5a), and require that it is zero except for the 36 positions $0, \ldots, 17, 64, \ldots, 81$. Now consider $d_1(c_0) = d_1(v) = \sigma_a(d_1(\bar{v}))$: σ_a rotates by $0, 110, 87$ bits to the left, or $0, 18, 41$ bits to the right. Thus, all non-zero elements in $\bar{v}$ are diffused to disjoint bit positions, namely $0 \ldots 17$ to $0 \ldots 17$, $18 \ldots 35$, $41 \ldots 59$ in the first half of the limb, and $64 \ldots 81$ similarly in the second half. This implies that the linear parts $d_1(\bar{v}), d_1(v''), d_1(v''')$ after 3 rounds are all masked selections from $d_1(v)$, and the XOR of all three limbs preserves this property. Now, by a similar argument as in Fig. 5a, the output of the AND gate is another selection from $d_1(v)$ and thus linear. In summary, if we select the linear part at the input as $d_1(b_0) = 0$ and $d_1(a_0) = d_1(c_0) = \sigma_c(\sigma_a(d_1(\bar{v})))$ with $d_1(\bar{v})$ zero except in positions $0, \ldots, 17, 64, \ldots, 81$, then we have an initial structure that linearizes 4 rounds of FRIT^{-1}.

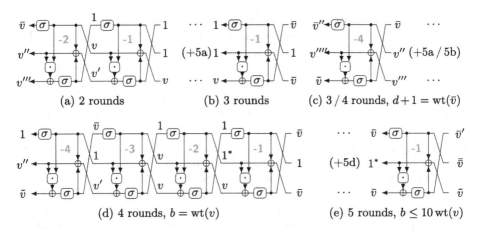

Fig. 5. Initial structures to (conditionally) linearize $s \leq 5$ rounds of FRIT^{-1}.

Alternatively, we can obtain a simpler 4-round structure by imposing bit conditions on the constant part, as illustrated in Fig. 5d: For the $\mathrm{wt}(\mathrm{d}_1(v))$ non-zero positions, we require that $\mathrm{d}_0(a_0 \oplus b_0 \oplus c_0) = 1$. Then, we get $\mathrm{d}_1(b_2) = \mathrm{d}_1(c_2)$ and thus $\mathrm{d}_1(b_3) = 0$. We can also prepend another round, at the cost of significantly more new conditions: In addition to the $\mathrm{wt}(\mathrm{d}_1(v))$ conditions on $\mathrm{d}_0(b_2)$ (b_1 in Fig. 5d), which we can satisfy by varying a_0 (and compensating in c_0 to keep b_1 constant), we need to fix the behaviour of the AND operation in the first round. For this purpose, we want to set b_1 to zero in all positions where $\mathrm{d}_1(b_0) = \mathrm{d}_1(\bar{\bar{v}})$ is non-zero, which imposes up to $9\,\mathrm{wt}(\mathrm{d}_1(v))$ additional conditions that can be controlled via c_0. As an example, for $s + r = 16$ we could target $d + 1 = 17$ and would need up to $17 + 92 = 109$ bit conditions for v with 17 consecutive linear bits.

Table 2. Degree after $s + r \leq 16$ rounds of FRIT^{-1} using the initial structures of Fig. 5. The last 3 rows list the degrees in $a_{s+r}, b_{s+r}, c_{s+r}$ based on an initial structure for the first s rounds, with $s \in \{0, 2, 3, 4, 5\}$.

FRIT^{-1}	$r + s$	–	0	1	2	3	4	5	6	7	8	9	10	11	12	13	14	15	16
	0–1 (Fig. 5a)	2	3	4	5	6	7	8	9	10	11	12	13	14	15	16			
	0–2 (Fig. 5b)	3	4	5	6	7	8	9	10	11	12	13	14	15	16				
	0–3 (Fig. 5c)	4	5	6	7	8	9	10	11	12	13	14	15	16					
	0–4 (Fig. 5e)	5	6	7	8	9	10	11	12	13	14	15	16						
a_{r+s}	Init.Str.	1	1	1	2	2	3	4	5	7	9	12	16	21	28	37	49	65	
b_{r+s}		1	1	2	2	3	4	5	7	9	12	16	21	28	37	49	65	86	
c_{r+s}		1	2	2	3	4	5	7	9	12	16	21	28	37	49	65	86	114	

Combined Inside-Out Structure. So far, we considered distinguishing properties of the (possibly keyed) permutation FRIT or FRIT^{-1}. When considering the permutation as an unkeyed primitive, we can also obtain distinguishing properties that are even less costly to test, but that will usually be less useful to exploit for key recovery or other attack goals. In particular, we can use inside-out computations and concatenate compatible initial structures to obtain a zero-sum partitioning of very low dimension as follows. The 2-round forward and backward structures of Figs. 4 and 5a obviously start from compatible structures $(1, 1, v)$. Furthermore, if we consider a low dimension, we can add a backward round for free as in Fig. 5c. As illustrated in Table 3, if we start from $(1, 1, v)$, the degree after 6 forward rounds is at most 8, and after 10 backward rounds at most 9 (for suitable v). Thus, if we fix a suitable v for dimension $d + 1 = 10$, and consider any affine space of this vector space, applying FRIT$_{10}^{-1}$ produces $2^{10} = 1024$ inputs to the permutation that sum to 0 while their outputs after FRIT$_{16}$ also sum to 0. Since we did not require any bit conditions, we can partition the entire input space of size 2^{384} into 2^{374} such zero-sum partitions of size 2^{10}.

Table 3. Inside-out degrees for 10-dimensional zero-sum partitioning of FRIT.

In-Out	r	1	2	3	4	5	6	7	8	9	10	11	12	13	14	15	16
	a_r	5	4	3	2	2	1	1	1					2	3	5	8
	b_r	7	5	4	3	2	2	1	Fig. 5a and c			Fig. 4a		1	2	3	5
	c_r	9	7	5	4	3	2	2						2	3	5	8

4   Key-Recovery Attacks on Keyed FRIT

In this section, we analyze the security of FRIT-based block ciphers. In the following attack descriptions, we consider FRIT in a single-key Even-Mansour construction to encrypt a 384-bit plaintext P under a 384-bit key K to $C = $ FRIT$(P \oplus K) \oplus K$. The attacks apply with identical complexities for a two-key construction, since the second key can be obtained trivially once the first key has been recovered. For a FRIT-like construction with a key schedule and round keys, the attack complexities would also only increase by a negligible amount.

We first propose a simple chosen-ciphertext attack that recovers the key with a very low complexity by exploiting the low effective degree of FRIT^{-1} with a 15-round integral distinguisher. However, since the implementation cost of FRIT^{-1} is higher than that of FRIT, we do not expect that FRIT would be used in a way that requires an implementation of the decryption algorithm and thus allows chosen-ciphertext attacks. For this reason, we also propose a chosen-plaintext attack with a higher complexity. While the 11-round integral distinguisher in this case is shorter and weaker due to the higher effective degree of FRIT, the key-recovery part can cover more rounds efficiently by applying optimized interpolation attacks that again profit from the low degree of FRIT^{-1}.

4.1   Simple Key-Recovery Attack Using Chosen Ciphertexts

Assume that we can query chosen ciphertexts C to receive the corresponding plaintexts $P = \text{FRIT}^{-1}(C \oplus K) \oplus K$. Here and in the following, we always "peel off" the final linear operation σ_a^{-1} by applying σ_a to limb a for all obtained plaintexts, and considering the corresponding equivalent key. If we query 2^{17} ciphertexts in an affine space constructed with the initial structure of Fig. 5c, we know that their values of limb a_{15} after decrypting 15 rounds must sum to 0. The relevant degrees after r rounds are summarized in Table 4, and the initial structure in Fig. 6. Moreover, if we continue decrypting another half-round, the same holds for the value of limb c between the mixing step σ_c^{-1} and the Toffoli gate, which we denote by c^*.

To verify this integral distinguishing property in one bit of c^*, we need to guess 3 bits of (equivalent) key information. Of all 2^3 key guesses, half (including the correct key) will satisfy the 1-bit distinguishing property. After repeating the test 3 or more times for different choices of the initial structure, we expect that only the correct key guess for the 3 bits will survive. The test can be applied in parallel on all 128 bit positions, thus recovering the complete 384-bit key. In order to collect enough data for 3 or more different initial structures, we can query 2^{18} chosen plaintexts and select different 17-dimensional subspaces. For each subspace and bit position, it is sufficient to count how often each of the 2^3 possible values of the 3 relevant plaintext bits occurs; or more specifically, whether it occurs an odd number of times. For each 3-bit key candidate, we can then test whether these $\leq 2^3$ ciphertext values with odd counters sum to the target constant. Overall, the time and data complexity is dominated by cost of querying 2^{18} chosen ciphertexts. An alternative trade-off with a slightly lower data complexity of 2^{14} chosen ciphertexts and a higher, but still practical time complexity can be obtained by using a 14-round distinguisher and guessing 27 key bits.

We practically implemented and verified the attack in C. It takes about 5 seconds to recover the full 384-bit key for the full-round primitive. However, the experiment showed that a minor tweak to the attack is necessary.

Let $K = (K_a, K_b, K_c)$ denote the key we want to recover. Since bit c^* depends linearly on the guessed key bits of K_c, the contribution of these key bits cancels when evaluating the sum, and the distinguishing property is independent of K_c.

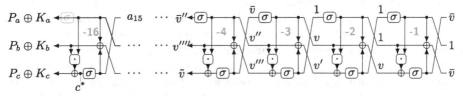

(a) Key recovery   (b) Initial structure to linearize 4 rounds (from Figure 5c)

Fig. 6. Key-recovery attack on FRIT^{-1}.

We can however correctly recover the bits of K_a and K_b one by one with 2 or more repetitions per bit position. To also recover K_c, we tweak the attack as follows. We first recover the full keys K_a, K_b as described above using 2 or more repetitions. Then, we peel off the first round, which is now linear in the remaining unknown key K_c, and repeat the attack for the partially encrypted plaintexts using dimension $12+1$ for 15-round FRIT^{-1}. This way, we will recover the "equivalent" keys $K'_a = \sigma_a(\sigma_c(K_c))$ and $K'_b = 0$ (though, again, not the part $K'_c = \sigma_c(K_c)$) and thus learn K_c to complete the key K.

Table 4. Key-recovery attacks on keyed FRIT in Even-Mansour construction using chosen-ciphertext (CCA) or chosen-plaintext (CPA) queries.

Keyed FRIT		r	1	2	3	4	5	6	7	8	9	10	11	12	13	14	15	16
CCA	a_r	K	16	12	9	7	5	4	3	2	2	1	1		5c = 6b			
	b_r		*	16	12	9	7	5	4	3	2	2	1					
	c_r		*	*	16	12	9	7	5	4	3	2	2					
CPA	a_r		4a		2	3	5	8	13	21	34	55	*		$f_K(C)$			
	b_r			1	2	3	5	8	13	21	34	55						
	c_r				2	3	5	8	13	21	34	55	*					

4.2 Optimized Interpolation Attack Using Chosen Plaintexts

When trying to develop similar key-recovery attacks using chosen plaintexts, we run into several limitations that prevent a full-round attack: First, the degree of FRIT grows much faster, so the core distinguisher can only cover fewer rounds. Second, the initial structures we identified in Fig. 4 are shorter and only cover two rounds (without additional conditions). Third, the diffusion of σ^{-1} is much better than that of σ, which may impact the size of the necessary key guess. However, we can use a different approach for key guessing to take advantage of the properties of the weaker inverse FRIT^{-1}: Jakobsen and Knudsen's interpolation attack [30] with Dinur et al.'s variable transformations [18].

In the following, we propose a chosen-plaintext attack that combines an 11-round integral distinguisher with a 5-round key recovery by interpolation, as illustrated in Table 4. We target the limb $b^* = b_{11}$ after 11 rounds, for which we can construct an integral distinguisher of dimension $55 + 1$ using an initial structure of $s = 2$ rounds and a core distinguisher for $r = 9$ rounds: the bits of b^* have degree 55 in the selected variables from the plaintext side.

On the other hand, the bits of b^* can also be written as a polynomial of the ciphertext bits with key-dependent coefficients. For 5 rounds, this polynomial can be obtained by considering the ANF of FRIT_5^{-1}, substituting the keyed ciphertext bits $(K_i \oplus C_i)$ for the FRIT output bits, and grouping the terms by the ciphertext monomials in C_i. According to the effective degree of FRIT^{-1}, this polynomial has degree at most 4 with respect to the variables C_i (see Table 2).

We want to recover the key-dependent coefficients of the ciphertext monomials to recover the key. To estimate the complexity of the resulting attack, we first need to analyze the structure and properties of this polynomial for FRIT.

Interpolation and Monomial Count. We write one bit of b^* as a polynomial $f(K, C)$ of degree 4 in the key $K = (K_0, \ldots, K_{383}) \in \mathbb{F}_2^{384}$ and ciphertext $C = (C_0, \ldots, C_{383}) \in \mathbb{F}_2^{384}$. This polynomial can be rewritten as a key-dependent polynomial in the ciphertext,

$$f_K(C) = \sum \alpha_u C^u \in \mathbb{F}_2[K][C],$$

with ciphertext monomials $C^u = \prod C_i^{u_i}$ for $u = (u_0, \ldots, u_{373}) \in \mathbb{F}_2^{384}$ and key-dependent coefficients $\alpha_u \in \mathbb{F}_2[K]$. We are interested in the number of monomials with non-zero coefficients. This number is generally upper-bounded by $\binom{384}{\leq 4} \approx 2^{29.7}$, but is significantly lower for FRIT^{-1}. The polynomial is not exactly identical (modulo variable indexing) for different bit positions due to the round constant addition, but the monomial count and structure with respect to the monomials C^u is the same for all bit positions. Also note that due to the Even-Mansour construction, the definition of the polynomial is entirely symmetric with respect to C and K, i.e., $f_K(C) = f_C(K)$.

For the monomial count, we can derive simple bounds by hand, but to obtain a more precise, tight result, we used Sage to symbolically evaluate the polynomial. More specifically, we derived the ANF of FRIT_r^{-1} for $r \leq 5$, substituted $(K_i \oplus C_i)$ to obtain $f(K, C)$, and counted the number of distinct ciphertext monomials C^u with (potentially) non-zero coefficients. We list the corresponding Sage code in Listing 1.1 in the appendix. For 5 rounds, this takes about 45 min, and an upper bound for 6 rounds can be obtained in comparable time. Table 5 lists the resulting exact monomial count $\bar{n}$ for $r \in \{2, 3, 4, 5\}$, grouped by the monomial degree. The polynomial is quite sparse: For FRIT_5^{-1}, only $\bar{n} = 60320 \approx 2^{15.88}$ out of the total $\approx 2^{29.7}$ monomials C^u have non-zero coefficients α_u.

Table 5. Number of monomials $\bar{n}$ and unknowns n of $f_K(C)$ per bit for FRIT_r^{-1}, derived using Listing 1.1.

Round	Degree	$\sum$	0	1	2	3	4
2	$\bar{n}$	69	1	67	1		
	n	69	1	68			
3	$\bar{n}$	230	1	163	66		
	n	165	1	164			
4	$\bar{n}$	7921	1	274	7519	127	
	n	550	1	274	275		
5	$\bar{n}$	60320	1	337	30768	25054	4160
	n	31444	1	337	30768	338	

We want to interpolate this polynomial and then recover the key bits from its key-dependent coefficients. We could do this with an interpolation attack by collecting $\bar{n}$ equations in the $\bar{n}$ unknown coefficients using $\bar{n}$ different zero-sum distinguishers for our target bit. To improve the complexity, we use the dual approach and variable transformation proposed by Dinur et al. [18] for the analysis of LowMC. The exact number of monomials of degrees $(0, 1, \ldots, 4)$ is $(1, 337, 30768, 25054, 4160)$. Since the overall degree of $f(K, C)$ is also $L = 4$, monomials C^u of higher degree $\mathrm{wt}(u)$ in C must have coefficients $\alpha_u = \sum_v \beta_{u,v} K^v$ of lower degree $\max_v \{\mathrm{wt}(v) \mid \beta_{u,v} \neq 0\} \leq L - \mathrm{wt}(u)$ in K. We can thus split the set of monomials C^u into those with degree lower than some limit $\ell \geq \mathrm{wt}(u)$, whose coefficients α_u we consider as unknowns, and those with higher degree $\mathrm{wt}(u) > \ell$. While there are many monomials with higher degree, they all have low-degree coefficients α_u involving the few available low-degree key monomials K^v, and we use those key monomials as unknowns. We thus rewrite the polynomial using fewer unknowns α_u and K^v as

$$
\begin{aligned}
f(K, C) &= \sum_{\mathrm{wt}(u) \leq \ell} \alpha_u C^u + \sum_{\mathrm{wt}(u) > \ell} \alpha_u C^u \\
&= \sum_{\mathrm{wt}(u) \leq \ell} \alpha_u C^u + \sum_{\mathrm{wt}(u) > \ell} \left(\sum_{\mathrm{wt}(v) \leq L - \ell} \beta_{u,v} K^v \right) C^u \\
&= \sum_{\mathrm{wt}(u) \leq \ell} \alpha_u C^u + \sum_{\mathrm{wt}(v) \leq L - \ell} \left(\sum_{\mathrm{wt}(u) > \ell} \beta_{u,v} C^u \right) K^v \\
&= \sum_{\mathrm{wt}(u) \leq \ell} \alpha_u C^u + \sum_{\mathrm{wt}(v) \leq L - \ell} \beta_v K^v .
\end{aligned}
$$

For FRIT_5^{-1}, we can use this approach to reduce the number of unknowns α_u, K^v by a factor of about 2:

- We keep the coefficients α_u of $n_p = 1 + 337 + 30768$ monomials C^u of degree $\mathrm{wt}(u) \leq \ell = 2$ in C_i.
- We transform the coefficients of the remaining $25054 + 4160$ monomials of degree $3, 4$ in C_i. These coefficients must be polynomials in the key bits of degree at most 1 or 0, respectively. Since the ANF is entirely symmetric in C and K, only 1 or $1 + 337$ key monomials, respectively, can be involved in these coefficients. If we consider FRIT with round keys and model them as independent new variables, the count would be higher, but still much smaller than n_p. By linearizing the key monomials, we can replace the $25054 + 4160$ coefficients with $n_k = 1 + 337$ new unknowns.

The reduced number of unknowns is then $n = n_p + n_k = 1 + 2 \cdot 337 + 30768 = 31444 \approx 2^{14.94}$.

Conveniently, the value of 337 of the new unknowns corresponds exactly to different key bits that can thus be trivially recovered from the interpolated polynomial. To recover the full key, it will be necessary to repeat the attack one more time with a different target bit position, which can be done with the same data.

4.3   Key Recovery and Attack Complexity

We state the memory complexity M in bits (bit), data complexity D in the number of queries, and time complexity T in bit operations (op) or encryptions (enc), where $1\,\text{enc} = 16 \cdot 128 \cdot (2 \cdot 2 + 3.5 \cdot 1) + 2 \cdot 384\,\text{op} \approx 2^{14}\,\text{op}$ (assuming 128-bit round constants).

For our attack, we use dimension $d+1 = 55+1$, $n = 31444 = 2^{14.94}$ unknowns, $\bar{n} = 60320 = 2^{15.88}$ monomials. Then we select t such that $\binom{d+1+t}{d+1} \geq n$, i.e., $t = 3$: $\binom{59}{56} \approx 2^{14.99} > 2^{14.94}$. The attack recovers 337 key bits, so a single repetition is sufficient and the remaining key bits can be recovered by brute force using about $2^{384-337} = 2^{47}$ trial encryptions (or the attack can be repeated once with the same data for a different bit position of b^*). The attack procedure and complexity is then as follows:

1. **Query** the encryption oracle with a set $\mathcal{P}$ of 2^{d+1+t} chosen plaintexts: $\mathcal{P}$ is defined by the initial structure in Fig. 4a, i.e., $d+1+t$ bits of limb c enumerate all possible values, the rest is set to an arbitrary constant. Denote by $\mathcal{P}_i \leq \mathcal{P}$, $0 \leq i < 2^{d+1+t}$ the subspace of dimension $\text{wt}(i)$, where the 1-bits of i select the basis vectors of $\mathcal{P}$. Fix a selection $\{\mathcal{P}_i\}$ of n subspaces with $\text{wt}(i) = d+1$. $(D = 2^{d+1+t})$
2. **Set up equation system**: Initialize $n \times n$ array; For each of the $\bar{n}$ monomials:
   (a) **Evaluate the monomial** for each ciphertext. $(M = D\,\text{bit},\ T = \bar{n} \cdot D\,\text{op})$
   (b) **Apply the Moebius transform** to this bit vector. Extract the $n \leq \binom{d+1+t}{d+1}$ bits that correspond to the n subspaces $\{\mathcal{P}_i\}$ of dimension $\text{wt}(i) = d+1$. $(M = n\,\text{bit},\ T = \bar{n} \cdot D \log_2 D\,\text{op})$
   (c) **Update equation system**: For the first n_p monomials, copy n-bit vector to an array column. For the others, update up to n_k columns. $(M = n^2\,\text{bit},\ T = n_p \cdot n + (\bar{n} - n_p) \cdot n_k \cdot n\,\text{op})$
3. **Solve** the equation system to recover the relevant unknowns and **derive the key bits**. $(T = n^3 / \log n\ [5])$

The total complexity is $D = 2^{d+1+t}$, and T may be dominated by step 1, 2b, 2c, or 3. For our parameters, this is $D = 2^{d+1+t} = 2^{59}$, $M = 2^{d+1+t} = 2^{59}$ bit, $T \approx \bar{n} \cdot D \log_2 D = 2^{80.76}\,\text{op} \approx 2^{66.76}\,\text{enc}$.

5   Conclusion

Our analysis of FRIT shows that the inverse permutation FRIT^{-1} has less efficient diffusion between its 128-bit limbs than FRIT, although the diffusion within each limb is much stronger. This leads to several properties that we can exploit in attacks on FRIT^{-1} and, to a much lesser extent, also on FRIT: First, the algebraic degree grows much slower over multiple rounds, with an effective degree of only $\alpha_0 \approx 1.325$. Second, by carefully selecting the variables, we can linearize up to 4 rounds of $\textsc{Frit}^{-1}$ and thus obtain efficient initial structures for an integral attack. Third, we can express intermediate state bits as a polynomial in the output bits (and key bits) with a relatively limited monomial count. As a consequence, we can provide efficient attacks on the full 16-round $\textsc{Frit}$ permutation if it is used as a block cipher, e.g., in an Even-Mansour mode with complexity 2^{67} when targeting the encryption, or 2^{18} when targeting the decryption. Furthermore, we provide very low-dimensional start-in-the-middle zero-sum partitioning distinguishers for the permutation.

If we consider the use of reduced-round $\textsc{Frit}$ in a sponge or duplex mode of operation, the provided observations may provide a good starting point for cube-like or conditional cube attacks. First results in this direction for reduced-round $\textsc{Frit}$ have been proposed by Qin et al. However, so far, we cannot exploit our observations if the full $\textsc{Frit}$ permutation is used in a sponge or duplex mode of operation. Hence, we consider the detailed analysis of these use cases an interesting future research topic.

Finally, we remark that our analysis does not indicate any intrinsic problem of the general design approach, but underline the necessity for a detailed algebraic analysis of such designs. The attacks would be made significantly harder by small changes to the specification, such as an additional diffusion step between the two uses of a limb as input to different AND gates. The combination of the Toffoli gate with rotations and XOR remains a very attractive approach for both hardware and software implementations, as illustrated by the implementation performance and security results by the $\textsc{Frit}$ team, but also by other related designs aimed at other platforms such as the CAESAR finalist MORUS, which targets high-performance software implementations. We hope that our results will provide useful tools for the security analysis of future designs that take advantage of this flexible approach.

Acknowledgements. We thank the $\textsc{Frit}$ team for their comments on preliminary versions of the attack.

A   Symbolic Evaluation with Sage

Listing 1.1. Sage script to count monomials in limb b after ≤ 5 rounds of $\textsc{Frit}^{-1}$.

```
varnames = sum([[v+str(i) for i in range(384)] for v in 'CK'], [])
R = BooleanPolynomialRing(len(varnames), varnames, order='deglex')
Cvar, Kvar = list(R.gens())[:384], list(R.gens())[384:]

AND  = lambda x, y: [xi*yi for xi, yi in zip(x, y)]
XOR  = lambda x, y: [xi+yi for xi, yi in zip(x, y)]
XOR3 = lambda x, y, z: [xi+yi+zi for xi, yi, zi in zip(x, y, z)]
ROTL = lambda x, r: x[-r:] + x[:-r]
invlist = lambda l: [r for r, xr in enumerate(matrix.circulant(
                         [GF(2)(1) if i in l else GF(2)(0) for i in range(128)]
                     ).inverse()[0]) if xr]
SIGMA = lambda x, l: reduce(lambda x, y: XOR(x, y), [ROTL(x, li) for li in l])
SIGMA_a = lambda x: XOR3(x, ROTL(x, 110), ROTL(x, 87))
SIGMA_c = lambda x: XOR3(x, ROTL(x, 118), ROTL(x, 88))
```

```
SIGMA_a_inv = lambda x: SIGMA(x, invlist([0,87,110]))
SIGMA_c_inv = lambda x: SIGMA(x, invlist([0,88,118]))
RC = [GF(2)(rc) for rc in reversed(0xF9A42BB1.binary().zfill(128))]
RCs = [i*[GF(2)(0)] + RC[i:] for i in range(16)]

texnum = lambda x: str(x) + "␣=␣2^{" + str(log(x,2).n(digits=5)) + "}"
def STATS(rnd, x):
    print "ROUND", rnd
    print "F[K,C]:",[len(x.graded_part(d)) for d in [0..8]],"=",texnum(len(x))
    subsdict = {ki:R.one() for ki in Kvar}
    x = sum(set([mon.subs(subsdict) for mon in x.monomials()]))
    print "F_K[C]:",[len(x.graded_part(d)) for d in [0..8]],"=",texnum(len(x))

nrounds = 5
a = XOR(Cvar[0:128],   Kvar[0:128])
b = XOR(Cvar[128:256], Kvar[128:256])
c = XOR(Cvar[256:384], Kvar[256:384])

c = XOR3(c, AND(a, b), RCs[0])
a = SIGMA_a_inv(a)
STATS("1b", b[0])

for r in [2..(nrounds-2)]:
    c, a, b = a, b, c
    b = XOR3(b, a, c)
    c = XOR3(SIGMA_c_inv(c), AND(a, b), RCs[r-1])
    a = SIGMA_a_inv(a)
    STATS(str(r)+"b", b[0])

c, a, b = a, b, c
b = XOR3(b[:1], a[:1], c[:1])
STATS(str(nrounds-1)+"b", b[0])
b0 = (SIGMA_a_inv(a)[0] + b[0] + SIGMA_c_inv(c)[0]) + b[0] * a[0]
STATS(str(nrounds)+"b", b0)
```

References

1. Albrecht, M.R., Rechberger, C., Schneider, T., Tiessen, T., Zohner, M.: Ciphers for MPC and FHE. In: Oswald, E., Fischlin, M. (eds.) EUROCRYPT 2015. LNCS, vol. 9056, pp. 430–454. Springer, Heidelberg (2015). https://doi.org/10.1007/978-3-662-46800-5_17

2. Ashur, T., et al.: Cryptanalysis of MORUS. In: Peyrin, T., Galbraith, S. (eds.) ASIACRYPT 2018. LNCS, vol. 11273, pp. 35–64. Springer, Cham (2018). https://doi.org/10.1007/978-3-030-03329-3_2

3. Aumasson, J.P., Meier, W.: Zero-sum distinguishers for reduced Keccak-f and for the core functions of luffa and hamsi. Presented at the rump session of Cryptographic Hardware and Embedded Systems – CHES 2009 (2009). https://131002.net/data/papers/AM09.pdf

4. Bar-On, A., Dinur, I., Dunkelman, O., Lallemand, V., Keller, N., Tsaban, B.: Cryptanalysis of SP networks with partial non-linear layers. In: Oswald, E., Fischlin, M. (eds.) EUROCRYPT 2015. LNCS, vol. 9056, pp. 315–342. Springer, Heidelberg (2015). https://doi.org/10.1007/978-3-662-46800-5_13

5. Bard, G.V.: Algorithms for solving linear and polynomial systems of equations over finite fields with applications to cryptanalysis. Ph.D. thesis, University of Maryland, College Park, MD, USA (2007). https://hdl.handle.net/1903/7202

6. Bernstein, D.J., et al.: GIMLI : a cross-platform permutation. In: Fischer, W., Homma, N. (eds.) CHES 2017. LNCS, vol. 10529, pp. 299–320. Springer, Cham (2017). https://doi.org/10.1007/978-3-319-66787-4_15

7. Bertoni, G., Daemen, J., Peeters, M., Van Assche, G.: Sponge functions. Ecrypt Hash Workshop 2007, May 2007
8. Bertoni, G., Daemen, J., Peeters, M., Van Assche, G.: On the indifferentiability of the sponge construction. In: Smart, N. (ed.) EUROCRYPT 2008. LNCS, vol. 4965, pp. 181–197. Springer, Heidelberg (2008). https://doi.org/10.1007/978-3-540-78967-3_11
9. Bertoni, G., Daemen, J., Peeters, M., Van Assche, G.: The Keccak SHA-3 submission (Version 3.0) (2011). http://keccak.noekeon.org/Keccak-submission-3.pdf
10. Bertoni, G., Daemen, J., Peeters, M., Van Assche, G.: Duplexing the sponge: single-pass authenticated encryption and other applications. In: Miri, A., Vaudenay, S. (eds.) SAC 2011. LNCS, vol. 7118, pp. 320–337. Springer, Heidelberg (2012). https://doi.org/10.1007/978-3-642-28496-0_19
11. Biham, E., Shamir, A.: Differential fault analysis of secret key cryptosystems. In: Kaliski, B.S. (ed.) CRYPTO 1997. LNCS, vol. 1294, pp. 513–525. Springer, Heidelberg (1997). https://doi.org/10.1007/BFb0052259
12. Boneh, D., DeMillo, R.A., Lipton, R.J.: On the importance of checking cryptographic protocols for faults. In: Fumy, W. (ed.) EUROCRYPT 1997. LNCS, vol. 1233, pp. 37–51. Springer, Heidelberg (1997). https://doi.org/10.1007/3-540-69053-0_4
13. Canteaut, A., et al.: Stream ciphers: a practical solution for efficient homomorphic-ciphertext compression. In: Peyrin, T. (ed.) FSE 2016. LNCS, vol. 9783, pp. 313–333. Springer, Heidelberg (2016). https://doi.org/10.1007/978-3-662-52993-5_16
14. Canteaut, A., et al.: Stream ciphers: a practical solution for efficient homomorphic-ciphertext compression. J. Cryptol. **31**(3), 885–916 (2018). https://doi.org/10.1007/s00145-017-9273-9
15. Chari, S., Jutla, C.S., Rao, J.R., Rohatgi, P.: Towards sound approaches to counteract power-analysis attacks. In: Wiener, M. (ed.) CRYPTO 1999. LNCS, vol. 1666, pp. 398–412. Springer, Heidelberg (1999). https://doi.org/10.1007/3-540-48405-1_26
16. Daemen, J., Hoffert, S., Van Assche, G., Van Keer, R.: The design of Xoodoo and Xoofff. IACR Trans. Symmetric Cryptol. **2018**(4), 1–38 (2018). https://doi.org/10.13154/tosc.v2018.i4.1-38
17. Daemen, J., Peeters, M., Van Assche, G., Rijmen, V.: Nessie Proposal: NOEKEON. First Open NESSIE Workshop (2000). http://gro.noekeon.org/Noekeon-spec.pdf
18. Dinur, I., Liu, Y., Meier, W., Wang, Q.: Optimized interpolation attacks on LowMC. In: Iwata, T., Cheon, J.H. (eds.) ASIACRYPT 2015. LNCS, vol. 9453, pp. 535–560. Springer, Heidelberg (2015). https://doi.org/10.1007/978-3-662-48800-3_22
19. Dinur, I., Morawiecki, P., Pieprzyk, J., Srebrny, M., Straus, M.: Cube attacks and cube-attack-like cryptanalysis on the round-reduced keccak sponge function. In: Oswald, E., Fischlin, M. (eds.) EUROCRYPT 2015. LNCS, vol. 9056, pp. 733–761. Springer, Heidelberg (2015). https://doi.org/10.1007/978-3-662-46800-5_28
20. Dinur, I., Shamir, A.: Cube attacks on tweakable black box polynomials. In: Joux, A. (ed.) EUROCRYPT 2009. LNCS, vol. 5479, pp. 278–299. Springer, Heidelberg (2009). https://doi.org/10.1007/978-3-642-01001-9_16
21. Dobraunig, C., et al.: Rasta: a cipher with low ANDdepth and few ANDs per bit. In: Shacham, H., Boldyreva, A. (eds.) CRYPTO 2018. LNCS, vol. 10991, pp. 662–692. Springer, Cham (2018). https://doi.org/10.1007/978-3-319-96884-1_22
22. Dobraunig, C., Eichlseder, M., Mendel, F.: Higher-order cryptanalysis of LowMC. In: Kwon, S., Yun, A. (eds.) ICISC 2015. LNCS, vol. 9558, pp. 87–101. Springer, Cham (2016). https://doi.org/10.1007/978-3-319-30840-1_6

23. Dobraunig, C., Eichlseder, M., Mendel, F., Schläffer, M.: Ascon v1.2. Submission to Round 3 of the CAESAR competition (2016). https://competitions.cr.yp.to/round3/asconv12.pdf

24. Dong, X., Li, Z., Wang, X., Qin, L.: Cube-like attack on round-reduced initialization of Ketje Sr. IACR Trans. Symmetric Cryptol. **2017**(1), 259–280 (2017). https://doi.org/10.13154/tosc.v2017.i1.259-280

25. Even, S., Mansour, Y.: A construction of a cipher from a single pseudorandom permutation. In: Imai, H., Rivest, R.L., Matsumoto, T. (eds.) ASIACRYPT 1991. LNCS, vol. 739, pp. 210–224. Springer, Heidelberg (1993). https://doi.org/10.1007/3-540-57332-1_17

26. Gérard, B., Grosso, V., Naya-Plasencia, M., Standaert, F.-X.: Block ciphers that are easier to mask: how far can we go? In: Bertoni, G., Coron, J.-S. (eds.) CHES 2013. LNCS, vol. 8086, pp. 383–399. Springer, Heidelberg (2013). https://doi.org/10.1007/978-3-642-40349-1_22

27. Goubin, L., Patarin, J.: DES and differential power analysis the "Duplication" method. In: Koç, Ç.K., Paar, C. (eds.) CHES 1999. LNCS, vol. 1717, pp. 158–172. Springer, Heidelberg (1999). https://doi.org/10.1007/3-540-48059-5_15

28. Guo, J., Liu, M., Song, L.: Linear structures: applications to cryptanalysis of round-reduced KECCAK. In: Cheon, J.H., Takagi, T. (eds.) ASIACRYPT 2016. LNCS, vol. 10031, pp. 249–274. Springer, Heidelberg (2016). https://doi.org/10.1007/978-3-662-53887-6_9

29. Huang, S., Wang, X., Xu, G., Wang, M., Zhao, J.: Conditional cube attack on reduced-round keccak sponge function. In: Coron, J.-S., Nielsen, J.B. (eds.) EURO-CRYPT 2017. LNCS, vol. 10211, pp. 259–288. Springer, Cham (2017). https://doi.org/10.1007/978-3-319-56614-6_9

30. Jakobsen, T., Knudsen, L.R.: The interpolation attack on block ciphers. In: Biham, E. (ed.) FSE 1997. LNCS, vol. 1267, pp. 28–40. Springer, Heidelberg (1997). https://doi.org/10.1007/BFb0052332

31. Knudsen, L., Wagner, D.: Integral cryptanalysis. In: Daemen, J., Rijmen, V. (eds.) FSE 2002. LNCS, vol. 2365, pp. 112–127. Springer, Heidelberg (2002). https://doi.org/10.1007/3-540-45661-9_9

32. Kocher, P.C.: Timing attacks on implementations of Diffie-Hellman, RSA, DSS, and other systems. In: Koblitz, N. (ed.) CRYPTO 1996. LNCS, vol. 1109, pp. 104–113. Springer, Heidelberg (1996). https://doi.org/10.1007/3-540-68697-5_9

33. Kocher, P., Jaffe, J., Jun, B.: Differential power analysis. In: Wiener, M. (ed.) CRYPTO 1999. LNCS, vol. 1666, pp. 388–397. Springer, Heidelberg (1999). https://doi.org/10.1007/3-540-48405-1_25

34. Lai, X.: Higher order derivatives and differential cryptanalysis. In: Blahut, R.E., Costello Jr., D.J., Maurer, U., Mittelholzer, T. (eds.) Communications and Cryptography: Two Sides of One Tapestry. International Series in Engineering and Computer Science, vol. 276, pp. 227–233. Kluwer Academic Publishers (1994). https://doi.org/10.1007/978-1-4615-2694-0_23

35. Leander, G., Minaud, B., Rønjom, S.: A generic approach to invariant subspace attacks: cryptanalysis of Robin, iSCREAM and Zorro. In: Oswald, E., Fischlin, M. (eds.) EUROCRYPT 2015. LNCS, vol. 9056, pp. 254–283. Springer, Heidelberg (2015). https://doi.org/10.1007/978-3-662-46800-5_11

36. Li, Z., Bi, W., Dong, X., Wang, X.: Improved conditional cube attacks on keccak keyed modes with MILP method. In: Takagi, T., Peyrin, T. (eds.) ASIACRYPT 2017. LNCS, vol. 10624, pp. 99–127. Springer, Cham (2017). https://doi.org/10.1007/978-3-319-70694-8_4

37. Li, Z., Dong, X., Wang, X.: Conditional cube attack on round-reduced ASCON. IACR Trans. Symmetric Cryptol. **2017**(1), 175–202 (2017). https://doi.org/10.13154/tosc.v2017.i1.175-202
38. Méaux, P., Journault, A., Standaert, F.-X., Carlet, C.: Towards stream ciphers for efficient FHE with low-noise ciphertexts. In: Fischlin, M., Coron, J.-S. (eds.) EUROCRYPT 2016. LNCS, vol. 9665, pp. 311–343. Springer, Heidelberg (2016). https://doi.org/10.1007/978-3-662-49890-3_13
39. Nikova, S., Rechberger, C., Rijmen, V.: Threshold implementations against side-channel attacks and glitches. In: Ning, P., Qing, S., Li, N. (eds.) ICICS 2006. LNCS, vol. 4307, pp. 529–545. Springer, Heidelberg (2006). https://doi.org/10.1007/11935308_38
40. Nikova, S., Rijmen, V., Schläffer, M.: Secure hardware implementation of non-linear functions in the presence of glitches. In: Lee, P.J., Cheon, J.H. (eds.) ICISC 2008. LNCS, vol. 5461, pp. 218–234. Springer, Heidelberg (2009). https://doi.org/10.1007/978-3-642-00730-9_14
41. Nikova, S., Rijmen, V., Schläffer, M.: Secure hardware implementation of nonlinear functions in the presence of glitches. J. Cryptol. **24**(2), 292–321 (2011). https://doi.org/10.1007/s00145-010-9085-7
42. Qin, L., Dong, X., Jia, K., Zong, R.: Key-dependent cube attack on reduced Frit permutation in Duplex-AE modes. IACR Cryptology ePrint Archive, Report 2019/170 (2019). https://eprint.iacr.org/2019/170
43. Rasoolzadeh, S., Ahmadian, Z., Salmasizadeh, M., Aref, M.R.: Total break of Zorro using linear and differential attacks. IACR Cryptology ePrint Archive, Report 2014/220 (2014). https://eprint.iacr.org/2014/220
44. Schneider, T., Moradi, A., Güneysu, T.: ParTI – towards combined hardware countermeasures against side-channel and fault-injection attacks. In: Robshaw, M., Katz, J. (eds.) CRYPTO 2016. LNCS, vol. 9815, pp. 302–332. Springer, Heidelberg (2016). https://doi.org/10.1007/978-3-662-53008-5_11
45. Shi, D., Sun, S., Sasaki, Y., Li, C., Hu, L.: Correlation of quadratic Boolean functions: cryptanalysis of all versions of full MORUS. IACR Cryptology ePrint Archive, Report 2019/172 (2019). https://eprint.iacr.org/2019/172
46. Simon, T., et al.: Towards lightweight cryptographic primitives with built-in fault-detection. IACR Cryptology ePrint Archive, Report 2018/729 (2018). https://eprint.iacr.org/2018/729
47. Song, L., Liao, G., Guo, J.: Non-full sbox linearization: applications to collision attacks on round-reduced KECCAK. In: Katz, J., Shacham, H. (eds.) CRYPTO 2017. LNCS, vol. 10402, pp. 428–451. Springer, Cham (2017). https://doi.org/10.1007/978-3-319-63715-0_15
48. Todo, Y.: Integral cryptanalysis on Full MISTY1. In: Gennaro, R., Robshaw, M. (eds.) CRYPTO 2015. LNCS, vol. 9215, pp. 413–432. Springer, Heidelberg (2015). https://doi.org/10.1007/978-3-662-47989-6_20
49. Todo, Y.: Structural evaluation by generalized integral property. In: Oswald, E., Fischlin, M. (eds.) EUROCRYPT 2015. LNCS, vol. 9056, pp. 287–314. Springer, Heidelberg (2015). https://doi.org/10.1007/978-3-662-46800-5_12
50. Wang, Y., Wu, W., Guo, Z., Yu, X.: Differential cryptanalysis and linear distinguisher of full-round zorro. In: Boureanu, I., Owesarski, P., Vaudenay, S. (eds.) ACNS 2014. LNCS, vol. 8479, pp. 308–323. Springer, Cham (2014). https://doi.org/10.1007/978-3-319-07536-5_19
51. Wu, H., Huang, T.: The authenticated cipher MORUS (v2). Submission to Round 3 of the CAESAR competition (2016). https://competitions.cr.yp.to/round3/morusv2.pdf

Improved Interpolation Attacks on Cryptographic Primitives of Low Algebraic Degree

Chaoyun Li$^{(\boxtimes)}$ and Bart Preneel

imec-COSIC, Department Electrical Engineering (ESAT), KU Leuven,
Leuven, Belgium
{chaoyun.li,bart.preneel}@esat.kuleuven.be

Abstract. Symmetric cryptographic primitives with low multiplicative complexity have been proposed to improve the performance of emerging applications such as secure Multi-Party Computation. However, primitives composed of round functions with low algebraic degree require a careful evaluation to assess their security against algebraic cryptanalysis, and in particular interpolation attacks. This paper proposes new low-memory interpolation attacks on symmetric key primitives of low degree. Moreover, we present generic attacks on block ciphers with a simple key schedule; our attacks require either constant memory or constant data complexity. The improved attack is applied to the block cipher MiMC which aims to minimize the number of multiplications in large finite fields. As a result, we can break MiMC-129/129 with 38 rounds with time and data complexity $2^{65.5}$ and $2^{60.2}$ respectively and with negligible memory; this attack invalidates one of the security claims of the designers. Our attack indicates that for MiMC-129/129 the full 82 rounds are necessary even with restrictions on the memory available to the attacker. For variants of MiMC with larger keys, we present new attacks with reduced complexity. Our results do not affect the security claims of the full round MiMC.

Keywords: Block cipher · Cryptanalysis · Interpolation attack · MiMC

1 Introduction

Symmetric cryptographic primitives have been widely employed to provide confidentiality and authenticity for communicated and stored data [24]. Recently, they find new applications in advanced cryptographic protocols for computing on encrypted data, such as secure Multi-Party Computation (MPC), Zero-Knowledge proofs (ZK) and Fully Homomorphic Encryption (FHE). The adoption of dedicated symmetric key primitives turns out to be vital to improve the efficiency of these protocols. The main design goal is to minimize the multiplicative complexity (MC), i.e., minimize the number of multiplications in a circuit

© Springer Nature Switzerland AG 2020
K. G. Paterson and D. Stebila (Eds.): SAC 2019, LNCS 11959, pp. 171–193, 2020.
https://doi.org/10.1007/978-3-030-38471-5_8

and/or to minimize the multiplicative depth of the circuit. However, traditional block ciphers, stream ciphers and hash functions are typically not designed to minimize these parameters; to the contrary, having high multiplicative depth is seen as an important requirement to achieve strong security.

Many new symmetric primitives have been proposed in the context of MPC, ZK, or FHE schemes [3,5,8,15]. The block cipher LowMC [5] is one of the earliest designs dedicated to FHE and MPC applications. With very small multiplicative size and depth, it outperforms AES-128 in computation and communication complexity for these applications. The stream ciphers Kreyvium [8] and FLIP [20] have been designed to minimize the AND-depth of the circuit. Indeed, they aim to provide practical solutions for efficient homomorphic-ciphertext compression [8,20]. A new family of stream ciphers Rasta [12] intends to achieve both minimum AND-depth and minimum number of AND gates per encrypted bit.

MiMC, proposed by Albrecht et al. [3,4], is dedicated to applications for which the total number of field multiplications in the underlying cryptographic primitive poses the largest performance bottleneck. More specifically, MiMC aims to minimize multiplications in the larger fields $\mathbb{F}_{2^n}$ and $\mathbb{F}_p$. Indeed, MiMC outperforms both AES and LowMC in applications such as MPC [15], Succinct Non-interactive Arguments of Knowledge (SNARKs) [7], and Scalable Transparent ARguments of Knowledge (STARKs) [6]. New variants of MiMC, such as GMiMC [2], have been constructed by inserting the original design into generalized Feistel structures.

However, the security of MiMC is not well understood. Due to the simple algebraic structure and the large number of rounds, the security evaluation of MiMC has been focusing on algebraic attacks such as interpolation attacks and Gröbner basis attacks [1,3]. In the design paper, the authors first consider the classical interpolation attack. Moreover, the so-called GCD attack has been introduced. With this new technique, new lower bounds on the number of rounds have been derived. However, there is a need for further work to assess the security of round-reduced MiMC and to find tighter lower bounds on the number of rounds.

Our Contributions. This paper presents novel attacks against primitives with low algebraic degree. The first new attack is based on an observation from Sun et al. [27]. It introduces novel interpolation attacks with constant memory complexity: some key-dependent terms of the interpolated polynomial are determined directly, without constructing the complete polynomial. Then we propose an algorithm with constant memory for recovering the second highest order coefficient resulting in an efficient key recovery attack.

The second new attack exploits a simple cyclic key schedule. The master key is $k_0||k_1||\cdots||k_{\ell-1}$ and the round keys are given by $k_i = k_{i \bmod \ell} + c_i$, where the c_i's are constants that are chosen independently. For this specific key schedule, we present generic attacks with either constant memory or constant data complexity. Our attacks follow a guess-and-determine strategy. After guessing $(\ell - 1)$ subkeys, we apply state-of-the-art key recovery attacks to the reduced cipher. The advantage of our strategy is that we can keep the data and memory complexity of the whole attack as low as those of the attack on the reduced cipher. The results of our attacks are summarized in Table 1.

As an illustration, we apply the new attacks to the block cipher MiMC. Specifically, we can break 38-round MiMC-129/129 with time complexity $2^{65.5}$, data complexity $2^{60.2}$ and *negligible* memory. Our results refute the claim of the MiMC designers who consider attacks with less than 2^{64} bytes memory and conclude [4, p. 17]: "38 rounds are sufficient to protect MiMC-129/129 against the interpolation, the GCD and the other attacks. Time-memory trade-offs might well be possible, and we leave this as a topic for future research." Our attack simply reduces memory while keeping the time complexity at the same value, hence we show that there is no trade-off. Further, our attack indicates that for MiMC-n/n over $\mathbb{F}_q$ the number of rounds cannot be smaller than $\lceil \frac{\log_2(q)}{\log_2(3)} \rceil$ even if there is a restriction on the memory available to the attacker.

For a two-key version of MiMC-n/n, the best attack described by the designers has complexity $O(3^{3r})$. The designers further claimed that the bound can be improved by a Meet-In-The-Middle (MITM) attack [4, p. 18], but they offer no details. By employing our generic attack to the concrete design, the complexity can be reduced to $O(r3^r)$ if $r \leq \lceil \frac{n}{\log_2(3)} \rceil - 1$ and $O(r3^{2r-1})$ if $r \geq \lceil \frac{n}{\log_2(3)} \rceil$. Our reduced bound is the first tighter bound based on specific attacks.

To the best of our knowledge, our analysis of MiMC is the first third party cryptanalysis of MiMC.

Table 1. Attacks on r-round key-alternating and Feistel network ciphers with round function of degree d over $\mathbb{F}_q$. For $\ell > 1$, we cyclically add ℓ independent subkeys in each round.

Type	Key size	Time	Memory	Data	Ref
Key-alternating	q	$O(rd^r)$	$O(rd^r)$	$d^r + 1$	[4]
	q	$O(r^2 d^r)$	$O(rd^r)$	3	[4]
	q	$O(rd^r)\sharp$	$O(1)$	$d^r + 1$	Sect. 3.3
	q^ℓ	$O(rd^r)\sharp$	$O(1)$	$d^r + 1$	Sect. 4.1
	q^ℓ	$O(R_{\mathrm{KA}}(r,\ell)d^{R_{\mathrm{KA}}(r,\ell)}q^{\ell-1})$ †$\sharp$	$O(1)$	$d^{R_{\mathrm{KA}}(r,\ell)} + 1$	Sect. 4.2
	q^ℓ	$O(R_{\mathrm{KA}}(r,\ell)^2 d^{R_{\mathrm{KA}}(r,\ell)}q^{\ell-1})$	$O(R_{\mathrm{KA}}(r,\ell)d^{R_{\mathrm{KA}}(r,\ell)})$	3	Sect. 4.2
Feistel network	q	$O(\lfloor \frac{r}{2}\rfloor^2 d^{\lfloor \frac{r}{2}\rfloor})$	$O(\lfloor \frac{r}{2}\rfloor d^{\lfloor \frac{r}{2}\rfloor})$	3	[4]
	q	$O(rd^{r-2})\P$	$O(1)$	$d^{r-2} + 1$	Sect. 3.3
	q^ℓ	$O(rd^{r-2})\P$	$O(1)$	$d^{r-2} + 1$	Sect. 4.1
	q^ℓ	$O(R_{\mathrm{FN}}(r,\ell)d^{R_{\mathrm{FN}}(r,\ell)-2}q^{\ell-1})\P\ddagger$	$O(1)$	$d^{R_{\mathrm{FN}}(r,\ell)-2} + 1$	Sect. 4.2
	q^ℓ	$O(\lfloor \frac{R_{\mathrm{FN}}(r,\ell)}{2}\rfloor^2 d^{\lfloor \frac{R_{\mathrm{FN}}(r,\ell)}{2}\rfloor}q^{\ell-1})$	$O(\lfloor \frac{R_{\mathrm{FN}}(r,\ell)}{2}\rfloor d^{\lfloor \frac{R_{\mathrm{FN}}(r,\ell)}{2}\rfloor})$	3	Sect. 4.2

$\sharp r \leq \lceil \log_d(q-1)\rceil + \ell - 2$
$\P r \leq \lceil \log_d(q-1)\rceil + \ell$
$\dagger R_{\mathrm{KA}}(r,\ell) = (\lfloor \frac{r+1}{\ell}\rfloor - 1)\ell$
$\ddagger R_{\mathrm{FN}}(r,\ell) = 1 + (\lfloor \frac{r}{\ell}\rfloor - 1)\ell$

Related Work. MiMC has a very a simple round function $F_i(x) := (x+k+c_i)^3$. This design is inspired by the KN cipher of Nyberg and Knudsen [22] and the $\mathcal{PURE}$ cipher of Jakobsen and Knudsen, which is a simplified variant of the KN cipher [16]. The KN cipher is a prototype cipher which is provably secure against linear and differential attacks. However, Jakobsen and Knudsen showed that the KN cipher is vulnerable to the higher-order differential attacks [16]. The same authors introduced interpolation attacks and applied the new method to assess the security of $\mathcal{PURE}$ [16,17].

However, neither the higher-order differential attack [18,19] nor the classical interpolation attack is applicable to MiMC. In both attacks, one needs to guess the last round key which is exactly the master key of MiMC. Thus, one already reaches the complexity of exhaustive key search. By contrast, our low-memory interpolation attack does not need to guess any round key; it is the first low-memory attack applicable to round-reduced MiMC.

Interpolation attacks are known to be efficient against primitives with operations over a large finite field. To improve the attack on bit-oriented primitives, Dinur *et al.* [10] proposed the optimized interpolation attack, which breaks the first version of LowMC. The optimized interpolation attacks exploit higher-order differential properties, building on Shimoyama *et al.* [25]. As pointed out by the designers of MiMC, the degree of any state bits rises quickly when the round function is viewed as a vectorial Boolean function. This makes it impossible to obtain higher-order differentials of MiMC after a few rounds. Hence, the optimized interpolation attacks on MiMC would be infeasible.

Recently, Rechberger *et al.* have introduced difference enumeration techniques to analyze the full LowMC v2 [23]. In order to counter this atack, a new version was proposed called LowMC v3 [5].

We conclude the related work by briefly recalling some recent work on the dedicated low MC stream ciphers Kreyvium and FLIP. Cube attacks [11] and guess-and-determine attacks are common techniques for the cryptanalysis of stream ciphers. Cube attacks based on the division property have been introduced by Todo *et al.* [28] and further improved by Wang *et al.* [29]. They yield the current best key recovery attack on round-reduced Kreyvium. A preliminary version of the stream cipher FLIP [20] has been broken by guess-and-determine attacks [13]. This has resulted in more conservative parameters of the design.

The remainder of this paper is organized as follows. In Sect. 2, we introduce iterated ciphers and recall some classical polynomial algorithms. In Sect. 3, new low-memory interpolation attacks are presented. Section 4 proposes attacks on ciphers with simple key schedules. Applications of our attacks to MiMC are provided in Sect. 5. The final section concludes the paper.

2   Preliminaries

In this section, alternating ciphers and Feistel ciphers are presented. We also recall some polynomial algorithms, which will be used in the sequel.

Notation. We will use the following notation in the sequel.

- Let $\mathbb{F}_q$ be the finite field with q elements, where q is a prime power.
- The symbol "+" stands for addition in the finite field $\mathbb{F}_q$. It can also denote integer addition; we trust that the meaning will be clear from the context.
- d is the degree of the round function $F(x)$, where $d > 1$
- r represents the number of rounds of a block cipher
- κ is the size of key space in bits
- $R(d, q) = \lceil \log_d(q - 1) \rceil$
- T/M/D represent time, memory and data complexities of an attack respectively

2.1 Basic Constructions for Block Ciphers

An r-round *key-alternating (KA) cipher* is constructed by iterating a round function r times where each round consists of a key addition and the application of a nonlinear function F. The ciphertext is obtained by adding a final key k_r to the output of the last round. Let the round function be $F_i(x) = F(x + k_i)$. Then the encryption process is given by

$$E_k(x) = (F_{r-1} \circ F_{r-2} \circ \cdots \circ F_0)(x) + k_r, \tag{1}$$

where k is the master key, k_i is the i-th round key derived from k by a key schedule algorithm, and x and $E_k(x)$ are plaintext and ciphertext, respectively. An r-round KA cipher is depicted in Fig. 1.

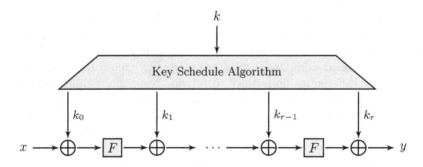

Fig. 1. A key-alternating cipher

An r-round *Feistel Network (FN) cipher* consists of the r-round repetition of a round function F and swap:

$$x_i^L = x_{i-1}^R, \tag{2}$$

$$x_i^R = F(k_i + x_{i-1}^R) + x_{i-1}^L, \tag{3}$$

where $x = x_0^L || x_0^R$ is the plaintext, and the ciphertext is $x_r^R || x_r^L$ since the swap operation is not applied in the last round. One round of an FN cipher is depicted in Fig. 2.

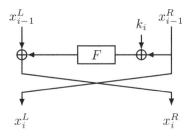

Fig. 2. One round of a Feistel network

In this paper, we always assume that the round function F is a monic polynomial of degree d over $\mathbb{F}_q$, i.e.,

$$F(x) = x^d + \sum_{i=0}^{d-1} a_i x^i,\tag{4}$$

where d is a positive integer and $a_i \in \mathbb{F}_q$.

We associate to the parameters q, κ, d, r (*cf. supra*) a KA cipher $\mathrm{KA}[q, \kappa, d, r]$. Similarly, we define the FN cipher $\mathrm{FN}[q, \kappa, d, r]$. Here q is the size of only half of the state, i.e., the whole state has size q^2. It should be pointed that we ignore the details of the polynomials since our attacks work on the generic constructions regardless of the concrete choice of the components.

How to Choose the Polynomial $F(x)$. Since a block cipher must have invertible round functions, $F(x)$ needs to be a permutation polynomial for KA ciphers. While for FN ciphers, there is no such restriction. It is readily seen that $F(x)$ is the only nonlinear component. For instance, $F(x)$ must have high nonlinearity and low differential uniformity to provide resistance against differential and linear attacks [9,21]. For FHE- and MPC-friendly ciphers, an additional requirement is to minimize the number of multiplications in the implementation of $F(x)$. This motivates the choice of $F(x)$ with very low algebraic degree, such as x^3 in MiMC.

The Number of Rounds. Since we focus on ciphers with low degree components, a large number of rounds is needed to protect against algebraic cryptanalysis. The design goal is to achieve the balance between security and performance. Thus we aim to deduce some lower bounds to preclude algebraic attacks.

2.2 Polynomial Algorithms

This paper measures the time complexity of polynomial algorithms in terms of field operations. Without loss of generality, we also assume that the underlying finite fields support Fast Fourier Transforms (FFTs). Similarly, the memory complexity is estimated with regard to field elements.

Polynomial Interpolation. Assume that $f(x) \in \mathbb{F}_q[x]$ has degree at most n, where n is a positive integer. Consider $(n+1)$ distinct points $\{(x_0, y_0), (x_1, y_1),$ $\cdots, (x_n, y_n)\}$ where $y_i = f(x_i)$ and $x_i \in \mathbb{F}_q$. Then $f(x)$ is uniquely determined by the following Lagrange interpolation formula

$$f(x) = \sum_{i=0}^{n} y_i \cdot \prod_{0 \leq j \leq n, j \neq i} \frac{x - x_j}{x_i - x_j} . \tag{5}$$

It has been shown in [14, 26] that the Lagrange interpolation polynomial can be constructed with time and memory complexity $O(n \log(n))$.

GCD Algorithms. Given two polynomials of degree n with coefficients from $\mathbb{F}_q$, the straightforward Euclidean Algorithm computes the Greatest Common Divisor (GCD) with $O(n^2)$ field operations. The Fast Euclidean Algorithm computes the same GCD in $O(M(n) \log(n))$ field operations, where $M(n)$ is the time to multiply two n-degree polynomials [14]. In this paper, we take $M(n) = O(n \log(n))$. Hence, the time complexity of the GCD algorithm is $O(n \log^2(n))$, which is exactly the estimate used by the MiMC designers [3].

3   Low-Memory Interpolation Attacks

This section presents novel interpolation attacks on primitives with low algebraic degree. Compared with classical interpolation attacks, our new attacks have very low memory complexities. Before giving our attacks, we first recall the classical interpolation attacks.

3.1   Interpolation Attacks

Interpolation attacks were introduced by Jakobsen and Knudsen [16,17]: one considers the (intermediate) ciphertext as a polynomial of plaintext. With sufficiently many plaintext/ciphertext pairs, one can reconstruct this polynomial. Since the polynomial is key-dependent, it is possible to recover some round keys by employing a guess-and-determine strategy.

Assume that a block cipher E has r rounds. First, one finds an upper bound N on the degree of the intermediate ciphertext after $(r-1)$ rounds, denoted with y^{r-1}. Next one guesses the last round key and obtains the corresponding value of y^{r-1}. With $(N+1)$ distinct plaintext/ciphertext pairs, one can construct the polynomial representation of y^{r-1} by Lagrange interpolation. Afterwards, the key guess can be confirmed with an additional plaintext/ciphertext pair. Specifically, one decrypts the last round and evaluates the polynomial in the corresponding plaintext. Then the key guess is considered as a valid key candidate if the decrypted and evaluated values match. Otherwise, the key guess is eliminated and we repeat the process until the correct key is found.

Let L denote the number of all possible last round keys of the cipher E. Then the above attack has time complexity $O(N \log(N) \cdot L)$, memory complexity $O(N)$ and data complexity $N + 2$.

The **meet-in-the-middle (MITM)** approach has also been introduced in [16]. One considers $h(x)$ and $g(y)$ as two polynomials describing the same intermediate state, where x and y denote the plaintext and ciphertext respectively, hence $h(x) = g(y)$. If one substitutes the values of x and y, this yields a linear equation in the unknown coefficients of h and g. By collecting a sufficient number of plaintext/ciphertext pairs, one can solve the linear system to recover these coefficients. Then one can mount a key recovery attack with a similar guess-and-determine strategy as in the original interpolation attack. The only difference is that here we test the key guess by checking if the plaintext/ciphertext pair satisfies the equation $h(x) = g(y)$.

If both the encryption and decryption round functions have low degree, the MITM attack can cryptanalyze more rounds than the original interpolation attack. Let $\deg(h) = N_1$ and $\deg(g) = N_2$. Then one needs to establish $O(N_1 + N_2 + 2)$ linear equations with $O(N_1 + N_2 + 2)$ data and solve these for each key guess. The time and memory complexities are $O((N_1 + N_2 + 2)^2 \cdot L)$ and $O((N_1 + N_2 + 2)^3)$ respectively, where L is the number of last round keys.

We briefly discuss the impact of the MITM attack on different constructions. For any permutation polynomial $g(x) \in \mathbb{F}_q[x]$ with $\deg(g) > 1$, let $g^{-1}(x)$ be the (compositional) inverse of $g(x)$, then

$$g^{-1}(g(x)) \equiv x \pmod{x^q - x}.$$

Hence we have $\deg(g) \cdot \deg(g^{-1}) \geq q$. Note that we always assume that $\deg(g)$ is small, so $\deg(g^{-1})$ can be quite large, i.e., close to q. Thus, for KA$[q, \kappa, d, r]$, there is no benefit to consider the MITM attacks. However, for Feistel networks, we need to take the MITM attack into account since the inverse of the round function has the same degree as the original one.

3.2 Leading Terms of the Output

We present some results on the leading terms, *i.e.*, terms with the highest and the second highest degrees, of the output of KA and FN ciphers. These results will be used in the sequel.

Proposition 1. *Let $f(x) = x^d + \sum_{i=0}^{d-1} a_i x^i$ be the round function of KA$[q, \kappa, d, r]$, where d is a positive integer with $d > 1$ and $a_i \in \mathbb{F}_q$. If $r \leq R(d, q) - 1$, then for KA$[q, \kappa, d, r]$, we have that (i) the algebraic degree of the output is d^r, and (ii) the leading terms of the output are $x^{d^r} + (d_p^r \cdot k_0 + d_p^{r-1} \cdot a_{d-1})x^{d^r - 1}$, where $d \equiv d_p \bmod p$, $0 \leq d_p \leq p-1$ and p is the characteristic of $\mathbb{F}_q$.*

Proof. The claim (i) is a direct corollary of (ii), so it suffices to prove (ii). We will show the result by induction on r. If $r = 1$, then the output is $f(x + k_0) + k_1$. By the binomial theorem, the output can be written as

$$x^d + d \cdot k_0 x^{d-1} + g_1(x) + a_{d-1} x^{d-1} + g_2(x),$$

where $\deg(g_1 + g_2) \leq d - 2$. Hence the leading terms are

$$x^d + (d_p \cdot k_0 + a_{d-1})x^{d-1} \, .$$

Assume that the claim holds for $t - 1$, where $1 \leq t - 1 \leq R(d, q) - 2$. Then the leading terms of the output of round $t - 1$ are

$$x^{d^{t-1}} + (d_p^{t-1} \cdot k_0 + d_p^{t-2} \cdot a_{d-1})x^{d^{t-1}-1} \, .$$

Again, by the binomial theorem, the leading terms of the round t output is

$$\left(x^{d^{t-1}}\right)^d + d \cdot \left(x^{d^{t-1}}\right)^{d-1} (d_p^{t-1} \cdot k_0 + d_p^{t-2} \cdot a_{d-1})x^{d^{t-1}-1}$$
$$= x^{d^t} + \left(d_p^t \cdot k_0 + d_p^{t-1} \cdot a_{d-1}\right) x^{d^t-1} \, ,$$

which implies that the claim is true for t. Therefore, the claim holds for any $r \leq R(d, q) - 1$. □

For $FN[q, \kappa, d, r]$, we consider plaintexts of the form $x\|C$, where C is a constant in $\mathbb{F}_q$. As shown in the following proposition, we can achieve two more rounds compared with KA ciphers.

Proposition 2. *Let* $f(x) = x^d + \sum_{i=0}^{d-1} a_i x^i$ *be the round function of* $FN[q, \kappa, d, r]$, *where d is a positive integer with $d > 1$ and $a_i \in \mathbb{F}_q$. Consider plaintexts of the form $x\|C$, where C is a constant in $\mathbb{F}_q$. If $3 \leq r \leq R(d, q) + 1$, then the leading terms of the right part of the output are $x^{d^{r-2}} + (d_p^{r-2} \cdot (k_1 + f(C + k_0)) + d_p^{r-3} \cdot a_{d-1})x^{d^{r-2}-1}$, where $d \equiv d_p \bmod p$, $0 \leq d_p \leq p - 1$ and p is the characteristic of $\mathbb{F}_q$.*

Proof. The output of the first round is $C\|(x + f(C + k_0))$. This leads to the output $(x + f(C + k_0))\|(f(x + k_1 + f(C + k_0)) + C)$ after the second round and output $(f(x+k_1+f(C+k_0))+C)\|(x+f(C+k_0)+f(f(x+k_1+f(C+k_0))+C+k_2))$ after the third round. Then similarly to Proposition 1, one can prove that the leading terms of the right part of the output are

$$x^{d^{r-2}} + (d_p^{r-2} \cdot (k_1 + f(C + k_0)) + d_p^{r-3} \cdot a_{d-1})x^{d^{r-2}-1}$$

when $3 \leq r \leq R(d, q) + 1$. □

Remark 1. Note that the special case $p = 2$, d odd and $P = x\|C$ or $C\|x$ has been described by Sun et al. [27].

3.3   New Attacks

One of the bottlenecks of classical interpolation attacks is that the attacker always needs to store the whole interpolated polynomial. Thus, the memory complexity can be very high if the degree of the polynomial is high. Based on the result in Sect. 3.2, for certain KA and FN ciphers, the key can be deduced from the second highest term of the interpolated polynomial. Hence, to recover the key, we only need to store the coefficient of the specific term rather than the whole polynomial. In this way, we can present our new interpolation attack with constant memory complexity.

Interpolating One Coefficient. Now we present the algorithm for recovering the coefficient of the second highest term of the interpolated polynomial.

Assume that $g(x) \in \mathbb{F}_q[x]$ has degree at most Δ. Also assume that we know $(\Delta+1)$ points $\{(x_0, y_0), (x_1, y_1), \cdots, (x_\Delta, y_\Delta)\}$, where $x_i = \alpha^i$ for some primitive element $\alpha \in \mathbb{F}_q$ and $y_i = g(x_i)$. Then by the Lagrange interpolation formula, $g(x)$ is uniquely determined by the formula

$$g(x) = \sum_{i=0}^{\Delta} g(\alpha^i) \cdot \prod_{0 \leq j \leq \Delta, j \neq i} \frac{x - \alpha^j}{\alpha^i - \alpha^j} .$$

Let $g(x) = \sum_{i=0}^{\Delta} a_i x^i$, then the coefficient of the second highest term is equal to

$$a_{\Delta-1} = \sum_{i=0}^{\Delta} \frac{-g(\alpha^i) \cdot \sum_{0 \leq j \leq \Delta, j \neq i} \alpha^j}{\prod_{0 \leq j \leq \Delta, j \neq i} (\alpha^i - \alpha^j)} = \sum_{i=0}^{\Delta} g(\alpha^i) \frac{\beta_i}{\gamma_i}, \tag{6}$$

where $\gamma_i = \prod_{0 \leq j \leq \Delta, j \neq i}(\alpha^i - \alpha^j)$ and $\beta_i = -\sum_{0 \leq j \leq \Delta, j \neq i} \alpha^j$. Note that

$$\gamma_{i+1} = \gamma_i \cdot \alpha^\Delta \cdot \frac{\alpha^i - \alpha^{-1}}{\alpha^i - \alpha^\Delta} \quad \text{and} \quad \beta_i = \alpha^i - \sum_{0 \leq j \leq \Delta} \alpha^j .$$

By combining these observations, we present the procedure for recovering only the coefficient of the second highest term in Algorithm 1.

Algorithm 1. Recover the coefficient of the second highest term

---

Input: The algebraic degree Δ of the polynomial, a primitive element $\alpha \in \mathbb{F}_q$, and the polynomial evaluation oracle $\mathcal{O}$
Output: The coefficient t of the second highest term
1: $t \leftarrow 0$
2: $s \leftarrow -\sum_{j=0}^{\Delta} \alpha^j$
3: $a \leftarrow \prod_{j=1}^{\Delta}(1 - \alpha^j)$
4: $b \leftarrow 1$
5: **for** i from 0 to Δ **do**
6:      $t \leftarrow t + \mathcal{O}(b) \cdot \frac{s+b}{a}$
7:      **if** $i < \Delta$ **then**
8:          $a \leftarrow a \cdot \alpha^\Delta \cdot \frac{b - \alpha^{-1}}{b - \alpha^\Delta}$
9:          $b \leftarrow b \cdot \alpha$
10:      **end if**
11: **end for**
12: **return** t

Proposition 3 describes the complexity of Algorithm 1.

Proposition 3. *Algorithm 1 has time complexity* $O(\Delta \log(\Delta))$ *and memory complexity* $O(1)$.

Proof. The time complexity of Algorithm 1 is exactly the time complexity of interpolating one coefficient in Lagrange interpolation, which is shown to be $O(\Delta \log(\Delta))$ in [26]. Due to the simplicity of the algorithm, one can immediately obtain that the memory complexity is $O(1)$.   □

New Attacks on KA. Assume that $d_p \neq 0$ and $r \leq R(d,q) - 1$. Then the attack on $\text{KA}[q, \kappa, d, r]$ is described below.

1. Let $\Delta = d^r$. Choose a primitive element $\alpha \in \mathbb{F}_q$, and the encryption oracle $\mathcal{E}$ as input to Algorithm 1.
2. Run Algorithm 1. Let t be the output.
3. By Proposition 1, we have $t = d_p^r \cdot k_0 + d_p^{r-1} \cdot a_{d-1}$. Therefore, k_0 can be determined from

$$k_0 = \frac{t - d_p^{r-1} \cdot a_{d-1}}{d_p^r} .$$

In the above attack, we need to query the encryption oracle $d^r + 1$ times. The time and memory complexity are dominated by Algorithm 1, which is $O(rd^r)$ and $O(1)$ respectively according to Proposition 3. In summary, the time/memory/data complexities of the attack on $\text{KA}[q, \kappa, d, r]$ are as follows:

$$T = O(rd^r), M = O(1), D = d^r + 1. \tag{7}$$

New Attacks on FN. Assume that $d_p \neq 0$ and $3 \leq r \leq R(d,q) + 1$. For $r \leq R(d,q) + 1$, the attack on $\text{FN}[q, \kappa, d, r]$ is shown below:

1. Let $\Delta = d^{r-2}$ and C_0 be a constant in $\mathbb{F}_q$. Take a primitive element $\alpha \in \mathbb{F}_q$, and the FN encryption oracle $\mathcal{E}$ as input to Algorithm 1. Note that the input of $\mathcal{E}$ is of the form $\alpha^i || C_0$.
2. Run Algorithm 1. Let t be the output.
3. By Proposition 1, we have $t = d_p^{r-2} \cdot (k_1 + f(C + k_0)) + d_p^{r-3} \cdot a_{d-1}$.
4. Pick two other distinct constants C_1 and C_2. Repeat Steps 1–3, assume that the results are t_1 and t_2 respectively. Now we have the system of equations with unknowns k_0 and k_1:

$$\begin{cases} t_0 = d_p^{r-2} \cdot (k_1 + f(C_0 + k_0)) + d_p^{r-3} \cdot a_{d-1}, \\ t_1 = d_p^{r-2} \cdot (k_1 + f(C_1 + k_0)) + d_p^{r-3} \cdot a_{d-1}, \\ t_2 = d_p^{r-2} \cdot (k_1 + f(C_2 + k_0)) + d_p^{r-3} \cdot a_{d-1}. \end{cases} \tag{8}$$

5. From Eq. (8), we obtain

$$f(C_i + k_0) - f(C_j + k_0) - \frac{t_i - t_j}{d_p^{r-2}} = 0,$$

where $0 \leq i < j \leq 2$. Then k_0 can be determined by computing the GCD of the three polynomials of k_0. Finally, one can obtain

$$k_1 = \frac{t_0 - d_p^{r-3} \cdot a_{d-1}}{d_p^{r-2}} - f(C_0 + k_0).$$

Note that $f(x)$ is assumed to have low degree in this paper. Thus, the complexity of Step 5 is negligible. Then similarly to the analysis of attacks on KA ciphers, the complexity of the above attack on $\text{FN}[q, \kappa, d, r]$ is:

$$T = O(rd^{r-2}), M = O(1), D = d^{r-2} + 1 .$$

Discussion. It is worth pointing out that our new attacks are chosen-plaintext attacks since we need to choose plaintexts of a specific form in Algorithm 1. As classical interpolation attacks are known-plaintext attacks, the low-memory interpolation attacks requires a stronger attack model.

Note that Sun *et al.* in [27] also present a low-memory higher-order integral attack which applies to both KA and FN ciphers. However, their attack needs to know the values of the interpolated polynomials over *all* elements in $\mathbb{F}_q$. That is, their attack has data complexity q. Under our assumption, we always have $d^r + 1 \leq q$. Hence, our attack has smaller data complexity than the higher-order integral attack in [27].

An interesting research direction is to break the barrier of the assumption, i.e., determine some key-dependent terms even with $r > R(d, q) + 1$.

4   Attacks on Block Ciphers with Simple Key Schedules

This section proposes attacks on block ciphers with simple key schedules. The first type of attacks are direction applications of the low-memory attack proposed in Sect. 3. The second class of attacks are based on the same strategy and are divided into two groups in terms of memory and data complexities.

We consider ciphers with key space size $\kappa = q^\ell$, i.e., $\text{KA}[q, q^\ell, d, r]$ and $\text{FN}[q, q^\ell, d, r]$, where $2 \leq \ell \leq r+1$. In this section, we assume a simple key schedule. The master key is $k_0 || k_1 || \cdots || k_{\ell-1}$ and the i-th round key is $k_{i \bmod \ell} + c_i$, i.e., the i-th round function is

$$F_i(x) := F(x + k_{i \bmod \ell} + c_i), \ 0 \leq i \leq r ,$$

where F has the form as in (4) and the c_i's are independently chosen constants.

4.1   Iterative Low-Memory Interpolation Attacks

This section presents attacks on block ciphers with simple key schedules by iteratively applying the low-memory attack proposed in Sect. 3.

Our attack is based on the observation that the low-memory interpolation attack is **independent of the key schedule**. Hence, one can recover the first subkey k_0 by the low-memory interpolation attack and then substitute the obtained subkey to peel off the first round. By repeating the process, the remaining subkeys can be determined, as illustrated in Algorithm 2. An interesting property of the attack is that the complexity of the whole attack is dominated by that of recovering the first subkey. Actually, the complexities of recovering the i-th subkey k_i are given by those of the low-memory interpolation attack on the $(r-i)$-round reduced cipher. Thus, by the analysis in Sect. 3.3, the i-th subkey k_i can be determined with complexities:

$$T_i = O(rd^{r-i}), M_i = O(1), D_i = d^{r-i} + 1, \ i = 0, 1, \cdots, \ell - 1.$$

Therefore, the total complexities of the full attack is dominated by those of recovering the subkey k_0, i.e.,

$$T = O(rd^r), M = O(1), D = d^r + 1.$$

Algorithm 2. Attacks on $KA[q, q^\ell, d, r]$ with $r \leq R(d,q) - 1$ and $FN[q, q^\ell, d, r]$ with $r \leq R(d,q) + 1$

---

1. Recover k_0 by the low-memory interpolation attack in Sect. 3.3.
2. Substitute k_0 in the cipher. Then repeat Step 1 to recover k_1.
3. Repeat Step 2 until the master key $k_0||k_1||\cdots||k_{\ell-1}$ is obtained.

Now we elaborate the above attack for the cipher $KA[q, q^2, d, r]$ with a simple key schedule. Assume that $d_p \neq 0$ and $r \leq R(d,q) - 1$. Then the attack is described below.

1. Let $\Delta = d^r$. Choose a primitive element $\alpha \in \mathbb{F}_q$, and the encryption oracle $\mathcal{E}$ as input to Algorithm 1.
2. Run Algorithm 1. Let t be the output.
3. By Proposition 1, we have $t = d_p^r \cdot k_0 + d_p^{r-1} \cdot a_{d-1}$. Therefore, k_0 can be determined from

$$k_0 = \frac{t - d_p^{r-1} \cdot a_{d-1}}{d_p^r}.$$

4. Substitute k_0 in the cipher. Then repeat Steps 1–3 with the minor change that $\Delta = d^{r-1}$. Finally, k_1 can be recovered.

Similar to the discussion in Sect. 3.3, it is readily seen that the time/memory/data complexities of the attack on $KA[q, q^2, d, r]$ are as follows:

$$T = O(rd^r), M = O(1), D = d^r + 1.$$

The following proposition summarize the results in this section.

Proposition 4. *Assume that $r \leq R(d,q) - 1$ for $KA[q, q^\ell, d, r]$ and $r \leq R(d,q) + 1$ for $FN[q, q^\ell, d, r]$. Then there exists an attack on $KA[q, q^\ell, d, r]$ with time complexity $O(rd^r)$, memory complexity $O(1)$, and data complexity $d^r + 1$ while there exists an attack on $FN[q, q^\ell, d, r]$, with time complexity $O(rd^{r-2})$, memory complexity $O(1)$, and data complexity $d^{r-2} + 1$.*

4.2   Attacks Based on Guess-and-Determine Strategies

This section explores the guess-and-determine strategies in the analysis of block ciphers with simple key schedules. We propose a generic attack and then implement the attack with existing techniques.

Based on a guess-and-determine strategy, a generic attack on $KA[q, q^\ell, d, r]$ and $FN[q, q^\ell, d, r]$ is presented in Algorithm 3. The main idea is that after guessing $(\ell - 1)$ subkeys $k_0, k_1, \cdots, k_{\ell-2}$, we can skip the first $(\ell - 1)$ rounds. If the last round key is not $k_{\ell-1}$, by decrypting with the guessed subkeys we can also skip several final rounds until we hit $k_{\ell-1}$. As a result, we only need to consider $R_{KA}(r, \ell)$ and $R_{FN}(r, \ell)$ rounds for $KA[q, q^\ell, d, r]$ and $FN[q, q^\ell, d, r]$ respectively, where

$$R_{KA}(r, \ell) = \left(\left\lfloor \frac{r+1}{\ell} \right\rfloor - 1 \right) \ell \text{ and } R_{FN}(r, \ell) = 1 + \left(\left\lfloor \frac{r}{\ell} \right\rfloor - 1 \right) \ell. \qquad (9)$$

Moreover, the reduced cipher can be regarded as a reduced-round cipher by replacing some key additions with constant additions. This fact allows us to extend the attack on the single key version to large key versions. The above observation has been summarized in the following.

Proposition 5. *Assume that there is an attack on $KA[q, q, d, r]$ or $FN[q, q, d, r]$ with time complexity $T(r)$, memory complexity $M(r)$, and data complexity $D(r)$. Then there exists an attack on $KA[q, q^\ell, d, r]$ or $FN[q, q^\ell, d, r]$ with time complexity $T(R_\lambda(r, \ell))q^{\ell-1}$, memory complexity $M(R_\lambda(r, \ell))$, and data complexity $D(R_\lambda(r, \ell))$, where $\lambda \in \{KA, FN\}$.*

Algorithm 3. Generic attacks on $KA[q, q^\ell, d, r]$ and $FN[q, q^\ell, d, r]$

---

1. Guess subkeys $k_0, k_1, \cdots, k_{\ell-2}$.
2. Mount a key recovery attack on the reduced cipher with $k_{\ell-1}$ the only unknown key. If it fails to recover the remaining $k_{\ell-1}$, then go back to Step 1. Otherwise, one obtains a candidate $k_{\ell-1}^*$.
3. Test the candidate master key $k_0 \| k_1 \| \cdots \| k_{\ell-1}^*$ with an additional random plaintext/ciphertext pair. If the test is passed, then $k_0 \| k_1 \| \cdots \| k_{\ell-1}^*$ is the right key. Otherwise, repeat Steps 1-3 until right keys are found.

We will implement Algorithm 3 with low-memory interpolation and GCD attacks.

Low-Memory Interpolation Attacks. Note that the attack in Sect. 3.3 can be directly applied to the reduced ciphers of $KA[q, q^\ell, d, r]$ and $FN[q, q^\ell, d, r]$. Then by Proposition 5, we have the following result.

Proposition 6. *Assume that $r \leq R(d,q) + \ell - 2$ for $KA[q, q^\ell, d, r]$ and $r \leq R(d,q) + \ell$ for $FN[q, q^\ell, d, r]$. There exists an attack on $KA[q, q^\ell, d, r]$ with time complexity $O(R_{KA}(r, \ell) d^{R_{KA}(r,\ell)} q^{\ell-1})$, memory complexity $O(1)$, and data complexity $d^{R_{KA}(r,\ell)} + 1$ and there exists an attack on $FN[q, q^\ell, d, r]$, with time complexity $O(R_{FN}(r, \ell) d^{R_{FN}(r,\ell)-2} q^{\ell-1})$, memory complexity $O(1)$, and data complexity $d^{R_{FN}(r,\ell)-2} + 1$.*

To illustrate the main procedure, we present an attack on $KA[q, q^2, d, r]$. Assume that $d_p \neq 0, r \leq R(d,q)$ and $r \equiv 0 \pmod 2$. Then the attack is given below.

1. Guess subkey k_0.
2. Let $\Delta = d^{r-2}$. Choose a primitive element $\alpha \in \mathbb{F}_q$, and the encryption oracle $\mathcal{E}$ as input to Algorithm 1.
3. In Line 6 of Algorithm 1, the oracle returns $F^{-1}(\mathcal{E}(F^{-1}(b) + k_0 + c_0) + k_0 + c_r)$, where F^{-1} is the compositional inverse of F. Thus, Algorithm 1 returns the coefficient of the second highest term of the polynomial representing the last $(r-2)$ rounds of the cipher. Run Algorithm 1.
4. Let t be the output of Algorithm 1. By Proposition 1, we have $t = d_p^{r-2} \cdot k_1 + d_p^{r-3} \cdot a_{d-1}$, where the notation is from Proposition 1. Therefore, k_1^* can be determined from $k_1^* = (t - d_p^{r-3} \cdot a_{d-1})/d_p^{r-2}$.
5. Test the candidate master key $k_0 || k_1^*$. If the test is passed, then $k_0 || k_1^*$ is the right key. Otherwise, repeat Steps 1–5 until the right keys are found.

Step 1 needs q guesses in the worst case; for each guess we execute Steps 2–4, that correspond to a low-memory interpolation attack on an $(r-2)$-round reduced cipher. From Eq. (7) the complexity of the above attack is given by

$$T = O(rd^{r-2}q), M = O(1), D = d^{r-2} + 1.$$

GCD Attacks. The GCD attack on MiMC was introduced by Albrecht *et al.* [3]: it deduces the key by computing the greatest common divisor of polynomials from known plaintext/ciphertext pairs. The GCD attack enjoys very low data complexity, which makes it appropriate in a low-data scenario. It is straightforward to plug the attack into the framework of Algorithm 3. We will present GCD attacks on $KA[q, q^\ell, d, r]$ and $FN[q, q^\ell, d, r]$.

Denote by $E(x)$ the encryption of plaintext x under the key $k_0 || k_1 || \cdots || k_{\ell-1}$. The GCD attack on $KA[q, q^\ell, d, r]$ proceeds as follows:

1. Guess subkey $k_0, k_1, \cdots, k_{\ell-2}$.
2. Denote by $E(k_{\ell-1}, x)$ the output of the $R_{KA}(r, \ell)$-round reduced cipher with input x. For any two different plaintext/ciphertext pairs, one can obtain the corresponding input/output pairs (x_i, y_i) for $i = 0, 1$.
3. Compute the univariate polynomial $E(K, x_i) - y_i$ explicitly for $i = 0, 1$. It is clear that these polynomials share $K - k_{\ell-1}$ as a factor if the key guess is correct. Indeed, in this case with high probability $\gcd(E(K, x_0) - y_0, E(K, x_1) - y_1) = K - k_{\ell-1}$.

4. Compute $\gcd(E(K, x_0) - y_0, E(K, x_1) - y_1)$. If the result is 1 or has only irreducible factors with degree larger than two, then the key guess is wrong and we go back to Step 1. Otherwise, the constant part of the linear factors of the result are candidates for $k_{\ell-1}$, denoted by $k_{\ell-1}^*$.
5. Test the candidate master key $k_0 || k_1 || \cdots || k_{\ell-1}^*$. If the test is passed, then $k_0 || k_1 || \cdots || k_{\ell-1}^*$ is the right key. Otherwise, repeat Steps 1–6 until the right keys are found.

As we show in Appendix A, Step 3 can be implemented with both time and memory complexities $O(R_{\mathsf{KA}}(r, \ell) d^{R_{\mathsf{KA}}(r,\ell)})$. Note that both of the polynomials $E(K, x_0) - y_0$ and $E(K, x_1) - y_1$ have degree $d^{R_{\mathsf{KA}}(r,\ell)}$. Then, by the estimation in Sect. 2.2, the complexity of computing greatest common divisors in Step 4 is $O(R_{\mathsf{KA}}(r, \ell)^2 d^{R_{\mathsf{KA}}(r,\ell)})$. Thus, the time complexity for each subkey guess is dominated by the computation of the greatest common divisor, i.e., $O(R_{\mathsf{KA}}(r, \ell)^2 d^{R_{\mathsf{KA}}(r,\ell)})$. Therefore, the total time complexity of the above attack is $O(R_{\mathsf{KA}}(r, \ell)^2 d^{R_{\mathsf{KA}}(r,\ell)} q^{\ell-1})$. Moreover, the memory consumption is around $O(R_{\mathsf{KA}}(r, \ell) d^{R_{\mathsf{KA}}(r,\ell)})$ since Step 3 dominates the memory complexity. Notably, we only need three plaintext/ciphertext pairs. To sum up, the time/memory/data complexities of the above attack are given by

$$T = O(R_{\mathsf{KA}}(r, \ell)^2 d^{R_{\mathsf{KA}}(r,\ell)} q^{\ell-1}), M = O(R_{\mathsf{KA}}(r, \ell) d^{R_{\mathsf{KA}}(r,\ell)}), D = 3.$$

With the MITM approach, one can mount an attack on $\mathrm{FN}[q, q^{\ell}, d, r]$ with similar complexity but double the number of rounds attainable. Now we sketch the main idea by the attack on $\mathrm{FN}[q, q, d, r]$. First, we construct two polynomials $G(K, x)$ and $H(K, y)$ representing the state after round $\lceil r/2 \rceil$ as a polynomial in the unknown key and the plaintext or ciphertext respectively. Then the key can be deduced by computing the greatest common divisor of two polynomials $G(K, x_0) - H(K, y_0)$ and $G(K, x_1) - H(K, y_1)$ whose degrees are upper bounded by $d^{\lfloor r/2 \rfloor}$. Hence, the time/memory/data complexities of the above attack are given by

$$T = O(\lfloor r/2 \rfloor^2 d^{\lfloor r/2 \rfloor}), M = O(\lfloor r/2 \rfloor d^{\lfloor r/2 \rfloor}), D = 3.$$

We can generalize the above attack to $\mathrm{FN}[q, q^{\ell}, d, r]$ with slight modifications. Note that we only need to consider the $R_{\mathsf{FN}}(r, \ell)$-round cipher after the subkey guessing. Next, we compute two polynomials $G(K, x)$ and $H(K, y)$ representing the state after round $\lceil R_{\mathsf{FN}}(r, \ell)/2 \rceil$ of the reduced cipher as a polynomial in the unknown $k_{\ell-1}$ and the input or output of the reduced cipher respectively. Then consider the two polynomials $G(K, x_0) - H(K, y_0)$ and $G(K, x_1) - H(K, y_1)$. The remaining steps of the GCD computation and key filtering are the same as in the case $\mathrm{KA}[q, q^{\ell}, d, r]$. Hence, we omit the details. Similar to the attack on $\mathrm{FN}[q, q, d, r]$, we have that the complexity of the attack on $\mathrm{FN}[q, q^{\ell}, d, r]$ equals

$$T = O(\lfloor R_{\mathsf{FN}}(r, \ell)/2 \rfloor^2 d^{\lfloor R_{\mathsf{FN}}(r,\ell)/2 \rfloor} q^{\ell-1}), M = O(\lfloor R_{\mathsf{FN}}(r, \ell)/2 \rfloor d^{\lfloor R_{\mathsf{FN}}(r,\ell)/2 \rfloor}), D = 3.$$

In this way, with similar complexities one can double the number of rounds attainable compared with the GCD attack on $\mathrm{KA}[q, q^{\ell}, d, r]$.

We summarize the discussion in the following result.

Proposition 7. *There exists an attack on* $KA[q, q^\ell, d, r]$ *with time complexity* $O(R_{KA}(r, \ell)^2 d^{R_{KA}(r,\ell)} q^{\ell-1})$, *memory complexity* $O(R_{KA}(r, \ell) d^{R_{KA}(r,\ell)})$, *and data complexity 3, and there exists an attack on for* $FN[q, q^\ell, d, r]$ *with time complexity* $O(\lfloor R_{FN}(r, \ell)/2 \rfloor^2 d^{\lfloor R_{FN}(r,\ell)/2 \rfloor} q^{\ell-1})$, *memory* *complexity* $O(\lfloor R_{FN}(r, \ell)/2 \rfloor d^{\lfloor R_{FN}(r,\ell)/2 \rfloor})$, *and data complexity 3.*

Remark 2. GCD attacks enjoy very low data complexity while they suffer large memory complexity since one needs to compute and store the two polynomials. Thus, the low-memory interpolation attack and low data GCD attacks are not superior to each other.

5   Applications to MiMC

In this section, we apply our new techniques to the block cipher MiMC. Using our new techniques, we can break a variant of MiMC with memory restriction on attacks and lower the attack complexity of the larger key versions.

5.1   Description of MiMC

MiMC is a family of block cipher designs operating entirely over the finite field $\mathbb{F}_q$; they can be seen as generalizations of the KN-cipher [22] and $\mathcal{PURE}$ [16]. The design aims to achieve an efficient implementation over a field $\mathbb{F}_q$ —especially the large prime field $\mathbb{F}_p$—by minimizing computationally expensive field operations, e.g. multiplications or exponentiations.

MiMC- n/n. Let q be a prime or power of 2 such that $\gcd(3, q - 1) = 1$. For a message $x \in \mathbb{F}_q$ and a secret key $k \in \mathbb{F}_q$, the encryption process of MiMC-n/n is constructed by iterating a round function r times. At round i, the round function is defined as

$$F_i(x) := (x + k + c_i)^3,$$

where the c_i's are random constants in $\mathbb{F}_q$ and $c_0 = c_r = 0$. Then the encryption process is given by

$$E_k(x) = (F_{r-1} \circ F_{r-2} \circ \cdots \circ F_0)(x) + k.$$

The number of rounds is given by $r = \lceil \frac{\log_2(q)}{\log_2(3)} \rceil$.

MiMC- $2n/n$ (Feistel). By employing the same permutation polynomial in FN, one can process larger blocks and have the same circuit for encryption and decryption. The round function of MiMC-$2n/n$ is defined by

$$x_i^L || x_i^R \leftarrow x_{i-1}^R + (x_{i-1}^L + k + c_i)^3 || x_{i-1}^L,$$

where the c_i's are random constants in $\mathbb{F}_q$ and $c_0 = c_r = 0$. The swap operation is not applied in the last round. The number of rounds is given by $r' = 2 \cdot \lceil \frac{\log_2(q)}{\log_2(3)} \rceil$.

5.2 Attacks on a Variant with Low Memory Complexity

This section presents an attack on an instantiation of MiMC where the memory available to the attacker is limited. Our results indicate that the number of rounds proposed by the designers is too optimistic.

In [3], the designers consider the case in which there is a restriction on the memory available to the attacker. In this setting, many memory-consuming attacks will be infeasible. According to the designers, this enables the reduction of the number of rounds to gain better performance. To be specific, the authors claim that this restriction has a great impact on interpolation attacks and GCD attacks. Indeed, the problem arises if the attacker is not able to store all the coefficients of the interpolation polynomial and similar for the GCD attack.

For MiMC-129/129, the number of rounds is $82 = \left\lceil \frac{129}{\log_2(3)} \right\rceil$ in the original design. A much more aggressive version with only 38 rounds is proposed under the assumption that the attacker is restricted to a memory of 2^{64} bytes.

The Attack. We note that the 38-round MiMC-129/129 fits into the model of $\text{KA}[2^{129}, 2^{129}, 3, 38]$. Additionally, we have $d_p = 1$ in this case. Then we can adapt the attack on $\text{KA}[q, \kappa, d, r]$ to this concrete cipher. The attack is given below.

1. Let $\Delta = 3^{38}$. Choose a primitive element $\alpha \in \mathbb{F}_{2^{129}}$, and the encryption oracle 38-round MiMC-129/129 as input to Algorithm 1.
2. Run Algorithm 1. Let t be the output.
3. By Proposition 1, we have $k = t$ since $c_0 = 0, d_p = 1$ and $a_{d-1} = 0$.

Complexity Analysis. In this attack, we need to query the encryption oracle $3^{38} + 1$ times, i.e, around $2^{60.23}$. Actually, the time complexity is dominated by the running time of Algorithm 1, which is around $38 \cdot (3^{38} + 1)$, i.e., $2^{65.48}$. The data complexity is also $3^{38} + 1$, i.e, around $2^{60.23}$. Finally, as we can see, the memory complexity is *negligible*.

Our low-memory interpolation attacks have the same time complexity as classical interpolation attack with negligible memory complexity. This implies that the number of round **cannot be smaller than** $\left\lceil \frac{\log_2(q)}{\log_2(3)} \right\rceil$ even if there is a restriction on the memory available to the attacker.

Discussion. It is worth pointing out that neither of the classical interpolation attacks nor higher-order differential attacks work on MiMC-n/n. In both attacks, one needs to guess the last round key which is exactly the master key of MiMC. This leads to an attack with complexity worse than exhaustive key search. By contrast, our low-memory interpolation attack does not need to guess any round key. Therefore, our attack is the first low-memory attack against MiMC.

5.3 Attacks on Larger Key Versions

This section shows attacks on variants of MiMC with a larger key size. Our results indicate that the security margin is less than claimed by the designers.

Instead of adding the same key in each round, a variant of MiMC is proposed with a key length that is equal to ℓ times the block length. In this case, we cyclically add ℓ independent keys. That is, at round i, the round function is defined as

$$F_i(x) := (x + k_{i \bmod \ell} + c_i)^3,$$

where the c_i's are random constants in $\mathbb{F}_q$ and $c_0 = c_r = 0$.

We note that the MiMC-n/n and MiMC-$2n/n$ with larger key size fit into the model of $KA[q, q^\ell, 3, r]$ and $FN[q, q^\ell, 3, r]$ respectively. Then by Propositions 4, 6 and 7, we have the following results.

Proposition 8. *Let $R_{KA}(r, \ell)$ and $R_{FN}(r, \ell)$ be given as in Eq. (9). (i) Assume that $r \leq \lceil \log_3(q - 1) \rceil - 1$ for $KA[q, q^\ell, 3, r]$ and $r \leq \lceil \log_3(q - 1) \rceil + 1$ for $FN[q, q^\ell, 3, r]$. There exists an attack on r-round MiMC-n/n with key size ℓn having complexity $T = O(r3^r), M = O(1), D = 3^r + 1$. While for MiMC-$2n/n$ with key size ℓn, there exists an attack with complexity $T = O(r3^{r-2}), M = O(1), D = 3^{r-2} + 1$.*

(ii) Assume that $r \leq \lceil \log_3(q-1) \rceil + \ell - 2$ for $KA[q, q^\ell, 3, r]$ and $r \leq \lceil \log_3(q - 1) \rceil + \ell$ for $FN[q, q^\ell, 3, r]$. There exists an attack on r-round MiMC-n/n with key size ℓn having complexity $T = O(R_{KA}(r, \ell)3^{R_{KA}(r,\ell)}q^{\ell-1}), M = O(1), D = 3^{R_{KA}(r,\ell)} + 1$. While for MiMC-$2n/n$ with key size ℓn, there exists an attack with complexity $T = O(R_{FN}(r, \ell)3^{R_{FN}(r,\ell)-2}q^{\ell-1}), M = O(1), D = 3^{R_{FN}(r,\ell)-2} + 1$.

(iii) There exists an attack on r-round MiMC-n/n having key size ℓn with complexity $T = O(R_{KA}(r, \ell)^2 3^{R_{KA}(r,\ell)} q^{\ell-1}), M = O(R_{KA}(r, \ell)3^{R_{KA}(r,\ell)}), D = 3$. While for r-round MiMC-$2n/n$ having key size ℓn, there exists attacks with complexity $T = O(\lfloor R_{FN}(r, \ell)/2 \rfloor^2 3^{\lfloor R_{FN}(r,\ell)/2 \rfloor} q^{\ell-1}), M = O(\lfloor R_{FN}(r, \ell)/2 \rfloor 3^{\lfloor R_{FN}(r,\ell)/2 \rfloor}), D = 3$.

The designers of MiMC-n/n analyze the case $\ell = 2$ [3]. By computing the Gröbner basis the time complexity equals $O(4 \cdot 3^{3r})$ while the resultant algorithms lead to a complexity of $O(3^{4.69r})$. By Proposition 8 (i), our attacks have time complexity $O(r3^r)$ if $r \leq \lceil \log_3(q-1) \rceil - 1$. While for $r \geq \lceil \log_3(q-1) \rceil$, by Proposition 8 (ii), our attacks have asymptotic time complexity $O(r3^{2r-1})$. Therefore, our analysis shows a smaller security margin of the MiMC-n/n instance with larger key size.

For MiMC-$2n/n$, by Proposition 8 (i) and (iii), our attacks have time complexity $O(r3^{r-2})$ if $r \leq \lceil \log_3(q-1) \rceil - 1$ and $O(r^2 3^{\lfloor \frac{3r-2}{2} \rfloor - 1})$ if $r \geq \lceil \log_3(q-1) \rceil$.

The MiMC designers claimed that their security bounds $O(4 \cdot 3^{3r})$ and $O(3^{4.69r})$ can be improved by an MITM approach [4, p. 18]. However, there were no details on the claim. Our reduced bound is the first tighter bound which is derived from a specific attack.

5.4   Verification on MiMC over Small Fields

We have verified our attack experimentally. For instance, we have implemented the low-memory interpolation attack on 10-round MiMC-17/17. As a result, we can recover the key in 1.3 s with Sage.

We have also implemented the GCD attacks on larger key versions. Take $\ell = 2$, for finite fields with small size, one can recover the master key in practical time with Sage. For example, one can recover the key in less than one hour for 7-round MiMC-11/11.

We have also carried out experiments to evaluate the behavior of the GCD value obtained after guessing certain round keys when the GCD attack is applied to the larger key version. Again we take $\ell = 2$. The experiments are performed in fields $\mathbb{F}_q$ with $q \leq 2^{17}$. We take random plaintext/ciphertext pairs to obtain the distribution of GCD values. Our experiments show the following results:

- When the key guess k_0 is correct, we can always obtain the GCD value $K - k_1$.
- When the key guess k_0 is wrong, mostly we get GCD value 1 hence we can eliminate the wrong key guess immediately. With small probability, say less than 1%, we can get nontrivial GCD values and even a linear factor $K - a$. In this case, a is considered as a valid candidate that can be filtered out with an additional test.

The above observations support the settings of the attack described in Sect. 4.2.

6   Concluding Remarks

This paper has shown that the memory requirements for classical interpolation attacks can be reduced substantially, resulting in practical attacks on primitives with low algebraic degrees. For a simple key schedule, we present generic attacks that have either constant memory or constant data complexity. To illustrate our techniques, we have applied the new attacks to the block cipher MiMC. As a result, we can break a round-reduced version of MiMC with low memory complexity and we can reduce the attack complexity of the larger key versions. However, our results do not affect the security claims of the full round MiMC. To the best of our knowledge, our analysis of MiMC is the first third-party cryptanalysis of MiMC.

For future research, it is of interest to assess the security of MiMC with original key size, i.e., a single key addition in all rounds. It remains unclear if the approaches in this paper can be applied to the new proposal GMiMC. Moreover, it is an open problem to analyze the security of the MiMC-based hash function MiMCHash.

Acknowledgement. The authors thank the anonymous reviewers for many helpful comments. The work is supported by the Research Council KU Leuven under the grant C16/15/058 and by the European Union's Horizon 2020 research and innovation programme under grant agreement No. H2020-MSCA-ITN-2014-643161 ECRYPT-NET.

A   Algorithm for Computing $E(K, x_i) - y_i$

This section describes the algorithm to obtain the explicit expression of $E(K, x_i) - y_i$ which is used in Step 3 of the GCD attacks in Sect. 4.2. Recall that here K is the variable and (x_i, y_i) is an input/output pair corresponding to some plaintext/ciphertext pair.

1. Select $d^{R_{\text{KA}}(r,\ell)} + 1$ different values $\alpha_0, \cdots, \alpha_{d^{R_{\text{KA}}(r,\ell)}} \in \mathbb{F}_q$.
2. Compute $\beta_j = E(\alpha_j, x_i) - y_i$ for $i = 0, 1$ and $0 \le j \le d^{R_{\text{KA}}(r,\ell)}$.
3. Interpolate the polynomial $g_i(x)$ such that $g_i(\alpha_j) = \beta_j$ for $i = 0, 1$ and $0 \le j \le d^{R_{\text{KA}}(r,\ell)}$.

First observe that the iterative structure of $E(K, x_i) - y_i$ enables us to evaluate $E(\alpha_j, x_i) - y_i$ round by round. In each round one needs to evaluate a polynomial with constant degree, which can be done in constant time. Hence, each β_j is obtained with complexity only $O(R_{\text{KA}}(r, \ell))$ though the degree is $d^{R_{\text{KA}}(r,\ell)}$. It follows that the second step has time complexity $O(R_{\text{KA}}(r, \ell)d^{R_{\text{KA}}(r,\ell)})$. The third step is a standard polynomial interpolation with complexity $O(R_{\text{KA}}(r, \ell)d^{R_{\text{KA}}(r,\ell)})$. Hence, the total time complexity is $O(R_{\text{KA}}(r, \ell)d^{R_{\text{KA}}(r,\ell)})$. The memory complexities of the algorithm is $O(R_{\text{KA}}(r, \ell)d^{R_{\text{KA}}(r,\ell)})$ due to the polynomial interpolation in the third step [14].

References

1. Albrecht, M.R., et al.: Algebraic cryptanalysis of STARK-friendly designs: application to MARVELlous and MiMC. Cryptology ePrint Archive, Report 2019/419 (2019). https://eprint.iacr.org/2019/419
2. Albrecht, M.R., et al.: Feistel structures for MPC, and more. Cryptology ePrint Archive, Report 2019/397 (2019). https://eprint.iacr.org/2019/397
3. Albrecht, M., Grassi, L., Rechberger, C., Roy, A., Tiessen, T.: MiMC: efficient encryption and cryptographic hashing with minimal multiplicative complexity. In: Cheon, J.H., Takagi, T. (eds.) ASIACRYPT 2016. LNCS, vol. 10031, pp. 191–219. Springer, Heidelberg (2016). https://doi.org/10.1007/978-3-662-53887-6_7
4. Albrecht, M.R., Grassi, L., Rechberger, C., Roy, A., Tiessen, T.: MiMC: efficient encryption and cryptographic hashing with minimal multiplicative complexity. Cryptology ePrint Archive, Report 2016/492 (2016). https://eprint.iacr.org/2016/492
5. Albrecht, M.R., Rechberger, C., Schneider, T., Tiessen, T., Zohner, M.: Ciphers for MPC and FHE. In: Oswald, E., Fischlin, M. (eds.) EUROCRYPT 2015. LNCS, vol. 9056, pp. 430–454. Springer, Heidelberg (2015). https://doi.org/10.1007/978-3-662-46800-5_17
6. Ben-Sasson, E., Bentov, I., Horesh, Y., Riabzev, M.: Scalable, transparent, and post-quantum secure computational integrity. Cryptology ePrint Archive, Report 2018/046 (2018). https://eprint.iacr.org/2018/046
7. Ben-Sasson, E., Chiesa, A., Genkin, D., Tromer, E., Virza, M.: SNARKs for C: verifying program executions succinctly and in zero knowledge. In: Canetti, R., Garay, J.A. (eds.) CRYPTO 2013. LNCS, vol. 8043, pp. 90–108. Springer, Heidelberg (2013). https://doi.org/10.1007/978-3-642-40084-1_6
8. Canteaut, A., et al.: Stream ciphers: a practical solution for efficient homomorphic-ciphertext compression. In: Peyrin, T. (ed.) FSE 2016. LNCS, vol. 9783, pp. 313–333. Springer, Heidelberg (2016). https://doi.org/10.1007/978-3-662-52993-5_16
9. Daemen, J., Rijmen, V.: The Design of Rijndael: AES - the advanced encryption standard. In: Information Security and Cryptography. Springer (2002)

10. Dinur, I., Liu, Y., Meier, W., Wang, Q.: Optimized interpolation attacks on LowMC. In: Iwata, T., Cheon, J.H. (eds.) ASIACRYPT 2015. LNCS, vol. 9453, pp. 535–560. Springer, Heidelberg (2015). https://doi.org/10.1007/978-3-662-48800-3_22

11. Dinur, I., Shamir, A.: Cube attacks on tweakable black box polynomials. In: Joux, A. (ed.) EUROCRYPT 2009. LNCS, vol. 5479, pp. 278–299. Springer, Heidelberg (2009). https://doi.org/10.1007/978-3-642-01001-9_16

12. Dobraunig, C., et al.: Rasta: a cipher with low ANDdepth and few ANDs per bit. In: Shacham, H., Boldyreva, A. (eds.) CRYPTO 2018. LNCS, vol. 10991, pp. 662–692. Springer, Cham (2018). https://doi.org/10.1007/978-3-319-96884-1_22

13. Duval, S., Lallemand, V., Rotella, Y.: Cryptanalysis of the FLIP family of stream ciphers. In: Robshaw, M., Katz, J. (eds.) CRYPTO 2016. LNCS, vol. 9814, pp. 457–475. Springer, Heidelberg (2016). https://doi.org/10.1007/978-3-662-53018-4_17

14. von zur Gathen, J., Gerhard, J.: Modern Computer Algebra, 3rd edn. Cambridge University Press (2013)

15. Grassi, L., Rechberger, C., Rotaru, D., Scholl, P., Smart, N.P.: MPC-friendly symmetric key primitives. In: Proceedings of the 2016 ACM SIGSAC Conference on Computer and Communications Security, Vienna, Austria, 24–28 October 2016, pp. 430–443 (2016)

16. Jakobsen, T., Knudsen, L.R.: The interpolation attack on block ciphers. In: Biham, E. (ed.) FSE 1997. LNCS, vol. 1267, pp. 28–40. Springer, Heidelberg (1997). https://doi.org/10.1007/BFb0052332

17. Jakobsen, T., Knudsen, L.R.: Attacks on block ciphers of low algebraic degree. J. Cryptol. **14**(3), 197–210 (2001)

18. Knudsen, L.R.: Truncated and higher order differentials. In: Preneel, B. (ed.) FSE 1994. LNCS, vol. 1008, pp. 196–211. Springer, Heidelberg (1995). https://doi.org/10.1007/3-540-60590-8_16

19. Lai, X.: Higher order derivatives and differential cryptanalysis. In: Communications and Cryptography. The Springer International Series in Engineering and Computer Science, vol. 276, pp. 227–233 (1994)

20. Méaux, P., Journault, A., Standaert, F.-X., Carlet, C.: Towards stream ciphers for efficient FHE with low-noise ciphertexts. In: Fischlin, M., Coron, J.-S. (eds.) EUROCRYPT 2016, Part I. LNCS, vol. 9665, pp. 311–343. Springer, Heidelberg (2016). https://doi.org/10.1007/978-3-662-49890-3_13

21. Nyberg, K.: Differentially uniform mappings for cryptography. In: Helleseth, T. (ed.) EUROCRYPT 1993. LNCS, vol. 765, pp. 55–64. Springer, Heidelberg (1994). https://doi.org/10.1007/3-540-48285-7_6

22. Nyberg, K., Knudsen, L.R.: Provable security against a differential attack. J. Cryptol. **8**(1), 27–37 (1995)

23. Rechberger, C., Soleimany, H., Tiessen, T.: Cryptanalysis of low-data instances of full LowMCv2. IACR Trans. Symmetric Cryptol. **2018**(3), 163–181 (2018). https://doi.org/10.13154/tosc.v2018.i3.163-181, https://tosc.iacr.org/index.php/ToSC/article/view/7300

24. Shannon, C.E.: Communication theory of secrecy systems. Bell Syst. Tech. J. **28**(4), 656–715 (1949)

25. Shimoyama, T., Moriai, S., Kaneko, T.: Improving the higher order differential attack and cryptanalysis of the KN cipher. In: Okamoto, E., Davida, G., Mambo, M. (eds.) ISW 1997. LNCS, vol. 1396, pp. 32–42. Springer, Heidelberg (1998). https://doi.org/10.1007/BFb0030406

26. Stoß, H.: The complexity of evaluating interpolation polynomials. Theor. Comput. Sci. **41**, 319–323 (1985)

27. Sun, B., Qu, L., Li, C.: New Cryptanalysis of block ciphers with low algebraic degree. In: Dunkelman, O. (ed.) FSE 2009. LNCS, vol. 5665, pp. 180–192. Springer, Heidelberg (2009). https://doi.org/10.1007/978-3-642-03317-9_11

28. Todo, Y., Isobe, T., Hao, Y., Meier, W.: Cube attacks on non-blackbox polynomials based on division property. In: Katz, J., Shacham, H. (eds.) CRYPTO 2017, Part III. LNCS, vol. 10403, pp. 250–279. Springer, Cham (2017). https://doi.org/10.1007/978-3-319-63697-9_9

29. Wang, Q., Hao, Y., Todo, Y., Li, C., Isobe, T., Meier, W.: Improved division property based cube attacks exploiting algebraic properties of superpoly. In: Shacham, H., Boldyreva, A. (eds.) CRYPTO 2018, Part I. LNCS, vol. 10991, pp. 275–305. Springer, Cham (2018). https://doi.org/10.1007/978-3-319-96884-1_10

A General Framework
for the Related-Key Linear Attack
Against Block Ciphers
with Linear Key Schedules

Jung-Keun Lee[(⊠)], Bonwook Koo, and Woo-Hwan Kim

The Affiliated Institute of ETRI, Daejeon, Republic of Korea
{jklee,bwkoo,whkim5}@nsr.re.kr

Abstract. We present a general framework for the related-key linear attack that can be applied to iterative block ciphers with linear key schedules. The attack utilizes a newly introduced *related-key linear approximation* that is obtained directly from a linear trail. The attack makes use of a known related-key data consisting of triplets of a plaintext, a ciphertext, and a key difference such that the ciphertext is the encrypted value of the plaintext under the key that is the xor of the key to be recovered and the specified key difference. If such a block cipher has a linear trail with linear correlation ϵ, it admits attacks with related-key data of size $O(\epsilon^{-2})$ just as in the case of classical Matsui's Algorithms. But since the attack makes use of a related-key data, the attacker can use a linear trail with the squared correlation less than 2^{-n}, n being the block size, in case the key size is larger than n. Moreover, the standard key hypotheses seem to be appropriate even when the trail is not dominant as validated by experiments.

The attack can be applied in two ways. First, using a linear trail with squared correlation smaller than 2^{-n}, one can get an effective attack covering more rounds than existing attacks against some ciphers, such as SIMON48/96, SIMON64/128 and SIMON128/256. Secondly, using a trail with large squared correlation, one can use related-key data for key recovery even when the data is not suitable for existing linear attacks.

Keywords: Related-key attack · Linear cryptanalysis · Linear key schedule · SIMON

1 Introduction

In recent years many lightweight block ciphers have been proposed targeting resource-constrained platforms. They adopt simple key schedules to get competitive performance figures in terms of the resource requirements. In this regard not a few of them have linear key schedules. (e.g. GIFT [3], SKINNY [6], MIDORI [2], SIMON [4], ZORRO [21], PRINCE [14], LED [22], PICCOLO [39], KATAN [15].) However, there are little cryptanalytic techniques that are applicable to general block

© Springer Nature Switzerland AG 2020
K. G. Paterson and D. Stebila (Eds.): SAC 2019, LNCS 11959, pp. 194–224, 2020.
https://doi.org/10.1007/978-3-030-38471-5_9

Table 1. Attack results on SIMON

Cipher (# rounds)	# attacked rounds	Computation	Data	$Pr_{success}$	Attack	Ref.
SIMON32/64 (32)	**23**	$2^{46.65}$	$2^{46.3}$	0.5	RKLC	Here
	23	$2^{56.3}$	$2^{31.19}$	0.28	LC	[16]
	21	$2^{55.25}$	2^{31}	0.51	DC	[41]
SIMON48/96 (36)	**28**	$2^{71.07}$	$2^{70.9}$	0.5	RKLC	Here
	25	$2^{88.28}$	$2^{47.92}$	0.445*	LC	[16]
	24	$2^{87.25}$	2^{47}	0.48	DC	[41]
SIMON64/128 (44)	**34**	$2^{95.5}$	$2^{95.32}$	0.5	RKLC	Here
	31	2^{120}	$2^{63.53}$	0.316*	LC	[16]
	29	$2^{116.25}$	2^{63}	0.46	DC	[41]
SIMON128/256 (72)	**62**	$2^{190.76}$	$2^{190.4}$	0.5	RKLC	Here
	55	2^{175}	$2^{174.73}$	0.5	RKLC	Here
	53	$2^{248.01}$	$2^{127.6}$	0.315*	LC	[16]
	50	$2^{247.25}$	2^{127}	0.48	DC	[41]

* Estimates based on [8] under an assumption on the distribution of correlations [19]

ciphers of such a kind. In this work, we will present a framework for the related-key linear attack that can be applied to generic iterative block ciphers with linear key schedules. Since the linear attack was publicized by Matsui [33], there have been many extensions such as attacks using linear hulls [34,36], multiple linear attacks [7,27], multidimensional linear attacks [17,23,25] and zero-correlation attacks [13]. Though there are lots of works regarding the related-key attacks against block ciphers using differential characteristics, there are not many dealing with the related-key linear attacks. The current work tries to address this issue.

1.1   Our Contributions

- We present a general framework for the related-key linear attack that is applicable to block ciphers with linear key schedules. It is based on classical Matsui's Algorithms and makes use of a related-key linear approximations that can be obtained from an ordinary linear trail in a straightforward way. We also provide a statistical model for the attack from which we derive estimates for the success probability and the attack complexities.
- We present experimental results that confirm the validity of our framework including the appropriateness of the statistical model we presume. We consider small-scale variants of SIMON and a variant of PRESENT with a linear key schedule for the experiments.
- We present related-key linear attacks on SIMON whose results are summarized in Table 1. The attacks cover more rounds than existing attacks and can be

regarded to be better than the generic related-key attack [28] with known key differences and random plaintexts in terms of the attack complexities.

1.2 Related Works

Related-Key Linear Attacks. The idea of using related keys in linear attacks appears in a small number of previous works. Vora et al. [40] described an attack against a round-reduced DES based on a coding theory framework claiming that using related keys one can marginally improve the single-key linear attacks. Hermelin et al. [24] claim a related-key linear attack against the full PRESENT-128 using very special types of chosen key differences based on some assumption regarding the capacity of multidimensional approximations. Bogdadov et al. [10] presented a key recovery attack using related-key linear distinguishers with chosen key differences. Their method works against block ciphers whose key schedules admit certain invariance property. The related-key attack presented in this work uses keys with known differences though it works against block ciphers with linear key schedules.

Linear Attacks Using a Linear Approximation with the Small Correlation. A linear approximation of a block cipher with correlation $<2^{-n/2}$ is usually considered not of much use except when it is exploited in a multiple linear attack together with other approximations. Beierle et al. [6] argue that the SKINNY ciphers are secure against related-tweakey linear attacks by presenting bounds on the correlations of linear trails as the number of rounds increases, taking into account the fact that the attacker may utilize the tweakey as the additional data source. Kranz et al. [31] show that the linear tweak trails in such ciphers which can be used in the linear attack are exactly those coming from the ordinary trails. Ashur et al. [1] described a χ^2 distinguisher detecting correlations smaller than $2^{-n/2}$ in the multi-key setting. But they were not able to use the distinguisher for key recovery.

Generic Related-Key Attacks. Kelsey et al. [28] mentioned a related-key attack that can be applied to any block cipher, referring to [42]. The attack uses keys with known differences and the product of the number of related keys and the computational complexity is 2^k in the attack. But the plaintexts are required to be the same regardless of the keys in the attack. So in the known plaintext setting the attacker needs to get about $M2^n$ pairs of key difference and plaintext to get $M \gg 1$ related keys with the same plaintext. Thus the product of the data size and the computational complexity is about 2^{k+n} in such a setting.

1.3 Organization of the Paper

In Sect. 2 we introduce the terminology and notations used in the paper. In Sect. 3 we describe the framework for the related-key linear cryptanalysis against block ciphers with linear key schedules. In Sect. 4 we present attack results on

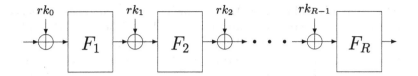

Fig. 1. A long-key cipher

SIMON obtained from the framework presented in Sect. 3 together with some dedicated analysis. In Sect. 5 we provide experimental results that corroborate the claims of the paper. In Sect. 6 we discuss the validity and the usefulness of the framework in more detail. We conclude in Sect. 7.

2   Terminology and Notations

$\mathbb{F}_2$ and $\mathbb{Z}$ denote the field with two elements and the ring of integers, respectively. A word is a bit string of the length $w = 12$, 16, 24, 32, or 64. For integers i, j with $i \leq j$, $[i..j]$ denotes the set of integers x such that $i \leq x \leq j$. The LSB (least significant bit) of a word is indexed as 0 and is located at the rightmost position. The $(i + 1)$-th rightmost bit of a word x is denoted by $x[i]$ so that $x[0]$ denotes the LSB of x. For a w-bit word x, $x[i]$ with $i \notin [0..(w - 1)]$ means $x[i \mod w]$. Also $x[i..j]$ denotes the bit string $x[j]\|\ldots\|x[i]$ for $0 \leq i \leq j < w$. $x \lll a$ and $x \ggg a$ denote the circular shift of a word x to the left and right by a bits, respectively. $\wedge$ represents the bitwise-and of two words. The inner product of a w-bit mask γ and a w-bit value x is defined to be $\oplus_{i=0}^{w-1} \gamma[i]x[i]$ and is denoted by $\langle \gamma, x \rangle$. For a Boolean function $G : \mathbb{F}_2^l \to \mathbb{F}_2$, the correlation of G is defined to be the imbalance $(|\{x : G(x) = 0\}| - |\{x : G(x) = 1\}|)/2^l$. For a vectorial Boolean function $F : \mathbb{F}_2^l \to \mathbb{F}_2^m$, an l-bit mask γ, and an m-bit mask λ, the (linear) correlation of F with respect to the mask pair (γ, λ) is defined to be the correlation of the Boolean function G given by $G(x) = \langle \gamma, x \rangle \oplus \langle \lambda, F(x) \rangle$ and is denoted by $\varepsilon_F(\gamma, \lambda)$. The Hamming weight of a word x, denoted by $\mathrm{wt}(x)$, is the number of the nonzero bits of x. For a bit string X with even length, X_{L} and X_{R} denote the left half and right half of X, respectively. The support of a w-bit word x is defined to be the set of indices $\{i \in [0..(w - 1)] : x[i] \neq 0\}$ and is denoted by $\mathsf{supp}(x)$. $\|$ denotes the concatenation of bit strings. Bit strings are expressed in the hexadecimal representations. For example, $\mathsf{c201}$ represents the bit string $1, 1, 0, 0, 0, 0, 1, 0, 0, 0, 0, 0, 0, 0, 0, 1$. For real numbers μ and $\sigma > 0$, $\mathcal{N}(\mu, \sigma^2)$ denotes the normal distribution with the mean μ and the standard deviation σ. $\varPhi$ denotes the cumulative distribution function of the standard normal distribution.

3   Description of the Framework

In our related-key linear attack, the attacker takes advantage of related-key data such that each entry in the data is a triplet $(P, C, \Delta K)$ of a plaintext P, a ciphertext C, and a key difference ΔK for which the ciphertext is the encrypted value $E_{K^* \oplus \Delta K}(P)$ of the plaintext under the key that is the xor of the unknown base key K^* to be recovered and the key difference ΔK. The attack proceeds as in the classical Matsui's Algorithms [33]. In the classical Algorithm 2 using a linear trail, for example, the attacker uses a linear approximation that involves masked intermediate values and a parity bit expressed as an xor of masked base round keys. But in our related-key linear attack, the attacker makes use of a *related-key linear approximation* that involves masked key differences together with the masked intermediate values and the parity bit. The related-key linear attack is based on the following features of the block ciphers with linear key schedules:

- When a key K is the xor of an unknown base key K^* and a known key difference ΔK, the difference of round keys derived from K and K^* can be computed directly from ΔK though two keys are unknown.
- The intermediate state obtained from a plaintext by performing several encryption rounds with a key K can be also computed using P, ΔK, and the round keys derived from K^*. The same holds for the decryption rounds.

3.1   A Related-Key Linear Approximation

Let R, r, and s be integers with $0 \le s \le s+r \le R$ and let $E : \mathbb{F}_2^k \times \mathbb{F}_2^n \to \mathbb{F}_2^n$ be an R-round key-alternating iterative block cipher with k-bit keys and n-bit blocks. Let $\tilde{E}$ be the long-key cipher corresponding to E and ψ be the key scheduling function that is linear. That is, $\tilde{E}$ is a function $\mathbb{F}_2^{Rn} \times \mathbb{F}_2^n \to \mathbb{F}_2^n$ defined by

$$\tilde{E}(rk_0 \| rk_1 \| \cdots \| rk_{R-1}, x) = F_R(rk_{R-1} \oplus \cdots F_2(rk_1 \oplus F_1(rk_0 \oplus x)) \cdots)$$

as in Fig. 1, where each F_i is a fixed n-bit permutation, ψ is a function $\mathbb{F}_2^k \to \mathbb{F}_2^{Rn}$, and $E(K, x) = \tilde{E}(\psi(K), x)$ for $(K, x) \in \mathbb{F}_2^k \times \mathbb{F}_2^n$. Suppose that we have an r-round linear trail $[\gamma_s, \gamma_{s+1}, \ldots, \gamma_{s+r}]$ for $\tilde{E}$ such that the correlation $\varepsilon_{F_{i+1}}(\gamma_i, \gamma_{i+1})$ for the $(i+1)$-th round is ϵ_i for each $i \in [s..(s+r-1)]$. It is well-known that the average of the correlations over long keys is $\epsilon = \epsilon_s \cdots \epsilon_{s+r-1}$. That is,

$$\Pr_{\mathbf{rk}, x}(\langle \gamma_s, x \rangle \oplus \langle \gamma_{s+r}, \tilde{E}_s^{s+r-1}(\mathbf{rk}, x) \rangle \oplus \bigoplus_{i=0}^{r-1} \langle \gamma_{s+i}, rk_{s+i} \rangle = 0) = \frac{1+\epsilon}{2}, \quad (1)$$

where $\mathbf{rk} = rk_0 \| rk_1 \| \cdots \| rk_{R-1}$ and $\tilde{E}_i^j$ is the subcipher of $\tilde{E}$ spanning from the $(i+1)$-th round to the $(j+1)$-th round. (See e.g. [35].) Let K^* be the fixed unknown key to be recovered. Let $\psi(K^*) = \mathbf{rk}^* = rk_0^* \| rk_1^* \| \cdots \| rk_{R-1}^*$. For each key K, let $\Delta K = K \oplus K^*$. Since ψ is linear, $\delta \mathbf{rk} := \psi(K) \oplus \psi(K^*)$ is determined by ΔK. Let $\delta \mathbf{rk} = \delta rk_0 \| \delta rk_1 \| \cdots \| \delta rk_{R-1}$. By (1),

$$\Pr_{\mathbf{rk} \in \mathrm{Im}(\psi), x}(\langle \gamma_s, x \rangle \oplus \langle \gamma_{s+r}, \tilde{E}_s^{s+r-1}(\mathbf{rk}, x) \rangle \oplus \bigoplus_{i=0}^{r-1} \langle \gamma_{s+i}, rk_{s+i} \rangle = 0) \approx \frac{1+\epsilon}{2},$$

which means that the correlation of the approximation

$$\langle \gamma_s, x \rangle \oplus \langle \gamma_{s+r}, E_s^{s+r-1}(K^* \oplus \Delta K, x) \rangle \oplus \bigoplus_{i=0}^{r-1} \langle \gamma_{s+i}, rk_{s+i}^* \oplus \delta rk_{s+i} \rangle, \quad (2)$$

i.e. the imbalance of the approximation as $(x, \Delta K)$ takes all the values in $\mathbb{F}_2^{n+k}$, is the same regardless of K^* and is very close to ϵ. Since ψ is linear, we have a linear function L_ψ and a constant C_ψ with $\psi(K) = L_\psi(K) \oplus C_\psi$ for each key K. So for each $i \in [0..(r-1)]$, we have a linear relation

$$\langle \bar{\gamma}_{s+i}, \Delta K \rangle \oplus \langle \gamma_{s+i}, \delta r k_{s+i} \rangle = 0 \tag{3}$$

where $\bar{\gamma}_{s+i}$ is a mask determined from γ_{s+i} and L_ψ. Now, using the approximation (2) and the relations (3), we get a linear approximation

$$\langle \gamma_s, x \rangle \oplus \langle \gamma_{s+r}, E_s^{s+r-1}(K^* \oplus \Delta K, x) \rangle \oplus \bigoplus_{i=0}^{r-1} (\langle \bar{\gamma}_{s+i}, \Delta K \rangle \oplus \langle \gamma_{s+i}, r k_{s+i}^* \rangle) = 0, \tag{4}$$

whose correlation, i.e. the imbalance of the approximation as $(x, \Delta K)$ takes all the values in $\mathbb{F}_2^{n+k}$, is very close to ϵ. We will call each of (2) and (4) a *related-key linear approximation*.

Assumption 1. The correlation of the related-key linear approximation (2) is ϵ.

We will also call $\bigoplus_{i=0}^{r-1} \langle \gamma_{s+i}, r k_{s+i}^* \rangle$ the *parity bit* of the approximation. In Matsui's Algorithm 1, the attacker tries to recover only the parity bit and the number of attacked rounds is the same as the number of the rounds that the linear approximation spans over. Matsui's Algorithm 2 tries to add outer rounds to the linear approximation and recover some outer round key bits and, if possible, the parity bits. We will describe the corresponding attacks in our related-key setting.

3.2   Description of Algorithm RKLC-1

In this variant of Matsui's Algorithm 1, we try to recover the parity bit without added outer rounds. So $s = 0$ and $r = R$. Suppose that we have a related-key linear approximation (4) with the correlation ϵ. Let a random related-key data $D = \{(P_i, C_i, \Delta K_i) : i = 1, \ldots, N\}$ for a key K^* be given. Compute

$$\tau_0(K^*, D) := |\{i : \langle \gamma_0, P_i \rangle \oplus \langle \gamma_R, C_i \rangle \oplus \bigoplus_{j=0}^{r-1} \langle \bar{\gamma}_{s+j}, \Delta K_i \rangle = 0\}|$$
$$- |\{i : \langle \gamma_0, P_i \rangle \oplus \langle \gamma_R, C_i \rangle \oplus \bigoplus_{j=0}^{r-1} \langle \bar{\gamma}_{s+j}, \Delta K_i \rangle = 1\}|.$$

If $\epsilon \tau_0(K^*, D) > 0$, then determine the parity bit to be 0 and otherwise determine it to be 1.

3.3   Description of Algorithm RKLC-2

Now we will describe the related-key attack that tries to add outer rounds to an r-round related-key linear approximation (4) and recover some of the outer round key bits together with the parity bit. Assume that we have the approximation (4) with the correlation ϵ. Let a random related-key data $D = \{(P_i, C_i, \Delta K_i) : i =$

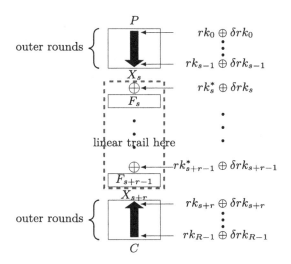

Fig. 2. The outline of RKLC-2

$1, \dots, N\}$ be given. We let $z_I^* = \bigoplus_{i=0}^{r-1} \langle \gamma_{s+i}, rk_{s+i}^* \rangle$ be the parity bit and z_I be the candidate value for z_I^*. We perform an attack using (4) as the distinguisher: We identify the positions of the outer round key bits that are required to compute $\langle \gamma_s, X_s^K \rangle \oplus \langle \gamma_{s+r}, X_{s+r}^K \rangle$ with the triplets of plaintext, ciphertext and the key difference where X_s^K and X_{s+r}^K are the intermediate states for the start of the s-th round and the end of the $(s + r - 1)$-th round, respectively, that is $X_s^K = E_0^{s-1}(K \oplus \Delta K, P)$ and $E_{s+r}^{R-1}(K \oplus \Delta K, X_{s+r}^K) = C$. (See Fig. 2. Here bits of δrk_i for outer rounds that are used in the computation are computable directly from ΔK.) By allocating a bit value in each of the positions and then concatenating, we get a candidate *outer key* z. Thus $\langle \gamma_s, X_s^K \rangle \oplus \langle \gamma_{s+r}, X_{s+r}^K \rangle \oplus \bigoplus_{i=0}^{r-1} \langle \bar{\gamma}_{s+i}, \Delta K \rangle$ can be expressed as $g(z, P, C, \Delta K)$ for some function g. We denote

$$|\{i : g(z, P_i, C_i, \Delta K_i) = 0\}| - |\{i : g(z, P_i, C_i, \Delta K_i) = 1\}|$$

by $\tau(K^*, D, z)$ and calll $\tau(K^*, D, z)/N$ the observed sample imbalance. Let z^* denote the correct outer key, i.e. the value of z obtained from K^*. Heuristically, if z is correct, then $\tau(K^*, D, z)/N$ is likely to be close to $(-1)^{z_I^*}\epsilon$ and otherwise the imbalance is likely to be close to 0. For the actual attack one usually performs the data compression first to reduce the computational complexity. The data compression in a linear attack is a process that collapses the data into a new data with multiplicity considering the outer round computations. It is part of the distillation [7] and is also called the linear compression by others [32]. But the data compression in our related-key setting needs to handle the key differences unlike that in the single-key linear attacks. So the "compression function" $H_c : \mathbb{F}_2^{2n+k} \rightarrow \mathbb{F}_2^d$ with $2^d \ll N$ we need to get for the data compression is one such that the computation of $g(z, P, C, \Delta K)$ can be carried out using z and $H_c(P, C, \Delta K)$ or such that there is a function h

---

Algorithm 1. Algorithm RKLC-2

---

1. Perform the data compression to get the compressed set of size 2^d and set $\tau(K^*, D, z) = 0$ for each z.
2. For each entry (v, n_v) in the compressed data,
   - For each z, compute $h(z, v)$ and increment or decrement $\tau(K^*, D, z)$ by n_v depending on whether $h(z, v)$ is 0 or 1.
3. For each (z, z_I) for which $(-1)^{z_I} \tau(K^*, D, z)\epsilon \geq tN\epsilon^2$, try to recover the whole key bits by trial encryption.

---

such that $g(z, P, C, \Delta K) = h(z, H_c(P, C, \Delta K))$ for any $(P, C, \Delta K)$. Once we have a compression function, we apply it to the data to get the compressed data $\{(v, n_v) \in \mathbb{F}_2^d \times \mathbb{Z} : n_v = |\{(P, C, \Delta K) \in D : H_c(P, C, \Delta K) = v\}|\}$. We determine whether (z, z_I) is correct or not by the decision rule $(-1)^{z_I} \tau(K^*, D, z)\epsilon \geq tN\epsilon^2$. Here t is the threshold parameter that enables us to get a tradeoff between the computational complexity and the success probability. To summarize, the attack proceeds as in Algorithm 1. If $h(z, v)$ can be expressed as $h'(z \oplus v)$, we can use the FWHT to reduce the computational complexity as described in [18]. Consider the list of (z, z_I)'s for which $(-1)^{z_I} \tau(K^*, D, z)\epsilon \geq tN\epsilon^2$ in the attack. The attack is successful if (z^*, z_I^*) is in the list, and the list may also contain many wrong entries that are called the false alarms.

3.4   Statistical Model, Success Probability and Attack Complexities

For our related-key attacks, we presume the "standard" key hypotheses that are similar to the ones accepted as valid in the ordinary linear attack using a dominant trail. But for that, we assume that the data D is random and that the round function of the cipher in consideration is not too simple. We will see in Sect. 5.2 that when the trail is not dominant and the number of plaintexts per each key difference in the data gets larger, such hypotheses get less pertinent. Under the standard hypotheses, we get the same estimates for the success probability and the attack complexities in terms of the data size and the correlation as in many previous works (e.g. [8,38]). But we will clarify our hypotheses in the related-key setting and elaborate on the details. We let $c_{N,\epsilon} := \sqrt{N}|\epsilon|$ for each $N > 0$ and ϵ.

Algorithm RKLC-1. Let us consider the attack in Sect. 3.2 that uses a random data D of size N. If we fix K^* and let D vary, $\tau_0(K^*, D)/N$ can be regarded as a random variable. For the attack, we presume the following:

Hypothesis 1. For each K^*, $\tau_0(K^*, D)/N$ follows $\mathcal{N}((-1)^b \epsilon, 1/N)$ where b is the parity bit.

With this hypothesis, the success probability of the attack is $\Phi(\sqrt{N}|\epsilon|)$ by Lemma 1.

Lemma 1. *Let $\sigma > 0, b, \mu$ be real numbers and let Y be a random variable with $Y \sim \mathcal{N}(\mu, \sigma^2)$. Then $\Pr(Y \geq b) = \Phi((\mu - b)/\sigma)$ and $\Pr(Y \leq b) = \Phi((b - \mu)/\sigma)$.*

Algorithm RKLC-2. Now we consider the attack in Sect. 3.3. We fix K^* and let z^* be the correct outer key. For each outer key z, we can regard $\tau(K^*, D, z)/N$ as a random variable letting D vary. The right key hypothesis and the wrong key hypothesis we presume are the following:

Hypothesis 2 (Right Key Hypothesis) . For each K^*, $\tau(K^*, D, z^*)/N$ follows $\mathcal{N}((-1)^{b^*}\epsilon, (1 - \epsilon^2)/N) \approx \mathcal{N}((-1)^b\epsilon, 1/N)$, where b^* is the parity bit.

Hypothesis 3 (Wrong Key Hypothesis) . For each K^*, $\tau(K^*, D, z)/N$ follows $\mathcal{N}(0, 1/N)$ when $z \neq z^*$.

We let $\mathcal{Z}$ be the set of the candidate outer keys and let $k_O = \log_2 |\mathcal{Z}|$. Let t be the threshold parameter. The success probability of the attack is $\Pr((-1)^{b^*}\tau(K^*, D, z^*)\epsilon \geq tN\epsilon^2)$, which equals $\Phi((1-t)c_{N,\epsilon})$ by Lemma 1 under Hypothesis 2. Using the same Lemma, we also have

- for (z, z_I) with $z \neq z^*$, the probability that $(-1)^{z_I}\tau(K^*, D, z)\epsilon \geq tN\epsilon^2$ is $\Phi(-tc_{N,\epsilon})$, and
- for (z, z_I) with $z = z^*$ and $z_I \neq z_I^*$, the probability that $(-1)^{z_I}\tau(K^*, D, z)\epsilon \geq tN\epsilon^2$ is $\Phi((-1 - t)c_{N,\epsilon})$.

under Hypothesis 3. So the false alarm probability is

$$\Pr(\mathbf{cond}, (z, z_I) \neq (z^*, z_I^*)) = \Pr(\mathbf{cond}, z \neq z^*) + \Pr(\mathbf{cond}, z = z^*, z_I \neq z_I^*)$$
$$= \Pr(\mathbf{cond} \mid z \neq z^*)\Pr(z \neq z^*) + \Pr(\mathbf{cond} \mid z = z^*, z_I \neq z_I^*)\Pr(z = z^*, z_I \neq z_I^*)$$
$$= (2^{k_O} - 1)\Phi(-tc_{N,\epsilon})/2^{k_O} + \Phi((-1 - t)c_{N,\epsilon})/2^{k_O+1},$$

where **cond** is short for the statement $(-1)^{z_I}\tau(K^*, D, z)\epsilon \geq tN\epsilon^2$.

Theorem 1. *With N, ϵ, t as described, the success probability of RKLC-2 is $\Phi((1-t)c_{N,\epsilon})$ and the false alarm probability $p_{\mathrm{fa}}(t)$ is $(2^{k_O} - 1)\Phi(-tc_{N,\epsilon})/2^{k_O} + \Phi((-1 - t)c_{N,\epsilon})/2^{k_O+1}$.*

Note that $p_{\mathrm{fa}}(t) \approx \Phi(-tc_{N,\epsilon})$ when k_O is not too small. To compare the computational complexity of the attack with that of the exhaustive key search, we say that the complexity of 1 encryption (including the key schedule) is 1. Let c_p be the complexity of 1 computation of H_c and c_o be the complexity of 1 computation of h using an entry in the compressed data and a candidate outer key. Then the computational complexity of RKLC-2 is $c_p N + c_o 2^{d+k_O} + 2^k p_{\mathrm{fa}}(t)$ by Theorem 1. The amount of memory required for the attack is $O(2^d)$. Let c_a be the complexity of addition or subtraction of two integers. In many cases, we can reduce the computational complexity by using FWHT:

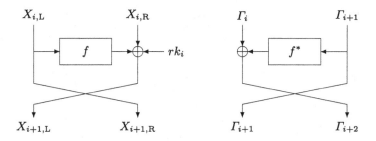

Fig. 3. A round of SIMON and a 1-round linear trail

Theorem 2. *The computational complexity of RKLC-2 using FWHT is*

$$c_p N + 3c_a k_O 2^{k_O+1} + 2^k p_{\text{fa}}(t),$$

with the success probability $\Phi((1-t)c_{N,\epsilon})$.

But in this case, the memory complexity is $O(2^{k_O})$. Here we have assumed that the restored outer key z and the parity bit reveal simple independent relations between the bits of K^*, meaning that using the $(k_O + 1)$-bit information that (z^*, z_I^*) reveals about K^*, we can recover the whole k bits of K^* using other simple $(k - k_O - 1)$ relations between the bits of K^*. This is mostly the case when the key schedule is linear.

4   Related-Key Linear Attacks on Round-Reduced Simon

The NSA published two families of lightweight block ciphers SIMON and SPECK [4]. They have remarkable performance figures on most software and hardware platforms and SIMON is the more hardware-oriented of the two. They have been the subject of intensive security analysis since their publication. The designers of SIMON expect that it is secure against related-key attacks [5].

4.1   The Simon Family of Block Ciphers

SIMONn/k is a block cipher of the classical Feistel structure with k-bit keys and n-bit blocks. Its round function f sends an $n/2$-bit input x onto $((x \lll 8) \land (x \lll 1)) \oplus (x \lll 2)$.(See Fig. 3.) It has a linear key schedule. We focus on the following ciphers whose key lengths are double the block lengths: SIMON32/64, SIMON48/96, SIMON64/128, and SIMON128/256. The details of this section can be applied equally well to the variant of SIMON to be used in Sect. 5.

4.2   Related-Key Linear Approximations of Simon

Since SIMONn/k has the classical Feistel structure, an r-round linear trail can be represented as a sequence of $(r+2)$ $n/2$-bit masks: $\Gamma_s.\Gamma_{s+1}.\cdots.\Gamma_{s+r+1}$ represents

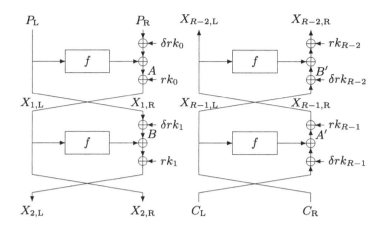

Fig. 4. 2-round computations of SIMON

a linear trail such that at the $(i + 1)$-th round, the input and output masks are $\Gamma_i \| \Gamma_{i+1}$ and $\Gamma_{i+1} \| \Gamma_{i+2}$, respectively, for each $i \in [s..(s + r - 1)]$. (See Fig. 3.) Such a linear trail leads to the related-key linear approximation

$$\langle \Gamma_s, X_{s,\mathrm{L}} \rangle \oplus \langle \Gamma_{s+1}, X_{s,\mathrm{R}} \rangle \oplus \langle \Gamma_{s+r}, X_{s+r,\mathrm{L}} \rangle \oplus \langle \Gamma_{s+r+1}, X_{s+r,\mathrm{R}} \rangle$$
$$\oplus \langle \Lambda, \Delta K \rangle \oplus \bigoplus_{i=0}^{r-1} \langle \Gamma_{s+i+1}, rk_{s+i}^* \rangle = 0 \qquad (5)$$

between X_s, ΔK, X_{s+r}, where Λ is a mask with $\langle \Lambda, \Delta K \rangle = \bigoplus_{i=0}^{r-1} \langle \Gamma_{s+i+1}, \delta rk_{s+i} \rangle$. Such a mask Λ can be easily obtained.

4.3   Adding Outer Rounds

One of the pivotal processes of the related-key attacks is to get effective data compression with the related-key linear approximation. For SIMON, we can get effective data compression for prepending and appending many rounds when both the initial mask and the final mask of the linear trail have small Hamming weights. In this subsection, we will explain in detail how to add 2+2 rounds, i.e., how to prepend 2 rounds and append 2 rounds at the same time. How to add $s + s$ rounds for $s = 3, 4, 5$ will be explained in Sect. C of the Appendix, from which how to add $s + s'$ rounds for $s \neq s'$ and $2 \leq s, s' \leq 5$ will be obvious. For simplicity $a + b$ and ab denote the XOR and AND of $a, b \in \mathbb{F}_2$ in this section, respectively.

2-round Computation. Let rk_0 and rk_1 be the round keys derived from the candidate key K for the first 2 rounds. For a plaintext $P = P_\mathrm{L} \| P_\mathrm{R}$ and a key difference ΔK, let δrk_0 and δrk_1 be the derived round key differences for the first 2 rounds. Note that δrk_0 and δrk_1 can be computed directly from ΔK.

We want to express each bit of $X_2 = X_{2,L}\|X_{2,R} = E_0^1(K \oplus \Delta K, P)$ in terms of P, rk_0, rk_1, δrk_0, and δrk_1. Let $A = f(P_L) \oplus P_R \oplus \delta rk_0$, and $B = P_L \oplus \delta rk_1$. (See Fig. 4.) Since $X_{2,R} = X_{1,L} = f(P_L) \oplus P_R \oplus \delta rk_0 \oplus rk_0 = rk_0 \oplus A$ and $X_{2,L} = f(X_{1,L}) \oplus P_L \oplus \delta rk_1 \oplus rk_1 = f(rk_0 \oplus A) \oplus B \oplus rk_1$,

$$
\begin{aligned}
X_{2,L}[i] &= (rk_0[i-1] + A[i-1])(rk_0[i-8] + A[i-8]) \\
&\quad + \underline{rk_0[i-2]} + A[i-2] + B[i] + \underline{rk_1[i]}, \\
X_{2,R}[i] &= \underline{rk_0[i]} + A[i]
\end{aligned}
$$

Here $X_{2,L}[i]$ can be computed in terms of $rk_0[i-1]+A[i-1], rk_0[i-8]+A[i-8]$, up to $A[i-2] + B[i]$ xored with a constant determined only by rk_0, rk_1. Note that the underlined terms do not mingle with the plaintext so that we will xor them with the parity bit to get an "adjusted parity bit" in RKLC-2. Otherwise the number of round key bits to restore and, hence, the attack complexity can be increased. By symmetry of the cipher structure, we get similar expressions for bits of $X_{R-2,R}$ and $X_{R-2,L}$ in terms of $A' = f(C_R) \oplus C_L \oplus \delta rk_{R-1}$, $B' = C_R \oplus \delta rk_{R-2}$, rk_{R-2}, and rk_{R-1}. (See Fig. 4.)

The Data Compression. The above arguments tell us how to compress the data when adding 2+2 rounds. Suppose that we want to make use of the related-key linear approximation represented as (5) with $s = 2$ and $s + r + 2 = R$. Let $w = n/2$ be the word size. Let $\mathcal{I}_L = \mathsf{supp}(\Gamma_s) = \{i \in [0..(w-1)] : \Gamma_s[i] \neq 0\}$, $\mathcal{I}_R = \mathsf{supp}(\Gamma_{s+1})$, $\mathcal{I}_L' = \mathsf{supp}(\Gamma_{R-2})$, and $\mathcal{I}_R' = \mathsf{supp}(\Gamma_{R-1})$. The compression function extracts the following values from each data entry $(P, C, \Delta K)$:

- $A[i]$ for i such that $(i+1) \bmod w \in \mathcal{I}_L$ or $(i+8) \bmod w \in \mathcal{I}_L$
- $A'[i]$ for i such that $(i+1) \bmod w \in \mathcal{I}_R'$ or $(i+8) \bmod w \in \mathcal{I}_R'$
- $\bigoplus_{i \in \mathcal{I}_L} (A[i-2] \oplus B[i]) \oplus \bigoplus_{i \in \mathcal{I}_R} A[i] \oplus \bigoplus_{i \in \mathcal{I}_R'} (A'[i-2] \oplus B'[i]) \oplus$ $\bigoplus_{i \in \mathcal{I}_L'} A'[i] \oplus \langle \Lambda, \Delta K \rangle$

The outer keys consists of the following outer round key bits that we need to guess:

- $rk_0[i]$ for i such that $(i+1) \bmod w \in \mathcal{I}_L$ or $(i+8) \bmod w \in \mathcal{I}_L$
- $rk_{R-1}[i]$ for i such that $(i+1) \bmod w \in \mathcal{I}_R'$ or $(i+8) \bmod w \in \mathcal{I}_R'$

The adjusted parity bit is $\bigoplus_{i=0}^{r-1} \langle \Gamma_{s+i+1}, rk_{s+i}^* \rangle \oplus \bigoplus_{i \in \mathcal{I}_L} (rk_0^*[i-2] \oplus rk_1^*[i]) \oplus$ $\bigoplus_{i \in \mathcal{I}_R} rk_0^*[i] \oplus \bigoplus_{i \in \mathcal{I}_R'} (rk_{R-1}^*[i-2] \oplus rk_{R-2}^*[i]) \oplus \bigoplus_{i \in \mathcal{I}_L'} rk_{R-1}^*[i]$. Note that the number k_O of guessed round key bits for outer rounds is at most $2\mathsf{wt}(\Gamma_s) + 2\mathsf{wt}(\Gamma_{R-1})$ and d, $\log_2$ of the size of the compressed data, is $k_O + 1$. Note also that using above data compression, we can use FWHT in RKLC-2.

4.4　Attacks on Round-Reduced Simon

Now we will present the attacks on round-reduced SIMON summarized in Table 1. Note that we compare our attacks with the current best linear attacks [16] and differential attacks [41] only since the differential/linear attacks are the most limiting attacks on SIMON as noted in [5]. Note also that there does not exist a related-key attack that is more efficient than such attacks yet (cf. [30]).

Each of our attacks is an instance of the RKLC-2 and we will specify the positions of the outer round key bits that will constitute the outer keys. We use the linear trails presented in Sect. B of the Appendix. Note that each of them has squared correlation somewhat larger than $2^{-(n+k)/2}$ and the product of the computational complexity and the data complexity of the presented attack using it is less than 2^{k+n}. So each presented attack is an effective one not covered by the generic attack in [28]. We set the threshold parameter t for each attack to 1 so that the success probabilities are all $\Phi(0) = 0.5$ by Theorem 1. Also we have $k_O \ll \log_2(N)$ and use FWHT in each attack so that we estimate the computational complexity as $c_p N + 2^k \Phi(-\sqrt{N}|\epsilon|)$ by Theorem 2. We use the estimate $c_p = R_{\text{add}}/R$, where R is the number of rounds of the round-reduced SIMON and R_{add} is the number of the added outer rounds. The attack method presented in this work can be applied to other SIMONn/k with $k > n$ in a straightforward manner.

Simon 32/64. We use a 16-round linear trail with the correlation 2^{-21} whose initial and final mask are 40000001 and 00400110, respectively. We can add 4+3 rounds to this linear trail with $k_O = 35$: The guessed outer round key bits are $rk_0[0, 2, 3, 4, 6, 7, 9, 10 \ 11, 12, 13, 14]$, $rk_1[4, 5, 6, 11, 12, 13, 14]$, $rk_2[6, 13]$, $rk_{21}[0, 3, 7, 12]$, and $rk_{22} \ [1,2,4,5,6,8,10,11,14,15]$. Letting $N = 2^{46.3}$, $c_{N,\epsilon} = 2^{2.15}$ so that the complexity of RKLC-2 on the 23-round reduced SIMON32/64 is $2^{46.65}$ by Theorem 2.

Simon 48/96. We use a 20-round linear trail with the correlation 2^{-33} whose initial and final mask are 400000000001 and 400000100001, respectively. We add 5+3 rounds to this linear trail with $k_O = 53$. Letting $N = 2^{70.9}$, $c_{N,\epsilon} = 2^{2.45}$ and the complexity of RKLC-2 on the 28-round reduced SIMON48/96 is $2^{71.07}$.

Simon 64/128. We use a 26-round linear trail with the correlation 2^{-45} whose initial mask is 0000000100004044 and final mask is 0000100000004400. We add 4+4 rounds to this linear trail with $k_O < 80$. Letting $N = 2^{95.32}$, $c_{N,\epsilon} = 2^{2.66}$ and the complexity of RKLC-2 on the 34-round reduced SIMON64/128 is $2^{95.5}$.

Simon 128/256. We use a 51-round linear trail with the correlation 2^{-92} whose initial and final mask are $00\ldots004\|00\ldots00$ and $00\ldots001\|400\ldots004$, respectively. We get an attack on the 62-round reduced SIMON128/256 with data complexity $2^{190.4}$ and computational complexity $2^{190.76}$ by adding 6+5 rounds. Also, using a 45-round subtrail with the correlation 2^{-84} whose initial and final mask are $100\ldots001\|4400\ldots004$ and $400\ldots004\|100\ldots00$, respectively, we get an attack on the 55-round reduced SIMON128/256 with data complexity $2^{174.73}$ and computational complexity 2^{175} by adding 5+5 rounds.

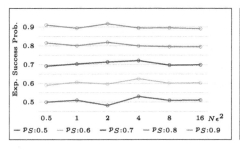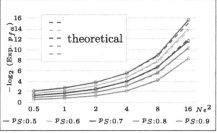

Fig. 5. Experimental results for 22-round key recovery on SIMON24

5   Experiments

In this section, we carry out experiments using three block ciphers. Two of them are small-scale variants of SIMON. The other is PRESENT-L that is a variant of PRESENT-128 that has a linear key schedule.

5.1   Experiments with Variants of Simon

Related-Key Attacks on the 22-round Simon24. We describe experimental results on SIMON24/48 that is a 22-round cipher with 48-bit keys and 24-bit blocks. The round function and the key schedule of the cipher are defined exactly in the same way as SIMON32/64. The 31-bit constant used in the key schedule is also the same. We try to add 2+2 rounds to the 18-round linear trail 001.000.001.410.001.000.001.410.001.000.001.410.001.000.001.410.00 1.000.001.400 with the correlation $\epsilon = 2^{-17}$. The guessed outer round key bits are $rk_0[4, 11], rk_{21}[2, 9]$, the number k_O of the guessed outer round key bits is 4, and the size of the compressed data is 2^5 by arguments in Sect. 4. The additional bit to be guessed is the adjusted parity bit $rk_0[10] \oplus rk_1[0] \oplus rk_{20}[10] \oplus rk_{21}[0] \oplus rk_{21}[8] \oplus \langle 000, rk_2 \rangle \oplus \langle 001, rk_3 \rangle \oplus \cdots \oplus \langle 001, rk_{19} \rangle$. In the experiment we repeat the key recovery tests using 1,000 different keys K^*. For each key, we generate data of size N for $N = 2^i \epsilon^{-2}$ with $i = -1, 0, 1, 2, 3$, and 4. The number ν of data entries per key difference was fixed to as large as 2^{16}. For each N, we compute the threshold parameters corresponding to $p_S = 0.5, 0.6, 0.7, 0.8$, and 0.9 using Theorem 1 and proceed as in Algorithm 1. We count the number of the successful attempts and measure the average of the number of false alarms for the 1,000 tests. The result is shown in Fig. 5 from which we can see that the experimental probabilities are close to the theoretical ones.

Related-Key Attacks on the 16-round Simon32. We try to add 2+2 round to the 12-round trail 0005.0000.0005.c001.1005.0110.0040.0100. 0000.0100.0040.0110.0004.0111 with the correlation $\epsilon = -2^{-17}$. The number k_O of guessed outer round key bits is 10 and we proceed as in the preceding section. Then we get the results as in Fig. 6.

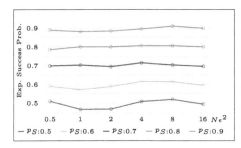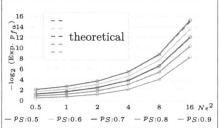

Fig. 6. Experimental results for 16-round key recovery on Simon32

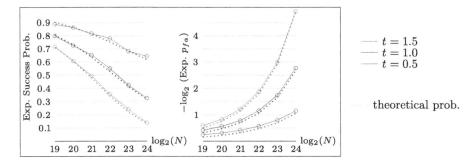

Fig. 7. Experimental results for 18-round single-key attack on Simon24

Single-Key Attacks on the 18-round Simon24. For comparison with the related-key linear attacks, we also perform a single-key linear attack using the linear hull containing the 14-round trail with correlation 2^{-13} represented as `001.000.001.410.001.000.001.410.001.000.001.410.001.000.001.400`. We try to add 2+2 rounds to the linear hull. By analyzing the distribution of the squared correlation of the linear hull over 1,000 keys, we noticed that the linear probability of the linear hull is about 2^{-23}. We also observed that the distribution of the correlation of the linear hull is close to $\mathcal{N}(0, 2^{-23})$ as predicted by arguments in [19]. So we assume that the linear probability ϵ_H^2 of the linear hull is 2^{-23} and the distribution of the correlation of the linear hull is $\mathcal{N}(0, \epsilon_H^2)$. Then we apply Matsui's Algorithm 2 presuming some adjusted key hypotheses for attacks using data sampled without replacement [8]: For the attack we let the data size N be $2^{19}, 2^{20}, \ldots, 2^{23}$, or 2^{24}. We use the decision rule $|\tau(K^*, D, z)/N| \geq t|\epsilon_H|$ with threshold parameters $t = 0.5, 1.0, 1.5$. The theoretical success probability and the false alarm probability for each (t, N) are $2\Phi(-t\sqrt{N}|\epsilon_H|/\sqrt{1 - N/2^n + N\epsilon_H^2})$ and $2\Phi(-t\sqrt{N}|\epsilon_H|)$, respectively [8,9]. We observe that the experimental probabilities are close to the theoretical ones as shown in Fig. 7, confirming the analyses in [8] with linear hulls. Considering the success probabilities for each fixed (a, N), where a is the advantage $-\log_2(p_{fa}(t))$ and N is the data size, the single-key linear attack using the linear hull with the linear probability 2^{-23} is not so advantageous compared with the related-key

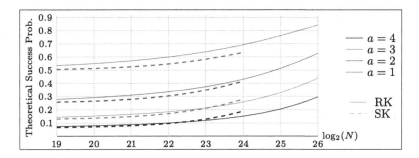

Fig. 8. Success probabilities for the single-key/related-key attack

linear attack (RKLC-2) using a linear trail with the linear correlation 2^{-13} as we see in Fig. 8.

5.2   Experiments with a Variant of Present-128

Let PRESENT-L be a block cipher that originates from the same long key cipher as PRESENT-128 and has a linear key schedule: The key schedule of PRESENT-L is the same as that of PRESENT-128 except that all the 4-bit S-boxes in the key schedule of PRESENT-128 are removed. So each key schedule round of PRESENT-L is just a rotation of the 128-bit state followed by xoring with a round constant. Let T-4R-B21 and T-4R-B42 be the 4-round trails with correlations 2^{-8} such that the input and output mask for each round is 0000000000200000 and 0000040000000000, respectively. Let T-6R-B21 and T-6R-B42 be the 6-round trails with correlations 2^{-12} defined similarly. Considering linear trails such that all the constituent masks have Hamming weight 1, we see that T-4R-B21 and T-4R-B42 have 2 and 1 other trails with the correlation $\pm 2^{-8}$ in their linear hulls, respectively (cf. [36]). We also see that T-6R-B21 and T-6R-B42 have at least 26 and 7 other trails with the correlation $\pm 2^{-12}$ in their linear hulls, respectively. In the experiments, we set the data size N to be ϵ^{-2}, $4\epsilon^{-2}$, or $16\epsilon^{-2}$. We also set the number ν of data entries per key difference to be 1, 8, or 64. We try to prepend 2 rounds before the 4-round trails or the 6-round trails. The results are as in Figs. 9 and 10. When ν is large, the experimental probabilities may deviate considerably from the estimates given by Theorem 1. But when ν is close to 1, as in the case of random sampling, they are close to the theoretically predicted ones. Rather surprisingly, results with 6-round trails are closer to predicted ones than with the 4-round ones, though the former are far less dominant in their linear hulls than the latter. We suspect that this has been caused by the nonrandomness of the data we have used. The details of the data are provided in the Appendix.

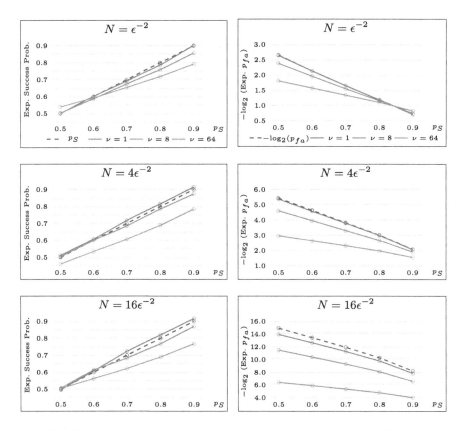

Fig. 9. Experimental results for 6-round key recovery using T-4R-B21

6   Discussions

6.1   Statistical Models

The standard key hypotheses are not adequate for most single-key linear attacks [8,9,11,12]. But we claim that the standard key hypotheses we presume are adequate for our attacks in the related-key scenario where the attacker has random related-key data though the results in Sect. 5.1 shows that sometimes such key hypotheses are suitable even when the trail is far from dominant and the number of data entries per key difference is quite large. First, the standard *right* key hypothesis is applicable in our related-key setting since the correlation of the related-key linear approximation is the same regardless of K^* as mentioned in Sect. 3 while that of the single-key linear approximation obtained from a linear trail varies greatly depending on the key if the trail is not dominant. We do not claim that the standard wrong key hypotheses are adequate in the related-key attack regardless of the round structure of the block cipher. But we claim that such hypotheses are appropriate in the related-key scenario with random data if the round function is not too simple. In the extreme nontypical case when we

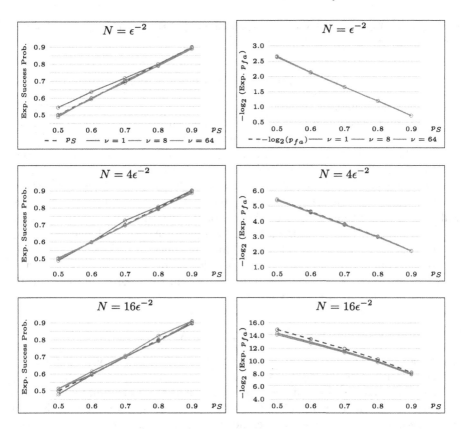

Fig. 10. Experimental results for 6-round key recovery using T-6R-B42

have only one related key, our attack would become one in the single-key setting and we might have to consider some adjusted wrong key hypotheses especially when the data size is large. The reason is that the distribution of the correlations for wrong keys in the single-key setting has deviation $O(2^{-n/2})$ [11] from Daemen and Rijmen's analysis [19] on the distribution of the correlations of linear approximations for n-bit permutations. But in our related-key setting where the data is random, we just need to consider $(k+n)$-bit-to-n-bit functions where the additional k bits come from key differences so the deviation of the distribution might be $O(2^{-(k+n)/2})$ that is negligible compared to $1/\sqrt{N}$ with the data size N being much smaller than 2^{k+n}. The standard wrong key hypothesis in Matsui's Algorithm 2 in the single-key linear attack is not so valid especially when the linear probability of the linear hull is close to 2^{-n}. But the experimental results in Sect. 5.1 using a linear trail with the correlation whose absolute value is considerably less than $2^{-n/2}$ corroborate our claims on the wrong key hypotheses as well as the right key hypotheses in our related-key attacks. We also note that the choice between sampling data with replacement and without replacement yields little difference in the success probability and the attack complexities due to the size of the whole data space.

6.2   Linear Trails, Linear Hulls, and Multiple Linear Approximations

The formulations in Sect. 3 indicate that in our related-key linear attacks it seems natural to use linear trails. The experimental results in Sect. 5 show that our estimates regarding the related-key linear attacks are accurate regardless of whether the trail is dominant or not when random data is used. In fact, none of the linear trail used in the experiments in Sect. 5 are dominant. For example, the linear correlation of the 18-round linear trail for SIMON24 is 2^{-17} whose square is quite less than the linear probability of the linear hull containing the trail that is larger than 2^{-30}. But the use of the key differences in our attacks seems to make it hard or inherently impossible to utilize the linear hulls. On the other hand, we would get related-key multiple linear attacks and related-key multidimensional attacks as straightforward derivations of the ones presented in [7,23]. We expect that the key dependency issue in the original attacks will be mitigated in our related-key setting.

6.3   Comparison with Single-Key Linear Attacks

Our attack has significance even when it requires slightly more computation and data than the single-key linear attacks since it can utilize related-key data that the single-key attacks cannot exploit. But it is more meaningful when it is more effective than the generic related-key attack and covers more rounds than the single-key attacks. For a block cipher with a linear key schedule whose key length k is larger than the block length n, we need to find a linear trail with the correlation $\approx \pm 2^{-(k+n)/4}$ considering the generic related-key attack. The attack will be likely to cover longer rounds than the single-key linear attack only when we can find such a trail that is longer than any single-key linear approximation with the linear probability $\approx 2^{-n}$. The advantage of the related-key linear attack will be more visible for block ciphers with linear key schedules such that the linear hulls exploited in the single-key linear attacks contain dominant trails. For each of SIMON ciphers, we could not cover much longer rounds with the related-key attacks than with the single-key attacks mainly because it admits considerably longer single-key linear characteristics with the linear probability $\approx 2^{-n}$ originating from linear hulls than single-key linear trails with the correlation $\approx \pm 2^{-n/2}$. For example, the linear attack on the 25-round reduced SIMON48/k in [16] exploits a 16-round linear hull with linear probability $2^{-42.92}$, while there does not exist a 16-round linear trail whose squared correlation is larger than 2^{-50}.

6.4   Application to Tweakable Blockciphers

The statistical model in this work can be slightly modified to provide a relevant framework for the linear attack on the tweakable blockciphers constructed from the tweakey framework [6,26]. Though the linear attack using a linear approximation with squared correlation much smaller than 2^{-n} against such a cipher is rather straightforward and was considered in [6,31], it requires suitable statistical models. It seems that Assumption 1 can be adjusted to provide an adequate right key hypothesis for the attack. For example, it may be assumed that the average of the correlations over (K^*, T) as the tweak T varies are very close to the correlation of the linear trail regardless of the base key K^*. Note that the correlations of the related-key linear approximations are the same regardless of K^*, and we just assume that they are the same as the correlation of the linear trail. A wrong key hypothesis that is similar to the one given in this work might be adopted for the attack.

7   Conclusions

We have introduced a general framework for the related-key linear cryptanalysis on block ciphers with linear key schedules. The attack is likely to cover more rounds than the existing linear attacks if the key length of the cipher is much larger than its block length. Using the framework, we are able to get effective related-key linear attacks on SIMON that cover longer rounds than the previous attacks. Experiments with small-scale variants of SIMON and a variant of PRESENT corroborate the validity of the attack together with the suitability of the statistical model concerning the right keys and wrong keys. Some lightweight ciphers do not consider security against related-key attacks in its design criteria and the attack may be hard to apply in practice due to the requirement of large related-key data. But the attack is certainly one that should be taken into account in the design of a block cipher with a small block length and a linear key schedule that might be used in circumstances where frequent key update is inevitable. An additional feature of our attack is that the complexity of the attack does not depend much on the detail of the key schedule once the key schedule is linear, in contrast with other related-key attacks. As further works, one may try to apply the framework presented in this work to various block ciphers with linear key schedules other than SIMON. Another important line of works would be to investigate the multiple linear attacks and multidimensional linear attacks in the related key setting to reduce the attack complexities.

Acknowledgements. We are grateful to the anonymous reviewers for their help in improving the quality of the paper. This work was supported by Institute for Information & Communications Technology Planning & Evaluation (IITP) grant funded by the Korean government (MSIT) (No. 2017-0-00267).

A   Searching Method for the Linear Trails of SIMON

Linear trails with the squared correlation less than 2^{-n} for SIMONn/k are not provided in the previous works. To find such trails, we apply an efficient search algorithm that we have designed by slightly modifying the searching method described in [32] that is based on Matsui's branch-and-bound algorithm. As noted before, an r-round linear trail of SIMONn/k can be represented as a sequence of $(r + 2)$ $n/2$-bit masks: $\Gamma_s.\Gamma_{s+1}.\cdots.\Gamma_{s+r+1}$ represents a linear trail such that at the $(i + 1)$-th round, the input and output masks are $\Gamma_i\|\Gamma_{i+1}$ and $\Gamma_{i+1}\|\Gamma_{i+2}$, respectively, for each $i \in [s..(s + r - 1)]$. Such a linear trail leads to the related-key linear approximation (5). The linear correlation of the round function of SIMON with respect to various input-output mask pairs can be easily computed as explained in [29] and [32]. Throughout this section, f denotes the round function of SIMONn/k that sends an $n/2$-bit input x onto $((x \lll 8) \wedge (x \lll 1)) \oplus (x \lll 2)$. Note that if $\Gamma_s.\cdots.\Gamma_{s+r+1}$ is a linear trail with the correlation ϵ, so are the reversed trail $\Gamma_{s+r+1}.\cdots.\Gamma_s$ and the rotated trail $(\Gamma_s \lll l).\cdots.(\Gamma_{s+r+1} \lll l)$ for each l.

For each $l \geq 0$, let $\mathcal{L}_l$ be the list of mask pairs (α, β) such that $|\varepsilon_f(\alpha, \beta)| = 2^{-l}$. We denote $- \log_2(|\varepsilon_f(\beta \ggg 2, \beta)|)$ by $\mathrm{lac}(\beta)$. Then the mask pairs in $\mathcal{L}_l$ are exactly those (α, β)'s for which $\mathrm{lac}(\beta) = l$ and $\varepsilon_f(\alpha, \beta) \neq 0$. A mask β is called a rotational representative if $(\beta \lll j) \geq \beta$ for each j. For each $l \geq 0$, let $\mathcal{L}_l^{\mathrm{red}}$ be the set of mask pairs (α, β) in $\mathcal{L}_l$ such that β is a rotational representative. For an r-round trail $T = \Gamma_0.\Gamma_1.\cdots.\Gamma_{r+1}$ and $l \leq r + 1$, T_l denotes Γ_l and $\mathrm{lac}(T)$ denotes $\sum_{l=1}^{r} \mathrm{lac}(\Gamma_l)$. Also for $l \leq r$, $T|_l$ denotes the l-round subtrail $\Gamma_0.\Gamma_1.\cdots.\Gamma_{l+1}$. When we search for an r-round trail T, we impose the following restrictions on the masks in the trail:

- $\mathrm{lac}(T_i) \leq 4$ for $i = 0, \ldots, r$.
- If $T_1 = 0$, T_0 is a rotational representative. Otherwise, T_1 is a rotational representative.

It turns out that these restrictions let us quickly find out the trails suitable for our purposes. For each r, let B_r be the minimum of $\mathrm{lac}(T)$ when T runs among all the r-round trails such that each mask in the trail except the last one has lac ≤ 4. It is easy to see that $B_1 = 0$, $B_2 = 1$, and $B_3 = 2$. In the search algorithm, for each $r \geq 4$, we get B_r and an r-round linear trail T with $\mathrm{lac}(T) = B_r$ assuming that we have already computed B_1, ..., B_{r-1}. The search algorithm is presented as Algorithm 2. Before running it, we prepare two lists of $n/2$-bit masks in advance for acceleration: One with β's such that $\mathrm{lac}(\beta) \leq 4$ and the other with β's such that $\mathrm{lac}(\beta) \leq 4$ *and* β is a rotational representative. B_r's we have obtained are the same as those presented in [32] for SIMONn/k with $n = 32$, 48, or 64 whenever $B_r \leq n$. We remark that by modifying Algorithm 2, we can also find many linear trails with various constraints on the intermediate masks and the correlation.

Algorithm 2. The search algorithm

Set $\bar{B} = B_{r-1} - 1$, and *found* = 0.
repeat
    $\bar{B}++$
    ProcessR1( )
until *found* == 1
Output T, $\bar{B}$

function ProcessR1( )
    ProcessR2A( )
    for $l \leftarrow 1$ **to** $\min(4, \bar{B} - B_{r-1})$ **do**
        for $(\alpha, \beta) \in \mathcal{L}_l^{\mathrm{red}}$ **do**
            ProcessR2(α, β)
        end for
    end for
    return
end function

function ProcessR2A( )
    for $l \leftarrow 1$ **to** $\min(4, \bar{B} - B_{r-2})$ **do**
        for $(\alpha, \beta) \in \mathcal{L}_l^{\mathrm{red}}$ **do**
            Set $T_0 = \beta$, $T_1 = 0$, $T_2 = \beta$, $T_3 = \alpha$.
            ProcessR(3)
        end for
    end for
    return
end function

function ProcessR2(α, β)
    Set $c = \mathrm{lac}(\beta)$.
    for $l \leftarrow 0$ **to** $\min(4, \bar{B} - c - B_{r-2})$ **do**
        for $(\alpha_1, \beta_1) \in \mathcal{L}_l$ for which $\mathrm{lac}(\alpha \oplus \beta_1) \leq 4$ **do**
            Set $T_0 = \alpha \oplus \beta_1$, $T_1 = \beta$, $T_2 = \beta_1$, $T_3 = \beta \oplus \alpha_1$.
            ProcessR(3)
        end for
    end for
    return
end function
function ProcessR(m)
    Set $\beta_m = T_m$, $c = \mathrm{lac}(\beta_m)$.
    if $m < r$ **then**
        if $(\mathrm{lac}(T|_{m-1}) + c + B_{r-m} > \bar{B})$ or $(c > 4)$ **then**
            return
        else
            for α_m for which $\varepsilon_f(\alpha_m, \beta_m) \neq 0$ **do**
                Set $T_{m+1} = \alpha_m \oplus T_{m-1}$.
                ProcessR$(m + 1)$
            end for
        end if
    else
        if $\mathrm{lac}(T|_{m-1}) + c == \bar{B}$ **then**
            Choose an α_m for which $\varepsilon_f(\alpha_m, \beta_m) \neq 0$.
            Set $T_{m+1} = \alpha_m \oplus T_{m-1}$.
            Set *found* = 1, and exit all the functions.
        else
            return
        end if
    end if
end function

B   Linear Trails of Simon

The linear trails we have used in Sect. 4.4 are as follows:

- a 16-round trail for SIMON32/64 with the correlation $\pm 2^{-21}$:
  4000.0001.0000.0001.4000.1001.0400.1101.4040.0111.0004.0110.
  0040.0100.0000.0100.0040.0110.
- a 20-round trail for SIMON48/96 with the correlation $\pm 2^{-33}$:
  400000.000001.000000.000001.400000.100001.040000.110001.404000.
  011001.018400.013001.40c000.110001.040000.100001.400000.00
  0001.000000.000001.400000.100001
- a 26-round trail for SIMON64/128 with the correlation $\pm 2^{-45}$:
  00000001.00004044.00001010.00004440.00000100.00004400.0000100
  0.00004000.00000000.00004000.00001000.00004400.00000100.00004
  440.00001010.00004044.00000061.0000404c.00001030.00004440.0000
  0100.00004400.00001000.00004000.00000000.00004000.00001000.00
  004400
- a 45(=32+13)-round trail for SIMON128/256 with the correlation $\pm 2^{-84}$:
  0100000000000001.0440000000000004.0610000000000000.04c00000
  00000004.····.0100000000000001.0440000000000004.0610000000000
  000.04c0000000000004.····.0000000000000001.4000000000000004.10
  00000000000000
- a 51(=48+3)-round trail for SIMON128/256 with the correlation $\pm 2^{-92}$:
  0000000000000004.0000000000000000.0000000000000004.0000000
  000000001.····.0000000000000004.0000000000000000.00000000000
  00004.0000000000000001.····.0000000000000004.0000000000000001.
  4000000000000004

Linear trails for SIMON32, SIMON48, SIMON64 were found by our search algorithm, but the trail for SIMON128 was obtained as a subtrail of an iterative trail in [32].

C   Adding More Rounds to Related-Key Linear Approximations of Simon

In this section, we will explain how to add $r_{\text{pre}} + r_{\text{post}}$ rounds for $(r_{\text{pre}}, r_{\text{post}}) = (3, 3)$, $(4, 4)$, or $(5, 5)$. For simplicity $a + b$ and ab (or $a \bullet b$) denote the XOR and AND of $a, b \in \mathbb{F}_2$, respectively. Let $w = n/2$ be the word size as before.

C.1   Adding 3+3 Rounds

3-round Computation. Let rk_0, rk_1, rk_2 be the round keys derived from the candidate key K for the first 3 rounds. For a plaintext $P = P_{\text{L}} \| P_{\text{R}}$ and a key difference ΔK, let $\delta rk_0, \delta rk_1, \delta rk_2$ be the derived round key differences for the first 3 rounds. Let $A = f(P_{\text{L}}) \oplus P_{\text{R}} \oplus \delta rk_0$, and $B = P_{\text{L}} \oplus \delta rk_1$ as before. Then using the relations $X_{3,\text{R}} = X_{2,\text{L}}$ and $X_{3,\text{L}} = f(X_{2,\text{L}}) \oplus X_{2,\text{R}} \oplus \delta rk_2 \oplus rk_2$, we can compute each bit of $X_3 = X_{3,\mathrm{L}} \| X_{3,\mathrm{R}} = E_0^2(K \oplus \Delta K, P)$ in terms of bits of $A, B, rk_0, rk_1, rk_2, \delta rk_0, \delta rk_1, \delta rk_2$ as follows:

$$
\begin{aligned}
X_{3,\mathrm{L}}[i] = &((rk_0 \oplus A)[i-9](rk_0 \oplus A)[i-2] + (rk_0 \oplus A)[i-3] + (rk_1 \oplus B)[i-1]) \bullet \\
&((rk_0 \oplus A)[i-16](rk_0 \oplus A)[i-9]) + (rk_0 \oplus A)[i-10] + (rk_1 \oplus B)[i-8]) \\
&+(rk_0 \oplus A)[i-10](rk_0 \oplus A)[i-3] + \underline{rk_0[i-4]} + A[i-4] + \underline{rk_0[i]} + A[i] \\
&+\underline{rk_1[i-2]} + B[i-2] + \underline{rk_2[i]} + \delta rk_2[i], \\
X_{3,\mathrm{R}}[i] = &\overline{X_{2,\mathrm{L}}[i]}.
\end{aligned}
$$

Thus

- $X_{3,\mathrm{L}}[i]$ can be computed in terms of $(rk_0 \oplus A)[i-2, i-3, i-9, i-10, i-16]$, $(rk_1 \oplus B)[i-1, i-8]$, xored with $A[i-4] + B[i-2] + A[i] + \delta rk_2[i]$ and the underlined terms determined only by rk_0, rk_1, rk_2.
- $X_{3,\mathrm{R}}[i]$ can be computed in terms of $(rk_0 \oplus A)[i-1]$, $(rk_0 \oplus A)[i-8]$, xored with $A[i-2] + B[i]$ and terms determined only by rk_0, rk_1, rk_2.

By symmetry of the cipher structure, we get similar expressions for bits of $X_{R-3,\mathrm{R}}$ and $X_{R-3,\mathrm{L}}$ in terms of $A' = f(C_\mathrm{R}) \oplus C_\mathrm{L} \oplus \delta rk_{R-1}$, $B' = C_\mathrm{R} \oplus \delta rk_{R-2}$, $\delta rk_{R-3}, rk_{R-1}, rk_{R-2}$, and rk_{R-3}.

The Data Compression. Suppose that we want to make use of the related-key linear approximation represented as (5) with $s = 3$ and $s + r + 3 = R$. Let $\mathcal{I}_\mathrm{L} = \mathsf{supp}(\Gamma_s)$, $\mathcal{I}_\mathrm{R} = \mathsf{supp}(\Gamma_{s+1})$, $\mathcal{I}'_\mathrm{L} = \mathsf{supp}(\Gamma_{R-3})$, and $\mathcal{I}'_\mathrm{R} = \mathsf{supp}(\Gamma_{R-2})$. The compression function extracts the following values from each data entry $(P, C, \Delta K)$:

- $A[i]$ for i such that one of $i+2, i+3, i+9, i+10, i+16 \bmod w$ is in $\mathcal{I}_\mathrm{L}$
- $B[i]$ for i such that one of $i+1, i+8 \bmod w$ is in $\mathcal{I}_\mathrm{R}$
- $A'[i]$ for i such that one of $i+2, i+3, i+9, i+10, i+16 \bmod w$ is in $\mathcal{I}'_\mathrm{R}$
- $B'[i]$ for i such that one of $i+1, i+8 \bmod w$ is in $\mathcal{I}'_\mathrm{L}$
- $\bigoplus_{i \in \mathcal{I}_\mathrm{L}} (A[i-4] + B[i-2] + A[i] + \delta rk_2[i]) \oplus \bigoplus_{i \in \mathcal{I}_\mathrm{R}} (A[i-2] + B[i]) \oplus$
  $\bigoplus_{i \in \mathcal{I}'_\mathrm{R}} (A'[i-4] + B'[i-2] + A'[i] + \delta rk_{R-3}[i]) \oplus \bigoplus_{i \in \mathcal{I}'_\mathrm{L}} (A'[i-2] + B'[i]) \oplus$
  $\langle \Lambda, \Delta K \rangle$

The outer round key bits we need to guess are as follows:

- $rk_0[i]$ for i such that one of $i+2, i+3, i+9, i+10, i+16 \bmod w$ is in $\mathcal{I}_\mathrm{L}$
- $rk_1[i]$ for i such that one of $i+1, i+8 \bmod w$ is in $\mathcal{I}_\mathrm{L}$
- $rk_0[i]$ for i such that one of $i+1, i+8 \bmod w$ is in $\mathcal{I}_\mathrm{R}$
- $rk_{R-1}[i]$ for i such that one of $i+2, i+3, i+9, i+10, i+16 \bmod w$ is in $\mathcal{I}'_\mathrm{R}$
- $rk_{R-2}[i]$ for i such that one of $i+1, i+8 \bmod w$ is in $\mathcal{I}'_\mathrm{R}$
- $rk_{R-1}[i]$ for i such that one of $i+1, i+8 \bmod w$ is in $\mathcal{I}'_\mathrm{L}$

Note that the number k_O of guessed round key bits for outer rounds is at most $7\mathrm{wt}(\Gamma_s) + 2\mathrm{wt}(\Gamma_{s+1}) + 2\mathrm{wt}(\Gamma_{R-3}) + 7\mathrm{wt}(\Gamma_{R-2})$ and d, $\log_2$ of the size of the compressed data, is $k_O + 1$.

C.2   Adding 4+4 Rounds

Let $A = f(P_L) \oplus P_R \oplus \delta rk_0$, and $B = P_L \oplus \delta rk_1$ as before. Using the relations $X_{4,R} = X_{3,L}$ and $X_{4,L} = f(X_{3,L}) \oplus X_{3,R} \oplus \delta rk_3 \oplus rk_3$, we see that $X_{4,L}[i]$ (up to a constant determined only by rk_0, rk_1, rk_2, rk_3) is a function of the following terms

- $(rk_0 \oplus A)[i-1, i-3, i-4, i-5, i-8, i-10, i-11, i-12, i-17, i-18, i-24]$
- $(rk_1 \oplus B)[i-2, i-3, i-9, i-10, i-16]$
- $(rk_2 \oplus \delta rk_2)[i-1, i-8]$

xored with $A[i-6] + B[i] + B[i-4] + \delta rk_2[i-2] + \delta rk_3[i]$. Note also that $X_{4,R}[i] = X_{3,L}[i]$ and the backward computations can be carried out similarly. So when we use a related-key linear approximation represented as (5) with $s = 4$ and $s + r + 4 = R$, we have a compression with $k_O \le 18\mathrm{wt}(\Gamma_s) + 7\mathrm{wt}(\Gamma_{s+1}) + 7\mathrm{wt}(\Gamma_{R-4}) + 18\mathrm{wt}(\Gamma_{R-3})$ and $d = k_O + 1$.

C.3   Adding 5+5 Rounds

Let $A = f(P_L) \oplus P_R \oplus \delta rk_0$, and $B = P_L \oplus \delta rk_1$. $X_{4,L}[i]$ (up to a constant determined only by $rk_0, rk_1, rk_2, rk_3, rk_4$) is a function of the following terms

- $(rk_0 \oplus A)[i-2, i-3, i-4, i-5, i-6, i-7, i-9, i-10, i-11, i-12, i-13, i-14, i-16, i-18, i-19, i-20, i-25, i-26, i-32]$
- $(rk_1 \oplus B)[i-1, i-3, i-4, i-5, i-8, i-10, i-11, i-12, i-17, i-18, i-24]$
- $(rk_2 \oplus \delta rk_2)[i-2, i-3, i-9, i-10, i-16]$
- $(rk_3 \oplus \delta rk_3)[i-1, i-8]$

xored with $A[i] + A[i-4] + A[i-8] + B[i-6] + \delta rk_2[i] + \delta rk_2[i-4] + \delta rk_3[i-2] + \delta rk_4[i]$. We also have $X_{5,R}[i] = X_{4,L}[i]$ and the backward computations can be carried out similarly. So when we use a related-key linear approximation represented as (5) with $s = 5$ and $s + r + 5 = R$, we have a compression with $k_O \le 39\mathrm{wt}(\Gamma_s) + 18\mathrm{wt}(\Gamma_{s+1}) + 18\mathrm{wt}(\Gamma_{R-5}) + 39\mathrm{wt}(\Gamma_{R-4})$ and $d = k_O + 1$.

D   Application of FWHT to Related-key Linear Attacks

We will explain how FWHT can be applied in our related-key linear attacks with an example presented in Sect. 5.2. Consider the 8-round attack on PRESENT-L prepending 2 rounds to the 6-round linear trail T-6R-B42 using RKLC-2. Suppose that we have a related-key data D obtained from a base key K^*. We set the compression function H_c as the 21(=16+4+1)-bit valued function defined by

$$(P, C, \Delta K) \mapsto (P \oplus \delta rk_0)[32..47] \| \delta rk_1[40..43] \| (\bigoplus_{i=2}^{8} \delta rk_i[42] \oplus C[42]).$$

The round key bits and the parity bit to recover are $rk_0^*[32..47] \| rk_1^*[40..43]$ and $\bigoplus_{i=2}^{8} rk_i^*[42]$, respectively. In Step 1, we perform the data compression to get the compressed set

$$\{(v, n_v) \in \mathbb{F}_2^{21} \times \mathbb{Z} : n_v = |\{(P, C, \Delta K) \in D : H_c(P, C, \Delta K) = v\}|\}.$$

Let h_1 be 4-bit valued function such that

$$h_1(x) = S(x[12..15])[2] \| S(x[8..11]))[2] \| S(x[4..7]))[2] \| S(x[0..3])[2]$$

for each $x \in \mathbb{F}_2^{21}$. Then let h' be the 1-bit valued function such that $h'(x) = S(h_1(x) \oplus x[16..19])[2] \oplus x[20]$ for each $x \in \mathbb{F}_2^{21}$. Then we have to compute $\sum_v n_v(-1)^{h'(z \oplus v)}$ for each $z \in \mathbb{F}_2^{21}$ in Step 2. This can be done by performing FWHTs three times with memory $O(2^{21})$ just as described in [18].

E   Additional Results with Present-L

In this section, we present some of the results obtained from the experiments in Sect. 5.2 not provided there due to the lack of space. They are results from the 6-round key recovery using T-4R-B42 (Fig. 11) and the 8-round key recovery using T-6R-B21 (Fig. 12).

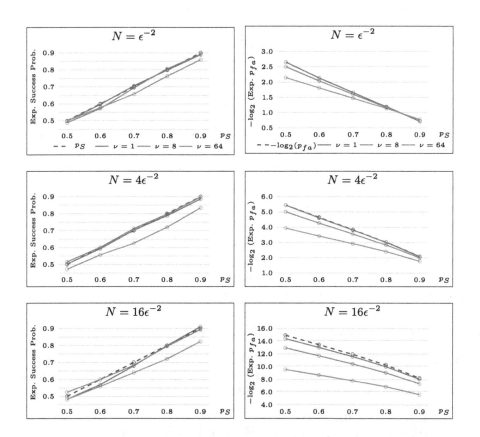

Fig. 11. Experimental results for 6-round key recovery using T-4R-B42

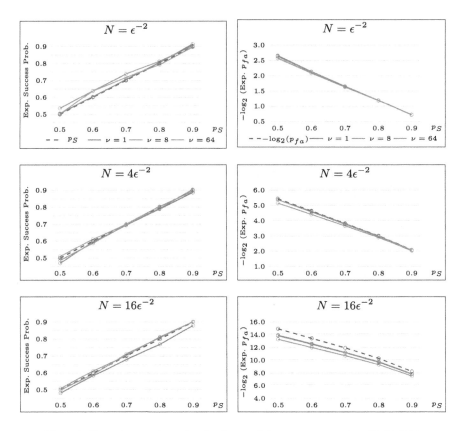

Fig. 12. Experimental results for 8-round key recovery using T-6R-B21

F   Keys and Data Used in the Experiments

For each cipher, linear trail, and data size, 1,000 keys were used as the targets for recovery. For variants of SIMON, we used a single GTX 1060 GPU and a Core i7-5820K CPU to generate the data and get the results. Experiment with each cipher took just a few days or less.

F.1   Experiments with the Small-scale Simon

For experiments with 22-round SIMON24 and 16-round SIMON32, the number ν of data entries per key difference was fixed at 2^{16} regardless of N. The following keys and data were used for 22-round SIMON24.

- base keys K^l ($l = 0, \ldots, 999$):
  - $K^l[36..47] = \text{0x012} + l \pmod{2^{12}}$, $K^l[24..35] = \text{0x345} + l \pmod{2^{12}}$
  - $K^l[12..23] = \text{0x678} + l \pmod{2^{12}}$, $K^l[0..11] = \text{0x9ab} + l \pmod{2^{12}}$
- $\Delta K_i^l = \text{0xfedcba987654321} \times (Nl/\nu + i) \pmod{2^{48}}$ ($i = 0, \ldots, N/\nu - 1$)
- $P_{i,j}^l = j$, $j = 0, \ldots, \nu - 1$

Similar keys and data were used for 16-round SIMON32:

- base keys K^l ($l = 0, \ldots, 999$):
  - $K^l[48..63] = \text{0x0123} + l \pmod{2^{16}}$, $K^l[32..47] = \text{0x4567} + l \pmod{2^{16}}$
  - $K^l[16..31] = \text{0x89ab} + l \pmod{2^{16}}$, $K^l[0..11] = \text{0xcdef} + l \pmod{2^{16}}$
- $\Delta K_i^l = \text{0xfedcba987654321} \times (Nl/\nu + i) \pmod{2^{64}}$ ($i = 0, \ldots, N/\nu - 1$)
- $P_{i,j}^l = j$, $j = 0, \ldots, \nu - 1$

F.2   Experiments with Present-L

The keys and data used are as follows regardless of the number of rounds or the linear trail:

- base keys K^l ($l = 0, \ldots, 999$):
  - $K^l[64..127] = \text{0x123456789abcdef} \times l \pmod{2^{64}}$
  - $K^l[0..63] = \text{0x123456789abcdef} \times (l + 1) \pmod{2^{64}}$
- key differences ΔK_i^l ($i = 0, \ldots, N/\nu - 1$):
  - $\Delta K_i^l[64..127] = \text{0xfedcba987654321} \times i \times \text{0x321321321321321} \pmod{2^{64}}$
  - $\Delta K_i^l[0..63] = \text{0xfedcba987654321} \times i \times \text{0x432405887348} \pmod{2^{64}}$
- plaintexts $P_{i,j}^l = j$, $j = 0, \ldots, \nu - 1$

References

1. Ashur, T., Bodden, D., Dunkelman, O.: Linear cryptanalysis using low-bias linear approximations. Cryptology ePrint Archive, Report 2017/204 (2017). http://eprint.iacr.org/2017/204
2. Banik, S., et al.: Midori: a block cipher for low energy. In: Iwata, T., Cheon, J.H. (eds.) ASIACRYPT 2015. LNCS, vol. 9453, pp. 411–436. Springer, Heidelberg (2015). https://doi.org/10.1007/978-3-662-48800-3_17
3. Banik, S., Pandey, S.K., Peyrin, T., Sasaki, Y., Sim, S.M., Todo, Y.: GIFT: a small present. In: Fischer, W., Homma, N. (eds.) CHES 2017. LNCS, vol. 10529, pp. 321–345. Springer, Cham (2017). https://doi.org/10.1007/978-3-319-66787-4_16
4. Beaulieu, R., Shors, D., Smith, J., Treatman-Clark, S., Weeks, B., Wingers, L.: The Simon and Speck families of lightweight block ciphers. Cryptology ePrint Archive, Report 2013/404 (2013). http://eprint.iacr.org/2013/404
5. Beaulieu, R., Shors, D., Smith, J., Treatman-Clark, S., Weeks, B., Wingers, L.: Notes on the design and analysis of Simon and Speck. Cryptology ePrint Archive, Report 2017/560 (2017)
6. Beierle, C., et al.: The SKINNY family of block ciphers and its low-latency variant MANTIS. In: Robshaw, M., Katz, J. (eds.) CRYPTO 2016. LNCS, vol. 9815, pp. 123–153. Springer, Heidelberg (2016). https://doi.org/10.1007/978-3-662-53008-5_5
7. Biryukov, A., De Cannière, C., Quisquater, M.: On multiple linear approximations. In: Franklin, M. (ed.) CRYPTO 2004. LNCS, vol. 3152, pp. 1–22. Springer, Heidelberg (2004). https://doi.org/10.1007/978-3-540-28628-8_1
8. Blondeau, C., Nyberg, K.: Improved parameter estimates for correlation and capacity deviates in linear cryptanalysis. IACR Trans. Symmetric Cryptol. **2016**(2), 162–191 (2016)

9. Blondeau, C., Nyberg, K.: Joint data and key distribution of simple, multiple, and multidimensional linear cryptanalysis test statistic and its impact to data complexity. Des. Codes Crypt. **82**(1–2), 319–349 (2017)

10. Bogdanov, A., Boura, C., Rijmen, V., Wang, M., Wen, L., Zhao, J.: Key difference invariant bias in block ciphers. In: Sako, K., Sarkar, P. (eds.) ASIACRYPT 2013. LNCS, vol. 8269, pp. 357–376. Springer, Heidelberg (2013). https://doi.org/10.1007/978-3-642-42033-7_19

11. Bogdanov, A., Tischhauser, E.: On the wrong key randomisation and key equivalence hypotheses in Matsui's Algorithm 2. In: Moriai, S. (ed.) FSE 2013. LNCS, vol. 8424, pp. 19–38. Springer, Heidelberg (2014). https://doi.org/10.1007/978-3-662-43933-3_2

12. Bogdanov, A., Vejre, P.S.: Linear cryptanalysis of DES with asymmetries. In: Takagi, T., Peyrin, T. (eds.) ASIACRYPT 2017. LNCS, vol. 10624, pp. 187–216. Springer, Cham (2017). https://doi.org/10.1007/978-3-319-70694-8_7

13. Bogdanov, A., Wang, M.: Zero correlation linear cryptanalysis with reduced data complexity. In: Canteaut, A. (ed.) FSE 2012. LNCS, vol. 7549, pp. 29–48. Springer, Heidelberg (2012). https://doi.org/10.1007/978-3-642-34047-5_3

14. Borghoff, J., et al.: PRINCE – a low-latency block cipher for pervasive computing applications. In: Wang, X., Sako, K. (eds.) ASIACRYPT 2012. LNCS, vol. 7658, pp. 208–225. Springer, Heidelberg (2012). https://doi.org/10.1007/978-3-642-34961-4_14

15. De Cannière, C., Dunkelman, O., Knežević, M.: KATAN and KTANTAN—a family of small and efficient hardware-oriented block ciphers. In: Clavier, C., Gaj, K. (eds.) CHES 2009. LNCS, vol. 5747, pp. 272–288. Springer, Heidelberg (2009). https://doi.org/10.1007/978-3-642-04138-9_20

16. Chen, H., Wang, X.: Improved linear hull attack on round-reduced SIMON with dynamic key-guessing techniques. In: Peyrin, T. (ed.) FSE 2016. LNCS, vol. 9783, pp. 428–449. Springer, Heidelberg (2016). https://doi.org/10.1007/978-3-662-52993-5_22

17. Cho, J.Y., Hermelin, M., Nyberg, K.: A new technique for multidimensional linear cryptanalysis with applications on reduced round serpent. In: Lee, P.J., Cheon, J.H. (eds.) ICISC 2008. LNCS, vol. 5461, pp. 383–398. Springer, Heidelberg (2009). https://doi.org/10.1007/978-3-642-00730-9_24

18. Collard, B., Standaert, F.-X., Quisquater, J.-J.: Improving the time complexity of matsui's linear cryptanalysis. In: Nam, K.-H., Rhee, G. (eds.) ICISC 2007. LNCS, vol. 4817, pp. 77–88. Springer, Heidelberg (2007). https://doi.org/10.1007/978-3-540-76788-6_7

19. Daemen, J., Rijmen, V.: Probability distributions of correlation and differentials in block ciphers. Cryptology ePrint Archive, Report 2005/212 (2005). http://eprint.iacr.org/2005/212

20. Gennaro, R., Robshaw, M. (eds.): CRYPTO 2015. LNCS, vol. 9215. Springer, Heidelberg (2015). https://doi.org/10.1007/978-3-662-47989-6

21. Gérard, B., Grosso, V., Naya-Plasencia, M., Standaert, F.-X.: Block ciphers that are easier to mask: how far can we go? In: Bertoni, G., Coron, J.-S. (eds.) CHES 2013. LNCS, vol. 8086, pp. 383–399. Springer, Heidelberg (2013). https://doi.org/10.1007/978-3-642-40349-1_22

22. Guo, J., Peyrin, T., Poschmann, A., Robshaw, M.J.B.: The LED block cipher. In: Preneel and Takagi [37], pp. 326–341
23. Hermelin, M., Cho, J.Y., Nyberg, K.: Multidimensional linear cryptanalysis. J. Cryptology **32**(1), 1–34 (2019)
24. Hermelin, M., Nyberg, K.: Linear cryptanalysis using multiple linear approximations. IACR Cryptology ePrint Archive 2011, 093 (2011). http://eprint.iacr.org/2011/093
25. Huang, J., Vaudenay, S., Lai, X., Nyberg, K.: Capacity and data complexity in multidimensional linear attack. In: Gennaro and Robshaw [20], pp. 141–160
26. Jean, J., Nikolić, I., Peyrin, T.: Tweaks and keys for block ciphers: the TWEAKEY framework. In: Sarkar, P., Iwata, T. (eds.) ASIACRYPT 2014. LNCS, vol. 8874, pp. 274–288. Springer, Heidelberg (2014). https://doi.org/10.1007/978-3-662-45608-8_15
27. Kaliski, B.S., Robshaw, M.J.B.: Linear cryptanalysis using multiple approximations. In: Desmedt, Y.G. (ed.) CRYPTO 1994. LNCS, vol. 839, pp. 26–39. Springer, Heidelberg (1994). https://doi.org/10.1007/3-540-48658-5_4
28. Kelsey, J., Schneier, B., Wagner, D.: Key-schedule cryptanalysis of IDEA, G-DES, GOST, SAFER, and Triple-DES. In: Koblitz, N. (ed.) CRYPTO 1996. LNCS, vol. 1109, pp. 237–251. Springer, Heidelberg (1996). https://doi.org/10.1007/3-540-68697-5_19
29. Kölbl, S., Leander, G., Tiessen, T.: Observations on the SIMON block cipher family. In: Gennaro and Robshaw [20], pp. 161–185
30. Kondo, K., Sasaki, Y., Todo, Y., Iwata, T.: Analyzing key schedule of SIMON: iterative key differences and application to related-key impossible differentials. In: Obana, S., Chida, K. (eds.) IWSEC 2017. LNCS, vol. 10418, pp. 141–158. Springer, Cham (2017). https://doi.org/10.1007/978-3-319-64200-0_9
31. Kranz, T., Leander, G., Wiemer, F.: Linear cryptanalysis: key schedules and tweakable block ciphers. IACR Trans. Symmetric Cryptol. **2017**(1), 474–505 (2017)
32. Liu, Z., Li, Y., Wang, M.: The security of Simon-like ciphers against linear cryptanalysis. Cryptology ePrint Archive, Report 2017/576 (2017). http://eprint.iacr.org/2017/576
33. Matsui, M.: Linear cryptanalysis method for DES cipher. In: Helleseth, T. (ed.) EUROCRYPT 1993. LNCS, vol. 765, pp. 386–397. Springer, Heidelberg (1994). https://doi.org/10.1007/3-540-48285-7_33
34. Nyberg, K.: Linear approximation of block ciphers. In: De Santis, A. (ed.) EUROCRYPT 1994. LNCS, vol. 950, pp. 439–444. Springer, Heidelberg (1995). https://doi.org/10.1007/BFb0053460
35. Nyberg, K.: Linear cryptanalysis. SAC Summer School (2015). http://sacworkshop.org/SAC2015/S3-linear-all.pdf
36. Ohkuma, K.: Weak keys of reduced-round PRESENT for linear cryptanalysis. In: Jacobson, M.J., Rijmen, V., Safavi-Naini, R. (eds.) SAC 2009. LNCS, vol. 5867, pp. 249–265. Springer, Heidelberg (2009). https://doi.org/10.1007/978-3-642-05445-7_16
37. Preneel, B., Takagi, T. (eds.): CHES 2011. LNCS, vol. 6917. Springer, Heidelberg (2011). https://doi.org/10.1007/978-3-642-23951-9
38. Selçuk, A.A.: On probability of success in linear and differential cryptanalysis. J. Cryptol. **21**(1), 131–147 (2008)
39. Shibutani, K., Isobe, T., Hiwatari, H., Mitsuda, A., Akishita, T., Shirai, T.: Piccolo: an ultra-lightweight blockcipher. In: Preneel and Takagi [37], pp. 342–357

40. Vora, P.L., Mir, D.J.: Related-key linear cryptanalysis. In: Proceedings of the 2006 IEEE International Symposium of Information Theory 2006, ISIT 2006, pp. 1609–1613, July 2006
41. Wang, N., Wang, X., Jia, K., Zhao, J.: Differential attacks on reduced SIMON versions with dynamic key-guessing techniques. Cryptology ePrint Archive, Report 2014/448 (2014). http://eprint.iacr.org/2014/448
42. Winternitz, R.S., Hellman, M.E.: Chosen-key attacks on a block cipher. Cryptologia **11**(1), 16–20 (1987)

Real-World Cryptography

Towards a Practical Cluster Analysis over Encrypted Data

Jung Hee Cheon, Duhyeong Kim$^{(\boxtimes)}$, and Jai Hyun Park

Department of Mathematical Sciences,
Seoul National University, Seoul, South Korea
{jhcheon,doodoo1204,jhyunp}@snu.ac.kr

Abstract. Cluster analysis is one of the most significant unsupervised machine learning methods, and it is being utilized in various fields associated with privacy issues including bioinformatics, finance and image processing. In this paper, we propose a practical solution for privacy-preserving cluster analysis based on homomorphic encryption (HE). Our work is the first HE solution for the mean-shift clustering algorithm. To reduce the super-linear complexity of the original mean-shift algorithm, we adopt a novel random sampling method called dust sampling approach, which perfectly suits with HE and achieves the linear complexity. We also substitute non-polynomial kernels by a new polynomial kernel so that it can be efficiently computed in HE.

The HE implementation of our modified mean-shift clustering algorithm based on the approximate HE scheme HEAAN shows prominent performance in terms of speed and accuracy. It takes approx. 30 min with 99% accuracy over several public datasets with hundreds of data, and even for the dataset with $262, 144$ data, it takes 82 min only when SIMD operations in HEAAN is applied. Our results outperform the previously best known result (SAC 2018) by over 400 times.

Keywords: Clustering · Mean-shift · Homomorphic encryption · Privacy

1 Introduction

For a decade, machine learning has garnered much attention globally in various fields due to its strong ability to resolve various real world problems. Since many fields of frequently-used data such as financial and biomedical data including personal or sensitive information, privacy-related issues are inevitable in the use of machine learning in such fields. There have been several non-cryptographic approaches for privacy-preserving machine learning including anonymization, perturbation, randomization and condensation [34,44]; however, these methods commonly accompany a potential loss of information which might degrade the utility of data.

On the other hand, Homomorphic Encryption (HE), which allows *computations over encrypted data* without any decryption process, is theoretically one

© Springer Nature Switzerland AG 2020
K. G. Paterson and D. Stebila (Eds.): SAC 2019, LNCS 11959, pp. 227–249, 2020.
https://doi.org/10.1007/978-3-030-38471-5_10

of the most ideal cryptographic primitives for privacy protection without the potential leakage of any information related to relevant data. There have been a number of studies on privacy-preserving machine learning based on HE, particularly supervised machine learning tasks such as classification and regression; including logistic regression [5,9,15,19,27,30,31,45] and (the prediction phase of) deep neural networks [6,25].

cluster analysis is one of the most significant unsupervised machine learning tasks, which aims to split a set of given data into several subgroups, called clusters, in which such data in the same cluster are "similar" to each other. As well as classification and regression, clustering is also widely used in various fields that engage the use of private information, including bioinformatics, image segmentation, finance, customer behavior analysis and forensics [20,22,36].

Contrary to classification and regression, there are only a few works [4,29] on privacy-preserving clustering based on HE, and even only one of these works provides a full HE solution, i.e., the whole procedure is done by HE operations without any decryption process or a trusted third-party setting. The main reason for the slow progress of the research on HE-based clustering is that there are many HE-unfriendly operations such as division and comparison. Recently, Cheon et al. [14] proposed efficient HE algorithms for division and comparison of numbers which are encrypted word-wise, and this work surely has its significance as it has initiated and called for active research on HE-based clustering.

1.1 This Work

In this paper, we propose a practical solution of privacy-preserving cluster analysis based on HE. Our solution is the *first* HE algorithm for *mean-shift clustering*, which is one of the representative algorithms for cluster analysis (Fig. 1). For given n-dimensional points $P_1, P_2, \ldots, P_p$ and a function called *kernel* $K : \mathbb{R}^n \times \mathbb{R}^n \to \mathbb{R}_{\geq 0}$, the mean-shift clustering utilizes the gradient descent algorithm which finds local maxima (called *modes*) of the kernel density estimator $F(\boldsymbol{x}) = \frac{1}{p} \cdot \sum_{i=1}^{p} K(\boldsymbol{x}, P_i)$, in which $K(\boldsymbol{x}, P_i)$ outputs a value close to 0 when $\boldsymbol{x}$ and P_i are far from each other.

Core Ideas. The major challenges for the original mean-shift algorithm to be applied on HE are (1) super-linear computational complexity $O(p^2)$ for each mean-shift process and (2) non-polynomial operations in kernel which are hard to be efficiently computed in HE. In order to overcome these challenges, we suggest several novel techniques to modify the original mean-shift algorithm into an *HE-friendly* form:

- Rather than mean-shifting every given point, we randomly sample several points called *dusts* and the mean-shift process will only be conducted for the *dusts*. As a result, the computational cost to seek the modes is reduced from $O(p^2)$ to $O(d \cdot p)$ where d is the number of dusts, which is much smaller than p.
- After the mode-seeking phase, one should match given points to the closest mode, which we call *point-labeling*. We suggest a carefully devised algorithm

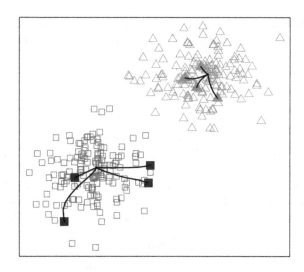

Fig. 1. Illustration of the mean-shift algorithm

for labeling points with the modes, which only consists of polynomial operations so that it can be implemented by HE efficiently.

- We propose a new *HE-friendly kernel* $K(\boldsymbol{x}, \boldsymbol{y}) = (1 - ||\boldsymbol{x} - \boldsymbol{y}||^2)^{2^\Gamma + 1}$. The most commonly used kernel functions in clustering are Gaussian kernel and Epanechnikov kernel. However, the derivatives of those functions, which we should compute for each mean-shift process, are either exponential or discontinuous. Our new kernel is a simple polynomial which only requires $\log(degree)$ complexity to compute its derivative, and the cluster analysis based on this HE-friendly kernel is very accurate in practice.

Practical Performance: Fast and Accurate. To the best of our knowledge, the work in [29] has been a unique full HE solution to privacy-preserving clustering so far. While their implementation takes as much as 619 h for 400 2-dimensional data, our algorithm takes only approx. 1.4 h for the same dataset, which is over 400 times faster than the previous result. Using a multi-threading option with 8 threads, its running time is even reduced to *half an hour*. The fast and accurate performance of our algorithm implies that the research on HE-based privacy-preserving clustering is approaching to a stage of practical application.

Why Mean-shift Clustering? K-means clustering is another representative algorithm for clustering, and many of the previous works on privacy-preserving clustering used the K-means clustering algorithm. However, there are some critical drawbacks in K-means clustering in the perspective of HE applications. Firstly, K-means clustering requires a user to pre-determine the exact number of clusters. However, there is no way to determine the number of clusters when the encrypted data are given only. Therefore, a data owner should additionally provide the number of clusters, but determining the exact number of clusters from a given dataset also requires a costly process even in an unencrypted state [41]. Secondly, K-means clustering often does not work when the shape of clusters is non-convex, but the shape of clusters is also non-predictable information from encrypted data.

1.2 Related Works

In the case of HE-based privacy-preserving clustering, to the best of our knowledge, there has been proposed only a single solution [29] which does not requires any decryption process during the analysis. They transform the K-means clustering algorithm into an HE algorithm based on the HE scheme TFHE [16,17], which encrypts data bit-wisely. One of their core ideas is to modify the original K-means clustering algorithm by substituting a homomorphic division of a ciphertext, which is very expensive, with a simple constant division. As a result, to run their modified algorithm with TFHE over 400 2-dimensional data, it takes approx. 619 h ($\approx$.26 days) on a virtual machine with an Intel i7-3770 processor with 3.4 GHz without parallelization options. Before this work, there has been an attempt [4] to perform K-means clustering based on HE with trusted third party; however, the HE scheme they used [32] was proved to be insecure [46].

Contrary to HE, there have been a number of works [7,21,28,33,38–40,43] on privacy-preserving clustering based on another cryptographic tool called Multi-party Computation (MPC), which is a protocol between several parties to jointly compute a function without revealing any information of their inputs. For more details on MPC-based privacy-preserving clustering algorithms, we refer the readers to a survey paper written by Meskine and Nait-Bahloul [35]. MPC is normally known to be much faster than HE; however, MPC requires *online* computation of data owners and it yields significantly large bandwidth. On the other hand, HE computation can be totally done *offline* after encrypted data are sent to a computing service provider. Since data owners do not need to participate in the computation phase, HE-based solutions can be regarded to be much more convenient and economic to data owners than MPC.

2 Backgrounds

2.1 Notations

We call each given datum of the clustering problem *a point*. Let n be the dimension of each point, and $P = \{P_1, P_2, \dots, P_p\}$ be the set of given points where p is the number of elements in P. We denote the set of dusts, which will be defined in Sect. 3, by $D = \{D_1, D_2, \dots, D_d\}$ where d is the number of dusts. There are several auxiliary parameters for our new algorithms in Sects. 2 and 3: ζ, t, Γ and T denote the number of iterations for Inv, MinIdx, Kernel and Mode-seeking, respectively. $\mathbb{R}$ denotes the real number field, and $\mathbb{R}_{\geq 0}$ is a subset of $\mathbb{R}$ which consists of non-negative real numbers. The set $\mathbb{B}_n(1/2)$ denotes the n-dimensional ball of the radius $1/2$ with center 0. For an n-dimensional vector $\boldsymbol{x} \in \mathbb{R}^n$, the

L_2-norm of x is denoted by $||x||$. For a finite set X, $x \leftarrow U(X)$ means that x is sampled uniformly at random from X, and $|X|$ denotes the number of elements in X. For (row) vectors $x \in \mathbb{R}^n$ and $y \in \mathbb{R}^m$, the concatenation of the two vectors is denoted by $(x||y) \in \mathbb{R}^{n+m}$. For a positive integer q, $[\cdot]_q$ denotes a residue modulo q in $[-q/2, q/2)$.

2.2   Approximate Homomorphic Encryption HEAAN

For privacy-preserving clustering, we apply an HE scheme called HEAAN proposed by Cheon et al. [12,13], which supports *approximate computation* of real numbers in encrypted state. Efficiency of HEAAN in the real world has been proved by showing its applications in various fields including machine learning [15,30,31] and cyber-physical systems [11]. After the solution [30] based on HEAAN won the first place in privacy-preserving genome data analysis competition called IDash in 2017, all the solutions for the next-year competition which aimed to develop a privacy-preserving solution for Genome-wide Association Study (GWAS) computation were constructed based on HEAAN.

In detail, let ct be a HEAAN ciphertext of a plaintext vector $m \in \mathbb{C}^{N/2}$. Then, the decryption process with a secret key sk is done as

$$\mathsf{Dec}_{\mathsf{sk}}(\mathsf{ct}) = m + e \approx m$$

where e is a small error attached to the plaintext vector m. For formal definitions, let L be a level parameter and $q_\ell := 2^\ell$ for $1 \le \ell \le L$. Let $R := \mathbb{Z}[X]/(X^N + 1)$ for a power-of-two N and R_q be a modulo-q quotient ring of R, i.e., $R_q := R/qR$. The distribution $\chi_{\mathsf{key}} := \mathsf{HW}(\mathsf{h})$ over R_q outputs a polynomial of $\{-1, 0, 1\}$-coefficients having h number of non-zero coefficients, and χ_{enc} and χ_{err} denote the discrete Gaussian distribution with some prefixed standard deviation. Finally, $[\cdot]_q$ denotes a component-wise modulo q operation on each element of R_q. Note that whether those parameters N, L and h are satisfying a certain security level can be determined by Albrecht's security estimator [2,3].

A plaintext vector $m \in \mathbb{C}^{n/2}$ is firstly encoded as a polynomial in R by applying a (field) isomorphism τ from $\mathbb{R}[X]/(X^N + 1)$ to $\mathbb{C}^{N/2}$ called canonical embedding. A naive approach is to transform the plaintext vector as $\tau^{-1}(m) \in \mathbb{R}[X]/(X^N + 1)$; however, the naive rounding-off can derive quite a large relative error on the plaintext. In order to control the error, we round the plaintext off after scaling up by p bits for some integer p, i.e., $\lfloor 2^p \cdot \tau^{-1}(m) \rceil$, so that the relative error can be reduced. The full scheme description of HEAAN is as following:

- KeyGen.
    - Sample $s \leftarrow \chi_{\mathsf{key}}$. Set the secret key as sk $\leftarrow (1, s)$.
    - Sample $a \leftarrow U(R_{q_L})$ and $e \leftarrow \chi_{\mathsf{err}}$. Set the public key as pk $\leftarrow (b, a) \in R_{q_L}^2$ where $b \leftarrow [-a \cdot s + e]_{q_L}$.
    - Sample $a' \leftarrow U(R_{q_L^2})$ and $e' \leftarrow \chi_{\mathsf{err}}$. Set the evaluation key as evk $\leftarrow (b', a') \in R_{q_L^2}^2$ where $b' \leftarrow [-a's + e' + q_L \cdot s^2]_{q_L^2}$.

- $\underline{\mathsf{Enc}_{\mathsf{pk}}(\boldsymbol{m})}$.
    - For a plaintext $\boldsymbol{m} = (m_0, ..., m_{N/2-1})$ in $\mathbb{C}^{N/2}$ and a scaling factor $p > 0$, compute a polynomial $\mathfrak{m} \leftarrow \lfloor 2^p \cdot \tau^{-1}(\boldsymbol{m}) \rceil \in R$
    - Sample $v \leftarrow \chi_{\mathsf{enc}}$ and $e_0, e_1 \leftarrow \chi_{\mathsf{err}}$. Output $\mathsf{ct} = [v \cdot \mathsf{pk} + (\mathfrak{m} + e_0, e_1)]_{q_L}$.
- $\underline{\mathsf{Dec}_{\mathsf{sk}}(\mathsf{ct})}$.
    - For a ciphertext $\mathsf{ct} = (c_0, c_1) \in R_{q_\ell}^2$, compute $\mathfrak{m}' = [c_0 + c_1 \cdot s]_{q_\ell}$.
    - Output a plaintext vector $\boldsymbol{m}' = 2^{-p} \cdot \tau(\mathfrak{m}') \in \mathbb{C}^{N/2}$.
- $\underline{\mathsf{Add}(\mathsf{ct}, \mathsf{ct}')}$. For $\mathsf{ct}, \mathsf{ct}' \in R_{q_\ell}^2$, output $\mathsf{ct}_{\mathsf{add}} \leftarrow [\mathsf{ct} + \mathsf{ct}']_{q_\ell}$.
- $\underline{\mathsf{Sub}(\mathsf{ct}, \mathsf{ct}')}$. For $\mathsf{ct}, \mathsf{ct}' \in R_{q_\ell}^2$, output $\mathsf{ct}_{\mathsf{sub}} \leftarrow [\mathsf{ct} - \mathsf{ct}']_{q_\ell}$.
- $\underline{\mathsf{Mult}_{\mathsf{evk}}(\mathsf{ct}, \mathsf{ct}')}$. For $\mathsf{ct} = (c_0, c_1), \mathsf{ct}' = (c_0', c_1') \in \mathcal{R}_{q_\ell}^2$, let $(d_0, d_1, d_2) = (c_0 c_0', c_0 c_1' + c_1 c_0', c_1 c_1')$. Compute $\mathsf{ct}_{\mathsf{mult}}' \leftarrow [(d_0, d_1) + \lfloor q_L^{-1} \cdot d_2 \cdot \mathsf{evk} \rceil]_{q_\ell}$, and output $\mathsf{ct}_{\mathsf{mult}} \leftarrow [\lfloor (1/p) \cdot \mathsf{ct}_{\mathsf{mult}}' \rceil]_{q_{\ell-1}}$.

We omitted the parameters (N, L, h, p) as an input of the above algorithms for convenience. Let ct_1 and ct_2 be ciphertexts of plaintext vectors $\boldsymbol{m}_1$ and $\boldsymbol{m}_2$. Then, the homomorphic evaluation algorithms Add and Mult satisfy

$$\mathsf{Dec}_{\mathsf{sk}}(\mathsf{Add}(\mathsf{ct}_1, \mathsf{ct}_2)) \approx \boldsymbol{m}_1 + \boldsymbol{m}_2,$$
$$\mathsf{Dec}_{\mathsf{sk}}(\mathsf{Mult}_{\mathsf{evk}}(\mathsf{ct}_1, \mathsf{ct}_2)) \approx \boldsymbol{m}_1 \odot \boldsymbol{m}_2$$

where $\odot$ denotes the Hadamard (component-wise) multiplication, i.e., addition and multiplication can be *internally* done in a Single Instruction Multi Data (SIMD) manner even in encrypted state. For more details of the scheme including the correctness and security analysis, we refer the readers to [13].

In order to manage a plaintext vector of the form $\boldsymbol{m} \in \mathbb{C}^K$ having length $K \leq N/2$ for some power-of-two divisor K of $N/2$, HEAAN encrypts $\boldsymbol{m}$ into a ciphertext of an $N/2$-dimensional vector $(\boldsymbol{m}||\cdots||\boldsymbol{m}) \in \mathbb{C}^{N/2}$. This implies that a ciphertext of $\boldsymbol{m} \in \mathbb{C}^K$ can be understood as a ciphertext of $(\boldsymbol{m}||\cdots||\boldsymbol{m}) \in \mathbb{C}^{K'}$ for powers-of-two K and K' satisfying $K \leq K' \leq N/2$.

Bootstrapping of HEAAN. Since the output ciphertext of a homomorphic multiplication has a reduced modulus by the scaling factor p compared to the input ciphertexts, the homomorphic operation should be stopped when the ciphertext modulus becomes so small that no more modulus reduction can be done. In other words, without some additional procedures, the HE scheme only supports polynomial operations with a bounded degree pre-determined by HEAAN parameters.

A *bootstrapping* algorithm, of which the concept was firstly proposed by Gentry [24], enables us to overcome the limitation on the depth of computation. The bootstrapping algorithm gets a ciphertext with the lowest modulus $\mathsf{ct} \in R_{q_1}^2$ as an input, and outputs a refreshed ciphertext $\mathsf{ct}' \in R_{q_{L'}}^2$ where L' is a pre-determined parameter smaller than L. The important fact is that the bootstrapping preserves the most significant bits of a plaintext, i.e., $\mathsf{Dec}_{\mathsf{sk}}(\mathsf{ct}) \approx \mathsf{Dec}_{\mathsf{sk}}(\mathsf{ct}')$. In 2018, a first bootstrapping algorithm for HEAAN was proposed by Cheon et al. [12], and later it was improved by several works concurrently [8,10].

Even though the performance of bootstrapping has been improved by active studies, the bootstrapping algorithm is still regarded as the most expensive part of HE. In the case of HEAAN, the performance of bootstrapping depends on the number of plaintext slots K; roughly the computational complexity is $O(\log K)$ considering SIMD operations of HEAAN.

2.3   Non-polynomial Operations in HEAAN

Since HEAAN basically supports homomorphic addition and multiplication, performing non-polynomial operations in HEAAN is clearly non-trivial. In this section we introduce how to perform the *division* and a comparison-related operation called *min-index* in word-wise HE including HEAAN, which are required for our mean-shift clustering algorithm. Note that the following methods are essentially efficient polynomial approximations for the target operations.

Division. The Goldschmidt's division algorithm [26] is an approximate algorithm to compute the inversion of a positive real number in $(0, 2)$, and has been used in various cryptographic applications [14, 18] to deal with inversion and division operations through a polynomial evaluation. The algorithm approximates the inversion of $x \in (0, 2)$ by

$$\frac{1}{x} = \prod_{i=0}^{\infty} \left(1 + (1 - x)^{2^i}\right) \approx \prod_{i=0}^{\zeta-1} \left(1 + (1 - x)^{2^i}\right)$$

where ζ is a parameter we choose considering the approximation error. If the range of an input is $(0, m)$ for large $m > 0$ which is known, then the Goldschmidt's division algorithm can be easily generalized by simply scaling down the input into the range $(0, 2)$ and scaling up the output after the whole process.

Algorithm 1. $\mathrm{Inv}(x; m, \zeta)$

Input: $0 < x < m$, $\zeta \in \mathbb{N}$
Output: an approximate value of $1/x$
1: $a_0 \leftarrow 2 - (2/m) \cdot x$
2: $b_0 \leftarrow 1 - (2/m) \cdot x$
3: **for** $i \leftarrow 0$ **to** $\zeta - 1$ **do**
4:     $b_{i+1} \leftarrow b_i^2$
5:     $a_{i+1} \leftarrow a_i \cdot (1 + b_{i+1})$
6: **end for**
7: **return** $(2/m) \cdot a_\zeta$

Min Index. In [14], Cheon et al. proposed the iterative algorithm MaxIdx to compute the max-index of an array of positive numbers that can be homomorphically computed by HEAAN efficiently. More precisely, for an input vector $\boldsymbol{x} = (x_1, x_2, .., x_m)$ where $x_i \in (0, 1)$ are distinct numbers, the output of the max-index algorithm is a vector $\left(x_i^{2^t} / (\sum_{j=1}^{m} x_j^{2^t})\right)_{1 \le i \le m}$ for sufficiently large $t > 0$, in which i-th component is close to 1 if x_i is the maximal element and is approximately 0 otherwise. If there are several maximal numbers, say $x_1, ..., x_\ell$ for $1 \le \ell \le m$ without loss of generality, the output vector is approximately $(1/\ell, 1/\ell, ..., 1/\ell, 0..., 0)$.

As a simple application of max-index, one can also compute the *min-index* of an array of positive numbers in $(0, 1)$ by running the `MaxIdx` algorithm for input $(1 - x_1, 1 - x_2, ..., 1 - x_m)$. The following algorithm describes the min-index algorithm denoted by `MinIdx`.

Algorithm 2. `MinIdx`$((x_i)_{i=1}^{m}; t, \zeta)$

Input: $(x_1, ..., x_m) \in (0, 1)^m$ where $\ell \ge 1$ elements are minimal, $t \in \mathbb{N}$
Output: $(y_1, ..., y_m)$ where $y_i \approx 1/\ell$ if x_i is a minimal element and $y_i \approx 0$
  otherwise;
1: $sum \leftarrow 0$
2: **for** $i \leftarrow 1$ **to** m **do**
3:   $y_i \leftarrow 1 - x_i$
4:   **for** $j \leftarrow 1$ **to** t **do**
5:     $y_i \leftarrow y_i \cdot y_i$
6:   **end for**
7:   $sum \leftarrow sum + y_i$
8: **end for**
9: $inv \leftarrow \text{Inv}(sum; m, \zeta)$
10: **for** $i \leftarrow 1$ **to** m **do**
11:   $y_i \leftarrow y_i \cdot inv$ $// \ y_i \simeq (1 - x_i)^{2^t} / \sum_{j=1}^{m} (1 - x_j)^{2^t}$
12: **end for**
13: **return** $(y_1, ..., y_m)$

2.4 Mean-Shift Clustering

The mean-shift clustering algorithm is a *non-parametric* clustering technique which does not restrict *the shape of the clusters* and not require prior knowledge of *the number of clusters*. The goal of the algorithm is to cluster the given points by finding the local maxima (called *modes*) of a density function called *Kernel Density Estimator* (KDE), and this process is essentially done by the gradient descent algorithm. For given n-dimensional points $P_1, P_2, ..., P_p$ and a function $K : \mathbb{R}^n \times \mathbb{R}^n \to \mathbb{R}_{\ge 0}$ so-called *kernel*, the KDE map $F : \mathbb{R}^n \to \mathbb{R}^n$ is defined as

$$F(\boldsymbol{x}) = \frac{1}{p} \cdot \sum_{i=1}^{p} K(\boldsymbol{x}, P_i).$$

The kernel K is defined by a profile $k : \mathbb{R} \to \mathbb{R}_{\ge 0}$ as $K(\boldsymbol{x}, \boldsymbol{y}) = c_k \cdot k(||\boldsymbol{x} - \boldsymbol{y}||^2)$ for some constant $c > 0$. Through a simple computation, one can check that

$\nabla F(\boldsymbol{x})$ is parallel to $\sum_{i=1}^{p} \frac{k'(||\boldsymbol{x}-P_i||^2) \cdot P_i}{\sum_{i=1}^{p} k'(||\boldsymbol{x}-P_i||^2)} - \boldsymbol{x}$ where k' is the derivative of k. As a result, the mean-shift process is to update the point $\boldsymbol{x}$ with

$$\boldsymbol{x} \leftarrow \boldsymbol{x} + \left(\sum_{i=1}^{p} \frac{k'(||\boldsymbol{x} - P_i||^2)}{\sum_{j=1}^{p} k'(||\boldsymbol{x} - P_j||^2)} \cdot P_i - \boldsymbol{x} \right) = \sum_{i=1}^{p} \frac{k'(||\boldsymbol{x} - P_i||^2)}{\sum_{j=1}^{p} k'(||\boldsymbol{x} - P_j||^2)} \cdot P_i,$$

which is the weighted mean of given points. The most usual choices of the kernel function are the Gaussian kernel $K_G(\boldsymbol{x}, \boldsymbol{y}) = c_{k_G} \cdot \exp\left(-||\boldsymbol{x} - \boldsymbol{y}||^2/\sigma^2\right)$ and the Epanechnikov kernel $K_E(\boldsymbol{x}, \boldsymbol{y}) = c_{k_E} \cdot \max(0, 1 - ||\boldsymbol{x} - \boldsymbol{y}||^2/\sigma^2)$ for $\boldsymbol{x}, \boldsymbol{y} \in \mathbb{R}^n$ with an appropriate parameter $\sigma > 0$ and constants c_{k_G} and c_{k_E}. Algorithm 3 is a full description of the original mean-shift clustering algorithm with Gaussian kernel.

Algorithm 3. MS-clustering-original$(P = \{P_1, ..., P_p\}, T; \sigma)$

Input: $P_1, P_2, \cdots, P_p \in \mathbb{R}^n$, the number of iterations $T \in \mathbb{N}$
Output: Label vector M of given points $P_1, ..., P_p$
1: **for** $i \leftarrow 1$ to p **do**
2:    $M_i \leftarrow P_i$
3: **end for**
4: **for** $i \leftarrow 1$ to T **do**
5:    **for** $j \leftarrow 1$ to p **do**
6:       $sum \leftarrow 0$
7:       $A \leftarrow 0^d$
8:       **for** $k \leftarrow 1$ to p **do**
9:          $a \leftarrow \exp(-||P_k - M_j||^2/\sigma^2)$
10:          $A \leftarrow A + a \cdot P_k$
11:          $sum \leftarrow sum + a$
12:       **end for**
13:       $M_j \leftarrow (1/sum) \cdot A$
14:    **end for**
15: **end for**
16: **return** $M = (M_1, ..., M_p)$

Freedman-Kisilev Mean-Shift. A decade ago, Freedman and Kisilev [23] proposed a novel fast mean-shifting algorithm based on the random sampling. As the first step, for the given set $P = \{P_1, P_2, ..., P_p\}$ which consists of n-dimensional points, they randomly choose a subset $P' \subset P$ of the cardinality p'. Here the cardinality p' is indeed smaller than p but *should not be too small* so that the subset P' approximately conserves the distribution of the points. For example, if the random sampling factor p/p' is too high, then Freedman-Kisilev mean-shift algorithm shows a quite different result compared to that of the original mean-shift algorithm. After the random sampling phase, the second step is to run the original mean-shift algorithm only on the randomly chosen subset P' and obtain the modes of KDE constructed by P', not P. Since only p' points are used for mean-shifting process, the computational complexity of this phase is $O(p'^2)$, not $O(p^2)$. The last step so-called "map-backwards" is to find the closest point in $P_j' \in P'$ for each point in $P_i \in P$ and then output the mode mean-shifted from P_j'. The last step takes $O(p' \cdot p)$ computational complexity, which is still smaller than $O(p^2)$. Note that the map-backwards, the last step in Freedman-Kisilev mean-shift algorithm, is not required in the original mean-shift algorithm, since every point converges to some mode which takes a role of the label in the original mean-shift algorithm.

2.5   Clustering Quality Evaluation Criteria

To evaluate the quality of our cluster analysis results, we bring two measures: accuracy and silhouette coefficient. The accuracy is measured by comparing the cluster analysis result and the given true label information. Let L_i and $C(P_i)$ be the true label and the label obtained by cluster analysis of the point P_i, respectively; then, the accuracy is calculated as

$$\mathsf{Accuracy} = \frac{|\{1 \leq i \leq p : L_i = C(P_i)\}|}{p}.$$

Note that the measure is valid only if the number of clusters of the given true label is equal to that of the cluster analysis result.

The silhouette coefficient [37] is another measure which evaluates the quality of cluster analysis, which does not require true label information to be given. Let $Q_1,...,Q_k$ be the clusters of the given dataset P obtained by cluster analysis. For each point P_i which belongs to the cluster Q_{k_i}, we first define two functions A and B as

$$A(P_i) = \frac{1}{|Q_{k_i}| - 1} \cdot \sum_{\substack{P_\ell \in Q_{k_i} \\ \ell \neq i}} \mathrm{dist}(P_i, P_\ell), \quad B(P_i) = \min_{j \neq i} \frac{1}{|Q_{k_j}|} \cdot \sum_{P_\ell \in Q_{k_j}} \mathrm{dist}(P_i, P_\ell).$$

Then, the silhouette coefficient is defined as

$$\mathsf{SilhCoeff} = \frac{1}{p} \cdot \sum_{i=1}^{p} \frac{B(P_i) - A(P_i)}{\max(B(P_i), A(P_i))}$$

which indicates how well the points are clustered. It is clear that $-1 \leq \mathsf{SilhCoeff} \leq 1$, and the silhouette coefficient closer to 1 implies the better result of clustering.

3   HE-Friendly Modified Mean-Shift Clustering

In this section, we introduce several modifications on the mean-shift algorithm which can be efficiently performed by HE. One big drawback of the original mean-shift algorithm to be implemented by HE is the evaluation of kernel functions. They usually contain non-polynomial operations, but these operations cannot be easily computed with HE algorithms. In order to overcome the problem, we suggest a new HE-friendly kernel function in Sect. 3.1 which is computationally efficient and shows a good performance.

Another big drawback of the original mean-shift algorithm to be implemented by HE is its high computational cost. The usual mean-shift process classifies data by seeking modes and mapping points to its corresponding mode at the same time. This strategy eventually forces us to perform mean-shift process on all data, so it is computationally inefficient to be implemented by HE which possibly accompanies more than hundreds or thousands times of overhead. In order to address this issue, we adopt a random sampling method called dust sampling and separate the total mean-shift clustering process into two phases: *mode-seeking phase* and *point-labeling phase*. One can check the details on these two phases in Sects. 3.2 and 3.3 respectively, and the full description of our modified mean-shift clustering algorithm is described in Sect. 3.4.

3.1 HE-Friendly Kernel

As described in Sect. 2.4, the most popular kernel functions for mean-shift algorithm are Gaussian kernel and Epanechnikov kernel. However, the derivatives of both kernel functions, which should be computed in the mean-shift clustering algorithm, are either exponential or discontinuous that cannot be directly computed with HE.

In order to overcome those drawbacks, we propose a new HE-friendly kernel function which is a polynomial. We aim to construct a kernel function that vanishes rapidly as its input goes far from the origin. Moreover, we also consider about reducing the number of multiplications during the computation of the kernel. For each $x \in [0,1]$, our new profile k is calculated as following:

$$k(x) = (1-x)^{2^\Gamma + 1}. \tag{1}$$

The degree was set $2^\Gamma + 1$ to reduce the computational complexity of the derivative function k', which should be computed for mean-shift. Using this profile, a new HE-friendly kernel is defined as following: For $x, y \in \mathbb{B}_n(1/2)$, the kernel function K based on the profile k is

$$K(x,y) = c \cdot \left(1 - ||x-y||^2\right)^{2^\Gamma + 1} \tag{2}$$

for some constant $c > 0$. The following algorithm, denoted by Kernel, shows a very simple computation of $k'(||x-y||^2)$ up to constant $-1/(2^\Gamma + 1)$. If one chooses bigger Γ, the kernel function will decrease more rapidly, so the mean-shift process will focus more on closer points. Conversely, if one chooses smaller Γ, the kernel function will decrease more slowly so that the mean-shift process references wider area.

Our new kernel function is composed of $(\Gamma + 1)$ multiplications and one constant addition, while Γ is relatively minute compared to the degree of the

---

Algorithm 4. Kernel($x, y; \Gamma$)

Input: $x, y \in \mathbb{B}_n(1/2)$, $\Gamma \in \mathbb{N}$
Output: HE-friendly kernel value between A and B
1: $a \leftarrow 1 - \|x - y\|^2$
2: **for** $i \leftarrow 1$ to Γ **do**
3:    $a \leftarrow a^2$
4: **end for**
5: **return** a

---

kernel polynomial ($\Gamma = \log(degree)$). Thus, our new kernel function is very HE-friendly. At the same time, it is non-negative and strictly decreasing, so it satisfies the core conditions of a kernel function for mean-shift algorithm. Moreover, its rapid decreasing property provides a high performance for mean-shift algorithm. The performance of our new kernel function is experimentally proved under various datasets (See Sect. 4). In an unencrypted state, the mean-shift clustering with our kernel function shows almost same performance with that with the Gaussian kernel function on same datasets described in Sect. 4.1.

3.2 Mode-Seeking Phase

The biggest drawback of the original mean-shift clustering algorithm is its high time complexity. It requires super-linear operations in the number of data points. Since HE consumes considerably long time to compute each operation, it is strongly demanded to modify mean-shift algorithm for practical implementation with HE.

In order to overcome those drawbacks, we use random sampling to reduce the total number of operations for each mean-shift process. Instead of performing mean-shift on every point, we perform the mean-shift process only on selected points, which we shall call *dusts*. Each mean-shift process references all the data so that dusts move to proper modes of the KDE map generated by given data. After sufficiently many iterations, each dust converges to a mode, so we can seek all modes if we selected enough number of dusts.

Advantage of the Dust Sampling Method. Our modification has a great advantage on the number of operations. In the original mean-shift clustering algorithm, every point shifts its position by referencing all of the other points. Hence, it needs $O(p^2)$ operations for each loop where p is the number of given points. However, in our approach, only selected dusts shift their positions, so we can complete each mean-shift iteration with $O(p \cdot d)$ operations, where d is the number of selected dusts. This decreases the total number of operations, because we select relatively negligible number of dusts among numerous points.

Even though our approach requires less operations, its performance is acceptable. Since we use the KDE map over all given points, the dusts converge to modes exactly in the same way with the original mean-shift algorithm. Consequently, we can seek all modes by selecting sufficiently many dusts.

How to Sample Dusts? There are many possible ways to set the initial position of dusts. We consider two candidates of initialization strategy of the dusts. One is to uniformly select dusts from the space (so that can form a *grid*), and the other is to select dusts among the given points. The first strategy is tempting because it guarantees high probability to seek all the modes. However, as the dimension of the data set becomes higher, it requires too many number of dusts, which directly increases the total time complexity. On the other hand, the second strategy provides a stable performance with less number of dusts even if the dimension and shape of the data vary. Moreover, it chooses more dusts from the denser regions, so we can expect that it succeeds in detecting all centers of clusters. Thus, we use the second strategy, selecting dusts among given points as described in Algorithm 5.

Comparison to Freedman-Kisilev's Method. At first glance, our approach looks similar to that of Freedman and Kisilev [23]. Remark that they pick p' random samples among the data, and run the mean-shift algorithm only on the sampled points by referencing the KDE map generated by the sampled points.

Compared to Freedman-Kisilev mean-shift, the number of selected dusts d in our mean-shift can be set smaller than the number of randomly sampled points p'. While our sampling method uses the original KDE map, Freedman-Kisilev algorithm uses the KDE map generated by the sampled points. As a consequence, Freedman and Kisilev have to select substantially many samples to preserve the original KDE structure, while we do not have such restriction on the number of dusts.

Algorithm 5. Mode-seeking($P = \{P_1, ..., P_p\}, d, T; \Gamma, \zeta$)

Input: Points $P_1, P_2, \cdots, P_p \in \mathbb{B}_n(1/2)$, the number of dusts $d \in \mathbb{N}$, the number of mean-shift iterations $T \in \mathbb{N}$

Output: Mean-shifted dusts $D_i \in \mathbb{B}_n(1/2)$ close to modes for $1 \le i \le d$

1: **for** $i \leftarrow 1$ **to** d **do**
2:    $D_i \leftarrow U(P)$ // selecting dusts among P_i's
3: **end for**
4: **for** $i \leftarrow 1$ **to** T **do**
5:    **for** $j \leftarrow 1$ **to** d **do**
6:      $sum \leftarrow 0$
7:      $A \leftarrow 0^d$
8:      **for** $k \leftarrow 1$ **to** p **do**
9:        $a \leftarrow \texttt{Kernel}(P_k, D_j; \Gamma)$
10:        $A \leftarrow A + a \cdot P_k$
11:        $sum \leftarrow sum + a$
12:      **end for**
13:      $D_j \leftarrow \texttt{Inv}(sum; p, \zeta) \cdot A$ // $D_j \leftarrow \sum_{i=1}^{p} \frac{k'(||D_j - P_i||^2)}{\sum_{\ell=1}^{p} k'(||D_j - P_\ell||^2)} \cdot P_i$
14:    **end for**
15: **end for**
16: **return** D

The computational complexity of each mean-shift process in Freedman and Kisilev's algorithm is $O(p'^2)$, while ours is $O(d \cdot p)$. If p' is large enough so that $d \cdot p < p'^2$, our mean-shift process might require even less computations. And even if p' has been set small enough so that $p'^2 < p \cdot d$, the computational complexity of the map-backwards process in Freedman-Kisilev mean-shift $O(p \cdot p')$ is still larger than corresponding point-labeling process in our mean-shift $O(p \cdot d)$ since $p' > d$. More importantly, the less number of selected dusts in our approach has a huge advantage on HE implementation. Bootstrapping is the most expensive part in HE, so minimizing the cost of bootstrapping, by reducing the number of bootstrappings or setting the number of plaintext slots as small as possible, is very important to optimize HE implementations. Since the mean-shift clustering algorithm requires very large amount of computations, we have to repeatedly execute bootstrapping on d dusts in the case of our algorithm and p' samples in the case of Freedman-Kisilev. Since $d < p'$, the total bootstrapping procedure takes much less time in our mean-shift algorithm than the Freedman-Kisilev mean-shift algorithm.

3.3   Point-Labeling Phase

Let us move on to the second phase, point-labeling. After finding all the modes, we should label each point by mapping it to its closest mode. A naive way to label a point P_i is as followings:

$$C_{\texttt{naive}}(P_i) = \texttt{argmin}_{1 \leq j \leq d}\texttt{dist}(D_j, P_i)$$

where each D_i denotes the mean-shifted dust after the mode-seeking phase. However, the $\texttt{argmin}$ function is very hard to compute in HE, and furthermore this naive approach would label the points in the same cluster with different indices. For example, let two dusts D_1 and D_2 converge to a same mode M after the mean-shift process, and P_1 and P_2 are unselected points of which the closed dusts are D_1 and D_2 respectively. We expect P_1 and P_2 to be classified as a same cluster because both points are close to the same mode M. However, with the naive way of point-labeling above, $C_{\texttt{naive}}(P_1) = 1$ does not match with $C_{\texttt{naive}}(P_2) = 2$ due to the slight difference between D_1 and D_2.

Fortunately, utilizing $\texttt{MinIdx}$ algorithm in Sect. 2.3 resolves both problems of the naive approach. Let us define a modified point-labeling function C' as

$$C'(P_i) = \texttt{MinIdx}\left((\|P_i - D_k\|^2)_{1 \leq k \leq d}; t, \zeta\right).$$

Since $\texttt{MinIdx}$ algorithm consists of polynomial operations, it can be evaluated by HE for sure. Moreover, with appropriate parameters t and ζ, $\texttt{MinIdx}((x_1, ..., x_m); t, \zeta)$ outputs a vector close to $\left(\frac{1}{2}, \frac{1}{2}, 0, ..., 0\right)$ when x_1 and x_2 are (approximately) minimal among x_i's, rather than $(1, 0, ..., 0)$ or $(0, 1, ..., 0)$. Therefore, in the same setting to above, we get $C'(P_1) \simeq C'(P_2) \simeq \left(\frac{1}{2}, \frac{1}{2}, 0, ..., 0\right)$.

However, C' cannot be a complete solution if we consider the case that a lot of D_i's converge to a same mode. Let $D_1, ..., D_\ell$ converged to the same mode M after the mean-shifting process. Then for a point P_i that is close to the mode

---

Algorithm 6. `Point-labeling`$(P = \{P_1, ..., P_p\}, D = \{D_1, ..., D_d\}; \Gamma, \zeta, t)$

Input: $P_1, .., P_p \in \mathbb{B}_n(1/2), D_1, ..., D_d \in \mathbb{B}_n(1/2), \Gamma \in \mathbb{N}$
Output: Cluster index $C_i \in [0,1]^d$ of each P_i for $1 \le i \le p$
 1: **for** $i \leftarrow 1$ **to** d **do**
 2:     $\text{NHBD}_i \leftarrow 0$
 3:     **for** $j \leftarrow 1$ **to** d **do**
 4:         $\text{NBHD}_i \leftarrow \text{NBHD}_i + \text{Kernel}(D_i, D_j; \Gamma)$
 5:     **end for**
 6: **end for**
 7: $\text{NBHD} \leftarrow (\text{NBHD}_i)_{1 \le i \le d}$ // $\text{NBHD}_i = \sum_{j=1}^d \text{Kernel}(D_i, D_j; \Gamma)$
 8: **for** $i \leftarrow 1$ **to** p **do**
 9:     $C_i' \leftarrow \text{MinIdx}\left(\left(||P_i - D_k||^2\right)_{1 \le k \le d}; t, \zeta\right)$
10:     $C_i \leftarrow C_i' \odot \text{NBHD}$
11: **end for**
12: **return** $C = (C_i)_{1 \le i \le p}$

M, it holds that $C'(P_i) \simeq (\frac{1}{\ell}, \frac{1}{\ell}, ..., \frac{1}{\ell}, 0, ..., 0)$. When ℓ is sufficiently large, we may not be able to distinguish between $\frac{1}{\ell}$ and an approximation error of MinIdx attached to 0. We refine this problem by adopting a vector $\text{NBHD} \in \mathbb{R}^d$ of which i-th component indicates the number of D_j's very close to D_i:

$$\text{NBHD} = \left(\sum_{k=1}^d \text{Kernel}(D_j, D_k; \Gamma)\right)_{1 \le j \le d}$$

for proper parameter $\Gamma \ge 1$, and we define our final point-labeling function C as

$$C(P_i) = C'(P_i) \odot \text{NBHD}.$$

Since $\text{Kernel}(D_j, D_k; \Gamma)$ outputs approximately 1 if $D_j \simeq D_k$ and 0 otherwise, the j-th component NBHD_i an approximate value of the number of dusts close to D_j. Therefore, each component of $C(P_i)$ is approximately 0 or 1 for $1 \le i \le p$. More precisely, for $1 \le j \le d$, $C(P_i)_j \simeq 1$ if and only if D_j is one of the closest dusts to P_i.

To sum up, with mean-shifted dusts $D = \{D_1, ..., D_d\}$, we label each point P_i by

$$C(P_i) = \text{MinIdx}\left(\left(||P_i - D_k||^2\right)_{1 \le k \le d}; t, \zeta\right) \odot \left(\sum_{k=1}^d \text{Kernel}(D_j, D_k; \zeta)\right)_{1 \le j \le d}.$$

Parameters t and ζ control the accuracy of MinIdx, and the parameter ζ control the accuracy of counting the number of converged dusts in each mode. Note that the return type of C is a d-dimensional vector, in which the i-th component C_i denotes $C(P_i)$.

Other Approaches of Point-Labeling. Another possible choice of the point-labeling function is *coordinate-of-dust* function that simply returns the dust closest to the input point, i.e., $C_{\text{coord}}(P_i) = D_{\text{argmin}_{1 \leq j \leq d} \text{dist}(D_j, P_i)}$. However, the minimum distance between $C_{\text{coord}}(P_i)$'s cannot be bounded by any constant. This limitation makes it unclear to determine whether two points P_i and P_j satisfying $C_{\text{coord}}(P_i) \simeq C_{\text{coord}}(P_i)$ in some sense belong to the same cluster or not. Since we are using several approximate algorithms including Mode-seeking, this obscure situation occurs quite often. Therefore, C_{coord} is not the best choice for point labeling.

Freedman and Kisilev [23] uses another strategy called the map-backwards strategy. In this strategy, we label points by referencing the initial position of dusts instead of their final position. For example, we can compute the label of each point $P_i \in P$ by a vector-matrix multiplication as followings:

$$C_{\text{back}}(P_i) = \texttt{MinIdx}\left((\|P_i - D_j^0\|^2)_{1 \leq j \leq d}; t, \zeta\right) \cdot (\texttt{Kernel}(D_j, D_k))_{1 \leq j, k \leq d}$$

where D_j^0 is the initial position of each $D_j \in D$. Note that we treat the first term as a $1 \times d$ matrix and the second term as $d \times d$ matrix, and multiply them by a matrix multiplication. As a result, the j-th entry of $C_{\text{back}}(P_i)$ would designate the set of dust-neighborhood of the dust closest to P_i at the initial state.

This strategy is also reasonable since the points close to the initial position of each dust are generally expected to move close to the same mode through the mean-shift process. We may regard this strategy as partitioning the points as several regions through the initial position of dusts. However, the map-backwards strategy shall be relatively inefficient compared to our point-labeling strategy in the perspective of HE implementation. In the map-backwards strategy with only small number of dusts, the sampled point in each partitioned regions might not completely represent the region. Thus, the map-backwards strategy essentially requires substantially many number of dusts. As we explained in Sect. 3.2, a less number of dusts is better for HE implementation. Furthermore, a vector-matrix multiplication in the map-backwards strategy is more expensive in HE compared to a Hadamard multiplication of two vectors in our point-labeling strategy.

3.4 Our Modified Mean-Shift Clustering Algorithm

In summary, our modified mean-shift clustering procedure is done by two phases: mode-seeking phase and point-labeling phase. In the first phase, we seek all the modes which are candidates for the centers of clusters, and in the second phase, we map each point to its closest mode with well-devised point-labeling function. Algorithm 7 describes our HE-friendly modified mean-shift clustering algorithm:

Complexity Analysis. In the mode-seeking phase, the mean-shift process is iterated for T times. For each iteration, we calculate the kernel value between all pairs of points and dusts. Note that the computational complexity of Kernel between two n-dimensional points is $O(n)$, so each mean-shift iteration takes $O(n \cdot d \cdot p)$; hence, the computational cost of Mode-seeking is $O(n \cdot d \cdot p \cdot T)$.

The point-labeling phase consists of calculating vectors NBHD and C_i', and Hadamard multiplications NBHD $\odot$ C_i' for $1 \leq i \leq p$. In order to obtain NBHD,

---

Algorithm 7. Mean-shift-clustering$(P = \{P_1, ..., P_p\}, d, T; \Gamma_1, \Gamma_2, \zeta_1, \zeta_2, t)$

Input: $P_1, P_2, \cdots, P_p \in \mathbb{B}_n(1/2),\ \Gamma_1\Gamma_2, d, T \in \mathbb{N}$
Output: A label vector of $P_1, P_2, ..., P_p$
 1: $D \leftarrow$ Mode-seeking$(P, d, T; \Gamma_1, \zeta_1)$
 2: $C \leftarrow$ Point-labeling$(P, D; \Gamma_2, \zeta_2, t)$
 3: **return** $C = (C_1, ..., C_p)$

---

we calculate the kernel values between all pairs of dusts, so it takes $O(n \cdot d^2)$ computations. Also, to calculate C_i', we measure the distances from the given point to dusts, so it requires $O(n \cdot d)$ computations. Note that the cost $O(n)$ of a Hadamard multiplication is negligible. As a result, the computational cost of Point-labeling is $O(n \cdot d \cdot p)$ because d is always strictly smaller than p. To sum up, the cost of mode-seeking phase is $O(n \cdot d \cdot p \cdot T)$, and that of point-labeling phase is $O(n \cdot d \cdot p)$. Consequently, the computational cost of our algorithm is $O(n \cdot d \cdot p \cdot T)$.

We can reduce the computational cost of Mean-shift-clustering by at most $N/2$, since HEAAN supports $N/2$ parallel computations in a SIMD manner where N is a HEAAN parameter. Fortunately, we can apply SIMD efficiently to our algorithm. The most heaviest parts of our algorithm are mean-shift process and MinIdx, both of which require $O(n \cdot p \cdot d)$ computations. For mean-shift process, we compute kernel values between all pairs of points and dusts. When we have one ciphertext of

$$(P_1 \parallel P_2 \parallel \cdots \parallel P_p \parallel P_1 \parallel P_2 \parallel \cdots \parallel P_p \parallel \cdots \parallel P_1 \parallel P_2 \parallel \cdots \parallel P_p)$$

and another ciphertext of

$$(D_1 \parallel D_1 \parallel \cdots \parallel D_1 \parallel D_2 \parallel D_2 \parallel \cdots \parallel D_2 \parallel \cdots \parallel D_k \parallel D_k \parallel \cdots \parallel D_k)$$

with $k = \frac{N}{2np}$, then we can compute $k \cdot p = \frac{N}{2n}$ kernel computations simultaneously, and the computational cost of each kernel reduces to $O(\log n)$. As a result, we can run Mode-seeking with $O\left(\frac{n^2 \cdot d \cdot p \cdot T}{\log n \cdot N}\right)$ computations in HEAAN. Similarly we can reduce the number of computations for Point-labeling as well. Thereby the total computational cost of our algorithm would be $O\left(\frac{n^2 \cdot d \cdot p \cdot T}{\log n \cdot N}\right)$.

4   Experimental Results

4.1   Dataset Description

In order to monitor the performance, we implement our algorithm over four datasets (Hepta, Tetra, TwoDiamonds, Lsun) with true labels which are publicly accessible from fundamental clustering problems suite (FCPS) [42] and one large-scale dataset (LargeScale) randomly generated by ourselves. LargeScale dataset consists of four clusters following Gaussian distributions with small variance and distinct centers. Table 1 describes the properties of each dataset (Fig. 2):

Table 1. Short descriptions of the datasets

Dataset	Dimension	# Data	# Clusters	Property
Hepta	3	212	7	`Different densities`
Tetra	3	400	4	`Big and touching clusters`
TwoDiamonds	2	800	2	`Touching clusters`
Lsun	2	400	3	`Different shapes`
LargeScale	4	262,144	4	`Numerous points`

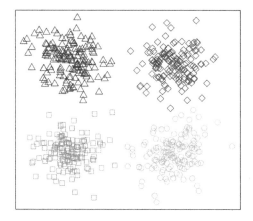

Fig. 2. A visualization of LargeScale dataset

4.2 Parameter Selection

Our implementation is based on the approximate HE library HEAAN [1,13]. We set HEAAN parameters (N, q_L, h, χ_{err}) to satisfy 128-bit security, where N is the ring dimension, q_L is the initial modulus of a ciphertext, h is a hamming weight of a secret polynomial, and χ_{err} is the error distribution. As mentioned in Sect. 2.2, we used Albrecht's security estimator [2,3] to estimate the bit security of those HEAAN parameters. Note that since the modulus of the evaluation key evk is q_L^2, the input on the security estimator is a tuple $(N, Q = q_L^2, h, \chi_{err})$. As a result, we set HEAAN parameters $N = 2^{17}$ and $\log q_L = 1480$, and we followed the default setting of HEAAN library [1] for error and secret distributions χ_{err}, χ_{enc} and χ_{key}.

We flexibly chose the clustering parameters T, Γ_1, Γ_2, ζ_1, ζ_2 and t for each dataset to optimize the implementation results. Let us denote the a tuple of parameters by $\mathsf{params} = (T, \Gamma_1, \Gamma_2, \zeta_1, \zeta_2, t)$. In the case of Hepta dataset, the best choice of parameters was $\mathsf{params} = (5, 6, 6, 4, 4, 6)$, while $\mathsf{params} = (7, 6, 6, 5, 6, 6)$ was the best for Tetra dataset, $\mathsf{params} = (8, 5, 5, 5, 6, 5)$ was the best for TwoDiamonds dataset, $\mathsf{params} = (5, 6, 5, 5, 8, 6)$ was the best for Lsun dataset, and $\mathsf{params} = (5, 5, 5, 3, 3, 5)$ was the best for LargeScale dataset. We set the number of dusts to be as small as possible (e.g., $d = 8$) to reduce the cost of bootstrapping.

Table 2. Experimental results for various datasets with 8 threads

Dataset	Comp. Time	Memory	Quality Evaluation	
			Accuracy	SilhCoeff
Hepta	25 min	10.7 GB	212/212	0.702 (0.702)
Tetra	36 min	10.7 GB	400/400	0.504 (0.504)
TwoDiamonds	38 min	9.6 GB	792/800	0.478 (0.485)
Lsun	24 min	9.4 GB	-	0.577 (0.443)
LargeScale	82 min	20.7 GB	262127/262144	0.781 (0.781)

4.3 Experimental Results

In this subsection, we present experimental results on our mean-shift clustering algorithm based on HEAAN. All experiments were performed on C++11 standard and implemented on Linux with Intel Xeon CPU E5-2620 v4 at 2.10 GHz processor.

In Table 2, we present the performance and quality of our algorithm on various datasets. We use 8 threads for all experiments here. We describe the accuracy value by presenting both the number of well-classified points and the total number of points. We present two silhouette coefficients; the one without bracket is the silhouette coefficient of our clustering results, and the other one with bracket is that of the true labels.

We complete the clustering on various datasets within a few dozens of minutes. In the case of FCPS datasets, their sizes are much smaller than the number of HEAAN plaintext slots we can manage. On the other hand, the size of LargeScale dataset is big enough so that we can use full slots; therefore, we can fully utilize SIMD of HEAAN for the LargeScale dataset. Consequently, the performance of our algorithm for LargeScale dataset is quite nice in spite of its huge size.

For all the five datasets, our algorithm achieves high accuracy. In the case of Hepta, Tetra and LargeScale datasets, we succeed in labeling all data points by its exact true label. For the TwoDiamonds dataset, we succeed in classifying 792 points out of 800 points properly. Even for the rest 8 points, the label vector of each point is close to its true label.

In the case of the Lsun dataset, our algorithm results in four clusters while there are only three clusters in the true labels. Thereby, it is impossible to measure the accuracy by comparing with the true labels, so one may doubt that our algorithm is inadequate to the Lsun dataset. However, it is also reasonable to classify the Lsun dataset with 4 clusters. In fact, our result shows even a better quality in aspect of the silhouette coefficient. The silhouette coefficient for our clustering result is 0.577, and that for the true labels is 0.443.

We also checked the performance of our algorithm with several numbers of threads for the Lsun dataset as described in Table 3. With a single thread, it consumes 9.4 GB memory and takes 83 min. This result is much faster than the result of the previous work in [29], which takes 25.79 days to complete a clustering process for the same Lsun dataset. Obviously we can speed up the performance by using much more number of threads. For example, the running time can be reduced to 16 min with just small overhead of memory when we use 20 threads.

Table 3. Experimental results for various # threads with the Lsun dataset

1 Thread		8 Threads		20 Threads	
Time	Memory	Time	Memory	Time	Memory
83 min	9.4 GB	24 min	9.4 GB	16 min	10.0 GB

Comparison to Freedman-Kisilev's Method. The experimental results of Freedman-Kisilev mean-shift clustering on the Tetra dataset under various p', the number of sampled points (see Sect. 2.4), shows how marginal p' may contaminate the performance. Note that our sampling method achieves $400/400$ accuracy on the Tetra dataset with only 8 dusts. In contrast, when p' is either 8 or 16, Freedman-Kisilev algorithm even fails to detect the correct modes from the original data. It detects only three clusters while there actually exist four clusters; it classifies two different clusters as a single cluster. Thus, the results on when p' is either 8 or 16 are not even comparable with the answer. This supports the argument that the KDE map of Freedman-Kisilev mean-shift may not fully represent the original KDE map unless p' is sufficiently big.

When p' is bigger than 16, Freedman-Kisilev algorithm succeed in detecting four clusters as expected. However, the accuracy under each $p' = 32, 64, 128, 256$ is $377/400, 368/400, 393/400, 399/400$ respectively, while our sampling method achieves $400/400$ with only 8 dusts. This implies that the approximate KDE map of Freedman-Kisilev mean-shift may indicate modes with possible errors.

As a consequence, Freedman and Kisilev have to select substantially many samples that can preserve the original KDE structure in some sense, while we do not have such restriction on the number of dusts.

Acknowledgement. This work was supported in part by the Institute for Information & Communications Technology Promotion (IITP) Grant through the Korean

Government (MSIT), (Development of lattice-based post-quantum public-key cryptographic schemes), under Grant 2017-0-00616, and in part by the National Research Foundation of Korea (NRF) Grant funded by the Korean Government (MSIT) (No. 2017R1A5A1015626). We also thank anonymous reviewers of SAC'19 for very usual comments.

References

1. HEAAN Library (2017). https://github.com/snucrypto/HEAAN
2. Albrecht, M.R.: A Sage Module for estimating the concrete security of Learning with Errors instances (2017). https://bitbucket.org/malb/lwe-estimator
3. Albrecht, M.R., Player, R., Scott, S.: On the concrete hardness of learning with errors. J. Math. Cryptol. **9**(3), 169–203 (2015)
4. Almutairi, N., Coenen, F., Dures, K.: K-means clustering using homomorphic encryption and an updatable distance matrix: secure third party data clustering with limited data owner interaction. In: Bellatreche, L., Chakravarthy, S. (eds.) DaWaK 2017. LNCS, vol. 10440, pp. 274–285. Springer, Cham (2017). https://doi.org/10.1007/978-3-319-64283-3_20
5. Bonte, C., Vercauteren, F.: Privacy-preserving logistic regression training. Cryptology ePrint Archive, Report 2018/233 (2018). https://eprint.iacr.org/2018/233
6. Bourse, F., Minelli, M., Minihold, M., Paillier, P.: Fast homomorphic evaluation of deep discretized neural networks. In: Shacham, H., Boldyreva, A. (eds.) CRYPTO 2018. LNCS, vol. 10993, pp. 483–512. Springer, Cham (2018). https://doi.org/10.1007/978-3-319-96878-0_17
7. Bunn, P., Ostrovsky, R.: Secure two-party k-means clustering. In: Proceedings of the 14th ACM Conference on Computer and Communications Security, CCS 2007, New York, NY, USA, pp. 486–497. ACM (2007)
8. Chen, H., Chillotti, I., Song, Y.: Improved bootstrapping for approximate homomorphic encryption. Cryptology ePrint Archive, Report 2018/1043 (2018). http://eprint.iacr.org/2018/1043. To appear EUROCRYPT 2019
9. Chen, H., et al.: Logistic regression over encrypted data from fully homomorphic encryption. Cryptology ePrint Archive, Report 2018/462 (2018). https://eprint.iacr.org/2018/462
10. Cheon, J.H., Han, K., Hhan, M.: Faster homomorphic discrete fourier transforms and improved FHE bootstrapping. Cryptology ePrint Archive, Report 2018/1073 (2018). https://eprint.iacr.org/2018/1073. To appear IEEE Access
11. Cheon, J.H., et al.: Toward a secure drone system: flying with real-time homomorphic authenticated encryption. IEEE Access **6**, 24325–24339 (2018)
12. Cheon, J.H., Han, K., Kim, A., Kim, M., Song, Y.: Bootstrapping for approximate homomorphic encryption. In: Nielsen, J.B., Rijmen, V. (eds.) EUROCRYPT 2018. LNCS, vol. 10820, pp. 360–384. Springer, Cham (2018). https://doi.org/10.1007/978-3-319-78381-9_14
13. Cheon, J.H., Kim, A., Kim, M., Song, Y.: Homomorphic encryption for arithmetic of approximate numbers. In: Takagi, T., Peyrin, T. (eds.) ASIACRYPT 2017. LNCS, vol. 10624, pp. 409–437. Springer, Cham (2017). https://doi.org/10.1007/978-3-319-70694-8_15
14. Cheon, J.H., Kim, D., Kim, D., Lee, H.H., Lee, K.: Numerical methods for comparison on homomorphically encrypted numbers. Cryptology ePrint Archive, Report 2019/417 (2019). https://eprint.iacr.org/2019/417, To appear ASIACRYPT 2019

15. Cheon, J.H., Kim, D., Kim, Y., Song, Y.: Ensemble method for privacy-preserving logistic regression based on homomorphic encryption. IEEE Access **6**, 46938–46948 (2018)
16. Chillotti, I., Gama, N., Georgieva, M., Izabachène, M.: Faster fully homomorphic encryption: bootstrapping in less than 0.1 seconds. In: Cheon, J.H., Takagi, T. (eds.) ASIACRYPT 2016. LNCS, vol. 10031, pp. 3–33. Springer, Heidelberg (2016). https://doi.org/10.1007/978-3-662-53887-6_1
17. Chillotti, I., Gama, N., Georgieva, M., Izabachène, M.: Faster packed homomorphic operations and efficient circuit bootstrapping for TFHE. In: Takagi, T., Peyrin, T. (eds.) ASIACRYPT 2017. LNCS, vol. 10624, pp. 377–408. Springer, Cham (2017). https://doi.org/10.1007/978-3-319-70694-8_14
18. Cho, H., Wu, D.J., Berger, B.: Secure genome-wide association analysis using multiparty computation. Nat. Biotechnol. **36**(6), 547 (2018)
19. Crawford, J.L., Gentry, C., Halevi, S., Platt, D., Shoup, V.: Doing real work with FHE: the case of logistic regression (2018)
20. Dhillon, I.S., Marcotte, E.M., Roshan, U.: Diametrical clustering for identifying anti-correlated gene clusters. Bioinformatics **19**(13), 1612–1619 (2003)
21. Doganay, M.C., Pedersen, T.B., Saygin, Y., Savaş, E., Levi, A.: Distributed privacy preserving k-means clustering with additive secret sharing. In: Proceedings of the 2008 International Workshop on Privacy and Anonymity in Information Society, PAIS 2008, New York, NY, USA, pp. 3–11. ACM (2008)
22. Duda, R.O., Hart, P.E., Stork, D.G.: Pattern Classification. Wiley, Hoboken (2012)
23. Freedman, D., Kisilev, P.: Fast mean shift by compact density representation. In: 2009 IEEE Conference on Computer Vision and Pattern Recognition, pp. 1818–1825. IEEE (2009)
24. Gentry, C.: A fully homomorphic encryption scheme. Ph.D. thesis, Stanford University (2009). http://crypto.stanford.edu/craig
25. Gilad-Bachrach, R., Dowlin, N., Laine, K., Lauter, K., Naehrig, M., Wernsing, J.: CryptoNets: applying neural networks to encrypted data with high throughput and accuracy. In: International Conference on Machine Learning, pp. 201–210 (2016)
26. Goldschmidt, R.E.: Applications of division by convergence. Ph.D. thesis, Massachusetts Institute of Technology (1964)
27. Han, K., Hong, S., Cheon, J.H., Park, D.: Logistic regression on homomorphic encrypted data at scale (2019)
28. Jagannathan, G., Wright, R.N.: Privacy-preserving distributed k-means clustering over arbitrarily partitioned data. In: Proceedings of the Eleventh ACM SIGKDD International Conference on Knowledge Discovery in Data Mining, KDD 2005, New York, NY, USA, pp. 593–599. ACM (2005)
29. Jäschke, A., Armknecht, F.: Unsupervised machine learning on encrypted data. In: Cid, C., Jacobson Jr., M. (eds.) SAC 2018. LNCS, vol. 11349, pp. 453–478. Springer, Cham (2018). https://doi.org/10.1007/978-3-030-10970-7_21
30. Kim, A., Song, Y., Kim, M., Lee, K., Cheon, J.H.: Logistic regression model training based on the approximate homomorphic encryption. BMC Med. Genomics **11**(4), 83 (2018)
31. Kim, M., Song, Y., Wang, S., Xia, Y., Jiang, X.: Secure logistic regression based on homomorphic encryption: design and evaluation. JMIR Med. Inform. **6**(2), e19 (2018)
32. Liu, D.: Practical fully homomorphic encryption without noise reduction. Cryptology ePrint Archive, Report 2015/468 (2015). https://eprint.iacr.org/2015/468

33. Liu, X., et al.: Outsourcing two-party privacy preserving k-means clustering protocol in wireless sensor networks. In: 2015 11th International Conference on Mobile Ad-Hoc and Sensor Networks (MSN), pp. 124–133. IEEE (2015)
34. Malik, M.B., Ghazi, M.A., Ali, R.: Privacy preserving data mining techniques: current scenario and future prospects. In: 2012 Third International Conference on Computer and Communication Technology (ICCCT), pp. 26–32. IEEE (2012)
35. Meskine, F., Nait-Bahloul, S.: Privacy preserving k-means clustering: a survey research. Int. Arab J. Inf. Technol. **9**, 03 (2012)
36. Pouget, F., Dacier, M., et al.: Honeypot-based forensics. In: AusCERT Asia Pacific Information Technology Security Conference (2004)
37. Rousseeuw, P.J.: Silhouettes: a graphical aid to the interpretation and validation of cluster analysis. J. Comput. Appl. Math. **20**, 53–65 (1987)
38. Sakuma, J., Kobayashi, S.: Large-scale k-means clustering with user-centric privacy preservation. In: Washio, T., Suzuki, E., Ting, K.M., Inokuchi, A. (eds.) PAKDD 2008. LNCS (LNAI), vol. 5012, pp. 320–332. Springer, Heidelberg (2008). https://doi.org/10.1007/978-3-540-68125-0_29
39. Samet, S., Miri, A., Orozco-Barbosa, L.: Privacy preserving k-means clustering in multi-party environment, January 2007
40. Su, C., Bao, F., Zhou, J., Takagi, T., Sakurai, K.: Privacy-preserving two-party k-means clustering via secure approximation. In: Proceedings of the 21st International Conference on Advanced Information Networking and Applications Workshops - Volume 01, AINAW 2007, Washington, DC, USA, pp. 385–391. IEEE Computer Society (2007)
41. Sugar, C.A., James, G.M.: Finding the number of clusters in a dataset: an information-theoretic approach. J. Am. Stat. Assoc. **98**(463), 750–763 (2003)
42. Ultsch, A.: Clustering with SOM: U*C. In: Proceedings of Workshop on Self-Organizing Maps, Paris, France, pp. 75–82 (2005). https://www.uni-marburg.de/fb12/arbeitsgruppen/datenbionik/data?language_sync=1
43. Vaidya, J., Clifton, C.: Privacy-preserving k-means clustering over vertically partitioned data. In: Proceedings of the Ninth ACM SIGKDD International Conference on Knowledge Discovery and Data Mining, KDD 2003, New York, NY, USA, pp. 206–215. ACM (2003)
44. Vinoth, K.J., Santhi, V.: A brief survey on privacy preserving techniques in data mining. IOSR J. Comput. Eng. (IOSR-JCE) **18**, 47–51 (2016)
45. Wang, S., et al.: HEALER: homomorphic computation of exact logistic regression for secure rare disease variants analysis in GWAS. Bioinformatics **32**(2), 211–218 (2016)
46. Wang, Y.: Notes on two fully homomorphic encryption schemes without bootstrapping. IACR Cryptology ePrint Archive, 2015:519 (2015)

Breaking the Bluetooth Pairing – The Fixed Coordinate Invalid Curve Attack

Eli Biham[✉] and Lior Neumann[✉]

Department of Computer Science,
Technion – Israel Institute of Technology, Haifa, Israel
{biham,lior.neumann}@cs.technion.ac.il

Abstract. Bluetooth is a widely deployed standard for wireless communications between mobile devices. It uses authenticated Elliptic Curve Diffie-Hellman for its key exchange. In this paper we show that the authentication provided by the Bluetooth pairing protocols is insufficient and does not provide the promised MitM protection. We present a new attack that modifies the y-coordinates of the public keys (while preserving the x-coordinates). The attack compromises the encryption keys of all of the current Bluetooth authenticated pairing protocols, provided both paired devices are vulnerable. Specifically, it successfully compromises the encryption keys of 50% of the Bluetooth pairing attempts, while in the other 50% the pairing of the victims is terminated. The affected vendors have been informed and patched their products accordingly, and the Bluetooth specification had been modified to address the new attack. We named our new attack the "Fixed Coordinate Invalid Curve Attack". Unlike the well known "Invalid Curve Attack" of Biehl et al. [2] which recovers the private key by sending multiple specially crafted points to the victim, our attack is a MitM attack which modifies the public keys in a way that lets the attacker deduce the shared secret.

1 Introduction

Bluetooth is a wireless communication standard for exchanging data over short distances. The protocol provides confidentiality and access authentication at the link layer. Thanks to its embedded security and flexibility Bluetooth has become one of the most popular communication protocols for mobile devices.

This paper presents a new cryptographic attack on the ECDH protocol and its application to all of the current Bluetooth versions. Our attack provides a new tool for attacking protocols with insufficient MitM authentication as we illustrate on Bluetooth.

As a result of our disclosure CVE-2018-5383 was assigned for this vulnerability in the Bluetooth protocol. All of the major Bluetooth vendors including Qualcomm, Broadcom, Intel, Google and Apple have addressed the issue and released

This research was partially supported by the Technion Hiroshi Fujiwara cyber security research center and the Israel national cyber directorate.

K. G. Paterson and D. Stebila (Eds.): SAC 2019, LNCS 11959, pp. 250–273, 2020.
https://doi.org/10.1007/978-3-030-38471-5_11

an update for their products either directly or through partner companies. Moreover, the Bluetooth Special Interest Group issued a mandatory requirement to the Bluetooth Core Specification in order to mitigate this vulnerability.

1.1   Bluetooth Versions

Bluetooth is a set of protocols evolved during many years of development. The two main Bluetooth protocols are *Bluetooth BR/EDR*, commonly used by audio peripheral and old Bluetooth equipment, and *Bluetooth Low Energy*, mainly used by IoT and smart devices.

In this paper we concentrate on the two associated pairing protocols, the *Secure Simple Pairing (SSP)* and the *LE Secure Connections (LE SC)*. The SSP protocol is used as part of the original Bluetooth BR/EDR protocol, while the recent LE SC protocol is used by the newer Bluetooth Low Energy protocol. The full list of Bluetooth protocols and sub-protocols is summarized in Appendix A.

1.2   The Elliptic Curve Diffie-Hellman Protocol

The *Elliptic Curve Diffie-Hellman (ECDH)* protocol, introduced in the 1980s by Miller [20] and Koblitz [13], is a variant of the Diffie-Hellman key exchange protocol [3]. It utilizes the algebraic structure of elliptic curves over finite fields in order to exchange cryptographic symmetric keys over a public compromised channel.

The domain parameters of ECDH consist of the order q of the underlying finite field $\mathbb{F}_q$, the equation of the elliptic curve $y^2 = x^3 + ax + b$ and a base point P with a prime order n. Examples of such parameters are the NIST domain parameters specified in the FIPS 186-2 standard [14], which are used by the Bluetooth pairing protocol.

Both parties should agree on the domain parameters $D = \{q, a, b, P, n\}$ in advance. For any integer x, denote $[x]P$ to be the repeated addition of point P to itself x times. The first step of the protocol is key-pair generation, in which each party generates an ECDH key-pair. A key-pair consists of a private scalar SK and a public point PK, such that $PK = [SK]P$. Both parties then send their public point to their correspondent. Finally both parties compute the shared-point by multiplying their private scalar by their correspondent's public point. A diagram of the protocol is outlined in Fig. 1.

Note that a scalar multiplication over elliptic curves is commutative. This fact ensures that both parties compute the same shared key

$$[SKa]PKb = [SKa]([SKb]P) = [SKb]([SKa]P) = [SKb]PKa.$$

A major advantage of DH based on elliptic curves over DH based on multiplicative modulus groups is the much lower communication complexity for a given security property. The best known attacks against the elliptic curve discrete logarithm problem for a general curve requires $O(\sqrt{n})$ group operations compared to sub-exponential complexity $O\left(e^{c(\log n)^{\frac{1}{3}}(\log \log n)^{\frac{2}{3}}}\right)$ in the modular

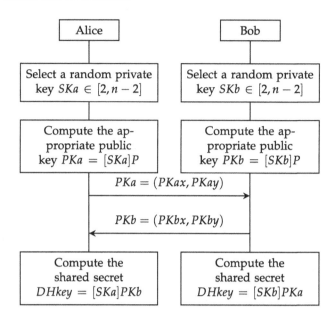

Fig. 1. Elliptic curve Diffie-Hellman protocol diagram

case. As a result the same security properties of multiplicative modulus groups can be achieved with much smaller group sizes, which makes ECDH far more space efficient than the original DH protocol. This property is making ECDH better suited for low-bandwidth radio based communication between embedded devices.

1.3   Previous Work

The first version of Bluetooth BR/EDR was not intended to be secure against MitM attacks. It used a short PIN code as its primary cryptographic secret. Bluetooth BR/EDR version 2.1 introduced SSP which added authenticated ECDH to achieve eavesdropping and MitM protection. A patent assigned by Landrock and Kjaersgaard [12] in 2008 describes how the Invalid Curve Attack could break SSP in cases where appropriate public key validation is not performed. It explains how a malicious attacker can extract the private ECDH key from a poorly implemented platform. The patent proposed multiple mitigations against the attack, which was adopted by the Bluetooth SIG. The protocol designers suggest three optional methods in order to "prevent an attacker from retrieving useful information about the device's private key using invalid public keys", as described in [7, Part H, Section 5.1]. The proposed methods are:

- "Change its private key after three failed attempts from any BD_ADDR and after 10 successful pairings from any BD_ADDR; or after a combination of these such that 3 successful pairings count as one failed pairing".

- "Verify that the received public keys from any BD_ADDR are on the correct curve".
- "Implement elliptic curve point addition and doubling using formulas that are valid only on the correct curve".

Most implementors chose the first mitigation.

The first version of the Bluetooth Low Energy pairing scheme also did not protect against MitM attacks. In an article called "With Low Energy Comes Low Security" [17] by Ryan, the author pointed out that BTLE "Legacy Pairing" is vulnerable to an eavesdropping attack. His article describes how an attacker with low resources can easily sniff BTLE traffic and decrypt it without any interaction with the victim. His attack relies on the same weakness that was found in the original Bluetooth pairing. Prior to the authentication phase a 6-digit decimal PIN is generated and displayed by the slave. The user then enters this PIN to the master device. The session key is exchanged encrypted using the PIN as a mutual temporary key. Ryan also provided an open-source software [16] that recovers the session key from captured Legacy Pairing traffic within a fraction of a second.

Bluetooth version 4.2 addressed the weaknesses found in the Legacy Pairing protocol by introducing LE Secure Connections, a new pairing protocol based on ECDH. Since the release of Core Specification 4.2 [7] no new security related issues regarding the pairing of Bluetooth Low Energy have been published.

Small-subgroups based attacks were described several times throughout history. In 2015, Jager, Schwenk and Somorovsky [11] presented practical Invalid Curve Attack on specific implementations of TLS which indicated that these attacks are still widely effective on modern software.

1.4 Our Results

In the Bluetooth core specification [7, Part A, Section 5.2.3], the protocol designers state that "Secure Simple Pairing protects the user from MitM attacks with a goal of offering a 1 in 1,000,000 chance that a MitM could mount a successful attack". Since LE SC is almost identical to SSP, it is safe to assume that the same goal was intended for it as well. We present a new MitM attack on both SSP and LE SC showing that this goal is not accomplished.

Our attack exploits improper validation of ECDH public keys by introducing the Fixed Coordinate Invalid Curve Attack. It is a MitM attack that modifies the public keys in a way that lets the attacker deduce the shared secret. Provided that both paired devices are vulnerable, our attack can compromise 50% of the Bluetooth pairing attempts, while in the rest the pairing fails.

In this paper we present two variations of our attack: semi-passive and fully-active. In both cases, our attack recovers the session encryption key on success, while on failure our attack causes a denial of service. The semi-passive attack requires packet interception and transmission only twice during the ECDH key exchange, and provides success probability of 25%. The fully-active attack generalizes the semi-passive attack by requiring packet interception and transmission throughout the entire connection. The fully-active attack provides a better success rate of 50%.

Finally, combining our attack with the already known weaknesses of Bluetooth pairing (Bluetooth BR/EDR) and "Legacy Pairing" (Bluetooth LE) insecurity against MitM, we show that all of the currently available Bluetooth pairing protocols (at the time of writing this paper) are insecure.

1.5   Structure of the Paper

This paper is organized as follows: in Sect. 2 we introduce the Bluetooth pairing schemes. Section 3 summarizes the original version of the Invalid Curve Attack. Section 4 is the core of our paper, where we describe our new attack. Section 5 describes the design flaws and suggests possible mitigations. Section 6 presents the platforms that are vulnerable to our attack, and our testing methods. Section 7 discusses the practicality of our attack. Finally, the paper is summarized in Sect. 8. The appendix summarizes the various versions of Bluetooth.

2   Bluetooth Pairing

The Bluetooth pairing protocol is the part of the Bluetooth link layer protocol that provides the encryption keys for the rest of the protocol. In this section we review the Bluetooth pairing protocols and their authentication mechanisms.

SSP and LE SC are very similar. Therefore, throughout this paper SSP and LE SC are interchangeable. We arbitrarily chose to elaborate LE SC, and then discuss the differences from SSP.

2.1   LE Secure Connections

Bluetooth Low Energy has two pairing schemes, "Legacy Pairing" and "LE Secure Connections". Oddly, Legacy Pairing was not intended to be protected against malicious eavesdroppers. The newer LE SC, introduced in Bluetooth version 4.2, promised to solve this problem and provide MitM protection using contemporary cryptographic primitives such as key exchange, commitments and MACs (message authentication codes).

The LE SC pairing scheme has four association models: "Just Works", "Numeric Comparison", "Passkey Entry" and "Out-Of-Band". The association model is chosen according to the IO capabilities of the participating devices. We do not address the "Out-Of-Band" mode in this paper since it requires a vendor specific protocol over a proprietary private channel, which is not fully-defined by [7]. Also, the Just Works mode is equivalent to Numeric Comparison, but without the user interaction, and therefore provides no authentication.

In the next subsections, after some required notations and definitions, we discuss the various phases of the Bluetooth LE SC pairing. The first phase of the pairing is feature exchange. We skip discussing this phase as its details are irrelevant in the context of this paper.

2.1.1   Notations and Definitions

Protocol variables:

- A, B (6 Bytes) – The BD_ADDR of each party.
- $IOcapA$, $IOcapB$ (1 Byte) – The advertised IO capabilities of each party (exchanged during the first phase).
- PKa, PKb (64 Bytes) – The public key of each party.
- SKa, SKb (32 Bytes) – The private key of each party.
- $PKax$, $PKbx$ (32 Bytes) – The x-coordinate of each party's public key.
- $DHKey$ (32 Bytes) – The shared Diffie-Hellman secret.
- Na, Nb (16 Bytes) – Nonces used for Numeric Comparison association model.
- Nai, Nbi (16 Bytes) – Nonces used for Passkey Entry association model.
- rai, rbi (1 Bytes) – Represents a single bit of the passkey.

Cryptographic functions (based on AES-CMAC [19]):

- **Function f4** – Commitment Value generation function, defined by:
  $f4(U, V, X, Y) = \text{AES-CMAC}_X(U \parallel V \parallel Y)$.
- **Function g2** – User Confirm Value generation function, defined by:
  $g2(U, V, X, Y) = \text{AES-CMAC}_X(U \parallel V \parallel Y) \pmod{2^{32}}$.
- **Function f5** – Key Derivation function, defined by:

$$f5(DHKey, N1, N2, A1, B2) =$$
$$\text{AES-CMAC}_T\Big(0 \parallel \text{`}btle\text{'} \parallel N1 \parallel N2 \parallel A1 \parallel A2 \parallel 256\Big) \parallel$$
$$\text{AES-CMAC}_T\Big(1 \parallel \text{`}btle\text{'} \parallel N1 \parallel N2 \parallel A1 \parallel A2 \parallel 256\Big),$$

where
$$T = \text{AES-CMAC}_{SALT}(DHKey),$$

and where $SALT$ is the 128-bit constant value defined in [7].
- **Function f6** – Check Value generation function, defined by:

$$f6(W, N1, N2, R, IOcap, A1, A2) =$$
$$\text{AES-CMAC}_W(N1 \parallel N2 \parallel R \parallel IOcap \parallel A1 \parallel A2).$$

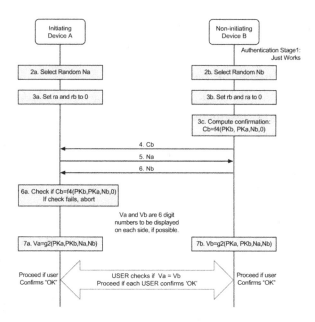

Fig. 2. Phase 3 – Authentication (Numeric Comparison)

2.1.2   Phase 2 – ECDH Key Exchange

Both participating devices exchange ECDH public keys using the standard NIST curve P-256 domain parameters. Each party computes the shared secret $DHKey$ as described in Subsect. 1.2.

2.1.3   Phase 3 – Authentication (Numeric Comparison)

The Numeric Comparison association model is used when both participating devices are capable of displaying a 6-digit decimal number and at least one of them can accept a "Confirm or Deny" input.

1. Each party selects a random 128-bit nonce Na and Nb.
2. The non-initiator commits (Cb) to Nb and public keys using Function f4, such that $Cb = \text{f4}(PKax, PKbx, Nb, 0)$.
3. Both parties reveal their nonces, first the initiator and then the non-initiator.
4. The initiator validates the commitment.
5. Both sides display the six least significant decimal digits of the User Confirm Value (Va and Vb), which are computed by $g2(PKax, PKbx, Na, Nb)$.
6. The user compares the values and confirms or denies accordingly.

Notice that the y-coordinates of the public keys are not authenticated during this phase. This observation is crucial to our attack.

The third phase using Numeric Comparison is outlined in Fig. 2 (taken from [7]).

Table 1. Function f6 inputs

	Numeric Comparison	Passkey Entry
Ea	$f6(MacKey, Na, Nb, 0, IOcapA, A, B)$	$f6(MacKey, Na20, Nb20, rb, IOcapA, A, B)$
Eb	$f6(MacKey, Nb, Na, 0, IOcapB, B, A)$	$f6(MacKey, Nb20, Na20, ra, IOcapB, B, A)$

2.1.4 Phase 3 – Authentication (Passkey Entry)

The Passkey Entry association model is used when at least one of the participating devices is capable of receiving numeric input from the user, while the other is capable of displaying a six-digit number.

1. The Passkey is generated and displayed on one device, and the user then types it into the other device.
2. Each party selects a 128-bit random nonce $Na1$ or $Nb1$.
3. Each party commits to its nonce, public keys and the first bit ($ra1$ and $rb1$) of the Passkey using Function f4, first the initiator by transmitting

$$f4(PKax, PKbx, Na1, ra1),$$

and then the non-initiator by transmitting

$$f4(PKbx, PKax, Nb1, rb1).$$

4. Both parties reveal their nonces and validate the commitments, first the initiator and then the non-initiator.
5. Steps 2–4 are repeated 20 times, where $ra1$ and $rb1$ are replaced with the next bit of the Passkey.

Notice that also here, the y-coordinates are not authenticated.

The third phase using Passkey Entry is outlined in Fig. 3 (taken from [7]).

2.1.5 Phase 4 – Session key derivation and validation

The fourth phase of the pairing is responsible for session key derivation.

1. Both parties derive the session keys ($MacKey$ and LTK) from the $DHKey$ using $f5(DHKey, Na, Nb, A, B)$.
2. Each device computes its Check Value (Ea and Eb) using Function f6. The inputs of Function f6 are listed in Table 1.
3. The initiator sends his Check Value to the non-initiator, which responds in turn with his Check Value.
4. Each side validates its correspondent's Check Value.

The fourth phase is outlined in Fig. 4 (taken from [7]).

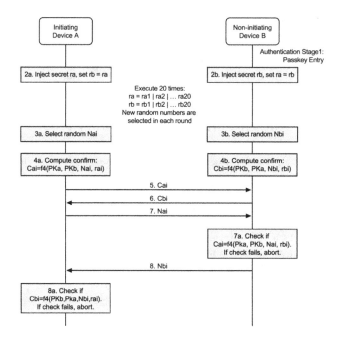

Fig. 3. Phase 3 – Authentication (Passkey Entry)

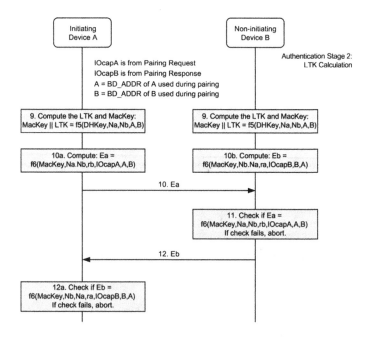

Fig. 4. Phase 4 – Session key derivation and validation

2.2   Secure Simple Pairing (SSP)

Secure Simple Pairing was the inspiration behind LE SC. There are two main differences between the two protocols. The first difference is the support of both P-192 and P-256 curves in the key exchange in SSP. The second difference is that SSP uses SHA-256 based HMAC functions, while LE SC uses AES-CMAC based functions. Other than those differences, SSP and LE SC are almost identical. Both of them have the same stages with similar functions and inputs. Due to these similarities they are interchangeable for the sake of this paper, and every statement regarding the security of one of them applies also to the other.

3   The Invalid Curve Attack

The Invalid Curve Attack, presented by Biehl et al. [2] and further described by Antipa et al. [1], exploits implementations of ECDH that improperly validate the received public keys. The invalid curve attack belongs to a larger family of attacks named *Small subgroup key recovery attacks*. This group of attacks utilizes small subgroups of finite groups in order to extract non-ephemeral secret information.

3.1   The Group Operation

Given domain parameters $D = \{q, a, b, P, n\}$ and two points $P = (P_x, P_y), Q = (Q_x, Q_y)$, the basic operations are defined as follows:

- Consider $Q = [-1]P$, where $[-1]P$ is defined by $[-1]P = (Px, -Py) \in E$. The sum $P + Q$ is defined to be the identity element $\infty \in E$. Note that $P_y \equiv 0$ (mod q) is a special case where $P = Q = [-1]P = (P_x, 0)$.
- Consider that $P \neq Q$ and $Q \neq [-1]P$. The point addition $R = P + Q$, is defined by drawing the line that intersects with P and Q. This line also intersects with a third point on the curve. The sum point R is the reflection of this third point across the x-axis. This computation is expressed by the following formulae:

$$s \equiv (Py - Qy)(Px - Qx)^{-1} \pmod{q}$$
$$Rx \equiv s^2 - Px - Qx \pmod{q}$$
$$Ry \equiv Py - s(Rx - Px) \pmod{q}$$

Notice that these formulae do not involve the curve parameters a and b.
- Consider $P = Q$ and $Q \neq [-1]P$. The point doubling $R = P + P = [2]P$, is defined by drawing the tangent line of the curve at point P. This line intersects with a second point on the curve. The sum point R is computed by reflecting this second point across the x-axis. This computation is expressed by the following formulae:

$$s \equiv (3Px^2 + a)(2Py)^{-1} \pmod{q}$$
$$Rx \equiv s^2 - 2Px \pmod{q}$$
$$Ry \equiv Py - s(Rx - Px) \pmod{q}$$

Notice that these formulae do not involve the curve parameter b.

3.2   Private Key Retrieval

Let E' be a different group with the curve equation $y^2 = x^3 + ax + b'$ (same a and a different b'), such that there exists a point $Q_1 \in E'$ with a small prime order p_1. The attacker provides Q_1 as his ECDH public-key. Denote the private key of the victim by SK, and denote the shared DH key from the victim's perspective by x_1. The victim then calculates $x_1 = [SK]Q_1$ and sends $H(x_1)$ to the attacker, where H is a publicly known function that follows the computation of the protocol regarding x_1. Given the output $H(x_1) = h_1^*$, the attacker can exhaustively search for the value a_1 that satisfies $H([a_1]Q_1) = h_1^*$. This search is computationally feasible since the order of Q_1 is low. The resultant discrete log a_1 provides the information $x = [a_1]Q_1 = [SK]Q_1$, and therefore it can be concluded that $SK \equiv a_1 \pmod{p_1}$. The attacker then repeats this process using a different point Q_i, which has a different small prime order p_i. This exchange repeats until the product of the primes satisfies $\prod_{i=1}^{k} p_i > n$. Finally, the attacker recovers the victim's private key using the Chinese Remainder Theorem.

4   Our Attack

In this section we introduce the Fixed Coordinate Invalid Curve Attack, which is MitM attack which modifies the y-coordinates of the transmitted public keys. Our attack exploits invalid-curve-points in a different way than Biehl et al.'s original Invalid curve attack. Specifically, we use the ability to forge low order ECDH public keys that preserve the x-coordinate of the original public-keys. Our attack is based on the observation that only the x-coordinate of each party is authenticated during the Bluetooth pairing protocol and on the fact that the protocol does not require its implementations to validate whether a given public-key satisfies the curve equation.[1] Our new attack can be applied to both SSP and LE SC.

As opposed to the classical Invalid Curve Attack our attack belongs to the family of attacks named *Small subgroup confinement attack*. In this family the attacker attempts to compromise the shared secret by forcing a key to be confined to an unexpectedly small subgroup.

4.1   A Semi-Passive Attack

Our attack exploits the fact that given an elliptic curve in Weierstrass notation $y^2 = x^3 + ax + b$, both point-doubling and point-addition operations are independent of b. Given an elliptic curve group E and a point $Q = (Qx, Qy) \in E$, let $Q' = (Qx, 0)$ be its projection on the x-axis. We can easily find a different curve E' with an equation $y^2 = x^3 + ax + b'$, such that $P' \in E'$, using the same curve parameter a and a different parameter b'. This manipulation is not detected by the protocol since the x-coordinates are left unchanged.

---

[1] Note that all of the implementations we tested did not add this validation voluntarily.

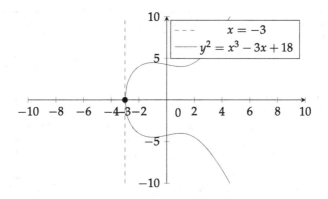

Fig. 5. Example of an elliptic curve with an order-two point at $(-3, 0)$

According to the group definition, given a point $Q = (Qx, Qy)$, the inverse of Q is found by reflecting it across the x-axis $[-1]Q = (Qx, -Qy)$. Therefore, every point of the form $(Qx, 0)$ equals its own inverse, and has order two. An example of such a point is outlined in Fig. 5. Since the y-coordinate is forced to zero on the given point, the new curve parameter b' on which $(Q_x, 0) \in E'$ can easily be calculated by

$$b' \equiv -Q_x^3 - a \cdot Q_x \pmod{q}.$$

Using this observation we introduce the Semi-Passive Fixed Coordinate Invalid Curve Attack. The semi-passive attack is thus as follows:

1. Eavesdrop both parties throughout the pairing protocol.
2. Let both parties perform the first phase of the pairing (feature exchange).
3. Let the parties transmit their ECDH public keys.
4. Modify the y-coordinates of the public keys to zero in both transmissions.
5. Conclude that both parties result with $DHKey = \infty$.
6. Do not intervene with rest the of the pairing protocol.
7. Observe if the pairing succeeds, otherwise, quit.
8. Derive the symmetric session keys (LTK and $MacKey$) using the expected $DHKey = \infty$ and the public parameters.
9. After the pairing is finished, forge or passively decrypt packets sent between the participating devices using the derived keys.

The message interception during the second phase is illustrated in Fig. 6. After the interception of the second phase the rest of the communication can be eavesdropped without further interaction, as outlined in Fig. 7.

Steps 7 and 8 above require elaboration: In step 4 the attacker confines each of the public keys to a sub-group of order two by projecting it on the x-axis. If both SK_a and SK_b are even, this confinement implies that the attack succeeds. In this case the computed $DHKey$ of both parties are equal: $DHKey_a = DHKey_b = \infty$. This result occurs with probability 0.25. In all other cases the parties compute different $DHKeys$, and thus the pairing protocol fails.

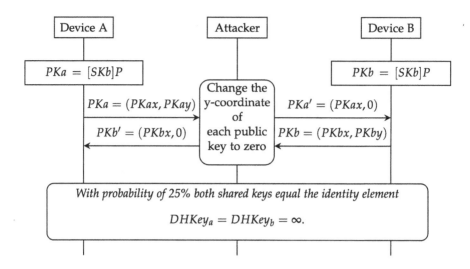

Fig. 6. Fixed Coordinate Invalid Curve Attack – Phase 2

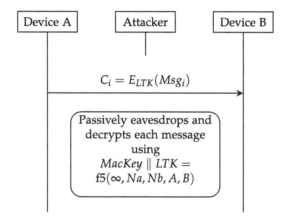

Fig. 7. Semi-passive MitM attack – passive eavesdropping

4.2 Fully-Active MitM Attack

The semi-passive attack requires a message interception only during the second phase of the pairing. The rest of the communication can be passively eavesdropped. We can further improve the attack success probability to 0.5 by also intercepting messages during the fourth phase. In order to achieve this better success rate we should consider the four possible values of $DHKey_x$ computed by each party after the interception of the second phase, as listed in Table 2. The first row in the table represents the success case of the semi-passive attack.

The session key is derived using the shared $DHKey$, ra, rb and several public parameters: nonce Na, nonce Nb, BD_ADDR of device A and BD_ADDR of device B. The values ra and rb differ between the Passkey Entry and the Numeric

Table 2. The possible values for $DHKey_a$ and $DHKey_b$

$DHKey_a$	$DHKey_b$
∞	∞
∞	PKa'
PKb'	∞
PKb'	PKa'

Comparison association models. In the Numeric Comparison model $ra = rb = 0$. In contrast, in the Passkey Entry model ra and rb are 6-digit decimal values expressed as 128-bit integers.

These values are not transmitted in plaintext but could still be retrieved with a small effort. The attacker could retrieve the passkey by exhaustively searching through the $10^6 \approx 2^{20}$ possible values. An even better solution for extracting the passkey is by iterating through all possible values of rai and rbi, which are used during the third phase as inputs for Function f4. Each value of rai and rbi represents a single bit of the passkey. The attacker can test each bit independently and thus he should iterate through at most $2 \cdot 20 = 40$ options to determine the correct values of ra and rb.

In the fourth phase both devices derive the session keys (see Subsect. 2.1.5). The first message of the fourth phase (Ea) reveals information about $DHKey_a$. The attacker uses this information to determine whether $DHKey_a$ equals PKb' or ∞. If $DHKey_a = \infty$, the attacker continues as in semi-passive attack, without further interception.

If $DHKey_a = PKb'$, the attacker guesses the yet unknown value of $DHKey_b$ to be either ∞ or PKa', and calculates the appropriate check-value Ea' accordingly. He then sends Ea' to the non-initiator instead of Ea. If the guess is incorrect, the non-initiator replies with the message "Pairing Failed (Check Value Failed)". Otherwise, the non-initiator replies with his check-value and the attacker concludes that the guess is correct. The fully-active attack is thus as follows:

1. Apply steps 1–3 as in the semi-passive attack.
2. Do not intervene with the third phase of the pairing protocol.
3. If the association model is Passkey Entry, find the correct value of ra and rb using one of the methods described above, otherwise, assume $ra = rb = 0$.
4. In the fourth phase of the pairing, receive the check-value (Ea), but distort it so it will not reach its destination (i.e., by destroying the checksum or preamble).
5. Use the check-value in order to validate whether $DHKey_a$ equals ∞ or PKb'.
   (a) If the $DHKey_a = \infty$, send the original check-value, and continue as with the semi-passive attack.
   (b) If $DHKey_a = PKb'$, randomly guess the value of $DHKey_b$ to be either ∞ or PKa'.

6. Compute and transmit the value of Ea' according to the guess of $DHKey_b$, instead of the distorted value from step 4.
7. If the guess is incorrect, the pairing protocol is terminated with a "Pairing Failed (Check Value Failed)" message.
8. Otherwise, Compute the session keys $LTK_a, MacKey_a$ and $LTK_b, MacKey_b$ associated with $DHKey_a$ and $DHKey_b$ and act as a relay between the participating devices by decrypting and re-encrypting each message, or send forged packets of your choice.

The message interception during the fourth phase considering $DHKey_a = PKb'$ is illustrated in Fig. 8. Note that using this improvement the attacker has to continually relay packets and act as MitM for the rest of the session: each message sent between the victim devices has to be intercepted by the attacker, decrypted using the sender's key, re-encrypted using the recipient's key, and sent to the recipient. The relay operation is illustrated in Fig. 9.

4.3   Success Rate

The success rate of our attack is calculated under the assumption that the private keys SK_x are chosen uniformly at random. For the semi-passive attack suppose that the shared keys computed by both parties are the point-at-infinity. Denote this event by $V = (DHKey_a = \infty) \cap (DHKey_b = \infty)$. As each of the terms is satisfied only when the corresponding SK is even, the probability of this event is $\Pr(V) = 25\%$.

For the fully-active attack suppose that the shared key as derived by the initiator is PKb', and that the attacker correctly guesses the shared key as derived by non-initiator. Denote this event by $U = (DHKey_a = PKb') \cap (DHKey_b' = DHKey_b)$. The probability of this event is also $\Pr(U) = 25\%$. Consequentially the success probability of the fully-active attack is $\Pr(U \cup V) = 25\% + 25\% = 50\%$.

The success probabilities of the various cases of our attack are summarized in Tables 3, 4 and 5.

Table 3. Success rate – semi-passive attack

$DHKey_a$ \ $DHKey_b$	∞	PKa'
∞	Success	Failure
PKb'	Failure	Failure

Total Semi-Passive Attack: **25%**

Table 4. Success rate – fully-active attack (when guessing $DHKey'_b = \infty$)

$DHKey_a$ \ $DHKey_b$	∞	PKa'
∞	Success	Failure
PKb'	Success	Failure

Total of this case: 50%

Table 5. Success rate – fully-active attack (when guessing $DHKey'_b = PKa'$)

$DHKey_a$ \ $DHKey_b$	∞	PKa'
∞	Success	Failure
PKb'	Failure	Success

Total of this case: 50%

5 Design Flaws and Mitigations

In this section we discuss multiple security flaws of the pairing protocol used in this paper, and point to which mitigations should be applied in order to protect a platform. We also warn from mitigations which are insufficient to protect against our attack.

5.1 Design Flaws

There are two major design flaws that make our attack possible. The first design flaw is sending both the x-coordinate and the y-coordinate during the public key exchange. This is unnecessary and highly inadvisable, since it greatly increases the attack surface, while calculating the y-coordinate from a given x-coordinate is simple.

The second major flaw is that although both coordinates of each public key are sent during the second phase of the pairing, the protocol authenticates only the x-coordinate. We are not aware of any reason why the designers decided to leave the y-coordinate unauthenticated, other than for saving a tiny computational effort. Even though the point validity should be checked by the implementation, our attack could have also been avoided if both coordinates were authenticated.

Another less significant flaw is that in [7, Part H, Section 5.1] the protocol designers state that "To protect a device's private key, a device should implement a method to prevent an attacker from retrieving useful information about the device's private key using invalid public keys. For this purpose, a device can use one of the following methods". In this quote, the specification uses the

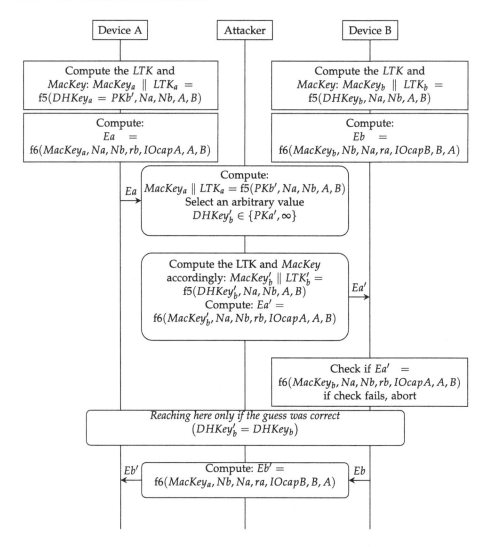

Fig. 8. Fully-Active MitM (Considering $DHKey_a = PKb'$) – Phase 4

term "should" (as opposed to "must"). Therefore, implementors may skip the instruction as it is not mandatory for compliance with the specification.

5.2 Mitigations

The obvious (and recommended) mitigation against our attack is to test if a given ECDH public-key satisfies the curve equation (i.e., the point is on the curve). This mitigation indeed became mandatory in the Bluetooth core specification as a response to our responsible disclosure.

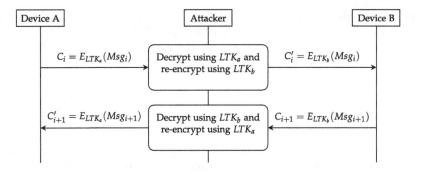

Fig. 9. Fully-Active MitM – Relay

In case that the order n of the base point P is prime, another acceptable mitigation is to validate whether the given public key (PK) satisfies $[n]PK = \infty$. This mitigation applies since it verifies the order of the given key, thus preventing public keys with smaller orders.

These mitigations are applicable to both LE SC and SSP.

5.3   Insufficient Mitigation

The commonly used mitigation proposed by the Bluetooth Core Specification [7] against Invalid Curve Attack is refreshing the ECDH key pair every pairing attempt. We stress that our attack applies even when this mitigation is applied.

We must also note that although checking whether the y-coordinate equals zero protects against our specific attack, it is not a sufficient mitigation. An extended version of our attack can still be devised using slightly higher order points with a decreased success probability. For example, given the same domain parameters $D = \{q, a, b, P, n\}$ and a valid public key $PK = (PKx, PKy)$, we can easily forge a public key $PK' = (PKx, PKy')$ with order four, such that $PKy' \neq 0$. Let $Q = (Qx, Qy)$ be the point defined by $Q = [2]PK'$. Such PK' point with order four can be generated by forcing $Qy = 0$. Substituting (PKx, PKy') into the point doubling equations we get

$$s \equiv (3PKx^2 + a)(2PKy')^{-1} \pmod{q}$$
$$Qx \equiv s^2 - 2PKx \pmod{q}$$
$$Qy \equiv PKy' - s(Qx - PKx) \equiv 0 \pmod{q}$$

from which we can deduce

$$PKy' \equiv (3PKx^2 + a)(2PKy')^{-1}(Qx - PKx) \pmod{q}$$
$$2PKy'^2 \equiv (3PKx^2 + a)(Qx - PKx) \pmod{q}$$
$$PKy' \equiv \pm\sqrt{(3PKx^2 + a)(Qx - PKx)2^{-1}} \pmod{q}.$$

Ignoring the negligible chance that $3PKx^2 + a \equiv 0 \pmod{q}$, we can assign any value Qx that satisfies $Qx \neq PKx$ for which $(3PKx^2 + a)(Qx - PKx)2^{-1}$ is a quadratic-residue modulo q. This generalized form of our attack provides success rate of 25%. Therefore, checking whether the y-coordinate equals zero is not a sufficient mitigation.

6   Vulnerable Platforms

We have tested the vulnerability of multiple devices from several manufacturers and discovered that almost all of the Bluetooth pairing implementations are vulnerable to our attack. Every vulnerable implementation we tested can be used in both master and slave roles, depending on the configuration.

Our tests used CY5677 programmable USB Bluetooth dongle by Cypress with modified dedicated firmware as our test platform. The following modifications were added to the dongle's Bluetooth stack:

1. We zeroize the y-coordinate of our public key just before transmission.
2. We zeroize the y-coordinate of the remote public key immediately after it is received.

We then examined the target responses, measured the pairing success rate and compared it to our expectations.

We used this "synthetic" validation method since it provides the most realistic setting while giving us enough flexibility to precisely test our attack. We stress that this validation proves that the target device is vulnerable since it performs exactly the same manipulations as a MitM implementation of the attack would do.

6.1   Vulnerable Bluetooth Low Energy Platforms

Since LE SC is implemented in the host, the vulnerability is found in the host's operating system, regardless of the Bluetooth adapter. We found the Android Bluetooth stack, "Bluedroid", to be vulnerable.[2] Note that Apple's iOS and MacOS implementations were also found to be vulnerable (as identified by Apple following our disclosure). On the other hand, Microsoft Windows did not support LE SC — the secure pairing was added to Windows 10 only after our disclosure.

6.2   Vulnerable Bluetooth BR/EDR Platforms

The vulnerability in SSP depends on the Bluetooth chip firmware implementation, since unlike LE SC, the key exchange is performed by the chip, rather than by the host. During our research we found that devices of most major chip vendors are affected. In particular, Qualcomm's, Broadcom's and Intel's chips[3]

---

[2] Tested on Nexus 5X devices with Android version 8.1.
[3] The examined Bluetooth adapters were: Qualcomm's QCA6174A, Broadcom's BCM4358 and Intel's 8265.

are vulnerable, which together constitute most of the Bluetooth chips market. We stress that every device (e.g., mobile phone, laptop or car) that uses such a chip is vulnerable.

7 Practical Considerations

In the following section we consider the requirements and obstacles facing attackers who wish to implement our attack in real-life environments.

7.1 Over the Air Implementation

Our attack requires the ability to manipulate the Bluetooth communication between two victim devices. In a wireless environment this is usually done by jamming the receiver while eavesdropping to the sender, before transmitting the modified message. Due to physical obstacles (such as frequency hopping and different clock synchronizations) Bluetooth eavesdropping and traffic interceptions are much more difficult than in other radio-based protocols (such as 802.11). Until recent years, in order to sniff Bluetooth traffic one had to purchase expensive equipment such as the "Ellisys Bluetooth Explorer", which costs in the range of 10K–20K US dollars.

In 2010 Ossman introduced an open-source project called "Project Ubertooth" [15], which introduced a highly accessible and inexpensive utility for Bluetooth sniffing, and costs only about $100. Moreover, Mike Ryan suggested in [17] how an attacker can break the frequency hopping parameters used in Bluetooth Low Energy allowing to easily sniff Bluetooth traffic using Ubertooth. A similar technique is used in Ubertooth in order to sniff Bluetooth Basic Rate traffic, but not yet intercept. It is therefore clear that frequency hopping is not a valid security mitigation against MitM.

After the success of Ubertooth a lot of new products were introduced improving the capabilities provided by Ubertooth and adding the ability to perform over the air MitM to Bluetooth LE traffic. One of the most popular solutions is "GATTack" [18] presented during Blackhat USA 2016. This tool is a software based framework providing over the air BLE MitM capabilities with equipment that costs about $10.

Unfortunately, all of the solutions we found are limited to Bluetooth 4.0 and do not support Bluetooth 4.2 due to its larger packet size. It is safe to assume that the next generation of these products will support Bluetooth 4.2 as it becomes more popular.

7.2 Public Key Manipulation

In addition to the straight-forward MitM technique, there is a much simpler technique for attacking SSP. Observe that the SSP packet size is limited to 16 bytes, while the ECDH public-key is either $192 \cdot 2 = 384bits = 48bytes$ or $256 \cdot 2 = 512bits = 64bytes$. To accompany this restriction the public key is divided into either 3 or 4 packets, allowing the attacker to forge the packet of the y-coordinate, without affecting the x-coordinate.

It is interesting to note that the P-192 variant is actually harder to forge than the P-256 variant, as the second packet in the P-192 variant contains data of both coordinates (x and y), while the P-256 variant separates the coordinates to different packets.

The maximal packet size in LE SC is much larger compared to SSP, limited by 256 bytes instead of 16. Thus both public key coordinates are encoded in the same packet.

7.3   Encoding of the Point-at-Infinity

In the description of our attack we repeatedly consider the point-at-infinity (aka. the identity element ∞) as a possible solution for the scalar multiplication. This requires a delicate discussion since the encoding of this point is not defined by the Bluetooth specification nor there is any standard encoding for it. If the encoding of the point-at-infinity is different between the master and the slave, the shared DH key will be different, even when both shared DH keys equals the point-at-infinity. This is of course a compatibility problem rather than just a theoretical issue. Nevertheless, our fully-active attack still applies in such a case by using the specific encoding for each of the victim devices. However, during our tests we found that all the popular implementations represent the point-at-infinity as $(0, 0)$, so this potential problem does not occur in practice.

8   Summary

In this paper we introduced the Fixed Coordinate Invalid Curve Attack which provides a new tool for attacking the ECDH protocols, and presented the application of our new attack to the Bluetooth pairing protocol.

During our research we discovered multiple design flaws in the Bluetooth specification. We then tested different Bluetooth implementations and found that a large majority of the Bluetooth devices are vulnerable.

Shortly after we discovered the attack we informed the affected vendors with the help of the Cert Coordination Center (CERT/CC). As a result, CVE-2018-5383 was assigned to this vulnerability in the Bluetooth protocol. In our responsible disclosure we recommended the Bluetooth Special Interest Group to fix the design flaws in future Bluetooth versions. We further suggested that the specification should require manufacturers to add the necessary validations, rather than having it optional. We also urged the manufacturers to add the proposed validations, even if it is not mandatory. Although we expect that most of the currently used Bluetooth peripherals will never be patched (as patching most devices is infeasible), patching all the mobile-phones and computers (where a software update is relatively easy) will greatly decrease the risk of this vulnerability.

Several months after our notification, all of the major vendors managed to coordinately patch their products which resulted in a vast amount of platforms that needed to be updated. The following vendors released a software update addressing our attack: Google (Android OS), Apple (MacOS), Apple (iOS), Intel, Broadcom, Qualcomm, Lenovo, Samsung, LG, Huawei and Dell.

Another implication of our disclosure was an update of the Bluetooth core specification which now mandates implementors to validate whether a given Diffie-Hellman public-key satisfies the curve equation. The update was released with the following announcement: "To remedy the vulnerability, the Bluetooth SIG has now updated the Bluetooth specification to require products to validate any public key received as part of public key-based security procedure".

A   Bluetooth Versions

Bluetooth has several versions. Each new version introduces extended capabilities or a complete new set of sub-protocols.

The initial releases of Bluetooth, versions 1.0 and 1.0B [9], had many problems, and manufacturers had difficulty making their products interoperable. The manufacturers included a mandatory Bluetooth hardware device address (BD_ADDR) for transmission in the connecting process, which made anonymity impossible at the protocol level. This was a major setback for certain services planned for use in Bluetooth environments.

Bluetooth versions 1.1 [10] introduced major improvements over their predecessors and addressed many of the errors found in v1.0B. New features were added, among them: RSSI for measurement of the power present in a received radio signal, faster connection, faster discovery, adaptive frequency-hopping and higher transmission speeds.

Version 2.0 [4] was released in 2004. It introduced an even faster data transfer with throughput of up to 3 Mbit/s. The throughput enhancement was due to the use of GFSK and PSK modulation. This new method of modulation is called *EDR*, or *Enhanced Data Rate*, while the older modulation is called *BR*, or *Basic Rate*. When both of the modulations are implemented together it is called *BR/EDR*.

Version 2.1 of the protocol added secured pairing named *Secure Simple Pairing (SSP)* to support *Man-in-the-Middle (MitM)* protection using authenticated Diffie-Hellman during the pairing stage.

Bluetooth 3.0 [5] introduced the support for an alternative MAC/PHY (AMP). AMP is a new feature, allowing the use of an alternative data channel. While the negotiation and establishment are still performed similarly to former versions, the data flow uses an alternative MAC PHY 802.11 (typically associated with Wi-Fi). The 802.11 standard defines different protocols for the physical layer and for the link layer. It is characterized by a high transfer-rate and a relatively high signal range. After the connection is established the 802.11 link encapsulates the data packets of the BT established connection. The result is a much higher transfer rate of up to 24 Mbit/s. This new feature was intended to allow streaming over Bluetooth, whose throughput was still poor compared to other protocols.

Bluetooth Core Specification version 4.0 [6] introduced a new modulation mode and link layer packet format called *Bluetooth Low Energy (BTLE)*. BTLE is intended for use in low power embedded devices. It was rapidly adopted by various consumer devices, such as smart phones, wearable technology, sports tracking devices and recently even health and medical equipment. BTLE PHY divides the RF spectrum into 40 channels, each of which is 2 MHz in width, from 2402 MHz to 2482MHz. Three of those 40 channels are labeled as advertising channels used for pairing and discovery packets. The rest are labeled as data channels, used for establishing connections and transmission of the data. The link layer was also redesigned and a new pairing protocol was added.

On December 2014, core specification 4.2 [7] was introduced, providing several new features to the BTLE protocol intended to make it the main protocol for the IoT (Internet of Things). These features include a new LE Secure Connections mode, as well as several security and privacy related features.

The latest version of Bluetooth, released on December 2016 was version 5.0 [8]. The new version added several performance features for Bluetooth Low Energy, most of them in the physical layer of the protocol. Among the new features were extended range, higher throughput and higher advertisement capacity.

In this paper we study the pairing protocols SSP used by Bluetooth BR/EDR and LE Secure Connections used by Bluetooth Low Energy. These are the only secure pairing protocols to date.

References

1. Antipa, A., Brown, D., Menezes, A., Struik, R., Vanstone, S.: Validation of elliptic curve public keys. In: Desmedt, Y.G. (ed.) PKC 2003. LNCS, vol. 2567, pp. 211–223. Springer, Heidelberg (2003). https://doi.org/10.1007/3-540-36288-6_16
2. Biehl, I., Meyer, B., Müller, V.: Differential fault attacks on elliptic curve cryptosystems. In: Bellare, M. (ed.) CRYPTO 2000. LNCS, vol. 1880, pp. 131–146. Springer, Heidelberg (2000). https://doi.org/10.1007/3-540-44598-6_8
3. Diffie, W., Hellman, M.E.: New directions in cryptography. Trans. Inf. Theory **IT–22**(6), 644–654 (1976)
4. Bluetooth Special Interest Group: Specification of the bluetooth system v2.0. 0 (2004)
5. Bluetooth Special Interest Group: Specification of the bluetooth system v3.0. 0 (2009)
6. Bluetooth Special Interest Group: Specification of the bluetooth system v4.0. 0 (2010)
7. Bluetooth Special Interest Group: Specification of the bluetooth system v4.2. 0 (2014)
8. Bluetooth Special Interest Group: Specification of the bluetooth system v5.0. 0 (2016)
9. IEEE: Specification of the bluetooth system v1.0b. 1 (1999)
10. IEEE: Specification of the bluetooth system v1.1. 1 (2001)

11. Jager, T., Schwenk, J., Somorovsky, J.: Practical invalid curve attacks on TLS-ECDH. In: Computer Security – ESORICS 2015, vol. 1880, pp. 407–425 (2000)
12. Landrock, P., Kjaersgaard, J.U.: Protecting against security attack. US Patent 8077866 B2 (2013)
13. Koblitz, N.: Elliptic curve cryptosystems. Math. Comput. **48**, 203–209 (1987)
14. National Institute of Standards and Technology: Federal information processing standards publication 186-2 (2000)
15. Ossmann, M.: Project Ubertooth. http://ubertooth.sourceforge.net
16. Ryan, M.: Crackle cracks BLE encryption. https://github.com/mikeryan/crackle
17. Ryan, M.: With low energy comes low security. In: USENIX WOOT, p. 4 (2013)
18. Securing. Gattack. http://gattack.io
19. Song, J.H., Poovendran, R., Lee, J., Iwata, T.: The AES-CMAC Algorithm (4493), pp. 1–20, June 2006
20. Miller, V.S.: Use of elliptic curves in cryptography. In: Williams, H.C. (ed.) CRYPTO 1985. LNCS, vol. 218, pp. 417–426. Springer, Heidelberg (1986). https://doi.org/10.1007/3-540-39799-X_31

Using TopGear in Overdrive: A More Efficient ZKPoK for SPDZ

Carsten Baum[1], Daniele Cozzo[2], and Nigel P. Smart[2,3]

[1] Department of Computer Science, Aarhus University, Aarhus, Denmark
cbaum@cs.au.dk
[2] imec-COSIC, KU Leuven, Leuven, Belgium
{daniele.cozzo,nigel.smart}@kuleuven.be
[3] Department of Computer Science, University of Bristol, Bristol, UK

Abstract. The HighGear protocol (Eurocrypt 2018) is the fastest currently known approach to preprocessing for the SPDZ Multi-Party Computation scheme. Its backbone is formed by an Ideal Lattice-based Somewhat Homomorphic Encryption Scheme and accompanying Zero-Knowledge proofs. Unfortunately, due to certain characteristics of High-Gear such current implementations limit the security parameters in a number of places. This is mainly due to memory and bandwidth consumption constraints.

In this work we present a new approach to the ZKPoKs for the SPDZ Multi-Party Computation scheme. We rigorously formalize the original approach of HighGear and show how to improve upon it using a different proof strategy. This allows us to increase the security of the underlying protocols, whilst simultaneously also increasing the performance in terms of memory and bandwidth consumption as well as overall throughput of the SPDZ offline phase.

1 Introduction

Multi-party computation (MPC) has turned in the last fifteen years from a mainly theoretical endeavor to one which is now practical, with a number of companies fielding products based on it. MPC comes in a number of flavours, depending on the underlying primitives (garbled circuits, secret sharing), number of parties (two or many parties) and security model (passive, covert, active). In this work we will focus on n-party secret sharing-based MPC for arithmetic circuits, secure against an active adversary corrupting a dishonest majority of parties. In this setting the most efficient protocol known is the SPDZ protocol [15] from 2012, along with its many improvements such as [14,24,25].

The SPDZ protocol family uses a form of authenticated secret sharing over a finite field $\mathbb{F}_p$ to perform the secure computation. The protocol is divided into two phases, an offline phase (which produces, among other things, multiplication triples) and an online phase (which uses these preprocessed multiplication triples to perform actual multiplications). In this work we will be focusing on the offline phase, specifically on how to increase its security level while keeping or increasing

© Springer Nature Switzerland AG 2020
K. G. Paterson and D. Stebila (Eds.): SAC 2019, LNCS 11959, pp. 274–302, 2020.
https://doi.org/10.1007/978-3-030-38471-5_12

the performance. The SPDZ protocol, among others, has been implemented in the SCALE-MAMBA system [2], which we refer to as a reference implementation allowing to measure and compare our contribution in practice.

To understand the difference of our approach in terms of efficiency and security we first consider the genesis of the problem we solve. The SPDZ protocol is itself based on an earlier work called BDOZ [7]. The BDOZ protocol used a form of pairwise MACs to authenticate a secret sharing amongst n-parties. At the heart of the offline phase for BDOZ is a pairwise multiplication protocol, using linearly homomorphic encryption. To ensure that active adversaries do not cheat in this phase pairwise zero-knowledge proofs are utilized to ensure active adversaries cannot deviate from the protocol without detection. In total $O(n^2)$ ZKPoKs need to be carried out per multiplication triple of BDOZ.

The main contribution of the SPDZ paper [15] over BDOZ was to replace the pairwise MACs with a global MAC. This was made possible by upgrading the linearly homomorphic encryption used in BDOZ to a limited form of Somewhat Homomorphic Encryption (SHE) based on the BGV encryption scheme [10]. This new scheme permits to reduce the number of ZK proofs per multiplication triple by a factor of n. At the same time, due to the Smart-Vercauteren SIMD packing underlying BGV plaintext spaces the overhead due to the ZKPoKs per multiplication triple was drastically reduced. This is because a single ZKPoK could be used to simultaneously prove statements for many thousands of multiplication triples.

However, BGV is a lattice based SHE scheme and ZKPoKs for these are relatively costly – due to the necessity of proving bounds on the size of plaintexts and randomness. For a single ciphertext, the basic Σ-protocol has challenge space $\{0,1\}$ and must thus be repeated many times to achieve reasonable security levels. Furthermore, to provide zero-knowledge one needs to "blow-up" the proven bounds, so the proven statement is strictly weaker than the honest parameter choice[1]. This introduces what is called the *soundness slack* between the honest language $\mathbb{L}$ and the proven language $\mathbb{L}'$.

To get around the problem of having to perform multiple proofs for the same ciphertext, SPDZ uses a standard amortization technique [12] to prove U statements at once, where U is the number of ciphertexts used in the protocol. This boosts the soundness security from $1/2$ to 2^{-U}, at the expense of introducing even more soundness slack, namely an additional factor of $2^{U/2}$. At the same time, [12] crucially needs to send $V = 2 \cdot U - 1$ auxiliary ciphertexts. In the implementation of this ZKPoK in the original, and subsequent works, the authors set U to be the same security level as the statistical zero-knowledge parameter ZK_sec.

Despite this use of amortization techniques, the ZKPoKs were for a long time considered too slow. This resulted in two new techniques based on cut-and-choose (being introduced in [14]). The first of these produced only covert security,

---

[1] There do exist ZKPoKs for lattice-based primitives which prove exact bounds. Unfortunately, their computation and communication overhead makes them no match in practice for protocols having soundness slack.

but was highly efficient, and thus for a number of years all implementations of the SPDZ offline phase only provided covert security. The second approach of [14] provided actively secure ZKPoK which seemed asymptotically more efficient than those provided in [15], but which due to large memory requirements were impossible to implement.

This inability to provide efficient actively secure offline phased based on SHE led to a temporary switch to an Oblivious Transfer-based offline phase, called MASCOT [24]. However, in 2018 Keller et al. [25] introduced the Overdrive suite of offline protocols. There, they revisited the original SPDZ offline phase and showed two interesting ways to optimize it. Firstly, in so-called LowGear, for a small number of parties the original pairwise ZKPoKs of the BDOZ methodology could be more efficient than that of SPDZ. They observe that an $O(n^2)$ algorithm can beat an $O(n)$ algorithm for small values of n and in addition improve the parameters of the SHE scheme. This was partially also enabled by using the same SIMD packing in BDOZ as was being used for SPDZ.

The second variant of Overdrive, called HighGear, works for larger values of n. Here, the original SPDZ ZKPoK was revisited and tweaked. While previously the ZKPoK was used so each party proved a statement to each other party, in HighGear the parties proved a single joint statement together for their secret inputs and an accumulated ciphertext. This did *not* provide an improvement in *communication efficiency*, but it did make the *computational* costs a factor of n smaller.

In the SCALE-MAMBA system (as of v1.2 in Nov 2018) only the HighGear variant of Overdrive is implemented for the case of dishonest majority MPC, even when $n = 2$. However, like all prior work the system adopts $U = \mathsf{ZK\_sec}$, and thus achieves the same soundness security $\mathsf{Snd\_sec}$ as zero-knowledge indistinguishability. This is neither as efficient, nor as secure, as one would want for two combined reasons.

1. The zero-knowledge security $\mathsf{ZK\_sec}$ is related to a statistical distance, whereas the soundness security $\mathsf{Snd\_sec}$ is related to the probability that an adversary can cheat in an interactive protocol. A low value for $\mathsf{Snd\_sec}$ is rather more acceptable than a low value for $\mathsf{ZK\_sec}$.
2. The practical complexity of the protocol, in particular the memory and computational consumption, is dominated by $\mathsf{Snd\_sec}$. It turns out that $\mathsf{ZK\_sec}$ has very virtually no effect on the overall execution time of the offline phase, for large values of p.

It is for this reason that [25] gives performance metrics for 40, 64 and 128-bit active security, and why v1.2 of SCALE-MAMBA utilizes only 40-bits of security for $\mathsf{Snd\_sec}$ and $\mathsf{ZK\_sec}$, since the execution time is highly dependent on $\mathsf{Snd\_sec}$.

Our Contribution. We first formalize the type of statement which the Overdrive ZKPoK tries to prove. The original treatment in [25] is relatively intuitive. We formalize the statement by presenting a generalization of standard Zero Knowledge-protocols to what we call an n-party Zero Knowledge-protocol. The formalization is tailored at the use of such proofs in preprocessing.

We then present a modified ZKPoK for the HighGear variant of Overdrive, which we denote TopGear. It treats the soundness security Snd_sec and the zero-knowledge security ZK_sec separately. This ZKPoK in its unamortized variant (i.e. only proving one statement at a time) uses a non-binary challenge space in a similar way as was done in [8]. Hence we obtain a challenge space of $2 \cdot N + 1$ in the "base" ZKPoK (where N is the ring dimension of the cryptosystem used). We then amortize this base ZKPoK by proving U statements in parallel using a technique from [3]. This enables us to achieve an arbitrary knowledge soundness of Snd_sec by selecting the number of auxiliary ciphertexts V such that $V \geq (\text{Snd\_sec} + 2)/\log_2(2 \cdot N + 1)$.

Since N is often $32768 = 2^{15}$, we are able to achieve a high soundness security, with a low value of V, e.g. we can obtain 128 bits of soundness security by setting V to be 8. This translates into a smaller amount of amortization than [25], and thus a smaller memory footprint and bandwidth for the same level of ZK_sec. Alternatively, we can select higher values of ZK_sec, if so desired, as this has little impact on the overall performance.

Concerning the slack we follow an approach similar to [25] but with a twist. In signature schemes based on lattices, such as BLISS, this issue is usually dealt with using rejection sampling, e.g. [18, 19, 26]. As the slack in TopGear will be removed due to the processing that happens after the ZKPoK is executed (during a modulus switch operation in the SHE scheme), we start with a simpler yet more efficient technique to achieve zero-knowledge called "noise drowning". We generally obtain a smaller slack and thus better SHE parameters due to the change of the ZKPoK from [12] to [3]. Due to our use of the larger challenge space of [8] we also cannot extract an "exact" preimage in the soundness proof, but only that of a related ciphertext. We will show that this can be corrected easily in the case of SPDZ preprocessing.

Other Related Work. Multiple techniques have been introduced to cope with the problem of amortized ZKPoK for lattice-based primitives. Multiple subsequent works [4, 13, 16] have introduced more and more efficient proofs of knowledge which have small (down to linear in Snd_sec) slack. Unfortunately, all of these require U to be in the multiple of 1000s to be efficient, which is far from practically feasible. Later, Baum and Lyubashevsky [5] showed how to build small-slack proofs for realistic sizes of U, though their idea was limited to structured lattices. The problem was only recently resolved in [3] which we therefore use as a building block in our work.

Another recent methodology to perform such ZKPoKs as needed in this paper is given in [17] based on bullet proofs. These give very short proofs but are not competitive with the approach in this paper. Firstly, we use amortization over the number of parties to produce a joint proof whereas the direct application of [17] would require pairwise proofs which would not scale well with the number of parties. The paper [17] also concentrates on the case of "small moduli q" of the SHE ciphertext space. In our case, we easily need this q to have a size of > 500 bits. Apart from the problem of constructing a secure DLP group of a given order at this size (leading to probably needing to use finite fields, or a group size larger than q to deal with integer overflow), this also leads to very large computational expenses. To sign and verify a proof from [17] requires *at least* $12 \cdot N \cdot \log_2 q$ exponentiations (where N again is the dimension of the rings used in the ideal lattice-based cryptosystem). In our case this would equate to around 2^{27} exponentiations for each proof.

2   Preliminaries

In this section we provide a recap of the BGV encryption scheme [10] as well as those building blocks of SPDZ that are used in combination with it. Most of the details about BGV can be found in [10,20–22], although we will employ a variant which supports circuits of multiplicative depth one only.

Notation. We generally let P_i denote a party, of which there are n in total. Those parties are modeled as probabilistic polynomial time (PPT) Turing machines. We let $[n]$ denote the interval $[1, \ldots, n]$. If M is a matrix then we write $M^{(r,c)}$ for the entry in the r-th row and c-th column. Vectors are (usually) written in bold, and their elements in non-bold with a subscript, thus $\boldsymbol{x} = (x_i)_{i \in [n]}$. We will write $\boldsymbol{x}[i]$ to denote the i-th element in the vector $\boldsymbol{x}$. All modular reduction operations $x \pmod q$ will be to the centered interval $(-q/2, q/2]$.

We let $a \leftarrow X$ denote randomly assigning a value a from a set X, where we assume a uniform distribution on X. If A is an algorithm, we let $a \leftarrow A$ denote assignment of the output, where the probability distribution is over the random tape of A; we also let $a \leftarrow b$ be a shorthand for $a \leftarrow \{b\}$, i.e. to denote normal variable assignment. If $\mathcal{D}$ is a probability distribution over a set X then we let $a \leftarrow \mathcal{D}$ denote sampling from X with respect to the distribution $\mathcal{D}$.

We will make use of the following standard lemma in a number of places

Lemma 1. *Let $\mathcal{D}$ be any distribution whose values are bounded by B. Then the distributions $\mathcal{D} + \mathcal{U}(0, \cdots, B')$ (by which we mean the distribution obtained from sampling from the two distributions and adding the result) is statistically close to the uniform distribution $\mathcal{U}(0, \cdots, B')$, with statistical distance bounded by $\frac{B}{B'}$.*

SPDZ Secret Sharing. This SPDZ protocol [15] processes data using an authenticated secret sharing scheme defined over a finite field $\mathbb{F}_p$, where p is prime. The secret sharing scheme is defined as follows: Each party P_i holds a share $\alpha_i \in \mathbb{F}_p$ of a global MAC key $\alpha = \sum_{i \in [n]} \alpha_i$. A data element $x \in \mathbb{F}_p$ is held in secret shared form as a tuple $\{x_i, \gamma_i\}_{i \in [n]}$, such that $x = \sum_i x_i$ and $\sum \gamma_i = \alpha \cdot x$. We denote a value x held in such a secret shared form as $\langle x \rangle$. The main goal of the SPDZ offline phase is to produce random triples $(\langle a \rangle, \langle b \rangle, \langle c \rangle)$ such that $c = a \cdot b$. If we wish to denote the specific value on which γ_i is a MAC share then we write $\gamma_i[x]$.

The Rings. The BGV encryption scheme, as we will use it, is built around the arithmetic of the cyclotomic ring $\mathcal{R} = \mathbb{Z}[X]/(\Phi_m(X))$, where $\Phi_m(X)$ is the m-th cyclotomic polynomial. For an integer $q > 0$, we denote by $\mathcal{R}_q$ the ring obtained as reduction of $\mathcal{R}$ modulo q. We take m to be a power of two, $m = 2^{n+1}$ and hence $\Phi_m(X) = X^N + 1$ where $N = 2^n$. Elements of $\mathcal{R}$ (resp. $\mathcal{R}_q$) can either be thought of as polynomials (of degree less than N) or as vectors of elements (of length N).

The canonical embedding of $\mathcal{R}$ is the mapping of $\mathcal{R}$ into $\mathbf{C}^{\phi(m)}$ given by $\sigma(x) = (x(\zeta_m^i))_{i \in [n]}$, where we think of x as a polynomial. We are interested in two norms of elements x in $\mathcal{R}$ (resp. $\mathcal{R}_q$). For the ∞-norm in the standard polynomial embedding we write $\|x\|_\infty$, whereas the ∞-norm in the canonical embedding we will write as $\|x\|_\infty^{\mathsf{can}} = \|\sigma(x)\|_\infty$. By standard inequalities we have $\|x \cdot y\|_\infty^{\mathsf{can}} \leq \|x\|_\infty^{\mathsf{can}} \cdot \|y\|_\infty^{\mathsf{can}}$, $\|x\|_\infty^{\mathsf{can}} \leq \|x\|_1$, $\|x\|_\infty^{\mathsf{can}} \leq \phi(m) \cdot \|x\|_\infty$ and $\|x\|_\infty \leq \|x\|_\infty^{\mathsf{can}}$; with the last two inequalities holding due to our specific choice of cyclotomic ring. Such norms can also be employed on elements of $\mathcal{R}_q$ by using the standard (centered) embedding of $\mathcal{R}_q$ into $\mathcal{R}$.

We will use the following two facts in a number of places.

Lemma 2. *Let m be a power of two. Then, for all $0 \leq i, j < 2 \cdot N$,*

$$\|2 \cdot (X^i - X^j)^{-1} \pmod{\phi_m(X)}\|_\infty \leq 1$$

Proof. Given in [8].

Lemma 3. *In the ring $\mathcal{R}$ defined by $\Phi_m(X)$ with m a power of two we have that for all $a \in \mathcal{R}$ that $\|a \cdot X^i\|_\infty = \|a\|_\infty$.*

Proof. This follows as X^i acts as a shift operation, with the wrap-around modulo $\phi(m)$ simply negating the respective coordinate.

Distributions as Used in BGV. Following [22, Full version, Appendix A.5] and [2] we use different distributions to define the BGV scheme, all of which produce vectors of length N which we consider as elements in $\mathcal{R}$.

- HWT(h, N): This generates a vector of length N with elements chosen at random from $\{-1, 0, 1\}$ subject to the condition that the number of non-zero elements is equal to h.
- ZO($0.5, N$): This generates a vector of length N with elements chosen from $\{-1, 0, 1\}$ such that the probability of each coefficient is $p_{-1} = 1/4$, $p_0 = 1/2$ and $p_1 = 1/4$. Thus if $x \leftarrow$ ZO($0.5, N$) then $\|x\|_\infty \leq 1$.
- dN(σ^2, N): This generates a vector of length N with elements chosen according to an approximation to the discrete Gaussian distribution with variance σ^2.
- RC($0.5, \sigma^2, N$): This generates a triple of elements (r_1, r_2, r_3) where r_3 is sampled from ZO$_s$($0.5, N$) and r_1 and r_2 are sampled from dN$_s$(σ^2, N).
- U(q, N): This generates a vector of length N with elements generated uniformly modulo q in a centred range. Thus $x \leftarrow$ U(q, N) implies $\|x\|_\infty \leq q/2$.

Following prior work on SPDZ we select $\sigma = 3.17$ and hence we can approximate the sampling from the discrete Gaussian distribution using a binomial distribution, as is done in NewHope [1]. In such a situation an element $x \leftarrow \mathsf{dN}(\sigma^2, N)$ is guaranteed to satisfy $\|x\|_\infty \leq 20$.

The Two-Level BGV Scheme. We consider a two-leveled homomorphic scheme, given by the algorithms $\{\mathsf{KeyGen}, \mathsf{Enc}, \mathsf{SwitchMod}, \mathsf{Dec}\}$. The plaintext space is the ring $\mathcal{R}_p$, for some prime modulus p, which is the same modulus used to define the SPDZ secret sharing scheme. The algorithms are parametrized by a *computational* security parameter κ and are defined as follows. First we fix two moduli q_0 and q_1 such that $q_1 = p_0 \cdot p_1$ and $q_0 = p_0$, where p_0, p_1 are prime numbers. Encryption generates level one ciphertexts, i.e. with respect to the largest modulo q_1, and level one ciphertexts can be moved to level zero ciphertexts via the modulus switching operation. We require $p_1 \equiv 1 \pmod{p}$ and $p_0 - 1 \equiv p_1 - 1 \equiv 0 \pmod{p}$. The first condition is to enable modulus switching to be performed efficiently, whereas the second is to enable fast arithmetic using Number Theoretic Fourier Transforms.

The algorithms of the BGV scheme are then as follows:

- $\underline{\mathsf{KeyGen}(1^\kappa)}$: The secret key $\mathfrak{st}$ is randomly selected from a distribution with Hamming weight h, i.e. $\mathsf{HWT}(h, N)$, much as in other systems, e.g. HELib [23] and SCALE [2]. The public key, $\mathfrak{pt}$, is of the form (a, b), such that $a \leftarrow \mathsf{U}(q_1, N)$ and $b = a \cdot \mathfrak{st} + p \cdot \epsilon \pmod{q_1}$, where $\epsilon \leftarrow \mathsf{dN}(\sigma^2, N)$. This algorithm also outputs the relinearization data $(a_{\mathfrak{st},\mathfrak{st}^2}, b_{\mathfrak{st},\mathfrak{st}^2})$ [11], where $a_{\mathfrak{st},\mathfrak{st}^2} \leftarrow \mathsf{U}(q_1, N)$ and $b_{\mathfrak{st},\mathfrak{st}^2} = a_{\mathfrak{st},\mathfrak{st}^2} \cdot \mathfrak{st} + p \cdot r_{\mathfrak{st},\mathfrak{st}^2} - p_1 \cdot \mathfrak{st}^2 \pmod{q_1}$, with $r_{\mathfrak{st},\mathfrak{st}^2} \leftarrow \mathsf{dN}(\sigma^2, N)$.

- $\underline{\mathsf{Enc}(m, \boldsymbol{r}; \mathfrak{pt})}$: Given a plaintext $m \in \mathcal{R}_p$, and randomness $\boldsymbol{r} = (r_1, r_2, r_3)$ chosen from $\mathsf{RC}(0.5, \sigma^2, n)$, i.e. we sample $r_1, r_2 \leftarrow \mathsf{dN}(\sigma^2, N)$ and $r_3 \leftarrow \mathsf{ZO}(0.5, N)$, this algorithm sets $c_0 = b \cdot r_3 + p \cdot r_1 + m \pmod{q_1}$ and $c_1 = a \cdot r_3 + p \cdot r_2 \pmod{q_1}$. Hence the initial ciphertext is $\mathfrak{ct} = (1, c_0, c_1)$, where the first index denotes the level (initially set to be equal to one). If the level ℓ is obvious we drop it in future discussions and refer to the ciphertext as an element in $\mathcal{R}_{q_\ell}^2$.

- $\underline{\mathsf{SwitchMod}((1, c_0, c_1))}$:   We define a modulus switching operation which allows us to move from a level one to a level zero ciphertext, *without altering* the plaintext polynomial, that is

$$(0, c_0', c_1') \leftarrow \mathsf{SwitchMod}((1, c_0, c_1)), \quad c_0', c_1' \in \mathcal{R}_{q_0}.$$

The effect of this operation is also to scale the noise term (see below) by a factor of $q_0/q_1 = 1/p_1$.

- $\underline{\mathsf{Dec}((c_0, c_1); \mathfrak{st})}$: Decryption is obtained by switching the ciphertext to level zero (if it is not already at level zero) and then decrypting $(0, c_0, c_1)$ via the equation $(c_0 - \mathfrak{st} \cdot c_1 \pmod{q_0}) \pmod{p}$, which results in an element of $\mathcal{R}_p$.

Homomorphic Operations. Ciphertexts at the same level ℓ can be added,

$$(\ell, c_0, c_1) \boxplus (\ell, c_0', c_1') = (\ell, (c_0 + c_0' \pmod{q_\ell}), (c_1 + c_1' \pmod{q_\ell})),$$

with the result being a ciphertext, which encodes a plaintext that is the sum of the two initial plaintexts. Ciphertexts at level one can be multiplied together to obtain a ciphertext at level zero, where the output ciphertext encodes a plaintext which is the product of the plaintexts encoded by the input plaintexts. We do not present the method here, although it is pretty standard consisting of a modulus-switch, tensor-operation, then relinearization (which we carry out in this order). We write the operation as

$$(1, c_0, c_1) \odot (1, c_0', c_1') = (0, c_0'', c_1''), \quad \text{with} \quad c_0'', c_1'' \in \mathcal{R}_{q_0},$$

or more simply as $(c_0, c_1) \odot (c_0', c_1') = (c_0'', c_1'')$ as the levels are implied.

Ciphertext Noise. The noise term associated with a ciphertext is the value $\|c_0 - \mathfrak{st} \cdot c_1\|_\infty^{\mathsf{can}}$. To derive parameters for the scheme we need to maintain a handle on this value. The term is additive under addition and is roughly divided by p_1 under a modulus switch. For the tensoring and relinearization in multiplication the terms roughly multiply. A ciphertext at level zero will decrypt correctly if we have $\|c_0 - \mathfrak{st} \cdot c_1\|_\infty \leq q_0/2$, which we can enforce by requiring $\|c_0 - \mathfrak{st} \cdot c_1\|_\infty^{\mathsf{can}} \leq q_0/2$.

We would like a ciphertext (adversarially chosen or not) to decrypt correctly with probability $1 - 2^{-\epsilon}$. In [22] ϵ is chosen to be around 55, but the effect of ϵ is only in producing the following constants: we define e_i such that $\mathsf{erfc}(e_i)^i \approx 2^{-\epsilon}$ and then we set $\mathfrak{c}_i = e_i^i$. This implies that $\mathfrak{c}_1 \cdot \sqrt{V}$, is a high probability bound on the canonical norm of a ring element whose coefficients are selected from a distribution with variance V, while $\mathfrak{c}_2 \cdot \sqrt{V_1 \cdot V_2}$ is a similar bound on a product of elements whose coefficient are chosen from distributions of variance V_1 and V_2 respectively.

With probability much greater than $1 - 2^{-\epsilon}$ the "noise" of an honestly generated ciphertext (given honestly generated keys) will be bounded by

$$
\begin{aligned}
\|c_0 - \mathfrak{st} \cdot c_1\|_\infty^{\mathsf{can}} &= \|((a \cdot \mathfrak{st} + p \cdot \epsilon) \cdot r_3 + p \cdot r_1 + m - (a \cdot r_3 + p \cdot r_2) \cdot \mathfrak{st}\|_\infty^{\mathsf{can}} \\
&= \|m + p \cdot (\epsilon \cdot r_3 + r_1 - r_2 \cdot \mathfrak{st})\|_\infty^{\mathsf{can}} \\
&\leq \|m\|_\infty^{\mathsf{can}} + p \cdot (\|\epsilon \cdot r_3\|_\infty^{\mathsf{can}} + \|r_1\|_\infty^{\mathsf{can}} + \|r_2 \cdot \mathfrak{st}\|_\infty^{\mathsf{can}}) \\
&\leq \phi(m) \cdot p/2 \\
&\quad + p \cdot \sigma \cdot \left(\mathfrak{c}_2 \cdot \phi(m)/\sqrt{2} + \mathfrak{c}_1 \cdot \sqrt{\phi(m)} + \mathfrak{c}_2 \cdot \sqrt{h \cdot \phi(m)} \right) \\
&= B_{\mathsf{clean}}.
\end{aligned}
$$

Recall this is the average case bound on the noise of honestly generated ciphertexts. In the preprocessing ciphertexts can be adversarially generated, and determining (and ensuring) a worst case bound on the resulting ciphertexts is the main focus of the HighGear and TopGear protocols.

Distributed Decryption. The BGV encryption scheme supports a form of distributed decryption, which is utilized in the SPDZ offline phase. A secret key $\mathfrak{sk} \in \mathcal{R}_q$ can be additively shared amongst n parties by giving each party a value $\mathfrak{sk}_i \in \mathcal{R}_q$ such that $\mathfrak{sk} = \mathfrak{sk}_1 + \ldots + \mathfrak{sk}_n$. We assume, as is done in most other works on SPDZ, that the key generation phase, including the distribution of the shares of the secret key to the parties, is done in a trusted setup.

To perform a distributed decryption of a ciphertext $\mathfrak{ct} = (c_0, c_1)$ at level zero, each party computes $d_i \leftarrow c_0 - c_1 \cdot \mathfrak{sk}_i + p \cdot R_i \pmod{q_0}$ where R_i is a uniformly random value selected from $[0, \ldots, 2^{\mathsf{DD\text{-}sec}} \cdot B/p]$ where B is an upper bound on the norm $\|c_0 - c_1 \cdot \mathfrak{sk}\|_\infty$. The values d_i are then exchanged between the players and the plaintext is obtained from $m \leftarrow (d_1 + \ldots + d_n \pmod{q_0}) \pmod{p}$. The statistical distance between the distribution of the *coefficients* of d_i and uniformly random elements of size $2^{\mathsf{DD\text{-}sec}} \cdot B$ is bounded by $2^{-\mathsf{DD\text{-}sec}}$ by Lemma 1. To ensure valid decryption we need the value of q_0 to satisfy $q_0 > 2 \cdot (1 + n \cdot 2^{\mathsf{DD\text{-}sec}}) \cdot B$ instead of $q_0 > 2 \cdot B$ for a scheme without distributed decryption, which implies parameter growth in the BGV scheme when using this distributed decryption procedure.

3 n-Prover Zero Knowledge-Protocols

The Overdrive ZKPoK is an $n + 1$ party protocol between n provers and one verifier[2]. Unlike traditional proofs of knowledge, there is a difference between the language used for completeness and the language that the soundness guarantees; much like the protocols considered in [9, Definition 2.2]. As the Overdrive paper does not formalize such proofs, our first contribution is to do precisely this. We give a generalized treatment of such proofs beyond regular Σ-protocols.

Let Samp be a PPT algorithm which, on input $n, i \in \mathbb{N}, 0 < i \leq n$ outputs a pair of values x_i, w_i where we consider x_i as the public and w_i as the private value. We require that if for all $i \in [n]$ we sample $(x_i, w_i) \leftarrow \mathsf{Samp}_n(i)$, then a given predicate $\mathbf{P}$ always holds, i.e. we have that $\mathbf{P}(x_1, \ldots, x_n, w_1, \ldots, w_n) = 1$. The predicate $\mathbf{P}$ defines a language $\mathbb{L}$ via the binary relation on the pairs ($\boldsymbol{x} = (x_1, \ldots, x_n), \boldsymbol{w} = (w_1, \ldots, w_n)$).

Consider a set of n provers $P_1, \ldots, P_n$, each with private input w_i and public input x_i. The provers wish to convince a verifier V (that could be one or all of the provers) that, for the public values $x_1, \ldots, x_n$ they know $w_1, \ldots, w_n$ such that $\mathbf{P}$ holds. The guarantee provided by our proof is, however, only that $\mathbf{P}'(x_1, \ldots, x_n, w_1, \ldots, w_n) = 1$ for some second language $\mathbb{L}'$, defined by a predicate $\mathbf{P}'$, with $\mathbb{L} \subseteq \mathbb{L}'$. This is still sufficient for the preprocessing of SPDZ.

Definition 1. *An n-party ZKPoK-protocol with challenge set $\mathcal{C}$ for the languages $\mathbb{L}, \mathbb{L}'$ and sampler Samp_n is defined as a tuple of algorithms* (Comm, Resp, Verify). *While* Comm *is a PPT algorithm, we assume that* Resp, Verify *are deterministic. The verifier V will have input $x_1, \ldots, x_n$. The protocol is executed in the following four phases:*

---

[2] In the way it is used each prover also acts as an independent verifier.

1. *Each prover P_i independently executes the algorithms*

$$(\mathsf{comm}_i, \mathsf{state}_i) \leftarrow \mathsf{Comm}(x_i, w_i)$$

   and sends (comm_i) to the verifier.
2. *The verifier selects a challenge value $c \in \mathcal{C}$ and sends it to each prover.*
3. *Each prover P_i, again independently, runs the algorithm*

$$\mathsf{resp}_i \leftarrow \mathsf{Resp}(\mathsf{state}_i, c)$$

   and sends resp_i to the verifier.
4. *The verifier accepts if $\mathsf{Verify}(\{\mathsf{comm}_i, \mathsf{resp}_i, x_i\}_{i \in [n]}, c) = \mathsf{true}$.*

Such a protocol should satisfy the following three properties

- **Correctness:**
  If all P_i, each on input $(x_i, w_i) \leftarrow \mathsf{Samp}_n(i)$ honestly follow the protocol, then an honest verifier will accept with probability one.
- **Computational Knowledge Soundness:** *Let $\mathcal{A} = (\mathcal{A}_1, \mathcal{A}_2)$ be a pair of PPT algorithms and $\epsilon \in [0, 1)$. Consider the following game:*
  1. *$\mathcal{A}_1$ is run and outputs $I \subseteq [n]$, $\{x_i\}_{i \in I}$ and $\mathsf{state}_1^{\mathcal{A}}$.*
  2. *Choose $(x_j, w_j) \leftarrow \mathsf{Samp}_n(j)$ honestly for each $P_j, j \notin I$.*
  3. *Compute $(\mathsf{comm}_j, \mathsf{state}_j) \leftarrow \mathsf{Comm}(x_j, w_j)$ for $j \notin I$.*
  4. *$\mathcal{A}_2$ on input of $\mathsf{state}_1^{\mathcal{A}}, \{x_j, \mathsf{comm}_j\}_{j \notin I}$ outputs $\mathsf{state}_2^{\mathcal{A}}$ and $\{\mathsf{comm}_i\}_{i \in I}$.*
  5. *Choose $c \in \mathcal{C}$ uniformly at random and compute $\mathsf{resp}_j \leftarrow \mathsf{Resp}(\mathsf{state}_j, c)$ for $j \notin I$.*
  6. *$\mathcal{A}_2$ on input $\mathsf{state}_2^{\mathcal{A}}, c, \{\mathsf{resp}_j\}_{j \notin I}$ outputs $\{\mathsf{resp}_i\}_{i \in I}$.*
  7. *We say that $\mathcal{A}_1, \mathcal{A}_2$ wins if $\mathsf{Verify}(\{\mathsf{comm}_i, \mathsf{resp}_i, x_i\}_{i \in [n]}, c)$ outputs true.*
  Assume that $\mathcal{A}$ wins the above game with probability $\delta > \epsilon$ where the probability is taken over the randomness of $\mathcal{A}_2$ and the choice of c.
  Then we say that the protocol is a computational proof of knowledge if there exists a PPT algorithm $\mathsf{Extract}$ which, for any fixed $I, \{x_i\}_{i \in I}$ generated by $\mathcal{A}_1$, with honestly generated $\{x_j, w_j, \mathsf{state}_j, \mathsf{comm}_j\}_{j \notin I}$ as input and black-box access to $\mathcal{A}_2(\mathsf{state}_2^{\mathcal{A}}, \{\mathsf{comm}_j, x_j\}_{j \notin I})$ outputs $\{w_i\}_{i \in I}$ such that $\mathbf{P}'(x_1, \ldots, x_n, w_1, \ldots, w_n) = 1$ in expected $q(\mathsf{Snd\_sec})/(\delta - \epsilon)$ steps where $q(\cdot)$ is a positive polynomial.
- **Honest Verifier Zero-Knowledge:** *There exists a PPT algorithm Sim_I indexed by a set $I \subset [n]$, which takes as input an element in the language $\mathbb{L}$ and a challenge $c \in \mathcal{C}$, and outputs tuples $\{\mathsf{comm}_i, \mathsf{resp}_i\}_{i \notin I}$. We require that for all such I the output of Sim_I is statistically indistinguishable from a valid execution of the protocol.*

Since the execution of the commitment and response phases are independent for each player, we only need to look at indistinguishability of the distribution of the values $(c, \{\mathsf{comm}_i, \mathsf{resp}_i\}_{i \notin I})$ produced in a valid and a simulated execution of the protocol. Whatever the adversary does cannot affect the zero-knowledge property, as the values sent by the honest provers are generated independently of those sent by adversarially-controlled parties. Our formalism for HV-ZK is therefore only to allow the simulator to be applied when some provers are honest.

The knowledge extraction follows the standard definition of a proof of knowledge, but also incorporates the slack-definition in [3] adapted to our situation of n-Prover ZKPoK-protocols: Note that we are not assuming a special soundness definition as is usual in Σ-protocols, since we allow the knowledge extractor to perform multiple rewind queries to the dishonest provers with correlated challenges. Also note that the knowledge extractor above outputs a witness for a predicate $\mathbf{P}'$ which is potentially different from the predicate that honest parties were using. In traditional ZK proofs-protocols we have that $\mathbf{P} = \mathbf{P}'$ but in many lattice based protocols these two predicates are distinct.

The above definitions imply two security parameters Snd_sec and ZK_sec. The soundness parameter Snd_sec controls the value ϵ from Definition 1. Usually we set $\epsilon = 2^{-\mathsf{Snd\_sec}}$, which then (loosely speaking) is the probability that an adversary with control over a set of provers $I \subseteq [n]$ can make an honest verifier accept for values $\{x_i\}_{i \in I}$ without actually having valid witnesses w_i. The second parameter is the zero-knowledge parameter ZK_sec, which defines the statistical distance between the distributions of genuine and simulated transcripts. We let this distance be bounded by $2^{-\mathsf{ZK\_sec}}$.

Relations to Other Definitions. It might seem that the above definition is related to multi-prover interactive proofs [6], but this is not true. Firstly, the provers in our definition may arbitrarily collude during the above protocol – which differs from multi-prover proofs where they cannot coordinate. Moreover, our definition can be seen as each P_i individually trying to convince the verifier about the correctness of an individual statement, but the soundness takes into account a combination of the individual statements as expressed by the language $\mathbb{L}$. Therefore, in an n-party ZK proof of knowledge it might happen that any subset of $n - 1$ successful provers cannot produce a correct witness for the overall statement $(x_1, \ldots, x_n)$ by pooling their w_i. In multi-prover interactive proofs, each P_i may itself have full knowledge of the complete witness.

Definition 1 also differs from just running n proofs in parallel, as the predicate $\mathbf{P}$ might introduce constraints over all x_i, w_i. This is exactly how [25] used it in their work, where they perform checks both on the individual ciphertexts and on all of them simultaneously, thus saving runtime.

4   A n-Prover ZKPoK for SPDZ

Our protocol, which we call TopGear, is given in Figs. 1 and 2. The protocol is a n-Prover ZKPoK-Protocol in which, in the way we have described it, the n players act both as a set of provers *and* individually as verifiers; as this is how the proof will be used in the SPDZ offline phase. In our description in Figs. 1 and 2 the challenge of the ZKPoK is produced via calling a random functionality $\mathcal{F}_{\mathsf{Rand}}$ which produces a single joint challenge between the players. Such a functionality is standard, see for example [15].

Protocol Π_{ZKPoK}: Sampling Algorithm, Commitment, Challenge and Response Phases

The protocol is parametrized by integer parameters U, V and $\mathsf{flag} \in \{\mathsf{Diag}, \perp\}$ as well as $\mathfrak{pk}$ and further parameters of the encryption scheme.

Sampling Algorithm: Samp

1. If $\mathsf{flag} = \perp$ then generate the plaintext $\boldsymbol{m} \in \mathcal{R}_p^U$ (considered as an element of $\mathcal{R}_{q_1}^U$) uniformly at random in $\mathcal{R}_p^U$. If $\mathsf{flag} = \mathsf{Diag}$ then instead for each $k \in [U]$ let $\boldsymbol{m}^{(k)}$ be a random "diagonal" message in $\mathcal{R}_p$.
2. Generate a randomness triple as $R \in \mathcal{R}_{q_1}^{U \times 3}$, each of whose rows is generated from $\mathsf{RC}\left(\sigma^2, 0.5, N\right)$.
3. Compute the ciphertexts by encrypting each row separately, thus obtaining $C \leftarrow \mathsf{Enc}(\boldsymbol{m}, R; \mathfrak{pk}) \in \mathcal{R}_{q_1}^{U \times 2}$.
4. Output $(x = (C), w = (\boldsymbol{m}, R))$.

Commitment Phase: Comm

1. Each P_i samples V pseudo-plaintexts $\boldsymbol{y}_i \in \mathcal{R}_{q_1}^V$ and pseudo-randomness vectors $S_i = (s_i^{(l,\ell)}) \in \mathcal{R}_{q_1}^{V \times 3}$ such that, for all $l \in [V]$, $\|\boldsymbol{y}_i^{(l)}\|_\infty \le 2^{\mathsf{ZK\_sec}-1} \cdot p$ and $\|s_i^{(l,\ell)}\|_\infty \le 2^{\mathsf{ZK\_sec}} \cdot \rho_\ell$. If $\mathsf{flag} = \mathsf{Diag}$ then each $\boldsymbol{y}_i$ contains the same value in each plaintext slot.
2. Party P_i computes $A_i \leftarrow \mathsf{Enc}(\boldsymbol{y}_i, S_i; \mathfrak{pk}) \in \mathcal{R}_{q_1}^{V \times 2}$.
3. The players broadcast $\mathsf{comm}_i \leftarrow A_i$.

Challenge Phase: Chall

1. Parties call $\mathcal{F}_{\mathsf{Rand}}$ to obtain a $V \times U$ challenge matrix W.
2. If $\mathsf{flag} = \perp$ this is a matrix with random entries in $\{X^i\}_{i=0\ldots,2\cdot N-1} \cup \{0\}$. If $\mathsf{flag} = \mathsf{Diag}$ then W is a random matrix in $\{0,1\}^{V \times U}$.

Response Phase: Resp

1. Each P_i computes $\boldsymbol{z}_i \leftarrow \boldsymbol{y}_i + W \cdot \boldsymbol{m}_i$ and $T_i \leftarrow S_i + W \cdot R_i$.
2. Party P_i sets $\mathsf{resp}_i \leftarrow (\boldsymbol{z}_i, T_i)$, and broadcasts resp_i.

Fig. 1. Protocol for global proof of knowledge of a set of ciphertexts: Part I

Recall from [15] that the proof is used in two ways. In the standard way, where $\mathsf{flag} = \perp$ there is no extra condition on the plaintext, however when $\mathsf{flag} = \mathsf{Diag}$ the underlying plaintexts are required to be the constant polynomial. To understand its workings and security, first we give the two languages and then a security proof for the standard case $\mathsf{flag} = \perp$. The reason for this flag is that in the SPDZ protocol [15], at one stage ciphertexts need to be proved to be "Diagonal", namely each plaintext slot component contains the same element. We will discuss this after giving the proof for the main protocol.

Protocol Π_{ZKPoK}: Verification Phase

Verification Phase: Verify

1. Each party P_i computes $D_i \leftarrow \mathsf{Enc}(z_i, T_i; \mathfrak{pe})$.
2. The parties compute $A \leftarrow \sum_{i=1}^{n} A_i$, $C \leftarrow \sum_{i=1}^{n} C_i$, $D \leftarrow \sum_{i=1}^{n} D_i$, $T \leftarrow \sum_{i=1}^{n} T_i$ and $z \leftarrow \sum_{i=1}^{n} z_i$.
3. The parties check whether $D = A + W \cdot C$, and then whether the following inequalities hold, for $l \in [V]$,

$$\|z^{(l)}\|_\infty \leq n \cdot 2^{\mathsf{ZK\_sec}} \cdot p, \quad \|T^{(l,\ell)}\|_\infty \leq 2 \cdot n \cdot 2^{\mathsf{ZK\_sec}} \cdot \rho_\ell \text{ for } \ell = 1, 2, 3.$$

4. If flag = Diag then the proof is rejected if $z^{(l)}$ is not a constant polynomial (i.e. a "diagonal" plaintext element).
5. If all checks pass, the parties accept, otherwise they reject.

Fig. 2. Protocol for global proof of knowledge of a set of ciphertexts: Part II

The Honest Language: In an honest execution of the preprocessing each party P_i first generates a set of U ciphertexts given by, for $k \in [U]$,

$$\mathfrak{ct}_i^{(k)} = \mathsf{Enc}\left(m_i^{(k)}, (r_i^{(k,1)}, r_i^{(k,2)}, r_i^{(k,3)}); \mathfrak{pe}\right).$$

Party P_i wishes to keep the values $m_i^{(k)}, r_i^{(k,1)}, r_i^{(k,2)}, r_i^{(k,3)}$ private, whereas the ciphertexts $\mathfrak{ct}_i^{(k)}$ are public. If we define $C_i = (\mathfrak{ct}_i^{(1)}, \ldots, \mathfrak{ct}_i^{(U)})$ and $\boldsymbol{m}_i, R_i$ equivalently, then we can instead say that P_i wishes to prove knowledge of $w_i = (\boldsymbol{m}_i, R_i)$ for a given $x_i = (C_i)$. By abuse of notation we relate to $\boldsymbol{m}_i, R_i, C_i$ via the equation $C_i \leftarrow \mathsf{Enc}(\boldsymbol{m}_i, R_i; \mathfrak{pe})$.

The proof shows a statement about $\boldsymbol{m} = \sum_{i=1}^{n} \boldsymbol{m}_i$, $R = \sum_{i=1}^{n} R_i$ and $C = \sum_{i=1}^{n} C_i$, i.e. when summed over all parties. It works over $\mathcal{R}$ (and not $\mathcal{R}_{q_1}$) to make $\|\cdot\|_\infty$ meaningful.

We define the "honest" language $\mathbb{L}$ as

$$\mathbb{L} = \Big\{((x_1, \ldots, x_n), (w_1, \ldots, w_n)):$$
$$x_i = C_i, \quad w_i = (\boldsymbol{m}_i, R_i),$$
$$C = \sum C_i, \quad \boldsymbol{m} = \sum \boldsymbol{m}_i, \quad R = \sum R_i,$$
$$C = \mathsf{Enc}(\boldsymbol{m}, R; \mathfrak{pe}) \text{ and for all } k \in [U]$$
$$\|\boldsymbol{m}^{(k)}\|_\infty \leq n \cdot p/2, \quad \|R^{(k,\ell)}\|_\infty \leq n \cdot \rho_\ell\Big\}.$$

where $\rho_1 = \rho_2 = 20$ and $\rho_3 = 1$. Note, the language says nothing about whether the initial witnesses encrypt to the initial public values C_i, it only considers a joint statement about all players' inputs. In the above definition we abuse notation by using Enc as a procedure irrespective of the distributions of the input variables (as $\boldsymbol{m}^{(k)}$ and $R^{(k,\ell)}$ are now elements in $\mathcal{R}$ and not necessarily in the correct domain). Here we simply apply the equations

$$b \cdot R^{(k,3)} + p \cdot R^{(k,1)} + \boldsymbol{m}^{(k)} \pmod{q_1}, \quad a \cdot R^{(k,3)} + p \cdot R^{(k,2)} \pmod{q_1}.$$

For dishonest provers (where we assume the worst case of all provers being dishonest) we will only be able to show that the inputs are from the language

$$\mathbb{L}_c' = \Big\{ ((x_1, \ldots, x_n), (w_1, \ldots, w_n)) :$$

$$x_i = C_i, \quad w_i = (\boldsymbol{m}_i, R_i),$$

$$C = \sum C_i, \quad \boldsymbol{m} = \sum \boldsymbol{m}_i, \quad R = \sum R_i,$$

$$C = \mathsf{Enc}(\boldsymbol{m}, R; \mathfrak{pk}) \text{ and for all } k \in [U]$$

$$\|c \cdot \boldsymbol{m}^{(k)}\|_\infty \le 2^{\mathsf{ZK\_sec}+1} \cdot n \cdot p,$$

$$\|c \cdot R^{(k,\ell)}\|_\infty \le 2^{\mathsf{ZK\_sec}+2} \cdot n \cdot \rho_\ell \Big\}.$$

Notice that not only the bounds on $\boldsymbol{m}^{(k)}, R^{(k)}$ have increased, but the values whose norms are determined have also been multiplied by a factor of c.

Thus we see that, at a high level, the bounds for the honest language are $|w_i| < B$, whilst the bounds for the proven language are $|c \cdot w_i| < 2^{\mathsf{ZK\_sec}+2} \cdot B$. This additional factor $2^{\mathsf{ZK\_sec}+2}$ is called the *soundness slack*. This soundness slack *could* be reduced by utilizing rejection sampling as in lattice signature schemes, but this would complicate the protocol (being an n-party proof), lead to a slowdown due to having to potentially rerun the protocol multiple times and (more importantly) it turns out that the soundness slack has no important effect on the parameters needed in practice.

There is an added complication arising from the language $\mathbb{L}_c'$, corresponding to the factor of c in Lemma 2. However, this can be side-stepped by a minor modification to how the ZKPoKs are used with the SPDZ offline phase (which we describe in Sect. 5).

Theorem 1. *Let* flag $= \perp$ *and* $V \ge (\mathsf{Snd\_sec} + 2)/\log_2(2N + 1)$, *then the algorithms in Figs. 1 and 2 are an n-party ZKPoK protocol according to Definition 1 for the languages $\mathbb{L}$ and $\mathbb{L}_2'$ with soundness error $2^{-\mathsf{Snd\_sec}}$ and statistical distance $2^{-\mathsf{ZK\_sec}}$ in the simulation.*

Proof. The proof is given in the full version of the paper.

For the ZKPoK of "diagonal" elements, the main difference is that soundness must ensure that the extracted $\boldsymbol{m}$ encodes a "diagonal" plaintext as well. Unfortunately, as we have to multiply with ring elements in the extraction process of the soundness argument, it cannot be guaranteed that the outcome is "diagonal". Instead, in such a case we fall back to a binary challenge matrix W (as depicted in Fig. 1), where the "diagonal" property follows as the extractor only performs additions and subtractions on the values z_i, T_i in the process, but no multiplications with inverses. As a side effect, the proof actually yields bounds on $\boldsymbol{m}^{(k)}, R^{(k,\ell)}$ for $c = 1$. One can easily show the following

Corollary 1. *Let* flag = Diag *and* $V \geq$ Snd_sec+2, *then the algorithms in Figs. 1 and 2 are an n-party ZKPoK protocol according to Definition 1 for the languages* $\mathbb{L}$ *and* $\mathbb{L}'_1$ *with soundness error* $2^{-\mathsf{Snd\_sec}}$ *and statistical distance* $2^{-\mathsf{ZK\_sec}}$ *in the simulation.*

5   SPDZ Offline Phase

We now show how to combine the ZKPoK from Sect. 4 with the offline phase of the SPDZ protocol. After a brief recap of it, we outline the necessary changes to the HighGear protocol of [25]. Recall that the offline phase of SPDZ primarily generates shared random triples $(\langle a \rangle, \langle b \rangle, \langle c \rangle)$ such that $c = a \cdot b$ where a, b are chosen uniformly at random from $\mathbb{F}_p$ (and no subset of parties either know a, b or c, or can affect their distribution). This is done, by each party P_i encoding $\phi(m)$ $\boldsymbol{a}_i$ and $\boldsymbol{b}_i$ values into two elements a_i and b_i in $\mathcal{R}_p$. These a_i and b_i are encrypted via the BGV scheme, and the parties obtain $\mathfrak{ct}_{a_i} = \mathsf{Enc}(a_i, \boldsymbol{r}_{a,i}; \mathfrak{pk})$ and $\mathfrak{ct}_{b_i} = \mathsf{Enc}(b_i, \boldsymbol{r}_{b,i}; \mathfrak{pk})$.

Using the homomorphic properties of the BGV encryption scheme the parties can then compute an encryption of the product $c \in \mathcal{R}_p$ via

$$\mathfrak{ct}_c = (\mathfrak{ct}_{a_1} \boxplus \cdots \boxplus \mathfrak{ct}_{a_n}) \odot (\mathfrak{ct}_{b_1} \boxplus \cdots \boxplus \mathfrak{ct}_{b_n}). \tag{1}$$

The product $\mathfrak{ct}_c$ is decrypted using a distributed decryption protocol which gives to each party a share $c_i \in \mathbb{F}_p$ of the plaintext of $\mathfrak{ct}_c$. To achieve security in the online phase, one furthermore needs to compute shares of the MACs $\gamma[a], \gamma[b]$ and $\gamma[c]$, which are obtained in a similar manner. In order to enforce input independence, the parties do not merely exchange $\mathfrak{ct}_{a_i}, \mathfrak{ct}_{b_i}$ but instead first commit to these ciphertexts before revealing them afterwards.

In the offline phase, the main attack vector is that dishonest parties could produce ciphertexts which contain maliciously chosen noise or a plaintext unbeknownst to the sending party. This would result in either selective failure attacks or information leakage during the distributed decryption procedure. Thus each ciphertext $\mathfrak{ct}_{a_i}$ needs to be accompanied by a ZKPoK showing that it is not too far from being an honestly generated ciphertext. As the ZKPoKs bound the noise term associated to every ciphertext, we use this bound to derive the parameters for the BGV encryption scheme. This in turn ensures that all ciphertexts will validly decrypt. Quite obviously we want to execute U such proofs in parallel such as to amortize.

As noticed in HighGear [25], the ciphertexts $\mathfrak{ct}_{a_i}$ are only ever used in a sum (as in Eq. 1). Therefore it is possible to replace n individual ZKPoKs for $\mathfrak{ct}_{a_i}$ by a single ZKPoK for the sum $\mathfrak{ct}_a = \mathfrak{ct}_{a_1} \boxplus \cdots \boxplus \mathfrak{ct}_{a_n}$ – which is exactly the strategy we outlined in the previous two sections. However, our proof comes at the expense of not obtaining guarantees about the original ciphertext sum $\mathfrak{ct}_a$, but instead of $2 \cdot \mathfrak{ct}_a = \mathfrak{ct}_a \boxplus \mathfrak{ct}_a$. Luckily this of no concern in preprocessing for SPDZ - we can simply later adjust some of the shares by a factor of two and continue as before. The modifications are explained in Fig. 3 for the case of triple

---

Protocol Π_{offline}

Init:

1. Each P_i locally runs $\mathsf{Samp}_n(i)$ with flag $=$ Diag and $U = 1$ to obtain $\alpha_i \in \mathbb{F}_p$ as well as the ciphertext $\mathfrak{ct}_{\alpha_i}$.
2. Each P_i broadcasts a commitment to $\mathfrak{ct}_{\alpha_i}$. Upon receiving all such commitments, each party broadcasts the opening to the commitment. If any such opening fails, then abort.
3. For $i = 1, \ldots, \mathsf{Snd\_sec}/16$
   (a) The parties perform the other phases of Π_{ZKPoK} with flag $=$ Diag, $U = 1$ and $V = 16$. If any proof rejects they abort.
4. The parties set $\mathfrak{ct}_\alpha \leftarrow (\mathfrak{ct}_{\alpha_1} \boxplus \cdots \boxplus \mathfrak{ct}_{\alpha_n})$.

Triples:

1. We set $V = (\mathsf{Snd\_sec} + 2)/\log_2(2 \cdot N + 1)$ and $U = 2 \cdot V$.
2. Each P_i runs $\mathsf{Samp}_n(i)$ for this value of U with flag $=\perp$. It thus obtains the plaintext vectors $\hat{\boldsymbol{a}}_i^{(k)}, \hat{\boldsymbol{b}}_i^{(k)}, \hat{\boldsymbol{f}}_i^{(k)} \in (\mathbb{F}_p)^{\phi(m)}$ as well as the ciphertexts $\mathfrak{ct}_{\hat{a}_i}^{(k)}, \mathfrak{ct}_{\hat{b}_i}^{(k)}$ and $\mathfrak{ct}_{\hat{f}_i}^{(k)}$ for $k \in [U]$.
3. Each P_i broadcasts commitments to $\mathfrak{ct}_{\hat{a}_i}^{(k)}, \mathfrak{ct}_{\hat{b}_i}^{(k)}$ and $\mathfrak{ct}_{\hat{f}_i}^{(k)}$ for $k \in [U]$. Upon receiving all such commitments, each party broadcasts the opening to the commitments. If any such opening fails, then abort.
4. The parties then run the remaining steps of the protocol Π_{ZKPoK} using U, V and flag $=\perp$. If any of the proofs fail, then they abort.
5. The parties set $\mathfrak{ct}_a^{(k)} \leftarrow 2 \cdot (\mathfrak{ct}_{\hat{a}_1}^{(k)} \boxplus \cdots \boxplus \mathfrak{ct}_{\hat{a}_n}^{(k)})$, $\mathfrak{ct}_b^{(k)} \leftarrow 2 \cdot (\mathfrak{ct}_{\hat{b}_1}^{(k)} \boxplus \cdots \boxplus \mathfrak{ct}_{\hat{b}_n}^{(k)})$ and $\mathfrak{ct}_f^{(k)} \leftarrow 2 \cdot (\mathfrak{ct}_{\hat{f}_1}^{(k)} \boxplus \cdots \boxplus \mathfrak{ct}_{\hat{f}_n}^{(k)})$ for $k \in [U]$.
6. The parties compute $\mathfrak{ct}_c^{(k)} \leftarrow \mathfrak{ct}_a^{(k)} \odot \mathfrak{ct}_b^{(k)}$ as well as $\mathfrak{ct}_{c+f}^{(k)} \leftarrow \mathfrak{ct}_c^{(k)} \boxplus \mathfrak{ct}_f^{(k)}$ for $k \in [U]$.
7. Using the distributed decryption operation of the BGV scheme they then decrypt $\mathfrak{ct}_{c+f}^{(k)}$ for $k \in [U]$, to obtain $\boldsymbol{\Delta}^{(k)}$.
8. P_1 sets $\hat{\boldsymbol{c}}_1^{(k)} \leftarrow \boldsymbol{\Delta}^{(k)} - \boldsymbol{f}_1^{(k)}$, while each remaining P_i sets $\hat{\boldsymbol{c}}_i^{(k)} \leftarrow -\boldsymbol{f}_i^{(k)}$ for $k \in [U]$.
9. The parties compute a fresh encryption of each $\hat{\boldsymbol{c}}^{(k)}$ via $\tilde{\mathfrak{ct}}_c^{(k)} \leftarrow \mathsf{Enc}(\boldsymbol{\Delta}^{(k)}, \boldsymbol{0}; \mathfrak{pk}) - \mathfrak{ct}_f^{(k)}$ with default random coins $\boldsymbol{0}$ for $k \in [U]$.
10. The parties compute $\mathfrak{ct}_{\alpha \cdot a}^{(k)} \leftarrow \mathfrak{ct}_\alpha \odot \mathfrak{ct}_a^{(k)}$, $\mathfrak{ct}_{\alpha \cdot b}^{(k)} \leftarrow \mathfrak{ct}_\alpha \odot \mathfrak{ct}_b^{(k)}$ and $\mathfrak{ct}_{\alpha \cdot c}^{(k)} \leftarrow \mathfrak{ct}_\alpha \odot \tilde{\mathfrak{ct}}_c^{(k)}$ for $k \in [U]$.
11. The MAC values $\gamma_i^{(k)}[\boldsymbol{a}], \gamma_i^{(k)}[\boldsymbol{b}], \gamma_i^{(k)}[\boldsymbol{c}]$ are obtained by applying the DistDec protocol in Figure 14 from [25] for $k \in [U]$.
12. Each party sets $\boldsymbol{a}_i^{(k)} \leftarrow 2 \cdot \hat{\boldsymbol{a}}_i^{(k)}$, $\boldsymbol{b}_i^{(k)} \leftarrow 2 \cdot \hat{\boldsymbol{b}}_i^{(k)}$ and $\boldsymbol{c}_i^{(k)} \leftarrow 4 \cdot \hat{\boldsymbol{c}}_i^{(k)}$. It then obtains the shares of the elements encoded in $\boldsymbol{a}_i^{(k)}, \boldsymbol{b}_i^{(k)}, \boldsymbol{c}_i^{(k)}$ as well as their MACs $\gamma_i^{(k)}[\boldsymbol{a}], \gamma_i^{(k)}[\boldsymbol{b}], \gamma_i^{(k)}[\boldsymbol{c}]$ by mapping the associated polynomials into the slot representation. They thus obtain $U \cdot \phi(m)$ shares.

Fig. 3. TopGear version of the SPDZ Offline Phase

production. The modifications to obtain other forms of preprocessed data such as those in [14] are immediate.

The overhead V for the ciphertexts encrypting α_i is quite big when compared to those of the triples and MAC shares. This is because our proof from Sect. 4 is not as efficient when flag = Diag (see Corollary 1). However, this is not an issue as we only produce one such ciphertext during the offline phase. To mitigate this we actually run the ZKPoK for a fixed value ($V = 16$) and then repeat this Snd_sec$/V$ times. This makes no difference to the overall running time, but keeps the memory requirements low for this part of the protocol.

In the protocol in Fig. 3 we have utilized the more efficient Distributed Decryption protocol from HighGear to obtain the MAC shares, and have merged in the ReShare protocol of [14, Figure 11]. This protocol is needed to obtain the shares of c and the fresh encryption of c.

The proof of security of this offline phase follows exactly as in the original SPDZ papers [14,15], all that changes is the bound on the noise of the resulting ciphertexts. Suppose (c_0, c_1) is a ciphertext corresponding to one of $\mathfrak{ct}_\alpha, \mathfrak{ct}_a, \mathfrak{ct}_b$ or $\mathfrak{ct}_f$ in our protocol. To prove security, it is necessary to obtain worst case bounds on the value $\|c_0 - \mathfrak{st} \cdot c_1\|_\infty^{\mathsf{can}}$. We know that

$$c_0 - \mathfrak{st} \cdot c_1 = 2 \cdot \sum_{i=1}^{n} (m_i + p \cdot (\epsilon \cdot r_i^{(3)} + r_i^{(1)} - r_i^{(2)} \cdot \mathfrak{st}))$$

where $(m_i, r_i^{(1)}, r_i^{(2)}, r_i^{(3)})$ are bounded due to the ZKPoK. From the soundness of it we can guarantee that the ciphertexts must satisfy

$$\left\| 2 \cdot \sum_{i \in [n]} m_i \right\|_\infty \leq 2^{\mathsf{ZK\_sec}+1} \cdot n \cdot p \quad \text{and} \quad \left\| 2 \cdot \sum_{i \in [n]} r_i^{(\ell)} \right\|_\infty \leq 2^{\mathsf{ZK\_sec}+2} \cdot n \cdot \rho_\ell.$$

Due to our assumption of an honest key generation phase, we also know that with probability $1 - 2^{-\epsilon}$ we have $\|\epsilon\|_\infty^{\mathsf{can}} \leq \mathfrak{c}_1 \cdot \sigma \cdot \sqrt{\phi(m)}$ and $\|\mathfrak{st}\|_\infty^{\mathsf{can}} \leq \mathfrak{c}_1 \cdot \sqrt{h}$. Using the inequality $\|x\|_\infty^{\mathsf{can}} \leq \phi(m) \cdot \|x\|_\infty$ we obtain

$$\|c_0 - \mathfrak{st} \cdot c_1\|_\infty^{\mathsf{can}}$$

$$\leq \sum_{i=1}^{n} \|2 \cdot m_i\|_\infty^{\mathsf{can}} + p \cdot \left(\|\epsilon\|_\infty^{\mathsf{can}} \cdot \|2 \cdot e_{2,i}\|_\infty^{\mathsf{can}} + \|2 \cdot e_{0,i}\|_\infty^{\mathsf{can}} + \|\mathfrak{st}\|_\infty^{\mathsf{can}} \cdot \|2 \cdot e_{1,i}\|_\infty^{\mathsf{can}} \right)$$

$$\leq 2 \cdot \phi(m) \cdot 2^{\mathsf{ZK\_sec}+1} \cdot n \cdot p/2$$

$$\quad + p \cdot \left(\mathfrak{c}_1 \cdot \sigma \cdot \phi(m)^{3/2} \cdot 2 \cdot 2^{\mathsf{ZK\_sec}+1} \cdot n + \phi(m) \cdot 2 \cdot 2^{\mathsf{ZK\_sec}+1} \cdot n \cdot 20 \right.$$

$$\quad \left. + \mathfrak{c}_1 \cdot \sqrt{h} \cdot \phi(m) \cdot 2 \cdot 2^{\mathsf{ZK\_sec}+1} \cdot n \cdot 20 \right)$$

$$= \phi(m) \cdot 2^{\mathsf{ZK\_sec}+2} \cdot n \cdot p \cdot \left(\frac{41}{2} + \mathfrak{c}_1 \cdot \sigma \cdot \phi(m)^{1/2} + 20 \cdot \mathfrak{c}_1 \cdot \sqrt{h} \right)$$

$$= B_{\mathsf{clean}}^{\mathsf{dishonest}}.$$

Using this bound we can then derive the parameters for the BGV system using exactly the same methodology as can be found in [2].

6   Results

Recall we have three different security parameters in play, apart from the computational security parameter κ of the underlying BGV encryption scheme. The main benefit of TopGear over HighGear is that it potentially enables higher values of the parameter Snd_sec to be obtained. Recall $2^{-\text{Snd\_sec}}$ is the probability that an adversary will be able to produce a convincing ZKPoK for an invalid input. The other two security parameters are ZK_sec and DD_sec, which measure the statistical distance of *coefficients* of ring elements generated in a protocol to the same coefficients being generated in the simulation of the security proof.

In the context of the HighGear ZKPoK in the Overdrive paper [25] the two security parameters are set to be equal, i.e. ZK_sec = Snd_sec. In practice the value of Snd_sec needs to be very low for the HighGear ZKPoK as it has a direct effect on the memory consumption of the underlying protocol. Thus in SCALE v1.2 the default value for Snd_sec is 40. This unfortunately translates into having a high probability of an adversary being able to get away with cheating in a ZKPoK and is therefore not desirable. The first goal that our work achieves, which will be validated with experiments in this section, is that Snd_sec can be taken to be as large as is desired, whilst also obtaining an efficiency saving.

We also aim to increase the values of ZK_sec and DD_sec. These measure statistical distances of *coefficients*. Picking ZK_sec and DD_sec at low values potentially introduces leakage about the plaintexts or the secret keys. Hence, after demonstrating the effect of our new protocol with respect to more secure choices of Snd_sec, we then turn to examining the effect of increasing the other security parameters as well. In Table 1 in the Appendix we give various parameter sizes for the degree N and moduli $q_0 = p_0, q_1 = p_0 \cdot p_1$ for different plaintext space sizes p, and different security levels ZK_sec, Snd_sec, DD_sec and computational security parameter κ, and two parties[3]. We selected parameters for which ZK_sec, DD_sec $\leq$ Snd_sec to keep the table managable. We use the methodology described in [2] to derive parameter sizes for both HighGear and TopGear; this maps the computational security parameter to lattice parameters using Albrecht's tool[4]. In the table a row with values of $\star$ in the ZK_sec columns means that the parameter values do not change when this parameter is to set either 40 or 80.

From the table we see that the values of ZK_sec and Snd_sec produce relatively little effect on the overall parameter sizes, especially for large values of the plaintext modulus p. This is because the modulus switch, within the homomorphic evaluation, squashes the noise by a factor of at least p. The values ZK_sec and Snd_sec only blow up the noise by a factor of $2^{\text{ZK\_sec}+\text{Snd\_sec}/2+2}$ (for HighGear) and $2^{\text{ZK\_sec}+2}$ (for TopGear), and hence a large p value cancels out this increase in noise due to the ZKPoK security parameters. In addition the

---

[3] Similar values can be obtained for other values of n, we selected $n = 2$ purely for illustration here, the effect of n on the values is relatively minor.

[4] https://bitbucket.org/malb/lwe-estimator.

parameter sizes are identical for both HighGear and TopGear, except in the case of some parameters for low values of $\log_2 p$.

We based our implementation and experiments on the SCALE-MAMBA system [2] which has an implementation of the HighGear protocol. To measure the improvement due to our new TopGear protocol we modified [2] to test against the old version. We focused on the case of 128-bit plaintext moduli in our experiments, being the recommended size in SCALE-MAMBA v1.2 to support certain MPC operations such as fixed-point arithmetic. We first baselined the implementation in SCALE-MAMBA of HighGear against the implementation reported in [25]. The experiments in [25] were executed on i7-4790 and i7-3770S CPUs, compared to our experiments which utilized i7-7700K CPUs. From a pure CPU point of view our machines should be roughly 30% faster. The ping time between our machines was 0.47 milliseconds, whereas that for [25] was 0.3 ms.

Keller et al. [25], in the case of 128-bit plaintext moduli, and with the security settings equivalent to our setting of DD_sec = ZK_sec = Snd_sec = 64, utilize a ciphertext modulus of 572 bits, whereas SCALE-MAMBA v1.2 utilizes a ciphertext modulus of 541 bits. In this setting [25] achieve a maximum throughput of 5600 triples per second, whereas SCALE-MAMBA's implementation of High-Gear obtains a maximum throughput of roughly 2900 triples per second. We suspect the reason for the difference in costs is that SCALE-MAMBA is performing other operations related to storing the triples for later consumption by online operations. This also means that memory utilization grows as more triples are produced, leading to a larger amount of non-local memory accesses. These effects decrease the measurable triple production rate in SCALE-MAMBA compared to the experiments presented in [25].

We now turn to examining the performance differences between HighGear and the new TopGear protocol within our modified version of SCALE-MAMBA. We first looked at two security settings so as to isolate the effect of increasing the Snd_sec parameter alone. Our first setting was the standard SCALE-MAMBA setting of DD_sec = ZK_sec = Snd_sec = 40, our second was the more secure setting of DD_sec = ZK_sec = 40 and Snd_sec = 128.

There are two main parameters in SCALE-MAMBA one can tweak which affect triple production; (i) the number of threads devoted to executing the zero-knowledge proofs and (ii) the number of threads devoted to taking the output of these proofs and producing triples. We call these two values t_{ZK} and t_{Tr}; we chose $t_{ZK}, t_{Tr} \in \{1, 2, 4, 8\}$ in the experiments. We focus here on triple production for simplicity, a similar situation to that described below occurs in the case of bit production. We examine memory consumption and triple production in these settings so as to see the effect of changing Snd_sec. After this we examine increasing all the security parameters, and the effect this has on memory and triple production.

Memory Consumption: We see from Table 1 that the parameters in TopGear for the underlying FHE scheme are generally identical to those in HighGear, the only difference being when the extra soundness slack in HighGear compared to

TopGear is not counter balanced by size of the ciphertext modulus. However, the real effect of TopGear comes in the amount of data one can simultaneously process. Running the implementation in SCALE-MAMBA for HighGear one sees immediately that memory usage is a main constraint of the system.

A rough (under-) estimation of the memory requirements of the ZKPoKs in HighGear and TopGear can be given by the sizes of the input and auxiliary ciphertexts of the ZKPoK. A single ciphertext can be represented by (roughly) $\phi(m) \cdot \log_2(p_0 \cdot p_1)$ bits. There are U input ciphertexts and V auxiliary ciphertexts per player (where V is set to $2 \cdot U - 1$ in HighGear). Hence, the total number of bits required to process a ZKPoK is at least $(U + V) \cdot n \cdot \phi(m) \cdot \log_2(p_0 \cdot p_1)$.

Now in HighGear we need to take $U = \mathsf{Snd\_sec}$, which is what limits the applicability of large soundness security parameters in the implementations of HighGear. Meanwhile, TopGear can take $V = (\mathsf{Snd\_sec} + 2)/\log_2(2 \cdot N + 1)$, and have arbitrary choice on U, although in practice we select $U = 2 \cdot V$. For the ZKPoKs for the encryptions of α we have $U = 1$ and set $V = 16$, simply to reduce memory costs, and then repeat the TopGear proof $\mathsf{Snd\_sec}/16$ times. Thus, all other things being equal (which Table 1 gives evidence for) TopGear should reduce the memory footprint by a factor of roughly $\log_2(2 \cdot N + 1)$. For the range of N under consideration (i.e. 8192 to 32768) this gives a memory saving of a factor of between 14 and 16. A similar saving occurs in the amount of data which needs to be transferred when executing the ZKPoK. Note that this is purely the saving for running the zero-knowledge proofs, the overall effect on the memory consumption of the preprocessing will be much less, as that will also include the memory needed to store the output of this offline process.

To see this in practice we examined the memory consumption of running HighGear and TopGear with the above settings (of $\mathsf{DD\_sec} = \mathsf{ZK\_sec} = \mathsf{Snd\_sec} = 40$, and $\mathsf{DD\_sec} = \mathsf{ZK\_sec} = 40$, $\mathsf{Snd\_sec} = 128$) the results being given in Tables 2 and 3 in the Appendix. We give the percentage memory consumption (given in terms of the percentage maximum resident set size obtained from /usr/bin/time -v). This is the maximum percentage memory consumed by the whole system when producing two million multiplication triples only. This value can vary from run to run as the different threads allocate and de-allocate memory, thus figures will inevitably vary. However, they do give an indication of memory overall consumption in a given configuration.

We find that for HighGear with the higher security parameters we are unable to perform some experiments ($t_{\mathsf{ZK}} > 2$) due to memory consumption producing an abort of the SCALE-MAMBA system. We see immediately that with TopGear the memory consumption drops by a factor 3–7 for identical security parameters. Furthermore, we are able to cope with a much larger value for the security parameter $\mathsf{Snd\_sec}$ and all our considered number of threads of the ZKPoK implementation. Even when running $t_{\mathsf{Tr}} = t_{\mathsf{ZK}} = 8$ and $\mathsf{Snd\_sec} = 128$ we still only utilize 70% of memory.

Triple Production Throughput: We now turn to looking at throughput of the overall triple production process where the metric to look at is the average time per triple. However due to the set up costs, (e.g. producing the zero-knowledge proofs for the ciphertext encrypting the MAC key α) this average time decreases as one runs the system. In the Appendix we provide graphs to show how this average time decreases as more triples are produced for various settings. The spikes in these graphs are due the main triple production threads having to wait for the zero-knowledge threads to complete a zero-knowledge proof before proceeding. Thus a spike indicates a waiting period for a zero-knowledge proofs to complete. As the number of proof threads increases (t_{ZK} increases), the effect of these spikes becomes less pronounced. To show the difference between HighGear and TopGear we keep the same y-axis in each graph.

We now look at the average number of triples per second we could obtain for the various settings, after computing two million triples (see Tables 4 and 5 in the Appendix for a summary). The TopGear protocol produces, all other parameters being equal, 2–5 times as many triples per second than HighGear. This improvement is due to reduced memory consumption (U and V are smaller), but also because the ratio of V to U in HighGear is larger than that in TopGear (2 vs 1/2 in general). In both security settings the TopGear protocol works best when we have $t_{Tr} \geq 2$.

Recommendations: Given that $2^{-\mathsf{Snd\_sec}}$ represents the *probability* that an adversary can pass of an invalid ZKPoK as valid, the default SCALE-MAMBA v1.2 setting of $\mathsf{Snd\_sec} = 40$ is arguably too low. Thus increasing it to 128 seems definitely prudent.

As mentioned above we also recommend using higher values for $\mathsf{ZK\_sec}$ and $\mathsf{DD\_sec}$. Despite these measuring statistical distances, and hence can be arguably smaller than $\mathsf{Snd\_sec}$, in practice they measure the statistical distance of distributions of coefficients from uniformly random. Each ZKPoK/distributed decryption produces tens of thousands of such coefficients, and thus having $\mathsf{DD\_sec} = \mathsf{ZK\_sec} = 40$ is also probably too low.

We therefore also give some experimental results using TopGear for settings of $\mathsf{DD\_sec} = \mathsf{ZK\_sec} = 80$, $\mathsf{Snd\_sec} = 128$. and $\mathsf{DD\_sec} = \mathsf{ZK\_sec} = \mathsf{Snd\_sec} = 128$. Again we focus on the two party case with a plaintext prime of 128 bits in length (with results giving in Tables 6 and 7 in the Appendix). We see that with $\mathsf{DD\_sec} = \mathsf{ZK\_sec} = 80$ we obtain a triple throughput which is often more than twice that of what SCALE-MAMBA v1.2 achieves using HighGear and $\mathsf{DD\_sec} = \mathsf{ZK\_sec} = \mathsf{Snd\_sec} = 40$. On the other hand with $\mathsf{DD\_sec} = \mathsf{ZK\_sec} = 128$ the performance improvement is less pronounced (improvement by a factor $1.5 - 2$), although still significant. We believe that $\mathsf{DD\_sec} = \mathsf{ZK\_sec} = 80$ gives a suitable compromise between security and performance.

Also notice in the tables the high memory consumption in the case of $t_{Tr} = 1$ and $t_{ZK} = 8$ compared to (say) $t_{Tr} = 2$ and $t_{ZK} = 8$. This is because in this case memory is increasing as the validated ciphertexts are being produced by the eight zero-knowledge proof threads *faster* than the single triple production thread can process them.

Acknowledgments. We thank Ivan Damgård for his helpful comments. The work of Carsten has been done at Bar Ilan University, Israel. This work has been supported by the BIU Center for Research in Applied Cryptography and Cyber Security in conjunction with the Israel National Cyber Bureau in the Prime Minister's Office, in part by the European Research Council (ERC) under the European Union's Horizon 2020 research and innovation programme under grant agreement No. 669255 (MPCPRO), in part by ERC Advanced Grant ERC-2015-AdG-IMPaCT, by the Defense Advanced Research Projects Agency (DARPA) and Space and Naval Warfare Systems Center, Pacific (SSC Pacific) under contract No. N66001-15-C-4070, and by the FWO under an Odysseus project GOH9718N.

A   Parameter Size Table

See Table 1 for the various FHE parameter sizes for our different security levels.

Table 1. SHE parameters sizes for various security parameters in HighGear and TopGear (two parties). With DD_sec, ZK_sec $\leq$ Snd_sec and DD_sec, ZK_sec, Snd_sec $\in$ $\{40, 80, 128\}$. The single checkmark for a row shows the default parameters used in SCALE-MAMBA v1.2. Two checkmarks denote the parameters we use in the experiments related to memory and throughput. The rows with three checkmarks show the parameters we would recommend.

| | $\log_2 p$ | κ | DD_sec | Snd_sec | ZK_sec | HighGear | | | TopGear | | | | |
						N	$\log_2 p_0$	$\log_2 p_1$	N	U	V	$\log_2 p_0$	$\log_2 p_1$
	64	80	40	40	40	8192	177	114	8192	6	3	176	115
	64	80	40	80	40	8192	177	114	8192	12	6	176	115
	64	80	40	128	40	8192	177	114	8192	18	9	176	115
	64	80	40	80	80	8192	177	144	8192	12	6	176	115
	64	80	40	128	80	16384	177	174	8192	18	9	167	115
	64	80	80	40	40	16384	218	163	16384	6	3	217	164
	64	80	80	80	40	16384	218	163	16384	12	6	217	164
	64	80	80	128	40	16384	218	163	16384	18	9	217	164
	64	80	80	80	80	16384	218	163	16384	12	6	217	164
	64	80	80	128	80	16384	218	173	16384	18	9	217	164
	64	80	128	40	40	16384	266	205	16384	6	3	265	206
	64	80	128	80	$\star$	16384	266	205	16384	12	6	265	206
	64	80	128	128	$\star$	16384	266	205	16384	18	9	265	206
✓	64	128	40	40	40	16384	178	123	16384	6	3	177	124
	64	128	40	80	40	16384	178	123	16384	12	6	177	124
	64	128	40	128	40	16384	178	133	16384	18	9	177	124
	64	128	40	80	80	16384	178	153	16384	12	6	177	124
	64	128	40	128	80	16384	178	173	16384	18	9	177	124
✓✓✓	64	128	80	40	40	16384	218	163	16384	6	3	217	164
	64	128	80	80	40	16384	218	163	16384	12	6	217	164
	64	128	80	128	40	16384	218	163	16384	18	9	217	164
	64	128	80	80	80	16384	218	163	16384	12	6	217	164
	64	128	80	128	80	16384	218	173	16384	18	9	217	164
✓✓✓	64	128	128	40	$\star$	32768	266	205	32768	6	3	266	205
	64	128	128	80	$\star$	32768	266	205	32768	10	5	266	205
	64	128	128	128	$\star$	32768	266	205	32768	16	8	266	205
	64	128	128	128	128	32768	266	225	32768	16	8	266	205

(continued)

Table 1. (*continued*)

	$\log_2 p$	κ	DD_sec	Snd_sec	ZK_sec	HighGear N	$\log_2 p_0$	$\log_2 p_1$	TopGear N	U	V	$\log_2 p_0$	$\log_2 p_1$
	128	80	40	40	40	16384	305	186	16384	6	3	305	186
	128	80	40	80	⋆	16384	305	186	16384	12	6	305	186
	128	80	40	128	⋆	16384	305	186	16384	18	9	305	186
	128	80	80	40	⋆	16384	345	226	16384	6	3	345	226
	128	80	80	80	⋆	16384	345	226	16384	12	6	345	226
	128	80	80	128	⋆	16384	345	226	16384	18	9	345	226
	128	80	128	40	⋆	16384	393	268	16384	6	3	393	268
	128	80	128	80	⋆	16384	393	268	16384	12	6	393	268
	128	80	128	128	⋆	16384	393	268	16384	18	9	393	268
✓	128	128	40	40	⋆	32768	306	185	32768	6	3	306	185
	128	128	40	80	⋆	32768	306	185	32768	10	5	306	185
✓✓	128	128	40	128	⋆	32768	306	185	32768	16	8	306	185
✓✓✓	128	128	80	40	⋆	32768	346	225	32768	6	3	346	225
	128	128	80	80	⋆	32768	346	225	32768	10	5	346	225
	128	128	80	128	⋆	32768	346	225	32768	16	8	346	225
✓✓✓	128	128	128	40	⋆	32768	394	277	32768	6	3	394	277
	128	128	128	80	⋆	32768	394	277	32768	10	5	394	277
	128	128	128	128	⋆	32768	394	277	32768	16	8	394	277
	128	128	128	128	128	32768	394	277	32768	16	8	394	277

B   Experimental Data

Table 2. Percentage memory consumption for HighGear for two players and $\log_2 p = 128$.

t_{Tr}	t_{ZK} 1	2	4	8
1	25	41	68	98
2	25	38	68	98
4	28	49	75	98
8	32	52	81	98

DD_sec = ZK_sec = Snd_sec = 40

t_{Tr}	t_{ZK} 1	2	4	8
1	70	98	-	-
2	72	98	-	-
4	73	98	-	-
8	76	98	-	-

DD_sec = ZK_sec = 40, Snd_sec = 128

Table 3. Percentage memory consumption for TopGear for two players and $\log_2 p = 128$.

t_{Tr}	t_{ZK} 1	2	4	8
1	7	9	15	27
2	8	10	15	26
4	10	12	17	28
8	14	17	21	33

DD_sec = ZK_sec = Snd_sec = 40

t_{Tr}	t_{ZK} 1	2	4	8
1	11	19	33	63
2	12	18	33	64
4	14	21	34	64
8	16	24	39	70

DD_sec = ZK_sec = 40, Snd_sec = 128

Table 4. Maximum Triples per Second for HighGear for two players and $\log_2 p = 128$, after computing two million triples.

t_{Tr}	t_{ZK} 1	2	4	8
1	1503	1602	1562	1335
2	1488	2347	2212	1976
4	1272	1876	2150	1865
8	976	1307	1464	1533

DD_sec = ZK_sec = Snd_sec = 40

t_{Tr}	t_{ZK} 1	2	4	8
1	1240	1369	-	-
2	1426	1834	-	-
4	1231	1612	-	-
8	940	1129	-	-

DD_sec = ZK_sec = 40, Snd_sec = 128

Table 5. Maximum Triples per Second for TopGear for two players and $\log_2 p = 128$, after computing two million triples.

t_{Tr}	t_{ZK} 1	2	4	8
1	2806	2829	2846	2752
2	3809	4851	4709	4540
4	5672	6086	6692	6293
8	4666	5635	6084	5636

DD_sec = ZK_sec = Snd_sec = 40

t_{Tr}	t_{ZK} 1	2	4	8
1	1743	2775	2692	2569
2	4251	4622	4572	4021
4	3943	3712	4955	5000
8	3265	3272	5254	5041

DD_sec = ZK_sec = 40, Snd_sec = 128

Table 6. Percentage memory consumption and triples per second for TopGear for two players with DD_sec = ZK_sec = 80 and $\log_2 p = $ Snd_sec $= 128$. We also give (in brackets) the percentage throughput compared to the (low security) standard SCALE-MAMBA v1.2 settings using HighGear.

t_{Tr}	t_{ZK} 1	2	4	8
1	12	19	35	75
2	13	19	33	65
4	15	21	36	67
8	18	26	40	76

Memory Consumption

t_{Tr}	t_{ZK} 1	2	4	8
1	2312 (153)	2378 (148)	2369 (151)	2178 (163)
2	3632 (244)	3980 (169)	3905 (176)	3354 (169)
4	3260 (256)	4709 (251)	4667 (217)	3976 (213)
8	2736 (280)	3959 (302)	4628 (316)	3703 (241)

Triples per Second

Table 7. Percentage memory consumption and triples per second for TopGear for two players with $\log_2 p = $ DD_sec = ZK_sec = Snd_sec $= 128$. Again, we also give (in brackets) the percentage throughput compared to the (low security) standard SCALE-MAMBA v1.2 settings using HighGear.

t_{Tr}	t_{ZK} 1	2	4	8
1	14	21	40	90
2	14	22	38	78
4	17	24	40	78
8	18	28	47	87

Memory Consumption

t_{Tr}	t_{ZK} 1	2	4	8
1	1604 (107)	1923 (120)	1921 (122)	1775 (132)
2	2945 (198)	3281 (139)	3265 (147)	2868 (145)
4	2605 (205)	2923 (155)	4046 (188)	3427 (183)
8	2080 (213)	2571 (196)	3516 (240)	3322 (216)

Triples per Second

C   Run Time Graphs

In Fig. 4 we provide graphs of the throughput for HighGear in our low security, Snd_sec = 40, setting, with the comparable graph for TopGear in Fig. 5 for two players; given graphs up to the production of 2 million triples. The fact that the graphs are not straight, they have bumps in them, is because the triple production threads are producing triples faster than the ciphertexts can be supplied by the threads doing the ZKPoKs. Thus the triple production threads often need to wait until a ZKPoK has been completed before they can proceed. In Figs. 6 and 7 we provide similar graphs of the throughput for HighGear and TopGear in our high security setting Snd_sec = 128.

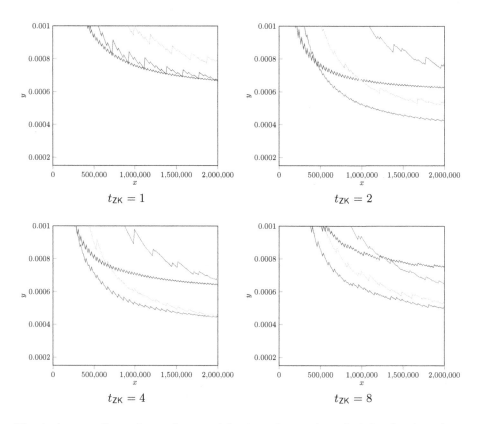

Fig. 4. Average time y to produce a triple given the number of triples that have been produced x for **HighGear** with parameters DD_sec = ZK_sec = Snd_sec = 40. Blue $t_{Tr} = 1$, Red $t_{Tr} = 2$, Green $t_{Tr} = 4$, Magenta $t_{Tr} = 8$ (Color figure online)

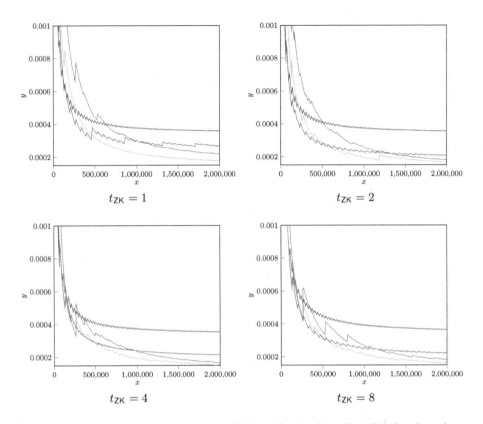

Fig. 5. Average time y to produce a triple given the number of triples that have been produced x for **TopGear** with parameters DD_sec = ZK_sec = Snd_sec = 40. Blue $t_{Tr} = 1$, Red $t_{Tr} = 2$, Green $t_{Tr} = 4$, Magenta $t_{Tr} = 8$ (Color figure online)

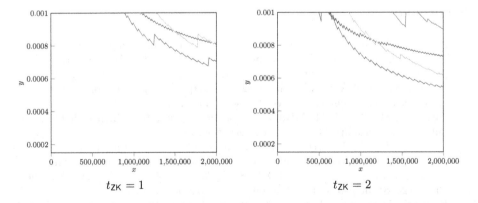

Fig. 6. Average time y to produce a triple given the number of triples that have been produced x for **HighGear** with parameters DD_sec = ZK_sec = 40 and Snd_sec = 128. Blue $t_{Tr} = 1$, Red $t_{Tr} = 2$, Green $t_{Tr} = 4$, Magenta $t_{Tr} = 8$ (Color figure online)

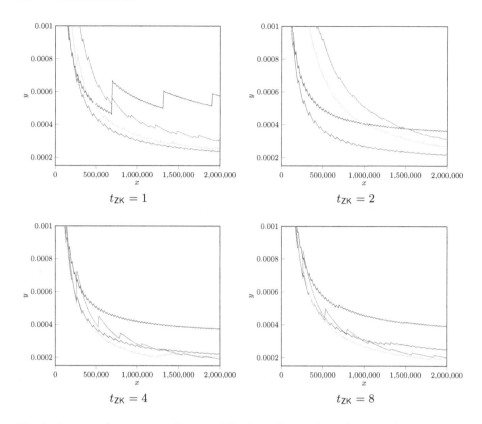

Fig. 7. Average time y to produce a triple given the number of triples that have been produced x for **TopGear** with parameters DD_sec = ZK_sec = 40 and Snd_sec = 128. Blue $t_{Tr} = 1$, Red $t_{Tr} = 2$, Green $t_{Tr} = 4$, Magenta $t_{Tr} = 8$ (Color figure online)

References

1. Alkim, E., Ducas, L., Pöppelmann, T., Schwabe, P.: Post-quantum key exchange - a new hope. In: Holz, T., Savage, S. (eds.) 25th USENIX Security Symposium, USENIX Security 2016, Austin, TX, USA, 10–12 August 2016, pp. 327–343. USENIX Association (2016). https://www.usenix.org/conference/usenixsecurity16/technical-sessions/presentation/alkim
2. Aly, A., et al.: SCALE-MAMBA v1.2: Documentation (2018). https://homes.esat.kuleuven.be/~nsmart/SCALE/Documentation.pdf
3. Baum, C., Bootle, J., Cerulli, A., del Pino, R., Groth, J., Lyubashevsky, V.: Sublinear lattice-based zero-knowledge arguments for arithmetic circuits. In: Shacham, H., Boldyreva, A. (eds.) CRYPTO 2018. LNCS, vol. 10992, pp. 669–699. Springer, Cham (2018). https://doi.org/10.1007/978-3-319-96881-0_23
4. Baum, C., Damgård, I., Larsen, K.G., Nielsen, M.: How to prove knowledge of small secrets. In: Robshaw, M., Katz, J. (eds.) CRYPTO 2016. LNCS, vol. 9816, pp. 478–498. Springer, Heidelberg (2016). https://doi.org/10.1007/978-3-662-53015-3_17

5. Baum, C., Lyubashevsky, V.: Simple amortized proofs of shortness for linear relations over polynomial rings. Cryptology ePrint Archive, Report 2017/759 (2017). http://eprint.iacr.org/2017/759
6. Ben-Or, M., Goldwasser, S., Kilian, J., Wigderson, A.: Multi-prover interactive proofs: how to remove intractability assumptions. In: 20th Annual ACM Symposium on Theory of Computing, pp. 113–131. ACM Press, Chicago, 2–4 May 1988
7. Bendlin, R., Damgård, I., Orlandi, C., Zakarias, S.: Semi-homomorphic encryption and multiparty computation. In: Paterson, K.G. (ed.) EUROCRYPT 2011. LNCS, vol. 6632, pp. 169–188. Springer, Heidelberg (2011). https://doi.org/10.1007/978-3-642-20465-4_11
8. Benhamouda, F., Camenisch, J., Krenn, S., Lyubashevsky, V., Neven, G.: Better zero-knowledge proofs for lattice encryption and their application to group signatures. In: Sarkar, P., Iwata, T. (eds.) ASIACRYPT 2014. LNCS, vol. 8873, pp. 551–572. Springer, Heidelberg (2014). https://doi.org/10.1007/978-3-662-45611-8_29
9. Benhamouda, F., Krenn, S., Lyubashevsky, V., Pietrzak, K.: Efficient zero-knowledge proofs for commitments from learning with errors over rings. In: Pernul, G., Ryan, P.Y.A., Weippl, E. (eds.) ESORICS 2015. LNCS, vol. 9326, pp. 305–325. Springer, Cham (2015). https://doi.org/10.1007/978-3-319-24174-6_16
10. Brakerski, Z., Gentry, C., Vaikuntanathan, V.: (Leveled) fully homomorphic encryption without bootstrapping. In: Goldwasser, S. (ed.) ITCS 2012: 3rd Innovations in Theoretical Computer Science, pp. 309–325. Association for Computing Machinery, Cambridge, 8–10 January 2012
11. Brakerski, Z., Vaikuntanathan, V.: Efficient fully homomorphic encryption from (standard) LWE. In: Ostrovsky, R. (ed.) 52nd Annual Symposium on Foundations of Computer Science, pp. 97–106. IEEE Computer Society Press, Palm Springs, 22–25 October 2011
12. Cramer, R., Damgård, I.: On the amortized complexity of zero-knowledge protocols. In: Halevi, S. (ed.) CRYPTO 2009. LNCS, vol. 5677, pp. 177–191. Springer, Heidelberg (2009). https://doi.org/10.1007/978-3-642-03356-8_11
13. Cramer, R., Damgård, I., Xing, C., Yuan, C.: Amortized complexity of zero-knowledge proofs revisited: achieving linear soundness slack. In: Coron, J.-S., Nielsen, J.B. (eds.) EUROCRYPT 2017. LNCS, vol. 10210, pp. 479–500. Springer, Cham (2017). https://doi.org/10.1007/978-3-319-56620-7_17
14. Damgård, I., Keller, M., Larraia, E., Pastro, V., Scholl, P., Smart, N.P.: Practical covertly secure MPC for dishonest majority – or: breaking the SPDZ limits. In: Crampton, J., Jajodia, S., Mayes, K. (eds.) ESORICS 2013. LNCS, vol. 8134, pp. 1–18. Springer, Heidelberg (2013). https://doi.org/10.1007/978-3-642-40203-6_1
15. Damgård, I., Pastro, V., Smart, N., Zakarias, S.: Multiparty computation from somewhat homomorphic encryption. In: Safavi-Naini, R., Canetti, R. (eds.) CRYPTO 2012. LNCS, vol. 7417, pp. 643–662. Springer, Heidelberg (2012). https://doi.org/10.1007/978-3-642-32009-5_38
16. del Pino, R., Lyubashevsky, V.: Amortization with fewer equations for proving knowledge of small secrets. In: Katz, J., Shacham, H. (eds.) CRYPTO 2017. LNCS, vol. 10403, pp. 365–394. Springer, Cham (2017). https://doi.org/10.1007/978-3-319-63697-9_13
17. del Pino, R., Lyubashevsky, V., Seiler, G.: Short discrete log proofs for FHE and ring-LWE ciphertexts. In: Lin, D., Sako, K. (eds.) PKC 2019. LNCS, vol. 11442, pp. 344–373. Springer, Cham (2019). https://doi.org/10.1007/978-3-030-17253-4_12

18. Ducas, L., Durmus, A., Lepoint, T., Lyubashevsky, V.: Lattice signatures and bimodal Gaussians. In: Canetti, R., Garay, J.A. (eds.) CRYPTO 2013. LNCS, vol. 8042, pp. 40–56. Springer, Heidelberg (2013). https://doi.org/10.1007/978-3-642-40041-4_3

19. Ducas, L., et al.: CRYSTALS-Dilithium: a lattice-based digital signature scheme. IACR Trans. Cryptogr. Hardw. Embedd. Syst. **2018**(1), 238–268 (2018). https://tches.iacr.org/index.php/TCHES/article/view/839

20. Gentry, C., Halevi, S., Smart, N.P.: Better bootstrapping in fully homomorphic encryption. In: Fischlin, M., Buchmann, J., Manulis, M. (eds.) PKC 2012. LNCS, vol. 7293, pp. 1–16. Springer, Heidelberg (2012). https://doi.org/10.1007/978-3-642-30057-8_1

21. Gentry, C., Halevi, S., Smart, N.P.: Fully homomorphic encryption with polylog overhead. In: Pointcheval, D., Johansson, T. (eds.) EUROCRYPT 2012. LNCS, vol. 7237, pp. 465–482. Springer, Heidelberg (2012). https://doi.org/10.1007/978-3-642-29011-4_28

22. Gentry, C., Halevi, S., Smart, N.P.: Homomorphic evaluation of the AES circuit. In: Safavi-Naini, R., Canetti, R. (eds.) CRYPTO 2012. LNCS, vol. 7417, pp. 850–867. Springer, Heidelberg (2012). https://doi.org/10.1007/978-3-642-32009-5_49

23. Halevi, S., Shoup, V.: Algorithms in HElib. In: Garay, J.A., Gennaro, R. (eds.) CRYPTO 2014. LNCS, vol. 8616, pp. 554–571. Springer, Heidelberg (2014). https://doi.org/10.1007/978-3-662-44371-2_31

24. Keller, M., Orsini, E., Scholl, P.: MASCOT: faster malicious arithmetic secure computation with oblivious transfer. In: Weippl, E.R., Katzenbeisser, S., Kruegel, C., Myers, A.C., Halevi, S. (eds.) ACM CCS 2016: 23rd Conference on Computer and Communications Security, pp. 830–842. ACM Press, Vienna, 24–28 October 2016

25. Keller, M., Pastro, V., Rotaru, D.: Overdrive: making SPDZ great again. In: Nielsen, J.B., Rijmen, V. (eds.) EUROCRYPT 2018. LNCS, vol. 10822, pp. 158–189. Springer, Cham (2018). https://doi.org/10.1007/978-3-319-78372-7_6

26. Lyubashevsky, V.: Fiat-Shamir with aborts: applications to lattice and factoring-based signatures. In: Matsui, M. (ed.) ASIACRYPT 2009. LNCS, vol. 5912, pp. 598–616. Springer, Heidelberg (2009). https://doi.org/10.1007/978-3-642-10366-7_35

On the Real-World Instantiability of Admissible Hash Functions and Efficient Verifiable Random Functions

Tibor Jager[1] and David Niehues[2(✉)]

[1] Bergische Universität Wuppertal, Wuppertal, Germany
tibor.jager@uni-wuppertal.de
[2] Paderborn University, Paderborn, Germany
david.niehues@upb.de

Abstract. *Verifiable random functions* (VRFs) are essentially digital signatures with additional properties, namely *verifiable uniqueness* and *pseudorandomness*, which make VRFs a useful tool, e.g., to prevent enumeration in DNSSEC Authenticated Denial of Existence and the CONIKS key management system, or in the random committee selection of the Algorand blockchain.

Most standard-model VRFs rely on *admissible hash functions* (AHFs) to achieve security against *adaptive* attacks in the standard model. Known AHF constructions are based on error-correcting codes, which yield *asymptotically* efficient constructions. However, previous works do not clarify how the code should be instantiated *concretely* in the real world. The *rate* and the *minimal distance* of the selected code have significant impact on the efficiency of the resulting cryptosystem, therefore it is unclear if and how the aforementioned constructions can be used in practice.

First, we explain inherent limitations of code-based AHFs. Concretely, we assume that even if we were given codes that achieve the well-known Gilbert-Varshamov or McEliece-Rodemich-Rumsey-Welch bounds, existing AHF-based constructions of verifiable random functions (VRFs) can only be instantiated quite inefficiently. Then we introduce and construct *computational* AHFs (cAHFs). While classical AHFs are information-theoretic, and therefore work even in presence of computationally unbounded adversaries, cAHFs provide only security against computationally bounded adversaries. However, we show that cAHFs can be instantiated significantly more efficiently. Finally, we use our cAHF to construct the currently most efficient verifiable random function with full adaptive security in the standard model.

Keywords: Admissible hash functions · Verifiable random functions · Error-correcting codes · Provable security

Tibor Jager: Supported by the European Research Council (ERC) under the European Union's Horizon 2020 research and innovation programme, grant agreement 802823.
David Niehues: Supported by the German Research Foundation (DFG) within the Collaborative Research Center "On-The-Fly Computing" (SFB 901/3).

K. G. Paterson and D. Stebila (Eds.): SAC 2019, LNCS 11959, pp. 303–332, 2020.
https://doi.org/10.1007/978-3-030-38471-5_13

1   Introduction

Verifiable random functions (VRFs), introduced by Micali, Rabin and Vadhan [35], are the public-key counterpart to Pseudorandom Functions (PRFs). The evaluation of a VRF $V_{sk}(X)$ can only be privately computed using the secret key sk. The evaluation at X yields a pseudorandom value Y together with a non-interactive proof π. The verifier can use the public verification key vk and π to confirm that Y was correctly computed as $V_{sk}(X)$. VRFs have recently found several interesting real-world applications. For instance, the Algorand blockchain uses a VRF to randomly select a committee for a Byzantine agreement [18]. Furthermore, VRFs can be used to prevent enumeration attacks against hash-based data structures, since the VRF can only be evaluated privately and the correctness of the computation can be publicly verified. This approach is used in the DNSSEC Authenticated Denial of Existence draft [38,46] to prevent offline DNS-enumeration attacks. Yet another application domain of VRFs are key management systems. For instance, CONIKS, a modern transparent key management system, uses a VRF in a similar way to prevent leaking private data of users [34]. Due to these numerous practical applications, the IETF is currently standardizing VRFs [20]. These VRFs are efficient, but the accompanying security proofs rely on the random oracle heuristic [5], which can not be instantiated in general [12]. In this work, we consider efficient practical constructions of VRFs in the standard model, meaning without the random oracle heuristic.

Partitioning is a technique which is commonly used to prove security of cryptographic constructions, and the only known way to construct verifiable random functions, both in the standard model and in the random oracle model. Essentially, a partitioning proof divides a certain considered set, such as for instance the message space of a digital signature scheme, the domain of a verifiable random function, or the identity space of an identity-based encryption (IBE) scheme, into two subsets:

1. A *"controlled"* set, which contains all elements for which the simulator in the security proof is able to efficiently simulate, e.g., digital signatures, and
2. an *"uncontrolled"* set, which contains elements where the simulator is able to efficiently embed an instance of a computationally hard problem, such that an efficient adversary on the considered cryptographic construction can be turned into an efficient algorithm solving the hard problem.

Partitioning is often used in the *random oracle model* [5], where an idealized cryptographic hash function can be adaptively "programmed" in order to enable a successful simulation. For instance, the well-known security proofs of Full-Domain Hash signatures [6], BLS signatures [11], or Boneh-Franklin IBE [10] use this approach. Furthermore, partitioning is the only known way to prove security of *unique signatures*[1] or *verifiable random functions* (VRFs) [35] against adaptive adversaries.

---

[1] That is, digital signatures where for any given (public key, message)-pair there exists only one unique string that is accepted as a signature by the verification algorithm.

Admissible hash functions (AHFs) are a generic and very useful tool to enable partitioning proofs in the *standard model*, that is, without random oracles. AHFs were formally introduced in [9,13,17], but have implicitly already been used by Lysyanskaya [31]. Essentially, the idea is that the AHF partitions the considered set "randomly" and invisible to the adversary, such that with noticeable probability exactly the "right" elements fall into the "controlled" set. For instance, the "right" message may be exactly those messages for which the adversary queries a signature in the EUF-CMA security experiment. At the same time, exactly the "right" other elements fall into the "uncontrolled" set, e.g., the message for which the adversary produces a signature forgery. AHFs ensure that this holds with sufficiently high probability, even if the adversary chooses these values adaptively and possibly maliciously. AHFs are an ubiquitous tool in public-key cryptography, and have been used to realize numerous cryptographic primitives with strong adaptive security and without random oracles, such as unique signatures [31], verifiable random functions [7,22,25,31], different variants of identity-based encryption [1,9], Bonsai trees [13], programmable hash functions [17], and constrained PRFs [2].

For some primitives AHF-based partitioning proofs (and variants thereof, such as those defined in [7,27,48]) are still the only known way to achieve provable adaptive security with an efficient polynomial-time reduction. For some other primitives, such as identity-based encryption [9], AHFs yielded the first constructions with adaptive security, and later more efficient constructions have been developed that apply other techniques that are specifically designed for a particular (class of) cryptosystem(s) and are not as generic as AHFs. We also view AHFs as an extremely useful generic tool that will most likely find applications to further advanced cryptographic constructions in the future.

Practical Instantiability of AHFs. Given the large number of cryptographic constructions based on AHFs, it is interesting and important to ask how AHF-based constructions can be instantiated in *practice*. Known constructions are based on different types of error-correcting codes with suitable minimal distance, which is required to be a *constant* fraction of the length of the code, in order to make the partitioning argument go through with noticeable success probability. There are many possible codes to choose from [19,42,45,49], which yield very different concrete instantiations with very different efficiency and security properties.

Most aforementioned works mention that one or another of these codes can be used to instantiate their AHFs in the *asymptotic* setting, but it is never clarified how their constructions can be instantiated *concretely*, by explaining how the underlying code and other cryptographic parameters must be chosen, taking into account the considered security parameter, deployment parameters such as the number of AHF evaluations by a realistic adversary, and the tightness of the security proof. The concrete choice of the code used to instantiate the AHF has a very significant impact on the efficiency of the resulting cryptosystem. Hence, while AHFs provide a powerful generic tool to achieve provable security *asymptotically*, it is completely unclear how efficiently they can be instantiated *concretely*.

Our Contributions. Our main objective is to clarify how AHFs can be securely and efficiently instantiated concretely in practice, and to develop new techniques that enable a more efficient instantiation of AHF-based cryptosystems. To this end, we make the following contributions:

- We assess how AHFs can be instantiated with error-correcting codes (ECC). We show that while AHFs are theoretically sufficient to obtain polynomial-time constructions and security against polynomial-time adversaries in the asymptotic setting, they yield only extremely inefficient concrete instantiations. By applying bounds on ECCs from classical coding theory, we point out inherent limitations of concrete instantiations of the AHFs presented in prior work. Concretely, we show that even with codes that meet the Gilbert-Varshamov or McEliece-Rodemich-Rumsey-Welch (MRRW) bound, even optimised variants [27,48] of known verifiable random functions [25,31] have only very inefficient practical instantiations.
- Our first main novel technical contribution is the introduction of the notion of *computational* AHFs (cAHFs). Standard AHFs based on error-correcting codes are essentially an *information-theoretic* primitive, which works unconditionally and even for computationally unbounded adversaries, which of course is stronger than necessary for most applications. cAHFs therefore relax this requirement, in the sense that they are only required to partition the considered set successfully in the presence of a *computationally bounded* adversary. This will make it possible to overcome the aforementioned limitations of AHFs. We also give a concrete instantiation of cAHFs, based on the notion of *truncation collision resistant hash functions* from [26].
- Finally, we show how cAHFs can be used to construct the currently most efficient verifiable random function (VRF) with full adaptive security and exponential-sized input space, based on a non-interactive complexity assumption, in the standard model.

Classical balanced admissible hash functions, and therefore also the security proofs of VRFs based on those, which include [25,27,48], require (reasonably close bounds on) the number of VRF *evaluation queries* and advantage of an adversary. Our instantiation of cAHFs inherits from [26] that security proofs require knowledge of (sufficiently close bounds on) the *running time* and advantage of an adversary.

Related Work. Boneh and Boyen [9] formally introduced AHFs to construct IBE without random oracles. *Balanced* AHFs were introduced in [25]. The balancedness makes it possible to apply AHF-based partitioning directly in security proofs considering "indistinguishability-based" security experiments, without requiring the *artificial abort* approach of Waters [47]. Balanced AHFs were used to construct verifiable random functions [7,22,25,48], IBE [48], constrained PRFs [3], and distributed PRFs [30]. We consider both standard and balanced AHFs below.

Several papers developed techniques to optimize schemes using AHFs. Yamada [48] and Katsumata [27] encode the information of the "controlled" set into shorter bit strings and employ the AHF on this shorter string. Recently, Kohl [29] applied such an approach to the VRF construction of [22] to obtain a VRF with strong security properties and shorter proofs.

Most previous applications of AHFs consider a setting where a polynomially-bounded number of Q elements $X^{(1)}, \ldots, X^{(Q)}$ must fall into the "controlled" set, while *one* "challenge" element X^* must fall into the "uncontrolled" set for the reduction in the security proof to be successful. This matches what is required for most common security experiments for primitives such as digital signatures, VRFs, IBE, and many others. Chen *et al.* [14] generalize this to AHFs that can handle more than one challenge element and ensure that $n > 1$ challenge elements $X^{(1)*}, \ldots, X^{(n)*}$ fall into the "uncontrolled" set, and give a construction with $n = 2$.

AHFs are related to *programmable hash functions* (PHFs) [23, 24], but are more general, in the sense that PHFs can generically be constructed from AHFs, but there exist cryptographic primitives, such as VRFs, for which only constructions based on AHFs are known to exist, but not on PHFs.

Notation. Following ususal conventions, we denote the natural numbers without zero by $\mathbb{N}$. Furthermore, we use $k \in \mathbb{N}$ as our security parameter and for $n \in \mathbb{N}$ we denote the set $\{1, \ldots, n\}$ by $[n]$ and the power set of a set S as 2^S. Given a finite set T, we write $x \xleftarrow{\$} T$ for drawing x uniformly at random from T. If $A(\cdot)$ is a probabilistic algorithm, we write $y \xleftarrow{\$} A(x)$ for executing A with input x and assigning the result of this execution to the variable y. For a vector $v \in T^n$ and $n \in \mathbb{N}$, we denote the i-th component of v as v_i. If not stated otherwise, all logarithms are to the base two and $\ln(x)$ denotes the natural logarithm of $x \in \mathbb{R}^{>0}$. We refer to a function $\epsilon : \mathbb{N} \to [0,1]$ as *negligible* if for all positive polynomials p and all $n \in \mathbb{N}$ large enough, it holds $\epsilon(n) < 1/p(n)$.

2   Admissible Hash Functions

Furthermore, let n, Q be polynomials over $\mathbb{N}$ and let $\mathcal{C} := \{C_k\}_{k \in \mathbb{N}}$ be a family of functions with $C_k : \Sigma^k \to \Sigma^{n(k)}$ for all $k \in \mathbb{N}$ and some finite alphabet Σ. Whenever it is clear from the context, we use n instead of $n(k)$ and Q instead of $Q(k)$. For a finite alphabet Σ with $\perp \notin \Sigma$, let $\Sigma_\perp := \Sigma \cup \{\perp\}$. For $d \in [n]$, we denote by $\Sigma_\perp^{(n,d)}$ the subset of $\Sigma_\perp^n$ containing all the elements of $\Sigma_\perp^n$ having exactly d components that are *not* $\perp$.

Binary Biased PRF. An essential building block to define AHFs is the binary biased PRF F_K, that was introduced by Boneh and Boyen [9].

Definition 1 (The Binary Biased PRF [9]). *Let $C : \Sigma^k \to \Sigma^n$ and $K \in \Sigma_\perp^n$, then define*

$$F_K(X) := \begin{cases} 0, & \text{if } \forall i \in [n] : C(X)_i = K_i \vee K_i = \perp \text{ holds} \\ 1, & \text{otherwise.} \end{cases} \tag{1}$$

Admissible Hash Functions. Now we are ready to define AHFs. Intuitively, an AHF realizes a partitioning of a set Σ^k into a "controlled" and an "uncontrolled" set, such that $X \in \Sigma^k$ lies in the "controlled" set *if and only if* $F_K(X) = 0$. For example, in a security proof for a digital signature scheme this would typically be used as follows:

- The reduction is able to simulate a signature for message $X \in \Sigma^k$ *if and only if* $F_K(X) = 1$.
- The reduction is able to extract the solution to a computationally hard problem from a signature for message $X^* \in \Sigma^k$ *if and only if* $F_K(X^*) = 0$.

This intuition yields the following generic definition of AHFs from [9].

Definition 2 (Admissible Hash Function [9]). *We call $\{C_\ell\}_{\ell \in \mathbb{N}}$ an $(n, Q, \gamma_{\min})$-admissible hash function family (AHF family) if there exists a PPT algorithm $K \xleftarrow{\$} \mathsf{AdmSmp}(1^k, Q)$ generating $K \in \Sigma_\perp^n$ such that for all $(X^{(1)}, \ldots, X^{(Q)}, X^*) \in (\Sigma^k)^{Q+1}$ with $X^* \neq X^{(i)}$ it holds*

$$\gamma_{\min}(k) \leq \Pr\left[F_K\left(X^{(1)}\right) = \cdots = F_K\left(X^{(Q(k))}\right) = 0 \wedge F_K\left(X^*\right) = 1\right], \quad (2)$$

where the probability is over the choice of $K \xleftarrow{\$} \mathsf{AdmSmp}(1^k, Q)$.

Note that $\gamma_{\min}(k) \in [0, 1]$ is a *lower* bound on the probability that the partitioning works as desired for any given sequence of values $(X^{(1)}, \ldots, X^{(Q)}, X^*)$.

Remark 1. There have been several slightly different definitions of AHFs. The first definition of AHFs by Boneh and Boyen [9] includes the application of a collision resistant hash function before applying the function C above, allowing to process inputs of arbitrary length. However, most applications of AHFs, for example in [7,17,22,25,27,29,48], only consider fixed length inputs and therefore do not apply a collision resistant hash function. For this reason, we define standard AHFs with a bounded length input space and view the application of a collision resistant hash function in [9] only as a generic way of processing arbitrary length inputs with an information-theoretic AHF.

Balanced AHFs. *Balanced* AHFs are an extension of standard AHFs, introduced in [25]. Intuitively, a balanced AHF provides both a *lower* bound $\gamma_{\min}$ and an *upper* bound $\gamma_{\max}$ on the probability that partitioning works as desired for any given sequence of values $(X^{(1)}, \ldots, X^{(Q)}, X^*)$. Furthermore, it is required that these bounds are *sufficiently close*. As shown in [25], this makes AHFs applicable in settings considering *indistinguishability-based* security experiments, such as indistinguishability of verifiable random functions. Balancedness makes it possible to avoid the "artificial abort" technique of Waters [47] and can be seen as an abstraction and adoption of a proof technique by Bellare and Ristenpart [4] to AHFs. Previous works [4,25] provide a detailed explanation of this.

Definition 3 (Balanced Admissible Hash Function [25]). *Let $\epsilon : \mathbb{N} \rightarrow [0, 1]$ be a non-negligible function. We call $\{C_k\}_{k \in \mathbb{N}}$ an $(n, Q, \gamma_{\min}, \gamma_{\max})$-balanced AHF family if there exists a PPT $\mathsf{AdmSmp}(1^k, Q, \epsilon)$ and functions $\gamma_{\max}, \gamma_{\min} : \mathbb{N} \rightarrow [0, 1]$, such that for all $(X^{(1)}, \ldots, X^{(Q(k))}, X^*) \in (\Sigma^k)^{Q(k)+1}$ with $X^* \neq X^{(i)}$*

$$\gamma_{\min}(k) \leq \Pr\left[F_K\left(X^{(1)}\right) = \cdots = F_K\left(X^{(Q(k))}\right) = 0 \wedge F_K\left(X^*\right) = 1 \right] \leq \gamma_{\max}(k)$$

holds, where the probability is over the choice of $K \xleftarrow{\$} \mathsf{AdmSmp}(1^k, Q(k), \epsilon(k))$. We require that

$$\tau(k) := \epsilon(k)\gamma_{\min}(k) - \frac{\gamma_{\max}(k) - \gamma_{\min}(k)}{2}. \tag{3}$$

is a non-negligible function.

The term $\tau(k)$ may appear overly specific. However, it turns out that this is exactly what is required in common proofs that use balanced AHFs. We refer to [4,25] for details. As long as it does not lead to ambiguities, we will refer to both balanced admissible hash functions and admissible hash functions as AHFs in the sequel.

2.1   Instantiating AHFs from Error Correcting Codes

Error Correcting Codes. To describe how AHFs are instantiated from error correcting codes, let us first recap some fundamental notions.

Definition 4 (Hamming Weight and Distance). *Let $n \in \mathbb{N}$, q a prime power and $x, y \in \mathbb{F}_q^n$, then $\mathrm{wt}(x)$ is defined as the number of components of x that are not zero. We call $\mathrm{wt}(x)$ the Hamming weight of x and $\Delta(x, y) := \mathrm{wt}(x - y)$ the Hamming distance between x and y.*

Definition 5 (Linear ECCs). *Let q be a prime power, $k, n \in \mathbb{N}$ with $k < n$ and $G \in \mathbb{F}_q^{k \times n}$. Then $C = \{xG \mid x \in \mathbb{F}_q^k\}$ is the linear q-ary error correcting code (ECC) generated by the generator matrix G. We say that C has minimal distance*

$$d := \min_{\substack{x, x' \in \mathbb{F}_q^k \\ x \neq x'}} (\Delta(xG, x'G)).$$

Furthermore we refer to $\delta(C) := d/n$ as the relative minimal distance and to $\mathcal{R}(C) := k/n$ as the rate of C. If C has a minimal distance of d, we say that C is a linear $[n, k, d]_q$ ECC.

As usual, we will also refer to the mapping $C : \mathbb{F}_q^k \rightarrow F_q^n, x \mapsto xG$ as an ECC. If the alphabet of the code is clear from the context, we drop the index q.

AHFs from ECCs. To the best of our knowledge, all constructions of AHFs and bAHFs use an algorithm AdmSmp that samples K as follows. First $d \in [n]$ is calculated as a function of a bound on Q and the advantage ϵ of a given adversary $\mathcal{A}$ (the latter only for bAHFs). Then K is chosen uniformly at random from $K \xleftarrow{\$} \Sigma_\perp^{(n,d)}$.

Theorem 1 (Instantiation of AHFs Using an ECC [17,25]). *Let q be a prime power and let $\{C_k\}_{k \in \mathbb{N}}$ be a family of $[n(k), k, n(k) \cdot \delta(k)]_q$ ECCs, where $\delta = \delta(k) \in [0, 1/2)$ denotes the relative distance of C_k. If $K \xleftarrow{\$} \mathbb{F}_q^{(n,d)}$ is chosen uniformly at random for some $d \in [n(k)]$, then*

$$\gamma_{\min}(k) \leq \Pr\left[F_K\left(X^{(1)}\right) = \cdots = F_K\left(X^{(Q)}\right) = 0 \wedge F_K\left(X^*\right) = 1 \right] \leq \gamma_{\max}(k)$$

holds for all $X^{(1)}, \ldots, X^{(Q)}, X^* \in \left(\mathbb{F}_q^k\right)^{(Q+1)}$ and

$$\gamma_{\min}(k) := (1 - Q \cdot (1 - \delta(k))^d) \cdot q^{-d} \quad and \quad \gamma_{\max}(k) := q^{-d}. \tag{4}$$

The proof is given in [25]. If

$$d := \log_{1-\delta}\left(\frac{-\ln(q)}{Q \cdot \ln\left(\frac{1-\delta}{q}\right)} \right) \tag{5}$$

is used, then $\gamma_{\min}$ is non-negligible as shown in [17]. Note that d in Eq. 5 maximizes $\gamma_{\min}$ from Eq. 4 compared the [17] and therefore yields slightly better parameters.

Balanced AHFs from ECCs. If the parameter d from Theorem 1 is set to

$$d := \log_{1-\delta}\left(\frac{-2 \cdot \epsilon \cdot \ln(q)}{(2 \cdot \epsilon + 1) \cdot Q \cdot \ln\left(\frac{1-\delta}{q}\right)} \right)$$

then one can also prove that the above construction is a *balanced* AHF [25]. Again, this value of d improves on that given in [25], in the sense that $\tau = \epsilon \cdot \gamma_{\min} - (\gamma_{\max} - \gamma_{\min})/2$ is maximised.

Remark. Note that the choices of d above, just as the choices from [17,25], can yield a d larger than n for some combinations of Q, ϵ and q. However, $d \in [n]$ holds for reasonable parameters as showcased in Sect. 4.2.

2.2   Efficiency Bounds on Admissible Hash Functions

In order to be able to efficiently instantiate the code-based AHFs, it is important to reduce the length of code words n. This is because applications usually embed the AHF in the public keys or public parameters of a cryptosystem, and the size of these depends on the length of code words. For example, the public key of the VRF of [25] contains one group element for every bit in the output of the ECC. The VRFs in [27,48] reduce this, but still contain at least logarithmically many group elements. Even though asymptotically logarithmic, the number may still be impractically large when instantiated concretely - we discuss this below in Sect. 4.2. In the following, we provide the first analysis of inherent limitations of instantiating AHFs with ECCs, by applying results from coding theory.

Gilbert-Varshamov Bound. In order to instantiate AHFs efficiently, we need a code that has both a high rate and a high relative minimal distance. Coding theorists worked on the construction of such codes and accompanying bounds for decades [32]. Asymptotically, the *Gilbert-Varshamov bound* guarantees the *existence* of well-suited families of binary ECCs, but we note that this result is *not constructive.*

Theorem 2 (Gilbert-Varshamov Bound [19,45]**).** *For all $n \in \mathbb{N}$ and $c \in (0, 1/2)$, there exists an ECC $C \subset \mathbb{F}_2^n$ with*

$$\delta(C) \geq c \quad and \quad R(C) \geq 1 - H_2(\delta).$$

H_2 *denotes the binary entropy, defined as*

$$H_2(p) := p \cdot \log(1/p) + (1 - p) \cdot \log(1/(1 - p)).$$

Even though the Gilbert-Varshamov (GV) bound guarantees the existence of families of binary ECCs with the parameters from above, no explicit construction of such a family attaining the GV bound is known so far. Random linear codes attain the GV bound [45]. However, as [16,44] show, there is no efficient algorithm that can compute or approximate the minimal distance of a random linear code, which would be necessary in order to instantiate the code concretely and efficiently. Also, algebraic geometric ECCs like [41] beat the GV bound, but only for larger, non-binary alphabets, which are not suitable for most constructions using AHFs.

Hence, when instantiating a family of (balanced) AHFs, we can treat the GV bound as an upper bound on what is possible with currently known families of binary ECCs. The GV bound yields that for $\delta = 0.2$, the best rate we can hope to achieve with known construction of families of ECCs is ≈ 0.28. For the VRF from [25], this would require a number of group elements in the public key that is at least about four times larger than the number of input bits. It is possible however to construct a family of binary ECCs that comes relatively close to this bound by concatenating algebraic geometry codes with binary error correcting codes as explained in [41, Section V].

In order to estimate the efficiency of code-based AHFs, we assumed a code family that achieves the GV bound, and computed the size of verification keys, secret keys, and proofs for different verifiable random functions that use AHFs to achieve adaptive security. See Sect. 4.2, Tables 1 and 2.

Remark 2. Our analysis based on the GV bound is somewhat conservative, in the sense that no efficient construction of a family of codes that achieves the GV bound asymptotically is known (even though they are known to exist).[2] Therefore our efficiency analysis of cryptosystems based on codes that meet the GV bound is currently overly optimistic, and any known code family would lead to even worse parameters.

McEliece-Rodemich-Rumsey-Welch (MRRW) bound. Things may improve when we consider instantiations for a specific input length k of the ECC.[3] For example for $k = 128$, there is a $[255, 128, 38]_2$ ECC C based on a BCH code [21]. Thus, this code beats the GV bound as $R(C) \approx 1/2$ and $\delta(C) \approx 0.15$, whereas the GV bound only allows for $R(C) \approx 0.39$ for $\delta(C) = 0.15$. However, even when considering concrete input sizes of ECCs, there are bounds on the relation between the rate and the relative minimal distance. The sharpest known bound for binary ECCs is the MRRW bound presented in Theorem 3.

Theorem 3 (MRRW Bound [33]**).** *Let C be an $[n, k, d]_2$ ECC with relative distance $\delta(C) \in (0, 1/2)$ and let $g(x) := H_2((1 - \sqrt{1 - x})/2)$. Then*

$$R(C) \leq \min_{0 \leq u \leq 1 - 2\delta} \{1 + g(u^2) - g(u^2 + 2\delta(C)u + 2\delta(C))\}$$

holds for the rate of C.

The MRRW-Bound once more yields limits on what can be achieved concretely. For example, every binary ECC C with $\delta(C) = 0.15$ inevitably has $R(C) < 0.58$. Analogously, any ECC C with $\delta(C) = 0.2$ has $R(C) < 0.47$.

Again, we estimate the efficiency of code-based AHFs by assuming a code that achieves the MRRW bound, and compute the size of verification keys, secret keys, and proofs for different AHF-based verifiable random functions. See Section Sect. 4.2, Tables 1 and 2.

3   Computational Admissible Hash Functions

In order to overcome the inherent limitations of (balanced) AHFs and their instantiation with ECCs, we *relax the constraints* and consider a *computational* setting. To this end, we allow C to have inputs $X, Y,$ $X \neq Y$, such that $\Delta(C(X), C(Y)) < \delta n$ or even $C(X) = C(Y)$. For an adversary, however, such inputs X and Y should be *computationally infeasible* to find. This relaxation allows us to reduce redundancy inherent to ECCs and thus the length of the output of C. We refer to this relaxed variant of AHFs as *computational admissible hash functions* (cAHFs).

Furthermore, we aim at defining cAHFs in a way that allows us to replace bAHFs in many construction like [2,22,25,27,30,48], while making only minor

---

[2] Codes based on expander graphs can get close to this bound, while not achieving it [43].

[3] For the VRFs in [22,25,27,29,48] this is identical to the input length.

modifications to the constructions or their accompanying security proofs. Since we instantiate cAHFs with families of hash functions in Sect. 3.1, we change the notation and use H for the computational setting instead of C in order to avoid confusion between the two settings.

Defining Computational Admissible Hash Functions. We keep using the binary biased PRF F_K from [9], since we strive to allow to *generically replace* bAHFs with cAHFs. Allowing H to have pairs of inputs X, Y with $X \neq Y$ and $H(X) = H(Y)$ comes with the problem that an adversary can have a collision for H hard coded. Therefore, we need to draw the function H from a *family of functions* $\mathcal{H}$. This requires us to incorporate H and do the following minor modification to the definition of F_K. Nevertheless, note that the definition of cAHFs is not syntactically bound to families of hash functions.

$$F_{K,H}(X) = \begin{cases} 0, & \text{if } \forall j \in [n] : H(X)_j = K_j \vee K_j = \bot \\ 1, & \text{otherwise.} \end{cases} \tag{6}$$

Definition 6 (Computational Admissible Hash Function). *Let* $\mathcal{H} = \{H : \{0,1\}^* \to \{0,1\}^n\}$ *be a family of functions and* $H \in \mathcal{H}$. *For* $K \in \{0,1,\bot\}^n$ *and all* $(X^{(1)}, \ldots, X^{(Q)}, X^*)$ *with* $X^{(i)}, X^* \in \{0,1\}^*$ *and* $X^{(i)} \neq X^*$ *for all* i, *we let* $X^{(Q+1)} := X^*$ *to ease notation and define the events* coll *and* badchal *as follows.*

$$\text{badchal} \iff F_{K,H}(X^*) \neq 0$$

$$\text{coll} \iff \exists i, j \text{ with } X^{(i)} \neq X^{(j)} \text{ s.t.}$$

$$\forall \ell \in [n] : H(X^{(i)})_\ell = H(X^{(j)})_\ell \vee K_\ell = \bot$$

Let $t_\mathcal{A} \in \mathbb{N}$ *and* $\epsilon_\mathcal{A} \in (0,1]$ *such that* $t_\mathcal{A}/\epsilon_\mathcal{A} < 2^k$, *where* k *is the security parameter. We say that* $\mathcal{H}$ *is a family of* computational admissible hash functions (cAHFs), *if there is an efficient algorithm* AdmSmp$(1^k, t_\mathcal{A}, \epsilon_\mathcal{A})$ *generating* $K \in \{0,1,\bot\}^n$ *such that for every adversary* $\mathcal{A}$ *running in time* $t_\mathcal{A}$ *outputting* $(X^{(1)}, \ldots, X^{(Q)}, X^*)$ *it holds that*

$$\tau(k) := \Pr[\neg \text{badchal}](\epsilon_\mathcal{A} - \Pr[\text{coll}]) \tag{7}$$

is non-negligible as a function in k. *The probabilities are over the randomness used by* $\mathcal{A}$, $H \overset{\$}{\leftarrow} \mathcal{H}$ *and* $K \overset{\$}{\leftarrow}$ AdmSmp$(1^k, t_\mathcal{A}, \epsilon)$.

Remark 3. The term τ in Eq. 7 is the equivalent of τ for bAHFs in Definition 3, in the sense that it conveniently describes a term that typically occurs in a reduction-based security proof that uses a computational AHF. Intuitively, it captures a security proof that in a first step aborts when coll occurs and in a second step aborts when badchal occurs. See Appendix B for a concrete application.

3.1   cAHFs from Truncation Collision Resistant Hash Functions

We show how to construct very efficient cAHFs based on *truncation collision-resistant hash functions* (TCRHFs), as introduced in [26].

Truncation Collision Resistant Hash Functions. Let $H : \{0,1\}^* \rightarrow \{0,1\}^n$ be a cryptographic hash function. We write $H_{:j} : \{0,1\}^* \rightarrow \{0,1\}^j$ to denote the hash function H, with outputs truncated to the first j bits. Essentially, a hash function is *truncation collision resistant*, if for every prefix of length $j \in [n]$ there is no significantly more efficient algorithm to find a collision for $H_{:j}$ than the birthday attack. Note that this property is likely satisfied by standard cryptographic hash functions, like SHA-3. Furthermore, as explained in [26], one can easily obtain a suitable *family* of hash functions from a standard hash function, e.g. by choosing a random key that is prefixed to all hash function inputs. We refer to such families of hash functions as families of *keyed hash functions*[4].

Definition 7 (Truncation Collision Resistance [26]). *Let* $\mathcal{H} = \{H : \{0,1\}^* \rightarrow \{0,1\}^n\}$ *be a family of keyed hash functions. For* $j \in [n]$, *we say that an adversary* $\mathcal{A}$ j-*breaks the truncation collision resistance of* $\mathcal{H}$, *if it runs in time* $t_\mathcal{A}$ *and*

$$\Pr_{H \xleftarrow{\$} \mathcal{H}} \left[\begin{matrix} (x_0, \dots x_q) \xleftarrow{\$} \mathcal{A}(H) : \\ \exists u, v \text{ s.t. } H_{:j}(x_u) = H_{:j}(x_v) \wedge x_u \neq x_v \end{matrix} \right] > \frac{t_\mathcal{A}(t_\mathcal{A} - 1)}{2^{j+1}}.$$

We say $\mathcal{H}$ *is* truncation collision resistant, *if there exists no adversary* $\mathcal{A}$ j-*breaking the truncation collision resistance of* H *for any* $j \in [n]$.

We deem truncation collision resistance a reasonable assumption since truncated versions of SHA-256 (to 224 bits) and SHA-512 (to 384 bits) have already been standardized by NIST in [36]. Furthermore, [37] defines *extendable-output functions* (XOF) based on SHA-3. These allow to extend the output of the hash function to an arbitrary length while maintaining collision resistance.

Useful Technical Lemma. The following lemma is a variant of [26, Lemma 1], tailored to our application and cAHFs, which yields better parameters than the corresponding result in [26]. The condition $t/\epsilon < 2^k$ captures that we consider an efficient adversary, i. e. one with a small time complexity, a high success probability or both. Chosing j as small as possible such that $(2t(2t-1))/2^j \leq \epsilon/2$ holds then yields the bounds on j and $1/2^j$ below. The lower bound on $1/2^j$ is important because this is the probability that a prefix of length j matches a random binary string of length j. A more thorough explanation can be found in [26].

Lemma 1. *Let* $t \in \mathbb{N}$, $\epsilon \in (0,1]$ *such that* $t/\epsilon < 2^k$, *and* $j := \lceil \log(4t(2t-1)/\epsilon) \rceil$. *Then it holds that*

$$j \in \{1, \dots, 2k+3\}, \qquad \frac{2t(2t-1)}{2^j} \leq \frac{\epsilon}{2}, \quad and \quad \frac{1}{2^j} \geq \frac{\epsilon}{16t^2 - 8t}.$$

---

[4] A detailed dicussion of keyed hash functions can be found in [28].

Proof. We start by proving $j \in \{1, \ldots, 2k+3\}$.

$$j = \lceil \log(4t(2t-1)/\epsilon) \rceil \leq \lceil \log\left(4 \cdot 2^k(2t-1)\right) \rceil$$
$$\leq \lceil \log\left(8 \cdot 2^k t\right) \rceil \leq \lceil \log\left(2^k 2^{k+3}\right) \rceil = 2k+3$$

Since $4t(2t-1) = 8t^2 - 4t > 1$ for all $t \in \mathbb{N}$ and $\epsilon \in (0,1]$, we have $\log(4t(2t-1)/\epsilon) > 0$ and therefore $j \geq 1$.

We proceed to prove $2t(2t-1)/2^j \leq \epsilon/2$.

$$\frac{2t(2t-1)}{2^j} = \frac{2t(2t-1)}{2^{\lceil \log(4t(2t-1)/\epsilon) \rceil}} \leq \frac{\epsilon 2t(2t-1)}{4t(2t-1)} = \frac{\epsilon}{2}$$

Finally, we have

$$\frac{1}{2^j} = \frac{1}{2^{\lceil \log(4t(2t-1)/\epsilon) \rceil}} \geq \frac{1}{2} \cdot \frac{\epsilon}{4t(2t-1)} = \frac{\epsilon}{16t^2 - 8t}.$$

Constructing cAHFs from TCRHFs. Lemma 1 enables us to prove that a family of TCRHFs is also a family of cAHFs. Note that even though the first definition of AHFs in [9] already incorporates collision resistant hash functions, they are only used to enable the processing of arbirtrary length inputs, while the core of the AHF in [9] is the error correcting code that yields an information-theoretic AHF, which we replace with TCRHFs.

Theorem 4. *Let* $\mathcal{H} = \{H : \{0,1\}^* \to \{0,1\}^{2k+3}\}$ *be a family of truncation collision resistant keyed hash functions in the sense of Definition 7. Then* $\mathcal{H}$ *is a family of computational AHFs. In particular, let* $t_\mathcal{A} \in \mathbb{N}$ *and* $\epsilon_\mathcal{A} \in (0,1]$ *such that* $t_\mathcal{A}/\epsilon_\mathcal{A} < 2^k$. *Then for every adversary* $\mathcal{A}$ *running in time* $t_\mathcal{A}$ *that, given* $H \xleftarrow{\$} \mathcal{H}$, *outputs* $X^{(1)}, \ldots, X^{(Q)}, X^* \in \{0,1\}^*$ *with* $X^{(i)} \neq X^*$, *there is an algorithm* $\mathsf{AdmSmp}(1^k, t, \epsilon)$ *such that*

$$\Pr[\neg\mathsf{badchal}](\epsilon - \Pr[\mathsf{coll}]) \geq \epsilon^2/(32t^2 - 16t).$$

In particular, if $t_\mathcal{A}$ *is polynomial in* k *and* ϵ *is non-negligible in* k, *then* $\epsilon_\mathcal{A}^2/(32t_\mathcal{A}^2)$ *is also non-negligible.*

Proof. Let $n := 2k + 3$. The algorithm $\mathsf{AdmSmp}(1^k, t, \epsilon)$ sets $j := \lceil \log(4t(2t-1)/\epsilon) \rceil$, samples $K' \xleftarrow{\$} \{0,1\}^j$, and defines $K := K' \| \perp^{n-j}$, where $\|$ denotes string concatenation and $\perp^{n-j}$ the string consisting of $(n-j)$-times the $\perp$-symbol. In total the key K consists of j uniformly random bits, padded to a string of length n in $\{0, 1, \perp\}^n$ by appending $\perp$-symbols. Note that $n \geq j$ by Lemma 1.

Recall that $\neg\mathsf{badchal}$ occurs iff $F_{K,H}(X^*) = 0$. For our construction, this means that the first j bits of $H(X^*)$ are *identical* to K', the first j bits of K. Since K' is chosen uniformly random, and independent of $H \xleftarrow{\$} \mathcal{H}$, this happens with probability 2^{-j}. We therefore have

$$\Pr[\neg\mathsf{badchal}] = \frac{1}{2^j} \geq \frac{\epsilon_\mathcal{A}}{16t_\mathcal{A}^2 - 8t},$$

where the inequality uses Lemma 1. Furthermore, recall that coll occurs, if the adversary outputs, as queries or as challenge, two values $X \neq Y$ such that $H(X)$ and $H(Y)$ are identical in all positions where K is not $\perp$. In particular, we then have $H_{:j}(X) = H_{:j}(Y)$. We therefore claim that we have

$$\Pr[\text{coll}] \leq \frac{\epsilon_{\mathcal{A}}}{2}.$$

We prove this upper bound on $\Pr[\text{coll}]$ by contradiction. Assume $\mathcal{A}$ outputs $X = (X^{(1)}, \dots, X^{(Q)}, X^*)$ such that $\Pr[\text{coll}] > \epsilon/2$. Then we can construct an adversary $\mathcal{B}$ that j-breaks the truncation collision resistance of $\mathcal{H}$. $\mathcal{B}$ runs $\mathcal{A}$, waits for $\mathcal{A}$ to output X and then outputs X itself. $\mathcal{B}$'s running time consists of the time to execute $\mathcal{A}$ plus the time to output X, yielding[5] $t_{\mathcal{B}} \leq 2 \cdot t_{\mathcal{A}}$. Thus, $\mathcal{B}$ is an algorithm with success probability at least $\epsilon_{\mathcal{A}}/2$ in j-breaking the truncation collision resistance of $\mathcal{H}$. We furthermore have

$$\Pr[\text{coll}] > \epsilon_{\mathcal{A}}/2 \geq \frac{2t_{\mathcal{A}}(2t_{\mathcal{A}} - 1)}{2^j} \geq \frac{2t_{\mathcal{A}}(2t_{\mathcal{A}} - 1)}{2^j} = \frac{t_{\mathcal{B}}(t_{\mathcal{B}} - 1)}{2^j} > \frac{t_{\mathcal{B}}(t_{\mathcal{B}} - 1)}{2^{j+1}},$$

where the second inequality follows from Lemma 1. This contradicts the truncation collision resistance of $\mathcal{H}$ and therefore proves the upper bound on $\Pr[\text{coll}]$. In conclusion, the following equation yields the theorem.

$$\Pr[\neg\text{badchal}](\epsilon_{\mathcal{A}} - \Pr[\text{coll}]) \geq \frac{\epsilon_{\mathcal{A}}}{16t_{\mathcal{A}}^2 - 8t} \left(\epsilon_{\mathcal{A}} - \frac{\epsilon_{\mathcal{A}}}{2} \right) = \frac{\epsilon_{\mathcal{A}}^2}{32t_{\mathcal{A}}^2 - 16t}$$

Note that if $t_{\mathcal{A}}$ is polynomial in k and $\epsilon_{\mathcal{A}}$ is non-negligible in k, then $\epsilon_{\mathcal{A}}^2/(32t_{\mathcal{A}}^2 - 16t)$ is also non-negligible.

4   Verifiable Random Functions from cAHFs

In this section, we show how to use *computational* AHFs (cAHFs) in a cryptographic scheme. To this end, we instantiate the verifiable random function of Jager [25], which uses an AHF based on error-correcting codes, with a cAHF and show how it is used in a proof in Appendix B. We chose the VRF from [25] as an example, because the construction is relatively simple, based on a *weak q-type* assumption, and satisfies *all desirable properties* of a VRF in the sense described by Hofheinz and Jager [22] in the standard model.

Bilinear Maps. In the sequel let $\mathbb{G}, \mathbb{G}_T$ be groups of order p with bilinear map $e : \mathbb{G} \times \mathbb{G} \to \mathbb{G}_T$. We assume that the groups and bilinear map are *certified* in the sense of [22], which essentially means that each group element has a unique representation and that group membership can be tested efficiently. This is required to achieve the *unique provability* property of a VRF: we do not prove this explicitly, as it follows immediately from [25].

---

[5] One could tighten the upper bound $t_{\mathcal{B}}$ to $t_{\mathcal{A}} + Q$. However, it would at most save a factor of two in the run time of $\mathcal{B}$ and would complicate the analysis. We therefore use the slightly less tight bound.

VRFs and Their Security. Intuitively, VRFs are the public-key counterpart of PRFs. A VRF can be evaluated on a value X using the secret key sk, yielding a pseudorandom value Y together with a unique proof π. Using the public verification key vk and π, everyone can verify that Y is the evaluation of the VRF on X. We recap the standard definitions of syntax and security of VRFs in Appendix A.

4.1 VRF Construction

Let $\mathcal{H} = \{H : \{0,1\}^* \to \{0,1\}^n\}$ be a family of keyed hash functions and let $\mathcal{VF} = (\mathsf{Gen}, \mathsf{Eval}, \mathsf{Vfy})$ be the following algorithms.

Key Generation. Gen chooses a random hash function $H \xleftarrow{\$} \mathcal{H}$ and random generators $g, h \xleftarrow{\$} \mathbb{G}$ and $\alpha_{i,j} \xleftarrow{\$} \mathbb{Z}_p$ for $(i,j) \in [n] \times \{0,1\}$, and defines $g_{i,j} := g^{\alpha_{i,j}}$. The keys are defined as

$$\mathsf{vk} := \big(H, g, h, (g_{i,j})_{(i,j)\in[n]\times\{0,1\}}\big) \in \mathbb{G}^{2n+2} \quad \mathsf{sk} := \{\alpha_{i,j} : (i,j) \in [n] \times \{0,1\}\}$$

Evaluation. On input $X \in \{0,1\}^k$, Eval computes $(H_1, \ldots, H_n) := H(X)$,

$$\alpha_X := \prod_{i=1}^{n} \alpha_{i,H_i} \qquad \text{and} \qquad Y = V_{\mathsf{sk}}(X) := e(g,h)^{\alpha_X}$$

To compute the proof, it sets $\pi_0 := g$ and then computes $(\pi_1, \ldots, \pi_n)$ as

$$\pi_i := \pi_{i-1}^{\alpha_{i,H_i}}$$

Finally, output $(Y, \pi_1, \ldots, \pi_n)$.

Verification. Given $X \in \{0,1\}^k$ and $(Y, \pi_1, \ldots, \pi_n)$, Vfy tests whether Y and π contain only valid group elements, and outputs 0 if not. Then it computes $(H_1, \ldots, H_n) := H(X) \in \{0,1\}^n$, defines $\pi_0 := g$, and outputs 1 if and only if

$$e(\pi_i, g) = e(\pi_{i-1}, g_{i,H_i}) \text{ for all } i \in [n] \qquad \text{and} \qquad Y = e(\pi_n, h)$$

Comparison to Jager's VRF. The construction given above is nearly identical to that from [25], except that above we sample a random hash function $H \xleftarrow{\$} \mathcal{H}$, while [25] uses an error-correcting code instead. It is also straightforward to verify *correctness* and *unique provability*, just as in [25].

Security Proof. We will prove security based on the q-decisional Diffie-Hellman assumption, also used in [25], with small $q = \lceil \log(4t_\mathcal{A}(2t_\mathcal{A} - 1)/\epsilon_\mathcal{A})) \rceil = \mathcal{O}(\log k)$.

Definition 8. *Let $G_\mathcal{B}^{q\mathsf{DDH}}$ be the following game. The experiment samples $g, h \xleftarrow{\$} \mathbb{G}$, $x \xleftarrow{\$} \mathbb{Z}_{|\mathbb{G}|}$, and $b \xleftarrow{\$} \{0,1\}$. Then it defines $T_0 := e(g,h)^{x^{q+1}}$ and $T_1 \xleftarrow{\$} \mathbb{G}_T$.*

Finally, it runs $b' \xleftarrow{\$} \mathcal{B}(g, g^x, \ldots, g^{x^q}, h, T_b)$, *and outputs* 1 *if* $b = b'$, *and* 0 *otherwise. We denote with*

$$\mathsf{Adv}_{\mathcal{B}}^{q\mathsf{DDH}}(k) := \Pr\left[G_{\mathcal{B}}^{q\mathsf{DDH}} = 1\right] - 1/2$$

the advantage *of* $\mathcal{A}$ *in breaking the* $q\mathsf{DDH}$-*assumption in* $(\mathbb{G}, \mathbb{G}_T)$.

Theorem 5. *If* $\mathcal{VF}$ *is instantiated with the computational admissible hash function from Theorem 4, then for any legitimate attacker* $\mathcal{A}$ *that breaks the pseudorandomness of* $\mathcal{VF}$ *in time* $t_{\mathcal{A}}$ *with advantage* $\epsilon_{\mathcal{A}} := \mathsf{Adv}_{\mathcal{A}}^{\mathsf{VRF}}(k)$ *by making at most* Q Eval-*queries, there exists an algorithm* $\mathcal{B}$ *that, given (sufficiently close approximations of)* $t_{\mathcal{A}}$ *and* $\epsilon_{\mathcal{A}}$, *breaks the* q-DDH *assumption with* $q = \lceil \log(4t_{\mathcal{A}}(2t_{\mathcal{A}} - 1)/\epsilon_{\mathcal{A}}) \rceil$ *in time* $t_{\mathcal{B}} \approx t_{\mathcal{A}}$ *and with advantage*

$$\mathsf{Adv}_{\mathcal{B}}^{q\mathsf{DDH}}(k) \geq \epsilon_{\mathcal{A}}^2/(32t_{\mathcal{A}}^2 - 16t_{\mathcal{A}}).$$

Due to space limitations, the proof is deferred to Appendix B. Remarkably, it is significantly simpler than the corresponding AHF-based proof from [25].

4.2   Comparison of VRF Instantiations

We compare the key sizes yielded by instantiating the VRFs from Jager [25], Yamada [48][6]and Katsumata [27] with ECCs with the key sizes yielded by instantiating the same VRFs with the cAHFs from Sect. 3.1. Table 1 shows the sizes of the verification key $|\mathsf{vk}|$, the secret key $|\mathsf{sk}|$ and the proof $|\pi|$ together with the advantage of the solver $\mathsf{Adv}_{\mathcal{B}}$ against the respective hard problem. For the VRFs of [27] and [48], this is the q-DBDHI assumption from [8]. Even though the assumptions differ, the numbers are comparable for the following reasons.

1. The algorithm from [15] is the most efficient known generic algorithm to solve both, the q-DDH assumption and the q-DBDHI assumption.
2. All schemes considered share almost the same q in the assumption, as can be verified in Table 2 and further comparisons in Appendix D.

$|\mathsf{vk}|, |\mathsf{sk}|$ and $|\pi|$ are given as the number of group elements they contain in dependence of k, Q, ϵ, δ and t. Table 1 and its caption explain how the key and proof sizes relate to these variables. We assume that the VRFs from [25,27,48] are instantiated to take inputs from $\{0, 1\}^*$ by first hashing the inputs with a collision resistant hash function $H : \{0, 1\}^* \to \{0, 1\}^\alpha$. We let $\alpha = 2k$, where k is the security parameter, to ensure the collision resistance of H against birthday attacks. Hence, the ECC C used in the instantiation of the VRFs from [25,27,48] maps from $\{0, 1\}^{2k}$ to n, where n denotes the length of the output of C.

---

[6] We do not consider the VRF in Appendix C of [48], because it relies on a polynomial q-type assumption.

Table 1. The sizes of vk, sk, π as the number of group elements and the advantage of the solver in the security proof for the instantiation of the VRFs from [25,27,48]. $d = \lfloor (2Q + Q/\epsilon)/\log(1-\delta) \rfloor$ is the number of positions in the key of the bAHF that are not $\bot$. Note that [25,27,48] all chose d in this way. For the VRFs from Katsumata [27], $\zeta = \lfloor \log(2n) \rfloor + 1$ is the number of bits required to encode an element from $[2n]$. τ is as in Definition 3 and describes the advantage of a solver against the underlying q-type assumption with $q := d$ for the instantiation using ECCs and $q := j$ using TCRHFs. stat represents statistically negligible values introduced in the security proofs in [27,48]. Note that for Yamadas VRFs [48], $n_1, n_2 \in \mathbb{N}$ can be chosen freely such that $n = n_1 n_2$. Analogously, we have $n^{\text{tcrh}} := 2k + 3$ as the output length of the truncation collision hash function, ζ^{tcrh} is the number of bits required to encode an element from $[n^{\text{tcrh}}]$. As in Theorem 4 the length of the prefix used for the TCRHFs is $j := \lceil 4t(2t-1)/\epsilon \rceil$. Again, $n_1^{\text{tcrh}}, n_2^{\text{tcrh}} \in \mathbb{N}$ can be chosen freely such that $n^{\text{tcrh}} = n_1^{\text{tcrh}} n_2^{\text{tcrh}}$. Finally, we have $\tau^{\text{tcrh}} = \epsilon^2/(32t^2 - 16t)$ from Theorem 4.

Construction	Instantiation	$|\text{vk}|$ #G	$|\text{sk}|$ #G	$|\pi|$ #G	$\text{Adv}_\mathcal{B}$
[27] Sec. 5.1	ECCs	$3 + \zeta d$	$d\zeta + 1$	$d + dn + \zeta + 1$	$\tau + \text{stat}$
	cAHF	$3 + \zeta^{\text{tcrh}} j$	$\zeta^{\text{tcrh}} + 1$	$j + j(n^{\text{tcrh}}) + \zeta^{\text{tcrh}} + 1$	$\tau^{\text{tcrh}} + \text{stat}$
[27] Sec. 5.3	ECCs	$3 + d(2^{\zeta/2+2} - 2)$	$d\zeta + 1$	$2d - 1$	$\tau + \text{stat}$
	cAHF	$3 + j(2^{\zeta^{\text{tcrh}}/2+2} - 2)$	$j\zeta^{\text{tcrh}} + 1$	$2j - 1$	$\tau^{\text{tcrh}} + \text{stat}$
[48] Sec. 6.1	ECCs	$dn_1 + 2$	d	dn_2	$\tau + \text{stat}$
	cAHF	$jn_1^{\text{tcrh}} + 2$	j	jn_2^{tcrh}	$\tau^{\text{tcrh}} + \text{stat}$
[48] Sec. 6.3	ECCs	$d + 2$	d	$d(n_1 + n_2 - 1)$	$\tau + \text{stat}$
	cAHF	$j + 2$	j	$j(n_1^{\text{tcrh}} + n_2^{\text{tcrh}} - 1)$	$\tau^{\text{tcrh}} + \text{stat}$
[25]	ECCs	$n + 2$	$2n$	$n + 1$	τ
	cAHFs	$n^{\text{tcrh}} + 2$	$2n^{\text{tcrh}}$	$n^{\text{tcrh}} + 1$	τ^{tcrh}

Key Sizes of VRFs. We list the key sizes of the different VRFs, instantiated with cAHFs and with ECCs in Table 2. Unfortunately, a comparison of the two instantiations is only possible to a limited degree because finding the best known ECC is non-trivial for larger parameters. Code tables [21], the to the best of our knowledge largest collection of best known codes for different parameters, only lists binary codes of length up to 256. Therefore, we compare the instantiation with cAHFs and TCRHFs to the instantiation with AHFs the following ECCs.

- We consider primitive BCH codes that we puncture to achieve the desired relative mininmal distance. Again, tables in for example [39, Table 9.1] only list codes for lengthes up to 1023. We therefore wrote a small programm that finds the most suited primitve BCH code for this purpose. It can be found at https://github.com/DavidNiehues/bch-code-search. Note that the programm considers the Bose distance of the BCH codes instead of the design distance. The caption of Table 2 states the used primituve BCH code explicitly.
- Furthermore, we present key and proof sizes under the assumptions that ECCs on the GV and MRRW bound can be efficiently instantiated.

For the instantiation of the VRFs from Yamada [48], we pick $n_1 = n_2$ as $\lceil \sqrt{n} \rceil$ in order to make the parameter sizes comparable. We make this choice, because Yamada [48] suggest to pick n_1 and n_2 close to $\sqrt{n}$ and because chosing actual divisors of n would make the results heavily depend on the factorization of n.

This would lead to incomparable results. Furthermore, we chose δ such that all instantiations achieve the same advantage of the solver. This makes the different instantiations comparable. Note that we did not incorporate the statistically negligible terms stat in the calculation of the advantage.

Table 2. Key and proof sizes for $k = 128, Q = 2^{25}, t = 2^{50}, \epsilon = 2^{-25}$ and $\delta = 0.235$. In consequence, we have $d = 129$. Puncturing a primitive $[2047, 264, 495]$ BCH-code 18 times to a $[2029, 264, 477]$ code yields $n^{\text{BCH}} = 2029, n_1^{\text{BCH}} = 46, n_2^{\text{BCH}} = 46$ and $\zeta^{\text{BCH}} = 12$. If an ECC on the GV bound is used, this implies $n^{\text{GV}} = 1200, n_1^{\text{GV}} = 35, n_2^{\text{GV}} = 35$ and $\zeta^{\text{GV}} = 12$. Analogously, if an ECC on the MRRW bound is used, this implies $n^{\text{MRRW}} = 664, n_1^{\text{MRRW}} = 26, n_2^{\text{MRRW}} = 26$ and $\zeta^{\text{MRRW}} = 11$. Finally, if the VRFs are instantiated with a cAHF using TCRHFs, we have $n^{\text{tcrh}} = 259, n_1^{\text{tcrh}} = 17, n_2^{\text{tcrh}} = 15, j = 128$ and $\zeta^{\text{tcrh}} = 10$.

Construction	Instantiation	|vk| #$\mathbb{G}$	|sk| #$\mathbb{G}$	|π|#$\mathbb{G}$	Adv$_{\mathcal{B}}$
[27] Sec. 5.1	BCH	1551	1549	261883	$\approx 2^{-155}$
	GV	1551	1549	154942	$\approx 2^{-155}$
	MRRW	1422	1420	85797	$\approx 2^{-155}$
	cAHF	1283	1281	33291	$\approx 2^{-155}$
[27] Sec. 5.3	BCH	32769	1549	257	$\approx 2^{-155}$
	GV	32769	1549	257	$\approx 2^{-155}$
	MRRW	23094	1420	257	$\approx 2^{-155}$
	cAHF	16131	1281	255	$\approx 2^{-155}$
[48] Sec. 6.1	BCH	5936	129	5934	$\approx 2^{-155}$
	GV	4517	129	4515	$\approx 2^{-155}$
	MRRW	3356	129	3354	$\approx 2^{-155}$
	cAHF	2178	128	1920	$\approx 2^{-155}$
[48] Sec. 6.3	BCH	131	129	11739	$\approx 2^{-155}$
	GV	131	129	8901	$\approx 2^{-155}$
	MRRW	131	129	6579	$\approx 2^{-155}$
	cAHF	130	128	3999	$\approx 2^{-155}$
[25]	BCH	2031	4058	2030	$\approx 2^{-155}$
	GV	1202	2400	1201	$\approx 2^{-155}$
	MRRW	666	1328	665	$\approx 2^{-155}$
	cAHF	261	518	260	$\approx 2^{-155}$

Results. Table 2 shows the concrete number of group elements of the different instantiations in the setting with $k = 128$, $Q = 2^{25}$, $t = 2^{50}$ and $\epsilon = 2^{-25}$. The instantiation of the VRFs with cAHFs improves the size of keys and proofs significantly, even compared to bAHFs instantiated with the best theoretically possible ECCs on the MRRW-bound. Concretely, we reduce the size of the proofs of the VRF in Section 5.1 in [27] by $\approx 61\%$ compared to the best theoretically possible instantiation with ECCs, in the setting of Table 2. Compared to an instantiation with ECCs on the GV-bound, we reduced the proof size by

$\approx 78\%$. Compared to the instanitation with punctured primitive BCH codes, the improvement is even $\approx 87\%$. Particularly, keys and proofs whose size depends linearly on n shrink when the VRFs are instantiated with cAHFs. Over all key and proof sizes affected by the improvement, the reduction amounts for at least 9% of the size of an instantiation with ECCs on the MRRW-bound. Note that the size of all keys and proofs stays at least the same. Hence, by making an additional (but from a practical point of view plausible and natural) hardness assumption, we can reduce the key and proof sizes significantly, which may be useful for many practical applications of VRF. We provide more comparisons with different k, ϵ in Appendix D to support this conclusion.

A   Verifiable Random Functions and Their Security

Verifiable random functions are essentially pseudorandom functions, where each function $V_{\sf sk}$ is associated with a secret key $\sf sk$ and a corresponding public verification key $\sf vk$. Given $\sf sk$ and an element X from the domain of $V_{\sf sk}$, one can efficiently compute a *non-interactive, publicly verifiable* proof π that $Y = V_{\sf sk}(X)$ was computed correctly. For security it is required that for each X only one unique value Y such that the statement "$Y = V_{\sf sk}(X)$" can be proven may exist (*unique provability*), and that $V_{\sf sk}(X)$ is indistinguishable from random, if no corresponding proof is given (*pseudorandomness*).

Syntax of VRFs. Formally, a VRF consists of algorithms $({\sf Gen}, {\sf Eval}, {\sf Vfy})$ with the following syntax.

- $({\sf vk}, {\sf sk}) \xleftarrow{\$} {\sf Gen}(1^k)$ takes as input a security parameter k and outputs a key pair $({\sf vk}, {\sf sk})$. We say that $\sf sk$ is the *secret key* and $\sf vk$ is the *verification key*.
- $(Y, \pi) \xleftarrow{\$} {\sf Eval}({\sf sk}, X)$ takes as input a secret key $\sf sk$ and $X \in \{0,1\}^k$, and outputs a function value $Y \in \mathcal{Y}$, where $\mathcal{Y}$ is a finite set, and a proof π. We write $V_{\sf sk}(X)$ to denote the function value Y computed by ${\sf Eval}$ on input $({\sf sk}, X)$.
- ${\sf Vfy}({\sf vk}, X, Y, \pi) \in \{0,1\}$ takes as input a verification key $\sf vk$, $X \in \{0,1\}^k$, $Y \in \mathcal{Y}$, and proof π, and outputs a bit.

Initialize :	Evaluate(X) :	Challenge(X^*) :	Finalize(b') :
$({\sf vk}, {\sf sk}) \xleftarrow{\$} {\sf Gen}(1^k)$	$(Y, \pi) \xleftarrow{\$} {\sf Eval}({\sf sk}, X)$	$(Y_0, \pi) \xleftarrow{\$} {\sf Eval}({\sf sk}, X^*)$	If $b = b'$ then
Return $\sf vk$	Return (Y, π)	$Y_1 \xleftarrow{\$} \mathcal{Y}$	Return 1
		Return Y_b	Return 0

Fig. 1. Procedures defining the VRF security experiment.

Definition 9. $({\sf Gen}, {\sf Eval}, {\sf Vfy})$ *is a* verifiable random function *(VRF) if all of the following hold.*

Correctness. *For all* $(\mathsf{vk}, \mathsf{sk}) \xleftarrow{\$} \mathsf{Gen}(1^k)$ *and* $X \in \{0,1\}^k$ *holds: if* $(Y, \pi) \xleftarrow{\$}$ $\mathsf{Eval}(\mathsf{sk}, X)$, *then* $\mathsf{Vfy}(\mathsf{vk}, X, Y, \pi) = 1$. *Algorithms* Gen, Eval, Vfy *are polynomial-time.*

Unique Provability. *For all* $(\mathsf{vk}, \mathsf{sk}) \xleftarrow{\$} \mathsf{Gen}(1^k)$ *and all* $X \in \{0,1\}^k$, *there does not exist any tuple* (Y_0, π_0, Y_1, π_1) *such that* $Y_0 \neq Y_1$ *and* $\mathsf{Vfy}(\mathsf{vk}, X, Y_0, \pi_0) = \mathsf{Vfy}(\mathsf{vk}, X, Y_1, \pi_1) = 1$.

Pseudorandomness. *Consider an attacker* $\mathcal{A}$ *with access (via oracle queries) to the procedures defined in Fig. 1. Let* $G^{\mathcal{A}}_{\mathsf{VRF}}$ *denote the game where* $\mathcal{A}$ *first queries* $\mathsf{Initialize}$, *then* $\mathsf{Challenge}$, *then* $\mathsf{Finalize}$. *The output of* $\mathsf{Finalize}$ *is the output of the game. Moreover,* $\mathcal{A}$ *may arbitrarily issue* $\mathsf{Evaluate}$-*queries, but only after querying* $\mathsf{Initialize}$ *and before querying* $\mathsf{Finalize}$. *We say that* $\mathcal{A}$ *is legitimate, if* $\mathcal{A}$ *never queries* $\mathsf{Evaluate}(X)$ *and* $\mathsf{Challenge}(X^*)$ *with* $X = X^*$ *throughout the game. We define the advantage of* $\mathcal{A}$ *in breaking the pseudorandomness as*

$$\mathsf{Adv}^{\mathsf{VRF}}_{\mathcal{A}}(k) := \Pr\left[G^{\mathcal{A}}_{\mathsf{VRF}} = 1\right] - 1/2$$

B   Proof of Theorem 5

We prove Theorem 5 with a sequence of games. In the sequel let us write X_i to denote the event that Game i outputs "1" (Fig. 2).

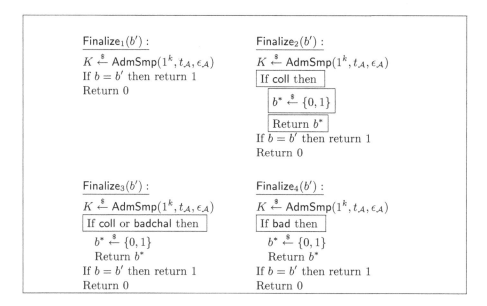

Fig. 2. Procedures used in the proof of Theorem 5. New or modified statements are highlighted in boxes.

Game 0. This is the original VRF security game, as described in Definition 9. By definition, we have

$$\Pr[X_0] = 1/2 + \mathsf{Adv}_{\mathcal{A}}^{\mathsf{VRF}}(k)$$

Game 1. Recall that Theorem 5 assumes knowledge of (sufficiently close approximations of) the running time $t_{\mathcal{A}}$ and the advantage $\epsilon_{\mathcal{A}}$. In this game we replace the Finalize procedure with $\mathsf{Finalize}_1$, which additionally uses $t_{\mathcal{A}}$ and $\epsilon_{\mathcal{A}}$ by running $K \xleftarrow{\$} \mathsf{AdmSmp}(t_{\mathcal{A}}, \epsilon_{\mathcal{A}})$, as depicted in Fig. 1. Note that K now defines the function $F_{K,H}(X)$ from Eq. 6 and events coll and badchal as

$$\mathsf{badchal} \iff F_{K,H}(X^*) \neq 0$$
$$\mathsf{coll} \iff \exists i, j \text{ with } X^{(i)} \neq X^{(j)} \text{ s.t.}$$
$$\forall \ell \in [n] : H(X^{(i)})_\ell = H(X^{(j)})_\ell \vee K_\ell = \bot$$

like in Definition 6. Note that we denote with $X^{(1)}, \ldots, X^{(Q)}$ the values queried by $\mathcal{A}$ to Evaluate, and with X^* the value queried to Challenge. These modifications are purely conceptual and perfectly hidden from $\mathcal{A}$, such that we have

$$\Pr[X_1] = \Pr[X_0].$$

Game 2. This game proceeds identically to Game 1, except that we replace $\mathsf{Finalize}_1$ with $\mathsf{Finalize}_2$ from Fig. 1. By applying Shoup's Difference Lemma [40], we get

$$\Pr[X_2] \geq \Pr[X_1] - \Pr[\mathsf{coll}].$$

Game 3. This game proceeds identically to Game 2, except that we replace $\mathsf{Finalize}_2$ with $\mathsf{Finalize}_3$, which outputs a random bit if badchal occurs. We have

$$
\begin{aligned}
\Pr[X_3] &= \Pr[X_3 \wedge \mathsf{badchal}] + \Pr[X_3 \wedge \neg\mathsf{badchal}] \\
&= \Pr[X_3 \mid \mathsf{badchal}](1 - \Pr[\neg\mathsf{badchal})]) + \Pr[X_3 \mid \neg\mathsf{badchal}]\Pr[\neg\mathsf{badchal}] \\
&= 1/2 + \Pr[\neg\mathsf{badchal}](\Pr[X_3 \mid \neg\mathsf{badchal}] - 1/2) \\
&= 1/2 + \Pr[\neg\mathsf{badchal}](\Pr[X_2 \mid \neg\mathsf{badchal}] - 1/2) \\
&= 1/2 + \Pr[\neg\mathsf{badchal}](\Pr[X_2] - 1/2)
\end{aligned}
$$

The third equality uses that $\Pr[X_3 \mid \mathsf{badchal}] = 1/2$, since a random bit is returned if badchal occurs, the fourth uses that by definition of the games it holds that $\Pr[X_3 \mid \neg\mathsf{badchal}] = \Pr[X_2 \mid \neg\mathsf{badchal}]$, and the last uses $\Pr[X_2 \mid \neg\mathsf{badchal}] = \Pr[X_2]$, since Game 2 is independent of badchal. This is because K is only sampled after $\mathcal{A}$ made all its queries and stated its challenge and K is therefore perfectly hidden from $\mathcal{A}$.

Game 4. We replace events badchal and coll with an equivalent event, in order to simplify the construction of adversary $\mathcal{B}$. We let bad denote the event that coll $\vee$ badchal. In Game 3 the experiment outputs a random bit $b^* \xleftarrow{\$} \{0,1\}$

if (badchal ∨ coll) occurs. Now we output a random bit if bad occurs, which is equivalent. Formally, we achieve this by replacing $\mathsf{Finalize}_3$ with $\mathsf{Finalize}_4$ as defined in Fig. 1, and get

$$\Pr[X_4] = \Pr[X_3]$$

Thus, summing up probabilities from Game 0 to Game 4, we get

$$\Pr[X_4] \geq 1/2 + \Pr[\neg\mathsf{badchal}]\,(\Pr[X_0] - 1/2 - \Pr[\mathsf{coll}])$$
$$= 1/2 + \Pr[\neg\mathsf{badchal}]\,(\epsilon_{\mathcal{A}} - \Pr[\mathsf{coll}])$$
$$\geq 1/2 + \tau(k) \tag{8}$$

for some non-negligible function $\tau(k)$, where the last inequality is due to the definition of cAHFs (see Eq. 7).

Reduction From the q-DDH Assumption. Now we are ready to describe our algorithm $\mathcal{B}$ that solves the q-DDH problem by *perfectly* simulating Game 4 for adversary $\mathcal{A}$. When instantiated with the computational AHF from Theorem 4, a q-DDH instance with $q = \lceil \log(4t_{\mathcal{A}}(2t_{\mathcal{A}} - 1)/\epsilon_{\mathcal{A}}) \rceil$ is sufficient.

The only minor difference between Game 3 and the simulation by $\mathcal{B}$ is that $\mathcal{B}$ aborts "as early as possible". That is, it samples the AHF key $K \xleftarrow{\$} \mathsf{AdmSmp}(1^k, t_{\mathcal{A}}, \epsilon_{\mathcal{A}})$ and random bit b^* already in the Initialize procedure, and checks whether bad occurs after each Evaluate or Challenge query of $\mathcal{A}$. If bad occurs, then it immediately outputs b^*, rather than waiting for the adversary to query Finalize. Obviously, this does not modify the probability of X_4. The proof proceeds now exactly as in [25], as described in Appendix C for completeness.

$\mathcal{B}$'s *Running Time.* The running time $t_{\mathcal{B}}$ of $\mathcal{B}$ consists essentially of the running time $t_{\mathcal{A}}$ of $\mathcal{A}$ plus a minor number of additional operations, thus we have $t_{\mathcal{B}} \approx t_{\mathcal{A}}$.

$\mathcal{B}$'s *Success Probability.* Let $c \in \{0,1\}$ denote the random bit chosen by the qDDH challenger. $\mathcal{B}$ perfectly simulates $G_{\mathsf{VRF}}^{\mathcal{A}}$ with $b = c$. Hence, by Eq. 8, we get

$$\mathsf{Adv}_{\mathcal{B}}^{q\mathsf{DDH}}(k) \geq \Pr[X_4] \geq 1/2 + \tau(k)$$

for a non-negligible function τ. In particular, when instantiated concretely with the computational AHF from Theorem 4, then we have

$$\mathsf{Adv}_{\mathcal{B}}^{q\mathsf{DDH}}(k) \geq 1/2 + \epsilon_{\mathcal{A}}^2/(32t_{\mathcal{A}}^2 - 16t_{\mathcal{A}})$$

C   Full Proof of VRF Security

We proceed by providing the the full proof of security of the VRF. For this purpose, let $\mathcal{B}$ be the following algorithm. $\mathcal{B}$ receives as input $(g, g^x, \ldots, g^{x^q}, h, T)$. Whenever $\mathcal{A}$ queries Initialize, Evaluate, Challenge, or Finalize, $\mathcal{B}$ executes the corresponding procedure from Fig. 3. Finally, it outputs either the random bit b^* if event bad occurs, or otherwise whatever Finalize returns. Note that $\mathcal{B}$ already outputs the random bit b^* if $\mathcal{A}$ makes a query $X^{(i)}$ with $F_{K,H}(X^{(i)}) = 0$ because then either coll or badchal must occur throughout the experiment.

Initialize :
_____

$K \stackrel{\$}{\leftarrow} \mathsf{AdmSmp}(1^k, t_{\mathcal{A}}, \epsilon_{\mathcal{A}})$

$b^* \stackrel{\$}{\leftarrow} \{0, 1\}$

For $(i, j) \in [n] \times \{0, 1\}$ do

    $\alpha_{i,j} \stackrel{\$}{\leftarrow} \mathbb{Z}_{|\mathbb{G}|}$

    If $K_i = j$ then $g_{i,j} := g^{x + \alpha_{i,j}}$

    Else $g_{i,j} := g^{\alpha_{i,j}}$

$\mathsf{vk} := \big(C, g, h, (g_{i,j})_{(i,j)}\big)$

Return vk

Evaluate(X) :
_____

If $F_K(X) = 0$ then output b^*

$Y := e(g^{P_{K,n,X}(x)}, h)$

For $j \in [n]$ do

    $\pi_j := g^{P_{K,j,X}(x)}$

$\pi := (\pi_1, \ldots, \pi_n)$

Return (Y, π)

Challenge(X^*) :
_____

If $F_K(X) = 1$ then output b^*

Compute $\gamma_0, \ldots, \gamma_{q+1}$ s.t.

    $P_{K,n,X^*}(x) = \sum_{i=0}^{q+1} \gamma_i x^i$

$Y^* := T^{\gamma_{q+1}} \cdot \prod_{i=1}^{q} e((g^{x^i})^{\gamma_i}, h)$

Return Y^*

Finalize$^{\mathsf{VRF}}(b')$:
_____

Return b'

Fig. 3. Procedures for the simulation of the VRF pseudorandomness experiment by $\mathcal{B}$.

Initialization. The values (g, h, g^x) in Initialize are from the qDDH-challenge. $\mathcal{B}$ computes the $g_{i,j}$-values exactly as in the original Gen-algorithm, by choosing $\alpha_{i,j} \stackrel{\$}{\leftarrow} \mathbb{Z}_{|\mathbb{G}|}$ and setting $g_{i,j} := g^{\alpha_{i,j}}$, but with the exception that

$$g_{i,K_i} := g^{x + \alpha_{i,K_i}}.$$

for all $(i, j) \in [n] \times \{0, 1\}$ with $K_i \neq \perp$. Due to our choice of a computational admissible hash function according to Theorem 5, there are *exactly* $q+1$ components K_i of K which are not equal to $\perp$. All g_{i,K_i}-values are distributed correctly.

Helping Definitions. To explain how $\mathcal{B}$ responds to Evaluate and Challenge queries made by $\mathcal{A}$, we define two sets $I_{K,w,X}$ and $J_{K,w,X}$, which depend on an AHF key K, a VRF input $X \in \{0, 1\}^k$, and integer $w \in \mathbb{N}$ with $1 \leq w \leq n$, as

$$I_{K,w,X} := \{i \in [w] : K_i = H(X)_i\} \quad \text{and} \quad J_{K,w,X} := [w] \setminus I_{K,w,X}$$

Note that $I_{K,w,X}$ denotes the set of all indices $i \in [w] \subseteq [n]$ such that $K_i = H(X)_i$, and $J_{K,w,X}$ denotes the set of all indices in $[w]$ which are not contained in $I_{K,w,X}$. Based on these sets, we define polynomials $P_{K,w,X}(x)$

$$P_{K,w,X}(x) = \prod_{i \in I_{K,w,X}} (x + \alpha_{i,K_i}) \cdot \prod_{i \in J_{K,w,X}} \alpha_{i,K_i} \in \mathbb{Z}_{|\mathbb{G}|}[x].$$

The following observations were described in [25]:

1. For all X with $F_K(X) = 1$, the set $I_{K,w,X}$ contains at most q elements, and thus the polynomial $P_{K,w,X}(x)$ has degree at most q. This implies that if $F_K(X) = 1$, then $\mathcal{B}$ can efficiently compute $g^{P_{K,w,X}(x)}$ for all $w \in [n]$. To this end, $\mathcal{B}$ first computes the coefficients $\gamma_0, \ldots, \gamma_q$ of the polynomial $P_{K,w,X}(x) = \sum_{i=0}^{q} \gamma_i x^i$ with degree at most q, and then

$$g^{P_{K,w,X}(x)} := g^{\sum_{i=0}^{q} \gamma_i x^i} = \prod_{i=0}^{q} (g^{x^i})^{\gamma_i}$$

   using the terms $(g, g^x, \ldots, g^{x^q})$ from the q-DDH challenge.

2. If $F_K(X) = 0$, then $P_{K,n,X}(x)$ has degree $q + 1$. We do not know how $\mathcal{B}$ can efficiently compute $g^{P_{K,n,X}(x)}$ in this case.

Responding to Evaluate-*Queries.* If $F_K(X) = 1$, then procedure Evaluate computes the group elements $g^{P_{K,w,X}(x)}$ as explained above. Note that in this case the response to the Evaluate(X)-query of $\mathcal{A}$ is correct. If $F_K(X) = 0$, then $\mathcal{B}$ outputs the random bit b^* and aborts.

Responding to the Challenge-*Query.* If $F_K(X^*) = 0$, then procedure Challenge computes

$$Y^* := T^{\gamma_{q+1}} \cdot \prod_{i=1}^{q} e((g^{x^i})^{\gamma_i}, h) = T^{\gamma_{q+1}} \cdot e(g^{\sum_{i=1}^{q} \gamma_i x^i}, h)$$

where $\gamma_0, \ldots, \gamma_{q+1}$ are the coefficients of the degree-$(q + 1)$-polynomial $P_{K,n,X^*}(x) = \sum_{i=0}^{q+1} \gamma_i x^i$. Note that if $T = e(g, h)^{x^{q+1}}$, then it holds that $Y^* = V_{\mathsf{sk}}(X^*)$. Moreover, if T is uniformly random, then so is Y^*. If $F_K(X) = 1$, then $\mathcal{B}$ outputs the random bit b^* and aborts.

D   Further comparisons

We provide further comparisons like in Table 2. The results we present are calculated using the formulas stated in Table 1. Compared to Table 2, we provide key and proof sizes for $k \in \{100, 128, 256\}$ and $\epsilon \in \{2^{-25}, 2^{-50}\}$. For every combination of k and ϵ, δ is chosen such that the advantages for the instantiation using ECCs and the instantiation using TCRHFs are approximately the same. All variables have the same semantics as in Sect. 4.2. The results show that using the cAHF instantiated with a TCRHF reduces key and proof sizes significantly (Tables 3, 4, 5, 6, 7 and 8).

Table 3. Key and proof sizes for $k = 100, Q = 2^{25}, t = 2^{50}, \epsilon = 2^{-50}$ and $\delta = 0.286$. In consequence, we have $d = 154$. Puncturing a primitive $[4095, 211, 1463]$ BCH-code 408 times to a $[3687, 211, 1055]$ code yields $n^{BCH} = 3687, n_1^{BCH} = 61, n_2^{BCH} = 61$ and $\zeta^{BCH} = 13$. If an ECC on the GV bound is used, this implies $n^{GV} = 1466, n_1^{GV} = 39, n_2^{GV} = 39$ and $\zeta^{GV} = 12$. Analogously, if an ECC on the MRRW bound is used, this implies $n^{MRRW} = 719, n_1^{MRRW} = 27, n_2^{MRRW} = 27$ and $\zeta^{MRRW} = 11$. Finally, if the VRFs are instantiated with a cAHF using TCRHFs, we have $n^{tcrh} = 203, n_1^{tcrh} = 15, n_2^{tcrh} = 13, j = 153$ and $\zeta^{tcrh} = 9$.

Construction	Instantiation	$|vk|$ #G	$|sk|$ #G	$|\pi|$ #G	Adv_B
[27] Sec. 5.1	BCH	2005	2003	567966	$\approx 2^{-205}$
	GV	1851	1849	225931	$\approx 2^{-205}$
	MRRW	1697	1695	110892	$\approx 2^{-205}$
	cAHF	1380	1378	31222	$\approx 2^{-205}$
[27] Sec. 5.3	BCH	55443	2003	307	$\approx 2^{-205}$
	GV	39119	1849	307	$\approx 2^{-205}$
	MRRW	27569	1695	307	$\approx 2^{-205}$
	cAHF	13467	1378	305	$\approx 2^{-205}$
[48] Sec. 6.1	BCH	9396	154	9394	$\approx 2^{-205}$
	GV	6008	154	6006	$\approx 2^{-205}$
	MRRW	4160	154	4158	$\approx 2^{-205}$
	cAHF	2297	153	1989	$\approx 2^{-205}$
[48] Sec. 6.3	BCH	156	154	18634	$\approx 2^{-205}$
	GV	156	154	11858	$\approx 2^{-205}$
	MRRW	156	154	8162	$\approx 2^{-205}$
	cAHF	155	153	4158	$\approx 2^{-205}$
[25]	BCH	3689	7374	3688	$\approx 2^{-205}$
	GV	1468	2932	1467	$\approx 2^{-205}$
	MRRW	721	1438	720	$\approx 2^{-205}$
	cAHF	205	406	204	$\approx 2^{-205}$

Table 4. Key and proof sizes for $k = 100, Q = 2^{25}, t = 2^{50}, \epsilon = 2^{-25}$ and $\delta = 0.235$. In consequence, we have $d = 129$. Puncturing a primitive $[2047, 209, 511]$ BCH-code 39 times to a $[2008, 209, 472]$ code yields $n^{BCH} = 2008, n_1^{BCH} = 45, n_2^{BCH} = 45$ and $\zeta^{BCH} = 12$. If an ECC on the GV bound is used, this implies $n^{GV} = 938, n_1^{GV} = 31, n_2^{GV} = 31$ and $\zeta^{GV} = 11$. Analogously, if an ECC on the MRRW bound is used, this implies $n^{MRRW} = 519, n_1^{MRRW} = 23, n_2^{MRRW} = 23$ and $\zeta^{MRRW} = 11$. Finally, if the VRFs are instantiated with a cAHF using TCRHFs, we have $n^{tcrh} = 203, n_1^{tcrh} = 15, n_2^{tcrh} = 13, j = 128$ and $\zeta^{tcrh} = 9$.

Construction	Instantiation	$|vk|$ #G	$|sk|$ #G	$|\pi|$ #G	Adv_B
[27] Sec. 5.1	BCH	1551	1549	259174	$\approx 2^{-155}$
	GV	1422	1420	121143	$\approx 2^{-155}$
	MRRW	1422	1420	67092	$\approx 2^{-155}$
	cAHF	1155	1153	26122	$\approx 2^{-155}$
[27] Sec. 5.3	BCH	32769	1549	257	$\approx 2^{-155}$
	GV	23094	1420	257	$\approx 2^{-155}$
	MRRW	23094	1420	257	$\approx 2^{-155}$
	cAHF	11267	1153	255	$\approx 2^{-155}$
[48] Sec. 6.1	BCH	5807	129	5805	$\approx 2^{-155}$
	GV	4001	129	3999	$\approx 2^{-155}$
	MRRW	2969	129	2967	$\approx 2^{-155}$
	cAHF	1922	128	1664	$\approx 2^{-155}$
[48] Sec. 6.3	BCH	131	129	11481	$\approx 2^{-155}$
	GV	131	129	7869	$\approx 2^{-155}$
	MRRW	131	129	5805	$\approx 2^{-155}$
	cAHF	130	128	3483	$\approx 2^{-155}$
[25]	BCH	2010	4016	2009	$\approx 2^{-155}$
	GV	940	1876	939	$\approx 2^{-155}$
	MRRW	521	1038	520	$\approx 2^{-155}$
	cAHF	205	406	204	$\approx 2^{-155}$

Table 5. Key and proof sizes for $k = 128, Q = 2^{25}, t = 2^{50}, \epsilon = 2^{-50}$ and $\delta = 0.286$. In consequence, we have $d = 154$. Puncturing a primitive $[4095, 259, 1399]$ BCH-code 319 times to a $[3776, 259, 1080]$ code yields $n^{\text{BCH}} = 3776, n_1^{\text{BCH}} = 62, n_2^{\text{BCH}} = 62$ and $\zeta^{\text{BCH}} = 13$. If an ECC on the GV bound is used, this implies $n^{\text{GV}} = 1876, n_1^{\text{GV}} = 44, n_2^{\text{GV}} = 44$ and $\zeta^{\text{GV}} = 12$. Analogously, if an ECC on the MRRW bound is used, this implies $n^{\text{MRRW}} = 920, n_1^{\text{MRRW}} = 31, n_2^{\text{MRRW}} = 31$ and $\zeta^{\text{MRRW}} = 11$. Finally, if the VRFs are instantiated with a cAHF using TCRHFs, we have $n^{\text{tcrh}} = 259, n_1^{\text{tcrh}} = 17, n_2^{\text{tcrh}} = 15, j = 153$ and $\zeta^{\text{tcrh}} = 10$.

Construction	Instantiation	$|vk|$ #$\mathbb{G}$	$|sk|$ #$\mathbb{G}$	$|\pi|$#$\mathbb{G}$	$\text{Adv}_\mathcal{B}$
[27] Sec. 5.1	BCH	2005	2003	581672	$\approx 2^{-205}$
	GV	1851	1849	289071	$\approx 2^{-205}$
	MRRW	1697	1695	141846	$\approx 2^{-205}$
	cAHF	1533	1531	39791	$\approx 2^{-205}$
[27] Sec. 5.3	BCH	55443	2003	307	$\approx 2^{-205}$
	GV	39119	1849	307	$\approx 2^{-205}$
	MRRW	27569	1695	307	$\approx 2^{-205}$
	cAHF	19281	1531	305	$\approx 2^{-205}$
[48] Sec. 6.1	BCH	9550	154	9548	$\approx 2^{-205}$
	GV	6778	154	6776	$\approx 2^{-205}$
	MRRW	4776	154	4774	$\approx 2^{-205}$
	cAHF	2603	153	2295	$\approx 2^{-205}$
[48] Sec. 6.3	BCH	156	154	18942	$\approx 2^{-205}$
	GV	156	154	13398	$\approx 2^{-205}$
	MRRW	156	154	9394	$\approx 2^{-205}$
	cAHF	155	153	4774	$\approx 2^{-205}$
[25]	BCH	3778	7552	3777	$\approx 2^{-205}$
	GV	1878	3752	1877	$\approx 2^{-205}$
	MRRW	922	1840	921	$\approx 2^{-205}$
	cAHF	261	518	260	$\approx 2^{-205}$

Table 6. Key and proof sizes for $k = 128, Q = 2^{25}, t = 2^{50}, \epsilon = 2^{-25}$ and $\delta = 0.235$. In consequence, we have $d = 129$. Puncturing a primitive $[2047, 264, 495]$ BCH-code 18 times to a $[2029, 264, 477]$ code yields $n^{\text{BCH}} = 2029, n_1^{\text{BCH}} = 46, n_2^{\text{BCH}} = 46$ and $\zeta^{\text{BCH}} = 12$. If an ECC on the GV bound is used, this implies $n^{\text{GV}} = 1200, n_1^{\text{GV}} = 35, n_2^{\text{GV}} = 35$ and $\zeta^{\text{GV}} = 12$. Analogously, if an ECC on the MRRW bound is used, this implies $n^{\text{MRRW}} = 664, n_1^{\text{MRRW}} = 26, n_2^{\text{MRRW}} = 26$ and $\zeta^{\text{MRRW}} = 11$. Finally, if the VRFs are instantiated with a cAHF using TCRHFs, we have $n^{\text{tcrh}} = 259, n_1^{\text{tcrh}} = 17, n_2^{\text{tcrh}} = 15, j = 128$ and $\zeta^{\text{tcrh}} = 10$.

Construction	Instantiation	$|vk|$ #$\mathbb{G}$	$|sk|$ #$\mathbb{G}$	$|\pi|$#$\mathbb{G}$	$\text{Adv}_\mathcal{B}$
[27] Sec. 5.1	BCH	1551	1549	261883	$\approx 2^{-155}$
	GV	1551	1549	154942	$\approx 2^{-155}$
	MRRW	1422	1420	85797	$\approx 2^{-155}$
	cAHF	1283	1281	33291	$\approx 2^{-155}$
[27] Sec. 5.3	BCH	32769	1549	257	$\approx 2^{-155}$
	GV	32769	1549	257	$\approx 2^{-155}$
	MRRW	23094	1420	257	$\approx 2^{-155}$
	cAHF	16131	1281	255	$\approx 2^{-155}$
[48] Sec. 6.1	BCH	5936	129	5934	$\approx 2^{-155}$
	GV	4517	129	4515	$\approx 2^{-155}$
	MRRW	3356	129	3354	$\approx 2^{-155}$
	cAHF	2178	128	1920	$\approx 2^{-155}$
[48] Sec. 6.3	BCH	131	129	11739	$\approx 2^{-155}$
	GV	131	129	8901	$\approx 2^{-155}$
	MRRW	131	129	6579	$\approx 2^{-155}$
	cAHF	130	128	3999	$\approx 2^{-155}$
[25]	BCH	2031	4058	2030	$\approx 2^{-155}$
	GV	1202	2400	1201	$\approx 2^{-155}$
	MRRW	666	1328	665	$\approx 2^{-155}$
	cAHF	261	518	260	$\approx 2^{-155}$

Table 7. Key and proof sizes for $k = 256, Q = 2^{25}, t = 2^{50}, \epsilon = 2^{-50}$ and $\delta = 0.286$. In consequence, we have $d = 154$. Puncturing a primitive $[8191, 521, 2731]$ BCH-code 543 times to a $[7648, 521, 2188]$ code yields $n^{BCH} = 7648, n_1^{BCH} = 88, n_2^{BCH} = 88$ and $\zeta^{BCH} = 14$. If an ECC on the GV bound is used, this implies $n^{GV} = 3751, n_1^{GV} = 62, n_2^{GV} = 62$ and $\zeta^{GV} = 13$. Analogously, if an ECC on the MRRW bound is used, this implies $n^{MRRW} = 1840, n_1^{MRRW} = 43, n_2^{MRRW} = 43$ and $\zeta^{MRRW} = 12$. Finally, if the VRFs are instantiated with a cAHF using TCRHFs, we have $n^{tcrh} = 515, n_1^{tcrh} = 23, n_2^{tcrh} = 22, j = 153$ and $\zeta^{tcrh} = 11$.

Construction	Instantiation	$|vk|$ #G	$|sk|$ #G	$|\pi|$#G	Adv_B
[27] Sec. 5.1	BCH	2159	2157	1177961	$\approx 2^{-205}$
	GV	2005	2003	577822	$\approx 2^{-205}$
	MRRW	1851	1849	283527	$\approx 2^{-205}$
	cAHF	1686	1684	78960	$\approx 2^{-205}$
[27] Sec. 5.3	BCH	78543	2157	307	$\approx 2^{-205}$
	GV	55443	2003	307	$\approx 2^{-205}$
	MRRW	39119	1849	307	$\approx 2^{-205}$
	cAHF	27390	1684	305	$\approx 2^{-205}$
[48] Sec. 6.1	BCH	13554	154	13552	$\approx 2^{-205}$
	GV	9550	154	9548	$\approx 2^{-205}$
	MRRW	6624	154	6622	$\approx 2^{-205}$
	cAHF	3521	153	3366	$\approx 2^{-205}$
[48] Sec. 6.3	BCH	156	154	26950	$\approx 2^{-205}$
	GV	156	154	18942	$\approx 2^{-205}$
	MRRW	156	154	13090	$\approx 2^{-205}$
	cAHF	155	153	6776	$\approx 2^{-205}$
[25]	BCH	7650	15296	7649	$\approx 2^{-205}$
	GV	3753	7502	3752	$\approx 2^{-205}$
	MRRW	1842	3680	1841	$\approx 2^{-205}$
	cAHF	517	1030	516	$\approx 2^{-205}$

Table 8. Key and proof sizes for $k = 256, Q = 2^{25}, t = 2^{50}, \epsilon = 2^{-25}$ and $\delta = 0.235$. In consequence, we have $d = 129$. Puncturing a primitive $[8191, 520, 2731]$ BCH-code 1053 times to a $[7138, 520, 1678]$ code yields $n^{BCH} = 7138, n_1^{BCH} = 85, n_2^{BCH} = 85$ and $\zeta^{BCH} = 14$. If an ECC on the GV bound is used, this implies $n^{GV} = 2400, n_1^{GV} = 49, n_2^{GV} = 49$ and $\zeta^{GV} = 13$. Analogously, if an ECC on the MRRW bound is used, this implies $n^{MRRW} = 1328, n_1^{MRRW} = 37, n_2^{MRRW} = 37$ and $\zeta^{MRRW} = 12$. Finally, if the VRFs are instantiated with a cAHF using TCRHFs, we have $n^{tcrh} = 515, n_1^{tcrh} = 23, n_2^{tcrh} = 22, j = 128$ and $\zeta^{tcrh} = 11$.

Construction	Instantiation	$|vk|$ #G	$|sk|$ #G	$|\pi|$#G	Adv_B
[27] Sec. 5.1	BCH	1809	1807	920946	$\approx 2^{-155}$
	GV	1680	1678	309743	$\approx 2^{-155}$
	MRRW	1551	1549	171454	$\approx 2^{-155}$
	cAHF	1411	1409	66060	$\approx 2^{-155}$
[27] Sec. 5.3	BCH	65793	1807	257	$\approx 2^{-155}$
	GV	46443	1678	257	$\approx 2^{-155}$
	MRRW	32769	1549	257	$\approx 2^{-155}$
	cAHF	22915	1409	255	$\approx 2^{-155}$
[48] Sec. 6.1	BCH	10967	129	10965	$\approx 2^{-155}$
	GV	6323	129	6321	$\approx 2^{-155}$
	MRRW	4775	129	4773	$\approx 2^{-155}$
	cAHF	2946	128	2816	$\approx 2^{-155}$
[48] Sec. 6.3	BCH	131	129	21801	$\approx 2^{-155}$
	GV	131	129	12513	$\approx 2^{-155}$
	MRRW	131	129	9417	$\approx 2^{-155}$
	cAHF	130	128	5676	$\approx 2^{-155}$
[25]	BCH	7140	14276	7139	$\approx 2^{-155}$
	GV	2402	4800	2401	$\approx 2^{-155}$
	MRRW	1330	2656	1329	$\approx 2^{-155}$
	cAHF	517	1030	516	$\approx 2^{-155}$

References

1. Abdalla, M., Fiore, D., Lyubashevsky, V.: From selective to full security: semi-generic transformations in the standard model. In: Fischlin, M., Buchmann, J., Manulis, M. (eds.) PKC 2012. LNCS, vol. 7293, pp. 316–333. Springer, Heidelberg (2012). https://doi.org/10.1007/978-3-642-30057-8_19
2. Attrapadung, N., Matsuda, T., Nishimaki, R., Yamada, S., Yamakawa, T.: Adaptively single-key secure constrained PRFs for NC1. IACR Cryptol. ePrint Arch. **2018**, 1000 (2018)
3. Attrapadung, N., Matsuda, T., Nishimaki, R., Yamada, S., Yamakawa, T.: Constrained PRFs for NC^1 in traditional groups. In: Shacham, H., Boldyreva, A. (eds.) CRYPTO 2018. LNCS, vol. 10992, pp. 543–574. Springer, Cham (2018). https://doi.org/10.1007/978-3-319-96881-0_19
4. Bellare, M., Ristenpart, T.: Simulation without the artificial abort: simplified proof and improved concrete security for waters' IBE scheme. In: Joux, A. (ed.) EUROCRYPT 2009. LNCS, vol. 5479, pp. 407–424. Springer, Heidelberg (2009). https://doi.org/10.1007/978-3-642-01001-9_24
5. Bellare, M., Rogaway, P.: Random oracles are practical: a paradigm for designing efficient protocols. In: Denning, D.E., Pyle, R., Ganesan, R., Sandhu, R.S., Ashby, V. (eds.) ACM CCS 93, pp. 62–73. ACM Press (November 1993)
6. Bellare, M., Rogaway, P.: The exact security of digital signatures-how to sign with RSA and Rabin. In: Maurer, U. (ed.) EUROCRYPT 1996. LNCS, vol. 1070, pp. 399–416. Springer, Heidelberg (1996). https://doi.org/10.1007/3-540-68339-9_34
7. Bitansky, N.: Verifiable random functions from non-interactive witness-indistinguishable proofs. In: Kalai, Y., Reyzin, L. (eds.) TCC 2017. LNCS, vol. 10678, pp. 567–594. Springer, Cham (2017). https://doi.org/10.1007/978-3-319-70503-3_19
8. Boneh, D., Boyen, X.: Efficient selective-ID secure identity-based encryption without random oracles. In: Cachin, C., Camenisch, J.L. (eds.) EUROCRYPT 2004. LNCS, vol. 3027, pp. 223–238. Springer, Heidelberg (2004). https://doi.org/10.1007/978-3-540-24676-3_14
9. Boneh, D., Boyen, X.: Secure identity based encryption without random oracles. In: Franklin, M. (ed.) CRYPTO 2004. LNCS, vol. 3152, pp. 443–459. Springer, Heidelberg (2004). https://doi.org/10.1007/978-3-540-28628-8_27
10. Boneh, D., Franklin, M.K.: Identity based encryption from the Weil pairing. SIAM J. Comput. **32**(3), 586–615 (2003)
11. Boneh, D., Lynn, B., Shacham, H.: Short signatures from the Weil pairing. J. Cryptol. **17**(4), 297–319 (2004)
12. Canetti, R., Goldreich, O., Halevi, S.: The random oracle methodology, revisited. J. ACM **51**(4), 557–594 (2004)
13. Cash, D., Hofheinz, D., Kiltz, E., Peikert, C.: Bonsai trees, or how to delegate a lattice basis. J. Cryptol. **25**(4), 601–639 (2012)
14. Chen, Y., Huang, Q., Zhang, Z.: Sakai-Ohgishi-kasahara identity-based non-interactive key exchange revisited and more. Int. J. Inf. Secur. **15**(1), 15–33 (2016)
15. Cheon, J.H.: Security analysis of the strong Diffie-Hellman problem. In: Vaudenay, S. (ed.) EUROCRYPT 2006. LNCS, vol. 4004, pp. 1–11. Springer, Heidelberg (2006). https://doi.org/10.1007/11761679_1
16. Dumer, I., Micciancio, D., Sudan, M.: Hardness of approximating the minimum distance of a linear code. In: 40th Annual Symposium on Foundations of Computer Science, FOCS 1999, 17–18 October, 1999, New York, NY, USA, pp. 475–485. IEEE Computer Society (1999)

17. Freire, E.S.V., Hofheinz, D., Paterson, K.G., Striecks, C.: Programmable hash functions in the multilinear setting. In: Canetti, R., Garay, J.A. (eds.) CRYPTO 2013. LNCS, vol. 8042, pp. 513–530. Springer, Heidelberg (2013). https://doi.org/10.1007/978-3-642-40041-4_28

18. Gilad, Y., Hemo, R., Micali, S., Vlachos, G., Zeldovich, N.: Algorand: scaling byzantine agreements for cryptocurrencies. In: Proceedings of the 26th Symposium on Operating Systems Principles, Shanghai, China, October 28–31, 2017, pp. 51–68. ACM (2017)

19. Gilbert, E.N.: A comparison of signalling alphabets. Bell Syst. Tech. J. **31**, 504–522 (1952)

20. Goldberg, S., Reyzin, L., Papadopoulos, D., Vcelak, J.: Verifiable random functions (VRFs). Internet-Draft draft-irtf-cfrg-vrf-04, IETF Secretariat, February 2019. http://www.ietf.org/internet-drafts/draft-irtf-cfrg-vrf-04.txt

21. Grassl, M.: Bounds on the minimum distance of linear codes and quantum codes (2007). http://www.codetables.de. Accessed 20 Jan 2019

22. Hofheinz, D., Jager, T.: Verifiable random functions from standard assumptions. In: Kushilevitz, E., Malkin, T. (eds.) TCC 2016. LNCS, vol. 9562, pp. 336–362. Springer, Heidelberg (2016). https://doi.org/10.1007/978-3-662-49096-9_14

23. Hofheinz, D., Jager, T., Kiltz, E.: Short signatures from weaker assumptions. In: Lee, D.H., Wang, X. (eds.) ASIACRYPT 2011. LNCS, vol. 7073, pp. 647–666. Springer, Heidelberg (2011). https://doi.org/10.1007/978-3-642-25385-0_35

24. Hofheinz, D., Kiltz, E.: Programmable hash functions and their applications. J. Cryptol. **25**(3), 484–527 (2012)

25. Jager, T.: Verifiable random functions from weaker assumptions. In: Dodis, Y., Nielsen, J.B. (eds.) TCC 2015. LNCS, vol. 9015, pp. 121–143. Springer, Heidelberg (2015). https://doi.org/10.1007/978-3-662-46497-7_5

26. Jager, T., Kurek, R.: Short digital signatures and ID-KEMs via truncation collision resistance. In: Peyrin, T., Galbraith, S. (eds.) ASIACRYPT 2018. LNCS, vol. 11273, pp. 221–250. Springer, Cham (2018). https://doi.org/10.1007/978-3-030-03329-3_8

27. Katsumata, S.: On the untapped potential of encoding predicates by arithmetic circuits and their applications. In: Takagi, T., Peyrin, T. (eds.) ASIACRYPT 2017. LNCS, vol. 10626, pp. 95–125. Springer, Cham (2017). https://doi.org/10.1007/978-3-319-70700-6_4

28. Katz, J., Lindell, Y.: Introduction to Modern Cryptography. Chapman and Hall/CRC Press, Boca Raton (2007)

29. Kohl, L.: Hunting and gathering – verifiable random functions from standard assumptions with short proofs. In: Lin, D., Sako, K. (eds.) PKC 2019. LNCS, vol. 11443, pp. 408–437. Springer, Cham (2019). https://doi.org/10.1007/978-3-030-17259-6_14

30. Libert, B., Stehlé, D., Titiu, R.: Adaptively secure distributed PRFs from LWE. In: Beimel, A., Dziembowski, S. (eds.) TCC 2018. LNCS, vol. 11240, pp. 391–421. Springer, Cham (2018). https://doi.org/10.1007/978-3-030-03810-6_15

31. Lysyanskaya, A.: Unique signatures and verifiable random functions from the DH-DDH separation. In: Yung, M. (ed.) CRYPTO 2002. LNCS, vol. 2442, pp. 597–612. Springer, Heidelberg (2002). https://doi.org/10.1007/3-540-45708-9_38

32. MacWilliams, F.J., Sloane, N.J.A.: The Theory of Error Correcting Codes, 10th edn. North Holland Mathematical Library, Amsterdam (1998)

33. McEliece, R.J., Rodemich, E.R., Rumsey Jr., H., Welch, L.R.: New upper bounds on the rate of a code via the Delsarte-MacWilliams inequalities. IEEE Trans. Inf. Theory **23**(2), 157–166 (1977)

34. Melara, M.S., Blankstein, A., Bonneau, J., Felten, E.W., Freedman, M.J.: CONIKS: bringing key transparency to end users. In: Jung, J., Holz, T. (eds.) USENIX Security 2015, pp. 383–398. USENIX Association (August 2015)
35. Micali, S., Rabin, M.O., Vadhan, S.P.: Verifiable random functions. In: 40th FOCS, pp. 120–130. IEEE Computer Society Press (October 1999)
36. National Institute of Standards and Technology. FIPS PUB 180–4: Secure hash standard, August 2015. https://doi.org/10.6028/NIST.FIPS.180-4
37. National Institute of Standards and Technology. FIPS PUB 202: SHA-3 standard: permutation-based hash and extendable-output functions, August 2015. https://doi.org/10.6028/NIST.FIPS.202
38. Papadopoulos, D., et al.: Making NSEC5 practical for DNSSEC. Cryptol. ePrint Arch. Rep. **2017**, 099 (2017). http://eprint.iacr.org/2017/099
39. Peterson, W.W., Weldon, E.J.: Error-Correcting Codes, 2nd edn. MIT Press, Cambridge (1988). 9 print edition
40. Shoup, V.: Sequences of games: a tool for taming complexity in security proofs. Cryptol. ePrint Arch. Rep. **2004**, 332 (2004). http://eprint.iacr.org/2004/332
41. Shum, K.W., Aleshnikov, I., Kumar, P.V., Stichtenoth, H., Deolalikar, V.: A low-complexity algorithm for the construction of algebraic-geometric codes better than the Gilbert-Varshamov bound. IEEE Trans. Inf. Theory **47**(6), 2225–2241 (2001)
42. Sipser, M., Spielman, D.A.: Expander codes. IEEE Trans. Inf. Theory **42**(6), 1710–1722 (1996)
43. Ta-Shma, A.: Explicit, almost optimal, epsilon-balanced codes. In: Hatami, H., McKenzie, P., King, V. (eds.) Proceedings of the 49th Annual ACM SIGACT Symposium on Theory of Computing, STOC 2017, Montreal, QC, Canada, June 19–23, 2017, pp. 238–251. ACM (2017)
44. Vardy, A.: The intractability of computing the minimum distance of a code. IEEE Trans. Inf. Theory **43**(6), 1757–1766 (1997)
45. Varshamov, R.R.: Estimate of the number of signals in error correcting codes. Docklady Acad. Nauk SSSR **117**(5), 739–741 (1957)
46. Vcelak, J., Goldberg, S., Papadopoulos, D., Huque, S., Lawrence, D.: NSEC5, DNSSEC authenticated denial of existence. Internet-Draft draft-vcelak-nsec5-08, IETF Secretariat, December 2018. http://www.ietf.org/internet-drafts/draft-vcelak-nsec5-08.txt
47. Waters, B.: Efficient identity-based encryption without random oracles. In: Cramer, R. (ed.) EUROCRYPT 2005. LNCS, vol. 3494, pp. 114–127. Springer, Heidelberg (2005). https://doi.org/10.1007/11426639_7
48. Yamada, S.: Asymptotically compact adaptively secure lattice IBEs and verifiable random functions via generalized partitioning techniques. In: Katz, J., Shacham, H. (eds.) CRYPTO 2017. LNCS, vol. 10403, pp. 161–193. Springer, Cham (2017). https://doi.org/10.1007/978-3-319-63697-9_6
49. Zémor, G.: On expander codes. IEEE Trans. Inf. Theory **47**(2), 835–837 (2001)

Stream Ciphers and Lightweight Cryptography

Tight Security Bounds for Generic Stream Cipher Constructions

Matthias Hamann[(✉)], Matthias Krause, and Alexander Moch

Universität Mannheim, Mannheim, Germany
{hamann,krause,moch}@uni-mannheim.de

Abstract. The design of modern stream ciphers is strongly influenced by the fact that Time-Memory-Data tradeoff (TMD-TO) attacks reduce their effective key length to half of the inner state length. The classical solution is to design the cipher in accordance with the LARGE-STATE-SMALL-KEY principle, which implies that the state length is at least twice as large as the session key length. In lightweight cryptography, considering heavily resource-constrained devices, a large amount of inner state cells is a big drawback for these type of constructions.

Recent stream cipher proposals like Lizard, Sprout, Plantlet and Fruit employ new techniques to avoid a large inner state size. However, when considering indistinguishability, none of the ciphers mentioned above provide a security above the birthday barrier with regard to the state length.

In this paper, we present a formal indistinguishability framework for proving lower bounds on the resistance of generic stream cipher constructions against TMD-TO attacks. In particular, we first present a tight lower bound on constructions underlying the LARGE-STATE-SMALL-KEY principle. Further, we show a close to optimal lower bound of stream cipher constructions continuously using the initial value during keystream generation. These constructions would allow to shorten the inner state size significantly and hence the resource requirements of the cipher. We thus believe that CONTINUOUS-IV-USE constructions are a hopeful direction of future research.

Keywords: Symmetric-key cryptography · Indistinguishability · Random oracle model · Provable security · Stream cipher · Lightweight cryptography

1 Introduction

STREAM CIPHERS. When considering symmetric encryption schemes one distinguishes two types: block ciphers and stream ciphers. The former work on large blocks of data simultaneously while the latter consider the data as a stream of individual bits and maintain an internal state to change the cipher at each step. The advantage of stream ciphers is that in many application scenarios, their resource requirements are lower than those of block ciphers. This makes them particularly useful in lightweight cryptography. Instances of stream ciphers

© Springer Nature Switzerland AG 2020
K. G. Paterson and D. Stebila (Eds.): SAC 2019, LNCS 11959, pp. 335–364, 2020.
https://doi.org/10.1007/978-3-030-38471-5_14

are used in the GSM cellular telephone standard (A5/1), Bluetooth (E0) and wireless networking (RC4).

Current stream ciphers are vulnerable to Time-Memory-Data tradeoff attacks. [6,8,19] These attacks reduce the effective security to one half of the inner state size. This influences the design of modern stream ciphers such that the inner state size is at least twice the size of the desired security level. We refer to these construction by LARGE-STATE-SMALL-KEY. This is in stark contrast to the lightweight principle of stream ciphers, since a larger state necessarily increases resource requirements. Stream ciphers that correspond to the LARGE-STATE-SMALL-KEY construction are the eSTREAM portfolio members Trivium [11] and Grain v1 [24].

RECENT WORK. Recently, efforts have been made to reduce the inner state size while still retaining a reasonable security level. Three generic constructions have been proposed: (1) the LIZARD construction [20], (2) the CONTINUOUS-KEY-USE construction, and (3) the CONTINUOUS-IV-USE construction. The LIZARD construction aims to prevent attacks that recover the secret inner state of the cipher. While the security to prevent inner state recovery is $2/3 \cdot$ SL, where SL is the state length, the security against distinguishing attacks remains at $1/2 \cdot$ SL. A stream cipher based on the LIZARD construction can be found in [22]. The CONTINUOUS-KEY-USE construction uses the non-volatile secret key not only for initialization, as is common, but also during the keystream generation. The stream ciphers Plantlet [28], Fruit [1], and Sprout [4] are based on the CONTINUOUS-KEY-USE construction. The CONTINUOUS-IV-USE construction similarly uses the initial value during keystream generation as well. It was first proposed in [21]. There are no stream ciphers based on the CONTINUOUS-IV-USE construction so far as this scheme is relatively new.

Very recently, it came to light that the CONTINUOUS-KEY-USE construction does not fulfill the expectations. By giving a corresponding attack, it was shown in [23] that the resistance of the CONTINUOUS-KEY-USE construction against generic TMD-TO distinguishing attacks is only half of the internal state's size. This once more emphasizes the importance of equipping serious proposals for new stream ciphers with lower bound proofs on their security against TMD-TO attacks, and we hope that our paper represents a valuable contribution in this context.

CONTRIBUTION. While, in the last decade, a large number of formal security bounds based on random oracle models (ROMs) have been shown for constructions like block ciphers [3,9,12,13,17,26], modes of operation of block ciphers [7,31,32], or message authentication codes [14–16,18,27,29], comparatively little is known about ROM-based approaches to provable stream cipher security.

In this paper, we present a ROM-based approach for analyzing the security of keystream generator-based (KSG-based) stream ciphers against generic attacks. Our focus is on indistinguishability. These lower bounds prove that generic attacks, in particular Time-Memory-Data tradeoff (TMD-TO) attacks, with a complexity lower than the bounds given cannot be successful. Specifically, we prove that the bound of $1/2 \cdot$ SL of the LARGE-STATE-SMALL-KEY construction is tight. Further, we provide a lower bound on the CONTINUOUS-IV-USE construction that is close to optimal with regard to key length but uses a smaller volatile state compared to the LARGE-STATE-SMALL-KEY construction. For future stream ciphers built upon the CONTINUOUS-IV-USE construction it may thus be possible to reduce the volatile state size significantly. As of writing of this paper, the idea of continuously using the IV during keystream generation has not yet been instantiated as the idea of this scheme is relatively new [21]. The purpose of the proof of security for the CONTINUOUS-IV-USE construction in this work is to provide guidance to the stream cipher designer as it will ensure the resistance of the stream cipher against generic attacks. We thus see the CONTINUOUS-IV-USE construction as a hopeful direction of future research and a possible paradigm for the instantiation of new stream ciphers.

OUTLINE. In Sect. 2 we provide the basics to stream ciphers. In Sect. 3 we present the basics of TMD-TO attacks to the reader. In Sect. 4 we give an overview of our model and state our results in detail. In Sect. 5 we introduce the random oracle model that we will be working with. In Sect. 6 we provide the analysis to establish the lower bounds. In Sect. 7 we conclude our analysis.

2 Stream Cipher Basics

Stream ciphers are symmetric encryption algorithms intended for the online encryption of plaintext bitstreams X which have to pass an insecure channel. The encryption is performed via bitwise addition of a keystream $S = S(k, \text{IV})$. The keystream S is generated in dependence of a secret symmetric session key k and, possibly, a public initial value IV. The legal recipient, who also knows the secret k, decrypts the encrypted bitstream $Y = X \oplus S$ by generating S and computing $X = Y \oplus S$. In this paper, we consider KSG-based stream ciphers, i.e., stream ciphers which generate the keystream using a so-called keystream generator (KSG).

KSGs are stepwise working devices which can be formally specified by finite automata. These finite automata are defined by an inner state length SL and the corresponding set of inner states $\{0,1\}^{\text{SL}}$, a state update function $\pi : \{0,1\}^{\text{SL}} \to \{0,1\}^{\text{SL}}$, and an output function $\text{out} : \{0,1\}^{\text{SL}} \to \{0,1\}$. Starting from an initial state q_0, in each clock cycle $i \geq 0$, the KSG produces a keystream bit $z_i = \text{out}(q_i)$ and changes the inner state according to $q_{i+1} = \pi(q_i)$. The output bitstream $S(q_0)$ is defined by concatenating all the outputs $z_1 z_2 z_3 \cdots$.

In the context of TMD-TO security, it is convenient to express the output behavior of a stream cipher by the function $\text{OUTBLOCK} : \{0,1\}^{\text{SL}} \to \{0,1\}^{\text{SL}}$, which is defined by π and out. OUTBLOCK assigns to each inner state $q \in \{0,1\}^{\text{SL}}$ the block of the first SL keystream bits generated on q:

$$\text{OUTBLOCK}(q) = \left(\text{out}(\pi^0(q)), \ldots, \text{out}(\pi^{\text{SL}-1}(q))\right).$$

2.1 Keystream Generation

The keystream generation process of a KSG-based stream cipher usually depends on a further parameter, the packet length PL $\geq$ SL. We will elaborate on the packet length further down. The keystream generation process can be divided into the following four phases:

(1) **The session key generation phase:** The secret session key $k \in \{0,1\}^{\text{KL}}$ is generated by running a key-exchange protocol between the legal communication partners. This phase will *not* be considered in this paper.

(2) **The loading phase:** The session key k, an initial value IV $\in \{0,1\}^{\text{IVL}}$, and, possibly, some constants are loaded into the inner state register cells of the KSG. This phase results in a state $q_{\text{load}} = q_{\text{load}}(\text{IV}, k) \in \{0,1\}^{\text{SL}}$.

(3) **The mixing phase:** Using a so-called mixing algorithm MIX : $\{0,1\}^{\text{SL}} \to \{0,1\}^{\text{SL}}$, the KSG transforms the loading state q_{load} into the initial state

$$q_{\text{init}}(\text{IV}, k) = \text{MIX}(q_{\text{load}}(\text{IV}, k)).$$

During this procedure, the KSG does not output any keystream bits. MIX aims to provide a sufficiently large amount of diffusion, confusion, and a high algebraic degree in the dependencies of the initial state bits from the session key and initial value bits.

(4) **The output phase:** The keystream packet corresponding to k and IV, consisting of the first PL bits of the keystream $S(q_{\text{init}}(\text{IV}, k))$, is generated in the way described above.

One distinguishes stream ciphers which work in one stream mode (like Trivium [11] or Grain v1 [24]) and stream ciphers that work in packet mode (like the GSM standard $A5/1$ [10] or LIZARD [22]). In the following differentiation, *session length* denotes the number of keystream bits that need to be encrypted under a single (session) key.

ONE-STREAM MODE. In the one-stream mode, the packet length is defined to be larger than the session length. So, the keystream for encrypting the communication of one session is the prefix of only one keystream packet and only one initial value per session is needed.

PACKET MODE. In the packet mode, the packet length is defined to be much shorter than the session length and the keystream is a concatenation of packets. For each packet, the initialization algorithm (phases (2) and (3)) has to be restarted with a new initial value. The motivation underlying this approach is that in many real-world communication scenarios (Ethernet, WLAN, Bluetooth, cellular networks etc.) data streams are transmitted packet-wise. It thus seems natural to consider stream ciphers running in packet mode and, in particular, to look for corresponding design optimizations.

2.2 Large-State-Small-Key Ciphers

To illustrate the LARGE-STATE-SMALL-KEY construction, we give a rough description of the stream ciphers Trivium and Grain v1, which belong to the final portfolio of the eSTREAM contest [5].

Trivium: The stream cipher Trivium has an inner state length of $L = 288$ bits, distributed over three nonlinear feedback shift registers (NFSRs) of lengths 93, 84, and 111 bits. The state update function consists of the corresponding three feedback functions. The feedback functions are quadratic and take their inputs from two of the three NFSRs. The linear output function produces one keystream bit per clock cycle. It XORs six inner state bits, two from each NFSR. The loading state $q_{\text{load}}(\text{IV}, k)$ is defined to be the concatenation of the 80-bit session key k, the 80-bit initial value IV, and a predefined 128-bit constant CONST. The MIX operation consists of clocking the KSG $4 \cdot 288$ times without producing output. We refer the interested reader to [11] for more details.

Grain v1: The stream cipher Grain v1 has an inner state length of $L = 160$ bits, distributed over one NFSR and one linear feedback shift register (LFSR), both of length 80 bits. The state update function consists of the corresponding two feedback functions, where the NFSR feedback function depends also on one of the LFSR bits. Again, the output function produces one keystream bit per clock cycle and depends nonlinearly on five LFSR bits and one NFSR bit and linearly on further seven NFSR bits. The loading state $q_{\text{load}}(\text{IV}, k)$ is defined to be the concatenation of the 80-bit session key k, the 64-bit initial value IV, and a predefined 16-bit constant CONST. In the mixing phase, the Grain-KSG is clocked 160 times, where, in each clock cycle, the corresponding output keystream bit is XORed to the result of each of the two feedback functions (see [24] for more details).

In both cases we obtain that the SL-block of bits r to $r + \text{SL} - 1$ of the keystream packet corresponding to k and IV can be expressed as

$$\text{OUTBLOCK}(\pi^r(\text{MIX}(\text{IV}, \text{CONST}, k))).$$

2.3 Continous-IV-Use Ciphers

For the CONTINUOUS-IV-USE construction, which is also treated in this paper, a concrete instantiation has yet do be designed. However, as a part of introducing the general idea of continuously using the IV during keystream generation, the authors of [21] conjecture that "cyclically XORing one IV bit per step to the volatile inner state" would already be sufficient. This actually corresponds to the way how the secret key is employed in the CONTINUOUS-KEY-USE stream cipher Plantlet. In each step, Plantlet cyclically XORs one of the 80 key bits to the register feedback of one of its two feedback shift registers.

3 Time-Memory-Data Tradeoff Attacks and Small State Ciphers

During the last decades, many different techniques for cryptanalyzing KSG-based stream ciphers have been developed; correlation attacks, fast correlation attacks, guess-and-verify attacks, BDD attacks, cube attacks, etc. Attacks on stream ciphers typically refer to a known-IV scenario: The attacker knows a set $\mathcal{S}$ of keystream blocks having their origin in one session with secret session key k. The keystream blocks were generated with respect to a set of known initial values. Typical goals of attacks on stream ciphers are to distinguish $\mathcal{S}$ from a set of blocks coming from a truly random source, to recover the inner state responsible for at least one keystream block contained in $\mathcal{S}$, or to predict a keystream packet corresponding to k and a new initial value IV.

TMD-TO attacks are generic in the sense that they have only black-box access to the component functions MIX and OUTBLOCK. TMD-TO attacks are often divided into a precomputation phase, in which some helping data structure is computed, and an online phase, in which on the basis of the keystream available for the attack and the helping data structure the goal of the attack is reached. The relevant costs of a TMD-TO attack are typically measured in the four cost dimensions D (the amount keystream/data available in the online phase), T (the time consumption of the online phase), P (the time consumption of the precomputation phase), and M (the memory consumption including the size of the helping data structure). The costs are expressed in a so-called tradeoff curve, consisting of all 4-tuples (T, M, D, P) of cost values, which allow to reach the goal of the attack with high probability. For attacks without a precomputation phase, the cost dimension P is not considered.

The first TMD-TO attacks against KSG-based stream ciphers go back to Babbage [6] and Golić [19]. They yield the tradeoff curve $T \cdot D = 2^{\text{SL}}$, containing the point $T = D = 2^{\text{SL}/2}$. We describe the idea of these attacks below. Biryukov and Shamir [8] combined the idea of the attacks of Babbage and Golić with the idea of Hellman's attack on block ciphers [25], yielding an attack with tradeoff curve $T \cdot M^2 \cdot D^2 = 2^{2 \cdot \text{SL}}$ with $P = 2^{\text{SL}}/D$. In [20], a TMD-TO key recovery attack without precomputation phase against the LIZARD construction is presented. This attack is successful with high probability for $T = D = M = 2^{2/3 \cdot \text{SL}}$ and matches the lower bound shown in the same paper.

In our security proofs, we derive lower bounds on the overall time consumption $T + P$. These bounds apply to all TMD-TO attacks against the respective construction. Note that $M, D \leq T+P$ always applies, as occupied memory blocks are the result of operations covered by P or T and, similarly, data blocks not treated by corresponding operations would be of no use. Furthermore, we refer to chosen-IV attackers. Chosen-IV attackers have access to blocks of keystream packets generated with respect to initial values of the attacker's choice.

3.1 The TMD-TO Attack of Babbage and Golić

For illustration purposes, we describe the classical TMD-TO attack of Babbage [6] and Golić [19]: Suppose that the attacker knows a set $\mathcal{S}$ of D keystream blocks of length SL. These blocks originate from one session with the secret session key k. Let $Q = \{q^1, \cdots, q^D\}$ denote the set of corresponding inner states. The attacker generates a set of T pairs $(y, \text{OUTBLOCK}(y))$ for randomly chosen inner states $y \in \{0, 1\}^{\text{SL}}$. If $D \cdot T \approx 2^{\text{SL}}$, there will be a collision with high probability, i.e., some y falls into Q, which implies that OUTBLOCK(y) falls into S. As a result, the attacker knows the inner state q^j corresponding to one keystream block of a packet generated with respect to a known initial value IV. This allows to compute the whole keystream packet corresponding to k and IV. It also allows to recover the initial state $q_{init}(IV, k)$ for this packet. Moreover, for Trivium, Grain v1, and many other ciphers, it is possible to efficiently recover k from $q_{init}(IV, k)$.

By choosing $D = T = 2^{SL/2}$, we obtain an attack which lowers the security level of the respective cipher to SL/2, as it consumes data, time, and memory of at most $2^{SL/2}$. Consequently, to reach the desired security level of the length of the secret session key, KL, classical stream ciphers have to use an inner state length SL of at least $2 \cdot$ KL.

In Sect. 6, we analyze a generic LARGE-STATE-SMALL-KEY construction with SL = VSL = IVL + CONSTL + KL, $q_{load}(IV, k) = (IV|CONST|k)$, and $q_{init}(IV, k) =$ MIX$(IV|CONST|k)$. For this construction, exhaustive key search and the Babbage-Golić attack yield an upper bound of min{KL, SL/2}. The first main result of this paper is to show a nearly tight[1] lower bound for this upper bound w.r.t. TMD-TO attacks. We refer the reader to inequality 3 in Sect. 4.

3.2 New Stream Cipher Constructions

As already mentioned, the search for constructions yielding a TMD-TO resistance beyond SL/2 has led to three generic constructions so far: the LIZARD-construction, the CONTINUOUS-KEY-USE construction, and the CONTINUOUS-IV-USE construction. We will briefly describe these constructions and how to perform the corresponding TMD-TO attacks.

LIZARD construction implies to run a stream cipher with SL = KL = IVL in packet mode with packet length PL, where the packet initial states are computed according to $q_{init}(IV, k) = $ MIX$(k \oplus IV) \oplus k$. This does not prevent recovering the initial state of *one* of at least $2^{SL/2}/$PL known keystream packets (i.e., $2^{SL/2}$ bits of known data in total) by applying the Babbage-Golić attack with TMD-cost $2^{SL/2}$. However, one can prove beyond-the-birthday-bound resistance against key recovery and packet prediction attacks. More precisely, by considering a random oracle model approach similar to the one employed here, a corresponding $2/3 \cdot$ SL lower bound was shown in [20]. This justified the proposal of the stream cipher LIZARD [22], which uses an inner state length of SL = 121.

CONTINUOUS-KEY-USE construction means that the secret session key is continuously employed during keystream generation and thus becomes a non-volatile part of the cipher's inner state. This principle underlies the stream cipher proposals Sprout [4] (SL = 167 and VSL = 87), Plantlet [28] (SL = 188 and VSL = 108), and Fruit [1] (SL = 167 and VSL = 87). Remember here that for CONTINUOUS-KEY-USE (and CONTINUOUS-IV-USE) constructions, we have to distinguish between SL, the size of the full inner state, and

---

[1] Up to a factor of $2 \cdot$ SL w.r.t. attack complexity $2^{SL/2}$.

VSL, the size of its volatile part. In particular, depending on the concrete instantiation, also (possibly secret) counters used, e.g., for key/IV bit selection, can become part of the volatile inner state if they influence the state update during keystream generation (see, e.g., [23] for further details).

Very recently, it could be shown in [23] that the resistance of CONTINUOUS-KEY-USE ciphers against generic TMD-TO distinguishing attacks does not exceed VSL/2. In the following, we give a rough description of the corresponding approach. Note that at the beginning of the corresponding oracle game, in the pseudorandom case, the oracle randomly and independently chooses a secret session key on the basis of which it henceforth provides its replies.

First, the attacker obtains $2^{VSL/2}$ consecutive keystream blocks (each of length $\tilde{n}$ slightly larger than VSL) from about $2^{VSL/2}$ bits of keystream provided by the oracle (possibly generated under a single IV) and stores these blocks in an efficiently searchable data structure.[2] Then, for $2^{VSL/2}$ randomly and independently chosen IVs, he obtains the corresponding $\tilde{n}$-bit keystream prefix from the oracle. Due to the birthday paradox, in the pseudorandom scenario, he is likely to find a collision of one of the keystream prefixes generated in the second step with one of the keystream blocks stored in the first step. This holds as the session key is fixed and thus all inner states differ only in the volatile part. Hence, with high probability, some *initial state* underlying one of the keystream prefixes of the second step will be identical to some *inner state* underlying one of the keystream blocks from the first step. As $\tilde{n} > VSL$, this allows to distinguish the cipher from a truly random source in a generic way. For a detailed description of this attack, we refer the reader to [23].

CONTINUOUS-IV-USE construction (as suggested in [21]) refers to a cipher working in packet mode with packet length PL where the IV is continuously employed during keystream generation and thus becomes a non-volatile, publicly known part of the cipher's inner state. It can be easily checked that the above attack against CONTINUOUS-KEY-USE ciphers cannot be applied to CONTINUOUS-IV-USE.

In Sect. 6, we will analyze a variant of the CONTINUOUS-IV-USE construction in which the cipher, as in the case of Trivium and Grain v1, uses besides the IV and the secret key a public constant $\{0,1\}$-string CONST of bitlength CONSTL. The concatenation of CONST and the secret key is loaded into the volatile part of the inner state.[3] The IV forms the non-volatile part of the inner state. The non-volatile part of the inner state remains unchanged during loading, mixing, and the generation of a keystream packet. Correspondingly, we set SL = IVL + VSL and VSL = CONSTL + KL. We assume that

$$CONSTL = \log_2(PL) \tag{1}$$

---

[2] That is, he slides an $\tilde{n}$-bit window over the given keystream.

[3] In a previous version of our construction, instead of using a constant CONST, the IV was extended by CONSTL bits and these bits were loaded into the volatile part of the inner state. This allowed a chosen-IV attacker to generate more utilizable keystream bits than intended and was exploited in [2]. The above specification of our construction fixes this issue and the approach from [2] is no longer applicable.

and
$$\text{IVL} \geq \text{VSL} - 2 \cdot \text{CONSTL} = \text{KL} - \text{CONSTL} = \text{KL} - \log_2(\text{PL}). \qquad (2)$$

For all keys $k \in \{0,1\}^{\text{KL}}$ and initial values $\text{IV} \in \{0,1\}^{\text{IVL}}$, it holds $q_{\text{load}}(\text{IV}, k) = (\text{IV}|\text{CONST}|k)$ and $q_{\text{init}}(\text{IV}, k) = \text{MIX}(\text{IV}|\text{CONST}|k)$. As pointed out above, we assume that MIX leaves the non-volatile part of the state constant. The reason for considering this particular variant of the CONTINUOUS-IV-USE construction will be explained now.

Note that there are two ways of applying the Babbage-Golić TMD-TO attack to this cipher. The first approach is to mount the attack in its original form, which does not take the special structure of inner states into account. This attack has the tradeoff curve $T \cdot D = 2^{\text{SL}}$, yielding the point $T = D = 2^{\text{SL}/2} = 2^{(\text{IVL}+\text{VSL})/2}$.

The second approach is to make use of the fact that the IVs for the keystream packets are publicly known. Let us hence assume that the keystream data consists of U keystream packets of length PL corresponding to the initial values $\text{IV}^{(1)}, \cdots, \text{IV}^{(U)}$. Note that U is variable, PL is constant, and the resulting data complexity is $D = U \cdot \text{PL}$. The attacker now generates at most S times a random state $z \in \{0,1\}^{\text{VSL}}$ and computes $\text{OUTBLOCK}(\text{IV}^{(u)}, z)$ for all $u, 1 \leq u \leq U$, until a collision with the data occurs. This attack has the time complexity $T = U \cdot S$ and, based on the birthday paradox, needs to satisfy $U \cdot \text{PL} \cdot S \geq 2^{\text{VSL}}$, i.e., $T \geq 2^{\text{VSL}}/\text{PL}$. The best choice for an attacker is thus $S = 2^{\text{VSL}}/\text{PL}$ and $U = 1$ (i.e., attacking only a single packet of length PL) as it leads to the optimal values $T = 2^{\text{VSL}}/\text{PL}$ and $D = \text{PL}$ for time and data complexity, respectively. This now also immediately shows that considering fewer than PL keystream bits per packet in the attack would lead to worse results. Together with the trivial exhaustive key search attack, we hence obtain an upper bound for the security level of $\min\{\text{KL}, \text{VSL} - \log_2(\text{PL}), (\text{IVL} + \text{VSL})/2\}$ on the resistance of this construction. Note that by the relations (1) and (2) we obtain $\text{KL} = \text{VSL} - \log_2(\text{PL})$ and $\text{KL} \leq (\text{IVL} + \text{VSL})/2$, which implies that none of the TMD-TO attacks beat exhaustive key search.

The second main result of this paper is to show a nearly matching (up to a factor of $2 \cdot \text{SL}$ w.r.t. attack complexity $2^{\text{VSL}-\log_2(\text{PL})}$) lower bound for this upper bound (see inequality 4 in Sect. 4).

In Appendix A we provide a table that compares the LARGE-STATE-SMALL-KEY and the CONTINUOUS-IV-USE construction and also provides an overview of the notation used throughout this paper.

4   Overview of the Model and Results

In this paper, we introduce a random oracle model (ROM) for KSG-based stream ciphers and prove tight security bounds on the resistance against TMD-TO attacks for two of the four generic stream cipher constructions discussed in the last subsection: the LARGE-STATE-SMALL-KEY construction and the CONTINUOUS-IV-USE construction.

Our ROM refers to a packet length parameter PL and a predefined bijective state transition function π, which is assumed to have a large period everywhere. The ROM is based on identifying the functions MIX and out (respectively, OUTBLOCK, which is determined by out and π) as the main components of the cipher.

We derive our security bounds by analyzing the maximal success probability of an attacker Eve in a distinguishing game with players Eve and Alice, where Alice holds the secret session key k and randomly chosen instantiations of the components MIX and out. Attacker Eve is allowed to pose oracle queries to the components MIX and OUTBLOCK, and construction oracle queries with inputs (IV, r), $0 \leq r \leq PL - SL$. The answer to a construction query with input (IV, r) is the block of bits $r, \cdots, r + SL - 1$ of the keystream packet corresponding to initial value IV.

The goal of the attacker Eve is to distinguish the pseudorandom scenario, in which the answers to the construction queries refer to keystream packets generated on k and IV in accordance to the stream cipher construction under consideration, from a random scenario, in which randomly and independently for each initial value IV a keystream packet of length PL is generated.

As usual, our security proofs have an information-theoretic nature, i.e., we consider Eve to be a randomized algorithm of unbounded computational power. Eve is allowed to pose a predefined number M of oracle queries to Alice and has to output $b = 0$ (pseudorandom case) or $b = 1$ (random case) after posing these M queries. The success of Eve is expressed by the advantage $\mathsf{Adv}(M)$, which is defined as

$$\mathsf{Adv}(M) = |\Pr[b = 0|\text{pseudorandom scenario}] - \Pr[b = 0|\text{random scenario}]|,$$

where the probabilities are taken w.r.t. Alice's random choice of the components and the internal randomization of Eve.

4.1   Main Results

Our main results are that in the game corresponding to the LARGE-STATE-SMALL-KEY construction it holds

$$\mathsf{Adv}(M) \leq \frac{M}{2^{KL} - M} + \frac{(2 \cdot SL + 1) \cdot M^2}{2^{SL} - (2 \cdot SL + 1) \cdot M^2} \tag{3}$$

and that in the game corresponding to the CONTINUOUS-IV-USE construction it holds that $\mathsf{Adv}(M)$ is bounded by

$$\mathsf{Adv}(M) \leq \frac{M}{2^{KL} - M} + \frac{(2 \cdot SL + 1) \cdot PL \cdot M}{2^{VSL} - (2 \cdot SL + 1) \cdot PL \cdot M}. \tag{4}$$

The first result says that no generic TMD-TO attack against LARGE-STATE-SMALL-KEY stream ciphers can be significantly better than the Babbage-Golić attack (if $SL < 2 \cdot KL$) or exhaustive key search (if $SL \geq 2 \cdot KL$). Note that our assumptions $\mathsf{PL} = 2^{\mathsf{CONSTL}}$ and $\mathsf{VSL} = \mathsf{CONSTL} + \mathsf{KL}$ imply that $2^{\mathsf{VSL}} = 2^{\mathsf{KL}} \cdot \mathsf{PL}$ which allows to simplify Relation (4) to

$$\mathsf{Adv}(M) \le \frac{M}{2^{\mathsf{KL}} - M} + \frac{(2 \cdot \mathsf{SL} + 1) \cdot M}{2^{\mathsf{KL}} - (2 \cdot \mathsf{SL} + 1) \cdot M} \le \frac{2 \cdot (2 \cdot \mathsf{SL} + 1) \cdot M}{2^{\mathsf{KL}} - (2 \cdot \mathsf{SL} + 1) \cdot M}. \qquad (5)$$

Thus, the second result says that under our assumptions no generic TMD-TO attack against CONTINUOUS-IV-USE stream ciphers is significantly better than exhaustive key search.

5   A Random Oracle Model for Stream Ciphers

In this section, we introduce the random oracle models for the LARGE-STATE-SMALL-KEY construction (underlying, e.g., Grain v1 [24] and Trivium [11]) and the CONTINUOUS-IV-USE construction introduced in [21], and start with the formal definitions for them.

Definition 1. *A stream cipher designed according to the* LARGE-STATE-SMALL-KEY *construction, resp. the* CONTINUOUS-IV-USE *construction, is defined in the following way:*

- *Both constructions depend on the parameters* KL *(the session key length),* IVL *(the initial value length),* PL *(the packet length),* CONSTL *(the length of a constant bitstring* CONST*), and* SL *(the inner state length). Inner states consist of a volatile part of length* VSL *and a non-volatile part of length* SL − VSL*. For all inner states* $y \in \{0,1\}^{\mathsf{SL}}$*, we denote by* $v(y) \in \{0,1\}^{\mathsf{VSL}}$ *and* $nv(y) \in \{0,1\}^{\mathsf{SL-VSL}}$ *the volatile, resp. the non-volatile part of* y*. It holds that* $y = nv(y) \| v(y)$*.*
- *For the* LARGE-STATE-SMALL-KEY *construction, it holds* $\mathsf{SL} = \mathsf{VSL}$ *(i.e., the whole inner state is volatile), and that* $\mathsf{SL} = \mathsf{IVL} + \mathsf{CONSTL} + \mathsf{KL}$*, i.e., the inner state corresponds to the concatenation of the initial value, the constant, and the secret key. For the* CONTINUOUS-IV-USE *construction we have* $\mathsf{SL} = \mathsf{IVL} + \mathsf{VSL}$ *and* $\mathsf{VSL} = \mathsf{CONSTL} + \mathsf{KL}$*, i.e., the non-volatile part corresponds to the initial value and the volatile part corresponds to the concatenation of* CONST *and the secret key. While for the* LARGE-STATE-SMALL-KEY *construction the length of the constant does not influence our analysis, for the* CONTINUOUS-IV-USE *construction we define that* $\mathsf{CONSTL} = \log_2(\mathsf{PL})$*.*
- ***State transition:*** *Both constructions refer to a bijective state transition function* $\pi : \{0,1\}^{\mathsf{SL}} \longrightarrow \{0,1\}^{\mathsf{SL}}$ *for which the period of the sequence* $(\pi^i(y))_{i \ge 0}$ *is greater than* PL *for all inner states* $y \in \{0,1\}^{\mathsf{SL}}$*. For the* CONTINUOUS-IV-USE *construction, the additional restriction holds that* π *leaves the non-volatile part of the state constant, i.e., for each* $z \in \{0,1\}^{\mathsf{VSL}}$ *and* $x \in \{0,1\}^{\mathsf{SL-VSL}}$*, there is some* $z' \in \{0,1\}^{\mathsf{VSL}}$ *such that*

$$\pi(x, z) = (x, z').$$

- **Loading:** In both constructions, the concatenation (IV|CONST|k) forms the loading state $q_{\text{load}}(\text{IV}, k)$ corresponding to the initial value IV and the session key k. In the case of the CONTINUOUS-IV-USE construction, the initial value forms the non-volatile part of the loading state, and the concatenation of the constant CONST and the session key k is loaded into the volatile part of the loading state.

- **Mixing and state initialization:** Both constructions use a bijective and efficiently invertible state mixing function MIX : $\{0,1\}^{\text{SL}} \longrightarrow \{0,1\}^{\text{SL}}$, which transforms the loading state into the packet initial state, i.e., $q_{\text{init}}(\text{IV}, k) = \text{MIX}(\text{IV}|\text{CONST}|k)$.

  For the CONTINUOUS-IV-USE construction, we assume again that MIX leaves the non-volatile part of the state constant, i.e., for each $z \in \{0,1\}^{\text{VSL}}$ and $x \in \{0,1\}^{\text{SL}-\text{VSL}}$, there is some $z' \in \{0,1\}^{\text{VSL}}$ such that

$$\text{MIX}(x, z) = (x, z').$$

- **Keystream generation:** Both constructions employ an output bit function out : $\{0,1\}^{\text{SL}} \longrightarrow \{0,1\}$, which defines, together with π, the corresponding output block function OUTBLOCK : $\{0,1\}^{\text{SL}} \longrightarrow \{0,1\}^{\text{SL}}$, where for each inner state $y \in \{0,1\}^{\text{SL}}$, $\text{OUTBLOCK}(y) = (z_0, \cdots, z_{\text{SL}-1})$ and $z_i = \text{out}(\pi^i(y))$, $i = 0, \ldots, \text{SL}-1$. The keystream packet $(z_0, \cdots, z_{\text{PL}-1})$ corresponding to a key-IV pair (k, IV) is defined by

$$z_i = \text{out}(\pi^i(q_{\text{init}}(\text{IV}, k))),$$

which implies that the output block starting at a position r, $0 \leq r \leq \text{PL} - \text{SL}$, is defined by

$$(z_r, \cdots, z_{r+\text{SL}-1}) = \text{OUTBLOCK}(\pi^r(q_{\text{init}}(\text{IV}, k))).$$

Each of the two constructions defines a distinguishing game between the two players Alice, the secret holder and legal user, and Eve, the attacker. Eve is assumed to have unbounded computational power and to have black-box access to the components of the cipher and to the output keystream, i.e., she is allowed to pose component oracle queries to the components MIX and OUTBLOCK and construction oracle queries for blocks of size SL of keystream packets corresponding to initial values x of Eve's choice. After a predefined number of oracle queries, Eve has to decide whether this keystream stems from a random source, i.e., a source which generates for each initial value a truly random bitstream of length PL, or whether it stems from a pseudorandom source, i.e., a stream cipher designed according to the construction under consideration.

Definition 2 (The Distinguishing Game). *The parameters* KL, IVL, CONSTL, CONST, PL, SL, *and* VSL *and the function* $\pi : \{0,1\}^{\text{SL}} \longrightarrow \{0,1\}^{\text{SL}}$ *have the same meaning as in Definition 1 and fulfill, for each of the two constructions, the respective conditions. We now describe the game:*

(i) *First, Alice chooses randomly and w.r.t. the uniform distribution a secret 5-tuple* $\omega = (b_\omega, k_\omega, P_\omega, f_\omega, e_\omega)$, *where*

- $b_\omega \in \{0,1\}$ *indicates pseudorandom case or random case,*
- $k_\omega \in \{0,1\}^{\mathrm{KL}}$ *is the secret key,*
- $P_\omega : \{0,1\}^{\mathrm{SL}} \longrightarrow \{0,1\}^{\mathrm{SL}}$ *is a valid permutation (definition see below) and corresponds to the mixing function,*
- $f_\omega : \{0,1\}^{\mathrm{SL}} \longrightarrow \{0,1\}$ *corresponds to the output bit function,*
- $e_\omega : \{0,1\}^{\mathrm{IVL}} \times \{0,\cdots,\mathrm{PL}-1\} \longrightarrow \{0,1\}$ *defines the random bitstream generator.*

Here, the definition of a valid permutation depends on the construction. In the LARGE-STATE-SMALL-KEY *case, each bijective mapping* $P_\omega : \{0,1\}^{\mathrm{SL}} \longrightarrow \{0,1\}^{\mathrm{SL}}$ *is a valid permutation. For the* CONTINUOUS-IV-USE *construction,* P_ω *is required to leave the non-volatile part of the state constant, i.e., for each* $z \in \{0,1\}^{\mathrm{VSL}}$ *and* $x \in \{0,1\}^{\mathrm{SL}-\mathrm{VSL}}$, *there is some* $z' \in \{0,1\}^{\mathrm{VSL}}$ *such that*

$$P_\omega(x,z) = (x,z').$$

This is equivalent to choosing a family $(P_\omega(x,\cdot))_{x \in \{0,1\}^{\mathrm{SL}-\mathrm{VSL}}}$ *of mutually independent random bijective mappings* $P_\omega(x,\cdot) : \{0,1\}^{\mathrm{VSL}} \longrightarrow \{0,1\}^{\mathrm{VSL}}$. *We denote by* Ω *the probability space consisting of all these 5-tuples together with the uniform distribution. Each elementary event* $\omega = (b_\omega, k_\omega, P_\omega, f_\omega, e_\omega)$ *defines one further component* F_ω, *corresponding to the output block function, and one further component* E_ω, *corresponding to the construction.*

(ii) *The function* F_ω *is for all inner states* $y \in \{0,1\}^{\mathrm{SL}}$ *defined by*

$$F_\omega(y) = (f_\omega(y), f_\omega(\pi(y)), \cdots, f_\omega(\pi^{\mathrm{SL}-1}(y))). \tag{6}$$

(iii) *The construction function* $E_\omega : \{0,1\}^{\mathrm{IVL}} \times \{0,\cdots,\mathrm{PL}-\mathrm{SL}\} \longrightarrow \{0,1\}^{\mathrm{SL}}$ *assigns to each initial value* x *and position value* r, $0 \le r \le \mathrm{PL}-\mathrm{SL}$, *the block*

$$E_\omega(x,r) = (e_r, \cdots, e_{r+\mathrm{SL}-1}) \tag{7}$$

of the keystream packet corresponding to x, *starting at position* r. *If* $b_\omega = 1$, *we are in the **random case** and it holds for all* $i = 0, \cdots, \mathrm{SL}-1$ *that*

$$e_{r+i} = e_\omega(x)_{r+i}. \tag{8}$$

If $b_\omega = 0$, *we are in the **pseudorandom case** and it holds that*

$$e_{r+i} = f_\omega(\pi^{r+i}(q_{\mathrm{init}}(x,k_\omega))), \tag{9}$$

which is equivalent to

$$E_\omega(x,r) = F_\omega(\pi^r(q_{\mathrm{init}}(x,k_\omega))). \tag{10}$$

Remember that $q_{\mathrm{init}}(x,k_\omega) = P_\omega(x,\mathrm{CONST},k_\omega)$.

(iv) *The distinguisher Eve is supposed to be a randomized oracle algorithm of potentially unbounded computational power. She aims to find out if* $b_\omega = 0$ *or* $b_\omega = 1$ *on the basis of oracle queries of the following types, which she submits to Alice and which will be answered honestly by Alice:*

- *Eve accesses the mixing component via P/P^{-1}-queries $P(u)$ =? or $P^{-1}(v)$ =? for inputs $u, v \in \{0,1\}^{\text{SL}}$, which are answered by Alice with $P_\omega(u)$, resp. $(P_\omega)^{-1}(v)$.*
- *Eve accesses the output component via F-queries $F(y)$ =? for inner states $y \in \{0,1\}^{\text{SL}}$, which are answered by Alice with the keystream block $F_\omega(y)$ as defined in Relation (6).*
- *Eve accesses the construction via E-queries for input pairs (x, r), where $x \in \{0,1\}^{\text{IVL}}$ and $0 \leq r \leq \text{PL} - \text{SL}$, which are answered by Alice with the keystream packet block $E_\omega(x, r)$ as defined by the relations (7), (8), (9), (10).*

(v) *We suppose that in each computation, Eve poses the same number M of oracle queries and finishes the computation with some output $b \in \{0,1\}$. The advantage $\mathsf{Adv}(M)$ reached by Eve with M oracle queries is defined to be*

$$\mathsf{Adv}(M) = \left| \Pr_{\omega \in_U \Omega}[\textit{Eve outputs } 1|b_\omega = 1] - \Pr_{\omega \in_U \Omega}[\textit{Eve outputs } 1|b_\omega = 0] \right|$$

$$= \left| \Pr_{\omega \in_U \Omega}[\textit{Eve outputs } 0|b_\omega = 1] - \Pr_{\omega \in_U \Omega}[\textit{Eve outputs } 0|b_\omega = 0] \right|.$$

Obviously, TMD-TO attacks against a generic stream cipher construction can be formulated in a straightforward way as strategies for Eve in the corresponding distinguishing game, where the overall number of oracle queries lower bounds the overall time consumption $P + T$ of the attack, and the number of construction queries corresponds to the data consumption D. Note that not only component but also construction queries contribute to either P or T, as the corresponding data blocks would be useless without processing them in some way.

In our lower bound proofs, we make use of the fact that the state transition function π defines an undirected graph structure $G_\pi = (V_\pi, E_\pi)$ on $V_\pi = \{0,1\}^{\text{SL}}$ with $E_\pi = \{(v, \pi(v)), v \in \{0,1\}^{\text{SL}}\}$. As π is bijective, the connected components of G_π, which we call π-components, are simple circuits of size at least PL. This graph structure implies the following distance metric on $\{0,1\}^{\text{SL}}$.

Definition 3

- *The π-distance $\text{dist}_\pi(v, v')$ of inner states $v, v' \in V_\pi = \{0,1\}^{\text{SL}}$ is defined to be ∞ if v and v' belong to different π-components. Otherwise, it is defined to be the number of edges of a shortest path connecting v and v' in G_π.*
- *For each $v \in V_\pi = \{0,1\}^{\text{SL}}$ and $s \geq 0$, we define the (π, s)-environment $\text{Env}_\pi^s(v) \subseteq \{0,1\}^{\text{SL}}$ of v as*

$$\text{Env}_\pi^s(v) = \{v' \in \{0,1\}^{\text{SL}} ; \text{dist}_\pi(v, v') \leq s\}.$$

Note that $\text{Env}_\pi^s(v) = \{\pi^{-s}(v), \cdots, \pi^{-1}(v), v, \pi(v), \cdots, \pi^s(v)\}$, which implies that $|\text{Env}_\pi^s(v)| = 2s + 1$ if $s \leq \text{PL}/2$.
- *For each set $Z \subseteq V_\pi = \{0,1\}^{\text{SL}}$ and $s \geq 0$, we define the (π, s)-environment $\text{Env}_\pi^s(Z) \subseteq \{0,1\}^{\text{SL}}$ of Z as*

$$\text{Env}_\pi^s(Z) = \bigcup_{z \in Z} \text{Env}_\pi^s(z).$$

Note that inputs v, v' belong to the same π-component if and only if there is some integer r such that $v' = \pi^r(v)$. Note that in this case

$$dist_\pi(v, v') = \min\{|r|, v' = \pi^r(v)\}.$$

6 Analysis

Theorem 1. *The advantage of Eve, $\mathsf{Adv}(M)$, in the distinguishing game described in Definition 2 with $M \geq 0$ oracle queries is bounded by*

(i)

$$\mathsf{Adv}(M) \leq \frac{M}{2^{\mathsf{KL}} - M} + \frac{(2 \cdot \mathsf{SL} + 1) \cdot M^2}{2^{\mathsf{SL}} - (2 \cdot \mathsf{SL} + 1) \cdot M^2}$$

in the case of the LARGE-STATE-SMALL-KEY *construction, and*
(ii)

$$\mathsf{Adv}(M) \leq \frac{M}{2^{\mathsf{KL}} - M} + \frac{(2 \cdot \mathsf{SL} + 1) \cdot \mathsf{PL} \cdot M}{2^{\mathsf{VSL}} - (2 \cdot \mathsf{SL} + 1) \cdot \mathsf{PL} \cdot M}$$

in the case of the CONTINUOUS-IV-USE *construction.*

In the remaining part of the section, we give the proof of Theorem 1. The proof is divided into subsections, where in the first two subsections, we introduce a number of notions and notations which are relevant in our context. This enables us to describe the idea of the proof in Subsect. 6.3.

6.1 Near Collision and the Friendly Alice

For arbitrary subsets A, B of Ω, we denote by $\Pr[A]$ and by $\Pr_B[A] = \Pr[A|B]$ the probability for the event $\omega \in A$, resp. the probability for the event $\omega \in A$ conditioned to the event $\omega \in B$, where ω is chosen w.r.t. the uniform distribution over Ω.

Definition 4 (Near Collisions). *Let $\omega = (b_\omega, k_\omega, P_\omega, f_\omega, e_\omega) \in \Omega$ be an elementary event and F_ω and E_ω be the output block function and the construction function defined by ω.*

– *A pair $((x, r), y)$, where $(x, r) \in \{0, 1\}^{\mathsf{IVL}} \times \{0, \cdots, \mathsf{PL} - \mathsf{SL}\}$ and $y \in \{0, 1\}^{\mathsf{SL}}$, is called a near EF-collision w.r.t. ω if*

$$dist_\pi(\pi^r(q_{\mathrm{init}}(x, k_\omega)), y) \leq \mathsf{SL} - 1.$$

– *A pair $((x, r), (x', r'))$, where $(x, r), (x', r') \in \{0, 1\}^{\mathsf{IVL}} \times \{0, \cdots, \mathsf{PL} - \mathsf{SL}\}$ and $x \neq x'$, is called a near EE-collision w.r.t. ω if*

$$dist_\pi(\pi^r(q_{\mathrm{init}}(x, k_\omega)), \pi^{r'}(q_{\mathrm{init}}(x', k_\omega))) \leq \mathsf{SL} - 1.$$

Note that in the case of the CONTINUOUS-IV-USE construction the existence of a near EF-collision $((x, r), y)$ implies that $nv(y) = x$, and that near EE-collision do not exist at all. In the following, we suppose that Alice behaves friendly in the sense that in certain situations she provides some additional information about her secret ω to Eve.

Definition 5 (The Friendly Alice). *Let* $\omega = (b_\omega, k_\omega, P_\omega, f_\omega, e_\omega)$ *denote the secret held by Alice.*

- *Whenever Eve poses a P-query with input* $u = (w, k_w)$ *or a* P^{-1}*-query with output* (w, k_w) *for some prefix* $w \in \{0, 1\}^{SL-KL}$, *then, besides giving the correct answer to this query, the friendly Alice makes a **key-recovery announcement**.*
- *Whenever Eve poses a query with some input which causes a near collision w.r.t.* ω *with some other input asked before, then, besides giving the correct answer to this query, the friendly Alice makes a **near-collision announcement**.*

From now on, we suppose that Alice behaves friendly. As the additional information provided by the friendly Alice does not lower Eve's chances to win the game, each security lower bound proved for the friendly Alice does also hold for the general Alice.

6.2   Formalizing Computations by Transcripts

As described in [13], we can assume that Eve is deterministic, i.e., Eve chooses new queries and the final decision deterministically in dependence of the answers of the queries asked before. Let Ω_0 and Ω_1 denote the subsets of Ω formed by all $\omega = (b_\omega, k_\omega, P_\omega, f_\omega, e_\omega) \in \Omega$ fulfilling $b_\omega = 0$, resp. $b_\omega = 1$. We identify computations by transcripts τ, which are defined to be the sequence of the M oracle queries posed during the computation, together with the corresponding answers, and followed by a single output bit $b(\tau)$ corresponding to Eve's final decision. Note that possible announcements about key recovery and near collisions are part of the corresponding oracle answers and, thus, part of the transcript. As Eve is deterministic, there is a unique transcript $\tau(\omega)$ for each $\omega \in \Omega$ corresponding to the computation of Eve under the condition that Alice has chosen ω. We denote by $\mathcal{T}^M$ the set of all transcripts τ of length M for which there is some $\omega \in \Omega$ with $\tau(\omega) = \tau$.

Let $\tau \in \mathcal{T}^M$ be a transcript and fix some index j, $1 \leq j \leq M$. Then $\tau^{\leq j}$ denotes the sub-transcript defined by the first j queries of τ. We denote by $\mathcal{T}^j$ the set of all sub-transcripts of length j of transcripts from $\mathcal{T}^M$. Moreover, we define $\mathcal{T} = \bigcup_{j=1}^{M} \mathcal{T}^j$. Each transcript $\tau \in \mathcal{T}$ will be associated with the following sets $\tau_E \subseteq \{0, 1\}^{IVL} \times \{r; 0 \leq r \leq PL - SL\}$, $\tau_F \subseteq \{0, 1\}^{SL}$, $\tau_P \subseteq \{0, 1\}^{SL}$, and $\tau_{P^{-1}} \subseteq \{0, 1\}^{SL}$ of the inputs of the oracle queries occurring in τ, and a set of keys $K(\tau) \subseteq \{0, 1\}^{KL}$:

- $\tau_E = \{(x, r) \in \{0, 1\}^{IVL} \times \{r; 0 \leq r \leq PL - SL\}; \tau$ contains E-query with input $(x, r)\}$,

- $\tau_F = \{y \in \{0,1\}^{SL}; \tau$ contains F-query with input $y\}$,
- $\tau_P = \{u \in \{0,1\}^{SL}; \tau$ contains P-query with input u or P^{-1}-query with output $u\}$,
- $\tau_{P^{-1}} = \{v \in \{0,1\}^{SL}; \tau$ contains P^{-1}-query with input v or P-query with output $v\}$.
- $K(\tau) \subseteq \{0,1\}^{KL}$ denotes the set of all keys k which occur in τ in the sense that τ_P contains an element $u \in \{0,1\}^{SL}$ for which the rightmost KL bits equal k.
- In the case of the CONTINUOUS-IV-USE construction, we denote for all initial values $x \in \{0,1\}^{IVL}$

$$\tau_F(x) = \{y \in \tau_F; nv(y) = x\}.$$

Let us denote by $\mathcal{T}_0^M$ and $\mathcal{T}_1^M$ the set of all transcripts of length M with output bit 0, resp. 1. For all computations $\tau \in \mathcal{T}^M$, we denote by $\Omega_0(\tau)$ and $\Omega_1(\tau)$ the sets of all elementary events $\omega \in \Omega_0$, resp. $\omega \in \Omega_1$, for which $\tau(\omega) = \tau$, and by $\Omega(\tau)$ the set $\Omega_0(\tau) \cup \Omega_1(\tau)$. Moreover, for $b \in \{0,1\}$ let Ω_b^0 and Ω_b^1 denote the set of elementary events from Ω_b for which $\tau(\omega)$ outputs 0, resp. 1, and let $\Omega^1 = \Omega_0^1 \cup \Omega_1^1$ and $\Omega^0 = \Omega_0^0 \cup \Omega_1^0$. For all $b \in \{0,1\}$ and transcripts $\tau \in \mathcal{T}^M$, we denote by

$$\Pr_b[\tau] = \Pr_{\Omega_b}[\Omega_b(\tau)]$$

the probabilities of the transcript τ in the pseudorandom case ($b = 0$) and the random case ($b = 1$). Note that the advantage $\mathsf{Adv}(M)$ can be written as

$$\mathsf{Adv}(M) = \left| \Pr_{\Omega_0}\left[\Omega_0^0\right] - \Pr_{\Omega_1}\left[\Omega_1^0\right] \right| = \left| \Pr_{\Omega_0}\left[\Omega_0^1\right] - \Pr_{\Omega_1}\left[\Omega_1^1\right] \right|$$

$$= \left| \sum_{\tau \in \mathcal{T}_1^M} \Pr_0[\tau] - \Pr_1[\tau] \right| = \left| \sum_{\tau \in \mathcal{T}_0^M} \Pr_0[\tau] - \Pr_1[\tau] \right|. \tag{11}$$

6.3 Bad Elementary Events and Bad Transcripts and the Idea of the Proof of Theorem 1

Definition 6 (Badness). *An elementary event ω is called bad if during the computation $\tau(\omega)$ the correct key k_ω or a near collision (i.e., a near EF-collision or a near EE-collision) is discovered. Here, the correct key k_ω is considered to be discovered during $\tau(\omega)$ if $\tau(\omega)$ contains a P-query with input u or a P^{-1}-query with output u such that the KL rightmost bits of u equal k_ω. An elementary event ω is called good if it is not bad. For all $b \in \{0,1\}$, we denote by Ω_b^{bad} and Ω_b^{good} the set of all elementary events in Ω_b which are bad, resp. good. Moreover, let $\Omega^{bad} = \Omega_0^{bad} \cup \Omega_1^{bad}$ and $\Omega^{good} = \Omega_0^{good} \cup \Omega_1^{good}$. A transcript is called bad if it contains some key-recovery announcement or some near-collision announcement. For all $b \in \{0,1\}$, we denote by $\mathcal{T}_b^{M,bad}$ and $\mathcal{T}_b^{M,good}$ the set of all transcripts in $\mathcal{T}_b^M$ which are bad, resp. good. Moreover, let $\mathcal{T}^{M,bad} = \mathcal{T}_0^{M,bad} \cup \mathcal{T}_1^{M,bad}$ and $\mathcal{T}^{M,good} = \mathcal{T}_0^{M,good} \cup \mathcal{T}_1^{M,good}$.*

The next lemma shows that with good transcripts, the random and the pseudorandom case cannot be distinguished.

Lemma 1. *For all transcripts* $\tau \in \mathcal{T}^{M,\text{good}}$, *it holds* $\Pr_0[\tau] - \Pr_1[\tau] = 0$.

Proof. Let us fix an arbitrary good transcript $\tau \in \mathcal{T}^{M,\text{good}}$. As τ does not contain near collisions, it holds that in both cases, from Eve's point of view, the answers to the E-queries with inputs (x, r) and (x', r'), $x \neq x'$, and the answers to the E-queries and to the F-queries are mutually independent random variables which are all distributed according to the uniform distribution over $\{0, 1\}^{\text{SL}}$. This allows to construct the following bijective mapping from $\Omega_0(\tau)$ to $\Omega_1(\tau)$, assigning to each elementary event $\omega = (0, k_\omega, P_\omega, f_\omega, e_\omega)$ an elementary event $\bar{\omega} = (1, k_{\bar{\omega}}, P_{\bar{\omega}}, f_{\bar{\omega}}, e_{\bar{\omega}})$ which is defined as follows:

- $k_\omega = k_{\bar{\omega}}$ and $P_\omega = P_{\bar{\omega}}$.
- For all $(x, r) \in \tau_E$, exchange the function values of $E_\omega(x, r)$ with the function values of $F_\omega(\pi^r(q_{\text{init}}(x, k_\omega)))$, i.e.,
  - $F_{\bar{\omega}}(\pi^r(q_{\text{init}}(x, k_\omega))) := E_\omega(x, r)$.
  - $E_{\bar{\omega}}(x, r) := F_\omega(\pi^r(q_{\text{init}}(x, k_\omega)))$.

From the fact that $k_\omega \notin K(\tau)$ for all $\omega \in \Omega_0(\tau) \cup \Omega_1(\tau)$ and as τ does not contain near-collision announcements, it follows that the mapping described above is correctly defined and bijective. The existence of a bijective mapping from $\Omega_0(\tau)$ to $\Omega_1(\tau)$ proves Lemma 1.   □

Lemma 2. $\text{Adv}(M) \leq \Pr_\Omega[\Omega^{\text{bad}}]$.

Proof. By Lemma 1 and Relation 11, it holds

$$
2 \cdot \text{Adv}(M) = \left| \sum_{\tau \in \mathcal{T}_1^M} \Pr_0[\tau] - \Pr_1[\tau] \right| + \left| \sum_{\tau \in \mathcal{T}_0^M} \Pr_0[\tau] - \Pr_1[\tau] \right|
$$

$$
= \left| \sum_{\tau \in \mathcal{T}_1^{M,\text{bad}}} \Pr_0[\tau] - \Pr_1[\tau] \right| + \left| \sum_{\tau \in \mathcal{T}_0^{M,\text{bad}}} \Pr_0[\tau] - \Pr_1[\tau] \right|
$$

$$
\leq \sum_{\tau \in \mathcal{T}^{M,\text{bad}}} \left| \Pr_0[\tau] - \Pr_1[\tau] \right|
$$

$$
\leq \sum_{\tau \in \mathcal{T}^{M,\text{bad}}} \Pr_0[\tau] + \Pr_1[\tau]
$$

$$
\leq \sum_{\tau \in \mathcal{T}^{M,\text{bad}}} 2 \cdot \Pr_\Omega[\tau] = 2 \cdot \Pr_\Omega[\Omega^{\text{bad}}].
$$

In the last line we used the fact that $\Pr_\Omega[\Omega_0] = \Pr_\Omega[\Omega_1] = \frac{1}{2}$.   □

Remark 1. The informed reader may have noticed that it would also have been possible to use the H-coefficient technique by Patarin [30]. In this particular case, the ratio between the probabilities of the occurrence of a good transcript in either world (real or ideal) would be 1, i.e. for a good transcript the real and the ideal world would be indistinguishable as shown in Lemma 1. It remains to upper bound the occurrence of a bad event in the ideal world, as shown in Lemma 2. This will provide the final bound.

To estimate the probability $\Pr_{\Omega}[\Omega^{\mathsf{bad}}]$ of bad elementary events, we slightly change the perspective of the computational behaviour of Eve. So far, each computation of Eve had $M+1$ rounds, i.e., M rounds in each of which Eve poses an oracle query, followed by round $M+1$ in which Eve propagates her final decision. We now assume that the computation stops immediately if Eve manages to pose a query in such a way that the corresponding answer makes the computation bad. This implies that $\Pr_{\Omega}[\Omega^{\mathsf{bad}}]$ equals the probability that Eve stops in some round j, $1 \le j \le M$.

We fix some arbitrary round j, $1 \le j \le M$. If Eve has completed the first $j-1$ rounds without stopping with some good transcript $\tau \in \mathcal{T}^{M,\mathsf{good}}$, then Eve chooses deterministically the j-th query $q(\tau)$ in dependence of τ. The computation stops with the answer to $q(\tau)$ with probability $\Pr_{\Omega(\tau)}[\mathsf{Bad}(\tau)]$, where $\mathsf{Bad}(\tau)$ denotes the set of all elementary events $\omega \in \Omega(\tau)$ for which the next query along $\tau(\omega)$ makes $\tau(\omega)$ bad (i.e., $\tau(\omega)^{\le j-1} = \tau$ is still good and $\tau(\omega)^{\le j}$ is bad). Consequently, the computation does not stop before round $M+1$, i.e., produces a transcript $\tau \in \mathcal{T}^{M,\mathsf{good}}$, if for all j, $1 \le j \le M$, the event $\mathsf{Bad}(\tau^{\le j-1})$ does not happen. This implies

Lemma 3. $\Pr_{\Omega}[\Omega^{\mathsf{bad}}] \le \max \left\{ \sum_{j=1}^{M} \Pr_{\Omega(\tau^{\le j-1})} \left[\mathsf{Bad}(\tau^{\le j-1}) \right] ; \tau \in \mathcal{T}^{M,\mathsf{good}} \right\}.$ □

We prove Theorem 1 by carefully bounding the probabilities $\Pr_{\Omega(\tau)}[\mathsf{Bad}(\tau)]$ for transcripts $\tau \in \mathcal{T}^{j-1,\mathsf{good}}$, $1 \le j \le M$. In particular, we show

Lemma 4. *For all j, $1 \le j \le M$, and all $\tau \in \mathcal{T}^{j-1,\mathsf{good}}$, the following holds:*

- *If query $q(\tau)$ is a P-query, then*

$$Pr_{\Omega(\tau)}[\mathsf{Bad}(\tau)] \le \frac{1}{2^{\mathsf{KL}} - (j-1)}. \tag{12}$$

- *If query $q(\tau)$ is a P^{-1}-query, then*

$$Pr_{\Omega(\tau)}[\mathsf{Bad}(\tau)] \le \frac{1}{2^{\mathsf{KL}} - (j-1)} + \frac{1}{2^{\mathsf{SL}} - (2 \cdot \mathsf{SL} + 1)(j-1)^2} \tag{13}$$

if the construction is LARGE-STATE-SMALL-KEY *and*

$$Pr_{\Omega(\tau)}[\mathsf{Bad}(\tau)] \le \frac{1}{2^{\mathsf{KL}} - (j-1)} + \frac{1}{2^{\mathsf{VSL}} - (2 \cdot \mathsf{SL} + 1) \cdot \mathsf{PL} \cdot (j-1)} \tag{14}$$

if the construction is CONTINUOUS-IV-USE.

- If query $q(\tau)$ is an E-query with input (x, r), then

$$Pr_{\Omega(\tau)}[\mathsf{Bad}(\tau)] \leq \frac{(2 \cdot \mathsf{SL} + 1)(j - 1)}{2^{\mathsf{SL}} - (2 \cdot \mathsf{SL} + 1)(j - 1)^2} \tag{15}$$

if the construction is LARGE-STATE-SMALL-KEY and

$$Pr_{\Omega(\tau)}[\mathsf{Bad}(\tau)] \leq \frac{(2 \cdot \mathsf{SL} + 1) \cdot |\tau_F(x)|}{2^{\mathsf{VSL}} - (2 \cdot \mathsf{SL} + 1) \cdot \mathsf{PL} \cdot (j - 1)}. \tag{16}$$

if the construction is CONTINUOUS-IV-USE.
- If query $q(\tau)$ is an F-query, then

$$Pr_{\Omega(\tau)}[\mathsf{Bad}(\tau)] \leq \frac{(2 \cdot \mathsf{SL} - 1)(j - 1)}{2^{\mathsf{SL}} - (2 \cdot \mathsf{SL} + 1)(j - 1)^2} \tag{17}$$

if the construction is LARGE-STATE-SMALL-KEY and

$$Pr_{\Omega(\tau)}[\mathsf{Bad}(\tau)] \leq \frac{(2 \cdot \mathsf{SL} - 1) \cdot \mathsf{PL}}{2^{\mathsf{VSL}} - (2 \cdot \mathsf{SL} + 1) \cdot \mathsf{PL} \cdot (j - 1)} \tag{18}$$

if the construction is CONTINUOUS-IV-USE.

We will prove Lemma 4 in the Subsects. 6.4 and 6.5. Together with Lemma 3, we obtain

$$Pr_{\Omega}[\Omega^{\mathsf{bad}}] \leq \frac{M}{2^{\mathsf{KL}} - M} + \frac{(2 \cdot \mathsf{SL} + 1) \cdot M^2}{2^{\mathsf{SL}} - (2 \cdot \mathsf{SL} + 1) \cdot M^2} \tag{19}$$

if the construction is LARGE-STATE-SMALL-KEY and

$$Pr_{\Omega}[\Omega^{\mathsf{bad}}] \leq \frac{M}{2^{\mathsf{KL}} - M} + \frac{(2 \cdot \mathsf{SL} + 1) \cdot \mathsf{PL} \cdot M}{2^{\mathsf{VSL}} - (2 \cdot \mathsf{SL} + 1) \cdot \mathsf{PL} \cdot M} \tag{20}$$

if the construction is CONTINUOUS-IV-USE.

Relation (20) holds as the sum of all values $|\tau_F(x)|$ induced by F-queries along τ is at most M. Together with Lemma 2, relations (19) and (20) prove Theorem 1.

6.4   The Structure of the Probability Space $\Omega(\tau)$

We fix some index j, $1 \leq j \leq M$, and a transcript $\tau \in T^{j-1, \mathsf{good}}$. We have to derive an upper bound for the probability $Pr_{\Omega(\tau)}[\mathsf{Bad}(\tau)]$ that an elementary event $\omega \in \Omega_b(\tau)$ becomes bad with the j-th query along $\tau(\omega)$. In this section, we will first analyze the structure of the probability space $\Omega(\tau)$. Note that an elementary event $\omega = (b_\omega, k_\omega, P_\omega, f_\omega, e_\omega)$ belongs to $\Omega(\tau)$ if and only if all of the following conditions are satisfied:

(a) $P_\omega|_{\tau_P}$ is consistent with the answers to all P, P^{-1}-queries contained in τ.
(b) $F_\omega|_{\tau_F}$ is consistent with the answers to all F-queries contained in τ.

(c) If $b = 1$ (random case), then $E_\omega|_{\tau_E}$ is consistent with the answers to all E-queries contained in τ.

(d) If $b = 0$ (pseudorandom case), then for all inputs $(x, r) \in \tau_E$ the answer is

$$F_\omega(\pi^r(q_{\text{init}}(x, k_\omega))).$$

(e) $k_\omega \notin K(\tau)$.

(f) For all $(x, r) \in \tau_E$ and $y \in \tau_F$, it holds

$$dist_\pi\left(\pi^r(q_{\text{init}}(x, k_\omega)), y\right) \geq \text{SL}.$$

(g) For all $(x, r), (x', r') \in \tau_E$ with $x \neq x'$ it holds

$$dist_\pi\left(\pi^r(q_{\text{init}}(x, k_\omega)), \pi^{r'}(q_{\text{init}}(x', k_\omega))\right) \geq \text{SL}.$$

For bounding the probability $\Pr_{\Omega(\tau)}[\text{Bad}(\tau)]$ we will first show that the probability space $\Omega(\tau)$ has a very regular structure. Note that the uniform distribution on $\Omega(\tau)$ induces a probability distribution on the set of keys $\{0, 1\}^{\text{KL}}$, given by

$$\Pr_{\Omega(\tau)}[k] := \Pr_{\Omega(\tau)}[\{\omega \in \Omega(\tau); k_\omega = k\}],$$

and a probability distribution on the set of all pairs (k, P) of keys $k \in \{0, 1\}^{\text{KL}}$ and valid permutations P over $\{0, 1\}^{\text{SL}}$, given by

$$\Pr_{\Omega(\tau)}[k, P] := \Pr_{\Omega(\tau)}[\{\omega \in \Omega(\tau); k_\omega = k, P_\omega = P\}].$$

The proof of Lemma 4 is based on the nontrivial observation that these two probability distributions have the following property:

Lemma 5. *For all keys $k, k' \in \{0, 1\}^{\text{KL}}$ and valid permutations $P, P' : \{0, 1\}^{\text{SL}} \longrightarrow \{0, 1\}^{\text{SL}}$ the following applies*

(I) From $\Pr_{\Omega(\tau)}[k] > 0$ and $\Pr_{\Omega(\tau)}[k'] > 0$ it follows $\Pr_{\Omega(\tau)}[k] = \Pr_{\Omega(\tau)}[k']$.

(II) From $\Pr_{\Omega(\tau)}[k, P] > 0$ and $\Pr_{\Omega(\tau)}[k', P'] > 0$ it follows

$$\Pr_{\Omega(\tau)}[k, P] = \Pr_{\Omega(\tau)}[k', P'].$$

(III) $\Pr_{\Omega(\tau)}[k] > 0$ if and only if $k \notin K(\tau)$.

The Proof of Lemma 5: We start the proof with some technical definitions.

Definition 7 (τ-consistency). *A valid permutation $P : \{0, 1\}^{\text{SL}} \longrightarrow \{0, 1\}^{\text{SL}}$ is called τ-consistent if for all inputs $u \in \tau_P$ it holds that $P(u)$ equals the answer of the P-query with input u, resp. the input of the P^{-1}-query with output u.*

Definition 8 (Environment). *For all inner states $y \in \{0, 1\}^{\text{SL}}$ we denote by $Env(y) \subseteq \{0, 1\}^{\text{SL}}$ the set of all inner states $y' \in \{0, 1\}^{\text{SL}}$ with $dist_\pi(y, y') \leq \text{SL} - 1$, i.e.,*

$$Env(y) = \{\pi^{-(\text{SL}-1)}(y), \pi^{-(\text{SL}-2)}(y), \cdots, \pi^{-1}(y), y, \pi(y), \cdots, \pi^{(\text{SL}-1)}(y)\}.$$

For all subsets $Y \subseteq \{0, 1\}^{\text{SL}}$ we denote by $Env(Y) \subseteq \{0, 1\}^{\text{SL}}$ the set $Env(Y) = \bigcup_{y \in Y} Env(y)$.

Note that $|Env(y)| = 2 \cdot \mathsf{SL} - 1$ and that $|Env(Y)| \leq (2 \cdot \mathsf{SL} - 1)|Y|$ for all $Y \subseteq \{0,1\}^{\mathsf{SL}}$. Let us denote by $X \subseteq \{0,1\}^{\mathsf{IVL}}$ the set of all $x \in \{0,1\}^{\mathsf{IVL}}$ for which there is some r, $0 \leq r \leq \mathsf{PL} - 1$, such that $(x, r) \in \tau_E$. For all $x \in X$ we denote

$$\rho(x) = \{r, (x, r) \in \tau_E\}.$$

The proof of Lemma 5 is based on a more detailed characterization of elementary events ω which fulfill conditions (e),(f),(g) formulated at the beginning of Subsect. 6.4. Remember that all $\omega \in \Omega(\tau)$ have the property that $k_\omega \notin K(\tau)$, otherwise τ would contain a key-recovery announcement. This implies that for all $x \in X$ τ_P does not contain any $u \in \{0,1\}^{\mathsf{SL}}$ with prefix x and suffix k_ω.

We will assign to each pair (k, P), where $k \in \{0,1\}^{\mathsf{KL}} \setminus K(\tau)$ and $P : \{0,1\}^{\mathsf{SL}} \longrightarrow \{0,1\}^{\mathsf{SL}}$ is a valid permutation, an injective mapping $V_{P,k} : X \longrightarrow \{0,1\}^{\mathsf{SL}}$, defined for all $x \in X$ by

$$V_{P,k}(x) := P(x, \mathsf{CONST}, k).$$

The proof of Lemma 5 is based on

Lemma 6. *For all τ-consistent valid permutations $P : \{0,1\}^{\mathsf{SL}} \longrightarrow \{0,1\}^{\mathsf{SL}}$ and keys $k \in \{0,1\}^{\mathsf{KL}}$, it holds that $\mathrm{Pr}_{\Omega(\tau)}[k, P] > 0$ if and only if $k \notin K(\tau)$ and $V_{P,k}$ is τ-collision free. Here, an injective mapping $V : X \longrightarrow \{0,1\}^{\mathsf{SL}}$ is called τ-collision free if $V(x) \notin \mathsf{Forbidden}_\tau(x, V)$ for all $x \in X$.*

The underlying definition of the sets $\mathsf{Forbidden}_\tau(x, V)$ for injective mappings $V : X \longrightarrow \{0,1\}^{\mathsf{SL}}$ are driven by the definition of near collisions in the sense that $V(x) \in \mathsf{Forbidden}_\tau(x, V)$ would imply a near collision. In particular, we define

$$\mathsf{Forbidden}_\tau(x, V) = \tau_{P^{-1}} \cup Coll_{EE}(x) \cup Coll_{EF}(x),$$

where the definitions of $Coll_{EE}(x)$ and $Coll_{EF}(x)$ depend on the construction.

Definition 9 (Forbidden Sets)

(i) *In the case of the* LARGE-STATE-SMALL-KEY *construction we have*

$$Coll_{EF}(x) = \bigcup_{r \in \rho(x)} \pi^{-r}\left(Env(\tau_F)\right),$$

and

$$Coll_{EE}(x) = \bigcup_{r \in \rho(x)} \pi^{-r}\left(Env(\{\pi^{r'}(V(x')); x' \in X \setminus \{x\}, r' \in \rho(x')\})\right).$$

(ii) *In the case of the* CONTINUOUS-IV-USE *construction let*

$$Coll_{EF}(x) = \bigcup_{r \in \rho(x)} \pi^{-r}\left(Env(\tau_F(x))\right),$$

and $Coll_{EE}(x) = \emptyset$.

Note that in the case of the LARGE-STATE-SMALL-KEY construction it holds

$$|\mathsf{Forbidden}_\tau(x, V)| \le (j-1) + (j-2) + |\rho(x)| \cdot (2 \cdot \mathsf{SL} - 1) \cdot (|\tau_E| + |\tau_F|)$$

$$\le |\rho(x)|(2 \cdot \mathsf{SL} + 1) \cdot (j-1) \le (2 \cdot \mathsf{SL} + 1) \cdot (j-1)^2. \tag{21}$$

In the case of the CONTINUOUS-IV-USE construction it holds

$$|\mathsf{Forbidden}_\tau(x, V)| \le (j-1) + (j-2) + |\rho(x)| \cdot (2 \cdot \mathsf{SL} - 1) \cdot |\tau_F(x)|$$

$$\le (2 \cdot \mathsf{SL} + 1) \cdot \mathsf{PL} \cdot |\tau_F(x)| \le (2 \cdot \mathsf{SL} + 1) \cdot \mathsf{PL} \cdot (j-1). \tag{22}$$

The second inequality is due to the fact that $|\rho(x)| \le \mathsf{PL}$.

The Proof of Lemma 6. We start with the if-direction and fix some $\omega \in \Omega(\tau)$. It holds $k_\omega \notin K(\tau)$, otherwise τ would contain a key-recovery announcement which would contradict the assumption that τ is good. Further we know that there do not occur near collisions during τ which implies that for all $x \in X$ it holds that V_{P_ω, k_ω} is (τ, k)-collision free.

To prove the only-if part let us fix some $b \in \{0, 1\}$, some key $k \in \{0, 1\}^{\mathsf{KL}} \setminus K(\tau)$ and some valid permutation $P : \{0, 1\}^{\mathsf{SL}} \longrightarrow \{0, 1\}^{\mathsf{SL}}$ such that P is τ-consistent and $V_{P,k}$ is τ-collision free. Note first that, as $k \notin K(\tau)$, it holds that for all $x \in X$, τ_P does not contain an element with prefix x and suffix k. The fact that $V_{P,k}$ is τ-collision free implies that the E-queries and the F-queries during τ do not produce any near collision.

The only thing which remains to do is to construct functions $f : \{0, 1\}^{\mathsf{SL}} \longrightarrow \{0, 1\}$ and $e : \{0, 1\}^{\mathsf{IVL}} \times \{0, \cdots, \mathsf{PL} - 1\} \longrightarrow \{0, 1\}$ in such a way the (b, k, P, f, e) belongs to $\Omega(\tau)$. We do this by constructing the corresponding block output functions $F : \{0, 1\}^{\mathsf{SL}} \longrightarrow \{0, 1\}^{\mathsf{SL}}$ and $E : \{0, 1\}^{\mathsf{IVL}} \times \{0, \cdots, \mathsf{PL} - \mathsf{SL}\} \longrightarrow \{0, 1\}^{\mathsf{SL}}$.

(1) First we define $F(y)$ for all $y \in \tau_F$ to be equal to the answer of the corresponding F-query during τ.
(2) If $b = 0$, the pseudorandom case, then we have to define for all $(x, r) \in \tau_E$ the value $F(\pi^r(P(x, \mathsf{CONST}, k)))$ to be equal to the answer of the E-query with input (x, r) during τ. This can be done without contradiction to F-queries in τ or to other E-queries in τ. This is because for all $y \in \tau_F$ the π-distance between y and $\pi^r(P(x, \mathsf{CONST}, k))$ is at least SL. Moreover, in the case of the LARGE-STATE-SMALL-KEY construction, for all $(x', r') \in \tau_E$, $x' \ne x$, the π-distance between $\pi^{r'}(P(x', \mathsf{CONST}, k))$ and $\pi^r(P(x, \mathsf{CONST}, k))$ is at least SL.
(3) If $b = 1$, the random case, we define $E(x, r)$ to be equal to the answer of the E-query with input (x, r) during τ for all $(x, r) \in \tau_E$.

At all positions which were not affected by (1), (2), (3) the functions e and f can be defined in an arbitrary way. This proves Lemma 6. □

To complete the proof of Lemma 5 it is sufficient to show the following two claims:

- **Claim 1:** For all $b \in \{0,1\}$, keys $k \in \{0,1\}^{\text{KL}} \setminus K(\tau)$ and valid permutations $P : \{0,1\}^{\text{SL}} \longrightarrow \{0,1\}^{\text{SL}}$ which are τ-consistent and for which $V_{P,k}$ is τ-collision free, the number of output bits of the functions e and f which have to be fixed for ensuring $(b, k, P, f, e) \in \Omega(\tau)$ is the same.
- **Claim 2:** For all keys $k \in \{0,1\}^{\text{KL}} \setminus K(\tau)$ the number of valid permutations $P : \{0,1\}^{\text{SL}} \longrightarrow \{0,1\}^{\text{SL}}$ which are τ-consistent, and for which $V_{P,k}$ is τ-collision free, is the same.

Note that Claim 1 follows straightforwardly from the construction rule described in items (2) and (3) above. Claim 2 is equivalent to

- **Claim 3** saying that for all keys $k \in \{0,1\}^{\text{KL}} \setminus K(\tau)$ the number of τ-collision free injective mappings $V : X \longrightarrow \{0,1\}^{\text{SL}}$ is the same.

The proof of Claim 3 is obvious as the definition of τ-collision freeness does not depend on k. $\square$

6.5   The Proof of Lemma 4

In the following we prove Lemma 4 with Lemma 5. Let us denote by q the query posed by Eve after τ. Note that the type of this query and the input of this query is determined by τ, while the answer depends on which $\omega \in \Omega(\tau)$ is held by Alice. This answer determines if the j-th query along τ_ω makes $\tau(\omega)$ and ω bad (i.e., $\omega \in \text{Bad}(\tau)$) or not. Corresponding to the possible types queries we distinguish four cases:

Case 1: The query q is a P-query with input $u \in \{0,1\}^{\text{SL}} \setminus \tau_P$. Let $k \in \{0,1\}^{\text{KL}}$ denote the string of the rightmost KL bits of u. It holds by definition that a P-query cannot cause a new near collision. Thus, the only possibility to generate badness with q is to have $k = k_\omega$. As τ is good, Eve knows that $k_\omega \notin K(\tau)$ and that all keys outside $K(\tau)$ are equally likely to be k_ω (see Lemma 5). As $|K(\tau)| \leq j - 1$ we obtain

$$\Pr_{\Omega(\tau)}\left[\text{Bad}(\tau)|q \text{ is } P\text{-query}\right] \leq \frac{1}{2^{\text{KL}} - (j-1)} \tag{23}$$

Case 2: The query q is a P^{-1}-query with input $v \in \{0,1\}^{\text{SL}} \setminus \tau_{P^{-1}}$. Then the only possibility to generate badness with q is to choose v in such a way that the answer to q has suffix k_ω. This event is the union of the following two events BadEv_1 and BadEv_2.

BadEv_1 corresponds to the case that q is a P^{-1}-query and that Eve manages to choose v in such a way that $v = P_\omega(x, \text{CONST}, k_\omega)$ for some $x \in X$. As in the proof of Lemma 5, we denote by X the set of all inputs $x' \in \{0,1\}^{\text{IVL}}$ for which there is some r', $0 \leq r' \leq \text{PL} - \text{SL}$, such that $(x', r') \in \tau_E$. We again denote by $V_{k_\omega, P_\omega} : X \longrightarrow \{0,1\}^{\text{SL}}$ the mapping assigning to each

$x' \in X$ the value $P_\omega(x', \text{CONST}, k_\omega)$. Lemma 5 implies that Eve knows that $P_\omega(x, \text{CONST}, k_\omega) \notin \text{Forbidden}_\tau(x, V_{k_\omega, P_\omega})$.

In the case of the LARGE-STATE-SMALL-KEY construction this set has at most $(2 \cdot \text{SL} + 1)(j-1)^2$ elements (see Relations (21)), while in case of the CONTINUOUS-IV-USE construction it has at most $(2 \cdot \text{SL} + 1) \cdot \text{PL} \cdot (j-1)$ elements (see Relations (22)). All values outside $\text{Forbidden}_\tau(x, V_{k_\omega, P_\omega})$ are equally likely to be equal to $P_\omega(x, \text{CONST}, k_\omega)$. This implies that

$$\Pr_{\Omega(\tau)}[\text{BadEv}_1] \leq \frac{1}{2^{\text{SL}} - (2 \cdot \text{SL} + 1)(j-1)^2} \tag{24}$$

if the construction is LARGE-STATE-SMALL-KEY, and

$$\Pr_{\Omega(\tau)}[\text{BadEv}_1] \leq \frac{1}{2^{\text{VSL}} - (2 \cdot \text{SL} + 1) \cdot \text{PL} \cdot (j-1)} \tag{25}$$

if the construction is CONTINUOUS-IV-USE.

BadEv_2 corresponds to the case that q is a P^{-1}-query and $v \neq P_\omega(x, \text{CONST}, k_\omega)$ for all $x \in \tau_E$ but that $P_\omega^{-1}(v)$ has suffix k_ω. Lemma 5 ensures that from Eve's point of view all values in $\{0,1\}^{\text{SL}} \setminus \tau_P$ are equally likely to be $P_\omega^{-1}(v)$. Consequently,

$$\Pr_{\Omega(\tau)}[\text{BadEv}_2] \leq \frac{2^{\text{SL}-\text{KL}}}{2^{\text{SL}} - (j-1)} \leq \frac{1}{2^{\text{KL}} - (j-1)}. \tag{26}$$

Case 3: The query q is an E-query for some input (x, r), where $0 \leq r \leq \text{PL} - \text{SL}$ and $x \in \{0,1\}^{\text{IVL}}$. We have to distinguish two subcases:

Subcase 3a: $x \notin X$. For all keys $k \in \{0,1\}^{\text{KL}}$, mappings $\tilde{V} : X \longrightarrow \{0,1\}^{\text{SL}}$, and valid permutation $P : \{0,1\}^{\text{SL}} \longrightarrow \{0,1\}^{\text{SL}}$, we denote by

$$(P, k)|_X \equiv \tilde{V}$$

the event that $P(x, \text{CONST}, k) = \tilde{V}(x)$ for all $x \in X$. We fix some $k \in \{0,1\}^{\text{KL}} \setminus K(\tau)$ (which implies that $(x, \text{CONST}, k) \notin \tau_P$) and some τ-collision free mapping $\tilde{V} : X \longrightarrow \{0,1\}^{\text{SL}}$ and estimate the probability that q makes $\omega \in \Omega(\tau)$ bad under the condition that $k_\omega = k$ and $(P_\omega, k)|_X \equiv \tilde{V}$. For all elementary events ω fulfilling this condition we denote by $\tilde{V}_\omega : X \cup \{x\} \longrightarrow \{0,1\}^{\text{SL}}$ the mapping $\tilde{V} \cup (x \rightarrow P_\omega(x, \text{CONST}, k))$. Query q makes ω bad if $P_\omega(x, \text{CONST}, k) \in \text{Forbidden}_{\tau(\omega) \leq j}(x, \tilde{V}_\omega)$ (see Lemma 6 and Definition 9). As $\rho(x)$ contains only one element w.r.t. $\tau(\omega)^{\leq j}$, relations (21) and (22) imply that

$$|\text{Forbidden}_{\tau(\omega) \leq j}(x, \tilde{V}_\omega)| \leq (2 \cdot \text{SL} + 1) \cdot j$$

for the LARGE-STATE-SMALL-KEY construction, and

$$|\text{Forbidden}_{\tau(\omega) \leq j}(x, \tilde{V}_\omega)| \leq (2 \cdot \text{SL} + 1) \cdot |\tau_F(x)|$$

for the CONTINUOUS-IV-USE construction. As all values outside τ_{P-1} are equally likely to be equal to $P_\omega(x, \text{CONST}, k)$ it holds

$$\Pr_{\Omega(\tau)}\left[P_\omega(x, \text{CONST}, k) \in \text{Forbidden}_\tau(x, \tilde{V}_\omega)|k_\omega = k, (P_\omega, k_\omega)|_X \equiv \tilde{V}\right]$$

$$\leq \frac{(2 \cdot \text{SL} + 1) \cdot j}{2^{\text{SL}} - (j-1)}, \tag{27}$$

if the construction is LARGE-STATE-SMALL-KEY, and

$$\Pr_{\Omega(\tau)}\left[P_\omega(x, \text{CONST}, k) \in \text{Forbidden}_\tau(x, \tilde{V}_\omega)|k_\omega = k, (P_\omega, k_\omega)|_X \equiv \tilde{V}\right]$$

$$\leq \frac{(2 \cdot \text{SL} + 1) \cdot |\tau_F(x)|}{2^{\text{VSL}} - (j-1)}, \tag{28}$$

if the construction is CONTINUOUS-IV-USE.

Subcase 3b $x \in X$. Note that $r \notin \rho(x)$, otherwise the same query q would have been posed already during τ. We denote $X' = X \setminus \{x\}$. Now we fix some $k \in \{0,1\}^{\text{KL}} \setminus K(\tau)$ (which implies that $(x, \text{CONST}, k) \notin \tau_P$) and some τ-collision free mapping $\tilde{V}' : X' \longrightarrow \{0,1\}^{\text{SL}}$ and denote by $\Omega(\tau, k, \tilde{V}')$ the set of all elementary events $\omega \in \Omega(\tau)$ for which $k_\omega = k$ and $(P_\omega, k)_{X'} = \tilde{V}'$. For all $\omega \in \Omega(\tau, k, \tilde{V}')$ we denote by $\tilde{V}'_\omega : X \longrightarrow \{0,1\}^{\text{SL}}$ the mapping $\tilde{V}' \cup \{(x \to P_\omega(x, \text{CONST}, k))\}$. We estimate the probability over $\Omega(\tau, k, \tilde{V}')$ of the event that q makes $\omega \in \Omega(\tau, k, \tilde{V}')$ bad. As $\tilde{V}'_\omega$ is τ-collision free we know that $P_\omega(x, \text{CONST}, k) \notin B := \text{Forbidden}_\tau(x, \tilde{V}'_\omega)$ and that, from Eve's point of view, all values outside of B are equally likely to be equal to $P_\omega(x, \text{CONST}, k)$. Moreover, we know that q makes $\omega \in \Omega(\tau, k, \tilde{V}')$ bad if $\tilde{V}'_\omega$ is not $\tau(\omega)^{\leq j}$-collision free, where $\tau(\omega)^{\leq j}$ denotes the transcript of length j obtained from τ by adding the E-query with input (x, r) as j-th query to τ, which corresponds to adding r to $\rho(x)$. This is equivalent to $P_\omega(x, \text{CONST}, k) \in A \setminus B$, where $A := \text{Forbidden}_{\tau(\omega)^{\leq j}}(x, \tilde{V}'_\omega)$. Note that by Relation (21)

$$|A \setminus B| \leq (2 \cdot \text{SL} + 1)(j-1), \text{ and}$$
$$|B| \leq (2 \cdot \text{SL} + 1)(j-1)^2,$$

in the case of the LARGE-STATE-SMALL-KEY construction, and that by Relation (22)

$$|A \setminus B| \leq (2 \cdot \text{SL} + 1) \cdot |\tau_F(x)|, \text{ and}$$
$$|B| \leq (2 \cdot \text{SL} + 1) \cdot \text{PL} \cdot (j-1).$$

in the case of the CONTINUOUS-IV-USE construction. Consequently, in the case of the LARGE-STATE-SMALL-KEY construction,

$$\Pr_{\Omega(\tau, k, \tilde{V}')}[\text{Bad}(\tau)|x \in X] \leq \frac{|A \setminus B|}{2^{\text{SL}} - |B|} \leq \frac{(2 \cdot \text{SL} + 1)(j-1)}{2^{\text{SL}} - (2 \cdot \text{SL} + 1)(j-1)^2}. \tag{29}$$

In the case of the CONTINUOUS-IV-USE construction it holds

$$\Pr_{\Omega(\tau, k, \tilde{V}')}[\text{Bad}(\tau)|x \in X] \leq \frac{(2 \cdot \text{SL} + 1) \cdot |\tau_F(x)|}{2^{\text{VSL}} - (2 \cdot \text{SL} + 1) \cdot \text{PL} \cdot (j-1)}. \tag{30}$$

Case 4: q is an F-query for some input $y \notin \tau_F$. We first consider the case of the LARGE-STATE-SMALL-KEY construction. We fix an arbitrary key $k \in \{0,1\}^{\text{KL}} \setminus K(\tau)$ and a τ-collision free mapping $V : X \longrightarrow \{0,1\}^{\text{SL}}$ and denote by $\Omega(\tau, k, V)$ the set of all $\omega \in \Omega(\tau)$ with $k_\omega = k$ and $(P_\omega, k)|_X \equiv V$. For all $\omega \in \Omega(\tau, k, V)$ it holds that q makes ω bad if and only if there is some $(x, r) \in \tau_E$ such that $P_\omega(x, \text{CONST}, k)$ belongs to $Env(\pi^{-r}(y))$, a set of size at most $2 \cdot \text{SL} - 1$. Moreover, from Eve's point of view, each point outside $\text{Forbidden}_\tau(x, V)$, a set of size at most $(2 \cdot \text{SL} + 1)(j - 1)^2$, is equally likely to be equal to $P_\omega(x, \text{CONST}, k)$. Consequently, the probability that q makes $\omega \in \Omega(\tau, k, V)$ bad is at most

$$\frac{(2 \cdot \text{SL} - 1)(j - 1)}{2^{\text{SL}} - (2 \cdot \text{SL} + 1)(j - 1)^2}.$$

Let us now consider the case of the CONTINUOUS-IV-USE construction. We write y as $y = (x, z)$ for $z \in \{0,1\}^{\text{VSL}}$ and $x \in \{0,1\}^{\text{IVL}}$. If $x \notin X$, then $\Pr_{\Omega(\tau)}[\text{Bad}(\tau)] = 0$. Otherwise, q makes an elementary event $\omega \in \Omega(\tau)$ bad if and only if

$$dist_\pi \left(\pi^r \left(P_\omega(x, \text{CONST}, k_\omega) \right), (x, z) \right) \leq \text{SL} - 1 \tag{31}$$

for some $r \in \rho(x)$. As $\tau_E(x)$ contains at most PL queries we obtain by the same arguments used in Subcase 3b that

$$\Pr_{\Omega(\tau)}[\text{Bad}(\tau)] \leq \frac{\text{PL} \cdot (2 \cdot \text{SL} - 1)}{2^{\text{VSL}} - (2 \cdot \text{SL} + 1) \cdot \text{PL} \cdot (j - 1)}. \tag{32}$$

$\square$

7 Conclusion

We considered two generic stream cipher construction in this paper: the LARGE-STATE-SMALL-KEY construction and the CONTINUOUS-IV-USE construction. Stream ciphers like Trivium and Grain v1 are based on the LARGE-STATE-SMALL-KEY construction whereas there are no stream ciphers based on the CONTINUOUS-IV-USE constructions so far. For both constructions, we showed a tight security bound. We provided a security bound of $\min\{\text{KL}, \text{SL}/2\}$ for the LARGE-STATE-SMALL-KEY construction and a security bound of $\min\{\text{KL}, \text{VSL} - \log_2(\text{PL}), (\text{IVL} + \text{VSL})/2\}$ on the resistance of the CONTINUOUS-IV-USE construction against time-memory-data tradeoff attacks. This would allow stream ciphers based on the CONTINUOUS-IV-USE principle to use significantly less state cells than current stream ciphers based on the LARGE-STATE-SMALL-KEY construction.

In particular, the latter bound provides design guidance for future instances of CONTINUOUS-IV-USE stream ciphers which realize the common security level of 80 bits w.r.t. TMD-TO attacks. A corresponding choice of parameters would be a volatile state length of $\text{VSL} = 100$ bits, an IV length of $\text{IVL} = 60$ bits, and a key length of $\text{KL} = 80$ bits, which implies an overall inner state length of $\text{SL} = 160$, a packet length of $PL = 2^{20}$ bits and a constant length of $CONSTL = \log_2(PL) = 20$ bits. The loading state to a key-IV pair (IV, k) would here be $(IV|CONST|k)$.

We consider the design of a corresponding practical instantiation a promising next step in the search for ultra-lightweight stream ciphers. In fact, it would be the first stream cipher with a volatile state length below 160 bits that still offers (even *provable*) 80-bit security against generic TMD-TO-based inner state recovery *and* distinguishing.

A   Comparison of the Two Schemes

For further clarification the following tables provide an overview of the parameters used in this paper. Additionally it is shown how the $(i + 1)$-th output bit z_i of the stream cipher is computed from the loading state q_{load}. Note that π^0 is the identity function.

	LARGE-STATE-SMALL-KEY	CONTINUOUS-IV-USE
State Length, SL	IVL + CONSTL + KL	IVL + CONSTL + KL
Vol. State Len., VSL	IVL + CONSTL + KL	CONSTL + KL
Non-Vol. State Len.	0	IVL
Loading State, q_{load}	$IV \,\|\, CONST \,\|\, k$	$IV \,\|\, CONST \,\|\, k$
$v(q_{load})$	$IV \,\|\, CONST \,\|\, k$	$CONST \,\|\, k$
$nv(q_{load})$	–	IV
Output Bit z_i		

References

1. Ghafari, V.A., Hu, H.: Fruit-80: a secure ultra-lightweight stream cipher for constrained environments. Entropy **20**(3), 180 (2018)

2. Ghafari, V.A., Hu, H., Lin, F.: On designing secure small-state stream ciphers against time-memory-data tradeoff attacks. Cryptology ePrint Archive, Report 2019/670 (2019). https://eprint.iacr.org/2019/670

3. Andreeva, E., Bogdanov, A., Dodis, Y., Mennink, B., Steinberger, J.P.: On the indifferentiability of key-alternating ciphers. In: Canetti, R., Garay, J.A. (eds.) CRYPTO 2013. LNCS, vol. 8042, pp. 531–550. Springer, Heidelberg (2013). https://doi.org/10.1007/978-3-642-40041-4_29

4. Armknecht, F., Mikhalev, V.: On lightweight stream ciphers with shorter internal states. In: Leander, G. (ed.) FSE 2015. LNCS, vol. 9054, pp. 451–470. Springer, Heidelberg (2015). https://doi.org/10.1007/978-3-662-48116-5_22

5. Babbage, S., Borghoff, J., Velichkov, V.: D.SYM.10 - The eSTREAM Portfolio in 2012. eSTREAM: The ECRYPT Stream Cipher Project (2012). http://www.ecrypt.eu.org/ecrypt2/documents/D.SYM.10-v1.pdf

6. Babbage, S.H.: Improved "exhaustive search" attacks on stream ciphers. In: European Convention on Security and Detection, May 1995, pp. 161–166 (1995)

7. Bellare, M., Rogaway, P., Wagner, D.: The EAX mode of operation. In: Roy, B., Meier, W. (eds.) FSE 2004. LNCS, vol. 3017, pp. 389–407. Springer, Heidelberg (2004). https://doi.org/10.1007/978-3-540-25937-4_25

8. Biryukov, A., Shamir, A.: Cryptanalytic time/memory/data tradeoffs for stream ciphers. In: Okamoto, T. (ed.) ASIACRYPT 2000. LNCS, vol. 1976, pp. 1–13. Springer, Heidelberg (2000). https://doi.org/10.1007/3-540-44448-3_1

9. Bogdanov, A., Knudsen, L.R., Leander, G., Standaert, F.-X., Steinberger, J., Tischhauser, E.: Key-alternating ciphers in a provable setting: encryption using a small number of public permutations. In: Pointcheval, D., Johansson, T. (eds.) EUROCRYPT 2012. LNCS, vol. 7237, pp. 45–62. Springer, Heidelberg (2012). https://doi.org/10.1007/978-3-642-29011-4_5

10. Briceno, M., Goldberg, I., Wagner, D.: A pedagogical implementation of A5/1 (1999). http://www.scard.org/gsm/a51.html

11. De Cannière, C., Preneel, B.: Trivium - Specifications. eSTREAM: The ECRYPT Stream Cipher Project (2005). http://www.ecrypt.eu.org/stream/p3ciphers/trivium/trivium_p3.pdf

12. Chen, S., Lampe, R., Lee, J., Seurin, Y., Steinberger, J.: Minimizing the two-round Even-Mansour cipher. In: Garay, J.A., Gennaro, R. (eds.) CRYPTO 2014. LNCS, vol. 8616, pp. 39–56. Springer, Heidelberg (2014). https://doi.org/10.1007/978-3-662-44371-2_3

13. Chen, S., Steinberger, J.: Tight security bounds for key-alternating ciphers. In: Nguyen, P.Q., Oswald, E. (eds.) EUROCRYPT 2014. LNCS, vol. 8441, pp. 327–350. Springer, Heidelberg (2014). https://doi.org/10.1007/978-3-642-55220-5_19

14. Cogliati, B., Lee, J., Seurin, Y.: New constructions of MACs from (tweakable) block ciphers. IACR Trans. Symmetric Cryptol. **2017**, 27–58 (2017)

15. Cogliati, B., Seurin, Y.: EWCDM: an efficient, beyond-birthday secure, nonce-misuse resistant MAC. In: Robshaw, M., Katz, J. (eds.) CRYPTO 2016. LNCS, vol. 9814, pp. 121–149. Springer, Heidelberg (2016). https://doi.org/10.1007/978-3-662-53018-4_5

16. Datta, N., Dutta, A., Nandi, M., Yasuda, K.: Encrypt or decrypt? To make a single-key beyond birthday secure nonce-based MAC. In: Shacham, H., Boldyreva, A. (eds.) CRYPTO 2018. LNCS, vol. 10991, pp. 631–661. Springer, Cham (2018). https://doi.org/10.1007/978-3-319-96884-1_21

17. Dunkelman, O., Keller, N., Shamir, A.: Minimalism in cryptography: the Even-Mansour scheme revisited. In: Pointcheval, D., Johansson, T. (eds.) EUROCRYPT 2012. LNCS, vol. 7237, pp. 336–354. Springer, Heidelberg (2012). https://doi.org/10.1007/978-3-642-29011-4_21
18. Dutta, A., Jha, A., Nandi, M.: Tight security analysis of EHtM MAC. IACR Trans. Symmetric Cryptol. **2017**, 130–150 (2017)
19. Golić, J.D.: On the security of nonlinear filter generators. In: Gollmann, D. (ed.) FSE 1996. LNCS, vol. 1039, pp. 173–188. Springer, Heidelberg (1996). https://doi.org/10.1007/3-540-60865-6_52
20. Hamann, M., Krause, M.: On stream ciphers with provable beyond-the-birthday-bound security against time-memory-data tradeoff attacks. Cryptogr. Commun. **10**(5), 959–1012 (2018)
21. Hamann, M., Krause, M., Meier, W.: A note on stream ciphers that continuously use the IV. Cryptology ePrint Archive, Report 2017/1172 (2017). https://eprint.iacr.org/2017/1172
22. Hamann, M., Krause, M., Meier, W.: LIZARD - a lightweight stream cipher for power-constrained devices. IACR Trans. Symmetric Cryptol. **2017**(1), 45–79 (2017)
23. Hamann, M., Krause, M., Meier, W., Zhang, B.: Design and analysis of small-state grain-like stream ciphers. Cryptogr. Commun. **10**, 803–834 (2017)
24. Hell, M., Johansson, T., Meier, W.: Grain - a stream cipher for constrained environments. eSTREAM: The ECRYPT Stream Cipher Project (2006). http://www.ecrypt.eu.org/stream/p3ciphers/grain/Grain_p3.pdf
25. Hellman, M.: A cryptanalytic time-memory trade-off. IEEE Trans. Inf. Theory **26**(4), 401–406 (1980)
26. Lampe, R., Patarin, J., Seurin, Y.: An asymptotically tight security analysis of the iterated Even-Mansour cipher. In: Wang, X., Sako, K. (eds.) ASIACRYPT 2012. LNCS, vol. 7658, pp. 278–295. Springer, Heidelberg (2012). https://doi.org/10.1007/978-3-642-34961-4_18
27. Mennink, B., Neves, S.: Encrypted Davies-Meyer and its dual: towards optimal security using mirror theory. In: Katz, J., Shacham, H. (eds.) CRYPTO 2017. LNCS, vol. 10403, pp. 556–583. Springer, Cham (2017). https://doi.org/10.1007/978-3-319-63697-9_19
28. Mikhalev, V., Armknecht, F., Müller, C.: On ciphers that continuously access the non-volatile key. IACR Trans. Symmetric Cryptol. **2016**(2), 52–79 (2017)
29. Moch, A., List, E.: Parallelizable MACs based on the sum of PRPs with security beyond the birthday bound. In: Deng, R.H., Gauthier-Umaña, V., Ochoa, M., Yung, M. (eds.) ACNS 2019. LNCS, vol. 11464, pp. 131–151. Springer, Cham (2019). https://doi.org/10.1007/978-3-030-21568-2_7
30. Patarin, J.: The "Coefficients H" technique. In: Avanzi, R.M., Keliher, L., Sica, F. (eds.) SAC 2008. LNCS, vol. 5381, pp. 328–345. Springer, Heidelberg (2009). https://doi.org/10.1007/978-3-642-04159-4_21
31. Pietrzak, K.: A leakage-resilient mode of operation. In: Joux, A. (ed.) EUROCRYPT 2009. LNCS, vol. 5479, pp. 462–482. Springer, Heidelberg (2009). https://doi.org/10.1007/978-3-642-01001-9_27
32. Rogaway, P., Bellare, M., Black, J.: OCB: a block-cipher mode of operation for efficient authenticated encryption. ACM Trans. Inf. Syst. Secur. (TISSEC) **6**(3), 365–403 (2003)

On the Data Limitation of Small-State Stream Ciphers: Correlation Attacks on Fruit-80 and Plantlet

Yosuke Todo[1(✉)], Willi Meier[2], and Kazumaro Aoki[1]

[1] NTT Secure Platform Laboratories, Tokyo 180-8585, Japan
{yosuke.todo.xt,kazumaro.aoki.ya}@hco.ntt.co.jp
[2] FHNW, Windisch, Switzerland
willimeier48@gmail.com

Abstract. Many cryptographers have focused on lightweight cryptography, and a huge number of lightweight block ciphers have been proposed. On the other hand, designing lightweight stream ciphers is a challenging task due to the well-known security criteria, i.e., the state size of stream ciphers must be at least twice the key size. The designers of Sprout addressed this issue by involving the secret key not only in the initialization but also in the keystream generation, and the state size of such stream ciphers can be smaller than twice the key size. After the seminal work, some small-state stream ciphers have been proposed such as Fruit, Plantlet, and LIZARD. Unlike conventional stream ciphers, these small-state stream ciphers have the limitation of keystream bits that can be generated from the same key and IV pair. In this paper, our motivation is to show whether the data limitation claimed by the designers is proper or not. The correlation attack is one of the attack methods exploiting many keystream bits generated from the same key and IV pair, and we apply it to Fruit-80 and Plantlet. As a result, we can break the full Fruit-80, i.e., the designers' data limitation is not sufficient. We can also recover the secret key of Plantlet if it allows about 2^{53} keystream bits from the same key and IV pair.

Keywords: Small-state stream cipher · Grain · Correlation attack

1 Introduction

Lightweight cryptography has been a hot topic in the past few years. The availability of low-area implementation is one of the most common metrics for the "lightweight," and many such block ciphers have been proposed [1–4]. On the other hand, designing lightweight stream ciphers is a challenging topic. A time-memory-data trade-off (TMDTO) attack is a powerful generic attack against stream ciphers, and the state size of stream ciphers must be at least twice of the key length to avoid the TMDTO attack [5–7]. It implies that designing stream ciphers whose state size is small is impossible.

© Springer Nature Switzerland AG 2020
K. G. Paterson and D. Stebila (Eds.): SAC 2019, LNCS 11959, pp. 365–392, 2020.
https://doi.org/10.1007/978-3-030-38471-5_15

Table 1. State size, security level, and data limitation of Sprout, Plantlet, and Fruit.

Cipher	Size of NFSR	Size of LFSR	Security level	Data limitation
Sprout	40 bits	40 bits	80 bits	2^{40}
Plantlet	40 bits	61 bits	80 bits	2^{30}
Fruit-80	37 bits	43 bits	80 bits	2^{43}
Fruit-128	63 bits	65 bits	128 bits	2^{65}

In FSE 2015, Armknecht and Mikhalev tackled this issue and designed a small-state stream cipher Sprout based on the Grain structure [8]. The claimed security level is 80 bits, although the state size of Sprout is 80 bits, which is not enough to be secure against the TMDTO attack. However, the designers of Sprout introduced a new idea, where the secret key is involved not only in the initialization but also in the keystream generation. Then, the immunity against the TMDTO attack is higher and small-state stream ciphers become possible.

Unfortunately, full Sprout was exposed to many attacks soon after its proposal [9–12]. On the other hand, the idea that the secret key is involved in the keystream generation is promising, and two new small-state stream ciphers were proposed by taking these attacks into account. Fruit is a series of new small-state stream ciphers, and the initial version denoted as Fruit-v1 was proposed in [13]. However, Fruit-v1 was also broken by the divide-and-conquer attack [14] and correlation attack [15]. The designers of Fruit then updated the version of Fruit to be secure against these attacks [16] and proposed a 128-bit security version called Fruit-128 [17]. Recently, the designers proposed Fruit-80 as the formal journal publication [18]. Plantlet is another new small-state stream cipher [19] and is conservatively designed compared with Sprout and Fruit. State sizes of Sprout and Fruit are the same as their key lengths, while the state size of Plantlet is 101 bits to achieve 80-bit security. On the other hand, Plantlet is more carefully designed such that it has high performance under the condition that the secret key is stored in non-volatile memory.

On the Data Limitation of Small-State Stream Ciphers. In this paper, our focus is the data limitation, and this part is significantly different from the original Grain ciphers. For example, Grain-v1 does not have such a data limitation, i.e., 2^{80}-bit keystream can be generated. On the other hand, the designers of small-state stream ciphers establish a limitation of keystream generated from the same key and IV pair. Table 1 summarizes the state size, security level, and the limitation of Sprout, Plantlet, Fruit-80, and Fruit-128. The data limitations of Sprout and Fruit are derived from the size of LFSR, and such a limitation is plausible from the aspect of the security because the same internal state of the LFSR is repeated when the limitation is exceeded. On the other hand, Plantlet allows to output at most 2^{30}-bit keystream. This limitation is significantly smaller than the data limitation derived from the LFSR size.

Table 2. Summary of our key-recovery attacks.

Cipher	Keystream	# IV	Time	Data	Note
Fruit-80	2^{46}	1	$2^{54.5985}$	2^{46}	Recovers 0.1501 bit of the weak key
	2^{43}	2^{21}	$2^{77.8702}$	2^{64}	Recovers the full key
Plantlet	2^{55}	1	$2^{65.9362}$	2^{55}	Recovers 1 bit of the key
	2^{53}	2^{6}	$2^{75.0990}$	2^{59}	Recovers the full key

The following question is naturally raised: If small-state stream ciphers output more keystream bits, can the secret key be recovered? The designers of Fruit said that *Fruit-80 is secure against all types of key recovery attacks without any limitation on the number of keystream bits* [18]. Moreover, the authors of Plantlet did not provide any plausible reason about the data limitation of Plantlet [19]. To show an answer for this question, we estimate a secure size of keystream against correlation attacks.

Our Contributions. A Grain-based structure is preferred to design lightweight stream ciphers because it is comparatively lightweight and had been believed to be secure. However, in CRYPTO 2018, Grain-v1 and the stream cipher mode of Grain-128a were broken by using the fast correlation attack [20], where the authors showed that there are too many linear approximations of the Grain-based structure. This is a potential vulnerability of the Grain-based structure, but the designers of small-state stream ciphers had not cared about security against correlation attacks seriously and it should be considered more carefully than the designers expected.

The goal of the correlation attack is to recover the initial state of the LFSR. Linear approximations are constructed, and many keystream bits generated from the same key and IV pair are used to distinguish the correct initial state of the LFSR. The more keystream is generated from the same key and IV pair, the easier the correlation attack. Therefore, the correlation attack is one of useful metrics to consider the impact of the data limitation.

A small-state stream cipher is a little different from the naive Grain-based structure, and this difference makes the correlation attack more difficult. The major difference is involving a round key during the keystream generation. Therefore, the constructed linear approximations also involve the round key like in linear cryptanalysis on block ciphers. We cannot exploit data where the involved round keys are different because the sign of the correlation depends on the involved round keys. This property surely enhances the security against correlation attacks. On the other hand, interestingly, involving the round key yields a new property that is useful for attackers. The conventional correlation attack does not recover the secret key directly because its goal is to recover the initial state of the LFSR. On the correlation attack on the small-state stream cipher, we can recover the secret key directly by observing the bias direction of its empirical correlation like Matsui's Algorithm 1 [21]. Moreover, since the bias

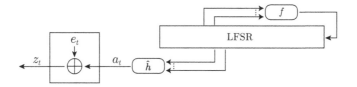

Fig. 1. Correlation attacks on Grain-based stream ciphers

direction does not depend on the IV, we show an extended correlation attack that uses keystream generated from the same key and different IVs.

We applied the correlation attacks to Fruit-80 and Plantlet, and Table 2 summarized the attack. The conventional correlation attack using the single IV can recover the secret key of Fruit-80 and Plantlet if they allow to output 2^{46}-bit and 2^{55}-bit keystream, respectively. The extended correlation attack using multiple IVs requires more data and time complexities, but it is useful to reduce the size of keystream generated from the same key and IV pair. The extended attack successfully breaks the full Fruit-80, and the secret key can be recovered with $2^{77.8702}$ time and 2^{43+21} data. Even if the extended attack is used, we cannot break the full Plantlet because it only allows to output at most 2^{30}-bit keystream. On the other hand, 2^{53}-bit keystream is enough to recover the secret key, and it is quite smaller than 2^{61} deduced by the size of the LFSR.

2   Correlation Attacks on Grain-Based Stream Ciphers

2.1   Notations

We first introduce some notations used in this paper. Let $B = \{\boldsymbol{b}_0, \boldsymbol{b}_1, \ldots, \boldsymbol{b}_{m-1}\}$ be a set of n-bit vectors. Then, $V(B) \subseteq \{0,1\}^n$ denotes a vector space spanned by B, i.e., $V(B) := \{\sum a_i \boldsymbol{b}_i : a_i \in \{0,1\}\}$.

Example 1. When B is given as $\{0100, 1101\}$, the vector space $V(B)$ is $\{0000, 0100, 1101, 1001\}$.

If all vectors in B are linearly independent, the cardinal number of $V(B)$ is 2^m, i.e., $|V(B)| = 2^m$.

2.2   Grain-Based Stream Ciphers

In this paper, we discuss the security of small-state stream ciphers, and many such ciphers adopt the so-called Grain structure. The Grain structure consists of an LFSR and NFSR, where the LFSR is updated independent of the NFSR and the NFSR is updated while involving the output of the LFSR. The keystream bit is generated as the output of a nonlinear filter function, and the domain of the filter function is made of tapping some bits from the LFSR and NFSR states. We focus on the correlation attack [22,23] against the Grain structure. The correlation attack exploits high correlation between the initial state of the

LFSR and corresponding keystream, and the goal is to recover the state of the LFSR. When we apply the correlation attack to the Grain structure, we simply regard the structure as the model described in Fig. 1. The difference from the classical LFSR-based stream ciphers is the existence of a linear function $\hat{h}$, which is generated by linearly approximating the nonlinear filter function. Let $\{a_0, a_1, \ldots, a_{N-1}\}$ be an N-bit output sequence of $\hat{h}$. Then, an N-bit keystream $\{z_0, z_1, \ldots, z_{N-1}\}$ is computed as $z_t = a_t \oplus e_t$, where e_t is a binary noise. Let

$$f(x) = c_0 + c_1 x^1 + c_2 x^2 + \cdots + c_{n-1} x^{n-1} + x^n$$

be the feedback polynomial of the LFSR and $L^{(t)} = (\ell_t, \ell_{t+1}, \ldots, \ell_{t+n-1})$ be an n-bit internal state of the LFSR in round t. Then, the state is updated as

$$L^{(t+1)} = L^{(t)} \times F = L^{(t)} \times \begin{pmatrix} 0 & \cdots & 0 & 0 & c_0 \\ 1 & \cdots & 0 & 0 & c_1 \\ \vdots & \ddots & \vdots & \vdots & \vdots \\ 0 & \cdots & 1 & 0 & c_{n-2} \\ 0 & \cdots & 0 & 1 & c_{n-1} \end{pmatrix},$$

where F is an $n \times n$ binary matrix that represents the feedback polynomial $f(x)$. In concrete Grain-based stream ciphers, the binary noise e_t is nonlinearly generated from the internal state in the LFSR and NFSR and the secret key.

2.3 Linear Approximations for Correlation Attacks

To understand the correlation attack, we first assume the simplest case, where there is $\hat{h}$ such that e_t itself is highly biased. Let p be the probability of $e_t = 1$, and the correlation c is defined as $c = 1 - 2p$. We guess the initial internal state $L^{(0)}$, calculate $\{a_0, a_1, \ldots, a_{N-1}\}$ from the guessed $L^{(0)}$ and $\hat{h}$, and evaluate $\sum_{t=0}^{N-1}(-1)^{a_t \oplus z_t}$, where the sum is computed over the set of integers. If the correct initial state is guessed, the sum is equal to $\sum_{t=0}^{N-1}(-1)^{e_t}$ and follows a normal distribution $\mathcal{N}(Nc, N)$[1]. On the other hand, assuming that the sum behaves at random when an incorrect initial state is guessed, it follows $\mathcal{N}(0, N)$. To distinguish their distributions, we need to collect $N \approx O(1/c^2)$ bits of keystream.

Since the $\hat{h}$ function is linear, there is a corresponding linear mask Λ_h satisfying $\hat{h}(L^{(t)}) = \langle L^{(t)}, \Lambda_h \rangle$. Then, the output a_t is linearly computed as

$$a_t = \hat{h}(L^{(0)} \times F^t) = \langle L^{(0)} \times F^t, \Lambda_h \rangle = \langle L^{(0)}, \Lambda_h \times {}^{\mathrm{T}}F^t \rangle.$$

Once a high-biased $\hat{h}$ is found, the aim of attackers is to find $L^{(0)}$ such that $\sum_{t=0}^{N-1}(-1)^{z_t \oplus \langle L^{(0)}, \Lambda_h \times {}^{\mathrm{T}}F^t \rangle} = \sum_{t=0}^{N-1}(-1)^{e_t}$ is far from 0.

Modern stream ciphers are usually designed such that the binary noise e_t is balanced, but we may be able to observe a high bias by summing optimally chosen binary noises. In other words, the following value

---

[1] If the correct initial state is guessed, it follows $\mathcal{N}(Nc, N - Nc^2)$. However, since N is huge and Nc^2 is small, $\mathcal{N}(Nc, N)$ is enough to approximate the distribution.

$$\bigoplus_{q \in \mathbb{T}_z} e_{t+q} = \bigoplus_{q \in \mathbb{T}_z} a_{t+q} \oplus \bigoplus_{q \in \mathbb{T}_z} z_{t+q}$$

$$= \bigoplus_{q \in \mathbb{T}_z} \langle L^{(0)}, \Lambda_{h,q} \times {}^{\mathrm{T}}F^{t+q} \rangle \oplus \bigoplus_{q \in \mathbb{T}_z} z_{t+q}$$

$$= \left\langle L^{(0)}, \left(\bigoplus_{q \in \mathbb{T}_z} \left(\Lambda_{h,q} \times {}^{\mathrm{T}}F^q \right) \right) \times {}^{\mathrm{T}}F^t \right\rangle \oplus \bigoplus_{q \in \mathbb{T}_z} z_{t+q}$$

could be biased. Note that the $\hat{h}$ function is generated by linearly approximating the filter function, and we do not need to use a common $\hat{h}$ function in all $q \in \mathbb{T}_z$. If a different $\hat{h}$ function is used, the corresponding linear mask is also different. Therefore, different linear masks $\Lambda_{h,q}$ can be used for each q in $\mathbb{T}_z$ in the equation above. For simplicity, we introduce Γ denoted by $\Gamma = \bigoplus_{q \in \mathbb{T}_z} (\Lambda_{h,q} \times {}^{\mathrm{T}}F^q)$. Then, we can introduce the following parity-check equations

$$e'_t(\Gamma) = \left\langle L^{(0)}, \Gamma \times {}^{\mathrm{T}}F^t \right\rangle \oplus \bigoplus_{q \in \mathbb{T}_z} z_{t+q}. \tag{1}$$

We redefine p as the probability satisfying $e'_t(\Gamma) = 1$ for all possible t, and the correlation c is also redefined from the corresponding p.

2.4   Key-Recovery Algorithm Based on FWHT

The most straightforward algorithm requires the time complexity of $O(N2^n)$ to recover $L^{(0)}$. Chose et al. showed that the guess and evaluation procedure can be regarded as a Walsh-Hadamard transform [24]. The fast Walsh-Hadamard transform (FWHT) can be successfully applied to accelerate the algorithm, and it reduces the time complexity to $O(N + n2^n)$.

Definition 1 (Walsh-Hadamard Transform (WHT)). *Given a function* $w : \{0,1\}^n \to \mathbb{Z}$, *the WHT of* w *is defined as* $\hat{w}(s) = \sum_{x \in \{0,1\}^n} w(x)(-1)^{\langle s, x \rangle}$.

When $s \in \{0,1\}^n$ is guessed, the empirical correlation $\sum_{t=0}^{N-1}(-1)^{e'_t}$ is rewritten as

$$\sum_{t=0}^{N-1}(-1)^{e'_t} = \sum_{t=0}^{N-1}(-1)^{\langle s, \Gamma \times {}^{\mathrm{T}}F^t \rangle \oplus \bigoplus_{q \in \mathbb{T}_z} z_{t+q}}$$

$$= \sum_{x \in \{0,1\}^n} \left(\sum_{t \in \{0,1,\dots,N-1 | \Gamma \times {}^{\mathrm{T}}F^t = x\}} (-1)^{\langle s, x \rangle \oplus \bigoplus_{q \in \mathbb{T}_z} z_{t+q}} \right)$$

$$= \sum_{x \in \{0,1\}^n} \left(\sum_{t \in \{0,1,\dots,N-1 | \Gamma \times {}^{\mathrm{T}}F^t = x\}} (-1)^{\bigoplus_{q \in \mathbb{T}_z} z_{t+q}} \right) (-1)^{\langle s, x \rangle}.$$

Therefore, from the following public function w given as

$$w(x) := \sum_{t \in \{0,1,\dots,N-1 | \Gamma \times {}^{\mathrm{T}}F^t = x\}} (-1)^{\bigoplus_{q \in \mathbb{T}_z} z_{t+q}},$$

we get $\hat{w}$ by using the FWHT, where $\hat{w}(s)$ is the empirical correlation when s is guessed.

2.5   Use of Multiple Linear Masks

In [20], Todo et al. showed that Grain-based stream ciphers have a huge number of high-biased linear masks.[2] The $\hat{h}$ function is generated by linearly approximating the filter function, and the filter function tends to have many linear approximate representations. For example, let us consider the following function

$$h(x) = x_0 x_1 + x_2 x_3 + x_4 x_5 + x_6 x_7 + x_0 x_4 x_8,$$

which is used in the filter function of Grain-128a [25] and Plantlet. Then, there are 2^8 linear masks Λ such that the correlation of $h(x) \oplus \langle x, \Lambda \rangle$ is $\pm 2^{-4}$. In other words, we can construct 2^8 high-biased linear masks, and each one generates a different linear mask Γ.

Assuming that there are m high-biased linear masks $(\Gamma_0, \Gamma_1, \ldots, \Gamma_{m-1})$ and letting c_i be the correlation when Γ_i is used, we compute

$$\sum_{i \in \{\{0,1,\ldots,m-1\} | c_i > 0\}} (-1)^{e'_t(\Gamma_i)} - \sum_{i \in \{\{0,1,\ldots,m-1\} | c_i < 0\}} (-1)^{e'_t(\Gamma_i)},$$

where $e'(\Gamma)$ is defined in Eq. (1). When we guess the initial state $L^{(0)}$, the value above follows a normal distribution $\mathcal{N}(mN\bar{c}, mN)$, where $\bar{c}$ is the average value of absolute values of c_i, i.e.,

$$\bar{c} = \frac{\sum_{i,c_i > 0} c_i - \sum_{i,c_i < 0} c_i}{m} = \frac{\sum_i |c_i|}{m}.$$

The key recovery algorithm based on the FWHT also works. Assuming that the data complexity (size of keystream) is N, the time complexity $O(N)$ is required to collect data. Then, we apply m high-biased linear masks for N data, and the time complexity is $O(mN)$. Finally, the FWHT is applied, and the time complexity is $O(n2^n)$. In total, the time complexity is $O(N + mN + n2^n)$.

3   Correlation Attacks on Small-State Stream Ciphers

Almost all small-state stream ciphers are based on the Grain structure, but it is modified from the original structure to avoid the time-memory-data trade-off (TMDTO) attack. Figure 2 shows the overview of Grain-based small-state stream ciphers. The major difference is involving the round key in the state update function g and filter function h.

In this paper, we apply the correlation attack to Grain-based small-state stream ciphers. The basic attack strategy is the same as the correlation attack described in Sect. 2, but some different strategy is used to be optimized for the small-state stream ciphers. In this section, we summarize three major differences from the original correlation attack against the Grain structure.

---

[2] Another contribution of [20] is to show the link between the parity-check equation and the multiplication over a finite field. This link is used to execute the correlation attack without guessing the whole of the initial state of the LFSR, but we do not use this technique because the size of the LFSR is small enough.

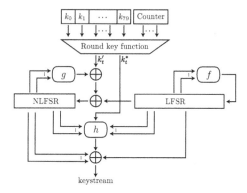

Fig. 2. Overview of Grain-based small-state stream ciphers

3.1   Involving Round Keys

Generally, involved round keys makes correlation attacks difficult because constructed linear approximations also involve the round key. In other words, involved round keys must be constant when we collect data used in the correlation attack. The sequence of round keys usually has a small cycle to avoid degradation in efficiency. Assuming that the cycle length is ϕ, the available data decreases to N/ϕ when N-bit keystream is used. For example, in Fruit-80, both k_t' and k_t^* are generated from the secret key and a 7-bit counter. Therefore, the same pair of round keys is used every 2^7 rounds, i.e., $\phi = 2^7$. In Plantlet, only k_t' is used and $k_t' = k_{t \bmod 80} + c_t$. Since the counter c_t is public and linear, we can remove c_t efficiently. Thus, $\phi = 80$.

On the attack procedure of the correlation attack, the only difference is the interval of data sampling. Therefore, we can use the same attack strategy described in Sect. 2. Then, the empirical correlation follows $\mathcal{N}(mN\bar{c}/\phi, mN/\phi)$ when the correct initial state is guessed. Otherwise, it follows $\mathcal{N}(0, mN/\phi)$. Since m linear masks are used every ϕ rounds, the data and time complexities are N and $O(N + mN/\phi + n2^n)$.

3.2   Finding Multiple Linear Approximations with High Correlation

The reason why the Grain structure has many high-biased linear masks comes from the fact that there are many linear approximations of the filter function. Therefore, Grain-based small-state stream ciphers also inherit the property. On the other hand, finding such concrete linear masks is still difficult. A systematic method was used to find high-biased linear masks of Grain-128 and Grain-128a in [20], but the correlation found by the method is too small to attack small-state stream ciphers. Therefore, we use a more heuristic method. Recalling Eq. (1), the linear approximation exploits the sum $\bigoplus_{q \in \mathbb{T}_z} z_{t+q}$, where we exhaustively evaluate preferable $\mathbb{T}_z$. Unfortunately, only considering $\mathbb{T}_z$ is not enough because the sum $\bigoplus_{q \in \mathbb{T}_z} z_{t+q}$ always involves new bits, which are computed from the g

function. Let $N_t = (n_t, n_{t+1}, \ldots, n_{t+m-1})$ be an internal state in the NFSR. Then, the new bit n_{t+m} is computed by $n_{t+m} = k'_t \oplus g_t \oplus \ell_t$, where g_t denotes the output of the g function and ℓ_t denotes the output of the LFSR in the tth round. We introduce a value b_t such that

$$b_t = n_{t+m} \oplus k'_t \oplus \ell_t \oplus g_t = 0.$$

Then, our linear approximations are constructed from $\bigoplus_{q \in \mathbb{T}_z} z_{t+q} \oplus \bigoplus_{i \in \mathbb{T}_b} b_{t+i}$.

Our task exhaustively evaluates preferable $\mathbb{T}_z$ and $\mathbb{T}_b$. To reduce the search space, we evaluate $\mathbb{T}_z$ and $\mathbb{T}_b$ such that the exploited number of rounds is small, i.e., the maximum number of values in $\mathbb{T}_z$ and $\mathbb{T}_b$ are not large.

3.3   Exploiting Keystream Generated from Different IVs

As shown in Sect. 3.1, the data must be sampled such that involved round keys are constant. While involved round keys are constant, they are still involved in the linear approximations. It implies that the bias direction depends on the involved round keys like in linear cryptanalysis on block ciphers.

We construct our linear approximations from $\bigoplus_{q \in \mathbb{T}_z} z_{t+q} \oplus \bigoplus_{i \in \mathbb{T}_b} b_{t+i}$, and the term $\bigoplus_{i \in \mathbb{T}_b} k'_{t+i}$ is included in $\bigoplus_{i \in \mathbb{T}_b} b_{t+i}$. Then, parity-check equations that we eventually construct change from Eq. (1) to

$$e'_t(\Gamma) \oplus \bigoplus_{i \in \mathbb{T}_b} k'_{t+i} = \left\langle L^{(0)}, \Gamma \times {}^{T}F^t \right\rangle \oplus \bigoplus_{q \in \mathbb{T}_z} z_{t+q}. \tag{2}$$

In other words, the bias direction is inverted if $\bigoplus_{i \in \mathbb{T}_b} k'_{t+i} = 1$. It implies that we can easily recover the involved round keys by observing the bias direction.

Another important observation is that the bias direction is preserved unless the secret key changes. This property is useful when we consider an attack in which the size of keystream generated from the same key and IV pair is limited. Let N be the available keystream size, m be the number of linear masks, $\bar{c}$ be the average number of absolute values of correlations, and ϕ be the cycle length. Once we execute the correlation attack, the empirical correlation follows

$$\begin{cases} \mathcal{N}(mN\bar{c}/\phi, mN/\phi) & \text{for correct initial state and } \bigoplus_{i \in \mathbb{T}_b} k'_{t+i} = 0, \\ \mathcal{N}(0, mN/\phi) & \text{for incorrect initial state,} \\ \mathcal{N}(-mN\bar{c}/\phi, mN/\phi) & \text{for correct initial state and } \bigoplus_{i \in \mathbb{T}_b} k'_{t+i} = 1. \end{cases}$$

We introduce a threshold th such that

$$\Pr[|X| > th \mid X \sim \mathcal{N}(0, mN/\phi)] \leq 2^{-n},$$

where 2^n denotes the number of candidates of the initial state of the LFSR. We pick initial states of the LFSR whose absolute value of empirical correlation is larger than the threshold th and store only the information whether its bias direction is positive or negative. Then, one incorrect initial state remains in average, where we assume that it behaves randomly, i.e., the probability that the bias direction is positive is $1/2$. Similarly, let ϵ be the probability that the correct initial state survives, i.e.,

$$\epsilon = \Pr[X > th \mid X \sim \mathcal{N}(mN\bar{c}/\phi, mN/\phi)].$$

In other words, the bias direction leans toward positive with probability $1/2 + \epsilon$ when $\bigoplus_{i \in \mathbb{T}_b} k'_{t+i} = 0$. Similarly, it leans toward positive with probability $1/2 - \epsilon$ when $\bigoplus_{i \in \mathbb{T}_b} k'_{t+i} = 1$. Assuming that we repeat the attack procedure above over N_{iv} IVs under the fixed key, the number that the bias direction is positive follows a binomial distribution $\mathcal{B}(N_{iv}, 1/2 + \epsilon)$. Since it follows $\mathcal{B}(N_{iv}, 1/2)$ in the case of random behavior, we can distinguish the correct bias direction by using $N_{iv} = O(1/\epsilon^2)$ and recover $\bigoplus_{i \in \mathbb{T}_b} k'_{t+i}$. Since we repeat the correlation attack N_{iv} times, the data and time complexities are $N \times N_{iv}$ and $O(N_{iv} \times (N + mN/\phi + n2^n))$, respectively.

Note that this technique does not improve both time and data complexities. In other words, if we can collect enough keystream such that ϵ is almost 1, we do not need to use this technique because the naive correlation attack is always more efficient than this technique. This technique is useful only when there are data limitations about the keystream generated from the same key and IV pair.

4   Cryptanalysis on Full Fruit-80

In this section, we apply the correlation attack to Fruit-80. As shown in Sects. 2 and 3, we can estimate the data and time complexities by enumerating linear masks with high correlation and estimating the average value of correlations.

4.1   Specification of Fruit-80

The keystream generation of Fruit-80 is depicted in Fig. 2, where the sizes of NFSR and LFSR are 37 and 43 bits, respectively. Let $L^{(t)} = (\ell_t, \ell_{t+1}, \ell_{t+2}, \ldots, \ell_{t+42})$ and $N^{(t)} = (n_t, n_{t+1}, n_{t+2}, \ldots, n_{t+36})$ be the internal state of t rounds after the initialization. Then, the state update function is defined as

$$\ell_{t+43} = \ell_{t+37} \oplus \ell_{t+28} \oplus \ell_{t+23} \oplus \ell_{t+18} \oplus \ell_{t+8} \oplus \ell_t,$$

$$n_{t+37} = k'_t \oplus \ell_t \oplus g_t,$$

$$g_t = n_t \oplus n_{t+10} \oplus n_{t+20} \oplus n_{t+12}n_{t+3} \oplus n_{t+14}n_{t+25}$$
$$\oplus n_{t+5}n_{t+23}n_{t+31} \oplus n_{t+8}n_{t+18} \oplus n_{t+28}n_{t+30}n_{t+32}n_{t+34},$$

$$z_t = h_t \oplus \bigoplus_{j \in \mathbb{A}} n_{t+j} \oplus \ell_{t+38},$$

$$h_t = k^*_t \cdot (n_{t+36} \oplus \ell_{t+19})$$
$$\oplus \ell_{t+6}\ell_{t+15} \oplus \ell_{t+1}\ell_{t+22} \oplus n_{t+35}\ell_{t+27} \oplus n_{t+1}n_{t+24} \oplus n_{t+1}n_{t+33}\ell_{t+42},$$

where $\mathbb{A} = \{0, 7, 19, 29, 36\}$.

The round keys k_t' and k_t^* are generated from the secret key and 7-bit counter $C^{(t)} = (c_t^0 \| c_t^1 \| \cdots \| c_t^6)$ as

$$k_t' = k_r \cdot k_{p+16} \cdot k_{q+48} \oplus k_r \cdot k_{p+16} \oplus k_{p+16} \cdot k_{q+48} \oplus k_r \cdot k_{q+48} \oplus k_{p+16},$$

$$k_t^* = k_r \cdot k_{p+16} \oplus k_{p+16} \cdot k_{q+48} \oplus k_r \cdot k_{q+48} \oplus k_r \oplus k_{p+16} \oplus k_{q+48},$$

where $p = (c_t^1 \| c_t^2 \| c_t^3 \| c_t^4 \| c_t^5)$, $q = (c_t^2 \| c_t^3 \| c_t^4 \| c_t^5 \| c_t^6)$, and $r = (c_t^0 \| c_t^1 \| c_t^2 \| c_t^3)$.

4.2   Enumerating Linear Masks with High Correlation

We exhaustively evaluated various $\mathbb{T}_z$ and $\mathbb{T}_b$ in the range that the maximum number of values in $\mathbb{T}_z$ and $\mathbb{T}_b$ are 8. As a result, $\mathbb{T}_z = \{0, 2, 3, 7\}$ and $\mathbb{T}_b = \{0, 1, 2, 6\}$ yielded the highest correlation.

Core Linear Approximate Representation. Let b_t be defined as $b_t = n_{t+37} \oplus k_t' \oplus \ell_t \oplus g_t = 0$, and let us consider the following sum of keystream.

$$\bigoplus_{q \in \{0,2,3,7\}} z_{t+q} = \bigoplus_{q \in \{0,2,3,7\}} z_{t+q} \oplus \bigoplus_{i \in \{0,1,2,6\}} b_{t+i}$$

$$= \bigoplus_{i \in \{0,1,2,6\}} k_{t+i}' \oplus \bigoplus_{i \in \{0,1,2,6\}} \ell_{t+i} \oplus \bigoplus_{q \in \{0,2,3,7\}} \ell_{t+38+q}$$

$$\oplus \bigoplus_{q \in \{0,2,3,7\}} \left(h_{t+q} \oplus \bigoplus_{j \in \mathbb{A}} n_{t+q+j} \right) \oplus \bigoplus_{i \in \{0,1,2,6\}} \left(n_{t+37+i} \oplus g_{t+i} \right).$$

Since the internal state of the LFSR can be guessed in the correlation attack, $\bigoplus_{i \in \{0,1,2,6\}} \ell_{t+i} \oplus \bigoplus_{q \in \{0,2,3,7\}} \ell_{t+38+q}$ is computed. Therefore, assuming that the following Boolean function

$$g_t' = \bigoplus_{q \in \{0,2,3,7\}} \left(h_{t+q} \oplus \bigoplus_{j \in \mathbb{A}} n_{t+q+j} \right) \oplus \bigoplus_{i \in \{0,1,2,6\}} \left(n_{t+37+i} \oplus g_{t+i} \right) \qquad (3)$$

is highly biased and the correlation of g_t' is c, the following approximation

$$\bigoplus_{q \in \{0,2,3,7\}} z_{t+q} \oplus \langle L^{(t)}, \Gamma_{base} \rangle = g_t' \oplus \bigoplus_{i \in \{0,1,2,6\}} k_t' \approx \bigoplus_{i \in \{0,1,2,6\}} k_t'$$

holds with the correlation c, where the linear mask Γ_{base} is defined as

$$\langle L^{(t)}, \Gamma_{base} \rangle = \bigoplus_{i \in \{0,1,2,6\}} \ell_{t+i} \oplus \bigoplus_{q \in \{0,2,3,7\}} \ell_{t+38+q}.$$

When we use the formula of Eq. (2), $e_t'(\Gamma_{base}) = g'$.

Generating Multiple Linear Approximations. Before we evaluate the correlation of g'_t, we first focus on the linear approximation of h_{t+q}, i.e., we focus on the correlation of the following function

$$h_{t+q} \oplus \langle L_{t+q}, \Lambda_{h,q} \rangle = k^*_{t+q} \cdot (n_{t+q+36} \oplus \ell_{t+q+19}) \oplus \ell_{t+q+6} \ell_{t+q+15}$$
$$\oplus \ell_{t+q+1} \ell_{t+q+22} \oplus n_{t+q+35} \ell_{t+q+27} \oplus n_{t+q+1} n_{t+q+24}$$
$$\oplus n_{t+q+1} n_{t+q+33} \ell_{t+q+42} \oplus \langle L_{t+q}, \Lambda_{h,q} \rangle.$$

When $k^*_{t+q} = 0$, six bits listed as ℓ_{t+q+1}, ℓ_{t+q+6}, ℓ_{t+q+15}, ℓ_{t+q+22}, ℓ_{t+q+27}, and ℓ_{t+q+42} are involved in h_{t+q}. Therefore, if other bits except for the six bits above are involved in $\langle L_{t+q}, \Lambda_{h,q} \rangle$, the correlation of $h_{t+q} \oplus \langle L_{t+q}, \Lambda_{h,q} \rangle$ is always 0. Therefore, $\Lambda_{h,q}$ must be chosen from the vector space $V(u_1, u_6, u_{15}, u_{22}, u_{27}, u_{42})$, where u_i denotes a unit vector whose $(i+1)$th element is 1 and the vector space $V(B)$ is defined in Sect. 2. When $k^*_t = 1$, $\Lambda_{h,q} \in u_{19} + V(u_1, u_6, u_{15}, u_{22}, u_{27}, u_{42})$ because ℓ_{t+q+19} is linearly involved.

Recall Eq. (3), where $\bigoplus_{q \in \{0,2,3,7\}} h_{t+q}$ is used. Therefore, we introduce a linear mask Λ such that the following equation

$$\bigoplus_{q \in \{0,2,3,7\}} h_{t+q} \oplus \langle L_t, \Lambda \rangle = \bigoplus_{q \in \{0,2,3,7\}} \left(h_{t+q} \oplus \langle L_{t+q}, \Lambda_{h,q} \rangle \right)$$

holds. Then, Λ can take a value from the set $k^*_t u_{19} + k^*_{t+2} u_{21} + k^*_{t+3} u_{22} + k^*_{t+7} u_{26} + V(B)$, where

$$B = \{u_1, u_3, u_4, u_6, u_8, u_9, u_{13}, u_{15}, u_{17}, u_{18}, u_{22}, u_{24}, u_{25}, u_{27}, u_{29}, u_{30}, u_{34}, u_{42},$$
$$u_{44} = u_{38} + u_{29} + u_{24} + u_{19} + u_9 + u_1,$$
$$u_{45} = u_{39} + u_{30} + u_{25} + u_{20} + u_{10} + u_2,$$
$$u_{49} = (u_{37} + u_{28} + u_{23} + u_{18} + u_8 + u_0) + u_{34} + u_{29} + u_{24} + u_{14} + u_6\}.$$

Since all vectors in B are linearly independent, $|V(B)| = 2^{21}$. Since the linear approximation involves k^*_t nonlinearly, the correlation depends on k^*_t. Therefore, we first assume weak keys as $(k^*_t, k^*_{t+2}, k^*_{t+3}, k^*_{t+7}) = (0, 1, 0, 0)$ because the use of this weak key yielded the highest correlation eventually. Note that this weak-key assumption can be removed in the attack procedure of the correlation attack. We substitute $(0, 1, 0, 0)$ for $(k^*_t, k^*_{t+2}, k^*_{t+3}, k^*_{t+7})$, and then, Λ takes a value from the set $u_{21} + V(B)$.

The internal state of the LFSR is guessed in the correlation attack. Namely, if $g'_t \oplus \langle L^{(t)}, \Lambda \rangle$ is biased for multiple Λ, we can construct multiple linear approximations. The following

$$\sum_{q \in \{0,2,3,7\}} z_{t+q} \oplus \langle L^{(t)}, \Gamma_{base} \rangle \oplus \langle L^{(t)}, \Lambda \rangle = \sum_{i \in \{0,1,2,6\}} k'_{t+i} \oplus g'_t \oplus \langle L^{(t)}, \Lambda \rangle$$
$$\approx \sum_{i \in \{0,1,2,6\}} k'_{t+i}$$

represents linear approximations for our correlation attack, and the correlation that this approximation holds coincides with the correlation of $g'_t \oplus \langle L^{(t)}, \Lambda \rangle$. We want to evaluate correlations of $g'_t \oplus \langle L^{(t)}, \Lambda \rangle$ for $\Lambda \in \boldsymbol{u}_{21} + V(B)$. To evaluate them simply, we extract independent terms from $g'_t \oplus \langle L^{(t)}, \Lambda \rangle$ as

$$g'_t \oplus \langle L^{(t)}, \Lambda \rangle$$

$$= \ell_{t+6}\ell_{t+15} \oplus \ell_{t+6} \cdot \Lambda[6] \oplus \ell_{t+15} \cdot \Lambda[15] \tag{4}$$

$$\oplus \ell_{t+9}\ell_{t+18} \oplus \ell_{t+9} \cdot \Lambda[9] \oplus \ell_{t+18} \cdot \Lambda[18] \tag{5}$$

$$\oplus \ell_{t+3}\ell_{t+24} \oplus \ell_{t+3} \cdot \Lambda[3] \oplus \ell_{t+24} \cdot \Lambda[24] \tag{6}$$

$$\oplus \ell_{t+4}\ell_{t+25} \oplus \ell_{t+4} \cdot \Lambda[4] \oplus \ell_{t+25} \cdot \Lambda[25] \tag{7}$$

$$\oplus \ell_{t+1}\ell_{t+22} \oplus \ell_{t+13}\ell_{t+22} \oplus \ell_{t+1} \cdot \Lambda[1] \oplus \ell_{t+13} \cdot \Lambda[13] \oplus \ell_{t+22} \cdot \Lambda[22] \tag{8}$$

$$\oplus n_{t+42}\ell_{t+34} \oplus \ell_{t+34} \cdot \Lambda[34]. $$

$$\oplus g''_t \oplus \langle L^{(t)}, \Lambda' \rangle, \tag{9}$$

where $g''_t \oplus \langle L^{(t)}, \Lambda' \rangle$ is the remaining term after extracting six lines. Equation (4) is independent of other terms, and each correlation is $\pm 2^{-1}$ for 2^2 linear masks $\Lambda[6, 15] \in \{00, 01, 10, 11\}$. Similarly, the correlations of Eqs. (5), (6), and (7) are also $\pm 2^{-1}$ for 2^2 linear masks. In Eq. (8), the correlation is $\pm 2^{-1}$ for $\Lambda[1, 13, 22] \in \{000, 001, 110, 111\}$. In Eq. (9), the correlation is 2^{-1} for any $\Lambda[34]$. In total, the correlation of the above six lines is $\pm 2^{-6}$, and their signs are determined by $\Lambda[1, 3, 4, 6, 9, 13, 15, 18, 22, 24, 25, 34]$, and the number of linear masks is $2^{2+2+2+2+2+1}$. In other words, there are 2^{11} linear masks $\Lambda[1, 3, 4, 6, 9, 13, 15, 18, 22, 24, 25, 34]$ satisfying $g'_t \oplus \langle \Lambda, L \rangle \approx g''_t \oplus \langle L^{(t)}, \Lambda' \rangle$ with correlation $\pm 2^{-6}$.

Finally, we want to evaluate the correlation of $g''_t \oplus \langle L^{(t)}, \Lambda' \rangle$, and it is calculated by using the brute force method. Eventually, we can find 12 Λ' whose absolute values of correlations are $2^{-17.415}$ and $2^{-17.8301}$, and please refer to Appendix A in detail. Since there are 2^{11} linear masks Λ satisfying $g'_t \oplus \langle L^{(0)}, \Lambda \rangle \approx g''_t + \langle L^{(0)}, \Lambda' \rangle$ with correlation $\pm 2^{-6}$, there are 12×2^{11} linear masks Λ such that the correlations of $g'_t \oplus \langle L^{(t)}, \Lambda \rangle$ are $\pm 2^{-23.415}$ and $\pm 2^{-23.8301}$.

4.3   Correlation Attack against Fruit-80

There are 12×2^{11} linear masks whose correlations are $\pm 2^{-23.415}$ and $\pm 2^{-23.8301}$, respectively. Thus, the attack parameter is

$$m = 24 \times 2^{11}, \quad \bar{c} = \frac{2^{-23.415} + 2^{-23.8301}}{2} = 2^{-23.6077}.$$

We assume that N keystream bits are observed. The linear approximation depends on k'_t and k^*_t, and the same (k'_t, k^*_t) is used every 2^7 rounds. Therefore, $\phi = 2^7$. As we already showed in Sect. 3, the empirical correlation follows $\mathcal{N}(mN\bar{c}/\phi, mN/\phi)$ if we guess the initial state correctly and $\sum_{i \in \{0,1,2,6\}} k'_t = 0$. When $\sum_{i \in \{0,1,2,6\}} k'_t = 1$, the bias direction is inverted, i.e., $\mathcal{N}(-mN\bar{c}/\phi, mN/\phi)$. Otherwise, we assume that the empirical correlation behaves randomly, i.e., $\mathcal{N}(0, mN/\phi)$.

Table 3. Success probability of correlation attack on Fruit-80.

Keystream	2^{40}	2^{41}	2^{42}	2^{43}	2^{44}	2^{45}	2^{46}	2^{47}	Threshold
Probability	0%	0%	0%	0.27%	18.36%	96.09%	100.00%	100.00%	$th_{2^{-42}}$
	0%	0%	0%	0.01%	3.76%	81.15%	100.00%	100.00%	$th_{2^{-52}}$

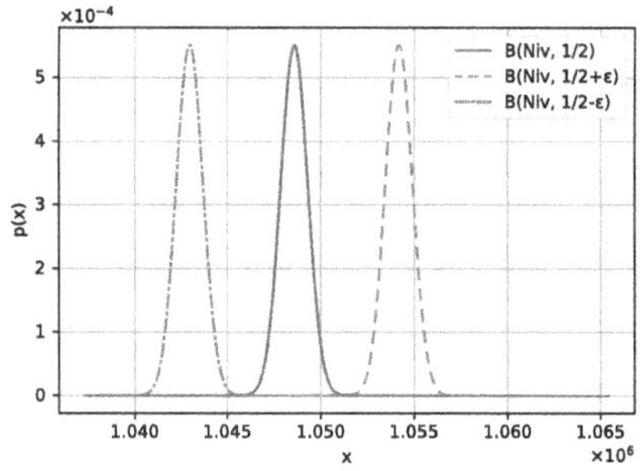

Fig. 3. Comparison of binomial distributions on Fruit-80

We introduce a threshold th_p satisfying $\Pr[|X| > th_p \mid X \sim \mathcal{N}(0, mN/\phi)] = p$, and pick initial states whose absolute value of the empirical correlation is greater than th_p. Table 3 summarizes the probability that the correct initial state survives. To avoid all-zero initial state of the LFSR, the leftmost bit of the initial state of the LFSR is forced to 1. Therefore, the number of candidates of the initial state of the LFSR is 2^{42}. Therefore, using 2^{46} keystream with $th_{2^{-52}}$ is enough to recover the initial state of the LFSR uniquely. Then, the data and time complexities are $N = 2^{46}$ and $N + mN/\phi + n2^n = 2^{54.5985}$.

Reducing Data Complexity and Removing Weak-Key Assumption. As explained in Table 3, using 2^{43} keystream is not enough to recover the initial state of the LFSR. Even if $th_{2^{-42}}$ is used, the survival probability is $\epsilon = 0.27\%$. Besides, it assumes the use of the weak key. To enhance the success probability and remove the weak-key assumption, we exploit the technique described in Sect. 3.3.

We use 2^{43} keystream generated from the same key and IV pair. We pick initial states of the LFSR whose absolute value of empirical correlation is larger than the threshold $th_{2^{-42}}$ and store only the information whether its bias direction is positive or negative. Then, we repeat this procedure while changing IVs, and let N_{iv} be the number of repetitions. If the secret key belongs to the weak key, the number that the bias direction is positive follows a binomial distribution $\mathcal{B}(N_{iv}, 1/2 + \epsilon)$. If the secret key is not weak key, it follows $\mathcal{B}(N_{iv}, 1/2)$.

Figure 3 shows the comparison of the binomial distributions $\mathcal{B}(N_{iv}, 1/2)$ and $\mathcal{B}(N_{iv}, 1/2 \pm \epsilon)$, where $N_{iv} = 2^{21}$ and $\epsilon = 0.27\% = 2^{-1.8890}$. We can distinguish three binomial distributions enough. As a result, the data and time complexities are

$$N \times N_{iv} = 2^{43} \times 2^{21} = 2^{64},$$

$$N_{iv} \times (N + mN/\phi + n2^n) = 2^{21} \times (2^{43} + 24 \times 2^{11+43-7} + 42 \times 2^{42}) \approx 2^{72.67},$$

respectively.

Finally, we analyze the round-key functions, which are not balanced. The probabilities satisfying $k_t^* = 1$ and $k_t^* = 0$ are $3/4$ and $1/4$, respectively. Moreover, the probabilities satisfying $k_t' = 1$ and $k_t' = 0$ are $3/8$ and $5/8$, respectively. Therefore, the probability satisfying weak keys is $(1/4)^3 \times (3/4) = 2^{-6.4150}$. In other words, we can recover $-\log_2(15/16)$, $4 - \log_2(3/8)$, $4 - \log_2(5/8)$ bits of information with probabilities $(1-2^{-6.4150})$, $2^{-6.4150} \times (3/8)$, and $2^{-6.4150} \times (5/8)$, respectively. Therefore, only 0.1501 bits of information is recovered. On the other hand, exploited rounds t are restricted as $t \in \mathbb{S}_i$, where $\mathbb{S}_i := \{2^7 \times j + i \mid j = \{0, 1, \ldots, N/2^7 - 1\}\}$. We can repeat this attack procedure for $\mathbb{S}_1, \mathbb{S}_2, \ldots, \mathbb{S}_i$. By taking the trade-off with the brute-force search into account, the time complexity is optimal when 27 sets are used, i.e., $27 \times 2^{72.67} + 2^{80-0.1501 \times 27} \approx 2^{77.8702}$. Note that we assume that the exhaustive search of the secret key can be immediately filtered by using the recovered round keys, and we believe that it is possible because the round key function is very simple.

5   Plantlet

5.1   Specification

Plantlet is another Grain-based small-state stream cipher and consists of a 61-bit LFSR and 40-bit NFSR. Let $L^{(t)}$ and $N^{(t)}$ be the internal state in round t after the initialization, and they are represented as

$$L^{(t)} = (\ell_t, \ell_{t+1}, \ell_{t+2}, \ldots, \ell_{t+60}),$$
$$N^{(t)} = (n_t, n_{t+1}, n_{t+2}, \ldots, n_{t+39}).$$

Then, the state update function is defined as

$$\ell_{t+61} = \ell_{t+54} \oplus \ell_{t+43} \oplus \ell_{t+34} \oplus \ell_{t+20} \oplus \ell_{t+14} \oplus \ell_t,$$

$$n_{t+40} = k_t' \oplus \ell_t \oplus g_t,$$

$$\begin{aligned} g_t = {} & n_t \oplus n_{t+13} \oplus n_{t+19} \oplus n_{t+35} \oplus n_{t+39} \oplus n_{t+2}n_{t+25} \oplus n_{t+3}n_{t+5} \\ & \oplus n_{t+7}n_{t+8} \oplus n_{t+14}n_{t+21} \oplus n_{t+16}n_{t+18} \oplus n_{t+22}n_{t+24} \oplus n_{t+26}n_{t+32} \\ & \oplus n_{t+33}n_{t+36}n_{t+37}n_{t+38} \oplus n_{t+10}n_{t+11}n_{t+12} \oplus n_{t+27}n_{t+30}n_{t+31}, \end{aligned}$$

$$z_t = h_t \oplus \ell_{t+30} \oplus \bigoplus_{j \in \mathbb{A}} n_{t+j},$$

$$h_t = n_{t+4}\ell_{t+6} \oplus \ell_{t+8}\ell_{t+10} \oplus \ell_{t+32}\ell_{t+17} \oplus \ell_{t+19}\ell_{t+23} \oplus n_{t+4}\ell_{t+32}n_{t+38},$$

where $\mathbb{A} = \{1, 6, 15, 17, 23, 28, 34\}$. Moreover, the round key k_t' is defined as

$$k_t' = k_{t \bmod 80} \oplus c_t,$$

where c_t is 0 and 1 when $0 \le (t \bmod 8) \le 3$ and $4 \le (t \bmod 8) \le 7$, respectively.

5.2   Enumerating Linear Masks with High Correlation

We heuristically searched for various $\mathbb{T}_z$ and $\mathbb{T}_b$, where we restricted the number of elements in $\mathbb{T}_z$ and the maximum number of values in $\mathbb{T}_z$ and $\mathbb{T}_b$ to 2 and 13, respectively. As a result, $\mathbb{T}_z = \{0, 12\}$ and $\mathbb{T}_b = \{1, 3, 5, 7, 8, 9, 10\}$ yielded the highest correlation.

Core Linear Approximate Representation. Let b_t be defined as $b_t = n_{t+40} \oplus k_t' \oplus \ell_t \oplus g_t = 0$, and let us consider the following sum of keystream bits.

$$
\bigoplus_{q \in \{0,12\}} z_{t+q} = \bigoplus_{q \in \{0,12\}} z_{t+q} \oplus \bigoplus_{i \in \{1,3,5,7,8,9,10\}} b_{t+i}
$$

$$
= \bigoplus_{i \in \{1,3,5,7,8,9,10\}} k_{t+i}' \oplus \bigoplus_{q \in \{0,12\}} \ell_{t+30+q} \oplus \bigoplus_{i \in \{1,3,5,7,8,9,10\}} \ell_{t+i}
$$

$$
\oplus \bigoplus_{q \in \{0,12\}} \left(h_{t+q} \oplus \bigoplus_{j \in \mathbb{A}} n_{t+q+j} \right) \oplus \bigoplus_{i \in \{1,3,5,7,8,9,10\}} \left(n_{t+40+i} \oplus g_{t+i} \right).
$$

Since the internal state of the LFSR can be guessed in the correlation attack, $\bigoplus_{q \in \{0,12\}} \ell_{t+30+q} \oplus \bigoplus_{i \in \{1,3,5,7,8,9,10\}} \ell_{t+i}$ is computed. Therefore, assuming that the following Boolean function

$$
g_t' = \bigoplus_{q \in \{0,12\}} \left(h_{t+q} \oplus \bigoplus_{j \in \mathbb{A}} n_{t+q+j} \right) \oplus \bigoplus_{i \in \{1,3,5,7,8,9,10\}} \left(n_{t+40+i} \oplus g_{t+i} \right) \qquad (10)
$$

is highly biased and the correlation of g_t' is c, the following linear approximation

$$
\bigoplus_{q \in \{0,12\}} z_{t+q} \oplus \langle L^{(t)}, \Gamma_{base} \rangle = \bigoplus_{i \in \{1,3,5,7,8,9,10\}} k_{t+i}' \oplus g_t' \approx \bigoplus_{i \in \{1,3,5,7,8,9,10\}} k_{t+i}'
$$

holds with the correlation c, where Γ_{base} is defined as

$$
\langle L^{(t)}, \Gamma_{base} \rangle = \bigoplus_{i \in \{1,3,5,7,8,9,10\}} \ell_{t+i} \oplus \bigoplus_{q \in \{0,12\}} \ell_{t+30+q}.
$$

Generating Multiple Linear Approximations. We first focus on the linear approximation of h_{t+q}, i.e., we focus on the correlation of the following function

$$
h_{t+q} \oplus \langle L_{t+q}, \Lambda_{h,q} \rangle = n_{t+q+4} \ell_{t+q+6} \oplus \ell_{t+q+8} \ell_{t+q+10} \oplus \ell_{t+q+32} \ell_{t+q+17}
$$
$$
\oplus \ell_{t+q+19} \ell_{t+q+23} \oplus n_{t+q+4} \ell_{t+q+32} n_{t+q+38} \oplus \langle L_{t+q}, \Lambda_{h,q} \rangle.
$$

Seven bits listed as ℓ_{t+q+6}, ℓ_{t+q+8}, ℓ_{t+q+10}, ℓ_{t+q+17}, ℓ_{t+q+19}, ℓ_{t+q+23}, and ℓ_{t+q+32} are involved in h_{t+q}. Therefore, $\Lambda_{h,q}$ must be chosen from the vector space

$V(\boldsymbol{u}_6, \boldsymbol{u}_8, \boldsymbol{u}_{10}, \boldsymbol{u}_{17}, \boldsymbol{u}_{19}, \boldsymbol{u}_{23}, \boldsymbol{u}_{32})$, where $\boldsymbol{u}_i$ denotes a unit vector whose $(i+1)$th element is 1 and the vector space $V(B)$ is defined in Sect. 2.

Recall Eq. (10), where $\bigoplus_{q \in \{0,12\}} h_{t+q}$ is used. Therefore, we introduce a linear mask Λ such that the following equation

$$\bigoplus_{q \in \{0,12\}} h_{t+q} \oplus \langle L_t, \Lambda \rangle = \bigoplus_{q \in \{0,12\}} \left(h_{t+q} \oplus \langle L_{t+q}, \Lambda_{h,q} \rangle \right)$$

holds. Then, Λ can take a value from the set $V(B)$, where

$$B = \{\boldsymbol{u}_6, \boldsymbol{u}_8, \boldsymbol{u}_{10}, \boldsymbol{u}_{17}, \boldsymbol{u}_{18}, \boldsymbol{u}_{19}, \boldsymbol{u}_{20}, \boldsymbol{u}_{22}, \boldsymbol{u}_{23}, \boldsymbol{u}_{29}, \boldsymbol{u}_{31}, \boldsymbol{u}_{32}, \boldsymbol{u}_{35}, \boldsymbol{u}_{44}\}.$$

Since all vectors in B are linearly independent, $|V(B)| = 2^{14}$.

The internal state of the LFSR is guessed in the correlation attack. Namely, if $g'_t \oplus \langle L^{(t)}, \Lambda \rangle$ is biased for multiple Λ, we can construct multiple linear approximations. The following

$$\bigoplus_{q \in \{0,12\}} z_{t+q} \oplus \langle L^{(t)}, \Gamma_{base} \rangle \oplus \langle L^{(t)}, \Lambda \rangle \approx \bigoplus_{i \in \{1,3,5,7,8,9,10\}} k'_{t+i}$$

represents linear approximations for our correlation attack, and the probability that this approximation holds coincides with the correlation of $g'_t \oplus \langle L^{(t)}, \Lambda \rangle$. We want to evaluate correlations of $g'_t \oplus \langle L^{(t)}, \Lambda \rangle$ for $\Lambda \in V(B)$. To evaluate them simply, we extract independent terms from $g'_t \oplus \langle L^{(t)}, \Lambda \rangle$ as

$$\begin{aligned} & g'_t \oplus \langle L^{(t)}, \Lambda \rangle \\ &= \ell_{t+8}\ell_{t+10} \oplus \ell_{t+8} \cdot \Lambda[8] \oplus \ell_{t+10} \cdot \Lambda[10] && (11) \\ & \oplus \ell_{t+19}\ell_{t+23} \oplus \ell_{t+19} \cdot \Lambda[19] \oplus \ell_{t+23} \cdot \Lambda[23] && (12) \\ & \oplus \ell_{t+20}\ell_{t+22} \oplus \ell_{t+20} \cdot \Lambda[20] \oplus \ell_{t+22} \cdot \Lambda[22] && (13) \\ & \oplus \ell_{t+31}\ell_{t+35} \oplus \ell_{t+31} \cdot \Lambda[31] \oplus \ell_{t+35} \cdot \Lambda[35] \\ & \oplus g''_t \oplus \langle L^{(t)}, \Lambda' \rangle, && (14) \end{aligned}$$

where $g''_t \oplus \langle L^{(t)}, \Lambda' \rangle$ is the remaining term after extracting four lines. The correlations of Eqs. (11), (12), (13), and (14) are $\pm 2^{-1}$ for 2^2 linear masks. In total, the correlation of the above four lines is $\pm 2^{-4}$, and their signs are determined by $\Lambda[8, 10, 19, 20, 22, 23, 31, 35]$, and the number of linear masks is $2^{2+2+2+2} = 2^8$. In other words, there are 2^8 linear masks $\Lambda[8, 10, 19, 20, 22, 23, 31, 35]$ satisfying $g'_t \oplus \langle \Lambda, L \rangle \approx g''_t \oplus \langle L^{(t)}, \Lambda' \rangle$ with correlation $\pm 2^{-4}$.

Finally, we want to evaluate the correlation of $g''_t \oplus \langle L^{(t)}, \Lambda' \rangle$, and it is calculated by using the brute force method. Eventually, we can find 12 Λ' whose absolute values of correlations are $2^{-22.142}$, and please refer to Appendix B in detail. Since there are 2^8 linear masks Λ satisfying $g'_t \oplus \langle L^{(0)}, \Lambda \rangle \approx g''_t \oplus \langle L^{(0)}, \Lambda' \rangle$ with correlation $\pm 2^{-4}$, there are 12×2^8 linear masks Λ such that the correlations of $g'_t \oplus \langle L^{(t)}, \Lambda \rangle$ are $\pm 2^{-26.142}$.

Table 4. Success probability of correlation attack on Plantlet.

Keystream	2^{50}	2^{51}	2^{52}	2^{53}	2^{54}	2^{55}	2^{56}	2^{57}	Threshold
Probability	0%	0%	0.06%	18.17%	99.14%	100.00%	100.00%	100.00%	th_{2-60}
	0%	0%	0%	4.93%	94.93%	100.00%	100.00%	100.00%	th_{2-70}

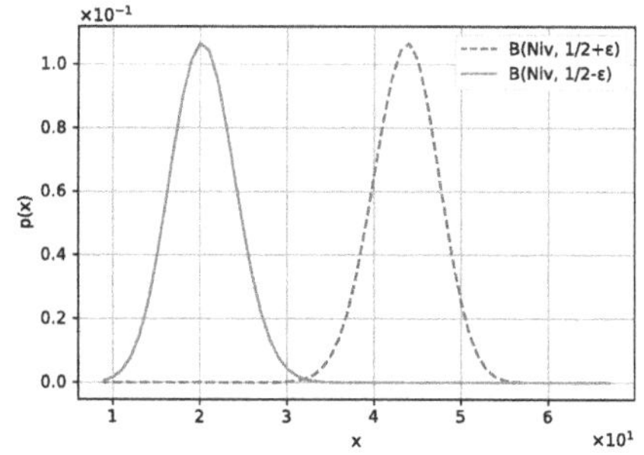

Fig. 4. Comparison of binomial distributions on Plantlet.

5.3 Correlation Attack Against Plantlet

There are 12×2^8 linear masks whose correlations are $\pm 2^{-26.142}$. Thus, the attack parameter is $m = 12 \times 2^8$ and $\bar{c} = 2^{-26.142}$. We assume that N keystream bits are observed. The linear approximation depends on $k'_t = k_{t \bmod 80} \oplus c_t$. Since the same $k_{t \bmod 80}$ is used every 80 rounds and c_t is public, $\phi = 80$.

As shown in Sect. 3, the empirical correlation follows $\mathcal{N}(mN\bar{c}/\phi, mN/\phi)$ if we guess the initial state correctly and $\bigoplus_{i \in \{1,3,5,7,8,9,10\}} k'_t = 0$. On the other hand, when $\bigoplus_{i \in \{1,3,5,7,8,9,10\}} k'_t = 1$, the bias direction is inverted, i.e., $\mathcal{N}(-mN\bar{c}/\phi, mN/\phi)$. Otherwise, we assume that the empirical correlation behaves randomly, i.e., $\mathcal{N}(0, mN/\phi)$.

We introduce th_p, which was defined in Sect. 4, and pick initial states whose absolute value of the empirical correlation is greater than th_p. Table 4 summarizes the probability that the correct initial state survives. Similarly to Fruit-80, one bit in the initial state of the LFSR is forced to 1. Therefore, the number of candidates of the initial state of the LFSR is 2^{60}. Therefore, using 2^{55} keystream with th_{2-70} is enough to recover the initial state of the LFSR uniquely. Then, the data and time complexities are $N = 2^{55}$ and $N + mN/\phi + n2^n = 2^{65.9362}$.

Reducing Data Complexity. Similarly to the application to Fruit-80, we exploit the technique described in Sect. 3.3. We use 2^{53} keystream generated from the same key and IV pair, and pick initial states of the LFSR whose absolute value of empirical correlation is larger than the threshold th_{2-60} and store the information whether its bias direction is positive or negative. We repeat this procedure while changing IVs, and let N_{iv} be the number of repetitions. When $\bigoplus_{i \in \mathbb{T}_b} k'_{t+i} = 0$, the number that the bias direction is positive follows a binomial distribution $\mathcal{B}(N_{iv}, 1/2+\epsilon)$, where $\epsilon = 18.17\% = 2^{-2.4604}$. When $\bigoplus_{i \in \mathbb{T}_b} k'_{t+i} = 1$, it follows $\mathcal{B}(N_{iv}, 1/2 - \epsilon)$.

Figure 4 shows the comparison of the binomial distributions when $N_{iv} = 2^6$, and we can distinguish two binomial distributions enough. As a result, the data and time complexities are

$$N \times N_{iv} = 2^{53} \times 2^6 = 2^{59},$$
$$N_{iv} \times (N + mN/\phi + n2^n) = 2^6 \times (2^{53} + 12 \times 2^{8+53}/80 + 60 \times 2^{60}) \approx 2^{71.92},$$

respectively. Unlike Fruit-80, it is very easy to analyze the time complexity to recover the secret key due to its simple round key function. Since all round keys are balanced, one procedure can recover 1 bit of information. Moreover, we can repeat this attack procedure for $\mathbb{S}_1, \mathbb{S}_2, \ldots, \mathbb{S}_i$, where $\mathbb{S}_i$ is defined in Sect. 4. By taking the trade-off with the brute-force search into account, the time complexity is optimal when 8 sets are used, i.e., $8 \times 2^{71.92} + 2^{80-8} \approx 2^{75.0990}$.

6   Conclusion

In this paper, we discussed the data limitation of keystream generated by stream ciphers using the same key and IV pair. We proposed correlation attacks for the small-state stream ciphers and applied them to two Grain-like small-state stream ciphers, Fruit-80 and Plantlet. The data limitation of Fruit-80 is derived by designers from the size of the component LFSR, but our correlation attack can successfully recover the secret key and break full Fruit-80. It implies that the claimed data limitation is not sufficient. On Plantlet, 2^{53}-bit keystream is required to recover the secret key. The data limitation is 2^{30} bits, which comes from the expectation that such a keystream length is sufficient for a current practical use. Thanks to this conservative claimed security, our correlation attack cannot break full Plantlet, but 2^{53} is quite smaller than the data limitation derived from the size of the LFSR.

The round key is involved in the state update function or filter function in the small-state stream ciphers. When involved round keys are distinct, the absolute value of the observed correlation is the same but the bias direction could be reversed. Therefore, in this paper, we used keystream bits in which involved round keys are common. On the other hand, similar circumstances often happen in a multi-dimensional linear attack for block cipher, and a chi-squared method is successfully used to improve the attack. Thus, adopting the chi-squared method is one of the future works to improve our attacks.

Acknowledgments. The authors thank the anonymous SAC 2019 reviewers for careful reading and many helpful comments.

A   Correlation of $g'_t \oplus \langle L^{(t)}, \Lambda \rangle$ on Fruit-80

In this section, we show the detailed method to evaluate the correlation of $g'_t \oplus \langle L^{(t)}, \Lambda \rangle$. As we already showed in Sect. 4, we first extract independent terms from $g'_t \oplus \langle L^{(t)}, \Lambda \rangle$ as

$$
\begin{aligned}
g'_t &\oplus \langle L^{(t)}, \Lambda \rangle \\
&= \ell_{t+6}\ell_{t+15} \oplus \ell_{t+6} \cdot \Lambda[6] \oplus \ell_{t+15} \cdot \Lambda[15] \\
&\oplus \ell_{t+9}\ell_{t+18} \oplus \ell_{t+9} \cdot \Lambda[9] \oplus \ell_{t+18} \cdot \Lambda[18] \\
&\oplus \ell_{t+3}\ell_{t+24} \oplus \ell_{t+3} \cdot \Lambda[3] \oplus \ell_{t+24} \cdot \Lambda[24] \\
&\oplus \ell_{t+4}\ell_{t+25} \oplus \ell_{t+4} \cdot \Lambda[4] \oplus \ell_{t+25} \cdot \Lambda[25] \\
&\oplus \ell_{t+1}\ell_{t+22} \oplus \ell_{t+13}\ell_{t+22} \oplus \ell_{t+1} \cdot \Lambda[1] \oplus \ell_{t+13} \cdot \Lambda[13] \oplus \ell_{t+22} \cdot \Lambda[22] \\
&\oplus n_{t+42}\ell_{t+34} \oplus \ell_{t+34} \cdot \Lambda[34]. \\
&\oplus g''_t \oplus \langle L^{(t)}, \Lambda' \rangle,
\end{aligned}
$$

where $g''_t \oplus \langle L^{(t)}, \Lambda' \rangle$ is the remaining term after extracting the first six lines. Then, there are 2^{11} linear masks $\Lambda[1, 3, 4, 6, 9, 13, 15, 18, 22, 24, 25, 34]$ satisfying $g'_t \oplus \langle \Lambda, L \rangle \approx g''_t \oplus \langle L^{(t)}, \Lambda' \rangle$ with correlation $\pm 2^{-6}$.

Our next goal is to evaluate the correlation of $g''_t \oplus \langle L^{(t)}, \Lambda' \rangle$, which is described as

$$
\begin{aligned}
g''_t &\oplus \langle L^{(t)}, \Lambda' \rangle \\
&= n_{t+38} \oplus \ell_{t+21} \\
&\oplus n_{t+35}\ell_{t+27} \oplus n_{t+1}n_{t+24} \oplus n_{t+1}n_{t+33}\ell_{t+42} \\
&\oplus \ell_{t+8}\ell_{t+17} \oplus n_{t+37}\ell_{t+29} \oplus n_{t+3}n_{t+26} \oplus n_{t+3}n_{t+35}\ell_{t+44} \\
&\oplus n_{t+38}\ell_{t+30} \oplus n_{t+4}n_{t+27} \oplus n_{t+4}n_{t+36}\ell_{t+45} \\
&\oplus \ell_{t+8}\ell_{t+29} \oplus n_{t+8}n_{t+31} \oplus n_{t+8}n_{t+40}\ell_{t+49} \\
&\oplus \bigoplus_{q \in \{0,2,3,7\}} \left(\bigoplus_{j \in \mathbb{A}} n_{t+q+j} \right) \oplus \bigoplus_{i \in \{0,1,2,6\}} \left(n_{t+37+i} \oplus g_{t+i} \right) \oplus \langle L^{(t)}, \Lambda' \rangle,
\end{aligned}
$$

where

$$
\begin{aligned}
\langle L^{(t)}, \Lambda' \rangle = (&\ell_{t+21} \oplus \Lambda'[8] \cdot \ell_{t+8} \oplus \Lambda'[17] \cdot \ell_{t+17} \oplus \Lambda'[27] \cdot \ell_{t+27} \oplus \Lambda'[29] \cdot \ell_{t+29} \\
&\oplus \Lambda'[30] \cdot \ell_{t+30} \oplus \Lambda'[42] \cdot \ell_{t+42} \oplus \Lambda'[44] \cdot \ell_{t+44} \oplus \Lambda'[45] \cdot \ell_{t+45} \oplus \Lambda'[49] \cdot \ell_{t+49}).
\end{aligned}
$$

Here, the indices 44, 45, and 49 exceeds the length of Λ, i.e., 43. Therefore, $\Lambda'[44, 45, 49]$ are computed by using the feedback function f as

$$
\begin{aligned}
\Lambda'[44] &= \Lambda'[38] \oplus \Lambda'[29] \oplus \Lambda'[24] \oplus \Lambda'[19] \oplus \Lambda'[9] \oplus \Lambda'[1], \\
\Lambda'[45] &= \Lambda'[39] \oplus \Lambda'[30] \oplus \Lambda'[25] \oplus \Lambda'[20] \oplus \Lambda'[10] \oplus \Lambda'[2] \\
\Lambda'[49] &= (\Lambda'[37] \oplus \Lambda'[28] \oplus \Lambda'[23] \oplus \Lambda'[18] \oplus \Lambda'[8] \oplus \Lambda'[t]) \\
&\oplus \Lambda'[34] \oplus \Lambda'[29] \oplus \Lambda'[24] \oplus \Lambda'[14] \oplus \Lambda'[6].
\end{aligned}
$$

We expand all terms in $g_t'' \oplus \langle L^{(t)}, \Lambda' \rangle$ as

$$g_t'' \oplus \langle L^{(t)}, \Lambda' \rangle$$
$$= n_{t+38} \oplus \ell_{t+21}$$
$$\oplus n_{t+35}\ell_{t+27} \oplus n_{t+1}n_{t+24} \oplus n_{t+1}n_{t+33}\ell_{t+42}$$
$$\oplus \ell_{t+8}\ell_{t+17} \oplus n_{t+37}\ell_{t+29} \oplus n_{t+3}n_{t+26} \oplus n_{t+3}n_{t+35}\ell_{t+44}$$
$$\oplus n_{t+38}\ell_{t+30} \oplus n_{t+4}n_{t+27} \oplus n_{t+4}n_{t+36}\ell_{t+45}$$
$$\oplus \ell_{t+8}\ell_{t+29} \oplus n_{t+8}n_{t+31} \oplus n_{t+8}n_{t+40}\ell_{t+49}$$
$$\oplus n_t \oplus n_{t+7} \oplus n_{t+19} \oplus n_{t+29} \oplus n_{t+36}$$
$$\oplus n_{t+2} \oplus n_{t+9} \oplus n_{t+21} \oplus n_{t+31} \oplus n_{t+38}$$
$$\oplus n_{t+3} \oplus n_{t+10} \oplus n_{t+22} \oplus n_{t+32} \oplus n_{t+39}$$
$$\oplus n_{t+7} \oplus n_{t+14} \oplus n_{t+26} \oplus n_{t+36} \oplus n_{t+43}$$
$$\oplus n_{t+37} \oplus (n_t \oplus n_{t+10} \oplus n_{t+20} \oplus n_{t+12}n_{t+3} \oplus n_{t+14}n_{t+25}$$
$$\oplus n_{t+5}n_{t+23}n_{t+31} \oplus n_{t+8}n_{t+18} \oplus n_{t+28}n_{t+30}n_{t+32}n_{t+34})$$
$$\oplus n_{t+38} \oplus (n_{t+1} \oplus n_{t+11} \oplus n_{t+21} \oplus n_{t+13}n_{t+4} \oplus n_{t+15}n_{t+26}$$
$$\oplus n_{t+6}n_{t+24}n_{t+32} \oplus n_{t+9}n_{t+19} \oplus n_{t+29}n_{t+31}n_{t+33}n_{t+35})$$
$$\oplus n_{t+39} \oplus (n_{t+2} \oplus n_{t+12} \oplus n_{t+22} \oplus n_{t+14}n_{t+5} \oplus n_{t+16}n_{t+27}$$
$$\oplus n_{t+7}n_{t+25}n_{t+33} \oplus n_{t+10}n_{t+20} \oplus n_{t+30}n_{t+32}n_{t+34}n_{t+36})$$
$$\oplus n_{t+43} \oplus (n_{t+6} \oplus n_{t+16} \oplus n_{t+26} \oplus n_{t+18}n_{t+9} \oplus n_{t+20}n_{t+31}$$
$$\oplus n_{t+11}n_{t+29}n_{t+37} \oplus n_{t+14}n_{t+24} \oplus n_{t+34}n_{t+36}n_{t+38}n_{t+40})$$
$$\oplus (\ell_{t+21} \oplus \Lambda'[8] \cdot \ell_{t+8} \oplus \Lambda'[17] \cdot \ell_{t+17} \oplus \Lambda'[27] \cdot \ell_{t+27} \oplus \Lambda'[29] \cdot \ell_{t+29}$$
$$\oplus \Lambda'[30] \cdot \ell_{t+30} \oplus \Lambda'[42] \cdot \ell_{t+42} \oplus \Lambda'[44] \cdot \ell_{t+44} \oplus \Lambda'[45] \cdot \ell_{t+45} \oplus \Lambda'[49] \cdot \ell_{t+49}).$$

There are 35 bits in the NFSR and 9 bits in the LFSR in $g_t'' \oplus \langle L^{(t)}, \Lambda' \rangle$, and the size of involved bits is too large to evaluate the correlation with brute force. Therefore, we decompose this Boolean function into six Boolean functions G_1, G_2, G_3, G_4, G_5, and G_6, i.e., $g_t'' \oplus \langle L^{(t)}, \Lambda' \rangle = G_1 \oplus G_2 \oplus G_3 \oplus G_4 \oplus G_5 \oplus G_6$.

$$G_1 = n_{t+20} \oplus n_{t+31} \oplus n_{t+10}n_{t+20} \oplus n_{t+20}n_{t+31},$$
$$G_2 = n_{t+1} \oplus n_{t+1}n_{t+24} \oplus n_{t+1}n_{t+33}\ell_{t+42} \oplus \Lambda'[42] \cdot \ell_{t+42},$$
$$G_3 = n_{t+14} \oplus n_{t+14}n_{t+25} \oplus n_{t+14}n_{t+5} \oplus n_{t+14}n_{t+24} \oplus n_{t+5}n_{t+23}n_{t+31} \oplus n_{t+7}n_{t+25}n_{t+33},$$
$$G_4 = n_{t+16} \oplus n_{t+4}n_{t+27} \oplus n_{t+13}n_{t+4} \oplus n_{t+16}n_{t+27} \oplus n_{t+4}n_{t+36}\ell_{t+45} \oplus \Lambda'[45] \cdot \ell_{t+45},$$
$$G_5 = n_{t+6} \oplus n_{t+32} \oplus n_{t+38} \oplus n_{t+9} \oplus n_{t+19} \oplus n_{t+18}n_{t+9} \oplus n_{t+9}n_{t+19} \oplus n_{t+38}\ell_{t+30}$$
$$\oplus n_{t+8}n_{t+18} \oplus n_{t+8}n_{t+40}\ell_{t+49} \oplus n_{t+6}n_{t+24}n_{t+32} \oplus n_{t+8}n_{t+31}$$
$$\oplus n_{t+28}n_{t+30}n_{t+32}n_{t+34} \oplus n_{t+30}n_{t+32}n_{t+34}n_{t+36} \oplus n_{t+34}n_{t+36}n_{t+38}n_{t+40}$$
$$\oplus \Lambda'[30] \cdot \ell_{t+30} \oplus \Lambda'[49] \cdot \ell_{t+49},$$
$$G_6 = n_{t+3} \oplus n_{t+11} \oplus n_{t+12} \oplus n_{t+29} \oplus n_{t+37} \oplus \ell_{t+8}\ell_{t+17} \oplus \ell_{t+8}\ell_{t+29} \oplus n_{t+37}\ell_{t+29}$$
$$\oplus n_{t+35}\ell_{t+27} \oplus n_{t+12}n_{t+3} \oplus n_{t+3}n_{t+26} \oplus n_{t+15}n_{t+26} \oplus n_{t+3}n_{t+35}\ell_{t+44}$$
$$\oplus n_{t+11}n_{t+29}n_{t+37} \oplus n_{t+29}n_{t+31}n_{t+33}n_{t+35} \oplus \Lambda'[29] \cdot \ell_{t+29} \oplus \Lambda'[27] \cdot \ell_{t+27}$$
$$\oplus \Lambda'[8] \cdot \ell_{t+8} \oplus \Lambda'[17] \cdot \ell_{t+17} \oplus \Lambda'[44] \cdot \ell_{t+44}.$$

Six Boolean functions G_1, G_2, G_3, G_4, G_5, and G_6 involve 3, 5, 8, 7, 18, and 20 bits, respectively. These involved bits are independent except for n_{t+24}, n_{t+31},

n_{t+33}, and n_{t+36}, where these four bits are colored by red. Therefore, we compute the conditional correlations of G_1, G_2, G_3, G_4, G_5, and G_6.

Definition 2 (Conditional correlation). *Let G be a Boolean function from n bits to 1 bit, and let x be the input of G. We add a condition for bits $x_i \in \mathbb{I}$, and these bits are fixed to v_i. Then, the conditional correlation of G is defined as*

$$\sum_{x \in \{\{0,1\}^n, x_i = v_i \text{ for all } x_i \in \mathbb{I}\}} (-1)^{G(x)}.$$

We add conditions for four bits n_{t+24}, n_{t+31}, n_{t+33}, and n_{t+36}. Then, we compute the conditional correlations of the six Boolean functions, and then, compute the conditional correlation of G by using the piling-up lemma. Finally, the correlation of G is computed by summing conditional correlations of G over all conditions.

Table 5. Case that $\Lambda'[8, 17, 27, 29, 30, 42, 44, 45, 49] = 000100000$.

n_{t+24}	n_{t+31}	n_{t+33}	n_{t+36}	G_1	G_2	G_3	G_4	G_5	G_6	Correlation
0	0	0	0	2^{-1}	0	2^{-1}	2^{-2}	0	-2^{-6}	0
0	0	0	1	2^{-1}	0	2^{-1}	2^{-2}	0	-2^{-6}	0
0	0	1	0	2^{-1}	2^{-1}	2^{-2}	2^{-2}	0	-2^{-6}	0
0	0	1	1	2^{-1}	2^{-1}	2^{-2}	2^{-2}	0	-2^{-6}	0
0	1	0	0	-2^{-1}	0	2^{-2}	2^{-2}	0	-2^{-6}	0
0	1	0	1	-2^{-1}	0	2^{-2}	2^{-2}	0	-2^{-6}	0
0	1	1	0	-2^{-1}	2^{-1}	0	2^{-2}	0	-2^{-6}	0
0	1	1	1	-2^{-1}	2^{-1}	0	2^{-2}	0	-2^{-6}	0
1	0	0	0	2^{-1}	1	2^{-1}	2^{-2}	$2^{-5.415}$	-2^{-6}	$-2^{-15.415} \times 2^{-4}$
1	0	0	1	2^{-1}	1	2^{-1}	2^{-2}	$2^{-5.415}$	-2^{-6}	$-2^{-15.415} \times 2^{-4}$
1	0	1	0	2^{-1}	2^{-1}	2^{-2}	2^{-2}	$2^{-5.415}$	-2^{-6}	$-2^{-17.415} \times 2^{-4}$
1	0	1	1	2^{-1}	2^{-1}	2^{-2}	2^{-2}	$2^{-5.415}$	-2^{-6}	$-2^{-17.415} \times 2^{-4}$
1	1	0	0	-2^{-1}	1	2^{-2}	2^{-2}	$-2^{-5.415}$	-2^{-6}	$-2^{-16.415} \times 2^{-4}$
1	1	0	1	-2^{-1}	1	2^{-2}	2^{-2}	$-2^{-5.415}$	-2^{-6}	$-2^{-16.415} \times 2^{-4}$
1	1	1	0	-2^{-1}	2^{-1}	2^{-2}	2^{-2}	$-2^{-5.415}$	-2^{-6}	$-2^{-17.415} \times 2^{-4}$
1	1	1	1	-2^{-1}	2^{-1}	2^{-2}	2^{-2}	$-2^{-5.415}$	-2^{-6}	$-2^{-17.415} \times 2^{-4}$
Sum										$-2^{-17.415}$

Table 5 shows the correlation of G when $\Lambda'[8, 17, 27, 29, 30, 42, 44, 45, 49] = 000100000$. Here, note that each conditional correlation must be divided by 2^4 because we add 4-bit condition. Finally, Table 6 summarizes each correlation, where we picked the case whose absolute values of correlation are greater than 2^{-18}.

Table 6. Correlations of $g_t'' \oplus \langle L^{(t)}, \Lambda' \rangle$.

$\Lambda'[8]$	$\Lambda'[17]$	$\Lambda'[27]$	$\Lambda'[29]$	$\Lambda'[30]$	$\Lambda'[42]$	$\Lambda'[44]$	$\Lambda'[45]$	$\Lambda'[49]$	Correlation
0	0	0	1	0	0	0	0	0	$-2^{-17.4150}$
0	0	0	1	0	0	0	0	1	$-2^{-17.4150}$
0	0	0	1	1	0	0	0	0	$2^{-17.4150}$
0	0	1	1	0	0	1	0	0	$-2^{-17.8301}$
0	0	1	1	0	0	1	0	1	$-2^{-17.8301}$
0	0	1	1	1	0	1	0	0	$2^{-17.8301}$
0	1	0	0	0	0	0	0	0	$-2^{-17.4150}$
0	1	0	0	0	0	0	0	1	$-2^{-17.4150}$
0	1	0	0	1	0	0	0	0	$2^{-17.4150}$
0	1	1	0	0	0	1	0	0	$-2^{-17.8301}$
0	1	1	0	0	0	1	0	1	$-2^{-17.8301}$
0	1	1	0	1	0	1	0	0	$2^{-17.8301}$
1	0	0	1	0	0	0	0	0	$-2^{-17.4150}$
1	0	0	1	0	0	0	0	1	$-2^{-17.4150}$
1	0	0	1	1	0	0	0	0	$2^{-17.4150}$
1	0	1	1	0	0	1	0	0	$-2^{-17.8301}$
1	0	1	1	0	0	1	0	1	$-2^{-17.8301}$
1	0	1	1	1	0	1	0	0	$2^{-17.8301}$
1	1	0	0	0	0	0	0	0	$2^{-17.4150}$
1	1	0	0	0	0	0	0	1	$2^{-17.4150}$
1	1	0	0	1	0	0	0	0	$-2^{-17.4150}$
1	1	1	0	0	0	1	0	0	$2^{-17.8301}$
1	1	1	0	0	0	1	0	1	$2^{-17.8301}$
1	1	1	0	1	0	1	0	0	$-2^{-17.8301}$

B   Correlation of $g_t'' \oplus \langle L^{(t)}, \Lambda' \rangle$ of Plantlet

Similarly to the case of Fruit-80, we compute the correlation of $g_t'' \oplus \langle L^{(t)}, \Lambda' \rangle$ of Plantlet. After extracting independent terms from $g_t' \oplus \langle L^{(t)}, \Lambda \rangle$, $g_t'' \oplus \langle L^{(t)}, \Lambda' \rangle$ is described as

$$\begin{aligned} g_t'' \oplus \langle L^{(t)}, \Lambda' \rangle = {} & n_{t+4}\ell_{t+6} \oplus \ell_{t+32}\ell_{t+17} \oplus n_{t+4}\ell_{t+32}n_{t+38} \\ & \oplus n_{t+16}\ell_{t+18} \oplus \ell_{t+44}\ell_{t+29} \oplus n_{t+16}\ell_{t+44}n_{t+50} \\ & \oplus \bigoplus_{j \in \mathbb{A}} n_{t+j} \oplus \bigoplus_{j \in \mathbb{A}} n_{t+12+j} \\ & \oplus \bigoplus_{i \in \{1,3,5,7,8,9,10\}} \left(n_{t+40+i} \oplus g_{t+i} \right) \oplus \langle L^{(t)}, \Lambda' \rangle, \end{aligned}$$

where

$$\langle L^{(t)}, \Lambda' \rangle = (\Lambda'[6]\ell_{t+6} \oplus \Lambda'[17]\ell_{t+17} \oplus \Lambda'[18]\ell_{t+18}$$
$$\oplus \Lambda'[29]\ell_{t+29} \oplus \Lambda'[32]\ell_{t+32} \oplus \Lambda'[44]\ell_{t+44}).$$

Now, let us expand all terms in $g_t'' \oplus \langle L^{(t)}, \Lambda' \rangle$ as

$g_t'' \oplus \langle L^{(t)}, \Lambda' \rangle$

$= n_{t+4}\ell_{t+6} \oplus \ell_{t+32}\ell_{t+17} \oplus n_{t+4}\ell_{t+32}n_{t+38}$

$\oplus n_{t+16}\ell_{t+18} \oplus \ell_{t+44}\ell_{t+29} \oplus n_{t+16}\ell_{t+44}n_{t+50}$

$\oplus \cancel{n_{t+1}} \oplus n_{t+6} \oplus n_{t+15} \oplus n_{t+17} \oplus \cancel{n_{t+23}} \oplus \cancel{n_{t+28}} \oplus n_{t+34}$

$\oplus n_{t+13} \oplus \cancel{n_{t+18}} \oplus \cancel{n_{t+27}} \oplus \cancel{n_{t+29}} \oplus n_{t+35} \oplus \cancel{n_{t+40}} \oplus \cancel{n_{t+46}}$

$\oplus n_{t+41} \oplus (\cancel{n_{t+1}} \oplus n_{t+14} \oplus \cancel{n_{t+20}} \oplus n_{t+36} \oplus \cancel{n_{t+40}} \oplus n_{t+3}n_{t+26} \oplus n_{t+4}n_{t+6}$

$\oplus n_{t+8}n_{t+9} \oplus n_{t+15}n_{t+22} \oplus n_{t+17}n_{t+19} \oplus \cancel{n_{t+23}n_{t+25}} \oplus n_{t+27}n_{t+33}$

$\oplus n_{t+34}n_{t+37}n_{t+38}n_{t+39} \oplus n_{t+11}n_{t+12}n_{t+13} \oplus n_{t+28}n_{t+31}n_{t+32})$

$\oplus \cancel{n_{t+43}} \oplus (n_{t+3} \oplus n_{t+16} \oplus \cancel{n_{t+22}} \oplus n_{t+38} \oplus \cancel{n_{t+42}} \oplus n_{t+5}n_{t+28} \oplus n_{t+6}n_{t+8}$

$\oplus n_{t+10}n_{t+11} \oplus n_{t+17}n_{t+24} \oplus n_{t+19}n_{t+21} \oplus \cancel{n_{t+25}n_{t+27}} \oplus n_{t+29}n_{t+35}$

$\oplus n_{t+36}n_{t+39}n_{t+40}n_{t+41} \oplus n_{t+13}n_{t+14}n_{t+15} \oplus n_{t+30}n_{t+33}n_{t+34})$

$\oplus \cancel{n_{t+45}} \oplus (n_{t+5} \oplus \cancel{n_{t+18}} \oplus n_{t+24} \oplus n_{t+40} \oplus \cancel{n_{t+44}} \oplus n_{t+7}n_{t+30} \oplus n_{t+8}n_{t+10}$

$\oplus n_{t+12}n_{t+13} \oplus n_{t+19}n_{t+26} \oplus n_{t+21}n_{t+23} \oplus n_{t+27}n_{t+29} \oplus n_{t+31}n_{t+37}$

$\oplus n_{t+38}n_{t+41}n_{t+42}n_{t+43} \oplus n_{t+15}n_{t+16}n_{t+17} \oplus n_{t+32}n_{t+35}n_{t+36})$

$\oplus \cancel{n_{t+47}} \oplus (n_{t+7} \oplus \cancel{n_{t+20}} \oplus n_{t+26} \oplus \cancel{n_{t+42}} \oplus \cancel{n_{t+46}} \oplus n_{t+9}n_{t+32} \oplus n_{t+10}n_{t+12}$

$\oplus n_{t+14}n_{t+15} \oplus n_{t+21}n_{t+28} \oplus \cancel{n_{t+23}n_{t+25}} \oplus n_{t+29}n_{t+31} \oplus n_{t+33}n_{t+39}$

$\oplus n_{t+40}n_{t+43}n_{t+44}n_{t+45} \oplus n_{t+17}n_{t+18}n_{t+19} \oplus n_{t+34}n_{t+37}n_{t+38})$

$\oplus \cancel{n_{t+48}} \oplus (n_{t+8} \oplus n_{t+21} \oplus \cancel{n_{t+27}} \oplus \cancel{n_{t+43}} \oplus \cancel{n_{t+47}} \oplus n_{t+10}n_{t+33} \oplus n_{t+11}n_{t+13}$

$\oplus n_{t+15}n_{t+16} \oplus n_{t+22}n_{t+29} \oplus n_{t+24}n_{t+26} \oplus n_{t+30}n_{t+32} \oplus n_{t+34}n_{t+40}$

$\oplus n_{t+41}n_{t+44}n_{t+45}n_{t+46} \oplus n_{t+18}n_{t+19}n_{t+20} \oplus n_{t+35}n_{t+38}n_{t+39})$

$\oplus \cancel{n_{t+49}} \oplus (n_{t+9} \oplus \cancel{n_{t+22}} \oplus \cancel{n_{t+28}} \oplus \cancel{n_{t+44}} \oplus \cancel{n_{t+48}} \oplus n_{t+11}n_{t+34} \oplus n_{t+12}n_{t+14}$

$\oplus n_{t+16}n_{t+17} \oplus n_{t+23}n_{t+30} \oplus \cancel{n_{t+25}n_{t+27}} \oplus n_{t+31}n_{t+33} \oplus n_{t+35}n_{t+41}$

$\oplus n_{t+42}n_{t+45}n_{t+46}n_{t+47} \oplus n_{t+19}n_{t+20}n_{t+21} \oplus n_{t+36}n_{t+39}n_{t+40})$

$\oplus n_{t+50} \oplus (n_{t+10} \oplus \cancel{n_{t+23}} \oplus \cancel{n_{t+29}} \oplus \cancel{n_{t+45}} \oplus \cancel{n_{t+49}} \oplus n_{t+12}n_{t+35} \oplus n_{t+13}n_{t+15}$

$\oplus n_{t+17}n_{t+18} \oplus n_{t+24}n_{t+31} \oplus n_{t+26}n_{t+28} \oplus n_{t+32}n_{t+34} \oplus n_{t+36}n_{t+42}$

$\oplus n_{t+43}n_{t+46}n_{t+47}n_{t+48} \oplus n_{t+20}n_{t+21}n_{t+22} \oplus n_{t+37}n_{t+40}n_{t+41})$

$\oplus (\Lambda'[6]\ell_{t+6} \oplus \Lambda'[32]\ell_{t+32} \oplus \Lambda'[17]\ell_{t+17}$

$\oplus \Lambda'[18]\ell_{t+18} \oplus \Lambda'[44]\ell_{t+44} \oplus \Lambda'[29]\ell_{t+29}).$

There are 46 bits in the NFSR and 6 bits in the LFSR in $g_t'' \oplus \langle L^{(t)}, \Lambda' \rangle$, and the size of involved bits is too large to evaluate the correlation with brute force. We decompose this Boolean function into four Boolean functions G_1, G_2, G_3, and G_4, i.e., $g_t'' \oplus \langle L^{(t)}, \Lambda' \rangle = G_1 \oplus G_2 \oplus G_3 \oplus G_4$.

$$G_1 = n_{t+6} \oplus n_{t+8} \oplus n_{t+9} \oplus n_{t+10} \oplus n_{t+21} \oplus n_{t+38} \oplus n_{t+4}\ell_{t+6} \oplus \ell_{t+32}\ell_{t+17}$$
$$\oplus\, n_{t+4}\ell_{t+32}n_{t+38} \oplus n_{t+4}n_{t+6} \oplus n_{t+8}n_{t+9} \oplus n_{t+6}n_{t+8}$$
$$\oplus\, n_{t+8}n_{t+10} \oplus n_{t+9}n_{t+32} \oplus \varLambda'[6]\ell_{t+6} \oplus \varLambda'[17]\ell_{t+17} \oplus \varLambda'[32]\ell_{t+32}$$

$$G_2 = n_{t+7} \oplus n_{t+34} \oplus n_{t+27}n_{t+33} \oplus n_{t+7}n_{t+30} \oplus n_{t+21}n_{t+23}$$
$$\oplus\, n_{t+27}n_{t+29} \oplus n_{t+29}n_{t+31} \oplus n_{t+33}n_{t+39}$$
$$\oplus\, n_{t+10}n_{t+33} \oplus n_{t+30}n_{t+32} \oplus n_{t+23}n_{t+30} \oplus n_{t+31}n_{t+33}$$
$$\oplus\, n_{t+30}n_{t+33}n_{t+34}$$

$$G_3 = n_{t+13} \oplus n_{t+14} \oplus n_{t+35} \oplus n_{t+36} \oplus n_{t+40} \oplus n_{t+41}$$
$$\oplus\, n_{t+10}n_{t+11} \oplus n_{t+29}n_{t+35} \oplus n_{t+12}n_{t+13} \oplus n_{t+31}n_{t+37} \oplus n_{t+10}n_{t+12}$$
$$\oplus\, n_{t+14}n_{t+15} \oplus n_{t+11}n_{t+34} \oplus n_{t+12}n_{t+14} \oplus n_{t+35}n_{t+41}$$
$$\oplus\, n_{t+12}n_{t+35} \oplus n_{t+13}n_{t+15} \oplus n_{t+36}n_{t+42} \oplus n_{t+11}n_{t+13}$$
$$\oplus\, n_{t+34}n_{t+40} \oplus n_{t+11}n_{t+12}n_{t+13} \oplus n_{t+13}n_{t+14}n_{t+15}$$
$$\oplus\, n_{t+32}n_{t+35}n_{t+36} \oplus n_{t+35}n_{t+38}n_{t+39} \oplus n_{t+36}n_{t+39}n_{t+40}$$
$$\oplus\, n_{t+37}n_{t+40}n_{t+41} \oplus n_{t+34}n_{t+37}n_{t+38}$$
$$\oplus\, n_{t+41}n_{t+44}n_{t+45}n_{t+46} \oplus n_{t+34}n_{t+37}n_{t+38}n_{t+39}$$
$$\oplus\, n_{t+36}n_{t+39}n_{t+40}n_{t+41} \oplus n_{t+40}n_{t+43}n_{t+44}n_{t+45}$$
$$\oplus\, n_{t+42}n_{t+45}n_{t+46}n_{t+47} \oplus n_{t+43}n_{t+46}n_{t+47}n_{t+48}$$
$$\oplus\, n_{t+38}n_{t+41}n_{t+42}n_{t+43}$$

$$G_4 = n_{t+3} \oplus n_{t+5} \oplus n_{t+15} \oplus n_{t+16} \oplus n_{t+17} \oplus n_{t+24} \oplus n_{t+26} \oplus n_{t+50}$$
$$\oplus\, n_{t+16}\ell_{t+18} \oplus \ell_{t+44}\ell_{t+29} \oplus n_{t+16}\ell_{t+44}n_{t+50} \oplus n_{t+3}n_{t+26}$$
$$\oplus\, n_{t+15}n_{t+22} \oplus n_{t+17}n_{t+19} \oplus n_{t+5}n_{t+28} \oplus n_{t+17}n_{t+24}$$
$$\oplus\, n_{t+19}n_{t+21} \oplus n_{t+19}n_{t+26} \oplus n_{t+21}n_{t+28} \oplus n_{t+15}n_{t+16}$$
$$\oplus\, n_{t+22}n_{t+29} \oplus n_{t+24}n_{t+26} \oplus n_{t+16}n_{t+17} \oplus n_{t+17}n_{t+18}$$
$$\oplus\, n_{t+24}n_{t+31} \oplus n_{t+26}n_{t+28} \oplus n_{t+32}n_{t+34}$$
$$\oplus\, n_{t+17}n_{t+18}n_{t+19} \oplus n_{t+18}n_{t+19}n_{t+20} \oplus n_{t+19}n_{t+20}n_{t+21}$$
$$\oplus\, n_{t+28}n_{t+31}n_{t+32} \oplus n_{t+15}n_{t+16}n_{t+17} \oplus n_{t+20}n_{t+21}n_{t+22}$$
$$\oplus\, \varLambda'[18]\ell_{t+18} \oplus \varLambda'[29]\ell_{t+29} \oplus \varLambda'[44]\ell_{t+44}$$

Four Boolean functions G_1, G_2, G_3, and G_4 involve 14, 12, 24, and 24 bits, respectively. These involved bits are independent except for n_{t+39}, n_{t+38}, n_{t+34}, n_{t+32}, n_{t+31}, n_{t+29}, n_{t+21}, n_{t+15}, and n_{t+10}, where these nine bits are colored by red. Therefore, we compute the conditional correlations of G_1, G_2, G_3, and G_4.

Table 7 shows the correlation of G when $\varLambda'[6, 17, 18, 29, 32, 44] = 001100$. Here, note that each conditional correlation must be divided by 2^9 because we add 9-bit condition. Table 8 summarizes each correlation, where we picked the case whose correlation is non-zero.

Table 7. Case that $\Lambda'[8, 17, 27, 29, 30, 42, 44, 45, 49] = 000100000$.

n_{t+10}	n_{t+15}	n_{t+29}	n_{t+31}	n_{t+34}	n_{t+38}	n_{t+39}	G_1	G_2	G_3	G_4	Correlation
0	0	0	0	0	0	0	2^{-3}	2^{-2}	$2^{-6.4150}$	2^{-6}	$2^{-17.4150-9}$
0	0	0	0	0	0	1	2^{-3}	2^{-2}	2^{-8}	2^{-6}	2^{-19-9}
0	0	0	0	0	1	0	-2^{-3}	2^{-2}	$2^{-6.4150}$	2^{-6}	$-2^{-17.4150-9}$
0	0	0	0	0	1	1	-2^{-3}	2^{-2}	-2^{-8}	2^{-6}	2^{-19-9}
0	0	0	1	0	1	1	-2^{-3}	2^{-2}	2^{-7}	-2^{-7}	2^{-19-9}
0	0	1	0	0	0	0	2^{-3}	2^{-2}	$-2^{-4.5406}$	2^{-7}	$-2^{-16.5406-9}$
0	0	1	0	0	0	1	2^{-3}	-2^{-2}	$-2^{-4.5406}$	2^{-7}	$2^{-16.5406-9}$
0	0	1	0	0	1	0	-2^{-3}	2^{-2}	-2^{-8}	2^{-7}	2^{-20-9}
0	0	1	0	0	1	1	-2^{-3}	-2^{-2}	2^{-8}	2^{-7}	2^{-20-9}
0	1	0	0	0	0	0	2^{-3}	2^{-2}	$-2^{-5.1926}$	2^{-7}	$-2^{-17.1926-9}$
0	1	0	0	0	0	1	2^{-3}	2^{-2}	$-2^{-5.4150}$	2^{-7}	$-2^{-17.4150-9}$
0	1	0	0	0	1	0	-2^{-3}	2^{-2}	-2^{-7}	2^{-7}	2^{-19-9}
0	1	0	0	0	1	1	-2^{-3}	2^{-2}	2^{-8}	2^{-7}	-2^{-20-9}
0	1	1	0	0	0	0	2^{-3}	2^{-2}	$2^{-5.1926}$	2^{-6}	$2^{-16.1926-9}$
0	1	1	0	0	0	1	2^{-3}	-2^{-2}	$2^{-5.4150}$	2^{-6}	$-2^{-16.4150-9}$
0	1	1	0	0	1	0	-2^{-3}	2^{-2}	2^{-7}	2^{-6}	-2^{-18-9}
0	1	1	0	0	1	1	-2^{-3}	-2^{-2}	-2^{-8}	2^{-6}	-2^{-19-9}
0	1	1	1	0	0	0	2^{-3}	2^{-2}	$-2^{-5.6781}$	2^{-7}	$-2^{-17.6781-9}$
0	1	1	1	0	0	1	2^{-3}	-2^{-2}	$-2^{-5.6781}$	2^{-7}	$2^{-17.6781-9}$
0	1	1	1	0	1	0	-2^{-3}	2^{-2}	-2^{-8}	2^{-7}	2^{-20-9}
0	1	1	1	0	1	1	-2^{-3}	-2^{-2}	2^{-8}	2^{-7}	2^{-20-9}
1	0	0	0	1	0	0	2^{-3}	-2^{-2}	$-2^{-3.6077}$	2^{-6}	$2^{-14.6077-9}$
1	0	0	0	1	0	1	2^{-3}	-2^{-2}	$-2^{-3.4764}$	2^{-6}	$2^{-14.4764-9}$
1	0	0	0	1	1	1	-2^{-3}	-2^{-2}	2^{-8}	2^{-6}	2^{-19-9}
1	0	0	1	1	1	0	-2^{-3}	-2^{-2}	$-2^{-3.6077}$	-2^{-7}	$2^{-15.6077-9}$
1	0	0	1	1	1	1	-2^{-3}	-2^{-2}	2^{-7}	-2^{-7}	-2^{-19-9}
1	0	1	0	1	0	0	2^{-3}	-2^{-2}	$2^{-4.5406}$	2^{-7}	$-2^{-16.5406-9}$
1	0	1	0	1	0	1	2^{-3}	2^{-2}	$2^{-4.5406}$	2^{-7}	$2^{-16.5406-9}$
1	0	1	0	1	1	0	-2^{-3}	-2^{-2}	2^{-7}	2^{-7}	2^{-19-9}
1	0	1	0	1	1	1	-2^{-3}	2^{-2}	$-2^{-3.4764}$	2^{-7}	$2^{-15.4764-9}$
1	1	0	0	1	0	0	2^{-3}	-2^{-2}	$2^{-5.6781}$	2^{-7}	$-2^{-17.6781-9}$
1	1	0	0	1	0	1	2^{-3}	-2^{-2}	$2^{-5.4150}$	2^{-7}	$-2^{-17.4150-9}$
1	1	0	0	1	1	0	-2^{-3}	-2^{-2}	-2^{-8}	2^{-7}	-2^{-20-9}
1	1	0	0	1	1	1	-2^{-3}	-2^{-2}	$2^{-4.5406}$	2^{-7}	$2^{-16.5406-9}$
1	1	1	0	1	0	0	2^{-3}	-2^{-2}	$2^{-5.6781}$	2^{-6}	$-2^{-16.6781-9}$
1	1	1	0	1	0	1	2^{-3}	2^{-2}	$2^{-5.4150}$	2^{-6}	$2^{-16.4150-9}$
1	1	1	0	1	1	0	-2^{-3}	-2^{-2}	-2^{-8}	2^{-6}	-2^{-19-9}
1	1	1	0	1	1	1	-2^{-3}	2^{-2}	$2^{-4.5406}$	2^{-6}	$-2^{-15.5406-9}$
1	1	1	1	1	0	0	2^{-3}	-2^{-2}	$-2^{-5.6781}$	2^{-7}	$2^{-17.6781-9}$
1	1	1	1	1	0	1	2^{-3}	2^{-2}	$-2^{-5.6781}$	2^{-7}	$-2^{-17.6781-9}$
1	1	1	1	1	1	0	-2^{-3}	-2^{-2}	$2^{-4.6781}$	2^{-7}	$2^{-16.6781-9}$
1	1	1	1	1	1	1	-2^{-3}	2^{-2}	-2^{-8}	2^{-7}	2^{-20-9}
Sum											$2^{-22.1420}$

When $n_{t+21} = 0$ or $n_{t+32} = 1$, the correlation is 0. Therefore, n_{t+21} must be 1, and n_{t+32} must be 0, and columns for n_{t+21} and n_{t+32} are omitted.

Table 8. Correlations of $g_t'' \oplus \langle L^{(t)}, \Lambda' \rangle$.

$\Lambda'[6]$	$\Lambda'[17]$	$\Lambda'[18]$	$\Lambda'[29]$	$\Lambda'[32]$	$\Lambda'[44]$	Correlation
0	0	1	1	0	0	$2^{-22.142}$
0	0	1	1	0	1	$-2^{-22.142}$
0	0	1	1	1	0	$2^{-22.142}$
0	0	1	1	1	1	$-2^{-22.142}$
0	1	1	1	0	0	$2^{-22.142}$
0	1	1	1	0	1	$-2^{-22.142}$
0	1	1	1	1	0	$-2^{-22.142}$
0	1	1	1	1	1	$2^{-22.142}$
1	0	1	1	0	0	$2^{-23.678}$
1	0	1	1	0	1	$-2^{-23.678}$
1	0	1	1	1	0	$2^{-23.678}$
1	0	1	1	1	1	$-2^{-23.678}$
1	1	1	1	0	0	$2^{-22.142}$
1	1	1	1	0	1	$-2^{-22.142}$
1	1	1	1	1	0	$-2^{-22.142}$
1	1	1	1	1	1	$2^{-22.142}$

References

1. Bogdanov, A., Knudsen, L.R., Leander, G., Paar, C., Poschmann, A., Robshaw, M.J.B., Seurin, Y., Vikkelsoe, C.: PRESENT: an ultra-lightweight block cipher. In: Paillier, P., Verbauwhede, I. (eds.) CHES 2007. LNCS, vol. 4727, pp. 450–466. Springer, Heidelberg (2007). https://doi.org/10.1007/978-3-540-74735-2_31
2. Guo, J., Peyrin, T., Poschmann, A., Robshaw, M.: The LED block cipher. In: Preneel, B., Takagi, T. (eds.) CHES 2011. LNCS, vol. 6917, pp. 326–341. Springer, Heidelberg (2011). https://doi.org/10.1007/978-3-642-23951-9_22
3. Beierle, C., Jean, J., Kölbl, S., Leander, G., Moradi, A., Peyrin, T., Sasaki, Y., Sasdrich, P., Sim, S.M.: The SKINNY family of block ciphers and its low-latency variant MANTIS. In: Robshaw, M., Katz, J. (eds.) CRYPTO 2016. LNCS, vol. 9815, pp. 123–153. Springer, Heidelberg (2016). https://doi.org/10.1007/978-3-662-53008-5_5
4. Banik, S., Pandey, S.K., Peyrin, T., Sasaki, Y., Sim, S.M., Todo, Y.: GIFT: a small Present. In: Fischer, W., Homma, N. (eds.) CHES 2017. LNCS, vol. 10529, pp. 321–345. Springer, Cham (2017). https://doi.org/10.1007/978-3-319-66787-4_16
5. Babbage, S.H.: Improved "exhaustive search" attacks on stream ciphers. In: European Convention on Security and Detection 1995, pp. 161–166 (1995)
6. Golić, J.D.: Cryptanalysis of alleged A5 stream cipher. In: Fumy, W. (ed.) EUROCRYPT 1997. LNCS, vol. 1233, pp. 239–255. Springer, Heidelberg (1997). https://doi.org/10.1007/3-540-69053-0_17
7. Biryukov, A., Shamir, A.: Cryptanalytic time/memory/data tradeoffs for stream ciphers. In: Okamoto, T. (ed.) ASIACRYPT 2000. LNCS, vol. 1976, pp. 1–13. Springer, Heidelberg (2000). https://doi.org/10.1007/3-540-44448-3_1

8. Armknecht, F., Mikhalev, V.: On lightweight stream ciphers with shorter internal states. In: Leander, G. (ed.) FSE 2015. LNCS, vol. 9054, pp. 451–470. Springer, Heidelberg (2015). https://doi.org/10.1007/978-3-662-48116-5_22

9. Lallemand, V., Naya-Plasencia, M.: Cryptanalysis of full Sprout. In: Gennaro, R., Robshaw, M. (eds.) CRYPTO 2015. LNCS, vol. 9215, pp. 663–682. Springer, Heidelberg (2015). https://doi.org/10.1007/978-3-662-47989-6_32

10. Esgin, M.F., Kara, O.: Practical cryptanalysis of full Sprout with TMD tradeoff attacks. In: Dunkelman, O., Keliher, L. (eds.) SAC 2015. LNCS, vol. 9566, pp. 67–85. Springer, Cham (2016). https://doi.org/10.1007/978-3-319-31301-6_4

11. Banik, S.: Some results on Sprout. In: Biryukov, A., Goyal, V. (eds.) INDOCRYPT 2015. LNCS, vol. 9462, pp. 124–139. Springer, Cham (2015). https://doi.org/10.1007/978-3-319-26617-6_7

12. Zhang, B., Gong, X.: Another tradeoff attack on Sprout-like stream ciphers. In: Iwata, T., Cheon, J.H. (eds.) ASIACRYPT 2015. LNCS, vol. 9453, pp. 561–585. Springer, Heidelberg (2015). https://doi.org/10.1007/978-3-662-48800-3_23

13. Ghafari, V.A., Hu, H., Xie, C.: Fruit: ultra-lightweight stream cipher with shorter internal state. Cryptology ePrint Archive, Report 2016/355 (2016). http://eprint.iacr.org/2016/355

14. Dey, S., Sarkar, S.: Cryptanalysis of full round Fruit. Cryptology ePrint Archive, Report 2017/087 (2017). http://eprint.iacr.org/2017/087

15. Zhang, B., Gong, X., Meier, W.: Fast correlation attacks on Grain-like small state stream ciphers. IACR Trans. Symm. Cryptol. **2017**(4), 58–81 (2017). https://doi.org/10.13154/tosc.v2017.i4.58-81

16. Ghafari, V.A., Hu, H., Chen, Y.: Fruit-v2: ultra-lightweight stream cipher with shorter internal state. IACR Cryptology ePrint Archive 2016, 355 (2016)

17. Ghafari, V.A., Hu, H., Alizadeh, M.: Necessary conditions for designing secure stream ciphers with the minimal internal states. Cryptology ePrint Archive, Report 2017/765 (2017). http://eprint.iacr.org/2017/765

18. Ghafari, V.A., Hu, H.: Fruit-80: a secure ultra-lightweight stream cipher for constrained environments. Entropy **20**(3), 180 (2018)

19. Mikhalev, V., Armknecht, F., Müller, C.: On ciphers that continuously access the non-volatile key. IACR Trans. Symm. Cryptol. **2016**(2), 52–79 (2016). https://doi.org/10.13154/tosc.v2016.i2.52-79

20. Todo, Y., Isobe, T., Meier, W., Aoki, K., Zhang, B.: Fast correlation attack revisited. In: Shacham, H., Boldyreva, A. (eds.) CRYPTO 2018. LNCS, vol. 10992, pp. 129–159. Springer, Cham (2018). https://doi.org/10.1007/978-3-319-96881-0_5

21. Matsui, M.: On correlation between the order of S-boxes and the strength of DES. In: De Santis, A. (ed.) EUROCRYPT 1994. LNCS, vol. 950, pp. 366–375. Springer, Heidelberg (1995). https://doi.org/10.1007/BFb0053451

22. Siegenthaler, T.: Correlation-immunity of nonlinear combining functions for cryptographic applications. IEEE Trans. Inf. Theory **30**(5), 776–780 (1984)

23. Meier, W., Staffelbach, O.: Fast correlation attacks on certain stream ciphers. J. Cryptol. **1**(3), 159–176 (1989)

24. Chose, P., Joux, A., Mitton, M.: Fast correlation attacks: an algorithmic point of view. In: Knudsen, L.R. (ed.) EUROCRYPT 2002. LNCS, vol. 2332, pp. 209–221. Springer, Heidelberg (2002). https://doi.org/10.1007/3-540-46035-7_14

25. Ågren, M., Hell, M., Johansson, T., Meier, W.: Grain-128a: a new version of Grain-128 with optional authentication. IJWMC **5**(1), 48–59 (2011)

A Lightweight Alternative to PMAC

Kazuhiko Minematsu[(⊠)]

NEC Corporation, Kawasaki, Japan
k-minematsu@nec.com

Abstract. PMAC is a parallelizable message authentication code (MAC) based on a block cipher. PMAC has many desirable features, such as parallelizability and essential optimality in terms of the number of block cipher calls, and the provable security. However, PMAC needs a pre-processing of one block cipher call taking all-zero block to produce the input masks to all subsequent block cipher calls. This incurs an overhead for both time and memory, which is often non-negligible. In particular, this makes PMAC's state size $3n$ bits. To address these issues, we propose a new parallelizable MAC as an alternative to PMAC, which we call LAPMAC. LAPMAC enables a high parallelizability, and unlike PMAC, it does not need a pre-processing to create an input mask. This leads to $2n$-bit state memory compared to PMAC's $3n$-bit state. Moreover, LAPMAC is highly optimized in terms of the number of block cipher calls, for example it requires *exactly* the same number of block cipher calls as PMAC when one pre-processing call is allowed, and achieves the same number of block cipher calls as the state-of-the-art serial MACs those do not need the pre-processing call.

We prove that LAPMAC is secure up to around $2^{n/2}$ queried blocks, under the standard pseudorandomness assumption of the underlying block cipher.

Keywords: Parallel MAC · PMAC · Block cipher mode · State size

1 Introduction

MAC Modes. Message authentication code (MAC) is a symmetric-key cryptographic function for ensuring the authenticity of a message. MAC functions can be realized by modes of block cipher operations. For example, XCBC by Black and Rogaway [9] and OMAC (a.k.a. CMAC [2]) by Iwata and Kurosawa [20], are popular MAC modes. They are provably secure, however, inherently serial due to the structural similarity to the classic CBC-MAC. For MACs that allow a parallel processing of the message blocks, PMAC is one of the most popular modes. It was first proposed by Black and Rogaway [10], and has been revised since then [23,36]. The core structure of PMAC has been employed by the seminal OCB mode of operation for authenticated encryption (AE) [36] for processing associated data (AD). Since then, many state-of-the-art AE schemes, including those proposed to the CAESAR competition [1], employed PMAC or its variant.

© Springer Nature Switzerland AG 2020
K. G. Paterson and D. Stebila (Eds.): SAC 2019, LNCS 11959, pp. 393–417, 2020.
https://doi.org/10.1007/978-3-030-38471-5_16

The mechanism also has been employed by cryptographic permutation-based schemes, such as OPP [19] and Farfalle [7].

PMAC. The security of PMAC was first proved by the designers [10, 23, 36], and has been deeply studied since then [13, 18, 24, 29, 33]. It is known that PMAC is secure as long as the total number of queried blocks is sufficiently smaller than $2^{n/2}$, which we call security up to the birthday bound, or birthday-bound security.

PMAC is highly efficient. For processing a message of m blocks, it needs m block cipher calls, which is minimum. The minimum number of calls is possible assuming the pre-processing of $E_K(0^n)$, i.e., the encryption of all-zero block by the underlying n-bit block cipher E_K. This $E_K(0^n)$ is used to produce *the input mask* applied to each block cipher input.

While this $E_K(0^n)$ plays a key role in computation efficiency and security, it also imposes an overhead for both time and memory. First, the computation of $E_K(0^n)$ is non-negligible when pre-processing is not possible. For example, as pointed out by Fischlin and Lehmann [17], a MAC in the conventional key exchange protocols takes a (usually short) transcript as message and the key is only known after the transcript. Hence the pre-computation of $E_K(0^n)$ is not possible and the computational overhead will be non-negligible. Second, the mask generated by $E_K(0^n)$ must kept in memory, thus it increases the state size by n bits. See Sect. 2 for details. This results in the $3n$-bit state memory for PMAC, while the main routine without the mask operates on $2n$-bit state. This is particularly significant for hardware: from the recent advances in lightweight cryptography, it is often the case that the n-bit state register (implemented by flip-flops) is comparable to an implementation of the core n-bit lightweight block cipher routine (i.e. except the registers). Hence, reducing state size by n bits can be equally valuable to reducing one block cipher core. We note that serial modes for authenticated encryption with small state size are recently actively studied [12, 21, 31], and serial MAC modes without pre-processing call of $E_K(0^n)$ are also studied [32], however, parallel MAC modes have been rather overlooked in this respect. We expect that the size of parallel modes will also be important in the forthcoming era of IoT, a heterogeneous network consisting of a wide variety of platforms, say because low-end edge devices may use parallel MAC in serial because the server side with high-end computers wants to run MAC in parallel for high throughput. Similar motivations have been often observed in the context of parallel modes/implementations of lightweight cryptographic primitive [25, 26].

Lightweight Alternative to PMAC. To address these issues around the input mask computation, we propose an alternative to PMAC, which we call LAPMAC (for Lightweight Alternative to PMAC). It accepts an arbitrarily long input as PMAC, and has a high parallelizability without using the input mask. It needs $2n$-bit state memory, which is smaller than $3n$ bits of PMAC. The number of on-line block cipher calls is minimum, i.e. m calls for m-block message, except the case $m = 1$ which needs two calls. The same property has also been achieved by GCBC by Nandi [32], however it is completely serial. Moreover, unlike GCBC, we can minimize the number of on-line calls for any m including the case $m = 1$ if off-line computation of $E_K(0^n)$ is allowed, which has been achieved by CMAC and PMAC. Table 1 shows a detailed comparison of LAPMAC with other MAC modes. For security, we prove LAPMAC is secure up to the birthday bound, hence LAPMAC has the same level of security as other popular modes. We note that permutation-based variants of PMAC, which use tweakable Even-Mansour (TEM) cipher [15,27] as a primitive, can reduce the total state size including the key, since the key does not need to be hold after the mask is computed. We here do not focus on this approach as it is based on a different security model of public random permutation. We also stress that our goal is different from dedicated lightweight MACs, such as Chaskey [30], which is permutation-based and completely serial.

Design Challenge. Some previous parallel MACs do not need input masks, such as Protected Counter Sum [6], XOR-MAC [5] (a predecessor of PMAC), and LightMAC [25]. However, they are not optimally efficient in terms of the number of on-line block cipher calls, since a part of the input to the cryptographic primitive is reserved for the index of message blocks. That is, they do not perform full-absorption.

Minematsu [28] showed the basic idea of parallel MAC without input mask, and he showed a parallel MAC using $2n$-bit state without input mask, called S2V-R. The core idea is an introduction of post-processing function applied to block cipher outputs, and an instantiation of post-processing function based on bit rotation (of special length). Unfortunately, S2V-R only accepts about n message blocks. Our work is based on [28], and essentially is an effort to derive an arbitrarily-long-input MAC from S2V-R via proper chaining of it. Although it sounds rather straightforward, a construction that fulfills multiple criterion such as the optimal number of on-line calls, parallelizability, and the $2n$-bit state size turns out to be surprisingly non-trivial. To solve the problem, we assume linearity and commutativity of the post-processing function, which are not needed for the case of S2V-R. Fortunately, one of the two proposals of post-processing function by [28] fulfills our requirements.

To our knowledge, LAPMAC is the first full-fledged MAC proposal to remove the computation and memory overhead of PMAC rooted in the need of mask, without sacrificing the efficiency. One drawback of LAPMAC is its limited parallelizability up to around $n/2$ to n blocks, where n is the length of a block. We nevertheless think this is acceptable for many practical cases. For example, modern high-end processors of Intel and AMD with AESNI instructions allow to encrypt 4 to 8 blocks in parallel. The bit-slice implementations of block ciphers take n or fewer, say $n/8$, blocks in parallel [3,8,22].

2   Preliminaries

Notations. Let $[\![n]\!] = \{1, \ldots, n\}$ and $(\![n]\!) = \{0, \ldots, n-1\}$. Let $\{0,1\}^n$ be the space of n-bit binary strings, and let $\{0,1\}^*$ be the space of all binary strings, including the empty string, ε. Let $(\{0,1\}^n)^+$ be the set of strings of length

Table 1. Comparison of MACs for processing m-block message M. All MACs have $n/2$-bit security with n-bit block cipher. Precomp denotes the pre-computation of $E_K(0^n)$. Maximum Parallelism denotes the maximum number of input blocks that can be processed in parallel. The function $\Delta(a, b)$ is 1 if $a \leq |M| \leq b$ and 0 otherwise. The empty message of length 0 is counted as 1 block. LightMAC accepts at most $2^s(n-s)$-bit message for some $s < n$.

Scheme	State size (bit)	# of keys	# of calls w/ precomp	# of calls w/o precomp	Parallel	Max. Parallelism	Reference
EMAC	n	2	$m+1$	$m+1$	No	1	[11]
CMAC	$2n$	1	m	$m+1$	No	1	[20]
PMAC	$3n$	1	m	$m+1$	Yes	$m-1$	[10]
GCBC1	n	1	$m + \Delta(0, n)$	$m + \Delta(0, n)$	No	1	[32]
GCBC2	n	1	$m + \Delta(n-3, n)$	$m + \Delta(n-3, n)$	No	1	[32]
LightMAC	$2n$	2	$m(n/(n-s))+1$	$m(n/(n-s))+1$	Yes	$m-1$	[25]
LAPMAC	$2n$	1	m	$m + \Delta(0, n)$	Yes	$n/2 \sim n$	This work

multiple of n. Bit length of $X \in \{0, 1\}^*$ is written as $|X|$, where $|\varepsilon| = 0$. The first (last) c bits of X is denoted by $\mathsf{msb}_c(X)$ ($\mathsf{lsb}_c(X)$).

A concatenation of two binary strings, X and Y, is written as $X \parallel Y$ or simply XY. A sequence of i zeros is written as 0^i. For $X \in \{0, 1\}^*$, "is-partial" function $\mathsf{isp}_n(X) = 0$ if $|X| \bmod n = 0$ and $\mathsf{isp}_n(X) = 1$ otherwise. We may simply write $\mathsf{isp}(X)$ if n is obvious. Let $\mathsf{pad}(X)$ be the "one-zero padding" function defined as $\mathsf{pad}(X) = X \parallel 10^{n-(|X| \bmod n)-1}$ if $\mathsf{isp}(X) = 1$ and $\mathsf{pad}(X) = X$ if $\mathsf{isp}(X) = 0$. A bit rotation of X to the left by i bits is denoted by $X \lll i$. Formally, when $|X| = x$ and $1 \leq i < x$, given $(X[1], X[2], \ldots, X[x]) \xleftarrow{1} X$ (i.e. $X[i]$ is the i-th bit of X), $X \lll i$ is written as $(X[i+1]X[i+2] \ldots X[x]X[1]X[2] \ldots X[i])$.

For $X, Y \in \{0, 1\}^*$, let $X \oplus_{\shortparallel} Y$ be the XOR of X and Y with zero-prepending to the shorter one. That is,

$$X \oplus_{\shortparallel} Y = \begin{cases} (0^{|Y|-|X|} \parallel X) \oplus Y & \text{if } |X| < |Y| \\ (0^{|X|-|Y|} \parallel Y) \oplus X & \text{if } |Y| < |X| \\ X \oplus Y & \text{if } |X| = |Y|. \end{cases} \quad (1)$$

If X is uniformly distributed over set $\mathcal{X}$, we write $X \xleftarrow{\$} \mathcal{X}$. The set of all functions of n-bit input and m-bit output is denoted by $\mathrm{Func}(n, m)$ and the set of all n-bit permutations is denoted by $\mathrm{Perm}(n)$. A keyed function F with key $K \in \mathcal{K}$, input domain $\mathcal{X}$, and output domain $\mathcal{Y}$ is written as $F : \mathcal{K} \times \mathcal{X} \to \mathcal{Y}$. We write $F_K(X)$ to denote $F(K, X)$ and write $F_K : \mathcal{X} \to \mathcal{Y}$ to denote a function $F(K, *)$.

Keyed Functions and Random Functions. For a keyed function F_K with $K \in \mathcal{K}$, let A be an adversary who queries F_K (i.e. A determines $X \in \mathcal{X}$ and receives $Y = F_K(X)$, where K is randomly sampled and is not given to A) and generates an output in $\{0, 1\}$ after all, possibly adaptively-chosen queries. The event that A makes output 1 is denoted by $\mathsf{A}^{F_K} \to 1$, and $\Pr[K \xleftarrow{\$} \mathcal{K} : \mathsf{A}^{F_K} \to 1]$ denotes the probability of that event under the uniform choice of key K. Here, the probability space is defined by the randomness of K and the random coin of A.

We define the uniform random function (URF) R : $\{0,1\}^n \to \{0,1\}^m$ as a keyed function with the key uniform over Func(n, m). The n-bit uniform random permutation (URP), P : $\{0,1\}^n \to \{0,1\}^n$ is a keyed permutation with the key uniform over Perm(n). Note that the notion of URF can be extended to the case that the input domain is an infinite set, say, $\{0,1\}^*$. The output such URF can be evaluated by the lazy sampling.

Pseudorandom Function and Pseudorandom Permutation. For a pair of keyed functions $F : \mathcal{K} \times \mathcal{X} \to \mathcal{Y}$ and $G : \mathcal{K}' \times \mathcal{X} \to \mathcal{Y}$ with $K \in \mathcal{K}$ and $K' \in \mathcal{K}'$ ($\mathcal{K}$ and $\mathcal{K}'$ may be different), and an adversary A who makes (possibly adaptive) chosen-plaintext queries and then makes a binary output, let

$$\mathbf{Adv}^{\mathrm{cpa}}_{F_K, G_{K'}}(\mathsf{A}) \stackrel{\mathrm{def}}{=} \Pr[K \stackrel{\$}{\leftarrow} \mathcal{K} : \mathsf{A}^{F_K} \to 1] - \Pr[K' \stackrel{\$}{\leftarrow} \mathcal{K}' : \mathsf{A}^{G_{K'}} \to 1]$$

denote the advantage of A in distinguishing F from G. In particular, using URF R : $\{0,1\}^n \to \{0,1\}^m$, we define

$$\mathbf{Adv}^{\mathrm{prf}}_{F_K}(\mathsf{A}) \stackrel{\mathrm{def}}{=} \mathbf{Adv}^{\mathrm{cpa}}_{F_K, \mathsf{R}}(\mathsf{A}) = \Pr[K \stackrel{\$}{\leftarrow} \mathcal{K} : \mathsf{A}^{F_K} \to 1] - \Pr[\mathsf{R} \stackrel{\$}{\leftarrow} \mathrm{Func}(n, m) : \mathsf{A}^{\mathsf{R}} \to 1]$$

as the pseudorandom function (PRF) advantage of A against F. In addition, when $E_K : \{0,1\}^n \to \{0,1\}^n$ is invertible for any $K \in \mathcal{K}$ (i.e. a block cipher), we define

$$\mathbf{Adv}^{\mathrm{prp}}_E(\mathsf{A}) \stackrel{\mathrm{def}}{=} \Pr[K \stackrel{\$}{\leftarrow} \mathcal{K} : \mathsf{A}^{F_K} \to 1] - \Pr[\mathsf{P} \stackrel{\$}{\leftarrow} \mathrm{Perm}(n) : \mathsf{A}^{\mathsf{P}} \to 1], \qquad (2)$$

which is called the pseudorandom permutation (PRP) advantage.

State Size Calculation. The state size is the maximum bit size of input-dependent data, where key is a part of input, that must be kept in memory to process the input. Following previous work on modes (e.g. [31]), we do not count the key from our count, as our focus is the memory needed beyond what is needed for the block cipher. We assume the input message is given by n-bit blocks from the interface (one block per one clock), where n is the bit size of the underlying block cipher. As an example, let us explain how state size is calculated for PMAC [37][1] of Fig. 1. If we see at line 5, the i-th message block $M[i]$ is encrypted by E_K with input mask $2^i L$, and the result $E_K(2^i L \oplus M[i])$ is added to the chaining value S, where $L = E_K(0^n)$. This computation needs three n-bit values, namely the chaining state S, the mask $2^i L$, and the n-bit state for block cipher encryption, $3n$ bits in total. The message parsing (line 3) is done by the interface so we do not have store the entire M inside PMAC circuit. Note that,

---

[1] This is a version from [29] which is slightly simplified from the version of [37], for L is initialized to $L \leftarrow E_K(0^n)$ instead of $3^2 L \leftarrow E_K(0^n)$, which was needed when PMAC is used as a component of OCB2. This does not harm the provable security of PMAC.

Algorithm $\text{PMAC}_{E_K}(M)$

1. $S \leftarrow 0^n$
2. $L \leftarrow E_K(0^n)$
3. $M[1], \ldots, M[m] \xleftarrow{n} M$
4. **for** $i \leftarrow 1$ **to** $m - 1$
5. $S \leftarrow S \oplus E_K(2^i L \oplus M[i])$
6. $S \leftarrow S \oplus \text{pad}(M[m])$
7. **if** $|M[m]| = n$
8. $T \leftarrow E_K(2^m 3L \oplus S)$
9. **else** $T \leftarrow E_K(2^m 3^2 L \oplus S)$
10. **return** T

Fig. 1. PMAC.

as well as many other work, we implicitly avoid inefficient operation in terms of block cipher calls, therefore we cache $2^i L$ instead of evicting from memory, so that $2^{i+1} L$ is immediately computed when $M[i+1]$ is given. Otherwise, we need two block cipher calls plus a (full) field multiplication for every block, which is significantly slower than the normal operation. In case of LightMAC [25], the corresponding operation is $S \leftarrow S \oplus E_K(i_s \parallel M[i])$, where i_s is an s-bit encoding of positive integer i for a fixed s, thus there is no mask and the state size is $2n$ bits. This comes with the cost of slowdown caused by the shorter input block $|M[i]| = n - s$ and the limit of maximum input length about $n2^s$ bits.

As described earlier, the state size of a mode of operation is usually an important factor for hardware footprint. For software this effect is usually small, but the omission of $E_K(0^n)$ may be useful in some scenario, as explained in Introduction.

3 Our Proposal

3.1 Description of LAPMAC

We describe LAPMAC. It uses an n-bit block cipher E_K and a tweak function $f : \{0,1\}^n \times \mathcal{I}_f \rightarrow \{0,1\}^n$ for integer set $\mathcal{I}_f = (I_{\max})$ with $I_{\max} \geq 7$. Let $2 \leq \mu \leq I_{\max} - 1$ be the parameter of maximum parallelism, i.e., the maximum number of n-bit input blocks that can be processed in parallel[2]. We also define positive integers $\alpha = 1$, $\beta = 3$, $\gamma = 5$, $\delta = 6$, all are members of $\mathcal{I}_f$ that are used for the domain separation of certain cases depending on the input length (the reason for the assignments will be described later). For simplicity, we assume that $f(*, 0)$ is the identity function.

Informally, LAPMAC proceeds as follows. For each i-th message block $M[i]$ (in n bits), we encrypt it by E_K and applies $f(*, (i-1) \bmod \mu)$, and take XOR

---

[2] More precisely, the first $\mu + 1$ blocks can be parallel, and each of the subsequent μ blocks can be parallel.

of all f-outputs to compute the state value. When $i - 1 = 0 \bmod \mu$, instead of the above procedure we directly take XOR of the message block and the current state value, and renew the state by E_K followed by $f(*, 0)$, i.e. a plain encryption. This is repeated until the last-but-one block. For the last block $M[m]$, we first pad it to n bits using the standard 10^* padding, then take an XOR with the state block, and apply $f(*, \alpha)$ to the state block when $|M[m]| < n$ and $f(*, \beta)$ when $|M[m]| = n$. Finally, we encrypt the state block to create the (untrancated) tag. In case of single block message, we do differently and take an XOR of $E_K(0^n)$ and the padded message, followed by $f(*, \gamma)$ or $f(*, \delta)$ and encryption.

The pseudocode of LAPMAC is shown in Fig. 3. See Fig. 4 for an illustration.

As Fig. 4 shows, the paralleizability is up to μ blocks, and there is no mask and no pre-computation of $E_K(0^n)$. For one-block message, the procedure is different. We first compute $E_K(0^n)$ and take a sum with $M = M[1]$. This $E_K(0^n)$ is not needed for longer inputs. The lack of input mask allows to reduce the state memory from PMAC's $3n$ to $2n$ bits.

Design Rationale and Trade-Off. We describe the design rationale behind our design. As mentioned in Introduction, the structure of LAPMAC is similar to a proposal of short-input PRF, called S2V-R [28]. Figure 2 depicts a slightly simplified form of S2V-R, where t is defined as the parameter of tweak function, which was about n in case of [28]. In S2V-R, the block cipher takes the full n-bit message block and the encryption result is tweaked depending on the block index, before added to the chaining state (S). This structure seems to be the sole option to achieve our goal, i.e. $2n$-bit-state parallel MAC mode of full absorption. Basically, we can build a parallel MAC for arbitrarily long inputs by a black-box composition of S2V-R, say using Merkle-Damgård. However, this forces block cipher calls that cannot be parallelized for every μ blocks (since the last block cipher call of each S2V-R invocation cannot be parallelizable), which is quite undesirable for parallel implementations.

Let us describe more details. Our problem is to modify S2V-R to extend the maximum input length more than tn bits. We basically chain the computations of S2V-R, i.e., we parse the message M into chunks of $\sim tn$ bits, $C[1], C[2], \ldots, C[\ell]$, and compute $Y[1] \leftarrow$ S2V-R$_{E_K}(C[1])$, add $Y[1]$ to $C[2]$ and compute $Y[2] \leftarrow$ S2V-R$_{E_K}(Y[1] \oplus C[2])$, and so on. Note that the addition $Y[1] \oplus C[2]$ may not be well-defined when $|Y[1]| \neq |C[2]|$, and in fact if we add $Y[1]$ to the first n bits of $C[2]$ then we will have a non-parallelizable E_K call per chunk, since the last block cipher call of S2V-R must be evaluated separately. Instead, we add $Y[1]$ to the last of $C[2]$, then this non-parallelizable E_K call disappears, because the last block cipher call of S2V-R is now evaluated in parallel with the block cipher calls of the next S2V-R instance. The actual chain rule is more involved, as we used several different instantiations of S2V-R to simplify the global presentation of the scheme (Fig. 3). We also remove the computation of $E_K(0^n)$ used by S2V-R, which is not used as an input mask, but only to make a difference at the last chunk. Our trick is somewhat similar to GCBC that tweaks the chaining value depending on the necessity of message padding just before the last message block, however due to the difference in the structure, this requires

---

Algorithm S2V-R$_{E_K}(M)$

1. $S \leftarrow 0^n$
2. $L \leftarrow E_K(0^n)$
3. $M[1], \ldots, M[m] \xleftarrow{n} M$
4. **for** $i \leftarrow 1$ **to** $m-1$
5. $S \leftarrow S \oplus f(E_K(M[i]), i)$
6. **if** $|M[m]| = n$
7. $S \leftarrow S \oplus f(L, t-1)$
8. **else** $S \leftarrow S \oplus f(L, t) \oplus \text{pad}(M[m])$
9. $T \leftarrow E_K(S)$
10. **return** T

Fig. 2. A slightly simplified form of S2V-R. We ignore the case of empty string input, and assume the underlying VIL-PRF is n-bit block cipher E_K. It can accept messages of at most $(t-1)$ n-bit blocks, and when f is based on bit rotation, t is about n.

more conditions for the tweak function than the case of S2V-R, particularly the condition 3 of Definition 1.

As shown in Table 1, our design imposes several trade-offs, that is, the limited parallelizability of up to μ blocks whereas PMAC has no such limitation. In addition, comparing with serial GCBC mode, the state size is increased.

3.2 Security of LAPMAC

We show that LAPMAC is provably secure if tweak function f satisfies certain conditions.

Definition 1. Let $f : \{0,1\}^n \times \mathcal{I}_f \rightarrow \{0,1\}^n$ be the tweak function described above. We say f is valid if

1. $|\mathcal{I}_f| \geq 7$
2. $f(*, i)$ for any $i \in \mathcal{I}_f$ is a permutation
3. $f(f(x, i), j) = f(x, i+j)$ for any $i, j \in \mathcal{I}_f$ such that $i + j \in \mathcal{I}_f$.

As mentioned, we fix $\alpha = 1$, $\beta = 3$, $\gamma = 5$, $\delta = 6$. This is to guarantee $\alpha, \alpha+1, \beta, \beta+1, \gamma$ and δ are distinct elements of $\mathcal{I}_f \setminus \{0\}^3$. The following property of tweak function by [28] plays a central role in our analysis.

Definition 2. For tweak function $f(*, *)$, if

$$\max_{\mathcal{I} \subseteq \mathcal{I}_f, \mathcal{I} \neq \emptyset, c \in \{0,1\}^n} \Pr\left[U \xleftarrow{\$} \{0,1\}^n : \bigoplus_{i \in \mathcal{I}} f(U, i) = c\right] \leq p_f$$

holds for some $0 < p_f \leq 1$, we say f is p_f-almost-subset-sum-uniform (p_f-ASSU).

---

[3] It may be possible to reduce the number of parameters which relaxes the minimum size of $\mathcal{I}_f$ but it can complicate the security analysis.

Algorithm $\text{LAPMAC}_{E_K}(M)$	**Algorithm** $\text{RotSum}_{E_K}(m, M)$
	$// \ |M| = nm$
1. **if** $|M| \leq n$ **then**	
2. $\quad T \leftarrow \text{Single}_{E_K}(M)$	1. $S \leftarrow 0^n$
3. $\quad$ **return** T	2. $M[1], \ldots, M[m] \xleftarrow{n} M$
4. **else** $\ S \leftarrow 0^n$	3. **for** $i = 1$ **to** m
5. $C[1], \ldots, C[\rho] \xleftarrow{n\mu} M$	4. $\quad S \leftarrow f(E_K(M[i]), i-1) \oplus S$
6. **for** $i \leftarrow 1$ **to** $\rho - 1$ **do**	5. **return** S
7. $\quad C[i] \leftarrow S \oplus_{||} C[i]$	
8. $\quad S \leftarrow \text{RotSum}_{E_K}(\mu, C[i])$	**Algorithm** $\text{Single}_{E_K}(M)$
9. $c \leftarrow |C[\rho]|_n$	$// \ 0 \leq |M| \leq n$
10. **if** $c > 1$ **then**	
11. $\quad (A, B) \xleftarrow{(c-1)n} C[\rho]$	1. $S \leftarrow E_K(0^n)$
12. $\quad A \leftarrow S \oplus_{||} A$	2. $S \leftarrow S \oplus \text{pad}(M)$
13. $\quad S \leftarrow \text{RotSum}_{E_K}(c-1, A)$	3. **if** $|M| < n$ **then**
14. **else** $B \leftarrow C[\rho]$	4. $\quad T \leftarrow \text{msb}_\tau(E_K(f(S, \gamma)))$
15. $S \leftarrow S \oplus \text{pad}(B)$	5. **else**
16. **if** $|B| = n$ **then**	6. $\quad T \leftarrow \text{msb}_\tau(E_K(f(S, \delta)))$
17. $\quad T \leftarrow \text{msb}_\tau(E_K(f(S, \alpha)))$	7. **return** T
18. **else**	
19. $\quad T \leftarrow \text{msb}_\tau(E_K(f(S, \beta)))$	
20. **return** T	

Fig. 3. LAPMAC.

The security of LAPMAC is proved as follows. For simplicity, we only provide information-theoretic results using n-bit random permutation P instead of PRP E_K throughout the paper. See below for the derivation of computational counterpart.

Theorem 1. *Suppose* $f : \{0,1\}^n \times \mathcal{I}_f \to \{0,1\}^n$ *is a valid tweak function and is* p_f-*ASSU. Let* A *be an adversary against LAPMAC using* q *queries with* σ *total blocks, i.e.,* $\sigma = \sum_{i=1,\ldots,q} |M_i|_n$ *where* $M_i \in \{0,1\}^*$ *denotes the* i-*th query. When* $\sigma \leq 2^n / 2$, *we have*

$$\mathbf{Adv}_{LAPMAC_P}^{\text{prf}}(A) \leq \left(\frac{3}{2^n} + p_f \right) \cdot \sigma^2.$$

The proof is given in Sect. 4. The computational counterpart, where a block cipher E_K is used instead of P, is easily obtained by the standard technique (see [4]). Specifically, assuming the time complexity of adversary A being t (under some computation model), we add a term $\mathbf{Adv}_{E_K}^{\text{prp}}(B)$ to the right hand side of the above bound, where B takes at most $(\sigma + q)$ queries with time complexity $t + O(\sigma)$.

3.3 Instantiations of Tweak Function

We provide some examples of tweak function. Minematsu [28] showed a class of universal hash functions based on bit rotations, called CLH, which directly

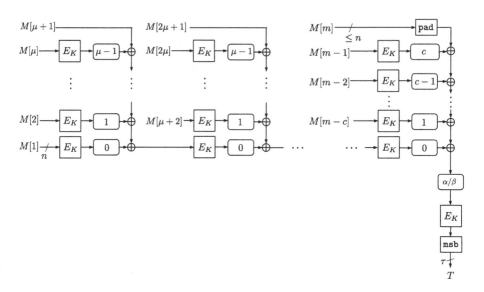

Fig. 4. LAPMAC for messages longer than n bits. The rounded box with label $i \in \{0, \ldots, \mu - 1\}$ denotes $f(*, i)$, and with label α/β denotes $f(*, \alpha)$ if $|M[m]| = n$ and $f(*, \beta)$ otherwise.

provides good tweak functions. The construction of [28] can be explained in the following lemma.

Lemma 1 *(Lemma 1 of [28]). Suppose n is a prime and 2 is the primitive root modulo n. Let $\mathcal{I}_f = (n - 1)$ and let $f : \{0, 1\}^n \times \mathcal{I}_f \rightarrow \{0, 1\}^n$ be defined as $f(U, i) = U \lll i$ for $i \in \mathcal{I}_f$. Then, f is $1/2^{n-1}$-ASSU.*

The proof is based on an old work of Daykin [16] on the rank of matrix defined over finite field [28]. The primes satisfying the above condition are called p-prime in [28], and they are easy to find by search. For example, $3, 5, 11, 13$ and 19 satisfy the condition, however 7 and 17 do not. Since prime n is not convenient to work with conventional block ciphers whose block size is a power of two, [28] also introduced two variants defined over power-of-two bits. Based on Lemma 1, we use the following tweak functions[4].

Corollary 1 *(A variant of Lemma 2 of [28]). For even n, let $n' < n$ and $n'' < n/2$ be p-primes. We define*

$$f_{n'}^1(U, i) \stackrel{\text{def}}{=} (\mathsf{msb}_{n'}(U) \lll i) \| \mathsf{lsb}_{n-n'}(U), \tag{3}$$

$$f_{n''}^2(U, i) \stackrel{\text{def}}{=} f_{n''}^1(\mathsf{msb}_{n/2}(U), i) \| f_{n''}^1(\mathsf{lsb}_{n/2}(U), i). \tag{4}$$

---

[4] In fact, [28] proposed another rotation-based function using p-prime larger than n, however it fails to fulfill our requirements, such as invertibility.

Then $f_{n'}^1$ is a tweak function of $2/2^{n'}$-ASSU with $\mathcal{I}_f = \{0, \ldots, n'-2\}$, and $f_{n''}^2$ is a tweak function of $4/2^{2n''}$-ASSU with $\mathcal{I}_f = \{0, \ldots, n''-2\}$.

Moreover, both tweak functions fulfill the last two conditions of Definition 1, hence both are valid when n' and n'' are not smaller than 8.

Clearly, the best strategy to build a highly-secure tweak function is to choose a p-prime close to n for f^1 and $n/2$ for f^2. When $n = 64$, $n' = 61$ is the largest p-prime smaller than n. For block size of n bits, we suggest f_{61}^1 for $n = 64$, and f_{61}^2 for $n = 128$. The resulting tweak functions are $1/2^{60}$-ASSU and $1/2^{120}$-ASSU respectively. When $n = 128$, the prime 127 is unfortunately not a p-prime, instead $n' = 107$ is the largest p-prime smaller than n.

As mentioned before, S2V-R [28] is a PRF construction similar to LAPMAC using bit rotation, however, it takes at most μ (hence around n) blocks, and needs a pre-computation of $E_K(0^n)$. Zhang et al. [39] also suggested to use a bit rotation for tweaking the last input block of CBC-MAC. However, it is defined over full n bits, hence cannot be directly used as a tweak function of reasonably large $\mathcal{I}_f$ when n is a power of two.

Corollary 2. *Let P be the n-bit URP. When $n = 64$, we use tweak function f_{61}^1 and we have*

$$\mathbf{Adv}_{LAPMAC_P}^{\mathrm{prf}}(A) \le \frac{17\sigma^2}{2^{64}},$$

for any A using queries of total blocks σ. When $n = 128$, we use f_{61}^2 and we have

$$\mathbf{Adv}_{LAPMAC_P}^{\mathrm{prf}}(A) \le \frac{259\sigma^2}{2^{128}},$$

for any A using queries of total blocks σ. Both cases have $\mu \le 60$, hence at most 60 blocks can be processed in parallel.

The proofs are obtained by Corollary 1 and Theorem 1. We remark that the implementation of these tweak functions are pretty simple, needing few logic operations.

Other Instantiations. We could also use a constant multiplication over $GF(2^n)$, e.g., $f(U, i) = 2^i U$, where $2U$ denotes a multiplication by polynomial x over $GF(2^n)$. This is also called *doubling* and is a popular tool for constructions of modes [20,36]. This will give us $1/2^n$-ASSU tweak function with μ being around n. The cost will sharply increase as i grows, though using Horner's rule we could reduce the computation so that we only need single doubling per input block, as in the same manner as S2V PRF by Rogaway and Shrimpton [38]. In that case, however, the computation of tweak function becomes serial. One might wonder if we could instantiate tweak function for μ much larger than n. This is in theory possible by combining multiplication and exponentiation over a finite field, however the cost will be quite high, thus is not suitable for our purpose. In general, the construction of efficient tweak functions with $\mu > n$ is open.

Discussion on Bounds. The security bounds of Corollary 2 show large constants, in particular for $n = 128$, which results in about $(n - 7)/2$-bit security. The constant 17 for $n = 64$ is smaller but still larger than others, say PMAC or CMAC. This comes from the relatively large p_f value of the tweak function. Developing a tweak function for $n = 64, 128$ with smaller p_f of similar μ and similar efficiency as bit rotation is another interesting future direction.

4 Security Proof

4.1 Proof of Theorem 1

Overview. Let LAPMAC$_R$ be the LAPMAC algorithm using an n-bit random function, R, as internal component. As well as previous work, we first prove the security bound of LAPMAC$_R$, and combine the result with standard PRP-PRF switching lemma to derive the security bound of LAPMAC$_P$. Here, we stress that proving the security of LAPMAC is much more involved than the case of S2V-R. This is because the message blocks of S2V-R are completely parallel and the domain separation for final block follows the standard way as was done by CMAC, i.e., tweak $E_K(0^n)$ depending on the $\mathrm{isp}(M[m])$ for any message. This implies that S2V-R can be proved as an instantiation of a classical Carter-Wegman MAC. To prove the security of LAPMAC$_R$, we first decompose it into a family of fixed-length functions, each uses the same R, then prove that it is hard to distinguish them from independent random functions. The analysis here can be seen as an extension of the proof of S2V-R. Then, we analyze the composition of the function family assuming each function is an independent random function. This turns out to be a variant of CBC-MAC collision analysis. These two results are combined via a standard hybrid argument, resulting in the final security bound of LAPMAC$_R$.

First Step: Decomposition of LAPMAC into Small FIL Functions. We show that LAPMAC$_R$ can be described as a composition (mode) of a set of fixed-input-length (FIL) functions taking integer blocks. They are

$$F_{h,1} : (\{0,1\}^n)^{\mu+1} \to \{0,1\}^n, \tag{5}$$

$$F_{h,2} : (\{0,1\}^n)^{\mu} \to \{0,1\}^n, \tag{6}$$

$$F_{f,i,w} : \{0,1\}^{ni} \to \{0,1\}^n, \text{ for } i = 1, \ldots, \mu+1, w \in \{0,1\}, \tag{7}$$

$$F_{g,j,w} : \{0,1\}^{nj} \to \{0,1\}^n, \text{ for } j = 1, \ldots, \mu, w \in \{0,1\}, \tag{8}$$

and defined at Fig. 5. Let $\mathcal{F}$ be the set of above functions. Each function in $\mathcal{F}$ uses URF R. In addition there is a random $U \xleftarrow{\$} \{0,1\}^n$ and some functions also use U (the sampling is shared by the functions). This U serves as a dummy and will be canceled in the composition. This technique is similar to the proof of OMAC [20]. We index functions in $\mathcal{F}$ by their subscripts, and let $\mathcal{Z}$ be the set of their indexes (subscripts), written as

$$\mathcal{Z} = \{(\mathsf{h}, 1), (\mathsf{h}, 2)\} \cup \{(\mathsf{f}, i, w)\}_{i=1,\ldots,\mu+1, w=0,1} \cup \{(\mathsf{g}, j, w)\}_{j=1,\ldots,\mu, w=0,1}.$$

Using $\mathcal{F}$, we build a function $\psi_{\mathcal{F}}$ which takes a binary string of any length to produce n-bit output. It is shown in Fig. 6. We observe that $Z \in \mathcal{Z}$ is uniquely determined by M.

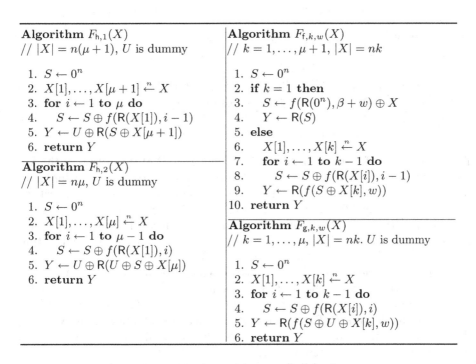

Algorithm $F_{h,1}(X)$
// $|X| = n(\mu + 1)$, U is dummy

1. $S \leftarrow 0^n$
2. $X[1], \ldots, X[\mu + 1] \xleftarrow{n} X$
3. **for** $i \leftarrow 1$ **to** μ **do**
4. $\quad S \leftarrow S \oplus f(\mathsf{R}(X[1]), i - 1)$
5. $Y \leftarrow U \oplus \mathsf{R}(S \oplus X[\mu + 1])$
6. **return** Y

Algorithm $F_{h,2}(X)$
// $|X| = n\mu$, U is dummy

1. $S \leftarrow 0^n$
2. $X[1], \ldots, X[\mu] \xleftarrow{n} X$
3. **for** $i \leftarrow 1$ **to** $\mu - 1$ **do**
4. $\quad S \leftarrow S \oplus f(\mathsf{R}(X[1]), i)$
5. $Y \leftarrow U \oplus \mathsf{R}(U \oplus S \oplus X[\mu])$
6. **return** Y

Algorithm $F_{f,k,w}(X)$
// $k = 1, \ldots, \mu + 1$, $|X| = nk$

1. $S \leftarrow 0^n$
2. **if** $k = 1$ **then**
3. $\quad S \leftarrow f(\mathsf{R}(0^n), \beta + w) \oplus X$
4. $\quad Y \leftarrow \mathsf{R}(S)$
5. **else**
6. $\quad X[1], \ldots, X[k] \xleftarrow{n} X$
7. $\quad$ **for** $i \leftarrow 1$ **to** $k - 1$ **do**
8. $\quad\quad S \leftarrow S \oplus f(\mathsf{R}(X[i]), i - 1)$
9. $\quad Y \leftarrow \mathsf{R}(f(S \oplus X[k], w))$
10. **return** Y

Algorithm $F_{g,k,w}(X)$
// $k = 1, \ldots, \mu$, $|X| = nk$. U is dummy

1. $S \leftarrow 0^n$
2. $X[1], \ldots, X[k] \xleftarrow{n} X$
3. **for** $i \leftarrow 1$ **to** $k - 1$ **do**
4. $\quad S \leftarrow S \oplus f(\mathsf{R}(X[i]), i)$
5. $Y \leftarrow \mathsf{R}(f(S \oplus U \oplus X[k], w))$
6. **return** Y

Fig. 5. Members of function family $\mathcal{F}$.

In $\psi_{\mathcal{F}}$, $F_{f,i,w}$ works as a MAC function for messages of at most $\mu + 1$ blocks, and for longer messages the MAC function is decomposed into two parts, message hashing function composed by $F_{h,1}$ and $F_{h,2}$, written as $\mathrm{CBC}[F_{h,1}, F_{h,2}]$, and the finalization taking the output of message hashing function to produce the output. The finalization takes the last $i \in [\![\mu]\!]$ blocks and processes with $F_{g,i,w}$. In addition, input M is first partitioned into *chunks* which consists of multiple n-bit blocks, written as $C[i]$. We write $C[1], \ldots, C[c] \leftarrow \mathsf{Parse}_{n,\mu}(M)$ to denote the partition of M into c chunks. It is defined as follows. First we pad M as $M \leftarrow \mathsf{ozp}(M)$ and perform block partition $M[1], \ldots, M[m] \xleftarrow{n} M$. When $m \leq \mu + 1$, let $c = 1$ and $C[1] = M$. When $m \geq \mu + 2$, we first extract its first $\mu + 1$ blocks and partition M into the chunks of block length μ, except the first chunk. The last chunk may be shorter, $i \in [\![\mu]\!]$ blocks. Here, $c = \lceil (m - 2)/\mu \rceil$ whenever $m > \mu + 2$ and $|C[i]|$ is $n(\mu + 1)$ for $i = 1$, $n\mu$ for $i = 2, \ldots, c - 1$, and we have $2 \leq |C[c]| \leq n\mu$. See Fig. 6 for the pseudocode.

We observe that $\psi_{\mathcal{F}}$ perfectly simulates $\mathrm{LAPMAC}_{\mathsf{R}}$.

Proposition 1. *For any* $M \in \{0,1\}^*$,

$$LAPMAC_R(M) = \psi_{\mathcal{F}}(M). \tag{9}$$

Proof is easy, just to check that the following cases, with $w = \text{isp}(M)$:

- the case of $|M|_n \in [\![\mu + 1]\!]$: $F_{f,|M|_n,w}$ is used.
- the case of $|M|_n \in \{\mu + 2, \ldots, 2\mu + 1\}$: two functions $F_{h,1}$ and $F_{g,i,w}$ for $i = |M|_n - (\mu + 1)$ are chained.
- the case of $2\mu + 1 < |M|_n$: after processing the first chunk (of $\mu + 1$ blocks) by $F_{h,1}$, the successive chunks except the last one is processed by $F_{h,2}$ in a chain. The last chunk is processed by $F_{g,i,w}$ to create a tag, where $i = \mu$ when $\gamma \stackrel{\text{def}}{=} (|M|_n - (\mu + 1)) \bmod \mu = 0$, and $i = \gamma$ otherwise.

For all cases, two functions are chained by taking XOR of the output of the former to the *last* input block to the latter. Observe that if two consecutive functions in a chain use U, it is always canceled, hence it maintains the original algorithm. For example, when $|M|_n = m = \mu + 2$ we first give $C[1] = (M[1], \ldots, M[\mu+1])$ to $F_{f,1}$ which outputs $U \oplus Y$ for some R-output Y, and it is added to the (padded, single) input block of $F_{g,1,w}$, for $w = \text{isp}(M)$. This yields the final output $R(f(U \oplus \text{pad}(M[m]) \oplus U \oplus Y, w)) = R(f(\text{pad}(M[m]) \oplus Y, w))$.

From Proposition 1, $\mathbf{Adv}_{LAPMAC_R}^{\text{prf}}(\mathsf{A}) = \mathbf{Adv}_{\psi_{\mathcal{F}}}^{\text{prf}}(\mathsf{A})$ holds for any A.

Let $\mathcal{R} = \{R_Z : Z \in \mathcal{Z}\}$ be a set of independent URFs compatible (i.e. having the same domain and range) to the corresponding $F_Z \in \mathcal{F}$. We show that $\mathcal{F}$ is indistinguishable from $\mathcal{R}$. By assuming $Z \in \mathcal{Z}$ as a part of input, let $\mathbf{Adv}_{\mathcal{F},\mathcal{R}}^{\text{cpa}}(\mathsf{A})$ denote the advantage of the adversary A in distinguishing $\mathcal{F}$ from $\mathcal{R}$. That is, a query to $\mathcal{F}$ can be written as $(X, Z) \in (\{0,1\}^+)^n \times \mathcal{Z}$ and if $Z = (h, 1)$ the oracle returns $F_{h,1}(X)$, and if $Z = (f, 2, 0)$ the oracle returns $F_{f,2,0}(X)$, and so on. For each query (X, Z), the length of X is implicitly determined by Z.

Lemma 2. *Let f be a valid, p_f-ASSU tweak function. Let A' be an adversary for distinguishing $\mathcal{F}$ and $\mathcal{R}$ by asking q queries, (X_i, Z_i) for $i = 1, \ldots, q$ with total σ blocks, i.e., $\sum_i |X_i|_n = \sigma$. Then*

$$\mathbf{Adv}_{\mathcal{F},\mathcal{R}}^{\text{cpa}}(\mathsf{A}') \leq q\sigma p_f.$$

The proof of Lemma 2 is in Sect. 4.2.

Let $\psi_{\mathcal{R}}$ be the procedure ψ using $\mathcal{R}$ as an internal module, instead of $\mathcal{F}$. Then, Lemma 2 tells that, for A trying to distinguish $\psi_{\mathcal{F}}$ from $\psi_{\mathcal{R}}$ using q queries and total σ message blocks, we have

$$\mathbf{Adv}_{\psi_{\mathcal{F}}, \psi_{\mathcal{R}}}^{\text{cpa}}(\mathsf{A}) \leq \sigma^2 p_f, \tag{10}$$

since q queries with σ total blocks to $\psi_{\mathcal{F}}$ can be simulated by at most σ queries with σ total blocks to $\mathcal{F}$.

Second Step: Security of $\psi_{\mathcal{R}}$. We consider the indistinguishability of $\psi_{\mathcal{R}}$ from variable-input-length (VIL) URF, $R^* : \{0,1\}^* \to \{0,1\}^n$. Here, $\psi_{\mathcal{R}}$ is

---

Algorithm $\psi_{\mathcal{F}}(M)$

    1. $w \leftarrow \mathsf{isp}(M)$
    2. $C[1], \ldots, C[c] \leftarrow \mathsf{Parse}_{n,\mu}(M)$
    3. $k \leftarrow |C[c]|_n$
    4. $V \leftarrow \mathrm{CBC}[F_{\mathsf{h},1}, F_{\mathsf{h},2}](C[1], \ldots, C[c])$
    5. **if** $c = 1$ **then** $T \leftarrow F_{\mathsf{f},k,w}(V)$
    6. **else** $T \leftarrow F_{\mathsf{g},k,w}(V)$
    7. **return** T

Algorithm $\mathrm{CBC}[F_{\mathsf{h},1}, F_{\mathsf{h},2}](C[1], \ldots, C[c])$ $// \ c \geq 1$ $//$ Input is an output of $\mathsf{Parse}_{n,\mu}$	**Algorithm** $\mathsf{Parse}_{n,\mu}(M)$ $// \ M \in \{0,1\}^*$

1. **if** $c = 1$ **then**
  2. $V[1] \leftarrow C[1]$
  3. **if** $c \geq 2$ **then**
  4. $Y[1] \leftarrow F_{\mathsf{h},1}(C[1])$
  5.   **for** $i \leftarrow 2$ **to** $c - 1$ **do**
  6. $V[i] \leftarrow C[i] \oplus_{\shortparallel} Y[i-1]$
  7. $Y[i] \leftarrow F_{\mathsf{h},2}(V[i])$
  8. $V[c] \leftarrow C[c] \oplus_{\shortparallel} Y[c-1]$
  9. $V \leftarrow V[c]$
 10. **return** V
	1. $M \leftarrow \mathsf{ozp}(M)$
	  2. $M[1], \ldots, M[m] \overset{n}{\leftarrow} M$
	  3. **if** $m \leq \mu + 1$ **then**
	  4. $c \leftarrow 1$
	  5. $C[c] \leftarrow M$ $//$ Given to $F_{\mathsf{f},m,w}$
	  6. **else**
	  7. $C[1] \leftarrow M[1] \parallel \ldots \parallel M[\mu+1]$
	  8. $\tilde{M} \leftarrow M[\mu+2] \parallel \ldots \parallel M[m]$
	  9. $C[2] \parallel \ldots \parallel C[c] \overset{n\mu}{\leftarrow} \tilde{M}$
	 10. **return** $C[1] \parallel \ldots \parallel C[c]$

Fig. 6. $\psi_{\mathcal{F}}$, an alternative representation of LAPMAC$_{\mathsf{R}}$. The operator $\oplus_{\shortparallel}$ is an XOR of two strings of different lengths (shorter one is prepended by zeros) as defined by (1).

obtained by replacing each $F_Z \in \mathcal{F}$ in Fig. 6 with $\mathsf{R}_Z \in \mathcal{R}$. Following Fig. 6, let $V_i[c_i]$ denote the last input chunk of message M_i having c_i chunks given to $\psi_{\mathcal{R}}$. We may also abbreviate $V_i[c_i]$ to V_i. As Fig. 6 shows, $\mathrm{CBC}[\mathsf{R}_{\mathsf{h},1}, \mathsf{R}_{\mathsf{h},2}]$ is the process that determines V_i from M_i. Clearly, $\psi_{\mathcal{R}}$ has a similar structure as the serial MAC modes with independent finalization. That is, the message M is first padded, and then hashed by sequentially applying $\mathsf{R}_{\mathsf{h},1}$ for the first chunk and $\mathsf{R}_{\mathsf{h},2}$ for the remaining, and the final hash value (of kn bits where $k = |C[c]|_n$) is processed by either $\mathsf{R}_{\mathsf{f},k,w}$ or $\mathsf{R}_{\mathsf{g},k,w}$, depending solely by (the length of) M. Let Z^* denote the final F-tweak value for the tag: $T = F_{Z^*}(V)$ where V is the output of $\mathrm{CBC}[F_{\mathsf{h},1}, F_{\mathsf{h},2}]$ in line 4 of Fig. 6. Since the value of Z^* is independent of the randomness of hashing ($\mathsf{R}_{\mathsf{h},1}$ and $\mathsf{R}_{\mathsf{h},2}$), the analysis can be reduced to a non-adaptive collision analysis.

We assume R^* to invoke $\mathrm{CBC}[\mathsf{R}_{\mathsf{h},1}, \mathsf{R}_{\mathsf{h},2}]$ as a dummy so that $V[c]$ in Fig. 6 is uniquely determined as well. Let $\mathbf{Adv}^{\mathsf{coll}}_{\mathsf{R}^*}(\mathsf{A})$ denote the probability $Z_i^* = Z_j^*$ and $V_i = V_j$ for some $1 \leq i < j \leq q$ when (possibly adaptive) A queries R^*. Here, the outputs of R^* are uniform and independent of the dummy hashing results, which implies the indistinguishability of $\psi_{\mathcal{R}}$ is bounded by the maximum of

$\mathbf{Adv}_{R^*}^{\text{coll}}(\overline{A})$ for any non-adaptive adversary $\overline{A}$, in the same manner to the proofs of block cipher-based MACs [9,20]. Thus, we have

$$\mathbf{Adv}_{\psi_{\mathcal{R}},R^*}^{\text{cpa}}(A) \le \mathbf{Adv}_{R^*}^{\text{coll}}(\overline{A}) \stackrel{\text{def}}{=} \Pr_{\overline{A},R^*}[\exists(i,j) : i < j, Z_i^* = Z_j^*, V_i = V_j], \quad (11)$$

holds for some non-adaptive adversary $\overline{A}$ using the same amount of queries as A. Since Z_i^*, Z_j^* are determined by the messages, the last term of the above equation can be simply bounded by the collision probability of CBC, that is,

$$\max_{\substack{C_1,\dots,C_q, \\ C_i \ne C_j, \sum_i |C_i|_n = \sigma}} \Pr[\exists(i,j) : i < j, \text{CBC}[\mathsf{R}_{h,1}, \mathsf{R}_{h,2}](C_i) = \text{CBC}[\mathsf{R}_{h,1}, \mathsf{R}_{h,2}](C_j)],$$

$$(12)$$

where the queries are of the form $C_i = (C_i[1], C_i[2], \dots, C_i[c_i])$ (rather than M_i) with $\sum_i |C_i|_n \le \sigma$. Note that $|M|_n = |C|_n$ holds when $C = \mathsf{Parse}_{n,\mu}(M)$.

Collision Probability of $\text{CBC}[\mathsf{R}_{h,1}, \mathsf{R}_{h,2}]$. We observe that $\text{CBC}[\mathsf{R}_{h,1}, \mathsf{R}_{h,2}]$ is similar to CBC-MAC, or more specifically, MOMAC-E function defined by [20], which is a variant of CBC-MAC using two independent URPs, P_1 and P_2, where P_1 is used for the first block and P_2 is used for the rest. The output of MOMAC-E is an XOR of the last output of URP and the last message block.

The major differences between $\text{CBC}[\mathsf{R}_{h,1}, \mathsf{R}_{h,2}]$ and MOMAC-E are (1) random functions in $\text{CBC}[\mathsf{R}_{h,1}, \mathsf{R}_{h,2}]$ take a chunk which is longer than n-bit chain and (2) MOMAC-E is defined over messages of at least two blocks, while $\text{CBC}[\mathsf{R}_{h,1}, \mathsf{R}_{h,2}]$ takes single chunk input, $C[1]$, with output being $C[1]$ itself. Nevertheless, the collision probability of $\text{CBC}[\mathsf{R}_{h,1}, \mathsf{R}_{h,2}]$ can be analyzed in the same manner as that of MOMAC-E. We count all non-trivial internal collisions between n-bit chain values in an amortized way among q messages, which is at most $\binom{\sigma}{2}$, and observe that each collision has probability $1/2^n$ given that there is no non-trivial collision before. We have the following lemma. The proof is given in Appendix A.

Lemma 3. *When $\sigma \le 2^n/2$, (12) is bounded by $\sigma^2/2^n$.*

From (10) to (12) and Lemma 3, we have

$$\mathbf{Adv}_{\text{LAPMAC}_{\mathsf{R}}}^{\text{prf}}(A) \le \mathbf{Adv}_{\psi_{\mathcal{F}},\psi_{\mathcal{R}}}^{\text{cpa}}(A) + \mathbf{Adv}_{\psi_{\mathcal{R}},R^*}^{\text{cpa}}(A) \le \sigma^2 p_f + \frac{\sigma^2}{2^n}. \quad (13)$$

From the PRP-PRF switching lemma (e.g. [4]),

$$\mathbf{Adv}_{\text{LAPMAC}_{\mathsf{P}},\text{LAPMAC}_{\mathsf{R}}}^{\text{cpa}}(A) \le \frac{(\sigma+1)^2}{2^{n+1}} \quad (14)$$

holds for any A using q queries and σ blocks, where $\sigma+1$ comes from the fact that the single-block input needs an evaluation of $E_K(0^n)$. The proof is completed by combining (13) and (14).

4.2   Proof of Lemma 2

Coefficients-H Technique. The proof uses Coefficients-H technique developed by Patarin [35], which is one of common tools for provable security analysis of symmetric-key cryptographic functions. We briefly describe the basics. See e.g. [34] or [14] for reference.

The task of adversary A is to play the game for distinguishing $\mathcal{F}$, which we call *real world*, from $\mathcal{R}$, which we call *ideal world*. The adversary A is assumed to have at most q queries but there is no computational limitation for A. In this game, let $\mathbf{X}_i$ be the i-th query and $\mathbf{Y}_i$ be the corresponding response from the oracle. The set of tuples of random variables $\{(\mathbf{X}_1, \mathbf{Y}_1), \ldots, (\mathbf{X}_q, \mathbf{Y}_q)\}$ is called *transcript*. Since the game is purely information-theoretic, we can (w.l.o.g) assume A is deterministic including the final binary decision. We fix such A. We also assume A never repeats queries.

Let $\Theta_{\mathcal{F}}$ ($\Theta_{\mathcal{R}}$) be the random variable denoting the transcript under the real world (ideal world). Since A is fixed and deterministic, the probability space of transcript is uniquely determined by the underlying world ($\mathcal{F}$ or $\mathcal{R}$).

We say a transcript is *attainable* if it has non-zero probability in $\mathcal{R}$ (i.e., a sampled value of the transcript θ is attainable if $\Pr[\Theta_{\mathcal{R}} = \theta] > 0$). Let AllT be the set of all attainable transcripts.

To evaluate the indistinguishability, we determine a set of *good* transcripts, which is a subset of attainable transcripts. The set of good transcripts is written as $\mathsf{GoodT} \subseteq \mathsf{AllT}$. A transcript that is not good is called *bad*, and the set of all bad transcripts are denoted by BadT. Here, $\mathsf{AllT} = \mathsf{GoodT} \cup \mathsf{BadT}$.

Suppose there are $0 \leq \epsilon_{\mathrm{bad}}, \epsilon_{\mathrm{ratio}} \leq 1$ such that

$$\Pr[\Theta_{\mathcal{R}} \in \mathsf{BadT}] \leq \epsilon_{\mathrm{bad}} \text{ and }, \tag{15}$$

$$\frac{\Pr[\Theta_{\mathcal{F}} = \theta]}{\Pr[\Theta_{\mathcal{R}} = \theta]} \geq 1 - \epsilon_{\mathrm{ratio}} \text{ holds for all good } \theta. \tag{16}$$

Then from the fundamental lemma of Patarin [35] (see e.g. [14] for proof), we have

$$\mathbf{Adv}^{\mathrm{cpa}}_{\mathcal{F},\mathcal{R}}(\mathsf{A}) \leq \epsilon_{\mathrm{bad}} + \epsilon_{\mathrm{ratio}}. \tag{17}$$

Therefore, Coefficients-H technique reduces the task of proving indistinguishability of $\mathcal{F}$ and $\mathcal{R}$ to finding the adequate definitions of good and bad transcripts such that ϵ_{bad} and $\epsilon_{\mathrm{ratio}}$ are proved to be sufficiently small.

Transcript. We start with the definition transcripts. In our game, the i-th query is $(M_i, Z_i) \in (\{0,1\}^n)^+ \times \mathcal{Z}$, and the oracle response is $T_i \in \{0,1\}^n$. We define m_i as $|M_i|_n$ and write $M_i = M_i[1], \ldots, M_i[m_i]$. First, we include random dummy U in the transcript. For $M_i = M_i[1], \ldots, M_i[m_i]$ with $m_i \geq 2$, let $X_i[j] = M_i[j]$ for $j = 1, \ldots, m_i - 1$, and let $Y_i[j] = \mathsf{R}(X_i[j])$. When $m_i = 1$ there is no $X_i[j]$. For convention, let $m_0 = 2$ and $X_0[m_0 - 1] = 0^n$ to denote the constant input used when $Z = (\mathsf{f}, 1, w)$. As an exception, when $Z = (\mathsf{g}, 1, w)$, we let $X_i = M_i$ but Y_i be an arbitrarily default constant const, since $\mathsf{R}(X)$ is not used by $F_{\mathsf{g},1,w}(M)$.

We write S_i to denote the input to final R for the i-th query. From the commutative property of valid f (Definition 1), it is written as follows.

- Case $Z = (\mathsf{f}, 1, 0)$: $|M| = n$.
  $S = f(\mathsf{R}(0^n), \gamma) \oplus X[1]$
- Case $Z = (\mathsf{f}, 1, 1)$: $0 < |M| < n$.
  $S = f(\mathsf{R}(0^n), \delta) \oplus \mathsf{pad}(X[1])$
- Case $Z = (\mathsf{f}, i, 0)$: $|M| = ni$.
  $S = \bigoplus_{j=1}^{i-1} f(\mathsf{R}(X[j]), j + \alpha - 1) \oplus f(X[i], \alpha)$
- Case $Z = (\mathsf{f}, i, 1)$: $n(i - 1) < |M| < ni$.
  $S = \bigoplus_{j=1}^{i-1} f(\mathsf{R}(X[j]), j + \beta - 1) \oplus f(\mathsf{pad}(X[i]), \beta)$
- Case $Z = (\mathsf{h}, 1)$: $|M| = n(\mu + 1)$.
  $S = \bigoplus_{j=1}^{\mu} f(\mathsf{R}(X[j]), j - 1) \oplus X[\mu + 1]$
- Case $Z = (\mathsf{h}, 2)$: $|M| = n\mu$.
  $S = \bigoplus_{j=1}^{\mu-1} f(\mathsf{R}(X[j]), j) \oplus X[\mu] \oplus U$
- Case $Z = (\mathsf{g}, 1, 0)$: $|M| = n$.
  $S = f(X[1] \oplus U, \alpha) = f(X[1], \alpha) \oplus f(U, \alpha)$
- Case $Z = (\mathsf{g}, 1, 1)$: $0 < |M| < n$.
  $S = f(\mathsf{pad}(X[1]) \oplus U, \beta) = f(\mathsf{pad}(X[1]), \beta) \oplus f(U, \beta)$
- Case $Z = (\mathsf{g}, i, 0)$: $|M| = ni$.
  $S = \bigoplus_{j=1}^{i-1} f(\mathsf{R}(X[j]), j + \alpha) \oplus f(X[i], \alpha)$
- Case $Z = (\mathsf{g}, i, 1)$: $n(i - 1) < |M| < ni$.
  $S = \bigoplus_{j=1}^{i-1} f(\mathsf{R}(X[j]), j + \beta) \oplus f(\mathsf{pad}(X[i]) \oplus U, \beta)$

Recall that we have set $\alpha = 1$, $\beta = 3$, $\gamma = 5$, and $\delta = 6$. Let $\mathbb{S} = \{S_i\}_{i=1,\ldots,q}$ and $\mathbb{X}_i = \{X_i[j]\}_{j=1,\ldots,m_i-1}$. We let $\mathbb{X} = \bigcup_{i=1,\ldots,q} \mathbb{X}_i$ be the set of all $X_i[j]$s. Since there are σ message blocks, we have $|\mathbb{X}| \le \sigma - q + 1$. For $\mathcal{R}$, we assume that, U, $X_i[j]$, $Y_i[j]$, and S_i are generated as dummy variables in the same manner to $\mathcal{F}$, using single URF R and a uniformly random source for U. This enables us to define $\mathbb{S}$ and $\mathbb{X}$ for $\mathcal{R}$. For instance, if $M_i = (M_i[1], M_i[2], M_i[3])$ with $Z_i = (\mathsf{f}, 3, 0)$, $X_i[1] = M_i[1]$, $X_i[2] = M_i[2]$, $Y_i[1] = \mathsf{R}(X_i[1])$, $Y_i[2] = \mathsf{R}(X_i[2])$, and $S_i = f(Y_i[1], 0) \oplus f(Y_i[2], \alpha) \oplus M_i[3]$ are defined for $\mathcal{F}$ and $\mathcal{R}$.

By convention, we assume U and all outputs of R are given to the adversary *after* all queries, including $\mathsf{R}(0^n)$ which is needed only for one-block query. This does not decrease the distinguishing advantage, hence we can extend transcript to include these URF outputs. Then, the transcript $\Theta_{\mathcal{F}}$ is written as the following sequence of I/O pairs of R.

$$((X_0[1], Y_0[1]), (X_1[1], Y_1[1]), (X_1[2], Y_1[2]), \ldots, (X_1[m_1 - 1], Y_1[m_1 - 1]),$$
$$\ldots, (X_q[1], Y_q[1]), (X_q[2], Y_q[2]), \ldots, (X_q[m_q - 1], Y_q[m_q - 1]), (S_1, T_1), \ldots, (S_q, T_q)),$$

where $X_0[1] = 0^n$ as described. For $\mathcal{R}$, the transcript $\Theta_{\mathcal{R}}$ is similarly defined due to the dummy calls of R to determine Y and S. Unlike $\mathcal{F}$, however, (S_i, T_i) is not an I/O pair of R.

We define the set of good transcripts GoodT as the set of transcripts such that $S_i \notin \mathbb{X}$ and $S_i \ne S_j$ for all $1 \le i < j \le q$. As defined, BadT = AllT \ GoodT is the set of bad transcripts.

Analysis of $\epsilon_{\mathsf{ratio}}$. Let θ be a good transcript, and let $u(\mathbb{X})$ denote the number of unique elements among $\mathbb{X}$ for this θ. Since $\mathbb{X} \wedge \mathbb{S} = \emptyset$ and all elements of $\mathbb{S}$ are distinct, we observe

$$\Pr[\Theta_{\mathcal{R}} = \theta] = \Pr[\Theta_{\mathcal{F}} = \theta] = \frac{1}{2^{n \cdot u(\mathbb{X})}} \cdot \frac{1}{2^{n \cdot q}}, \tag{18}$$

which implies

$$\epsilon_{\mathsf{ratio}} = 0. \tag{19}$$

Analysis of ϵ_{bad}. We need to evaluate the probabilities of $S_i = S_j$ for some $1 \leq i < j \leq q$ and $S_i = X$ for an element of $X \in \mathbb{X}$, and for $1 \leq i \leq q$, under the oracle $\mathcal{R}$. For a query (M, Z), let $\mathcal{I}(Z)$ be the list of the second arguments to f used inside R_Z. Figure 5 shows that

$$\mathcal{I}(Z) = \begin{cases} (0, 1, \ldots, \mu - 1) & \text{when } Z = (\mathsf{h}, 1) \\ (1, 2, \ldots, \mu - 1) & \text{when } Z = (\mathsf{h}, 2) \\ \gamma & \text{when } Z = (\mathsf{f}, 1, 0) \\ \delta & \text{when } Z = (\mathsf{f}, 1, 1) \\ (\alpha, 1 + \alpha, \ldots, (i - 2) + \alpha) & \text{when } Z = (\mathsf{f}, i, 0) \text{ for } 2 \leq i \leq \mu + 1 \\ (\beta, 1 + \beta, \ldots, (i - 2) + \beta) & \text{when } Z = (\mathsf{f}, i, 0) \text{ for } 2 \leq i \leq \mu + 1 \\ \emptyset & \text{when } Z = (\mathsf{g}, 1, 0) \\ \emptyset & \text{when } Z = (\mathsf{g}, 1, 1) \\ (1 + \alpha, 2 + \alpha, \ldots, (i - 1) + \alpha) & \text{when } Z = (\mathsf{g}, k, 0) \text{ for } 2 \leq k \leq \mu \\ (1 + \beta, 2 + \beta, \ldots, (i - 1) + \beta) & \text{when } Z = (\mathsf{g}, k, 0) \text{ for } 2 \leq k \leq \mu \end{cases} \tag{20}$$

From Definition 1 and the setting $(\alpha, \beta, \gamma, \delta) = (1, 3, 5, 6)$, the above shows that, when $Z \notin \mathcal{G}_1 \overset{\text{def}}{=} \{(\mathsf{g}, 1, 0), (\mathsf{g}, 1, 1)\}$, $\mathcal{I}(Z)$ is always non-empty, and $\mathcal{I}(Z) \neq \mathcal{I}(Z')$ holds for any $Z \neq Z'$, for any valid f.

We want to evaluate the probability of $S_i = S_j$ for two distinct queries, (M_i, Z_i) and (M_j, Z_j). First consider the case that $Z_i, Z_j \notin \mathcal{G}_1$. For $V \in \{0, 1\}^n$, let $\mathsf{Sum}(V)$ to denote $\bigoplus_{s \in \mathcal{I}} f(\mathsf{R}(V), s)$ for some non-empty $\mathcal{I} \subseteq \mathcal{I}_f$, and let $\mathsf{Others}(V)$ denote a function of $\{\mathsf{R}(X)\}_{Z \in \mathcal{X}}$ for some $\mathcal{X} \subseteq \{0, 1\}^n \setminus \{V\}$. Here, when $\mathcal{X} = \emptyset$, $\mathsf{Others}(V)$ is defined as 0^n. Note that $\mathsf{Sum}(V)$ is independent of $\mathsf{Others}(V)$ from the property of URF, thus we have

$$\Pr[\mathsf{Sum}(V) \oplus \mathsf{Others}(V) \oplus c = 0^n] \leq p_f \tag{21}$$

for any constant $c \in \{0, 1\}^n$ as f is p_f-ASSU. When $Z_i \neq Z_j$, we have $\mathcal{I}(Z_i) \neq \mathcal{I}(Z_j)$ from (20). Thus, there exists an element $V \in \{0^n\} \cup \mathbb{X}_i \cup \mathbb{X}_j$ such that $S_i \oplus S_j$ can be represented as $\mathsf{Sum}(V) \oplus \mathsf{Others}(V) \oplus c$ for some constant $c \in \{0, 1\}^n$. For example, if $Z_i = (\mathsf{f}, 3, 0)$ and $Z_j = (\mathsf{g}, 3, 0)$, we can set $V = X_i[1]$ since 0 is contained only in $\mathcal{I}(Z_i)$. If $Z_i = (\mathsf{f}, 3, 0)$ and $Z_j = (\mathsf{f}, 4, 0)$, we can set $V = X_i[2]$ since 1 is contained only in $\mathcal{I}(Z_j)$.

When $Z_i = Z_j$, we have $M_i \neq M_j$ and $m_i = m_j$. Let $m = m_i = m_j$. There are two possibilities such that (1) there exists $X_i[h] \neq X_j[h]$ for some $h < m$ or (2) $X_i[h] = X_j[h]$ for all $1 \leq h \leq m - 1$ and the difference is only in the last blocks, i.e. $X_i[m] \neq X_j[m]$. For the first case, $S_i \oplus S_j$ can be represented as $\texttt{Sum}(V) \oplus \texttt{Others}(V) \oplus c$ for $V = X_i[h]$ and $c = X_i[m-1] \oplus X_j[m-1]$. The second case makes $S_i \oplus S_j = X_i[m] \oplus X_j[m]$, which is non-zero with probability one. Therefore, $S_i \oplus S_j$ is always represented as $\texttt{Sum}(V) \oplus \texttt{Others}(V) \oplus c$ or is a non-zero constant, hence the probability of $S_i = S_j$ is bounded by p_f from (21). In a similar manner, the probability of $S_i = X_j[h]$ is bounded by p_f for any $1 \leq i, j \leq q$, $1 \leq h \leq m_j - 1$, and the probability of $S_i = 0^n$ is bounded by p_f for any $1 \leq i \leq q$.

The remaining case is that one of Z_i or Z_j is in $\mathcal{G}_1$, which can be analyzed in a similar manner as above. When $Z_i \in \mathcal{G}_1$ and $Z_j \notin \mathcal{G}_1$, then the fact that only S_i contains $f(U, \alpha)$ or $f(U, \beta)$ implies that $\Pr[S_i = S_j] \leq p_f$ from the property of f. Consider the case $Z_i, Z_j \in \mathcal{G}_1$, which needs further analysis. If $Z_i = Z_j = (\mathbf{g}, 1, 0)$, we have $M_i = X_i[1]$ and $M_j = X_j[1]$ (both single blocks), and $S_i \oplus S_j = f(X_i[1], \alpha) \oplus f(X_j[1], \alpha) = f(X_i[1] \oplus X_j[1], \alpha)$ which must be non-zero since $M_i \neq M_j$ and $f(*, \alpha)$ is a permutation. If $Z_i = Z_j = (\mathbf{g}, 1, 1)$, we have $\texttt{pad}(X_i[1]) \neq \texttt{pad}(X_j[1])$ (as both are partial) thus $S_i \oplus S_j = f(\texttt{pad}(X_i[1]), \beta) \oplus f(\texttt{pad}(X_j[1]), \beta) = f(\texttt{pad}(X_j[1]) \oplus \texttt{pad}(X_j[1]), \beta)$ is non-zero. If $Z_i = (\mathbf{g}, 1, 0)$ and $Z_j = (\mathbf{g}, 1, 1)$, $S_i \oplus S_j$ contains $f(U, \alpha) \oplus f(U, \beta)$, thus collision probability is at most p_f.

Thus, by counting the number of sub-events, we have

$$\Pr[\Theta_\mathcal{R} \in \texttt{BadT}] \leq \Pr_\mathcal{R}[\exists i, j : S_i = S_j, 1 \leq i < j \leq q]$$
$$+ \Pr_\mathcal{R}[\exists i, j, h : S_i = X_j[h], 1 \leq i, j \leq q, 1 \leq h \leq m_j - 1]$$
$$+ \Pr_\mathcal{R}[\exists i : S_i = 0^n, 1 \leq i \leq q] \tag{22}$$

$$\leq \binom{q}{2} p_f + (\sigma - q) \cdot q \cdot p_f + q \cdot p_f \leq q\sigma p_f, \tag{23}$$

which gives

$$\epsilon_{\text{bad}} \leq q\sigma p_f. \tag{24}$$

Combining (17) and (19) and (24), we conclude the proof.

5 Conclusions

We have described a parallelizable MAC mode of $2n$-bit state for arbitrarily long inputs, which, to the best of our knowledge, is the first proposal of this kind. It has a birthday-bound security as well as the previous MAC modes such as CMAC or PMAC, however it does not need an input block mask needed for them, which contributes to a reduced state size and computational overhead.

An interesting question is about the maximum parallelism (μ) achieved by our proposal: we adopted the bit rotation-based tweak function by Minematsu [28], which provides μ to be close to n if we use n-bit block cipher. However, we could not think of a tweak function that enables $\mu > n$ efficiently.

Acknowledgements. The author would like to thank Jean Paul Degabriele for shepherding and the anonymous reviewers for their insightful comments.

A   Proof of Lemma 3

In Fig. 7, we build the game to bound the probability of collision of $CBC[R_{h,1}, R_{h,2}]$. The game and the subsequent analysis are essentially the same as the proof of Lemma 4.2 of [20]. First we give some notations for the game, which are mostly taken from [20]. We implement $R_{h,1}$ and $R_{h,2}$ by lazy sampling, where they are expressed as lists. For $i = 1, 2$, we maintain the lists of input and output to $R_{h,i}$ determined in the game. In particular, $\text{Domain}(R_{h,i})$ denotes the list of inputs and $R_{h,i}(x)$ denotes the output corresponding to input x. Initially $\text{Domain}(R_{h,i})$ is set to empty, and $R_{h,i}(x)$ is undefined if $x \notin \text{Domain}(R_{h,i})$. We maintain the flags, bad_1 and bad_2, which are initialized to false. We also introduce two sets for chain blocks, BAD_1 and BAD_2, to determine whether the flags are set (to true) or not. We observe that the output collision of $CBC[R_{h,1}, R_{h,2}]$ only occurs when bad_1 is set at line 22, or bad_2 is set at line 44. Thus, (12) is at most the sum of $\Pr[\text{bad}_1 \leftarrow \text{true}]$ and $\Pr[\text{bad}_2 \leftarrow \text{true}]$.

Following [20], for the t-th process of line 13, let l_t denote the size of BAD_2 after line 21, assuming bad_1 is false for the first $t - 1$ process of line 13. The probability of $\text{bad}_1 \leftarrow \text{true}$ is bounded as follows. Let $V(t)$ denote the probability of $\text{bad}_1 \leftarrow \text{true}$ at the t-th choice of $Y_i[1]$ (at line 13) conditioned by the even that bad_1 is false before choosing $Y_i[1]$. Then

$$V(t) \leq \frac{(l_1 + \cdots + l_{t-1})l_t}{2^n}$$

holds since sampling at line 13 is uniform over n bits and BAD_1 has $(l_1 + \cdots + l_{t-1})$ points and BAD_2 has l_t points. Let s denote the total number of process line 13. Then we have

$$\Pr[\text{bad}_1 \leftarrow \text{true}] \leq \sum_{1 \leq t \leq s} V(t) = \sum_{1 \leq t \leq s} \frac{(l_1 + \cdots + l_{t-1})l_t}{2^n} \tag{25}$$

$$\leq \frac{1}{2^n} \cdot \frac{{l_0'}^2 - (l_1^2 + \cdots + l_s^2)}{2} \leq \frac{{l_0'}^2}{2^n} \tag{26}$$

where ${l_0'}^2 = l_1 + \cdots + l_s$.

The probability of $\text{bad}_2 \leftarrow \text{true}$ is similarly bounded. Let $l_{t'}'$ denote the size of BAD_2 after line 43, at the t'-th process of line 35, assuming bad_2 is false for the first $t' - 1$ process of line 35. Let s' denote the total number of process line 35 in the game. Here, $s' \leq \sigma$. Let $V'(t)$ denote the probability of $\text{bad}_2 \leftarrow \text{true}$ at

Initialization:

1. **for** $i \leftarrow 1$ **to** q **do** $X_i[1] \leftarrow C_i[1]$
2. **for all** x **do** $R_{h,1}(x) \leftarrow$ undefined
3. **for all** x **do** $R_{h,2}(x) \leftarrow$ undefined
4. $\mathsf{bad}_1, \mathsf{bad}_2 \leftarrow$ false
5. **for all** $i = 1$ **to** q **do** $\mathrm{BAD}_1 \leftarrow \{X_i[1]\}$

Computation of $X_1[2], \ldots, X_q[2]$**:**

11. **for** $i \leftarrow 1$ **to** q **do** $X_i[1] \leftarrow C_i[1]$
12.   **if** $X_i[1] \notin \mathrm{Domain}(R_{h,1})$ **then**
13. $Y_i[1] \xleftarrow{\$} \{0,1\}^n$
14. $R_{h,1}(X_i[1]) \leftarrow Y_i[1]$
15. $X_i[2] \leftarrow C_i[2] \oplus_{\shortparallel} Y_i[1]$
16. $\mathrm{BAD}_2 \leftarrow \{X_i[2]\}$
17. $\mathrm{Index} \leftarrow \{k \mid i+1 \le k \le q \text{ and } X_i[1] = X_k[1]\}$
18.   **for all** $k \in \mathrm{Index}$ **do**
19. $Y_k[1] \leftarrow Y_i[1]$
20. $X_k[2] \leftarrow C_k[2] \oplus_{\shortparallel} Y_k[1]$
21. $\mathrm{BAD}_2 \leftarrow \mathrm{BAD}_2 \cup \{X_k[2]\}$
22.   **if** $\mathrm{BAD}_2 \cap \mathrm{BAD}_1 \neq \emptyset$ **then** $\mathsf{bad}_1 \leftarrow$ true
23.   **else** $\mathrm{BAD}_1 \leftarrow \mathrm{BAD}_1 \cup \mathrm{BAD}_2$

Computation of $X_1[c_1], \ldots, X_q[c_q]$**:**

31. **for** $j \leftarrow 2$ **to** σ **do**
32.   **for** $i \leftarrow 1$ **to** q **do**
33.   **if** $j < c_i$ **then**
34.   **if** $X_i[j] \notin \mathrm{Domain}(R_{h,2})$ **then**
35. $Y_i[j] \xleftarrow{\$} \{0,1\}^n$
36. $R_{h,2}(Y_i[j]) \xleftarrow{\$} \{0,1\}^n$
37. $X_i[j+1] \leftarrow C_i[j+1] \oplus_{\shortparallel} Y_i[j]$
38. $\mathrm{BAD}_2 \leftarrow \{X_i[j+1]\}$
39. $\mathrm{Index} \leftarrow \{k \mid i+1 \le k \le q, j < c_k \text{ and } X_i[j] = X_k[j]\}$
40.   **for all** $k \in \mathrm{Index}$ **do**
41. $Y_k[j] \leftarrow Y_i[j]$
42. $X_k[j+1] \leftarrow C_k[j+1] \oplus_{\shortparallel} Y_k[j]$
43. $\mathrm{BAD}_2 \leftarrow \mathrm{BAD}_2 \cup \{X_k[j+1]\}$
44.   **if** $\mathrm{BAD}_2 \cap \mathrm{BAD}_1 \neq \emptyset$ **then** $\mathsf{bad}_2 \leftarrow$ true
45.   **else** $\mathrm{BAD}_1 \leftarrow \mathrm{BAD}_1 \cup \mathrm{BAD}_2$

Fig. 7. Game for collision analysis of $\mathrm{CBC}[R_{h,1}, R_{h,2}]$.

the t'-th choice of $Y_i[j]$ (at line 35) conditioned by the event that bad_2 is false before choosing $Y_i[j]$. Then we have

$$V'(t') \leq \frac{(l'_0 + l'_1 + \cdots + l'_{t'-1})l'_{t'}}{2^n},$$

and

$$\Pr[\mathsf{bad}_2 \leftarrow \mathsf{true}] \leq \sum_{1 \leq t' \leq s'} V'(t') \leq \sum_{1 \leq t' \leq s'} \frac{(l'_0 + l'_1 + \cdots + l'_{t'-1})l'_{t'}}{2^n} \leq \frac{\sigma^2 - l'_0{}^2}{2^n} \tag{27}$$

as we have $\sigma \geq l'_0 + l'_1 + \cdots + l'_{t'-1}$, $s' \leq \sigma$ which is at most $2^n/2$ by assumption. From (26) and (27), the proof is concluded as

$$\Pr[\mathsf{bad}_1 \leftarrow \mathsf{true}] + \Pr[\mathsf{bad}_2 \leftarrow \mathsf{true}] \leq \frac{\sigma^2}{2^n}. \tag{28}$$

References

1. CAESAR: Competition for Authenticated Encryption: Security, Applicability, and Robustness. http://competitions.cr.yp.to/caesar.html
2. Recommendation for Block Cipher Modes of Operation: the CMAC Mode for Authentication. NIST Special Publication 800-38B. National Institute of Standards and Technology (2005)
3. Beierle, C., et al.: The SKINNY family of block ciphers and its low-latency variant MANTIS. In: Robshaw, M., Katz, J. (eds.) CRYPTO 2016. LNCS, vol. 9815, pp. 123–153. Springer, Heidelberg (2016). https://doi.org/10.1007/978-3-662-53008-5_5
4. Bellare, M., Desai, A., Jokipii, E., Rogaway, P.: A concrete security treatment of symmetric encryption. In: 38th FOCS, pp. 394–403. IEEE Computer Society Press, October 1997. https://doi.org/10.1109/SFCS.1997.646128
5. Bellare, M., Guérin, R., Rogaway, P.: XOR MACs: new methods for message authentication using finite pseudorandom functions. In: Coppersmith, D. (ed.) CRYPTO 1995. LNCS, vol. 963, pp. 15–28. Springer, Heidelberg (1995). https://doi.org/10.1007/3-540-44750-4_2
6. Bernstein, D.J.: How to stretch random functions: the security of protected counter sums. J. Cryptol. 12(3), 185–192 (1999). https://doi.org/10.1007/s001459900051
7. Bertoni, G., Daemen, J., Hoffert, S., Peeters, M., Assche, G.V., Keer, R.V.: Farfalle: parallel permutation-based cryptography. IACR Trans. Symm. Cryptol. 2017(4), 1–38 (2017). https://doi.org/10.13154/tosc.v2017.i4.1-38
8. Biham, E.: A fast new DES implementation in software. In: Biham, E. (ed.) FSE 1997. LNCS, vol. 1267, pp. 260–272. Springer, Heidelberg (1997). https://doi.org/10.1007/BFb0052352
9. Black, J., Rogaway, P.: CBC MACs for arbitrary-length messages: the three-key constructions. In: Bellare, M. (ed.) CRYPTO 2000. LNCS, vol. 1880, pp. 197–215. Springer, Heidelberg (2000). https://doi.org/10.1007/3-540-44598-6_12
10. Black, J., Rogaway, P.: A block-cipher mode of operation for parallelizable message authentication. In: Knudsen, L.R. (ed.) EUROCRYPT 2002. LNCS, vol. 2332, pp. 384–397. Springer, Heidelberg (2002). https://doi.org/10.1007/3-540-46035-7_25

11. Bosselaers, A., Preneel, B. (eds.): Integrity Primitives for Secure Information Systems. LNCS, vol. 1007. Springer, Heidelberg (1995). https://doi.org/10.1007/3-540-60640-8
12. Chakraborti, A., Iwata, T., Minematsu, K., Nandi, M.: Blockcipher-based authenticated encryption: how small can we go? In: Fischer, W., Homma, N. (eds.) CHES 2017. LNCS, vol. 10529, pp. 277–298. Springer, Cham (2017). https://doi.org/10.1007/978-3-319-66787-4_14
13. Chakraborty, D., Sarkar, P.: A general construction of tweakable block ciphers and different modes of operations. IEEE Trans. Inf. Theory **54**(5), 1991–2006 (2008)
14. Chen, S., Steinberger, J.: Tight security bounds for key-alternating ciphers. In: Nguyen, P.Q., Oswald, E. (eds.) EUROCRYPT 2014. LNCS, vol. 8441, pp. 327–350. Springer, Heidelberg (2014). https://doi.org/10.1007/978-3-642-55220-5_19
15. Cogliati, B., Lampe, R., Seurin, Y.: Tweaking even-mansour ciphers. In: Gennaro, R., Robshaw, M. (eds.) CRYPTO 2015. LNCS, vol. 9215, pp. 189–208. Springer, Heidelberg (2015). https://doi.org/10.1007/978-3-662-47989-6_9
16. Daykin, D.E.: On the rank of the matrix f(A) and the enumeration of certain matrices over a finite field. J. Lond. Math. Soc. **s1–35**(1), 36–42 (1960)
17. Fischlin, M., Lehmann, A.: Delayed-key message authentication for streams. In: Micciancio, D. (ed.) TCC 2010. LNCS, vol. 5978, pp. 290–307. Springer, Heidelberg (2010). https://doi.org/10.1007/978-3-642-11799-2_18
18. Gazi, P., Pietrzak, K., Rybár, M.: The exact security of PMAC. IACR Trans. Symm. Cryptol. **2016**(2), 145–161 (2016). https://doi.org/10.13154/tosc.v2016.i2.145-161. http://tosc.iacr.org/index.php/ToSC/article/view/569
19. Granger, R., Jovanovic, P., Mennink, B., Neves, S.: Improved masking for tweakable blockciphers with applications to authenticated encryption. In: Fischlin, M., Coron, J.-S. (eds.) EUROCRYPT 2016. LNCS, vol. 9665, pp. 263–293. Springer, Heidelberg (2016). https://doi.org/10.1007/978-3-662-49890-3_11
20. Iwata, T., Kurosawa, K.: OMAC: one-key CBC MAC. In: Johansson, T. (ed.) FSE 2003. LNCS, vol. 2887, pp. 129–153. Springer, Heidelberg (2003). https://doi.org/10.1007/978-3-540-39887-5_11
21. Iwata, T., Minematsu, K., Guo, J., Morioka, S.: CLOC: authenticated encryption for short input. In: Cid, C., Rechberger, C. (eds.) FSE 2014. LNCS, vol. 8540, pp. 149–167. Springer, Heidelberg (2015). https://doi.org/10.1007/978-3-662-46706-0_8
22. Käsper, E., Schwabe, P.: Faster and timing-attack resistant AES-GCM. In: Clavier, C., Gaj, K. (eds.) CHES 2009. LNCS, vol. 5747, pp. 1–17. Springer, Heidelberg (2009). https://doi.org/10.1007/978-3-642-04138-9_1
23. Krovetz, T., Rogaway, P.: The software performance of authenticated-encryption modes. In: Joux, A. (ed.) FSE 2011. LNCS, vol. 6733, pp. 306–327. Springer, Heidelberg (2011). https://doi.org/10.1007/978-3-642-21702-9_18
24. Luykx, A., Preneel, B., Szepieniec, A., Yasuda, K.: On the influence of message length in PMAC's security bounds. In: Fischlin, M., Coron, J.-S. (eds.) EUROCRYPT 2016. LNCS, vol. 9665, pp. 596–621. Springer, Heidelberg (2016). https://doi.org/10.1007/978-3-662-49890-3_23
25. Luykx, A., Preneel, B., Tischhauser, E., Yasuda, K.: A MAC mode for lightweight block ciphers. In: Peyrin, T. (ed.) FSE 2016. LNCS, vol. 9783, pp. 43–59. Springer, Heidelberg (2016). https://doi.org/10.1007/978-3-662-52993-5_3
26. Matsuda, S., Moriai, S.: Lightweight cryptography for the cloud: exploit the power of bitslice implementation. In: Prouff, E., Schaumont, P. (eds.) CHES 2012. LNCS, vol. 7428, pp. 408–425. Springer, Heidelberg (2012). https://doi.org/10.1007/978-3-642-33027-8_24

27. Mennink, B.: XPX: generalized tweakable even-mansour with improved security guarantees. In: Robshaw, M., Katz, J. (eds.) CRYPTO 2016. LNCS, vol. 9814, pp. 64–94. Springer, Heidelberg (2016). https://doi.org/10.1007/978-3-662-53018-4_3

28. Minematsu, K.: A short universal hash function from bit rotation, and applications to blockcipher modes. In: Susilo, W., Reyhanitabar, R. (eds.) ProvSec 2013. LNCS, vol. 8209, pp. 221–238. Springer, Heidelberg (2013). https://doi.org/10.1007/978-3-642-41227-1_13

29. Minematsu, K., Matsushima, T.: New bounds for PMAC, TMAC, and XCBC. In: Biryukov, A. (ed.) FSE 2007. LNCS, vol. 4593, pp. 434–451. Springer, Heidelberg (2007). https://doi.org/10.1007/978-3-540-74619-5_27

30. Mouha, N., Mennink, B., Van Herrewege, A., Watanabe, D., Preneel, B., Verbauwhede, I.: Chaskey: an efficient MAC algorithm for 32-bit microcontrollers. In: Joux, A., Youssef, A. (eds.) SAC 2014. LNCS, vol. 8781, pp. 306–323. Springer, Cham (2014). https://doi.org/10.1007/978-3-319-13051-4_19

31. Naito, Y., Matsui, M., Sugawara, T., Suzuki, D.: SAEB: a lightweight blockcipher-based AEAD mode of operation. IACR TCHES 2018(2), 192–217 (2018). https://doi.org/10.13154/tches.v2018.i2.192-217. https://tches.iacr.org/index.php/TCHES/article/view/885

32. Nandi, M.: Fast and secure CBC-type MAC algorithms. In: Dunkelman, O. (ed.) FSE 2009. LNCS, vol. 5665, pp. 375–393. Springer, Heidelberg (2009). https://doi.org/10.1007/978-3-642-03317-9_23

33. Nandi, M.: A unified method for improving PRF bounds for a class of blockcipher based MACs. In: Hong, S., Iwata, T. (eds.) FSE 2010. LNCS, vol. 6147, pp. 212–229. Springer, Heidelberg (2010). https://doi.org/10.1007/978-3-642-13858-4_12

34. Patarin, J.: New results on pseudorandom permutation generators based on the des scheme. In: Feigenbaum, J. (ed.) CRYPTO 1991. LNCS, vol. 576, pp. 301–312. Springer, Heidelberg (1992). https://doi.org/10.1007/3-540-46766-1_25

35. Patarin, J.: The "coefficients H" technique. In: Avanzi, R.M., Keliher, L., Sica, F. (eds.) SAC 2008. LNCS, vol. 5381, pp. 328–345. Springer, Heidelberg (2009). https://doi.org/10.1007/978-3-642-04159-4_21

36. Rogaway, P.: Efficient instantiations of tweakable blockciphers and refinements to modes OCB and PMAC. In: Lee, P.J. (ed.) ASIACRYPT 2004. LNCS, vol. 3329, pp. 16–31. Springer, Heidelberg (2004). https://doi.org/10.1007/978-3-540-30539-2_2

37. Rogaway, P.: Efficient instantiations of tweakable blockciphers and refinements to modes OCB and PMAC. Full version of [36] (2004). http://www.cs.ucdavis.edu/~rogaway/papers/

38. Rogaway, P., Shrimpton, T.: A provable-security treatment of the key-wrap problem. In: Vaudenay, S. (ed.) EUROCRYPT 2006. LNCS, vol. 4004, pp. 373–390. Springer, Heidelberg (2006). https://doi.org/10.1007/11761679_23

39. Zhang, L., Wu, W., Zhang, L., Wang, P.: CBCR: CBC MAC with rotating transformations. Sci. China Inf. Sci. 54(11), 2247–2255 (2011)

Post-quantum Analysis

An Improved Security Analysis on an Indeterminate Equation Public Key Cryptosystem by Evaluation Attacks

Akifumi Muroi[1], Shinya Okumura[1(✉)], and Atsuko Miyaji[1,2]

[1] Graduate School of Engineering, Osaka University, Suita, Japan
muroi@cy2sec.comm.eng.osaka-u.ac.jp,
{okumura,miyaji}@comm.eng.osaka-u.ac.jp
[2] Japan Advanced Institute of Science and Technology, Nomi, Japan

Abstract. Akiyama, Goto, Okumura, Takagi, Nuida and Hanaoka introduced an indeterminate equation analogue of learning with errors (IE-LWE) problem as a new computationally hard problem and constructed a candidate of post-quantum cryptosystem, called "Giophantus". Giophantus satisfies the indistinguishability under chosen plaintext attack (IND-CPA) if IE-LWE problem is computationally infeasible. Akiyama et al., Shimizu and Ikematsu proposed improved Giophantus to the post-quantum standardization project. Beullens, Castryck and Vercauteren proposed an evaluation at one attack against IND-CPA security of Giophantus. However, Akiyama et al. assert that recommended parameters can resist Vercauteren et al.'s attack. Therefore, the security analysis on Giophantus is still needed.

In this paper, we propose a new kind of evaluation attack against IND-CPA security of Giophantus. Our attack solves IE-LWE problem by combining a part of Vercauteren et al.'s attack with a lattice attack on low rank lattices, e.g., 6-rank lattices for recommended parameters. Moreover, we investigate a way to avoid our attack and some variants of our attack. We give some remarks on modification of the IE-LWE problem. Our experimental analysis shows that our attack can solve IE-LWE problem efficiently, and that Giophantus does not satisfy IND-CPA security unless IE-LWE problem is modified appropriately.

Keywords: IE-LWE problem · Evaluation at one attack · Closest vector problem

1 Introduction

Post-quantum cryptography now becomes a central role in cryptography as can be seen from the post-quantum cryptography standardization project (PQC project) by the National Institute of Standards and Technology (NIST) [15]. Some computationally hard problems arising from lattice theory, coding theory and algebraic geometry (solving multivariate polynomial systems) have successfully provided various candidates of post-quantum cryptographic protocols

© Springer Nature Switzerland AG 2020
K. G. Paterson and D. Stebila (Eds.): SAC 2019, LNCS 11959, pp. 421–436, 2020.
https://doi.org/10.1007/978-3-030-38471-5_17

[7,11,14,18]. However, the development of attacks on known computationally hard problems make difficult constructing efficient and practical post-quantum cryptographic protocols. Therefore, finding new computationally hard problems, which are also hard even by using sufficiently large scale quantum computers, is an important task in post-quantum cryptography.

At SAC 2017, Akiyama, Goto, Okumura, Takagi, Nuida and Hanaoka [1] introduced the smallest solution problem and an indeterminate equation analogue of learning with errors (IE-LWE) problem as new computationally hard problems. The smallest solution problem is that given a polynomial $F \in R_p[x, y]$, where $R_p := \mathbb{F}_p[t]/(t^n - 1)$ for a prime p, find a solution $(x, y) = (u_x, u_y) \in R_p^2$ with small coefficients to $F = 0$. IE-LWE problem is roughly described as follows: Given a pair (X, Y) of polynomials in $R_p[x, y]$, distinguish whether (X, Y) is chosen from a 'noisy' set in $R_p[x, y] \times R_p[x, y]$ or not. For more detail, see Sects. 2.2 and 3.1. The smallest solution problem and the IE-LWE problem are expected to be computationally infeasible even by large scale quantum computers because these problems are reduced to the (approximate) closest vector problem (CVP) on lattices with large rank, which is usually used as a computational hard problem to construct candidates of post-quantum cryptographic protocols.

Akiyama et al. constructed a candidate of post-quantum cryptosystem, which was named "Giophantus^{TM}" later, based on the small solution problem [1]. (We refer to Akiyama et al.'s cryptosystem as "Giophantus" for short.) Giohantus is not only a candidate of post-quantum cryptosystem but also a multi-bit somewhat homomorphic encryption scheme (cf. [3, Section 11.1]). The smallest solution problem is (almost) equivalent to the recovering secret key problem of Giophantus, and Akiyama et al. proved that Giophantus satisfies the indistinguishability under chosen plaintext attack (IND-CPA) under the assumption that IE-LWE problem is computationally infeasible (cf. [1, Theorem 1]). Akiyama et al. described a key recovery attack and a linear algebra attack, which are based on lattice attacks, and experimentally analyzed their difficulty. Akiyama et al. set recommended parameters according to their experimental analysis and concluded that sizes of public/secret keys of Giophantus are relatively small among well-known candidates of post-quantum cryptosystems, e.g., LWE base [13] and NTRU base [16] cryptosystems (cf. [1, Table 4]). The two properties are important in post-quantum cryptography.

However, at PQCrypto 2018, Xagawa [17] proposed some attacks on Giophantus and firstly succeeded in recovering (partial/full) messages and secret keys of Giophantus for recommended parameters by lattice attacks. Xagawa's attacks decrease ranks of lattices occurring in lattice attacks by applying Gentry's technique for attacking NTRU [10] to recover partial messages and partial secret keys of Giophantus. Xagawa also applied subring technique, which also decreases ranks of lattices by substituting 0 for a variable x (or y) of multivariate polynomials occurring in Giophantus, and succeeded in recovering messages in the case of $\deg(X) = 2$. In order to avoid Xagawa's attacks, a parameter n (degree of modulus polynomial $t^n - 1$) must be increased and should be a prime number, and thus Akiyama et al. modified recommended parameters of Giophantus by executing many experiments and by using "2016 Estimate" [4].

After modifying parameters and security analysis, Akiyama et al., Shimizu and Ikematsu submitted Giophantus [2] to NIST's PQC project. Akiyama et al.'s experiments show that Giophantus with modified parameters is expected to resist Xagawa's attacks. However, Vercauteren, Beullens and Castryck [5] submitted a distinguishing attack for breaking IND-CPA security of Giophantus to official comments of NIST's PQC project. Their attack is based on the fact that a map $\varphi : \mathbb{F}_p[t]/(t^n - 1) \longrightarrow \mathbb{F}_p$ by $f(t) \pmod{t^n - 1} \mapsto f(1) \pmod{p}$ is a ring homomorphism, which is similar to an attack on the Poly-LWE problem [8]. Vercauteren et al.'s attack tries to recover partial messages by substituting 1 for a variable t of ciphertext and by searching small secret elements in small range (see Sect. 3.3 for more detail). We refer to a kind of this attack as an evaluation attack.

Akiyama et al. [3, Section 7.3] analyzed Vercauteren et al.'s attack by many experiments and concluded that recommended parameters of Giophantus can resist Vercauteren et al.'s attack. However, Vercauteren et al.'s attack suggests that there would exist evaluation (at one or at other special values) attacks which can break IND-CPA security of Giophantus. We investigate such evaluation attacks.

1.1 Our Contribution

Our contribution in this paper is summarized as follows:

1. **Breaking IND-CPA Security of Giophantus**
   We propose a new and practical evaluation at one attack on IND-CPA security of Giophantus. Our attack reduces the IE-LWE problem to the closest vector problem (CVP) on low rank lattices, e.g., 6-rank lattices for recommended parameters, by substituting 1 for a variable occurring in the IE-LWE problem, which is similar to the first step of Vercauteren et al.'s attack and an attack on Poly-LWE problem [8]. We note that the dimension of lattices occurring in our attack is also low, e.g., 9-dimensional lattices (with 6-rank) for recommended parameters. We can use exact CVP algorithm which can solve CVP exactly for such lattices. This is an advantage of our attack. Another advantage of our attack is that our attack does not require to search small secret elements, and thus our attack is efficient. We conducted many experiments on our attack by using exact CVP algorithm in computational algebra system Magma [6] and conclude that our attack is efficient (within 4 s in average) and can break IND-CPA security with high probability (about 99%). Our implementation of our attack is available at https://github.com/Shinya-Okumura/S.O..git.

2. **Modification of Giophantus**
   We investigate a way to modify Giophantus to avoid our attack. The IE-LWE problem is characterized by two modulus parameters (a prime number p and a univariate polynomial $t^n - 1$) and by multivariate polynomials. An easy way to avoid our attack is to change the modulus polynomial from $t^n - 1$ to

other polynomials $f \in \mathbb{F}_p[t]$ satisfying $f(1) \not\equiv 0$ (mod. p). We, however, show that if the modulus polynomial f satisfies $f(\alpha) = 0$ for a small order $\alpha \in \mathbb{F}_{p^d}$ with any d, i.e., $\alpha^k = 1$ for a small $k \ll n$, then the difficulty of the IE-LWE problem w.r.t. f is decreased as in the Poly-LWE problem [9,12]. We note that the extension degree d should be small, e.g., $1 \le d \le 3$, in the case of attacking the Poly-LWE problem, but the condition on d is not required in the case of attacking the (modified) IE-LWE problem (see Sect. 6). This means that the condition $f(1) \not\equiv 0$ (mod. p) is not enough to construct IND-CPA secure Giophantus. As a result, we recommend to use polynomials f with small coefficients, which has roots of large order, e.g., the q-th cyclotomic polynomial with prime power integers q.

1.2 Remark

We remark that Giophantus could not move on to the second round of NIST's PQC project [15], which is mainly due to Vercauteren et al.'s attack. As we mentioned above, the effectiveness of Vercauteren et al.'s attack is still unclear (there is no verification that Akiyama et al.'s analysis is enough). To our best knowledge, our attack is the first attack that determines the correctness of NIST's PQC project members. However, we believe that the study of the IE-LWE problem (and its variants) is still important and interesting for post-quantum cryptography.

1.3 Organization

This paper is organized as follows: Sect. 2 gives some notation used in this paper. Section 3 describes Giophantus, the IE-LWE problem and some possible attacks on Giophantus. Section 4 describes our evaluation attack. Section 5 gives our experimental results on our attack. Section 6 discusses the modification of the IE-LWE problem and variants of our attack. Section 7 concludes our work.

2   Preliminary

We define some notation used in this paper. Let p be a prime number and $\mathbb{Z}$ the (rational) integer ring. Suppose that any element in $\mathbb{F}_p := \mathbb{Z}/p\mathbb{Z}$ is represented by integers in $\{0, \ldots, p-1\}$. Set $R_p = \mathbb{F}_p[t]/(t^n - 1)$. For an integer $\ell \ll p$, let R_ℓ be the subset of R_p consisting of all polynomials with coefficients represented by integers in $\{0, \ldots, \ell - 1\}$. For a commutative ring R, we write a two-variable polynomial $A(x, y)$ over R as

$$A(x, y) = \sum_{(i,j) \in \Gamma_A} a_{ij} x^i y^j (a_{ij} \in R),$$

where Γ_A is a finite subset of $\mathbb{Z}_{\ge 0}^2$.

2.1   IE-LWE Problem

We explain the IE-LWE problem in this section. For finite sets Γ_r, $\Gamma_{Xr} \subset \mathbb{Z}_{\geq 0}$, we define

$$\mathfrak{F}_{\Gamma_r/R_p} := \left\{ \sum_{(i,j) \in \Gamma_r} a_{ij} x^i y^j \,\middle|\, a_{ij} \in R_p \right\},$$

$$\mathfrak{F}_{\Gamma_{X_r}/R_\ell} := \left\{ \sum_{(i,j) \in \Gamma_{X_r}} a_{ij} x^i y^j \,\middle|\, a_{ij} \in R_\ell \right\},$$

$$\mathfrak{X}(\Gamma_X, \ell)/R_p := \{ X \in \mathfrak{F}_{\Gamma_X}/R_p \mid \exists u_x, u_y \in R_\ell, \ X(u_x, u_y) = 0 \}.$$

We assume

$$(0,0) \in \Gamma_X, (0,0) \in \Gamma_r.$$

For given polynomial sets $\mathfrak{X}(\Gamma_X, \ell)/R_p$, $\mathfrak{F}_{\Gamma_r}/R_p$ and $\mathfrak{F}_{\Gamma_{X_r}}/R_\ell$, we define the IE-LWE problem as follows:

Definition 1 (IE-LWE Problem). *Write U_X and T_X as follows:*

$$U_X = \mathfrak{X}(\Gamma_X, \ell)/R_p \times \mathfrak{F}_{\Gamma_{X_r}}/R_p,$$
$$T_X = \{(X, Xr + e) | X \in \mathfrak{X}(\Gamma_X, \ell)/R_p, r \in \mathfrak{F}_{\Gamma_r}/R_p, \ e \in \mathfrak{F}_{\Gamma_{X_r}}/R_\ell\}.$$

The IE-LWE problem is a problem that for a given pair of polynomials $(X, Y) \in U_X$, determine whether (X, Y) is in T_X or not.

For a set A, the notation $a \overset{U}{\leftarrow}$ means that an element a is sampled from A according to the uniform distribution on A.

Definition 2 (IE-LWE Assumption). *Let p, ℓ, n, $\mathfrak{X}(\Gamma_X, \ell)/R_p$, $\mathfrak{F}_{\Gamma_r}/R_p$ and $\mathfrak{F}_{\Gamma_{X_r}}/R_\ell$ be as above. The IE-LWE assumption is the assumption that for a security parameter k and any probabilistic polynomial-time algorithm $\mathfrak{A}$ for the IE-LWE problem, the advantage of $\mathfrak{A}$ defined as*

$$Adv_{\mathfrak{A}}^{IE\text{-}LWE}(k) :=$$

$$\left| Pr\left[\mathfrak{A}(p, \ell, n, \Gamma_r, \Gamma_X, X, Y) \to 1 \,\middle|\, \begin{array}{l} (p, \ell, n, \Gamma_X, \Gamma_r, X) \leftarrow Gen(1^k); \\ r \overset{U}{\leftarrow} \mathfrak{F}_{\Gamma_r}/R_p; e \overset{U}{\leftarrow} \mathfrak{F}_{\Gamma_{X_r}}/R_\ell; \\ Y := Xr + e \end{array} \right] \right.$$

$$\left. -Pr\left[\mathfrak{A}(p, \ell, n, \Gamma_r, \Gamma_X, X, Y) \to 1 \,\middle|\, \begin{array}{l} (p, \ell, n, \Gamma_X, \Gamma_r, X) \leftarrow Gen(1^k); \\ Y \overset{U}{\leftarrow} \mathfrak{F}_{\Gamma_{X_r}}/R_p \end{array} \right] \right|$$

is negligible, where $Gen(1^k)$ is a function that outputs parameters p, ℓ, n, Γ_X, Γ_r and $X \in \mathfrak{X}(\Gamma_X, \ell)/R_p$ for input k.

2.2 Smallest-Solution Problem

For a given $X \in \mathfrak{X}(\Gamma_X, \ell)/R_p$, let us express a solution $u = (u_x, u_y) \in R_\ell^2$ of an indeterminate equation $X = 0$ as

$$u_x = \sum_{i=0}^{n-1} \overline{\alpha}_i t^i, \ u_y = \sum_{i=0}^{n-1} \overline{\beta}_i t^i \ (\overline{\alpha}_i, \overline{\beta} \in R_\ell).$$

Let α_i and β_i be integers representing $\overline{\alpha}_i$ and $\overline{\beta}_i$, respectively, for $0 \leq i \leq n - 1$. Then, we define the norm of the solution $u := (u_x, u_y)$ as follows:

$$\mathrm{Norm}(u) = \max\{\alpha_i, \beta_i \in \{0, ..., \ell - 1\} \mid 0 \leq i \leq n - 1\}.$$

The smallest solution problem is defined as follows:

Definition 3 (Smallest Solution Problem). *Let $X \in R_p[x, y]$ be as above. If $X(x, y) = 0$ is an indeterminate equation over the ring R_p, then a problem of finding a solution $(x, y) = (u_x, u_y)$ to $X = 0$ over R_p with the smallest norm is called a smallest solution problem on X.*

The IE-LWE problem is not more difficult than the smallest solution problem. In fact, let $(X, Y) \in \mathfrak{X}(\Gamma_X, \ell)/R_p \times \mathfrak{F}_{\Gamma_{X_r}}/R_p$ be a sample, which we want to distinguish, and $(u_x, u_y) \in R_\ell$ a solution to the smallest solution problem on X. If (X, Y) is an IE-LWE instance, i.e., $(X, Y) \in T_X$, and the Eq. (1) below is true, then all coefficients of

$$\ell \cdot Y(u_x, u_y) = \ell \cdot e(u_x, u_y)$$

are less than p and multiples of ℓ (note that we regard all coefficients of $\ell \cdot Y(u_x, u_y)$ as integers, and that any integer $> p$ is reduced by modulo p). If Y is sampled from $\mathfrak{F}_{\Gamma_{X_r}}/R_p$ uniformly at random, then the probability that all coefficients of $\ell \cdot Y(u_x, u_y)$ are less than p and multiples of ℓ (as integers) is about $1 - 1/\ell^n$ which is non-negligible. Therefore, if the smallest solution problem can be solved, then we can solve the IE-LWE problem by checking whether all coefficients of $\ell \cdot Y(u_x, u_y)$ are less than p and multiples of ℓ or not.

3 Description of Giophantus and Known Attacks

In this section, we briefly review Akiyama et al.'s encryption scheme "Giophantus" [1–3] and some possible attacks on Giophantus.

3.1 Giophantus and IE-LWE Problem

Here we describe Giophantus, which is IND-CPA secure under the IE-LWE assumption, proposed by Akiyama et al. at SAC 2017. Let p and ℓ be a prime number and a positive integer, respectively, that satisfy $\ell \ll p$ (as in Sect. 2). Furthermore, for $X, r \in R_p[x, y]$, w_X and w_r denote the total degrees of X and

r, respectively. In order to decrypt any ciphertext correctly, it is necessary to satisfy the following relation for p and ℓ:

$$p > \#\Gamma_{X_r} \cdot \ell(\ell-1) \cdot (n(\ell-1))^{w_X + w_r}. \tag{1}$$

Next, we describe procedures of key generation, encryption and decryption processes.

- Key Generation
  Choose u_x, $u_y \in R_\ell$ uniformly at random with $\deg(u_x) = \deg(u_y) = n-1$ and generate $X(x,y) \in R_p[x,y]$ satisfying $X(u_x, u_y) = 0$ as follows:
  1. Choose a finite set $\Gamma_X \subset (\mathbb{Z}_{\geq 0})^2$ with $(0,0) \in \Gamma_X$.
  2. For each $(i,j) \in \Gamma_X \setminus \{(0,0)\}$, choose $a_{ij} \in R_p$ uniformly at random.
  3. Put $a_{00} = -\sum_{(i,j) \in \Gamma_X \setminus \{(0,0)\}} a_{ij} u_x^i u_y^j$.
  4. Put $X(x,y) = \sum_{(i,j) \in \Gamma_X} a_{ij} x^i y^j$.
  The $X(x,y)$ is a public key, and (u_x, u_y) is a secret key of Giophantus, respectively.
- Encryption
  1. Embed a plaintext M in the coefficients of the plaintext polynomial $m \in R_\ell$.
  2. Choose a polynomial $r(x,y) \in \mathfrak{F}_{\Gamma_r}/R_p$ uniformly at random.
  3. Choose a polynomial $e(x,y) \in \mathfrak{F}_{X_r}/R_\ell$ uniformly at random.
  4. We set a cipher polynomial $c(x,y)$ as follows:

  $$c(x,y) = m + X(x,y)r(x,y) + \ell \cdot e(x,y).$$

- Decryption
  1. Substitute the smallest solution (u_x, u_y) into $c(x,y)$ and obtain

  $$c(u_x, u_y) = m + \ell \cdot e(u_x, u_y).$$

  2. If p and ℓ satisfy the condition of (1), then all coefficients of $m + \ell \cdot e(u_x, u_y) \in \mathbb{Z}[t]/(t^n - 1)$ are in the range $\{0, \ldots, p-1\}$. Compute $m' = c(u_x, u_y) \pmod{\ell}$ (note that we regard the coefficients of $c(u_x, u_y)$ as integers). If p and ℓ satisfy the condition of (1), then all coefficients of $c(u_x, u_y) = m + \ell e(u_x, u_y)$ are smaller than p. Thus we have $m = m'$.
  3. Recover the plaintext M from the coefficients of m.

Akiyama et al. proved that Giophantus is IND-CPA secure if the IE-LWE problem is computationally infeasible. More precisely, the following theorem holds true [3, Theorem 2].

Theorem 1. *We denote by Σ the Giophantus encryption scheme. For a security parameter k, let $\mathrm{Adv}_{\mathfrak{A}}^{\mathrm{IE\text{-}LWE}}(k)$ be as in Definition 2. Similarly, we denote by $\mathrm{Adv}_{\mathfrak{B},\Sigma}^{\mathrm{IND\text{-}CPA}}(k)$ the advantage of the probabilistic polynomial time algorithm $\mathfrak{B}$ for breaking IND-CPA security of Giophantus. Then we have*

$$\mathrm{Adv}_{\mathfrak{B},\Sigma}^{\mathrm{IND\text{-}CPA}}(k) = 2\mathrm{Adv}_{\mathfrak{A}}^{\mathrm{IE\text{-}LWE}}(k).$$

Akiyama et al., Xagawa and Vercauteren et al. proposed some possible attacks on Giophantus. In Sects. 3.2 and 3.3, we briefly review Akiyama et al.'s linear algebra attack and Vercauteren et al.'s evaluation attack because these two attacks are closely related to our new attack.

3.2   Linear Algebra Attack

For a given polynomial pair (X, Y), we can determinate that (X, Y) is sampled from T_X if we find $r \in \mathfrak{F}_{\Gamma_r}/R_p$ and $e \in \mathfrak{F}_{\Gamma_{X_r}}/R_\ell$ such that $Y = Xr + e$. The problem of finding such polynomials r and e can be solved by comparing the coefficients of $x^i y^j$. To make a linear equation, put $X = \sum_{(i,j) \in \Gamma_X} a_{ij} x^i y^j$, $r = \sum_{(i,j) \in \Gamma_r} r_{ij} x^i y^j$, $e = \sum_{(i,j) \in \Gamma_e} e_{ij} x^i y^j$ and $Y = \sum_{(i,j) \in \Gamma_Y} d_{ij} x^i y^j$, where r_{ij} and e_{ij} are variables. We have

$$\sum_{(i,j) \in \Gamma_{X_r}} d_{ij} x^i y^j = \left(\sum_{(i,j) \in \Gamma_X} a_{ij} x^i y^j \right) \left(\sum_{(i,j) \in \Gamma_r} r_{ij} x^i y^j \right) + \left(\sum_{(i,j) \in \Gamma_{X_r}} e_{ij} x^i y^j \right).$$

Consider the case of $\deg X = \deg r = 1$. Write the polynomials X, r, e and Y as

$$X(x, y) = a_{10}x + a_{01}y + a_{00},$$
$$r(x, y) = r_{10}x + r_{01}y + r_{00},$$
$$e(x, y) = e_{20}x^2 + e_{11}xy + e_{02}y^2 + e_{10}x + e_{01}y + e_{00},$$
$$Y(x, y) = d_{20}x^2 + d_{11}xy + d_{02}y^2 + d_{10}x + d_{01}y + d_{00}.$$

From the above equation

$$X(x, y)r(x, y) = a_{10}r_{10}x^2 + (a_{10}r_{01} + a_{01}r_{10})xy + a_{01}r_{01}y^2 + $$
$$(a_{10}r_{00} + a_{00}r_{10})x + (a_{01}r_{00} + a_{00}r_{01})y + a_{00}r_{00},$$

we get a linear equation

$$\begin{aligned}
a_{10}r_{10} + e_{20} &= d_{20}, \\
a_{10}r_{01} + a_{01}r_{10} + e_{11} &= d_{11}, \\
a_{01}r_{01} + e_{02} &= d_{02}, \\
a_{10}r_{00} + a_{00}r_{10} + e_{10} &= d_{10}, \\
a_{01}r_{00} + a_{00}r_{01} + e_{01} &= d_{01}, \\
a_{00}r_{00} + e_{00} &= d_{00}.
\end{aligned} \tag{2}$$

If an R_ℓ-valued solution $\{e_{ij}\}_{(i,j) \in \Gamma_{X_r}}$ is found, then (X, Y) is sampled from T_X. In order to avoid a typical brute force attack on polynomial e, the form $\#\Gamma_{X_r}$ is necessary to satisfy

$$((\ell - 1)\ell^{n-1})\#\Gamma_{X_r} > 2^k,$$

where k is a security parameter. Next we use a lattice reduction attack to find a small e_{ij}. Represent a_{10} as follows:

$$a_{10} = a_{n-1}^{(10)}t^{n-1} + \cdots + a_0^{(10)}.$$

When $r_{10}, d_{20} \in R_p$ and $e_{20} \in R_\ell$ are represented in the same way as a_{10}, then $a_{10}r_{10} + e_{20} = d_{20}$ can be represented as follows:

$$
\begin{pmatrix}
a_{n-1}^{(10)} & a_{n-2}^{(10)} & \cdots & a_1^{(10)} & a_0^{(10)} \\
a_{n-2}^{(10)} & a_{n-3}^{(10)} & \cdots & a_0^{(10)} & a_{n-1}^{(10)} \\
a_{n-3}^{(10)} & a_{n-4}^{(10)} & \cdots & a_{n-1}^{(10)} & a_{n-2}^{(10)} \\
\vdots & \vdots & \vdots & \vdots & \vdots \\
a_0^{(10)} & a_{n-1}^{(10)} & \cdots & a_2^{(10)} & a_1^{(10)}
\end{pmatrix}
\begin{pmatrix}
r_0^{(10)} \\
r_1^{(10)} \\
\vdots \\
r_{n-2}^{(10)} \\
r_{n-1}^{(10)}
\end{pmatrix}
+
\begin{pmatrix}
e_{n-1}^{(20)} \\
e_{n-2}^{(20)} \\
\vdots \\
e_1^{(20)} \\
e_0^{(20)}
\end{pmatrix}
=
\begin{pmatrix}
d_{n-1}^{(20)} \\
d_{n-2}^{(20)} \\
\vdots \\
d_1^{(20)} \\
d_0^{(20)}
\end{pmatrix}.
$$

Thus the first Eq. (2) can be written as

$$
A_{10} r_{10} + e_{20} = d_{20}, \tag{3}
$$

where

$$
A_{10} =
\begin{pmatrix}
a_{n-1}^{(10)} & a_{n-2}^{(10)} & \cdots & a_1^{(10)} & a_0^{(10)} \\
a_{n-2}^{(10)} & a_{n-3}^{(10)} & \cdots & a_0^{(10)} & a_{n-1}^{(10)} \\
a_{n-3}^{(10)} & a_{n-4}^{(10)} & \cdots & a_{n-1}^{(10)} & a_{n-2}^{(10)} \\
\vdots & \vdots & \vdots & \vdots & \vdots \\
a_0^{(10)} & a_{n-1}^{(10)} & \cdots & a_2^{(10)} & a_1^{(10)}
\end{pmatrix}, \quad
r_{10} =
\begin{pmatrix}
r_0^{(10)} \\
r_1^{(10)} \\
\vdots \\
r_{n-2}^{(10)} \\
r_{n-1}^{(10)}
\end{pmatrix},
$$

$$
e_{20} =
\begin{pmatrix}
e_{n-1}^{(20)} \\
e_{n-2}^{(20)} \\
\vdots \\
e_1^{(20)} \\
e_0^{(20)}
\end{pmatrix}, \quad
d_{20} =
\begin{pmatrix}
d_{n-1}^{(20)} \\
d_{n-2}^{(20)} \\
\vdots \\
d_1^{(20)} \\
d_0^{(20)}
\end{pmatrix}.
$$

The Eq. (3) is an equation over $\mathbb{F}_p$, and we lift the Eq. (3) to an equation over $\mathbb{Z}$ by adding an integer vector g_{20} to the left-hand side of (3):

$$
A_{10} r_{10} + e_{20} + p g_{20} = d_{20}.
$$

We consider the integer lattice $\mathcal{L}$ with the basis matrix $(A_{10} \ p I_n)$. If $v \in \mathcal{L}$ is a vector closest to d_{20}, then we can expect that a short vector $\pm e_{20}$ is found by calculating $d_{20} - v$. In order to find all e_{ij}, one needs to deal with all equations of (2) simultaneously. See [3] for more detail. This means that the IE-LWE problem can be reduced to the closest vector problem (CVP) on the lattice $\mathcal{L}$. This attack is called the linear algebra attack.

3.3   Vercauteren et al.'s Evalution Attack

In this section, we describe Vercauteren et al.'s evaluation attack that tries to break IND-CPA security of Giophantus. This attack uses the fact that a map $R_p = \mathbb{F}_p[t]/(t^n - 1) \longrightarrow \mathbb{F}_p$ by $a(t) \mapsto a(1)$ is a well-defined ring homomorphism. Let $X(x, y) \in R_p[x, y]$ and $(u_x(t), u_y(t)) \in R_\ell^2$ be the public key and the secret key of Giophantusas, respectively, in Sect. 3.1. The detailed description is as follows:

1. We obtain the equation $X(x, y, 1) = 0$ over $\mathbb{F}_p$, where $X(x, y, 1)$ means the image of $X(x, y)$ under a map $R_p[x, y] \longrightarrow \mathbb{F}_p[x, y]$ by $\sum f_{ij}(t)x^i y^j \mapsto \sum f_{ij}(1)x^i y^j$.
2. Perform exhaustive search to find a solution (u'_x, u'_y) to $X(x, y, 1) = 0$ over $\mathbb{F}_p$ such that u'_x and u'_y are represented by integers in $\{0, \ldots, n(\ell - 1)\}$. The existence of such a solution is guaranteed by $X(u_x(1), u_x(1), 1) = 0$. In fact, if the secret key is represented as

$$(u_x, u_y) = \left(\sum_{i=0}^{n-1} \overline{\alpha}_i t^i, \sum_{i=0}^{n-1} \overline{\beta}_i t^i \right) \quad (0 \leq \alpha_i, \beta_i \leq \ell - 1),$$

then we have

$$0 \leq \max \left\{ \sum \alpha_i, \sum \beta_i \right\} \leq n(\ell - 1),$$

where α_i and β_i are integers representing $\overline{\alpha}_i$ and $\overline{\beta}_i$, respectively. The smallest solution (u'_x, u'_y) can be found in two ways.
   - Choose $\overline{\alpha}_x, \overline{\alpha}_y \in \{\overline{0}, \ldots, \overline{n(\ell - 1)}\} \subset \mathbb{F}_p$ and check whether $X(\overline{\alpha}_x, \overline{\alpha}_y, 1) = 0$ or not.
   - Choose $\overline{\alpha} \in \{\overline{0}, \ldots, \overline{n(\ell - 1)}\} \subset \mathbb{F}_p$ and check whether $X(\overline{\alpha}, y, 1)$ has a factor of the form $(y - \overline{\beta})$ with $0 \leq \beta \leq n(\ell - 1)$ or not.
3. Let m_0 and m_1 be plaintext polynomials in R_ℓ with $m_0(1) \not\equiv m_1(1) \pmod{\ell}$. Randomly choose $b \in 0, 1$ and put $c(x, y) = m_b + X(x, y)r(x, y) + \ell e(x, y)$. Substitute (u'_x, u'_y) for x and y of $c(x, y)$, respectively, and calculate

$$c(u'_x, u'_y, 1) \equiv m_b(1) + \ell \cdot e(u'_x, u'_y, 1) \pmod{\ell}.$$

4. Calculate $m'_b \equiv c(u'_x, u'_y, 1) \pmod{\ell}$.
5. Under the condition $m_0(1) \not\equiv m_1(1) \pmod{\ell}$, we determine the value of b by comparing $m_0(1)$, $m_1(1)$ and $m'_b \pmod{\ell}$.

To get $m_b(1) \pmod{\ell}$ in Step 4, the modulus p needs to satisfy

$$p > \max\{c(u'_x, u'_y, 1) \mid 0 \leq u'_x, u'_y \leq n(\ell - 1)\}.$$

To estimate the value of $c(u'_x, u'_y, 1)$, we consider

$$c(u'_x, u'_y, 1) = m_b(1) + \ell \cdot e(u'_x, u'_y)$$
$$= m_b(1) + \ell \cdot \sum_{(i,j) \in \Gamma_e} e_{ij}(1)(u'_x)^i (u'_y)^j.$$

Since

$$0 \leq m_b(1), e_{ij}(1) \leq n(\ell - 1),$$

We have

$$\max\{c(u'_x, u'_y, 1) \mid 0 \leq u'_x, u'_y \leq n(\ell - 1)\}$$
$$\leq n(\ell - 1) + \ell \cdot \sum_{(i,j) \in \Gamma_e} (n(\ell - 1))^{i+j+1}$$
$$\leq n(\ell - 1) + \ell \cdot \sum_{k=0}^{dX+dr} (k + 1)(n(\ell - 1))^{k+1},$$

which is much larger than p if p is the smallest prime number satisfying the inequality (1). Therefore, the above attack does not work well. However, Vercauteren et al. pointed out that the distribution of $c(u'_x, u'_y, 1)$ over the integers would leak information of $m_b(1)$, and thus Akiyama et al. conducted many experiments on the distribution of $c(u'_x, u'_y, 1)$. As a result of their experiments, the distribution of $c(u'_x, u'_y, 1)$ does not leak any information of plaintext polynomials for recommended parameters of Giophantus.

4   Our Evaluation Attack

In this section, we describe our new evaluation attack. An idea of our evaluation attack is similar to Vercauteren et al.'s evaluation attack in Sect. 3.3 and a known attack on Poly-LWE [8]. The main difference between our attack and those attacks is that our attack does not require to search some partial information of secret keys. In our attack, we reduce the IE-LWE problem to CVP on low rank lattices, e.g., 6-rank for recommended parameters. We can solve such CVP efficiently. The detailed description of our attack is as follows: Let (X, Y) be as in Sect. 3.2. By substituting $t = 1$ for the Eq. (2) and by adding ph_{ij} ($h_{ij} \in \mathbb{Z}$ to each equation of (2), we obtain a new linear equation over $\mathbb{Z}$

$$a_{10}(1)r_{10}(1) + e_{20}(1) + ph_{20} = d_{20}(1),$$
$$a_{10}(1)r_{01}(1) + a_{01}(1)r_{10}(1) + e_{11}(1) + ph_{11} = d_{11}(1),$$
$$a_{01}(1)r_{01}(1) + e_{02}(1) + ph_{01} = d_{02}(1),$$
$$a_{10}(1)r_{00}(1) + a_{00}(1)r_{10}(1) + e_{10}(1) + ph_{10} = d_{10}(1),$$
$$a_{01}(1)r_{00}(1) + a_{00}(1)r_{01}(1) + e_{01}(1) + ph_{01} = d_{01}(1),$$
$$a_{00}(1)r_{00}(1) + e_{00}(1) + ph_{00} = d_{00}(1).$$

We write $a_{ij}(1)$ as a_{ij} for simplicity. By regarding $r_{ij}(1)$ and $e_{ij}(1)$ as variables, we have the linear equations:

$$
\begin{pmatrix}
a_{10} & 0 & 0 & p & 0 & 0 & 0 & 0 & 0 \\
a_{01} & a_{10} & 0 & 0 & p & 0 & 0 & 0 & 0 \\
0 & a_{01} & 0 & 0 & 0 & p & 0 & 0 & 0 \\
a_{00} & 0 & a_{10} & 0 & 0 & 0 & p & 0 & 0 \\
0 & a_{00} & a_{01} & 0 & 0 & 0 & 0 & p & 0 \\
0 & 0 & a_{00} & 0 & 0 & 0 & 0 & 0 & p
\end{pmatrix}
\begin{pmatrix}
r_{10} \\ r_{01} \\ r_{00} \\ h_{20} \\ h_{11} \\ h_{02} \\ h_{10} \\ h_{01} \\ h_{00}
\end{pmatrix}
+
\begin{pmatrix}
e_{20} \\ e_{11} \\ e_{02} \\ e_{10} \\ e_{01} \\ e_{00}
\end{pmatrix}
=
\begin{pmatrix}
d_{20} \\ d_{11} \\ d_{02} \\ d_{10} \\ d_{01} \\ d_{00}
\end{pmatrix}.
$$

If (X, Y) is an IE-LWE instance, then we have $0 \le e_{ij} \le n(\ell - 1)$. We see that $n(\ell - 1)$ is much smaller than p from the inequality (1). Thus if we can find a vector closest to $(d_{20}\ d_{11}\ d_{02}\ d_{10}\ d_{01}\ d_{00})^{\mathrm{T}}$ in the lattice generated by the column vectors of

$$\begin{pmatrix} a_{10} & 0 & 0 & p & 0 & 0 & 0 & 0 & 0 \\ a_{01} & a_{10} & 0 & 0 & p & 0 & 0 & 0 & 0 \\ 0 & a_{01} & 0 & 0 & 0 & p & 0 & 0 & 0 \\ a_{00} & 0 & a_{10} & 0 & 0 & 0 & p & 0 & 0 \\ 0 & a_{00} & a_{01} & 0 & 0 & 0 & 0 & p & 0 \\ 0 & 0 & a_{00} & 0 & 0 & 0 & 0 & 0 & p \end{pmatrix}.$$

We obtain a short vector $(e'_{20}, \ldots, e'_{00})^T$ (not necessarily $(e_{20}, \ldots, e_{00})^T$). As a result of solving CVP, if all e'_{ij} are equal or smaller than $n(\ell - 1)$, then we determine that (X, Y) is an IE-LWE instance. In other words, the IE-LWE problem is reduced to CVP on 6-rank lattices.

5 Experiments on Our Attack

In this section, we report experimental results on our new evaluation attack described in the Sect. 4. The procedure of our experiments is as follows:

- Randomly sample IE-LWE instances and determine whether they are IE-LWE instance or not by our attack.
- Randomly sample pairs of polynomials from U_X. Determine whether they are IE-LWE instances or not by our attack.

In our experiments, we set $\ell = 4$, i.e., the coefficients of the secret keys (u_x, u_y) are in the range $\{0, ..., 3\}$. The number of attack experiments is 100,000 times. The computer environment is shown below.

- CPU: Intel(R)XeonCPU E7-4830 v4@2.00 GHz,
- RAM:3 TB,
- OS: Ubuntu 10.04.5 LTS,
- Software: Magma [6].

We show our experimental results in Tables 1 and 2. In Tables 1 and 2, "num. of success" means the number of successes, respectively. From the above results, we see that our attack can efficiently solve the IE-LWE problem within 4 s for security parameters $k = 143, 207, 272$. When given a pair of polynomials (X, Y), it is possible to determine whether the pair is an IE-LWE instance or not, and to break the IND-CPA security of Giophantus.

6 Modification of IE-LWE Problem

In this section, we discuss how to modify the IE-LWE problem to avoid our attack and its variant described below. An easy way to avoid our attack is to use other modulus polynomials $f \in \mathbb{F}_p[t]$ satisfying $f(1) \not\equiv 0 \pmod{p}$. However, the following argument implies that the condition is not enough.

If there is a root $\alpha \in \mathbb{F}_{p^d}$ of f, i.e., $f(\alpha) = 0$, then a map $\mathbb{F}_p[t]/(f) \longrightarrow \mathbb{F}_{p^d}$ by $a(t) \mapsto a(\alpha)$ is a well-defined ring homomorphism. We assume that $\alpha^w = 1$

Table 1. Attack for IE-LWE instances

k	n	p	Num. of success	Success probability	Average time (sec)
143	1201	467424413	100000	1	0.32235
207	1733	973190461	100000	1	0.61882
272	2267	1665292879	100000	1	3.20274

Table 2. Attack for random samples

k	n	p	Num. of success	Success probability	Average time (sec)
143	467424413	130	99870	0.99870	0.22551
207	973190461	151	99849	0.99849	0.43368
272	1665292879	142	99858	0.99858	2.23923

for $w < n - 1$. For simplicity, we also assume $w \mid (n-1)$, say $n - 1 = ww'$. Put $n_f := \deg(f)$ and $R_p^{(f)} := \mathbb{F}_p[t]/(f)$. Let $R_\ell^{(f)}$ be the subset of $R_p^{(f)}$ defined by the same way as R_ℓ. A variant of the IE-LWE problem is defined by replacing R_p and R_ℓ in Definition 1 by $R_p^{(f)}$ and $R_\ell^{(f)}$, respectively. We call the variant of the IE-LWE problem the IE-LWE$_f$ problem. We try to solve the IE-LWE$_f$ problem by combining the linear algebra attack in Sect. 3.2 and evaluation attack at $t = \alpha$. For a given sample $(X_f, Y_f = X_f r_f + e_f)$ from the IE-LWE$_f$ problem, put $X_f = \sum_{(i,j)\in\Gamma_{X_f}} a_{ij}^{(f)} x^i y^j, r_f = \sum_{(i,j)\in\Gamma_{r_f}} r_{ij}^{(f)} x^i y^j, e_f = \sum_{(i,j)\in\Gamma_{e_f}} e_{ij}^{(f)} x^i y^j$ and $Y_f = \sum_{(i,j)\in\Gamma_{Y_f}} d_{ij}^{(f)} x^i y^j$, where $r_{ij}^{(f)}$ and $e_{ij}^{(f)}$ are variables. If we find that all $e_{ij}^{(f)}$ are $R_\ell^{(f)}$-values variables, then (X_f, Y_f) is an IE-LWE$_f$ instance.

Put $e_{ij}^{(f)}$ as

$$e_{n-1}^{(ij,f)} t^{n-1} + \cdots + e_0^{(ij,f)}.$$

From the assumption $\alpha^w = 1$, we have

$$\begin{aligned}
e_{ij}^{(f)}(\alpha) = &(e_{w-1}^{(ij,f)} + \cdots + e_{w'w-1}^{(ij,f)})\alpha^{w-1} \\
& + (e_{w-2}^{(ij,f)} + \cdots + e_{w'w-2}^{(ij,f)})\alpha^{w-2} \\
& + \cdots + (e_0^{(ij,f)} + \cdots + e_{ww'}^{(ij,f)}).
\end{aligned}$$

If $e_{ij}^{(f)}$ is in $R_\ell^{(f)}$, then we can regard $e_{ij}^{(f)}(\alpha)$ as a polynomial with small coefficients within $\{0, \ldots, w'(\ell - 1)\}$ of degree $w - 1 < n - 2$. The above argument can be also applied to $a_{ij}^{(f)}$, $r_{ij}^{(f)}$ and $d_{ij}^{(f)}$, i.e., $a_{ij}^{(f)}(\alpha)$, $r_{ij}^{(f)}(\alpha)$ and $d_{ij}^{(f)}(\alpha)$ can be regarded as polynomials of degree $w - 1$. We see that $w'(\ell - 1) < n(\ell - 1)$ is much smaller than p from the inequality (1). Thus, by applying the linear algebra attack, we can expect that the IE-LWE$_f$ problem is solved by solving the (approximate) CVP on lattices with smaller rank. The rank of lattice is reduced by applying Xagawa's method (cf. [3]). We note that $1, \alpha, \ldots, \alpha^{w-1}$ would be $\mathbb{F}_p$-

linearly dependent elements. Thus, we need to slightly modify the linear algebra attack.

The above attack is similar to attacks on Poly-LWE problem [9,12]. However, in the case of attacking Poly-LWE problem, the extension degree d should be small, e.g., $1 \le d \le 3$, because one needs to find secret elements in $\mathbb{F}_{p^d}$ by exhaustive search. On the other hand, the above attack does not require to search secret elements and would work for any d.

From the above argument, we need to use modulus polynomials f whose roots have large order $(> n)$ to avoid our attack in Sect. 4 and its variant above. For instance, all roots of the m-th cyclotomic polynomial (mod. p) have order m (see [9]). Moreover, we should use modulus polynomials with small coefficients, e.g., the q-th cyclotomic polynomials with prime power integers q, so that the coefficients of $e(u_x(t), u_y(t))$ does not become so large.

Remark 1. At Symposium on Cryptography and Information Security 2019, which is a big symposium in Japan, Akiyama, Yuntao Wang, Ikematsu and Takagi announced the modified IE-LWE problem and proposed Giophantus$^+$ which is IND-CPA secure if the modified IE-LWE problem is computationally infeasible. Their modification is to use $t^k + 1$ for 2-power integer k, i.e., the $2k$-th cyclotomic polynomial, as a modulus polynomial. Akiyama et al.'s modified IE-LWE problem cannot be solved by our evaluation attack and its variant. However, Akiyama et al.'s analysis is only based on lattice attacks, and the value of k is very limited even though k is closely related to the sizes of public/secret keys and ciphertexts. Therefore, one should also consider other modifications as in our argument above.

7 Conclusion

In this paper, we proposed a new and practical evaluation attack on IND-CPA security of an indeterminate equation public key post-quantum cryptosystem, called "Giophantus". The Giophantus satisfies IND-CPA security under the assumption that an indeterminate equation analogue of learning with errors (IE-LWE) problem is computationally infeasible. However, our attack efficiently succeeded in solving the IE-LWE problem with probability about 99% within 4 s in average. Moreover, we investigate how to modify the IE-LWE problem to avoid our attack. We gave the notable argument and a variant of our evaluation attack. As a result, we conclude that one should use polynomials f with small coefficients, which have roots of large order, e.g., the q-th cyclotomic polynomial with prime power integers q.

Although our attack is cleary solve the IE-LWE problem with high probability, we could not give the theoretical estimate of the success probability of our attacks. Moreover, our approach for solving the IE-LWE problem is similar to known attacks on Poly-LWE problem. Therefore, our future work is to estimate the theoretical success probability and to investigate attacks of other approaches.

Acknowledgement. This work is partially supported by JSPS KAKENHI Grant(B) (JP17K18450), Grant (C)(JP15K00183), Microsoft Research Asia, CREST(JPMJCR1-404) at Japan Science and Technology Agency, the Japan-Taiwan Collaborative Research Program at Japan Science and Technology Agency, and Project for Establishing a Nationwide Practical Education Network for IT Human Resources Development, Education Network for Practical Information Technologies.

References

1. Akiyama, K., Goto, Y., Okumura, S., Takagi, T., Nuida, K., Hanaoka, G.: A public-key encryption scheme based on non-linear indeterminate equations. In: Adams, C., Camenisch, J. (eds.) SAC 2017. LNCS, vol. 10719, pp. 215–234. Springer, Cham (2018). https://doi.org/10.1007/978-3-319-72565-9_11

2. Akiyama, K., et al.: Indeterminate equation publickey cryptosystem (Giophantus^tm), in the round-1-submissions of NIST PQC standardization (2017). https://csrc.nist.gov/Projects/Post-Quantum-Cryptography/

3. Akiyama, K., et al.: A public-key encryption scheme based on non-linear indeterminate equations (Giophantus). IACR Cryptology ePrint Archive 2017, 1241 (2017). http://eprint.iacr.org/2017/1241

4. Albrecht, M.R., Göpfert, F., Virdia, F., Wunderer, T.: Revisiting the expected cost of solving uSVP and applications to LWE. In: Takagi, T., Peyrin, T. (eds.) ASIACRYPT 2017. LNCS, vol. 10624, pp. 297–322. Springer, Cham (2017). https://doi.org/10.1007/978-3-319-70694-8_11

5. Beullens, W., Castryck, W., Vercauteren, F.: IND-CPA attack on Giophantus, in the official-comments to Giophantus for NIST round-1-submissions (2018). https://csrc.nist.gov/CSRC/media/Projects/Post-Quantum-Cryptography/documents/round-1/official-comments/Giophantus-official-comment.pdf

6. Bosma, W., Cannon, J.J., Playoust, C.: The MAGMA algebra system I: the user language. J. Symb. Comput. **24**(3/4), 235–265 (1997). https://doi.org/10.1006/jsco.1996.0125

7. Ding, J., Schmidt, D.: Rainbow, a new multivariable polynomial signature scheme. In: Ioannidis, J., Keromytis, A., Yung, M. (eds.) ACNS 2005. LNCS, vol. 3531, pp. 164–175. Springer, Heidelberg (2005). https://doi.org/10.1007/11496137_12

8. Eisenträger, K., Hallgren, S., Lauter, K.: Weak instances of PLWE. In: Joux, A., Youssef, A. (eds.) SAC 2014. LNCS, vol. 8781, pp. 183–194. Springer, Cham (2014). https://doi.org/10.1007/978-3-319-13051-4_11

9. Elias, Y., Lauter, K.E., Ozman, E., Stange, K.E.: Provably weak instances of Ring-LWE. In: Gennaro, R., Robshaw, M. (eds.) CRYPTO 2015. LNCS, vol. 9215, pp. 63–92. Springer, Heidelberg (2015). https://doi.org/10.1007/978-3-662-47989-6_4

10. Gentry, C.: Key recovery and message attacks on NTRU-composite. In: Pfitzmann, B. (ed.) EUROCRYPT 2001. LNCS, vol. 2045, pp. 182–194. Springer, Heidelberg (2001). https://doi.org/10.1007/3-540-44987-6_12

11. Hoffstein, J., Pipher, J., Silverman, J.H.: NTRU: a ring-based public key cryptosystem. In: Buhler, J.P. (ed.) ANTS 1998. LNCS, vol. 1423, pp. 267–288. Springer, Heidelberg (1998). https://doi.org/10.1007/BFb0054868

12. Kudo, M.: Attacks against search Poly-LWE. IACR Cryptology ePrint Archive 2016, 1153 (2016). http://eprint.iacr.org/2016/1153

13. Lindner, R., Peikert, C.: Better key sizes (and attacks) for LWE-based encryption. In: Kiayias, A. (ed.) CT-RSA 2011. LNCS, vol. 6558, pp. 319–339. Springer, Heidelberg (2011). https://doi.org/10.1007/978-3-642-19074-2_21

14. McEliece, R.J.: A public-key cryptosystem based on algebraic coding theory. The Deep Space Network Progress Report, DSN PR 42-44, January and February 1978, pp. 114–116 (1987)
15. NIST: Post-quantum cryptography standardization. https://csrc.nist.gov/Projects/Post-Quantum-Cryptography/Post-Quantum-Cryptography-Standardization
16. Stehlé, D., Steinfeld, R.: Making NTRU as secure as worst-case problems over ideal lattices. In: Paterson, K.G. (ed.) EUROCRYPT 2011. LNCS, vol. 6632, pp. 27–47. Springer, Heidelberg (2011). https://doi.org/10.1007/978-3-642-20465-4_4
17. Xagawa, K.: Practical cryptanalysis of a public-key encryption scheme based on non-linear indeterminate equations at SAC 2017. IACR Cryptology ePrint Archive 2017, 1224 (2017). http://eprint.iacr.org/2017/1224
18. Yasuda, T., Sakurai, K.: A multivariate encryption scheme with rainbow. In: Qing, S., Okamoto, E., Kim, K., Liu, D. (eds.) ICICS 2015. LNCS, vol. 9543, pp. 236–251. Springer, Cham (2016). https://doi.org/10.1007/978-3-319-29814-6_19

Ternary Syndrome Decoding with Large Weight

Rémi Bricout[1,2], André Chailloux[2(✉)], Thomas Debris-Alazard[1,2],
and Matthieu Lequesne[1,2]

[1] Sorbonne Universités, UPMC Univ Paris 06, Paris, France
[2] Inria, Paris, France
{remi.bricout,andre.chailloux,thomas.debris,matthieu.lequesne}@inria.fr

Abstract. The Syndrome Decoding problem is at the core of many code-based cryptosystems. In this paper, we study ternary Syndrome Decoding in large weight. This problem has been introduced in the Wave signature scheme but has never been thoroughly studied. We perform an algorithmic study of this problem which results in an update of the Wave parameters. On a more fundamental level, we show that ternary Syndrome Decoding with large weight is a really harder problem than the binary Syndrome Decoding problem, which could have several applications for the design of code-based cryptosystems.

Keywords: Post-quantum cryptography · Syndrome decoding problem · Subset sum algorithms

1 Introduction

Syndrome decoding is one of the oldest problems used in coding theory and cryptography [McE78]. It is known to be NP-complete [BMvT78] and its average case variant is still believed to be hard forty years after it was proposed, even against quantum computers. This makes code-based cryptography a credible candidate for post-quantum cryptography. There has been numerous proposals of post-quantum cryptosystems based on the hardness of the Syndrome Decoding (SD) problem, some of which were proposed for the NIST standardization process for quantum-resistant cryptographic schemes. Most of them are qualified for the second round of the competition [ABB+17,ACP+17,AMAB+17,BBC+19, BCL+17]. It is therefore a significant task to understand the computational hardness of the Syndrome Decoding problem.

Informally, the Syndrome Decoding problem is stated as follows. Given a matrix $\mathbf{H} \in \mathbb{F}_q^{(n-k)\times n}$, a vector $\mathbf{s} \in \mathbb{F}_q^{n-k}$ and a weight $w \in [\![0, n]\!]$, the goal is to find a vector $\mathbf{e} \in \mathbb{F}_q^n$ such that $\mathbf{He}^\mathsf{T} = \mathbf{s}^\mathsf{T}$ and $|\mathbf{e}| = w$, where $|\mathbf{e}|$ denotes the Hamming weight, namely $|\mathbf{e}| = |\{i : \mathbf{e}_i \neq 0\}|$. The binary case, *i.e.* when $q = 2$ has been extensively studied. Even before this problem was used in cryptography, Prange [Pra62] constructed a clever algorithm for solving the binary problem using a method now referred to as Information Set Decoding (ISD).

© Springer Nature Switzerland AG 2020
K. G. Paterson and D. Stebila (Eds.): SAC 2019, LNCS 11959, pp. 437–466, 2020.
https://doi.org/10.1007/978-3-030-38471-5_18

1.1   Binary vs. Ternary Case

The binary case of the SD problem has been thoroughly studied. Its complexity is always studied for relative weight $W := \frac{w}{n} \in [0, 0.5]$ because the case $W > 0.5$ is equivalent (see Remark 2 in Sect. 2). However, this argument is no longer valid in the general case ($q \geq 3$). Indeed, the large weight case does not behave similarly to the small weight case, as we can see on Fig. 1.

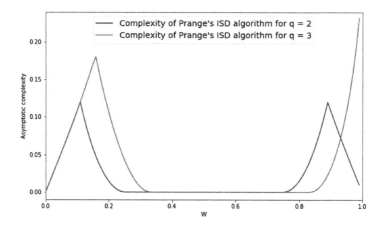

Fig. 1. Asymptotic complexity of Prange's ISD algorithm for $R := \frac{k}{n} = 0.5$.

The general case $q \geq 3$ has received much less attention than the binary case. One possible explanation for this is that there were no cryptographic applications for the general case. This has recently changed. Indeed, a new signature scheme named Wave was recently proposed in [DST18], based on the difficulty of SD on a ternary alphabet and with large weight. This scheme makes uses of the new regime of large weight induced by the asymmetry of the ternary case. Therefore, in addition to the algorithmic interest of studying the general syndrome decoding problem, the results of this study can be applied to a real cryptosystem.

Another reason why the general case $q \geq 3$ has been less studied is that the Hamming weight measure becomes less meaningful as q grows larger. Indeed, the Hamming weight only counts the number of non-zero elements but not their repartition. Hence, the weight loses a significant amount of information for large values of q. Therefore, $q = 3$ seems to be the best candidate to understand the structure of the non-binary case without losing too much information.

1.2   State of the Art for $q \geq 3$

Still, there exist some interesting results concerning the SD problem in the general q-ary case. Coffey and Goodman [CG90] were the firsts to propose a generalization of Prange's ISD algorithm to $\mathbb{F}_q$. Following this seminal work, most existing ISD algorithms were extended to cover the q-ary case. In 2010, Peters [Pet10] generalized Stern's algorithm. In his dissertation thesis, Meurer [Meu17] generalized the BJMM algorithm. Hirose [Hir16] proposed a generalization of Stern's algorithm with May-Ozerov's approach (using nearest neighbors) and showed that for $q \geq 3$ this does not improve the complexity compared to Stern's classical approach. Later, Gueye, Klamti and Hirose [GKH17] extended the BJMM algorithm with May-Ozerov's approach and improved the complexity of the general SD problem. A result from Canto-Torres [CT17] proves that all ISD-based algorithms converge to the same asymptotic complexity when $q \to \infty$. Finally, a recent work [IKR+18] proposed a generalization of the ball-collision decoding over $\mathbb{F}_q$.

All these papers focus solely on the SD problem for relative weight $W <$ 0.5. None of them mentions the case of large weight. The claimed worst case complexities in these papers should be understood as the worst case complexity for the SD problem with relative weight $W < 0.5$, but as we can see on Fig. 1 the highest complexity is actually reached for large relative weight.

1.3 Our Contributions

Our contribution consists in a general study of ternary syndrome decoding with large weight. We first focus on the Wave signature scheme [DST18] and present the best known algorithmic attack on this scheme. We then look more generally at the hardest instances of the ternary syndrome decoding with large weight and show that this problem seems significantly harder than the binary variant, making it a potentially very interesting problem for code-base cryptography.

The PGE+SS Framework. A first minor contribution consists in a modular description of most ISD-based algorithms. All these algorithms contain two steps. First, performing a partial Gaussian elimination (PGE), and then, solving a variant of the Subset Sum problem (SS). This was already implicitly used in previous papers but we want to make it explicit to simplify the analysis and hopefully make those algorithms easier to understand for non-specialists.

Ternary SD with Large Weight. We then study specifically the SD problem in the ternary case and for large weights. From our modular description, we can focus only on finding many solutions of a specific instance of the Subset Sum problem. At a high level, we combine Wagner's algorithm [Wag02] and representation techniques [BCJ11, BJMM12] to obtain our algorithm. Our first takeaway is that, while representations are very useful to obtain a unique solution (as in [BCJ11]), there are some drawbacks in using them to obtain many solutions. These drawbacks are strongly mitigated in the binary case as in [BJMM12] but it becomes much harder for larger values of q. We manage to partially compensate this by changing the moduli size, the place and the number of representations. For instance, for the Wave [DST18] parameters, we derive an algorithm that is a Wagner tree with seven floors where the last two floors have partial representations and the others have none.

New Parameters for Wave. We then use our algorithms to study the complexity of the Wave signature scheme, for which we significantly improve the original analysis. We show that the key sizes of the original scheme presented for 128 bits of security have to be more than doubled, going roughly from 1Mb to 2.2Mb, to achieve the claimed security. This requires to study the Decode One Out of Many (DOOM) problem, on which Wave actually relies. This problem corresponds to a multiple target SD problem. More precisely, given N syndromes $(\mathbf{s}_1, \ldots, \mathbf{s}_N)$ (N can be large, for example $N = 2^{64}$) the goal is to find an error $\mathbf{e}$ of Hamming weight w and an integer i such that $\mathbf{e}\mathbf{H}^\mathsf{T} = \mathbf{s}_i$.

Hardest Instances of the Ternary SD with Large Weight. Next, we look at the hardest instances of the ternary SD with large weight problem. We study the standard ISD algorithms and show that for all of them, the hardest instances occur for $R \approx 0.369$ and $W = 1$ (still in the case $q = 3$). Unsurprisingly, for equivalent code length and dimension, ternary syndrome decoding is harder than its binary counterpart. But this is due to the fact that the input matrix contains more information, since its elements are in $\mathbb{F}_3$, hence the input size is $\log_2(3)$ times larger than a binary matrix with equivalent dimensions.

A more surprising conclusion of our work is that ternary syndrome decoding is significantly harder than the binary case *for equivalent input size*, that is, when normalizing the exponent by a factor $\log_2(q)$. This new result is in sharp contrast with all the previous work on q-ary syndrome decoding that showed that the problem becomes simpler as q increases. This is due to the fact that all the previous literature only considered the small weight case while we now take large weights into account.

Table 1 represents the minimum input size for which the underlying syndrome decoding problem offers 128 bits of security, *i.e.* the associated algorithm needs at least 2^{128} operations to solve the problem.

Table 1. Minimum input sizes (in kbits) for a time complexity of 2^{128}.

Algorithm	$q = 2$	$q = 3$ and $W > 0.5$
Prange	275	44
Dumer/Wagner	295	83
BJMM/Our algorithm	374	99

We want to stress again that those input sizes in the ternary case take into account the fact that the matrix elements are in $\mathbb{F}_3$. So the increase in efficiency is quite significant and the ternary SD could efficiently replace its binary counterpart when looking for a hard code-based problem.

1.4 Notations

We define here some notations that will be used throughout the paper. The notation $x \stackrel{\triangle}{=} y$ means that x is defined to be equal to y. We denote by

$\mathbb{F}_q = \{0, 1, \cdots, q - 1\}$ the finite field of size q. Vectors will be written with bold letters (such as $\mathbf{e}$) and uppercase bold letters will be used to denote matrices (such as $\mathbf{H}$). Vectors are in row notation. Let $\mathbf{x}$ and $\mathbf{y}$ be two vectors, we will write $(\mathbf{x}, \mathbf{y})$ to denote their concatenation. Finally, we denote by $[\![a, b]\!]$ the set $\{\tilde{a}, \tilde{a} + 1, \ldots, \tilde{b}\}$ where $\tilde{a} = \lfloor a \rfloor$ and $\tilde{b} = \lfloor b \rfloor$.

2   A General Framework for Solving the Syndrome Decoding Problem

2.1   The Syndrome Decoding Problem

The goal of this paper is to study the Syndrome Decoding problem, which is at the core of most code-based cryptosystems.

Problem 1. [Syndrome Decoding - SD(q, R, W)]

Instance: $\mathbf{H} \in \mathbb{F}_q^{(n-k) \times n}$ of full rank,
$\qquad\quad$ $\mathbf{s} \in \mathbb{F}_q^{n-k}$ (usually called the *syndrome*).
Output: $\mathbf{e} \in \mathbb{F}_q^n$ such that $|\mathbf{e}| = w$ and $\mathbf{e}\mathbf{H}^{\mathsf{T}} = \mathbf{s}$,

where $k \overset{\triangle}{=} \lceil Rn \rceil$, $w \overset{\triangle}{=} \lceil Wn \rceil$ and $|\mathbf{e}| \overset{\triangle}{=} |\{i : \mathbf{e}_i \neq 0\}|$.

The problem SD(q, R, W) is parametrized by the field size q, the rate $R \in [0, 1]$ and the relative weight $W \in [0, 1]$. We are always interested in the average case complexity (as a function of n) of this problem, where $\mathbf{H}$ is chosen uniformly at random and $\mathbf{s}$ is chosen uniformly from the set $\{\mathbf{e}\mathbf{H}^{\mathsf{T}} : |\mathbf{e}| = w\}$. This ensures the existence of a solution for each input and corresponds to the typical situation in cryptanalysis. More generally, the following proposition gives the average expected number of solutions

Proposition 1. *Let n, k, w be integers with $k \leq n$ and $\mathbf{s} \in \mathbb{F}_q^{n-k}$. The expected number of solutions of $\mathbf{e}\mathbf{H}^{\mathsf{T}} = \mathbf{s}$ in $\mathbf{e}$ of weight w when $\mathbf{H}$ is chosen uniformly at random in $\mathbb{F}_q^{(n-k) \times n}$ is given by:*

$$\frac{\binom{n}{w}(q - 1)^w}{q^{n-k}}.$$

Proof. This is simple combinatorics. The numerator corresponds to the number of vectors $\mathbf{e}'$ of weight w. The denominator corresponds to the inverse of the probability over $\mathbf{H}$ that $\mathbf{e}\mathbf{H}^{\mathsf{T}} = \mathbf{s}^{\mathsf{T}}$ for $\mathbf{e} \neq \mathbf{0}$. $\qquad\qquad\square$

Remark 1. The matrix length n is not considered as a parameter of the problem since we are only interested in the asymptopic complexity, that is the coefficient $F(q, R, W)$ (which does not depend on n) such that the complexity of the Syndrome Decoding problem for a matrix of size n can be expressed as $2^{n(F(q,R,W)+o(1))}$.

State of the Art on $\mathbb{F}_2$. This problem was mostly studied in the case $q = 2$. Depending on the parameters R and W, the complexity of the problem can greatly vary. Let us fix a value R, and let W_{GV} denote the Gilbert-Varshamov bound, that is $W_{GV} \overset{\triangle}{=} h_2^{-1}(1 - R)$ where h_2 is the binary entropy function restricted to the input space $\left[0, \frac{1}{2}\right]$. For $W \in \left[0, \frac{1}{2}\right]$, there exist three different regimes.

1. $W \approx W_{GV}$. When W is close to W_{GV}, there is on average a small number of solutions. This is the regime where the problem is the hardest and where it is the most studied. To the best of our knowledge, we only know two code-based cryptosystems in this regime, namely the CFS signature scheme [CFS01] and the authentication scheme of Stern [Ste93].
2. $W \gg W_{GV}$. In this case, there are on average exponentially many solutions and this makes the problem simpler. When W reaches $\frac{1-R}{2}$, the problem can be solved in average polynomial time using Prange's algorithm [Pra62]. There is a cryptographic motivation to consider W much larger than W_{GV}, for instance to build signatures schemes following the [GPV08] paradigm as it was done in [DST17] but one has to be careful to not make SD too simple.
3. $W \ll W_{GV}$. In this regime, we have with high probability a unique solution. However, the search space, *i.e.* the set of vectors $\mathbf{e}$ st. $|\mathbf{e}| = \lceil Wn \rceil$ is much smaller than in the other regimes. The original McEliece system [McE78] or the QC-MDPC systems [MTSB12] are in this regime.

Remark 2. Solving $SD(2, R, W)$ for $W \in \left[\frac{1}{2}, 1\right]$ and the instance $(\mathbf{H}, \mathbf{s})$ can be reduced to one of the above-mentioned cases using $SD(2, R, 1 - W)$ and the instance $(\mathbf{H}, \mathbf{s} + \mathbf{1H^T})$ where $\mathbf{1}$ denotes the vector with all its components equal to 1.

Remark 3. Contrary to the binary case, when $q \geq 3$ the case of large relative weight can not be reduced to that of small relative weight using the trick of Remark 2. In fact, the problem has a quite different behavior in small and large weights, see Fig. 1.

2.2   The PGE+SS Framework in $\mathbb{F}_q$

The SD problem has been extensively studied in the binary case. Most algorithms designed to solve this problem [Dum91, MMT11, BJMM12] follow the same framework:

1. perform a partial Gaussian elimination (PGE);
2. solve the Subset Sum problem (SS) on a reduced instance.

We will see how we can extend this framework to the non-binary case. Our goal here is to describe the PGE+SS framework for solving $SD(q, R, W)$. Fix $\mathbf{H} \in \mathbb{F}_q^{(n-k) \times n}$ of full rank and $\mathbf{s} \in \mathbb{F}_q^{n-k}$. Recall that we want to find $\mathbf{e} \in \mathbb{F}_q^n$ such that $|\mathbf{e}| = w \overset{\triangle}{=} \lceil Wn \rceil$ and $\mathbf{He^T} = \mathbf{s^T}$. Let us introduce ℓ and p, two parameters of the system, that we will consider fixed for now. In this framework, an algorithm for solving $\mathrm{SD}(q, R, W)$ will consist of 4 steps: a permutation step, a partial Gaussian Elimination step, a Subset Sum step and a test step.

1. *Permutation step.* Pick a random permutation π. Let $\mathbf{H}_\pi$ be the matrix $\mathbf{H}$ where the columns have been permuted according to π. We now want to solve the problem $\mathrm{SD}(q, R, W)$ on inputs $\mathbf{H}_\pi$ and $\mathbf{s}$.

2. *Partial Gaussian Elimination step.* If the top left square submatrix of $\mathbf{H}_\pi$ of size $n - k - \ell$ is not of full rank, go back to step 1 and choose another random permutation π. This happens with constant probability. Else, if this submatrix is of full rank, perform a Gaussian elimination on the rows of $\mathbf{H}_\pi$ using the first $n - k - \ell$ columns. Let $\mathbf{S} \in \mathbb{F}_q^{(n-k) \times (n-k)}$ be the invertible matrix corresponding to this operation. We now have two matrices $\mathbf{H}' \in \mathbb{F}_q^{(n-k-\ell) \times (k+\ell)}$ and $\mathbf{H}'' \in \mathbb{F}_q^{\ell \times (k+\ell)}$ such that:

$$\mathbf{SH}_\pi = \begin{pmatrix} 1_{n-k-\ell} & \mathbf{H}' \\ 0 & \mathbf{H}'' \end{pmatrix}.$$

The error $\mathbf{e}$ can be written as $\mathbf{e} = (\mathbf{e}', \mathbf{e}'')$ where $\mathbf{e}' \in \mathbb{F}_q^{n-k-\ell}$ and $\mathbf{e}'' \in \mathbb{F}_q^{k+\ell}$, and one can write $\mathbf{sS}^\mathsf{T} = (\mathbf{s}', \mathbf{s}'')$ with $\mathbf{s}' \in \mathbb{F}_q^{n-k-\ell}$ and $\mathbf{s}'' \in \mathbb{F}_q^\ell$.

$$\mathbf{H}_\pi \mathbf{e}^\mathsf{T} = \mathbf{s}^\mathsf{T} \iff \mathbf{SH}_\pi \mathbf{e}^\mathsf{T} = \mathbf{Ss}^\mathsf{T}$$

$$\iff \begin{pmatrix} 1_{n-k-\ell} & \mathbf{H}' \\ 0 & \mathbf{H}'' \end{pmatrix} \begin{pmatrix} \mathbf{e}'^\mathsf{T} \\ \mathbf{e}''^\mathsf{T} \end{pmatrix} = \begin{pmatrix} \mathbf{s}'^\mathsf{T} \\ \mathbf{s}''^\mathsf{T} \end{pmatrix}$$

$$\iff \begin{cases} \mathbf{e}'^\mathsf{T} + \mathbf{H}' \mathbf{e}''^\mathsf{T} = \mathbf{s}'^\mathsf{T} \\ \mathbf{H}'' \mathbf{e}''^\mathsf{T} = \mathbf{s}''^\mathsf{T} \end{cases} \tag{1}$$

To solve the problem, we will try to find a solution $(\mathbf{e}', \mathbf{e}'')$ to the above system such that $|\mathbf{e}''| = p$ and $|\mathbf{e}'| = w - p$.

3. *The Subset Sum step.* Compute a set $\mathcal{S} \subseteq \mathbb{F}_q^{k+\ell}$ of solutions $\mathbf{e}''$ of $\mathbf{H}'' \mathbf{e}''^\mathsf{T} = \mathbf{s}''^\mathsf{T}$ such that $|\mathbf{e}''| = p$. We will solve this problem by considering it as a Subset Sum problem as it is described in Subsect. 2.4.

4. *The test step.* Take a vector $\mathbf{e}'' \in \mathcal{S}$ and let $\mathbf{e}'^\mathsf{T} = \mathbf{s}'^\mathsf{T} - \mathbf{H}' \mathbf{e}''^\mathsf{T}$. Equation (1) ensures that $\mathbf{H}_\pi (\mathbf{e}', \mathbf{e}'')^\mathsf{T} = \mathbf{s}^\mathsf{T}$. If $|\mathbf{e}'| = w - p, \mathbf{e} = (\mathbf{e}', \mathbf{e}'')$ is a solution of $\mathrm{SD}(q, R, W)$ on inputs $\mathbf{H}_\pi$ and $\mathbf{s}$, which can be turned into a solution of the initial problem by permuting the indices, as detailed in Eq. (2). Else, try again for other values of $\mathbf{e}'' \in \mathcal{S}$. If no element of $\mathcal{S}$ gives a valid solution, go back to step 1.

At the end of protocol, we have a vector $\mathbf{e}$ such that $\mathbf{H}_\pi \mathbf{e}^\mathsf{T} = \mathbf{s}^\mathsf{T}$ and $|\mathbf{e}| = w$. Let $\mathbf{e}_{\pi^{-1}}$ be the vector $\mathbf{e}$ where we permute all the coordinates according to π^{-1}. Hence,

$$\mathbf{He}_{\pi^{-1}}^\mathsf{T} = \mathbf{H}_\pi \mathbf{e}^\mathsf{T} = \mathbf{s}^\mathsf{T} \quad \text{and} \quad |\mathbf{e}_{\pi^{-1}}| = |\mathbf{e}| = w. \tag{2}$$

Therefore, $\mathbf{e}_{\pi^{-1}}$ is a solution to the problem.

2.3   Analysis of the Algorithm

In order to analyse this algorithm, we rely on the following two propositions.

Notation 1. *An important quantity to understand the complexity of this algorithm is the probability of success at step 4. On an input $(\mathbf{H}, \mathbf{s})$ uniformly drawn at random, suppose that we have a solution to the Subset Sum problem, i.e. a vector $\mathbf{e}''$ such that $\mathbf{H}''\mathbf{e}''^{\mathsf{T}} = \mathbf{s}''^{\mathsf{T}}$ and $|\mathbf{e}''| = p$. Let $\mathbf{e}'^{\mathsf{T}} = \mathbf{s}'^{\mathsf{T}} - \mathbf{H}'\mathbf{e}''^{\mathsf{T}}$. We will denote:*

$$\mathcal{P}_{p,\ell} \triangleq \mathbb{P}\left(|\mathbf{e}'| = w - p \mid |\mathbf{e}''| = p\right).$$

Proposition 2. *We have, up to a polynomial factor,*

$$\mathcal{P}_{p,\ell} = \frac{\binom{n-k-\ell}{w-p}(q-1)^{w-p}}{\min\left(q^{n-k-\ell}, \binom{n}{w}(q-1)^{w}q^{-\ell}\right)}.$$

Proof. The proof of this statement is simple combinatorics. The numerator corresponds to the number of vectors $\mathbf{e}'$ of weight $w - p$. The denominator corresponds to the inverse of the probability that $\mathbf{e}'^{\mathsf{T}} = \mathbf{s}'^{\mathsf{T}} - \mathbf{H}'\mathbf{e}''^{\mathsf{T}}$. For a typical random behavior, this is equal to $q^{n-k-\ell}$. But here we know that there is at least one solution. Therefore, we know that the number of vectors of weight $w - p$ is bounded from above by the number of vectors $\mathbf{e}$ such that $\mathbf{H}''\mathbf{e}''^{\mathsf{T}} = \mathbf{s}''^{\mathsf{T}}$. This explains the second term of the minimum.   □

Proposition 3. *Assume that we have an algorithm that finds a set $\mathcal{S}$ of solutions of the Subset Sum problem in time T. The average running time of the algorithm is, up to a polynomial factor,*

$$T \cdot \max\left(1, \frac{1}{|\mathcal{S}| \cdot \mathcal{P}_{p,\ell}}\right).$$

As we can see, all the parameters are entwined. The success probability $\mathcal{P}_{p,\ell}$ depends of p and ℓ, as well as the time T to find the set $\mathcal{S}$ of solutions.

In this work, we will focus on a family of parameters useful in the analysis of the Wave signature scheme [DST18]. More precisely, we will study the following regime:

$$q = 3; \quad R \in [0.5, 0.9]; \quad W \in [0.9, 0.99].$$

One consequence of working with a very high relative weight W is that our best algorithms will work with:

$$\ell = \Theta(n); \quad p = k + \ell. \tag{3}$$

Here, ℓ is $\Theta(n)$ for the following reason: if $\ell = o(n)$ then it is readily verified that, asymptotically in n, the average running time of the PGE+SS framework will be bounded from below (up to a polynomial factor) by $1/\mathcal{P}_{p,0}$. This exactly corresponds to the complexity of the simplest generic algorithm to solve SD, namely Prange's ISD algorithm [Pra62].

2.4   Reduction to the Subset Sum Problem

In step 3 of the PGE+SS framework, we have a matrix $\mathbf{H}'' \in \mathbb{F}_q^{\ell \times (k+\ell)}$, a vector $\mathbf{s}'' \in \mathbb{F}_q^{\ell}$ and we want to compute a set $\mathcal{S} \subseteq \mathbb{F}_q^{k+\ell}$ of solutions $\mathbf{e}''$ of $\mathbf{H}''\mathbf{e}''^{\mathsf{T}} = \mathbf{s}''^{\mathsf{T}}$ such that $|\mathbf{e}''| = p$. At first sight, this looks exactly like a Syndrome Decoding problem with inputs $\mathbf{H}''$ and $\mathbf{s}''$ so we could just recursively apply the best SD algorithm on this subinstance. But the main difference is that, in this case, we want to find many solutions to the problem and not just one. One possibility to solve this problem is to reduce it to the Subset Sum problem on vectors in $\mathbb{F}_q^{\ell}$.

Problem 2. [Subset Sum problem - $\mathrm{SS}(q, n, m, L, p)$]

Instance: n vectors $\mathbf{x}_i \in \mathbb{F}_q^m$ for $1 \leq i \leq n$, a target vector $\mathbf{s} \in \mathbb{F}_q^m$.
  Output: L solutions $\mathbf{b}^{(j)} = (b_1^{(j)}, \ldots, b_n^{(j)}) \in \{0,1\}^n$ for $1 \leq j \leq L$,
     such that for all j, $\sum_{i=1}^n b_i^{(j)} \mathbf{x}_i = \mathbf{s}$ and $|\mathbf{b}^{(j)}| = p$.

We can consider the same problem with elements b in $\mathbb{F}_q$ instead of $\{0,1\}$.

Problem 3. [Subset Sum with non-zero characteristic - $\mathrm{SSNZC}(q, n, m, L, p)$]

Instance: n vectors $\mathbf{x}_i \in \mathbb{F}_q^m$ for $1 \leq i \leq n$, a target vector $\mathbf{s} \in \mathbb{F}_q^m$.
  Output: L solutions $\mathbf{b}^{(j)} = (b_1^{(j)}, \ldots, b_n^{(j)}) \in \mathbb{F}_q^n$ for $1 \leq j \leq L$,
     such that for all j, $\sum_{i=1}^n b_i^{(j)} \mathbf{x}_i = \mathbf{s}$ and $|\mathbf{b}^{(j)}| = p$.

Notation 2. *We will denote* $\mathrm{SS}(q, n, m, L, \emptyset)$ *(resp.* SSNZC*) the* SS *problem (resp.* SSNZC *problem) without any constraint on the weight.*

Again, we will be interested in the average case, where all the inputs are taken uniformly at random. Notice that the problem that needs to be solved at step 3 of the PGE+SS framework reduces exactly to $\mathrm{SSNZC}(q, k + \ell, \ell, |\mathcal{S}|, p)$.

There is an extensive literature [HJ10, BCJ11] about the Subset Sum problem for specific parameter ranges, typically when $L = 1, q = 2, n = m$ and $p = \frac{m}{2}$. This is the hardest case where there is on average a single solution. There are several regimes of parameters, each of which lead to different algorithms. For instance, when $m = O(n^\varepsilon)$ for $\varepsilon < 1$, there are many solutions on average and we are in the high density setting for which we have sub-exponential algorithm [Lyu05]. Table 2 summarizes the complexity of algorithms to solve the Subset Sum problem for some different regimes of parameters when only one solution is required ($L = 1$) and for $q = 2$.

In our case, m will be a small, but constant, fraction of n, which leads to multiple solutions but exponentially complex algorithms to find them. We will be in a moderate density situation. Furthermore, the case $L = 1$ and $L \gg 1$ require quite different algorithms. When $q = 2$, authors of [BJMM12] show how to optimize this whole approach to solve the original Syndrome Decoding problem using better algorithms for the Subset Sum problem.

Table 2. Complexity of best known algorithms to solve $SS(2, n, m, 1, \emptyset)$.

Value of m	Complexity	Reference
$O(\log(n))$	$\text{poly}(n)$	[GM91, CFG89]
$O(\log(n)^2)$	$\text{poly}(n)$	[FP05]
$O(n^\varepsilon)$ for $\varepsilon < 1$	$2^{O\left(\frac{n^\varepsilon}{\log(n)}\right)}$	[Lyu05]
n	$2^{O(n)}$	[HJ10, BCJ11]

2.5 Application to the PGE+SS Framework with High Weight

There are quite a lot of interesting regimes that could be studied with this approach and have not been studied yet. Indeed, very few papers tackle the case $q \geq 3$ and they only cover a small fraction of the possible parameters. In this work we focus on the problem $SSNZC(3, k+\ell, \ell, |\mathcal{S}|, k+\ell)$ given by the PGE+SS framework for high weights in $\mathbb{F}_3$. The choice of $p = k + \ell$ for large weights is explained in Eq. (3). This is quite convenient because this problem is actually equivalent to solving $SS(3, k + \ell, \ell, |\mathcal{S}|, \emptyset)$ as shown by the following lemma.

Lemma 1. *If we have an algorithm that solves $SS(3, k+\ell, \ell, |\mathcal{S}|, \emptyset)$ then we have an algorithm that solves $SSNZC(3, k + \ell, \ell, |\mathcal{S}|, k + \ell)$ with the same complexity.*

Proof. Let $\mathcal{A}$ be an algorithm that solves $SS(3, k + \ell, \ell, |\mathcal{S}|, \emptyset)$ and consider an instance $(\mathbf{x}_1, \ldots, \mathbf{x}_{k+\ell}), \mathbf{s}$ of $SSNZC(3, k + \ell, \ell, |\mathcal{S}|, k + \ell)$. We want to find $b_1, \ldots, b_{k+\ell} \in \{1, 2\}$ (see $\mathbb{F}_3 = \{0, 1, 2\}$) such that $\sum_{i=1}^{k+\ell} b_i \mathbf{x}_i = \mathbf{s}$. Let $\mathbf{s}' = 2\mathbf{s} + \sum_i \mathbf{x}_i$ and let us run $\mathcal{A}$ on input $(\mathbf{x}_1, \ldots, \mathbf{x}_{k+\ell}), \mathbf{s}'$. We obtain $b_1', \ldots, b_{k+\ell}' \in \{0, 1\}$ such that $\sum_{i=1}^{k+\ell} b_i' \mathbf{x}_i = \mathbf{s}'$. Take $b_i = \frac{b_i' - 1}{2}$ for $1 \leq i \leq k + \ell$, where the division is done in $\mathbb{F}_3$ and return $(b_1, \ldots, b_{k+\ell})$.

Indeed, this gives a valid solution to the problem: the elements b_i belong to $\{1, 2\}$ and we have:

$$\sum_{i=1}^{k+\ell} b_i \mathbf{x}_i = \sum_{i=1}^{k+\ell} \frac{b_i' - 1}{2} \mathbf{x}_i = \frac{\mathbf{s}'}{2} - \frac{\sum_{i=1}^{k+\ell} \mathbf{x}_i}{2} = \mathbf{s}.$$

$\square$

Hence, in the context of the PGE+SS framework for solving SD with high weights, it is enough to solve $SS(3, k + \ell, \ell, |\mathcal{S}|, \emptyset)$. However, as explained at the end of Subsect. 2.2, we will have to choose $\ell = \Theta(n) = \Theta(k)$ (because $k = \lceil Rn \rceil$). Therefore, we are in a regime where solving the Subset Sum problem requires exponential complexity, as explained in the previous subsection. However, as we will see in the next session, we will be able to choose ℓ as a small fraction of k. In this case, generic algorithms as Wagner's [Wag02] perform exponentially better compared to Prange's algorithm [Pra62] (case $\ell = 0$) or Subset Sum algorithms [BCJ11] (case $\ell = n - k$).

3 Ternary Subset Sum with the Generalized Birthday Algorithm

We show in this section how to solve $SS(3, k + \ell, \ell, L, \emptyset)$, first with Wagner's algorithm [Wag02]. Parameters k and ℓ will be free. We will focus on the values L for which we can find L solutions to $SS(3, k + \ell, \ell, L, \emptyset)$ in time $O(L)$. In such a case, we say that we can find solutions in *amortized time* $O(1)$.

3.1 A Brief Description of Wagner's Algorithm

Recall that we are here in the context of the Subset Sum step of the PGE+SS framework described in Subsect. 2.2. Given $k + \ell$ vectors $\mathbf{x}_1, \cdots, \mathbf{x}_{k+\ell} \in \mathbb{F}_3^\ell$ (columns of the matrix $\mathbf{H}''$) and a target vector $\mathbf{s} \in \mathbb{F}_3^\ell$, our goal is to find L solutions of the form $\mathbf{b}^{(j)} = (b_1^{(j)}, \cdots, b_{k+\ell}^{(j)}) \in \{0, 1\}^{k+\ell}$ such that for all $1 \leq j \leq L$,

$$\sum_{i=1}^{k+\ell} b_i^{(j)} \mathbf{x}_i = \mathbf{s}. \tag{4}$$

Here, we are interested in the average case, which means that all the vectors $\mathbf{x}_i$ are independent and follow a uniform law over $\mathbb{F}_3^\ell$. In order to apply Wagner's algorithm [Wag02], let $a \in \mathbb{N}^*$ be some integer parameter. For $i \in [\![1, 2^a]\!]$, denote by $\mathcal{I}_i$ the sets $\mathcal{I}_i \stackrel{\triangle}{=} [\![1 + \frac{(i-1)(k+\ell)}{2^a}, \frac{i(k+\ell)}{2^a}]\!]$. The sets $\mathcal{I}_i$ form a partition of $[\![1, k + \ell]\!]$.

The first step of Wagner's algorithm is to compute 2^a lists $(\mathcal{L}_i)_{1 \leq i \leq 2^a}$ of size L such that:

$$\forall i \in [\![1, 2^a]\!], \ \mathcal{L}_i \subseteq \left\{ \sum_{j \in \mathcal{I}_i} b_j \mathbf{x}_j \ : \ \forall j \in \mathcal{I}_i, \ b_j \in \{0, 1\} \right\} \text{ and } |\mathcal{L}_i| = L. \tag{5}$$

Each list $\mathcal{L}_i$ consists of L random elements of the form $\sum_{j \in \mathcal{I}_i} b_j \mathbf{x}_j$ where the randomness is on $b_j \in \{0, 1\}$. By construction, we make sure that given $\mathbf{y} \in \mathcal{L}_i$ we have access to the coefficients $(b_j)_{j \in \mathcal{I}_i}$ such that $\mathbf{y} = \sum_{j \in \mathcal{I}_i} b_j \mathbf{x}_j$. In other words, we have divided the vectors $\mathbf{x}_1, \ldots, \mathbf{x}_{k+\ell}$ in 2^a stacks of $(k + \ell)/2^a$ vectors and for each stack we have computed a list of L random linear combinations of the vectors in the stack. The running time to build theses lists is $O(L)$. Once we have computed these lists we can use the main idea of Wagner to solve (4). In our case we would like to find solutions in amortized time $O(1)$. For this, Wagner's algorithm requires the lists $\mathcal{L}_i$ to be all of the same size:

$$\forall i \in [\![1, 2^a]\!], \ |\mathcal{L}_i| = L = 3^{\ell/a}.$$

This gives a first constraint on the parameters k, ℓ and a, namely:

$$3^{\ell/a} \leq 2^{(k+\ell)/2^a} \quad \text{(number of vectors } \mathbf{b}^{(j)} \text{ in each stack)}.$$

which puts a constraint on a since k, ℓ are fixed. With these lists at hand, Wagner's idea is to merge the lists in the following way. For every $p \in \{1, 3, \cdots, 2^a - 3\}$, create a list $\mathcal{L}_{p,p+1}$ from $\mathcal{L}_p$ and $\mathcal{L}_{p+1}$ such that:

$$\mathcal{L}_{p,p+1} \overset{\triangle}{=} \{\mathbf{y}_p + \mathbf{y}_{p+1} : \mathbf{y}_i \in \mathcal{L}_i \text{ and the last } \ell/a \text{ bits of } \mathbf{y}_p + \mathbf{y}_{p+1} \text{ are 0s.}\}.$$

A list $\mathcal{L}_{2^a-1,2^a}$ is created from $\mathcal{L}_{2^a-1}$ and $\mathcal{L}_{2^a}$ in the same way except that the last ℓ/a bits have to be equal to those of $\mathbf{s}$. As the elements of the lists $\mathcal{L}_p$ are drawn uniformly at random in $\mathbb{F}_3^\ell$, it is easily verified that by merging them on ℓ/a bits, the new lists $\mathcal{L}_{p,p+1}$ are typically of size $|\mathcal{L}_i|^2/3^{\ell/a} = (3^{\ell/a})^2/3^{\ell/a} = 3^{\ell/a}$. Therefore, the cost in time and in space of such a merging (by using classical techniques such as hash tables or sorted lists) will be $O(3^{\ell/a})$ on average. This way, we obtain 2^{a-1} lists of size L. It is readily seen that we can repeat this process $a - 1$ times, with each time a cost of $O(3^{\ell/a})$ for merging on ℓ/a new bits. After a steps, we obtain a list of solutions to the Eq. (4) containing $L = 3^{\ell/a}$ elements on average.

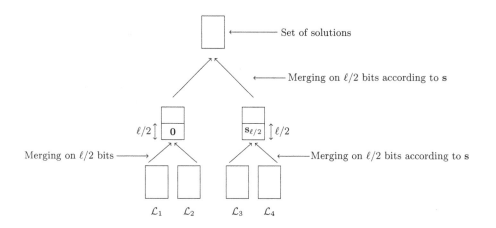

Fig. 2. Wagner's algorithm with $a = 2$.

Let us summarize the previous discussion with the following theorem.

Theorem 1. *Fix $k, \ell \in \mathbb{N}^*$ and let a be any non zero integer such that*

$$3^{\ell/a} \leq 2^{(k+\ell)/2^a}.$$

The associated $SS(3, k + \ell, \ell, 3^{\ell/a}, \emptyset)$ problem can be solved in average time and space $O(3^{\ell/a})$.

This theorem indicates for which value L it is possible to find L solutions in time $O(L)$ using Wagner's approach.

3.2   Smoothing of Wagner's Algorithm

Wagner's algorithm as stated above shows how to find L solutions in amortized time $O(1)$ for $L = 3^{\ell/a}$. If we want more than L solutions, we can repeat this algorithm and find all those solutions also in amortized time $O(1)$. So the smaller L is, the better the algorithm performs. So the idea is to take the largest integer a such that $3^{\ell/a} < 2^{(k+\ell)/2^a}$ and take $L = 3^{\ell/a}$, as explained in Theorem 1. But this induces a discontinuity in the optimal value of L and on the complexity: when the input parameters change continuously, the optimal value of a (which has to be an integer) evolves discontinuously, therefore the slope of the complexity curve is discontinuous, as we can see on Figs. 8 and 9. We show here a refinement of Theorem 1 that reduces the discontinuity.

Proposition 4. *Let a be the largest integer such that $3^{\ell/(a-1)} < 2^{(k+\ell)/2^{a-1}}$. If $a \geq 3$, the above algorithm can find 2^λ solutions in time $O(2^\lambda)$ with*

$$\lambda = \frac{\ell \log(3)}{a-2} - \frac{k+\ell}{(a-2)2^{a-1}}.$$

We see that we retrieve the result of Theorem 1 when $3^{\ell/a} = 2^{(k+\ell)/2^a}$. We have not found any statement of this form in the literature, which is surprising because Wagner's algorithm has a variety of applications. We now prove the proposition.

Proof. Parameters k and ℓ are fixed. Let a be the largest integer such that $3^{\ell/(a-1)} < 2^{(k+\ell)/2^{a-1}}$ and we suppose that $a \geq 3$. We will consider Wagner's algorithm on a levels but the merging at the bottom of the tree will be performed with a lighter constraint: we want the sums to agree on less than ℓ/a bits. Indeed, we consider the following list sizes. At the bottom of the trees, we take lists of size $2^{\frac{k+\ell}{2^a}}$ (the maximal possible size); at all other levels, we want lists of size 2^λ. We run Wagner's algorithm by firstly merging on m bits. In order to obtain lists of size 2^λ at the second step, we have to choose m such that

$$\frac{\left(2^{(k+\ell)/2^a}\right)^2}{3^m} = 2^\lambda \quad i.e. \quad \frac{2(k+\ell)}{2^a} - m\log_2(3) = \lambda. \tag{6}$$

The other $(a-1)$ merging steps are designed such that merging two lists of size 2^λ gives a new list of size 2^λ, which means that we merge on $\lambda/\log_2(3)$ bits. However, in the final list we want to obtain solutions to the problem, which means that in total we have to put a constraint on all bits. Therefore, λ and m have to verify:

$$m + (a-1)\frac{\lambda}{\log_2(3)} = \ell. \tag{7}$$

By combining Eqs. (6) and (7) we get:

$$\lambda = \frac{\ell \log_2(3)}{a-2} - \frac{k+\ell}{(a-2)2^{a-1}}.$$

It is easy to check that under the conditions $3^{\ell/(a-1)} < 2^{(k+\ell)/2^{a-1}}$ and $a \geq 3, \lambda$ and m are positive which concludes the proof. $\qquad\square$

4 Ternary Subset Sum Using Representations

4.1 Basic Idea

In the list tree of Wagner's algorithm (see Fig. 2), we split each list in two, according to what is called the *left-right* procedure. This means that if we start from a set $S = \{\sum_{j \in [\![A,B]\!]} b_j \mathbf{x}_j : |b_j| = p\}$, we decompose each element of $\mathbf{y} \in S$ as $\mathbf{y} = \mathbf{y}_1 + \mathbf{y}_2$ where $\mathbf{y}_1 \in S_1$ and $\mathbf{y}_2 \in S_2$, where

$$S_1 \triangleq \left\{ \sum_{j \in [\![A, \lfloor \frac{B+A}{2} \rfloor]\!]} b_j \mathbf{x}_j : b_j \in \{0,1\}, \ |\mathbf{b}| = p/2 \right\}$$

$$S_2 \triangleq \left\{ \sum_{j \in [\![\lfloor \frac{B+A}{2} \rfloor +1, B]\!]} b_j \mathbf{x}_j : b_j \in \{0,1\}, \ |\mathbf{b}| = p/2 \right\}.$$

Such a decomposition does not always exist, but it exists with probability at least $\frac{1}{p}$. Indeed, the probability that a vector of weight p can be split this way is

$$\frac{\binom{n/2}{p/2}^2}{\binom{n}{p}} \geq \frac{1}{p}.$$

Wagner's algorithm uses this principle. When looking for vectors $\mathbf{b}$ containing the same number of 0's and 1's, it looks for $\mathbf{b}$ in the form $\mathbf{b} = \mathbf{b}_1 + \mathbf{b}_2$, where the second half of $\mathbf{b}_1$ and the first half of $\mathbf{b}_2$ are only zeros. The first half of $\mathbf{b}_1$ and the second half of $\mathbf{b}_2$ are expected to have the same number of 0s and 1s.

The idea of representations is to follow Wagner's approach of list merging while allowing more possibilities to write $\mathbf{b}$ as the sum of two vectors $\mathbf{b} = \mathbf{b}_1 + \mathbf{b}_2$. We remove the constraint that $\mathbf{b}_1$ has zeros on its right half and $\mathbf{b}_2$ has zeros on its left half. We replace it by a less restrictive constraint: we fix the number of 0s, 1s and 2s (see $\mathbb{F}_3 = \{0,1,2\}$) in $\mathbf{b}_1$ and $\mathbf{b}_2$.

More precisely, we consider the set

$$S' = \left\{ \sum_{j \in [\![A,B]\!]} b_j \mathbf{x}_j : b_j \in \mathbb{F}_3, \ |\{b_j = 1\}| = p_1 \text{ and } |\{b_j = 2\}| = p_2 \right\} \tag{8}$$

for some weights p_1 and p_2 and we want to decompose each $\mathbf{y}$ into $\mathbf{y}_1 + \mathbf{y}_2$ such that $\mathbf{y}_1, \mathbf{y}_2 \in S'$. On the example of Fig. 3, we have $p = 4, p_1 = 3$ and $p_2 = 1$.

At first sight, this approach may seem unusual. Indeed, except for very specific values of p_1 and p_2, the sum $\mathbf{y}_1 + \mathbf{y}_2$ will rarely match the desired weight p to be in S. Such a sum $\mathbf{y}_1 + \mathbf{y}_2$, which matches the targeted bits for merging but not the weight constraint, will be called *badly-formed*. Those *badly-formed* sums cannot be used for the remaining of the algorithm and must be discarded. However, the positive aspect is that each element $\mathbf{y} \in S$ accepts many decompositions (the so-called *representations*) $\mathbf{y}_1 + \mathbf{y}_2$ where $\mathbf{y}_1, \mathbf{y}_2 \in S'$. The results

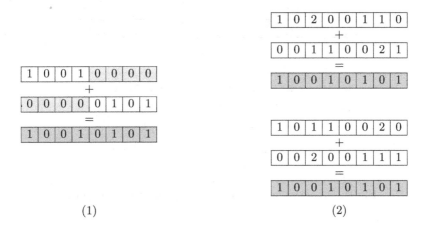

(1) (2)

Fig. 3. Same vector (1) using left-right split and (2) using representations.

from [HJ10, BCJ11, BJMM12] show that this large number of ways to represent each element can compensate the fact that most decompositions do not belong to S. One can slightly lower the number of agreement bits when merging the lists, in order to obtain on average the desired number of elements in the merged list.

Notice that in this definition of S', the elements b_j belong to the set $\mathbb{F}_3$ and not $\{0, 1\}$, even though we want to obtain a binary solution. The ternary structure also increases the number of representations as shown in Fig. 3. It is actually natural to consider representations of binary strings using three elements $\{0, 1, 2\}$, as in [BCJ11].

4.2 Partial Representations

If we relieve too many constraints and allow too many representations of a solution, it may happen that we end up with multiple copies of the same solution. In order to avoid this situation, we use *partial representations*, which is an intermediate approach between *left-right* splitting and using *representations*, as illustrated in Fig. 4.

4.3 Presentation of Our Algorithm

Plugging representations in Wagner's algorithm can be done in a variety of ways. The way we achieved our best algorithm was mostly done by trial and error. We present here the main features of our algorithm.

- In the regime we consider, the number of floors a varies from 5 to 7. Notice that this is quite larger than in other similar algorithms and is mostly due to the fact that we have many solutions to our Subset Sum problem.

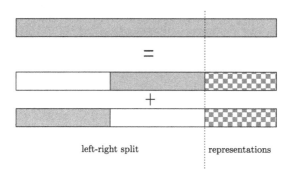

Fig. 4. Decomposing a vector using partial representations.

- Because we want to find many solutions, representations become less efficient. Indeed, the fact that we obtain many *badly-formed* elements makes it harder to find solutions in amortized time $O(1)$ (or even just in small time).
- However, we show that representations can still be useful. For most parameters, the optimal algorithm consists of a left-right split at the bottom level of the tree, then 2 layers of partial representation and from there to the top level, left-right splits again.

Figure 5 illustrates an example for $a = 7$. When we increase the number of floors, we just add some left-right splits.

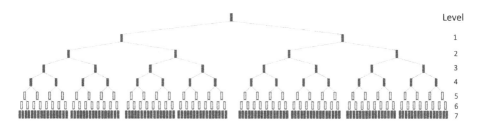

Fig. 5. Wagner tree for $a = 7$. Yellow list correspond to representations and blue list to left-right splits. (Color figure online)

In the next section, we present the different parameters for a particular input to show how our algorithm behaves.

4.4   Application to the Syndrome Decoding Problem

We embedded in the PGE+SS framework the three above-described algorithms, namely the classical Wagner algorithm, the smoothed one in Sect. 3 and the one using the representation technique in Sect. 4. By using Proposition 2, we derived the exponents given in Figs. 8 and 9.

We present here the details of our algorithm for the $SD(3, R, W)$ with $R = 0.676$ and $W = 0.948366$. These are the parameters which are used for the analysis of Wave. For this set of parameters, we claim that the complexity of our algorithm is $2^{0.0176n}$. In the PGE+SS framework (see Sect. 2.2), we needed to choose to parameters p and ℓ. We take $\ell = 0.060835n$ and $p = k + \ell$.

The best algorithm we found uses $a = 7$, which means that the associated Wagner tree has 7 levels, and therefore 128 leaves (Fig. 5). From level 0 to level 6, the lists have size $L = 2^{0.0176}$ (*i.e.* equal to the overall complexity of the Subset Sum problem). As we have more than the required number of solutions for 6 levels, but not enough for 7 levels, we use the smoothing method described in Sect. 3.2, which gives a size of the leaves equal to $2^{0.01039}$.

We present below in more detail how we construct the different lists of the Wagner tree.

- Levels 1 to 4 consist of left-right splits. For instance, at level 4, we have 16 lists

$$\forall i \in [\![1, 16]\!], \; \mathcal{L}_i \subseteq \left\{ \sum_{j \in \mathcal{I}_i} b_j \mathbf{x}_j \; : \; \forall j \in \mathcal{I}_i, \; b_j \in \{0, 1\} \right\} \text{ and } |\mathcal{L}_i| = L.$$

with $\mathcal{I}_i \overset{\triangle}{=} [\![1 + \frac{(i-1)(k+\ell)}{16}, \frac{i(k+\ell)}{16}]\!]$.
- In levels 5 and 6, we use partial representations. Going from level 4 to level 5, on a proportion $\lambda_1 = 0.7252$ of the vector, we use representations for level 5 and left-right split for level 6. On the remaining fraction of the vector, we use representations on both levels. More precisely, for each interval $\mathcal{I}_i$, we split it in 2 according to Fig. 6. For each part, we use Eq. 8 with the following densities:
  - for the part with only one level of representations, ρ_1 consists on 74.8% of 0s, 25.1% of 1s and 0.1% of 2s;
  - for the part with two levels of representations, we have ρ_2, composed of 74.2% of 0s, 25.4% of 1s and 0.4% of 2s for level 5, and ρ_3 composed of 86.9% of 0s, 13.1% of 1s and 0.0% of 2s for level 6.
- In order to construct level 7, we start from each list of level 6 and perform again a left-right split.

The choice of the densities and all the calculi related to the representations can be quite complicated. We perform a full analysis in Appendix A, see in particular Proposition 5.

As explained in Sect. 4.1, most of the elements we build at floors 5 and 4 are *badly-formed* and do not match the desired densities of 0s, 1s and 2s. We only keep the well-formed elements and lower the number of bits on which we merge, so that the merged lists have again L elements. In our case, as the expected number of well-formed elements in level-4 lists is $2^{0.0116n}$, we merge on $2^{0.0055n}$ bits to compute the level-3 lists (instead of $2^{0.0176n}$ bits.) Similarly, we merge on $2^{0.0173n}$ bits to compute the level-4 lists because level-5 lists have $2^{0.0174n}$ well-formed elements. This is represented in Fig. 7.

Level

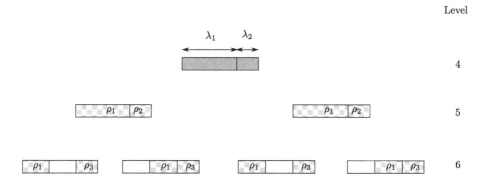

Fig. 6. Detail of the floors where we use partial representations.

Finally, level 7 is a left-right split with smaller lists (because of the smoothing). The leaves have size $2^{0.01039n}$, so we merge on $2^{0.0032n}$ bits to build the level-6 lists.

The numbers of well-formed elements per list are thus (from level 0 to level 7):

$$2^{0.0176n}, 2^{0.0176n}, 2^{0.0176n}, 2^{0.0176n}, 2^{0.0116n}, 2^{0.0174n}, 2^{0.0176n}, 2^{0.01039n},$$

and the numbers of bits we merge on:

$$2^{0.0176n}, 2^{0.0176n}, 2^{0.0176n}, 2^{0.0055n}, 2^{0.0173n}, 2^{0.0176n}, 2^{0.0032n}.$$

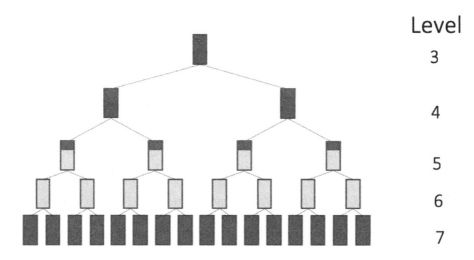

Level

3

4

5

6

7

Fig. 7. Detail of the bottom floors. Red elements are badly-formed elements. (Color figure online)

One can check that we merge on a total of $2^{0.0964n}$ bits, which is exactly equal to $2^{\ell \log_2(3)}$, meaning that the level-0 list is entirely composed of solutions of the Subset Sum problem.

One can also check that the Subset Sum problem has $2^{\ell+k-\ell \log_2(3)} = 2^{0.6404n}$ solutions, that one solution has $2^{0.4915n}$ representations (see Appendix A), and that the merging constraints waste $2^{1.1143n}$ solution representations. We are thus left with $2^{0.0176n}$ solutions, which are exactly the solutions we get on the level-0 list.

4.5 Summary of Our Results

We present here 2 plots that illustrate the performance of our different algorithms. What we show is that, in this parameter range, the gain obtained by using representations is relatively small. This is quite surprising because, in the binary case, representations are very efficient. One explanation we have is that, in a regime where there are naturally many solutions, Wagner's algorithm is very efficient while the representation technique has difficulties in finding solutions in amortized time $O(1)$. In Sect. 6, we study the hardest instances, and show that representations turn out to be more efficient.

5 New Parameters for the WAVE Signature Scheme

Wave is a new code-based signature scheme proposed in [DST18]. It uses a *hash-and-sign* approach and follows the GPV paradigm [GPV08] with the instantiation of a code-based preimage sampleable family of functions.

Forging a signature in the Wave scheme amounts to solving the SD problem. Roughly speaking, the public key is a specific pseudo-random parity-check matrix $\mathbf{H}$ of size $(n-k) \times n$ and the signature of a message $\mathbf{m}$ is an error $\mathbf{e}$ of weight w such that $\mathbf{e}\mathbf{H}^\mathsf{T} = h(\mathbf{m})$ with h a hash function. However, instead of trying to forge a signature for one message of our choice, a natural idea is to try to forge one message among a selected set of messages. This context leads directly to a slight variation of the classical SD problem. Instead of having one syndrome, there is a list of possible syndromes and the goal is to decode one of them. This problem is known as the *Decoding One Out of Many* (DOOM) problem.

Problem 4. [Decoding One Out of Many - $\text{DOOM}(n, z, q, R, W)$]

Instance: $\mathbf{H} \in \mathbb{F}_q^{(n-k) \times n}$ of full rank,
$\quad\quad\quad \mathbf{s}_1, \cdots, \mathbf{s}_z \in \mathbb{F}_q^{n-k}$.

Output: $\mathbf{e} \in \mathbb{F}_q^n$ and $i \in [\![1, z]\!]$ such that $|\mathbf{e}| = w$ and $\mathbf{e}\mathbf{H}^\mathsf{T} = \mathbf{s}_i$,

where $k \overset{\triangle}{=} \lceil Rn \rceil$, $w \overset{\triangle}{=} \lceil Wn \rceil$ and $|\mathbf{e}| \overset{\triangle}{=} |\{i : \mathbf{e}_i \neq 0\}|$.

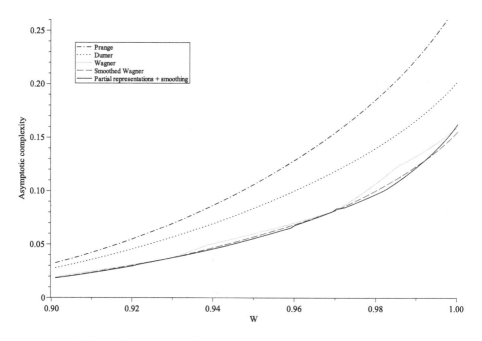

Fig. 8. Comparison of the exponent complexities for $R = 0.5$

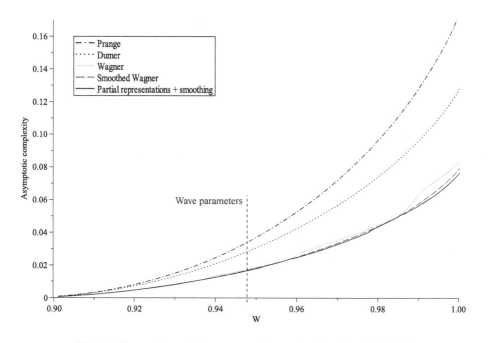

Fig. 9. Comparison of the exponent complexities for $R = 0.676$

This problem was first considered in [JJ02] and later analyzed for the binary case ($q = 2$) in [Sen11, DST17]. These papers show that one can solve the DOOM problem with an exponential speed-up compared to the SD problem with equivalent parameters.

The difference induced by DOOM on the PGE+SS framework is that it increases the search space. Namely, instead of searching a solution $\mathbf{e}$ of weight w in the space $\{\mathbf{e} : \mathbf{e}\mathbf{H}^{\mathsf{T}} = \mathbf{s}\}$ we search in $\cup_{i=1}^{z} \{\mathbf{e} : \mathbf{e}\mathbf{H}^{\mathsf{T}} = \mathbf{s}_i\}$.

The idea to solve this problem with Wagner's approach is to take $z \geq 3^{\ell/a}$ and replace the bottom-right list of the tree $\mathcal{L}_{2^a}$ by a list containing all the syndromes. Hence, there are only $2^a - 1$ lists to generate from the search space. Therefore, the constraint of Theorem 1 becomes

$$3^{\ell/a} \leq 2^{(k+\ell)/(2^a-1)}.$$

For the practical parameters, we have $a = 6$ or $a = 7$ so the change from 2^a to $2^a - 1$ has a negligible impact when we adapt the representation technique to the DOOM problem.

The DOOM parameters stated in [DST18] are derived from the complexity of a key attack detailed in the Wave paper. Our result stated in Sect. 4.4 provides another attack to consider. We computed the minimal parameters for the Wave scheme so that both attacks would have a time complexity of at least 2^{128}. They are stated in Table 3 where n is the length of code used in Wave, k its dimension and w the weight of the signature. These should be considered as the new parameters to use for the Wave scheme.

Table 3. New parameters of the Wave signature scheme for 128 bits of security.

(n, k, w)	Public key size (in MB)	Signature length (in kB)
$(7236, 4892, 6862)$	2.27	1.434

6   Hardest Instances of Ternary Syndrome Decoding

In the previous sections, we tried to optimize our algorithms for the regime of parameters used in the Wave signature scheme. The corresponding Syndrome Decoding problem uses $R = 0.676$ and $w \approx 0.948$. This corresponds to a regime where there are many solutions to the problem and hence Wagner's algorithm with a large number of floors was efficient. However, this is not the setting where the problem is the hardest.

We will now look at the hardest instances of the ternary Syndrome Decoding in large weight. As we already pointed out in the introduction, ternary SD is much harder in large weights than in small weights. In the two examples we considered, namely $R = 0.5$ and $R = 0.676$, the problem was the hardest for

$W = 1$. As we will see, there are some lower rates for which the complexity of the Syndrome Decoding problem is maximal for $W < 1$.

Consider an instance $(\mathbf{H}, \mathbf{s})$ of SD$(3, R, W)$ with $W \geq \frac{2}{3}$. We have $\mathbf{H} \in \mathbb{F}_3^{(n-k) \times n}$ of full rank and $\mathbf{s} \in \mathbb{F}_3^{n-k}$. As in the binary case, the problem is the hardest when it has a unique solution on average, if such a regime exists.

Let $R_{\max} \triangleq \frac{\log_2(3) - 1}{\log_2(3)} \approx 0.36907$. For $R \in [0, R_{\max}]$, we define $W_{\mathrm{GV}}^{\mathrm{high}}(R)$ as the only value in $[2/3, 1]$ such that

$$W_{\mathrm{GV}}^{\mathrm{high}}(R) + h_2(W_{\mathrm{GV}}^{\mathrm{high}}(R)) = (1 - R) \log_2(3),$$

where $h_2(x) \triangleq -x \log_2(x) - (1 - x) \log_2(1 - x)$.

The rate $R_{\max}$ was defined such that $W_{\mathrm{GV}}^{high}(R_{\max}) = 1$, while this quantity is not defined for $R > R_{\max}$. This is why Figs. 8 and 9 do not show a high peak for $R = 0.5$ and $R = 0.676$ but an increasing function up to $W = 1$. By Proposition 1, quantity $W_{\mathrm{GV}}^{\mathrm{high}}(R)$ corresponds to the relative weight for which we expect one solution to SD with rate R and $q = 3$.

In order to study the above problem for hard high weight instances, we compared the performance of 3 standard algorithms: Prange's algorithm, Dumer's algorithm and the BJMM algorithm (Table 4).

We performed a case study and showed that, for all the above-mentioned algorithms, the hardest case is reached for $R = R_{\max} \approx 0.36907$ and $W = 1$. We obtain the following results.

Table 4. Best exponents with associated rates.

Algorithm	$q = 2$	$q = 3$ and $W > 0.5$
Prange	0.121 ($R = 0.454$)	0.369 ($R = 0.369$)
Dumer/Wagner	0.116 ($R = 0.447$)	0.269 ($R = 0.369$)
BJMM/our algorithm	0.102 ($R = 0.427$)	0.247 ($R = 0.369$)

In both the binary and the ternary case, we can see that Prange's algorithm performs very poorly, but that Dumer's algorithm already gives much better results and that BJMM's Subset Sum techniques, using representations, increases the gain. The analysis of Prange and Dumer for $q = 3$ is quite straightforward and follows closely the binary case. For BJMM (*i.e.* Wagner's algorithm with representations), the exponent 0.247 comes from a 2-levels Wagner tree that includes 1 layer of representations. We tried using a larger Wagner trees but this did not give any improvement.

The ternary SD appears significantly harder than its binary counterpart. This was expected to some extent because in the ternary case, the input matrices have elements in $\mathbb{F}_3$ and not $\mathbb{F}_2$, which means that matrices of the same dimension contain more information.

In order to confirm this idea, we define the following metric: what is the smallest input size for which the algorithms need at least 2^{128} operations to decode? We use the value 128, as 128 security bits is a cryptographic standard. The input matrix $\mathbf{H} \in \mathbb{F}_3^{n(1-R) \times n}$ is represented in systematic form. This means that we write

$$\mathbf{H} = \left(\mathbf{1}_{n(1-R)} \ \mathbf{H}' \right).$$

The only relevant part that needs to be specified is $\mathbf{H}'$. This requires $R(1 - R)n^2 \log_2(q)$ bits. We show that, even in this metric, the ternary syndrome decoding problem is much harder, *i.e.* requires 2^{128} operations to decode inputs of much smaller sizes. Our results are summarized in the Table 5 below.

Table 5. Minimum input sizes (in Kbits) for a time complexity of 2^{128}.

Algorithm	$q = 2$	$q = 3$ and $W > 0.5$
Prange	275 ($R = 0.384$)	44 ($R = 0.369$)
Dumer/Wagner	295 ($R = 0.369$)	83 ($R = 0.369$)
BJMM/our algorithm	374 ($R = 0.326$)	99 ($R = 0.369$)

Notice that in this metric, in the binary case, it is worth reducing the rate R, as this reduces the input size. But in the ternary case, we do not observe this behavior, which shows that the problem quickly becomes simpler, as R decreases.

The work we present here is very preliminary but opens many new perspectives. It seems there are many cases in code-based cryptography, from encryption schemes to signatures, where this problem could replace the binary Syndrome Decoding problem to get smaller key sizes.

7 Conclusion

In this work, we stressed a strong difference between the cases $q = 2$ and $q \geq 3$ of the Syndrome Decoding problem. Namely, the symmetry between the small weight and the large weight cases, which occurs in the binary case, is broken for larger values of q. The large weight case of the general Syndrome Decoding problem had never been studied before. We proposed two algorithms to solve the Syndrome Decoding problem in this new regime in the context of the *Partial Gaussian Elimination and Subset Sum* framework. Our first algorithm uses a q-ary version of Wagner's approach to solve the underlying Subset Sum problem. We proposed a second algorithm making use of representations as in the BJMM approach. We studied both algorithms and proposed a first application for cryptographic purposes, namely for the Wave signature scheme. Considering our complexity analysis, we proposed new parameters for this scheme. Furthermore, we showed that the worst case complexity of Syndrome Decoding in large weight is higher than in small weight. This implies that it should be possible to develop new code-based cryptographic schemes using this regime of parameters that reach the same security level with smaller key sizes.

A   Appendix: Ternary Representations

In this section, we explain how to compute the number of representations as well as the number of badly-formed vectors when using ternary representations.

A.1   Notations

The notation $\begin{pmatrix} n \\ k_1, \ldots, k_i \end{pmatrix}$ will denote the multinomial coefficient $\dfrac{n!}{k_1! \ldots k_i!}$, assuming that $n = k_1 + \cdots + k_i$.

Let us denote $g : (n, k_1, k_2) \rightarrow n \log_2(n) - k_1 \log_2(k_1) - k_2 \log_2(k_2) - (n - k_1 - k_2) \log_2(n - k_1 - k_2)$. We have:

$$\begin{pmatrix} n \\ k_1, k_2, n - k_1 - k_2 \end{pmatrix} = \tilde{O}\left(2^{g(n,k_1,k_2)}\right).$$

The function g satisfies:

- $g(n, k_1, k_2) = g(n, k_2, k_1)$,
- $g(n, k_1, k_2) = g(n, k_1, n - k_1 - k_2)$,
- $g(\lambda n, \lambda k_1, \lambda k_2) = \lambda g(n, k_1, k_2)$,
- $g(n, k_1, k_2) = n h_2\left(\frac{k_1 + k_2}{n}\right) + (k_1 + k_2) h_2\left(\frac{k_1}{k_1 + k_2}\right)$, where h_2 stands for the binary entropy.

We denote by $T(n, \alpha, \beta)$ the set of all vectors of length n composed with αn 1s, βn 2s and $(1 - \alpha - \beta)n$ 0s. There exist $\begin{pmatrix} n \\ \alpha n, \beta n, (1 - \alpha - \beta)n \end{pmatrix} = \tilde{O}\left(2^{ng(1,\alpha,\beta)}\right)$ such vectors.

A.2   Main Result

The goal of this section is to prove the following result.

Proposition 5. *For* $\mathbf{b} \in T(n, \alpha_0, \beta_0)$, *the number of ways one can decompose* $\mathbf{b}$ *as the sum of two vectors from* $T(n, \alpha_1, \beta_1)$ *is given by:*

$$\tilde{O}\left(2^{n(g(1-\alpha_0-\beta_0, \overline{x}_{12}, \overline{x}_{12}) + g(\alpha_0, \overline{x}_{01}, \overline{x}_{01}) + g(\beta_0, \overline{x}_{02}, \overline{x}_{02}))}\right),$$

where

$$\overline{x}_{01} = \frac{2\alpha_0 + \beta_0 - \alpha_1 - 2\beta_1}{3} + z$$

$$\overline{x}_{02} = \frac{\alpha_0 + 2\beta_0 - 2\alpha_1 - \beta_1}{3} + z$$

$$\overline{x}_{12} = z$$

and z is the real root of

$$\frac{(2\alpha_0 + \beta_0 - \alpha_1 - 2\beta_1 + 3z)(\alpha_0 + 2\beta_0 - 2\alpha_1 - \beta_1 + 3z)z}{(1 - \alpha_0 - \beta_0 - 2z)(-2\alpha_0 - \beta_0 + 4\alpha_1 + 2\beta_1 - 6z)(-\alpha_0 - 2\beta_0 + 2\alpha_1 + 4\beta_1 - 6z)} = 1.$$

A.3   A Simple Example

Let us consider a very simple case: we want to decompose a balanced vector of size n (the number of 0s, 1s and 2s is $n/3$) in two balanced vectors (*i.e.* $\alpha_0 = \beta_1 = \alpha_1 = \beta_1 = 1/3$). There are several ways to achieve this. One solution is that each 0 is obtain by $0 + 0$, each 1 by $2 + 2$, and each 2 by $1 + 1$. There is exactly only one way to build the vector in this way. Another possibility is that each case $(0 + 0, 1 + 2, 2 + 1, 1 + 0, 2 + 2, 0 + 1, 2 + 0, 0 + 2$ and $1 + 1)$ happens $n/9$ times. This is the scenario admitting the maximal number of decompositions: $\tilde{O}(3^n)$. There are many more possibilities.

The number of representations is the sum of all decompositions for all the possible scenarios. There are only a polynomial number of different scenarios. The total number of representations (which is what we want to determine) is determined, up to a polynomial factor, by the scenario which gives the maximal number of decompositions. In this case, there are $\tilde{O}(3^n)$ representations.

Let us check that this is the result given by Proposition 5. Indeed, in this case, z must satisfy the equation

$$\frac{(3z)(3z)z}{(1/3 - 2z)(1 - 6z)(1 - 6z)} = 1, \text{ or equivalently } 27z^3 = (1 - 6z)^3.$$

The real root of this equation is $1/9$. Thus we obtain $\overline{x}_{01} = \overline{x}_{02} = \overline{x}_{12} = 1/9$. Finally, the number of representations is

$$\tilde{O}\left(2^{3ng(1/3, 1/9, 1/9)}\right) = \tilde{O}\left(2^{3n \times (\log_2(3)/3)}\right) = \tilde{O}(3^n).$$

A.4   Typical Case

In general, we have a vector $\mathbf{b} \in T(n, \alpha_0, \beta_0)$. We want to decompose it into two vectors of $T(n, \alpha_1, \beta_1)$. Let us call $x_{00}, \ldots, x_{22}$ the density of the nine cases $(0 + 0, 0 + 1, \ldots, 2 + 2)$ as shown in the following table:

	0	1	2
0	x_{00}	x_{01}	x_{02}
1	x_{10}	x_{11}	x_{12}
2	x_{20}	x_{21}	x_{22}

We denote by $\mathcal{A}$ the set of possible such tuples $x_{00}, \ldots, x_{22}$.

Given the target vector $\mathbf{b}$, there are $\binom{n(1 - \alpha_0 - \beta_0)}{nx_{00}, nx_{12}, nx_{21}} \binom{n\alpha_0}{nx_{01}, nx_{10}, nx_{22}}$ $\binom{n\beta_0}{nx_{02}, nx_{11}, nx_{20}}$ ways of decomposing this $\mathbf{b}$ according to $(x_{00}, \ldots, x_{22})$.

Indeed, a 0 in $\mathbf{b}$ can be decomposed as $0 + 0$ (this happens nx_{00} times), $1 + 2$ (nx_{12} times) or $2 + 1$ (nx_{21} times). As the number of 0s in $\mathbf{b}$ is $n(1 - \alpha_0 - \beta_0)$, there are $\begin{pmatrix} n(1 - \alpha_0 - \beta_0) \\ nx_{00}, nx_{12}, nx_{21} \end{pmatrix}$ ways to choose the decomposition of each 0 of $\mathbf{b}$. The choices of the decompositions of the 1s and the 2s give the other two factors.

For given $\alpha_0, \beta_0, \alpha_1$ and β_1, the number of possible decompositions is

$$\sum_{(x_{00},\ldots,x_{22})\in\mathcal{A}} \begin{pmatrix} n(1 - \alpha_0 - \beta_0) \\ nx_{00}, nx_{12}, nx_{21} \end{pmatrix} \begin{pmatrix} n\alpha_0 \\ nx_{01}, nx_{10}, nx_{22} \end{pmatrix} \begin{pmatrix} n\beta_0 \\ nx_{02}, nx_{11}, nx_{20} \end{pmatrix}.$$

Up to a polynomial factor this is equal to

$$\sum_{(x_{00},\ldots,x_{22})\in\mathcal{A}} 2^{n(g(1-\alpha_0-\beta_0,x_{21},x_{12})+g(\alpha_0,x_{01},x_{10})+g(\beta_0,x_{02},x_{20}))}.$$

The largest term (or eventually one of the largest terms) of this sum is

$$2^{n(g(1-\alpha_0-\beta_0,\overline{x}_{21},\overline{x}_{12})+g(\alpha_0,\overline{x}_{01},\overline{x}_{10})+g(\beta_0,\overline{x}_{02},\overline{x}_{20}))},$$

where $(\overline{x}_{00},\ldots,\overline{x}_{22})$ is called the *typical case*.

We are interested in this typical case because it gathers a polynomial fraction of all the possible decompositions. The asymptotic exponent of the total number of representations is then simply given by the exponent of the typical case.

A.5   Computation of the Typical Case

Given $\alpha_0, \beta_0, \alpha_1$ and β_1, the following constraints exist on $x_{00},\ldots,x_{22}$.

$$x_{00} + x_{01} + x_{02} = 1 - \alpha_1 - \beta_1$$
$$x_{10} + x_{11} + x_{12} = \alpha_1$$
$$x_{20} + x_{21} + x_{22} = \beta_1$$

$$x_{00} + x_{10} + x_{20} = 1 - \alpha_1 - \beta_1$$
$$x_{01} + x_{11} + x_{21} = \alpha_1$$
$$x_{02} + x_{12} + x_{22} = \beta_1$$

$$x_{00} + x_{12} + x_{21} = 1 - \alpha_0 - \beta_0$$
$$x_{01} + x_{10} + x_{22} = \alpha_0$$
$$x_{02} + x_{11} + x_{20} = \beta_0$$

However, these equations are not independent. Each of the three sets of three equations implies $x_{00} + \cdots + x_{22} = 1$. We are actually left with two degrees of freedom, and any solution can be written as

$$x_{00} = \frac{1 - \alpha_0 - \beta_0}{} \qquad\qquad - 2z$$

$$x_{01} = \frac{2\alpha_0 + \beta_0 - \alpha_1 - 2\beta_1}{3} \qquad + z + w$$

$$x_{02} = \frac{\alpha_0 + 2\beta_0 - 2\alpha_1 - \beta_1}{3} \qquad + z - w$$

$$x_{10} = \frac{2\alpha_0 + \beta_0 - \alpha_1 - 2\beta_1}{3} \qquad + z - w$$

$$x_{11} = \frac{-2\alpha_0 - \beta_0 + 4\alpha_1 + 2\beta_1}{3} \qquad - 2z$$

$$x_{12} = 0 \qquad\qquad\qquad\qquad\quad + z + w$$

$$x_{20} = \frac{\alpha_0 + 2\beta_0 - 2\alpha_1 - \beta_1}{3} \qquad + z + w$$

$$x_{21} = 0 \qquad\qquad\qquad\qquad\quad + z - w$$

$$x_{22} = \frac{-\alpha_0 - 2\beta_0 + 2\alpha_1 + 4\beta_1}{3} \qquad - 2z.$$

Thus, $\mathcal{A} = \{(x_{00}(w, z), \ldots, x_{22}(w, z)) \mid \forall(i, j), x_{ij} \geqslant 0\}$.

Determining w. In a first step, we will show that the typical case must be symmetric (*i.e.* $\overline{x}_{01} = \overline{x}_{10}$, $\overline{x}_{02} = \overline{x}_{20}$ and $\overline{x}_{12} = \overline{x}_{21}$), which means that w must be 0. To do so, we consider a pair (w, z) such that the corresponding $(x_{00}, \ldots, x_{22})$ is in $\mathcal{A}$, and we call $(\tilde{x}_{00}, \ldots, \tilde{x}_{22})$ the solution with the same z but 0 instead of w.

As $(x_{00}, \ldots, x_{22})$ is in $\mathcal{A}$, all x_{ij} are positive or zero. This implies that all $\tilde{x}_{ij}$ are positive or zero. For example, for $\tilde{x}_{01}$ we have:

$$0 \leqslant \min(x_{01}, x_{10}) = \tilde{x}_{01} - \mathrm{abs}(w) \leqslant \tilde{x}_{01}.$$

Therefore, $(\tilde{x}_{00}, \ldots, \tilde{x}_{22})$ is in $\mathcal{A}$ and we obtain

$$\frac{\mathrm{Nrep}(\tilde{\mathbf{x}})}{\mathrm{Nrep}(\mathbf{x})} = \frac{2^{n(g(1-\alpha_0-\beta_0,\tilde{x}_{21},\tilde{x}_{12})+g(\alpha_0,\tilde{x}_{01},\tilde{x}_{10})+g(\beta_0,\tilde{x}_{02},\tilde{x}_{20}))}}{2^{n(g(1-\alpha_0-\beta_0,x_{21},x_{12})+g(\alpha_0,x_{01},x_{10})+g(\beta_0,x_{02},x_{20}))}}. \tag{9}$$

But we have the following equality.

$$\begin{aligned} g(1 - \alpha_0 - \beta_0, x_{21}, x_{12}) &= g(1 - \alpha_0 - \beta_0, \tilde{x}_{12} + w, \tilde{x}_{12} - w) \\ &= g(1 - \alpha_0 - \beta_0, \tilde{x}_{12}, \tilde{x}_{12}) + 2\tilde{x}_{21}\left(h(1/2 + w/\tilde{x}_{12}) - h(1/2)\right). \end{aligned}$$

Similarly, we obtain two other formulas.

$$g(\alpha_0, x_{01}, x_{10}) = g(\alpha_0, \tilde{x}_{01}, \tilde{x}_{10}) + 2\tilde{x}_{01}\left(h(1/2 + w/\tilde{x}_{01}) - h(1/2)\right),$$

$$g(\beta_0, x_{02}, x_{20}) = g(\beta_0, \tilde{x}_{02}, \tilde{x}_{20}) + 2\tilde{x}_{02}\left(h(1/2 + w/\tilde{x}_{02}) - h(1/2)\right).$$

Therefore, we can reduce Eq. 9 to

$$\frac{\mathrm{Nrep}(\tilde{\mathbf{x}})}{\mathrm{Nrep}(\mathbf{x})} = 2^{2n\left(\tilde{x}_{01}\left(1 - h\left(\frac{1}{2} + \frac{w}{\tilde{x}_{01}}\right)\right) + \tilde{x}_{02}\left(1 - h\left(\frac{1}{2} + \frac{w}{\tilde{x}_{02}}\right)\right) + \tilde{x}_{12}\left(1 - h\left(\frac{1}{2} + \frac{w}{\tilde{x}_{12}}\right)\right)\right)}.$$

So $\mathrm{Nrep}(\mathbf{x}) \leqslant \mathrm{Nrep}(\tilde{\mathbf{x}})$ and these two quantities are equal if and only $w = 0$, *i.e.* $\mathbf{x} = \tilde{\mathbf{x}}$.

Determining z. To get the typical case, we now have to find the value of z that maximises the expression

$$g(1 - \alpha_0 - \beta_0, x_{21}, x_{12}) + g(\alpha_0, x_{01}, x_{10}) + g(\beta_0, x_{02}, x_{20}).$$

Notice that this expression is equivalent, up to an additive constant, to $-\sum_{i,j} x_{ij} \log_2(x_{ij})$.

This function is concave and thus admit a single maximum. The differentiation of this function with respect to z gives

$$-2 \log_2 \left(\frac{\left(\frac{2\alpha_0 + \beta_0 - \alpha_1 - 2\beta_1}{3} + z \right)\left(\frac{\alpha_0 + 2\beta_0 - 2\alpha_1 - \beta_1}{3} + z \right) z}{(1 - \alpha_0 - \beta_0 - 2z)\left(\frac{-2\alpha_0 - \beta_0 + 4\alpha_1 + 2\beta_1}{3} - 2z \right)\left(\frac{-\alpha_0 - 2\beta_0 + 2\alpha_1 + 4\beta_1}{3} - 2z \right)} \right),$$

which is equal to zero if and only if

$$\frac{(2\alpha_0 + \beta_0 - \alpha_1 - 2\beta_1 + 3z)(\alpha_0 + 2\beta_0 - 2\alpha_1 - \beta_1 + 3z)z}{(1 - \alpha_0 - \beta_0 - 2z)(-2\alpha_0 - \beta_0 + 4\alpha_1 + 2\beta_1 - 6z)(-\alpha_0 - 2\beta_0 + 2\alpha_1 + 4\beta_1 - 6z)} = 1.$$

This explains why z is the root of a polynomial of degree 3.

A.6   Number of Representations and Badly-formed Elements

There are $\tilde{O}\left(2^{ng(1,\alpha_0,\beta_0)}\right)$ vectors in $T(n, \alpha_0, \beta_0)$. For each of these vectors, there are by definition $\mathrm{Nrep}(\alpha_0, \beta_0, \alpha_1, \beta_1)$ ways of decomposing it as the sum of two vectors of $T(n, \alpha_1, \beta_1)$. Moreover, the number of vectors in $T(n, \alpha_1, \beta_1)$ is $\tilde{O}\left(2^{ng(1,\alpha_1,\beta_1)}\right)$. There are then $\tilde{O}\left(2^{2ng(1,\alpha_1,\beta_1)}\right)$ pairs of vectors of $T(n, \alpha_1, \beta_1)$, but only $\tilde{O}\left(\mathrm{Nrep}(\alpha_0, \beta_0, \alpha_1, \beta_1)2^{ng(1,\alpha_0,\beta_0)}\right)$ of these pairs give a valid representation of a vector of $T(n, \alpha_0, \beta_0)$. All the other pairs give badly-formed elements. Thus, when we merge two L-sized lists of elements of $T(n, \alpha_1, \beta_1)$ on L bits, we obtain $\tilde{O}\left(L\,\mathrm{Nrep}(\alpha_0, \beta_0, \alpha_1, \beta_1)2^{ng(1,\alpha_0,\beta_0)-2ng(1,\alpha_1,\beta_1)}\right)$ vectors of $T(n, \alpha_0, \beta_0)$, the remaining consisting on badly-formed vectors.

References

[ABB+17] Aragon, N., et al.: BIKE. NIST Round 1 submission for Post-Quantum Cryptography, December 2017

[ACP+17] Albrecht, M., Cid, C., Paterson, K.G., Tjhai, C.J., Tomlinson, M.: NTS-KEM. First round submission to the NIST post-quantum cryptography call, December 2017

[AMAB+17] Melchor, C.A., et al.: HQC. NIST Round 1 submission for Post-Quantum Cryptography, December 2017

[BBC+19] Baldi, M., Barenghi, A., Chiaraluce, F., Pelosi, G., Santini, P.: LEDAcrypt. Second round submission to the NIST post-quantum cryptography call, January 2019

[BCJ11] Becker, A., Coron, J.-S., Joux, A.: Improved generic algorithms for hard knapsacks. In: Paterson, K.G. (ed.) EUROCRYPT 2011. LNCS, vol. 6632, pp. 364–385. Springer, Heidelberg (2011). https://doi.org/10.1007/978-3-642-20465-4_21

[BCL+17] Bernstein, D.J., et al.: Classic McEliece: conservative code-based cryptography. First round submission to the NIST post-quantum cryptography call, November 2017. https://csrc.nist.gov/CSRC/media/Projects/Post-Quantum-Cryptography/documents/round-1/submissions/Classic-McEliece.zip

[BJMM12] Becker, A., Joux, A., May, A., Meurer, A.: Decoding random binary linear codes in $2^{n/20}$: how $1 + 1 = 0$ improves information set decoding. In: Pointcheval, D., Johansson, T. (eds.) EUROCRYPT 2012. LNCS, vol. 7237, pp. 520–536. Springer, Heidelberg (2012). https://doi.org/10.1007/978-3-642-29011-4_31

[BMvT78] Berlekamp, E., McEliece, R., van Tilborg, H.: On the inherent intractability of certain coding problems. IEEE Trans. Inf. Theory 24(3), 384–386 (1978)

[CFG89] Chaimovich, M., Freiman, G., Galil, Z.: Solving dense subset-sum problems by using analytical number theory. J. Complex. 5(3), 271–282 (1989)

[CFS01] Courtois, N.T., Finiasz, M., Sendrier, N.: How to achieve a McEliece-based digital signature scheme. In: Boyd, C. (ed.) ASIACRYPT 2001. LNCS, vol. 2248, pp. 157–174. Springer, Heidelberg (2001). https://doi.org/10.1007/3-540-45682-1_10

[CG90] Coffey, J.T., Goodman, R.M.: The complexity of information set decoding. IEEE Trans. Inf. Theory 36(5), 1031–1037 (1990)

[CT17] Torres, R.C.: Asymptotic analysis of ISD algorithms for the $q-$ary case. In: Proceedings of the Tenth International Workshop on Coding and Cryptography WCC 2017, September 2017

[DST17] Debris-Alazard, T., Sendrier, N., Tillich, J.-P.: Surf: a new code-based signature scheme. Preprint, September 2017. arXiv:1706.08065v3

[DST18] Debris-Alazard, T., Sendrier, N., Tillich, J.-P.: Wave: a new code-based signature scheme. Cryptology ePrint Archive, Report 2018/996, October 2018. https://eprint.iacr.org/2018/996

[Dum91] Dumer, I.: On minimum distance decoding of linear codes. In: Proceedings of the 5th Joint Soviet-Swedish International Workshop Information Theory, Moscow, pp. 50–52 (1991)

[FP05] Flaxman, A.D., Przydatek, B.: Solving medium-density subset sum problems in expected polynomial time. In: Diekert, V., Durand, B. (eds.) STACS 2005. LNCS, vol. 3404, pp. 305–314. Springer, Heidelberg (2005). https://doi.org/10.1007/978-3-540-31856-9_25

[GKH17] Gueye, C.T., Klamti, J.B., Hirose, S.: Generalization of BJMM-ISD using May-Ozerov nearest neighbor algorithm over an arbitrary finite field $\mathbb{F}_q$. In: El Hajji, S., Nitaj, A., Souidi, E.M. (eds.) C2SI 2017. LNCS, vol. 10194, pp. 96–109. Springer, Cham (2017). https://doi.org/10.1007/978-3-319-55589-8_7

[GM91] Galil, Z., Margalit, O.: An almost linear-time algorithm for the dense subset-sum problem. SIAM J. Comput. 20(6), 1157–1189 (1991)

[GPV08] Gentry, C., Peikert, C., Vaikuntanathan, V.: Trapdoors for hard lattices and new cryptographic constructions. In: Proceedings of the Fortieth Annual ACM Symposium on Theory of Computing, pp. 197–206. ACM (2008)

[Hir16] Hirose, S.: May-Ozerov algorithm for nearest-neighbor problem over $\mathbb{F}_q$ and its application to information set decoding. In: Bica, I., Reyhanitabar, R. (eds.) SECITC 2016. LNCS, vol. 10006, pp. 115–126. Springer, Cham (2016). https://doi.org/10.1007/978-3-319-47238-6_8

[HJ10] Howgrave-Graham, N., Joux, A.: New generic algorithms for hard knapsacks. In: Gilbert, H. (ed.) EUROCRYPT 2010. LNCS, vol. 6110, pp. 235–256. Springer, Heidelberg (2010). https://doi.org/10.1007/978-3-642-13190-5_12

[IKR+18] Interlando, C., Khathuria, K., Rohrer, N., Rosenthal, J., Weger, V.: Generalization of the ball-collision algorithm. arXiv preprint arXiv:1812.10955 (2018)

[JJ02] Johansson, T., Jönsson, F.: On the complexity of some cryptographic problems based on the general decoding problem. IEEE Trans. Inf. Theory **48**(10), 2669–2678 (2002)

[Lyu05] Lyubashevsky, V.: On random high density subset sums. Electronic Colloquium on Computational Complexity (ECCC), 1(007) (2005)

[McE78] McEliece, R.J.: A public-key system based on algebraic coding theory, pp. 114–116. Jet Propulsion Lab, DSN Progress Report 44 (1978)

[Meu17] Meurer, A.: A coding-theoretic approach to cryptanalysis. Ph.D. thesis, Ruhr University Bochum, November 2017

[MMT11] May, A., Meurer, A., Thomae, E.: Decoding random linear codes in $\tilde{\mathcal{O}}(2^{0.054n})$. In: Lee, D.H., Wang, X. (eds.) ASIACRYPT 2011. LNCS, vol. 7073, pp. 107–124. Springer, Heidelberg (2011). https://doi.org/10.1007/978-3-642-25385-0_6

[MTSB12] Misoczki, R., Tillich, J.-P., Sendrier, N., Barreto, P.S.L.M.: MDPC-McEliece: new McEliece variants from moderate density parity-check codes. IACR Cryptology ePrint Archive, Report 2012/409, 2012 (2012)

[Pet10] Peters, C.: Information-set decoding for linear codes over $\mathbf{F}_q$. In: Sendrier, N. (ed.) PQCrypto 2010. LNCS, vol. 6061, pp. 81–94. Springer, Heidelberg (2010). https://doi.org/10.1007/978-3-642-12929-2_7

[Pra62] Prange, E.: The use of information sets in decoding cyclic codes. IRE Trans. Inf. Theory **8**(5), 5–9 (1962)

[Sen11] Sendrier, N.: Decoding one out of many. In: Yang, B.-Y. (ed.) PQCrypto 2011. LNCS, vol. 7071, pp. 51–67. Springer, Heidelberg (2011). https://doi.org/10.1007/978-3-642-25405-5_4

[Ste93] Stern, J.: A new identification scheme based on syndrome decoding. In: Stinson, D.R. (ed.) CRYPTO 1993. LNCS, vol. 773, pp. 13–21. Springer, Heidelberg (1994). https://doi.org/10.1007/3-540-48329-2_2

[Wag02] Wagner, D.: A generalized birthday problem. In: Yung, M. (ed.) CRYPTO 2002. LNCS, vol. 2442, pp. 288–304. Springer, Heidelberg (2002). https://doi.org/10.1007/3-540-45708-9_19

Exploring Trade-offs in Batch Bounded Distance Decoding

Martin R. Albrecht[1], Benjamin R. Curtis[1(✉)], and Thomas Wunderer[2]

[1] Information Security Group, Royal Holloway, University of London, Egham, UK
martin.albrecht@royalholloway.ac.uk, benjamin.curtis.2015@rhul.ac.uk
[2] Bundesamt für Sicherheit in der Informationstechnik (BSI), Bonn, Germany
thomas.wunderer@bsi.bund.de

Abstract. Algorithms for solving the Bounded Distance Decoding problem (BDD) are used for estimating the security of lattice-based cryptographic primitives, since these algorithms can be employed to solve variants of the Learning with Errors problem (LWE). In certain parameter regimes where the target vector is small and/or sparse, batches of BDD instances emerge from a combinatorial approach where several components of the target vector are guessed before decoding. In this work we explore trade-offs in solving "Batch-BDD", and apply our techniques to the small-secret Learning with Errors problem. We compare our techniques to previous works which solve batches of BDD instances, such as the hybrid lattice-reduction and meet-in-the-middle attack. Our results are a mixed bag. We show that, in the "enumeration setting" and with BKZ reduction, our techniques outperform a variant of the hybrid attack which does not consider time-memory trade-offs in the guessing phase for certain Round5 (17-bits out of 466), Round5-IoT (19-bits out of 240), and NTRU LPrime (23-bits out of 385) parameter sets. On the other hand, our techniques do not outperform the Hybrid Attack under standard, albeit unrealistic, assumptions. Finally, as expected, our techniques do not improve on previous works in the "sieving setting" (under standard assumptions) where combinatorial attacks in general do not perform well.

Keywords: Bounded distance decoding · Cryptanalysis · Hybrid attack · Lattice-based cryptography · LWE · NTRU

1 Introduction

The *Bounded Distance Decoding* problem with parameter $0 < \alpha$ asks to find the closest vector in some lattice $\Lambda \subset \mathbb{R}^d$ to some target vector $\mathbf{t} \in \mathbb{R}^d$

The research of Albrecht was supported by the European Union PROMETHEUS project (Horizon 2020 Research and Innovation Program, grant 780701) and EPSRC grants EP/S02087X/1 and EP/S020330/1. The research of Curtis was supported by the EPSRC and the UK government as part of the Centre for Doctoral Training in Cyber Security at Royal Holloway, University of London (EP/K035584/1).

© Springer Nature Switzerland AG 2020
K. G. Paterson and D. Stebila (Eds.): SAC 2019, LNCS 11959, pp. 467–491, 2020.
https://doi.org/10.1007/978-3-030-38471-5_19

under the guarantee that the distance between the lattice and $\mathbf{t}$ is at most $\alpha \cdot \lambda_1(\Lambda)$, where $\lambda_1(\Lambda)$ is the length of a shortest vector in Λ. Establishing the concrete cost of solving BDD has received renewed attention in recent years because algorithms for solving this problem give rise to cryptanalytic attacks on schemes based on the hardness of the *Learning with Errors* problem (LWE) [Reg05] as well as the NTRU problem [HPS96]. These problems have been established as popular building blocks for realising post-quantum secure primitives such as public key encryption [HPS96, Reg05], key encapsulation [SAB+17, SHRS17], key exchange [LP11, DXL12, ADPS16] and digital signatures [BAA+17, PFH+17] as well as advanced primitives such as fully homomorphic encryption (FHE) [GSW13, BGV14].

Informally, LWE challenges an adversary to determine the secret vector $\mathbf{s} \in \mathbb{Z}_q^n$ given $(\mathbf{A}, \mathbf{b}) \in (\mathbb{Z}_q^{m \times n} \times \mathbb{Z}_q^n)$ from a noisy linear system $\mathbf{b} = \mathbf{As} + \mathbf{e}$, where $\mathbf{A} \in \mathbb{Z}_q^{m \times n}$ is uniformly random, and the error vector $\mathbf{e} \in \mathbb{Z}_q^m$ is drawn from some distribution χ producing small entries. In what follows, we will assume that the vector $\mathbf{s}$ also has short entries. If $\mathbf{s}$ follows χ then this is known as *normal form* LWE and is no easier than if $\mathbf{s}$ is uniformly random [ACPS09].

Similarly, NTRU challenges an adversary to recover (small multiples of) f, g in some polynomial quotient ring R, given $h = f^{-1} \cdot g$, where f is sampled to have an inverse and f, g are sampled from some distributions χ_f, χ_g producing small entries.

Both of these problems can be solved using an algorithm solving the *unique Shortest Vector Problem* (uSVP) and this approach is often considered in the literature. For LWE, we consider the lattice

$$\{(\mathbf{x}, \mathbf{y}, c) \in \mathbb{Z}^{n+m+1} \mid \mathbf{A} \cdot \mathbf{x} + \mathbf{y} - c \cdot \mathbf{b} \equiv \mathbf{0} \bmod q\},$$

for NTRU we consider the lattice

$$\{(\mathbf{x}, \mathbf{y}) \in \mathbb{Z}^{2n} \mid \mathbf{H} \cdot \mathbf{x} - \mathbf{y} \equiv \mathbf{0} \bmod q\}$$

where $\mathbf{H}$ is the matrix produced by considering $h \cdot x^i$ for $0 \le i < n$ with n being the degree of the ring R. These lattices contain $(\mathbf{s}, \mathbf{e}, 1)$ resp. $(\mathbf{f}, \mathbf{g})$ – the coefficient vectors of f and g – which are, for typical choices of parameters, unusually short. To solve uSVP, we may employ a lattice reduction algorithm such as BKZ [SE94, CN11] to find this unusually short vector using the success condition

$$\sqrt{\beta/d} \cdot \lambda_1(\Lambda) \le \delta^{2\beta-d} \cdot \det(\Lambda)^{1/d}$$

from [ADPS16], which was experimentally verified in [AGVW17].

The lattice considered in the case of LWE is an embedding lattice for solving BDD via uSVP. We may also tackle BDD directly by first running lattice reduction to find a basis of sufficiently good quality for the lattice

$$\{(\mathbf{x}, \ \mathbf{A} \cdot \mathbf{x} \bmod q) \mid \mathbf{x} \in \mathbb{Z}^n\}$$

followed by either Babai's Nearest Plane algorithm [Bab86] or pruned enumeration [LP11, LN13]. This is known as the *decoding attack* in the cryptographic literature. Note that we may think of Babai's Nearest Plane algorithm as a form of pruned enumeration where all pruning coefficients are small enough to enforce the "Babai branch" of the search tree.

In the case of NTRU, BDD instances emerge from the *Hybrid Attack* [How07, GvVW17, Wun19] which combines guessing some coefficients of f or g and Babai's Nearest Plane algorithm. Due to the low cost, this algorithmic choice is natural as the adversary has to perform many calls to the BDD oracle: one for each guess. Thus, the algorithm has two phases: (a) a *lattice reduction phase* producing a sufficiently orthogonal basis used later and (b) a *guess and verify phase* where guesses are verified by running a BDD solver against the previously reduced basis and a target vector derived from the particular guess. The second step can – and is typically considered to – be realised using a meet-in-the-middle (mitm) or time-memory trade-off approach. The Hybrid Attack can be extended to LWE [BGPW16].

Contribution. From the discussion above we may consider the Hybrid Attack as a form of batched (candidate) BDD enumeration, where many points need to be decoded against the same lattice. Furthermore, we may consider the uSVP embedding approach and the Nearest Plane algorithm as endpoints of a continuum of strategies for solving (batch) BDD: the final enumeration is either (essentially) as expensive as the initial lattice reduction or optimised to be as cheap as possible to decode a large number of points. In this work we explore this continuum of strategies for solving LWE instances with small (and sparse) secrets **s** such as [GHS12, GZB+19, BCLv19]. That is, we trade lattice-reduction preprocessing cost with BDD enumeration cost to reduce the overall cost of BDD. We note that in our parameterisation our algorithm solves many BDD-like instances with $\alpha \approx 1$ where a unique solution is not guaranteed to exist. In other words, we actually solve many instances of CVP.

In more detail, we present a *guess-and-verify* decoding approach which, like the Hybrid Attack, makes use of a guessing approach to reduce the dimension of the BDD problem. However, in our guess-and-verify decoding, we employ a more expensive BDD solver than Babai's Nearest Plane, i.e. we enumerate candidate solutions rather than just following the 'Babai branch'. To establish the dimension in which we perform enumeration, we deploy (a slight variant of) the success condition from [ADPS16], i.e. we pick parameters so that the distance between our target and the projected sub-lattice is slightly smaller than the expected shortest vector in that sub-lattice. Therefore, as opposed to applying a low probability BDD solver on a large number of (candidate) BDD instances, our technique applies heavier enumeration, with a higher probability of success, to a smaller number of (candidate) BDD instances.

Findings. Our results are presented in Tables 1 and 2 (see also Tables 3 and 4). We apply our techniques on parameter sets for NTRU LPrime [BCLv19], Round5 [GZB+19] and HElib [Hal18].

Table 1 considers the enumeration setting, where the SVP oracle is realised using lattice-point enumeration [FP85,Kan83] and highlights that our non-mitm variant outperforms the non-mitm variant of the Hybrid Attack for the Round5, Round5-IoT and NTRU LPrime parameter sets by 17-bits, 19-bits and 23-bits respectively. These results assume the basis shape after lattice reduction exhibits an HKZ-shape in the last block, as observed in practice for BKZ reduction and predicted by the BKZ simulator [CN11], instead of a "line" as predicted by the Geometric Series Assumption (GSA). We also include estimates assuming the GSA holds also in the last block. In this setting, the non-mitm variant of the Hybrid Attack outperforms our techniques. We further note that for HElib our approach closes the gap between the dual and the primal attack observed in [Alb17]. Note that here, since β is relatively small, the output basis shape from the BKZ Simulator is very close to the Geometric Series Assumption (GSA), and thus the results are similar in each case.

Table 2 considers the sieving setting, where the SVP oracle is instanti-ated using a lattice sieving algorithm [AKS01,BDGL16]. Here, combinatorial approaches (i.e. guessing components of the secret) do not improve the run-ning time of a BDD approach for the Round5, Round5-IoT, and NTRU LPrime parameter sets. Thus, our approach only marginally outperforms the uSVP attack by decoupling β and η, i.e. our approach reduces to the usual "decoding" approach [LP11,LN13] translated to the sieving setting (see also [ADH+19]). Such estimates are marked by † in all tables.

We stress that a "g-v decoding" estimate that is lower than a "hybrid" esti-mate does not necessarily imply an invalidation of any security claim made by the designers of the schemes considered in our work, and to highlight this point we consider the (pre-quantum) security claim of each scheme, denoted by λ, in all of our tables. In particular, there are several points within our analysis in which we have had to make assumptions, and, whilst the assumptions we have chosen are reasonable based on currently known techniques, designers have made different assumptions to ours, and this can change the ordering of attack complexities. We consider a spectrum of such assumptions and their effect in Appendix B.

Limitations and Future Work. The Hybrid Attack is defined as a hybrid of a meet-in-the-middle guess-and-verify step and lattice reduction. For a guess $\mathbf{v}_g$ we can decode using Babai's Nearest Plane algorithm in the hope of finding the remaining components of the secret $\mathbf{v}_l$. In a meet-in-the-middle step, the guessed part of the secret $\mathbf{v}_g$ is split into two sub-guesses $\mathbf{v}_g = \mathbf{v}'_g + \mathbf{v}''_g$, and we in turn have *two* applications of Babai's Nearest Plane: one for each "half" of the original guess. Then, each decoded vector is stored in a hash table using a locality sensitive hash function [Wun19] which permits to find collisions in this table which, with some probability, correspond to $\mathbf{v}_g$. Whilst this approach allows the correct vector $\mathbf{v}_g$ to be found more quickly by reducing the search space for guessing, it also introduces an additional probability of failure. That is, we have to hope that the output of our BDD solver is homomorphic: if the guess $\mathbf{v}'_g$

Table 1. Estimates in enumeration setting.

Attack	τ	β	η	BDD cost	$|S|$	Repeats	d	#pp	$\log_2(\text{rop})$
NTRU LPrime: $n = 761, q = 4591, \sigma = \sqrt{2/3}, h = 250$									$\lambda = 222$
uSVP (GSA)	92	458	458	n/a	1	$2^{57.2}$	1220	n/a	384.6
Dual (GSA)	69	495	n/a	n/a	n/a	$2^{320.9}$	1281	11	374.0
g-v decoding (GSA)	285	430	102	$2^{336.1}$	$2^{252.8}$	$2^{34.1}$	1026	55	337.6
Non mitm hybrid (GSA)	275	400	n/a	$2^{324.1}$	$2^{255.6}$	$2^{49.6}$	1036	57	**325.7**
g-v decoding	225	435	272	$2^{360.9}$	$2^{146.4}$	$2^{53.9}$	1086	28	**362.1**
Non mitm hybrid	305	395	n/a	$2^{384.3}$	$2^{252.3}$	$2^{113.1}$	1006	53	385.3
Round5: $n = 756, q = 2^{12}, \sigma \approx 4.61, h = 242$									$\lambda = 270$
uSVP (GSA)	230	449	449	n/a	1	$2^{160.1}$	936	n/a	478.9
Dual (GSA)	63	626	n/a	n/a	n/a	$2^{413.5}$	1227	19	489.2
g-v decoding (GSA)	365	490	117	$2^{415.2}$	$2^{297.9}$	$2^{60.2}$	814	62	416.9
Non mitm hybrid (GSA)	335	445	n/a	$2^{391.0}$	$2^{295.7}$	$2^{76.8}$	844	64	**392.5**
g-v decoding	290	490	320	$2^{448.2}$	$2^{157.2}$	$2^{92.6}$	889	28	**449.6**
Non mitm hybrid	365	420	n/a	$2^{465.5}$	$2^{274.2}$	$2^{172.9}$	814	55	466.6
Round5 (IoT): $n = 372, q = 2^{11}, \sigma \approx 4.61, h = 178$									$\lambda = 129$
uSVP (GSA)	0	335	335	n/a	n/a	1	682	n/a	220.0
Dual (GSA)	32	334	n/a	n/a	n/a	$2^{174.7}$	661	14	221.7
g-v decoding (GSA)	65	315	224	$2^{213.1}$	$2^{79.2}$	$2^{9.0}$	616	22	214.3
Non mitm hybrid (GSA)	115	270	n/a	$2^{203.6}$	$2^{149.5}$	$2^{36.9}$	566	43	**205.5**
g-v decoding	50	320	266	$2^{220.4}$	$2^{51.6}$	$2^{12.8}$	631	13	**221.4**
Non mitm hybrid	120	270	n/a	$2^{239.6}$	$2^{150.8}$	$2^{71.5}$	561	42	240.6
HElib-1024: $n = 1024, q = 2^{47}, \sigma \approx 3.19, h = 64$									
uSVP (GSA)	140	105	105	n/a	1	$2^{14.0}$	1670	n/a	75.5
Dual (GSA)	189	107	n/a	n/a	n/a	$2^{22.3}$	1680	7	68.4
g-v decoding (GSA)	185	100	48	$2^{66.7}$	$2^{29.5}$	$2^{9.9}$	1624	4	69.1
Non mitm hybrid (GSA)	210	100	n/a	$2^{67.5}$	$2^{36.6}$	$2^{10.7}$	1599	5	69.9

τ is the (fixed) guessing dimension, β is the blocksize used in lattice reduction, η is the enumeration dimension considered, BDD cost is the cost of solving BDD (via enumeration) in the dimension η projected sublattice, $|S|$ is the size of the search space considered, i.e the number of points on which we decode (chosen as a union $\cup_{i=0}^{\#pp} S_i$ of sets S_i containing all length τ vectors with Hamming weight i), d is the dimension of the lattice considered, #pp denotes the maximal hamming weight considered in the search space, and rop is the cost of running the algorithm in CPU cycles; "g-v decoding" is the technique described in this work. Best in class are highlighted in bold where meaningful. "λ" values outline the security claims of each scheme, considering similar (pre-quantum) cost models and (pre-quantum) attacks; we note that such values of λ can be generated using vastly different assumptions.

Table 2. Estimates in the sieving setting, where BKZ and the BDD solver are instantiated with sieving algorithms. Notation as in Table 1. Estimates marked with [†] correspond to standard BDD decoding.

Attack	τ	β	η	BDD cost	$\lvert S\rvert$	Repeats	d	#pp	$\log_2(\mathrm{rop})$
NTRU LPrime: $n = 761, q = 4591, \sigma = \sqrt{2/3}, h = 250$									$\lambda = 155$
uSVP (GSA)	0	532	532	n/a	n/a	1	1352	n/a	185.1
Dual (GSA)	45	586	n/a	n/a	n/a	$2^{148.0}$	1383	14	203.1
g-v decoding (GSA)	0	515	549	$2^{179.7}$	1	1	1351	n/a	**181.0**[†]
Non mitm hybrid (GSA)	170	580	n/a	$2^{218.9}$	$2^{178.1}$	$2^{21.4}$	1181	43	220.8
g-v decoding	0	530	562	$2^{183.5}$	1	1	1351	n/a	**185.3**[†]
Non mitm hybrid	230	615	n/a	$2^{302.1}$	$2^{189.6}$	$2^{93.3}$	1121	40	303.3
Round5: $n = 756, q = 2^{12}, \sigma \approx 4.61, h = 242$									$\lambda = 193$
uSVP (GSA)	0	664	664	n/a	n/a	1	1266	n/a	223.6
Dual (GSA)	46	748	n/a	n/a	n/a	$2^{198.6}$	1325	13	251.0
g-v decoding (GSA)	0	645	679	$2^{217.7}$	1	1	1265	n/a	**218.9**[†]
Non mitm hybrid (GSA)	225	705	n/a	$2^{273.7}$	$2^{215.4}$	$2^{39.3}$	1040	49	275.2
g-v decoding	0	660	699	$2^{223.5}$	1	1	1265	n/a	**224.1**[†]
Non mitm hybrid	290	700	n/a	$2^{393.9}$	$2^{214.8}$	$2^{160.3}$	975	43	394.9
Round5 (IoT): $n = 372, q = 2^{11}, \sigma \approx 4.61, h = 178$									$\lambda = 96$
uSVP (GSA)	0	335	335	n/a	n/a	1	682	n/a	126.6
Dual (GSA)	22	396	n/a	n/a	n/a	$2^{104.2}$	710	1	145.0
g-v decoding (GSA)	0	315	349	$2^{121.6}$	1	1	681	n/a	**122.4**[†]
Non mitm hybrid (GSA)	85	375	n/a	$2^{155.2}$	$2^{119.5}$	$2^{18.3}$	596	38	156.9
g-v decoding	0	320	358	$2^{123.9}$	1	1	681	n/a	**124.3**[†]
Non mitm hybrid	95	380	n/a	$2^{204.5}$	$2^{122.1}$	$2^{65.1}$	586	35	205.6
HElib-1024: $n = 1024, q = 2^{47}, \sigma \approx 3.19, h = 64$									
uSVP (GSA)	0	137	137	n/a	n/a	1	1939	n/a	70.3
Dual (GSA)	80	115	n/a	n/a	n/a	$2^{19.6}$	1741	7	67.1
g-v decoding (GSA)	85	125	50	$2^{66.6}$	$2^{30.0}$	$2^{2.6}$	1853	5	69.8
Non mitm hybrid (GSA)	155	115	n/a	$2^{66.2}$	$2^{40.1}$	$2^{5.6}$	1783	6	69.8

corresponds to $\mathbf{v}'_l$ and $\mathbf{v}''_g$ corresponds to $\mathbf{v}''_l$, then we hope that $\mathbf{v}'_l + \mathbf{v}''_l = \mathbf{v}_l$. The probability that this occurs has been analysed in the case that the BDD solver is Babai's Nearest Plane in [Wun19]. However, this refined model is not employed e.g. in submissions to the NIST PQC process [BCLv17,SHRS17,ZCHW17].

Our techniques share the same genealogy as the Hybrid Attack. However, in the main body of this work we consider only a setting where the guess-and-verify step is executed without the time-memory trade-off. In Appendix A, then, we also consider a meet-in-the-middle approach or time-memory trade-off where we (a) assume that collisions occur with probability one, (b) assume a square-root speed-up in the search phase and (c) ignore the memory cost.

Although our work uses preprocessing to control the dimension of the CVP problems we then have to solve in batch, we do not make specific use of techniques for solving the *Closest Vector Problem with Preprocessing* (CVPP) [Mic01]. In particular, the works [Laa16, DLdW16] discuss a time-memory trade-off in the sieving setting. After lattice reduction a *preprocessing* step can be deployed, generating a list of short vectors in some projected sublattice which can then be used to carry out many, typically cheaper, *query* steps (one for each guess). In the enumeration setting, pre-computing many reduced lattice bases allows lattice-point enumeration to be run many times, each with a low probability of success, and without incurring an additional cost for preprocessing. Thus, these techniques offer the potential for improvements to our techniques when used instead of our assumption that the cost of solving CVP is the same as the cost of solving SVP.

We also note that this work naturally gives rise to a quantum variant where quantum algorithms are used for enumeration and for the guess-and-verify phase.

In summary, we note that any analysis of variants of the Hybrid Attack requires usage of several assumptions: (a) usage of a sieving-based, or enumeration-based, SVP oracle in the lattice reduction phase (of which we consider both), (b) an output lattice basis shape, namely GSA, Z-shaped, or usage the BKZ Simulator (of which we consider the BKZ Simulator and the GSA), (c) the guessing strategy, namely brute-force, meet-in-the-middle, or quantum (of which we assume brute-force, and also consider a square-root-style meet-in-the-middle search in Appendix A), (d) the choice of BDD/CVP solver i.e Babai's algorithm, pruned enumeration, or sieving (of which we consider all three possibilities) with or without preprocessing (which we do not consider). Thus, while our work explores trade-offs in batch BDD solving it still leaves many possible variants of such trade-offs unexplored and a full investigation of the concrete cost of solving this problem is still outstanding.

Related Work. The hardness of small-secret LWE was considered in [BLP+13], which gives a reduction from LWE in dimension n with secrets sampled from $\mathbb{Z}_q^n$ to LWE in dimension $n \log q$ with a secret sampled uniformly over $\{0, 1\}^n$. This reduction has recently been revisited in [Mic18]. Several of the NTRU and LWE-based schemes submitted to the NIST standardisation process make use of small secrets [CPL+17, GZB+19, SPL+17, BCLv19].

As mentioned above, several works have explored the cost of solving CVP with Preprocessing such as [Mic01, Laa16, DLdW16].

Algorithmically, our work clearly builds on the line of works exploring hybrids of combinatorial and lattice reduction algorithms such as [MS01, How07, BGPW16, Alb17, GvVW17, Wun19]. We may also consider this work as a parameter space exploration for a specialisation of [LN13] to the case of batch BDD where many (candidate) BDD instances need to be solved. We note that the "decoding attack" is one of the three attacks considered by default in the LWE Estimator [APS15]. Thus, this work may also be considered as an investigation into the effectiveness of this attack compared to the other two considered there ("uSVP" and "Dual").

2   Preliminaries

Notation. We denote columns vectors by lower case bold letters, e.g. $\mathbf{b}$. Matrices are represented by upper case bold letters, e.g. $\mathbf{B}$. We denote the ith component of the vector $\mathbf{b}$ by b_i, where i begins at one, and similarly the $(i, j)^{th}$ entry of a matrix by $B_{i,j}$. We write $\mathbf{B}_i$ for the ith column of $\mathbf{B}$. Abusing notation, we denote by $(\mathbf{v}_1, \mathbf{v}_2, c)$ the vector formed by concatenating the entries of $\mathbf{v}_1$, $\mathbf{v}_2$ and the scalar c. We denote the ith unit vector as $\mathbf{u}_i$. A *lattice* $\Lambda = \Lambda(\mathbf{B})$ is a discrete subgroup of $\mathbb{R}^n$ which can be characterised by a (column) basis $\mathbf{B}$: $\{\mathbf{b}_1, \mathbf{b}_2, \ldots, \mathbf{b}_d\}$ which can itself be represented in matrix form $\mathbf{B} = [\mathbf{b}_1 \mid \mathbf{b}_2 \mid \cdots \mid \mathbf{b}_d]$. When $d = n$, the lattice has full rank. We denote the corresponding Gram-Schmidt orthogonalised (GSO) vectors by $\mathbf{b}_i^*$. We write $\mathbf{B}_{(\tau)}$ to represent the $d \times (d - \tau)$ submatrix of $\mathbf{B}$ constructed via dropping τ random columns of $\mathbf{B}$, i.e. $\mathbf{B}_{(\tau)} = [\mathbf{b}_{i_1} \mid \mathbf{b}_{i_2} \mid \cdots \mid \mathbf{b}_{i_{d-\tau}}]$ for some indices $1 \leq i_1 < i_2 < \cdots < i_{d-\tau} \leq d$. We similarly write $\mathbf{b}_{(\tau)}$ to denote dropping the corresponding τ components of the vector $\mathbf{b}$. We write $\pi_i(\mathbf{x})$ to denote the orthogonal projection of $\mathbf{x}$ onto the space spanned by the set of vectors $\{\mathbf{b}_1, \mathbf{b}_2, \ldots, \mathbf{b}_{i-1}\}$. We denote by $\lambda_i(\Lambda)$ the ith successive minima of the lattice Λ, i.e. the radius of the smallest ball, centred at the origin, containing at least i linearly independent lattice vectors. Unless stated otherwise, our logarithms are to base two.

$T_{\mathsf{bdd}}(\eta)$ denotes the cost of solving BDD in a dimension η projected lattice (typically $\pi_{d-\eta+1}(\Lambda)$). This process has probability p_{bdd} of returning the projection $\pi_{d-\eta+1}(\mathbf{v})$ of a closest (in the projected sublattice) lattice vector $\mathbf{v}$ to our target $\mathbf{t}$. Typically, we will have $p_{\mathsf{bdd}} \approx 1$. We denote the probability of correctly guessing τ random zeros of the LWE secret (where τ is the fixed guessing dimension) by p_0. The probability p_i for $1 \leq i \leq \min(\tau, h)$ represents the probability that the guessed components of the LWE secret contain i non-zero components. $\mathcal{S}_j$ is the set of all ternary vectors of length τ with Hamming weight j. Furthermore,

$$p_{\mathsf{babai}} \approx \prod_{1 \leq i \leq d} \left(1 - \frac{2}{B(\frac{d-1}{2}, \frac{1}{2})} \int_{\min(r_i, 1)}^{1} (1 - t^2)^{(d-3)/2} \, dt \right)$$

is the (heuristic) probability of Babai's algorithm lifting the projected short vector (found via solving BDD) to the full lattice [Wun19]. Here d is the number of dimensions we have to lift the projected solution through, and $r_i = \|\mathbf{b}_i^*\|/2\|\mathbf{v}\|$ where $\|\mathbf{v}\|$ is the (expected) norm of the target vector, and $B(\cdot, \cdot)$ denotes the Beta function. We cost this lifting process as in [Wun19] to be $T_{\mathsf{lift}} = d^2/2^{1.06}$.

Our work is concerned with the following computational problem:

Definition 1 (α-Bounded Distance Decoding (BDD$_\alpha$)). *Given a lattice basis $\mathbf{B}$, a vector $\mathbf{t}$, and a parameter $0 < \alpha$ such that the Euclidean distance* $dist(\mathbf{t}, \mathbf{B}) < \alpha\lambda_1(\mathbf{B})$, *find the lattice vector $\mathbf{v} \in \Lambda(\mathbf{B})$ which is closest to $\mathbf{t}$.*

As discussed above, we can use a BDD_α solver for solving the NTRU and LWE problems. In this case we have $\alpha < 1/2$ which guarantees unique decoding (up to signs and rotations in the case of NTRU). To solve these instances, we may repeatedly call a BDD solver on smaller lattices where $\alpha \approx 1$. When solving the instances with $\alpha \approx 1$ we do not have a guarantee of unique decoding, only an expectation. In this case, we might more appropriately refer to the instances as CVP instances.

Definition 2 (NTRU [HPS96]). *Let n, q be positive integers, $\phi \in \mathbb{Z}[x]$ be a monic polynomial of degree n, and $\mathbb{R}_q = \mathbb{Z}_q[x]/(\phi)$. Let $f \in \mathbb{R}_q^\times, g \in \mathbb{R}_q$ be small polynomials (i.e. having small coefficients) and $h = g \cdot f^{-1} \bmod q$.*
Search-NTRU *is the problem of recovering f or g given h.*
Decision-NTRU *is the problem of deciding if h is of the form $h = g \cdot f^{-1}$ or is chosen uniformly at random.*

Definition 3 (LWE [Reg05]). *Let n, q be positive integers, χ be a probability distribution on $\mathbb{Z}$ and $\mathbf{s}$ be a secret vector in $\mathbb{Z}_q^n$. We denote the LWE Distribution $L_{\mathbf{s},\chi,q}$ as the distribution on $\mathbb{Z}_q^n \times \mathbb{Z}_q$ given by choosing $\mathbf{a} \in \mathbb{Z}_q^n$ uniformly at random, choosing $e \in \mathbb{Z}$ according to χ and considering it as an element of $\mathbb{Z}_q$, and outputting $(\mathbf{a}, \langle \mathbf{a}, \mathbf{s} \rangle + e) \in \mathbb{Z}_q^n \times \mathbb{Z}_q$.*
Search-LWE *is the problem of recovering the vector $\mathbf{s}$ from a collection $\{(\mathbf{a}_i, b_i)\}_{i=1}^m$ of samples drawn according to $L_{\mathbf{s},\chi,q}$.*
Decision-LWE *is the problem of distinguishing whether samples $\{(\mathbf{a}_i, b_i)\}_{i=1}^m$ are drawn from the LWE distribution $L_{\mathbf{s},\chi,q}$ or uniformly from $\mathbb{Z}_q^n \times \mathbb{Z}_q$.*

LWE, as defined in [Reg05], makes use of a rounded Gaussian distribution for the error distribution χ. However, LWE is typically considered with a discrete Gaussian distribution [LP11]. In practice, many schemes choose bounded uniform error distributions $\mathcal{U}_{[a,b]}$ [LDK+17] or binomial distributions [PAA+17].

Many constructions in the literature make use of Ring-LWE [SSTX09, LPR10] or Module-LWE [LS15] where the vectors $\mathbf{a}_i$ are not uniformly random, but have structure induced by a ring or module. We can treat these problems as LWE by ignoring this additional structure. Since our work does not exploit this additional structure, this is how we will proceed.

Secret Distributions. LWE, as defined, samples a secret $\mathbf{s}$ uniformly at random from $\mathbb{Z}_q^n$. In practice, many schemes choose to restrict the space of potential secrets by sampling secrets which are *small* and/or *sparse* by sampling from some *secret distribution* χ_s. Below we outline typical choices for these secret distributions, extending the notation from [Alb17].

Definition 4 (Small Secret Distributions). *Let n, q be positive integers.*

$\mathcal{B}^-$ *is the probability distribution on $\mathbb{Z}_q^n$ where each component is independently sampled uniformly at random from $\{-1, 0, 1\}$.*
$\mathcal{B}_h^-$ *is the probability distribution on $\mathbb{Z}_q^n$ where components are sampled uniformly at random from $\{-1, 0, 1\}$ with the additional guarantee that exactly h components are non-zero.*

$\mathcal{B}^-_{(h_1,h_2)}$ is the probability distribution on $\mathbb{Z}^n_q$ where components are sampled uniformly at random from $\{-1, 0, 1\}$ with the additional guarantee that exactly h_1 components are equal to -1 and exactly h_2 components are equal to 1.

We refer to a *small-secret LWE instance* as an LWE instance which samples secrets from one of the distributions outlined in Definition 4. Examples of such parameter choices are seen in homomorphic encryption libraries HElib ($\mathcal{B}^-_{64}$) [Hal18] and SEAL ($\mathcal{B}^-$) [SEA18]. In the NTRU domain, f is typically drawn from the distribution $\mathcal{B}^-_h$ for some h. The NTRUPrime submission to the NIST PQC standardisation process considers the distributions $\mathcal{B}^-_{250}$ and $\mathcal{B}^-_{286}$ [BCLv19]. Some other schemes in the NTRU domain make use of the secret distribution $\mathcal{B}^-_{(\frac{h}{2},\frac{h}{2})}$, where h is the Hamming weight of the secret.

Lattice Reduction and BDD Solver Costs. We consider lattice reduction when instantiated with either enumeration or sieving for solving the shortest vector problem. In particular, we consider the BKZ algorithm [SE94] parametrised by a block size β which determines the running time (at least exponential in β) and output quality. For enumeration [FP85,Kan83], we consider the cost of lattice reduction using blocksize β on a lattice of dimension d to be

$$T_{\mathsf{BKZ}}(\beta, d) = 8\, d \cdot 2^{0.18728\beta \log(\beta) - 1.019\beta + 16.1} \text{ enum. nodes}$$

which is taken from [APS15] based on experiments from [CN11]. To translate from the number of nodes visited during enumeration to CPU cycles, the literature typically assumes one node ≈ 100 CPU cycles [dt16]. For sieving [AKS01,BDGL16], we consider the cost of lattice reduction using blocksize β on a lattice of dimension d to be:

$$T_{\mathsf{BKZ}}(\beta, d) = 8\, d \cdot 2^{0.292\beta + 16.4} \tag{1}$$

where the constant term is somewhat arbitrarily picked as in [APS15].

"Core"-style BKZ cost models used in e.g [ADPS16], where the cost of BKZ is equated to the cost of a single SVP call and lower order terms are simply set to zero, are not considered in our work. There are several reasons for this: first, these estimates do not claim to capture the running time but constitute explicit lower bounds. Second, as a consequence, these costs suggest, in contrast to the state-of-the-art, that combinatorial techniques do not perform as well, especially in the sieving setting [ACD+18]. Third, since we are using the BKZ simulator from [CN11] to emulate the effect of lattice reduction more precisely, the number of tours has an effect on the output basis shape.

We also make use of both enumeration-based, and sieving-based, $\mathrm{BDD}_1/\mathrm{CVP}$ solvers. When using enumeration to solve $\mathrm{BDD}_1/\mathrm{CVP}$ in dimension η, we assume a cost of:

$$T_{\mathsf{bdd}}(\eta) = 2^{0.18728\eta \log(\eta) - 1.019\eta + 16.1} \text{ enum. nodes}$$

where again we assume that one node ≈ 100 CPU cycles [dt16]. Such an enumeration is assumed to succeed with probability close to one, i.e. $p_{\text{bdd}} \approx 1$. When using sieving to solve BDD_1/CVP in dimension η, we assume a cost of:

$$T_{\text{bdd}}(\eta) = 2^{0.292\eta + 16.4}$$

based on the results of [Laa16], which suggest that without preprocessing (see the discussion in the introduction) sieving for short vectors has the same asymptotic cost as sieving for close vectors. We assume that this sieving process suceeds with probability close to one, i.e $p_{\text{bdd}} \approx 1$. We note that it is always clear from context whether an enumeration-based, or a sieving-based, BDD_1/CVP solver is being deployed.

2.1   The Geometric Series Assumption and 'Z-Shaped' Bases

To determine the performance of the algorithms considered in this work, we are interested in the lengths of the GSO vectors after lattice reduction has taken place. We briefly recall the notion of the *root-Hermite factor* δ, which describes the quality of a basis after lattice reduction.

Definition 5 (root-Hermite factor). *For a basis* $\mathbf{B}$ *of a lattice* Λ *of dimension* d, *the root-Hermite factor is defined to be:*

$$\delta = \left(\frac{\|\mathbf{b}_1\|}{\det(\Lambda)^{1/d}} \right)^{1/d}.$$

For BKZ blocksizes considered in this work ($\beta \geq 40$), this value is well approximated [Che13] by $\delta^{2(\beta-1)} = \frac{\beta}{2\pi e}(\beta\pi)^{1/\beta}$. This value decreases towards 1 as the lattice reduction blocksize β increases.

In the context of the decoding attack, the lengths of the GSO vectors will determine the success probability of our BDD solvers. These lengths may be approximated the Geometric Series Assumption (GSA) [Sch03]:

Definition 6 (Geometric Series Assumption). *Let* $\{\mathbf{b}_1, \mathbf{b}_2, \ldots, \mathbf{b}_d\}$ *be a basis of a lattice* Λ, *of quality* δ, *that is output by some lattice reduction algorithm. Then the lengths* $\|\mathbf{b}_i^*\|$ *for* $(1 \leq i \leq d)$ *of the Gram-Schmidt vectors of this basis are approximated by* $\|\mathbf{b}_i^*\| = \alpha^{i-1}\|\mathbf{b}_1\|$ *for some* $0 < \alpha < 1$.[1]

We can combine this assumption with $\|\mathbf{b}_1\| = \delta^d \cdot \det(\Lambda)^{1/d}$ and $\prod \|\mathbf{b}_i^*\| = \det(\Lambda)$ to determine $\alpha \approx \delta^{-2}$.

There are several models in the literature for the behaviour of the BKZ algorithm on q-ary lattices. In most of the literature on solving LWE via BDD, we use the public LWE matrix $\mathbf{A} \in \mathbb{Z}_q^{(m \times n)}$ to construct a lattice basis $\mathbb{Z}^{(n+m) \times (n+m)}$

---

[1] Note that, following the literature, we are overloading notation here: this α is unrelated to the BDD approximation factor α. It will always be clear from context which α we are referring to.

for which it is commonly assumed that the Geometric Series Assumption is relatively accurate after running BKZ-β with $\beta \ll m+n$. The literature on analysing the Hybrid Attack considers lattice bases of the form

$$\begin{pmatrix} q\mathbf{I}_m & \mathbf{A} \\ 0 & \mathbf{I}_n \end{pmatrix}. \tag{2}$$

This form of writing the basis immediately suggests that the GSA might not hold. Specifically, when the GSA predicts that $\|\mathbf{b}_1\| > q$, this is longer than the first vector already in the basis before lattice reduction and thus we will obtain $\|\mathbf{b}_1\| = q$. As a consequence, lattice reduction is expected to produce a "Z-shaped" basis [How07], comprised of leading qs, trailing ones and a middle part approximated by the GSA.

In Fig. 1 we give an illustrative example, chosen to highlight the effect, of the output of lattice reduction as implemented in FPLLL [dt16] which clearly illustrates the Z-shape.

To model this Z-shape, we can insist on no vector after lattice reduction having norm $> q$ [Wun19]. Let k be the number of lattice vectors which follow a GSA-style behaviour, and the other $(d - k)$ vectors remain as q. Explicitly, we have:

$$\|\mathbf{b}_i^*\| = \begin{cases} q & \text{if } i \leq d - k \\ \delta^{-2(i-(d-k)-1)+k} q^{\frac{k-n}{k}} & \text{otherwise.} \end{cases}$$

Making the assumption that $\|\mathbf{b}_{(d-k+1)}^*\| \approx q$ [Wun19], it is possible to compute a value for k, namely $k = \min\left(\left\lfloor \sqrt{\frac{n}{\log_q(\delta)}} \right\rfloor, d\right)$. Indeed, running the BKZ simulator from [Che13] will output a predicted shape closely resembling this prediction for $\beta \ll m + n$. On the other hand, [Wun19] makes no attempt to model the number of trailing ones. Indeed, while some works pick the length of this part by choosing a sublattice to reduce [HPS+15], no work in the literature offers a way of predicting the number of trailing ones.

For this reason, in this work we assume that the q-ary structure of the lattice does not impact the shape of the basis after lattice reduction, i.e. we do not assume leading qs or trailing 1s. This assumption can be made to hold by rerandomising the input basis for lattice reduction. Considering the techniques in this work in a setting exploiting the q-ary structure is an interesting area for future work.

2.2   Decoding Small-Secret LWE

The decoding approach for solving small-secret LWE instances [BG14] $\mathbf{b} = \mathbf{A} \cdot \mathbf{s} + \mathbf{e}$ constructs a lattice for which the vector $(\mathbf{b}, \mathbf{0})$ is separated by the short vector $(-\mathbf{e}, \mathbf{s})$ to the lattice point $(\mathbf{A} \cdot \mathbf{s} \bmod q, \mathbf{s})$. The basis of the lattice is given by the columns of the matrix $\mathbf{B}$, where

$$\mathbf{B} = \begin{pmatrix} q\mathbf{I}_m & \mathbf{A} \\ 0 & \mathbf{I}_n \end{pmatrix}.$$

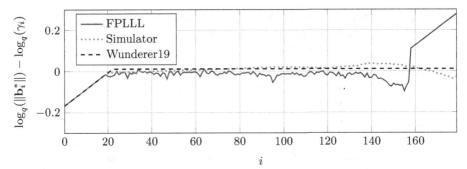

We define $\gamma_i = \alpha^{i-1}\delta^d \det(\Lambda)^{1/d}$ and thus the GSA corresponds to the line at $y = 0$.

Fig. 1. Example of BKZ-60 reduction on a q-ary lattice of dimension $d = 180$ with $q = 17$ and volume 17^{80} for bases constructed as in (2), along with the output of BKZ simulation and the heuristic from [Wun19].

In more detail, we have that

$$\begin{pmatrix} q\mathbf{I}_m & \mathbf{A} \\ \mathbf{0} & \mathbf{I}_n \end{pmatrix} \begin{pmatrix} * \\ \mathbf{s} \end{pmatrix} = \begin{pmatrix} q* + \mathbf{A} \cdot \mathbf{s} \\ \mathbf{s} \end{pmatrix} = \begin{pmatrix} \mathbf{b} \\ \mathbf{0} \end{pmatrix} + \begin{pmatrix} -\mathbf{e} \\ \mathbf{s} \end{pmatrix} \bmod q.$$

After lattice reduction on the lattice spanned by $\mathbf{B}$, we perform enumeration around the target point $(\mathbf{b}, \mathbf{0})$, which is close to a unique lattice point. With some probability, this enumeration will return this unique closest lattice point, enabling recovery of the LWE secret. As noted in [MS01] we can combine this attack with *dimension reduction techniques*, where τ components of the secret are guessed (as zero) and the associated decoding problem is solved in dimension $(d - \tau)$. We refer to this variant as *drop-and-solve decoding*.

2.3 The Hybrid Meet-in-the-Middle and Lattice Reduction Attack

The Hybrid meet-in-the-middle and lattice reduction strategy was introduced by Howgrave-Graham in [How07]. It leverages small and sparse target vectors by combining a lattice reduction phase with a guess and verify phase. As opposed to solving BDD in a dimension d lattice, the Hybrid Attack sets a guessing dimension τ, carries out lattice reduction in dimension $(d - \tau)$ and solves BDD on a dimension $(d - \tau)$ lattice by decoding on various points corresponding to guesses in the τ-dimensional guessing space. When $s \leftarrow_{\$} \mathcal{B}^-$, the coefficients s_i of the secret vector are contained within the set $\{-1, 0, 1\}$. We then observe that

$$\mathbf{A} \cdot \mathbf{s} = \sum_{\{i|s_i=1\}} \mathbf{A}_i - \sum_{\{j|s_j=-1\}} \mathbf{A}_j. \tag{3}$$

We begin by choosing a guessing dimension τ and generate the lattice basis determined by the columns of the matrix

$$\mathbf{X} = \begin{pmatrix} q\mathbf{I}_m & \mathbf{A}_{(\tau)} \\ \mathbf{0} & \mathbf{I}_{n-\tau} \end{pmatrix}$$

where $\mathbf{A}_{(\tau)}$ denotes the matrix $\mathbf{A}$ with τ random columns dropped. We then reduce this basis to $\tilde{\mathbf{X}} = \mathsf{BKZ}_\beta(\mathbf{X})$, and use it to carry out decoding using Babai's Nearest Plane [Bab86] on vectors in the τ-dimensional guessing space. We have:

$$\begin{pmatrix} q\mathbf{I}_m & \mathbf{A}_{(\tau)} \\ 0 & \mathbf{I}_{n-\tau} \end{pmatrix} \begin{pmatrix} * \\ \mathbf{s}_{(\tau)} \end{pmatrix} = \begin{pmatrix} q* + \mathbf{A}_{(\tau)} \cdot \mathbf{s}_{(\tau)} \\ \mathbf{s}_{(\tau)} \end{pmatrix}.$$

If we correctly guess zero components then we have $\mathbf{A}_{(\tau)} \cdot \mathbf{s}_{(\tau)} = \mathbf{A} \cdot \mathbf{s}$, allowing us to decode on the point $(\mathbf{b}, \mathbf{0})$. Otherwise, assuming without loss of generality that the last τ components of $\mathbf{s}$ were the guessed components, we can make a new guess $\mathbf{v}_g = \sum_{k=d-\tau+1}^{d} c_k \cdot \mathbf{u}_k$ for some values $c_k \in \{-1, 0, 1\}$. For this new guess, we can decode on the point $(\mathbf{b} - \sum_{k=n-\tau+1}^{n} c_k \cdot \mathbf{A}_k, 0)$. For the correct guess $\mathbf{v} = \sum_{k=n-\tau+1}^{n} s_k \cdot \mathbf{u}_k$ we have

$$\mathbf{b} - \sum_{k=n-\tau+1}^{n} s_k \cdot \mathbf{A}_k = \mathbf{A}_{(\tau)} \cdot \mathbf{s}_{(\tau)} + \mathbf{e} \bmod q.$$

Therefore, we have that $(\mathbf{b} - \sum_{k=d-\tau+1}^{d} s_k \cdot \mathbf{A}_k, 0)$ is separated from the lattice point $(\mathbf{A}_{(\tau)} \cdot \mathbf{s}_{(\tau)} \bmod q, \mathbf{s}_{(\tau)})$ by the vector $(-\mathbf{e}, \mathbf{s}_{(\tau)})$, as is required. Typically, this guessing is realised via the usage of a time-memory trade-off approach. As previously mentioned, throughout this work we do not consider any meet-in-the-middle techniques, except for compatibility with previous works in Appendix A.

3   A Spectrum of Decoding Approaches

In this section we outline the expected costs of: (i) the classical "decoding" approach in the LWE literature, (i) the "drop-and-solve decoding" approach, which is a combination of zero-guessing and solving a single BDD instance in a reduced dimension, and (ii) our *guess-and-verify* decoding approach, where multiple BDD instances are solved per lattice reduction step. Our attack parameters are chosen such that $p_{\mathsf{bdd}} \approx 1$ and $p_{\mathsf{babai}} \approx 1$, although for clarity we include these probabilities in the running times presented in this section. Recall that p_{bdd} corresponds to the probability of solving BDD in the dimension η projected sublattice, where η is chosen in our work such that the probability of lifting the solution to the full lattice is $p_{\mathsf{babai}} \approx 1$. Exploring trade-offs which arise by varying these probabilities is interesting future work.

Running Example. Throughout this section we make use of a running example to illustrate the behaviour of the approaches under consideration. We consider the small-secret LWE parameter set $n = 653, q = 4621, \sigma \approx \sqrt{2/3}, \chi_s = \mathcal{B}_{100}^-$ and use this parameter set as a reference throughout. We note that for this parameter set, a combinatorial dual attack costs $2^{214.9}$ CPU cycles ($\beta = 210$), and a combinatorial uSVP attack, assuming use of the GSA, costs $2^{209.6}$ CPU cycles ($\beta = 223$), according to the LWE Estimator [APS15][2], under the enumeration-based BKZ cost model mentioned in Sect. 2.

---

[2] All estimates use the LWE Estimator as of commit **3019847**.

Decoding. We start by outlining the expected running time of the decoding approach described in Sect. 2.2. Typically, the cost of lattice reduction and decoding are balanced, and the output BDD probability determines the number of times the algorithm is repeated. The total expected running time is

$$T_{\mathsf{Dec}} = \frac{T_{\mathsf{BKZ}}(\beta_{\mathsf{Dec}}, d) + T_{\mathsf{bdd}}(\eta_{\mathsf{Dec}})}{p_{\mathsf{babai}} \cdot p_{\mathsf{bdd}}}.$$

Lattice reduction is carried out on the full lattice with block size β_{Dec}, and a BDD_1 solver is used on a projected sub-lattice of dimension η_{Dec}, which is determined by (a variant of) the success condition in [ADPS16]. Here p_{babai} is the probability of lifting the candidate solution from $\pi_{d-\eta_{\mathsf{Dec}}+1}(\Lambda)$ to the full lattice. Since η_{Dec} is determined using the condition from [ADPS16] we have $p_{\mathsf{babai}} \approx 1$ [AGVW17]. For our running example parameter set, assuming the GSA, this approach has a cost of $2^{293.0}$ CPU cycles with an optimal blocksize $\beta_{\mathsf{Dec}} = 419$, where $\eta_{\mathsf{Dec}} = 429$. Note that when $\eta_{\mathsf{Dec}} = \beta_{\mathsf{Dec}}$ then this is equivalent to the uSVP approach in [ADPS16].

Drop-and-Solve Decoding. In this approach, we guess τ zero components of **s** and then run the decoding attack in dimension $(d - \tau)$ [MS01, Alb17, ACD+18]. If we are unsuccessful, we restart with a fresh guess for the positions of zeroes. The core idea is that the lower running time of the dimension-reduced problem will trade-off positively against the probability of guessing zero components. If we correctly guess, for example, the first τ zeros, then $(s_{\tau+1}, \ldots, s_n, \mathbf{e})$ can be found via solving BDD_1 in the dimension-reduced problem. The total expected running time of this strategy is

$$T_{\mathsf{dsDec}} = \frac{T_{\mathsf{BKZ}}(\beta_{\mathsf{dsDec}}, d - \tau) + T_{\mathsf{bdd}}(\eta_{\mathsf{dsDec}})}{p_{\mathsf{babai}} \cdot p_{\mathsf{bdd}} \cdot p_0}.$$

Here p_0 denotes the probability of correctly guessing τ random zeros of the LWE secret. Lattice reduction is carried out on a lattice of dimension $(d - \tau)$ with block size β_{dsDec}, and enumeration is carried out in the projected sub-lattice whose dimension corresponds again to (a variant of) the [ADPS16] success condition. The meaning of p_{babai} is as above. For our running example parameter set, assuming the GSA, this attack returns a complexity of $2^{208.2}$ CPU cycles with optimal values of $\beta_{\mathsf{dsDec}} = 170$ and $\tau = 315$.

Guess-and-Verify Decoding. There is no a priori reason to restrict the decoding algorithm in any guess-and-verify decoding attack to Babai's Nearest Plane algorithm (as in the hybrid attack). Instead, we may employ stronger BDD_1 solvers which in turn permits a reduction in the cost of preprocessing, or the usage of a lower guessing dimension. In this *g-v decoding* attack, we consider a BDD_1 dimension as defined by (a variant of) the success condition from [ADPS16]. The overall expected cost of this approach then becomes

$$T_{\mathsf{gvDec}} = \frac{T_{\mathsf{BKZ}}(\beta_{\mathsf{gvDec}}, d - \tau) + \|S_{t_{\mathsf{gvDec}}}\| \cdot T_{\mathsf{bdd}}(\eta_{\mathsf{gvDec}})}{p_{\mathsf{babai}} \cdot p_{\mathsf{bdd}} \cdot \left(\sum_{i=0}^{t_{\mathsf{gvDec}}} p_i\right)}.$$

where the probabilities p_i for $1 \leq i \leq t_{\mathsf{gvDec}}$ represents the probability that the guessed components of the LWE secret contain i non-zero components. For our running example parameter set, assuming the GSA, this attack returns a complexity of $2^{186.1}$ CPU cycles with $\beta_{\mathsf{gvDec}} = 225$ and $\tau = 335$, with optimal choices of $\eta_{\mathsf{gvDec}} = 49$ $t_{\mathsf{gvDec}} = 16$ so that $\|\mathcal{S}_{t_{\mathsf{gvDec}}}\| = \sum_{i=0}^{16} \binom{335}{i} \cdot 2^i \approx 2^{105.5}$.

We note that "guess-and-verify" decoding encompasses the usual decoding strategy ($\tau = 0, \|\mathcal{S}_{t_{\mathsf{gvDec}}}\| = 1, \sum p_i = 1$) and the "drop-and-solve" strategy ($\tau > 0, \|\mathcal{S}_{t_{\mathsf{gvDec}}}\| = 1, t_{\mathsf{gvDec}} = 0$). On the other hand, as specified here, it does not encompass the hybrid attack (even without time-memory trade-offs) since we insist on picking β, η such that $p_{\mathsf{babai}} \approx 1$ which is not the case for the Hybrid Attack in general.

4   Estimates

In this section we apply our techniques to parameter sets from the NTRU-LPrime [BCLv19] and Round5 [BGL+18] submissions to the NIST PQC standardisation process, as well as a parameter set used in the homomorphic encryption library HElib [Hal18]. We compare our results against the LWE estimator under the same assumptions, i.e. considering the cost models in Sect. 2 and the Geometric Series Assumption. We also present our results considering usage of the BKZ simulator, which estimates the shape of the basis after BKZ reduction. Our results are given in Tables 1 and 2.

NTRU LPrime. We consider one of the three NTRU LPrime parameter sets from [BCLv19]. The construction is based on LWE with a ternary, fixed Hamming weight, secret and a random ternary error. Specifically, the parameter set considered is:

$$n = 761, q = 4591, \sigma \approx \sqrt{2/3}, \chi_s = \mathcal{B}_{250}^-.$$

Round5. For Round5, we consider the NIST level 3 parameter set from [GZB+19]. Round 5 is based on the Learning with Rounding problem (LWR) [BPR12] with a ternary, fixed hamming weight, secret. In the case of LWR, we have an additional parameter p which is an additional modulus considered in the deterministic rounding process. In this case, we have $\sigma \approx \sqrt{\frac{(q/p)^2-1}{12}}$ as in [ACD+18]. We can therefore model this parameter set as LWE with

$$n = 756, \sigma \approx 4.61, q = 2^{12}, p = 2^8, \chi_s = \mathcal{B}_{242}^-.$$

We also consider the IoT specific use-case parameter set from [GZB+19]. We can model this parameter set as LWE with

$$n = 372, \sigma \approx 4.61, q = 2^{11}, p = 2^7, \chi_s = \mathcal{B}_{178}^-.$$

HElib. We also consider our approach in the context of the homomorphic encryption library HElib. To compare with previous works, we consider the sparse-secret parameter set outlined in [Alb17]. Specifically, the parameter set we consider is:

$$n = 1024, q = 2^{47}, \sigma \approx 3.19, \chi_s = \mathcal{B}_{64}^-.$$

Acknowledgements. The authors thank the anonymous SAC reviewers for their feedback, which has been used to improve this work.

A   Meet-in-the-Middle

We consider a meet-in-the-middle approach where we assume (a) that collisions occur with probability 1, and (b) a square-root speed-up in the search phase. As discussed above, this modelling has been shown to be not correct [Wun19]. We include it here for compatibility with previous works which make similar assumptions, e.g [BCLv19]. On the other hand, we assume "free memory" here, i.e. we do not take the cost of memory into account. As illustrated in Table 3 under these assumptions and in the enumeration setting the Hybrid Attack and "g-v decoding" are essentially on par; in the sieving setting, BDD decoding is the most efficient.

Table 3. Estimates in enumeration setting considering a "meet-in-the-middle" approach which does not consider probabilities of failure in the meet-in-the-middle phase. Such an approach considers a square-root speed-up in the guessing phase. Notation as in Table 1.

Attack	τ	β	η	BDD cost	$|S|$	Repeats	d	#pp	$\log_2(\text{rop})$
NTRU LPrime: $n = 761, q = 4591, \sigma = \sqrt{2/3}, h = 250$									$\lambda = 222$
sqrt g-v decoding (GSA)	370	350	43	$2^{243.5}$	$2^{412.2}$	$2^{11.5}$	941	102	245.0
sqrt hybrid (GSA)	360	335	n/a	$2^{240.1}$	$2^{402.8}$	$2^{20.0}$	951	100	**241.3**
sqrt g-v decoding	370	380	119	$2^{273.6}$	$2^{400.0}$	$2^{15.5}$	941	97	**274.7**
sqrt hybrid	395	350	n/a	$2^{274.9}$	$2^{428.3}$	$2^{42.1}$	916	104	275.9
Round5: $n = 756, q = 2^{12}, \sigma \approx 4.61, h = 242$									$\lambda = 270$
sqrt g-v decoding (GSA)	445	395	37	$2^{283.9}$	$2^{490.0}$	$2^{14.1}$	734	120	285.5
sqrt hybrid (GSA)	425	365	n/a	$2^{277.0}$	$2^{453.9}$	$2^{32.0}$	754	109	**278.0**
sqrt g-v decoding	450	430	131	$2^{324.8}$	$2^{474.6}$	$2^{22.7}$	729	113	325.9
sqrt hybrid	460	390	n/a	$2^{320.5}$	$2^{496.6}$	$2^{54.3}$	719	120	**321.6**
Round5 (IoT): $n = 372, q = 2^{11}, \sigma \approx 4.61, h = 178$									$\lambda = 129$
sqrt g-v decoding (GSA)	175	250	48	$2^{156.7}$	$2^{250.8}$	$2^{4.0}$	506	80	157.8
sqrt hybrid (GSA)	165	225	n/a	$2^{151.6}$	$2^{234.5}$	$2^{17.4}$	516	74	**152.9**
g-v decoding	170	270	101	$2^{174.3}$	$2^{237.2}$	$2^{6.5}$	511	73	175.4
non mitm hybrid	180	240	n/a	$2^{172.2}$	$2^{256.4}$	$2^{27.1}$	501	81	**173.4**
HElib-1024: $n = 1024, q = 2^{47}, \sigma \approx 3.19, h = 64$									
sqrt g-v decoding (GSA)	210	95	36	$2^{59.9}$	$2^{59.7}$	$2^{5.2}$	1599	9	62.0
sqrt hybrid (GSA)	270	85	n/a	$2^{60.8}$	$2^{63.1}$	$2^{9.1}$	1539	9	61.8

Table 4. Estimates in sieving setting for a "meet-in-the-middle" approach as in Table 3. Notation as in Table 1. Estimates marked with † correspond to standard BDD decoding.

Attack	τ	β	η	BDD cost	$|S|$	Repeats	d	#pp	$\log_2(\mathsf{rop})$
NTRU LPrime: $n = 761, q = 4591, \sigma = \sqrt{2/3}, h = 250$									$\lambda = 155$
sqrt g-v decoding (GSA)	0	515	549	$2^{179.7}$	1	1	1351	0	$\mathbf{181.0}^\dagger$
sqrt hybrid (GSA)	260	475	n/a	$2^{181.3}$	$2^{296.5}$	$2^{13.9}$	1091	75	182.7
sqrt g-v decoding	0	530	562	$2^{183.5}$	1	1	1351	0	$\mathbf{185.3}^\dagger$
sqrt hybrid	315	550	n/a	$2^{230.4}$	$2^{341.1}$	$2^{40.9}$	1036	83	231.7
Round5: $n = 756, q = 2^{12}, \sigma \approx 4.61, h = 242$									$\lambda = 193$
sqrt g-v decoding (GSA)	0	645	679	$2^{217.7}$	1	1	1265	0	$\mathbf{218.9}^\dagger$
sqrt hybrid (GSA)	320	565	n/a	$2^{216.4}$	$2^{350.7}$	$2^{22.3}$	945	86	**217.5**
sqrt g-v decoding	0	660	699	$2^{223.5}$	1	1	1265	0	$\mathbf{224.1}^\dagger$
sqrt hybrid	390	660	n/a	$2^{288.4}$	$2^{405.8}$	$2^{67.0}$	875	96	289.6
Round5 (IoT): $n = 372, q = 2^{11}, \sigma \approx 4.61, h = 178$									$\lambda = 96$
sqrt g-v decoding (GSA)	0	315	349	$2^{121.6}$	1	1	681	0	$\mathbf{122.4}^\dagger$
sqrt hybrid (GSA)	135	300	n/a	$2^{126.9}$	$2^{196.9}$	$2^{11.4}$	546	65	128.2
sqrt g-v decoding	0	320	358	$2^{123.9}$	1	1	681	0	$\mathbf{124.3}^\dagger$
sqrt hybrid	155	335	n/a	$2^{155.2}$	$2^{218.1}$	$2^{29.2}$	526	68	156.3
HElib-1024: $n = 1024, q = 2^{47}, \sigma \approx 3.19, h = 64$									
sqrt g-v decoding (GSA)	195	100	31	$2^{63.1}$	$2^{53.4}$	$2^{5.3}$	1743	8	65.1
sqrt hybrid (GSA)	235	95	n/a	$2^{61.7}$	$2^{72.1}$	$2^{5.2}$	1703	11	63.6

B   Case Study: NTRU LPrime

We consider NTRU LPrime [BCLv19] as a case study of assumptions within the Hybrid Attack. This issue has recently been discussed on the "pqc-forum" associated to the NIST standardisation process [Duc19]. In the NTRUPrime Round 2 submission document [BCLv19] an updated security evaluation is provided based on the analysis of [Wun19]. The security evaluation considers uSVP and Hybrid approaches, and does not consider dual attacks. The Hybrid Attack analysis is made using the following assumptions:

– The modified GSA for q-ary lattices [Wun19] is considered as the output basis shape of BKZ, based on the technique of reducing a sublattice of dimension $d - k$, where k is the number of "untouched" q-vectors.
– The use of the formula from [Wun19] for the success of Babai's Nearest Plane algorithm, i.e

$$p_{\mathsf{np}} \approx \prod_{1 \leq i \leq d} \left(1 - \frac{2}{B\left(\frac{d-1}{2}, \frac{1}{2}\right)} \int_{\min(r_i, 1)}^{1} (1 - t^2)^{(d-3)/2} \, dt \right)$$

where $r_i = \frac{\|\mathbf{b}_i^*\|}{2\|\mathbf{v}\|}$, $\|\mathbf{v}\|$ is the expected length of the target vector, i.e $\|\mathbf{v}\| = \sqrt{\sigma^2 \cdot m + \frac{n-\tau}{n} \cdot h}$, and $B(\cdot, \cdot)$ is the Beta function.

- The cost of Babai's Nearest Plane algorithm is considered to be one operation.
- In the meet-in-the-middle variant of the Hybrid Attack, the probability of collisions is one.
- In the quantum variant of the Hybrid Attack, the techniques from [GvVW17] are considered, which improves the search compared to Grover's algorithm.
- Lattice scaling is considered for the uSVP attack, but not for the hybrid attack.
- Drop-and-solve style techniques are considered in the uSVP attack.
- Memory consumption for the meet-in-the-middle step is considered.
- Core-style BKZ cost models are considered, i.e $2^{0.292\beta}$ (no lower order terms) in the sieving setting, and $2^{0.18728\beta \log(\beta) - 1.019\beta + 16.1}$ in the enumeration setting.

We modified the script for estimating security accompanying [BCLv19] to provide *individual* estimates for a Hybrid Attack with "classical" guessing, and a Hybrid Attack with a meet-in-the-middle approach (as opposed to only outputting the estimate for the fastest attack) to retrieve the estimates in Table 5.

Table 5. Estimates from the NTRU LPrime Round 2 security script, best in class is highlighted in bold. Based on [BCLv19, Table 2].

BKZ model	Pre-quantum				Post-quantum			
Memory cost	Enum		Sieving		Enum		Sieving	
	free	"Real"	Free	"Real"	Free	"Real"	Free	"Real"
uSVP	364	364	**155**	**210**	187	**187**	140	**210**
Hybrid (classical)	307	307	194	235	219	219	183	235
Hybrid (mitm)	**222**	**275**	159	216	**170**	213	149	216

Pre-quantum enumeration corresponds to $T_{\mathsf{BKZ}}(\beta, d) = 2^{0.18728\beta \log(\beta) - 1.019\beta + 16.1}$, post-quantum enumeration corresponds to $T_{\mathsf{BKZ}}(\beta, d) = 2^{\frac{1}{2}(0.18728\beta \log(\beta) - 1.019\beta + 16.1)}$. Pre-quantum sieving corresponds to $T_{\mathsf{BKZ}}(\beta, d) = 2^{0.292\beta}$, post-quantum sieving corresponds to $T_{\mathsf{BKZ}}(\beta, d) = 2^{0.265\beta}$. In both sieving cases, *real memory* reverts the cost of lattice reduction to $T_{\mathsf{BKZ}}(\beta, d) = 2^{0.396\beta}$. In the *real memory* cases, memory requirements of the meet-in-the-middle phase (if applicable) are considered.

Bridging Assumptions

As discussed above, there are several points during a Hybrid Attack-based security analysis where assumptions are required. In order to cross-check our hybrid attack estimates, we align our code with the assumptions made in the NTRU

LPrime security script. That is, we consider the set of assumptions $\mathcal{A}_0$ outlined in Table 6. Explicitly, we assume core-style BKZ models ("pre-quantum sieving" (i.e $2^{0.292\beta}$) and "pre-quantum enumeration" (i.e $2^{0.18728\beta \log(\beta)-1.019\beta+16.1}$), both with "free memory", in the language of [BCLv19]), we assume the formula for the success probability of Babai's Nearest Plane algorithm from [Wun19] with a cost of one operation, we assume the q-ary GSA, a meet-in-the-middle guessing phase, with associated collision probability of one, we assume the target norm of the vector recovered via the BDD algorithm has Euclidean length $\sqrt{\sigma^2 \cdot m + h \cdot \frac{n-\tau}{n}}$ and we do not consider memory requirements[3], or lattice scaling.

After considering the assumption set $\mathcal{A}_0$, we move through assumptions until we reach those used in our work. In particular, assumption set $\mathcal{A}_1$ corresponds to $\mathcal{A}_0$ with the q-ary GSA swapped for the BKZ simulator, since this is a more accurate measure of the output of BKZ, assumption set $\mathcal{A}_2$ corresponds to $\mathcal{A}_1$ with the cost of Babai's Nearest Plane algorithm altered from one operation to be polynomial in the dimension of the lattice, i.e $\frac{d^2}{2^{1.06}}$ operations as in [Wun19], assumption set $\mathcal{A}_3$ corresponds to $\mathcal{A}_2$ with the core- style cost models changed to cost models which consider eight tours, and assumption set $\mathcal{A}_4$ corresponds to $\mathcal{A}_3$ with the guessing strategy changed from a meet-in-the-middle to a classical guessing strategy, thus dropping the innacurate assumption that collisions occur with probability one. Finally, the only difference between assumptions set $\mathcal{A}_4$ and the assumptions considered in our work is that we consider lattice scaling.

Table 6. Sets of Assumptions Considered in this Appendix. There are many other alternative assumptions considered throughout the literature which we do not consider in this work.

Technique	Assumption	$\mathcal{A}_0$	$\mathcal{A}_1$	$\mathcal{A}_2$	$\mathcal{A}_3$	$\mathcal{A}_4$	Our work
BKZ SVP calls	1	✓	✓	✓			
	$8d$				✓	✓	✓
p_{babai}	$\prod_{1 \leq i \leq d} \left(1 - \frac{2}{B(\frac{d-1}{2},\frac{1}{2})} \int_{\min(r_i,1)}^{1} (1-t^2)^{(d-3)/2}\right)$	✓	✓	✓	✓	✓	✓
T_{babai}	1	✓	✓				
	$\frac{d^2}{2^{1.06}}$			✓	✓	✓	✓
BKZ output shape	q-ary GSA	✓					
	BKZ Simulator		✓	✓	✓	✓	✓
Guessing strategy	MiTM	✓	✓	✓	✓		
	Classic					✓	✓
Target norm	$\sqrt{\sigma^2 \cdot m + h \cdot \frac{n-\tau}{n}}$	✓	✓	✓	✓	✓	✓
Lattice scaling	$\mathbf{s} \mapsto \eta\mathbf{s} : \|\mathbf{s}\| \approx \|\mathbf{e}\|$						✓
MiTM probability	1	✓	✓	✓	✓	✓	✓
Memory considered?	Yes						

---

[3] Note that [BCLv19] does contain estimates which consider memory, however we do not compare against them in our work, since we do not consider memory costs.

We present results for each assumption set in Tables 7 and 8. To continue matching the assumptions in the NTRUPrime script, we searched for optimal values of β and τ over the sets $\tau \in \{0, 40, 80, \dots\}$, $\beta \in \{40, 80, 120, \dots\}$, we note that, in both our script and the NTRUPrime script, lower estimates can be found by performing a more granular search.

Table 7. Enumeration-based estimates, each section corresponds to a set of assumptions outlined in Table 6, "$-$" denotes a value which is not compatible with our notation (for example, our script considers a simple sqrt speed-up in the search space, the NTRUPrime script considers splitting the search space as in a meet-in-the-middle approach).

Ass	Alg	τ	β	η	BDD cost	$\lvert S \rvert$	Repeats	d	#pp	$\log_2(\mathrm{rop})$
	NTRU LPrime: $n = 761, q = 4591, \sigma = \sqrt{2/3}, h = 250$									
	NTRUPrime script	360	320	n/a	$2^{220.9}$	$-$	$2^{32.5}$	881	$-$	222.1
$\mathcal{A}_0$	Our script (hybrid)	360	320	n/a	$2^{221.3}$	$2^{375.4}$	$2^{33.6}$	951	89	**222.9**
	Our script (g-v decoding)	360	360	83	$2^{239.0}$	$2^{380.5}$	$2^{18.1}$	951	91	240.5
$\mathcal{A}_1$	Our script (hybrid)	400	360	n/a	$2^{257.6}$	$2^{442.8}$	$2^{36.2}$	911	109	**258.7**
	Our script (g-v decoding)	360	400	139	$2^{270.1}$	$2^{390.6}$	$2^{14.4}$	951	95	271.2
$\mathcal{A}_2$	Our script (hybrid)	400	360	n/a	$2^{273.0}$	$2^{404.5}$	$2^{52.2}$	911	94	274.5
	Our script (g-v decoding)	360	400	139	$2^{270.1}$	$2^{390.6}$	$2^{14.4}$	951	95	**271.2**
$\mathcal{A}_3$	Our script (hybrid)	400	360	n/a	$2^{276.2}$	$2^{442.8}$	$2^{36.2}$	911	109	**277.9**
	Our script (g-v decoding)	360	400	139	$2^{283.6}$	$2^{409.8}$	$2^{8.7}$	951	103	284.9
$\mathcal{A}_4$	Our script (hybrid)	320	400	n/a	$2^{386.9}$	$2^{256.3}$	$2^{111.8}$	991	53	388.1
	Our script (g-v decoding)	240	440	280	$2^{376.0}$	$2^{141.3}$	$2^{68.1}$	1071	26	**380.0**

Table 8. Sieving Estimates. Estimates marked with † correspond to standard BDD decoding.

Ass	Alg	τ	β	η	BDD cost	$\lvert S \rvert$	Repeats	d	#pp	$\log_2(\mathrm{rop})$
	NTRU LPrime: $n = 761, q = 4591, \sigma = \sqrt{2/3}, h = 250$									
	NTRUPrime script	240	480	n/a	$2^{156.0}$	$-$	$2^{18.8}$	1081	$-$	159.4
$\mathcal{A}_0$	Our script (hybrid)	240	480	n/a	$2^{158.1}$	$2^{279.7}$	$2^{18.3}$	1111	72	**159.4**
	Our script (g-v decoding)	0	560	562	$2^{164.1}$	1	1	1351	0	$165.0^\dagger$
$\mathcal{A}_1$	Our script (hybrid)	320	600	n/a	$2^{209.9}$	$2^{348.2}$	$2^{35.8}$	1031	85	211.5
	Our script (g-v decoding)	0	560	593	$2^{173.2}$	1	1	1351	0	$\mathbf{173.2}^\dagger$
$\mathcal{A}_2$	Our script (hybrid)	360	320	n/a	$2^{221.3}$	$2^{375.4}$	$2^{33.6}$	951	89	222.9
	Our script (g-v decoding)	0	560	593	$2^{173.2}$	1	1	1351	0	$\mathbf{173.2}^\dagger$
$\mathcal{A}_3$	Our script (hybrid)	320	600	0	$2^{227.2}$	$2^{338.2}$	$2^{39.1}$	1031	81	228.3
	Our script (g-v decoding)	0	560	593	$2^{176.2}$	1	1	1351	0	$\mathbf{177.8}^\dagger$
$\mathcal{A}_4$	Our script (hybrid)	200	640	0	$2^{297.6}$	$2^{180.7}$	$2^{97.6}$	1151	40	298.6
	Our script (g-v decoding)	0	560	593	$2^{176.2}$	1	1	1351	0	$\mathbf{177.8}^\dagger$

References

[ACD+18] Albrecht, M.R., et al.: Estimate all the LWE, NTRU schemes!. In: Catalano, D., De Prisco, R. (eds.) SCN 2018. LNCS, vol. 11035, pp. 351–367. Springer, Cham (2018). https://doi.org/10.1007/978-3-319-98113-0_19

[ACPS09] Applebaum, B., Cash, D., Peikert, C., Sahai, A.: Fast cryptographic primitives and circular-secure encryption based on hard learning problems. In: Halevi, S. (ed.) CRYPTO 2009. LNCS, vol. 5677, pp. 595–618. Springer, Heidelberg (2009). https://doi.org/10.1007/978-3-642-03356-8_35

[ADH+19] Albrecht, M.R., Ducas, L., Herold, G., Kirshanova, E., Postlethwaite, E.W., Stevens, M.: The general sieve kernel and new records in lattice reduction. Cryptology ePrint Archive, Report 2019/089 (2019). https://eprint.iacr.org/2019/089

[ADPS16] Alkim, E., Ducas, L., Pöppelmann, T., Schwabe, P.: Post-quantum key exchange - a new hope. In: Holz, T., Savage, S. (ed.) 25th USENIX Security Symposium, USENIX Security 16, pp. 327–343. USENIX Association (2016)

[AGVW17] Albrecht, M.R., Göpfert, F., Virdia, F., Wunderer, T.: Revisiting the expected cost of solving uSVP and applications to LWE. In: Takagi, T., Peyrin, T. (eds.) ASIACRYPT 2017. LNCS, vol. 10624, pp. 297–322. Springer, Cham (2017). https://doi.org/10.1007/978-3-319-70694-8_11

[AKS01] Ajtai, M., Kumar, R., Sivakumar, D.: A sieve algorithm for the shortest lattice vector problem. In: 33rd ACM STOC, pp. 601–610. ACM Press, July 2001

[Alb17] Albrecht, M.R.: On dual lattice attacks against small-secret LWE and parameter choices in HElib and SEAL. In: Coron, J.-S., Nielsen, J.B. (eds.) EUROCRYPT 2017. LNCS, vol. 10211, pp. 103–129. Springer, Cham (2017). https://doi.org/10.1007/978-3-319-56614-6_4

[APS15] Albrecht, M.R., Player, R., Scott, S.: On the concrete hardness of learning with errors. J. Math. Cryptol. 9(3), 169–203 (2015)

[BAA+17] Bindel, N., et al.: qTESLA. Technical report, National Institute of Standards and Technology (2017). https://csrc.nist.gov/projects/post-quantum-cryptography/round-1-submissions

[Bab86] Babai, L.: On lovász lattice reduction and the nearest lattice point problem. Combinatorica 6(1), 1–13 (1986)

[BCLv17] Bernstein, D.J., Chuengsatiansup, C., Lange, T., van Vredendaal, C.: NTRU prime. Technical report, National Institute of Standards and Technology (2017). https://csrc.nist.gov/projects/post-quantum-cryptography/round-1-submissions

[BCLv19] Bernstein, D.J., Chuengsatiansup, C., Lange, T., van Vredendaal, C.: NTRU prime. Technical report, National Institute of Standards and Technology (2019). https://csrc.nist.gov/projects/post-quantum-cryptography/round-2-submissions

[BDGL16] Becker, A., Ducas, L., Gama, N., Laarhoven, T.: New directions in nearest neighbor searching with applications to lattice sieving. In: Krauthgamer, R. (ed.) 27th SODA, pp. 10–24. ACM-SIAM, January 2016

[BG14] Bai, S., Galbraith, S.D.: Lattice decoding attacks on binary LWE. In: Susilo, W., Mu, Y. (eds.) ACISP 2014. LNCS, vol. 8544, pp. 322–337. Springer, Cham (2014). https://doi.org/10.1007/978-3-319-08344-5_21

[BGL+18] Bhattacharya, S., et al.: Round5: compact and fast post-quantum public-key encryption. Cryptology ePrint Archive, Report 2018/725 (2018). https://eprint.iacr.org/2018/725

[BGPW16] Buchmann, J., Göpfert, F., Player, R., Wunderer, T.: On the hardness of LWE with binary error: revisiting the hybrid lattice-reduction and meet-in-the-middle attack. In: Pointcheval, D., Nitaj, A., Rachidi, T. (eds.) AFRICACRYPT 2016. LNCS, vol. 9646, pp. 24–43. Springer, Cham (2016). https://doi.org/10.1007/978-3-319-31517-1_2

[BGV14] Brakerski, Z., Gentry, C., Vaikuntanathan, V.: (Leveled) fully homomorphic encryption without bootstrapping. ACM Trans. Comput. Theory (TOCT) **6**(3), 13 (2014)

[BLP+13] Brakerski, Z., Langlois, A., Peikert, C., Regev, O., Stehlé, D.: Classical hardness of learning with errors. In: Boneh, D., Roughgarden, T., Feigenbaum, J. (eds.) 45th ACM STOC, pp. 575–584. ACM Press, June 2013

[BPR12] Banerjee, A., Peikert, C., Rosen, A.: Pseudorandom functions and lattices. In: Pointcheval, D., Johansson, T. (eds.) EUROCRYPT 2012. LNCS, vol. 7237, pp. 719–737. Springer, Heidelberg (2012). https://doi.org/10.1007/978-3-642-29011-4_42

[Che13] Chen, Y.: Réduction de réseau et sécurité concrète du chiffrement complètement homomorphe. Ph.D. thesis, Paris 7 (2013)

[CN11] Chen, Y., Nguyen, P.Q.: BKZ 2.0: better lattice security estimates. In: Lee, D.H., Wang, X. (eds.) ASIACRYPT 2011. LNCS, vol. 7073, pp. 1–20. Springer, Heidelberg (2011). https://doi.org/10.1007/978-3-642-25385-0_1

[CPL+17] Cheon, J.H., et al.: Lizard. Technical report, National Institute of Standards and Technology (2017). https://csrc.nist.gov/projects/post-quantum-cryptography/round-1-submissions

[DLdW16] Doulgerakis, E., Laarhoven, T., de Weger, B.: Finding closest lattice vectors using approximate Voronoi cells. Cryptology ePrint Archive, Report 2016/888 (2016). https://eprint.iacr.org/2016/888

[dt16] The FPLLL development team. FPLLL, a lattice reduction library (2016). https://github.com/fplll/fplll

[Duc19] Ducas, L.: Thread on PQC-forum (2019). https://groups.google.com/a/list.nist.gov/forum/#!topic/pqc-forum/JwR0_fpNujc

[DXL12] Ding, J., Xie, X., Lin, X.: A simple provably secure key exchange scheme based on the learning with errors problem. Cryptology ePrint Archive, Report 2012/688 (2012). http://eprint.iacr.org/2012/688

[FP85] Fincke, U., Pohst, M.: Improved methods for calculating vectors of short length in a lattice, including a complexity analysis. Math. Comput. **44**(170), 463–463 (1985)

[GHS12] Gentry, C., Halevi, S., Smart, N.P.: Homomorphic evaluation of the AES circuit. In: Safavi-Naini, R., Canetti, R. (eds.) CRYPTO 2012. LNCS, vol. 7417, pp. 850–867. Springer, Heidelberg (2012). https://doi.org/10.1007/978-3-642-32009-5_49

[GSW13] Gentry, C., Sahai, A., Waters, B.: Homomorphic encryption from learning with errors: conceptually-simpler, asymptotically-faster, attribute-based. In: Canetti, R., Garay, J.A. (eds.) CRYPTO 2013. LNCS, vol. 8042, pp. 75–92. Springer, Heidelberg (2013). https://doi.org/10.1007/978-3-642-40041-4_5

[GvVW17] Göpfert, F., van Vredendaal, C., Wunderer, T.: A hybrid lattice basis reduction and quantum search attack on LWE. In: Lange, T., Takagi, T. (eds.) PQCrypto 2017. LNCS, vol. 10346, pp. 184–202. Springer, Cham (2017). https://doi.org/10.1007/978-3-319-59879-6_11

[GZB+19] Garcia-Morchon, O., et al.: Round5. Technical report, National Institute of Standards and Technology (2019). https://csrc.nist.gov/projects/post-quantum-cryptography/round-2-submissions

[Hal18] Halevi, S.: HElib (2018). https://github.com/shaih/HElib

[How07] Howgrave-Graham, N.: A hybrid lattice-reduction and meet-in-the-middle attack against NTRU. In: Menezes, A. (ed.) CRYPTO 2007. LNCS, vol. 4622, pp. 150–169. Springer, Heidelberg (2007). https://doi.org/10.1007/978-3-540-74143-5_9

[HPS96] Hoffstein, J., Pipher, J., Silverman, J.H.: NTRU: a new high speed public key cryptosystem. Draft Distributed at Crypto 1996 (1996). http://web.securityinnovation.com/hubfs/files/ntru-orig.pdf

[HPS+15] Hoffstein, J., et al.: Choosing parameters for NTRUEncrypt. Cryptology ePrint Archive, Report 2015/708 (2015). http://eprint.iacr.org/2015/708

[Kan83] Kannan, R.: Improved algorithms for integer programming and related lattice problems. In: 15th ACM STOC, pp. 193–206. ACM Press, April 1983

[Laa16] Laarhoven, T.: Sieving for closest lattice vectors (with preprocessing). In: Avanzi, R., Heys, H. (eds.) SAC 2016. LNCS, vol. 10532, pp. 523–542. Springer, Cham (2017). https://doi.org/10.1007/978-3-319-69453-5_28

[LDK+17] Lyubashevsky, V., et al.: CRYSTALS-DILITHIUM. Technical report, National Institute of Standards and Technology (2017). https://csrc.nist.gov/projects/post-quantum-cryptography/round-1-submissions

[LN13] Liu, M., Nguyen, P.Q.: Solving BDD by enumeration: an update. In: Dawson, E. (ed.) CT-RSA 2013. LNCS, vol. 7779, pp. 293–309. Springer, Heidelberg (2013). https://doi.org/10.1007/978-3-642-36095-4_19

[LP11] Lindner, R., Peikert, C.: Better key sizes (and attacks) for LWE-based encryption. In: Kiayias, A. (ed.) CT-RSA 2011. LNCS, vol. 6558, pp. 319–339. Springer, Heidelberg (2011). https://doi.org/10.1007/978-3-642-19074-2_21

[LPR10] Lyubashevsky, V., Peikert, C., Regev, O.: On ideal lattices and learning with errors over rings. In: Gilbert, H. (ed.) EUROCRYPT 2010. LNCS, vol. 6110, pp. 1–23. Springer, Heidelberg (2010). https://doi.org/10.1007/978-3-642-13190-5_1

[LS15] Langlois, A., Stehlé, D.: Worst-case to average-case reductions for module lattices. Des. Codes Cryptogr. **75**(3), 565–599 (2015)

[Mic01] Micciancio, D.: The hardness of the closest vector problem with preprocessing. IEEE Trans. Inf. Theory **47**(3), 1212–1215 (2001)

[Mic18] Micciancio, D.: On the hardness of LWE with binary error. Technical report, February 2018. http://cseweb.ucsd.edu/~daniele/papers/BinLWE.pdf

[MS01] May, A., Silverman, J.H.: Dimension reduction methods for convolution modular lattices. In: Silverman, J.H. (ed.) CaLC 2001. LNCS, vol. 2146, pp. 110–125. Springer, Heidelberg (2001). https://doi.org/10.1007/3-540-44670-2_10

[PAA+17] Poppelmann, T., et al.: NewHope. Technical report, National Institute of Standards and Technology (2017). https://csrc.nist.gov/projects/post-quantum-cryptography/round-1-submissions

[PFH+17] Prest, T., et al.: FALCON. Technical report, National Institute of Standards and Technology (2017). https://csrc.nist.gov/projects/post-quantum-cryptography/round-1-submissions

[Reg05] Regev, O.: On lattices, learning with errors, random linear codes, and cryptography. In: Gabow, H.N., Fagin, R. (eds.) 37th ACM STOC, pp. 84–93. ACM Press, May 2005

[SAB+17] Schwabe, P., et al.: CRYSTALS-KYBER. Technical report, National Institute of Standards and Technology (2017). https://csrc.nist.gov/projects/post-quantum-cryptography/round-1-submissions

[Sch03] Schnorr, C.P.: Lattice reduction by random sampling and birthday methods. In: Alt, H., Habib, M. (eds.) STACS 2003. LNCS, vol. 2607, pp. 145–156. Springer, Heidelberg (2003). https://doi.org/10.1007/3-540-36494-3_14

[SE94] Schnorr, C.-P., Euchner, M.: Lattice basis reduction. Improved practical algorithms and solving subset sum problems. Math. Program. **66**, 181–199 (1994)

[SEA18] Simple Encrypted Arithmetic Library (release 3.1.0). Microsoft Research, Redmond, WA, December 2018 https://github.com/Microsoft/SEAL

[SHRS17] Schanck, J.M., Hulsing, A., Rijneveld, J., Schwabe, P.: NTRU-HRSS-KEM. Technical report, National Institute of Standards and Technology (2017). https://csrc.nist.gov/projects/post-quantum-cryptography/round-1-submissions

[SPL+17] Seo, M., Park, J.H., Lee, D.H., Kim, S., Lee, S.-J.: EMBLEM and R.EMBLEM. Technical report, National Institute of Standards and Technology (2017). https://csrc.nist.gov/projects/post-quantum-cryptography/round-1-submissions

[SSTX09] Stehlé, D., Steinfeld, R., Tanaka, K., Xagawa, K.: Efficient public key encryption based on ideal lattices. In: Matsui, M. (ed.) ASIACRYPT 2009. LNCS, vol. 5912, pp. 617–635. Springer, Heidelberg (2009). https://doi.org/10.1007/978-3-642-10366-7_36

[Wun19] Wunderer, T.: A detailed analysis of the hybrid lattice-reduction and meet-in-the-middle attack. J. Math. Cryptol. **13**(1), 1–26 (2019)

[ZCHW17] Zhang, Z., Chen, C., Hoffstein, J., Whyte, W.: NTRUEncrypt. Technical report, National Institute of Standards and Technology (2017). https://csrc.nist.gov/projects/post-quantum-cryptography/round-1-submissions

On Quantum Slide Attacks

Xavier Bonnetain[1,2]([⊠]), María Naya-Plasencia[2], and André Schrottenloher[2]

[1] Collège Doctoral, Sorbonne Université, 75005 Paris, France
xavier.bonnetain@inria.fr
[2] Inria, Paris, France

Abstract. At Crypto 2016, Kaplan *et al.* proposed the first quantum exponential acceleration of a classical symmetric cryptanalysis technique: they showed that, in the superposition query model, Simon's algorithm could be applied to accelerate the slide attack on the alternate-key cipher. This allows to recover an n-bit key with $\mathcal{O}(n)$ queries.

In this paper we propose many other types of quantum slide attacks, inspired by classical techniques including *sliding with a twist, complementation slide* and *mirror slidex*. We also propose four-round self-similarity attacks for Feistel ciphers when using XOR operations. Some of these variants combined with whitening keys (FX construction) can also be successfully attacked. We present a surprising new result involving composition of quantum algorithms, that allows to combine some quantum slide attacks with a quantum attack on the round function, allowing an efficient key-recovery even if this function is strong classically.

Finally, we analyze the case of quantum slide attacks exploiting cycle-finding, whose possibility was mentioned in a paper by Bar-On *et al.* in 2015, where these attacks were introduced. We show that the speed-up is smaller than expected and less impressive than the above variants, but nevertheless provide improved complexities on the previous known quantum attacks in the superposition model for some self-similar SPN and Feistel constructions.

Keywords: Quantum cryptanalysis · Slide attacks · Feistel networks · Simon's algorithm · Kuperberg's algorithm · Slidex attacks · Cycle finding

1 Introduction

For a long time, symmetric primitives were believed easy to protect against quantum adversaries, by simply doubling the key length. As Grover's algorithm allows to perform an exhaustive search in the square root of the classical time, this counter measure was supposed to provide an equivalent ideal security as before.

Today, many new results have appeared on dedicated quantum attacks, like quantum generic meet-in-the-middle attacks on iterative block ciphers [22], quantum linear and differential attacks [24], an analysis of the FX construct against

© Springer Nature Switzerland AG 2020
K. G. Paterson and D. Stebila (Eds.): SAC 2019, LNCS 11959, pp. 492–519, 2020.
https://doi.org/10.1007/978-3-030-38471-5_20

quantum adversaries [29], new algorithms for collisions or multicollisions [9,20] and [6,27,28] that respectively analyze the security of 3-round Feistel schemes, the Even-Mansour construction and quantumly break the AEZ primitive for authenticated encryption.

Related Work. In [23], Kaplan *et al.* considered the superposition query model and, amongst other results, provided for the first time an exponential acceleration of a classical cryptanalysis. Using Simon's algorithm [32] the complexity of quantum slide attacks on the alternate-key cipher with bit-wise additions was shown to be of $\mathcal{O}(n)$ in that model. Simon's algorithm was also used in an independent work [31]. In [1] it was proposed to counter these attacks by using another group law, especially modular additions. In this setting Kuperberg's algorithm [25] replaces Simon's. Detailed cost estimates of attacks were done in [8], in which the authors also propose an algorithm for the case of several parallel modular additions.

In an independent and very recent result [13], quantized versions of some advanced slide attacks on 2k- and 4k-Feistel schemes were proposed (we will define all these schemes in Sect. 2). They correspond respectively to Sect. 3.4 and a small part of Sect. 5. The authors also propose a quantum attack on GOST, which is unrelated to quantum slide attacks. In [14], the three round distinguisher of [27] is exploited to reduce by three the number of keys to search for in a Feistel cipher with independent keys. In [19], some meet-in-the-middle attacks on Feistel constructions are proposed and the same observation as [14] is presented.

Summary of Our Results. In this paper we propose the quantized version of several advanced slide attacks from [4], like slide attacks on Feistel constructions, the *complementation slide* attack and the *slide with a twist* technique. We also show that quantum attacks can be composed, allowing for instance to perform efficient key-recovery attacks even when the round function is classically strong. We provide the complexities of these attacks when the key is inserted with bitwise-addition or with modular additions. We also propose a quantum version of mirror slide attacks from [12], and quantum slide attacks exploiting cycle finding, as was proposed in [2]. We show that the quantum speedup of the latter is smaller than expected by the authors.

We display in Table 1 all quantum improvements of existing slide attacks that we know of, including our new results. The costs are given asymptotically in n, in number of superposition queries. In order to give meaningful bounds, we estimate that one quantum query costs $\Omega(n^2)$ quantum gates, as we are considering block ciphers of block size n, for which we want a dependency between all the input and output bits. The classical and quantum memory complexities are at most subexponential. Simon's algorithm requires $\mathcal{O}(n)$ qubits and $\mathcal{O}(n^2)$ bits when used alone, $\mathcal{O}(n^2)$ qubits if used inside a Grover search. Grover's algorithm needs only $\mathcal{O}(n)$ qubits. The only non-polynomial memory requirements for these attacks appear when we use Kuperberg's sieving algorithm.

Table 1. Quantum slide attacks. They all allow a complete key-recovery, except for three distinguishing attacks. We label the 4k-Feistel attack of [13] as a distinguisher, as it can recover the keys only if the round function is weak.

Cipher	Attack details	Queries	Decryption oracle	Source
1k-Feistel (XOR)	Basic slide	$n/2$		[13]
1k-Feistel (additions)	Basic slide	$2^{1.2\sqrt{n}}$		Sect. 3.2
1k-Feistel (any)	Composed slide	$n/2$ to $2^{2.4\sqrt{n}}$		Sect. 4
2k-Feistel (XOR)	Complementation	$n2^{n/4}$		Sect. 3.3
2k-Feistel (XOR)	Sliding with a twist	$n/2$	Yes	[13]
2k-Feistel (XOR)	Composed slide	n		Sect. 4
2k-Feistel (additions)	Complementation	$2^{1.2\sqrt{n}+n/4}$		Sect. 3.3
2k-Feistel (additions)	Composed slide	$2^{1.8\sqrt{n}}$		Sect. 4
3k-Feistel (any)	Cycle finding	$2^{n/2}$		Sect. 6
4k-Feistel (XOR)	Complementation, sliding with a twist	n (Dist.)	Yes	[13]
4k-Feistel (XOR)	Complementation, sliding with a twist	$4n^2$	Yes	Sect. 5.2
4k-Feistel (XOR)	Enhanced reflection	$2^{n/4}$		Sect. 5.3
4k-Feistel (any)	Cycle finding	$2^{n/2}$		Sect. 6
2k-Whitened Feistel (DESX)	Mirror slidex	$n2^{n/4}$		Sect. 5.1
4k-Whitened Feistel (DESX) (XOR)	Complementation, sliding with a twist	$n^2 2^{n/4}$ $n2^{n/4}$ (Dist.)	Yes	Sect. 5.2
4k-Whitened Feistel (DESX) (variant) (XOR)	Mirror slidex	n (Dist.)	Yes	Sect. 5.2
1k-SPN (XOR)	Basic slide	n		[23]
1k-SPN (additions)	Basic slide	$2^{1.8\sqrt{n}}$		Sect. 3.1
2k-SPN (any)	Grover-meet-Simon	$n2^{n/2}$		[29]
2k-SPN (any)	Cycle finding	$2^{n/2}$		Sect. 6

Organization. The paper is organized as follows. Section 2 presents some preliminaries: the quantum algorithms used in the paper and the general principle of slide attacks. Section 3 proposes new quantum advanced slide attacks on Feistel networks, which are quantized versions of [4] and [15]. Section 4 shows how to compose a quantum slide attack with a quantum attack on the round function. Section 5 combines the principles of the previous sections to attack 4-round self-similar Feistel ciphers. Finally, Sect. 6 describes quantum slide attacks exploiting cycle finding.

2   Preliminaries

In this section we provide a brief introduction to classical and quantum slide attacks, the considered quantum adversary model, and some quantum algorithms used throughout the paper. We describe the results from [23] regarding quantum slide attacks using Simon's algorithm.

2.1   Classical Slide Attacks

Slide attacks were introduced in [3]. Their common principle is to leverage the structural properties of the cipher, especially self-similarity, to attack an iterated cipher independently of its number of rounds. A summary of the classical attacks we considered can be found in the Appendix.

Notations. We consider a cipher E_k : $\{0,1\}^n \rightarrow \{0,1\}^n$, constructed from a round function $F(x,k)$: $\{0,1\}^n \times \{0,1\}^m \rightarrow \{0,1\}^n$ applied a certain number of times. There are r rounds and they use round subkeys $k_1, \ldots k_r$ derived from the master key K of the cipher. In such constructions, we consider mainly two group operations: the bitwise XOR addition, denoted $\oplus$, and the modular addition, denoted $+$.

Basic Slide Property. Suppose that all the round subkeys are equal. The cipher is *one-round self-similar*: it applies r times the same permutation $x \mapsto F(x,k)$. We can write a simple equality, the *slide property*: $E_K(F(x,k)) = F(E_K(x),k)$.

Basic Slide Attack. The goal of the attacker is to find two pairs x,y satisfying $F(x,k) = y$. The birthday paradox implies that, among $\mathcal{O}(2^{n/2})$ plaintext-ciphertext couples P,C, there exists a *slide pair*: P_0, C_0 and P_1, C_1 such that $F(P_0, k) = P_1$. In that case, we also have: $F(C_0, k) = C_1$. If F is supposed *weak*, these two equations suffice to retrieve the key k. Hence, the simplest attack setting consists in performing $\mathcal{O}(2^{n/2})$ queries, then checking for each pair P_0, C_0 and P_1, C_1 if it is a slide pair; and in that case returning the key k. This requires $\mathcal{O}(2^{n/2})$ memory and $\mathcal{O}(2^n)$ time independently of the length of k.

Example of Weak Round Function. In the case of a keyed permutation $F(x,k) = k \oplus \Pi(x)$, as shown in Fig. 1, a slide pair $(P_0, C_0), (P_1, C_1)$ satisfies $F(P_0, k) = P_1$ i.e. $P_1 = k \oplus \Pi(P_0)$, which is equivalent to $C_1 = k \oplus \Pi(C_0)$. Hence it suffices to check if $P_1 \oplus C_1 = \Pi(P_0) \oplus \Pi(C_0)$.

Slide attacks have been successfully applied to the TREYFER cipher, variants of DES and Blowfish and Feistel constructions [3]. We do not study stream ciphers in this paper and focus on block ciphers.

Some Definitions. We define quickly some generic constructions mentioned in the rest of this paper.

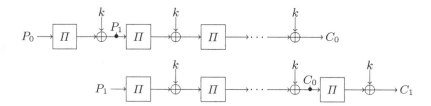

Fig. 1. Example of slide attack on a cipher with a weak round function

rk-Feistel and rk-SPN. We name rk-Feistel and rk-SPN versions of those ciphers where the round keys form a periodic sequence of period r. In particular, 1k-Feistel denotes the case where all subkeys are equal.

Whitened Feistels. In this paper, the notation rk-WFeistel refers to a rk-Feistel scheme augmented by key whitenings (sometimes called DESX in the literature). This is an example of the FX construction, which consists in applying key whitenings to a block cipher:

$$WFeistel : \begin{matrix} \{0,1\}^k \times (\{0,1\}^n)^3 & \to & \{0,1\}^n \\ (\quad k \quad , \quad k_x, k_y, m \quad) & \mapsto & Feistel(k, m \oplus k_x) \oplus k_y \end{matrix} \cdot$$

2.2 The Attack Model

In this paper we consider the model of *superposition queries*, as defined *e.g.* in [5,11,34]. The adversary is not only allowed local computations on a quantum computer, but also *superposition queries* to a remote quantum cryptographic oracle. Given a superposition of inputs to this oracle, it returns the superposition of the outputs.

This model implies security in all possible intermediate scenarios and appears naturally in quantum security proofs of symmetric cryptographic constructions (which assume ideal building blocks). It has been considered in many previous cryptanalysis results, like [6,23,27–29] We refer to [17] and [16] for further discussion on the relevance of this model.

2.3 Quantum Slide Attacks

Quantum Slide Attacks are built upon classical ones and they reduce drastically their cost, thanks to the use of quantum algorithms and the model of superposition queries. Classically, the general layout of a slide attack is to perform a certain amount of queries, among which, thanks to the analysis, we expect one or more slide pairs to occur. Sometimes these pairs can be detected; sometimes one merely tries all possibilities. Using these pairs, one can then break a smaller component of the cipher (*e.g.* its weak round function $F(\cdot, k)$) and retrieve some secret material (*e.g.* some subkeys).

In the quantum setting, an exponential speedup can be obtained by the use of a quantum Hidden Shift Algorithm. In turn, this puts heavier constraints on the structure of the attack. Instead of merely promising that some slide pairs will be found, we must ensure that a Hidden Shift property holds, that must be valid for all inputs. When rewriting classical into quantum slide attacks, we will call this property a *slide-shift* property.

Generically, it consists in a functional equality, $g_0(x) = g_1(x + s)$, with two functions g_0 and g_1 depending on the encryption scheme and some publicly known parameters or components, and s a secret value (generally a subkey) that we seek. This is not always doable (in particular, it requires that all the inputs belong to a slide pair), which explains why some slide attacks have a more efficient quantum counterpart than others. Moreover, the cost depends on the group law $+$.

Quantum Slide Attacks were first introduced in [23], where the authors show that such rewriting is doable for Fig. 1. Their slide-shift property is the equality, for all x:

$$\Pi(E_k(x)) \oplus k = E_k(\Pi(x \oplus k)) \implies \Pi(E_k(x)) \oplus x = E_k(\Pi(x \oplus k)) \oplus (x \oplus k) \ .$$

Hence $g_0(x) = g_1(x \oplus k)$ where $g_0(x) = \Pi(E_k(x)) \oplus x$ and $g_1(x) = E_k(\Pi(x)) \oplus x$, and since superposition queries to E_k are authorized, we can use Simon's algorithm (which is recalled below).

Composing Algorithms. The previous method recovers a value s, which depends on the instance. This value can be fixed, but it can depend on some context parameters, becoming $s(y)$ for a given y, independent of the inputs of g_0 and g_1. In that case, we can see the quantum algorithm as a classical oracle to the function $y \mapsto s(y)$. Classically, the function s is often assumed to be *weak*: a few input-output pairs, in practice a few slide pairs, suffice to find the secrets.

But we can go further, and do all the computation reversibly on the quantum computer. This means we can make a *quantum* oracle to the function s, and call it in any quantum algorithm. The relevant security notion for s becomes its *quantum security*, and not only the classical one.

As we want to make a proper quantum circuit that computes reversibly the function $y \mapsto s(y)$, the cost is doubled with uncomputations (all intermediate computations need to be erased). This is a case of quantum algorithm composition, as the Grover-meets-Simon technique of [29]. Examples of compositions are presented in Sect. 4 and 5.

2.4   Quantum Hidden Shift Algorithms

Simon's Algorithm. Simon's algorithm [32] solves the following problem:

Problem 1 (Simon's Problem). Let $G : \{0,1\}^n \to \{0,1\}^n$. Given the promise that there exists $s \in \{0,1\}^n$ such that for any $(x,y) \in \{0,1\}^n$, $[G(x) = G(y)] \Leftrightarrow [x \oplus y \in \{0^n, s\}]$, find s.

This problem is a *hidden subgroup problem* in the group $((\mathbb{Z}/(2))^n, \oplus)$. Due to the structure of the group, it can also solve a problem of *hidden shift* in it, which is as follows:

Problem 2 (Simon's Problem, Hidden Shift Version). Let $g_0, g_1 : \{0,1\}^n \to \{0,1\}^n$ two permutations such that there exists $s \in \{0,1\}^n$ such that, for all x, $g_0(x) = g_1(x \oplus s)$. Find s.

Proof (Reduction from Problem 2 to Problem 1). Let G be a function from $\{0,1\} \times \{0,1\}^n$ to $\{0,1\}^n$ such that: $G(b,x) = g_0(x)$ if $b = 0$ and $G(b,x) = g_1(x)$ if $b = 1$. G satisfies $G(b_0, x_0) = G(b_1, x_1)$ if and only if $g_{b_0}(x_0) = g_{b_1}(x_1)$, that is, $b_0 = b_1$ and $x_0 = x_1$, or $b_0 \neq b_1$ and $x_0 = x_1 \oplus s$. Hence, $G(b_0, x_0) = G(b_1, x_1)$ if and only if $(b_0 \oplus b_1, x_0 \oplus x_1) \in \{(0,0),(1,s)\}$, so Simon's algorithm will recover the hidden period $(1,s)$ of G. More precisely, a single superposition query to G (hence a superposition query to g_0 and g_1) allows to obtain a random value $v \in \{0,1\}^n$ satisfying $v \cdot (1,s) = 0$. After $\mathcal{O}(n)$ such queries, and by solving a linear system of equations, s can be obtained with high probability.

With Random Functions. In cryptanalysis, this function G is built from a block cipher and possibly public components; we suppose that all can be queried in quantum superposition. The implication: $[G(x) = G(y)] \Rightarrow [x \oplus y \in \{0^n, s\}]$ might not be true; some additional random collisions can occur.

As shown in [6,23,29], Simon's algorithm is still very efficient in that case. There is a fixed multiplicative overhead estimated to be close to 3 [23], around 2 [29] or less than 1.2 [6], the algorithm being less efficient if some differentials occurs with a high probability.

This motivates us to consider a cost of n queries. The failure rate of this algorithm decreases exponentially with the number of queries once the threshold is passed, hence we will also neglect the failure probability of the algorithm when we use it as a routine for another quantum algorithm. We estimate each query to cost $\Omega(n^2)$ gates, so the gate complexity of sampling the random values v and solving the linear system for s are roughly equivalent. In this paper, we choose to count in queries, hence a total n for Simon's algorithm, or $2n$ if it is implemented as a quantum subroutine (to take into account the uncomputation of intermediate values).

Kuperberg's Algorithm and Variants. Kuperberg's Algorithm aims at solving the *abelian* hidden shift problem, defined as:

Problem 3 (Abelian Hidden shift problem). Let $(\mathbb{G}, +)$ an abelian group, $g_0, g_1 : \mathbb{G} \to \mathbb{G}$ two permutations such that there exists $s \in \mathbb{G}$ such that, for all x, $g_0(x) = g_1(x + s)$. Find s.

Many variants of Kuperberg's algorithm have been proposed, and studied asymptotically [25,26,30]. As we consider symmetric primitives, we're mainly interested in the case of addition modulo a power of two, which is fairly common.

Moreover, we want concrete estimates for given parameters. This case has been studied in [8], where various algorithms and explicit costs for groups of the form $(\mathbb{Z}/(2^w))^p$ are proposed.

Concretely, their cost estimate (in quantum memory, time and queries) is $2^{\sqrt{2\log_2(3)n}} \simeq 2^{1.8\sqrt{n}}$ for the group $\mathbb{Z}/(2^n)$. The authors also propose some more efficient algorithms in the case of parallel modular additions. As the worst case is for $\mathbb{Z}/(2^n)$, we will consider this complexity in our cost estimates. As before, for a purely quantum implementation, we estimate that the cost is doubled.

As for Simon's algorithm, Kuperberg's algorithm still works if g_0 and g_1 are not permutations, with a small overhead in queries [8]. As the cost is subexponential, we neglect this overhead.

Memory Complexities. Simon's algorithm only requires $\mathcal{O}(n)$ qubits, but $\mathcal{O}(n^2)$ bits to solve the n-dimensional linear system. If implemented as a fully quantum procedure (for example, if we use it as a testing procedure in a Grover search), the quantum memory requirement then becomes $\mathcal{O}(n^2)$, as the linear system solving needs also to be performed in superposition.

Among the variants of Kuperberg's sieve, the one we consider requires a subexponential quantum memory. However, variants with polynomial quantum and classical memory exist [7,10], although they have higher time complexities.

Grover search requires only $\mathcal{O}(n)$ qubits. When combining these different algorithms, the quantum memory requirements only sum up, which is why they remain polynomial unless Kuperberg's sieve is part of the procedure.

3 Quantum Slide-Shift Attacks

In this section, we first present a quantum slide attack on an iterated keyed permutation, similar to the one in [23], but with modular additions instead of XOR. Next, we present new advanced quantum slide attacks on Feistel networks, with slide attacks based on one-round self-similarity and advanced sliding techniques from [4], applied to Feistel variants.

3.1 Key-Alternating Cipher with Modular Additions

We reuse the notations of Fig. 1 for a key-alternating cipher with a public permutation Π and a repeated secret key k. We replace the bitwise addition $\oplus$ by a modular addition $+$. It is still possible to write a slide-shift equation, with the following function:

$$G : \{0,1\} \times \{0,1\}^n \to \{0,1\}^n$$

$$b, x \mapsto \begin{cases} g_0(x) = \Pi(E_k(x)) - x & \text{if } b = 0, \\ g_1(x) = E_k(\Pi(x)) - x & \text{if } b = 1. \end{cases}$$

As in the previous attack, we know that all x satisfy $\Pi(E_k(x)) + k = E_k(\Pi(x+k))$ because of the sliding property. Then we can see that G verifies the conditions of the hidden shift problem as $g_0(x) = g_1(x + k)$:

$$G(0, x) = \Pi(E_k(x)) - x = E_k(\Pi(x + k)) - k - x = G(1, x + k).$$

We reasonably assume that both $E_k \circ \Pi$ and $\Pi \circ E_k$ are indistinguishable from a random permutation, and we can apply Kuperberg's algorithm. This way we can recover k with a complexity of $2^{1.8\sqrt{n}}$ quantum time and queries, using the result of [8].

3.2 Feistel Scheme with One Round Self-similarity and Modular Additions

We consider from now on Feistel schemes, like the one represented on Fig. 2a. The cipher iterates the following transformation: the block message is decomposed in two branches, one branch has a round key added, and a round function f applied to it, and is next added (by a XOR or a modular addition) to the other branch before the two branches swap places. We denote by E_k the encryption function, and by $Trunc_L$ and $Trunc_R$ the functions that truncate a Feistel state to its left or right part respectively.

For a Feistel construction, if we consider a slide attack over one round, the right part of the first plaintext R (left side in Fig. 2a) will be the same as the left part of the second plaintext, L'. Classical adversaries could use a fixed right part, and take random plaintexts for the left part. For our quantum attack, we fix a known value $R_0 = R = L'$. We can consider the variable $k' = f(R_0 + k)$, represented on Fig. 2a, as an equivalent key, and this will be the value retrieved by Kuperberg's algorithm.

We use the following function:

$$G : \{0,1\} \times \{0,1\}^{n/2} \to \{0,1\}^{n/2}$$

$$b, x \mapsto \begin{cases} g_0(x) = Trunc_R(E_k(x, R_0)) & \text{if } b = 0, \\ g_1(x) = Trunc_L(E_k(R_0, x)) & \text{if } b = 1. \end{cases}$$

From Fig. 2a we can verify the slide shift equation $g_0(x) = g_1(x+k')$. By applying Kuperberg's algorithm we will recover the value of $k' = f(R_0 + k)$ for the value of R_0 that we fixed in the beginning. Since we know R_0, we can retrieve the actual value of k when f is weak. The cost of this attack with modular additions is $2^{1.2\sqrt{n}}$. With XORs, the analysis is quite similar, and the time complexity is reduced to around n. This basic attack is generalized to any non-degenerate function f in Sect. 4 (it works as long as the key k is added or xored as on Fig. 2a).

3.3 The Quantum Complementation Slide Attack

We illustrate the *complementation slide attack* [4] on a Feistel cipher with 2-round self-similarity, like for instance 2k-DES, introduced in [3]. We only describe the attack with modular additions in the key insertions and round combinations.

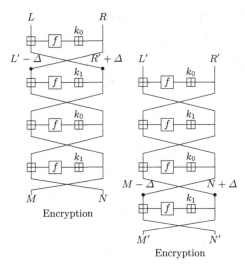

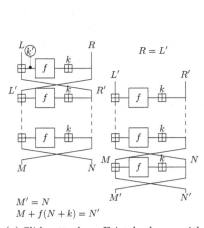

(a) Slide attack on Feistel scheme with one round self-similarity and modular addition

(b) Representation of the complementation slide attack

Fig. 2. Slide attacks on self-similar Feistels

The main idea of this attack, described in Fig. 2b, is to slide by one round only. This implies that the round-keys of the middle rounds are not the same, which can be compensated by adding a relative difference between the complemented slide pairs. As can be seen on the figure, if we denote by $\Delta = k_0 - k_1$ and if the following equations are verified: $R = L' - \Delta$ and $L + f(R + k_0) = R' + \Delta$, then, the outputs of both plaintexts, (M, N) and (M', N') verify $N = M' - \Delta$ and $N' = M + f(k_1 + N + \Delta) - \Delta$. With such inputs, all the transformations through the f functions will be the same pairwise through all the slid pairs. The combination of both halves ensures that the input round difference stays as wanted.

In this case, we propose to combine an exhaustive search with Grover's algorithm and Kuperberg's algorithm for solving the hidden shift problem.

We perform an exhaustive search on Δ. The size of a block and of the whole key is n. Considering the value of R fixed to a chosen and known one, we can redefine an equivalent round-key $k_0' = f(R + k_0)$: the correspondence between k_0 and k_0' is bijective, and when we recover k_0' we can immediately deduce k_0. The exhaustive search can be combined with Kuperberg's algorithm applied to the following function (keeping in mind that R and Δ are known):

$$G : \{0,1\} \times \{0,1\}^{n/2} \to \{0,1\}^{n/2}$$

$$b, x \mapsto \begin{cases} g_0(x) = Trunc_R(E_k(x, R)) + \Delta & \text{if } b = 0, \\ g_1(x) = Trunc_L(E_k(R - \Delta, x + \Delta)) & \text{if } b = 1. \end{cases}$$

From Fig. 2b we can verify that $g_0(x) = g_1(x + k'_0)$. For each of the tested values for Δ, by applying Kuperberg's algorithm we will recover the value of k'_0 for the fixed value of R that we fixed in the beginning, R_0. From k'_0 and R_0 we directly recover k_0 because f is weak, and with Δ, this implies the value of k_1. When the tested value for Δ is the correct one, we should also obtain a collision given by $N' = M + f(k_1 + N + \Delta) - \Delta$, which happens with a random probability $2^{-n/2}$. When this is the case, this implies that we have recovered the correct values of k_0 and k_1.

The cost for this if all the transformations were XORs would be of $n2^{n/4}$, compared to $2^{n/2}$ from the quantum accelerated exhaustive search of the key. If we have modular additions instead, the cost becomes $2^{1.2\sqrt{n}+n/4}$, which is still better than generic exhaustive search. We show in Sect. 4 how to do better if the key and branch addition are exactly the same.

3.4 Sliding with a Twist

A further improved variant of the slide attacks is the *sliding with a twist*, also introduced in [4], that can be applied against some Feistel constructions (Fig. 3). The quantum version can be applied as long as the two branches are added with a XOR. We will describe the attack considering key insertions and round combinations by XOR, the addition of the key being irrelevant for the complexity.

The key idea is that encryption of a two-round self similarity Feistel cipher is a slid version of its decryption, modulo the final twists, that are easily taken into account. For (L, R), (M, N) as inputs and outputs of the encryption function and $(M'N')$, (L', R') as inputs and outputs of the decryption one, we have that if $R = N'$ and $M' = L \oplus f(R \oplus k_0)$, then $R' = N$ and $L' = M \oplus f(N \oplus k_0)$.

We can consider now $R = N'$ as a fixed chosen value. Like the previous attack, if we consider an equivalent key $k'_0 = f(R \oplus k_0)$, we can apply Simon's algorithm. Let us denote the decryption function D_k.

$$G : \{0,1\} \times \{0,1\}^{n/2} \to \{0,1\}^{n/2}$$

$$b, x \quad \mapsto \quad \begin{cases} g_0(x) = Trunc_R(E_k(x, R)) = N & \text{if } b = 0, \\ g_1(x) = Trunc_R(D_k(x, R)) = R' & \text{if } b = 1. \end{cases}$$

From Fig. 3 we can verify the slide shift equation $g_0(x) = g_1(x \oplus k'_0)$. Simon's algorithm recovers the value of k'_0, and from it, also the one of k_0 with negligible complexity because f is easy to invert. We can repeat a similar attack peeling off one layer in order to recover also k_1 with comparable complexity.

The cost when all the transformations are XORs is n, compared to $2^{n/2}$ for the quantum accelerated exhaustive search. If we have modular additions between branches, this attack does not apply, as the decryption scheme has subtractions instead of additions.

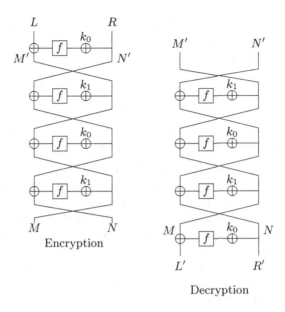

Fig. 3. Representation of the sliding with a twist technique

4 Composing Quantum Attacks: Key-Recovery with Strong Round Functions

In this section, we propose efficient key-recovery attacks on self-similar Feistel constructions with a classically strong round function. We first describe the generic case and show an even more efficient attack when the round function has the form $f(x + k)$ (with f strong as, for instance, a hash function) and the branch and key additions are the same.

4.1 General Attack

In the attacks presented in the previous section, the round function was supposed to be weak. Indeed, the quantum Hidden Shift Algorithm recovers the equivalent round key $k' = f_k(R_0)$. We are left with the task of finding k. Exhaustive search requires time $2^{n/2}$, Grover's algorithm requires time $2^{n/4}$. But there are some common cases in which we can quantumly attack the round function. In the previous attacks, the value of R_0 was fixed to a random chosen value. This means that we can repeat the same operation for several values R_i.

Case $f(x+k)$. We consider here that the round function is a key addition composed with a public function f, as this is a fairly common design. We use the attack of Sect. 3.2, which, given a value R_0, produces $f(R_0 + k)$. As presented in Sect. 2.3, we consider this attack as a quantum black box H, that takes an input x, and produces $f(x + k)$. Given this H, we can construct the following function G, whose hidden shift is k:

$$G : \{0, 1\} \times \{0, 1\}^{n/2} \rightarrow \{0, 1\}^{n/2}$$

$$b, x \quad \mapsto \quad \begin{cases} g_0(x) = H(x) = f(x + k) & \text{if } b = 0, \\ g_1(x) = f(x) & \text{if } b = 1. \end{cases}$$

The cost of the attack is summarized in Table 2 for a Feistel scheme with one-round self-similarity, and it is easy to extend it to other scenarios.

Generalization. We described the attack for a Feistel round function of the form $F(x, k) = f(x + k)$, but we can use this for any keyed function vulnerable to quantum key recovery, like the Even-Mansour construction in Fig. 4. The total cost of the attack is the cost to attack the round function multiplied by the cost of the slide attack. This means that the one-round self-similar Feistel construct offers essentially the security of its inner round function.

For the example in Fig. 4, the exhaustive search is classically in $2^{n/2}$, quantumly in $2^{n/4}$. The classical slide attack can find a pair $(x, f_k(x))$ in $2^{n/4}$ queries. Once this is done, we can easily retrieve some other slide pairs using the slide pairs at the output of the cipher, and do the classical slide attack to break Even-Mansour in $2^{n/4}$ more queries and time. In comparison, the quantum slide attack performs in $n2^{1.2\sqrt{n}}$ queries.

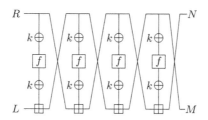

Fig. 4. Example of a vulnerable Feistel

4.2 With the Same Branch and Key Addition

If the round function is $f(x + k)$ and the branch and the key addition both use the same law, the attack can be made more efficient. We can consider a Feistel construct E_k composed of a certain number of iterations of the function $f_k(x, y) = y, x + f(y + k)$. In that case, we have $f_k(x, y) + (k, k) = f_0(x + k, y + k)$, hence $E_k(x, y) + (k, k) = E_0(x + k, y + k)$. We can then consider this function, with hidden shift k:

$$G : \{0, 1\} \times \{0, 1\}^{n/2} \rightarrow \{0, 1\}^n$$

$$b, x \quad \mapsto \quad \begin{cases} g_0(x) = E_k(x, x) + (x, x) & \text{if } b = 0, \\ g_1(x) = E_0(x, x) + (x, x) & \text{if } b = 1. \end{cases}$$

Case $f(x + k)$, 2-rounds Self-Similarity. If the Feistel has two alternating keys (k_0, k_1), we can use

$$G : \{0,1\} \times \left(\{0,1\}^{n/2}\right)^2 \to \{0,1\}^n$$

$$b, x, y \quad \mapsto \quad \begin{cases} g_0(x) = E_{k_0,k_1}(x, y) + (x, y) & \text{if } b = 0, \\ g_1(x) = E_{0,0}(x, y) + (x, y) & \text{if } b = 1. \end{cases}$$

As we have the same property $E_{k_0,k_1} + (k_0, k_1) = E_0(x + k_0, y + k_1)$, the hidden shift is (k_0, k_1).

Table 2 presents a summary of the costs of this attack, depending on the group operation for the branch addition, and the key addition. $+$ can represent a modular addition, or multiple additions in parallel, as long as it is the same operation at each round. It can be different for the branch and the key, except for the sixth and last attack in the table.

Table 2. Summary of the slide attack costs, n is the block size.

Branch and key addition	Round function	Quantum query cost	Remark
$\oplus$, any	Weak	$n/2$	
$\oplus, \oplus$	$f(x \oplus k)$	$n/2$	
$\oplus, \oplus$	$f_k(x)$	$n^2/2$	Simon calls purely quantum Simon
$\oplus, +$	$f_k(x)$	$n2^{1.2\sqrt{n}}$	Kuper. Calls purely quantum Simon
$+$, any	Weak	$2^{1.2\sqrt{n}}$	
$+, +$	$f(x + k)$	$2^{1.2\sqrt{n}}$	Need the exact same addition
$+, \oplus$	$f_k(x)$	$n2^{1.2\sqrt{n}}$	Simon calls purely quantum Kuper
$+, +$	$f_k(x)$	$2^{2.4\sqrt{n}+1}$	Kuper. Calls purely quantum Kuper
$\oplus, \oplus$	$f(x \oplus k)$	n	2-Round self-similarity
$+, +$	$f(x + k)$	$2^{1.8\sqrt{n}}$	2-Round self-similarity, Need the exact same addition

5 Advanced Quantum Slide Attacks on Feistels

In this section, we give our best attacks on self-similar Feistel schemes, most of them based on *slide shift* properties. These attacks reach up to four rounds of self-similarity, they run very efficiently and also concern whitened versions, but the operations used (branch or key addition, whitenings) are limited to XORs.

5.1   Mirror Slidex Attack on 2k-WFeistel

The *mirror slidex* attack [15] applies to any cipher that can be decomposed as $E = E_2 \circ E_1 \circ E_0$ where E_1 is an involution ($E_1 \circ E_1 = Id$). It is in fact a generalization of the *sliding with a twist*, which corresponds to the case where $E_2 = Id$. The slide equation is: $E_0^{-1} \circ E_2^{-1} \circ E(P) = E^{-1} \circ E_2(E_0(P))$, which turns into a slide shift property if E_0 and E_2 have a good form. A classical mirror slidex does not necessarily give rise to a quantum one.

2k-WFeistel. We follow [15, Section 7.3] (2K-DESX in the paper). We denote $E(x) = k_{post} \oplus E_k(k_{pre} \oplus x)$ where E is the full cipher, k_{pre} and k_{post} are the pre and post-whitening keys, of size n each (they are xored to the full state of the cipher), and E_k is a 2k-Feistel scheme of alternating keys k_0, k_1 of size $\frac{n}{2}$ each.

We have $E_k(x) = k_{post} \oplus E(k_{pre} \oplus x)$. We also denote $k_{post}^L, k_{post}^R, k_{pre}^L, k_{pre}^R$ the respective left and right sides of the whitening keys. The whole key of E is $k_0, k_1, k_{pre}, k_{post}$ of size $3n$. We note $\Delta = k_0 \oplus k_1$. Recall the slide shift property coming from the *complementation slide* technique:

$$Trunc_R(E_k(x, R)) \oplus \Delta = Trunc_L(E_k(R \oplus \Delta, x \oplus f(R \oplus k_0) \oplus \Delta)).$$

We replace calls to E_k by E, which is our oracle, and obtain that:

$$Trunc_R(E(x \oplus k_{pre}^L, R \oplus k_{pre}^R)) \oplus k_{post}^R \oplus \Delta =$$
$$Trunc_L(E(R \oplus \Delta \oplus k_{pre}^L, x \oplus k_{pre}^R \oplus f(R \oplus k_0) \oplus \Delta)) \oplus k_{post}^L.$$

Let us denote $\Delta' = \Delta \oplus k_{pre}^L \oplus k_{pre}^R$ as an adapted value of Δ, we rewrite:

$$Trunc_R(E(x, R)) \oplus \Delta' \oplus (k_{pre}^L \oplus k_{pre}^R \oplus k_{post}^L \oplus k_{post}^R) =$$
$$Trunc_L(E(R \oplus \Delta', x \oplus \Delta' \oplus f(R \oplus k_0))).$$

Our new slide function is:

$$G : \{0,1\} \times \left(\{0,1\}^{n/2} \right)^2 \to \{0,1\}^{n/2}$$

$$b, x, y \longmapsto \begin{cases} g_0(x,y) = Trunc_R(E_k(x,R)) \oplus y & \text{if } b = 0, \\ g_1(x,y) = Trunc_L(E_k(R \oplus \Delta', x \oplus \Delta')) \oplus \Delta' \oplus y & \text{if } b = 1. \end{cases}$$

where we guess the value of Δ'. Then G verifies the slide shift property $g_0(x,y) = g_1(x \oplus f(R \oplus k_0), y \oplus (k_{pre}^L \oplus k_{pre}^R \oplus k_{post}^L \oplus k_{post}^R))$.

Now, as we did in Sect. 4, we can consider this whole slide attack as a black box, that, given an input R, outputs $f(R \oplus k_0)$. As f is public, we can create a quantum oracle to the function $G'(R) = f(R) \oplus f(R \oplus k_0)$. This function has k_0 as a hidden period, which can be recovered, by reusing Simon's algorithm.

Since Δ' is guessed, we deduce $k_1 \oplus k_{pre}^L \oplus k_{pre}^R$. There now remains only one unknown subkey in the Feistel. We can apply the quantum attack on the FX construction [29] to recover it and the whitening keys in $\mathcal{O}(n2^{n/4})$ queries and time.

This attack still works if we replace XORs by modular additions both inside the Feistel and for the whitenings (we reuse the complementation slide equation of the previous section). Its complexity becomes $\mathcal{O}\left(2^{1.2\sqrt{n}+n/4}\right)$ queries. Different group operations will not commute anymore; in that case we are unable to write a slide-shift property as above.

5.2   Attacking 4k-Feistel and 4k-WFeistel

Combining twist and complementation slides enables the authors in [4] to attack a 4k-Feistel. In this section we show how to efficiently quantize this attack and extend it to 4k-WFeistel. The main idea is that the sequence of keys for encryption is $k_0 k_1 k_2 k_3 \dots$ and for decryption, $k_3 k_2 k_1 k_0 \dots$ (see Fig. 6). If we slide by one round, we make the keys k_0 and k_2 coincide, whereas the keys in the other rounds always have a constant difference $\Delta = k_1 \oplus k_3$, similarly to the *complementation slide* technique. Let E_k and D_k be the encryption and decryption oracles.

We gather from [4] that a slide pair $(P, C) = (L, R), (M, N)$ (in input to E_k), $(P', C') = (L', R'), (M', N')$ (in input to D_k) satisfies the following properties:

$$L', R' = M \oplus \Delta \oplus f(k_0 \oplus N), N$$
$$M', N' = L \oplus f(R \oplus k_0) \oplus \Delta, R$$

For all $P = (x, R)$ we write $D_k(M', N') = (L', R')$, $M = Trunc_L(E_k(x, R))$, $N = Trunc_R(E_k(x, R))$, which gives:

$$D_k(x \oplus f(R \oplus k_0) \oplus \Delta, R) = M \oplus \Delta \oplus f(k_0 \oplus N), N$$
$$\implies Trunc_R(D_k(x \oplus f(R \oplus k_0) \oplus \Delta, R)) = Trunc_R(E_k(x, R))$$

Hence, for a fixed R, we have the following function G:

$$G : \{0,1\} \times \{0,1\}^{n/2} \to \{0,1\}^{n/2}$$
$$b, x \mapsto \begin{cases} g_0(x) = Trunc_R(D_k(x, R)) & \text{if } b = 0, \\ g_1(x) = Trunc_R(E_k(x, R)) & \text{if } b = 1. \end{cases}$$

The hidden shift between g_0 and g_1 is $f(R \oplus k_0) \oplus \Delta$. As in Sect. 4, we remark that the function $R \mapsto f(R \oplus k_0) \oplus \Delta \oplus f(R)$ has k_0 as hidden period, which can be recovered with Simon's algorithm. Contrary to [13], we do not need to assume that f is weak.

The total cost is around $n^2/2$ queries (the input space is of size $n/2$, the inner Simon needs uncomputation), for recovering k_0. Once k_0 is known, we can directly use the first attack to get $\Delta = k_1 \oplus k_3$, at a negligible cost of $n/2$.

Moreover, we can "shift" the cipher, that is, suppress the first round of encryption, and add it at the last round, in order to get access to the same cipher, but with keys (k_1, k_2, k_3, k_0) instead of (k_0, k_1, k_2, k_3). Hence, we can repeat the same attack, to get k_1, and $\Delta' = k_2 \oplus k_0$. With k_1 and Δ, we obtain k_3, and with k_0 and Δ', we obtain k_2. The total cost is around n^2, for a total key size of $2n$ bits.

Attacking 4k-WFeistel. Building on the previous 4k-Feistel attack, we can further extend it to 4k-WFeistel, with key whitenings k_{pre} and k_{post}. Indeed, if we rewrite the slide shift equation:

$$Trunc_R(D_k(x \oplus f(R \oplus k_0) \oplus \Delta, R)) = Trunc_R(E_k(x, R))$$

using the whole primitive $E(\cdot) = k_{post} \oplus E_k(k_{pre} \oplus \cdot)$, we obtain:

$$Trunc_R(D(x \oplus k_{post}^L \oplus f(R \oplus k_0) \oplus \Delta, R \oplus k_{post}^R)) \oplus k_{pre}^R =$$
$$Trunc_R(E(x \oplus k_{pre}^L, R \oplus k_{pre}^R)) \oplus k_{post}^R$$

which we rewrite:

$$Trunc_R(D(x \oplus \delta_L \oplus f(R \oplus k_0 \oplus k_{post}^R), R)) = Trunc_R(E(x, R \oplus \delta_R)) \oplus \delta_R$$

where $\delta_R = k_{pre}^R \oplus k_{post}^R$ and $\delta_L = k_{pre}^L \oplus k_{post}^L \oplus k_1 \oplus k_3$.

Now, we can use the function

$$G : \{0,1\} \times \left(\{0,1\}^{n/2}\right)^2 \to \{0,1\}^{n/2}$$

$$b, x, y \quad \mapsto \begin{cases} g_0(x, y) = Trunc_R(D(x \oplus f(y \oplus (k_{post}^R \oplus k_0)), y) \oplus y & \text{if } b = 0, \\ g_1(x, y) = Trunc_R(E(x, y)) & \text{if } b = 1. \end{cases}$$

We have $g_0(x, y) = g_1(x \oplus \delta_L, y \oplus \delta_R)$. However, to implement g_0, we need to know the value $(k_{post}^R \oplus k_0)$. Hence, we first guess the value of $(k_{post}^R \oplus k_0)$ using Grover's algorithm, and combine it with Simon's algorithm. In time and queries $2n2^{n/4}$, this attack recovers δ_L, δ_R and $(k_{post}^R \oplus k_0)$. Now, we can perform the analogue of the classical attack: swapping the encryption and the decryption, we obtain $k_{pre}^L \oplus k_{post}^L$ and $k_{pre}^R \oplus k_{post}^R \oplus k_0 \oplus k_2$, which allows to obtain $k_0 \oplus k_2$, $k_1 \oplus k_3$ and $k_{pre} \oplus k_{post}$. This step costs $n2^{n/4}$.

But we can also move differently δ_R in the slide shift property:

$$Trunc_R(D(x \oplus \delta_L \oplus f(R \oplus k_0 \oplus k_{pre}^R), R \oplus \delta_R)) = Trunc_R(E(x, R)) \oplus \delta_R.$$

We now interpret this as a hidden shift equation on x only and, given an arbitrary R, we can recover $f(R \oplus k_0 \oplus k_{pre}^R)$. In turn, this gives us the value $k_0 \oplus k_{pre}^R$ for a total of n^2 queries.

Since we have already guessed $(k_{post}^R \oplus k_0)$, we deduce $k_0, k_{pre}^R, k_{post}^R$, and k_2 from $k_0 \oplus k_2$. Only $\frac{n}{2}$ bits of key material remain unknown in the Feistel scheme, as $k_1 \oplus k_3$ has been previously obtained. We can break the complete cipher and finish the key-recovery by applying the Grover-meet-Simon attack on the FX construction of [29], in $n2^{n/4}$ queries.

If we replace all operations by modular additions, we stumble upon the same problem as in Sect. 3.4: modular additions are not involutions, and the decryption oracle is not a slid version of the encryption one.

A variant of 4k-WFeistel. We follow [15, Section 7.4] and consider the 4k-WFeistel scheme (4K-DESX in the paper), with two whitening keys k_{pre} and k_{post} and four alternating keys k_0, k_1, k_2, k_3 scheduled in $4m + 1$ rounds as: $(k_0, k_1, k_2, k_3)^m, k_0$.

Slide pairs $(P, C), (P', C')$ have the properties:

$$P \oplus C' = k_{pre} \oplus k_{post} \oplus (k_1 \oplus k_3 || 0)$$

$$E_k(P \oplus k_{pre}) = E_k^{-1}(C' \oplus k_{post}) \oplus (k_1 \oplus k_3 || 0)$$

where the term $\Delta = k_1 \oplus k_3$ intervenes as in the *complementation slide* to correct the inversion of E_k. We can rewrite this as a slide shift equation holding for all input x:

$$E_k(x) = E_k^{-1}(x \oplus (\Delta || 0)) \oplus (\Delta || 0)$$

$$\implies E(x \oplus k_{pre}) \oplus k_{post} = E^{-1}(x \oplus k_{post} \oplus (\Delta || 0)) \oplus k_{pre} \oplus (\Delta || 0)$$

$$\implies E(x) \oplus x = E^{-1}(x \oplus \Delta') \oplus x \oplus \Delta'$$

where $\Delta' = k_{pre} \oplus k_{post} \oplus (\Delta || 0)$, a slide shift equation holding for all x. We can retrieve Δ' in only n queries, achieving a very efficient distinguisher. Contrary to the previous attack, while Δ' depends on some key material, we did not manage to make an efficient key recovery based on it.

5.3   Enhanced Reflection Attack

The *enhanced reflection attack* was introduced in [12], improving the mirror slidex attack for ciphers of the form $E = E_2 \circ E_1 \circ E_0$ where E_1 is an involution. It requires to find P such that $E_0(P)$ is a *fixpoint* of E_1. This happens with probability $2^{-n/2}$. In this case we get directly $C = E_2(E_0(P))$.

In the case of 4-key-alternating Feistels, in this section, multiple pairs (P, C) are needed but the fixpoints can be detected. Notice that these attacks do not use a slide shift property as above.

Enhanced Reflection Attack on 4k-Feistel. In [12], the authors use a reflection attack on 4k-Feistel (which they name 4k-DES), where the four alternating sub-keys are denoted k_0, k_1, k_2, k_3. They prove (4.1.3, Property 3) that if (P, C) is a plaintext-ciphertext pair for $4m$-round 4k-Feistel, such that in the encryption process of P we have $X_{2m-1}^L = X_{2m+1}^L \oplus \Delta$ where $\Delta = k_1 \oplus k_3$, then $P^L = C^L$ and $P^R = C^R \oplus Out_{4m} \oplus \Delta$.

Out_{4m} is the output of the internal mixing function f at the $4m$-th step, so $Out_{4m} = f(X_{4m}^R \oplus k_3) = f(C^R \oplus k_3)$.

Reflection points, that satisfy these properties, can be detected by $P^L = C^L$. Only $\mathcal{O}(2^{n/2})$ known plaintexts are required. Given at least three of them, the adversary guesses Δ, then tries to obtain k_3 from the equation: if Δ is good, this works and both k_1 and k_3 can be obtained.

To complete the attack, the authors note that a similar reflection property holds with the equation $P^R = C^R$ to detect reflection points, and $P^L = C^L \oplus Out_1 \oplus (k_0 \oplus k_2)$.

In a quantum setting, only $\mathcal{O}(2^{n/4})$ superposition queries are enough to retrieve the reflection points, using Grover search over all plaintexts P. Again, trying all values of Δ requires $\mathcal{O}(2^{n/4})$ work. All subkeys are recovered in time $\mathcal{O}(2^{n/4})$.

Enhanced Reflection Attack on 4k-WFeistel. The reflection attack on 4k-Feistel can be classically turned into an attack for 4k-WFeistel. Suppose that $E(x) = k_{post} \oplus E'(k_{pre} \oplus x)$ where E' is a 4k-Feistel procedure. The adversary first has to guess $k_{pre}^L \oplus k_{post}^L$. To do this, remark that reflection points for E' of the form P', C' turn into reflection points for E that satisfy $P^L \oplus C^L = k_{pre}^L \oplus k_{post}^L$.

In this, the correct value of $k_{pre}^L \oplus k_{post}^L$ appears with probability $2 \cdot 2^{-n/2}$, whereas all incorrect values have probability $2^{-n/2}$ of appearance. This allows to retrieve $k_{pre}^L \oplus k_{post}^L$ using $\mathcal{O}(n2^{n/2})$ memory and time, the bottleneck of the attack.

We leave a quantization of this attack as an open problem. Indeed, we do not know of a quantum algorithm that would solve this problem (among $n2^{n/2}$ arbitrary values, finding the one that appears twice more often than the others) with more than a constant speedup.

Targeting More Rounds. The attacks we proposed on 2k- and 4k-Feistels have some similarities with the quantum distinguishers based on Simon's algorithm on 3 and 4 rounds of Feistel [21,27]. As 4 rounds of Feistel cannot be attacked if a decryption oracle is not available [18], it would be surprising to have a quantum slide attack on 4k-Feistel that does not require a decryption oracle. The security of Feistels with at least 5 rounds when a decryption oracle is available is an open problem, and a quantum distinguisher on such a Feistel may pave the way to a quantum slide attack on Feistels with a longer period in their key schedule.

6   On Quantum Attacks Exploiting Cycle Finding

A generic framework of cycle-based slide attacks is presented in [2, Section 4.1]. The authors suggest that it could be accelerated in a similar way as the slide attacks from [23], expecting for instance exponential speedups. In this section we study these attacks. As they do not seem to have a slide-shift structure, we find smaller improvements than expected.

6.1   Definition of a Cycle Slide Attack

We suppose that $E_k = f_k^\ell$ for some function f_k, which happens to be immune to simpler slide attacks such as those presented above for 1k-, 2k- and 4k-Feistel schemes. Consider a message P and the cycle built from P by iterating E_k: $P, E_k(P), E_k^2(P), \ldots$ Let m_2 be the period of this cycle. Let also m_1 be the period of the f_k-cycle, that is, the smallest integer such that $f_k^{m_1}(P) = P$. Then one has $m_2 = m_1/gcd(m_1, \ell)$. Moreover, suppose that $gcd(m_1, \ell) = 1$, then $m_1 = m_2 = m$. This condition cannot be checked directly by the attacker, since he does not have access to f_k.

By Bezout's theorem, there exists d_1, d_2 such that $d_1 m - d_2 \ell = 1$. This gives:

$$f_k^{d_1 m - d_2 \ell + 1}(P) = P$$
$$f_k^{d_1 m + 1} = f_k^{d_2 \ell}(P) = E_k^{d_2}(P)$$
$$f_k(P) = E_k^{d_2}(P)$$

Hence $(P, E_k^{d_2}(P))$ is a slide pair. Moreover, $(E_k^t(P), E_k^{d_2+t}(P))$ is one for every t. This gives a certain number of slide pairs "for free", up to the length of the cycle. Once they have been obtained, we can use them to perform an attack on f_k and try to recover the key material.

General Cycle Size. We assume that E_k is a random permutation. In that case, the i-th largest cycle has size $e^{-i+1}(1 - 1/e)\, 2^n$ (on average), the largest having size $(1 - 1/e)\, 2^n$. In particular, on average, half of the points lie on the largest cycle. Finding a cycle of E_k then requires $c2^n$ chosen plaintext queries for some $c < 1$, which is a little less than the entire codebook.

The main interest is the time complexity: suppose that the attack on f_k needs time $\mathcal{O}(t)$, then the total time complexity is $\mathcal{O}(t + 2^n)$ and not $\mathcal{O}(t2^n)$ as would require a standard slide attack (see [2, Section 4.1]).

Combining Cycles. It is important to note that the probability of success (i.e, m_1 is prime with ℓ) is strictly smaller than one, exactly $\phi(\ell)/\ell$ where ϕ is Euler's totient function. The only way to check that the slide pairs obtained were good is to try to attack f_k. Hence, it may be difficult to combine (when needed) the data obtained from multiple cycles.

In particular, if one is not able to tell if a given cycle is a good one (i.e, m_1 is prime with ℓ), the complexity can increase dramatically, since we would require all cycles to be good at the same time: it happens only with probability $(\phi(\ell)/\ell)^t$ if there are t of them.

6.2   Quantization of a Cycle-Based Slide Attack

At the end of [2, Section 4.1], the authors suggest that a quantum period-finding algorithm could be applied to cycle-based slide attacks. The issue that we found when trying to do this is that, given a point P, the period of interest is the one of the function $G : d \in \mathbb{Z} \mapsto E_k^d(P)$. If G is implemented using a quantum circuit, we can indeed use Shor's period-finding algorithm to retrieve the cycle length. But this requires to call E_k^d in superposition over d. As E_k is a permutation only accessed through queries $x \to E_k(x)$, the best way to compute E_k^d is still to perform d *successive calls* to E_k: there is no quantum speedup.

Quantization. What is quantumly easier is to find a fixpoint of E_k using Grover search; or a point lying on a small cycle. In a random permutation, there are on average $1/d$ cycles of length d; and d points of period less than or equal to d (among 2^n). Finding if a point lies on such a cycle can be done with d queries to E_k. So using Grover's algorithm, one can find a superposition of points that lie on a cycle of length less than d in $\mathcal{O}\left(d\sqrt{2^n/d}\right) = \mathcal{O}\left(\sqrt{d2^n}\right)$ queries to E_k (and time).

In the classical case, we do not have much choice: the cycle slide pairs found will fall on a large cycle, with high probability. On the contrary, in the quantum setting, we can *specifically* look for points lying on a short cycle. Surprisingly, finding fixed points (or points on very short cycles) costs less than finding points on bigger cycles, due to the cost of iterating E_k. But the smaller the cycle, the less slide pairs we can get from it. Consequently, cycle-based slide attacks seem to be eligible to an interesting quantum speedup when the cipher $E_k = f_k^r$ does not enjoy a slide-shift property as before, but has a sufficiently weak round function f_k, so that a small number of slide pairs suffice to get the subkey material. Examples from [2] are given in Table 1 and detailed in Appendix B.

7 Conclusion

In this paper, we presented various quantum slide attacks, against self-similar Feistel ciphers and SPN variants. In general, quantum superposition access is devastating for these structures, but we found a number of dependencies which do not occur classically. We showed that the relevant security notion for the inner function in a quantum slide-shift attack is its quantum security, which demonstrates a very powerful chaining property of some quantum attacks. This enables to recover the key of a 4-round self-similar Feistel at a cost quadratic in the block size. We provided a detailed analysis of cycle-based slide attacks.

Classical slide attacks have shown the importance of a good key schedule, as self-similarity in a cipher allows for powerful breaks. In the quantum setting, these results seem to put even more weight on this design principle, as the attacks become much more efficient. Furthermore, as their cost is very low, a possible future direction for improvement would be to consider new attack patterns, intrinsically unfeasible in a classical setting, with stronger functions relating the slide pairs.

Acknowledgments. We thank Xiaoyang Dong for communicating some independent work on the 4-round Feistel quantum slide attack to us. This project has received funding from the European Research Council (ERC) under the European Union's Horizon 2020 research and innovation programme (grant agreement n° 714294 - acronym QUASYModo).

A   Summary of Classical Slide Attacks

We provide in Tables 3 and 4 a (certainly non exhaustive) list of classical slide attacks that we studied for quantum improvements. They are not ordered by efficiency. We refer to the corresponding source for a presentation of the attack principle. Table 3 contains attacks on specific constructions, while Table 4 contains attacks on generic constructions (n is the block size of the cipher attacked; for a Feistel network, round keys have size $n/2$). Note that memory usage and required access to a decryption device play a role in the usefulness of these slide attacks.

Table 3. Classical slide attacks on specific constructions

Cipher attacked	Attack details	Encryption queries	Time	Memory	Source
2K-DES (64-bit blocks)		2^{32}	2^{50}	2^{32}	[3, Section 4]
TREYFER (64-bit blocks)		2^{32}	2^{40}	2^{32}	[3, Section 5]
DESX (64-bit blocks)	Slide with a twist, known-plaintext only	$2^{32.5}$	$2^{87.5}$	$2^{32.5}$	[4, Section 4]
GOST (20 rounds)	Slide with a twist	2^{33}	2^{70}	2^{65}	[4, Section 5]
2K-AES (128-bit blocks)		2^{69}	2^{69}	2^{69}	[2, Section 2.3]
3K-AES (128-bit blocks)		2^{81}	2^{81}	2^{81}	[2, Section 2.3]
24-round GOST, unknown S-Boxes	Slide and truncated differential	2^{63}	2^{63}	2^{63}	[2, Section 5.3]
Palindromic GOST, unknown S-Boxes		2^{40}	2^{40}	2^{40}	[2, Section 5.4]

B   Quantum Cycle-Based Slide Attacks

We are inspired by [2] and the attacks against the SA construction and weak variants of AES. In the classical as in the quantum versions, most of the computation time required is due to finding the actual slide pairs (via the cycle).

Two Keys and Two Permutations. Consider a cipher with alternating keys k_0, k_1, xored or modularly added, and two permutations Π_1, Π_2 (Fig. 5). In the case of a SPN, $\Pi_1 = \Pi_2 = \Pi$ are the same.

   This scheme resists to the basic slide attack, but we can write $E_k \circ \Pi_2 = f_k^{\tau}(x)$ where $f_k(x) = \Pi_2(k_1 \oplus \Pi_1(k_0 \oplus x))$, and apply the cycle-finding technique. In $\mathcal{O}(2^{n/2})$ superposition queries to E_k and computations, we can recover a small

Table 4. Classical slide attacks on generic constructions. We omit $\mathcal{O}$ notations.

Cipher attacked	Attack details	Encr. queries	Time	Dec. queries	Memory	Source
1k-cipher, weak round function	Exhaustive search of slide pairs	$2^{n/2}$	2^n		$2^{n/2}$	[3, Sec. 2]
1k-Feistel	Chosen-plaintext search of slide pairs	$2^{n/4}$	$2^{n/2}$		$2^{n/4}$	[3, Sec. 3]
2k-Feistel	Complementation slide	$2^{n/2}$	$2^{n/2}$		$2^{n/2}$	[4, Sec. 3.1]
2k-Feistel	Sliding with a twist	$2^{n/4}$	$2^{n/4}$	$2^{n/4}$	$2^{n/4}$	[4, Sec. 3.2]
4k-Feistel	Complementation and slide with a twist	$2^{n/4}$	$2^{n/4}$	$2^{n/4}$	$2^{n/4}$	[4, Sec. 3.3]
Even-Mansour construction	Known-plaintext only	$2^{(n+1)/2}$	$2^{(n+1)/2}$		$2^{(n+1)/2}$	[4, Sec. 4]
1k-SPN		$2^{n/2}$	$2^{n/2}$		$2^{n/2}$	[2, Sec. 2.1]
3k-Feistel		$2^{5n/6}$	$2^{5n/6}$		$2^{2n/3}$	[2, Sec. 3]
Palindromic-scheduled Feistel[†]		$2^{n/2}$	$2^{n/2}$			[2, Sec. 4.2]
Generic* $E_k = f_k^l$	Cycle structure	2^{n-1}	$t + 2^{n-1}$		2^{n-1}	[2, Sec. 4.1]
2k-WFeistel	Complementation slide and mirror slidex	$2^{n/2}$	$2^{n/2}$	$2^{n/2}$	$2^{n/2}$	[15, Sec. 7.3]
4k-Feistel	Enhanced reflection	$2^{n/2}$	$2^{n/2}$		n	[12, Sec. 4]
4k-WFeistel	Enhanced reflection	$n2^{n/2}$	$n2^{n/2}$		$n2^{n/2}$	[12, Sec. 4]
4k-WFeistel (variant)	Complementation slide and mirror slidex	$2^{n/2}$	$2^{n/2}$	$2^{n/2}$	$2^{n/2}$	[15, Sec. 7.4]

*t is the time needed to attack f_k.

† at best (depends in practice on attacking the palindromic round function)

number of slide pairs, say two, from small cycles of $E_k \circ \Pi_2$. Recall that n is the block size here; the key length is $2n$. Therefore we obtain two equations:

$$y = \Pi_2(k_1 \oplus \Pi_1(k_0 \oplus x))$$
$$y' = \Pi_2(k_1 \oplus \Pi_1(k_0 \oplus x'))$$

Since the permutations can be inverted, we find:

$$\Pi_2^{-1}(y) \oplus \Pi_2^{-1}(y') = \Pi_1(k_0 \oplus x) \oplus \Pi_1(k_0 \oplus x')$$

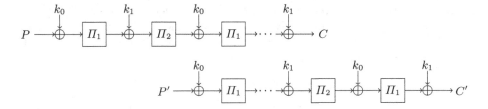

Fig. 5. Slide attack against a key- and permutation-alternating cipher

Solving this equation on k_0, if Π_1 has no specific property, can be done in $\mathcal{O}(2^{n/2})$ time using Grover's algorithm, the same complexity as the first stage. This improves on the Grover-meets-Simon technique of [29], which would perform in $\mathcal{O}(n2^{n/2})$ queries and more time (the Grover oracle requires to solve linear systems in superposition).

Attacking 3k-SPN. Cycle-finding can further be applied on a 3k-SPN construction, where there is a unique permutation $\Pi = A \circ S$, with A a linear layer and S a non-linear layer of S-Boxes. Still using $\mathcal{O}(2^{n/2})$ queries, we now write the slide equations as:

$$y = \Pi(k_2 \oplus \Pi(k_1 \oplus \Pi(k_0 \oplus x)))$$
$$y' = \Pi(k_2 \oplus \Pi(k_1 \oplus \Pi(k_0 \oplus x')))$$
$$\implies \Pi^{-1}(y) \oplus \Pi^{-1}(y') = \Pi(k_1 \oplus \Pi(k_0 \oplus x)) \oplus \Pi(k_1 \oplus \Pi(k_0 \oplus x'))$$

To solve efficiently this equation in k_0 and k_1, we first guess k_0 using Grover's algorithm. The equation on k_1 becomes:

$$A^{-1}(\Pi^{-1}(y) \oplus \Pi^{-1}(y')) = S(k_1 \oplus \Pi(k_0 \oplus x)) \oplus S(k_1 \oplus \Pi(k_0 \oplus x'))$$

Furthermore, we may consider each S-Box separately and solve the equation on k_1, S-Box by S-Box. if s is the bit size of an S-Box, the final complexity of this attack is $\mathcal{O}(2^{(n+s)/2})$ computations, with $\mathcal{O}(2^{n/2})$ oracle queries.

Attacking 4k-AES. In the case of AES, we can add one more round. Suppose that, by the cycle, we obtain four equations of the form:

$$A^{-1}(\Pi^{-1}(y) \oplus \Pi^{-1}(y')) =$$
$$S(k_2 \oplus \Pi(k_1 \oplus \Pi(k_0 \oplus x))) \oplus S(k_2 \oplus \Pi(k_1 \oplus \Pi(k_0 \oplus x')))$$

We use the fact that a column of $\Pi(x)$ does only depend on a diagonal of x. Since we need only to guess k_2 byte per byte, we need also only to guess k_1 column by column, assuming that the full k_0 is guessed. The cycle step has a complexity of approximately 2^{64} queries (usually, queries to an AES-like black-box should cost a non-negligible quantum time). The equation step has a complexity of approximately $2^{64} \times (2^{16}(2^4 \times 4) \times 4) \simeq 2^{84}$ calls to Π: each guess of k_0 is tested by searching the good k_1 (column by column) and k_2 (byte per byte).

Against 3k-Feistel. A Feistel scheme with a mixing function f, alternating three keys k_0, k_1, k_2, xored or modularly added, is immune to the *complementation slide* and *sliding with a twist* techniques. It seems difficult to write a slide shift property for this cipher. Let us write the round function g as:

$$L, R \mapsto R + f(k_1 + L + f(k_0 + R)),$$
$$L + f(k_0 + R) + f(k_2 + f(k_1 + L + f(k_0 + R)))$$

and suppose that we can invert f. In $\mathcal{O}(2^{n/2})$ queries, we can find two slide equations $g(L, R) = L', R'$, which imply $f(k_1 + L + f(k_0 + R)) = L' - R$. Regardless of the function f, we can invert it in time $\mathcal{O}(2^{n/4})$ using Grover and recover two equations $k_1 + L + f(k_0 + R) = X$. We take the difference (or sum if we replace $+$ by $\oplus$) to eliminate k_1, and we can solve the remaining equation on k_0 using Grover in $\mathcal{O}(2^{n/4})$ time. Once this is done, k_1 can be found via the relation $k_1 = f^{-1}(L' - R) - L - f(k_0 + R)$ and k_2 via $L + f(k_0 + R) + f(k_2 + f(k_1 + L + f(k_0 + R))) = R'$.

The whole attack requires $\mathcal{O}(2^{n/2})$ time and queries due to the cycle finding, with any function f.

Against 4k-Feistel. If we append one more round key k_3, the round function g becomes:

$$L, R \mapsto L + f(k_0 + R) + f(k_2 + f(k_1 + L + f(k_0 + R))),$$
$$R + f(k_1 + L + f(k_0 + R)) + f(k_3 + L + f(k_0 + R) + f(k_2 + f(k_1 + L + f(k_0 + R))))$$

Again, we can find some slide equations $g(L, R) = L', R'$ from a cycle in $\mathcal{O}(2^{n/2})$ queries. We guess the subkey k_0. For each guess, we can rewrite the equations as if there were only 3 subkeys, and solve them in time $\mathcal{O}(2^{n/4})$ using multiple Grover instances, as seen above, regardless of the properties of f. The whole attack requires $\mathcal{O}(2^{n/2})$ time and queries, the two steps (cycle finding and solving equations) are now balanced. The time complexity is greater than the other 4k-Feistel attacks seen above, but there is no restriction on the function f and the operations used; furthermore, we only use encryption queries, not decryption queries (which is the case of the twist).

C   Slide Attack on a Four-Round Self-similar Feistel

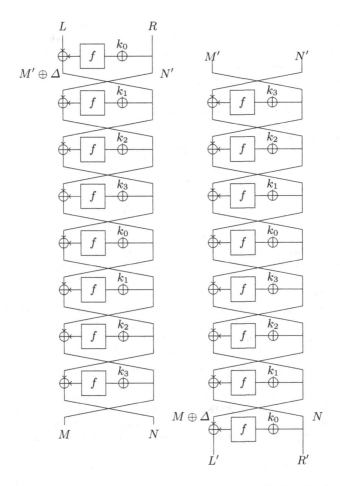

Fig. 6. Complementation and twist combined on a 4k-Feistel scheme

References

1. Alagic, G., Russell, A.: Quantum-secure symmetric-key cryptography based on hidden shifts. In: Coron, J.-S., Nielsen, J.B. (eds.) EUROCRYPT 2017. LNCS, vol. 10212, pp. 65–93. Springer, Cham (2017). https://doi.org/10.1007/978-3-319-56617-7_3
2. Bar-On, A., Biham, E., Dunkelman, O., Keller, N.: Efficient slide attacks. J. Cryptol. **31**(3), 641–670 (2018). https://doi.org/10.1007/s00145-017-9266-8
3. Biryukov, A., Wagner, D.: Slide attacks. In: Knudsen, L. (ed.) FSE 1999. LNCS, vol. 1636, pp. 245–259. Springer, Heidelberg (1999). https://doi.org/10.1007/3-540-48519-8_18

4. Biryukov, A., Wagner, D.: Advanced slide attacks. In: Preneel, B. (ed.) EURO-CRYPT 2000. LNCS, vol. 1807, pp. 589–606. Springer, Heidelberg (2000). https://doi.org/10.1007/3-540-45539-6_41

5. Boneh, D., Zhandry, M.: Secure signatures and chosen ciphertext security in a quantum computing world. In: Canetti, R., Garay, J.A. (eds.) CRYPTO 2013. LNCS, vol. 8043, pp. 361–379. Springer, Heidelberg (2013). https://doi.org/10.1007/978-3-642-40084-1_21

6. Bonnetain, X.: Quantum key-recovery on full AEZ. In: Adams, C., Camenisch, J. (eds.) SAC 2017. LNCS, vol. 10719, pp. 394–406. Springer, Cham (2018). https://doi.org/10.1007/978-3-319-72565-9_20

7. Bonnetain, X.: Improved low-qubit hidden shift algorithms. CoRR (2019). http://arxiv.org/abs/1901.11428

8. Bonnetain, X., Naya-Plasencia, M.: Hidden shift quantum cryptanalysis and implications. In: Peyrin, T., Galbraith, S. (eds.) ASIACRYPT 2018. LNCS, vol. 11272, pp. 560–592. Springer, Cham (2018). https://doi.org/10.1007/978-3-030-03326-2_19

9. Chailloux, A., Naya-Plasencia, M., Schrottenloher, A.: An efficient quantum collision search algorithm and implications on symmetric cryptography. In: Takagi, T., Peyrin, T. (eds.) ASIACRYPT 2017. LNCS, vol. 10625, pp. 211–240. Springer, Cham (2017). https://doi.org/10.1007/978-3-319-70697-9_8

10. Childs, A.M., Jao, D., Soukharev, V.: Constructing elliptic curve isogenies in quantum subexponential time. J. Math. Cryptol. 8(1), 1–29 (2014). https://doi.org/10.1515/jmc-2012-0016

11. Damgård, I., Funder, J., Nielsen, J.B., Salvail, L.: Superposition attacks on cryptographic protocols. In: Padró, C. (ed.) ICITS 2013. LNCS, vol. 8317, pp. 142–161. Springer, Cham (2014). https://doi.org/10.1007/978-3-319-04268-8_9

12. Dinur, I., Dunkelman, O., Keller, N., Shamir, A.: Reflections on slide with a twist attacks. Des. Codes Crypt. 77(2–3), 633–651 (2015). https://doi.org/10.1007/s10623-015-0098-y

13. Dong, X., Dong, B., Wang, X.: Quantum attacks on some Feistel block ciphers. Cryptol. ePrint Arch. Rep. 2018, 504 (2018). https://eprint.iacr.org/2018/504

14. Dong, X., Wang, X.: Quantum key-recovery attack on Feistel structures. Sci. China Inf. Sci. 61(10), 102501:1–102501:7 (2018). https://doi.org/10.1007/s11432-017-9468-y

15. Dunkelman, O., Keller, N., Shamir, A.: Slidex attacks on the Even-Mansour encryption scheme. J. Cryptol. 28(1), 1–28 (2015). https://doi.org/10.1007/s00145-013-9164-7

16. Gagliardoni, T.: Quantum security of cryptographic primitives. Ph. D. thesis, Darmstadt University of Technology, Germany (2017). http://tuprints.ulb.tu-darmstadt.de/6019/

17. Gagliardoni, T., Hülsing, A., Schaffner, C.: Semantic security and indistinguishability in the quantum world. In: Robshaw, M., Katz, J. (eds.) CRYPTO 2016. LNCS, vol. 9816, pp. 60–89. Springer, Heidelberg (2016). https://doi.org/10.1007/978-3-662-53015-3_3

18. Hosoyamada, A., Iwata, T.: Tight quantum security bound of the 4-round luby-rackoff construction. IACR Cryptol. ePrint Arch. 2019, 243 (2019). https://eprint.iacr.org/2019/243

19. Hosoyamada, A., Sasaki, Y.: Quantum Demiric-Selçuk meet-in-the-middle attacks: applications to 6-round generic Feistel constructions. In: Catalano, D., De Prisco, R. (eds.) SCN 2018. LNCS, vol. 11035, pp. 386–403. Springer, Cham (2018). https://doi.org/10.1007/978-3-319-98113-0_21

20. Hosoyamada, A., Sasaki, Y., Xagawa, K.: Quantum multicollision-finding algorithm. In: Takagi, T., Peyrin, T. (eds.) ASIACRYPT 2017. LNCS, vol. 10625, pp. 179–210. Springer, Cham (2017). https://doi.org/10.1007/978-3-319-70697-9_7
21. Ito, G., Hosoyamada, A., Matsumoto, R., Sasaki, Y., Iwata, T.: Quantum chosen-ciphertext attacks against Feistel ciphers. In: Matsui, M. (ed.) CT-RSA 2019. LNCS, vol. 11405, pp. 391–411. Springer, Cham (2019). https://doi.org/10.1007/978-3-030-12612-4_20
22. Kaplan, M.: Quantum attacks against iterated block ciphers. CoRR (2014). http://arxiv.org/abs/1410.1434
23. Kaplan, M., Leurent, G., Leverrier, A., Naya-Plasencia, M.: Breaking symmetric cryptosystems using quantum period finding. In: Robshaw, M., Katz, J. (eds.) CRYPTO 2016. LNCS, vol. 9815, pp. 207–237. Springer, Heidelberg (2016). https://doi.org/10.1007/978-3-662-53008-5_8
24. Kaplan, M., Leurent, G., Leverrier, A., Naya-Plasencia, M.: Quantum differential and linear cryptanalysis. IACR Trans. Symmetric Cryptol. **2016**(1), 71–94 (2016). http://tosc.iacr.org/index.php/ToSC/article/view/536
25. Kuperberg, G.: A subexponential-time quantum algorithm for the dihedral hidden subgroup problem. SIAM J. Comput. **35**(1), 170–188 (2005). https://doi.org/10.1137/S0097539703436345. http://dblp.uni-trier.de/rec/bib/journals/siamcomp/Kuperberg05
26. Kuperberg, G.: Another subexponential-time quantum algorithm for the dihedral hidden subgroup problem. In: Severini, S., Brandão, F.G.S.L. (eds.) 8th Conference on the Theory of Quantum Computation, Communication and Cryptography, TQC 2013, May 21–23, 2013, Guelph, Canada. LIPIcs, vol. 22, pp. 20–34. Schloss Dagstuhl - Leibniz-Zentrum fuer Informatik (2013). https://doi.org/10.4230/LIPIcs.TQC.2013.20
27. Kuwakado, H., Morii, M.: Quantum distinguisher between the 3-round Feistel cipher and the random permutation. In: 2010 IEEE International Symposium on Information Theory Proceedings (ISIT), pp. 2682–2685 (June 2010)
28. Kuwakado, H., Morii, M.: Security on the quantum-type Even-Mansour cipher. In: 2012 International Symposium on Information Theory and its Applications (ISITA), pp. 312–316 (October 2012)
29. Leander, G., May, A.: Grover Meets Simon – quantumly attacking the FX-construction. In: Takagi, T., Peyrin, T. (eds.) ASIACRYPT 2017. LNCS, vol. 10625, pp. 161–178. Springer, Cham (2017). https://doi.org/10.1007/978-3-319-70697-9_6
30. Regev, O.: A subexponential time algorithm for the dihedral hidden subgroup problem with polynomial space. CoRR (2004). http://arxiv.org/abs/quant-ph/0406151
31. Santoli, T., Schaffner, C.: Using Simon's algorithm to attack symmetric-key cryptographic primitives. Quantum Inf. Comput. **17**(1&2), 65–78 (2017). http://www.rintonpress.com/xxqic17/qic-17-12/0065-0078.pdf
32. Simon, D.R.: On the power of quantum computation. In: 35th Annual Symposium on Foundations of Computer Science, Santa Fe, New Mexico, USA, 20–22 November 1994, pp. 116–123. IEEE Computer Society (1994). https://doi.org/10.1109/SFCS.1994.365701
33. Takagi, T., Peyrin, T. (eds.): ASIACRYPT 2017. LNCS, vol. 10625. Springer, Cham (2017). https://doi.org/10.1007/978-3-319-70697-9
34. Zhandry, M.: How to construct quantum random functions. In: 53rd Annual IEEE Symposium on Foundations of Computer Science, FOCS 2012, New Brunswick, NJ, USA, October 20–23, 2012, pp. 679–687 (2012)

Post-quantum Implementations

XMSS and Embedded Systems
XMSS Hardware Accelerators for RISC-V

Wen Wang[1]([✉]), Bernhard Jungk[2], Julian Wälde[3], Shuwen Deng[1],
Naina Gupta[4], Jakub Szefer[1]([✉]), and Ruben Niederhagen[3]([✉])

[1] Yale University, New Haven, CT, USA
{wen.wang.ww349,shuwen.deng,jakub.szefer}@yale.edu
[2] Munich, Germany
[3] Fraunhofer SIT, Darmstadt, Germany
ruben@polycephaly.org
[4] Fraunhofer Singapore, Singapore, Singapore
naina.gupta@fraunhofer.sg

Abstract. We describe a software-hardware co-design for the hash-based post-quantum signature scheme XMSS on a RISC-V embedded processor. We provide software optimizations for the XMSS reference implementation for SHA-256 parameter sets and several hardware accelerators that allow to balance area usage and performance based on individual needs. By integrating our hardware accelerators into the RISC-V processor, the version with the best time-area product generates a key pair (that can be used to generate 2^{10} signatures) in 3.44 s, achieving an over 54× speedup in wall-clock time compared to the pure software version. For such a key pair, signature generation takes less than 10 ms and verification takes less than 6 ms, bringing speedups of over 42× and 17× respectively. We tested and measured the cycle count of our implementation on an Intel Cyclone V SoC FPGA. The integration of our XMSS accelerators into an embedded RISC-V processor shows that it is possible to use hash-based post-quantum signatures for a large variety of embedded applications.

Keywords: XMSS · Hash-based signatures · Post-quantum cryptography · Hardware accelerator · FPGA · RISC-V

1 Introduction

Due to the continued computerization and automation of our society, more and more systems from consumer products and Internet-of-Things (IoT) devices to cars, high-speed trains, and even nuclear power plants are controlled by embedded computers that often are connected to the Internet. Such devices can have a severe impact not only on our information security but increasingly also on our physical safety. Therefore, embedded devices must provide a high level of protection against cyber attacks—despite their typically restricted computing

B. Jungk—Independent Researcher.

K. G. Paterson and D. Stebila (Eds.): SAC 2019, LNCS 11959, pp. 523–550, 2020.
https://doi.org/10.1007/978-3-030-38471-5_21

resources. If an attacker is able to disrupt the authenticity of transmitted data, he or she can undermine the security of the system in many ways, e.g., malicious firmware can be loaded or contents of a digital document can be changed without being detected. Authenticity of the data is commonly ensured using digital signature schemes, often based on the DSA and ECDSA algorithms [22].

Such currently used asymmetric cryptographic algorithms, however, are vulnerable to attacks using quantum computers: Shor's algorithm [24,25] is able to factor integers and compute discrete logarithms in polynomial time and Grover's algorithm [10] provides a quadratic speedup for brute-force search. In light of recent advances in quantum-computer development and increased research interest in bringing practical quantum computers to life, a new field of post-quantum cryptography (PQC) has evolved [4], which provides cryptographic algorithms that are believed to be secure against attacks using quantum computers. This paper focuses on one of these algorithms, the eXtended Merkle Signature Scheme (XMSS), which has been standardized by the IETF [15].

XMSS is a stateful hash-based signature scheme proposed in 2011 by Buchmann, Dahmen and Hülsing [6]. It is based on the Merkle signature scheme [19] and proven to be a forward-secure post-quantum signature scheme with minimal security assumptions: Its security is solely based on the existence of a second pre-image resistant hash function family and a pseudorandom function (PRF) family. Both of these function families can be efficiently constructed even in the presence of large quantum computers [6]. Therefore, XMSS is considered to be a practical post-quantum signature scheme. Due to its minimal security assumptions and its well understood security properties, XMSS is regarded as one of the most confidence-inspiring post-quantum signature schemes.

Embedded devices will need to use algorithms such as XMSS to make them future-proof and to ensure their security even in the light of practical quantum computers. One of the increasingly popular processor architectures for embedded devices is the RISC-V architecture. It is an open and free architecture that is proving to be a practical alternative to close-source designs. Consequently, this work uses a RISC-V-based system on chip (SoC) (see Sect. 3) as a representative for embedded system architectures and shows how to efficiently deploy the post-quantum signature scheme XMSS on an embedded device, with the help of new hardware accelerators.

Hash-based signature schemes such as XMSS have relatively high resource requirements. They need to perform thousands of hash-computations for key generation, signing and verification and need sufficient memory for their relatively large signatures. Therefore, running such post-quantum secure signature schemes efficiently on a resource-constrained embedded system is a difficult task. This work introduces a number of hardware accelerators that provide a good time-area trade-off for implementing XMSS on RISC-V.

Our Contributions. Our work describes a software-hardware co-design of XMSS achieving 128 bit post-quantum security in an embedded systems setting To speed up the XMSS computations, we first provide SHA-256-specific software optimizations for the XMSS reference implementation. Based on the optimized

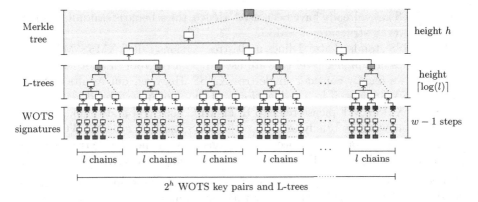

Fig. 1. XMSS tree with binary Merkle hash tree and WOTS instances with L-trees as leaves. Red nodes are the WOTS private key and blue nodes are the WOTS public key values. Green nodes are the L-tree roots and the gray node is the XMSS public key. (Color figure online)

XMSS software implementation, we then develop several hardware accelerators to speed up the most compute-intensive operations in XMSS. Our experimental results show a significant speedup of running XMSS on our software-hardware co-design compared to the pure (optimized) reference software version.

The source code for our work is publicly available under the open source GPLv3 license at https://caslab.csl.yale.edu/code/xmsshwswriscv/. An extended version of this work is available as Cryptology ePrint Archive, Report 2018/1225 [28].

2   Preliminaries

In this section, we give an introduction to the relevant aspects of the XMSS signature scheme and briefly recapitulate the functionalities of SHA-256.

2.1   XMSS

XMSS [15] is a stateful digital signature scheme based on the Merkle signature scheme [19]. Similar to the Merkle signature scheme, XMSS uses a variant of the Winternitz one-time signature scheme (WOTS or Winternitz-OTS) to sign individual messages. One private/public WOTS key pair is used to sign one single message (with the private secret key) and to verify the signature (with the corresponding public verification key). To be able to sign up to 2^h messages, XMSS uses 2^h pairs of WOTS secret and verification keys. To reduce the size of the public key, a Merkle hash tree of height h and binary L-trees are used to reduce the authenticity of many WOTS verification keys to one XMSS public key. Since each WOTS key must only be used once, the signer needs to remember which WOTS keys already have been used. Hence, the scheme is stateful. Figure 1 shows the overall structure of XMSS.

The XMSS standard also defines multi-tree versions called XMSS^MT where the leaf nodes of a higher-level tree are used to sign the root of another tree. In this paper, we mainly consider single-tree XMSS. However, our results apply to multi-tree XMSS as well in a straightforward way. For a detailed description of XMSS and XMSS^MT please refer to IETF RFC 8391 [15] and to [6].

In the following we briefly introduce the XMSS address scheme, WOTS, the L-tree construction, and the procedure for constructing the Merkle tree. We also give an introduction to XMSS key generation, signing, and verification.

Address Scheme. XMSS uses a hash-function address scheme throughout the Merkle tree, L-tree, and WOTS computations to uniquely identify each individual step in the overall graph. These addresses are used to derive keys for keyed hash functions that are unique for each specific location in the graph. Each address is composed of eight 32 bit fields, with fields for, e.g., the level within a tree and the leaf index. In total, an XMSS address has a size of 256 bit. For more details about the hash function address scheme, please refer to IETF RFC 8391 [15, Sect. 2.5].

Winternitz OTS. The WOTS scheme was first mentioned in [19]. For signing a message digest D of n-byte length, WOTS uses a cryptographically secure hash function with n-byte output strings to compute hash chains. The message digest is interpreted as binary representation of an integer d. First, d is split into $l_1 = \lceil 8n/\log_2(w) \rceil$ base-w words $d_i, 0 \le i < l_1$ and a checksum $c = \sum_{i=0}^{l_1} w - 1 - d_i$ is computed for these base-w words (w is called the "Winternitz parameter"). The checksum c is split into $l_2 = \lfloor \log_2(l_1(w-1))/\log_2(w)+1 \rfloor$ base-w words $c_i, 0 \le i < l_2$ as well. WOTS key generation, signing, and verification are performed as follows:

- To *create* a private/public WOTS key pair, Alice computes $l = l_1 + l_2$ secret strings $s_{0,i}$ for $0 \le i < l$, each of n-byte length (for example using a secret seed and a PRF). These l n-byte strings are the private WOTS key. Then, Alice uses a chaining function to compute l hash chains of length $w - 1$, hashing each $s_{0,i}$ iteratively $w - 1$ times. The resulting chain-head values $s_{w-1,i}, 0 \le i < l$ of n-byte length are the public WOTS key of Alice.
- To *sign* a message digest, d is split into l_1 base-w words together with l_2 base-w checksum values computed as described above, Alice (re-)computes the intermediate chain values $(s_{d_0,0}, s_{d_1,1}, \ldots, s_{d_{l_1-1},l_1-1}, s_{c_0,0}, s_{c_1,1}, \ldots, s_{c_{l_2-1},l_2-1})$ starting from her private key values. These $l = l_1 + l_2$ values are the signature.
- When Bob wants to *verify* the signature, he recomputes the remaining chain steps by applying $w - 1 - d_i$ hash-function iterations to signature value $s_{d_i,0}$ and compares the results with the corresponding public key values. If all chain-head values match the public WOTS key, the signature is valid.

XMSS uses a modified WOTS scheme, sometimes referred to as WOTS+ or as W-OTS+ [13]; we use the term WOTS+ only when a explicit distinction from "original" WOTS is required for clarification. WOTS+ uses a function chain() as chaining function that is a bit more expensive than the simple hash-chain function described above. The function chain() uses a keyed pseudo-random function $\text{prf}_k : \{0,1\}^{256} \mapsto \{0,1\}^{8n}$ and a keyed hash-function $f_{k'} : \{0,1\}^{8n} \mapsto \{0,1\}^{8n}$. Within each chain step, the function chain() first computes a unique n-byte key k' and a unique n-byte mask using the $\text{prf}_k()$ function. The input to $\text{prf}_k()$ is the hash function address of the current step (including the chain step and a marker for the usage as key or as mask). The key k for $\text{prf}_k()$ is a seed that is part of the XMSS public key. The mask is then XOR-ed with the n-byte output from the previous chain-function call (or the initial WOTS+ chain n byte input string) and the result is used as input for the hash-function $f()$ under the key k', which gives the n-byte output of the chaining function chain() in the last iteration step.

The WOTS+ secret key consists of l (l is defined as described above for WOTS) pseudo-random strings of n-bytes in length. The XMSS specification does not demand a certain function to compute the WOTS+ private key. In the XMSS reference implementation, they are generated using the $\text{prf}_k()$ function with the local address (including the chain index) as input and keyed with the XMSS secret key seed. Each WOTS+ secret key maps to one corresponding WOTS+ public key, which is computed by calling the chaining function chain() with $w - 1$ iteration steps. Signing and verification in WOTS+ work as described above for WOTS using the WOTS+ chaining function. The more complex structure of the chaining function of WOTS+ compared to WOTS is required for multi-target resistance and within the XMSS security proof.

L-tree. The leaf nodes of an XMSS tree are computed from the WOTS+ public keys by using an unbalanced binary tree of l leaf nodes (one leaf node for each WOTS+ public key value), hence called L-tree. The nodes on each level of the L-tree are computed by hashing together two nodes from the lower level. A tree hash function $\text{hash}_{\text{rand}} : \{0,1\}^{8n} \times \{0,1\}^{8n} \mapsto \{0,1\}^{8n}$ is used for this purpose.

The function $\text{hash}_{\text{rand}}()$ uses the keyed pseudo-random function $\text{prf}_k()$ and a keyed hash-function $h_{k''} : \{0,1\}^{16n} \mapsto \{0,1\}^{8n}$. First, an n-byte key k'' and two n-byte masks are computed using the $\text{prf}_k()$ with the address (including the L-tree level and node index) as input and the same public seed as used for WOTS+ as key. The masks are then each XOR-ed to the two n-byte input strings representing the two lower-level nodes and the results are concatenated and used as input for the hash-function $h()$ keyed with k'', which gives the n-byte output of the tree hash function $\text{hash}_{\text{rand}}()$.

To be able to handle the pairwise hashing at levels with an odd number of nodes, the last node on these levels is lifted to a higher level until another single node is available. The root of the L-tree gives one single hash-value, combining the l WOTS+ public keys into one WOTS+ verification key.

XMSS Merkle Tree. In order to obtain a small public key, the authenticity of many WOTS verification keys (i.e., L-tree root keys) is reduced to one XMSS public key using a binary Merkle tree. Similar to the L-tree construction, on each level of the binary tree, neighbouring nodes are pairwise hashed together to obtain one single root node that constitutes the XMSS public key (see Fig. 1).

XMSS Key Generation. XMSS key generation is quite expensive: In order to compute the XMSS public key, i.e., the root node of the Merkle tree, the entire XMSS tree needs to be computed. Depending on the height h of the tree, thousands to millions of hash-function calls need to be performed. XMSS key generation starts by generating 2^h leaf nodes of the Merkle tree. Each leaf node consists of an WOTS instance together with an L-tree. For each WOTS instance, first l WOTS private keys are generated. These are then used to compute the l WOTS chains to obtain l WOTS public keys and then the L-trees on top of these. Once all 2^h L-tree root nodes have been computed, the Merkle tree is computed to obtain the XMSS public key.

The XMSS public key consists of the n-byte Merkle tree root node and an n-byte public seed required by the verifier to compute masks and public hash-function keys using the function $\mathrm{prf}_k()$ within the WOTS-chain, L-tree, and Merkle tree computations. The XMSS standard does not define a format for the XMSS private key. In the XMSS reference implementation that accompanies the standard, an n-byte secret seed is used to generate the WOTS secrets using a pseudo random function (e.g., $\mathrm{prf}_k()$).

XMSS Signature Generation. XMSS is a stateful signature scheme: Each WOTS private/public key pair must be used only once; otherwise, the scheme is not secure. To determine which WOTS key pair already has been used, an n-byte leaf index (the state) is stored with the private key. The index defines which WOTS key pair will be used for the next signature; after each signature generation, the index must be increased.

Similar to most signature schemes, for signing an arbitrary-length message or a document M, first a message digest of M is computed; details can be found in [15, Sect. 4.1.9]. The digest M' is then signed using the selected WOTS instance. This results in l n-byte values corresponding to the base-w decomposition of M' including the corresponding checksum. Furthermore, in order to enable the verifier to recompute the XMSS public root key from a leaf node of the Merkle tree, the signer needs to provide the verification path in the Merkle tree, i.e., h n-byte nodes that are required for the pairwise hashing in the binary Merkle tree, one node for each level in the Merkle tree.

Therefore, in the worst case, the signer needs to recompute the entire XMSS tree in order to select the required nodes for the verification path. There are several optimization strategies using time-memory trade-offs to speed up signature generation. The BDS tree traversal algorithm [7] targets at reducing the worst case runtime of signature generation by computing a certain amount of nodes in the Merkle tree at each signature computation and storing them alongside the XMSS state.

XMSS Signature Verification. Compared to key generation, XMSS signature verification is fairly inexpensive: An XMSS public key contains the Merkle root node and the public seed. An XMSS signature contains the WOTS leaf index, l

WOTS-signature chain values, and the verification path consisting of h Merkle-tree pair values, one for each level in the tree. The verifier computes the message digest M' and then recomputes the WOTS verification key by completing the WOTS chains and computing the L-tree. The verifier then uses the Merkle-tree pair values to compute the path through the Merkle tree and finally compares the Merkle tree root node that was obtained with the root node of the sender's public key. If the values are equal, verification succeeds and the signature is sound; otherwise verification fails and the signature is rejected.

Parameter Set. RFC 8391 defines parameter sets for the hash functions SHA-2 and SHAKE targeting classical security levels of 256 bit with $n = 32$ and 512 bit with $n = 64$ in order to provide 128 bit and 256 bit of security respectively against attackers in possession of a quantum computer [15, Sect. 5]. The *required* parameter sets, as specified in [15, Sect. 5.2], all use SHA-256 to instantiate the hash functions (SHA-512 and SHAKE are optional). Therefore, for this work, we focus on the SHA-256 parameter sets with $n = 32$.

For SHA-256, three different parameter sets are provided in RFC 8391 [15, Sect. 5.3], all with $n = 32$ and $w = 16$ but with $h = 10$, $h = 16$, or $h = 20$. In general, a bigger tree height h leads to an exponential growth in the run time of key generation. For verification the run time is only linearly impacted. The naive approach for signing requires one to recompute the entire tree and thus is as expensive as key generation. However, by use of the BDS tree traversal algorithm [7], the tree height has only a modest impact on the run time. Multi-tree versions of XMSS can be used to speed up the computations at the cost of larger signature sizes (e.g., to improve key generation and signing performance or to achieve a larger h). We are using $h = 10$ throughout our experiments; however, our implementation is not restricted to this value.

2.2   SHA-256

The hash function SHA-256 [21] computes a 256 bit hash value from a variable-length input. SHA-256 uses a 256 bit internal state that is updated with 512 bit blocks of the input. SHA-256 defines a padding scheme for extending variable-length inputs to a multiple of 512 bit. SHA-256 works as follows:

1. Initialize the internal state with a well-defined IV (see [21, Sect. 4.2.2]).
2. Extend the ℓ-bit input message with a padding to make the length of the padded input a multiple of 512 bit:
   - append a single 1 bit to the input message, then
   - append $0 \le k$ 0 bit such that $\ell + 1 + k + 64$ is minimized and is a multiple of 512, and finally
   - append ℓ as a 64 bit big-endian integer.
3. Iteratively apply a compression function to all 512 bit blocks of the padded input and the current internal state to obtain the next updated internal state.
4. Once all 512 bit blocks have been processed, output the current internal state as the hash value.

The compression function uses the current internal state and a 512 bit input block and outputs an updated internal state. For SHA-256, the compression function is composed of 64 rounds.

3   RISC-V

Software-hardware co-design has been adopted as a common discipline for designing embedded system architectures since the 1990s [27]. By combining both software and hardware in an embedded system, a trade-off between software flexibility and hardware performance can be achieved depending on the user's needs. To accelerate XMSS computations, we developed a software-hardware co-design of XMSS by moving the most compute-intensive operations to hardware while keeping the rest of the operations running in software. Our software-hardware co-design of XMSS is developed based on a RISC-V platform.

RISC-V. The RISC-V instruction set architecture (ISA) is a free and open architecture, overseen by the RISC-V Foundation with more than 100 member organizations[1]. The RISC-V ISA has been designed based on well-established reduced instruction set computing (RISC) principles. It has a modular design, consisting of base sets of instructions with optional instruction set extensions. Due to its modular design, the RISC-V ISA is an increasingly popular architecture for embedded systems. It is used, e.g., as a control processor in GPUs and in storage devices [11], for secure boot and as USB security dongle [20], and for building trusted execution environments (TEE) with secure hardware enclaves[2].

Since the RISC-V ISA is an open standard, researchers and industry can easily extend and adopt it in their designs without IP constraints.

VexRiscv. First-prize winner in the RISC-V Soft-Core CPU Contest of 2018[3], VexRiscv[4] is a 32-bit RISC-V CPU implementation written in SpinalHDL[5], which is a Scala-based high-level hardware description language. It supports the RV32IM instruction set and implements a five-stage in-order pipeline. The design of VexRiscv is very modular: All complementary and optional components are implemented as plugins and therefore can easily be integrated and adapted into specific processor setups as needed. The VexRiscv ecosystem provides memories, caches, IO peripherals, and buses, which can be optionally chosen and combined as required.

Murax SoC. The VexRiscv ecosystem also provides a complete predefined processor setup called "Murax SoC" that has a compact and simple design and aims at small resource usage. The Murax SoC integrates the VexRiscv CPU with a shared on-chip instruction and data memory, an Advanced Peripheral

---

[1] https://riscv.org/.

[2] https://keystone-enclave.org/.

[3] https://riscv.org/2018/10/risc-v-contest/.

[4] https://github.com/SpinalHDL/VexRiscv/.

[5] https://spinalhdl.github.io/SpinalDoc/.

Bus (APB), a JTAG programming interface, and a UART interface. It has very low resource requirements (e.g., only 1350 ALMs on a Cyclone V FPGA) and can operate on its own without any further external components.

The performance of the Murax SoC is comparable to an ARM Cortex-M3: A multi-tree version of XMSS has been implemented on an embedded ARM Cortex-M3 platform in [16] (see also Sect. 7). We compiled a pure C-version of the code from [16] for both an ARM Cortex-M3 processor and the Murax SoC and compared their performance (see the bottom lines of Table 7). In terms of cycle count, the Cortex-M3 is only about 1.5× faster than the Murax SoC. Therefore, we conclude that the Murax SoC is a good representative for an embedded system processor with low resources. As opposed to an ARM Cortex-M3 platform, however, the Murax SoC is fully free, open, and customizable and thus is an ideal platform for our work.

Extending the Murax SoC with new hardware accelerators can be implemented easily in a modular way using the APB bus. We used this feature for our XMSS accelerators. Depending on different use cases, our open-source software-hardware co-design of XMSS can be migrated to other RISC-V or embedded architectures with small changes to the interface.

Setup. We evaluated our design using a DE1-SoC evaluation board from Terasic as test-platform. This board has an Intel (formerly Altera) Cyclone V SoC 5CSEMA5F31C6 device. We used Intel Quartus Software Version 16.1 (Standard Edition) for synthesis. On the DE1-SoC, we are running the Murax SoC described above with additional accelerators that will be described in Sect. 5. The DE1-SoC board is connected to a host computer by a USB-JTAG connection for programming the FPGA, a USB-serial connection for IO of the Murax SoC, and a second USB-JTAG connection for programming and debugging the software on the Murax SoC.

We configured the on-chip RAM size of the Murax SoC to 128 kB, which is sufficient for all our experiments. We tested our implementations on the DE1-SoC board at its default clock frequency of 50 MHz; however, to achieve a fair comparison, our speedup reports presented in the following sections are based on the maximum frequency reported by the synthesis tool. Our implementation is neither platform-specific nor dependent on a specific FPGA vendor.

4 Software Implementation and Optimization

We used the official XMSS reference implementation[6] with the BDS algorithm [7] for tree traversal as software-basis for this work. We applied minor modifications to the XMSS reference code to link against the mbed TLS library[7] instead of OpenSSL, because mbed TLS generally is more suitable for resource-restricted

---

[6] https://github.com/joostrijneveld/xmss-reference/, commit 06281e057d9f5d.

[7] https://tls.mbed.org/.

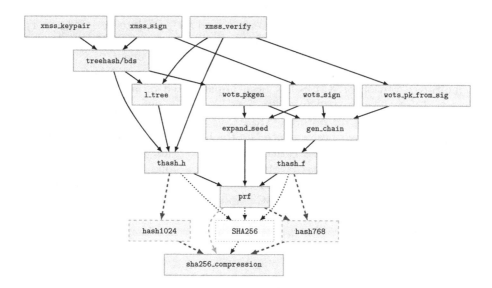

Fig. 2. Simplified XMSS call graph. Function calls that have been removed during software optimization are displayed with dotted nodes and arrows, added calls are dashed. The "fixed input length" optimization is marked in blue, the "pre-computation" optimization is marked in green. (Color figure online)

embedded platforms such as the Murax SoC platform and its SHA-256 implementation has less library-internal dependencies than that of OpenSSL, which simplifies stand-alone usage of SHA-256.

To have a fair reference point for the comparison of a pure software implementation with our hardware accelerators, we implemented two software optimizations for the XMSS reference software implementation as described in the following paragraphs. These optimizations are also helpful on other processor architectures but only work for SHA-256 parameter sets, because they depend on the specific SHA-256 block size and padding scheme. We are going to provide our software optimizations to the maintainers of the XMSS reference implementation so they can integrate them if they wish to.

Figure 2 shows a simplified XMSS call graph for both the original source code version and the changes that we applied for optimizations as described below.

Fixed Input Length. In the XMSS software reference implementation, around 90% of the time is spent inside the hash-function calls. Therefore, the SHA-256 function is most promising for optimization efforts. In particular for short-length inputs, a significant overhead is caused by computing the SHA-256 padding. However, within the XMSS scheme, the inputs of almost all SHA-256 calls have a well-known, fixed length: A general, arbitrary-length SHA-256 computation is only required when computing the actual hash digest of the input message, which is called only once for signing and once for verifying. For all the other SHA-256 calls, the length of the input data is either 768 bit or 1024 bit depending on

256-bit `hash768`-padding:

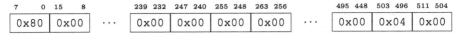

512-bit `hash1024`-padding:

Fig. 3. Fixed padding for `hash768` and `hash1024`.

where SHA-256 is called within the XMSS scheme: An input length of 768 bit is required within the PRF and within the WOTS-chain computation; an input length of 1024 bit is required within the Merkle tree and the L-trees to hash two nodes together. Therefore, we can eliminate the overhead for the padding computation of the SHA-256 function by "hardcoding" the two required message paddings, given that their lengths are known beforehand.

We implemented two specialized SHA-256 functions: The function `hash768` targeting messages with a fixed length of 768 bit and `hash1024` targeting messages with fixed length of 1024 bit. Figure 3 shows the padding for `hash768` and `hash1024`. Since SHA-256 has a block size of 512 bit, two blocks are required to hash a message of length 768 bit. Therefore, we need to hardcode a 256 bit padding for `hash768` to fill up the second block to 512 bit. When a 768 bit message is fed to the `hash768` function, the 256 bit padding is appended to the message. Then, the new 1024 bit padded message is divided into two 512 bit blocks and the compression function is performed on each of them one by one. Once the compression function on the second message block has finished, the internal state is read out and returned as the output. The SHA-256 standard always demands to append a padding even if the input length is a multiple of 512 bit. Therefore, for the `hash1024` function a 512 bit padding is hardcoded similarly to `hash768` and three calls to the compression function are performed.

Table 1 shows a comparison of the original XMSS reference implementation with an optimized version making use of the "fixed input length" optimization on the Murax SoC with parameters $n = 32$, $w = 16$ and $h = 10$. The speedup for 768 bit inputs is about $1.07\times$ and for 1024 bit inputs is about $1.04\times$. The use of 768 bit inputs is more common during the XMSS computations. Therefore, we see an about $1.06\times$ speedup for WOTS computations as well as the key generation, signing, and verification operations in XMSS.

Pre-computation. Pre-computation is commonly referred to as the act of performing an initial computation before runtime to generate a lookup table to avoid repeated computations during runtime. This technique is useful in improving real-time performance of algorithms at the expense of extra memory and extra preparatory computations [3]. In XMSS, a variant of this idea can be applied to improve the performance of the hash functions. Within XMSS, SHA-256 is used to implement four different keyed hash-functions, the function `thash_f`

Table 1. Cycle count and speedup of the "fixed input length" optimization and for both, the "fixed input length" and the "pre-computation" optimizations, on the Murax SoC with parameters $n = 32$, $w = 16$ and $h = 10$.

	"original"	+ "fixed input length"		+ "pre-computation"		
	Cycles (A)	Cycle (B)	Speedup (AB)	Cycles (C)	Speedup (BC)	Speedup (AC)
hash768	11.5×10^3	10.7×10^3	1.07	5.87×10^3	1.83	1.95
hash1024	16.2×10^3	15.6×10^3	1.04	—	—	—
WOTS-chain	571×10^3	530×10^3	1.08	371×10^3	1.43	1.54
XMSS-leaf	42.2×10^6	39.8×10^6	1.06	27.7×10^6	1.44	1.53
key generation	43.3×10^9	40.8×10^9	1.06	28.3×10^9	1.44	1.53
signing	58.3×10^6	55.0×10^6	1.06	38.4×10^6	1.43	1.52
verification	26.7×10^6	25.2×10^6	1.06	17.4×10^6	1.45	1.54

for computing f() in the WOTS-chains, the function thash_h for h() in the tree hashing, and the function prf for computing the prf(), generating masks and hash-function keys. Furthermore, SHA-256 is used to compute the message digest that is signed using a WOTS private key. The domain separation and the keying for these four functions are achieved by computing the input to SHA-256 as the concatenation of a 256 bit domain separator value (distinct for these four functions), the 256 bit hash key, and the hash-function input. Since SHA-256 operates on 512 bit blocks, one entire block is required for domain separation and keying of the respective hash function.

In case of the prf, for all public-key operations when generating masks and hash-function keys for the WOTS chain, the L-tree and Merkle tree operations, the key to the prf is the 256 bit XMSS public seed. Thus, both the 256 bit domain separator and the 256 bit hash-function key are the same for all these calls for a given XMSS key pair. These two parts fit exactly into one 512 bit SHA-256 block. Therefore, the internal SHA-256 state after processing the first 512 bit block is the same for all these calls to the prf and based on this fact, we can save one SHA-256 compression function call per prf-call by pre-computing and replaying this internal state. The internal state can either be computed once and stored together with the XMSS key or each time an XMSS operation (key generation, signing, verification) is performed. This saves the computation on one of the two input blocks in hash768 used in the prf. For hash1024, this optimization is not applicable since the fixed input block pattern does not exist.

At the first call to prf, we store the SHA-256 context of mbed TLS for later usage after the first compression function computation. The state includes the internal state and further information such as the length of the already processed data. When the prf is called during XMSS operations, we first create a copy of the initially stored prf SHA-256 context and then perform the following prf() operations based on this state copy, skipping the first input block. The cost for the compression function call on the first SHA-256 block within the `prf` is therefore reduced to a simple and inexpensive memory-copy operation.

Performance measurements and speedup for our pre-computation optimization are shown in Table 1. For `hash768` we achieve a 1.83× speedup over the "fixed input length" optimization, because only one SHA-256 block needs to be processed instead of two. For WOTS-chain computations we obtain a 1.43× speedup and for the overall XMSS leaf computations an about 1.44× speedup. The expected speedup for Merkle tree computations is about the same as for the L-tree computations since the trees are constructed in a similar way. Table 1 shows that we achieve an overall speedup of more than 1.5× including both optimizations also for the complete XMSS operations, i.e., key generation, signing, and verification. We observed a similar speedup on an Intel i5 CPU. Similar speedups can be achieved on other architectures as well, e.g., ARM processors.

5   Hardware Acceleration

To further accelerate the XMSS computations, we developed several dedicated hardware modules together with software interfaces for the XMSS software. As shown in Fig. 4, the Murax SoC uses an APB for connecting peripherals to the main CPU core. The peripheral can be accessed by the software running on the Murax SoC via control and data registers that are mapped into the address space. Therefore, the software interface can simply use read and write instructions to communicate with a hardware module. Due to the modularity of the VexRiscv implementation, dedicated hardware modules can be easily added to and removed from the APB before synthesis of the SoC (see Sect. 3).

The hardware accelerators are connected to the APB using a bridge module: The `Apb3Bridge` module connects on one side to the 32 bit data bus and the control signals of the APB and on the other side to the hardware accelerator. It provides a 32 bit control register, which is mapped to the control and state ports of the hardware accelerator, and data registers for buffering the input data, which are directly connected to the input ports of the hardware accelerator. The control and data registers are mapped to the APB as 32 bit words using a multiplexer, selected by the APB address port on APB write; the control register and the output ports of the hardware accelerator are connected in the same way to be accessed on APB read. This allows the software to communicate with the accelerators via memory-mapped IO using simple load and store instructions.

We modified the corresponding software functions in the optimized XMSS implementation to replace them with function calls to our hardware accelerators as follows: The function first sets control bits (e.g., RESET, INIT) to high in the control register. When these bits are received as high by the `Apb3Bridge` module, it raises the corresponding input signals of the hardware accelerator. Similarly, the input data is sent to the corresponding hardware accelerator via the APB bus in words of width 32 bit. Then the hardware accelerator is triggered using the control register, performs its computation, and raises a done signal when it finishes. Once the software is ready to read the result, it keeps polling

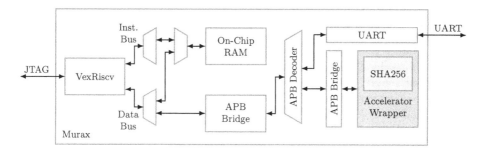

Fig. 4. Schematic of the Murax SoC. Hardware accelerators are connected to the APB. Details on the hardware accelerators are shown in Fig. 5.

the control register until the DONE bit is set high. The software then can read the results via the APB in words of 32 bit.

5.1   General-Purpose SHA-256 Accelerator

The first hardware module we developed is the SHA256 module, which is a general-purpose hash accelerator that accepts variable length inputs. The SHA256 module is used as the building block in the XMSS-specific hardware accelerators described in the following sub-sections. It has a similar interface as the generic SHA-256 compression function in software: It receives a 512 bit data block as input and computes the compression function, updating an internal 256 bit state. This state can be read out as the 256 bit digest when the SHA-256 computation is finished. Padding is performed in software as before.

We developed the module SHA256 by implementing an iterative version of SHA-256 by computing one round of SHA-256 in one clock cycle. Therefore, we require 64 clock cycles to process one SHA-256 data block. This provides a good trade-off between throughput and area consumption similar to [12]. The SHA256 module is a generic hash core without platform-specific optimizations that runs on any FPGA platform. Users can easily use a platform-optimized SHA-256 core within our hardware modules, e.g., [8,17,23].

Hardware Support for Software Optimizations. The software optimization of SHA-256 exploiting fixed input lengths of the SHA-256 function described in Sect. 4 can be mapped in a straightforward way to the SHA256 module. The software prepares the SHA-256 input chunks with pre-defined paddings just as before and then transfers each chunk to the SHA256 module for processing. Therefore, the speedup achieved for the pure software version can also be exploited for this hardware accelerator.

In order to support the "pre-computation" optimization, (Sect. 4), we added an interface to the SHA256 module that allows to set the internal state of the SHA256 module from software. Reading the internal state is the same as reading the SHA-256 message digest at the end of the hash computation. While the hardware is performing the hash computation, the software can go on transferring

Table 2. Performance of the hardware module SHA256 and comparisons of performing the SHA-256 compression function on different numbers of 512 bit blocks when called from the RISC-V software on a Murax SoC and on a Murax SoC with a SHA256 accelerator (all using the "fixed input length" optimization in software, i.e., cost for SHA-256 padding is not included).

Design	Cycles	Area (ALM)	Reg.	Fmax (MHz)	Time (μs)	Time×Area (relative)	Speedup
one 512 bit block							
SHA256	64	1180	1550	100	0.639	—	—
hash768 with pre-computation (one 512 bit block)							
Murax	4950	1350	1660	152	32.6	9.22	1.00
+ SHA256	253	2860	3880	99.9	2.53	1.00	12.9
hash768 without pre-computation (two 512 bit blocks)							
Murax	10,700	1350	1660	152	70.4	8.76	1.00
+ SHA256	576	2860	3880	99.9	5.77	1.00	12.2
hash1024 (three 512 bit blocks)							
Murax	15,600	1350	1660	152	102	10.5	1.00
+ SHA256	700	2860	3880	99.9	7.01	1.00	14.6

the next data block to the SHA256 module. This reduces the communication overhead and increases the efficiency of the SHA256 module.

Evaluation. Table 2 shows performance, resource requirements, and maximum frequency of the SHA256 module. The module requires 64 cycles (one cycle per round) for computing the compression function on one 512 bit input block.

Table 2 also shows a comparison of computing one SHA-256 compression function call in software (design Murax) with calling the hardware module from the software (design "Murax + SHA256"). Transferring data to the SHA256 accelerator module and reading back the results contribute a significant overhead: The entire computation on a 512 bit input block (without SHA-256 padding computation) requires 253 cycles. This overhead is due to the simple bus structure of the Murax SoC; a more sophisticated bus (e.g., an AXI bus) may have a lower overhead—at a higher cost of resources. However, we achieve an almost 13× speedup over the software implementation of the SHA-256 compression function.

Table 6 shows the performance impact of the SHA256 module on XMSS computations (designs Murax and "Murax + SHA256", including both "fixed input length" and "pre-computation" software optimizations). For the key generation, signing and verification operations, the SHA256 module accounts for an about 3.8× speedup in the XMSS scheme.

To further accelerate the XMSS computations in an efficient way, in the following we describe the XMSS-specific hardware accelerators that we developed. We first describe an XMSS-specific SHA-256 accelerator, which performs fixed-length SHA-256 padding and provides optional internal storage for one pre-computed state in hardware. Then, we describe how we use this XMSS-specific SHA-256 accelerator as building-block for larger hardware accelerators: An accelerator for WOTS-chain computations and an accelerator for XMSS-leaf generation including WOTS and L-tree computations.

5.2   XMSS-Specific SHA-256 Accelerator

In Sect. 4, we proposed two software optimizations for the XMSS scheme: "fixed input length" for accelerating SHA-256 computations on 768 bit and 1024 bit inputs and "pre-computation" for acceleration of the function prf(). For hardware acceleration, we introduced a general-purpose SHA-256 hardware module in Sect. 5.1, which replaces the SHA-256 compression function and thus naturally supports the "fixed input length" optimization and the "pre-computation" optimization of the software implementation. However, both of the optimizations require to repeatedly transfer the same data, i.e., padding or the pre-computed state, to the SHA256 module. To eliminate this overhead and as building block for the hardware accelerator modules described in the following sub-sections, we developed an XMSS-specific SHA-256 accelerator, the SHA256XMSS module. It has a similar functionality as the general SHA256 module; however, the SHA256XMSS module supports both of the software optimizations internally: It only accepts complete input data blocks of size 768 bit or 1024 bit and adds the SHA-256 padding in hardware. In addition, it provides an optional internal 256 bit register for storing and replaying a pre-computed state.

Implementation. We used the SHA256 module as building block for the implementation of the SHA256XMSS module. All the SHA-256 compression computations in SHA256XMSS are done by interacting with the SHA256 module. In order to handle larger input blocks, the data_in port of the SHA256XMSS module is 1024 bit wide. The SHA256XMSS module has an additional state machine to autonomously perform two or three compression-function iterations (depending on the input length). The state machine also takes care of appending the pre-computed SHA-256 padding to the input data before the last compression function computation. To select between different input lengths, the SHA256XMSS module has a message_length input signal (low for 768 bit, high for 1024 bit). To support the "pre-computation" optimization, the SHA256XMSS module has a similar interface as described for the SHA256 module in Sect. 5.1, which allows to set the internal state from software.

To further support the pre-computation functionality in hardware, a 256 bit register can optionally be activated at synthesis time to the SHA256XMSS module for storing the fixed internal state. An input signal store_intermediate is added for requesting to store the result of the first compression-function iteration in the internal 256 bit register. An input signal continue_intermediate is added for requesting to use the previously stored internal state instead of the first compression iteration. The pre-computation functionality can be enabled

Table 3. Performance of hardware module SHA256XMSS and performance comparisons of SHA-256 computations for 768 bit and 1024 bit (functions hash768 and hash1024) when called from the RISC-V software on a Murax SoC and on a Murax SoC with a SHA256XMSS accelerator.

Design	Cycles	Area (ALM)	Reg.	Fmax (MHz)	Time (μs)	Time×Area (relative)	Speedup
			two 512 bit blocks				
SHA256XMSS	128	1680	2070	89.7	1.43	1.77	1.00
+ PRECOMP	64	1900	2320	98.3	0.651	1.00	2.19
			three 512 bit blocks				
SHA256XMSS	192	1680	2070	89.7	2.14	—	—
			hash768				
Murax	10,700	1350	1660	152	70.4	16.0	1.00
+ SHA256XMSS	274	3490	4890	97.8	2.80	1.06	25.1
+ PRECOMP	247	3660	5170	97.6	2.53	1.00	27.8
			hash1024				
Murax	15,600	1350	1660	152	102	13.1	1.00
+ SHA256XMSS	458	3490	4890	97.8	4.68	1.00	21.9

(marked as "+ PRECOMP" in the tables) or disabled at synthesis time in order to save hardware resources for a time-area trade-off.

To reduce the latency of data transfer between the SHA256XMSS module and the software, the SHA256XMSS module starts computation once the first input data block (512 bit) is received. While the SHA256XMSS module is operating on the first input block, the software sends the rest of the input data.

When the SHA256XMSS module is added to the Murax SoC as a hardware accelerator, it provides a SHA256 accelerator as well since the SHA256 module is used as its building block. To achieve this, a hardware wrapper is designed (as shown in Fig. 5) which includes both the SHA256XMSS module and the SHA256 module. Apart from the control signals and input data, the bridge module Apb3Bridge also takes care of forwarding a 3 bit cmd signal from the software to the hardware wrapper. Depending on the value of cmd, the hardware wrapper further dispatches the signals to the corresponding hardware module (SHA256XMSS or SHA256) and triggers the computation. Similarly, based on the cmd value, the output data from the corresponding module is returned. The design of the hardware wrapper brings the flexibility that the SHA256XMSS module can not only accelerate XMSS-specific SHA-256 function calls, but also general SHA-256 function calls that accept variable length inputs, which may be helpful for some other applications running in the system.

Evaluation. Table 3 shows the performance, resource requirements, and maximum frequency of the SHA256XMSS module. When the pre-computation functionality is not enabled, it requires 128 cycles and 192 cycles respectively (one cycle per round) for computing the hash digests for input messages of size 768 bit and 1024 bit. When the pre-computation functionality of the SHA256XMSS module is enabled, the cycle count for computing the hash digests for input messages of size 768 bit is halved, because only one 512 bit block needs to be compressed instead of two. However, storing the pre-computed state to achieve this speedup increases ALM and register requirements. When the pre-computation functionality of the SHA256XMSS module is enabled, one hash768 call within design "Murax + SHA256XMSS + PRECOMP" obtains a speedup of around 27.8 × over the plain Murax design.

Table 6 shows the performance impact of the SHA256XMSS module on XMSS key generation, signing, and verification (design Murax compared to "Murax + SHA256XMSS" and "Murax + SHA256XMSS + PRECOMP"). For these operations, the SHA256XMSS module accounts for an about 5.4× speedup with pre-computation enabled. Compared to adding a SHA256 module to the Murax SoC, this gives an over 1.4× speedup in accelerating XMSS computations.

5.3   WOTS-chain Accelerator

The SHA256XMSS module provides a significant speedup to the XMSS computations. However, since inputs and outputs need to be written to and read from the SHA256XMSS module frequently, the raw speedup of the SHA-256 accelerator cannot fully be exploited: It actually takes more time to send the inputs to and to read the results from the accelerator than the accelerator requires for the SHA-256 operations. This overhead can significantly be reduced by performing several SHA-256 operations consecutively in hardware. In this case, the hardware accelerator needs to be able to prepare some of the inputs by itself.

The WOTS chain computations are an ideal candidate for such an optimization, because the prf() computations performed in each chain step share a large amount of their inputs (only a few bytes are modified in the address fields for each prf() computation) and the f() computations use previous hash-function outputs. Therefore, we implemented the hardware module Chain as dedicated hardware accelerator for the WOTS chain computations to accelerate the work of the software function gen_chain (see Fig. 2).

Implementation. One building block of the Chain module is the Step module, which implements the prf() and the keyed hash-function f() in hardware. The Step module takes in a 256 bit XMSS public seed, a 256 bit data string and a 256 bit address string as input and returns a 256 bit output. Within Step, two prf() computations and one f() computation are carried out in sequence using the hardware modules PRF and F. PRF and F are both implemented by interfacing with a SHA256XMSS module described in Sect. 5.2. The result generated by the first prf() computation is buffered in a 256 bit register and used later as hash-function key. Similarly the second prf() computation result is buffered in a 256 bit register MASK. The 256 bit input data then gets XOR-ed with MASK and sent to the final f() computation together with the previously computed hash key. The result of the f() computation is returned as the output of the Step module.

Table 4. Performance of the hardware module Chain and performance comparisons of calling the gen_chain function from the RISC-V software on a Murax SoC and on a Murax SoC with a Chain accelerator, with parameters $n = 32$ and $w = 16$.

Design	Cycles	Area (ALM)	Reg.	Fmax (MHz)	Time (µs)	Time×Area (relative)	Speedup
Chain	5960	1940	3060	91.0	65.5	1.30	1.00
+ PRECOMP	4100	2170	3320	96.0	42.7	1.00	1.53
Murax	530,000	1350	1660	152	3490	31.4	1.00
+ Chain	6910	4350	6220	91.6	75.4	1.32	46.2
+ PRECOMP	4990	4560	6460	95.2	52.4	1.00	66.5

The hardware module Chain repeatedly uses the Step module. It has two input ports chain_start and chain_end, defining the start and end step for the WOTS chain computation respectively, e.g., 0 and $w - 1$ when used in WOTS key generation. Each step in the Chain module uses its step index as its input address and the output from the previous step as its input data. The result from the last step is returned as the result of the Chain module. The "pre-computation" optimization (see Sect. 4) can be optionally enabled for the SHA256XMSS module before synthesis. To enable the optimization, the store_intermediate port of the SHA256XMSS module is set to high for the very first prf() computation to request the SHA256XMSS module to store the result of the first compression-function in its internal 256 bit register. For all the following prf() computations, the input port continue_intermediate of the SHA256XMSS module is raised high to request the usage of the previously stored internal state.

When the Chain module is added to the Murax SoC as a hardware accelerator, it provides a SHA256XMSS and a SHA256 accelerator as well since these modules are used as building blocks in Chain. A similar hardware wrapper as described for the SHA256XMSS accelerator in Sect. 5.2 is used.

Evaluation. Table 4 shows performance, resource requirements, and maximum frequency of the Chain module. Enabling the "pre-computation" optimization ("+ PRECOMP") results in a 1.53× speedup for the chain computations.

A comparison between the pure software and the software/hardware performance of the function gen_chain is also provided in Table 4. When gen_chain is called in the design "Murax + Chain + PRECOMP", a speedup of around 66.5× is achieved compared to the pure software implementation using the Murax design.

Table 6 shows the performance impact of the Chain module on XMSS key generation, signing, and verification (Murax compared to "Murax + Chain" and "Murax + Chain + PRECOMP"). Note that since the Chain accelerator provides a SHA256XMSS accelerator as well, when a Chain module is added to the Murax SoC, apart from the function gen_chain, the hash768 and hash1024 functions are also accelerated. The acceleration of the Chain module leads to a 23.9× speedup for both key generation and signing and a 17.5× speedup for verification when the pre-computation functionality is enabled. These speedups achieved are much higher compared to those achieved in the design with a SHA256XMSS/SHA256 accelerator, as shown in Table 6.

5.4   XMSS-leaf Generation Accelerator

When the Chain module is used to compute WOTS chains, the IO requirements are still quite high: For each WOTS key generation, the 256 bit WOTS private key and a 256 bit starting address need to be transferred to the Chain module for l times, although their inputs only differ in a few bytes of the address, and l WOTS chain public keys each of 256 bit need to be transferred back.

To reduce this communication overhead, we implemented an XMSS-leaf accelerator module, replacing the software function treehash (see Fig. 2). The Leaf module only requires a 256 bit address (leaf index), a 256 bit secret seed, and a 256 bit XMSS public seed as input. After the Leaf module finishes computation, the 256 bit L-tree root hash value is returned as the output.

Implementation. As shown in Fig. 5, the Leaf module is built upon two sub-modules: a WOTS module and an L-tree module. The WOTS module uses the Chain module described in Sect. 5.3 to compute the WOTS chains and returns l 256 bit strings as the WOTS public key. Then, these l values are pairwise hashed together as described in Sect. 2.1 by the L-tree module. Finally, the output of the L-tree module (the root of the L-tree) is returned as the output of the Leaf module.

The WOTS module first computes the secret keys for each WOTS chain using a PRF_priv module iteratively for l times. As opposed to the prf() computations during the WOTS chain, L-tree, and Merkle tree computations, the PRF_priv module takes a private, not a public seed as input. For each iteration, the corresponding address is computed and sent to the PRF_priv module as input as well. When the PRF_priv module finishes, its output is written to a dual-port memory mem, which has depth l and width 256 bit. Once the secret keys for the l WOTS chains have been computed and written to mem, the WOTS public key computation begins. This is done by iteratively using the Chain module (see Sect. 5.3) for l times. The output of the Chain module is written back to mem, overwriting the previously stored data.

Once the WOTS public key computation finishes, the L-tree module begins its work. The building block of the L-tree module is a RAND_HASH module which implements the tree-hash function as described in Sect. 2.1. It takes in a 256 bit XMSS public seed, two 256 bit data strings, and a 256 bit address string as input and returns a 256 bit output. Within the hardware module RAND_HASH, three prf() and one h() computations are carried out in sequence using the modules PRF and H. The result generated by the first prf() computation is buffered as the 256 bit key while the results from the following prf() computations are buffered as the two 256 bit masks. The two 256 bit input data strings then get each XOR-ed with a mask and sent to the final h() computation together

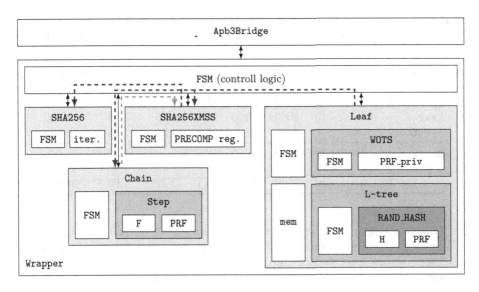

Fig. 5. Diagram of the Leaf accelerator wrapper including all the accelerator modules. (control logic is simplified). The SHA256XMSS module uses SHA256, the Chain module uses SHA256XMSS, and the Leaf module uses Chain and SHA256XMSS.

with the previously computed key. The result of the h() computation is returned as the output of the RAND_HASH module.

The L-tree module constructs the nodes on the first level by first reading out two adjacent leaf nodes from the dual-port memory mem by issuing two simultaneous read requests to adjacent memory addresses. The memory outputs are sent to the RAND_HASH module as input data. Once RAND_HASH finishes computation, the result is written back to mem in order (starting from memory address 0). Since the L-tree is not a complete binary hash tree, it occasionally happens that there is a last node on one level that does not have a sibling node. This node is read out from mem and immediately written back to the next available memory address. This pattern of computation is repeated until the root of the L-tree is reached. This root is returned as the output of the Leaf module.

In order to minimize the resource usage of the Leaf module, all the hash computations are done by interfacing with the same SHA256XMSS module. Figure 5 shows a diagram of the main building blocks of the Leaf module. The "pre-computation" optimization for the prf() computations again can be enabled for the SHA256XMSS module before synthesis. When the Leaf module is added to the Murax SoC as a hardware accelerator, it also provides a Chain, a SHA256XMSS, and a SHA256 accelerator since these modules are all used as building blocks in the Leaf module.

Evaluation. Table 5 shows performance, resource requirements, and maximum frequency of the Leaf module. Enabling the "pre-computation" optimization

Table 5. Performance of the hardware module Leaf and performance comparisons of calling the treehash function from the RISC-V software on a Murax SoC and on a Murax SoC with a Leaf accelerator, with parameters $n = 32$ and $w = 16$.

Design	Cycles	Area (ALM)	Reg.	FMax (MHz)	Time (ms)	Time×Area (relative)	Speedup
Leaf	447×10^3	4060	6270	86.1	5.20	1.23	1.00
+ PRECOMP	306×10^3	4820	6840	92.8	3.30	1.00	1.58
Murax	27.7×10^6	1350	1660	152	182	18.5	1.00
+ Leaf	450×10^3	6460	9270	86.6	5.19	1.45	35.0
+ PRECOMP	309×10^3	6500	9540	93.1	3.32	1.00	54.8

("+ PRECOMP") gives a 1.58× speedup at the cost of a small area overhead. Calling the accelerator in function treehash in the design "Murax + Leaf + PRECOMP" brings a 54.8× speedup over the pure software implementation on the plain Murax design. More importantly, as we can see from the Table (row "Leaf + PRECOMP" and "Murax + Leaf + PRECOMP"), the IO overhead is no longer impacting the performance of the hardware accelerator Leaf.

Table 6 shows the performance impact of the Leaf module on XMSS key generation, signing and verification (Murax compared with "Murax + Leaf" and "Murax + Leaf + PRECOMP"). When a Leaf module is added in the Murax SoC, it accelerates the functions treehash, gen_chain, hash768 and hash1024 in XMSS. For the key-generation operation, the Leaf module accounts for a 54.1× speedup with "PRECOMP" enabled. The Leaf module is not used during verification and hence does not affect its execution time. The BDS algorithm [7] for signing does make use of the Leaf accelerator: For signing the first 16 XMSS leaves, on average a 42.8× speedup is achieved.

6   Performance Evaluation

Table 6 shows performance, resource requirements, and maximum frequency of different designs for the XMSS operations: key generation, signing, and verification. Since the runtime of the BDS signature algorithm [7] varies depending on the leaf index, we report the average timing for the first 16 signature leaves of the XMSS tree. To accelerate the key generation, signing and verification operations in the XMSS scheme, our hardware accelerators ("SHA256", "SHA256XMSS", "Chain" and "Leaf") can be added to the Murax SoC, which leads to good speedups as shown in Table 6. In general, the more computations we delegate to hardware accelerators, the more speedup we can achieve in accelerating XMSS computations. However, at the same time, more overhead is introduced in the hardware resource usage, which is a trade-off users can choose depending on their needs. The best time-area product for the expensive key generation and the signing operations is achieved in design "Murax + Leaf" with "PRECOMP" enabled. For the less expensive verification operation, the "Murax + Chain + PRECOMP" design gives the best time-area product.

Table 6. Time and resource comparison for key generation, signing and verification on a Cyclone V FPGA (all values rounded to three significant figures with $n = 32$, $w = 16$ and $h = 10$). "Time" is computed as quotient of "Cycles" and"FMax"; "Time×Area" is computed based on "Area" and "Time" relative to the time-area product of the respective most efficient design (gray rows); "Speedup" is computed based on "Time" relative to the respective Murax design.

Design	Cycles	Reg.	Area (ALM)	BRAM (Blocks)	FMax (MHz)	Time		Time× Area	Speedup
			key generation						
Murax	28,300,000,000	1660	1350	132	152	186	s	11.2	1.00
+ SHA256	4,870,000,000	3880	2860	132	99.9	48.8	s	6.23	3.82
+ SHA256XMSS	3,810,000,000	4890	3490	132	97.8	39.0	s	6.09	4.78
+ PRECOMP	3,350,000,000	5170	3660	132	97.6	34.3	s	5.60	5.43
+ Chain	912,000,000	6220	4350	132	91.6	9.96	s	1.93	18.7
+ PRECOMP	742,000,000	6460	4560	132	95.2	7.80	s	1.59	23.9
+ Leaf	466,000,000	9270	6460	145	86.6	5.38	s	1.55	34.6
+ PRECOMP	320,000,000	9540	6500	145	93.1	3.44	s	1.00	54.1
			signing (average of the first 16 XMSS leaf signatures)						
Murax	64,800,000	1660	1350	132	152	426	ms	8.85	1.00
+ SHA256	11,200,000	3880	2860	132	99.9	112	ms	4.93	3.81
+ SHA256XMSS	8,750,000	4890	3490	132	97.8	89.5	ms	4.83	4.76
+ PRECOMP	7,700,000	5170	3660	132	97.6	78.8	ms	4.45	5.40
+ Chain	2,070,000	6220	4350	132	91.6	22.6	ms	1.52	18.9
+ PRECOMP	1,700,000	6460	4560	132	95.2	17.8	ms	1.26	23.9
+ Leaf	1,250,000	9270	6460	145	86.6	14.4	ms	1.44	29.5
+ PRECOMP	926,000	9540	6500	145	93.1	9.95	ms	1.00	42.8
			verification						
Murax	15,200,000	1660	1350	132	152	99.6	ms	5.17	1.00
+ SHA256	2,610,000	3880	2860	132	99.9	26.1	ms	2.88	3.81
+ SHA256XMSS	2,060,000	4890	3490	132	97.8	21.1	ms	2.84	4.73
+ PRECOMP	1,800,000	5170	3660	132	97.6	18.5	ms	2.61	5.39
+ Chain	649,000	6220	4350	132	91.6	7.08	ms	1.19	14.1
+ PRECOMP	541,000	6460	4560	132	95.2	5.68	ms	1.00	17.5
+ Leaf	649,000	9270	6460	145	86.6	7.49	ms	1.87	13.3
+ PRECOMP	541,000	9540	6500	145	93.1	5.80	ms	1.46	17.2

The maximum frequency for the designs is heavily impacted by our hardware accelerators (which is accounted for in our speedup and time-area product reports), dropping from 152 MHz down to as low as 86.6 MHz. If a high instruction throughput of the Murax SoC is required for an embedded application that is using our XMSS accelerators, a clock-frequency bridge between the APB and our accelerators might be necessary to enable independent clocks; however, this does not have an impact on the wall-clock speedup of our accelerators.

For a tree height of $h = 10$, i.e., a maximum number of $2^h = 1024$ signatures per key pair, the time for XMSS key generation can be as short as only 3.44 s using our hardware accelerators. Even more signatures per key pair are conceivably possible using multi-tree XMSS, as shown in Table 7 (row "XMSS^MT^b").

By use of our hardware accelerators, we expect a similar speedup in accelerating XMSS^MT as we achieved in XMSS. Signing and verification computations are very efficient on our hardware-software co-design for all the SHA-256 parameter sets, i.e., $n = 32, w = 16, h = \{10, 16, 20\}$: For $h = 10$, signing takes only 9.95 ms and verification takes only 5.80 ms. For a bigger tree height, e.g., $h = 20$, signing and verification are only slightly more expensive: Signing takes 11.1 ms and verification takes 6.25 ms, as shown in Table 7 (row "XMSS^o with $(n, h, w) = (32, 20, 16)$"). Our experiments show that running XMSS is very much feasible on a resource restricted embedded device such as the Murax SoC with the help of efficient dedicated hardware accelerators.

7   Related Work

We first compare our work with a very recent work [9] which shows a similar software-hardware co-design for XMSS. Then, we summarize all the existing FPGA-based implementations on other hash-based signature schemes. Finally, comparisons with implementations of XMSS on other platforms are provided. Detailed comparison results are shown in Table 7.

In 2019, Ghosh, Misoczki and Sastry [9] proposed a software-hardware co-design of XMSS based on a 32-bit Intel Quark microcontroller and a Stratix IV FPGA. WOTS computations are offloaded to a WOTS hardware engine which uses a general-purpose Keccak-400 hash core as building block. In their design, generating one WOTS key pair takes 355,925 cycles, consuming 2963 combinational logic cells and 2337 register cells. This hardware engine has the same functionality as our WOTS module described in Sect. 5.4. In our design, the WOTS module (with "+ PRECOMP") takes 279,388 cycles for generating a key pair. The synthesis result of our WOTS module on the same FPGA reports a usage of 2397 combinatorial logic cells and 3294 register cells. However, as shown in [9], keccak-400 has a 6× smaller Time×Area compared to SHA-256 when implemented on a 14 nm technology. Given such big differences in the building hash core, a fair comparison between the two WOTS designs is not possible.

By use of the WOTS hardware engine, running the XMSS reference implementation on their software-hardware co-design with $n = 32, h = 16, w = 16$ takes 4.8×10^6 cycles in verification on average (key generation and complete signature generation are not included in their tests). To achieve a better comparison, we run a full XMSS test with the same parameter set on the "Murax + Leaf + PRECOMP" design. As shown in Table 7, in terms of cycle count, our design achieves an over 8.5× bigger speedup compared to [9] in accelerating the verification operation in XMSS. However, a fair comparison between our work and [9] is not feasible due to the differences in the platforms, the hardware accelerators, the building hash cores, etc.

There are currently only a few publications focusing on FPGA hardware implementations of hash-based signature schemes: In 2011, Shoufan, Huber and Molter presented a cryptoprocessor architecture for the chained Merkle signature scheme (CMSS) [26], which is a successor of the classic Merkle signature

Table 7. Comparison with related work. All the tests running on Murax SoC with SW-HW feature is based on the "Murax + Leaf + PRECOMP" design. ^{b} shows our benchmarks and ^{o} means our work.

Design	Parameters (n,h,w)	Hash	Feature	Platform	Freq. MHz	KeyGen $\times 10^9$cyc.	Sign $\times 10^6$cyc.	Verify $\times 10^6$cyc.
CMSS [26]	32,(10x3),8	SHA-512	HW	Virtex-5	170	1.2	3.7	2.2
SPHINCS [1]	—	ChaCha-12	HW	Kintex-7	525	—	0.80	0.035
XMSS [14]	16,10,16	AES-128	AES	SLE78	33	0.62	3.3	0.56
XMSS^b	32,10,16	SHA-256	SW	Intel i5	3200	5.6	13	3.0
XMSS^o	32,10,16	SHA-256	SW-HW	Murax SoC	93	0.32	0.93	0.54
XMSS^b	32,16,16	SHA-256	SW	Intel i5	3200	360	14	3.1
XMSS [9]	32,16,16	Keccak-400	SW	Quark (Q)	32	—	—	26
XMSS [9]	32,16,16	Keccak-400	SW-HW	Q+Stratix IV	32	—	—	4.8
XMSS^o	32,16,16	SHA-256	SW	Murax SoC	152	1800	70	15
XMSS^o	32,16,16	SHA-256	SW-HW	Murax SoC	93	21	0.99	0.56
XMSS^b	32,20,16	SHA-256	SW	Intel i5	3200	5700	15	3.2
XMSS^o	32,20,16	SHA-256	SW-HW	Murax SoC	93	330	1.0	0.58
XMSS^MT^b	32,(10x2),16	ChaCha-20	SW	Cortex-M3	32	9.6	18	5.7
XMSS^MT^b	32,(10x2),16	ChaCha-20	SW	Murax SoC	152	14	28	8.2

scheme (MSS). All the operations, i.e., key generation, signing, and verification are implemented on an FPGA platform. The performance of their design is shown in Table 7. Their implementation, however, is no longer state-of-the-art: They provide none of the additional security features that have been developed for modern hash-based signature schemes like XMSS, LMS [18], and the SPHINCS family [5]. The straightforward hash-based operations are all replaced with more complex operations involving masks and keys computed by pseudorandom functions. Therefore, direct comparisons between the hardware modules among MSS and XMSS cannot be fairly done. For modern hash-based signature schemes, an implementation of the stateless hash-based signature scheme SPHINCS-256 [5] was proposed in [1] in 2018. This signature scheme is closely related to XMSS. SPHINCS-256 requires the cryptographic primitives BLAKE-256, BLAKE-512, and ChaCha-12. The source code of all these works [1,26] is not freely available. The detailed performance data for the main hardware modules is not provided in the paper either. Lack of access to the source code and detailed performance results make comparisons unfruitful.

Table 7 also shows comparisons of our work with implementations of XMSS on other platforms. We first benchmarked the original XMSS software implementation (linked against the OpenSSL library) for all the SHA-256 parameter sets on an Intel i5-4570 CPU. The performance results in Table 7 show that running the optimized XMSS software implementation on our software-hardware co-design leads to an over 15× speedup in terms of clock cycles compared to running the implementation on an off-the-shelf Intel i5 CPU. In 2012, Hülsing, Busold, and Buchmann presented an XMSS-based implementation [14] on a 16-bit Infineon SLE78 microcontroller. The hash functions are implemented by use of the embedded AES-128 co-processor. Performance results for XMSS with $n = 16, h = 10$ and $w = 16$ maintaining a classical security level of 78 bit is provided. However, a fair comparison between our work and [14] is not feasible since the security parameters used in [14] are already outdated. The practicability of running SPHINCS [5] on a 32-bit ARM Cortex-M3 processor is demonstrated in [16]. For comparison, they also implemented the multi-tree version of XMSS on the same platform. Chacha-20 is used as the building hash function in their design. We duplicated the same test with a pure C-version of the code on the Murax SoC. As shown in Table 7, running XMSS^MT with a big tree height $h = 20$ on the Murax SoC is feasible.

8   From XMSS to SPHINCS

The *stateful* hash-based signature scheme XMSS is closely related to the *stateless* hash-based signature scheme SPHINCS. In a nutshell, SPHINCS is similar to multi-tree XMSS with the addition of a few-time signature scheme (HORST or FORS) replacing the one-time signature scheme at the lowest level in the hypertree. There are several versions of SPHINCS, e.g. the original SPHINCS-256 [5] instantiation and the improved SPHINCS+ [2] from the NIST submission.

The software optimizations and hardware accelerators presented in this work can be directly used to accelerate most of the hash-based computations in SPHINCS as well. Some implementation details, for example the address scheme, might need to be adapted depending on the specific SPHINCS version. To further accelerate the SPHINCS computations, dedicated hardware accelerators can be developed to accelerate the respective few-time signature operations in the targeted SPHINCS version.

9   Conclusion

In this paper, we presented the first software-hardware co-design for XMSS on a RISC-V-based embedded system. We first proposed two software optimizations targeting the SHA-256 function for the XMSS reference software implementation, and then developed several hardware accelerators to speed up the most expensive operations in XMSS, including a general-purpose SHA-256 accelerator, an XMSS-specific SHA-256 accelerator, a WOTS-chain accelerator and an XMSS-leaf accelerator. The integration of these hardware accelerators to the RISC-V processor brings a significant speedup in running XMSS on our software-hardware co-design compared to the pure software version. Our work shows that embedded devices can remain future-proof by using algorithms such as XMSS to ensure their security, even in the light of practical quantum computers.

Acknowledgments. This work was supported in part by NSF grant 1716541. Part of the research was performed when the second author was affiliated with Fraunhofer Singapore.

References

1. Amiet, D., Curiger, A., Zbinden, P.: FPGA-based accelerator for post-quantum signature scheme SPHINCS-256. Crypt. Hardw. Embed. Syst. (CHES) **2018**(1), 18–39 (2018). Open Access
2. Aumasson, J.P., et al.: SPHINCS+ – submission to the 2nd round of the NIST post-quantum project. Technical report (2019), specification document (part of the submission package). https://sphincs.org/data/sphincs+-round2-specification.pdf
3. Aysu, A., Schaumont, P.: Precomputation methods for faster and greener post-quantum cryptography on emerging embedded platforms. IACR ePrint Archive, Report 2015/288 (2015)
4. Bernstein, D.J., Buchmann, J., Dahmen, E. (eds.): Post-Quantum Cryptography. Springer, Heidelberg (2009). https://doi.org/10.1007/978-3-540-88702-7
5. Bernstein, D., et al.: SPHINCS: practical stateless hash-based signatures. In: Oswald, E., Fischlin, M. (eds.) EUROCRYPT 2015. LNCS, vol. 9056, pp. 368–397. Springer, Heidelberg (2015). https://doi.org/10.1007/978-3-662-46800-5_15
6. Buchmann, J., Dahmen, E., Hülsing, A.: XMSS - a practical forward secure signature scheme based on minimal security assumptions. In: Yang, B.-Y. (ed.) PQCrypto 2011. LNCS, vol. 7071, pp. 117–129. Springer, Heidelberg (2011). https://doi.org/10.1007/978-3-642-25405-5_8. second Version, IACR ePrint Archive, Report 2011/484
7. Buchmann, J., Dahmen, E., Schneider, M.: Merkle tree traversal revisited. In: Buchmann, J., Ding, J. (eds.) PQCrypto 2008. LNCS, vol. 5299, pp. 63–78. Springer, Heidelberg (2008). https://doi.org/10.1007/978-3-540-88403-3_5
8. García, R., Algredo-Badillo, I., Morales-Sandoval, M., Feregrino-Uribe, C., Cumplido, R.: A compact FPGA-based processor for the secure hash algorithm SHA-256. Comput. Electr. Eng. **40**(1), 194–202 (2014)
9. Ghosh, S., Misoczki, R., Sastry, M.R.: Lightweight post-quantum-secure digital signature approach for IoT motes. IACR ePrint Archive, Report 2019/122 (2019)
10. Grover, L.K.: A fast quantum mechanical algorithm for database search. In: Symposium on the Theory of Computing (STOC), pp. 212–219. ACM (1996)
11. Higginbotham, S.: The rise of RISC - [opinion]. IEEE Spectr. **55**(8), 18 (2018)
12. Homsirikamol, E., Rogawski, M., Gaj, K.: Throughput vs. area trade-offs in high-speed architectures of five round 3 SHA-3 candidates implemented using Xilinx and altera FPGAs. In: Preneel, B., Takagi, T. (eds.) CHES 2011. LNCS, vol. 6917, pp. 491–506. Springer, Heidelberg (2011). https://doi.org/10.1007/978-3-642-23951-9_32
13. Hülsing, A.: W-OTS+ – shorter signatures for hash-based signature schemes. In: Youssef, A., Nitaj, A., Hassanien, A.E. (eds.) AFRICACRYPT 2013. LNCS, vol. 7918, pp. 173–188. Springer, Heidelberg (2013). https://doi.org/10.1007/978-3-642-38553-7_10
14. Hülsing, A., Busold, C., Buchmann, J.: Forward secure signatures on smart cards. In: Knudsen, L.R., Wu, H. (eds.) SAC 2012. LNCS, vol. 7707, pp. 66–80. Springer, Heidelberg (2013). https://doi.org/10.1007/978-3-642-35999-6_5
15. Hülsing, A., Butin, D., Gazdag, S., Rijneveld, J., Mohaisen, A.: XMSS: eXtended Merkle signature scheme. RFC **8391**, 1–74 (2018)
16. Hülsing, A., Rijneveld, J., Schwabe, P.: ARMed SPHINCS. In: Cheng, C.-M., Chung, K.-M., Persiano, G., Yang, B.-Y. (eds.) PKC 2016. LNCS, vol. 9614, pp. 446–470. Springer, Heidelberg (2016). https://doi.org/10.1007/978-3-662-49384-7_17

17. Kahri, F., Mestiri, H., Bouallegue, B., Machhout, M.: Efficient FPGA hardware implementation of secure hash function SHA-256/Blake-256. In: Systems, Signals and Devices (SSD), pp. 1–5. IEEE (2015)
18. McGrew, D., Curcio, M., Fluhrer, S.: Hash-based signatures. cfrg draft-mcgrew-hash-sigs-1, pp. 1–60 (2018)
19. Merkle, R.C.: A certified digital signature. In: Brassard, G. (ed.) CRYPTO 1989. LNCS, vol. 435, pp. 218–238. Springer, New York (1990). https://doi.org/10.1007/0-387-34805-0_21
20. Merritt, R.: Microsoft and Google planning silicon-level security. EE Times Asia, August 2018. https://www.eetasia.com/news/article/18082202-microsoft-and-google-planning-silicon-level-security
21. NIST: FIPS PUB 180-4: Secure Hash Standard. National Institute of Standards and Technology (2012)
22. NIST: FIPS PUB 186-4: Digital Signature Standard. National Institute of Standards and Technology (2013)
23. Padhi, M., Chaudhari, R.: An optimized pipelined architecture of SHA-256 hash function. In: Embedded Computing and System Design (ISED), pp. 1–4. IEEE (2017)
24. Shor, P.W.: Algorithms for quantum computation: discrete logarithms and factoring. In: Foundations of Computer Science (FOCS), pp. 124–134. IEEE (1994)
25. Shor, P.W.: Polynomial-time algorithms for prime factorization and discrete logarithms on a quantum computer. SIAM Rev. 41(2), 303–332 (1999)
26. Shoufan, A., Huber, N., Molter, H.G.: A novel cryptoprocessor architecture for chained Merkle signature scheme. Microprocess. Microsyst. 35(1), 34–47 (2011)
27. Teich, J.: Hardware/software codesign: the past, the present, and predicting the future. Proc. IEEE 100, 1411–1430 (2012)
28. Wang, W., et al.: XMSS and embedded systems – XMSS hardware accelerators for RISC-V. IACR ePrint Archive, Report 2018/1225 (2018)

A Timing Attack on the HQC
Encryption Scheme

Thales Bandiera Paiva$^{(\boxtimes)}$ (iD) and Routo Terada

Universidade de São Paulo, São Paulo, Brazil
{tpaiva,rt}@ime.usp.br

Abstract. The HQC public-key encryption scheme is a promising code-based submission to NIST's post-quantum cryptography standardization process. The scheme is based on the decisional decoding problem for random quasi-cyclic codes. One problem of the HQC's reference implementation submitted to NIST in the first round of the standardization process is that the decryption operation is not constant-time. In particular, the decryption time depends on the number of errors decoded by a BCH decoder. We use this to present the first timing attack against HQC. The attack is practical, requiring the attacker to record the decryption time of around 400 million ciphertexts for a set of HQC parameters corresponding to 128 bits of security. This makes the use of constant-time decoders mandatory for the scheme to be considered secure.

Keywords: HQC · Post-quantum cryptography · Timing attack · BCH decoding

1 Introduction

Hamming Quasi-Cyclic (HQC) [18] is a code-based public-key encryption scheme. It is based on the hardness of the quasi-cyclic syndrome decoding problem, a conjectured hard problem from Coding Theory. It offers reasonably good parameters, with better key sizes than the classical McEliece scheme [2,5,17], but without relying on codes with a secret sparse structure, such as QC-MDPC [19] and QC-LDPC [3].

One of the most interesting features HQC provides is a detailed analysis of the decryption failure probability, which makes it possible to choose parameters that provably avoid reaction attacks [9,12] that compromise the security of QC-LDPC and QC-MDPC encryption schemes. This makes it one of the most promising code-based candidates in NIST's Post-Quantum standardization process. However, the negligible probability of decoding failure comes at the expense of low encryption rates.

The scheme uses an error correction code $\mathcal{C}$ as a public parameter. The secret key is a sparse vector, while the public key is its syndrome with respect to a

---

T. B. Paiva is supported by CAPES. R. Terada is supported by CNPq grant number 442014/2014-7.

K. G. Paterson and D. Stebila (Eds.): SAC 2019, LNCS 11959, pp. 551–573, 2020.
https://doi.org/10.1007/978-3-030-38471-5_22

systematic quasi-cyclic matrix chosen at random, together with the description of this matrix. To encrypt a message, the sender first encodes it with respect to the public code $\mathcal{C}$, then adds to it a binary error vector which appears to be random for anyone who is not the intended receiver. The receiver, using the sparseness of her secret key, is able transform the ciphertext in such a way to significantly reduce the weight of the error vector. Then, the receiver can use the efficient decoding procedure for $\mathcal{C}$ to correct the remaining errors of the transformed ciphertext to recover the message.

The code $\mathcal{C}$ proposed by Aguilar-Melchor et al. [18] is a tensor code between a BCH code and a repetition code. One drawback of the HQC implementation submitted to NIST is that the decoder [14] for the BCH code is not constant-time, and depends on the weight of the error it corrects. This makes the decryption operation vulnerable to timing attacks.

The use of non-constant-time decoders has been exploited to attack code-based schemes such as QC-MDPC [8], and recently, RQC [1], which is a variant of HQC in the rank metric that uses Gabidulin codes [10], was shown vulnerable to timing attacks [6]. However, timing attacks exploiting non-constant-time decoders are not exclusive to code-base schemes, and the use of BCH codes in LAC [16] has been shown to leak secret information from timing [7].

Contributions. We present the first timing attack on HQC. The attack follows Guo et al. [12] idea: first we show how to obtain information, which is called the spectrum, on the secret key by timing a large number of decryptions, and then use the information gathered to reconstruct the key. We analyze in detail the reason behind the information leakage. As a minor contribution, we show that a randomized variant of Guo's et al. algorithm for key reconstruction is better than their recursive algorithm when the attacker has partial information on the secret key's spectrum. This is useful to reduce the number of decryption timings the attacker needs to perform.

Shortly after this paper was accepted for publication, Wafo-Tapa et al. [24] published a preprint in the Cryptology ePrint Archive in which they also present a timing attack against HQC. Our attack is stronger in the sense that we target the CCA secure version of HQC, while they target only the CPA secure version. However, their paper comes with a countermeasure, which consists of a constant-time BCH decoder with a low overhead.

Paper Organization. In Sect. 2, we review some background concepts for understanding HQC and our attack. The HQC is described in Sect. 3. The attack is presented in Sect. 4. Some mathematical and algorithmic aspects of the attack are analyzed in detail in Sect. 5. In Sect. 6, we analyze the practical performance of the attack against concrete HQC parameters. We conclude in Sect. 8.

2 Background

Definition 1 (Linear codes). *A binary $[n, k]$-linear code is a k-dimensional linear subspace of $\mathbb{F}_2^n$, where $\mathbb{F}_2$ denotes the binary field.*

Definition 2 (Generator and parity-check matrices). *Let C be a binary $[n, k]$-linear code. If C is the linear subspace spanned by the rows of a matrix $\mathbf{G}$ of $\mathbb{F}_2^{k \times n}$, we say that $\mathbf{G}$ is a generator matrix of C. Similarly, if C is the kernel of a matrix $\mathbf{H}$ of $\mathbb{F}_2^{(n-k) \times n}$, we say that $\mathbf{H}$ is a parity-check matrix of C.*

Definition 3 (Weight). *The Hamming weight of a vector $\mathbf{v}$, denoted by $\mathrm{w}(\mathbf{v})$, is the number of its non-null entries.*

Definition 4 (Support). *The support of a vector $\mathbf{v}$, denoted by $\mathrm{supp}(\mathbf{v})$, is the set of indexes of its non-null entries.*

We use zero-based numbering for the vectors indexes as we believe it allows more concise descriptions in some of the algorithms and analysis.

Definition 5 (Cyclic matrix). *The cyclic matrix defined by a vector $\mathbf{v} = [v_0, \ldots, v_{n-1}]$, is the matrix*

$$\mathrm{rot}(\mathbf{v}) = \begin{bmatrix} v_0 & v_{n-1} & \cdots & v_1 \\ v_1 & v_0 & \cdots & v_2 \\ \vdots & \vdots & \ddots & \vdots \\ v_{n-1} & v_{n-2} & \cdots & v_0 \end{bmatrix}.$$

Definition 6 (Vector product). *The product of two vectors $\mathbf{u}, \mathbf{v} \in \mathbb{F}_2^n$ is given as*

$$\mathbf{u} \cdot \mathbf{v} = \mathbf{u} \, \mathrm{rot}(\mathbf{v})^T = \left(\mathrm{rot}(\mathbf{v}) \mathbf{u}^T \right)^T = \mathbf{v} \, \mathrm{rot}(\mathbf{u})^T = \mathbf{v} \cdot \mathbf{u}.$$

Definition 7 (Syndrome decoding problem). *Consider the following input: a random binary matrix $\mathbf{H} \in \mathbb{F}_2^{k \times n}$, a random vector $\mathbf{s} \in \mathbb{F}_2^k$, and an integer $w > 0$. The syndrome decoding problem asks for a $\mathbf{v}$ of weight w such that $\mathbf{v}\mathbf{H}^T = \mathbf{s}$.*

The quasi-cyclic syndrome decoding problem is a restriction of the syndrome decoding problem, in which $\mathbf{H}$ is a block matrix consisting of cyclic blocks.

The syndrome decoding problem is proven to be **NP**-hard [4]. Despite no complexity result on the quasi-cyclic variant, it is considered hard since all known decoding algorithms that exploit the cyclic structure have only a small advantage over general decoding algorithms for the non-cyclic case.

Definition 8 (Circular distance). *The circular distance between the indexes i and j in a vector of length n is*

$$\mathrm{dist}_n(i, j) = \begin{cases} |i - j| & \text{if } |i - j| \leq \lfloor n/2 \rfloor, \\ n - |i - j| & \text{otherwise.} \end{cases}$$

We next define the spectrum of a vector, which is a crucial concept for the rest of the paper. The importance of the spectrum for the attack comes from the fact that it is precisely the spectrum of the key that can be recovered by the timing attack. Intuitively, the spectrum of a binary vector $\mathbf{v}$ is the set of circular distances that occur between two non-null entries of $\mathbf{v}$.

Definition 9 (Spectrum of a vector). *Let* $\mathbf{v} = [v_0, v_1, \ldots, v_{n-1}]$ *be an element of* $\mathbb{F}_2^n$. *Then the* spectrum *of* $\mathbf{v}$ *is the set*

$$\sigma(\mathbf{v}) = \{\text{dist}_n(i,j) : i \neq j, \ v_i = 1, \ and \ v_j = 1\}.$$

In some cases, it is important to consider the multiplicity of each distance d, that is the number of pairs of non-null entries that are at distance d apart. In such cases, we abuse notation and write $(d : m) \in \sigma(\mathbf{v})$ *to denote that d appears with multiplicity m in vector* $\mathbf{v}$.

Definition 10 (Mirror of a vector). *Let* $\mathbf{v} = [v_0, v_1, \ldots, v_{n-1}]$ *be an element of* $\mathbb{F}_2^n$. *Then the* mirror *of* $\mathbf{v}$ *is the vector*

$$\text{mirror}(\mathbf{v}) = [v_{n-1}, v_{n-2}, \ldots, v_0].$$

We sometimes abuse notation and write $\text{mirror}(V)$, *where V is the support of a vector* $\mathbf{v}$, *to represent the support of the mirror of* $\mathbf{v}$.

Notice that the spectrum of a vector is invariant with respect to its circular shifts and its mirror.

Guo et al. [12] showed that it is possible to reconstruct a sparse vector from its spectrum. To solve this problem, they propose an algorithm that consists of a simple pruned depth-first search. Its description is given as Algorithm 1.[1] The main argument by Guo et al. for the efficiency of their algorithm is that unfruitful branches are pruned relatively early in the search.

Let α be the fraction of the $\lfloor n/2 \rfloor$ possible distances that are not in D, that is $\alpha = 1 - |D|/\lfloor n/2 \rfloor$. For each new level in the search tree, it is expected that a fraction α of the possible positions in the previous level survive the sieve imposed by line 10. Let MAXPATHS be the total number of paths that Guo's et al. [12] algorithm can explore. Then

$$\text{MAXPATHS} = \prod_{\ell=2}^{w-1} \max\left(1, \lfloor n/2 \rfloor \alpha^\ell\right) = \lfloor n/2 \rfloor^\phi \alpha^{\phi(\phi+3)/2},$$

where ℓ represents the level in the search tree, and ϕ is the level at which each node has an expected number of child nodes lower than or equal to 1. Notice that, on average, the mirror test in line 5 cuts in half the number of paths the algorithm needs to explore until it finds the key. From the remaining paths, we expect that half of them have to be taken until the key is found. Therefore, considering $\mathbf{WF}_{\text{GJS}}$ to be the average number of paths the algorithm explores until a key is found, we have

$$\mathbf{WF}_{\text{GJS}} = \frac{1}{4}\text{MAXPATHS} = \frac{1}{4}\lfloor n/2 \rfloor^\phi \alpha^{\phi(\phi+3)/2}.$$

---

[1] Here we present a slightly more general version of Guo's et al. reconstruction algorithm that does not require the key's spectrum to be completely determined, but the idea is the same.

Algorithm 1. GJS key reconstruction algorithm [12]

Data: n, w the length and weight of the secret vector $\mathbf{y}$
$\quad\quad$ D a set of distances outside $\sigma(\mathbf{y})$
$\quad\quad$ s a distance inside $\sigma(\mathbf{y})$
$\quad\quad$ V the partially recovered support of a shift of $\mathbf{y}$ (initially set to $\{0, s\}$,
$\quad\quad$ where $s \in \sigma(\mathbf{y})$) is known
Result: V the support of some shift of $\mathbf{y}$, or $\perp$ if $\sigma(\mathbf{y})$ is an invalid spectrum

```
1  begin
2  |  if |V| = w then
3  |  |  if V is the support of a shift of y then
4  |  |  |  return V
5  |  |  else if mirror(V) is the support of a shift of y then
6  |  |  |  return mirror(V)
7  |  |  else
8  |  |  |  return ⊥
9  |  for each position j = 1, ..., n − 1 which are not in V do
10 |  |  if distₙ(v, j) ∉ D for all v in V then
11 |  |  |  Add j to V
12 |  |  |  ret ← recursive call with the updated set V
13 |  |  |  if ret ≠⊥ then
14 |  |  |  |  return V
15 |  |  |  Remove j from V
16 |  return ⊥
```

---

3 The HQC Encryption Scheme

3.1 Setup

On input 1^λ, where λ is the security parameter, the setup algorithm returns the public parameters $n, k, \delta, w, w_\mathbf{r}, w_\mathbf{e}$, from parameters table such as Table 1. For these parameters, an $[n, k]$ linear code $\mathcal{C}$, with an efficient decoding algorithm Ψ capable of correcting random errors of weight up to δ with overwhelming probability, is fixed. Parameters $w, w_\mathbf{r}$ and $w_\mathbf{e}$ correspond to the weights of the sparse vectors defined and used in the next sections.

3.2 Key Generation

Let $\mathbf{H} \in \mathbb{F}_2^{n \times 2n}$ be a quasi-cyclic matrix selected at random, in systematic form, that is $\mathbf{H} = [\,\mathbf{I}\,|\,\mathrm{rot}(\mathbf{h})\,]$, for some vector $\mathbf{h}$. Let $\mathbf{x}, \mathbf{y} \in \mathbb{F}_2^n$ be sparse vectors with weight $\mathrm{w}(\mathbf{x}) = \mathrm{w}(\mathbf{y}) = w$. Compute

$$\mathbf{s} = [\mathbf{x}|\mathbf{y}]\mathbf{H}^T = \mathbf{x} + \mathbf{y} \cdot \mathrm{rot}(\mathbf{h})^T = \mathbf{x} + \mathbf{y} \cdot \mathbf{h}.$$

The public and secret key are $K_{\mathrm{PUB}} = [\mathbf{s}|\mathbf{h}]$ and $K_{\mathrm{SEC}} = [\mathbf{x}|\mathbf{y}]$, correspondingly.

From this construction, it is easy to see the relation between recovering the secret key from the public key and the quasi-cyclic syndrome decoding problem.

Table 1. Suggested parameters for some security levels [1].

Instance	Security	n_1	n_2	$n \approx n_1 n_2{}^a$	$k = k_1$	w	$w_{\mathbf{r}} = w_{\mathbf{e}}$	p_{fail}
Basic-I	128	766	29	22,229	256	67	77	2^{-64}
Basic-II	128	766	31	23,747	256	67	77	2^{-96}
Basic-III	128	796	31	24,677	256	67	77	2^{-128}
Advanced-I	192	796	51	40,597	256	101	117	2^{-64}
Advanced-II	192	766	57	43,669	256	101	117	2^{-128}
Advanced-III	192	766	61	46,747	256	101	117	2^{-192}
Paranoiac-I	256	766	77	59,011	256	133	153	2^{-64}
Paranoiac-II	256	766	83	63,587	256	133	153	2^{-128}
Paranoiac-III	256	796	85	67,699	256	133	153	2^{-192}
Paranoiac-IV	256	796	89	70,853	256	133	153	2^{-256}

^{a} The value of n is the smallest prime number greater than $n_1 n_2$.

3.3 Encryption

Let $\mathbf{m} \in \mathbb{F}_2^k$ be the message to be encrypted. First, choose two random sparse vectors $\mathbf{r}_1, \mathbf{r}_2 \in \mathbb{F}_2^n$ such that $w(\mathbf{r}_1) = w(\mathbf{r}_2) = w_{\mathbf{r}}$. Then choose a random sparse vector $\mathbf{e} \in \mathbb{F}_2^n$ such that $w(\mathbf{e}) = w_{\mathbf{e}}$. Let

$$\mathbf{u} = [\mathbf{r}_1|\mathbf{r}_2]\mathbf{H}^T = \mathbf{r}_1 + \mathbf{r}_2 \cdot \mathbf{h}, \text{ and } \mathbf{v} = \mathbf{m}\mathbf{G} + \mathbf{s} \cdot \mathbf{r}_2 + \mathbf{e}.$$

Return the ciphertext $\mathbf{c} = [\mathbf{u}|\mathbf{v}]$.

3.4 Decryption

Compute $\mathbf{c}' = \mathbf{v} + \mathbf{u} \cdot \mathbf{y}$. Notice that

$$\begin{aligned}
\mathbf{c}' &= \mathbf{m}\mathbf{G} + \mathbf{s} \cdot \mathbf{r}_2 + \mathbf{e} + (\mathbf{r}_1 + \mathbf{r}_2 \cdot \mathbf{h}) \cdot \mathbf{y} \\
&= \mathbf{m}\mathbf{G} + (\mathbf{x} + \mathbf{y} \cdot \mathbf{h}) \cdot \mathbf{r}_2 + \mathbf{e} + (\mathbf{r}_1 + \mathbf{r}_2 \cdot \mathbf{h}) \cdot \mathbf{y} \\
&= \mathbf{m}\mathbf{G} + \mathbf{x} \cdot \mathbf{r}_2 + \mathbf{r}_1 \cdot \mathbf{y} + \mathbf{e}.
\end{aligned}$$

Intuitively, since $\mathbf{x}, \mathbf{y}, \mathbf{r}_1, \mathbf{r}_2$, and $\mathbf{e}$ all have low weight, we expect $\mathbf{e}' = \mathbf{x} \cdot \mathbf{r}_2 + \mathbf{r}_1 \cdot \mathbf{y} + \mathbf{e}$ to have a relatively low weight. This is made precise by Aguilar-Melchor et al. [1], where they propose the public parameters to ensure that $w(\mathbf{e}')$ is sufficiently low for it to be corrected out of $\mathbf{c}'$ with overwhelming probability.

Therefore we can use the decoder Ψ to correct the errors in $\mathbf{c}'$ and obtain $\mathbf{c}'' = \Psi(\mathbf{c}') = \mathbf{m}\mathbf{G}$. We finally get $\mathbf{m}$ by solving the overdetermined linear system $\mathbf{m}\mathbf{G} = \mathbf{c}''$.

3.5 Security and Instantiation

In general, schemes based on syndrome decoding have to take care to avoid generic attacks based on Information Set Decoding [20, 22, 23]. Furthermore, the quasi-cyclic structure of the code used to secure the secret key can make the scheme vulnerable to DOOM [21], or other structural attacks [11,15].

To instantiate the scheme, the authors propose parameters for which they prove very low decryption error probability and resistance to the attacks mentioned. This error analysis allows the HQC to achieve IND-CCA2 security using the transformation of Hofheinz et al. [13].

Of particular interest for our timing attack, is the way that code $\mathcal{C}$ is chosen. Their proposal is to build the tensor code $\mathcal{C} = \mathcal{C}_1 \otimes \mathcal{C}_2$, where the auxiliary codes are chosen as follows. $\mathcal{C}_1$ is a BCH(n_1, k_1, δ_1) code of length n_1, dimension k_1. $\mathcal{C}_2$ is a repetition code of length n_2 and dimension 1, that can decode up to $\delta_2 = \lfloor \frac{n_2-1}{2} \rfloor$. Therefore, to encode a message $\mathbf{m}$ with respect to $\mathcal{C}$ is equivalent to first encode it using the BCH code $\mathcal{C}_1$, and then encode *each bit* of the resulting codeword with the repetition code $\mathcal{C}_2$.

The suggested parameters for this instantiation are shown in Table 1. In this table, column p_{fail} contains an upper bound for the probability of a decryption failure for each instance of the scheme. The size of the public keys and ciphertexts correspond to $2n$ bits.

4   Timing Attack Against HQC

In the decryption algorithm, the decoder Ψ is used to correct the errors in the word

$$\mathbf{c}' = \mathbf{m}\mathbf{G} + \mathbf{x} \cdot \mathbf{r}_2 + \mathbf{r}_1 \cdot \mathbf{y} + \mathbf{e},$$

where the attacker knows every element, except for the secret key consisting of $\mathbf{x}$ and $\mathbf{y}$. For the original instantiation, where $\mathcal{C}$ is the tensor product of a BCH code and a repetition code, the decoder Ψ consists of a sequence of two operations: first apply a repetition code decoder Ψ_2, and then apply the BCH code decoder Ψ_1. That is $\Psi(\mathbf{c}') = \Psi_1(\Psi_2(\mathbf{c}'))$.

The timing attack is based on the fact the BCH decoder implemented by Aguilar-Melchor et al. [18] is not constant-time, and is slower when there are more errors to be corrected. In other words, the decryption time leaks the number of errors that the repetition code (RC) decoder Ψ_2 was not able to correct.

Figure 1 shows the essentially linear relation between the decryption time and the number of errors corrected by the BCH decoder. We emphasize that the time considered is for complete decryption, not only the BCH decoding step. The weight distribution is centered between 9 and 10, thus error weights larger than 22 are rare (around 1%).

Let $\mathbf{e}'$ be the error vector that Ψ_2 will try to correct, that is $\mathbf{e}' = \mathbf{x}\cdot\mathbf{r}_2 + \mathbf{r}_1\cdot\mathbf{y} + \mathbf{e}$. We note that it is useful to consider Guo's et al. [12] observation, used in their attack on QC-MDPC, that the weight of the product of two binary sparse vectors $\mathbf{a} \cdot \mathbf{b}$ is lower when the spectrums of $\mathbf{a}$ and $\mathbf{b}$ share more entries. However, this observation is not sufficient to enable us to accurately distinguish between distances in and out of the spectrum, because we are not just interested in the weight of $\mathbf{e}'$, but mainly in the probability that it has enough non-null entries in the same repetition blocks to cause Ψ_2 to leave decoding errors.

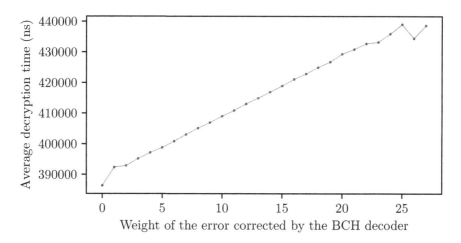

Fig. 1. The average decryption time for different weights of the errors corrected by the BCH decoder, considering 10 million decryption operations.

When the number of RC decoding errors for $\Psi_2(\mathbf{mG} + \mathbf{e}')$ is high, it means that $\mathbf{e}'$ has a lot of non-null entries that are at a distance lower than the repetition block size n_2. Therefore, if we understand how $\mathbf{r}_1$ and $\mathbf{y}$ influence the number of entries lower than n_2 in $\sigma(\mathbf{r}_1 \cdot \mathbf{y})$, we can use our knowledge on $\mathbf{r}_1$ together with the decryption time to obtain information on $\mathbf{y}$.[2]

We make three observations that relate the spectrum of $\mathbf{e}'$ to the spectrums of $\mathbf{r}_1$ and $\mathbf{y}$, (alternatively $\mathbf{r}_2$ and $\mathbf{x}$). These are presented in the next section based on empirical data, and their mathematical nature is explained in Sect. 5.1.

The timing attack then consists of two parts. In the first part, called the spectrum recovery, the attacker sends Alice a great number of ciphertexts and records the decryption times for each one. This step runs until it is gathered sufficient information on the spectrums of $\mathbf{y}$ (or $\mathbf{x}$) for him to build a large set D of distances outside the spectrum, and to obtain a distance $s \in \sigma(\mathbf{y})$ (respectively, $\sigma(\mathbf{x})$). In the second part, the set D and distance s are passed to the key reconstruction algorithm.

It is important to notice that the the attacker needs only to recover one of $\mathbf{x}$ or $\mathbf{y}$, because he can use the linear relation $\mathbf{s} = \mathbf{x} + \mathbf{y} \cdot \mathbf{h}$ to easily recover one from the other.

In the next sections, the two parts are presented in detail.

4.1 Spectrum Recovery

This is the part where timing information is used. Let Alice be the target secret key holder. The attacker sends Alice valid ciphertexts, and records the time she takes to decrypt each challenge. Since the attacker generated all ciphertexts, then, for each one of them, he knows $\mathbf{r}_1$ and $\mathbf{r}_2$. The idea is that the attacker

---

[2] This sentence remains valid if we substitute $\mathbf{y}$ and $\mathbf{r}_1$ by $\mathbf{x}$ and $\mathbf{r}_2$, respectively.

iteratively builds two arrays, $\mathbf{T_x}$ and $\mathbf{T_y}$, such that $\mathbf{T_x}[d]$ ($\mathbf{T_y}[d]$) is the average of the decryption time when d is in the spectrum of r_2 (resp. r_1).

The algorithm for spectrum recovery is given as Algorithm 2. Notice that we are not choosing the vectors r_1, r_2, which are assumed to be random. Therefore CCA2 conversions [13] do not protect the scheme against this attack.

Algorithm 2. Estimating the decryption time for each possible distance in $\sigma(\mathbf{x})$ and $\sigma(\mathbf{y})$

Data: The HQC public parameters and Alice's public key
$\mathcal{T}$ returns the target's decryption time for the challenge passed as argument
M number of decoding challenges
Result: $\mathbf{T_x}, \mathbf{T_y}$ average decryption time for candidate distances in $\sigma(\mathbf{x})$ and $\sigma(\mathbf{y})$, respectively

1 **begin**
2       $\mathbf{a}_y, \mathbf{b}_y, \mathbf{a}_x, \mathbf{b}_x \leftarrow$ zero-initialized arrays with $\lfloor n/2 \rfloor$ entries each
3   **for** *each decoding trial* $i = 1, 2, \ldots, M$ **do**
4           $\mathbf{m} \leftarrow$ a random message in $\mathbb{F}_2^k$
5           $\mathbf{c} \leftarrow$ encryption of $\mathbf{m}$ using vectors r_1 and r_2 randomly chosen
6           $t = \mathcal{T}(\mathbf{c})$
7   **for** *each distance* d *in* $\sigma(r_1)$ **do**
8               $\mathbf{a}_y[d] \leftarrow \mathbf{a}_y[d] + t$
9               $\mathbf{b}_y[d] \leftarrow \mathbf{b}_y[d] + 1$
10   **for** *each distance* d *in* $\sigma(r_2)$ **do**
11              $\mathbf{a}_x[d] \leftarrow \mathbf{a}_x[d] + t$
12              $\mathbf{b}_x[d] \leftarrow \mathbf{b}_x[d] + 1$
13      $\mathbf{T_x}, \mathbf{T_y} \leftarrow$ zero-initialized array with $\lfloor n/2 \rfloor$ positions
14   **for** *each distance* d *in* $\{1, 2, \ldots, \lfloor n/2 \rfloor\}$ **do**
15          $\mathbf{T_x}[d] \leftarrow \mathbf{a}_x[d]/\mathbf{b}_x[d]$
16          $\mathbf{T_y}[d] \leftarrow \mathbf{a}_y[d]/\mathbf{b}_y[d]$
17   **return** $\mathbf{T_x}$ *and* $\mathbf{T_y}$

To maximize the information obtained from each decryption timing, the proposed spectrum recovery procedure targets $\sigma(\mathbf{x})$ and $\sigma(\mathbf{y})$ simultaneously. This is interesting for the attacker since it may be the case that, after a number of challenges, the output $\mathbf{T_x}$ does not have sufficient information on $\mathbf{x}$ for it to be reconstructed, but $\mathbf{T_y}$ is sufficient to recover $\mathbf{y}$.

Figure 2 shows the output of the spectrum recovery algorithm $\mathbf{T_y}$ for $M = 1$ billion decryption challenges. On the left of the figure, we see that distances lower than n_2 have a significantly higher average decryption time. The figure shows that, in general, distances inside the spectrum of $\mathbf{y}$ appears to have lower average decryption time. However, there is no clear line to classify a distance d as inside or outside $\sigma(\mathbf{y})$, based only on $\mathbf{T_y}[d]$, since this value appears to also depend on the neighbors of d.

Figure 3 shows another interval of the same data, but with one vertical line for each distance in the spectrum. This enables us to see that regions where there are more distances inside the spectrum appear to have higher average decryption time.

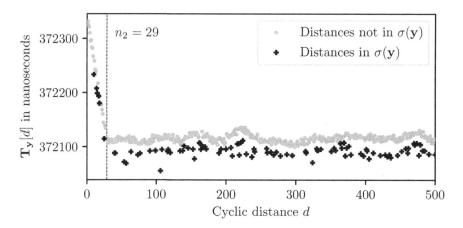

Fig. 2. The average decryption time $\mathbf{T_y}[d]$ for each distance d that can occur in $\mathbf{r_1}$, for $M = 1$ billion.

Summarizing the analysis of the figures, we make the following three informal observations that allow us to distinguish between distances inside and outside the spectrums.

1. When d decreases from $d = n_2 - 1$ to $d = 1$, the value of $\mathbf{T_y}[d]$ increases, getting significantly higher than the rest of the values in $\mathbf{T_y}$.
2. When $d \in \sigma(\mathbf{y})$, the value of $\mathbf{T_y}[d]$ is lower than the average in the neighborhood of d.
3. When d has a large number of neighbors in $\sigma(\mathbf{y})$, the value of $\mathbf{T_y}[d]$ tends to be higher.

The reasons why we observe such behavior are analyzed in detail in Sect. 5.1.

Similarly to the GJS algorithm (Algorithm 1), our key reconstruction algorithm for the next part of the attack works with two inputs: a set D of distances outside the spectrum, and a distance s inside the spectrum. Figure 2 suggests that, when a sufficiently large number of decryption challenges are timed, it is easy to get a distance inside the spectrum with high probability by just taking the distance s such that $\mathbf{T_y}[s]$ is the minimum value in the array. However, it is not trivial to find a sufficiently large set D from $\mathbf{T_y}$. For this, we propose a routine called BUILDD, which is describe next.

BuildD: Building the Set of Distances not in $\sigma(\mathbf{y})$ from $\mathbf{T_y}$. We propose to use the following simple algorithm, that takes as input a value μ and the decryption times estimation $\mathbf{T_y}$, and outputs μ distances which it classifies as

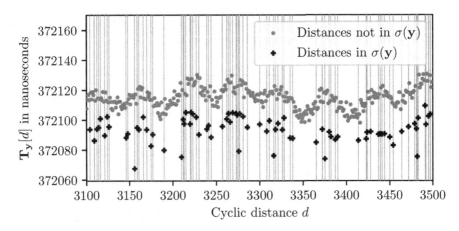

Fig. 3. A closer look at the behavior of $\mathbf{T_y}[d]$ for each distance d. The gray vertical lines represent distances inside $\sigma(\mathbf{y})$.

out of $\sigma(\mathbf{y})$. The idea is to select the μ values of d such that $\mathbf{T_y}[d]$ are among the highest of their corresponding neighborhood.

Let η be some small positive integer for which the probability that $\{d, d + 1, \ldots, d + \eta - 1\} \subset \sigma(\mathbf{y})$ is negligible for all values of d. The value η will be the size of the neighborhood, which must contain at least one distance outside the spectrum. This value can be estimated by generating N random vectors, then computing the minimum value η for which η consecutive distances always contain at least one distance not in the vectors corresponding spectrums. For the Basic-I parameters, we obtained $\eta = 11$ for $N = 10000$.

For each d, we compute the difference between $\mathbf{T_y}$ $[d]$ and the highest value of $\mathbf{T_y}$ in the window $\{d - \lfloor \eta/2 \rfloor, \ldots, d + \lceil \eta/2 \rceil - 1\}$. If the window contains invalid distances, we just truncate it to exclude them. In other words

$$\rho(d) = \left(\max_{i \in W_d} \mathbf{T_y}[i] \right) - \mathbf{T_y}[d],$$

where W_d is the intersection between $\{d - \lfloor \eta/2 \rfloor, \ldots, d + \lceil \eta/2 \rceil - 1\}$ and the set of possible distances. The algorithm sorts the possible distances with respect to $\rho(d)$, and returns the μ values of d such that $\rho(d)$ are the lowest ones.

Let BUILDD$(\mathbf{T_y}, \mu)$ be the output of the algorithm just described for the given inputs. Since the key reconstruction only works if D is a large set of distances not in the spectrum, it is natural to define the quality of the input $\mathbf{T_y}$ as

$$\text{QUALITY}(\mathbf{T_y}) = \max \{\mu : \text{BUILDD}(\mathbf{T_y}, \mu) \cap \sigma(\mathbf{y}) = \emptyset\}.$$

Figure 4 helps us visualize why this algorithm works. For $M = 1$ billion decryptions, it is easy to see that the distances between $\mathbf{T_y}[d]$ and $\max_{i \in W_d} \mathbf{T_y}[i]$ should be smaller when d is not in the spectrum of $\mathbf{y}$. However, it is not clear yet how many decryptions are necessary for the algorithm to be able to build sufficiently large sets D, that is, to obtain high values for QUALITY($\mathbf{T_y}$). This is considered in the experimental analysis in Sect. 6.2.

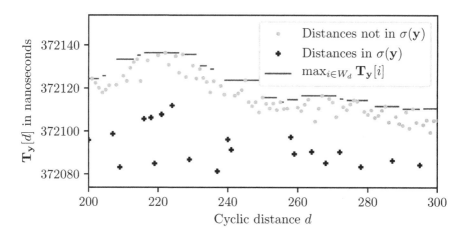

Fig. 4. Illustration of the values $\max_{i \in W_d} \mathbf{T_y}[i]$ for each distance d, considering windows of size $\eta = 11$, after $M = 1$ billion decryptions.

4.2 Reconstructing y from Partial Information on Its Spectrum

We propose the key reconstruction algorithm given as Algorithm 3, which is a simple randomized extension of Guo's et al. algorithm. Instead of performing a depth-first search for the key, at each level of the search tree, the algorithm chooses the next node at random.

We give a brief description of the algorithm. Parameters s, which must be a distance inside the spectrum of $\mathbf{y}$, and D, which is a set of distances outside the spectrum of $\mathbf{y}$, are obtained in the first part of the attack. At each iteration, the algorithm starts with the set $V = \{0, s\}$ and tries to complete it with $w - 2$ indexes. To complete the support V, the algorithm chooses at random an index inside the auxiliary set Γ_ℓ, which contains, for each level l, the possible positions to complete the support. That is, Γ_ℓ consists of all the elements from $\{0, \ldots, n - 1\}$ which are not in V, and whose circular distance to any index in V is not in D.

Notice that it is easy to perform the tests in lines 12 and 14 without knowing the secret key. Let $\overline{\mathbf{y}}$ be the vector with support V found in the algorithm's main loop. Consider all possible cyclic shifts of $\overline{\mathbf{y}}$, denoted by $\mathbf{y}^0, \ldots, \mathbf{y}^{n-1}$. To test if $\overline{\mathbf{y}}$ is a shift of $\mathbf{y}$, we look for a shift $\mathbf{y}^i$ such that the weight of the vector $\overline{\mathbf{x}} = \mathbf{s} + \mathbf{y}^i \cdot \mathbf{h}$ is $w(\overline{\mathbf{x}}) = w$. If we find one, then $\overline{\mathbf{y}}$ is a shift of $\mathbf{y}$ (high probability), or we have found an equivalent secret key for the given public key $(\mathbf{h}, \mathbf{s})$. If we do not find one, then we start a new iteration.

The complexity of the algorithm is analyzed in Sect. 5.2, while its practical performance is shown in Sect. 6.1.

Algorithm 3. Randomized key reconstruction algorithm

Data: The HQC public parameters and Alice's public key
      s a distance inside $\sigma(\mathbf{y})$
      D a set of distances which are not in $\sigma(\mathbf{y})$
Result: V the support of a rotation of $\mathbf{y}$

1 **begin**
2   **do**
3        $V \leftarrow \{0, s\}$
4        $\Gamma_2 \leftarrow \{i \in \{1, \ldots, \lfloor n/2 \rfloor\} - V : \mathrm{dist}_n(i, v) \notin D \text{ for all } v \in V\}$
5        $\ell \leftarrow 2$
6   **while** $|V| < w$ *and* $|\Gamma_\ell| > 0$ **do**
7           $p \leftarrow$ a random element from Γ_ℓ
8           $V \leftarrow V \cup \{p\}$
9           $\Gamma_{\ell+1} \leftarrow \{i \in \Gamma_\ell : \mathrm{dist}_n(i, v) \notin D \text{ for all } v \in V\}$
10          $\ell \leftarrow \ell + 1$
11   **while** *Both* V *and* $\mathrm{mirror}(V)$ *are not the support of a rotation of* $\mathbf{y}$;
12   **if** V *is the support of a shift of* $\mathbf{y}$ **then**
13   **return** V
14   **else if** $\mathrm{mirror}(V)$ *is the support of a shift of* $\mathbf{y}$ **then**
15   **return** $\mathrm{mirror}(V)$

---

5 Analysis

In this section we analyze two aspects of the attack. First we explain why it is possible to distinguish between distances inside and outside the spectrum based on decryption time. Then we analyze the complexity of the randomized key reconstruction algorithm, and how it compares to the one presented by Guo et al. [12].

5.1 Distinguishing Distances Inside and Outside the Spectrum

We know that the decryption time is related to the number of errors left by the repetition code (RC) decoder. Our main observation is that the number of RC decoding errors depends on how the spectrums of $\mathbf{r}_1$ and $\mathbf{r}_2$ relate to those of $\mathbf{y}$ and $\mathbf{x}$, respectively.

Consider the error to be corrected by the RC decoder, given by

$$\mathbf{e}' = \mathbf{r}_1 \cdot \mathbf{y} + \mathbf{r}_2 \cdot \mathbf{x} + \mathbf{e}.$$

An RC decoding error occurs when $\mathbf{e}'$ contains more than $(n_2 - 1)/2$ nonzero errors in the same repetition block. Therefore, an RC decoding error has higher probability of occurring when the spectrum of $\mathbf{e}'$ contains small distances with high multiplicity, and in particular, when $\sigma(\mathbf{e}')$ contains a lot of distances lower than the repetition block length n_2. We also expect that $\sigma(\mathbf{e}')$ contains small distances when $\sigma(\mathbf{r}_2 \cdot \mathbf{x})$ and $\sigma(\mathbf{r}_1 \cdot \mathbf{y})$ also contain small distances. In the following discussion, we focus on $\mathbf{r}_1 \cdot \mathbf{y}$, but we could have used $\mathbf{r}_2 \cdot \mathbf{x}$ without any difference.

The above paragraph motivates us to better understand what causes the spectrum of $r_1 \cdot y$ to contain small distances. Unfortunately, the strong dependency between the rows of $\text{rot}(y)^T$ can make it very hard to perform a satisfactory statistical analysis on the product $r_1 \cdot y$.

Therefore, we study a simpler problem, namely to describe $\sigma(r_1 \cdot y)$ as a function of $\sigma(r_1)$ and $\sigma(y)$, but restricted to the case where $w(r_1) = w(y) = 2$. Even though it is not the general case, it can give us a good intuition on why the attack works. The analysis is given in the following lemma. First we discuss the implications of the lemma and how it can be used to distinguish between distances inside and outside the spectrums of the secret key, and then we prove it.

Lemma 1. *Let* $y, r \in \mathbb{F}_2^n$ *be two binary vectors of weight 2, where n is an odd prime. Let α and β be the only distances in $\sigma(y)$ and $\sigma(r)$, respectively. Then, we have the following possibilities.*[3]
If $\alpha = \beta$, then

$$\sigma(r \cdot y) = \{\text{dist}_n(0, 2\alpha) : 1\} = \{\text{dist}_n(0, 2\beta) : 1\}. \tag{1}$$

If $\alpha \neq \beta$, then

$$\sigma(r \cdot y) = \{\alpha : 2, \tag{2}$$
$$\beta : 2, \tag{3}$$
$$|\beta - \alpha| : 1, \tag{4}$$
$$\text{dist}_n(0, \beta + \alpha) : 1\}. \tag{5}$$

Interpreting Lemma 1. Intuitively, α represents distances inside the spectrum of the secret vector y, while β represents distances inside the spectrum of r_1. We now restate the observations from Sect. 4.1 with brief discussions on why they happen, using the lemma to help us.

1. When β decreases from $\beta = n_2 - 1$ to $\beta = 1$, the value of $T_y[\beta]$ increases, getting significantly higher than the rest of the values in T_y.

   From (3), distance β in $\sigma(r_1)$ can cause $\sigma(r_1 \cdot x)$ to contain β with multiplicity 2. Therefore when $\beta < n_2$, it can be responsible for more RC errors than values of $\beta \geq n_2$. The reason why $T_y[\beta]$ gets increasingly higher when β approaches 1 is that, we get an increasing incidence of $\beta + \alpha < n_2$, where $\alpha \in \sigma(y)$. Therefore, from (5), these values of β tend to cause more distances lower than n_2 in $\sigma(r_1 \cdot y)$.

2. When $\beta \in \sigma(y)$, the value of $T_y[\beta]$ is lower than the average in the neighborhood of β.

   Comparing both cases considered by the lemma, we see that values of $\beta = \alpha$ for some $\alpha \in \sigma(y)$ (Case 1) are expected to produce a lower number of small distances in $\sigma(r_1 \cdot x)$ than values of $\beta \neq \alpha$ for all $\alpha \in \sigma(y)$ (Case 2).

---

[3] Recall that we use $(\gamma : m) \in \sigma(y)$ to denote that cyclic distance γ occurs m times between non-null entries of y.

3. When β has a large number of neighbors in $\sigma(\mathbf{y})$, the value of $\mathbf{T_y}[\beta]$ tends to be higher.

Using (4), we have that $\mathbf{T_y}[\beta]$ tends to be higher when more values of $\alpha \in \sigma(\mathbf{y})$ satisfy $|\beta - \alpha| < n_2$. In fact, the lemma even helps us formalize the neighborhood of β as the distances d between $\beta - n_2 < d < \beta + n_2$.

We now proceed with the proof of Lemma 1.

Proof (Lemma 1). Let α_1, α_2 and β_1, β_2 be the positions of the two ones in $\mathbf{y}$ and $\mathbf{r}$, respectively. We can suppose without loss of generality that

$$\alpha_2 = \alpha_1 + \alpha \bmod n, \text{ and } \beta_2 = \beta_1 + \beta \bmod n,$$

since if this is not the case, we can just swap the corresponding values.

The product $\mathbf{r} \cdot \mathbf{y}$ consists of the sum of two circular shifts of $\mathbf{y}$: one by β_1, and the other of β_2 positions, denoted by $\mathrm{shift}_{\beta_1}(\mathbf{y})$ and $\mathrm{shift}_{\beta_2}(\mathbf{y})$, respectively. More formally

$$\mathbf{r} \cdot \mathbf{y} = \mathbf{r} \, \mathrm{rot}(\mathbf{y})^T = \mathrm{shift}_{\beta_1}(\mathbf{y}) + \mathrm{shift}_{\beta_2}(\mathbf{y}),$$

where

$$\begin{aligned} \mathrm{supp}(\mathrm{shift}_{\beta_1}(\mathbf{y})) &= \{\alpha_1 + \beta_1 \bmod n, \alpha_2 + \beta_1 \bmod n\} \\ &= \{\alpha_1 + \beta_1 \bmod n, \alpha_1 + \alpha + \beta_1 \bmod n\}, \end{aligned}$$

and

$$\begin{aligned} \mathrm{supp}(\mathrm{shift}_{\beta_2}(\mathbf{y})) &= \{\alpha_1 + \beta_2 \bmod n, \alpha_2 + \beta_2 \bmod n\} \\ &= \{\alpha_1 + \beta_1 + \beta \bmod n, \alpha_1 + \alpha + \beta_1 + \beta \bmod n\}. \end{aligned}$$

Therefore the weight of $\mathbf{r} \cdot \mathbf{y}$ is at most 4, but can be lower if the supports above share some of their entries. We consider separately the cases when $\alpha = \beta$ and $\alpha \neq \beta$. These cases are illustrated in Fig. 5.

Case $\alpha = \beta$. In this case, we have:

$$\mathrm{supp}(\mathrm{shift}_{\beta_1}(\mathbf{y})) = \{\alpha_1 + \beta_1 \bmod n, \alpha_1 + \alpha + \beta_1 \bmod n\},$$

and

$$\mathrm{supp}(\mathrm{shift}_{\beta_2}(\mathbf{y})) = \{\alpha_1 + \beta_1 + \alpha \bmod n, \alpha_1 + 2\alpha + \beta_1 \bmod n\}.$$

The supports of the shifts share the entry $\alpha_1 + \beta_1 + \alpha \bmod n$. But notice that this is the only shared entry, since the fact that n is odd implies $\alpha_1 + \beta_1 \neq \alpha_1 + \beta_1 + 2\alpha \bmod n$. Then, summing the shifts of $\mathbf{y}$ we get

$$\mathrm{supp}(\mathbf{r} \cdot \mathbf{y}) = \{\alpha_1 + \beta_1 \bmod n, \alpha_1 + 2\alpha + \beta_1 \bmod n\}.$$

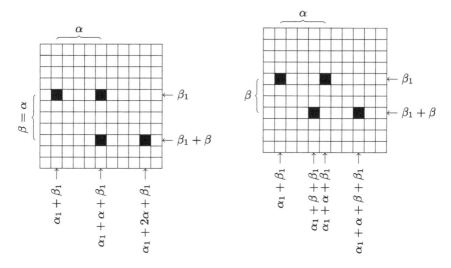

Fig. 5. The cases when $\alpha = \beta$ (left), and $\alpha \neq \beta$ (right).

Therefore, using the facts that $\alpha \leq \lfloor n/2 \rfloor$ and n is odd, we get

$$\sigma(\mathbf{r} \cdot \mathbf{y}) = \{\mathrm{dist}_n(\alpha_1 + \beta_1 \bmod n, \alpha_1 + 2\alpha + \beta_1 \bmod n) : 1\}$$
$$= \{\mathrm{dist}_n(0, 2\alpha \bmod n) : 1\}$$
$$= \{\mathrm{dist}_n(0, 2\alpha) : 1\}.$$

Case $\alpha \neq \beta$. We begin by showing that the supports of the shifts do not share any entry. It is clear that $\alpha_1 + \beta_1$ is not equivalent to $\alpha_1 + \beta_1 + \beta$ nor $\alpha_1 + \alpha + \beta_1 + \beta$ $(\bmod\,n)$ since $1 < \alpha, \beta \leq (n-1)/2$. The same can easily be seen for $\alpha_1 + \alpha + \beta_1$.

Therefore, spectrum of $\mathbf{r} \cdot \mathbf{y}$ consists of the following distances.

1. $\mathrm{dist}_n(\alpha_1 + \beta_1, \alpha_1 + \beta_1 + \beta) = \mathrm{dist}_n(0, \beta) = \beta$.
2. $\mathrm{dist}_n(\alpha_1 + \beta_1, \alpha_1 + \alpha + \beta_1) = \mathrm{dist}_n(0, \alpha) = \alpha$.
3. $\mathrm{dist}_n(\alpha_1 + \beta_1, \alpha_1 + \alpha + \beta_1 + \beta) = \mathrm{dist}_n(0, \alpha + \beta)$.
4. $\mathrm{dist}_n(\alpha_1 + \beta_1 + \beta, \alpha_1 + \alpha + \beta_1) = \mathrm{dist}_n(\beta, \alpha) = \mathrm{dist}_n(0, \alpha - \beta) = |\alpha - \beta|$.
5. $\mathrm{dist}_n(\alpha_1 + \beta_1 + \beta, \alpha_1 + \alpha + \beta_1 + \beta) = \mathrm{dist}_n(0, \alpha) = \alpha$.
6. $\mathrm{dist}_n(\alpha_1 + \alpha + \beta_1, \alpha_1 + \alpha + \beta_1 + \beta) = \mathrm{dist}_n(0, \beta) = \beta$.

Counting the multiplicities of these distances, we get the desired result. $\square$

5.2   Probabilistic Analysis of the Key Reconstruction Algorithm

In this section, we first analyze our randomized variant of the key reconstruction algorithm, given as Algorithm 3 in Sect. 4.2. We then compare it to Guo's et al. recursive algorithm, described as Algorithm 1 in the end of Sect. 2.

In each iteration, the algorithm performs a random walk down the search tree, starting from the root $\{0, s\}$, corresponding to $\ell = 2$, and ending in one of its leaves. Therefore, for the algorithm to succeed in finding $\mathbf{y}$, it has to choose, in each level of the search, an element in $\text{supp}(\mathbf{y})$.

Let s be a distance in $\sigma(\mathbf{y})$. Suppose the search is at level ℓ, and the algorithm has chosen, until now, the elements $V_\ell = \{v_1 = 0, v_2 = s, \ldots v_\ell\}$, all in the support of $\mathbf{y}$. Let Γ_ℓ be the set of possible choices at level ℓ, then

$$\Gamma_\ell = \{p \in (\{0, \ldots, n-1\} - V_\ell) : \text{dist}_n(p, v) \notin D \text{ for all } v \in V\}.$$

We now have exactly $w - |V_\ell|$ good choices for the next level, which gives us

$$\Pr(v_{\ell+1} \in \text{supp}(\mathbf{y}) \mid V_\ell \subset \text{supp}(\mathbf{y})) = \frac{w - |V_\ell|}{|\Gamma_\ell|} = \frac{w - \ell}{|\Gamma_\ell|}.$$

Remember that the spectrum recovery algorithm can find either $\mathbf{y}$ or $\text{mirror}(\mathbf{y})$, and both are of interest to the attacker. Therefore, we can write the probability that the algorithm successfully finds the key as

$$\Pr(\text{Success}) = 2 \prod_{\ell=2}^{w-1} \frac{w - \ell}{|\Gamma_\ell|},$$

where the product starts at level $\ell = 2$ since the search begins with $V_2 = \{0, s\}$, and it ends at level $\ell = w - 1$ because this is the last level in which a choice is made. The factor 2 comes from the mirror test.

Unfortunately, it is not easy to compute the distribution of $|\Gamma_\ell|$, because of the dependency between distances in D and elements in V_ℓ. However, we can approximate its expected value using an argument similar to the one used by Guo et al. [12]. Let α be the probability that a distance is not in D, that is $\alpha = 1 - |D|/\lfloor n/2 \rfloor$. At level ℓ, there are $w - \ell$ choices that are in $\text{supp}(\mathbf{y})$, and ℓ positions already in V_ℓ. For the other $n - w$ positions that are not in the support of $\mathbf{y}$, we expect a fraction of α^ℓ of them to have survived the sieves of each level. Therefore, we have

$$\mathbb{E}|\Gamma_\ell| \approx (n - w)\alpha^\ell + w - \ell.$$

We define the work factor $\mathbf{WF}_{\text{RAND}}$ of this algorithm as the expected number of paths it needs to explore until it finds the secret key. Then, using the approximation above, its value is

$$\mathbf{WF}_{\text{RAND}} = \frac{1}{\Pr(\text{Success})}$$

$$\approx \frac{1}{2} \prod_{\ell=2}^{w-1} \frac{(n-w)\alpha^\ell + w - \ell}{w - \ell} = \frac{1}{2} \prod_{\ell=2}^{w-1} \left(\frac{(n-w)\alpha^\ell}{w - \ell} + 1 \right).$$

Looking at the term in each level ℓ, they appear to be lower than the corresponding ones for Guo's et al. algorithm. However, just looking at the expressions, it is not clear how they compare.

To better understand how they compare, consider Fig. 6, which shows a concrete comparison of the work factors for both algorithms when the input D has an increasing number of distances outside the spectrum. We considered parameters for three HQC variants. Since the range of $|D|$ varies according to the parameters n and w, we normalized its value with respect to the average of the total number of distances outside the spectrum, denoted by Δ. To estimate Δ for each pair (n, w), we generated 1000 different random vectors and computed the average number of distances outside the spectrums. We can see that the work factor of the randomized algorithm is typically more than 3 orders of magnitude lower than Guo's et al. [12] recursive one.

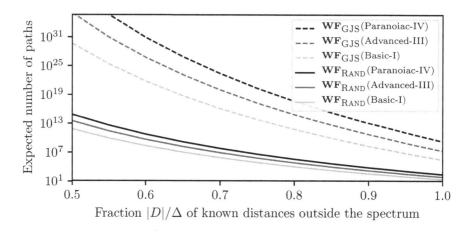

Fig. 6. Comparison between Guo's et al. [12] key reconstruction algorithm and our randomized variant with respect to the expected number of paths until the secret key is found. For each set of parameters (n, w) the value of $|D|$ is normalized using the average number of distances outside the spectrum, denoted by Δ.

6   Experimental Results

In this section, we present our results for the timing attack against the Basic-I parameters of the HQC. We consider the two parts of the attack separately. First we run experiments on the key reconstruction algorithm to find out how much information on the spectrum it needs to run efficiently. We then run simulations to estimate how many decryptions timings an attacker needs to perform to be able to reconstruct the key. The source code and data are available at www.ime. usp.br/tpaiva.

6.1   Performance of the Key Reconstruction Algorithm

We want to determine how many entries outside the spectrum of the secret vector **y** the attacker needs to know for the key reconstruction algorithm to efficiently reconstruct the vector. In other words, we are interested in how large the set D needs to be. Figure 6 gives us a hint on this matter, but it does not give us a concrete estimation of the key reconstruction algorithm's performance.

Table 2 shows the performance of both key reconstruction algorithms, the GJS and our randomized variant, when given sets D of different sizes for the Basic-I HQC parameters. For each considered size for the set D, we generated 10 random secret keys and considered D as a random set of $|D|$ distances outside the spectrum. The distance s was selected at random from the secret key spectrum. For a more clear interpretation of the results, we considered, in the second column, the approximate average number $\Delta = 9104$ of distances not in the spectrum, to normalize the values $|D|$. We then ran C implementations of the algorithms with parameters D and s. This experiment was performed on an Intel i7-8700 CPU at 3.20 GHz, using its 12 hyperthreads.

Table 2. Performance of the key reconstruction algorithms when input D has different sizes, for the Basic-I HQC parameters.

$|D|$	$|D|/\Delta$	Randomized variant of GJS reconstruction algorithm			GJS reconstruction algorithm
		$\mathbf{WF}_{\mathrm{RAND}}$	Median of the number of paths	Median of the CPU time (s)	Median of the CPU time (s)
9104	100%	28	63	0.51	0.98
8648	95%	99	80	0.51	10.78
8192	90%	407	232	0.50	772.64
7736	85%	1957	1714	0.75	6801.10
7280	80%	11394	9995	1.96	−
6824	75%	83670	54721	10.02	−
6368	70%	816671	365604	75.63	−
5912	65%	11355108	8472060	2767.90	−
5456	60%	246873607	−	−	−

We can see that our randomized algorithm performs much better than Guo's et al. [12] one. This not only implies that the randomized algorithm allows faster key reconstruction, but also that it allows the attacker to recover the key with less interaction with the secret key holder. The estimates for the number of paths $\mathbf{WF}_{\mathrm{RAND}}$ appear to be sufficiently accurate for our purposes, with only a minor discrepancy when $D/\Delta = 100\%$ that happens because of the concurrent hyperthreads. From $D/\Delta = 60\%$ down, the randomized algorithm starts taking too long to finish. Therefore, we consider that we are able to efficiently reconstruct the key when $D/\Delta \geq 65\%$.

6.2   Communication Cost

We now analyze how many decryption challenges an attacker needs to send to the secret key holder for a successful attack. In this paper, we only considered the Basic-I HQC parameters, but this experiment can easily be extended for the other parameters.

For the analysis, 10 secret keys were generated at random, and for each of them we ran the spectrum recovery algorithm for $M = 700$ million challenges. For each number challenges i, consider the quality of the decryption time estimates $\mathbf{T}_\mathbf{x}^i$ and $\mathbf{T}_\mathbf{y}^i$, given by

$$\text{QUALITY}(\mathbf{T}_\mathbf{x}^i) = \max\left\{\mu : \text{BUILDD}(\mathbf{T}_\mathbf{x}^i, \mu) \cap \sigma(\mathbf{x}) = \emptyset\right\}, \text{ and}$$
$$\text{QUALITY}(\mathbf{T}_\mathbf{y}^i) = \max\left\{\mu : \text{BUILDD}(\mathbf{T}_\mathbf{y}^i, \mu) \cap \sigma(\mathbf{y}) = \emptyset\right\},$$

where BUILDD is the algorithm described in the end of Sect. 4.1. For the BUILDD procedure, we considered the window size $\eta = 11$, which was obtained by the independent simulation described in the end of Sect. 4.1.

Based on the results from the previous section, we consider that the key reconstruction algorithm can efficiently recover $\mathbf{x}$ or $\mathbf{y}$, when either $\text{QUALITY}(\mathbf{T}_\mathbf{x}^i)$ or $\text{QUALITY}(\mathbf{T}_\mathbf{y}^i)$ is greater than 5912, correspondingly.

Figure 7 shows the result of the experiment. We can see that with about 400 million of challenges, efficient key reconstruction is possible. After 600 million challenges, almost all distances outside the spectrum can be correctly identified.

7   Discussion on Countermeasures

The most obvious countermeasure against this timing attack is to use constant-time BCH decoders [24, 25]. However, these decoders were proposed recently and they are not well studied yet. As such, their security against other types of side-channel attacks needs further investigation.

Walters and Sinha Roy [25] studied constant-time BCH decoders in the context of LAC [16]. Their decoder yields overheads between 10% and 40% when used in LAC. The optimized decoder proposed by Wafo-Tapa et al. [24] can yield reasonable overheads, between 3% and 11%, for the different security levels provided by the HQC instances. Hopefully, with further study on constant-time BCH decoders, lower overheads can be achieved.

If the slowdown factor is a problem, one could try to add a number of errors to the partially decoded vector right before the BCH decoding procedure. Next, we explain the rationale behind this idea. Consider the vector $\mathbf{c}' = \mathbf{mG} + \mathbf{x} \cdot \mathbf{r}_2 + \mathbf{r}_1 \cdot \mathbf{y} + \mathbf{e}$. When applying the repetition code decoder to each block of n_2 elements of $\mathbf{c}'$, we can estimate the probability of a repetition decoding error from the number of ones (or zeros) in the block. For example, if the number of 1's and 0's in a block are similar (both close to $n_2/2$), then the probability of a decoding error to occur is high. This might make it possible to estimate, within some statistical margin, the number of errors that the repetition code decoder has left for the BCH decoder. Then, one can add intentional errors to the partially decoded vector $\mathbf{c}'' = \Psi_2(\mathbf{c}')$, for it to have a weight W, where W is a constant error weight which the BCH decoder can correct. Further study and a careful probabilistic analysis is needed to understand if a decoder using this idea is secure.

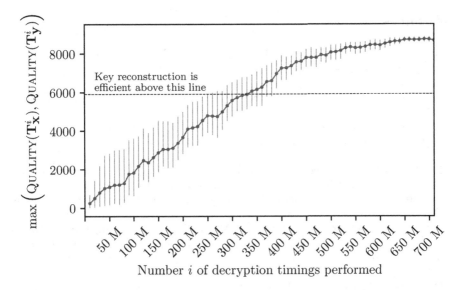

Number i of decryption timings performed

Fig. 7. Number of decryption timings an attacker needs to perform before the key can be successfully reconstructed. A confidence level of 95% was considered for the error bars.

8   Conclusion

In this paper, we present the first timing attack on the HQC encryption scheme. The attack depends on the choice of the parameter code C and its decoder implementation. We show that the attack is practical, requiring about 400 million decryption timings to be performed. This makes the use of constant-time decoders for C mandatory.

We discuss possible countermeasures against this timing attack, with the preferred one being to use constant-time BCH decoders [25]. However, further study is needed for the secure and efficient adoption of these decoders. Other solution would be to use codes for which efficient constant-time decoders are known. One interesting future work would be to find alternatives for the code C that admit compact keys and efficient constant-time decoders, and for which we can prove negligible decryption failure probability.

Acknowledgments. This study was financed in part by the Coordenação de Aperfeiçoamento de Pessoal de Nível Superior - Brasil (CAPES) - Finance Code 001. This research is part of the INCT of the Future Internet for Smart Cities funded by CNPq proc. 465446/2014-0, Coordenação de Aperfeiçoamento de Pessoal de Nível Superior – Brasil (CAPES) – Finance Code 001, FAPESP proc. 14/50937-1, and FAPESP proc. 15/24485-9.

References

1. Aguilar-Melchor, C., Blazy, O., Deneuville, J.C., Gaborit, P., Zémor, G.: Efficient encryption from random quasi-cyclic codes. IEEE Trans. Inf. Theory **64**(5), 3927–3943 (2018)
2. Albrecht, M., Cid, C., Paterson, K.G., Tjhai, C.J., Tomlinson, M.: NTS-KEM (2018)
3. Baldi, M.: QC-LDPC code-based cryptosystems. QC-LDPC Code-Based Cryptography. SECE, pp. 91–117. Springer, Cham (2014). https://doi.org/10.1007/978-3-319-02556-8_6
4. Berlekamp, E.R., McEliece, R.J., Van Tilborg, H.C.: On the inherent intractability of certain coding problems. IEEE Trans. Inf. Theory **24**(3), 384–386 (1978)
5. Bernstein, D.J., et al.: Classic McEliece: conservative code-based cryptography (2019)
6. Bettaieb, S., Bidoux, L., Gaborit, P., Marcatel, E.: Preventing timing attacks against RQC using constant time decoding of Gabidulin codes. In: Ding, J., Steinwandt, R. (eds.) PQCrypto 2019. LNCS, vol. 11505, pp. 371–386. Springer, Cham (2019). https://doi.org/10.1007/978-3-030-25510-7_20
7. D'Anvers, J.P., Tiepelt, M., Vercauteren, F., Verbauwhede, I.: Timing attacks on error correcting codes in post-quantum secure schemes. Cryptology ePrint Archive, Report 2019/292 (2019). https://eprint.iacr.org/2019/292
8. Eaton, E., Lequesne, M., Parent, A., Sendrier, N.: QC-MDPC: a timing attack and a CCA2 KEM. In: Lange, T., Steinwandt, R. (eds.) PQCrypto 2018. LNCS, vol. 10786, pp. 47–76. Springer, Cham (2018). https://doi.org/10.1007/978-3-319-79063-3_3
9. Fabšič, T., Hromada, V., Stankovski, P., Zajac, P., Guo, Q., Johansson, T.: A reaction attack on the QC-LDPC McEliece cryptosystem. In: Lange, T., Takagi, T. (eds.) PQCrypto 2017. LNCS, vol. 10346, pp. 51–68. Springer, Cham (2017). https://doi.org/10.1007/978-3-319-59879-6_4
10. Gabidulin, E.M.: Theory of codes with maximum rank distance. Probl. Peredachi Inform. **21**(1), 3–16 (1985)
11. Guo, Q., Johansson, T., Löndahl, C.: A new algorithm for solving Ring-LPN with a reducible polynomial. IEEE Trans. Inf. Theory **61**(11), 6204–6212 (2015)
12. Guo, Q., Johansson, T., Stankovski, P.: A key recovery attack on MDPC with CCA security using decoding errors. In: Cheon, J.H., Takagi, T. (eds.) ASIACRYPT 2016. LNCS, vol. 10031, pp. 789–815. Springer, Heidelberg (2016). https://doi.org/10.1007/978-3-662-53887-6_29
13. Hofheinz, D., Hövelmanns, K., Kiltz, E.: A modular analysis of the Fujisaki-Okamoto transformation. In: Kalai, Y., Reyzin, L. (eds.) TCC 2017. LNCS, vol. 10677, pp. 341–371. Springer, Cham (2017). https://doi.org/10.1007/978-3-319-70500-2_12
14. Joiner, L.L., Komo, J.J.: Decoding binary BCH codes. In: Proceedings IEEE Southeastcon 1995. Visualize the Future, pp. 67–73. IEEE (1995)
15. Löndahl, C., Johansson, T., Shooshtari, M.K., Ahmadian-Attari, M., Aref, M.R.: Squaring attacks on mceliece public-key cryptosystems using quasi-cyclic codes of even dimension. Des. Codes Crypt. **80**(2), 359–377 (2016)
16. Lu, X., et al.: LAC: Practical Ring-LWE based public-key encryption with byte-level modulus. Cryptology ePrint Archive, Report 2018/1009 (2018). https://eprint.iacr.org/2018/1009

17. McEliece, R.J.: A public-key cryptosystem based on algebraic coding theory. Deep Space Netw. Prog. Rep. **44**, 114–116 (1978)
18. Melchor, C.A., et al.: Hamming quasi-cyclic (HQC). Technical report, National Institute of Standards and Technology 2017 (2018)
19. Misoczki, R., Tillich, J.P., Sendrier, N., Barreto, P.S.: MDPC-McEliece: new McEliece variants from moderate density parity-check codes. In: 2013 IEEE International Symposium on Information Theory Proceedings (ISIT), pp. 2069–2073. IEEE (2013)
20. Prange, E.: The use of information sets in decoding cyclic codes. IRE Trans. Inf. Theory **8**(5), 5–9 (1962)
21. Sendrier, N.: Decoding one out of many. In: Yang, B.-Y. (ed.) PQCrypto 2011. LNCS, vol. 7071, pp. 51–67. Springer, Heidelberg (2011). https://doi.org/10.1007/978-3-642-25405-5_4
22. Stern, J.: A method for finding codewords of small weight. In: Cohen, G., Wolfmann, J. (eds.) Coding Theory 1988. LNCS, vol. 388, pp. 106–113. Springer, Heidelberg (1989). https://doi.org/10.1007/BFb0019850
23. Canto Torres, R., Sendrier, N.: Analysis of information set decoding for a sub-linear error weight. In: Takagi, T. (ed.) PQCrypto 2016. LNCS, vol. 9606, pp. 144–161. Springer, Cham (2016). https://doi.org/10.1007/978-3-319-29360-8_10
24. Wafo-Tapa, G., Bettaieb, S., Bidoux, L., Gaborit, P.: A practicable timing attack against HQC and its countermeasure. Cryptology ePrint Archive, Report 2019/909 (2019). https://eprint.iacr.org/2019/909
25. Walters, M., Roy, S.S.: Constant-time BCH error-correcting code. Cryptology ePrint Archive, Report 2019/155 (2019). https://eprint.iacr.org/2019/155

Block-Anti-Circulant Unbalanced Oil and Vinegar

Alan Szepieniec[1,2]($\boxtimes$) and Bart Preneel[1]

[1] imec-COSIC KU Leuven, Leuven, Belgium
{alan.szepieniec,bart.preneel}@esat.kuleuven.be
[2] Nervos Foundation, Panama City, Panama
alan@nervos.org

Abstract. We introduce a new technique for compressing the public keys of the UOV signature scheme that makes use of block-anti-circulant matrices. These matrices admit a compact representation as for every block, the remaining elements can be inferred from the first row. This space saving translates to the public key, which as a result of this technique can be shrunk by a small integer factor. We propose parameters sets that take into account the most important attacks, and present performance statistics derived from a C implementation along with a comparison to LUOV.

Keywords: Multivariate quadratic · Post-quantum · Unbalanced oil and vinegar

1 Introduction

Unbalanced Oil and Vinegar (UOV) is one of the longest-standing multivariate quadratic (MQ) signature schemes [10]. While the signatures are rather small, the public keys tend to be huge—they scale with the *cube* of the security parameter. Two notable improvements address this drawback in part.

First, the compression technique due to Petzoldt *et al.* allows most of the public key to be set arbitrarily; the remaining part is then computed with the secret key [14]. Since the arbitrary first part can be the output of a pseudo-random generator, the public key can be compressed to a short seed and the uncompressible second part.

Second, the field lifting technique due to Beullens and Preneel defines the public key over $\mathbb{F}_2$ but solves the signature equation and produces a signature over an extension of $\mathbb{F}_2$ [1]. As a result, the direct attack is more complex as it must be performed over a larger field; this allows a smaller number of equations for the same security level. At the same time, however, the public key admits a representation of just one bit for every polynomial coefficient as it was constructed that way.

We propose a third compression technique, relying on structured matrices to compactly represent objects of large size. In particular, the other rows of a

© Springer Nature Switzerland AG 2020
K. G. Paterson and D. Stebila (Eds.): SAC 2019, LNCS 11959, pp. 574–588, 2020.
https://doi.org/10.1007/978-3-030-38471-5_23

circulant or anti-circulant matrix can be inferred from the first. Moreover, these matrices guarantee that $B^\top AB$ is anti-circulant if both A and B are, or if A is anti-circulant and B is circulant. This property lends naturally to constructions of MQ public keys, where the matrix representation of the ith component's quadratic form can be presented as $S^\top F_i S$. As a result, the public key consists of block-anti-circulant matrices if the matrices of the secret key are block-anti-circulant. It can therefore be represented compactly by the list of first rows of each component block.

The obvious question raised by this design concerns its impact on security. We analyze empirically the complexity of a direct algebraic attack. With respect to the UOV Reconciliation Attack [5], our analysis assumes pessimistically that a successful attack need only consider each block to be its own variable living in the quotient ring $\mathbb{F}_q[x]/\langle x^\ell - 1\rangle$. Building on the insights gleaned from this empiricism and pessimistic analysis, we propose parameters for various security levels. Despite the conservative parameter choices, our compression technique achieves a notable size reduction of the public key and signatures—roughly half at all security levels compared to its immediate predecessor, LUOV.

2   Preliminaries

We use pythonic notation to slice submatrices from matrices: $A_{[i:j,k:l]}$ represents the $(j - i) \times (l - k)$ block of A whose upper left element has index (i, j), with indices starting as they should at zero. Furthermore we denote by $0_{[0:v,0:v]}$ the $v \times v$ zero matrix.

A square matrix A is *anti-cirulant*, and a square matrix B is *circulant*, if they are fully determined by their first rows $(a_{\ell-1}, a_{\ell-2}, \ldots, a_0)$ and $(b_0, b_1, \ldots, b_{\ell-1})$ via

$$A = \begin{pmatrix} a_{\ell-1} & a_{\ell-2} & \cdots & a_1 & a_0 \\ a_{\ell-2} & a_{\ell-3} & \cdots & a_0 & a_{\ell-1} \\ \vdots & \vdots & & \vdots & \vdots \\ a_1 & a_0 & \cdots & a_3 & a_2 \\ a_0 & a_{\ell-1} & \cdots & a_2 & a_1 \end{pmatrix} \quad \text{and} \quad B = \begin{pmatrix} b_0 & b_1 & \cdots & b_{\ell-2} & b_{\ell-1} \\ b_{\ell-1} & b_0 & \cdots & b_{\ell-3} & b_{\ell-2} \\ \vdots & \vdots & & \vdots & \vdots \\ b_2 & b_3 & \cdots & b_0 & b_1 \\ b_1 & b_2 & \cdots & b_{\ell-1} & b_0 \end{pmatrix}. \quad (1)$$

Circulant matrices are multiplication matrices of elements of the quotient ring $R[x]/\langle x^\ell - 1\rangle$, where R is the base ring of the matrix. Denote by J the $90°$ degree rotation of the identity matrix, *i.e.*, with the ones on the perpendicular diagonal. Then left or right multiplication by J makes a circulant matrix anti-circulant and vice versa. We make use of the following lemmata.

Lemma 1. *Let A be circulant and B anti-circulant. Then AB and BA are anti-circulant.*

Proof. There must be elements $a, b, b' \in R[x]/\langle x^\ell - 1\rangle$ with multiplication matrices M_a, M_b and $M_{b'}$ such that $A = M_a$ and $B = M_b J = J M_{b'}$. Then $AB = M_a M_b J = M_{ab} J$ and $BA = J M_{b'} M_a = J M_{b'a}$ are anti-circulant.   □

Lemma 2. *The sum of circulant matrices is circulant. The sum of anti-circulant matrices is anti-circulant.*

Proof. The sum of circulant matrices $\sum_i B_i$ corresponds to the sum of elements $b_i \in R[x]/\langle x^\ell - 1 \rangle$ and thus results in the multiplication matrix $M_{\sum_i b_i} = \sum_i M_{b_i}$, which is circulant as well. The sum of anti-circulant matrices $\sum_i A_i = \sum_i J M_{a_i} = J \sum_i M_{a_i} = J M_{\sum_i a_i}$.   □

3   Multivariate Quadratic Signature Schemes

The public key in a hash-and-sign multivariate signature scheme is given by a list of m quadratic polynomials $\mathbf{P} \in (\mathbb{F}_q[x_0, \ldots, x_{n-1}]_{\leq 2})^m$ in n variables over a finite field $\mathbb{F}_q$. To verify a signature $\mathbf{s} \in \mathbb{F}_q^n$ on a document $d \in \{0,1\}^*$, the user evaluates $\mathbf{P}(\mathbf{s})$ and tests if it is equal to the hash $\mathsf{H}(d) \in \mathbb{F}_q^m$. To generate a signature, the signer uses the secret decomposition of the public key $\mathbf{P} = T \circ \mathbf{F} \circ S$ where T and S are affine and where $\mathbf{F}$ is also quadratic but easy to invert. With this decomposition, the signer can compute sequentially $\mathbf{h} = \mathsf{H}(d)$ and $\mathbf{y} = T^{-1}\mathbf{h}$, followed by sampling an inverse $\mathbf{x}$ under $\mathbf{F}$ (as there may be many), and finally $\mathbf{s} = S^{-1}\mathbf{x}$. The key challenge for the design of multivariate quadratic (MQ) schemes is how to find a quadratic map $\mathbf{F}$ that simultaneously admits efficient inverse sampling and is also hard to recover from $\mathbf{P} = T \circ \mathbf{F} \circ S$ for random and unknown affine transforms T, S.

3.1   Unbalanced Oil and Vinegar

The Unbalanced Oil and Vinegar (UOV) scheme answers this question by partitioning the variables of $\mathbf{F}$ into two sets: the *vinegar* variables $x_0, \ldots, x_{v-1}$ which are multiplied with each other and all other variables, and the *oil* variables $x_v, \ldots, x_{v+o-1}$ which do not mix with other oil variables. Phrased differently, every term that is quadratic in the oil variables has coefficient equal to zero. This gives rise to quadratic forms with the following matrix silhouette:

$$F^{(i)} = \begin{pmatrix} & & \\ & & \\ & & \end{pmatrix} . \tag{2}$$

The black coefficients are chosen at random; the white coefficients are zero. The shape (2) anticipates the descriptor "unbalanced", as the number of vinegar variables is typically larger than the number of oil variables.

  Since all the quadratic forms of $\mathbf{F}$ have the same silhouette, the transform T hides nothing and therefore it is set to the identity transform. For the present description we will drop linear and constant terms so that $\mathbf{F}$ can be described as $\mathbf{F}(\mathbf{x}) = (\mathbf{x}^\mathsf{T} F^{(i)} \mathbf{x})_{i=0}^{m-1}$ and $S \overset{\$}{\leftarrow} \mathsf{GL}_n(\mathbb{F}_q)$ with $n = o + v$ and $m = o$. Here and elsewhere we use the shorthand $\mathbf{x}^\mathsf{T} = (x_0, \ldots, x_{n-1})$.

To sign a document $d \in \{0,1\}^*$, the signer computes the hash $\mathbf{h} = \mathsf{H}(d)$ and selects a random assignment to the vinegar variables $\mathbf{x}_{[0:v]} \xleftarrow{\$} \mathbb{F}_q^v$. This produces a system of m equations of the form

$$\mathbf{x}_{[0:v]}^{\mathsf{T}} \left(F^{(i)}_{[0:v,v:(v+o)]} + F^{(i)\mathsf{T}}_{[v:(v+o),0:v]} \right) \mathbf{x}_{[v:(v+o)]} = h_i - \mathbf{x}_{[0:v]}^{\mathsf{T}} F^{(i)}_{[0:v,0:v]} \mathbf{x}_{[0:v]} , \quad (3)$$

which is linear in the $o = m$ oil variables $\mathbf{x}_{[v:(v+o)]}$. Solving this system completes $\mathbf{x}$ and from this inverse the user computes the signature $\mathbf{s} = S^{-1}\mathbf{x}$ straightforwardly.

3.2 Petzoldt's Compression Technique

Petzoldt's compression technique [14] rests on the observation that the composition with S is a *linear* action on the quadratic forms $F^{(i)}$. In particular, let $\overrightarrow{F^{(i)}}$ denote the row-vector of all $n(n+1)/2$ coefficients in accordance with any standard monomial order; then $\overrightarrow{P^{(i)}} = \overrightarrow{F^{(i)}}A$ for some matrix $A \in \mathbb{F}_q^{\frac{n(n+1)}{2} \times \frac{n(n+1)}{2}}$ whose coefficients are given by

$$A_{[\mathsf{mo}(i,j),\mathsf{mo}(r,s)]} = \begin{cases} S_{[r,i]}S_{[s,j]} + S_{[r,j]}S_{[s,i]} & \text{if } i \neq j \\ S_{[r,i]}S_{[s,i]} & \text{otherwise,} \end{cases} \quad (4)$$

where $\mathsf{mo} : \mathbb{N}^2 \to \mathbb{N}$ sends the pair (i,j) to the index of the monomial $x_i x_j$ in the given monomial order.

As the $o(o+1)/2$ oil coefficients are zero, the $\overrightarrow{F^{(i)}}$ must live in a subspace of $\mathbb{F}_q^{n(n+1)/2}$ of dimension $n(n+1)/2 - o(o+1)/2$. As a result, the $\overrightarrow{P^{(i)}}$ must lie in a subspace of the same dimension. In particular, this means that the first $v(v+1)/2 + ov$ coefficients of every $\overrightarrow{P^{(i)}}$ can be set arbitrarily, after which the remaining $o(o+1)/2$ coefficients are fixed as a function of S.

The public key, represented as a Macaulay matrix whose rows are $\overrightarrow{P^{(i)}}$, is thus divisible into two blocks, of dimensions $m \times (v(v+1)/2 + vo)$, and $m \times o(o+1)/2$, respectively. The first block can be generated by a pseudorandom generator, after which point the user can find the second only if he knows S. The public key can therefore be reduced to a short seed and the second block. Note that this size is independent of the number of vinegar variables.

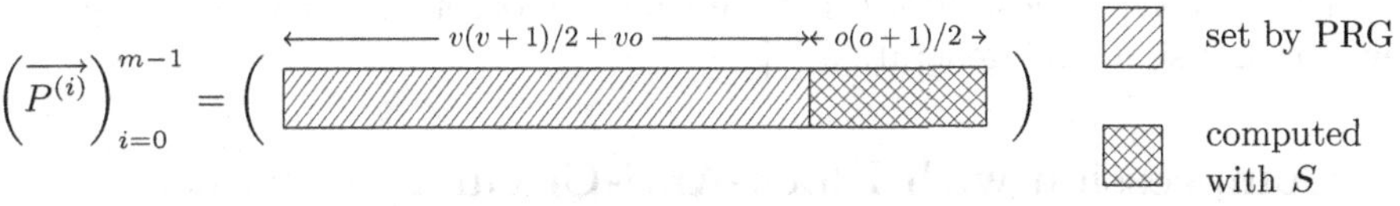

Fig. 1. Petzoldt's compression technique.

3.3   Field Lifting

Field lifting is another method of compressing the public key, although in this case it comes at the cost of a larger signature [1]. The secret and public keys are defined over a small base field, typically $\mathbb{F}_2$. However, the hash function $\mathsf{H} : \{0,1\}^* \to \mathbb{F}_{2^r}^m$ maps to a vector of *extension field elements*, and the signature is generated—and verified—using arithmetic over the extension field.

   This distinction allows the designer to ignore direct algebraic attacks performed over the base field. The number of equations needs only be large enough to guarantee the targeted level of security against a direct algebraic attack over the extension field. This number can be smaller as a result, which in turn leads to a much smaller public key. However, the base field must be taken into account for the UOV Reconciliation Attack [5], which solves a system of polynomial equations in order to recover the secret key from the public key. The complexity of this attack is accounted for by the increased number of vinegar variables. Since the field lifting technique is compatible with Petzoldt's technique, this increase does not affect the size of the public key. However, the signature size does grow as n is larger and as each component takes r bits to represent.

3.4   Irredundant S

It is always possible to find an equivalent secret key $(\mathbf{F}, S)$ for a given UOV public key, where S has the shape

$$
S = \begin{pmatrix} \diagdown & \blacksquare \\ & \diagdown \end{pmatrix} , \tag{5}
$$

where the white spaces are zero, the diagonal contains ones, and the nonzero block has dimensions $v \times o$. To see this, consider that only the rightmost o columns of S^{-1}—which has the same shape, just negate the rectangle—are capable of making the oil-oil coefficients of $S^{-1^\mathsf{T}} P^{(i)} S^{-1}$ equal to zero. Moreover, within the equivalence class of matrices S^{-1} with this property, it is always possible to choose one where the bottom right $o \times o$ block is the identity matrix.

   The UOV Reconciliation Attack is a search for a matrix S of form (5) regardless of whether the public key was actually constructed with such an S. Therefore, one might as well choose S of this form from the onset. This choice accelerates key pair and signature generation [4].

4   Compression with Block-Anti-Circulant Matrices

Let $\ell \in \mathbb{N}$ denote the height (and width) of the blocks on block matrices; from now on we refer to this parameter as the *degree of circulancy*. A matrix is *block-anti-circulant*, or *block-circulant*, if every $\ell \times \ell$ block represents an anti-circulant matrix, or a circulant matrix, respectively. Our compression technique arises from the following observation.

Theorem 1. *Let A, C be block-circulant matrices, and B be a block-anti-circulant matrix, all with square blocks of height (and width) ℓ. Then ABC is block-anti-circulant for blocks of the same size.*

Proof. The $\ell \times \ell$ blocks of BC represent the sum of products of anti-circulant matrices with circulant ones. Via lemmata 1 and 2 one observes that these blocks are circulant. The same argument shows that the $\ell \times \ell$ blocks of $A(BC)$ are anti-circulant. The matrix ABC is thus block-anti-circulant.   □

4.1   Description

Let $v = V \times \ell$, $o = O \times \ell$ and $N = O + V$. We choose S to be block-circulant; this does not affect the overall shape (5) but does imply that the top right $V \times O$ block must be block-circulant.

Likewise, the matrices $F^{(i)}$ are chosen to be $\ell \times \ell$ block-anti-circulant matrices $F^{(i)}$ in the shape of (2). One observes via Theorem 1 that the matrices $P^{(i)}$ are block-anti-circulant as well. These matrices can therefore be represented by only the first row of every block. This requires only $N^2\ell$ elements per matrix as opposed to the highly redundant $n^2 = N^2\ell^2$ elements associated with an explicit representation.

Matrices that represent quadratic forms, such as $F^{(i)}$ and $P^{(i)}$, are invariant under addition of skew-symmetric matrices. Over odd-characteristic fields[1] one can therefore always choose $F^{(i)}$ and $P^{(i)}$ to be symmetric, even when they are block-anti-circulant (but not necessarily when they are (block-)circulant). This reduces the storage requirement to $N(N+1)\ell/2$ field elements, down from $n(n+1)/2$. For fields of even characteristic, upper-triangular matrix representatives of the quadratic forms are preferred, and in this case the same compression argument applies. However, this means that the $\ell \times \ell$ blocks on the diagonal must be either identity or zero matrices.

We depart from the Macaulay matrix representation of the public key **P** or of the secret map **F** traditionally used in Petzoldt's compression technique. Instead, both **P** and **F** are represented as lists of symmetric block-anti-circulant matrices. Nevertheless, Petzoldt's compression technique still applies. The pseudorandom generator is used to generate the first row of every $\ell \times \ell$ block in the upper-triangular part, except for the bottom-most $O \times (O+1)/2$ blocks which are computed using S. Figure 2 elaborates.

More explicitly, let $S = \left(\begin{array}{c|c} I_{[0:v,0:v]} & S' \\ \hline 0_{[0:o,0:v]} & I_{[0:o,0:o]} \end{array} \right)$ for some block-circulant $v \times o$ matrix S'. The bottom right $o \times o$ block of $P^{(i)}$ is given by

$$P^{(i)}_{[v:n,v:n]} = {S'}^\mathsf{T} F^{(i)}_{[0:v,0:v]} S' + F^{(i)}_{[v:n,0:v]} S' + {S'}^\mathsf{T} F^{(i)}_{[0:v,v:n]} . \tag{6}$$

---

[1] We restrict focus to odd-characteristic fields because the use of even-characteristic fields induces a security degradation, as shown in Sect. 4.2.

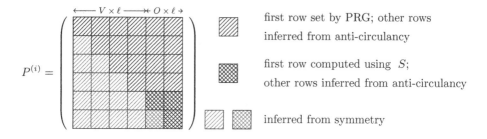

Fig. 2. Petzoldt's compression technique with $\ell \times \ell$ block-anti-circulant matrices.

The nonzero blocks of $F^{(i)}$ are given by

$$F^{(i)}_{[0:v,0:v]} = P^{(i)}_{[0:v,0:v]} \tag{7}$$

$$F^{(i)}_{[0:v,v:n]} = -P^{(i)}_{[0:v,0:v]}S' + P^{(i)}_{[0:v,v:n]} \tag{8}$$

$$F^{(i)}_{[v:n,0:v]} = -S'^{\mathsf{T}}P^{(i)}_{[0:v,0:v]} + P^{(i)}_{[v:n,0:v]} . \tag{9}$$

Altogether, if Petzoldt's technique is used in conjunction with our block-anti-circulant compression, then the public key is given by $m\ell O(O+1)/2$ field elements and a short seed.

4.2   Security

This section evaluates to which extent the additional structure in the public key facilitates attacks; based on this analysis, we propose parameters later on. The following attacks are considered: Direct Algebraic Attack, Kipnis-Shamir Attack, and UOV Reconciliation Attack.

The Kipnis-Shamir Attack and the UOV Reconciliation Attack can be accelerated by performing arithmetic in the quotient ring $\mathbb{F}_q[x]/\langle x^\ell - 1\rangle$. (We assume, optimistically from the point of view of the attacker, that the overhead of converting between circulant and anti-circulant matrices is negligible.) Arithmetic in the quotient ring can in turn be accelerated using the Chinese Remainder Theorem and the factorization $\frac{\mathbb{F}_q[x]}{\langle x^\ell - 1\rangle} \cong \frac{\mathbb{F}_q[x]}{\langle f_0(x)\rangle} \oplus \cdots \oplus \frac{\mathbb{F}_q[x]}{\langle f_t(x)\rangle}$, where $\prod_{i=0}^t f_i(x) = x^\ell - 1$. For the purpose of estimating attack complexity, we assume the cost is dominated by arithmetic over the largest component ring in this direct sum, associated with f_0, the largest-degree[2] irreducible factor of $x^\ell - 1$.

Embedded in this assumption is the assertion that if the attack should succeed over a smaller ring, say $\mathbb{F}_q[x]/\langle f_j(x)\rangle$ with $\deg(f_j) < \deg(f_0)$, this success does not help the attacker. Indeed, if successful, such a partial attack outputs

---

[2] Or any one of the irreducible factors of largest degree, if there are more than one.

the representative of S in $\mathbb{F}_q[x]/\langle f_j(x) \rangle$. However, the attacker needs the matching representative in $\mathbb{F}_q[x]/\langle f_0(x) \rangle$ for a complete attack, and this component is independent of the previous one.

Direct Attack. A direct algebraic attack involves deploying Gröbner basis type algorithms [6, 7, 11, 12] in order to solve for $\mathbf{s} \in \mathbb{F}_q$ the system of multivariate quadratic polynomial equations given by $\left(\mathbf{s}^\mathsf{T} P^{(i)} \mathbf{s} \right)_{i=0}^{m-1} = \mathbf{h}$, where $\mathbf{h} = \mathsf{H}(d) \in \mathbb{F}_q^m$ is the hash of a target document. The question is whether the introduction of the blockwise anti-circulant structure in order to compress the public key decreases the complexity of such an attack. We implemented the scheme with and without block-anti-circulant compression in Magma in order to test empirically whether this is the case.

In particular, we instantiate two systems of polynomials:

1. m equations in n variables without block-anti-circulant compression; this corresponds to $\ell = 1$.
2. m equations in $n = N \times \ell$ variables with block-anti-circulant compression; this corresponds to $\ell > 1$.

In both cases, the first $n - m$ variables were assigned random values that still guarantee that a solution exists. Figure 3 shows the running time of these attacks as a function of ℓ, for various values of (q, m), as performed by Magma's implementation of F_4 on an eight core 2.9 GHz machine. The plots suggest that over fields of even characteristic, block-anti-circulant matrices come with a security degradation proportional to the degree of circulancy. In contrast, the security of the same construction but over fields of odd characteristic seems largely unaffected by the degree of circulancy, except possibly at the extremal point where $\ell = m$.

Given the correspondence between anti-circulant matrices and the ring $\frac{\mathbb{F}_q[x]}{\langle x^\ell - 1 \rangle}$, another natural question is whether arithmetic in this ring can help mount a direct attack. Solutions might be found in each component term of $\frac{\mathbb{F}_q[x]}{\langle x^\ell - 1 \rangle} \cong \frac{\mathbb{F}_q[x]}{\langle f_0(x) \rangle} \oplus \frac{\mathbb{F}_q[x]}{\langle f_1(x) \rangle} \oplus \cdots$ before being joined together using the Chinese Remainder Theorem. However, finding even one such solution still requires solving a system of m equations in N variables; and since $N > m$, the complexity of this task is already captured by Fig. 3.

Kipnis-Shamir Attack. The present proposal is not the first time circulant matrices have been considered in conjunction with UOV. Peng and Tang recently proposed choosing the secret quadratic forms $F^{(i)}$ to have a specific structure such that during signature generation, the coefficient matrix becomes circulant [13]. This embedded structure not only shrinks the secret key, but it also speeds up signature generation. However, Hashimoto shows that this scheme is vulnerable to a Kipnis-Shamir attack, despite the numbers of vinegar and oil variables being unbalanced [9].

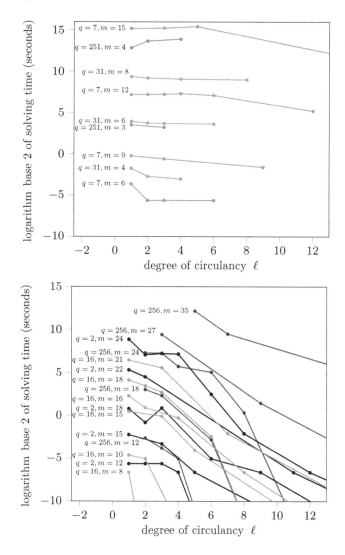

Fig. 3. Running time of direct algebraic attack for odd and even characteristic.

The circulancy in the scheme of Peng and Tang arises as a result of recycling oil-vinegar coefficients across the quadratic forms $F^{(i)}$. The algebraic relation that describes this recycling, is exactly the algebraic property that gives rise to the attack. If the $F^{(i)}$ are chosen independently, the required relation does not hold and the attack fails — or rather, the attack works only with the exponential complexity $O(q^{v-o})$ of regular unbalanced oil and vinegar.

The $F^{(i)}$ in our construction do have structure, but do not have algebraic properties relating $F^{(i)}$ for various i. The coefficient matrix obtained while generating a signature does not have a circulant or block-anti-circulant structure.

The attack can be performed over the constituent terms of $\mathbb{F}_q[x]/\langle x^\ell - 1\rangle$, after which the partial solutions are joined together with the Chinese Remainder Theorem. The number V of vinegar *blocks* must be chosen accordingly, *i.e.*, such that the targeted security level is reached by $(q^{\deg(f_0)})^{V-O}$, where $f_0(x)$ is the largest degree irreducible factor of $x^\ell - 1$. In fact, we consider $(q^{\deg(f_0)})^{(V-O)/2}$ instead, to account for a speedup on quantum computers due to Grover's algorithm [8].

UOV Reconciliation Attack. The UOV Reconciliation Attack [5] is an algebraic key recovery attack that mounts a search for the matrix S by treating its elements as variables and solving the system of equations obtained by equating $\left(S^{-1^\mathsf{T}} P^{(i)} S^{-1}\right)_{[v:n,v:n]} = 0_{[0:o,0:o]}$ for all $i \in \{0, \ldots, m-1\}$. Ding *et al.* argue that the search can be decomposed into a series of steps of which the first dominates the complexity of the entire procedure [5]. This first step requires solving a system of m quadratic equations in v variables, originating from the number of polynomials, *i.e.*, m, and the number of unknowns in the rightmost column of S, *i.e.*, v. In the case of UOV where $v > m$ it is tempting to use a result by Thomae and Wolf showing how to reduce solving a system of m quadratic equations in $n = \alpha m$ variables to solving one of $m - \lfloor \alpha \rfloor + 1$ equations in as many variables [15]. However, Beullens and Preneel argue that this reduction does not apply to this first step of the UOV Reconciliation Attack because it finds an arbitrary solution and not necessarily one that is consistent with the other steps [1]. Instead, Beullens and Preneel estimate the complexity of this attack as strictly larger than that of solving a system of v equations in v variables.

With respect to our construction, an attack performed over the quotient ring $\frac{\mathbb{F}_q[x]}{\langle x^\ell - 1\rangle} = \frac{\mathbb{F}_q[x]}{\langle f_0(x)\rangle} \oplus \cdots$ suffices to break the scheme. In this case the attack represents a search for the $V \times O$ unknown ring elements of the matrix S. In particular, the last column of S has only $V = v/\ell$ unknowns. However, the number m of equations remains unaffected by this ring switch. Therefore, as long as $V \geq m$, we can argue that the complexity of the Reconciliation Attack is lower-bounded by solving a system of V equations in V variables over $\mathbb{F}_q[x]/\langle f_0(x)\rangle$.

4.3 Parameters and Comparison

We advise against using fields of even characteristic in light of the poor resilience of our block-anti-circulant compression against direct algebraic attacks, as shown in Fig. 3. However, we note that using odd characteristic fields does not preclude using the field lifting technique of Beullens and Preneel, although it does make it less effective. Denote by r the extension degree, *i.e.*, the signature equation is defined over $\mathbb{F}_{q^r}$ instead of $\mathbb{F}_q$.

We estimate the complexity of algebraic system solving using the Wiedemann method [12] along with Groverized fixing of variables [1,3]. This makes for a complexity of

$$C_{m,n,k} = O\left(q^{k/2} \cdot \binom{n-k+2}{2}\binom{d_{reg}(k)+n-k}{n-k}^2\right), \tag{10}$$

where k is the number of variables that are quantumly guessed, and the degree of regularity d_{reg} is given by the degree of the first non-positive term in the formal power series expansion of

$$HS(z) = \frac{(1 - z^2)^m}{1 - z^n} . \tag{11}$$

To obtain one concrete number, we take the minimum of $C_{m,n,k}$ over all k and pretend as though the constant hidden by the Landau notation is equal to 1.

Table 1 presents a selection of parameter sets designed to meet various target levels of post-quantum security, measured in terms of the base 2 logarithm of the best attack's complexity. For convenience, it also offers comparisons with variants of UOV, namely:

- LUOV—UOV with Petzoldt's compression technique and field lifting [1].
- PCT—UOV with Petzoldt's compression technique [14].
- Plain—Plain UOV with no compression [10].

Table 1. Proposed parameter sets and comparison to other variants of UOV.

Scheme	Parameters	$|pk|$	$|sig|$	sec. lvl
Plain	$q = 256, v = 106, m = o = 53$	658.36 kB	159 bytes	128.85
PCT	$q = 256, v = 106, m = o = 53$	74.07 kB	159 bytes	128.85
LUOV	$q = 2, v = 296, m = o = 40, r = 68$	4.00 kB	2.79 kB	128.17
BACUOV	$q = 3, V = 49, O = 7, \ell = 7, r = 12$	2.34 kB	1.14 kB	129.32
Plain	$q = 256, v = 164, m = o = 82$	2.38 MB	246 bytes	191.89
PCT	$q = 256, v = 164, m = o = 82$	272.5 kB	246 bytes	191.89
LUOV	$q = 2, v = 444, m = o = 60, r = 84$	13.40 kB	5.16 kB	190.00
BACUOV	$q = 3, V = 76, O = 10, \ell = 7, r = 18$	6.58 kB	2.65 kB	192.08
Plain	$q = 256, v = 224, m = o = 112$	6.05 MB	336 bytes	256.50
PCT	$q = 256, v = 224, m = o = 112$	692.13 kB	336 bytes	256.50
LUOV	$q = 2, v = 600, m = o = 82, r = 90$	34.06 kB	7.49 kB	256.13
BACUOV	$q = 3, V = 104, O = 14, \ell = 7, r = 11$	17.59 kB	2.22 kB	256.68

Note that the choice $q = 3$, which minimizes the total size of public key and signature, is not represented in Fig. 3. In fact, this choice has a poor resilience against algebraic attack—its complexity decreases with increasing circulancy, albeit much slower than when q is even. Nevertheless, we argue that this subtle degradation is an artifact of the small coefficient field over which the system of equations is defined. In particular, extending this field by setting $r > 1$ reduces the degradation or even halts it completely. Figure 4 shows a similar plot except for $q = 3$ and various r. There is much less degradation when $r = 3$ and it seems to vanish entirely for $r = 5$, which incidentally understates the recommended

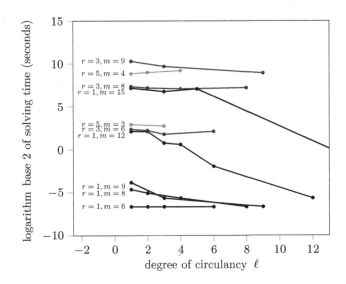

Fig. 4. Running time of direct algebraic attack for various r when $q = 3$.

parameters by a large factor. A complete argument would run the toy attack for $q = 3, r = 5$ and greater degrees of circulancy, but sadly this experiment is impossible with the available hardware and time.

4.4 Implementation

A full working proof of concept implementation was developed in Sage, and a mildly optimized version in C for the purpose of comparison, see below. The direct attack timings were obtained from a Magma implementation that only generates block-anti-cyclic public keys but does not do compression of any kind. The security levels are estimated using a Sage script. All source code is available under the Community Research and Academic Programming License (CRAPL) from github: https://github.com/aszepieniec/bacuov.

For the purpose of an apples-to-apples comparison, we use the reference implementation of the round 2 NIST candidate LUOV [2] with the recommended parameter sets for a balanced public key and signature size. On the part of the block-anti-circulant scheme, we adapt the parameters to minimize the combined size of the public key and signature, subject to meeting the same security level as their LUOV counterpart. This implementation uses arithmetic over $\mathbb{F}_q/\langle x^\ell - q \rangle$ as well as delayed modular reduction for various matrix operations, but exploits no parallelism. The performance numbers are given by the kilocycles (kc, first line), and milliseconds (ms, second line) in Table 2. These numbers are the average of 100 executions run on a 4-core Intel(R) Core(TM) i3-7100U CPU @ 2.40GHz with 3072 kB cache.

Table 2. Performance comparison between LUOV and block-anti-circulant UOV.

Scheme	Parameters	$|pk|$	$|sig|$	sec. lvl	Keygen	Sign	Verify
LUOV	$q = 2$, $r = 48$	5 kB	1.57 kB	NIST II	14 795 kc	54 831 kc	35 748 kc
	$m = 43$, $v = 222$				6.165 ms	22.846 ms	14.895 ms
BACUOV	$q = 3$, $V = 56$	3.45 kB	1.31 kB	NIST II	682 436 kc	332 498 kc	593 693 kc
	$O = 8$, $\ell = 7$, $r = 12$				284.323 ms	138.527 ms	247.355 ms
BACUOV	$q = 7$, $V = 60$	4.64 kB	1.55 kB	NIST II	2 685 130 kc	611 928 kc	1 265 715 kc
	$O = 5$, $\ell = 13$, $r = 5$				1118.648 ms	254.956 ms	527.364 ms
LUOV	$q = 2$, $r = 64$	14.1 kB	2.84 kB	NIST IV	40 039 kc	163 638 kc	90 331 kc
	$m = 61$, $v = 302$				16.683 ms	68.182 ms	37.638 ms
BACUOV	$q = 3$, $V = 84$	8.69 kB	2.60 kB	NIST IV	2 354 156 kc	1 402 365 kc	2 452 899 kc
	$O = 11$, $\ell = 7$, $r = 16$				980.803 ms	584.275 ms	1021.961 ms
BACUOV	$q = 7$, $V = 76$	8.70 kB	5.35 kB	NIST IV	4 801 991 kc	2 260 414 kc	3 740 856 kc
	$O = 7$, $\ell = 11$, $r = 16$				2000.665 ms	941.775 ms	1558.526 ms
LUOV	$q = 2$, $r = 80$	27.1 kB	4.29 kB	NIST V	176 100 kc	527 341 kc	248 874 kc
	$m = 76$, $v = 363$				73.374 ms	219.723 ms	103.696 ms
BACUOV	$q = 3$, $V = 104$	17.60 kB	2.42 kB	NIST V	5 096 796 kc	2 804 193 kc	4 758 999 kc
	$O = 14$, $\ell = 7$, $r = 16$				2123.658 ms	1168.403 ms	1982.899 ms
BACUOV	$q = 7$, $V = 97$	17.95 kB	3.41 kB	NIST V	12 019 482 kc	2 399 406 kc	5 401 021 kc
	$O = 9$, $\ell = 11$, $r = 8$				5007.974 ms	999.722 ms	2250.364 ms

5   Conclusion

We propose to introduce a block-anti-circulant structure into the secret and private keys of the UOV signature scheme. While the addition of structure may accelerate some attacks, we argue that it is possible to either offset this acceleration or block it entirely by choosing parameters appropriately. The resulting public key is smaller than the variant of UOV that uses only Petzoldt's compression trick by a factor ℓ which determines the block size. For typical values of this parameter, *i.e.* between 7 and 13, the resulting public keys are tens of kilobytes in size for all security levels.

With respect to the certificate metric $|pk| + |sig|$ (*i.e.*, the size of a link in a chain of signatures and public keys in a certificate), our scheme represents a small improvement over LUOV. As a result of this small improvement our scheme achieves the smallest combined size of public key and signature across all MQ signature schemes. While the size difference with respect to LUOV is marginal at the 128 bit security level, this difference increases noticeably for higher security levels and thus provides empirical evidence of the improved scaling behavior promised by the insertion of an anti-circulant structure.

The comparison between UOV with block-anti-circulant structure and LUOV shows that the bandwidth improvement comes at a significant performance penalty. In some cases, the block-anti-circulant algorithms are up to $70\times$ slower than their LUOV counterparts. Nevertheless, it should be noted that the algorithms stand to benefit from instruction-level parallelism, which the current implementation does not employ. In contrast, bitwise parallelism is native to the fields over which LUOV operates. We expect aggressive optimization to shrink this performance penalty significantly, but ultimately leave this task to future work. Regardless, the smaller bandwidth requirement may justify the computational overhead depending on the context. The present construction provides the protocol designer with a greater flexibility in choosing parameters, thus enabling him to better finetune the cryptosystem to the constraints of his problem.

Performance is not the only penalty associated with introducing a block-anti-circulant structure. Indeed, the security argument hinges on two new assumptions. First, a Kipnis-Shamir or UOV Reconciliation attack that exploits the block-anti-circulant structure is dominated by the cost of arithmetic in the largest ring in the decomposition $\frac{\mathbb{F}_q[x]}{\langle x^\ell - 1 \rangle} \cong \frac{\mathbb{F}_q[x]}{\langle f_0(x) \rangle} \oplus \frac{\mathbb{F}_q[x]}{\langle f_1(x) \rangle} \oplus \cdots$. Second, the block-anti-circulant structure does not speed up a direct algebraic attack for large enough fields of odd order. These two new assumptions are in addition to the assumption introduced by LUOV, namely that defining the public key over a subfield does not speed up a direct algebraic attack. We invite the community to help scrutinize these assumptions.

We close by posing two questions. The first is prompted by the observation that the inserted structure by which public key compression is achieved, is highly specific. We used block-anti-circulant structure because it is straightforward and simultaneously compatible with both the construction of $P^{(i)}_{[v:n,v:n]}$ from $P^{(i)}_{[0:v,0:v]}$ and $P^{(i)}_{[0:v,v:n]}$, and with the canonical representation of quadratic forms as symmetric matrices. Nevertheless, it might be possible that an alternative to circulant and anti-circulant matrices is also compatible with the necessary arithmetic, possibly at the expense of a less straightforward instantiation. For instance, instead of using the matrices of multiplication of polynomials modulo $x^\ell - 1$, one might opt for the same matrices of multiplication but modulo an irreducible polynomial. The advantage of this alternative structure would be the impossibility of decomposing the resulting ring into smaller components. However, the question remains whether this alternative algebra is compatible with the construction of $P^{(i)}_{[v:n,v:n]}$ from $P^{(i)}_{[0:v,0:v]}$ and $P^{(i)}_{[0:v,v:n]}$, and with the symmetric matrix representation of quadratic forms — or if it is not, which compromises can still confer a net benefit.

Lastly, an interesting question is raised by our empirical results: why is there a significant security degradation associated with a larger degree of circulancy specifically for fields of characteristic two? We conjecture that this degradation is related to the impossibility of representing quadratic forms over an even characteristic field by symmetric matrices. As a result, a block-anti-circulant representation of such a quadratic form necessarily contains blocks of zeros on its diagonal, thus greatly reducing the number of nonzero coefficients.

Acknowledgements. This work was supported in part by the Research Council KU Leuven: C16/15/058. In addition, this work was supported by the European Commission through the Horizon 2020 research and innovation programme under grant agreement H2020-DS-LEIT-2017-780108 FENTEC, by the Flemish Government through FWO SBO project SNIPPET S007619N and by the IF/C1 on Cryptanalysis of postquantum cryptography. Alan Szepieniec was supported by a doctoral grant from Flemish Agency for Innovation and Entrepreneurship (VLAIO, formerly IWT) and is supported by Nervos Foundation. Lastly, the authors would like to thank Ward Beullens for useful feedback.

References

1. Beullens, W., Preneel, B.: Field lifting for smaller UOV public keys. In: Patra, A., Smart, N.P. (eds.) INDOCRYPT 2017. LNCS, vol. 10698, pp. 227–246. Springer, Cham (2017). https://doi.org/10.1007/978-3-319-71667-1_12
2. Beullens, W., Preneel, B., Szepieniec, A., Vercauteren, F.: LUOV signature scheme proposal for NIST PQC project (Round 2 version). https://github.com/WardBeullens/LUOV
3. Chen, M.-S., Hülsing, A., Rijneveld, J., Samardjiska, S., Schwabe, P.: From 5-pass $\mathcal{MQ}$-based identification to $\mathcal{MQ}$-based signatures. In: Cheon, J.H., Takagi, T. (eds.) ASIACRYPT 2016. LNCS, vol. 10032, pp. 135–165. Springer, Heidelberg (2016). https://doi.org/10.1007/978-3-662-53890-6_5
4. Czypek, P., Heyse, S., Thomae, E.: Efficient implementations of MQPKS on constrained devices. In: Prouff, E., Schaumont, P. (eds.) CHES 2012. LNCS, vol. 7428, pp. 374–389. Springer, Heidelberg (2012). https://doi.org/10.1007/978-3-642-33027-8_22
5. Ding, J., Yang, B.-Y., Chen, C.-H.O., Chen, M.-S., Cheng, C.-M.: New differential-algebraic attacks and reparametrization of rainbow. In: Bellovin, S.M., Gennaro, R., Keromytis, A., Yung, M. (eds.) ACNS 2008. LNCS, vol. 5037, pp. 242–257. Springer, Heidelberg (2008). https://doi.org/10.1007/978-3-540-68914-0_15
6. Faugère, J.C.: A new efficient algorithm for computing Gröbner bases without reduction to zero (F_5). In: ISSAC 2002, pp. 75–83. ACM (2002)
7. Faugàre, J.C.: A new efficient algorithm for computing Gröbner bases (F4). J. Pure Appl. Algebra 139(1–3), 61–88 (1999)
8. Grover, L.K.: A fast quantum mechanical algorithm for database search. In: Miller, G.L. (ed.) ACM STOC 1996, pp. 212–219. ACM (1996)
9. Hashimoto, Y.: On the security of Circulant UOV/Rainbow. IACR Cryptology ePrint Archive 2018, p. 947 (2018). https://eprint.iacr.org/2018/947
10. Kipnis, A., Patarin, J., Goubin, L.: Unbalanced oil and vinegar signature schemes. In: Stern, J. (ed.) EUROCRYPT 1999. LNCS, vol. 1592, pp. 206–222. Springer, Heidelberg (1999). https://doi.org/10.1007/3-540-48910-X_15
11. Mohamed, M.S.E., Cabarcas, D., Ding, J., Buchmann, J., Bulygin, S.: MXL3: an efficient algorithm for computing Gröbner bases of zero-dimensional ideals. In: Lee, D., Hong, S. (eds.) ICISC 2009. LNCS, vol. 5984, pp. 87–100. Springer, Heidelberg (2010). https://doi.org/10.1007/978-3-642-14423-3_7
12. Mohamed, W.S.A., Ding, J., Kleinjung, T., Bulygin, S., Buchmann, J.: PWXL: a parallel Wiedemann-XL algorithm for solving polynomial equations over GF(2). In: Cid, C., Faugère, J. (eds.) Conference on Symbolic Computation and Cryptography, pp. 89–100 (2010)
13. Peng, Z., Tang, S.: Circulant UOV: a new UOV variant with shorter private key and faster signature generation. TIIS 12(3), 1376–1395 (2018)
14. Petzoldt, A., Buchmann, J.A.: A multivariate signature scheme with an almost cyclic public key. IACR Cryptology ePrint Archive 2009, p. 440 (2009). http://eprint.iacr.org/2009/440
15. Thomae, E., Wolf, C.: Solving underdetermined systems of multivariate quadratic equations revisited. In: Fischlin, M., Buchmann, J., Manulis, M. (eds.) PKC 2012. LNCS, vol. 7293, pp. 156–171. Springer, Heidelberg (2012). https://doi.org/10.1007/978-3-642-30057-8_10

Symmetric Cryptography

A DFA Attack on White-Box Implementations of AES with External Encodings

Alessandro Amadori[1(✉)], Wil Michiels[1,2], and Peter Roelse[3]

[1] Department of Mathematics and Computer Science,
Eindhoven University of Technology, Eindhoven, The Netherlands
a.amadori@tue.nl
[2] NXP Semiconductors, Eindhoven, The Netherlands
wil.michiels@nxp.com
[3] Irdeto B.V., Hoofddorp, The Netherlands
peter.roelse@irdeto.com

Abstract. Attacks based on DFA are an important threat to the security of white-box AES implementations. DFA typically requires that the output of AES is known. The use of external encodings that obfuscate this output is therefore a straightforward and well-known measure against such attacks. This paper presents a new DFA attack on a class of white-box implementations of AES that use a specific type of external encoding on the output. The expected work factor of the new attack is dominated by 2^{32} executions of the white-box implementation.

Keywords: White-box cryptography · AES · Differential fault analysis

1 Introduction

In 2002, Chow et al. introduced the concept of white-box cryptography in [1]. White-box cryptography aims to protect the secret key of a cryptographic algorithm in a white-box environment. Such an environment assumes that the adversary has full access to the implementation of the algorithm and full control over its execution environment. For example, the adversary can execute the algorithm to inspect or modify intermediate results of the computations. To protect the secret key, white-box implementations obfuscate, or encode, the intermediate results of the algorithm during its computations. Nowadays, white-box implementations of cryptographic algorithms are widely used in practice, e.g. in payment applications and in digital rights management systems.

Attacks on white-box implementations can be divided into two types: algebraic attacks and Side Channel Analysis (SCA) attacks. The first type of attack exploits mathematical relations between encoded and non-encoded results of the cryptographic algorithm to reverse-engineer the encodings. A prominent example of an algebraic attack is the BGE attack on a white-box implementation of the

K. G. Paterson and D. Stebila (Eds.): SAC 2019, LNCS 11959, pp. 591–617, 2020.
https://doi.org/10.1007/978-3-030-38471-5_24

Advanced Encryption Standard (AES) [2]. The second type of attack exploits information leakage during the execution of the implementation, and includes attacks based on Differential Computation Analysis (DCA) [3] and Differential Fault Analysis (DFA) [4–6]. Compared to algebraic attacks, advantages of SCA attacks are that they require little to no understanding of the implementation and that they can easily be automated. SCA attacks are nowadays considered to be the main threat to the security of white-box implementations of cryptographic algorithms. The use of encodings on the input and the output of the algorithm is a well-known measure against SCA attacks since these attacks typically require access to either the input or the output of the algorithm.

This paper presents a new DFA attack on a class of white-box implementations of AES with a specific type of external encoding on its output, referred to as a byte external encoding. The attack combines DFA techniques with techniques from the BGE attack [2] to remove the external encoding and extract the AES key. The class of white-box implementations is defined by two assumptions on the encoding of the intermediate results of the AES computations. These two assumptions are, for instance, satisfied by the white-box AES implementations specified in [1,7,8]. The expected work factor of the new attack is dominated by 2^{32} executions of the white-box implementation. This shows that the use of a byte external encoding on the output will not offer an adequate level of security in itself for this class of white-box AES implementations.

This paper is structured as follows: Sect. 2 contains a short description of AES and presents the assumptions on the white-box AES implementation. The new attack is presented in Sect. 3 and conclusions can be found in Sect. 4.

2 Preliminaries

2.1 The Advanced Encryption Standard

AES is a block cipher that takes a 128-bit plaintext and a key as inputs to produce a 128-bit ciphertext. The key size is either 128, 192 or 256 bits. Without loss of generality, this paper assumes that a 128-bit key is used. An intermediate result of AES is referred to as a state and is represented as a 4×4 array of bytes. The bytes in a state u are defined as:

u_0	u_4	u_8	u_{12}
u_1	u_5	u_9	u_{13}
u_2	u_6	u_{10}	u_{14}
u_3	u_7	u_{11}	u_{15}

with $u_i \in \mathbb{F}_{2^8}$ for $i = 0, 1, \ldots, 15$. As in [9], an element of $\mathbb{F}_{2^8}$ is represented as a 2-digit hexadecimal number. Its binary equivalent corresponds to the polynomial representation of the field that uses $x^8 + x^4 + x^3 + x + 1 \in \mathbb{F}_2[x]$ as the irreducible polynomial. For details, the reader is referred to [9]. The state u is also denoted by $(u_0, u_1, \ldots, u_{15})$ in the following text. AES consists of 10 rounds, and each of the first 9 rounds of the encryption operation comprises the following four invertible operations on a state:

- **SubBytes** applies an invertible function $S : \mathbb{F}_{2^8} \rightarrow \mathbb{F}_{2^8}$, referred to as the AES S-box, to each byte of the state.
- **ShiftRows** cyclically shifts the second, third, and fourth row of the state. If u is defined as above, then after applying ShiftRows to u, the second, third, and fourth row of the new state equal (u_5, u_9, u_{13}, u_1), $(u_{10}, u_{14}, u_2, u_6)$ and $(u_{15}, u_3, u_7, u_{11})$, respectively. The ShiftRows operation is denoted by SR.
- **MixColumns** multiplies each column of the state with a 4×4 matrix over $\mathbb{F}_{2^8}$. The matrix is denoted by $\mathcal{MC}$ and is defined as:

$$\mathcal{MC} = \begin{pmatrix} 02 \ 03 \ 01 \ 01 \\ 01 \ 02 \ 03 \ 01 \\ 01 \ 01 \ 02 \ 03 \\ 03 \ 01 \ 01 \ 02 \end{pmatrix} .$$

- **AddRoundKey** adds each byte of the state to the corresponding byte of the AES round key; the round key bytes are derived from the 128-bit AES key using the AES key scheduling algorithm.

Before the first round, the AES key is added to the plaintext. The last round is similar to the first 9 rounds; the only difference is that the MixColumns operation is omitted in the last round. Note that the ShiftRow operation of the last round only re-orders the bytes of the ciphertext and does not affect their values. For ease of exposition, this operation will be omitted in the following text.

2.2   Assumptions

An external encoding is a function that is kept secret and that is applied to the plaintext (input) or to the ciphertext (output) of AES. In case of an input encoding, the inverse external encoding is merged with operations of the first round of the cipher in the implementation. In case of an output encoding, the external encoding is merged with operations of the final round of the cipher. Next, software obfuscation techniques [10, 11] are applied to protect the external encodings against reverse-engineering. This ensures that the plaintext and the ciphertext can be kept obfuscated in the white-box implementation. The use of external encodings is a measure against a range of attacks and was already proposed in [1]. In particular, as indicated in Sect. 1, the use of external encodings is a measure against SCA attacks since these attacks typically assume that the adversary has access to the plaintext or to the ciphertext. SCA attacks are considered to be the main threat to white-box implementations since they don't require any reverse-engineering effort.

The first assumption relates to the type of external encoding that is used on the output of the AES operation. Without loss of generality, this paper assumes throughout that the white-box implementation of the AES encryption operation is available to the adversary and that the value of the AES key k is fixed.

Assumption 1. *Let $E_i : \mathbb{F}_{2^8} \rightarrow \mathbb{F}_{2^8}$ be bijective functions, and let the bytes of the AES ciphertext C associated with plaintext P be denoted by c_i for*

$i = 0, 1, \ldots, 15$. *The output encoding* $E : \mathbb{F}_{2^{128}} \rightarrow \mathbb{F}_{2^{128}}$ *is defined as:* $E(C) = (E_0(c_0), E_1(c_1), \ldots, E_{15}(c_{15}))$.

In the following text, E is also referred to as a byte external encoding, and Enc_k is used to denote the algorithm implementing AES with external encodings and key k. Note that no assumption is made on the external encoding on the input; this encoding is discussed in Sect. 3.6. The reason for focusing on byte external encodings is two-fold. First, external encodings that operate on a byte level can be added to an AES implementation without a performance penalty. If the external encodings operate on a larger state then typically the implementation size increases; for example, in the implementation of Chow et al. [1] this increase is around 20%. Second, the analysis of the security offered by byte external encodings can be seen as a first step. A future research direction is to analyze the security offered by a more generic class of external encodings.

The white-box model assumes that the adversary has full control over the execution environment of the white-box AES implementation. In particular, the adversary can execute the implementation using different inputs and observe the corresponding outputs and all the intermediate results of the computations. In addition, the adversary can halt an execution at any point, modify one or more intermediate results, and then continue the execution. The functions that are used to hide, or obfuscate, the intermediate results of AES in a white-box implementation are referred to as internal encodings. The second assumption relates to the internal encodings of the white-box AES implementation. To describe the assumption, we define AES ciphertext $C_{r,i,j}^{\text{in}}$ as the ciphertext that is produced by AES for plaintext P when the value of the input byte to S-box i with $i = 0, 1, \ldots, 15$ of Round r with $r \in \{7, 8, 9\}$ is set to $j \in \mathbb{F}_{2^8}$, and we define $C_{r,i,j}^{\text{out}}$ accordingly with the value of the S-box output set to j. For instance, for plaintext P, the ciphertext $C_{9,0,05}^{\text{in}}$ is the "altered" ciphertext obtained by setting the input of the first S-box of Round 9 to the byte value 05 during the encryption of P. If the value of the input byte of S-box i of Round r is modified to any of its possible values $j \in \mathbb{F}_{2^8}$ during 2^8 executions of AES with output encoding E and plaintext P, then the resulting encoded ciphertexts are the 2^8 elements of the set $\{E(C_{r,i,j}^{\text{in}}) \mid j \in \mathbb{F}_{2^8}\}$. The 2^8 elements of $\{E(C_{r,i,j}^{\text{out}}) \mid j \in \mathbb{F}_{2^8}\}$ are produced as encoded ciphertexts if the value of the output byte of this S-box is modified instead of the value of its input byte.

In a white-box implementation, the intermediate results are encoded, and it depends on the type of encoding used if modifying one intermediate S-box input or output to all its 2^8 possible values without modifying any other intermediate result can be achieved by modifying the value of one encoded byte in the white-box implementation. Since our attack requires this property for all S-boxes of Rounds 7, 8, and 9, we need the following assumption on the internal encodings:

Assumption 2. *For each combination of* $i = 0, 1, \ldots, 15$ *and* $r \in \{7, 8, 9\}$, *there is a byte in the execution of the white-box implementation associated with* P, *referred to as an encoded byte, with the following property: if the value of the encoded byte is modified to any of its* 2^8 *possible values during* 2^8 *executions of* *the white-box implementation associated with P, then the implementation outputs all 2^8 elements of the set $\{E(C_{r,i,j}^{in}) \mid j \in \mathbb{F}_{2^8}\}$ or all 2^8 elements of the set $\{E(C_{r,i,j}^{out}) \mid j \in \mathbb{F}_{2^8}\}$.*

The assumption holds true for implementations based on the encoding-techniques of Chow et al. [1] since such implementations use bijective functions on $\mathbb{F}_2^8$ to encode the S-box inputs. However, Assumption 2 is not limited to such implementations. For example, the masking techniques proposed in [7,8,12] also satisfy Assumption 2. In masking, a value x is pseudo-randomly split into d shares $x_0, x_1, \ldots, x_{d-1}$ with $d \geq 2$, such that $x = x_0 \oplus x_1 \oplus \ldots \oplus x_{d-1}$. The attacker then needs all d shares to recover x. A white-box variant of this approach uses the input message as the seed for the pseudo-random number generator. The combination of such a scheme with bijective functions on $\mathbb{F}_{2^8}$ to encode the shares (or at least one share) is also covered by the assumption above.

The assumption does not hold true for the implementations presented in [13–15] since intermediate bytes of these implementations are either merged or split into bits. For example, the implementation in [13] considers the inputs of 2 parallel S-boxes, concatenates these values, and encodes the resulting 16-bit value to a 16-bit encoded value using a secret bijective function. Modifying one byte of such a 16-bit encoded value to any of its 2^8 possible values will generally not result in modifying exactly one non-encoded S-box input (or output) of the round to all its 2^8 possible values. Similar reasoning applies to the 32-bit encoded S-box outputs in this implementation. A drawback of the implementations in [13–15] is that merging intermediate bytes or splitting bytes into bits make the resulting implementation considerably slower or larger. In practice it may not be possible to use a larger or slower implementation because it does not satisfy the requirements of the application. For example, a speed of several Mbits/second is typically required for the decryption of a video stream.

Obviously, Assumption 2 may also not hold true if the white-box implementation contains one or more other measures against DFA attacks (i.e. in addition to using the output encoding defined in Assumption 1). For example, the implementation may contain a measure that can detect a modification of an encoded intermediate result and output a value that is not an element of either of the two sets in Assumption 2 if such a modification is detected. In fact, the implementation of additional measures against DFA attacks will typically be necessary to prevent our attack if a byte encoding is used on the output of AES.

Note that, in contrast to the setting assumed in the BGE attack [2], the location of a byte in Assumption 2 may vary depending on the value of the input. That is, if we construct a collection of computational traces containing the memory addresses accessed during executions, as is for instance done in [3], then these traces do not need to be aligned.

Although Assumption 2 implies the existence of an encoded byte, it does not present a way to find one. To this end, consider an encoded byte that is associated with an S-box input or output of Round 9. It follows from the definition of the AES MixColumns operation that there is a bijection between this encoded byte and any of the four bytes in one of the output columns, while the values of the bytes in the other three output columns remain constant. The third assumption uses this property to find encoded bytes. To describe the assumption, we choose an AES plaintext P, and we denote the output of AES Round $r + 1$ with $r \in \{7, 8, 9\}$ by $x^{(r+1)}$. Further, let $E^{(r+1)}(x^{(r+1)})$ be a byte encoded version of $x^{(r+1)}$. We choose $E^{(10)} = E$ (see also Assumption 1), and we will derive byte encoded functions $E^{(8)}$ and $E^{(9)}$ during the attack. Finally, if we assign all possible values to an encoded byte at location ℓ_i in the white-box execution, then we define $V_i^{(r+1)}$ as the set of byte-encoded outputs of Round $r + 1$.

Assumption 3. *A first encoded byte associated with an S-box in Round r with $r \in \{7, 8, 9\}$ can be found by searching for the earliest location ℓ_0 in the execution satisfying the following condition: there is a bijective relation between the byte values at ℓ_0 and the values of each of the four bytes in a single column of $E^{(r+1)}(x^{(r+1)})$, while the values of the bytes of the other three columns of $E^{(r+1)}(x^{(r+1)})$ remain constant. Next, an encoded byte can be found for the other 15 S-boxes in Round r by executing the following step for $i = 1, 2, \ldots, 15$: find the earliest location ℓ_i after ℓ_{i-1} that satisfies the above-mentioned condition on the columns of $E^{(r+1)}(x^{(r+1)})$ for ℓ_i instead of ℓ_0 and for which $|V_i^{(r+1)} \cap V_j^{(r+1)}| = 1$ for $j = 0, 1, \ldots, i - 1$.*

The first part of the assumption indicates that the above-mentioned property of having bijective relations between an encoded byte and any of the 4 bytes in the associated output column is a valid check on whether we are changing an S-box input or output. The second part of the assumption indicates that, by using this property, we can also find the input or output bytes that are associated with the other 15 S-boxes of the round; the condition $|V_i^{(r+1)} \cap V_j^{(r+1)}| = 1$ is added to check if a new S-box is targeted. The implementations in [1, 7, 8, 12] also satisfy Assumption 3. This assumption also does not assume that computational traces are aligned.

3 The New Attack

3.1 Overview of the Attack

The attack is structured in 5 steps and it combines DFA techniques with techniques from the BGE attack [2]. Step 1 of the attack pre-computes sets of inputs to the white-box implementation. Step 2 uses these sets as inputs to a fault attack to derive the output of AES Round 9 up to 15 unknown affine bijections on $\mathbb{F}_2^8$, instead of the general byte bijections E_i for $i = 0, 1, \ldots, 15$ on the output of Round 10. In this step, we apply a fundamental theorem used in the BGE attack to the set of faulty output values to obtain the output of Round 9 encoded by affine functions over $\mathbb{F}_2^8$. In Step 3 we inject additional faults and apply other techniques from the BGE attack to further reduce this to 16 unknown affine bijections on $\mathbb{F}_{2^8}$. Step 4 uses fault injections to derive the non-encoded output of the SubBytes operation of Round 9. After this, a standard DFA attack is applied in Step 5 to extract the AES key. The 5 steps are detailed in the next sections, and the work factor of each step and the overall work factor are presented in Appendix C. In particular, the appendix shows that the overall work factor is dominated by 2^{32} executions of the white-box implementation in Step 1 of the attack.

3.2   Step 1: Pre-compute Sets of Inputs

Let m_{ref} be an arbitrary, fixed input to the white-box implementation. In order to find the output of Round 9 up to an affine bijection on $\mathbb{F}_2^8$ in Step 2 of the attack, we need to find sets $\mathcal{M}_i$ for $i = 0, 1, \ldots, 15$, each $\mathcal{M}_i$ consisting of 256 inputs to the white-box implementation with the following two properties: (1) $m_{\text{ref}} \in \mathcal{M}_i$ and (2) if we apply Enc_k to all elements from $\mathcal{M}_i$, then the value of output byte i is unique for each $m \in \mathcal{M}_i$ while the values of two other bytes in the same column of the output's state remain constant. In the following text, we assume that the indices of this other two bytes have been selected for every value of i. We denote these two indices by $r(i)$ and $s(i)$.

Algorithm 1 describes how the set $\mathcal{M}_i$ is computed. The inputs to the algorithm are m_{ref}, i, $Enc_k(m_{\text{ref}})$, and the set of all possible inputs to Enc_k, denoted by $\mathcal{M}$. In the description, selecting a random element of $\mathcal{M}$ is denoted by $\xleftarrow{\$} \mathcal{M}$.

Algorithm 1. Compute $\mathcal{M}_i$

> **Input** : m_{ref}, i, $Enc_k(m_{\text{ref}})$, and $\mathcal{M}$.
> **Output:** $\mathcal{M}_i$.
> $\mathcal{M}_i \leftarrow \{m_{\text{ref}}\}$;
> $x = (x_0, x_1, \ldots, x_{15}) \leftarrow Enc_k(m_{\text{ref}})$;
> $B_i \leftarrow \{x_i\}$;
> **while** $|\mathcal{M}_i| < 256$ **do**
> $\quad \overline{m} \xleftarrow{\$} \mathcal{M}$;
> $\quad \overline{x} = (\overline{x}_0, \overline{x}_1, \ldots, \overline{x}_{15}) \leftarrow Enc_k(\overline{m})$;
> $\quad$ **if** $\overline{x}_i \notin B_i \wedge \overline{x}_{r(i)} = x_{r(i)} \wedge \overline{x}_{s(i)} = x_{s(i)}$ **then**
> $\quad\quad B_i \leftarrow B_i \cup \{\overline{x}_i\}$;
> $\quad\quad \mathcal{M}_i \leftarrow \mathcal{M}_i \cup \{\overline{m}\}$;
> $\quad$ **else**
> $\quad$ **end**
> **end**
> **return** $\mathcal{M}_i$

The following text assumes without loss of generality that $i = 0$, $r(0) = 1$ and $s(0) = 2$. This attack on the first output byte can then be applied to each of the other 15 output bytes by adapting the value of i accordingly.

3.3   Step 2: Determine a State up to Affine Functions

Step 2 derives the output of Round 9 up to 16 unknown affine bijections on $\mathbb{F}_2^8$ from the encoded output of Round 10. Figure 1 depicts the last two rounds of Enc_k. The 16 round key bytes of Round j are denoted by $k_i^{(j)}$ for $i = 0, 1, \ldots, 15$ and $j = 9, 10$ in the figure. As indicated before, the ShiftRows operation of the final round is omitted. Step 2 starts in the same way as a standard DFA attack. That is, the attacker injects a fault in an execution by modifying an encoded byte, targeting the input or the output of an S-box in Round 9. A proper location is found as described in Assumption 3.

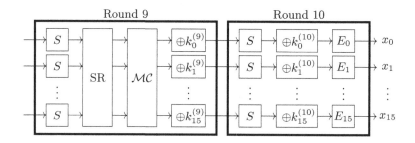

Fig. 1. Last 2 rounds of Enc_k.

We now assume that we inject a fault in the input or output byte of the first S-box operation in Round 9 and we will use this to derive the encodings on the bytes in the first output column. The approach can easily be adapted to the input or output of any of the other S-boxes and the corresponding output column. Let x_0, x_1, x_2, x_3 be the four bytes in the first column of $Enc_k(m_{\mathrm{ref}})$ and let X_0, X_1, X_2 and X_3 be the corresponding faulty bytes. Similar to a standard DFA, we can set up the following three equations:

$$S^{-1}(E_0^{-1}(x_0) \oplus k_0^{(10)}) \oplus S^{-1}(E_0^{-1}(X_0) \oplus k_0^{(10)}) = \\ 02(S^{-1}(E_1^{-1}(x_1) \oplus k_1^{(10)}) \oplus S^{-1}(E_1^{-1}(X_1) \oplus k_1^{(10)})), \tag{1}$$

$$S^{-1}(E_2^{-1}(x_2) \oplus k_2^{(10)}) \oplus S^{-1}(E_2^{-1}(X_2) \oplus k_2^{(10)}) = \\ S^{-1}(E_1^{-1}(x_1) \oplus k_1^{(10)}) \oplus S^{-1}(E_1(X_1) \oplus k_1^{(10)}), \tag{2}$$

$$S^{-1}(E_3^{-1}(x_3) \oplus k_3^{(10)}) \oplus S^{-1}(E_3^{-1}(X_3) \oplus k_3^{(10)}) = \\ 03(S^{-1}(E_1^{-1}(x_1) \oplus k_1^{(10)}) \oplus S^{-1}(E_1^{-1}(X_1) \oplus k_1^{(10)})). \tag{3}$$

Define $g_i^{-1}(x_i) = S^{-1}(E_i^{-1}(x_i) \oplus k_i^{(10)})$ for $i = 0, 1, 2, 3$. Note that $g_i^{-1}(x_i)$ equals the i-th output byte of Round 9 or, equivalently, the i-th input byte of Round 10. Equation 1 can now be written as:

$$g_0^{-1}(x_0) \oplus g_0^{-1}(X_0) = 02(g_1^{-1}(x_1) \oplus g_1^{-1}(X_1)),$$

or, by isolating X_0, as:

$$X_0 = g_0 \left(g_0^{-1}(x_0) \oplus 02(g_1^{-1}(x_1) \oplus g_1^{-1}(X_1)) \right). \tag{4}$$

We now define:

$$h_{g_j,x_j}^{\mu}(X_j) = \mu \left(g_j^{-1}(x_j) \oplus g_j^{-1}(X_j) \right). \tag{5}$$

with $\mu \in \{01, 02, 03\}$. Substituting this in Eq. 4 yields:

$$X_0 = g_0 \left(g_0^{-1}(x_0) \oplus h_{g_1,x_1}^{02}(X_1) \right). \tag{6}$$

Before proceeding with Eq. 6, we first recall a theorem from [2]. In the following text, $\circ$ denotes a composition of two functions, and $\oplus_a : \mathbb{F}_2^n \to \mathbb{F}_2^n$ with $a \in \mathbb{F}_2^n$ is defined as $\oplus_a(x) = x \oplus a$.

Theorem 1 ([2]). *Given a set of functions $\mathcal{S}_Q = \{Q \circ \oplus_\beta \circ Q^{-1}\}_{\beta \in \mathbb{F}_2^n}$, each defined by a look-up table, where Q is a permutation on $\mathbb{F}_2^n$, it is possible to construct a particular function $\tilde{Q}$ such that there exists an affine mapping A over $\mathbb{F}_2^n$ such that $\tilde{Q} = Q \circ A^{-1}$.*

Consider Eq. 6 with $Q = g_0$ and $\beta = h_{g_1,x_1}^{02}(X_1)$. Note that h_{g_1,x_1}^{02} is a bijective function (see also Eq. 5); however, the definition of h_{g_1,x_1}^{02} assumes that x_1 is constant. This means that all outputs of the functions in $\mathcal{S}_{g_0}$ can be generated by ranging x_0 and X_1 over all possible values, under the condition that x_1 is constant. Recall from Sect. 3.2 that the value of x_1 is constant and that the value of x_0 is unique for every $m \in \mathcal{M}_0$. Now suppose that, for each $m \in \mathcal{M}_0$, we can locate the encoded byte in the execution that is associated with the input or output of the first S-box of Round 9. Since there are bijective relations between this first S-box input or output and the first as well as the second output byte of the considered column, it follows that for any $m \in \mathcal{M}_0$, we can modify the value of this encoded byte during the execution of the white-box implementation with m as input to obtain all possible values of X_0 and X_1 associated with m. The functions in $\mathcal{S}_{g_0}$, defined by look-up tables, can now be obtained by repeating this step for every $m \in \mathcal{M}_0$ since x_1 is constant for all these elements.

Next, Theorem 1 implies that we can find a $\tilde{g}_0$ for which there exists an unknown affine bijective function A_0 on $\mathbb{F}_2^8$ such that $\tilde{g}_0 = g_0 \circ A_0^{-1}$. Finally, we can apply $\tilde{g}_0^{-1}$ to x_0 to obtain the first output byte of Round 9, encoded by A_0. The problem of Step 2 is now reduced to finding the location of the encoded byte for all $m \in \mathcal{M}_0$. This problem is addressed in Appendix A. Recall that we assumed that the first S-box of Round 9 was targeted. However, in practice we may also have targeted one of the three other S-boxes associated with the same MixColumns operation (see also Assumption 3). Lemma 3 in Appendix A shows that targeting one of these S-boxes would still yield the correct result.

The functions $\tilde{g}_i$ for $i = 1, 2, \ldots, 15$ can be computed in a similar way, taking the set $\mathcal{M}_i$ as input. Algorithm 2 describes Step 2 of the attack in pseudo-code, assuming that Tolhuizen's algorithm [16] is used to compute $\tilde{g}_i$ from $\mathcal{S}_{g_i}$.

Algorithm 2. Determine $\tilde{g}_i$

Input : i, $\mathcal{M}_i$, and Enc_k.
Output: $\tilde{g}_i$.
$\mathcal{S}[256][256] \leftarrow [[\,],[\,],\ldots,[\,]]$;

$m \xleftarrow{\$} \mathcal{M}_i$;
$x = (x_0, x_1, \ldots, x_{15}) \leftarrow Enc_k(m)$;
$\mathcal{S}[x_{r(i)}][x_i] \leftarrow x_i$;
for $\forall \varepsilon \in \mathbb{F}_{2^8}^*$ **do**
  $\quad X^\varepsilon \xleftarrow{\varepsilon} Enc_k(m)$ (Inject a fault ε during the encryption of m);
  $\quad \mathcal{S}[X_{r(i)}][x_i] \leftarrow X_i$;
  $\quad$ Store $(X_{r(i)}, X_{s(i)})$;
end
for $\forall \overline{m} \in \mathcal{M}_i \setminus \{m\}$ **do**
  $\quad \overline{x} = (\overline{x}_0, \overline{x}_1, \ldots, \overline{x}_{15}) \leftarrow Enc_k(\overline{m})$;
  $\quad \mathcal{S}[\overline{x}_{r(i)}][\overline{x}_i] \leftarrow \overline{x}_i$;
  $\quad$ **for** $\forall \varepsilon \in \mathbb{F}_{2^8}^*$ **do**
  $\quad\quad \overline{X}^\varepsilon \xleftarrow{\varepsilon} Enc_k(\overline{m})$;
  $\quad\quad$ **if** $\exists (X_{r(i)}, X_{s(i)})$ *such that* $X_{r(i)} = \overline{X}_{r(i)} \wedge X_{s(i)} = \overline{X}_{s(i)}$ **then**
  $\quad\quad\quad \mathcal{S}[\overline{X}_{r(i)}][\overline{x}_i] \leftarrow \overline{X}_i$;
  $\quad\quad$ **else**
  $\quad\quad\quad$ Choose another location to inject;
  $\quad\quad$ **end**
  $\quad$ **end**
end
return $\tilde{g}_i \leftarrow$ Tolhuizen's Algorithm($\mathcal{S}$)

3.4 Step 3: From Functions over $\mathbb{F}_2^8$ to Functions over $\mathbb{F}_{2^8}$

We denote the output bytes of Round 9 associated with x_i by y_i for $i = 0, 1, \ldots, 15$. After Step 2, we have access to $\tilde{x}_i = A_i(y_i) = \tilde{g}_i^{-1}(x_i)$ (see also Fig. 2). In the third step of the attack, we reduce this unknown affine encoding over $\mathbb{F}_2^8$ to an unknown affine encoding over $\mathbb{F}_{2^8}$. Hence, the linear part of the function is reduced to a scalar multiplication in $\mathbb{F}_{2^8}$. In the following text, we focus without loss of generality on the first output column of Round 9. In addition, for $i = 0, 1, 2, 3$, we represent A_i by an invertible matrix $G_i \in \mathbb{F}_2^{8 \times 8}$ and a vector $b_i \in \mathbb{F}_2^8$ such that $A_i(x) = G_i x \oplus b_i$ for all $x \in \mathbb{F}_2^8$. It follows that $y_i = G_i^{-1}(\tilde{x}_i \oplus b_i)$.

As in Step 2, consider a fault that has been injected at the input or output of the first S-box in Round 9. As before, for an element of $\mathcal{M}_0$, we denote the output values of a correct execution by $\tilde{x}_i$ for $i = 0, 1, 2, 3$ and the corresponding output bytes of the faulty execution by $\tilde{X}_i$. DFA now gives the following three relations:

$$02(G_1^{-1}(\tilde{x}_1 \oplus \tilde{X}_1)) = G_0^{-1}(\tilde{x}_0 \oplus \tilde{X}_0), \tag{7}$$

$$02(G_2^{-1}(\tilde{x}_2 \oplus \tilde{X}_2)) = G_0^{-1}(\tilde{x}_0 \oplus \tilde{X}_0), \tag{8}$$

$$02(G_3^{-1}(\tilde{x}_3 \oplus \tilde{X}_3)) = 03(G_0^{-1}(\tilde{x}_0 \oplus \tilde{X}_0)). \tag{9}$$

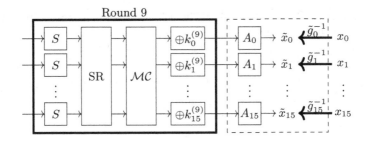

Fig. 2. Affine functions over $\mathbb{F}_2^8$ at the end of Round 9.

We now first recall a result from [2]:

Proposition 1 ([2]). *Given an element $\gamma \in \mathbb{F}_{2^8}$ that is not in any subfield of $\mathbb{F}_{2^8}$ and a linear function $L = M \circ \otimes_\gamma \circ M^{-1}$ over $\mathbb{F}_2^8$, with all functions being represented by invertible matrices, we can compute in less than 2^{16} steps, a function $\overline{M}$ represented by a matrix in $\mathbb{F}_2^{8 \times 8}$, such that there exists a unique non-zero constant $\lambda \in \mathbb{F}_{2^8}$ with $\overline{M} = M \circ \otimes_\lambda^{-1}$.*

Proposition 1 states that we can achieve the objective of this step of the attack if we can construct a function $L_{\gamma,i}$ defined as $L_{\gamma,i} = G_i \circ \otimes_\gamma \circ G_i^{-1}$ for which we know the value of γ. First, we rewrite Eqs. 7, 8 and 9 as:

$$\tilde{x}_1 \oplus \tilde{X}_1 = G_1 \circ \otimes_{02^{-1}} \circ G_0^{-1}(\tilde{x}_0 \oplus \tilde{X}_0), \tag{10}$$

$$\tilde{x}_2 \oplus \tilde{X}_2 = G_2 \circ \otimes_{02^{-1}} \circ G_0^{-1}(\tilde{x}_0 \oplus \tilde{X}_0), \tag{11}$$

$$\tilde{x}_3 \oplus \tilde{X}_3 = G_3 \circ \otimes_{02^{-1}.03} \circ G_0^{-1}(\tilde{x}_0 \oplus \tilde{X}_0). \tag{12}$$

In Step 2 of the attack, we changed the input or output of the first S-box to all its 256 possible values. These faults all result in a different value of X_0, and thus also in a different value of $\tilde{X}_0$ (see also Fig. 2). Since the value of x_0, and consequently, the value of $\tilde{x}_0$ are fixed, we can construct look-up table representations of the three functions $G_1 \circ \otimes_{02^{-1}} \circ G_0^{-1}$, $G_2 \circ \otimes_{02^{-1}} \circ G_0^{-1}$ and $G_3 \circ \otimes_{02^{-1}.03} \circ G_0^{-1}$.

Let the 4 S-boxes of Round 9 that influence the output column we are targeting be numbered from 0 to 3. Suppose now that we affected an S-box input or output with number $\ell_0 \in \{0, 1, 2, 3\}$. Using the same fault-injection results, we can rearrange the terms in Eqs. 10, 11 and 12 to construct look-up table representations of

$$G_j \circ \otimes_{\gamma_{i,j}^{(\ell_0)}} \circ G_i^{-1} \tag{13}$$

for all $i, j = 0, 1, 2, 3$ with $i \neq j$, where $\gamma_{i,j}^{(\ell_0)} = \mathcal{MC}_{j,\ell_0} \cdot (\mathcal{MC}_{i,\ell_0})^{-1}$. In other words, we are rewriting Eqs. 10, 11 and 12 with respect to any pair of indices. It follows that $\gamma_{i,j}^{(\ell_0)} \in \Lambda = \{01, 02, 03, 02^{-1}, 03^{-1}, 02^{-1}03, 03^{-1}02\}$. With this notation, $\gamma_{i,j}^{(0)}$, $\gamma_{i,j}^{(1)}$, $\gamma_{i,j}^{(2)}$ and $\gamma_{i,j}^{(3)}$ are the coefficients occurring in Eq. 13 using fault injections to affect the first, second, third and fourth S-box in the same column, respectively. Additionally, from Eq. 13, we define the set

$\Lambda_{i,j} = \{\gamma_{i,j}^{(\ell_0)} | \ \ell_0 \in \{0,1,2,3\}\} \subset \Lambda$ as the set of all coefficients occurring in the mappings from byte i to byte j.

As in the example for $i = 0$ above, we also have the generic case in which $G_j \circ \otimes_{\gamma_{i,j}^{(\ell_0)}} \circ G_i^{-1}$ defines the mapping between $\tilde{x}_i \oplus \tilde{X}_i$ and $\tilde{x}_j \oplus \tilde{X}_j$. Hence, we get look-up table representations of the elements of the following family of linear functions:

$$\mathcal{F}^{(\ell_0)} = \{w_{i,j}^{(\ell_0)} \mid w_{i,j}^{(\ell_0)} = G_j \circ \otimes_{\gamma_{i,j}^{(\ell_0)}} \circ G_i^{-1} \wedge j \in \left[4\lfloor\frac{i}{4}\rfloor, 4\lfloor\frac{i}{4}\rfloor + 3\right] \wedge i \neq j\}.$$

In order to apply Proposition 1, we need a function as in Eq. 13 with $i = j$, i.e. we need to derive, for some γ_i:

$$L_{\gamma_i,i} = G_i \circ \otimes_{\gamma_i} \circ G_i^{-1}. \tag{14}$$

However, no function in $\mathcal{F}^{(\ell_0)}$ occurs in this form. To this end, we derive a second family of linear functions. Using the same input as for $\mathcal{F}^{(\ell_0)}$, we target an S-box with number ℓ_1 that is different from the S-box we targeted for $\mathcal{F}^{(\ell_0)}$, i.e., $\ell_0 \neq \ell_1$, but which contributes to the same output column. We can now construct the second family of linear functions $\mathcal{F}^{(\ell_1)}$, analogously as for $\mathcal{F}^{(\ell_0)}$, in the form of Eq. 13 in which $\gamma_{i,j}^{(\ell_1)}$ is an element from Λ, meaning that $\gamma_{i,j}^{(\ell_1)}$ is also derived from two MixColumns coefficients. Next, we select two indices i and j such that $|i - j| \neq 2$, consider $w_{i,j}^{(\ell_0)} \in \mathcal{F}^{(\ell_0)}$ and $w_{i,j}^{(\ell_1)} \in \mathcal{F}^{(\ell_1)}$ and define

$$L_{\gamma_i,i}^{(j,\ell_0,\ell_1)} = \left(w_{i,j}^{(\ell_1)}\right)^{-1} \circ w_{i,j}^{(\ell_0)} = G_i \circ \otimes_{\gamma_i^{(j,\ell_0,\ell_1)}} \circ G_i^{-1} \tag{15}$$

with $\gamma_i^{(j,\ell_0,\ell_1)} = \gamma_{i,j}^{(\ell_0)} \cdot \left(\gamma_{i,j}^{(\ell_1)}\right)^{-1}$. In order to apply Proposition 1, we need to show that $\gamma_i^{(j,\ell_0,\ell_1)}$ is not in any sub-field of $\mathbb{F}_{2^8}$ and we need an algorithm for deriving the value of $\gamma_i^{(j,\ell_0,\ell_1)}$ from the function $L_{\gamma_i,i}^{(j,\ell_0,\ell_1)}$. To achieve these goals we introduce the following lemma.

Lemma 1. *Let $\mathcal{F}^{(\ell_0)}$ and $\mathcal{F}^{(\ell_1)}$ be two families of functions as defined above, constructed by targeting the input or output of two different S-boxes ℓ_0 and ℓ_1 that target the same output column. Let $i \in \{0,1,\ldots,15\}$ and $j \in [4\lfloor\frac{i}{4}\rfloor, 4\lfloor\frac{i}{4}\rfloor + 3]$ with $i \neq j$, and let $L_{\gamma_i,i}^{(j,\ell_0,\ell_1)} = \left(w_{i,j}^{(\ell_1)}\right)^{-1} \circ w_{i,j}^{(\ell_0)} = G_i \circ \otimes_{\gamma_i^{(j,\ell_0,\ell_1)}} \circ G_i^{-1}$ with $\gamma_i^{(j,\ell_0\ell_1)} = \gamma_{i,j}^{(\ell_0)} \cdot \left(\gamma_{i,j}^{(\ell_1)}\right)^{-1}$, $w_{i,j}^{(\ell_0)} \in \mathcal{F}^{(\ell_0)}, w_{i,j}^{(\ell_1)} \in \mathcal{F}^{(\ell_1)}$ and $\gamma_{i,j}^{(\ell_0)}, \gamma_{i,j}^{(\ell_1)} \in \Lambda_{i,j}$. Then, the following statements are true for $\gamma_i^{(j,\ell_0\ell_1)} \in \Gamma_{i,j}$ with $\Gamma_{i,j} =$*

$$\left\{\gamma_{i,j}^{(\ell_0)} \cdot \left(\gamma_{i,j}^{(\ell_1)}\right)^{-1} \mid \ell_0, \ell_1 \in \{0,1,2,3\} \wedge \ell_0 \neq \ell_1 \wedge \gamma_{i,j}^{(\ell_0)}, \gamma_{i,j}^{(\ell_1)} \in \Lambda_{i,j}\right\}$$

1. $\gamma_i^{(j,\ell_0,\ell_1)}$ *is not in any sub-field of $\mathbb{F}_{2^8}$.*
2. *If $|i-j| \neq 2$, then $\left(\gamma_i^{(j,\ell_0\ell_1)}\right)^{2^k} \in \Gamma_{i,j}$ with $k = 0,1,\ldots,7$ if and only if $k = 0$.*

3. If $|i - j| \neq 2$, then there exists a unique pair $(\gamma_{i,j}^{(\ell_0)}, \gamma_{i,j}^{(\ell_1)}) \in \Lambda_{i,j}^2$ such that
$$\gamma_i^{(j,\ell_0,\ell_1)} = \gamma_{i,j}^{(\ell_0)} \cdot \left(\gamma_{i,j}^{(\ell_1)}\right)^{-1}.$$

Proof. Choose $i \in \{0, 1, \ldots, 15\}$ and $j \in \left[4\lfloor\frac{i}{4}\rfloor, 4\lfloor\frac{i}{4}\rfloor + 3\right]$ with $i \neq j$. Using that the set $\Lambda_{i,j}$ in the definition of $\Gamma_{i,j}$ is defined by $\Lambda_{i,j} = \{\gamma_{i,j}^{(\ell)}| \gamma_{i,j}^{(\ell)} = \mathcal{MC}_{j,\ell} \cdot (\mathcal{MC}_{i,\ell})^{-1} \wedge \ell \in \{0, 1, 2, 3\}\}$ and by using the definition of the MixColumn matrix, one can verify that every element in $\Gamma_{i,j}$ has an order larger than 2^4, from which Statement 1 follows.

Next, consider statement 2. If $|i - j| \neq 2$, then it can be verified that all conjugates of an element from $\Gamma_{i,j}$ are not in that set, which is what the statement claims.

Lastly, we prove 3 for $i = 0$ and $j = 1$ (the proof is analogous for any other pair of values i, j satisfying $|i - j| \neq 2$). Consider the set $\Lambda_{0,1}$, which consists of the elements $\gamma_{0,1}^{(0)} = 02^{-1}$, $\gamma_{0,1}^{(1)} = 02 \cdot 03^{-1}$, $\gamma_{0,1}^{(02)} = 03$ and $\gamma_{0,1}^{(3)} = 01$. Since the elements in $\Gamma_{0,1}$ are obtained by multiplying an element from $\Lambda_{0,1}$ with the inverse of a different element from $\Lambda_{0,1}$, the set $\Gamma_{0,1}$ consists of at most $|\Lambda_{0,1}| \cdot (|\Lambda_{0,1}| - 1) = 12$ elements. Hence, if $\Gamma_{0,1}$ contains exactly 12 elements, then the pair of elements from $\Lambda_{0,1}$ that need to be multiplied to get a given element from $\Gamma_{0,1}$ is unique. For $\Gamma_{0,1}$ this is the case as it can be verified that it consists of the following 12 distinct elements: $02^{-2} \cdot 03, 02^{-1} \cdot 03^{-1}, 02^{-1}, 02 \cdot 03^{-2}, 02 \cdot 03^{-1}, 03, 02^2 \cdot 03^{-1}, 02 \cdot 03, 02, 02^{-1}03^2, 02^{-1} \cdot 03, 03^{-1}$. It is easy to check that only if $|i - j| = 2$, which case is excluded in statement 3, we have that $|\Gamma_{i,j}| < 12$. □

We will now show how an attacker can determine the value of γ_i from the function $L_{\gamma_i,i}$. The reasoning is obtained from Sect. 3.3 of [2]. After the attacker has constructed the function $L_{\gamma_i,i}^{(j,\ell_0,\ell_1)}$ for i, j with $|i - j| \neq 2$, he can compute $\gamma_i^{(j,\ell_0,\ell_1)}$ by checking the eigenvalues of $L_{\gamma_i,i}^{(j,\ell_0,\ell_1)}$, as we will now show. One of them is exactly the sought coefficient $\gamma_i^{(j,\ell_0,\ell_1)}$. Matrices $\otimes_{\gamma_i^{(j,\ell_0,\ell_1)}}$ and $L_{\gamma_i,i}^{(j,\ell_0,\ell_1)}$ are so-called similar matrices, which means that they share the same eigenvalues. In particular, those eigenvalues are exactly

$$\gamma_i^{(j,\ell_0,\ell_1)}, \left(\gamma_i^{(j,\ell_0,\ell_1)}\right)^2, \left(\gamma_i^{(j,\ell_0,\ell_1)}\right)^{2^2}, \ldots, \left(\gamma_i^{(j,\ell_0,\ell_1)}\right)^{2^7} \quad (16)$$

because $\gamma_i^{(j,\ell_0,\ell_1)}$ is a root of the characteristic polynomial of $\otimes_{\gamma_i^{(j,\ell_0,\ell_1)}}$ by Cayley-Hamilton's theorem and because of Theorem 2.14 from [17], the other values in Eq. 16 are the remaining roots of the characteristic polynomial. The attacker has now eight candidates for $\gamma_i^{(j,\ell_0,\ell_1)}$. However, due to 2 of Lemma 1, there is only one value which can be constructed from combining two different families $\mathcal{F}^{(\ell_0)}$ and $\mathcal{F}^{(\ell_1)}$ after having fixed the indices i and j with $|i - j| \neq 2$. We have now constructed the function $L_{\gamma_i,i}^{(j,\ell_0,\ell_1)}$ and computed the value $\gamma_i^{(j,\ell_0,\ell_1)}$, so we can now apply Proposition 1.

By applying Proposition 1 to $L_{\gamma_i,i}^{(j,\ell_0,\ell_1)} = G_i \circ \otimes_{\gamma_i^{(j,\ell_0,\ell_1)}} \circ G_i^{-1}$ with $|i-j| \neq 2$, we can construct a matrix $\overline{G}_i$ such that $\overline{G}_i = G_i \circ \otimes_{\lambda_i^{-1}}$, where the value of $\lambda_i \in \mathbb{F}_{2^8}^*$ is unknown. We only need $L_{\gamma_i,i}^{(j,\ell_0,\ell_1)}$ for one choice of j. We take $j = i+1$. Concerning the encoding A_i, if we apply $\overline{G}_i^{-1}$ to $\tilde{x}_i = A_i(y_i)$, we get $\hat{x}_i = \lambda_i y_i \oplus \hat{b}_i$, where $\hat{x}_i = \overline{G}_i^{-1}(\tilde{x}_i)$ and $\hat{b}_i = \overline{G}_i^{-1}(b_i)$. This results in 32 unknown values: the values of λ_i and $\hat{b}_i$ for $i = 0, 1, \ldots, 15$. In Appendix B we show how to reduce the number of unknown λ_i's to 4 (i.e. to one per column). Algorithm 3 describes an algorithm that performs Step 3.

Algorithm 3. Determine $\overline{G}_i$

Input   : $\tilde{g} \circ Enc_k$, the set of the coefficients Γ as in Lemma 1, indices i, j
          associated with the same column.

Output: $\overline{G}_i$.

$w_{i,j} \leftarrow [\ ];$

$\overline{w}_{i,j} \leftarrow [\ ];$

$m \xleftarrow{\$} \mathcal{M};$

$\tilde{x} = (\tilde{x}_0, \tilde{x}_1, \ldots, \tilde{x}_{15}) \leftarrow \tilde{g}^{-1} \circ Enc_k(m);$

for $\forall \varepsilon \in \mathbb{F}_{2^8}^*$ **do**

  $\hat{X}^\varepsilon \xleftarrow{\varepsilon} \tilde{g}^{-1} \circ Enc_k(m);$

  $w_{i,j}[\tilde{x}_i \oplus \hat{X}_i] \leftarrow \tilde{x}_j \oplus \hat{X}_j;$

end

for $\forall \overline{\varepsilon} \in \mathbb{F}_{2^8}^*$ **do**

  $\overline{X}^{\overline{\varepsilon}} \xleftarrow{\overline{\varepsilon}} \tilde{g}^{-1} \circ Enc_k(m);$

  $\overline{w}_{i,j}[\tilde{x}_i \oplus \overline{X}_i] \leftarrow \tilde{x}_j \oplus \overline{X}_j;$

end

$L_{\gamma_i,i} \leftarrow \overline{w}_{i,j}^{-1} \circ w_{i,j};$

if Eigenvalues$(L_{\gamma_i,i}) = \{\gamma_i, \gamma_i^2, \ldots, \gamma_i^{2^7}\} \wedge (\gamma_i$ *satisfies Lemma 1*) **then**

  return $\overline{G}_i \leftarrow$ a function $\overline{G}_i$ such that $L_{\gamma_i,i} = \overline{G}_i \circ \otimes_{\gamma_i} \circ \overline{G}_i^{-1}$;

else

  Choose another location to inject faults

end

3.5   Step 4: Determine a Non-encoded State

This section describes how the affine functions over $\mathbb{F}_{2^8}$, encoding the output of Round 9, can be retrieved by injecting faults. As shown in Fig. 3, these functions are denoted by q_i for $i = 0, 1, \ldots, 15$. If y_i denotes the i-th output byte of Round 9 for $i = 0, 1, \ldots, 15$, then from the reduction in Appendix B it follows that $y_i = q_i^{-1}(\hat{x}_i) = c_i \lambda_{4\lfloor \frac{i}{4} \rfloor}^{-1}(\hat{x}_i \oplus \hat{b}_i)$ in which the values of $c_i \in \mathbb{F}_{2^8}^*$ are known and in which the values of $\lambda_{4\lfloor \frac{i}{4} \rfloor}^{-1} \in \mathbb{F}_{2^8}^*$ and $\hat{b}_i \in \mathbb{F}_{2^8}$ are unknown. We now show

how these values can be derived by injecting faults at the beginning of Round 8 and by setting up a system of equations. As before, we will consider the first column of the AES state in the descriptions.

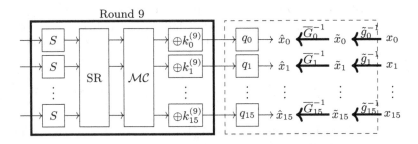

Fig. 3. Affine functions over $\mathbb{F}_{2^8}$ at the end of Round 9.

Consider the encoded Round 9 output $\hat{x} = (\hat{x}_0, \hat{x}_1, \ldots, \hat{x}_{15})$ as given in Eq. 26. If $k_i^{(9)}$ denotes the i-th round key byte as depicted in Fig. 3, and if $\underline{b}_i = c_i \lambda_{4\lfloor\frac{i}{4}\rfloor}^{-1} \hat{b}_i \oplus k_i^{(9)}$ for $i = 0, 1, \ldots, 15$, then the state after the MixColumns operation of Round 9 equals:

$c_0\lambda_0^{-1}\hat{x}_0 \oplus \underline{b}_0$	$c_4\lambda_4^{-1}\hat{x}_4 \oplus \underline{b}_4$	$c_8\lambda_8^{-1}\hat{x}_8 \oplus \underline{b}_8$	$c_{12}\lambda_{12}^{-1}\hat{x}_{12} \oplus \underline{b}_{12}$
$c_1\lambda_0^{-1}\hat{x}_1 \oplus \underline{b}_1$	$c_5\lambda_4^{-1}\hat{x}_5 \oplus \underline{b}_5$	$c_9\lambda_8^{-1}\hat{x}_9 \oplus \underline{b}_9$	$c_{13}\lambda_{12}^{-1}\hat{x}_{13} \oplus \underline{b}_{13}$
$c_2\lambda_0^{-1}\hat{x}_2 \oplus \underline{b}_2$	$c_6\lambda_4^{-1}\hat{x}_6 \oplus \underline{b}_6$	$c_{10}\lambda_8^{-1}\hat{x}_{10} \oplus \underline{b}_{10}$	$c_{14}\lambda_{12}^{-1}\hat{x}_{14} \oplus \underline{b}_{14}$
$c_3\lambda_0^{-1}\hat{x}_3 \oplus \underline{b}_3$	$c_7\lambda_4^{-1}\hat{x}_7 \oplus \underline{b}_7$	$c_{11}\lambda_8^{-1}\hat{x}_{11} \oplus \underline{b}_{11}$	$c_{15}\lambda_{12}^{-1}\hat{x}_{15} \oplus \underline{b}_{15}$

Define $\hat{z}^T = \mathcal{MC}^{-1} \cdot (c_0\hat{x}_0, c_1\hat{x}_1, \ldots, c_{15}\hat{x}_{15})^T$ and $\beta^T = \mathcal{MC}^{-1} \cdot \underline{b}^T$. The state after the S-boxes and before the ShiftRows and MixColumns operations of Round 9 is given by:

$$
\begin{array}{|c|c|c|c|}
\hline
\lambda_0^{-1}\hat{z}_0 \oplus \beta_0 & \lambda_4^{-1}\hat{z}_4 \oplus \beta_4 & \lambda_8^{-1}\hat{z}_8 \oplus \beta_8 & \lambda_{12}^{-1}\hat{z}_{12} \oplus \beta_{12} \\
\hline
\lambda_{12}^{-1}\hat{z}_{13} \oplus \beta_{13} & \lambda_0^{-1}\hat{z}_1 \oplus \beta_1 & \lambda_4^{-1}\hat{z}_5 \oplus \beta_5 & \lambda_8^{-1}\hat{z}_9 \oplus \beta_9 \\
\hline
\lambda_8^{-1}\hat{z}_{10} \oplus \beta_{10} & \lambda_{12}^{-1}\hat{z}_{14} \oplus \beta_{14} & \lambda_0^{-1}\hat{z}_2 \oplus \beta_2 & \lambda_4^{-1}\hat{z}_6 \oplus \beta_6 \\
\hline
\lambda_4^{-1}\hat{z}_7 \oplus \beta_7 & \lambda_8^{-1}\hat{z}_{11} \oplus \beta_{11} & \lambda_{12}^{-1}\hat{z}_{15} \oplus \beta_{15} & \lambda_0^{-1}\hat{z}_3 \oplus \beta_3 \\
\hline
\end{array}
\tag{17}
$$

If the attacker has injected a fault that affects the input or output of the first S-box of Round 8 then, similar to a standard DFA attack, the following three equations can be derived:

$$
02^{-1}S^{-1}(\lambda_0^{-1}\hat{z}_0 \oplus \beta_0) \oplus 02^{-1}S^{-1}(\lambda_0^{-1}\hat{Z}_0 \oplus \beta_0) =
$$
$$
S^{-1}(\lambda_{12}^{-1}\hat{z}_{13} \oplus \beta_{13}) \oplus S^{-1}(\lambda_{12}^{-1}\hat{Z}_{13} \oplus \beta_{13}),
\tag{18}
$$

$$
S^{-1}(\lambda_8^{-1}\hat{z}_{10} \oplus \beta_{10}) \oplus S^{-1}(\lambda_8^{-1}\hat{Z}_{10} \oplus \beta_{10}) =
$$
$$
S^{-1}\left(\lambda_{12}^{-1}\hat{z}_{13} \oplus \beta_{13}\right) \oplus S^{-1}\left(\lambda_{12}^{-1}\hat{Z}_{13} \oplus \beta_{13}\right),
\tag{19}
$$

$$03^{-1}S^{-1}(\lambda_4^{-1}\hat{z}_7 \oplus \beta_7) \oplus 03^{-1}S^{-1}(\lambda_4^{-1}\hat{Z}_7 \oplus \beta_7) =$$
$$S^{-1}\left(\lambda_{12}^{-1}\hat{z}_{13} \oplus \beta_{13}\right) \oplus S^{-1}\left(\lambda_{12}^{-1}\hat{Z}_{13} \oplus \beta_{13}\right). \tag{20}$$

The eight unknowns of Eqs. 18, 19 and 20 are $\lambda_0^{-1}, \lambda_4^{-1}, \lambda_8^{-1}, \lambda_{12}^{-1}, \beta_0, \beta_7, \beta_{10}, \beta_{13}$. We now describe a meet-in-the-middle approach to find the correct solution to this system of equations. First, collect α faulty output bytes $\hat{Z}_{13}^{(w)}$ for $w = 0, 1, \ldots, \alpha-1$ for output byte $\hat{z}_{13}$ by injecting different faults at the same location. Next, define the function $R_{\hat{\lambda}_R^{-1}, \hat{\beta}_R}$ as:

$$R_{\hat{\lambda}_R^{-1}, \hat{\beta}_R}(\hat{z}_{13}, \hat{Z}_{13}^{(w)}) = S^{-1}\left(\hat{\lambda}_R^{-1}\hat{z}_{13} \oplus \hat{\beta}_R\right) \oplus S^{-1}\left(\hat{\lambda}_R^{-1}\hat{Z}_{13}^{(w)} \oplus \hat{\beta}_R\right).$$

Note that this function, parametrized by $\hat{\lambda}_R^{-1}$ and $\hat{\beta}_R$, equals the right-hand side of Eqs. 18, 19 and 20. Then, for all $\hat{\lambda}_R^{-1} \in \mathbb{F}_{2^8}^*$ and $\hat{\beta}_R \in \mathbb{F}_{2^8}$, we compute:

$$R_{\hat{\lambda}_R^{-1}, \hat{\beta}_R}(\hat{z}_{13}, \hat{Z}_{13}^{(0)})\|R_{\hat{\lambda}_R^{-1}, \hat{\beta}_R}(\hat{z}_{13}, \hat{Z}_{13}^{(1)})\|\ldots\|R_{\hat{\lambda}_R^{-1}, \hat{\beta}_R}(\hat{z}_{13}, \hat{Z}_{13}^{(\alpha-1)}) \tag{21}$$

where $\|$ denotes the concatenation of values. We now apply a hash function to each of these values and store the hash value associated with the pair $(\hat{\lambda}_R^{-1}, \hat{\beta}_R)$ in a hash table HT, indexed by its hash value. Since HT has an entry for every pair (λ^{-1}, β), the maximum number of entries is 2^{16}. We therefore assume that the size of the output of the hash function is larger than 2^{16} to avoid collisions. Next, define the functions $L^{(0)}_{\tilde{\lambda}_{L(0)}^{-1}, \tilde{\beta}_{L(0)}}(\hat{z}_0, \hat{Z}_0^{(w)})$, $L^{(1)}_{\tilde{\lambda}_{L(1)}^{-1}, \tilde{\beta}_{L(1)}}(\hat{z}_{10}, \hat{Z}_{10}^{(w)})$, and $L^{(2)}_{\tilde{\lambda}_{L(2)}^{-1}, \tilde{\beta}_{L(2)}}(\hat{z}_7, \hat{Z}_7^{(w)})$ as

$$02^{-1}\left(S^{-1}\left(\tilde{\lambda}_{L(0)}^{-1}\hat{z}_0 \oplus \tilde{\beta}_{L(0)}\right) \oplus S^{-1}\left(\tilde{\lambda}_{L(0)}^{-1}\hat{Z}_0^{(w)} \oplus \tilde{\beta}_{L(0)}\right)\right),$$

$$S^{-1}\left(\tilde{\lambda}_{L(1)}^{-1}\hat{z}_{10} \oplus \tilde{\beta}_{L(1)}\right) \oplus S^{-1}\left(\tilde{\lambda}_{L(1)}^{-1}\hat{Z}_{10}^{(w)} \oplus \tilde{\beta}_{L(1)}\right), \text{ and}$$

$$03^{-1}\left(S^{-1}\left(\tilde{\lambda}_{L(2)}^{-1}\hat{z}_7 \oplus \tilde{\beta}_{L(2)}\right) \oplus S^{-1}\left(\tilde{\lambda}_{L(2)}^{-1}\hat{Z}_7^{(w)} \oplus \tilde{\beta}_{L(2)}\right)\right),$$

respectively. Note that these three functions, parametrized by $\hat{\lambda}_{L(i)}^{-1}$ and $\hat{\beta}_{L(i)}$, equal the left-hand side of Eqs. 18, 19 and 20, respectively. Using the same pairs of correct and faulty outputs as for Eq. 21, we now compute for all $\tilde{\lambda}_{L(0)}^{-1} \in \mathbb{F}_{2^8}^*$ and $\tilde{\beta}_{L(0)} \in \mathbb{F}_{2^8}$ the value

$$L^{(0)}_{\tilde{\lambda}_{L(0)}^{-1}, \tilde{\beta}_{L(0)}}(\hat{z}_0, \hat{Z}_0^{(0)})\|L^{(0)}_{\tilde{\lambda}_{L(0)}^{-1}, \tilde{\beta}_{L(0)}}(\hat{z}_0, \hat{Z}_0^{(1)})\|\ldots\|L^{(0)}_{\tilde{\lambda}_{L(0)}^{-1}, \tilde{\beta}_{L(0)}}(\hat{z}_0, \hat{Z}_0^{(\alpha-1)}).$$

We compute the hash of these values and verify if HT has an entry for this hash value. If so, we add the corresponding values of $\tilde{\lambda}_{L(0)}^{-1}, \tilde{\beta}_{L(0)}$ and $\tilde{\lambda}_R^{-1}, \tilde{\beta}_R$ to the set of candidate solutions for $\tilde{\lambda}_0^{-1}, \tilde{\beta}_0$ and $\tilde{\lambda}_{12}^{-1}, \tilde{\beta}_{13}$. We proceed in a similar way

for $L^{(1)}_{\tilde{\lambda}^{-1}_{L(1)},\tilde{\beta}_{L(1)}}$ and $L^{(2)}_{\tilde{\lambda}^{-1}_{L(2)},\tilde{\beta}_{L(2)}}$. That is, we compute for all $\tilde{\lambda}^{-1}_{L(1)}, \tilde{\lambda}^{-1}_{L(2)} \in \mathbb{F}^*_{2^8}$
and $\tilde{\beta}_{L(1)}, \tilde{\beta}_{L(1)} \in \mathbb{F}_{2^8}$ the values

$$L^{(1)}_{\tilde{\lambda}^{-1}_{L(1)},\tilde{\beta}_{L(1)}}(\hat{z}_{10}, \hat{Z}^{(0)}_{10}) || L^{(1)}_{\tilde{\lambda}^{-1}_{L(1)},\tilde{\beta}_{L(1)}}(\hat{z}_{10}, \hat{Z}^{(1)}_{10}) || \ldots || L^{(1)}_{\tilde{\lambda}^{-1}_{L(1)},\tilde{\beta}_{L(1)}}(\hat{z}_{10}, \hat{Z}^{(\alpha-1)}_{10}),$$

$$L^{(2)}_{\tilde{\lambda}^{-1}_{L(2)},\tilde{\beta}_{L(2)}}(\hat{z}_7, \hat{Z}^{(0)}_7) || L^{(2)}_{\tilde{\lambda}^{-1}_{L(2)},\tilde{\beta}_{L(2)}}(\hat{z}_7, \hat{Z}^{(1)}_7) || \ldots || L^{(2)}_{\tilde{\lambda}^{-1}_{L(2)},\tilde{\beta}_{L(2)}}(\hat{z}_7, \hat{Z}^{(\alpha-1)}_7)$$

and check whether the hash of these values have an entry in HT. If this is the
case, the former expression gives a candidate solution for $\tilde{\lambda}^{-1}_8, \tilde{\beta}_{10}$ and $\tilde{\lambda}^{-1}_{12}, \tilde{\beta}_{13}$
and the latter for $\tilde{\lambda}^{-1}_4, \tilde{\beta}_7$ and $\tilde{\lambda}^{-1}_{12}, \tilde{\beta}_{13}$. At the end, we take the intersection of
all three sets of candidate solutions w.r.t. the values of $\tilde{\lambda}^{-1}_{12}, \tilde{\beta}_{13}$. This gives us
a collection of solutions $(\tilde{\lambda}^{-1}_0, \tilde{\lambda}^{-1}_4, \tilde{\lambda}^{-1}_8, \tilde{\lambda}^{-1}_{12})$ and $(\tilde{\beta}_0, \tilde{\beta}_7, \tilde{\beta}_{10}, \tilde{\beta}_{13})$ that for all
α pairs of correct and faulty outputs we derived results in a valid solution for
Eqs. 18, 19 and 20. By taking α large enough, only a single solution remains;
see Appendix C. A similar approach can be used to find the values of λ^{-1} and
β associated with different columns of the state depicted in Eq. 17.

Remark 1. By Assumption 3, we can identify whether we are targeting an S-box.
However, after we located an S-box, we don't know which one of the four possible
S-boxes it is. This results in 4 different systems of equations. In practice, only
one of these systems will have a solution.

After a unique solution is found for $(\hat{\lambda}^{-1}_0, \hat{\lambda}^{-1}_4, \hat{\lambda}^{-1}_8, \hat{\lambda}^{-1}_{12})$ and $(\hat{\beta}_0, \hat{\beta}_1, \ldots, \hat{\beta}_{15})$,
the attacker is able to compute the non-encoded state after the Round 9 S-box
as $z_i = \lambda^{-1}_{4\lfloor \frac{i}{4} \rfloor} \hat{z}_i \oplus \beta_i$ for $i = 0, 1, \ldots, 15$. Algorithm 4 describes an algorithm that
performs Step 4.

3.6 Step 5: Standard DFA

In this section we describe the final step of the attack. This step retrieves
the round key $k^{(8)} = (k^{(8)}_0, k^{(8)}_1, \ldots, k^{(8)}_{15})$ from the non-encoded S-box output bytes z_i for $i = 0, 1, \ldots, 15$ as obtained in the previous step. To this
end, assume that faults are injected at the beginning of Round 7, and that
the attacker has access to the S-box outputs of Round 8. Next, define $\tilde{w}^T =$

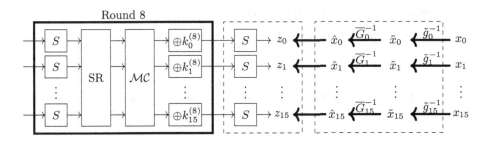

Fig. 4. Non-encoded S-box output of Round 9.

Algorithm 4. Determine $\hat{\lambda}_0^{-1}, \hat{\lambda}_4^{-1}, \hat{\lambda}_8^{-1}, \hat{\lambda}_{12}^{-1}, \hat{\beta}_0, \hat{\beta}_7, \hat{\beta}_{10}, \hat{\beta}_{13}$

Input : $\overline{G}^{-1} \circ \tilde{g}^{-1} \circ Enc_k$, $\{c_0, c_1, \ldots, c_{15}\}$, and $\alpha > 1$.

Output: $\hat{\lambda}_0^{-1}, \hat{\lambda}_4^{-1}, \hat{\lambda}_8^{-1}, \hat{\lambda}_{12}^{-1}, \hat{\beta}_0, \hat{\beta}_7, \hat{\beta}_{10}, \hat{\beta}_{13}$.

$m \xleftarrow{\$} \mathcal{M}$;

$\hat{x} = (\hat{x}_0, \hat{x}_1, \ldots, \hat{x}_{15}) \leftarrow \overline{G}^{-1} \circ \tilde{g}^{-1} \circ Enc_k(m)$;

$\hat{z}^T \leftarrow \mathcal{MC}^{-1} \cdot (c_0 \hat{x}_0, c_1 \hat{x}_1, \ldots, c_{15} \hat{x}_{15})^T$;

for $\forall w \in \{0, 1, \ldots, \alpha - 1\}$ **do**

  $\varepsilon \xleftarrow{\$} \mathbb{F}_{2^8}^*$ without repetitions;

  $\hat{X}^{(w)} \xleftarrow{\varepsilon} \overline{G}^{-1} \circ \tilde{g}^{-1} \circ Enc_k(m)$;

  $(\hat{Z}^{(w)})^T \leftarrow \mathcal{MC}^{-1} \cdot (c_0 \hat{X}_0^{(w)}, c_1 \hat{X}_1^{(w)}, \ldots, c_{15} \hat{X}_{15}^{(w)})^T$;

end

for $\forall \lambda_R^{-1}, \beta_R \in \mathbb{F}_{2^8}$ **do**

  $h_{\lambda_R^{-1}, \beta_R} \leftarrow$
  $\text{Hash}(\text{R}_{\lambda_R^{-1}, \beta_R}(\hat{z}_{13}, \hat{Z}_{13}^{(0)}) \| \text{R}_{\lambda_R^{-1}, \beta_R}(\hat{z}_{13}, \hat{Z}_{13}^{(1)}) \| \ldots \| \text{R}_{\lambda_R^{-1}, \beta_R}(\hat{z}_{13}, \hat{Z}_{13}^{(\alpha-1)}))$;

  Store $(h_{\lambda_R^{-1}, \beta_R}, \lambda_R^{-1}, \beta_R)$;

end

for $\forall \lambda_L^{-1}, \beta_L \in \mathbb{F}_{2^8}$ **do**

  Look for separate solutions $\lambda_R^{-1}, \beta_R, \lambda_L^{-1}, \beta_L$ to;

  $h_{\lambda_{L(0)}^{-1}, \beta_{L(0)}} =$
  $\text{Hash}(\text{L}_{\lambda_L^{-1}, \beta_L}^{(0)}(\hat{z}_0, \hat{Z}_0^{(0)}) \| \text{L}_{\lambda_L^{-1}, \beta_L}^{(0)}(\hat{z}_0, \hat{Z}_0^{(1)}) \| \ldots \| \text{L}_{\lambda_L^{-1}, \beta_L}^{(0)}(\hat{z}_0, \hat{Z}_0^{(\alpha-1)}))$;

  or $h_{\lambda_{L(1)}^{-1}, \beta_{L(1)}} =$
  $\text{Hash}(\text{L}_{\lambda_L^{-1}, \beta_L}^{(1)}(\hat{z}_{10}, \hat{Z}_{10}^{(0)}) \| \text{L}_{\lambda_L^{-1}, \beta_L}^{(1)}(\hat{z}_{10}, \hat{Z}_{10}^{(1)}) \| \ldots \| \text{L}_{\lambda_L^{-1}, \beta_L}^{(1)}(\hat{z}_{10}, \hat{Z}_{10}^{(\alpha-1)}))$;

  or $h_{\lambda_{L(2)}^{-1}, \beta_{L(2)}} =$
  $\text{Hash}(\text{L}_{\lambda_L^{-1}, \beta_L}^{(2)}(\hat{z}_7, \hat{Z}_7^{(0)}) \| \text{L}_{\lambda_L^{-1}, \beta_L}^{(2)}(\hat{z}_7, \hat{Z}_7^{(1)}) \| \ldots \| \text{L}_{\lambda_L^{-1}, \beta_L}^{(2)}(\hat{z}_7, \hat{Z}_7^{(\alpha-1)}))$;

end

if *all separate solutions have* λ_R^{-1}, β_R *in common* **then**

  if *# solutions > 1* **then**

   restart with $\alpha \leftarrow \alpha + 1$;

  else

   return $(\hat{\lambda}_0^{-1}, \hat{\lambda}_4^{-1}, \hat{\lambda}_8^{-1}, \hat{\lambda}_{12}^{-1}, \hat{\beta}_0, \hat{\beta}_7, \hat{\beta}_{10}, \hat{\beta}_{13}) \leftarrow$
   $(\lambda_{L(0)}^{-1}, \lambda_{L(2)}^{-1}, \lambda_{L(1)}^{-1}, \lambda_R^{-1}, \beta_{L(0)}, \beta_{L(2)}, \beta_{L(1)}, \beta_R)$;

  end

else

  Choose another location to inject faults

end

$\mathcal{MC}^{-1} \cdot (S^{-1}(z_0), S^{-1}(z_1), \ldots, S^{-1}(z_{15}))^T$ and $(\tilde{k}^{(8)})^T = \mathcal{MC}^{-1} \cdot (k^{(8)})^T$. If we assume that a fault is injected in the input or output of the first S-box, then the DFA equations are (Fig. 4):

$$S^{-1}(\tilde{w}_0 \oplus \tilde{k}_0^{(8)}) \oplus S^{-1}(\tilde{W}_0 \oplus \tilde{k}_0^{(8)}) = \\ 02S^{-1}(\tilde{w}_{13} \oplus \tilde{k}_{13}^{(8)}) \oplus 02S^{-1}(\tilde{W}_{13} \oplus \tilde{k}_{13}^{(8)}), \tag{22}$$

$$S^{-1}(\tilde{w}_{10} \oplus \tilde{k}_{10}^{(8)}) \oplus S^{-1}(\tilde{W}_{10} \oplus \tilde{k}_{10}^{(8)}) = \\ S^{-1}(\tilde{w}_{13} \oplus \tilde{k}_{13}^{(8)}) \oplus S^{-1}(\tilde{W}_{13} \oplus \tilde{k}_{13}^{(8)}), \tag{23}$$

$$S^{-1}(\tilde{w}_7 \oplus \tilde{k}_7^{(8)}) \oplus S^{-1}(\tilde{W}_7 \oplus \tilde{k}_7^{(8)}) = \\ 03S^{-1}(\tilde{w}_{13} \oplus \tilde{k}_{13}^{(8)}) \oplus 03S^{-1}(\tilde{W}_{13} \oplus \tilde{k}_{13}^{(8)}). \tag{24}$$

One can use a meet-in-the-middle approach as discussed in Sect. 3.5 to solve this system of equations and find the values of $\tilde{k}^{(8)}$. After $\tilde{k}^{(8)}$ has been computed, we can obtain the 8-th AES round key via $(k^{(8)})^T = \mathcal{MC} \cdot (\tilde{k}^{(8)})^T$. From this, and the AES key-schedule algorithm, we can retrieve the 128-bit AES key.

From the AES key and the known state after the Round 9 S-box layer for every input to the white-box implementation, the attacker can obtain known input-output pairs for both external encodings. The output encoding is then easy to retrieve since this problem reduces to 16 coupon collectors problems [18], one for each byte of the output of the white-box implementation. Recall that we did not make any assumption on the external encoding on the input; however, typically such encodings are weak if considered as an encryption algorithm. In other words, most of them will be easy to retrieve with known input-output pairs or with a chosen input attack.

4   Conclusions

Section 3 presented a new attack on a class of white-box AES implementations. The attack assumes that external encodings are used, and that the external encoding on the output of AES is a byte encoding. The class of white-box implementations is defined by two assumptions on the internal encodings that are used to obfuscate the S-box inputs or outputs. The attack combines techniques from the BGE attack with techniques used in DFA attacks, and it was shown that its expected work factor is dominated by 2^{32} executions of the white-box implementation. This shows that the use of a byte encoding on the output of AES does not provide an adequate level of security for this class of white-box implementations.

The new attack can be mitigated by ensuring that at least one of the assumptions does not hold true. In case of Assumption 1, one could use a more complicated type of encoding on the output of AES. An example is the concatenation of a linear function over $\mathbb{F}_2^{128}$, mixing the values of the bytes of the AES output, and a byte encoding as assumed in this paper. To ensure that Assumption 2 does not hold true, one could embed the bits of the S-box inputs and outputs into larger encoded values or use bit-slicing techniques to implement AES before applying the white-box encodings. Alternatively, one could perform parts of the computation multiple times, compare their results, and only output an encoded ciphertext if these results are equal. In case of Assumption 3, one could try to construct a white-box AES implementation that produces false positives for the checks listed in the assumption.

Acknowledgment. The authors would like to thank the anonymous reviewers for their useful and valuable comments.

A   Finding the Location to Inject Faults in Step 2

In this section we answer the following question. Given two pairs of correct and faulty outputs, where the inputs are elements of $\mathcal{M}_0$, if for both inputs we inject faults in the input or output of an S-box in Round 9, how can we determine whether we are targeting the same S-box? To this end, we make use of the additional output x_2 of which the value is fixed in the definition of $\mathcal{M}_0$. Let $m, \overline{m} \in \mathcal{M}_0$ with $m \neq \overline{m}$ and let the first column of their output states be denoted by (x_0, x_1, x_2, x_3) and $(\overline{x}_0, \overline{x}_1, \overline{x}_2, \overline{x}_3)$, respectively. The definition of $\mathcal{M}_0$ implies that

$$x_0 \neq \overline{x}_0, \quad x_1 = \overline{x}_1, \quad x_2 = \overline{x}_2. \tag{25}$$

Let ℓ and $\overline{\ell}$ be locations in the executions of the white-box implementation for m and $\overline{m}$, respectively, for which the adversary assumes they relate to the input or output of the same S-box. Then, the theorem below states that for every change we make at ℓ for m, there exists a change in $\overline{\ell}$ for $\overline{m}$ such that the values of the two fixed output bytes considered (in our example, the ones with index 1 and 2) are the same. Hence, by comparing outputs for all 256 possible values associated with ℓ and $\overline{\ell}$, we get a check on whether ℓ and $\overline{\ell}$ relate to the same S-box output.

Lemma 2. *Let $m, \overline{m} \in \mathcal{M}_i$ be different inputs that produce output bytes $x_i, x_{r(i)}$, $x_{s(i)}$ and $\overline{x}_i, \overline{x}_{r(i)}, \overline{x}_{s(i)}$ respectively with $x_{r(i)} = \overline{x}_{r(i)}$ and $x_s(i) = \overline{x}_{s(i)}$. Let (ε, ℓ) be the fault affecting a Round 9 S-box input or output with value ε injected at location ℓ during the encryption of m and define $(\overline{\varepsilon}, \overline{\ell})$ similarly for $\overline{m}$. Then, ℓ and $\overline{\ell}$ affect the same S-box input or output if and only if for all non-zero ε injected at ℓ, there exist a non-zero $\overline{\varepsilon}$ injected at $\overline{\ell}$ so that for all faulty output bytes $X_i, X_{r(i)}, X_{s(i)}$, there exist $\overline{X}_i, \overline{X}_{r(i)}, \overline{X}_{s(i)}$ such that $X_i \neq \overline{X}_i, X_{r(i)} = \overline{X}_{r(i)}$ and $X_{s(i)} = \overline{X}_{s(i)}$.*

Proof. We first prove that if two locations ℓ and $\overline{\ell}$ refer to the same S-box input or output, then for all faulty values ε that output the bytes $X_i, X_{r(i)}, X_{s(i)}$, there exists a fault $\overline{\varepsilon}$ that produces $\overline{X}_i, \overline{X}_{r(i)}, \overline{X}_{s(i)}$ such that $X_i \neq \overline{X}_i, X_{r(i)} = \overline{X}_{r(i)}$ and $X_{s(i)} = \overline{X}_{s(i)}$. Without loss of generality, we prove this statement for $i = 0$, $r(0) = 1$, and $s(0) = 2$. Let $z = (z_0, z_1, z_2, z_3)$ and $\overline{z} = (\overline{z}_0, \overline{z}_1, \overline{z}_2, \overline{z}_3)$ be the bytes at the beginning of the MixColumns operation of Round 9 that contribute to the computations of (x_0, x_1, x_2, x_3) and $(\overline{x}_0, \overline{x}_1, \overline{x}_2, \overline{x}_3)$ respectively. Let $\mathcal{MC}_j$ with $j \in \{0, 1, 2, 3\}$ denote the j-th row of $\mathcal{MC}$. Then Eq. 25 is equivalent to:

$$\mathcal{MC}_0 \cdot z^T \neq \mathcal{MC}_0 \cdot \overline{z}^T$$
$$\mathcal{MC}_1 \cdot z^T = \mathcal{MC}_1 \cdot \overline{z}^T$$
$$\mathcal{MC}_2 \cdot z^T = \mathcal{MC}_2 \cdot \overline{z}^T.$$

Suppose that the injections ε and $\overline{\varepsilon}$ affect the first byte of the state (for other bytes in the same column, the proof is analogous), so that the input to the MixColumns equals (Z_0, z_1, z_2, z_3) and $(\overline{Z}_0, \overline{z}_1, \overline{z}_2, \overline{z}_3)$, respectively. It follows that for all $\varepsilon \in \mathbb{F}_{2^8}^*$, there exists a unique $\delta \in \mathbb{F}_{2^8}^*$ such that $Z_0 = z_0 \oplus \delta$ (and, analogously, that for all $\overline{\varepsilon} \in \mathbb{F}_{2^8}^*$, there exists a unique $\overline{\delta} \in \mathbb{F}_{2^8}^*$ such that $\overline{Z}_0 = \overline{z}_0 \oplus \overline{\delta}$). From this it follows that for all ε there exist $\overline{\varepsilon} \in \mathbb{F}_{2^8}^*$ such that $\delta = \overline{\delta}$. Let $y = (y_0, y_1, y_2, y_3)$ and $\overline{y} = (\overline{y}_0, \overline{y}_1, \overline{y}_2, \overline{y}_3)$ be such that $\mathcal{MC} \cdot z^T = y^T$ and $\mathcal{MC} \cdot \overline{z}^T = \overline{y}^T$. By assumption, it holds that $x_0 \neq \overline{x}_0$, $x_1 = \overline{x}_1$ and $x_2 = \overline{x}_2$, hence that $y_0 \neq \overline{y}_0$, $y_1 = \overline{y}_1$, $y_2 = \overline{y}_2$.
Thus, we have for $\delta = \overline{\delta}$:

$$\mathcal{MC} \cdot \begin{pmatrix} z_0 \oplus \delta \\ z_1 \\ z_2 \\ z_3 \end{pmatrix} = \begin{pmatrix} y_0 \oplus 02\delta \\ y_1 \oplus \delta \\ y_2 \oplus \delta \\ y_3 \oplus 03\delta \end{pmatrix}, \quad \mathcal{MC} \cdot \begin{pmatrix} \overline{z}_0 \oplus \overline{\delta} \\ \overline{z}_1 \\ \overline{z}_2 \\ \overline{z}_3 \end{pmatrix} = \begin{pmatrix} \overline{y}_0 \oplus 02\overline{\delta} \\ \overline{y}_1 \oplus \overline{\delta} \\ \overline{y}_2 \oplus \overline{\delta} \\ \overline{y}_3 \oplus 03\overline{\delta} \end{pmatrix},$$

with $y_0 \oplus 2\delta \neq \overline{y}_0 \oplus 2\overline{\delta}$, $y_1 \oplus \delta = \overline{y}_1 \oplus \overline{\delta}$, $y_2 \oplus \delta = \overline{y}_2 \oplus \overline{\delta}$. This yields $X_i \neq \overline{X}_i$, $X_1 = \overline{X}_1$ and $X_2 = \overline{X}_2$.

Next, we prove the converse statement: if two injections ε and $\overline{\varepsilon}$ during the encryption of m and $\overline{m}$ produce outputs $X_i, X_{r(i)}, X_{s(i)}$, and $\overline{X}_i, \overline{X}_{r(i)}, \overline{X}_{s(i)}$ such that $X_i \neq \overline{X}_i$, $X_{r(i)} = \overline{X}_{r(i)}$ and $X_{s(i)} = \overline{X}_{s(i)}$, then ε and $\overline{\varepsilon}$ are affecting the same S-box output. As before, we set $i = 0$, $r(0) = 1$ and $s(0) = 2$ without loss of generality. Now suppose that for input m we inject a fault affecting z_0 and for $\overline{m}$ we inject a fault affecting $\overline{z}_1$, however the same proof works analogously if we inject faults affecting any two bytes in the same column. Thus, we construct two separate equations:

$$g_2^{-1}(x_2) \oplus g_2^{-1}(X_2) = g_1^{-1}(x_1) \oplus g_1^{-1}(X_1)$$

for an injection affecting z_0 during the encryption of m, and

$$02(g_2^{-1}(\overline{x}_2) \oplus g_2^{-1}(\overline{X}_2)) = g_1^{-1}(\overline{x}_1) \oplus g_1^{-1}(\overline{X}_1)$$

for an injection affecting $\overline{z}_1$ during the encryption of $\overline{m}$. By adding these two equations, and substituting $x_1 = \overline{x}_1$, $x_2 = \overline{x}_2$, $X_1 = \overline{X}_1$, $X_2 = \overline{X}_2$, we get:

$$03(g_2^{-1}(x_2) \oplus g_2^{-1}(X_2)) = 0$$

which implies $x_2 = X_2$, leading to a contradiction. $\square$

Lemma 2 provides a criterion to inspect whether injected faults affect the same output byte. Note that Lemma 2 does not allow us to understand which S-box input or output has been modified. By affecting a different S-box, the attacker would construct systems of equations similar to Eqs. 1, 2, and 3, with a function h_{g_i, x_i}^{μ} which may have different multiplicative coefficients μ and different fixed output bytes. However, this does not complicate the attack. Since h_{g_i, x_i}^{μ} assumes all possible values, the resulting set of functions $\mathcal{S}_{g_i}$ would be the same regardless of the S-box output that the fault is affecting. Since the set $\mathcal{S}_{g_i}$ would be the same, Theorem 1 applies to all cases, as shown by the following lemma:

Lemma 3. *If* $\mathcal{S}_1 = \{g_0 \circ \oplus_{h^\mu_{g_i,x_i}(X_i)} \circ g_0^{-1}\}_{X_i \in \mathbb{F}_{2^8}}$ *and* $\mathcal{S}_2 = \{g_0 \circ \oplus_{h^{\overline{\mu}}_{g_j,\overline{x}_j}(\overline{X}_j)} \circ g_0^{-1}\}_{\overline{X}_j \in \mathbb{F}_{2^8}}$ *be two sets of functions constructed by injecting faults affecting two different S-box input or outputs, then* $\mathcal{S}_1 = \mathcal{S}_2$.

Proof. An injection affecting an S-box input or output allows us to derive the following equation:

$$g_0^{-1}(x_0) \oplus g_0^{-1}(X_0) = h^\mu_{g_i,x_i}(X_i)$$

Since $h^\mu_{g_i,x_i}$ is bijective and X_i ranges over all possible values, $h^\mu_{g_i,x_i}(X_1)$ also ranges over all possible values. By injecting faults that affect another S-box input or output, we derive the following equation:

$$g_0^{-1}(\overline{x}_0) \oplus g_0^{-1}(\overline{X}_0) = h^{\overline{\mu}}_{g_j,\overline{x}_j}(\overline{X}_j).$$

By the same argument also $h^{\overline{\mu}}_{g_j,\overline{x}_j}(\overline{X}_j)$ assumes all possible values. By construction of $\mathcal{S}_1$ and $\mathcal{S}_2$, x_i and $\overline{x}_j$ are fixed, therefore the function

$$\otimes_{\overline{\mu}} \circ \oplus_{g_j(\overline{x}_j)} \circ g_j \circ g_i^{-1} \circ \oplus_{g_i(x_i)} \circ \otimes_{\mu^{-1}}$$

is a bijection that maps $h^\mu_{g_i,x_i}$ to $h^{\overline{\mu}}_{g_j,\overline{x}_j}$, hence $\mathcal{S}_1 = \mathcal{S}_2$.   □

B   Reducing the Number of Variables

In this section we reduce the number of unknown λ_i's to one per column. Let i be the first output byte of a column. By *3* in Lemma 1, we can decompose $\gamma_i^{(i+1,\ell_0,\ell_1)}$ from $L_{\gamma_i,i}^{(i+1,\ell_0,\ell_1)}$ uniquely into $\gamma_{i,i+1}^{(\ell_0)}$ and $\gamma_{i,i+1}^{(\ell_1)}$. Similarly, we can also decompose $\gamma_i^{(i+3,\ell_0,\ell_1)}$ from $L_{\gamma_i,i}^{(i+3,\ell_0,\ell_1)}$ uniquely into $\gamma_{i,i+3}^{(\ell_0)}$ and $\gamma_{i,i+3}^{(\ell_1)}$. Since we have $\gamma_{i,j}^{(\ell_0)} = \mathcal{MC}_{j,\ell_0} \cdot (\mathcal{MC}_{i,\ell_0})^{-1}$, we can derive the value of ℓ_0 from this. Having this value, we can next compute value $\gamma_{i,j}^{\ell_0}$ for all i,j (hence, also for i,j with $|i-j| = 2$). That is, for any $G_j \circ \otimes_{\gamma_{i,j}^{(\ell_0)}} \circ G_i^{-1}$ from $\mathcal{F}^{(\ell_0)}$ we now have the value of $\gamma_{i,j}^{(\ell_0)}$. By applying $\overline{G}_i^{-1}$ to the input and $\overline{G}_j^{-1}$ to the output of these functions, the attacker obtains a new family of functions, given by values:

$$\otimes_{\lambda_j} \circ \otimes_{\gamma_{i,j}^{(\ell_0)}} \circ \otimes_{\lambda_i^{-1}},$$

or, equivalently $\otimes_{\lambda_j \gamma_{i,j}^{(\ell_0)} \lambda_i^{-1}}$. Hence, if the value of λ_i is known, one can compute all other values λ_j associated with the same output column. In fact, given $\overline{x}_i = \overline{G}_i^{-1}(\tilde{x}_i \oplus \tilde{X}_i)$ and $\overline{x}_j = \overline{G}_j^{-1}(\tilde{x}_j \oplus \tilde{X}_j)$, it follows that $\overline{x}_j = \lambda_j \gamma_{i,j}^{(\ell_0)} \lambda_i^{-1} \overline{x}_i$ which can be rewritten as $\overline{x}_j^{-1} \overline{x}_i \gamma_{i,j}^{(\ell_0)} \lambda_i^{-1} = \lambda_j^{-1}$. For each column, we write λ_j^{-1} with respect to the one with the lowest index, that is, with respect to $\lambda_0^{-1}, \lambda_4^{-1}, \lambda_8^{-1}, \lambda_{12}^{-1}$

for the first, second, third, and fourth column respectively. Given λ_i^{-1} with i mod $4 = 0$, we can compute any other $\lambda_j^{-1} = c_i \lambda_i^{-1}$, with $c_i = 1$ and $c_j = \overline{y}^{-1} \overline{x} \gamma_{i,j}^{\ell_0}$, where $j > i$ and $j \in [4\lfloor \frac{i}{4} \rfloor, 4\lfloor \frac{i}{4} \rfloor + 3]$. It follows that, given $\hat{x}_i = \overline{G}_i^{-1}(\tilde{x}_i)$, the non-encoded output of Round 9 can be written as $c_i \lambda_{4\lfloor \frac{i}{4} \rfloor}^{-1}(\hat{x}_i \oplus \hat{b}_i)$ for a known constant $c_i \in \mathbb{F}_{2^8}^*$ and unknown $\lambda_{4\lfloor \frac{i}{4} \rfloor}^{-1} \in \mathbb{F}_{2^8}^*$ and $\hat{b}_i \in \mathbb{F}_{2^8}$. The state corresponding to the non-encoded output of Round 9 equals:

$$
\begin{array}{|c|c|c|c|}
\hline
c_0\lambda_0^{-1}(\hat{x}_0 \oplus \hat{b}_0) & c_4\lambda_4^{-1}(\hat{x}_4 \oplus \hat{b}_4) & c_8\lambda_8^{-1}(\hat{x}_8 \oplus \hat{b}_8) & c_{12}\lambda_{12}^{-1}(\hat{x}_{12} \oplus \hat{b}_{12}) \\
\hline
c_1\lambda_0^{-1}(\hat{x}_1 \oplus \hat{b}_1) & c_5\lambda_4^{-1}(\hat{x}_5 \oplus \hat{b}_5) & c_9\lambda_8^{-1}(\hat{x}_9 \oplus \hat{b}_9) & c_{13}\lambda_{12}^{-1}(\hat{x}_{13} \oplus \hat{b}_{13}) \\
\hline
c_2\lambda_0^{-1}(\hat{x}_2 \oplus \hat{b}_2) & c_6\lambda_4^{-1}(\hat{x}_6 \oplus \hat{b}_6) & c_{10}\lambda_8^{-1}(\hat{x}_{10} \oplus \hat{b}_{10}) & c_{14}\lambda_{12}^{-1}(\hat{x}_{14} \oplus \hat{b}_{14}) \\
\hline
c_3\lambda_0^{-1}(\hat{x}_3 \oplus \hat{b}_3) & c_7\lambda_4^{-1}(\hat{x}_7 \oplus \hat{b}_7) & c_{11}\lambda_8^{-1}(\hat{x}_{11} \oplus \hat{b}_{11}) & c_{15}\lambda_{12}^{-1}(\hat{x}_{15} \oplus \hat{b}_{15}) \\
\hline
\end{array}
\tag{26}
$$

The constants c_0, c_1, c_2, c_3 can now be computed as follows: $c_0 = 1$ and $c_i = [\overline{G}_i^{-1}(\tilde{x}_i \oplus \tilde{X}_i)]^{-1} \cdot \overline{G}_0^{-1}(\tilde{x}_0 \oplus \tilde{X}_0) \cdot \gamma_{0,i}$ for $i = 1, 2, 3$.

C   Work Factor

Step 1
Note that Algorithm 1 is closely related to the coupon collector's problem. To compute the expected number of iterations, we define the state of the algorithm as the cardinality of $\mathcal{M}_i$. Further, if the algorithm is in State j with $1 \leq j < 256$, then we define p_j as the probability that the algorithm transitions to State $j+1$ in one iteration. It follows that $p_j = \frac{2^8 - j}{2^8} \cdot \left(\frac{1}{2^8}\right)^2$, and that the expected total number of iterations for all 16 sets $\mathcal{M}_i$ equals

$$
16 \sum_{j=1}^{2^8-1} \frac{1}{p_j} = 2^{28} \sum_{j=1}^{2^8-1} \frac{1}{2^8 - j} < 2^{28} \cdot 2^3 = 2^{31}.
$$

The expected number of executions of the white-box implementation equals the expected number of iterations $+1$ since $Enc_k(m_{\text{ref}})$ needs to be computed only once.

Step 2
Algorithm 2 can be interpreted as follows: for all 256 elements of $\mathcal{M}_i$, we execute the white-box implementation and collect the output bytes of the functions in $\mathcal{S}_{g_i}$. For each input, it is necessary to inject $2^8 - 1$ different values and there are 16 sets $\mathcal{M}_i$. Therefore, the total number of executions of the white-box implementation equals $16 \cdot 2^8 \cdot 2^8$. The final step of the algorithm applies Tolhuizen's algorithm. The work factor of this algorithm is bounded above by 2^{14} (refer to [16] for details), implying an upper bound of $16 \cdot 2^{14}$ for all 16 sets.

Step 3

Similar reasoning applies to Step 3. The work factor of this step is defined by the effort to compute the 16 functions $\overline{G}_i^{-1}$ as described in Algorithm 3. The algorithm encrypts a plaintext and injects $2^8 - 1$ values that target an S-Box. The same procedure is repeated but now focusing on a different S-box. These steps require $2^8 + 2^8 - 1$ white-box executions in total. After this, the function L_i is constructed. Then, we apply Proposition 1 to the functions derived from the output bytes of the white-box implementation in order to construct the functions $\overline{G}_i^{-1}$. The work factor of this last step is bounded above by 2^{16}. This procedure is repeated for all affine byte encodings. Therefore, the number of executions of the white-box implementation equals $16(2^8 + 2^8 - 1)$ and the number of operations to compute all functions $\overline{G}_i^{-1}$ is bounded above by $16 \cdot 2^{16}$.

The intermediate part between Steps 3 and 4 computes the coefficients $c_0, c_1, \ldots, c_{15}$ as described in Appendix B. For each of the 4 columns of the AES state, the algorithm fixes a value of j, computes the 3 functions $\{G_i^{-1} \circ \otimes_{\gamma_{i,j}} \circ G_j\}$, and retrieves the value of $\gamma_{i,j}$. Then, it applies $\overline{G}_j$ to the input and $\overline{G}_i$ to the output of these functions. Then, for the 3 new functions, it performs a division in $\mathbb{F}_{2^8}$ to compute the values c_i as shown in Sect. 3.4. As a result, the number of operations required for this intermediate step is $4(3 + 3)$.

Step 4

Algorithm 4 solves 4 different systems of equations, each system defined by Eqs. 18, 19 and 20. We can choose $\alpha < 8$ as suggested by Table 1. We are required to inject α different faults and we perform 2 more operations within this loop. After this, we are using a meet-in-the-middle approach. The complexity for solving one system of equations is given by the sum of the work factors of the two main for-loops, and equals $8 \cdot 2^{16}$. Finally, we need to check the common solutions to the single equations. This procedure is repeated 4 times, once for every column of the AES state. Therefore, the number of executions of the white-box implementation is $4 \cdot \alpha$ and the number of operations required to find the solutions for the systems of equations is bounded above by $4 \cdot 2^3 \cdot 2 \cdot 2^{16}$.

We tested the performance of Algorithm 4 on a 9 round AES implementation with affine encodings over $\mathbb{F}_{2^8}$ on the output bytes. The experiments were performed with SageMath 8.2 on an Intel® Core™ i7-6700HQ rated at 2.60 GHz. In the experiments, we varied the value of α and recorded the average time to compute HT (referred to as time HT), the minimum size of HT (referred to as size HT), the maximum number of solutions to a single equation in the system (referred to as # matches), and the maximum number of solutions for several different output bytes (referred to as # solutions). Table 1 lists the values of these parameters for our experiments. The experiments suggest that for $\alpha = 2, 3$, the size of HT is small compared to its maximum number of 2^{16} entries. This is due to the fact that for some different pairs (λ^{-1}, β), the values derived from the Eq. 21 result in equal values, and therefore just one of them occurs in HT. For $\alpha > 3$ the hash-table HT starts to reach its maximum number of entries, and the average number of solutions is very small. In particular, starting from $\alpha = 6$, the number of solutions for the system did not exceed 1.

Table 1. Implementation of Algorithm 4.

α	Time HT (s)	Size HT	# matches	# solutions
2	≈ 19	$\approx 39030 < 2^{16}$	88803	64597
3	≈ 26	$\approx 39023 < 2^{16}$	50582	28688
4	≈ 38	$\approx 65107 < 2^{16}$	412	48
5	≈ 45	$\approx 65130 < 2^{16}$	305	2
6	≈ 59	$\approx 65279 < 2^{16}$	1	1
7	≈ 65	$\approx 65279 < 2^{16}$	1	1

In addition, we need to take into consideration the probability that two different values of Eq. 21 are mapped to the same hash value. If such a collision occurs, then there is a possibility that an entry in the table HT or a candidate solution gets discarded. To estimate the probability of a collision, we used hash tables implemented in SageMath 8.2 with a hash function that maps a bit-string to a 64-bit integer. Since $65280 < 2^{16}$ different hash values of Eq. 21 are computed, the probability that at least two of them collide is approximately

$$1 - \exp\left(-\frac{\left(2^{16}\right)^2}{2 \cdot 2^{64}}\right) = 1 - \exp\left(-2^{-33}\right) \approx 2^{-33}.$$

This implies that collisions are unlikely to occur in practice.

Step 5

This step uses standard DFA to solve 4 different systems of equations, each system defined by Eqs. 22, 23 and 24. If a meet-in-the-middle based approach as in Step 4 is used for this, then the required number of executions of the white-box implementation equals 4α (in our experiments, $\alpha = 4$ already yielded a unique solution in Step 5), and the required number of operations to find a solution to Eqs. 22, 23 and 24 is around $4 \cdot \alpha \cdot 2^9$.

Overall Work Factor

The overall work factor is the sum of the work factors of Steps 1–5. This work factor is dominated by 2^{32} executions of the white-box implementation. In Table 2, we report the total amount of white-box executions and the computational effort needed to analyze the faulty ciphertexts (work-factor of BGE Theorems and Meet-in-the-middle approaches) which are required to perform each step. Note that the number of faulty ciphertexts is approximately equal to the number of white-box executions because, per plaintext, only one additional white-box encryption is required to compute a non-faulty ciphertext.

Table 2. Number of white-box executions and analysis work-load.

	WB executions	Work-load analysis of ciphertext
Step 1	$< 2^{31}$	Negligible
Step 2	2^{20}	$< 2^{18}$
Step 3	$< 2^{13}$	$< 2^{20}$
Step 4	≤ 28	$< 2^{22}$
Step 5	≤ 20	$< 2^{13}$

References

1. Chow, S., Eisen, P., Johnson, H., Van Oorschot, P.C.: White-box cryptography and an AES implementation. In: Nyberg, K., Heys, H. (eds.) SAC 2002. LNCS, vol. 2595, pp. 250–270. Springer, Heidelberg (2003). https://doi.org/10.1007/3-540-36492-7_17
2. Billet, O., Gilbert, H., Ech-Chatbi, C.: Cryptanalysis of a white box AES implementation. In: Handschuh, H., Hasan, M.A. (eds.) SAC 2004. LNCS, vol. 3357, pp. 227–240. Springer, Heidelberg (2004). https://doi.org/10.1007/978-3-540-30564-4_16
3. Bos, J.W., Hubain, C., Michiels, W., Teuwen, P.: Differential computation analysis: hiding your white-box designs is not enough. In: Gierlichs, B., Poschmann, A.Y. (eds.) CHES 2016. LNCS, vol. 9813, pp. 215–236. Springer, Heidelberg (2016). https://doi.org/10.1007/978-3-662-53140-2_11
4. Biham, E., Shamir, A.: Differential fault analysis of secret key cryptosystems. In: Kaliski, B.S. (ed.) CRYPTO 1997. LNCS, vol. 1294, pp. 513–525. Springer, Heidelberg (1997). https://doi.org/10.1007/BFb0052259
5. Jacob, M., Boneh, D., Felten, E.: Attacking an obfuscated cipher by injecting faults. In: Feigenbaum, J. (ed.) DRM 2002. LNCS, vol. 2696, pp. 16–31. Springer, Heidelberg (2003). https://doi.org/10.1007/978-3-540-44993-5_2
6. Sanfelix, E., de Haas, J., Mune, C.: Unboxing the white-box: practical attacks against obfuscated ciphers. Presentation at BlackHat Europe 2015. https://www.blackhat.com/eu-15/briefings.html
7. Lee, S., Jho, N., Kim, M.: A key leakage preventive white-box cryptographic implementation. IACR Cryptology ePrint Archive, 2018/1047 (2018)
8. Lee, S., Kim, T., Kang, Y.: A masked white-box implementation for protecting against differential computation analysis. IEEE Trans. Inf. Forensics Secur. **13**(10), 2602–2615 (2018)
9. NIST, Advanced Encryption Standard (AES). FIPS PUB 197 (2001)
10. Banik, S., Bogdanov, A., Isobe, T., Jepsen, M.B.: Analysis of software countermeasures for whitebox encryption. IACR Trans. Symmetric Cryptol. **2017**(1), 307–328 (2017)
11. Collberg, C., Thomborson, C., Low, D.: A taxonomy of obfuscating transformations. Computer Science Technical Reports 148 (1997)
12. Mangard, S., Oswald, E., Popp, T.: Power Analysis Attacks: Revealing the Secrets of Smart Cards. Springer, Heidelberg (2008). https://doi.org/10.1007/978-0-387-38162-6
13. Xiao, Y., Lai, X.: A secure implementation of white-box AES. In: 2009 2nd International Conference on Computer Science and its Applications. IEEE (2009)

14. Biryukov, A., Udovenko, A.: Attacks and countermeasures for white-box designs. In: Peyrin, T., Galbraith, S. (eds.) ASIACRYPT 2018. LNCS, vol. 11273, pp. 373–402. Springer, Cham (2018). https://doi.org/10.1007/978-3-030-03329-3_13

15. Baek, C.H., Cheon, J.H., Hong, H.: White-box AES implementation revisited. J. Commun. Netw. **18**(3), 273–287 (2016)

16. Tolhuizen, L.: Improved cryptanalysis of an AES implementation. In: Proceedings of the 33rd WIC Symposium on Information Theory in the Benelux, Boekelo, The Netherlands (2012)

17. Lidl, R., Niederreiter, H.: Introduction to Finite Fields and Their Applications. Cambridge University Press, Cambridge (1986)

18. Feller, W.: An Introduction to Probability Theory and Its Applications, vol. 1, 3rd edn. Wiley, Hoboken (1968)

Parallelizable Authenticated Encryption with Small State Size

Akiko Inoue$^{(\boxtimes)}$ and Kazuhiko Minematsu$^{(\boxtimes)}$

NEC Corporation, Kawasaki, Japan
{a_inoue,k-minematsu}@nec.com

Abstract. Authenticated encryption (AE) is a symmetric-key encryption function that provides confidentiality and authenticity of a message. One of the evaluation criteria for AE is state size, which is memory size needed for encryption. State size is especially important when cryptosystem is implemented in constrained devices, while trivial reduction by using a small primitive is not generally acceptable as it leads to a degraded security.

In these days, the state size of AE has been very actively studied and a number of small-state AE schemes have been proposed, but they are inherently serial. It would be a natural question if we come up with a parallelizable AE with a smaller state size than the state-of-the-art.

In this paper, we study the seminal OCB mode for parallelizable AE and propose a method to reduce its state size without losing the bit security of it. More precisely, while (the most small-state variant of) OCB has $3n$-bit state, by carefully treating the checksum that is halved, we can achieve $2.5n$-bit state, while keeping the $n/2$-bit security as original. We also propose an inverse-free variant of it based on OTR. While the original OTR has $4n$-bit state, ours has $3.5n$-bit state. To our knowledge these numbers are the smallest ones achieved by the blockcipher modes for parallel AE and inverse-free parallel AE.

Keywords: Authenticated encryption · State size · OCB · OTR · Phash

1 Introduction

Authenticated encryption (AE) is a symmetric-key cryptographic scheme that provides confidentiality and authenticity of a message simultaneously. For example, GCM [19] and CCM [20] are the current NIST standard AE modes and used in TLS [37,40] and many other protocols. Among many criteria, the *state size* of AE has become an important one as well as the speed, since it is a key factor determining the size of hardware implementation. It is the memory size needed to implement the cryptosystem, in which we exclude core implementation (*e.g.* blockcipher) including key register. Thus we only count the memory size for the implementation of the mode of operation itself.

© Springer Nature Switzerland AG 2020
K. G. Paterson and D. Stebila (Eds.): SAC 2019, LNCS 11959, pp. 618–644, 2020.
https://doi.org/10.1007/978-3-030-38471-5_25

With the rise of lightweight cryptography, a number of small-state AE schemes have been proposed. CLOC and SILC proposed by Iwata *et al.* [25,26] in 2014 have $2n$-bit state using n-bit blockcipher. In 2017, Chakraborti *et al.* proposed COFB [16] which has $1.5n$-bit state size. Finally, Naito *et al.* proposed SAEB [36] and achieved n-bit state size which is essentially minimum as a mode of n-bit blockcipher. In the realm of permutation-based cryptography, the sponge AE schemes are known to have small state size [13]. However, these AEs are essentially serial to achieve small state size. Ideally, we want an AE scheme to perform good on a wide range of platforms, and parallelizability is very effective particularly for software on high-end to middle-end platforms. For example, AES runs about $4 \sim 8$ times faster in parallel on CPUs with AES instructions (AESNI), and the bitslice implementation of lightweight blockciphers typically run significantly (often by a order of magnitude) faster than the single-block implementation [12,29] on modern CPUs with SIMD instructions. This observation and the current research trend in serial AEs of small-state size suggest a natural question: *can we reduce the state size of a parallel AE?*

To answer the above question, we study the seminal OCB mode of operation from the state size perspective. OCB has been known to be the most efficient parallel AE. It consists of three versions, namely OCB1 [39], OCB2 [38] and OCB3 [27], and the latest OCB3 is in the final portfolio of CAESAR competition and was standardized in RFC [1]. In the submissions to the NIST Lightweight Cryptography Standardization project [2], the structure of OCB has been adopted by a number of schemes. Among the three versions of OCB, OCB2 has the smallest state size (*e.g.* OCB3 needs around n blocks in memory for internal mask generation). Note that OCB2 has been shown to be insecure by Inoue *et al.* [23]; we employed the fix of OCB2 suggested in [23] called OCB2f (for convention, we use "OCB2" to mean this fix unless otherwise stated). The original OCB2 needs $3n$-bit state, consisting of the blockcipher state and the mask applied to the blockcipher, and the checksum value to create the authentication tag. The last one is essentially a sum of the n-bit plaintext blocks.

We propose a way to reduce OCB's state size. In our method, we halve the length of checksum and we can reduce $0.5n$-bit state size from the original OCB. An important feature of our method is that it does not lose efficiency (the number of blockcipher calls needed) nor the essential bit security of OCB. When our method is instantiated with n-bit blockcipher, it needs $m + O(1)$ blockcipher calls to encrypt m-block input (this feature is called rate-1). Moreover, it has $n/2$-bit security despite of the trade-off relationship between the state size and security. We find that halving the checksum value does not harm the bit security of OCB2, and with a careful (though simple) handling of last block, we actually achieve $2.5n$-bit state size with our proposal called OCB-hc (for half-checksum).

One of the factors that increases the implementation size is the need of blockcipher inverse in its circuit. OCB needs the inverse, while Minematsu's OTR [31] derived from OCB is inverse-free. The state size of OTR is $4n$ bits as its operates on $2n$-bit blocks, thus larger than OCB2. However, thanks to the inverse-freeness, the total implementation size is expected to be smaller, which is also beneficial to high-throughput implementation (see the results of ATHENA benchmark[1] and [41]). Using a similar technique as OCB-hc, we propose OTR-hc that has $3.5n$-bit state with $n/2$-bit security.

We remark that improving OCB in any metric without losing the essential properties is already very tough. All versions of OCB have been extensively studied from various perspective, such as the provable security perspective [7,14] or the efficiency of mask generation scheme [22,33], or the misuse resistance [4,8] or the security beyond $O(2^{n/2})$ queries [21]. However, its general structure which determines the state size profile is already considered to be optimal since the inception. To the best of our knowledge, there is no previous work to reduce the state size, and $2.5n$-bit state of OCB-hc is the smallest among the known parallel AE modes. Likewise, $3.5n$-bit state size of OTR-hc is the smallest among the known inverse-free, parallel AE modes, to our knowledge. See Table 1.

Our technique can be applied to some variants of OCB as well, such as OPP [22] which has a much larger block size than OCB-AES and thus the gain is larger.

Table 1. Comparison of existing schemes and ours. State size excludes the key register. Rate is the number of input blocks processed in one primitive call.

Scheme	State size (bit)	Security	Rate	Inverse free	Parallelizable
OCB [27,38,39]	$3n$	$O(2^{n/2})$	1	-	✓
OTR [31]	$4n$	$O(2^{n/2})$	1	✓	✓
CLOC, SILC [25,26]	$2n$	$O(2^{n/2})$	1/2	✓	-
COFB [16]	$1.5n$	$O(2^{n/2})$	1	✓	-
SAEB [36]	n	$O(2^{n/2})$	1/2	✓	-
OCB-hc (Ours)	$2.5n$	$O(2^{n/2})$	1	-	✓
OTR-hc (Ours)	$3.5n$	$O(2^{n/2})$	1	✓	✓

2   Preliminaries

2.1   Notation

Let $\mathbb{N}$ be the set of natural numbers. For $n \in \mathbb{N}$, we define $\{0,1\}^n$ as the set of n-bit strings and $\{0,1\}^*$ as the set of all binary strings, including the empty string ε. For $A, B \in \{0,1\}^*$, $A \parallel B$ denotes the concatenation of A and B. The bit length of a string A is denoted by $|A|$, and $|A|_n := \lceil |A|/n \rceil$. Dividing a string A into blocks of n bits is denoted by $A[1] \parallel \cdots \parallel A[m] \xleftarrow{n} A$, where $m = |A|_n$ and $|A[i]| = n$, $|A[m]| \le n$ for $1 \le i \le m-1$. For $t \in \mathbb{N}$ and $t \le |A|$, $\mathtt{msb}_t(A)$ denotes the first t bits of A and $\mathtt{lsb}_t(A)$ denotes the last t bits of A. A sequence of i zeros (ones) is

---

[1] https://cryptography.gmu.edu/athena.

written as 0^i (1^i). When $|A| = n' < n$, we define $\mathsf{ozp}(A) := A \,\|\, 10^{n-n'-1}$, where $10^0 = 1$. When $|A| = n' = n$, $\mathsf{ozp}(A) := A$. When the element K is uniformly and randomly chosen from the set $\mathcal{K}$, it is denoted by $K \xleftarrow{\$} \mathcal{K}$.

2.2 (Tweakable) Blockcipher

Let $\mathcal{K}$ and $\mathcal{M}$ be the set of keys and messages, respectively. Let $\mathcal{T}$ be the set of tweaks, where a tweak is a public parameter. A tweakable blockcipher (TBC) [28] is a function $\widetilde{E} : \mathcal{K} \times \mathcal{T} \times \mathcal{M} \to \mathcal{M}$ s.t. $\widetilde{E}(K,T,\cdot)$ is a permutation on $\mathcal{M}$ for $\forall (K,T) \in \mathcal{K} \times \mathcal{T}$. It is also denoted by $\widetilde{E}_K^T$, $\widetilde{E}^T$ or $\widetilde{E}$, where $K \in \mathcal{K}$ and $T \in \mathcal{T}$. If $\mathcal{T}$ is singleton (and we thus omit it from the notation) it means a plain blockcipher. Namely, a blockcipher E is defined as $E : \mathcal{K} \times \mathcal{M} \to \mathcal{M}$ s.t. $E(K,\cdot)$ is a permutation on $\mathcal{M}$ for $\forall K \in \mathcal{K}$ and also denoted by E_K or E.

Let $\mathsf{Perm}(n)$ denote the set of all permutations on $\{0,1\}^n$. A tweakable permutation is a function $\pi : \{0,1\}^t \times \{0,1\}^n \to \{0,1\}^n$ s.t. for $\forall T \in \{0,1\}^t$, $\pi(T,\cdot) \in \mathsf{Perm}(n)$. Let $\widetilde{\mathsf{Perm}}(t,n)$ denote the set of above all functions π. Let P s.t. $\mathsf{P} \xleftarrow{\$} \mathsf{Perm}(n)$ be a uniform random permutation (URP) and $\widetilde{\mathsf{P}}$ s.t. $\widetilde{\mathsf{P}} \xleftarrow{\$} \widetilde{\mathsf{Perm}}(t,n)$ be a tweakable URP (TURP). A blockcipher E or a TBC $\widetilde{E}$ is said to be secure if it is computationally hard to distinguish from the ideal primitive with oracle access. More precisely, let $\mathcal{A}$ be an adversary who (possibly adaptively) queries to an oracle O and subsequently outputs a bit. We write $\Pr[\mathcal{A}^O \to 1]$ to denote the probability that this bit is 1. We define the notions of advantage of $\mathcal{A}$ as

$$\mathbf{Adv}_E^{\mathrm{prp}}(\mathcal{A}) := |\Pr[\mathcal{A}^E \to 1] - \Pr[\mathcal{A}^\mathsf{P} \to 1]|,$$
$$\mathbf{Adv}_E^{\mathrm{sprp}}(\mathcal{A}^{\pm}) := |\Pr[(\mathcal{A}^{\pm})^{E,E^{-1}} \to 1] - \Pr[(\mathcal{A}^{\pm})^{\mathsf{P},\mathsf{P}^{-1}} \to 1]|,$$
$$\mathbf{Adv}_{\widetilde{E}}^{\mathrm{tprp}}(\mathcal{A}) := |\Pr[\mathcal{A}^{\widetilde{E}} \to 1] - \Pr[\mathcal{A}^{\widetilde{\mathsf{P}}} \to 1]|,$$
$$\mathbf{Adv}_{\widetilde{E}}^{\mathrm{tsprp}}(\mathcal{A}^{\pm}) := |\Pr[(\mathcal{A}^{\pm})^{\widetilde{E},\widetilde{E}^{-1}} \to 1] - \Pr[(\mathcal{A}^{\pm})^{\widetilde{\mathsf{P}},\widetilde{\mathsf{P}}^{-1}} \to 1]|,$$

where the first and the third notions are for adversaries with encryption oracle (thus chosen-plaintext queries), and the second and the fourth are for adversaries with encryption and decryption oracles (thus chosen-ciphertext queries).

When the advantage is sufficiently low, E or $\widetilde{E}$ is said to be secure against the underlying adversary.

2.3 Authenticated Encryption

Let $\mathcal{K}$, $\mathcal{M}_{ae}$ and $\mathcal{N}_{ae}$ be the set of keys, messages and nonce, respectively. Let $\mathcal{A}_{ae}$ be the set of associated data (AD), which is data not encrypted but authenticated, and it can be empty. For convention, by saying AE we may mean AEAD. If we want to explicitly mean AE with no AD, (*i.e.* $\mathcal{A}_{ae}$ is empty) we call it *plain* AE. Suppose AE.$\mathcal{E}$ and AE.$\mathcal{D}$ as an encryption function and a decryption function of AE, respectively. We suppose that AE.$\mathcal{E}$ and AE.$\mathcal{D}$ share the key $K \in \mathcal{K}$

as input. For encryption, the sender inputs a nonce $N \in \mathcal{N}_{ae}$, an associated data $A \in \mathcal{A}_{ae}$ and a message $M \in \mathcal{M}_{ae}$ to AE.$\mathcal{E}_K$. Then she gets a ciphertext $C \in \mathcal{M}_{ae}$ and a tag $T \in \{0,1\}^{\tau}$ as the output, where τ is the length of tag. The sender sends the tuple (N, A, C, T), and the receiver inputs them to AE.$\mathcal{D}_K$ for decryption. AE.$\mathcal{D}_K$ outputs a message M' if the verification is success, otherwise outputs $\perp$, which means that the verification failed.

The security of AE scheme can be evaluated by two criteria: privacy and authenticity. Following the existing work [11,38,39], we use the term *privacy* to mean confidentiality. For privacy, we define the privacy advantage as the probability that the adversary successfully distinguishes the encryption function of AE from the *random-bit oracle*, \$($*, *, *$)$, which returns random bits of length $|M|+|T|$ for any query (N, A, M): $\mathbf{Adv}_{AE}^{priv}(\mathcal{A}) := |\Pr[\mathcal{A}^{AE.\mathcal{E}} \to 1] - \Pr[\mathcal{A}^{\$} \to 1]|$. Here, we assume $\mathcal{A}$ is nonce-respecting, that is, $\mathcal{A}$ does not repeat nonce N in the encryption queries. For authenticity, we define the authenticity advantage as the probability that the adversary creates a successful forgery by accessing encryption and decryption functions of AE. It is defined as $\mathbf{Adv}_{AE}^{auth}(\mathcal{A}) := \Pr[\mathcal{A}^{AE.\mathcal{E},AE.\mathcal{D}}$ forges.$]$, where $\mathcal{A}^{AE.\mathcal{E},AE.\mathcal{D}}$ forges if $\mathcal{A}$ receives $M' \neq \perp$ from AE.$\mathcal{D}$ by querying (N', A', C', T') while (N', A', M') has never been queried to AE.$\mathcal{E}$. As well as the privacy case, $\mathcal{A}$ is assumed to be nonce-respecting in its encryption queries, however no restriction on the nonce values in the decryption queries.

2.4   Computation on Galois Field

Let $\mathbb{F}_{p^n}$ be a finite filed, where characteristic p is prime and extension degree $n \in \mathbb{N}$. We focus on the case $n = 128$. Following [24,38], we use the lexicographically-first polynomial for defining the field and thus $\mathbb{F}_{2^{128}} := \mathbb{F}_2[x]/(x^{128}+x^7+x^2+x+1)$ and obtain $\mathbb{F}_{2^{128}} = \langle x \rangle$. We regard an element of $\mathbb{F}_{2^{128}}$ as a polynomial of x. For $\forall a \in \{0,1\}^{128}$, we also regard it as a coefficient vector of an element in $\mathbb{F}_{2^{128}}$. Thus, the primitive root x is interpreted as 2 in the decimal representation. For $a \in \mathbb{F}_{2^{128}}$, let $2a$ denote a multiplication by x and a, which is called doubling [38]. In $\mathbb{F}_{2^{128}}$, $2a := (a \ll 1)$ if $\mathtt{msb}_1(a) = 0$ and $2a := (a \ll 1) \oplus (0^{120}10^41^3)$ if $\mathtt{msb}_1(a) = 1$, where $(a \ll 1)$ is the left-shift of one bit. For $c \in \mathbb{N}$, we can calculate $2^c a$ by repeating doubling of a for c-times, and $3a = 2a \oplus a$.

3   Review of OCB and OTR

3.1   OCB

OCB is a blockcipher mode of operation for AE scheme proposed at [27,38,39]. It is parallelizable, and is a rate-1 scheme which needs one blockcipher call to process one message block. It also has provable security based on the pseudorandomness of underlying blockcipher. The security bound of OCB is $O(\sigma^2/2^n)$, which is called birthday-bound security, where σ is the number of access to n-bit blockcipher. OCB encrypts a message in a mode similar to ECB, where the blockcipher has input and output masks, and computes the sum of message blocks, called checksum. The authentication tag is an encryption of the checksum. Although OCB was initially proposed as a plain AE [39], it can be converted into AEAD by using PMAC [38] or Phash [27] for AD and taking the XOR of the output and the tag of (plain-AE) OCB. There are three versions for OCB: OCB1 [39], OCB2 [38], OCB3 [27]. Among them, OCB2 has the smallest state size of $3n$ bits, consisting of n-bit memory for processing of one message block, the value of the mask, and the checksum. As described before, since OCB2 has shown to be insecure by Inoue et al. [23], this paper focuses on the fix suggested by [23] called OCB2f, which has the same $3n$-bit state. We simply call it OCB2 or even OCB as the version of OCB that we study, if no confusion is possible. OBC2 can be interpreted as a TBC mode for AE, which we call ΘCB. The TBC used in ΘCB is a blockcipher mode called XEX*.

Let us review the specific (information-theoretic) security bound of OCB2 when it is instantiated with an n-bit URP P. Throughout the paper, we use a subscript to denote the underlying component, hence OCB2$_P$ is the target scheme. We write ΘCB$_{\widetilde{P}}$ to denote ΘCB using TURP $\widetilde{P}$. For n-bit tag case, and for the privacy-adversary $\mathcal{A}$ and the authenticity-adversary $\mathcal{A}^{\pm}$, the security bounds of OCB2$_P$ ($\mathbf{Adv}^{\mathrm{priv}}_{\mathrm{OCB2_P}}(\mathcal{A})$, $\mathbf{Adv}^{\mathrm{auth}}_{\mathrm{OCB2_P}}(\mathcal{A}^{\pm})$) are given as follows [23,30,38]:

$$\mathbf{Adv}^{\mathrm{priv}}_{\mathrm{OCB2_P}}(\mathcal{A}) \leq \mathbf{Adv}^{\mathrm{tprp}}_{\mathrm{XEX^*_P}}(\mathcal{B}) + \mathbf{Adv}^{\mathrm{priv}}_{\Theta\mathrm{CB}_{\widetilde{P}}}(\mathcal{A}) \leq \frac{4.5\sigma^2_{\mathrm{priv}}}{2^n} + 0,$$

$$\mathbf{Adv}^{\mathrm{auth}}_{\mathrm{OCB2_P}}(\mathcal{A}^{\pm}) \leq \mathbf{Adv}^{\mathrm{tsprp}}_{\mathrm{XEX^*_P}}(\mathcal{B}^{\pm}) + \mathbf{Adv}^{\mathrm{auth}}_{\Theta\mathrm{CB}_{\widetilde{P}}}(\mathcal{A}^{\pm}) \leq \frac{4.5\sigma^2_{\mathrm{auth}}}{2^n} + \frac{q_d}{2^n - 1},$$

where $\mathcal{B}$ (resp. $\mathcal{B}^{\pm}$) is the adversary performing chosen-plaintext attack (resp. chosen-ciphertext attack), σ_{priv} (resp. σ_{auth}) is the total number of queried blocks in privacy (resp. authenticity) game and q_d is the number of queries to verification (decryption) oracle. Since OCB3 can be also interpreted as a TBC mode, we can derive similar security bounds to OCB2 as above [27].

3.2   OTR

OTR is an AEAD blockcipher mode of operation proposed by Minematsu [31]. It is a parallelizable, rate-1 scheme. Whereas OCB needs blockcipher decryption for the entire decryption, OTR does not need it for both encryption and decryption, hence it is called inverse-free. As well as OCB, it has provable security based on the pseudorandomness of blockcipher, with security bound of $O(\sigma^2/2^n)$, where σ is the number of access to n-bit blockcipher[2]. OTR encrypts a message by using two-round Feistel permutation based on a blockcipher with an input mask, and computes the checksum as a sum of even-numbered message blocks. The authentication tag is an encryption of the checksum. The state size of OTR is $4n$ bits. It is composed of $2n$-bit memory for processing two message blocks

---

[2] Bost and Sanders [15] pointed a problem of the first version of OTR [31] regarding its instantiation of XE. Therefore we here refer OTR of the fixed versions [32].

(*i.e.* one Feistel chunk), and each n-bit memory for the value of the mask and the checksum. As well as OCB, OTR can be interpreted as a mode of TBC, which we call ΘTR (originally $\mathbb{OTR}$). The TBC used in ΘTR is a blockcipher mode called XE [38]. The security bound of OTRP can be bounded by a hybrid argument similar to OCBP. A tweakable uniform random function (TURF) is denoted by $\widetilde{\mathsf{R}} : \mathcal{T} \times \{0,1\}^n \to \{0,1\}^n$, where $\mathcal{T}$ is the same tweak space as XE. It is essentially a random function on the whole input domain.

For n-bit tag and for the privacy-adversary $\mathcal{A}$ and the authenticity-adversary $\mathcal{A}^\pm$, the security bounds of OTRP ($\mathbf{Adv}_{\mathrm{OTR_P}}^{\mathrm{priv}}(\mathcal{A})$, $\mathbf{Adv}_{\mathrm{OTR_P}}^{\mathrm{auth}}(\mathcal{A}^\pm)$) are given as follows:

$$\mathbf{Adv}_{\mathrm{OTR_P}}^{\mathrm{priv}}(\mathcal{A}) \leq \mathbf{Adv}_{\mathrm{XE_P},\widetilde{\mathsf{R}}}^{\mathrm{cpa}}(\mathcal{B}) + \mathbf{Adv}_{\Theta\mathrm{TR}_{\widetilde{\mathsf{R}}}}^{\mathrm{priv}}(\mathcal{A}) \leq \frac{6\sigma_{\mathrm{priv}}^2}{2^n} + 0,$$

$$\mathbf{Adv}_{\mathrm{OTR_P}}^{\mathrm{auth}}(\mathcal{A}^\pm) \leq \mathbf{Adv}_{\mathrm{XE_P},\widetilde{\mathsf{R}}}^{\mathrm{cpa}}(\mathcal{B}) + \mathbf{Adv}_{\Theta\mathrm{TR}_{\widetilde{\mathsf{R}}}}^{\mathrm{auth}}(\mathcal{A}^\pm) \leq \frac{6\sigma_{\mathrm{auth}}^2}{2^n} + \frac{q_d}{2^n},$$

where $\mathbf{Adv}_{\mathrm{XE_P},\widetilde{\mathsf{R}}}^{\mathrm{cpa}}(\mathcal{B})$ is the probability which the adversary $\mathcal{B}$ performing chosen-plaintext attack can distinguish $\mathrm{XE_P}$ from $\widetilde{\mathsf{R}}$. The parameter σ_{priv} (resp. σ_{auth}) is the total number of queried blocks in privacy (resp. authenticity) game and q_d is the number of queries to the decryption oracle.

4 Our Proposals

4.1 Overview

As we mentioned in Sect. 3, the security bounds of OCB and OTR are evaluated using the hybrid argument: the bound of OCB is a sum of the bound of XEX* and that of ΘCB. Similarly, the bound of OTR is a sum of the bound of XE and that of ΘTR. One can find that ΘCB and ΘTR have beyond-birthday-bound security (namely perfect privacy and n-bit authenticity), however the total security of OCB and OTR are $n/2$ bits because of the birthday bounds of XEX* and XE. This gap implies a potential improvement in size, by trading the state size of ΘCB and ΘTR for security, while maintaining the overall $n/2$-bit security of OCB and OTR. We found that such a trading-off is indeed possible by reducing the length of checksum by $n/2$ bits, which we call half-checksum method.

Actually, this gap has been exploited in the literature. For example, Naito's XKX [34,35] provides a beyond-birthday-bound secure implementation of TBC and he proposed it to be used within a mode similar to ΘCB so that the resulting AE has beyond-birthday-bound security.

4.2 OCB-hc

We apply the half-checksum method mentioned in Sect. 4.1 to OCB. The resultant scheme is denoted by OCB-hc. While we first propose OCB-hc as a plain

AE with $n/2$-bit tag length, we will extend it to an AEAD in Sect. 5. In the following, we fix the tag length to be $n/2$ bits as it is essentially minimum to achieve $n/2$-bit security. In case a longer tag is required, Sect. 5 will also provide an extension to the case of the arbitrary tag length up to n bits.

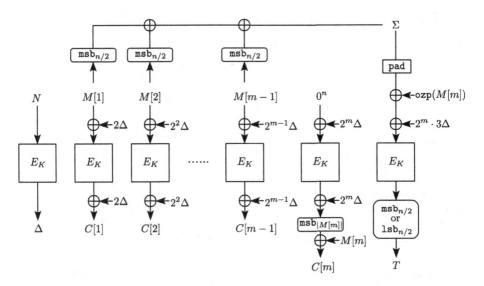

Fig. 1. The encryption of OCB-hc$_{E_K}$, where E_K is any n-bit blockcipher. The function pad denotes the zero padding to n bits.

Specification. We show OCB-hc in Figs. 1 and 2. As mentioned, the tag is $n/2$ bits and AD is empty. Let E_K be an n-bit blockcipher. We define the encryption function of OCB-hc$_{E_K}$ as OCB-hc.$\mathcal{E}_{E_K} : (N, M) \mapsto (C, T)$, where $(N, M) \in \{0,1\}^n \times \{0,1\}^*$ and $(C, T) \in \{0,1\}^* \times \{0,1\}^{n/2}$. We also define the decryption function as OCB-hc.$\mathcal{D}_{E_K} : (N, C, T) \mapsto M$ or $\perp$, where $(N, C, T) \in \{0,1\}^n \times \{0,1\}^* \times \{0,1\}^{n/2}$ and $M \in \{0,1\}^*$. The structure of OCB-hc is generally the same as OCB, except that it computes the $n/2$-bit checksum of message blocks (say the first $n/2$ bits; in fact any bits would work fine). This is also different in the last message block $M[m]$, which may be partial. Following OCB, we take an XOR of $M[m]$ and the checksum padded to n bits, which is needed for security.

State Size. Since the checksum is halved, it is easy to see that the state size of OCB-hc is reduced to $2.5n$ bits until the last message block. If $0 < M[m] \le n/2$, the state size remains $2.5n$ bits since the checksum needs only $n/2$-bit memory. However if $n/2 < M[m] \le n$, the state size seemingly increases to at most $3n$ bits, implying no gain. We can avoid this by only changing the computation procedure described above: we add $M[m]$ (more precisely, $\mathtt{ozp}(M[m])$) not to the checksum, but to the mask used in the last block for the tag (See line 10, 11 in Algorithm: OCB-hc.$\mathcal{E}$ and Algorithm: OCB-hc.$\mathcal{D}$ in Fig. 2). This will not change the algorithm. Since the mask is consistently n bits, this will not increase the size. Therefore, OCB-hc works with $2.5n$-bit state for any plaintext.

Algorithm: OCB-hc.$\mathcal{E}_{E_K}(N, M)$	**Algorithm:** OCB-hc.$\mathcal{D}_{E_K}(N, C, T)$
1. $M[1] \parallel \cdots \parallel M[m-1] \parallel M[m] \xleftarrow{n} M$	1. $C[1] \parallel \cdots \parallel C[m-1] \parallel C[m] \xleftarrow{n} C$
2. $\Delta \leftarrow 2E_K(N), \ \Sigma \leftarrow 0^{n/2}$	2. $\Delta \leftarrow 2E_K(N), \ \Sigma \leftarrow 0^{n/2}$
3. **for** $i \leftarrow 1$ **to** $m-1$ **do**	3. **for** $i \leftarrow 1$ **to** $m-1$ **do**
4. $C[i] \leftarrow E_K(M[i] \oplus \Delta) \oplus \Delta$	4. $M[i] \leftarrow D_K(C[i] \oplus \Delta) \oplus \Delta$
5. $\Sigma \leftarrow \Sigma \oplus \mathtt{msb}_{n/2}(M[i])$	5. $\Sigma \leftarrow \Sigma \oplus \mathtt{msb}_{n/2}(M[i])$
6. $\Delta \leftarrow 2\Delta$	6. $\Delta \leftarrow 2\Delta$
7. $\mathrm{Pad} \leftarrow E_K(0^n \oplus \Delta) \oplus \Delta$	7. $\mathrm{Pad} \leftarrow E_K(0^n \oplus \Delta) \oplus \Delta$
8. $\Delta \leftarrow 3\Delta$	8. $\Delta \leftarrow 3\Delta$
9. $C[m] \leftarrow \mathtt{msb}_{\lvert M[m] \rvert}(\mathrm{Pad} \oplus \mathtt{ozp}(M[m]))$	9. $M[m] \leftarrow \mathtt{msb}_{\lvert C[m] \rvert}(\mathrm{Pad}) \oplus C[m]$
10. $\Delta \leftarrow \Delta \oplus \mathtt{ozp}(M[m])$	10. $\Delta \leftarrow \Delta \oplus \mathtt{ozp}(M[m])$
11. $\mathrm{Tag} \leftarrow E_K(\Sigma \parallel 0^{n/2} \oplus \Delta)$	11. $\mathrm{Tag} \leftarrow E_K(\Sigma \parallel 0^{n/2} \oplus \Delta)$
12. **if** $\lvert M[m] \rvert = n$ **then** $T \leftarrow \mathtt{msb}_{n/2}(\mathrm{Tag})$	12. **if** $\lvert M[m] \rvert = n$ **then** $T' \leftarrow \mathtt{msb}_{n/2}(\mathrm{Tag})$
13. **else** $T \leftarrow \mathtt{lsb}_{n/2}(\mathrm{Tag})$	13. **else** $T' \leftarrow \mathtt{lsb}_{n/2}(\mathrm{Tag})$
14. **return** $(C[1] \parallel \cdots \parallel C[m], T)$	14. **if** $T = T'$ **then return** $M[1] \parallel \cdots \parallel M[m]$
	15. **else return** $\perp$

Fig. 2. The algorithm of OCB-hc. E_K is any n-bit blockcipher, and D_K is the decryption of E_K.

4.3   Security of OCB-hc

The security bounds of OCB-hc are shown below. We assume the underlying blockcipher is an n-bit URP, P. When the underlying blockcipher is a PRP, the security bounds are derived from ours using a standard technique [9], thus we omitted.

Theorem 1.

$$\mathbf{Adv}_{\text{OCB-hc}_P}^{\text{priv}}(\mathcal{A}) \leq \frac{4.5\sigma_{\text{priv}}^2}{2^n}, \quad \mathbf{Adv}_{\text{OCB-hc}_P}^{\text{auth}}(\mathcal{A}^{\pm}) \leq \frac{4.5\sigma_{\text{auth}}^2}{2^n} + \frac{4q_d}{2^{n/2}},$$

where $\mathcal{A}$, $\mathcal{A}^{\pm}$ are the adversaries against OCB-hc$_P$ and σ_{priv}, σ_{auth} and q_d are the parameters for $\mathcal{A}$ and $\mathcal{A}^{\pm}$. The parameter σ_{priv} (resp. σ_{auth}) is the number of accesses to P in privacy (resp. authenticity) game. The parameter q_d is the number of queries to the decryption oracle in authenticity game.

Proof. Let $i \in \mathbb{N}$, $j \in \{0, 1, 2, 3\}$. We define two TBCs XEX_{E_K} and XE_{E_K} as follows.

$$\mathrm{XEX}_{E_K}^{N,i}(M) = E_K(M \oplus 2^i E_K(N)) \oplus 2^i E_K(N),$$
$$\mathrm{XE}_{E_K}^{N,i,j}(M) = E_K(M \oplus 2^i 3^j E_K(N)).$$

Algorithm: $\Theta\text{CB-hc.}\mathcal{E}_{\tilde{E}}(N, M)$	**Algorithm:** $\Theta\text{CB-hc.}\mathcal{D}_{\tilde{E}}(N, C, T)$
1. $M[1] \,\|\, \cdots \,\|\, M[m-1] \,\|\, M[m] \overset{n}{\leftarrow} M$	1. $C[1] \,\|\, \cdots \,\|\, C[m-1] \,\|\, C[m] \overset{n}{\leftarrow} C$
2. $\Sigma \leftarrow 0^{n/2}$	2. $\Sigma \leftarrow 0^{n/2}$
3. **for** $i \leftarrow 1$ **to** $m-1$ **do**	3. **for** $i \leftarrow 1$ **to** $m-1$ **do**
4. $C[i] \leftarrow \tilde{E}^{N,1,i,0}(M[i])$	4. $M[i] \leftarrow \tilde{D}^{N,1,i,0}(C[i])$
5. $\Sigma \leftarrow \Sigma \oplus \text{msb}_{n/2}(M[i])$	5. $\Sigma \leftarrow \Sigma \oplus \text{msb}_{n/2}(M[i])$
6. $\text{Pad} \leftarrow \tilde{E}^{N,1,m,0}(0^n)$	6. $\text{Pad} \leftarrow \tilde{E}^{N,1,m,0}(0^n)$
7. $C[m] \leftarrow M[m] \oplus \text{msb}_{|M[m]|}(\text{Pad})$	7. $M[m] \leftarrow C[m] \oplus \text{msb}_{|C[m]|}(\text{Pad})$
8. $\text{Checksum} \leftarrow (\Sigma \,\|\, 0^{n/2}) \oplus \text{ozp}(M[m])$	8. $\text{Checksum} \leftarrow (\Sigma \,\|\, 0^{n/2}) \oplus \text{ozp}(M[m])$
9. $\text{Tag} \leftarrow \tilde{E}^{N,0,m,1}(\text{Checksum})$	9. $\text{Tag} \leftarrow \tilde{E}^{N,0,m,1}(\text{Checksum})$
10. **if** $|M[m]| = n$ **then** $T \leftarrow \text{msb}_{n/2}(\text{Tag})$	10. **if** $|M[m]| = n$ **then** $T' \leftarrow \text{msb}_{n/2}(\text{Tag})$
11. **else** $T \leftarrow \text{lsb}_{n/2}(\text{Tag})$	11. **else** $T' \leftarrow \text{lsb}_{n/2}(\text{Tag})$
12. **return** $(C[1] \,\|\, \cdots \,\|\, C[m], T)$	12. **if** $T = T'$ **then return** $M[1] \,\|\, \cdots \,\|\, M[m]$
	13. **else return** $\perp$

Fig. 3. The algorithm of $\Theta\text{CB-hc}$. $\tilde{E}$ is any TBC which has the same arguments as XEX^*, and $\tilde{D}$ is the decryption of $\tilde{E}$.

Then we combine them to one TBC denoted by $\text{XEX}^*_{E_K}$. $\text{XEX}^{*\,N,b,i,j}_{E_K}(M) = \text{XEX}^{N,i}_{E_K}(M)$ if $b = 1$, $\text{XEX}^{*\,N,b,i,j}_{E_K}(M) = \text{XE}^{N,i,j}_{E_K}(M)$ if $b = 0$. We also define $\Theta\text{CB-hc}_{\tilde{E}}$ as a TBC mode for plain AE in Fig. 3 for the security proof of OCB-hc. When $\tilde{E}$ is XEX^*_E, $\Theta\text{CB-hc}_{\tilde{E}}$ is equivalent to OCB-hc$_E$. Let $\widetilde{\mathsf{P}}$ denote a TURP which has the same arguments as XEX^*. We define $\mathbf{Adv}^{\text{cpa-nr}}_{F,G}(\mathcal{A})$ (resp. $\mathbf{Adv}^{\text{cca-nr}}_{F,G}(\mathcal{A})$) as the probability that the chosen-plaintext attack (resp. chosen-ciphertext attack) adversary $\mathcal{A}$, who is nonce-respecting in encryption queries, can distinguish F from G. Then we obtain

$$\mathbf{Adv}^{\text{priv}}_{\text{OCB-hc}_\mathsf{P}}(\mathcal{A}) \leq \mathbf{Adv}^{\text{cpa-nr}}_{\text{OCB-hc}_\mathsf{P}, \Theta\text{CB-hc}_{\tilde{\mathsf{P}}}}(\mathcal{A}) + \mathbf{Adv}^{\text{priv}}_{\Theta\text{CB-hc}_{\tilde{\mathsf{P}}}}(\mathcal{A})$$

$$= \mathbf{Adv}^{\text{tprp}}_{\text{XEX}^*_\mathsf{P}}(\mathcal{B}) + \mathbf{Adv}^{\text{priv}}_{\Theta\text{CB-hc}_{\tilde{\mathsf{P}}}}(\mathcal{A})$$

$$\leq \frac{4.5\sigma^2_{\text{priv}}}{2^n} + 0 \quad \text{and} \tag{1}$$

$$\mathbf{Adv}^{\text{auth}}_{\text{OCB-hc}_\mathsf{P}}(\mathcal{A}^\pm) \leq \mathbf{Adv}^{\text{cca-nr}}_{\text{OCB-hc}_\mathsf{P}, \Theta\text{CB-hc}_{\tilde{\mathsf{P}}}}(\mathcal{A}^\pm) + \mathbf{Adv}^{\text{auth}}_{\Theta\text{CB-hc}_{\tilde{\mathsf{P}}}}(\mathcal{A}^\pm)$$

$$= \mathbf{Adv}^{\text{tsprp}}_{\text{XEX}^*_\mathsf{P}}(\mathcal{B}^\pm) + \mathbf{Adv}^{\text{auth}}_{\Theta\text{CB-hc}_{\tilde{\mathsf{P}}}}(\mathcal{A}^\pm)$$

$$\leq \frac{4.5\sigma^2_{\text{auth}}}{2^n} + \frac{4q_d}{2^{n/2}}, \tag{2}$$

where $\mathcal{B}$ (resp. $\mathcal{B}^\pm$) is the adversary which can simulate $\mathcal{A}$ (resp. $\mathcal{A}^\pm$). The first terms of (1), (2) are derived from [38] and [33]. The derivations of the second terms of (1), (2) are described below.

Privacy. Every TURP invoked in the privacy game has the different tweak since the adversary is nonce-respecting. Thus, we have $\mathbf{Adv}^{\text{priv}}_{\Theta\text{CB-hc}_{\tilde{\mathsf{P}}}}(\mathcal{A}) = 0$.

Authenticity.

Lemma 1. *The authenticity advantage of $\Theta\text{CB-hc}_{\tilde{\mathsf{P}}}$ is*

$$\mathbf{Adv}^{\text{auth}}_{\Theta\text{CB-hc}_{\tilde{\mathsf{P}}}}(\mathcal{A}^{\pm}) \leq \frac{4q_d}{2^{n/2}},$$

where q_d denotes the number of verification (decryption) queries.

Proof. We start with the case $q_d = 1$. Without loss of generality, the adversary performs the decryption query after all encryption queries. Suppose that she obtains the transcript $z = \{(N_1, M_1, C_1, T_1), \ldots, (N_q, M_q, C_q, T_q)\}$ in encryption query, and she queries (N', C', T') in decryption query. Let Z be the set of all transcripts, and T^* be the valid tag for (N', C'). We define the function $\text{ifPad} : \{0,1\}^* \to \{0,1\}$ as follows.

$$\text{ifPad}(M) = \begin{cases} 0 & \text{if } |M| = 0 \bmod n; \\ 1 & \text{otherwise.} \end{cases}$$

Then we obtain the following equations.

$$\begin{aligned} \mathbf{Adv}^{\text{auth}}_{\Theta\text{CB-hc}_{\tilde{\mathsf{P}}}}(\mathcal{A}^{\pm}) &= \Pr[T' = T^*] \\ &= \sum_z \Pr[T' = T^*, Z = z] \\ &= \sum_z \Pr[T' = T^* \mid Z = z] \Pr[Z = z]. \end{aligned}$$

We define $\text{FP}_z := \Pr[T' = T^* \mid Z = z]$ and evaluate $\max_z \text{FP}_z$ as below.

1. Let $N' \neq N_i$ for $1 \leq \forall i \leq q$. Since the TURP which returns valid T^* takes a new tweak, the adversary has no information about T^*. Thus $\text{FP}_z \leq 1/2^{n/2}$ holds.
2. Let $N' = N_\alpha$, $\alpha \in \{1, 2, \ldots, q\}$, $C' \neq C_\alpha$. We divide the cases with the value of $|C'|$ as follows.
   (a) Let $|C'|_n \neq |C_\alpha|_n$. The tweak of the TURP which outputs T^* is different from that of TURPs which are invoked in encryption query. Thus $\text{FP}_z \leq 1/2^{n/2}$ holds.
   (b) Let $|C'|_n = |C_\alpha|_n$ and $\text{ifPad}(C') \neq \text{ifPad}(C_\alpha)$. Suppose that Checksum^* and M^* are the valid checksum and message for (N', C'), respectively, and Checksum_α is the value of the checksum for $(N_\alpha, M_\alpha, C_\alpha, T_\alpha)$. The adversary can make Checksum^* equal to Checksum_α by using padding. When $\text{Checksum}^* \neq \text{Checksum}_\alpha$, $\text{FP}_z \leq 2^{n/2}/(2^n - 1)$ holds. When $\text{Checksum}^* = \text{Checksum}_\alpha$, $\text{FP}_z \leq 1/(2^{n/2})$ holds since $\text{ifPad}(C') \neq \text{ifPad}(C_\alpha)$ and the adversary obtains no information about T^* from T_α.
   (c) Let $|C'|_n = |C_\alpha|_n$ and $\text{ifPad}(C') = \text{ifPad}(C_\alpha)$. Suppose $|C'|_n = |C_\alpha|_n = m$. We consider the following cases.
   Case e_1: When $C' \neq C_\alpha$, $\text{Checksum}^* = \text{Checksum}_\alpha$ holds.

Case e_2: When $C' \neq C_\alpha$, $T' = T^*$ holds.

We first evaluate $\Pr[e_1 \mid Z = z] = \Pr[\mathtt{Checksum}^* = \mathtt{Checksum}_\alpha \mid Z = z]$. When $C'[m] \neq C_\alpha[m]$ and $C'[i] = C_\alpha[i]$ for $\forall i \in \{1, \ldots, m-1\}$, we obtain $\Pr[e_1 \mid Z = z] = 0$ since $\mathtt{ozp}(M^*[m]) \neq \mathtt{ozp}(M_\alpha[m])$ holds. Then suppose $C'[u] \neq C_\alpha[u]$ for $\exists u\{1, \ldots, m-1\}$. We obtain following evaluation.

$$
\begin{aligned}
&\Pr[e_1 \mid Z = z] \\
&= \Pr\left[\left(\mathtt{msb}_{n/2}(M^*[u]) \,\|\, 0^{n/2}\right) \oplus \left(\mathtt{msb}_{n/2}(M_\alpha[u]) \,\|\, 0^{n/2}\right) = \delta \mid Z = z\right] \\
&\leq \frac{2^{n/2}}{2^n - 1},
\end{aligned}
$$

where $\delta = \left(\mathtt{msb}_{n/2}(M^*[u]) \,\|\, 0^{n/2}\right) \oplus \left(\mathtt{msb}_{n/2}(M_\alpha[u]) \,\|\, 0^{n/2}\right) \oplus \mathtt{Checksum}^* \oplus \mathtt{Checksum}_\alpha$. Thus, $\Pr[e_1 \mid Z = z] \leq 2/2^{n/2}$ is obtained. Then we evaluate $\Pr[e_2 | \bar{e}_1, Z = z]$. In this case, the TURP outputting T^* and the TURP outputting T_α take the same tweak, and ifPad$(C') = $ ifPad(C_α) holds. However, $\mathtt{Checksum}^* \neq \mathtt{Checksum}_\alpha$ holds, and we obtain $\Pr[e_2 | \bar{e}_1, Z = z] \leq 2^{n/2}/(2^n - 1)$.

From above, we obtain the following evaluation.

$$
\begin{aligned}
\mathrm{FP}_z &= \Pr[e_2 | Z = z] \\
&\leq \Pr[e_2 \cap \bar{e}_1 | Z = z] + \Pr[e_1 | Z = z] \\
&\leq \Pr[e_2 | \bar{e}_1, Z = z] + \Pr[e_1 | Z = z] \\
&\leq \frac{2^{n/2}}{2^n - 1} + \frac{2^{n/2}}{2^n - 1} \leq \frac{4}{2^{n/2}}.
\end{aligned}
$$

From the evaluations of the above cases, we obtain

$$
\mathbf{Adv}^{\mathrm{auth}}_{\Theta\mathrm{CB\text{-}hc}}(\mathcal{A}^\pm) \leq \sum_z \max_z \mathrm{FP}_z \cdot \Pr[Z = z] \leq \frac{4}{2^{n/2}}.
$$

For the case $q_d > 1$, we apply the generic conversion from $q_d = 1$ to $q_d > 1$ as shown by [10], which multiplies q_d to the above. This concludes the proof.

4.4 OTR-hc

We propose another plain AE scheme denoted by OTR-hc which is obtained by applying half-checksum method to OTR. As well as OCB-hc, we first propose OTR-hc as a plain AE with $n/2$-bit tag. The extension to AEAD with possibly longer tag is possible with a method applied to OCB-hc (See Sect. 5).

Specification. We show OTR-hc in Figs. 4 and 5. Let E_K be an n-bit block-cipher. We define the encryption function of OTR-hc$_{E_K}$ as OTR-hc.$\mathcal{E}_{E_K}$:

$(N, M) \mapsto (C, T)$, where $(N, M) \in \{0,1\}^n \times \{0,1\}^*$ and $(C, T) \in \{0,1\}^* \times \{0,1\}^{n/2}$. We also define the decryption function as OTR-hc.$\mathcal{D}_{E_K} : (N, C, T) \mapsto M$ or $\perp$, where $(N, C, T) \in \{0,1\}^n \times \{0,1\}^* \times \{0,1\}^{n/2}$ and $M \in \{0,1\}^*$. OTR-hc encrypts message with 2-round Feistel based on XE. An input to $2n$-bit Feistel permutation is called a chunk. The checksum is computed by XORing the most significant $n/2$ bits of the right halves of the chunk (*i.e.* the even-numbered message blocks) except the last chunk. When the number of message blocks, m, is odd, we take an XOR of $M[m]$ and the padded checksum. When m is even, we will take an XOR of $\mathtt{msb}_{n/2}(\mathcal{Z})$ and the checksum in the last chunk so that any small difference in $C[m-1]$ or $C[m]$ (typically between the encryption and decryption queries sharing the nonce) will yield the n-bit difference of $\mathcal{Z}$.

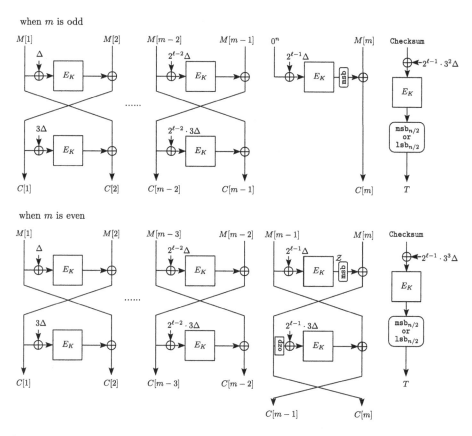

Fig. 4. The encryption of OTR-hc$_{E_K}$, where E_K is any n-bit blockcipher and $\Delta = E_K(N)$. When the number of input blocks m is an odd number, $\mathtt{Checksum} = (\Sigma \| 0^{n/2}) \oplus \mathtt{ozp}(M[m])$, where $\Sigma = \bigoplus_{i=1}^{(m-1)/2} \mathtt{msb}_{n/2}(M[2i])$. Otherwise, $\mathtt{Checksum} = \left(\bigoplus_{i=1}^{(m-2)/2} \mathtt{msb}_{n/2}(M[2i]) \oplus \mathtt{msb}_{n/2}(\mathcal{Z})\right) \| 0^{n/2}$.

State Size. When m is odd, OTR-hc has $3.5n$-bit state size following the procedure described above because the last chunk has only one block. When m is even, it also has $3.5n$-bit state size since the checksum can be computed in $n/2$ bits. Thus, the state size of OTR-hc is $3.5n$ bits. Unlike OCB-hc, we do not have to derive an alternative procedure for the last chunk.

Algorithm: OTR-hc.$\mathcal{E}_{E_K}(N, M)$	**Algorithm: OTR-hc.$\mathcal{D}_{E_K}(N, C, T)$**
1. $M[1] \,\|\, \cdots \,\|\, M[m-1] \,\|\, M[m] \xleftarrow{n} M$	1. $C[1] \,\|\, \cdots \,\|\, C[m-1] \,\|\, C[m] \xleftarrow{n} C$
2. $\Delta \leftarrow E_K(N),\ \ell \leftarrow \lceil \frac{m}{2} \rceil,\ \Sigma \leftarrow 0^{n/2}$	2. $\Delta \leftarrow E_K(N),\ \ell \leftarrow \lceil \frac{m}{2} \rceil,\ \Sigma \leftarrow 0^{n/2}$
3. **for** $i \leftarrow 1$ **to** $\ell - 1$ **do**	3. **for** $i \leftarrow 1$ **to** $\ell - 1$ **do**
4. $C[2i-1] \leftarrow E_K(M[2i-1] \oplus \Delta) \oplus M[2i]$	4. $M[2i-1] \leftarrow E_K(C[2i-1] \oplus 3\Delta) \oplus C[2i]$
5. $C[2i] \leftarrow E_K(C[2i-1] \oplus 3\Delta) \oplus M[2i-1]$	5. $M[2i] \leftarrow E_K(M[2i-1] \oplus \Delta) \oplus C[2i-1]$
6. $\Sigma \leftarrow \Sigma \oplus \mathrm{msb}_{n/2}(M[2i])$	6. $\Sigma \leftarrow \Sigma \oplus \mathrm{msb}_{n/2}(M[2i])$
7. $\Delta \leftarrow 2\Delta$	7. $\Delta \leftarrow 2\Delta$
8. **if** m **is odd**	8. **if** m **is odd**
9. $C[m] \leftarrow \mathrm{msb}_{|M[m]|}(E_K(0^n \oplus \Delta)) \oplus M[m]$	9. $M[m] \leftarrow \mathrm{msb}_{|C[m]|}(E_K(0^n \oplus \Delta)) \oplus C[m]$
10. $\mathrm{Checksum} \leftarrow \Sigma \,\|\, 0^{n/2} \oplus \mathrm{ozp}(M[m])$	10. $\mathrm{Checksum} \leftarrow \Sigma \,\|\, 0^{n/2} \oplus \mathrm{ozp}(M[m])$
11. **else**	11. **else**
12. $\mathcal{Z} \leftarrow E_K(M[m-1] \oplus \Delta),\ \Delta \leftarrow 3\Delta$	12. $M[m-1] \leftarrow E_K(\mathrm{ozp}(C[m]) \oplus 3\Delta) \oplus C[m-1]$
13. $\Sigma \leftarrow \Sigma \oplus \mathrm{msb}_{n/2}(\mathcal{Z})$	13. $\mathcal{Z} \leftarrow E_K(M[m-1] \oplus \Delta),\ \Delta \leftarrow 3\Delta$
14. $C[m] \leftarrow \mathrm{msb}_{|M[m]|}(\mathcal{Z}) \oplus M[m]$	14. $\Sigma \leftarrow \Sigma \oplus \mathrm{msb}_{n/2}(\mathcal{Z})$
15. $C[m-1] \leftarrow E_K(\mathrm{ozp}(C[m]) \oplus \Delta) \oplus M[m-1]$	15. $M[m] \leftarrow \mathrm{msb}_{|C[m]|}(\mathcal{Z}) \oplus C[m]$
16. $\mathrm{Checksum} \leftarrow \Sigma \,\|\, 0^{n/2}$	16. $\mathrm{Checksum} \leftarrow \Sigma \,\|\, 0^{n/2}$
17. $\mathrm{Tag} \leftarrow E_K(\mathrm{Checksum} \oplus 3^2\Delta)$	17. $\mathrm{Tag} \leftarrow E_K(\mathrm{Checksum} \oplus 3^2\Delta)$
18. **if** $|M[m]| = n$ **then** $T \leftarrow \mathrm{msb}_{n/2}(\mathrm{Tag})$	18. **if** $|M[m]| = n$ **then** $T' \leftarrow \mathrm{msb}_{n/2}(\mathrm{Tag})$
19. **else** $T \leftarrow \mathrm{lsb}_{n/2}(\mathrm{Tag})$	19. **else** $T' \leftarrow \mathrm{lsb}_{n/2}(\mathrm{Tag})$
20. **return** $(C[1] \,\|\, \cdots \,\|\, C[m], T)$	20. **if** $T = T'$ **then return** $M[1] \,\|\, \cdots \,\|\, M[m]$
	21. **else return** $\perp$

Fig. 5. The algorithm of OTR-hc. E_K is any n-bit blockcipher.

4.5   Security of OTR-hc

We here show the security bounds of OTR-hc. As in the security proof of OCB-hc, we assume the underlying blockcipher is an n-bit URP, P and omit the case when the underlying blockcipher is a PRP.

Theorem 2. *The security bounds of* OTR-hcP *are evaluated as follows:*

$$\mathbf{Adv}^{\mathrm{priv}}_{\mathrm{OTR\text{-}hcP}}(\mathcal{A}) \leq \frac{5\sigma^2_{\mathrm{priv}}}{2^n}, \quad \mathbf{Adv}^{\mathrm{auth}}_{\mathrm{OTR\text{-}hcP}}(\mathcal{A}^{\pm}) \leq \frac{5\sigma^2_{\mathrm{auth}}}{2^n} + \frac{2.5 q_d}{2^{n/2}},$$

where $\mathcal{A}$, $\mathcal{A}^{\pm}$ *are the adversaries against* OTR-hc *and* σ_{priv}, σ_{auth}, q_d *are the parameters for* $\mathcal{A}$, $\mathcal{A}^{\pm}$. *The parameter* σ_{priv} *(resp.* σ_{auth}*) is the number of accesses to* P *in privacy game (resp. authenticity game) and* q_d *is the number of queries to the decryption oracle in authenticity game.*

Algorithm: ΘTR-hc.$\mathcal{E}_{\widetilde{E}}(N, M)$	Algorithm: ΘTR-hc.$\mathcal{D}_{\widetilde{E}}(N, C, T)$
1. $M[1] \| \cdots \| M[m-1] \| M[m] \xleftarrow{n} M$	1. $C[1] \| \cdots \| C[m-1] \| C[m] \xleftarrow{n} C$
2. $\ell \leftarrow \lceil \frac{m}{2} \rceil, \Sigma \leftarrow 0^{n/2}$	2. $\ell \leftarrow \lceil \frac{m}{2} \rceil, \Sigma \leftarrow 0^{n/2}$
3. for $i \leftarrow 1$ to $\ell - 1$ do	3. for $i \leftarrow 1$ to $\ell - 1$ do
4. $\quad C[2i-1] \leftarrow \tilde{E}^{N,i-1,0}(M[2i-1]) \oplus M[2i]$	4. $\quad M[2i-1] \leftarrow \tilde{E}^{N,i-1,1}(C[2i-1]) \oplus C[2i]$
5. $\quad C[2i] \leftarrow \tilde{E}^{N,i-1,1}(C[2i-1]) \oplus M[2i-1]$	5. $\quad M[2i] \leftarrow \tilde{E}^{N,i-1,0}(M[2i-1]) \oplus C[2i-1]$
6. $\quad \Sigma \leftarrow \Sigma \oplus \mathtt{msb}_{n/2}(M[2i])$	6. $\quad \Sigma \leftarrow \Sigma \oplus \mathtt{msb}_{n/2}(M[2i])$
7. if m is odd	7. if m is odd
8. $\quad C[m] \leftarrow \mathtt{msb}_{|M[m]|}(\tilde{E}^{N,\ell-1,0}(0^n)) \oplus M[m]$	8. $\quad M[m] \leftarrow \mathtt{msb}_{|C[m]|}(\tilde{E}^{N,\ell-1,0}(0^n)) \oplus C[m]$
9. $\quad \mathtt{Checksum} \leftarrow (\Sigma \| 0^{n/2}) \oplus \mathtt{ozp}(M[m])$	9. $\quad \mathtt{Checksum} \leftarrow (\Sigma \| 0^{n/2}) \oplus \mathtt{ozp}(M[m])$
10. else	10. else
11. $\quad \mathcal{Z} \leftarrow \tilde{E}^{N,\ell-1,0}(M[m-1])$	11. $\quad M[m-1] \leftarrow \tilde{E}^{N,\ell-1,1}(\mathtt{ozp}(C[m])) \oplus C[m-1]$
12. $\quad \Sigma \leftarrow \Sigma \oplus \mathtt{msb}_{n/2}(\mathcal{Z})$	12. $\quad \mathcal{Z} \leftarrow \tilde{E}^{N,\ell-1,0}(M[m-1])$
13. $\quad C[m] \leftarrow \mathtt{msb}_{|M[m]|}(\mathcal{Z}) \oplus M[m]$	13. $\quad M[m] \leftarrow \mathtt{msb}_{|C[m]|}(\mathcal{Z}) \oplus C[m]$
14. $\quad C[m-1] \leftarrow \tilde{E}^{N,\ell-1,1}(\mathtt{ozp}(C[m])) \oplus M[m-1]$	14. $\quad \Sigma \leftarrow \Sigma \oplus \mathtt{msb}_{n/2}(\mathcal{Z})$
15. $\quad \mathtt{Checksum} \leftarrow \Sigma \| 0^{n/2}$	15. $\quad \mathtt{Checksum} \leftarrow \Sigma \| 0^{n/2}$
16. if m is odd then $\mathtt{Tag} \leftarrow \tilde{E}^{N,\ell-1,2}(\mathtt{Checksum})$	16. if m is odd then $\mathtt{Tag} \leftarrow \tilde{E}^{N,\ell-1,2}(\mathtt{Checksum})$
17. else $\mathtt{Tag} \leftarrow \tilde{E}^{N,\ell-1,3}(\mathtt{Checksum})$	17. else $\mathtt{Tag} \leftarrow \tilde{E}^{N,\ell-1,3}(\mathtt{Checksum})$
18. if $|M[m]| = n$ then $T \leftarrow \mathtt{msb}_{n/2}(\mathtt{Tag})$	18. if $|M[m]| = n$ then $T' \leftarrow \mathtt{msb}_{n/2}(\mathtt{Tag})$
19. else $T \leftarrow \mathtt{lsb}_{n/2}(\mathtt{Tag})$	19. else $T' \leftarrow \mathtt{lsb}_{n/2}(\mathtt{Tag})$
20. return $(C[1] \| \cdots \| C[m]) \| T$	20. if $T = T'$ then return $M[1] \| \cdots \| M[m]$
	21. else return $\perp$

Fig. 6. The algorithm of ΘTR-hc. $\widetilde{E}$ is any TBC which has the same arguments as XE.

Proof. To evaluate the security bound of OTR-hc, we define the TBC mode for plain AE, which is denoted by ΘTR-hc$_{\widetilde{E}}$ in Fig. 6. When $\widetilde{E}$ is XE$_E$, ΘTR-hc$_{\widetilde{E}}$ is equivalent to OTR-hc$_E$. Let $\widetilde{R}$ denote a TURF which has the same arguments as XE. For privacy-adversary $\mathcal{A}$ and authenticity-adversary $\mathcal{A}^{\pm}$, we obtain following security bounds of OTR-hc$_P$.

$$\mathbf{Adv}_{\text{OTR-hc}_P}^{\text{priv}}(\mathcal{A}) \leq \mathbf{Adv}_{\text{OTR-hc}_P, \Theta\text{TR-hc}_{\widetilde{R}}}^{\text{cpa-nr}}(\mathcal{A}) + \mathbf{Adv}_{\Theta\text{TR-hc}_{\widetilde{R}}}^{\text{priv}}(\mathcal{A})$$

$$= \mathbf{Adv}_{\text{XE}_P, \widetilde{R}}^{\text{cpa-nr}}(\mathcal{B}) + \mathbf{Adv}_{\Theta\text{TR-hc}_{\widetilde{R}}}^{\text{priv}}(\mathcal{A})$$

$$\leq \frac{5\sigma_{\text{priv}}^2}{2^n} + 0 \quad \text{and} \tag{3}$$

$$\mathbf{Adv}_{\text{OTR-hc}_P}^{\text{auth}}(\mathcal{A}^{\pm}) \leq \mathbf{Adv}_{\text{OTR-hc}_P, \Theta\text{TR-hc}_{\widetilde{R}}}^{\text{cca-nr}}(\mathcal{A}^{\pm}) + \mathbf{Adv}_{\Theta\text{TR-hc}_{\widetilde{R}}}^{\text{auth}}(\mathcal{A}^{\pm})$$

$$= \mathbf{Adv}_{\text{XE}_P, \widetilde{R}}^{\text{cpa-nr}}(\mathcal{B}^{\pm}) + \mathbf{Adv}_{\Theta\text{TR-hc}_{\widetilde{R}}}^{\text{auth}}(\mathcal{A}^{\pm})$$

$$\leq \frac{5\sigma_{\text{auth}}^2}{2^n} + \frac{2.5 q_d}{2^{n/2}}, \tag{4}$$

where $\mathcal{B}$ (resp. $\mathcal{B}^{\pm}$) is the adversary which can simulate $\mathcal{A}$ (resp. $\mathcal{A}^{\pm}$). The first terms of (3), (4) are derived from [31]. The second terms of (3), (4) are described below.

Privacy. As in the case of ΘCB-hc, every TURF invoked in the privacy game has a different tweak because the adversary is nonce-respecting. Therefore, we have $\mathbf{Adv}^{\mathrm{priv}}_{\Theta\mathrm{TR}\text{-hc}_{\tilde{\mathsf{R}}}}(\mathcal{A}) = 0$.

Authenticity.

Lemma 2. *The authenticity advantage of* $\Theta\mathrm{TR}\text{-hc}_{\tilde{\mathsf{R}}}$ *is*

$$\mathbf{Adv}^{\mathrm{auth}}_{\Theta\mathrm{TR}\text{-hc}_{\tilde{\mathsf{R}}}}(\mathcal{A}^{\pm}) \leq \frac{2.5q_d}{2^{n/2}},$$

where q_d denotes the number of decryption queries.

Proof. We start with the case $q_d = 1$. Without loss of generality, we assume that the adversary performs decryption query after all encryption queries. As in the security proof of OCB-hc, suppose that she obtains the transcript $z = \{(N_1, M_1, C_1, T_1), \ldots, (N_q, M_q, C_q, T_q)\}$ in encryption query, and then she queries (N', C', T') in decryption query. Let Z be the set of all transcripts, and T^* be the valid tag for (N', C'). We define $\mathrm{FP}_z := \Pr[T' = T^* \mid Z = z]$ and evaluate $\max_z \mathrm{FP}_z$ as below.

1. Let $N' \neq N_i$, $1 \leq \forall i \leq q$. Since the TURF which returns valid T^* takes a new tweak, the adversary has no information about T^*. Thus $\mathrm{FP}_z \leq 1/2^{n/2}$ holds.

2. Let $N' = N_\alpha$, $\alpha \in \{1, 2, \ldots, q\}$, $C' \neq C_\alpha$. We divide the cases with the value of $|C'|$ as follows.

   (a) Let $|C'|_{2n} \neq |C_\alpha|_{2n}$. The tweak of TURF which outputs T^* is different from that of TURFs which are invoked in encryption query. Thus $\mathrm{FP}_z \leq 1/2^{n/2}$ holds.

   (b) Let $|C'|_{2n} = |C_\alpha|_{2n}$ and $|C'|_n \neq |C_\alpha|_n$. As above, the tweak of TURF which outputs T^* is different from that of TURFs which are invoked in encryption query. Thus $\mathrm{FP}_z \leq 1/2^{n/2}$ holds.

   (c) Let $|C'|_n = |C_\alpha|_n$ and $\mathrm{ifPad}(C') \neq \mathrm{ifPad}(C_\alpha)$. Let $|C'|_n = |C_\alpha|_n = m$. We first consider the case that m is odd. Suppose that $\mathrm{Checksum}^*$ and M^* are the valid checksum and message for (N', C'), respectively, and $\mathrm{Checksum}_\alpha$ is the value of the checksum for $(N_\alpha, M_\alpha, C_\alpha, T_\alpha)$. The adversary can make $\mathrm{Checksum}^*$ equal to $\mathrm{Checksum}_\alpha$ by using padding. However, we obtain $\mathrm{FP}_z \leq 1/2^{n/2}$ no matter if $\mathrm{Checksum}^* \neq \mathrm{Checksum}_\alpha$ holds or not since $\mathrm{ifPad}(C') \neq \mathrm{ifPad}(C_\alpha)$ and the adversary obtains no information about T^* from T_α. Regarding to the case that m is even, we can discuss in the same way as above.

   (d) Let $|C'|_n = |C_\alpha|_n$ and $\mathrm{ifPad}(C') = \mathrm{ifPad}(C_\alpha)$. Suppose $|C'|_n = |C_\alpha|_n = m$ and $CC[1] \parallel CC[2] \parallel \cdots \parallel CC[\ell] \xleftarrow{2n} C$. We consider the following cases.
   Case e_1: When $CC'[i] \neq CC_\alpha[i]$ for $\exists i \in \{1, \ldots, \ell\}$, $M^*[2i - 1] = M_\alpha[2i - 1]$ holds.
   Case e_2: When $C' \neq C_\alpha$, $\mathrm{Checksum}^* = \mathrm{Checksum}_\alpha$ holds.
   Case e_3: When $C' \neq C_\alpha$, $T' = T^*$ holds.

We first evaluate $\Pr[e_1 \mid Z = z] = \Pr[M^*[2i-1] = M_\alpha[2i-1] \mid Z = z]$. Let $i \in \{1, \ldots, \ell-1\}$. When $C'[2i-1] = C_\alpha[2i-1]$, $C'[2i] \neq C_\alpha[2i]$ has to hold. Thus we obtain $\Pr[e_1 \mid Z = z] = 0$ since $\widetilde{R}^{N,i-1,1}(C'[2i-1]) \oplus C'[2i] \neq \widetilde{R}^{N,i-1,1}(C_\alpha[2i-1]) \oplus C_\alpha[2i]$ always holds. Then let $C'[2i-1] \neq C_\alpha[2i-1]$. $\Pr[e_1 \mid Z = z] \leq 1/2^n$ holds because $\widetilde{R}^{N,i-1,1}(C'[2i-1])$ is unpredictable for the adversary. When $i = \ell$ and m is even, $\Pr[e_1 \mid Z = z] \leq 1/2^n$ holds from the almost same discussion as above. When $i = \ell$ and m is odd, $\Pr[e_1 \mid Z = z] = 0$ holds.

Secondly, we evaluate $\Pr[e_2 \mid \bar{e}_1, Z = z]$. Let m is odd. When $C'[m] \neq C_\alpha[m]$ and $CC'[i] = CC_\alpha[i]$ for $\forall i \in \{1, \ldots, \ell-1\}$, we obtain $\Pr[e_2 \mid \bar{e}_1, Z = z] = 0$ since $\mathsf{ozp}(M^*[m]) \neq \mathsf{ozp}(M_\alpha[m])$ holds. Then, suppose $CC'[u] \neq CC_\alpha[u]$ for $\exists u \in \{1, \ldots, \ell-1\}$. We obtain the following evaluation.

$$\Pr[e_2 \mid \bar{e}_1, Z = z]$$
$$= \Pr[\mathsf{msb}_{n/2}(M^*[2u]) \parallel 0^{n/2} \oplus \mathsf{msb}_{n/2}(M_\alpha[2u]) \parallel 0^{n/2} = \delta \mid \bar{e}_1, Z = z],$$

where $\delta = \mathsf{msb}_{n/2}(M^*[2u]) \parallel 0^{n/2} \oplus \mathsf{msb}_{n/2}(M_\alpha[2u]) \parallel 0^{n/2} \oplus \mathsf{Checksum}^* \oplus \mathsf{Checksum}_\alpha$,

$$= \Pr[\mathsf{msb}_{n/2}(\widetilde{R}^{N,u-1,0}(M^*[2u-1]) \oplus C'[2u-1]) \parallel 0^{n/2}$$
$$\oplus \mathsf{msb}_{n/2}(\widetilde{R}^{N,u-1,0}(M_\alpha[2u-1]) \oplus C_\alpha[2u-1]) \parallel 0^{n/2} = \delta \mid \bar{e}_1, Z = z]$$
$$\leq 1/2^{n/2}.$$

The last line is derived since $\bar{e}_1$ and $\widetilde{R}^{N,u-1,0}(M^*[2u-1])$ is unpredictable. Thus, we obtain $\Pr[e_2 \mid \bar{e}_1, Z = z] \leq 1/2^{n/2}$ when m is odd. When m is even, $\Pr[e_2 \mid \bar{e}_1, Z = z] \leq 1/2^{n/2}$ also holds from the almost same discussion as above. Then we evaluate $\Pr[e_3 \mid \bar{e}_2, \bar{e}_1, Z = z]$. In this case, the TURF outputting T^* and the TURF outputting T_α take the same tweak, and $\mathsf{ifPad}(C') = \mathsf{ifPad}(C_\alpha)$ holds. However $\mathsf{Checksum}^* \neq \mathsf{Checksum}_\alpha$ holds, and we obtain $\Pr[e_3 \mid \bar{e}_2, \bar{e}_1, Z = z] \leq 1/2^{n/2}$.

From above, we obtain the following evaluation.

$$\begin{aligned}
\mathrm{FP}_z &= \Pr[e_3 \mid Z = z] \\
&\leq \Pr[e_3 \cap (\overline{e_1 \cup e_2}) \mid Z = z] + \Pr[e_2 \cap \bar{e}_1 \mid Z = z] + \Pr[e_1 \mid Z = z] \\
&\leq \Pr[e_3 \mid \bar{e}_2, \bar{e}_1, Z = z] + \Pr[e_2 \mid \bar{e}_1, Z = z] + \Pr[e_1 \mid Z = z] \\
&\leq \frac{1}{2^{n/2}} + \frac{1}{2^{n/2}} + \frac{1}{2^n} \leq \frac{2.5}{2^{n/2}}
\end{aligned}$$

From the evaluations of above cases, we obtain

$$\mathbf{Adv}^{\mathrm{auth}}_{\Theta\mathrm{TR\text{-}hc}}(\mathcal{A}^\pm) \leq \sum_z \max_z \mathrm{FP}_z \cdot \Pr[Z = z] \leq \frac{2.5}{2^{n/2}}.$$

For the case $q_d > 1$, we use [10] again. This completes the proof.

5   Extensions

In this section, we show extensions of our proposals. First, we show how to extend the tag length of OCB-hc to up to n bits. Second, we propose an extension of OCB-hc to AEAD, denoted by OCB-hc-AD, which is the mode of operation for AEAD with $2.5n$-bit state size. OCB-hc-AD is a combination of OCB-hc and a variant of Phash [27] with half-checksum method. OTR-hc can be extended to have arbitrary tag length up to n bits and AEAD in the same manner as OCB-hc, which we omit here.

5.1   Arbitrary Tag Length

When tag length τ is less than $n/2$ bits, we can change line 12 and 13 of OCB-hc.$\mathcal{E}$ in Fig. 2 as follows.

line 12 :   **if** $|M[m]| = n$ **then** $T \leftarrow \mathtt{msb}_\tau(\mathrm{Tag})$,
line 13 :   **else** $T \leftarrow \mathtt{lsb}_\tau(\mathrm{Tag})$.

For decryption, we can change OCB-hc.$\mathcal{D}$ accordingly. When $\tau > n/2$, we can change line 8 and 12–14 of OCB-hc.$\mathcal{E}$ in Fig. 2 as follows.

line 8 :   **if** $|M[m]| = n$ **then** $\Delta \leftarrow 3\Delta,$ **else** $\Delta \leftarrow 3^2\Delta$,
line 12–14 :   **return**$(C[1] \| \cdots \| C[m], \mathtt{msb}_\tau(\mathrm{Tag}))$.

For decryption, we can change OCB-hc.$\mathcal{D}$ accordingly. Thus, we have to use the different masks in the encryption of the checksum, depending on whether the message is full n bits or partial, which is the same as the original OCB and OTR.

5.2   OCB-hc with AD

Our extension of OCB-hc to AEAD, denoted by OCB-hc-AD, is shown in Fig. 7. OCB-hc-AD consists of the plain-AE core OCB-hc$'$ and the authentication core Phash-hc (Fig. 8 in Appendix A). The way of combination is similar to ΘCB3† proposed by Naito [34]. In OCB-hc-AD, Phash-hc processes AD and then OCB-hc$'$ processes a message using the output of Phash-hc as the initial value of the checksum. Note that the initial value of the checksum was $0^{n/2}$ in the case of OCB-hc. This way of combination is suitable when AD is processed first. If the message is processed before AD, one can combine OCB-hc$'$ and Phash-hc by XORing the tag of plain-AE OCB-hc$'$ and the output of Phash-hc. This combination is similar to OCB3 or AEM [27,38].

Specification. We show OCB-hc-AD in Fig. 7. For simplicity, the tag is $n/2$ bits. Let E_K be an n-bit blockcipher. We define the encryption function of OCB-hc-AD$_{E_K}$ as OCB-hc-AD.$\mathcal{E}_{E_K} : (N, A, M) \mapsto (C, T)$, where $(N, A, M) \in \{0,1\}^{\leq n-1} \times \{0,1\}^* \times \{0,1\}^*$ and $(C, T) \in \{0,1\}^* \times \{0,1\}^{n/2}$. We also define the decryption function as OCB-hc-AD.$\mathcal{D}_{E_K} : (N, A, C, T) \mapsto M$ or $\perp$, where $(N, A, C, T) \in \{0, 1\}^{\leq n-1} \times \{0, 1\}^* \times \{0, 1\}^* \times \{0, 1\}^{n/2}$ and $M \in \{0, 1\}^*$. OCB-hc$'$ is the same algorithm as OCB-hc except the length of nonce and the initial value of the checksum. We restrict the length of nonce to less than n bits because Phash-hc always uses 0^n as a nonce and so OCB-hc$'$ cannot use 0^n as a nonce. The initial value of the checksum of OCB-hc$'$ is an output of Phash-hc. Phash-hc computes the sum of the most significant $n/2$ bits of encrypted massage by XE.

State Size. OCB-hc$'$ has $2.5n$-bit state size as OCB-hc$'$ and OCB-hc are almost the same. Phash-hc also has $2.5n$-bit state size, which includes n-bit memory for message block and mask, and $0.5n$-bit memory for sum of encrypted message. Therefore, the state size of OCB-hc-AD is $2.5n$ bits.

5.3   Security of OCB-hc-AD

We here show the security bounds of OCB-hc-AD. For security analysis of OCB-hc-AD, we define ΘCB-hc-AD as a TBC mode for AEAD in Fig. 7. We also define ΘCB-hc$'$ and $\mathbb{P}$hash-hc as TBC versions of OCB-hc$'$ and Phash-hc, respectively in Fig. 7. When $\widetilde{E}$ is instantiated by XE$_E$, $\mathbb{P}$hash-hc$_{\widetilde{E}}$ is equivalent to Phash-hc$_E$. In this subsection, we first show the security of $\mathbb{P}$hash-hc. Then we evaluate the security bounds of OCB-hc-AD using hybrid argument.

Lemma 3. Let $\forall A, A' \in \{0, 1\}^*$ and $A \neq A'$. Suppose the underlying TBC of $\mathbb{P}$hash-hc is a TURP denoted by $\widetilde{\mathsf{P}}$, which has the same arguments as XE. $\mathbb{P}$hash-hc$_{\widetilde{\mathsf{P}}}$ has a following property.

$$\max_{\forall \delta \in \{0,1\}^{n/2}} \Pr\left[\mathbb{P}\text{hash-hc}_{\widetilde{\mathsf{P}}}(A) \oplus \mathbb{P}\text{hash-hc}_{\widetilde{\mathsf{P}}}(A') = \delta\right] \leq \frac{2}{2^{n/2}}.$$

The proof is described in Appendix A.

Then we show the security bounds of OCB-hc-AD. As in the security proofs of OCB-hc and OTR-hc, we assume the underlying blockcipher is an n-bit URP denoted by P and omit the case when the underlying blockcipher is a PRP.

Theorem 3. The security bounds of OCB-hc-AD$_{\mathsf{P}}$ are evaluated as follows:

$$\mathbf{Adv}^{\mathrm{priv}}_{\mathrm{OCB\text{-}hc\text{-}AD}_{\mathsf{P}}}(\mathcal{A}) \leq \frac{4.5\sigma^2_{\mathrm{priv}}}{2^n}, \quad \mathbf{Adv}^{\mathrm{auth}}_{\mathrm{OCB\text{-}hc\text{-}AD}_{\mathsf{P}}}(\mathcal{A}^{\pm}) \leq \frac{4.5\sigma^2_{\mathrm{auth}}}{2^n} + \frac{4q_d}{2^{n/2}},$$

where $\mathcal{A}, \mathcal{A}^{\pm}$ are the adversaries against OCB-hc-AD and $\sigma_{\mathrm{priv}}, \sigma_{\mathrm{auth}}, q_d$ are the parameters for $\mathcal{A}, \mathcal{A}^{\pm}$. The parameter σ_{priv} (resp. σ_{auth}) is the number of accesses to P in privacy game (resp. authenticity game) and q_d is the number of queries to the decryption oracle in the authenticity game.

We prove Theorem 3 in Appendix B.

Algorithm: OCB-hc-AD.$\mathcal{E}_{E_K}(N, A, M)$	**Algorithm:** OCB-hc-AD.$\mathcal{D}_{E_K}(N, A, C, T)$
1. Auth $\leftarrow$ Phash-hc$_{E_K}(A)$,	1. Auth $\leftarrow$ Phash-hc$_{E_K}(A)$,
2. **return** OCB-hc'.$\mathcal{E}_{E_K}(N, \text{Auth}, M)$	2. **return** OCB-hc'.$\mathcal{D}_{E_K}(N, \text{Auth}, C, T)$

Algorithm: OCB-hc'.$\mathcal{E}_{E_K}(N, \text{Auth}, M)$	**Algorithm:** OCB-hc'.$\mathcal{D}_{E_K}(N, \text{Auth}, C, T)$
1. $M[1] \| \cdots \| M[m-1] \| M[m] \xleftarrow{n} M$	1. $C[1] \| \cdots \| C[m-1] \| C[m] \xleftarrow{n} C$
2. $\Delta \leftarrow 2E_K(\text{ozp}(N))$, $\Sigma \leftarrow \text{Auth}$	2. $\Delta \leftarrow 2E_K(\text{ozp}(N))$, $\Sigma \leftarrow \text{Auth}$
3. **for** $i \leftarrow 1$ **to** $m-1$ **do**	3. **for** $i \leftarrow 1$ **to** $m-1$ **do**
4. $\quad C[i] \leftarrow E_K(M[i] \oplus \Delta) \oplus \Delta$	4. $\quad M[i] \leftarrow D_K(C[i] \oplus \Delta) \oplus \Delta$
5. $\quad \Sigma \leftarrow \Sigma \oplus \text{msb}_{n/2}(M[i])$	5. $\quad \Sigma \leftarrow \Sigma \oplus \text{msb}_{n/2}(M[i])$
6. $\quad \Delta \leftarrow 2\Delta$	6. $\quad \Delta \leftarrow 2\Delta$
7. Pad $\leftarrow E_K(0^n \oplus \Delta) \oplus \Delta$	7. Pad $\leftarrow E_K(0^n \oplus \Delta) \oplus \Delta$
8. $\Delta \leftarrow 3\Delta$	8. $\Delta \leftarrow 3\Delta$
9. $C[m] \leftarrow \text{msb}_{\text{len}(M[m])}(\text{Pad} \oplus \text{ozp}(M[m]))$	9. $M[m] \leftarrow \text{msb}_{\text{len}(C[m])}(\text{Pad}) \oplus C[m]$
10. $\Delta \leftarrow \Delta \oplus \text{ozp}(M[m])$	10. $\Delta \leftarrow \Delta \oplus \text{ozp}(M[m])$
11. Tag $\leftarrow E_K(\Sigma \| 0^{n/2} \oplus \Delta)$	11. Tag $\leftarrow E_K(\Sigma \| 0^{n/2} \oplus \Delta)$
12. **if** $|M[m]| = n$ **then** $T \leftarrow \text{msb}_{n/2}(\text{Tag})$	12. **if** $|M[m]| = n$ **then** $T' \leftarrow \text{msb}_{n/2}(\text{Tag})$
13. **else** $T \leftarrow \text{lsb}_{n/2}(\text{Tag})$	13. **else** $T' \leftarrow \text{lsb}_{n/2}(\text{Tag})$
14. **return** $(C[1] \| \cdots \| C[m], T)$	14. **if** $T = T'$ **then return** $M[1] \| \cdots \| M[m]$
	15. **else return** $\bot$

Algorithm: Phash-hc$_{E_K}(A)$	**Algorithm:** $\mathbb{P}$hash-hc$_{\widetilde{E}}(A)$
1. **if** $A = \varepsilon$ **then** Auth $\leftarrow 0^{n/2}$, **return** Auth	1. **if** $A = \varepsilon$ **then** Auth $\leftarrow 0^{n/2}$, **return** Auth
2. $A[1] \| \cdots \| A[a-1] \| A[a] \xleftarrow{n} A$	2. $A[1] \| \cdots \| A[a-1] \| A[a] \xleftarrow{n} A$
3. $\Delta \leftarrow 2E_K(0^n)$, Auth $\leftarrow 0^{n/2}$	3. Auth $\leftarrow 0^{n/2}$
4. **for** $i \leftarrow 1$ **to** $a-1$ **do**	4. **for** $i \leftarrow 1$ **to** $a-1$ **do**
5. $\quad$ Auth $\leftarrow$ Auth $\oplus \text{msb}_{n/2}(E_K(A[i] \oplus \Delta))$	5. $\quad$ Auth $\leftarrow$ Auth $\oplus \text{msb}_{n/2}(\widetilde{E}^{0^n,0,i,0}(A[i]))$
6. $\quad \Delta \leftarrow 2\Delta$	6. $Y \leftarrow \widetilde{E}^{0^n,0,a,0}(\text{ozp}(A[a]))$
7. $Y \leftarrow E_K(\text{ozp}(A[a]) \oplus \Delta)$	7. **if** $|A[a]| = n$ **then** Auth $\leftarrow$ Auth$\oplus \text{msb}_{n/2}(Y)$
8. **if** $|A[a]| = n$ **then** Auth $\leftarrow$ Auth$\oplus \text{msb}_{n/2}(Y)$	8. **else** Auth $\leftarrow \text{lsb}_{n/2}(Y)$
9. **else** Auth $\leftarrow$ Auth $\oplus \text{lsb}_{n/2}(Y)$	9. **return** Auth
10. **return** Auth	

Algorithm: ΘCB-hc-AD.$\mathcal{E}_{\widetilde{E}}(N, A, M)$	**Algorithm:** ΘCB-hc-AD.$\mathcal{D}_{\widetilde{E}}(N, A, C, T)$
1. Auth $\leftarrow \mathbb{P}$hash-hc$_{\widetilde{E}}(A)$,	1. Auth $\leftarrow \mathbb{P}$hash-hc$_{\widetilde{E}}(A)$,
2. **return** ΘCB-hc'.$\mathcal{E}_{\widetilde{E}}(N, \text{Auth}, M)$	2. **return** ΘCB-hc'.$\mathcal{D}_{\widetilde{E}}(N, \text{Auth}, C, T)$

Algorithm: ΘCB-hc'.$\mathcal{E}_{\widetilde{E}}(N, \text{Auth}, M)$	**Algorithm:** ΘCB-hc.$\mathcal{D}_{\widetilde{E}}(N, \text{Auth}, C, T)$
1. $M[1] \| \cdots \| M[m-1] \| M[m] \xleftarrow{n} M$	1. $C[1] \| \cdots \| C[m-1] \| C[m] \xleftarrow{n} C$
2. $\Sigma \leftarrow \text{Auth}$, $N \leftarrow \text{ozp}(N)$	2. $\Sigma \leftarrow \text{Auth}$, $N \leftarrow \text{ozp}(N)$
3. **for** $i \leftarrow 1$ **to** $m-1$ **do**	3. **for** $i \leftarrow 1$ **to** $m-1$ **do**
4. $\quad C[i] \leftarrow \widetilde{E}^{N,1,i,0}(M[i])$	4. $\quad M[i] \leftarrow \widetilde{D}^{N,1,i,0}(C[i])$
5. $\quad \Sigma \leftarrow \Sigma \oplus \text{msb}_{n/2}(M[i])$	5. $\quad \Sigma \leftarrow \Sigma \oplus \text{msb}_{n/2}(M[i])$
6. Pad $\leftarrow \widetilde{E}^{N,1,m,0}(0^n)$	6. Pad $\leftarrow \widetilde{E}^{N,1,m,0}(0^n)$
7. $C[m] \leftarrow M[m] \oplus \text{msb}_{|M[m]|}(\text{Pad})$	7. $M[m] \leftarrow C[m] \oplus \text{msb}_{|C[m]|}(\text{Pad})$
8. Checksum $\leftarrow (\Sigma \| 0^{n/2}) \oplus \text{ozp}(M[m])$	8. Checksum $\leftarrow (\Sigma \| 0^{n/2}) \oplus \text{ozp}(M[m])$
9. Tag $\leftarrow \widetilde{E}^{N,0,m,1}(\text{Checksum})$	9. Tag $\leftarrow \widetilde{E}^{N,0,m,1}(\text{Checksum})$
10. **if** $|M[m]| = n$ **then** $T \leftarrow \text{msb}_{n/2}(\text{Tag})$	10. **if** $|M[m]| = n$ **then** $T' \leftarrow \text{msb}_{n/2}(\text{Tag})$
11. **else** $T \leftarrow \text{lsb}_{n/2}(\text{Tag})$	11. **else** $T' \leftarrow \text{lsb}_{n/2}(\text{Tag})$
12. **return** $(C[1] \| \cdots \| C[m], T)$	12. **if** $T = T'$ **then return** $M[1] \| \cdots \| M[m]$
	13. **else return** $\bot$

Fig. 7. The algorithms of OCB-hc-AD and ΘCB-hc-AD. E_K is any blockcipher and D_K is the decryption of E_K. $\widetilde{E}$ is any TBC which has the same arguments as XEX* and $\widetilde{D}$ is the decryption of $\widetilde{E}$. Note that $\widetilde{E}$ in **Algorithm:** $\mathbb{P}$hash-hc$_{\widetilde{E}}(A)$ can also be interpreted as a TBC which has the same arguments as XE.

6   Discussion on the Security Bounds of Proposals

In the preceding section, we proved OCB-hc and OTR-hc keep the birthday-bound security as their originals (OCB and OTR). We here compare the security bounds of our proposals when the security parameters (*e.g.* the number of queries) are less than $2^{n/2}$.

For privacy-adversary, our proposals and originals have the exactly same security bounds, respectively, thus we focus on the authenticity-adversary.

We first compare the security bound of OCB-hc to that of OCB. For arbitrary tag length τ up to n, the security bound of $\mathbf{Adv}^{\mathrm{auth}}_{\mathrm{OCB\text{-}hcp}}(\mathcal{A}^{\pm})$ is evaluated to $4.5\sigma^2_{\mathrm{auth}}/2^n + 2^{n-\tau}q_d/(2^n-1) + 2^{n/2}q_d/(2^n-1)$ in the same manner as the proof in Sect. 4.3. The security bound of $\mathbf{Adv}^{\mathrm{auth}}_{\mathrm{OCB_P}}(\mathcal{A}^{\pm})$ is evaluated to $4.5\sigma^2_{\mathrm{auth}}/2^n + 2^{n-\tau}q_d/(2^n-1)$. In the case of $\tau = n/2$, OCB-hc and OCB have the same security bounds except the constant factor. Therefore, $\mathbf{Adv}^{\mathrm{auth}}_{\mathrm{OCB\text{-}hcp}}(\mathcal{A}^{\pm})$ and $\mathbf{Adv}^{\mathrm{auth}}_{\mathrm{OCB_P}}(\mathcal{A}^{\pm})$ grow with the same rate except the constant factor when $0 < \sigma_{\mathrm{auth}}, q_d < 2^{n/2}$. In the case of $\tau < n/2$ and $\sigma_{\mathrm{auth}} \approx q_d$, the security bounds of OCB-hc and OCB are $O(q_d/2^\tau)$. Therefore, there is no difference in their bounds except the constant factor when $0 < \sigma_{\mathrm{auth}}, q_d < 2^{n/2}$ similarly to the case of $\tau = n/2$. In the case of $n/2 < \tau \le n$, the security bound of OCB-hc still has the term $O(q_d/2^{n/2})$, which is not included by that of OCB. If we assume $\sigma_{\mathrm{auth}} \approx q_d$ and $0 < \sigma_{\mathrm{auth}}, q_d < 2^{n/2}$, we obtain $O(\sigma^2/2^n) < O(q_d/2^{n/2})$. Therefore, $\mathbf{Adv}^{\mathrm{auth}}_{\mathrm{OCB_P}}(\mathcal{A}^{\pm}) < \mathbf{Adv}^{\mathrm{auth}}_{\mathrm{OCB\text{-}hcp}}(\mathcal{A}^{\pm})$ always holds when $0 < \sigma_{\mathrm{auth}} \approx q_d < 2^{n/2}$. It indicates the security bound of OCB is better when $n/2 < \tau \le n$ and $0 < \sigma_{\mathrm{auth}} \approx q_d < 2^{n/2}$. The comparison of OTR-hc with OTR will be similar as above, thus we omit the details.

7   Conclusion

In this paper, we have proposed the half-checksum method to reduce the state size of parallel AE mode of operations having birthday-bound security. It maintains the bit security and overall efficiency. We have applied it to two representative parallel AE modes, OCB and OTR, to derive the concrete instantiations, OCB-hc and OTR-hc. They have almost same properties of OCB and OTR (*e.g.* parallelizability, efficiency, bit security, etc) except the reduced state size. When n is block length of the underlying blockcipher, OCB-hc has $2.5n$-bit state size, and OTR-hc has $3.5n$-bit state size. To the best of our knowledge, they achieve the smallest state size among the parallel, rate-1 AE modes of birthday security. Our method is applicable to other schemes having a similar structure as OCB or OTR, such as OPP [22]. While OCB-hc and OTR-hc are plain AE of fixed $n/2$-bit tag length, we presented the natural extensions of them to AEAD with arbitrary tag length up to n bits, without loss of security and increase of state size. It would be interesting to consider if we can apply the same method to other types of parallel AE, such as parallel online AE including COLM [3], COPA [5,6] and ELmD [17,18]. In addition, further study in hardware are required to evaluate actual circuit gain of our proposals. Finally, it would be natural to ask if the state size figures of our proposals are the theoretical minimum for parallel AE mode of birthday-bound security.

Acknowledgements. We would like to thank the anonymous reviewers for their comments and suggestions.

A   Proof of Security of $\mathbb{P}$hash-hc

We here show the proof of Lemma 3. Note that the underlying TURP $\widetilde{\mathsf{P}}$ has the same arguments as XE in Lemma 3, however we here write $\widetilde{\mathsf{P}}$ with the arguments of XEX* following Fig. 7. Thus we always use $\widetilde{\mathsf{P}}^{*,0,*,*}$ in this proof.

Proof. We define $\mathrm{XorColl}_\delta := \Pr\left[\mathbb{P}\mathrm{hash\text{-}hc}_{\widetilde{\mathsf{P}}}(A) \oplus \mathbb{P}\mathrm{hash\text{-}hc}_{\widetilde{\mathsf{P}}}(A') = \delta\right]$.

1. Let $A = \varepsilon$ and $A' \neq \varepsilon$.
   (i) We first consider the case of $|A'|_n = 1$. Suppose ifPad$(A') = 0$ without loss of generality. In this case,

   $$\mathbb{P}\mathrm{hash\text{-}hc}_{\widetilde{\mathsf{P}}}(A) \oplus \mathbb{P}\mathrm{hash\text{-}hc}_{\widetilde{\mathsf{P}}}(A') = \mathbb{P}\mathrm{hash\text{-}hc}_{\widetilde{\mathsf{P}}}(A')$$
   $$= \mathtt{msb}_{n/2}(\widetilde{\mathsf{P}}^{0^n,0,1,0}(\mathtt{ozp}(A'[1])))$$

   holds. Thus we obtain $\mathrm{XorColl}_{\forall\delta} \leq 1/2^{n/2}$.
   (ii) Let $|A'|_n > 1$. $\mathbb{P}\mathrm{hash\text{-}hc}(A')$ is a sum of the most (or least) significant $n/2$ bits of message blocks encrypted by TURPs which are invoked with respective different tweaks. Thus $\mathrm{XorColl}_{\forall\delta} = \Pr\left[\mathbb{P}\mathrm{hash\text{-}hc}_{\widetilde{\mathsf{P}}}(A') = \delta\right] \leq 1/2^{n/2}$. This discussion can be applied to the case that $A \neq \varepsilon$ and $A' = \varepsilon$. In following cases, we suppose $A \neq \varepsilon$ and $A' \neq \varepsilon$.
2. Let $|A|_n = |A'|_n$ and ifPad$(A) = $ ifPad(A'). Suppose $|A|_n = |A'|_n = a$. Without loss of generality, we suppose ifPad$(A) = $ ifPad$(A') = 0$. Since $A \neq A'$, there exists $u \in \{1, \ldots, a\}$ such that $A[u] \neq A'[u]$. For $\exists \gamma \in \{0,1\}^{n/2}$, $\mathbb{P}\mathrm{hash\text{-}hc}_{\widetilde{\mathsf{P}}}(A) \oplus \mathbb{P}\mathrm{hash\text{-}hc}_{\widetilde{\mathsf{P}}}(A') = \mathtt{msb}_{n/2}\left(\widetilde{\mathsf{P}}^{0^n,0,u,0}(\mathtt{ozp}(A[u]))\right) \oplus \mathtt{msb}_{n/2}\left(\widetilde{\mathsf{P}}^{0^n,0,u,0}(\mathtt{ozp}(A'[u]))\right) \oplus \gamma$ holds. Then we obtain

   $$\mathrm{XorColl}_\delta$$
   $$= \Pr\left[\mathtt{msb}_{n/2}\left(\widetilde{\mathsf{P}}^{0^n,0,u,0}(\mathtt{ozp}(A[u])) \oplus \widetilde{\mathsf{P}}^{0^n,0,u,0}(\mathtt{ozp}(A'[u]))\right) = \delta \oplus \gamma\right]$$
   $$\leq 2^{n/2}/(2^n - 1) \leq 2/2^{n/2}.$$

3. Let $|A|_n = |A'|_n$ and ifPad$(A) \neq$ ifPad(A'). Suppose $|A|_n = |A'|_n = a$. Without loss of generality, we suppose ifPad$(A) = 0$. Since ifPad$(A) \neq$ ifPad(A') holds, the case which satisfies $A[a] \neq A'[a]$ and $A[a] = \mathtt{ozp}(A'[a])$ can occur. When $A[a] = \mathtt{ozp}(A'[a])$, we obtain the following evaluation.

   $$\mathrm{XorColl}_{\forall\delta}$$
   $$= \Pr\left[\mathtt{msb}_{n/2}\left(\widetilde{\mathsf{P}}^{0^n,0,a,0}(A[a])\right) \oplus \mathtt{lsb}_{n/2}\left(\widetilde{\mathsf{P}}^{0^n,0,a,0}(\mathtt{ozp}(A'[a]))\right) = \delta \oplus \gamma\right]$$
   $$\leq 1/2^{n/2},$$

where $\gamma = \mathbb{P}\text{hash-hc}(A) \oplus \mathbb{P}\text{hash-hc}(A') \oplus \mathtt{msb}_{n/2}\left(\widetilde{\mathsf{P}}^{0^n,0,a,0}(A[a])\right) \oplus$
$\mathtt{lsb}_{n/2}\left(\widetilde{\mathsf{P}}^{0^n,0,a,0}(\mathtt{ozp}(A'[a]))\right)$. When $A[a] \neq \mathtt{ozp}(A'[a])$, we also obtain

$$\text{XorColl}_{\forall\delta}$$
$$= \Pr\left[\mathtt{msb}_{n/2}\left(\widetilde{\mathsf{P}}^{0^n,0,a,0}(A[a])\right) \oplus \mathtt{lsb}_{n/2}\left(\widetilde{\mathsf{P}}^{0^n,0,a,0}(\mathtt{ozp}(A'[a]))\right) = \delta \oplus \gamma\right]$$
$$\leq 2^{n/2}/(2^n - 1) \leq 2/2^{n/2}.$$

From these discussions, $\text{XorColl}_{\forall\delta} \leq 2/2^{n/2}$ holds.
4. Let $|A|_n \neq |A'|_n$. Suppose $|A|_n = a$ and $|A'|_n = a'$. We also suppose $|A|_n < |A'|_n$ and $\text{ifPad}(A') = 0$ without loss of generality. There exists $u \in \mathbb{N}$ such that $a + 1 \leq u \leq a'$ and we obtain the following evaluation.

$$\text{XorColl}_{\forall\delta} = \Pr\left[\mathtt{msb}_{n/2}\left(\widetilde{\mathsf{P}}^{0^n,0,u,0}(\mathtt{ozp}(A'[u]))\right) = \delta \oplus \gamma\right] \leq 1/2^{n/2},$$

where $\gamma = \mathbb{P}\text{hash-hc}(A) \oplus \mathbb{P}\text{hash-hc}(A') \oplus \mathtt{msb}_{n/2}\left(\widetilde{\mathsf{P}}^{0^n,0,u,0}(\mathtt{ozp}(A'[u]))\right)$.

From above four cases, $\max_{\forall\delta\in\{0,1\}^{n/2}} \Pr\left[\mathbb{P}\text{hash-hc}_{\widetilde{\mathsf{P}}}(A) \oplus \mathbb{P}\text{hash-hc}_{\widetilde{\mathsf{P}}}(A') = \delta\right] \leq 2/2^{n/2}$ holds.

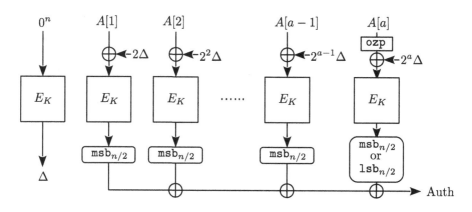

Fig. 8. The algorithm of Phash-hc$_{E_K}$, where E_K is any blockcipher.

B   Proof of the Security of OCB-hc-AD

We here show the proof of Theorem 3.

Proof. We obtain the following evaluations using hybrid argument.

$$\mathbf{Adv}^{\mathrm{priv}}_{\Theta\mathrm{CB\text{-}hc\text{-}AD_P}}(\mathcal{A}) \leq \mathbf{Adv}^{\mathrm{cpa\text{-}nr}}_{\Theta\mathrm{CB\text{-}hc\text{-}AD_P},\Theta\mathrm{CB\text{-}hc\text{-}AD_{\tilde{P}}}}(\mathcal{A}) + \mathbf{Adv}^{\mathrm{priv}}_{\Theta\mathrm{CB\text{-}hc\text{-}AD_{\tilde{P}}}}(\mathcal{A})$$

$$= \mathbf{Adv}^{\mathrm{tprp}}_{\mathrm{XEX}^*_{\tilde{P}}}(\mathcal{B}) + \mathbf{Adv}^{\mathrm{priv}}_{\Theta\mathrm{CB\text{-}hc\text{-}AD_{\tilde{P}}}}(\mathcal{A})$$

$$\leq \frac{4.5\sigma^2_{\mathrm{priv}}}{2^n} + 0, \tag{5}$$

$$\mathbf{Adv}^{\mathrm{auth}}_{\Theta\mathrm{CB\text{-}hc\text{-}AD_P}}(\mathcal{A}^{\pm}) \leq \mathbf{Adv}^{\mathrm{cca\text{-}nr}}_{\Theta\mathrm{CB\text{-}hc\text{-}AD_P},\Theta\mathrm{CB\text{-}hc\text{-}AD_{\tilde{P}}}}(\mathcal{A}^{\pm}) + \mathbf{Adv}^{\mathrm{auth}}_{\Theta\mathrm{CB\text{-}hc\text{-}AD_{\tilde{P}}}}(\mathcal{A}^{\pm})$$

$$= \mathbf{Adv}^{\mathrm{tsprp}}_{\mathrm{XEX}^*_{\tilde{P}}}(\mathcal{B}^{\pm}) + \mathbf{Adv}^{\mathrm{auth}}_{\Theta\mathrm{CB\text{-}hc\text{-}AD_{\tilde{P}}}}(\mathcal{A}^{\pm})$$

$$\leq \frac{4.5\sigma^2_{\mathrm{auth}}}{2^n} + \frac{4q_d}{2^{n/2}}, \tag{6}$$

where $\mathcal{B}$ (resp. $\mathcal{B}^{\pm}$) is the adversary which can simulate $\mathcal{A}$ (resp. $\mathcal{A}^{\pm}$). The first terms of (5), (6) are derived from [33,38]. The second terms of (5), (6) are described below.

Privacy. Similarly to $\Theta\mathrm{CB\text{-}hc}$ and $\Theta\mathrm{TR\text{-}hc}$, $\mathbf{Adv}^{\mathrm{priv}}_{\Theta\mathrm{CB\text{-}hc\text{-}AD_{\tilde{P}}}}(\mathcal{A}) = 0$ holds since the adversary follows nonce-respecting.

Authenticity. For simplicity, we suppose that the adversary can query to the decryption oracle only once. Without loss of generality, the adversary performs decryption query after all encryption queries. Suppose that she obtains the transcript $z = \{(N_1, M_1, A_1, C_1, T_1), \ldots, (N_q, M_q, A_q, C_q, T_q)\}$ in encryption query, and she queries (N', A', C', T') in decryption query. Let Z be the set of all transcripts, and T^* be the valid tag for (N', A', C'). Then we define $\mathrm{FP}_z := \Pr[T' = T^* \mid Z = z]$ and evaluate $\max_z \mathrm{FP}_z$ as below.

1. Let $N' \neq N_i$, $1 \leq \forall i \leq q$. As in the proof of $\Theta\mathrm{CB\text{-}hc}$, $\mathrm{FP}_z \leq 1/2^{n/2}$ holds.
2. Let $N' = N_\alpha$, $\alpha \in \{1, 2, \ldots, q\}$, $A' = A_\alpha$, $C' \neq C_\alpha$. In this case, we can evaluate FP_z in the same manner as the proof of $\Theta\mathrm{CB\text{-}hc}$. Thus $\mathrm{FP}_z \leq 4/2^{n/2}$ holds.
3. Let $N' = N_\alpha$, $\alpha \in \{1, 2, \ldots, q\}$, $A' \neq A_\alpha$. We suppose that $\mathtt{Checksum}^*$ is the valid checksum corresponding to (N', A', C') and that $\mathtt{Checksum}_\alpha$ is the value of the checksum corresponding to $(N_\alpha, A_\alpha, C_\alpha)$. Let e_1 is the event which $\mathtt{Checksum}^* = \mathtt{Checksum}_\alpha$ holds. Recall that

$$\mathtt{Checksum} = \left(\left(\mathbb{P}\mathrm{hash\text{-}hc}(A) \oplus \bigoplus_{i=1}^{m-1} \mathtt{msb}_{n/2}(M[i])\right) \| 0^{n/2}\right) \oplus \mathtt{ozp}(M[m]).$$

From the property of $\mathbb{P}\mathrm{hash\text{-}hc}$ mentioned in Lemma 3, we obtain the following evaluation.

$$\Pr[e_1 \mid Z = z] = \Pr[\mathbb{P}\mathrm{hash\text{-}hc}(A') \| 0^{n/2} \oplus \mathbb{P}\mathrm{hash\text{-}hc}(A_\alpha) \| 0^{n/2} = \gamma \mid Z = z]$$

$$\leq \frac{2}{2^{n/2}},$$

where $\gamma = \left(\bigoplus_{i=1}^{m'-1} \mathrm{msb}_{n/2}(M^*[i]) \right) \| 0^{n/2} \right) \oplus \left(\bigoplus_{i=1}^{m_\alpha-1} \mathrm{msb}_{n/2}(M_\alpha[i]) \right) \|$
$0^{n/2}) \oplus \mathrm{ozp}(M^*[m']) \oplus \mathrm{ozp}(M_\alpha[m_\alpha])$. Then we can evaluate a forgery probability as follows:

$$\mathrm{FP}_z \leq \Pr[T' = T^* \mid \bar{e}_1, Z = z] \Pr[e_1 \mid Z = z]$$
$$\leq \frac{2^{n/2}}{2^n - 1} + \frac{2}{2^{n/2}} \leq \frac{4}{2^{n/2}}.$$

From the evaluations of above cases, we obtain

$$\mathbf{Adv}_{\Theta\mathrm{CB\text{-}hc\text{-}AD}}^{\mathrm{auth}}(\mathcal{A}^\pm) \leq \sum_z \max_z \mathrm{FP}_z \cdot \Pr[Z = z] \leq \frac{4}{2^{n/2}}.$$

When the adversary queries to the decryption oracle q_d times, we obtain

$$\mathbf{Adv}_{\Theta\mathrm{CB\text{-}hc\text{-}AD}}^{\mathrm{auth}}(\mathcal{A}^\pm) \leq \frac{4q_d}{2^{n/2}}$$

by using a technique from [10].

References

1. The OCB Authenticated-Encryption Algorithm. IRTF RFC 7253 (2014)
2. NIST Lightweight Cryptography Standardization (2019). https://csrc.nist.gov/Projects/Lightweight-Cryptography
3. Andreeva, E., et al.: COLM v1. Submission to CAESAR competition (2015)
4. Andreeva, E., Bogdanov, A., Luykx, A., Mennink, B., Mouha, N., Yasuda, K.: How to securely release unverified plaintext in authenticated encryption. In: Sarkar, P., Iwata, T. (eds.) ASIACRYPT 2014. LNCS, vol. 8873, pp. 105–125. Springer, Heidelberg (2014). https://doi.org/10.1007/978-3-662-45611-8_6
5. Andreeva, E., Bogdanov, A., Luykx, A., Mennink, B., Tischhauser, E., Yasuda, K.: Parallelizable and authenticated online ciphers. In: Sako, K., Sarkar, P. (eds.) ASIACRYPT 2013. LNCS, vol. 8269, pp. 424–443. Springer, Heidelberg (2013). https://doi.org/10.1007/978-3-642-42033-7_22
6. Andreeva, E., Bogdanov, A., Luykx, A., Mennink, B., Tischhauser, E., Yasuda, K.: AES-COPA vol 2. Submission to CAESAR competition (2015)
7. Aoki, K., Yasuda, K.: The security of the OCB mode of operation without the SPRP assumption. In: Susilo, W., Reyhanitabar, R. (eds.) ProvSec 2013. LNCS, vol. 8209, pp. 202–220. Springer, Heidelberg (2013). https://doi.org/10.1007/978-3-642-41227-1_12
8. Ashur, T., Dunkelman, O., Luykx, A.: Boosting authenticated encryption robustness with minimal modifications. In: Katz, J., Shacham, H. (eds.) CRYPTO 2017. LNCS, vol. 10403, pp. 3–33. Springer, Cham (2017). https://doi.org/10.1007/978-3-319-63697-9_1
9. Bellare, M., Desai, A., Jokipii, E., Rogaway, P.: A concrete security treatment of symmetric encryption. In: FOCS, pp. 394–403. IEEE Computer Society (1997)
10. Bellare, M., Goldreich, O., Mityagin, A.: The power of verification queries in message authentication and authenticated encryption. Cryptology ePrint Archive, Report 2004/309 (2004). https://eprint.iacr.org/2004/309

11. Bellare, M., Namprempre, C.: Authenticated encryption: relations among notions and analysis of the generic composition paradigm. In: Okamoto, T. (ed.) ASIACRYPT 2000. LNCS, vol. 1976, pp. 531–545. Springer, Heidelberg (2000). https://doi.org/10.1007/3-540-44448-3_41

12. Benadjila, R., Guo, J., Lomné, V., Peyrin, T.: Implementing lightweight block ciphers on x86 architectures. In: Lange, T., Lauter, K., Lisoněk, P. (eds.) SAC 2013. LNCS, vol. 8282, pp. 324–351. Springer, Heidelberg (2014). https://doi.org/10.1007/978-3-662-43414-7_17

13. Bertoni, G., Daemen, J., Peeters, M., Van Assche, G.: Duplexing the sponge: single-pass authenticated encryption and other applications. In: Miri, A., Vaudenay, S. (eds.) SAC 2011. LNCS, vol. 7118, pp. 320–337. Springer, Heidelberg (2012). https://doi.org/10.1007/978-3-642-28496-0_19

14. Bhaumik, R., Nandi, M.: Improved security for OCB3. In: Takagi, T., Peyrin, T. (eds.) ASIACRYPT 2017. LNCS, vol. 10625, pp. 638–666. Springer, Cham (2017). https://doi.org/10.1007/978-3-319-70697-9_22

15. Bost, R., Sanders, O.: Trick or tweak: on the (In)security of OTR's tweaks. In: Cheon, J.H., Takagi, T. (eds.) ASIACRYPT 2016. LNCS, vol. 10031, pp. 333–353. Springer, Heidelberg (2016). https://doi.org/10.1007/978-3-662-53887-6_12

16. Chakraborti, A., Iwata, T., Minematsu, K., Nandi, M.: Blockcipher-based authenticated encryption: how small can we go? In: Fischer, W., Homma, N. (eds.) CHES 2017. LNCS, vol. 10529, pp. 277–298. Springer, Cham (2017). https://doi.org/10.1007/978-3-319-66787-4_14

17. Datta, N., Nandi, M.: ELmE: a misuse resistant parallel authenticated encryption. In: Susilo, W., Mu, Y. (eds.) ACISP 2014. LNCS, vol. 8544, pp. 306–321. Springer, Cham (2014). https://doi.org/10.1007/978-3-319-08344-5_20

18. Datta, N., Nandi, M.: ELMD v2.0. Submission to CAESAR competition (2015)

19. Dworkin, M.: Recommendation for Block Cipher Modes of Operation: Galois/Counter Mode (GCM) and GMAC. NIST-SP 800-38D (2007)

20. Dworkin, M.: Recommendation for Block Cipher Modes of Operation: the CCM Mode for Authentication and Confidentiality. NIST-SP 800-38C (2007)

21. Ferguson, N.: Collision attacks on OCB. Comments to NIST (2002)

22. Granger, R., Jovanovic, P., Mennink, B., Neves, S.: Improved masking for tweakable blockciphers with applications to authenticated encryption. In: Fischlin, M., Coron, J.-S. (eds.) EUROCRYPT 2016. LNCS, vol. 9665, pp. 263–293. Springer, Heidelberg (2016). https://doi.org/10.1007/978-3-662-49890-3_11

23. Inoue, A., Iwata, T., Minematsu, K., Poettering, B.: Cryptanalysis of OCB2: attacks on authenticity and confidentiality. Cryptology ePrint Archive, Report 2019/311 (2019). https://eprint.iacr.org/2019/311

24. Iwata, T., Kurosawa, K.: OMAC: one-key CBC MAC. In: Johansson, T. (ed.) FSE 2003. LNCS, vol. 2887, pp. 129–153. Springer, Heidelberg (2003). https://doi.org/10.1007/978-3-540-39887-5_11

25. Iwata, T., Minematsu, K., Guo, J., Morioka, S.: CLOC: authenticated encryption for short input. In: Cid, C., Rechberger, C. (eds.) FSE 2014. LNCS, vol. 8540, pp. 149–167. Springer, Heidelberg (2015). https://doi.org/10.1007/978-3-662-46706-0_8

26. Iwata, T., Minematsu, K., Guo, J., Morioka, S., Kobayashi, E.: CLOC and SILC v3. Submission to the CAESAR competition (2016)

27. Krovetz, T., Rogaway, P.: The software performance of authenticated-encryption modes. In: Fast Software Encryption - 18th International Workshop, FSE 2011, Lyngby, Denmark, 13–16 February 2011, Revised Selected Papers, pp. 306–327 (2011). https://doi.org/10.1007/978-3-642-21702-9_18

28. Liskov, M., Rivest, R.L., Wagner, D.: Tweakable block ciphers. In: Yung, M. (ed.) CRYPTO 2002. LNCS, vol. 2442, pp. 31–46. Springer, Heidelberg (2002). https://doi.org/10.1007/3-540-45708-9_3

29. Matsuda, S., Moriai, S.: Lightweight cryptography for the cloud: exploit the power of bitslice implementation. In: Prouff, E., Schaumont, P. (eds.) CHES 2012. LNCS, vol. 7428, pp. 408–425. Springer, Heidelberg (2012). https://doi.org/10.1007/978-3-642-33027-8_24

30. Minematsu, K.: Improved security analysis of XEX and LRW modes. In: Biham, E., Youssef, A.M. (eds.) SAC 2006. LNCS, vol. 4356, pp. 96–113. Springer, Heidelberg (2007). https://doi.org/10.1007/978-3-540-74462-7_8

31. Minematsu, K.: Parallelizable rate-1 authenticated encryption from pseudorandom functions. In: Nguyen, P.Q., Oswald, E. (eds.) EUROCRYPT 2014. LNCS, vol. 8441, pp. 275–292. Springer, Heidelberg (2014). https://doi.org/10.1007/978-3-642-55220-5_16

32. Minematsu, K.: AES-OTR v3. Submission to CAESAR competition (2016)

33. Minematsu, K., Matsushima, T.: Generalization and extension of XEX* mode. IEICE Trans. **92-A**(2), 517–524 (2009). http://search.ieice.org/bin/summary.php?id=e92-a_2_517&category=A&year=2009&lang=E&abst=

34. Naito, Y.: Improved XKX-based AEAD scheme: removing the birthday terms. In: Lange, T., Dunkelman, O. (eds.) LATINCRYPT 2017. LNCS, vol. 11368, pp. 228–246. Springer, Cham (2019). https://doi.org/10.1007/978-3-030-25283-0_13

35. Naito, Y.: Tweakable blockciphers for efficient authenticated encryptions with beyond the birthday-bound security. IACR Trans. Symmetric Cryptol. **2017**(2), 1–26 (2017)

36. Naito, Y., Matsui, M., Sugawara, T., Suzuki, D.: SAEB: a lightweight blockcipher-based AEAD mode of operation. IACR Trans. Cryptogr. Hardw. Embed. Syst. **2018**(2), 192–217 (2018). https://doi.org/10.13154/tches.v2018.i2.192-217

37. Rescorla, E.: The Transport Layer Security (TLS) Protocol Version 1.3. RFC 8446 (2018). https://doi.org/10.17487/RFC8446, https://rfc-editor.org/rfc/rfc8446.txt

38. Rogaway, P.: Efficient instantiations of tweakable blockciphers and refinements to modes OCB and PMAC. In: Advances in Cryptology - ASIACRYPT 2004, 10th International Conference on the Theory and Application of Cryptology and Information Security, Jeju Island, Korea, 5–9 December 2004, pp. 16–31 (2004). https://doi.org/10.1007/978-3-540-30539-2_2

39. Rogaway, P., Bellare, M., Black, J., Krovetz, T.: OCB: a block-cipher mode of operation for efficient authenticated encryption. In: CCS 2001, Proceedings of the 8th ACM Conference on Computer and Communications Security, Philadelphia, Pennsylvania, USA, 6–8 November 2001, pp. 196–205 (2001). https://doi.org/10.1145/501983.502011

40. T. Dierks, E.R.: The Transport Layer Security (TLS) Protocol Version 1.2. IETF, RFC 5246 (2008)

41. Ueno, R., Homma, N., Iida, T., Minematsu, K.: High throughput/gate FN-based hardware architectures for AES-OTR. In: 2019 IEEE International Symposium on Circuits and Systems (ISCAS), pp. 1–4 (2019)

Deep Neural Network Attribution Methods for Leakage Analysis and Symmetric Key Recovery

Benjamin Hettwer[1,2(✉)], Stefan Gehrer[1], and Tim Güneysu[2]

[1] Robert Bosch GmbH, Corporate Sector Research, Stuttgart, Germany
{benjamin.hettwer,stefan.gehrer}@de.bosch.com
[2] Horst Görtz Institute for IT-Security, Ruhr University Bochum, Bochum, Germany
tim.gueneysu@rub.de

Abstract. Deep Neural Networks (DNNs) have recently received significant attention in the side-channel community due to their state-of-the-art performance in security testing of embedded systems. However, research on the subject mostly focused on techniques to improve the attack efficiency in terms of the number of traces required to extract secret parameters. What has not been investigated in detail is a constructive approach of DNNs as a tool to evaluate and improve the effectiveness of countermeasures against side-channel attacks. In this work, we close this gap by applying attribution methods that aim for interpreting Deep Neural Network (DNN) decisions in order to identify leaking operations in cryptographic implementations. In particular, we investigate three different approaches that have been proposed for feature visualization in image classification tasks and compare them regarding their suitability to reveal Points of Interest (POIs) in side-channel traces. We show by experiments with four separate data sets that the three methods are especially interesting in the context of side-channel protected implementations and misaligned measurements. Finally, we demonstrate that attribution can also serve as a powerful side-channel distinguisher leading to a successful retrieval of the secret key with at least five times fewer traces compared to standard key recovery in DNN-based attack setups.

Keywords: Side-Channel Attacks · Deep Learning · Machine Learning · Leakage analysis

1 Introduction

Side-Channel Analyis (SCA) is a technique by which an adversary circumvents the security assumptions of a cryptographic system by analyzing its physical properties. In this regard, timing [19], power consumption [18], and Electromagnetic (EM) emanation [3] have been investigated to reveal secret parameters. In order to decrease the information leakage of cryptographic implementations,

© Springer Nature Switzerland AG 2020
K. G. Paterson and D. Stebila (Eds.): SAC 2019, LNCS 11959, pp. 645–666, 2020.
https://doi.org/10.1007/978-3-030-38471-5_26

researchers and industry came up with dedicated countermeasures which can be roughly classified into *Masking* and *Hiding* [21]. However, more powerful attacks demonstrated that even side-channel protected implementations may still be vulnerable [23].

A new line of work that deals with the application of DNNs for side-channel evaluation of protected and unprotected cryptographic implementations has been presented recently. In general, DNNs provide a powerful method for a variety of different real-world problems such as image classification [16], natural language processing [31], and medical applications [10]. In the context of SCA, especially Convolutional Neural Networks (CNNs) have shown to be advantageous over standard analyzing tools like TAs in different settings (for example in case of desynchronized traces or an unknown leakage model) [8,17,20,30].

Due to the black-box nature of DNNs, understanding the operation of Deep Learning (DL) models is an active area of research. It is evident that safety critical applications such as medicine or autonomously driving cars need to be validated exhaustively prior to their actual release. Regarding image classification, several so-called *attribution* or *heatmapping* methods have been proposed to explain the predictions of DNNs. The idea is to visualize the pixels of an input image which had the greatest influence of classifying it into a certain category. By doing so, it is possible to make the decisions of a DNN more transparent and explainable as it helps to identify if a DNN was able to learn the "correct" features during training.

In this work, we analyze different attribution methods of DNNs for their suitability in SCA. More specifically, we investigate *saliency maps* [28], *occlusion* [32], and *Layer-wise Relevance Propagation (LRP)* [6] to extract the features or POIs from a trained DNN which are most informative for symmetric key recovery. Proper POI detection is commonly considered as crucial for the success of profiled SCA (i.e. attacks which assume an adversary with access to a profiling device which is similar to the target) and usually performed as a preprocessing step ahead of the actual attack [24]. Here, we take another perspective and show a technique to compute the relevance of sample points in side-channel traces after the profiling step, which is applicable even in case of employed countermeasures. This can be seen as a constructive method for evaluators to identify the operations of the implementation under test causing the highest leakage. Furthermore, we demonstrate that attribution methods can also be used as a distinguisher in DNN-based SCA.

1.1   Contribution

The contributions of this paper are manifold:

1. We show a generic technique that can be used to calculate the POIs from a trained DNN. It is generic in a sense that it is independent of the actual used attribution method.
2. Based on the commonly known Key Guessing Entropy (KGE), we define two novel metrics tailored to the specifics of DNNs in order to quantitatively asses how well the selection of POIs is done.

3. We compare three attribution methods on four different data sets: a hardware implementation (with and without jitter in the traces) and two protected software implementations of the Advanced Encryption Standard (AES). Our results confirm that attribution methods are more suitable to extract POIs from protected implementations than a standard technique from the side-channel domain.
4. We show how LRP can be embedded in profiled attack setups to distinguish between correct and incorrect key hypotheses. We demonstrate by practical experiments that our proposed method is more efficient than using the network predictions directly for key recovery.

1.2 Related Work

Identifying POIs in side-channel traces has been traditionally studied in the context of TAs introduced by Chari et al. [9], in order to reduce the computational overhead during calculation of the covariance matrices. In particular, *Difference of Means (DOM)* [9], *Sum Of Squared pairwise T-differences (SOST)*, *Sum Of Squared Differences (SOSD)* [14], and *Principal Component Analysis (PCA)* [5] have been proposed for that purpose. Another common strategy for POIs selection is based on Pearson correlation, whereby the importance of sample points is measured by the correlation coefficient of the actual power consumption and some key-dependent target intermediate value [21]. Picek et al. investigated the so-called Wrapper and Hybrid methods stemming from the machine learning domain to determine a suitable subset of features in order to boost the efficiency of side-channel attacks [24].

In contrast to most of the aforementioned approaches, leakage detection techniques such as *Test Vector Leakage Assessment (TVLA)* aim for revealing data-dependent information leakage independent of any power model or intermediate value [11]. It can thus be considered as a complementary tool to identifying leaking operations in a first step, then performing an actual attack to check whether the found leakage can be exploited for a successful key extraction.

Very recently, Masure et al. came up with an idea similar to our work: POIs visualization after successful training of a neural network [22]. Their method based on sensitivity analysis is related to the saliency technique. In this work, we conduct a more comprehensive study of DNN attribution methods for side-channel analysis by comparing different techniques using a novel framework for POIs selection and evaluation. We additionally present, to the best of our knowledge, the first SCA distinguisher based on DNN attribution.

1.3 Structure of the Paper

The structure of the paper is as follows: In Sect. 2, we shortly recap DL-based SCA and give an introduction to DNN attribution methods. In Sect. 3, we present our approach for POIs visualization and apply them to four data sets for leakage analysis. In Sect. 4, we evaluate the quality of side-channel heatmaps. In Sect. 5, we describe our attribution-based technique for key recovery and use them to attack an unprotected and a protected implementation of the AES. The last section summarizes the paper and gives insights on possible future work.

2 Preliminaries

This section outlines the foundations of DL-based SCA. Furthermore, background and motivation of DNN attribution methods is provided.

2.1 Deep Learning-Based Profiled Side-Channel Analysis

Profiled SCA is divided in two stages: profiling phase and key recovery phase. In the former, the adversary takes advantage of a profiling device on which he can fully control input and secret key parameters of the cryptographic algorithm. He uses this to acquire a set of N_P profiling side-channel traces $\mathbf{x} \in \mathbb{R}^D$, where D denotes the number of sample points in the measurements. Let $V = g(p, k)$ be a random variable representing the result of an intermediate operation of the target cipher which depends partly on public information p (plaintext or ciphertext chunk) and secret key $k \in \mathcal{K}$, where $\mathcal{K}$ is the set of possible key values. V is assumed to have an influence on the deterministic part of the side-channel measurements. In the context of DL or Machine Learning (ML) in general, the goal of the attacker during the profiling phase is to construct a classifier that estimates the probability distribution $f(\mathbf{x}) \approx \mathrm{P}[V|\mathbf{x}]$ using the training set $\mathcal{D}_{Train} = \{\mathbf{x}_i, v_i\}_{i=1,\dots,N_P}$.

During the key recovery phase, the adversary generates a new set $\mathcal{D}_{Attack}$ with N_A attack traces from the actual target device (which is structurally identical to the profiling device) whereby the secret key k is fixed and unknown. In order to retrieve it, Log-likelihood (LL) scores over all possible key candidates $k^* \in \mathcal{K}$ are computed and combined to:

$$\mathbf{d}^{LL}(\mathcal{D}_{Attack}, f) = \sum_{i=1}^{N_A} \log f(\mathbf{x}_i)[g(p_i, k^*)] \tag{1}$$

The k-th entry in score vector $\mathbf{d}^{LL}$ corresponds to the correct key candidate [25]. A commonly known metric in profiled SCA is the so-called KGE or key rank function which quantifies the difficulty to retrieve the correct value of the key regarding the required number of traces from $\mathcal{D}_{Attack}$ [29]. It is computed by performing a ranking of $\mathbf{d}$ after the evaluation of each attack trace. Intuitively, the faster the key rank converges to one, the more powerful is the attack.

2.2 Deep Neural Network Attribution Methods

In recent years there has been a growing interest in neural networks having several layers of neurons stacked upon each other, which are commonly referred to as DNNs. They represent a particular powerful type of ML techniques that are able to represent the learning task as a nested hierarchy of concepts, where more abstract concept representations are built from simpler ones. Throughout the paper we assume a DNN as a classification function that takes an input vector $\mathbf{x} = [x_1, \ldots, x_D] \in \mathbb{R}^D$ and produces an output $f(\mathbf{x}, \mathbf{W}) = [f_1(\mathbf{x}), \ldots, f_C(\mathbf{x})]$, where C denotes the number of output neurons (=number of categories). The parameters $\mathbf{W}$ are learned during training to approximate f from a broad class of functions to map $\mathbf{x}$ to the desired output. Training a DNN is usually done in an iterative, multi-step process by which the parameters of the network are optimized to minimize a loss function, which depicts the difference between the expected output (i.e. labels) and the prediction result. In practice, optimizer algorithms such as Stochastic Gradient Descent (SGD) or ADAM are employed for that purpose [15].

Given a specific class c, attribution methods for DNNs aim to determine the influence $\mathbf{r}^c = [r_1^c, \ldots, r_D^c] \in \mathbb{R}^D$ of each data point x_i of an input vector (sometimes also called features) with respect to the output neuron f_c [4]. The result can be visualized, e.g., as a heatmap that indicates the features that contributed positively and/or negatively to the activation of the target output. In the following, we briefly summarize three recent attribution methods that have been proposed for calculating heatmaps for 2D images, which we later apply to 1D side-channel traces. We have chosen these three methods for two reasons: First, they are not designed for a specific type of DNN architecture (as for example Grad-CAM [27] and deconvolution [32] for CNNs) but generally applicable to several types of DNN and activation units. Second, we intend to compare techniques coming from different classes of attribution methods, i.e., a gradient-based method (saliency maps), a LRP-based method, and one that is based on the perturbation of the input (occlusion).

Saliency Maps. Simonyan et al. established saliency maps in 2013 in order to highlight class discriminative areas of images captured by CNNs [28]. To this end, the norm value $\|\cdot\|_\infty$ over partial derivatives of the output category is computed with respect to the input features:

$$r_i^c = \left\| \frac{\partial f_c(\mathbf{x})}{\partial x_i} \right\|_\infty \tag{2}$$

Partial derivatives are found by running the back-propagation algorithm throughout the layers of the network. Intuitively, the magnitude of the derivative indicates which features need to be modified the least to affect the class score the most. However, since the sign of the derivative is lost when using the norm, only positive attributions of input features can be detected with the saliency method. It consequently provides only local explanations, e.g., by indicating the features that make a car more/less a car, but no global explanations which features compose a car [26].

Layer-wise Relevance Propagation (LRP) was introduced by Bach et al. as a general concept to achieve a pixel-wise decomposition of the prediction $f(\mathbf{x})$ as a term of the separate input dimensions [6]:

$$f(\mathbf{x}) \approx \sum_{i=1}^{N} r_i \tag{3}$$

where $r_i > 0$ can be interpreted as positive evidence for the presence of a structure in the picture, and $r_i < 0$ as evidence for its absence. The algorithm follows a conservation principle that proceeds layer by layer, by which the prediction score f_c is propagated recursively through the network until the input layer is reached. For redistributing a layers relevance onto the preceding layer, Bach et al. proposed the following propagation rule:

$$r_i^{(l)} = \sum_j \frac{z_{ij}}{\sum_{i'} z_{i'j} + \epsilon \cdot sign(\sum_{i'} z_{i'j})} r_j^{(l+1)} \tag{4}$$

Here, $r_i^{(l)}$ denotes the relevance associated with the ith neuron in layer l received from the jth neuron in the layer $l + 1$, and $z_{ij} = a_i^{(l)} w_{ij}^{(l,l+1)}$ the weighted activation of neuron i onto neuron j in the next layer. The ϵ term is added in order to cope with numerical instabilities in case the denominator tends to zero. The idea of the propagation rule is that neurons of the preceding layer that gave an larger activation to neurons of the higher layer in the forward pass get more relevance on the backward pass.

Compared to gradient-based attribution methods such as saliency, LRP is applicable to any network with monotonous activation units (even non-continuous). LRP furthermore provides a clear interpretation by indicating the features for and against a category [26]. We will see later in the paper that this property can be exploited to construct a side-channel distinguisher.

Occlusion sensitivity analysis as proposed by Zeiler and Vergus attempts to identify the location of objects in images by systematically occluding different regions of the input with a grey square, and monitoring the classification result [32]. Therefore, the relevance of input features can be described as probability drop of the correct class with respect to the position of the grey patch. It is evident that the runtime and result of the algorithm heavily depends on the number of features that are removed together per iteration.

In the remainder of the paper, we refer to the *1-occlusion* approach given in [4]. In 1-occlusion, exactly one feature of the input data is set to zero per time, while the effect on the output is measured. More formally, the attribution of a single feature can be calculated as:

$$r_i^c = f_c(\mathbf{x}) - f_c(\mathbf{x}[i] = 0) \tag{5}$$

where $\mathbf{x}[i] = v$ indicates an input vector whose ith data point has been replaced with the value v. We have chosen 1-occlusion since the leakage information present in side-channel traces is often concentrated in a small number of sample points [24].

3   Attribution for POI Analysis

In this section, we describe a method to generate heatmaps for side-channel traces using DNN attribution and apply it to four data sets.

3.1   Side-Channel Heatmaps

DNN-based SCA aimed mainly for symmetric key recovery in the past. In this context, especially CNNs have shown to be a suitable tool due to the fact that they are able to automatically extract the areas in the side-channel traces which contain the most information [8,20]. Furthermore, CNNs are able to detect POIs that would normally not be considered by an attacker. These can be used by the network in conjunction with the areas that contain a lot of leakage to make the attack even more efficient, i.e., requiring less/smaller traces for a successful attack. When using established SCA techniques such as TAs, the selection of POIs has to be done manually as a preprocessing step ahead of the actual attack. This is not only tedious, but also error prone as proper POI selection has shown to have a significant impact on the attack efficiency [33]. Furthermore, in case of first-order secure implementations without access to the mask values during the profiling step, the adversary has to combine the leakage location of the mask and the masked target intermediate value when considering a second-order Correlation Power Analysis (CPA) for POIs detection. This requires to combine all possible combination of sample points and the overhead grows roughly quadratically with the size of the traces [21].

In this section, we go one step further and describe a way to extract the POIs from a trained Convolutional Neural Network (CNN) (or any type of DNN) that have been considered as most discriminative to reveal the correct key, based on the attribution methods presented in the previous section. The approach works as follows and is summarized in (6): Given a trained DNN f, the relevance $\mathbf{r}^{C_k}$ for an input trace $\mathbf{x}$ is found by using one of the attribution methods mentioned in Sect. 2. C_k represents the output class under the correct key, i.e., the labels that have been used for training of f. This procedure is conducted for a set of N_{Attr} traces and the average relevance $\bar{\mathbf{r}} \in \mathbb{R}^D$ is calculated.

$$\bar{\mathbf{r}} = \frac{1}{N_{Attr}} \sum_{i=1}^{N_{Attr}} \mathbf{r}^{C_k}(\mathbf{x}_i, f) \tag{6}$$

Because $\bar{\mathbf{r}}$ has the same dimensionality as $\mathbf{x}$, it can be visualized as 1D side-channel heatmap plot. The information can be used, for example, to determine leaking operations in cryptographic implementations since it is easily possible to trace which operations are performed at which time intervals (at least in white-box evaluation settings). Another use case would be to identify relevant regions in the side-channel traces using only a subset of the available traces in a first step, in order to decrease the number of data points for the actual attack with the complete data set (and thus speed up calculations).

3.2   Experimental Results

We consider four data sets for the experiments of the paper: An unprotected hardware AES with and without jitter in the traces (denoted as AES-Serial and AES-Serial-Desync), and two protected software implementations of the AES (denoted as ASCAD and AES-RSM). An overview about the data sets is given in Table 1. We have created attribution heatmaps for all data sets according to (6) using the Python frameworks Keras [2] and DeepExplain [1]. Additionally, we have computed Pearson correlations as a baseline. The same DNN architecture has been used in all experiments in order to allow an unbiased evaluation. The employed network is a CNN which consists of four blocks of convolution and max-pooling operations followed by two fully-connected layers. Details about the network structure along with related training parameters are described in detail in Table 2 in the Appendix. As a preprocessing step ahead of training the CNN, we transformed the traces of all data sets to have zero mean and unit variance (sometimes referred to as data standardization).

Table 1. Overview of data sets

Data set	Sample points	Traces (Profiling)	KGE < 3
AES-Serial	1000	25 000	750
AES-Serial-Desync	950	50 000	100
ASCAD	700	50 000	500
AES-RSM	10 000	100 000	20

AES-Serial. AES-Serial denotes a set of power traces of an unprotected AES hardware design that have been acquired from a Xilinx ZYNQ UltraScale+ evaluation board. A single measurement contains 1000 data points representing approximately the time interval when the first AES round is calculated. Since it is commonly known that the most leakage in a hardware implementation is caused by register transitions, we have used the XOR of two consecutive S-Box outputs in the first round as target operation and consequently as labels for training. We have trained the network using 25 000 traces and subsequently calculated heatmaps with a subset of $N_{Attr} = 1000$ measurements for each of the attribution methods introduced in Sect. 2. N_{Attr} was set to this value since we observed no improvements when using more than 1000 traces for the calculation. The resulting heatmaps along with the corresponding correlation for the correct key hypothesis are shown in the first row of Fig. 1. From there, one can observe that the region around sample point 800 is considered as most informative by all three attribution methods as well as by the Pearson correlation. Interestingly, the saliency heatmap indicates a wider range of samples as important and additionally shows a second peak in the first half of the heatmap which

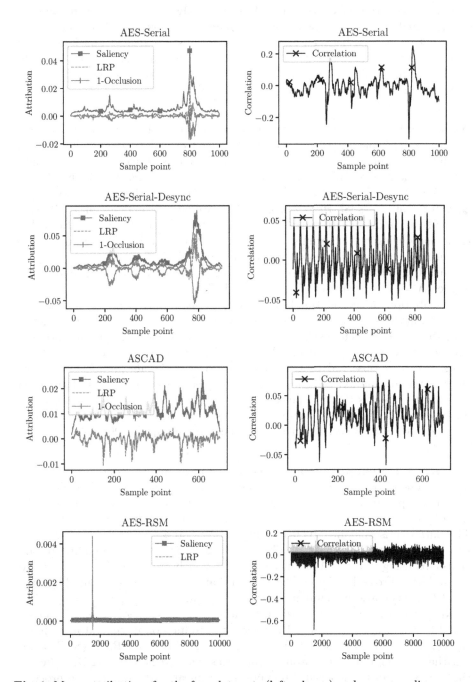

Fig. 1. Mean attributions for the four data sets (left column) and corresponding correlation analysis result (right column). Each curve has been calculated with 1000 traces.

is also visible in the correlation plot. We could easily backtrack by examining the implemented hardware layout that the found leakage is caused by unintended high routing fanouts between four registers of the state array. Considering this, it seems that correlation analysis gives better results than the attribution methods in this data set as four peaks are clearly visible in the correlation plot. We will see later in the paper that this assumption is correct.

AES-Serial-Desync. This data set is similar to the former one except that the traces have been artificially desynchronized in order to simulate jitter in the measurement setup. To this end, we have shifted each trace to the right with a random offset in the range [0, 50]. Cagli et al. demonstrated that CNNs are robust to such misalignments due to the spatial invariance property of the convolutional layers [8]. Here, our goal is to evaluate if the different attribution methods are still able to extract POIs in case of desynchronized traces. We examined during the experiments that our CNN architecture is indeed capable to learn a meaningful representation from the misaligned traces. However, more training traces have been required for a successful key recovery compared to the aligned AES-Serial data set (50 000 instead of 25 000).

Attribution and correlation heatmaps for the AES-Serial-Desync data set can be found in the second row of Fig. 1. One can notice that the attribution curves look similar to the curves for the aligned traces, while the correlation-based feature extraction totally fails in this case. Taking a closer look on the lefthand plots, it can be observed that the four expected peaks are even better visible than in the attribution heatmaps for the aligned traces. A second observation that can be made is that the peaks are broader compared to the curves plotted directly above. This due to the misalignment of the sample points and the fact that we have calculated then mean relevance over $N_{Attr} = 1000$ traces.

ASCAD is a public database of side-channel measurements and related metadata obtained from a first-order secured software AES implementation [25]. Each trace is composed of 700 sample points and the targeted intermediate result is the third byte of the masked S-Box output that is processed during the first round. The database is split in 50 000 training and 10 000 attack traces and we have used the complete former set for CNN training. Next, we calculated attribution heatmaps using $N_{Attr} = 1000$ measurements which are illustrated in the third row in Fig. 1. From there, it can be noticed that the heatmaps computed by LRP and 1-Occlusion are very similar in most areas, while the saliency heatmap shows a different characteristic with several peaks in regions where no attribution is found by the other techniques. However, the results look in general more noisy than for the former data sets. Considering the Signal-to-Noise Ratio (SNR) analysis that is given in [25], one would expect to see four regions with POIs: One for the processing of the masked S-box output in linear parts, one for the processing of the S-Box output masked with the output mask, and for the processing of the two masks each. This is mostly reflected by the LRP and 1-occlusion heatmaps. The example demonstrates that attribution methods may also help to reverse-engineer internal structures of protected cryptographic implementations. As expected, correlation analysis without sample point combination fails to extract a meaningful pattern from the first-order secure implementation.

AES-RSM. The fourth data set we have analyzed is based on a secured software AES implementation which originates from the DPA Contest v4.2 [7]. It is equipped with two SCA countermeasures: a first-order secure masking scheme called *Rotating Sbox Masking (RSM)*, and shuffling of the S-Box execution order. All traces are composed of 10 000 sample points representing approximately the first one and a half rounds of an encryption operation and have been acquired on a ChipWhisperer-Lite board. Previous work showed that the implementation can be attacked very efficiently using a CNN with Domain Knowledge (DK), where the profiling is done directly regarding a byte of the secret key (i.e. key is used as label) and the related plaintext byte is given to the network alongside the trace [17]. We slightly adapted our CNN architecture used in the former experiments to this setting. The network was trained using 100 000 traces with random keys and once again, we calculated attribution heatmaps using a subset of 1000 measurements. Since the DeepExplain framework does not support occlusion analysis for DNNs having multiple inputs, we only report results for saliency and LRP. In the last row of Fig. 1, it can be seen that both methods consider only a small fraction of sample points as most important. Same applies to correlation analysis. However, the remaining part of the correlation curve looks very noisy compared to the attribution-based methods. When examining the pseudo code of the implementation that is given in [7], it becomes evident that the high peak in the plots represent the time window when the key is masked before the actual AES round transformation. The second smaller peak, which appears a bit later in the saliency heatmap, is likely due to the XOR of the plaintext with the masked key. In RSM, the mask values are fixed to carefully chosen constants which are rotated for every cipher execution. The results show that such a construction is not secure enough to resist DNN-based attacks. That is why we recommend to employ masking schemes that provide a higher level of entropy.

DNN attribution mechanisms are especially interesting in combination with the DK approach, since here no specific assumption about the leakage behavior of the implementation under test is assumed. This means, an evaluator using the method out-of-the-box is only able to validate if the implementation is vulnerable to such kinds of attacks. Attribution-based leakage analysis supports this process by identifying which parts of the implementation need to be fixed in order to increase the SCA resistance.

4   Evaluating Side-Channel Heatmaps

As discussed in the previous section, side-channel heatmaps of the same data set can vary a lot depending on the used attribution method. A natural question is therefore which technique for computing DNN attributions is most suitable in the context of SCA for leakage analysis. In image classification tasks, heatmaps are often evaluated qualitatively by human experts. This is supported through highlighting the important pixels in the ground truth. It is trivial to see that this process cannot be applied for side-channel traces, as it is not always possible to judge whether a 1D heatmap indicates the 'important' sample points only by visual inspection. Because of that, we introduce two novel quantitative metrics in the following to assess the quality of side-channel heatmaps.

Given an attribution heatmap $\bar{\mathbf{r}}$, we can derive an ordered sequence $\mathbf{s} \in \mathbb{N}^D = [s_1, \ldots, s_D]$ that sorts the values of $\bar{\mathbf{r}}$ according to its relevance such that the property holds:

$$(i < j) \Leftrightarrow (|\bar{r}_i| > |\bar{r}_j|) \tag{7}$$

That means, values at the beginning of $\mathbf{s}$ indicate the sample points with the highest relevance, while values at end of the vector can be considered of less importance. We use absolute values for the comparison since a side-channel heatmap can also contain negative attribution values as illustrated in Fig. 1. However, the sign of the attribution can be disregarded in this case since both positive as well as negative evidence can be considered as important for POI detection. Based on the ordering $\mathbf{s}$, we can define our heatmap metrics called Key Rank Perturbation Curve (KRPC) and Zero-Baseline Key Guessing Entropy (ZB-KGE).

4.1   KRPC

The KRPC is inspired by the region perturbation method proposed in [26] and measures how the key rank calculated in the recovery phase of a profiled attack increases when we progressively replace sample points in the traces with Gaussian noise. Algorithm 1 summarizes the procedure to compute the KRPC.

Algorithm 1. KRPC

Inputs: Sorted heatmap indices $\mathbf{s}$, attack (sub-)set $\mathcal{D}_{Attack}$, correct key k, trained DNN f, number of perturbation (replacement) steps N_{Pert}

1: Initialize perturbation counter: $i = 1$
2: **while** $i < N_{Pert}$ **do**
3:     Get index of sample points to perturb: $ip = \mathbf{s}[i]$
4:     **for all** $\mathbf{x} \in \mathcal{D}_{Attack}$ **do**
5:         Replace sample point with Gaussian noise: $\mathbf{x}[ip] = \mathcal{N}(0, 1)$
6:     **end for**
7:     Calculate key rank with updated traces: $\mathbf{kr}[i] = \mathbf{d}^{LL}(\mathcal{D}_{Attack}, f)[k]$
8:     Increase perturbation counter: $i = i + 1$
9: **end while**
return: Key rank vector $\mathbf{kr}$ for key k

We have decided to use a Gaussian noise with mean $\mu = 0$ and standard deviation $\sigma = 1$ (denoted as $\mathcal{N}(0, 1)$ in Algorithm 1) as perturbation procedure,

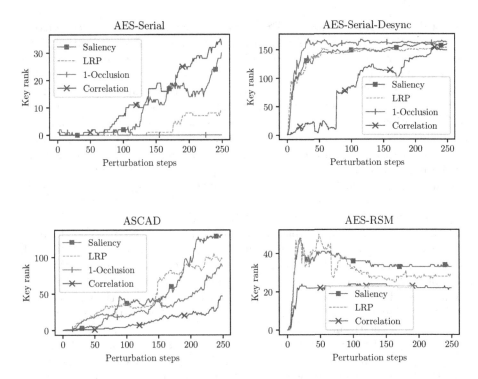

Fig. 2. Mean KRPC curves of four data sets

since the injected values lie within the same distribution as our standardized inputs. The KRPC can be interpreted as noise that is present in the attack traces, but not in the training traces. Replacing the most sensitive samples first (i.e. the sample points containing the most information regarding the classification) should imply a fast decrease of the key rank.

We have computed KRPC curves for all four data sets with $N_{Pert} = 250$ perturbation steps. This number was chosen since it represents at least 25% of the sample points in three of the four data sets. For computational reasons, and since we did not see a substantial change in the KRPC curves set when applying more than 250 perturbation steps, we used the same value of N_{Pert} for the AES-RSM data set. Additionally, we have restricted the number of attack traces that are used in Algorithm 1 to a value that led to a stable key rank below three without perturbation (The exact numbers are given in Table 1). In order to decrease the bias that is induced by a fix choice of the attack traces, we have repeated each experiment five times and used a different subset of the attack traces for every run. Finally, we calculated average KRPC curves which are illustrated as a function of perturbation steps in Fig. 2.

From there, we can generally observe that the correlation analysis reaches the highest key rank after perturbing 250 sample points in the unprotected hardware setting (AES-Serial), whereas the attribution methods perform better in case of desynchronized traces (AES-Serial-Desync) and the protected software implementations (ASCAD, AES-RSM). Looking at the three attribution methods exclusively, one can see that there is no clear winner over all data sets. For example, the heatmaps computed by LRP and 1-occlusion better identifies the most relevant POIs in the ASCAD data set in the beginning, while saliency performs far better than the two other techniques on the unprotected hardware implementation. We assume that this is due to the fact that saliency is only able to provide local explanations and thus is less suitable for POI detection in settings with highly multivariate leakage (i.e. implementations with masking countermeasures). The unprotected hardware implementation, in contrast, exhibits several independent leakage locations due to its serial architecture, which can be better detected by the saliency method.

Comparing the plots of AES-Serial with AES-Serial-Desync, it is notable that the results for the jitter-based setting are almost similar, while there are significant differences between the attribution methods for the aligned traces. It seems furthermore that the injected jitter is beneficial for identifying the most relevant areas in the traces as the corresponding curves rise stronger. However, we cannot exclude that this is solely due to the misalignment in the traces forcing the DNN to learn spatially invariant features, or just the fact that we had to use more traces in the training phase.

Results for AES-RSM again look very similar for Saliency and LRP, which is not surprising when looking at the corresponding attributions in Fig. 1. Although AES-RSM is also equipped with a lightweight masking countermeasure, the exploited leakage is rather of univariate nature since there is only a single peak visible in the heatmaps that is detected by saliency and LRP likewise. Same applies to a certain degree also for correlation, but the corresponding KRPC curve runs a bit flatter than the previous two mentioned.

4.2 ZB-KGE

Using ZB-KGE, we are able to determine how fast the key rank estimated with a zero-baseline attack set $\mathcal{D}_{Baseline}$ (i.e. an attack set where all sample points in the traces are set to zero) converges when we continuously add relevant sample points from the actual attack set $\mathcal{D}_{Attack}$ to $\mathcal{D}_{Baseline}$. The procedure for calculating a ZB-KGE curve is described in Algorithm 2. Intuitively, the steeper a ZB-KGE graph decreases, the more POIs have been identified by the related side-channel heatmap. Since the ZB-KGE simulates the absence of features, it furthermore provides insights on how many POIs should approximately be conserved in case of a dimensionality reduction.

Figure 3 displays the ZB-KGE as function of the number of added POIs for the four data sets. As in the previous experiment, we have calculated mean curves over five independent subsets of $\mathcal{D}_{Attack}$. From Fig. 3, it can be noticed that the results are close to, but not equivalent to those computed with Algorithm 1. For instance, correlation analysis again performs best on the AES-Serial dataset but is defeated by the attention methods for the remaining three data sets. What we find interesting is the fact that 1-occlusion identifies almost equally good relevant sample points as LRP and Saliency in the AES-Serial-Desync and ASCAD data sets, but a bit worse in the AES-Serial data set. This is an indicator that the information contained in a single sample point of the unprotected hardware traces is rather small. A greater occlusion factor might be more suitable in such cases where the univariate leakage is distributed over a large range of connected sample points. Furthermore, it can be noticed, that the random shifting of the data points in the AES-Serial-Desync data set has a very positive effect on 1-occlusion. Intuitively, the random shifting induces a varying occlusion factor which seems to be beneficial taking the results of the two previous sections into account. This makes the technique interesting for different setups where traces are not perfectly aligned, be it due to an unstable measurement setup, or because of some delay-based countermeasure (e.g. [12]).

The attribution curves for the AES-RSM data set are again very similar and show that roughly 150 out of 10 000 data points are sufficient to reveal the correct key. In contrast, the correlation curve decreases very slowly for this data set. We assume this is due to the noisy result of the correlation analysis shown above.

Algorithm 2. ZB-KGE

Inputs: Sorted heatmap indices $\mathbf{s}$, attack (sub-)set $\mathcal{D}_{Attack}$, correct key k, trained DNN f, number of sample points to add N_{Add}

  1: Initialize status counter: $i = 1$
  2: Initialize zero-baseline attack set: $\mathcal{D}_{Baseline}$
  3: **while** $i < N_{Add}$ **do**
  4:     Get index of sample points to add: $ia = \mathbf{s}[i]$
  5:     **for all** $\mathbf{x}^A \in \mathcal{D}_{Attack}, \mathbf{x}^B \in \mathcal{D}_{Baseline}$ **do**
  6:       Replace zero sample point with actual value: $\mathbf{x}^B[ia] = \mathbf{x}^A[ia]$
  7:     **end for**
  8:     Calculate key rank with updated traces: $\mathbf{kr}[i] = \mathbf{d}^{LL}(\mathcal{D}_{Baseline}, f)[k]$
  9:     Increase status counter: $i = i + 1$
10: **end while**
return: Key rank vector $\mathbf{kr}$ for key k

4.3 Limitations

We have seen that DNN-based attribution methods are superior to classical correlation analysis (except for the unprotected data set). However, there is a necessary precondition one have to consider: Meaningful POIs can only be extracted from the network when the training was successful, i.e., when the network was able to learn the target function f of the training set and generalize to new data. Since we were able to drive a successful key recovery on all data sets, we were certain about the network's performance. However, performing key recovery is not necessary to evaluate the training procedure. In order to monitor the learning

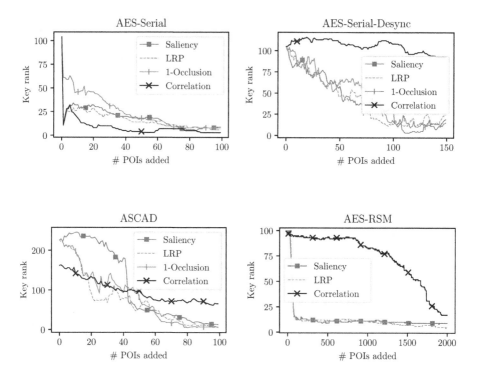

Fig. 3. Mean ZB-KGE curves for the four data sets.

progress, usually a small amount of the training set is used to verify the model's performance on unseen data (i.e. validation set) at the end of each epoch (i.e. an iteration over the complete training dataset [15]). An increasing training and validation accuracy along with a decreasing training and validation loss indicates that the DNN model is able to approximate f. If this is not case, the network either underfits the data (meaning model is not able to obtain a sufficiently low error on training and validation set), or runs into overfitting (model performs well on the training set, but not on the validation set). Overfitting and under-fitting is primarily influenced by the number of parameters of the model, which reveals another issue of DNN-based POI visualization compared to parameter-less methods like correlation or DOM: A suitable network architecture has to be determined which encompasses, amongst others, the number of layers, the number of neurons per layer, etc. For this paper, we derived our final network mainly from related work [17,25]. However, there are several methods available to automatically search for a suitable set of parameters like genetic algorithms or Bayesian optimization [13]. This facilitates also non-experts in the field an easy access to DNN-based methods.

5   Attribution as a Distinguisher

As explained earlier in the paper, LRP provides signed explanations that allow to distinguish between input features that support the classification decision, and features speaking against the prediction result. This property is very helpful in image classification tasks as LRP heatmaps can be easily interpreted, e.g., to debug which pixels of an image led to a misclassification. In this section, we exploit the ability of LRP to provide negative and positive evidence to distinguish between correct and incorrect key hypothesis in the key recovery phase of a profiled attack. The basic idea is that there should be a measurable difference between heatmaps calculated with the attack traces under the correct key guess, and heatmaps for which the wrong output neuron of the DNN (i.e. label) has been chosen. Furthermore, the difference should be most distinct in areas which have been identified as relevant during profiling. The procedure of the complete attack is as follows:

1. Perform DNN training as in a usual profiled attack according to Sect. 2.1 in order to build device model f.
2. Create side-channel heatmap $\bar{r}$ using (6) and a subset of $\mathcal{D}_{Train}$. Next, build ordered sequence $\mathbf{s}$ that fulfills (7).
3. For each key hypothesis $k^* \in \mathcal{K}$, calculate attribution vector $\mathbf{r}^{C_{k^*}}$ using LRP and sum up those values that correspond to the N_{POI} highest ranked components in $\mathbf{s}$. Repeat for complete attack set $\mathcal{D}_{Attack}$ composed of N_A attack traces such that:

$$\mathbf{d}^{AT}(\mathcal{D}_{Attack}, f) = \sum_{i=1}^{N_A} \sum_{j=1}^{N_{POI}} \mathbf{r}^{C_{k^*}}(\mathbf{x}_i, f)[\mathbf{s}[j]] \tag{8}$$

The attack is successful if $k = \arg\max(\mathbf{d}^{AT})$

We have performed the attack on the AES-Serial and ASCAD data sets with $N_{POI} = 50$ (The number of relevant POIs was roughly estimated by inspecting the corresponding plots in Fig. 1). The remaining parameters as well as the DNN architecture have been the same as in the previous experiments. Figure 4 shows the evolution of the average key rank as a function of the number of attack traces computed from ten independent attacks (using 1000 traces per attack). For comparison, we have done the key recovery also according to (1) using the same DNN models and exactly the same attack traces. From Fig. 4, one can see that our proposed attribution-based attack converges faster to a key rank of one than the LL-based attack in both data sets. More concretely, for the unprotected hardware AES, our method needs less than ten traces to enter a key rank below five and stabilizes after roughly 50 attack traces. The LL-based attack, in contrast, reaches a stable key rank of one only after 750 traces. Results for the protected software AES differ not to such an extent. However, the attribution-based attack manages a stable key rank of one using approximately 85 traces while the attack based on LL distinguisher needs around 500 traces more to pass that mark.

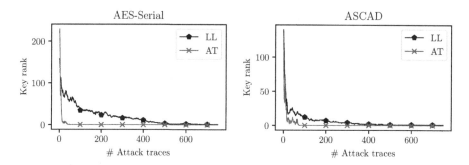

Fig. 4. Mean key ranks for the unprotected hardware AES (left) and the protected software AES (right). The attribution-based attack (AT) needs less traces for a successful key recovery than the LL-based attack in both setups.

In summary, our experiments demonstrate that attribution methods and especially LRP are able to use the information that is captured during DNN training more efficiently for key recovery than the standard LL approach. This is because to the fact that the attribution-based attack considers only the crucial parts in the traces during the attack phase, while complete traces are used to calculate the LL scores. Drawback of the method is the increased time complexity due to the need of computing attributions over all key hypothesis. However, we stress that time is often not a limiting factor for an adversary. We were able to do a successful key recovery on a single Nvidia GeForce GTX 1080 GPU in under 5 min (compared to approximately 15 seconds using the LL approach) which is still practical. This further confirms that our attribution-based distinguisher is a promising alternative when performing profiled SCA especially in settings where the adversary is able to acquire only a limited number of attack traces.

6   Conclusion

In this work we have studied DNN attribution methods as a tool for leakage analysis in DL-based side-channel attacks. In particular, we have presented a technique to compute heatmaps of side-channel traces in order to find leaking operations in unprotected and protected cryptographic implementations. We proposed two metrics to evaluate the quality of side-channel heatmaps and used them to assess saliency analysis, LRP, and 1-occlusion for their suitability to detect sensitive sample points in side-channel traces. Furthermore, we have compared the three methods with the widely-used Pearson correlation for POI analysis. As a summary, we can conclude that the attribution methods are beneficial especially with regard to secured implementations and in case of desynchronized traces. For standard unprotected settings, there seems to be no advantage over standard Pearson correlation especially when taking in consideration that training a DNN is much more time and computation intensive than a standard CPA. However, as also demonstrated in the paper, the LRP attribution method can also be used to build an effective distinguisher for key recovery.

Future work might investigate other DNN attribution methods in the context of SCA, such as prediction difference analysis [34] or Deconvolution [32]. Another interesting path could be to explore the usage of DNN visualization techniques for network debugging and architecture optimization.

A   Network Parameters

Table 2. Network configuration of CNN

Layer Type	Hyperparameters
Trace input	-
Convolution 1D	filters = 8, filter length = 8, activation = ReLU
Max-pooling	pool length = 2
Dropout	$P_{Drop} = 0.3$
Convolution 1D	filters = 16, filter length = 8, activation = ReLU
Batch normalization	-
Max-pooling	pool length = 2
Dropout	$P_{Drop} = 0.3$
Convolution 1D	filters = 32, filter length = 8, activation = ReLU
Batch normalization	-
Max-pooling	pool length = 2
Dropout	$P_{Drop} = 0.3$
Convolution 1D	filters = 64, filter length = 8, activation = ReLU
Batch normalization	-
Max-Pooling	pool length = 2
Dropout	$P_{Drop} = 0.3$
Flatten	-
(optional) Domain input	neurons = 256
(optional) Concatenate	-
Fully-connected	neurons = 20, activation = ReLU
Batch normalization	-
Dropout	$P_{Drop} = 0.2$
Output	neurons = 256

In all experiments, we trained the network using Adam optimizer and a learning rate of 0.0001 (AES-Serial & AES-Serial-Desync) or 0.001 (ASCAD & AES-RSM).

References

1. DeepExplain: attribution methods for Deep Learning. https://github.com/marcoancona/DeepExplain
2. Keras Documentation. https://keras.io/
3. Agrawal, D., Archambeault, B., Rao, J.R., Rohatgi, P.: The EM side—channel(s). In: Kaliski, B.S., Koç, K., Paar, C. (eds.) CHES 2002. LNCS, vol. 2523, pp. 29–45. Springer, Heidelberg (2003). https://doi.org/10.1007/3-540-36400-5_4
4. Ancona, M., Ceolini, E., Öztireli, C., Gross, M.: Towards better understanding of gradient-based attribution methods for Deep Neural Networks. ArXiv e-prints, November 2017
5. Archambeau, C., Peeters, E., Standaert, F.-X., Quisquater, J.-J.: Template attacks in principal subspaces. In: Goubin, L., Matsui, M. (eds.) CHES 2006. LNCS, vol. 4249, pp. 1–14. Springer, Heidelberg (2006). https://doi.org/10.1007/11894063_1
6. Bach, S., Binder, A., Montavon, G., Klauschen, F., Müller, K.R., Samek, W.: On pixel-wise explanations for non-linear classifier decisions by layer-wise relevance propagation. PLoS ONE **10**, 1–46 (2015)
7. Bhasin, S., Bruneau, N., Danger, J.-L., Guilley, S., Najm, Z.: Analysis and improvements of the DPA contest v4 implementation. In: Chakraborty, R.S., Matyas, V., Schaumont, P. (eds.) SPACE 2014. LNCS, vol. 8804, pp. 201–218. Springer, Cham (2014). https://doi.org/10.1007/978-3-319-12060-7_14
8. Cagli, E., Dumas, C., Prouff, E.: Convolutional neural networks with data augmentation against jitter-based countermeasures. In: Fischer, W., Homma, N. (eds.) CHES 2017. LNCS, vol. 10529, pp. 45–68. Springer, Cham (2017). https://doi.org/10.1007/978-3-319-66787-4_3
9. Chari, S., Rao, J.R., Rohatgi, P.: Template attacks. In: Kaliski, B.S., Koç, K., Paar, C. (eds.) CHES 2002. LNCS, vol. 2523, pp. 13–28. Springer, Heidelberg (2003). https://doi.org/10.1007/3-540-36400-5_3
10. Ching, T., et al.: Opportunities and obstacles for deep learning in biology and medicine. J. R. Soc. Interface **15**(141), 20170387 (2018). https://doi.org/10.1098/rsif.2017.0387
11. Cooper, J., Goodwill, G., Jaffe, J., Kenworthy, G., Rohatgi, P.: Test vector leakage assessment (TVLA) methodology in practice. In: International Cryptographic Module Conference (ICMC). Holiday Inn Gaithersburg, Gaithersburg (2013)
12. Coron, J.S., Kizhvatov, I.: An efficient method for random delay generation in embedded software. Cryptology ePrint Archive, Report 2009/419 (2009). https://eprint.iacr.org/2009/419
13. Elsken, T., Hendrik Metzen, J., Hutter, F.: Neural Architecture Search: A Survey. arXiv e-prints arXiv:1808.05377, August 2018
14. Gierlichs, B., Lemke-Rust, K., Paar, C.: Templates vs. stochastic methods. In: Goubin, L., Matsui, M. (eds.) CHES 2006. LNCS, vol. 4249, pp. 15–29. Springer, Heidelberg (2006). https://doi.org/10.1007/11894063_2
15. Goodfellow, I., Bengio, Y., Courville, A.: Deep Learning. MIT Press, Cambridge (2016). http://www.deeplearningbook.org
16. He, K., Zhang, X., Ren, S., Sun, J.: Deep residual learning for image recognition. In: The IEEE Conference on Computer Vision and Pattern Recognition (CVPR), June 2016

17. Hettwer, B., Gehrer, S., Güneysu, T.: Profiled power analysis attacks using convolutional neural networks with domain knowledge. In: Selected Areas in Cryptography - SAC 2018–25th International Conference, Calgary, AB, Canada, 15–17 August 2018, Revised Selected Papers, pp. 479–498 (2018). https://doi.org/10.1007/978-3-030-10970-7_22

18. Kocher, P., Jaffe, J., Jun, B.: Differential power analysis. In: Wiener, M. (ed.) CRYPTO 1999. LNCS, vol. 1666, pp. 388–397. Springer, Heidelberg (1999). https://doi.org/10.1007/3-540-48405-1_25

19. Kocher, P.C.: Timing attacks on implementations of Diffie-Hellman, RSA, DSS, and other systems. In: Koblitz, N. (ed.) CRYPTO 1996. LNCS, vol. 1109, pp. 104–113. Springer, Heidelberg (1996). https://doi.org/10.1007/3-540-68697-5_9

20. Maghrebi, H., Portigliatti, T., Prouff, E.: Breaking cryptographic implementations using deep learning techniques. In: Carlet, C., Hasan, M.A., Saraswat, V. (eds.) SPACE 2016. LNCS, vol. 10076, pp. 3–26. Springer, Cham (2016). https://doi.org/10.1007/978-3-319-49445-6_1

21. Mangard, S., Oswald, E., Popp, T.: Power Analysis Attacks: Revealing the Secrets of Smart Cards, 1st edn. Springer, Boston (2010). https://doi.org/10.1007/978-0-387-38162-6

22. Masure, L., Dumas, C., Prouff, E.: Gradient visualization for general characterization in profiling attacks. In: Polian, I., Stöttinger, M. (eds.) COSADE 2019. LNCS, vol. 11421, pp. 145–167. Springer, Cham (2019). https://doi.org/10.1007/978-3-030-16350-1_9

23. Moradi, A., Guilley, S., Heuser, A.: Detecting hidden leakages. In: Boureanu, I., Owesarski, P., Vaudenay, S. (eds.) ACNS 2014. LNCS, vol. 8479, pp. 324–342. Springer, Cham (2014). https://doi.org/10.1007/978-3-319-07536-5_20

24. Picek, S., Heuser, A., Jovic, A., Batina, L., Legay, A.: The secrets of profiling for side-channel analysis: feature selection matters. Cryptology ePrint Archive, Report 2017/1110 (2017). https://eprint.iacr.org/2017/1110

25. Prouff, E., Strullu, R., Benadjila, R., Cagli, E., Dumas, C.: Study of deep learning techniques for side-channel analysis and introduction to ASCAD database. Cryptology ePrint Archive, Report 2018/053 (2018). https://eprint.iacr.org/2018/053

26. Samek, W., Binder, A., Montavon, G., Lapuschkin, S., Müller, K.: Evaluating the visualization of what a deep neural network has learned. IEEE Trans. Neural Networks Learn. Syst. 28(11), 2660–2673 (2017). https://doi.org/10.1109/TNNLS.2016.2599820

27. Selvaraju, R.R., Cogswell, M., Das, A., Vedantam, R., Parikh, D., Batra, D.: Grad-CAM: visual explanations from deep networks via gradient-based localization. In: 2017 IEEE International Conference on Computer Vision (ICCV), pp. 618–626, October 2017. https://doi.org/10.1109/ICCV.2017.74

28. Simonyan, K., Vedaldi, A., Zisserman, A.: Deep Inside Convolutional Networks: Visualising Image Classification Models and Saliency Maps. arXiv:1312.6034 [cs], December 2013

29. Standaert, F.-X., Malkin, T.G., Yung, M.: A unified framework for the analysis of side-channel key recovery attacks. In: Joux, A. (ed.) EUROCRYPT 2009. LNCS, vol. 5479, pp. 443–461. Springer, Heidelberg (2009). https://doi.org/10.1007/978-3-642-01001-9_26

30. Timon, B.: Non-profiled deep learning-based side-channel attacks. Cryptology ePrint Archive, Report 2018/196 (2018). https://eprint.iacr.org/2018/196

31. Young, T., Hazarika, D., Poria, S., Cambria, E.: Recent trends in deep learning based natural language processing [review article]. IEEE Comput. Intell. Mag. 13(3), 55–75 (2018). https://doi.org/10.1109/MCI.2018.2840738

32. Zeiler, M.D., Fergus, R.: Visualizing and understanding convolutional networks. CoRR abs/1311.2901 (2013). http://arxiv.org/abs/1311.2901
33. Zheng, Y., Zhou, Y., Yu, Z., Hu, C., Zhang, H.: How to compare selections of points of interest for side-channel distinguishers in practice? In: Hui, L.C.K., Qing, S.H., Shi, E., Yiu, S.M. (eds.) ICICS 2014. LNCS, vol. 8958, pp. 200–214. Springer, Cham (2015). https://doi.org/10.1007/978-3-319-21966-0_15
34. Zintgraf, L.M., Cohen, T.S., Adel, T., Welling, M.: Visualizing Deep Neural Network Decisions: Prediction Difference Analysis. arXiv:1702.04595 [cs], February 2017

Post-quantum Constructions

.

BBQ: Using AES in Picnic Signatures

Cyprien Delpech de Saint Guilhem[1,2]🆔, Lauren De Meyer[1]🆔,
Emmanuela Orsini[1]🆔, and Nigel P. Smart[1,2(✉)]🆔

[1] imec-COSIC, KU Leuven, Leuven, Belgium
{cyprien.delpechdesaintguilhem,lauren.demeyer,
emmanuela.orsini,nigel.smart}@kuleuven.be
[2] Department of Computer Science, University of Bristol, Bristol, UK

Abstract. This works studies the use of the AES block-cipher for Picnic-style signatures, which work in the multiparty-computation-in-the-head model. It applies advancements to arithmetic circuits for the computation of the AES S-box over multiparty computation in the pre-processing model to obtain an improvement of signature sizes of 40% on average compared to using binary circuits for AES-128, AES-192 and AES-256 in combination with previous techniques. This work also discusses other methods for the computation of the S-box and provides insights into the reaches and limits of the multiparty-computation-in-the-head paradigm.

1 Introduction

With the possible advent of a quantum computer, cryptographers have turned their attention to building "post-quantum" variants of standard cryptographic functionalities such as public key encryption and digital signatures. Among the various paradigms for producing post-quantum signatures, one of the most promising is that of MPC-in-the-head (MPCitH), which was introduced in [17]. In this paradigm, the security of signatures is based on the security of a semi-honest multiparty computation (MPC) protocol against a dishonest majority, and of a given PRF family $F_k(\cdot)$, such as a block-cipher. Given the nature of the MPC protocol, the concrete security of the resulting signature scheme relies on the underlying PRF.

The secret key for such signature schemes is the key k used to select the PRF $F_k(\cdot)$, with the public key being an input-output pair of the PRF, i.e. values (x, y) such that $y = F_k(x)$. The signature itself is then a non-interactive zero-knowledge proof of knowledge (NIZKPoK) of the secret key k produced using the MPCitH paradigm. To do so, the signer first computes a commitment to an execution of an MPC evaluation of the PRF on input x, which constitutes the first component of the signature; then they hash the commitment to obtain the NIZKPoK challenge, according to the Fiat-Shamir heuristic, and include the message to be signed in the hash of the commitment; finally they respond to this challenge by outputting the views of a subset of parties as the final component of the signature. That this process reveals nothing about the secret key k follows

ⓒ Springer Nature Switzerland AG 2020
K. G. Paterson and D. Stebila (Eds.): SAC 2019, LNCS 11959, pp. 669–692, 2020.
https://doi.org/10.1007/978-3-030-38471-5_27

from the security of the MPC protocol, and the security of the PRF. That it also convinces a verifier that the signer knows k follows from [17].

While originally considered as a theoretical construction, MPCitH has been used to successfully create practical NIZKPoKs. ZKBoo [16], ZKBoo++ [9] and Ligero [2] are examples of such schemes. While ZKBoo and Ligero provide schemes for proofs of knowledge for SHA-256 pre-images, the ZKBoo++ paper makes use of the LowMC cipher [1], which was designed as a cipher optimized for evaluation in FHE and MPC applications. This construction (ZKBoo++ and LowMC) is the main idea behind the submission to the NIST Post-Quantum Cryptography project [20] titled Picnic [8].

The first applications of MPCitH drew inspiration from traditional MPC protocols. In recent years many practical improvements to these have been made in the so-called preprocessing model (such as VIFF, BDOZ and SPDZ [4,11,14]). Following the paradigm of MPC with preprocessing, an adaptation of the MPCitH paradigm to use the preprocessing model was presented recently in [18]. This technique allows for both smaller and more compact signatures together with faster verification and signing times. It is this later technique which, combined with the LowMC cipher, is used in the Round 2 updated Picnic submission [7].

The choice of the LowMC block-cipher as the PRF was made as it has a particularly simple circuit design. However, using LowMC comes with a risk. It is a less studied cipher, compared to standardized ones such as AES, and thus it is possible that future cryptanalytic attacks be developed which would then render the above digital signature schemes insecure. However, using a standard block cipher such as AES comes with a penalty. For example, the standard circuit for AES is far more complex than that for LowMC in terms of non-linear AND gates, and this results in larger signature sizes and computation times.

However, the above intuitive comparison assumes that a binary circuit for AES would be used within the MPCitH. There are however other ways to evaluate AES over MPC, see for example [12,13,19]. Many of these approaches use arithmetic circuits, and thus exploit the algebraic structure of the AES block cipher.

Contributions. In this work, we show how one can use the MPCitH with preprocessing paradigm of [18] for arithmetic circuits over $\mathbb{F}_{2^8}$ to define a signature scheme whose security rests on AES as opposed to LowMC. We estimate that our approach produces signatures that are on average 40% smaller than those that would be obtained using a binary circuit for AES. Our estimates are $2.5, 3.1$ and 2.8 times larger than the Picnic signatures using on LowMC for the L1, L3 and L5 security levels of the NIST project respectively. Thus our technique enables one to achieve security based on a block-cipher component which is better understood, with a better-than-expected penalty in terms of signature size.

To achieve this improvement compared to binary circuits, we make use of MPC techniques to compute the AES S-box. The problem is in computing the only non-linear component in AES is the S-Box inversion, namely the computation of $s \mapsto s^{254}$ in the finite field $\mathbb{F}_{2^8}$, which is well known to be equal to the function $s \mapsto 1/s$ when $s \neq 0$. This inversion function is easy to evaluate in MPC but different methods to capture the $s = 0$ case require more or less communication between parties, which directly translates to signature size.

Our main solution to the problem of zero S-box inputs is for the signer to select his private key k and the x component of the public key so that the computation of $y = F_k(x)$ (when F_k is the AES function) involves no zero-inputs to any S-Box. While this may seem restrictive, it in fact only reduces the key space by approximately 1.1, 2.4 and 2.9 bits for the AES-128, AES-192 and AES-256 circuits respectively. Thus, making this reduction in the key-space bypasses the problem one faces in producing an inverse of zero. This provides our most efficient solution and we obtain signature size estimates of 31.6 kB, 86.9 kB and 133.7 kB for circuits achieving L1, L3 and L5 security levels respectively.

Interestingly, we can observe that scaling up the key size of AES (and using AES-192 or AES-256) does not automatically scale up the security parameter when used in the MPCitH paradigm. The problem lies in the fact that the block-length of the circuit stays the same (128 bits in all AES versions), resulting in spurious keys if only single block input/output pairs are used in the public key. To solve this and achieve the L3 and L5 security levels, we come up with a way to construct simple circuits with appropriate block-lengths out of the AES cipher. We also consider the use of the original Rijndael block-cipher on which AES is based and which has parametrisable block-length.

Finally, we also discuss other solutions to address the case of $s = 0$ during the inversion computation. These would enable the use of any k and x for the signature key and therefore not reduce the bit-security of the cipher, but they would require significantly more communication in the MPC protocol and thus produce longer signatures. However, these alternative solutions provide insights on the added capabilities of the MPCitH paradigm could direct the design of more appropriate MPC protocols for this purpose.

2 Preliminaries

We let κ denote the computational security parameter. We also let H denote a collision-resistant hash function with co-domain $\{0,1\}^{2\kappa}$ and let com be a non-interactive commitment scheme where x is committed to by sampling a random $r \in \{0,1\}^{\kappa}$ and computing $\gamma = \text{com}(x, r)$; decommitment is done by opening x and r. (The Picnic scheme [7] uses a hash function to instantiate com.) We use bold lower case letters for tuples, overset small arrow to indicate elements of a vector space, like $\vec{v}$, and bold upper case letters for matrices. We also write $[n] = \{1, \ldots n\}$.

2.1 Efficient NIZKPoK in the MPC-in-the Head Paradigm

In 2007, Ishai et al. [17] showed how to use any MPC protocol to construct a zero-knowledge (ZK) proof for an arbitrary NP relation $\mathcal{R}$. The high level idea is the following: zero knowledge can be seen as a special function evaluation, and hence as a two-party computation between a prover $\mathcal{P}$ and a verifier $\mathcal{V}$, with common input the statement x, and $\mathcal{P}$'s private input w, which is a witness to the assertion that x belongs to a given NP language $\mathcal{L}$. The function they want to compute is then $f_x(w) = \mathcal{R}(x, w)$, which checks if w is a valid witness or not. The verifier $\mathcal{V}$ will accept the proof if $f_x(w) = \mathcal{R}(x, w) = 1$.

In the MPCitH paradigm the prover $\mathcal{P}$ simulates an n-party MPC protocol Π in "its head": $\mathcal{P}$ first samples n random values $w^{(1)}, \ldots, w^{(n)}$, subject to the condition $\sum_{i \in [n]} w^{(i)} = w$, as private inputs to the parties, and then emulates the evaluation of $f(w^{(1)}, \ldots, w^{(n)}) = \mathcal{R}(x, w^{(1)} + \cdots + w^{(n)})$ by choosing uniformly random coins $r^{(i)}$ for each party P_i, $i \in [n]$. Note that, once the inputs and random coins are fixed, for each round j of communication of the protocol Π and for each party P_i, the messages sent by P_i at round j are deterministically specified as a function of the internal state of P_i, i.e. P_i's private inputs $w^{(i)}$ and randomness $r^{(i)}$, and the messages $\mathsf{msg}^{(i)}$ that P_i received in previous rounds. The set with the state and all messages received by party P_i during the execution of the protocol constitutes the view of P_i, denoted as View_{P_i}.

After the evaluation, the prover $\mathcal{P}$ commits to the views of each party and sends them to $\mathcal{V}$. At this point, the verifier "corrupts" a random subset of parties, challenging the prover to open their committed views and finally verifies that the computation was done correctly from the perspective of these corrupt parties, by checking that the opened views are all consistent with each other. To obtain the desired soundness it is often necessary to iterate the above procedure many times.

Using the MPCitH paradigm, some recent works [2,9,16] have constructed efficient NIZKPoK for Boolean circuits and signature schemes [9,18]. In particular, the work of Katz et al. [18] constructs an (HVZKPoK) by instantiating the MPCitH paradigm using an MPC protocol designed in the preprocessing model. We now describe their protocol adapted for arithmetic circuits.

Arithmetic MPCitH in the Preprocessing Model. We consider some finite field $\mathbb{F}$. The honest-verifier zero-knowledge (HVZK) protocol we introduce here provides a proof of knowledge of a witness $\boldsymbol{w} \in \mathbb{F}^\iota$ such that $C(\boldsymbol{w}) = \boldsymbol{y} \in \mathbb{F}^o$, for a given circuit $C : \mathbb{F}^\iota \to \mathbb{F}^o$ and output $\boldsymbol{y}$.

As the underlying protocol Π_C is designed in the preprocessing model (and therefore has a preprocessing phase followed by an online phase), the HVZK proof also happens in two stages. In the first stage, $\mathcal{P}$ commits to a number of preprocessing executions (which consist only of input-independent randomness). Then $\mathcal{V}$ requests that some of these are opened, and checks that they are consistent preprocessing computations. In the second stage, the prover uses the unopened preprocessing material to execute parallel and independent executions of the online phase of the MPC protocol Π_C. It then commits to these executions and, for each of them, is challenged by the verifier to open a random selection of $n - 1$ parties' views. By receiving these views, $\mathcal{V}$ is able to perform checks to ensure that the prover did not falsify the executions of Π_C.

Since we will make use of an arithmetic circuit C over a field $\mathbb{F}$, C is composed of addition and multiplication gates operating on values in $\mathbb{F}$. This is a generalization of [18] as that work considers circuits operating on only bits with XOR and AND gates. The online evaluation of C is done by a SPDZ-like [14] protocol, simplified as we only require security against semi-honest adversaries (notably, we use broadcast as the only communication channel).

This protocol is executed by n parties. For every value $x \in \mathbb{F}$ in the arithmetic circuit C, the protocol uses an additive secret sharing $\langle x \rangle$ which denotes the sharing $x^{(1)}, \ldots, x^{(n)}$, such that $\sum_{i=1}^{n} x^{(i)} = x$ and every party P_i holds $x^{(i)}$.

To reconstruct, or "open", a shared value $\langle x \rangle$, each party P_i broadcasts its share $x^{(i)}$ and each party P_j can then reconstruct $x = \sum_{i=1}^{n} x^{(i)}$. With such a secret sharing, the following operations can be performed locally, i.e. without communication between parties:

- *Addition with public constant:* To compute $\langle z \rangle \leftarrow \langle x + a \rangle$ given $\langle x \rangle$ and a public value a, party P_1 sets his share to be $z^{(1)} \leftarrow x^{(1)} + a$ and every other party P_i ($i \neq 1$) sets $z^{(i)} := x^{(i)}$.
- *Addition of two shared values:* To compute $\langle z \rangle \leftarrow \langle x + y \rangle$ given $\langle x \rangle$ and $\langle y \rangle$, every party P_i sets his share to be $z^{(i)} \leftarrow x^{(i)} + y^{(i)}$.
- *Multiplication by public constant:* To compute $\langle z \rangle \leftarrow \langle a \cdot x \rangle$ given $\langle x \rangle$ and a, every party P_i sets his share to be $z^{(i)} \leftarrow a \cdot x^{(i)}$.

However, computing the multiplication of two shared values, i.e. $\langle z \rangle \leftarrow \langle x \cdot y \rangle$ given $\langle x \rangle$ and $\langle y \rangle$, cannot be done locally; it requires both preprocessing material and communication during the online phase. Namely, given a precomputed triple $(\langle a \rangle, \langle b \rangle, \langle c \rangle)$, such that $c = a \cdot b$, the parties can compute $\langle z \rangle$ as follows:

1. Locally compute $\langle \alpha \rangle := \langle x - a \rangle$ and $\langle \beta \rangle := \langle y - b \rangle$.
2. Open α and β.
3. Locally compute $\langle z \rangle = \langle c \rangle - \alpha \cdot \langle b \rangle - \beta \cdot \langle a \rangle + \alpha \cdot \beta$.

This technique is due to [3] and is easily checked to be correct:

$$\begin{aligned} z &= c - \alpha \cdot b - \beta \cdot a + \alpha \cdot \beta \\ &= a \cdot b - (x - a) \cdot b - (y - b) \cdot a + (x - a) \cdot (y - b) \\ &= x \cdot y. \end{aligned}$$

Before we describe the HVZK protocol of [18], we present the execution of both phases of Π_C that the prover will have to simulate; namely the preprocessing and online phases.

(1) Preprocessing Phase. The only preprocessing required is the generation of random multiplication triples $\{(\langle a_m \rangle, \langle b_m \rangle, \langle c_m \rangle)\}_{m \in [\mathsf{mult}]}$, where mult is the number of multiplication gates in C. As noted in [18] for its preprocessing computation, for each triple, the i-th share of $\langle a \rangle$ and $\langle b \rangle$ is uniform and therefore can be generated by party P_i applying a pseudorandom generator (PRG) to a short random seed $\mathsf{seed}^{(i)}$. Each share of $\langle c \rangle$ can also be generated in that way,

but then the actual generated value $\tilde{c} = \sum_{i=1}^{n} c^{(i)}$ would not equal $a \cdot b$ with very high probability. Instead, for each triple $(\langle a_m \rangle, \langle b_m \rangle, \langle c_m \rangle)$, party P_n is given a "correction value" $\Delta_m = a \cdot b - \sum_{i=1}^{n-1} c^{(i)}$ and directly sets $c^{(n)} \leftarrow \Delta_m$.

In summary, the outcome of the preprocessing is that every party P_i is given a κ-bit seed $\mathsf{seed}^{(i)} \in \{0,1\}^{\kappa}$ and P_n is also given mult values $\{\Delta_m\}$ denoted by $\mathsf{aux}^{(n)}$. This information is called the *state* of party P_i and is denoted by $\mathsf{state}^{(i)}$.

PARAMETERS: Let $H : \{0,1\}^* \to \{0,1\}^{2\kappa}$ and G be collision-resistant hash functions and com be a commitment scheme. Note G is only used in the non-interactive variant of the protocol.

Other parameters are T and τ, that indicate the total number of preprocessing executions emulated by $\mathcal{P}$ and the number of online executions, respectively.

INPUTS: Both parties hold a description of C over $\mathbb{F}$, the value $\boldsymbol{y} \in \mathbb{F}^o$. The prover $\mathcal{P}$ also holds $\boldsymbol{w} \in \mathbb{F}^\iota$ such that $C(\boldsymbol{w}) = \boldsymbol{y}$.

Round 1: *Protocol execution emulation.*

1. For each $t \in [T]$, $\mathcal{P}$ emulates the preprocessing phase as follows:
   (a) Sample a uniform master seed $\mathsf{seed}_t \in \{0,1\}^{\kappa}$ and use it to generate $\mathsf{seed}_t^{(1)}, \ldots, \mathsf{seed}_t^{(n)} \in \{0,1\}^{\kappa}$ and $r_t^{(1)}, \ldots, r_t^{(n)} \in \{0,1\}^{\kappa}$ used in the commitments.
   (b) For each multiplication gate $m \in [\mathsf{mult}]$:
      i. Use $\mathsf{seed}_j^{(i)}$ to sample $a_{t,m}^{(i)}, b_{t,m}^{(i)}$ and also $c_{t,m}^{(i)}$ for $i = 1, \ldots, n-1$.
      ii. Compute $a_{t,m} = \sum_{i=1}^{n} a_{t,m}^{(i)}$ and $b_{t,m}$ similarly.
      iii. Compute the offset $\Delta_{t,m} = a_{t,m} \cdot b_{t,m} - \sum_{i=1}^{n-1} c_{t,m}^{(i)}$.
   (c) Set $\mathsf{aux}_t^{(n)} = (\Delta_{t,m})_{m \in [\mathsf{mult}]}$.
   (d) Set $\mathsf{state}_t^{(i)} = \mathsf{seed}_t^{(i)}$ for $i \in [n-1]$ and set $\mathsf{state}_t^{(n)} = (\mathsf{seed}_t^{(n)}, \mathsf{aux}_t^{(n)})$.
   (e) For each $i \in [n]$, compute $\gamma_{\mathsf{s},t}^{(i)} = \mathsf{com}(\mathsf{state}_t^{(i)}, r_t^{(i)})$.
   (f) Compute $h_{\mathsf{s},t} = H(\gamma_{\mathsf{s},t}^{(1)}, \ldots, \gamma_{\mathsf{s},t}^{(n)})$.
2. For each $t \in [T]$, given $\boldsymbol{w} = (w_1, \ldots, w_\iota)$, $\mathcal{P}$ emulates the online phase as follows:
   (a) Generate the input offsets for each $j \in [\iota]$:
      1. Use $\mathsf{seed}_t^{(i)}$ to sample $w_{t,j}^{(i)}$ for $i \in [n]$.
      2. Compute $\tilde{w}_{t,j} = \sum_{i=1}^{n} w_{t,j}^{(i)}$.
      3. Compute $\Lambda_{t,j} = w_j - \tilde{w}_{t,j}$.
   (b) Compute C by proceeding through the gates in topological order. For each party P_i, record each broadcast message in $\mathsf{msg}_t^{(i)}$.
   (c) Compute $h_{\mathsf{m},t} = H(\{\Lambda_{t,j}\}_{j \in [\iota]}, \mathsf{msg}_t^{(1)}, \ldots, \mathsf{msg}_t^{(n)})$.
3. Compute $h_{\mathsf{s}} = H(h_{\mathsf{s},1}, \ldots, h_{\mathsf{s},T})$, $h_{\mathsf{m}} = H(h_{\mathsf{m},1}, \ldots, h_{\mathsf{m},T})$ and send $h^* = H(h_{\mathsf{s}}, h_{\mathsf{m}})$ to $\mathcal{V}$.

Fig. 1. 3-round HVZK proof (part 1).

(2) Online Phase. The online computation can itself be divided into three components: *input distribution*, *computation* and *output reconstruction*.

Round 2: *Challenge.*

$\mathcal{V}$ challenges $\mathcal{P}$ on the executions indexed by a set $\mathcal{T} \subset [T]$, with $|\mathcal{T}| = \tau$. For each of these, it chooses a party that remains honest, i.e. it chooses a vector $(i_t)_{t \in \mathcal{T}} \in [n]^\tau$. It then sends $(\mathcal{T}, (i_t)_{t \in \mathcal{T}})$ to $\mathcal{P}$.

In the NIZKPoK variant, $\mathcal{P}$ locally computes $(\mathcal{T}, (i_t)_{t \in \mathcal{T}}) = G(h^*)$.

Round 3: *Opening.*

$\mathcal{P}$ sends $(\text{seed}_t, h_{m,t})_{t \in \overline{\mathcal{T}}}$ and $((\text{state}_t^{(i)}, r_t^{(i)})_{i \in [n] \setminus \{i_t\}}, \gamma_{s,t}^{(i_t)}, \{\Lambda_{t,j}\}_{j \in [\iota]}, \text{msg}_t^{(i_t)})_{t \in \mathcal{T}}$, to $\mathcal{V}$.

Verification:

1. For each $t \in \mathcal{T}$, use $(\text{state}_t^{(i)}, r_t^{(i)})_{i \in [n] \setminus \{i_t\}}$ to reconstruct $\gamma_{s,t}^{(i)}$ for $i \in [n] \setminus \{i_t\}$. Then compute $h'_{s,t} = H(\gamma_{s,t}^{(1)}, \ldots, \gamma_{s,t}^{(n)})$ using $\gamma_{s,t}^{(i_t)}$ sent by $\mathcal{P}$.

2. For $t \in \overline{\mathcal{T}}$, use seed_t to compute $h'_{s,t}$ as an honest $\mathcal{P}$ would.

3. Then compute $h'_s = H(h'_{s,1}, \ldots, h'_{s,T})$.

4. For each $t \in \mathcal{T}$, use $\{\text{state}_t^{(i)}\}_{i \in [n] \setminus \{i_t\}}$, $(\Lambda_{t,j})_{j \in [\iota]}$ and $\text{msg}_t^{(i_t)}$ to recompute the online phase. Check that the output reconstruction yields the correct value of $\boldsymbol{y}$, and compute $h'_{m,t} = H(\{\Lambda_{t,j}\}_{j \in [\iota]}, \text{msg}_t^{(1)}, \ldots, \text{msg}_t^{(n)})$.

5. Then compute $h'_m = H(h'_{m,1}, \ldots, h'_{m,T})$ using $(h'_{m,t})_{t \in \overline{\mathcal{T}}}$ sent by $\mathcal{P}$.

6. Check that $h^* \stackrel{?}{=} H(h'_s, h'_m)$.

Fig. 2. 3-round HVZK proof (part 2).

Unlike for real MPC, the input $\boldsymbol{w} = (w_1, \ldots, w_\iota)$ is global and must be distributed by the prover, outside of the view of any $n-1$ parties. To do so, each party P_i uses $\text{seed}^{(i)}$ to generate a random share $w_j^{(i)}$, for $j \in [\iota]$. Identically to the generation of multiplication triple, a correction value Λ_j must then be computed so that $w_j = \Lambda_j + \sum_{i=1}^n w_j^{(i)}$. The values $(w_j^{(1)}, \ldots, w_j^{(n)}, \Lambda_j)$ now constitute an n-out-of-$(n+1)$ sharing of w_j and therefore it is safe for $\mathcal{P}$ to communicate the Λ_j values to $\mathcal{V}$ in addition to $n-1$ of the seeds $\text{seed}^{(i)}$. Before the computation begins, we let P_n be the one to set $w_j^{(n)} \leftarrow w_j^{(n)} + \Lambda_j$, for $j \in [\iota]$.

Next, the parties compute the intermediary values in the computation of $C(\boldsymbol{w})$. Whenever multiplication gate m is encountered, each party P_i recalls their share of the next unused triple $a_m^{(i)}, b_m^{(i)}, c_m^{(i)}$ from the preprocessing phase. This yields the triple $(\langle a_m \rangle, \langle b_m \rangle, \langle c_m \rangle)$ which can then be used to compute multiplication gate m. Whenever P_i needs to sample a random value, it does so using $\text{seed}^{(i)}$.

Once the parties have computed the shared output values $\langle y_1 \rangle, \ldots, \langle y_o \rangle$, they jointly reconstruct $\boldsymbol{y} = C(\boldsymbol{w})$. To do so, they open each value y_j, for $j \in [o]$, by having each party broadcast its share $y_j^{(i)}$.

As noted above during the description of the MPCitH paradigm, this online phase is entirely deterministic. In particular, the next broadcast message of party P_i at a given time in Π_C depends only on $\text{state}^{(i)}$ and the messages received by P_i so far. Denoting by A the set of "corrupt" parties, this implies that when the verifier $\mathcal{V}$ checks the views of these $n-1$ parties in the execution of Π_C, they only need to be given the $n-1$ states of parties in A together with the messages broadcast by the unopened party during each multiplication gate; they can then recompute the internal values of $C(\boldsymbol{w})$ since they can infer the broadcast messages sent by the opened parties. This means that instead of sending View_{P_i}, for each $i \in A$, $\mathcal{P}$ only needs to send $\mathsf{View}_A = \{\mathsf{state}^{(i)}\}_{i \in A} \cup \{\mathsf{msg}^{(j)}\}_{j \notin A}$, where $\{\mathsf{msg}^{(j)}\}_{j \notin A}$ are the messages sent by the "honest" parties.

The HVZKPoK Protocol. In Figs. 1 and 2, we give a slightly modified version of the 3-round protocol presented by Katz et al. [18] to compute their proof of knowledge, so that it can use our Π_C protocol for an arithmetic circuit C over $\mathbb{F}$. We refer the reader to the original paper [18] for a more in-depth explanation of the protocol. We adopt their optimization of performing a more general cut-and-choose by having the prover run T independent preprocessing phases and the verifier choosing τ of them to be used for independent online phases. For each of these online phases, $\mathcal{V}$ challenges $\mathcal{P}$ on $n-1$ parties which it then checks, together with the $T - \tau$ preprocessing phases that were not used.

From the 3-round protocol, it is possible to obtain a non-interactive ZKPoK by applying the Fiat-Shamir [15] transform, as indicated in the description of **Round 2** in Fig. 2. The system we obtain in this way consists of two stages, Prove and VerifyProof.

- Prove$(\boldsymbol{y}, \boldsymbol{w})$ takes as input $(\boldsymbol{y}, \boldsymbol{w})$ and consists of **Round 1, 2** and **3** of Figs. 1 and 2; i.e. $\mathcal{P}$ computes the first round message and then *locally* computes the challenge by hashing this message using a collision-resistant hash function G. The resulting proof, σ, consists of the concatenation of the first-round message and the response to the challenge.
- VerifyProof$(\boldsymbol{y}, \sigma)$ does the **Verification** step (Fig. 2) and returns $b \in \{0, 1\}$.

To obtain a formula for our proof size estimates we analyze each of the elements communicated by the prover in Rounds 1 and 3. We present and incorporate the optimizations discussed in [18] and thus obtain a formula very close to theirs. At the end of Round 1, $\mathcal{P}$ sends $h^* = H(h_\mathsf{s}, h_\mathsf{m})$ to $\mathcal{V}$, which contributes 2κ bits to the proof size. In Round 3, $\mathcal{P}$ sends two sets of elements; the first corresponds to the $T - \tau$ opened preprocessing executions and the second corresponds to the τ executions of the online phase of the protocol. By generating the master seeds as the leaves of a binary tree expanding from a single root, all-but-τ of the seeds can be sent by only sending $\tau \cdot \log(T/\tau)$ elements, each of κ bits. By computing the hash h_m in a similar way, i.e. as the root of a tree where the $h_{\mathsf{m},t}$ values are the leaves, then it also suffices to send at most $\tau \cdot \log(T/\tau)$ values, each of 2κ bits. This implies that the opening of the $T - \tau$ preprocessing executions adds $\tau \cdot \log(T/\tau) \cdot 3\kappa$ to the proof size. To open the τ online executions, $\mathcal{P}$ sends, for each execution, the commitment $\gamma_{\mathsf{s},t}^{(i_t)}$ of 2κ bits, the input correction values $\{\varLambda_{\mathsf{t},j}\}_{j \in [\ell]}$ of size $|\boldsymbol{w}|$ bits, the messages of the unopened party of size $|\mathsf{msg}^{(i)}|$ and the states of the opened parties. To reduce the communication here, it is observed in [18] that there is sufficient entropy contained in $\mathsf{state}_t^{(i)}$ to not require a separate randomness $r_t^{(i)}$. Combining this with a tree-like structure thus reduces the communication to only $\kappa \cdot \log n$ for the states. In the worst case when party P_n is opened, the prover also has to send the auxiliary information of size $|\mathsf{aux}^{(n)}|$. This results in the following estimate for the proof sizes.

$$2 \cdot \kappa + \tau \cdot \log\left(T/\tau\right) \cdot 3 \cdot \kappa + \tau \cdot (\kappa \cdot \log n + 2 \cdot \kappa + |\mathsf{aux}^{(n)}| + |\boldsymbol{w}| + |\mathsf{msg}^{(i)}|). \quad (1)$$

We have $\mathsf{aux}^{(n)} = \{\Delta_m\}_{m \in [\mathrm{mult}]}$ and typically, the majority of messages in $\mathsf{msg}^{(i)}$ are the openings of α and β during the multiplications. We see that when κ, n, T and τ are fixed, the final proof size is strongly correlated with the number of multiplications in the circuit.

2.2   The Picnic Signature Scheme

It is straightforward to use the NIZKPoK described in the previous section to obtain the Picnic signature scheme [9]. Given a block cipher $F_k(\boldsymbol{x}) : \mathcal{K} \times \mathcal{X} \to \mathcal{Y}$, presented as a binary circuit, the scheme is described by three algorithms:

- Gen(1^κ): Sample $\boldsymbol{x}$ in $\mathcal{X} = \{0,1\}^\kappa$, and $k \in \mathcal{K} = \{0,1\}^\kappa$ and then compute $\boldsymbol{y} = F_k(\boldsymbol{x})$. The public key pk is given by $(\boldsymbol{y}, \boldsymbol{x})$ and the secret key is sk $= k$.
- Sign(sk, m): Given a message m to be signed, compute $\sigma \leftarrow$ Prove(pk, k). Compute the challenge internally as $H(\tilde{\sigma}, m)$, where $\tilde{\sigma}$ denotes the message sent in **Round 1** of the proof.
- Verify(pk, m, σ) : Compute VerifyProof(pk, σ) and the challenge as $H(\tilde{\sigma}, m)$. Return 1 if the result of VerifyProof is 1 and 0 otherwise.

The Picnic signature scheme is thus a NIZKPoK of k realized with the HVZKPoK protocol of [18] for binary circuits. The size of the proof σ then depends on the number of AND gates required for the evaluation of the symmetric primitive F. In the submission to the NIST's Post-Quantum Cryptography project [8,20], F is instantiated with LowMC [1], an "MPC friendly" block-cipher explicitly designed to have low AND depth and lower multiplication complexity. LowMC is a very parametrizable scheme, the number s of 3-bits S-boxes per round and the number of rounds r can both be modified to favor either low round complexity or low multiplication complexity. The block-size and key-size κ does not affect the number of S-boxes, it only imposes the condition that $3s \leq \kappa$; bits of the state that are not affected by the S-box layer are left unchanged. In [7], the Picnic submission team provides parameters (κ, s, r) for the LowMC block-cipher and parameters $(n = 64, \kappa, T, \tau)$ for the NIZKPoK. We reproduce these parameters in Table 1 together with the number of AND gates in each circuit and the estimated signature size using the formula given in (1). As per the MPC protocol for binary circuits given in [18], we use $|\mathsf{aux}^{(n)}| = |\mathsf{msg}^{(i)}| = (\#\mathrm{ANDs})$ and $|\boldsymbol{w}| = \kappa$ in our estimates. We note that these estimated proof sizes consistently fall in between the maximum and averages sizes reported in the Picnic submission [7] and we will therefore compare our estimations to these.

Table 1. Picnic parameters and estimated proof sizes.

Scheme	κ	s	r	#ANDs	T	τ	est. size
picnic2-L1-FS	128	10	20	600	343	27	12.7 kB
picnic2-L3-FS	192	10	30	900	570	39	28.1 kB
picnic2-L5-FS	256	10	38	1140	803	50	47.9 kB

Key Generation Security. As discussed in [9, Appendix D], the security of the key generation relies on the assumption that the block cipher $F_k(x)$ is a one-way function with respect to k. That is, for a fixed plaintext block $x \in \mathcal{X}$, the function $f_x : \mathcal{K} \to \mathcal{Y}$ defined by $f_x : k \mapsto F_k(x)$ is a OWF. This is indeed the correct assumption since x and y as part of the public-key, thus fixing the function f_x and posing the challenge of recovering a suitable pre-image $\tilde{k} \in \mathcal{K}$ such that $f_x(\tilde{k}) = F_{\tilde{k}}(x) = y$. This also shows that first picking x and then picking k during key generation is the natural way of first fixing the function f_x and then computing the challenge image y.

In the full version of the original Picnic work [9], the authors go on to prove that if the block cipher $F_k(x)$ is a PRF family *with respect to* x (that is for a fixed k, the function $F_k : \mathcal{X} \to \mathcal{Y}$ is a PRF) then it is also a OWF *with respect to* k.

2.3   The Advanced Encryption Standard

AES is a 128-bit block-cipher based on a substitution-permutation network (SPN). It allows key lengths of 128, 192 or 256 bits and the corresponding number of rounds for the SPN is respectively 10, 12 or 14. The state always consists of 128 bits and can be considered as a 4×4 matrix of elements in $\mathbb{F}_{2^8}$. The cipher can thus be considered either as a Boolean circuit over $\mathbb{F}_2$ or as an arithmetic circuit over $\mathbb{F}_{2^8}$. We consider the latter. The round function is composed of four operations on the state, of which only one is non-linear: SubBytes.

AddRoundKey takes the 128-bit round key produced by the key schedule and performs an exclusive-or (XOR) operation with the current state to obtain the new state. As $\mathbb{F}_{2^8}$ has characteristic 2, the XOR operation can be computed by simply adding two elements together.

SubBytes is the only non-linear block of the round function, which transforms each of the 16 bytes of the state by means of a substitution function, known as the S-box. The AES S-box is a multiplicative inverse in the field $\mathbb{F}_{2^8}$, followed by an invertible affine transformation. In some sense, the S-box can be seen as

$$S : s \mapsto \phi^{-1}\left(\mathbf{A} \cdot \phi\left(s^{-1}\right) + \vec{b}\right) \tag{2}$$

where $\phi : \mathbb{F}_{2^8} \to (\mathbb{F}_2)^8$ is an isomorphism of vector spaces (mapping bytes in $\mathbb{F}_{2^8}$ to vectors of eight bits in $\mathbb{F}_2$) and $\mathbf{A} \in (\mathbb{F}_2)^{8 \times 8}$ and $(\vec{b} \in (\mathbb{F}_2)^8)$ are the public parameters of the affine transformation.

ShiftRows is a permutation of the 16 state bytes, obtained by rotating row i of the state by i bytes to the left. Hence, the first row (row zero) remains the same, the second row is rotated to the left by one byte, etc.

MixColumns is the final phase and linear component. It consists of a mixing operation that is applied to each column of the state separately. Column i is transformed by a matrix multiplication with a 4×4 matrix defined over $\mathbb{F}_{2^8}$.

Key Schedule. The key schedule is mostly linear except for the application of the same AES S-box to up to four bytes of the round key.

As the S-box is the only non-linear block, Table 2 presents how many times it needs to be computed for each AES circuit.

Table 2. Number of S-boxes in the AES circuits.

AES-	128	192	256
# Rounds	10	12	14
# Round S-boxes	160	192	224
# Key schedule S-boxes	40	32	52
Total # S-boxes	200	224	276

Rijndael. The AES is the standardized version of the Rijndael cipher [10]. The most prominent difference between the two is that Rijndael allows both a variable key size κ and a variable block-length β. The round transformations are the same, with SubBytes performing S-box on each of the $\frac{\beta}{8}$ state bytes and MixColumns transforming each of the $\frac{\beta}{32}$ state columns. The key schedule is identical to that of AES-κ, but keep in mind that the expanded key is larger in the former case and hence the number of S-box calculations also differs. We summarize the number of S-boxes in Rijndael-κ circuits with $\kappa = \beta$ in Table 3.

Table 3. Number of S-boxes in the Rijndael circuits.

Rijndael-	128	192	256
# Rounds	10	12	14
# Round S-boxes	160	288	448
# Key schedule S-boxes	40	48	112
Total # S-boxes	200	336	560

3   Computing the S-Box

To design an MPC protocol for the circuit $f_x(k) := \mathsf{AES}_k(x)$ over $\mathbb{F}_{2^8}$, we design a communication-efficient computation of the non-linear S-box in a distributed way using the advantages of MPCitH. This computation happens in two stages: first an *inversion* stage described by the map

$$
s \mapsto \begin{cases} s^{-1} & \text{if } s \neq 0, \\ 0 & \text{if } s = 0, \end{cases} \quad \text{over } \mathbb{F}_{2^8}; \tag{3}
$$

and second, an *affine* stage where $s^{-1} \mapsto \phi^{-1}(\mathbf{A} \cdot \phi(s^{-1}) + \vec{b})$ in $(\mathbb{F}_2)^8$ as described in Eq. (2). As the second stage is in fact local, we present it first and then address the inversion stage in Sect. 3.1.

The affine transformation (being linear) can be applied by each party independently. Since it operates on individual bits, the parties must first derive a sharing of the bit-decomposition of s. As we only require semi-honest security for our protocol, this can be also be achieved locally. Given the isomorphism $\phi : \mathbb{F}_{2^8} \to (\mathbb{F}_2)^8$, each party can locally obtain $\vec{s}^{(i)} = \phi(s^{(i)})$ which then corresponds to a sharing $\langle \vec{s} \rangle = \phi(\langle s \rangle)$. Each party can then locally compute the affine transformation $\vec{t}^{(i)} := \mathbf{A} \cdot \vec{s}^{(i)} + \vec{b}$; indeed, as $\mathbf{A}$ and $\vec{b}$ are both public values, the transformation can be computed as a series of multiplications by and additions with public constants during the online phase.. Finally, they can recompose $\langle t \rangle = \phi^{-1}(\langle \vec{t} \rangle)$. Thus the affine phase of the S-box can be computed entirely locally.

3.1   Computing the Inversion

To perform the Galois field inversion within the MPCitH paradigm, we use a masked inversion method. Namely, given $\langle s \rangle \in \mathbb{F}_{2^8}$ and a randomly sampled $\langle r \rangle \in \mathbb{F}_{2^8}$ (where each party samples $r^{(i)}$ at random from $\mathsf{seed}^{(i)}$), we run the following:

1. Compute $\langle s \cdot r \rangle$ (by using a preprocessed triple $(\langle a \rangle, \langle b \rangle, \langle c \rangle)$ and opening $s - a$ and $r - b$).
2. $\mathsf{Open}(s \cdot r)$.
3. Compute $(s^{-1} \cdot r^{-1})$ (done locally by each P_i).
4. Compute $\langle s^{-1} \rangle = (s^{-1} \cdot r^{-1}) \cdot \langle r \rangle$.

Performing the multiplication and the opening of $\langle s \cdot r \rangle$ results in every party broadcasting three elements of $\mathbb{F}_{2^8}$ for each inversion. This implies that we have a base communication cost of 3 bytes per party per inversion in the online phase; i.e. for each P_i,

$$
|\mathsf{msg}^{(i)}| = 8 \cdot (3 \cdot \#(\text{S-boxes}) + o),
$$

where the additional o bytes come from the opening of the output values as f_x outputs tuples in $(\mathbb{F}_{2^8})^o$.

Also considering the inclusion of the offset value $\Delta \in \mathbb{F}_{2^8}$ in the auxiliary information $\mathsf{aux}^{(n)}$, for the triple that is used for the inversion, we also have that

$$|\mathsf{aux}^{(n)}| = 8 \cdot \#(\text{S-boxes}).$$

There are however two complications with this method: when either $r = 0$ or $s = 0$. We first present how to deal with the first one, assuming that the second does not happen. We then discuss how to mitigate the second one.

Need for Non-Zero Randomness. Indeed, assuming that $s \neq 0$, we see that if $r = 0$, then $s \cdot r = 0$ as well and the inversion computation cannot proceed. However, this does not leak any information regarding s, so when the parties observe that $\mathsf{Open}(s \cdot r)$ yields 0, they can restart the computation of the inversion with a fresh $\langle r' \rangle$ and a new multiplication triple.

While this would not be a problem for real MPC executions of this protocol, here we are restricted because of the commitment to $\mathsf{aux}^{(n)}$, and therefore to the number of preprocessed triples, that the prover $\mathcal{P}$ of the HVZKPoK must make before it emulates the online phase of the protocol. The prover does emulate the online phase for every preprocessing phase, and it would therefore be possible for them to observe exactly how many triples are required for an execution. However, this would ultimately be dependent on the input.

In order to commit to the preprocessing, the prover would have to indicate how many triples were generated and using which bits of randomness, given that those bits produced from $\mathsf{seed}^{(i)}$ would be mixed with bits used to produce other randomness, such as the input sharings. We do not discuss here the design of a protocol which accounts for this flexible verification and the evaluation of whether this would leak information regarding the input to the verifier.

Instead, we design our protocol to generate a fixed number m of additional triples for every execution. In the rare cases that this additional number is not enough, we say that the prover aborts the proof and restarts. Table 4 shows the probability that a proof aborts for each of the AES circuits depending on the number of additional triples provided by $\mathcal{P}$. If we want the probability of needing to abort a proof to be less than $10^{-8} \approx 2^{-20}$, then adding $m = 9$ additional triples is sufficient.

Table 4. Probability of abort of each circuit (assuming $\Pr[r = 0] = \frac{1}{256}$).

m	0	1	2	3	4	5	6	7	8	9	10
AES-128	$2^{-0.9}$	$2^{-2.4}$	$2^{-4.5}$	$2^{-6.9}$	$2^{-9.7}$	$2^{-12.7}$	$2^{-15.9}$	$2^{-19.3}$	$2^{-22.9}$	$2^{-26.6}$	$2^{-30.5}$
AES-192	$2^{-0.8}$	$2^{-2.2}$	$2^{-4.1}$	$2^{-6.4}$	$2^{-9.0}$	$2^{-11.8}$	$2^{-14.8}$	$2^{-18.1}$	$2^{-21.5}$	$2^{-25.1}$	$2^{-28.8}$
AES-256	$2^{-0.6}$	$2^{-1.8}$	$2^{-3.4}$	$2^{-5.4}$	$2^{-7.7}$	$2^{-10.2}$	$2^{-13.0}$	$2^{-15.9}$	$2^{-19.0}$	$2^{-22.3}$	$2^{-25.7}$

The addition of these m additional triples then implies that, for each execution, the auxiliary information contains $(\#(\text{S-boxes}) + m)$ elements in $\mathbb{F}_{2^8}$ and we therefore have

$$|\mathsf{aux}^{(n)}| = 8 \cdot (\#(\text{S-boxes}) + m).$$

Similarly, since parties are susceptible to repeat the computation of up to m inversions during the protocol and therefore broadcast more than 3 bytes per inversion, we have that for each P_i

$$|\mathsf{msg}^{(i)}| \leq 8 \cdot (3 \cdot (\#(\text{S-boxes}) + m) + o).$$

One advantage of restricting the number of triples produced in this way is that it guarantees a maximum proof size, independently of the randomness used.

3.2   Need for Non-Zero Input

In the previous section we assumed that $s \neq 0$ to say that if $s \cdot r = 0$, then it must be that $r = 0$. However, in general, it is possible for the input s to the AES S-box to be 0. If the inversion was computed as above, with this possibility, then opening $s \cdot r = 0$ would in fact reveal information about s since r is not allowed to be zero in a correct inversion.

To avoid this leakage, we restrict our protocol to only prove knowledge of values of k for which there is no zero as input to any S-box in the computation of $f_x(k)$. We write $\mathcal{K}_x \subset \mathcal{K}$ to denote the subset of such keys. While this reduces the number of applications of this protocol as a general HVZKPoK for AES keys, this is not so significant in the context of Picnic signatures. Indeed, the values x and k for which the proof must be given are fixed during key generation and used for all signatures. It is therefore feasible to restrict the Keygen algorithm to first select a random x and then sample values of k until one from $\mathcal{K}_x$ is found.

We note that a malicious prover could intentionally generate a key for which some zeroes do appear in the computation of the circuit. However, in the context of PKI, users typically present a signature of their certificate under their public-key as a proof of possession. Check such a signature would immediately reveal whether a key was malformed and thus prevent verifiers from accepting further signatures.

Loss of Security. This particular design of the Keygen procedure naturally affects the assumption that $f_x(k) := \text{AES}_k(x)$ is still a OWF family as required for Picnic signatures. While the random selection of x still ensures that a random function f_x is selected from the family, the restricted selection of $k \in \mathcal{K}_x$ reduces the image space of f_x and also the pre-image space for a given y.

We can first estimate this security loss by assuming that, for a given block x and a randomly sampled key $k \in \mathcal{K}$, the S-boxes are independent from one another and each has a probability of $\frac{1}{256}$ of receiving 0 as input. Table 5 presents the proportion of keys that would also belong to $\mathcal{K}_x$ for the three different AES circuits, *i.e.* $(255/256)^{\# \text{ S-boxes}}$. For AES-256, we see that approximately $\frac{1}{3}$ of keys possess this property, which, from an attacker's perspective, reduces by only $\log_2(3) \approx 1.4$ the bit-security of the problem of inverting the OWF f_x and recovering $k \in \mathcal{K}_x$. The assumption that the S-boxes are independent is justified by the PRF-behaviour or AES. Moreover, our experiments confirmed that, for a fixed x, the same proportions of keys as shown in Table 5 yielded no zero-inputs.

Table 5. Probabilities of no zero-inputs to S-boxes.

Circuit	AES-128	AES-192	AES-256
Number of S-boxes	200	224	276
No-zeroes probability	45.7%	41.6%	34.0%

This also shows that it is not very computationally expensive for Keygen to re-sample k as it will only have to do so three times on average. To emphasize the low cost of this, we also recall that during Keygen, the signer samples and verifies that $k \in \mathcal{K}_x$ for a given x. While they do this, they do not have to execute the AES circuit using the MPC protocol, the S-box inputs can be verified using an un-shared execution.

A More Formal Analysis. In [9, Appendix D], the authors show that if an adversary $\mathcal{A}$, on input y has a high probability of inverting the OWF $f_x(k) = y$, then one can build a distinguisher $\mathcal{D}$ which has a high probability of distinguishing F_k from a random function. Recall that in our case, F_k is the usual AES$_k$ PRF family and that f_x is the AES function family considered on k indexed by x.

Let us now assume that the adversary $\mathcal{A}$ has a high probability p of inverting $f_x(k)$ only if $k \in \mathcal{K}_x$. In the reduction proof, $\mathcal{D}$ queries the PRF oracle $\mathcal{O}$ on input x to receive y as its image either under the PRF F_k for a random $k \in \mathcal{K}$ or under a random function. It then queries $\mathcal{A}$ on input y in the hope of receiving the correct key k. The only difference between our situation and theirs is that the key space $\mathcal{K}_x$ for which $\mathcal{A}$ is capable of returning the correct key is smaller than the whole of $\mathcal{K}$. In the case where $\mathcal{O}$ is indeed computing the PRF, there is then a probability of $|\mathcal{K}_x|/|\mathcal{K}|$ that the sampled hidden key will belong to the reduced key space and therefore $\mathcal{A}$ will return the correct key with smaller probability $p \cdot |\mathcal{K}_x|/|\mathcal{K}|$. All other aspects of the proof are the same as in [9] and therefore, under the assumption that AES, over any key $k \in \mathcal{K}$, is a PRF with respect to x, it holds that it also is a OWF with respect to $k \in \mathcal{K}_x$ with a tightness gap proportional to $|\mathcal{K}_x|/|\mathcal{K}|$ for a given x.

We can therefore say that if our AES circuit with restricted keys would yield a weak OWF, then there would be a similar proportion of keys for which it would be easy to distinguish the AES function from a random one, thus contradicting the assumed and observed PRF behaviour of the AES. Furthermore our experiments confirm that this proportion of keys is non-negligible, further increasing confidence in our OWF construction.

3.3 Application to Picnic Signatures

We now estimate the signature size if our arithmetic circuit $C_x(k) = \text{AES}_k(x)$ were to be used instead of the LowMC binary circuit in Picnic signatures and also present the interesting conclusion that a naive application of AES-192 or AES-256 is not sufficient to achieve stronger levels of security.

Table 6. Estimates for Picnic signatures with AES-128 circuit.

Level	Circuit	κ	T	τ	$|\mathsf{aux}^{(n)}|$	$|w|$	$|\mathsf{msg}^{(i)}|$	Est. size
L1	picnic2-AES-128-bin	128	343	27	6400	128	6400	51.9 kB
	picnic2-AES-128-inv				1664	128	5120	**31.6 kB**

AES-128: Table 6 presents our estimates using the AES-128 circuit instead of the LowMC circuit with parameters ($k = 128, s = 10, r = 20$), specified by the Picnic submission [7] as achieving AES-128-like security. For the picnic2-AES-128-bin circuit, we used the state-of-the-art figure of 32 AND gates per AES S-box reported in the inversion circuit of [6], thus yielding $|\mathsf{aux}^{(n)}| = |\mathsf{msg}^{(i)}| = 200 \cdot 32 = 6400$. We note that this differs from the figure of 5440 AND gates stated in [9, Section 6.1]. While we cite the same work [6], a figure of 5440 would make sense if the AES-128 circuit contained only 170 S-boxes, or 160 S-boxes with 34 AND gates per S-box. Our Table 2 shows that if the full circuit is considered, including the key schedule, then 200 S-boxes are necessary. Moreover, removing the key schedule is not possible as a fraudulent prover would then be able to create a forgery by selecting a final round key which would make the second-to-last state agree with the public key value y. Finally, for our picnic2-AES-128-inv circuit, we used our costs of $|\mathsf{aux}^{(n)}| = 8 \cdot (200 + 8) = 1664$ and $|\mathsf{msg}^{(i)}| = 8 \cdot (3 \cdot (200 + 8) + 16) = 5120$ accounting for $m = 8$ additional inversion operations and $o = 16$ bytes of communication per party for output reconstruction.

We see that implementing AES-128 using the best current binary circuit would increase the signature size by a factor of 4.07 compared to the estimated signature size for picnic2-L1-FS given in Table 1. However, our inversion technique yields an increase only by a factor of 2.48, thus a reduction of 39% over the binary circuit. We note that this improvement comes with the caveat that our technique of Sect. 3.2 reduces the key-space for k by $|\log_2(0.457)| = 1.13$ bits from the 128 bit-security level.

AES-192 and AES-256: Such a direct comparison as the one presented above is not possible for the AES-192 and AES-256 circuits. While these two algorithms are believed to provide respectively 192 and 256 classical bit-security when used as block-ciphers, this does not hold in this paradigm due to the requirement for a one-way function for the key generation of Picnic-like signatures.

Indeed, as remarked in [9, Appendix D], the security of the key generation requires the block-size and the key-size of the underlying block-cipher to be equal – in part to prevent quantum attacks which benefit from a square-root speedup over the block-size. This is not the case for AES-192 and AES-256 and therefore, interestingly, the shift to longer keys, without an accompanying shift to longer blocks, does not translate into increased security against forgery attacks for the signature scheme. Here, the standardized 128 bit block-length of the AES cipher becomes an obstacle to easily achieving both stronger security and optimal efficiency. For AES-192, for example, a single block of encryption would result in (an expected) 2^{64} spurious keys per single block $\boldsymbol{x}$, $\boldsymbol{y}$ pair. Thus the probability of guessing a valid key, with a single block pair $\boldsymbol{x}$, $\boldsymbol{y}$ will be 2^{-128} and not 2^{-192} as desired, and in addition applying Grover's search for a valid key would only be slightly more complex than in the AES-128 case.

This fixed block-length was actually not a part of the original Rijndael design [10]. Hence, to obtain L3 (resp. L5) constructions, one could alternatively use the Rijndael cipher with 192-bit (resp. 256-bit) blocks and key. Since these are not standardized, we first discuss some constructions using AES.

To design a circuit suitable for 192 (resp. 256) bit-security level Picnic signatures, we therefore combine two copies of an AES-192 (resp. AES-256) circuit, keyed with the same key. To realize such a cipher with longer block- and key-length, we propose to use AES in ECB mode. For our L3 construction using AES-192, we only require $\boldsymbol{x}$ and $\boldsymbol{y}$ to be 192 bits long. We therefore pad $\boldsymbol{x}$ with 64 0s to reach two full blocks, and then truncate the resulting ECB-mode encryption to its first 192 bits (one and a half blocks) to produce the output $\boldsymbol{y}$. For our L5 construction using AES-256, we use an $\boldsymbol{x}$ value of 256 bits, encrypted as two blocks in ECB mode, to produce a two-block value $\boldsymbol{y}$ of 256 bits.

One side-effect of using ECB is that we have the problem of malleable public keys, for example the public key $(\boldsymbol{x}_0\|\boldsymbol{x}_1, \boldsymbol{y}_0\|\boldsymbol{y}_1)$ would be equivalent to $(\boldsymbol{x}_1\|\boldsymbol{x}_0, \boldsymbol{y}_1\|\boldsymbol{y}_0)$. Whilst this does not break the security of the signature scheme in the standard security game, this could be a problem in practice. However, we can tie signatures to a specific public key by including it in the hash used to generate the challenge in the NIZKPoK.

The security of key generation now depends on the ECB construction which is clearly not a PRF family, but we can instead rely on the assumption that ECB mode is OW-CPA and we provide a similar argument as in [9] to formalise this assumption.

Claim. If $F_k(x)$ is OW-CPA then $f_x(k)$ is a OWF.

Proof (sketch). The proof follows similarly to the proof in [9, Appendix D]. Indeed, given an adversary $\mathcal{A}$ that can return k on input $y = f_x(k)$, we can build a adversary $\mathcal{B}$ against the OW-CPA challenger for F_k as follows. First, $\mathcal{B}$ submits x to the encryption oracle and receives $y = F_k(x)$ for random $k \in \mathcal{K}$ chosen by the oracle. Then $\mathcal{B}$ runs $\mathcal{A}$ on input y to obtain k with high probability. Finally, $\mathcal{B}$ requests the challenge ciphertext y^* and uses k to compute $x^* = F_k^{-1}(y^*)$ and return it as its answer to the OW-CPA challenge. With high probability, $\mathcal{B}$ returns the correct pre-image.

Both of the ECB-mode circuits result in executing two AES circuits but this drawback is inherent to the fixed block-length of the AES block-cipher and therefore applies equally to our inversion approach and the naive binary approach. We estimate the proof sizes obtained with these designs in Table 7.

For the binary circuits, we use the same figure of 32 AND gates per S-box [6]. In the case of the picnic2-AES-192-bin and picnic2-AES-256-bin circuits, we double the number of round S-boxes presented in Table 2 to obtain figures for $|\text{aux}^{(n)}|$

and $|\mathsf{msg}^{(i)}|$. We keep the same number of key-schedule S-boxes as both circuits use the same key $\boldsymbol{k}$ and therefore the key-schedule needs to be computed only once. For the inversion circuits, we also double the number of round S-boxes in our formulæ for $|\mathsf{aux}^{(n)}|$ and $|\mathsf{msg}^{(i)}|$ but we must also change number m of additional triples due to the increased risk of sampling zero randomness during the inversion computation. A quick calculation similar to the one used for Table 4 shows that our doubled-up circuits for AES-192 and AES-256 require $m = 11$ and $m = 12$ respectively to have a probability of abort below 2^{-20}.

We see that implementing our doubled-up AES-192 and AES-256 using the best current binary circuit would increase the signature sizes by a factor of 5.30 and 4.87 respectively compared to the estimated signature size for picnic2-L3-FS and picnic2-L5-FS given in Table 1. However, our inversion technique yields increases only by a factor of 3.09 and 2.79 respectively, thus reductions of 41.7% and 42.8% over the binary circuits. We note that this improvement comes with the caveat that our technique of Sect. 3.2 reduces the key-space for $\boldsymbol{k}$ by $|\log_2(0.196)| = 2.35$ bits and $|\log_2(0.141)| = 2.83$ bits from the 192 and 256 bit-security levels respectively.

Rijndael-192 and -256. To avoid the reliance on ECB mode and on a slightly different security assumption, we also provide estimates of proof sizes that make use of the original Rijndael-192 and -256 circuits which use an equal block and key size with the same S-box as AES. The number of rounds in Rijndael-192 (resp. Rijndael-256) is the same as in AES-192 (resp. AES-256), i.e. 12 (resp. 14)[1].

We use the figures of Table 3 to obtain figures for $|\mathsf{aux}^{(n)}|$ and $|\mathsf{msg}^{(i)}|$, presented in Table 7. As above, we calculate that values of $m = 10$ and $m = 12$ are required by the Rijndael-192 and -256 circuits respectively to have a probability of abort below 2^{-20}.

We see that implementing the Rijndael-192 and -256 circuits using the best current binary circuit would increase the signature sizes by a factor of 4.42 and 5.38 respectively compared to the estimated signature size for picnic2-L3-FS and picnic2-L5-FS given in Table 1. However, our inversion technique yields increases only by a factor of 2.64 and 3.12 respectively, thus reductions of 40.2% and 41.8% over the binary circuits. We note that this improvement comes with the caveat that our technique of Sect. 3.2 reduces the key-space for $\boldsymbol{k}$ by $|\log_2(0.268)| = 1.90$ bits and $|\log_2(0.112)| = 3.16$ bits from the 192 and 256 bit-security levels respectively.

It is not surprising that the Rijndael-192 results are overall better those with AES-192, since the ECB construction with extra padding performs more work than it should. On the other hand, the AES-256 construction is more efficient than the Rijndael-256 design since the latter has a larger key schedule.

---

[1] See   https://csrc.nist.gov/csrc/media/projects/cryptographic-standards-and-guidelines/documents/aes-development/rijndael-ammended.pdf.

Table 7. Estimates for Picnic signatures with AES-192, AES-256 and Rijndael circuits.

Level	Circuit	κ	T	τ	$|\mathsf{aux}^{(n)}|$	$|w|$	$|\mathsf{msg}^{(i)}|$	Est. size
L3	picnic2-AES-192-bin	192	570	39	13312	192	13312	149.1 kB
	picnic2-Rijndael-192-bin				10752	192	10752	124.2 kB
	picnic2-AES-192-inv				3416	192	10440	**86.9 kB**
	picnic2-Rijndael-192-inv				2768	192	8496	**74.2 kB**
L5	picnic2-AES-256-bin	256	803	50	16000	256	16000	233.7 kB
	picnic-Rijndael-256-bin				17920	256	17920	257.7 kB
	picnic2-AES-256-inv				4096	256	12544	**133.7 kB**
	picnic2-Rijndael-256-inv				4576	256	13984	**149.7 kB**

4   Alternative Computations of the AES S-Box

Representing the AES S-box as the map $s \mapsto s^{-1}$ (with $0 \mapsto 0$) over $\mathbb{F}_{2^8}$ is one of three methods described by Damgård and Keller [12] for this task in standard MPC. In fact, it is the most efficient method of that work to compute the AES arithmetic circuit in real-world MPC. However, their treatment of the $s = 0$ difficulty differs from ours, and they also present two alternative methods to compute the inversion operation. We discuss these methods and their cost here, along with other methods, to study the possibilities for computing the AES circuit in the MPCitH paradigm.

Square-and-Multiply. The first method of [12] is not to compute $s \mapsto s^{-1}$ but rather $s \mapsto s^{254}$. As $\mathrm{ord}(\mathbb{F}_{2^8}^{*}) - 1 = 255 - 1 = 254$, this achieves the same result with the additional advantage of not requiring a special case for $s = 0$ which maps to 0 naturally. However, s^{254} requires a square-and-multiply chain to be computed. The shortest such chain given in [12] requires 11 multiplications. Combining the cost of the openings and the auxiliary information required for triple generation, this method would cost $11 \cdot 3 = 33$ bytes per S-box, compared to only 4 bytes per S-box for our method in Sect. 3.

Masked Exponentiation. This second method of [12] computes the same map $s \mapsto s^{254}$ but using the fact that $(a+b)^{2^i} = a^{2^i} + b^{2^i}$ in fields of characteristic 2. Here, they are able to take advantage of the preprocessing model; they first precompute the squares $\langle r \rangle, \langle r^2 \rangle, \langle r^4 \rangle, \ldots, \langle r^{128} \rangle$ for a random value $r \in \mathbb{F}_{2^8}$. Then, to invert $\langle s \rangle$, they additively mask $\langle s \rangle + \langle r \rangle$, open $(s + r)$ and square locally to obtain $(s+r)^2, (s+r)^4, \ldots, (s+r)^{128}$. Finally, they unmask each power-of-two with the corresponding shared power-of-two of r, $(s+r)^{2^i} + \langle r^{2^i} \rangle = \langle s^{2^i} \rangle$ and then perform an online multiplication chain to obtain $\prod_{i=1}^{7} \langle s^{2^i} \rangle = \langle s^{254} \rangle$.

Unlike in [12], the requirement on the MPC protocol for only semi-honest security means that the successive shared powers of $\langle r \rangle$ can be computed locally.

Indeed, in characteristic 2, $r^2 = (\sum_{i=1}^{n} r^{(i)})^2 = \sum_{i=1}^{n} (r^{(i)})^2$, so each party can compute their shares locally. Therefore the cost of this method in our paradigm is the opening of $(s+r)$ and the six multiplications required for the computation of $\langle s^{128} \rangle$. This would still amount to $1 + 6 \cdot 3 = 19$ bytes per S-box (broadcast and auxiliary information put together).

Masked Inversion. In [12], Damgård and Keller also conclude that the masked inversion method that we presented in Sect. 3 is the most efficient. Indeed, at its core it only requires 3 bytes in the online phase and 1 triple in the preprocessing phase. However, the leakage that occurs when $s = 0$ must be prevented. While it is possible in our application to Picnic signatures to generate the public-/private-key pairs so that this leakage does not take place, this is not possible for generic computations of the AES circuit.

The solution given in [12] is to have the parties compute a shared "zero-indicator" value $\langle \delta(s) \rangle$ defined as

$$\delta(s) = \begin{cases} 1 & \text{if } s = 0, \\ 0 & \text{otherwise.} \end{cases}$$

It is then easily verified that the inversion mapping of (3) is equivalent to

$$s \mapsto (s + \delta(s))^{-1} + \delta(s)$$

When $\delta(s)$ is computed in shared form, then the parties can perform the inversion computation with $\langle s + \delta(s) \rangle$ instead of $\langle s \rangle$. Once $\langle (s + \delta(s))^{-1} \rangle$ is obtained, the parties can locally compute $\langle (s + \delta(s))^{-1} \rangle + \langle \delta(s) \rangle$. This ensures that if $s = 0$ then $s + \delta(s) = 1$ is instead inverted to $(s + \delta(s))^{-1} = 1$ and that the second addition of $\delta(s)$ returns the value to 0, as $\mathbb{F}_{2^8}$ has characteristic 2.

This technique could be applied to our MPCitH circuit for AES to avoid the loss of generality and security that come with the efficient method presented in the previous section. We present here two methods to compute the zero-indicator $\delta(s)$ in secret-shared form.

Method 1. In [12], the value $\langle \delta(s) \rangle$ is computed by first bit-decomposing $\langle s \rangle$, then NOT-ing each bit and finally computing the joint AND of the eight bits of s. This joint AND requires 7 bit-wise AND gates to output the final value. If these gates are performed so that each party eventually holds $\delta(s)^{(i)} \in \mathbb{F}_2$, then each party can embed its share into $\mathbb{F}_{2^8}$ to obtain its share of $\langle \delta(s) \rangle$.

As before, bit-decomposition is trivially obtained by each party locally bit-decomposing its share into $\vec{s}^{(i)} = \phi(s^{(i)})$. The NOT gates are then also performed locally by each party. For the AND gates, we make use of the same technique of preprocessed multiplication triples, but over $\mathbb{F}_2$ instead of $\mathbb{F}_{2^8}$. For each AND gate, 1 bit then needs to be added to $\mathsf{aux}^{(n)}$ to correct the triple and 2 bits need to be opened in the online phase to compute the multiplication.

This method therefore results in $7 \cdot 3 = 21$ bits per S-box in addition to the 4 bytes required for the inversion of $\langle s + \delta(s) \rangle$. This results in approximately

6.6 bytes per S-box which is only 17.5% less than implementing the best binary circuit for AES in the model of [18].

Method 2. In the world of MPC, the computation of the shared zero-indicator $\langle \delta(s) \rangle$ can be seen as an n-party functionality which takes $\langle s \rangle$ as input and distributes $\langle \delta(s) \rangle$ to all the parties. As we are in the MPCitH setting, the Prover can observe the value of s and act as this functionality by providing each party with their share of $\delta(s)$. To further optimize this, we can assume that P_i, for $i = 1 \to n - 1$, samples their share of $\delta(s)$ pseudo-randomly and that the Prover only give P_n a correction value which makes the reconstructed value equal to $\delta(s)$.

This approach is the first here that deviates from a normal MPC scenario and exploits the MPCitH paradigm to reduce the cost. However, it comes with the caveat that a malicious Prover is able to select an arbitrary correction value for P_n. This implies that they have the freedom to arbitrarily modify the computation of the circuit. A partial fix for this is to specify that the shares of $\delta(s)$ must be either 0 or 1 within $\mathbb{F}_{2^8}$. This is only natural, as $\delta(s)$ can only take either of these values and the sum of such values is again 0 or 1. In this way, the prover can at most substitute a 1 for a 0 or vice-versa thus greatly limiting their ability to cheat arbitrarily. They can only inject an arbitrary $\mathbb{F}_{2^8}$ value into P_n and not get caught if P_n is the party that is not revealed to the Verifier, which corresponds exactly to their usual cheating capability in Picnic. Furthermore, this approach means that the additional auxiliary input required for P_n is only one bit of information, as opposed to one byte.

The remaining drawback is then that a malicious Prover can arbitrarily change the value of $\delta(s)$ from 0 to 1 in the computation. Note that this 1-bit fault can only be injected in the least significant bit of the input of the AES inversion, and if injected, the same fault is automatically applied to the inversion output as well, corresponding to the second XOR with $\delta(s)$. Unfortunately, it remains as an open question to compute what the soundness would be of a proof which used this technique for the computation of the AES circuit. This kind of fault injections have not been studied in the side-channel analysis literature, since a fault attacker typically injects faults in order to obtain an exploitable (non-zero) output difference in the ciphertext (*i.e.* Differential Fault Analysis [5]). A malicious prover in MPCitH on the other hand would be trying to modify an execution yielding a wrong ciphertext into an apparently correct one.

In the normal MPCitH scenario, a malicious prover who does not have knowledge of the secret key k, has a probability $2^{-\kappa}$ to produce a valid signature by guessing the key, where $\kappa \in \{128, 192, 256\}$ is the key and block size. In this adapted scenario with very specific 1-bit faults, the size of the prover's search space increases to $2^\kappa \cdot 2^{\# \text{ S-boxes}}$, since they can guess both a key and a fault configuration by selecting which of the S-box computations to infect. Let $\tilde{k}$ be the key guess and $\tilde{F}$ be the circuits of Sect. 3 with injected faults; then the prover succeeds if the correct ciphertext is output at the end, *i.e.* for a public key (x, y), $\tilde{F}_{\tilde{k}}(x) = y$. We again assume that all S-box calculations are independent and treat AES as a PRF, hence we assume that each of the 2^{κ} possible outputs are equiprobable. We thus estimate that the number of correct choices is

$$\# \text{ correct choices} \approx \frac{\text{total } \# \text{ choices}}{\# \text{ outputs}} = \frac{2^{\kappa + \#\text{S-boxes}}}{2^{\kappa}} = 2^{\#\text{S-boxes}}.$$

This results in the following success probability for a malicious prover:

$$\Pr[\tilde{F}_{\tilde{k}}(\boldsymbol{x}) = \boldsymbol{y}] \approx \frac{\# \text{ correct choices}}{\text{total } \# \text{ choices}} = \frac{2^{\#\text{S-boxes}}}{2^{\kappa + \#\text{S-boxes}}} = 2^{-\kappa}$$

which corresponds exactly to the success probability in the MPCitH scenario without fault injections.

This methods originates from using an n-party functionality within the MPCitH paradigm, which is normally not permitted as a malicious Prover is then able to cheat arbitrarily. However our analysis shows that, for this particular application, this additional freedom does not seem to give the Prover further advantages to forge a signature. Therefore, while n-party functionalities may not be permitted in general, this shows that case-by-case analysis may reveal that they do not affect the soundness for specific proofs. This then raises the question of what other proofs may be realized by taking advantage of such functionalities, which are in fact "free", in terms of communication between parties, as they can be computed outside of the MPC protocol by the Prover themselves. We leave such a study for further work.

Acknowledgments. The authors would like to thank the referees for a number of comments which improved the quality of the paper. This work has been supported in part by ERC Advanced Grant ERC-2015-AdG-IMPaCT, by the Defense Advanced Research Projects Agency (DARPA) and Space and Naval Warfare Systems Center, Pacific (SSC Pacific) under contract No. N66001-15-C-4070, and by the Fund for Scientific Research Flanders (FWO) under an Odysseus project GOH9718N. Lauren De Meyer is funded by a PhD fellowship of the FWO. Any opinions, findings and conclusions or recommendations expressed in this material are those of the author(s) and do not necessarily reflect the views of the ERC, United States Air Force, DARPA or FWO.

References

1. Albrecht, M.R., Rechberger, C., Schneider, T., Tiessen, T., Zohner, M.: Ciphers for MPC and FHE. In: Oswald, E., Fischlin, M. (eds.) EUROCRYPT 2015. LNCS, vol. 9056, pp. 430–454. Springer, Heidelberg (2015). https://doi.org/10.1007/978-3-662-46800-5_17
2. Ames, S., Hazay, C., Ishai, Y., Venkitasubramaniam, M.: Ligero: Lightweight sublinear arguments without a trusted setup. In: Thuraisingham et al. [21], pp. 2087–2104
3. Beaver, D.: Efficient multiparty protocols using circuit randomization. In: Feigenbaum, J. (ed.) CRYPTO 1991. LNCS, vol. 576, pp. 420–432. Springer, Heidelberg (1992). https://doi.org/10.1007/3-540-46766-1_34

4. Bendlin, R., Damgård, I., Orlandi, C., Zakarias, S.: Semi-homomorphic encryption and multiparty computation. In: Paterson, K.G. (ed.) EUROCRYPT 2011. LNCS, vol. 6632, pp. 169–188. Springer, Heidelberg (2011). https://doi.org/10.1007/978-3-642-20465-4_11

5. Biham, E., Shamir, A.: Differential fault analysis of secret key cryptosystems. In: Kaliski, B.S. (ed.) CRYPTO 1997. LNCS, vol. 1294, pp. 513–525. Springer, Heidelberg (1997). https://doi.org/10.1007/BFb0052259

6. Boyar, J., Matthews, P., Peralta, R.: Logic minimization techniques with applications to cryptology. J. Cryptol. **26**(2), 280–312 (2013)

7. Chase, M., et al.: The picnic signature algorithm: specification version 2.1 (2019). https://github.com/Microsoft/Picnic/blob/master/spec/spec-v2.1.pdf. Accessed 3 May 2019

8. Chase, M., et al.: The picnic signature scheme (2019). https://microsoft.github.io/Picnic/. Submission to NIST Post-Quantum Cryptography project

9. Chase, M., et al.: Post-quantum zero-knowledge and signatures from symmetric-key primitives. In: Thuraisingham et al. [21], pp. 1825–1842

10. Daemen, J., Rijmen, V.: AES proposal: rijndael (1999). https://web.archive.org/web/20070203204845/csrc.nist.gov/CryptoToolkit/aes/rijndael/Rijndael.pdf. Accessed 3 May 2019

11. Damgård, I., Geisler, M., Krøigaard, M., Nielsen, J.B.: Asynchronous multiparty computation: theory and implementation. In: Jarecki, S., Tsudik, G. (eds.) PKC 2009. LNCS, vol. 5443, pp. 160–179. Springer, Heidelberg (2009). https://doi.org/10.1007/978-3-642-00468-1_10

12. Damgård, I., Keller, M.: Secure multiparty AES. In: Sion, R. (ed.) FC 2010. LNCS, vol. 6052, pp. 367–374. Springer, Heidelberg (2010). https://doi.org/10.1007/978-3-642-14577-3_31

13. Damgård, I., Keller, M., Larraia, E., Miles, C., Smart, N.P.: Implementing AES via an actively/covertly secure dishonest-majority MPC protocol. In: Visconti, I., De Prisco, R. (eds.) SCN 2012. LNCS, vol. 7485, pp. 241–263. Springer, Heidelberg (2012). https://doi.org/10.1007/978-3-642-32928-9_14

14. Damgård, I., Pastro, V., Smart, N., Zakarias, S.: Multiparty computation from somewhat homomorphic encryption. In: Safavi-Naini, R., Canetti, R. (eds.) CRYPTO 2012. LNCS, vol. 7417, pp. 643–662. Springer, Heidelberg (2012). https://doi.org/10.1007/978-3-642-32009-5_38

15. Fiat, A., Shamir, A.: How to prove yourself: practical solutions to identification and signature problems. In: Odlyzko, A.M. (ed.) CRYPTO 1986. LNCS, vol. 263, pp. 186–194. Springer, Heidelberg (1987). https://doi.org/10.1007/3-540-47721-7_12

16. Giacomelli, I., Madsen, J., Orlandi, C.: ZKBoo: faster zero-knowledge for boolean circuits. In: Holz, T., Savage, S. (eds.) USENIX Security 2016, pp. 1069–1083. USENIX Association, Austin, 10–12 August 2016

17. Ishai, Y., Kushilevitz, E., Ostrovsky, R., Sahai, A.: Zero-knowledge from secure multiparty computation. In: Johnson, D.S., Feige, U. (eds.) 39th ACM STOC, pp. 21–30. ACM Press, San Diego, 11–13 June 2007

18. Katz, J., Kolesnikov, V., Wang, X.: Improved non-interactive zero knowledge with applications to post-quantum signatures. In: Lie, D., Mannan, M., Backes, M., Wang, X. (eds.) ACM CCS 2018, pp. 525–537. ACM Press, Toronto, 15–19 October 2018

19. Keller, M., Orsini, E., Rotaru, D., Scholl, P., Soria-Vazquez, E., Vivek, S.: Faster secure multi-party computation of AES and DES using lookup tables. In: Gollmann, D., Miyaji, A., Kikuchi, H. (eds.) ACNS 2017. LNCS, vol. 10355, pp. 229–249. Springer, Cham (2017). https://doi.org/10.1007/978-3-319-61204-1_12

20. National Insitute of Standards and Technology: Post-Quantum Cryptography project (2016). https://csrc.nist.gov/projects/post-quantum-cryptography. Accessed 3 May 2019
21. Thuraisingham, B.M., Evans, D., Malkin, T., Xu, D. (eds.): ACM CCS 2017. ACM Press, Dallas, 31 October– 2 November 2017

Towards Practical GGM-Based PRF
from (Module-)Learning-with-Rounding

Chitchanok Chuengsatiansup[1](✉) and Damien Stehlé[2](✉)

[1] Inria and ENS de Lyon, Lyon, France
chitchanok.chuengsatiansup@ens-lyon.org
[2] ENS de Lyon, Laboratoire LIP (U. Lyon, CNRS, ENSL, INRIA, UCBL),
Lyon, France
damien.stehle@ens-lyon.fr

Abstract. We investigate the efficiency of a (module-)LWR-based PRF built using the GGM design. Our construction enjoys the security proof of the GGM construction and the (module-)LWR hardness assumption which is believed to be post-quantum secure. We propose GGM-based PRFs from PRGs with larger ratio of output to input. This reduces the number of PRG invocations which improves the PRF performance and reduces the security loss in the GGM security reduction. Our construction bridges the gap between practical and provably secure PRFs. We demonstrate the efficiency of our construction by providing parameters achieving at least 128-bit post-quantum security and optimized implementations utilizing AVX2 vector instructions. Our PRF requires, on average, only 39.4 cycles per output byte.

Keywords: Pseudorandom function · Post-quantum security · (Module-)learning-with-rounding · Efficient implementation · Karatsuba multiplication

1 Introduction

A pseudorandom function (PRF) is a keyed function whose outputs are pseudorandom, i.e., no probabilistic polynomial-time adversary can distinguish, with non-negligible advantage, between the outputs of the pseudorandom function for chosen inputs and those of a truly random function. The pseudorandom function should also be efficiently and deterministically computable.

Pseudorandom functions are essential tools in designing protocols. PRFs are used as building blocks in many cryptographic primitives especially in symmetric-key cryptography, for example, message authentication codes and block ciphers.

This work was supported in part by BPI-France in the context of the national project RISQ (P141580), by the European Union PROMETHEUS project (Horizon 2020 Research and Innovation Program, grant 780701).

© Springer Nature Switzerland AG 2020
K. G. Paterson and D. Stebila (Eds.): SAC 2019, LNCS 11959, pp. 693–713, 2020.
https://doi.org/10.1007/978-3-030-38471-5_28

Banerjee, Peikert and Rosen (BPR) [7] proposed theoretical provably-secure constructions of pseudorandom functions based on conjectured hard learning-with-error lattice problems and "rounded-subset products". They also introduced a "derandomization" technique in order to generate the error terms deterministically. Despite interesting proofs and new techniques, the main drawback of their constructions is that the parameters are too large for practicality.

Later on, Banerjee, Brenner, Leurent, Peikert and Rosen [6] proposed concrete and practical instantiations of PRFs called "SPRING" (for subset-product with rounding over a ring), which are based on the BPR design [7]. However, SPRING instantiations [6] do not adhere to the parameters suggested by the security proof of the BPR design, namely, they relax the condition requiring the modulus q to be exponentially large in the PRF input length ℓ. More precisely, they use a very small modulus q to obtain good performance.

Even though it has been stated in [6] (and also referred to the original comments in BPR [7]) that the exponentially large q might be a proof artifact, SPRING instantiations do not inherit the security guarantees from BPR [7]. Those instantiations can be viewed as heuristic. If SPRING [6] had set parameters according to the proofs in [7], it would have resulted in a huge performance penalty.

In this work, we investigate the practicality of the pseudorandom function construction of Goldreich, Goldwasser, and Micali (GGM) [22] and show that the GGM-based PRF can lead to a reasonably efficient scheme enjoying a proof under a reasonable assumption. Note that the GGM construction is elementary; it can be constructed from any length-doubling pseudorandom generator (PRG) and can be depicted as a binary tree. However, there is a significant disadvantage with this construction, namely, it requires ℓ *sequential* invocations to the underlying PRG for input length ℓ which corresponds to the number of levels in the binary tree. The reason why it is not possible to parallelize between different level of the tree is that one needs the output of the PRG at level i to be used as the input of the PRG at level $i + 1$. For many applications (in particular when used as building components of advanced cryptographic primitives), this can be a significant drawback. For this reason, the BPR construction and follow-up works do not rely on the GGM framework.

Even though the sequential invocation can be viewed as a crucial disadvantage, we can use this construction in applications which evaluate PRF using consecutive inputs such as in a counter mode. In such a case, the average number of invocations to the underlying PRG is approximately only 2 (as opposed to ℓ in the worst case). The reason why the number of invocations can be very low is that we do not always need to traverse the tree from the root to one of the leaves; we may backtrack only one level up. Recall the GGM construction: we use only half of the PRG's output for the next input. If the current evaluation uses the left half, then the next consecutive evaluation would use the right half which has already been computed, thus involving no PRG invocation at all.

To construct an efficient and post-quantum secure PRG, we rely on the hardness assumption of the (module-)learning-with-rounding ((module-)LWR) problem. We demonstrate the practicality of our lattice-based PRF by deriving parameters achieving at least 128-bit security and providing optimized implementations together with timing results.

1.1 Tools and Techniques

Our intention is to construct an efficient post-quantum secure PRF based on a provably secure construction and broadly studied conjectures which are believed to be hard problems. The main tools we used are the GGM construction and the hardness assumption of the (module-)LWR problem. Other tools that we used to obtain fast implementations are Karatsuba's multiplication and the vector instructions (AVX2). In the following, we briefly explain how we utilized and combined these tools.

GGM Construction. One of the main reasons that we chose the GGM construction is its simplicity: the construction requires only a length-doubling PRG and can be depicted using a binary tree. Moreover the GGM construction has a rigorous security proof, namely, so long as the underlying PRG is secure, the GGM-based PRF construction is secure. This means that we can restrict to building a secure length-doubling PRG.

We further observed that the *binary* tree in the GGM construction corresponds to the length-*doubling* requirement for the PRG. However, there is no restriction why we should use a *binary* tree. For example, we could use a *ternary* tree and use a length-*tripling* PRG. We could even push further and use a *4-ary* tree with a length-*quadrupling* PRG. In this work, we generalize to an ω-ary tree with a length-ω-fold PRG. Using higher expansion rate is the main technique in our construction to obtain a lower-depth tree, fewer number of calls to the underlying PRG, and improvements in the efficiency.

(M)LWR. Note that the security of the GGM-based PRFs relies on the security of the underlying PRG. Therefore, the next question that we need to answer is what to use for the secure expansion-rate-ω PRG. Note also that computing this PRG should be efficient because the performance of the PRF heavily depends on the performance of the underlying PRG.

Since we aim at constructing a post-quantum secure PRF, lattice-based constructions seem to be the most appealing especially in terms of efficiency. For this reason, we decided to rely on the (module-)LWR hardness assumption. Informally, the small-secret variant of the (module-)LWR problem states that multiplying a uniformly random matrix $\mathbf{A}$ with a "small" uniformly random vector $\mathbf{s}$ then performing rounding operations leads to a resulting vector that looks uniformly random, i.e., indistinguishable, with non-negligible probability, from a truly uniform vector.

Note that there also exist other variants such as ring-LWR, learning-with-errors (LWE), ring-LWE, and module-LWE. The main reason that we chose to focus on (module-)LWR variants instead of the ring variants is the flexibility in the parameter setting. Note that with the plain LWR, it allows even better adjustment of parameters and involves no polynomial reduction. However, one drawback of the plain LWR is that it requires rather huge memory for the public parameter, i.e., $\mathbf{A} \in \mathbb{Z}_q^{n \times n}$. For the completeness, we include the plain LWR variant in Appendix A.

We could have decided to construct the PRG relying on the hardness assumption of the (module-)LWE problem (instead of the (module-)LWR one). However, our analysis suggested that using learning-with-rounding provides more efficiency in terms of parameter selection and implementation. Since the input to the PRG (in our context) is the secret vector $\mathbf{s}$, if we were using (module-)LWE we would also need the error vector $\mathbf{e}$ as part of the input. This means that the output of the matrix-vector multiplication $\mathbf{As}$ plus an error vector $\mathbf{e}$ needs to provide enough bits to be used as the next input. In case we use (module-)LWR (which we do), we only need that the output has enough bits for the secret vector $\mathbf{s}$. We do not need the error vector $\mathbf{e}$ because we use deterministic rounding instead. This also means that we can set our parameters slightly smaller. Moreover, the rounding operation is simply cutting bits; this operation is arguably easier to implement than generating and adding errors.

Karatsuba's Multiplication. Our construction with module-LWR consists of matrix-vector multiplication and rounding operations. Since rounding is simply ignoring bits and can be done relatively fast, the bottleneck operation is the matrix-vector multiplication which is basically polynomial multiplication. Since we also aim at having efficient implementations, we wish to use a polynomial multiplication algorithm which gives better time complexity than that of the schoolbook multiplication. One of commonly used multiplications is the number-theoretic transform (NTT). However, this multiplication requires an NTT-friendly prime which we view as quite a strong restriction. Therefore, we opt for more flexible multiplication algorithms such as Karatsuba and Toom-Cook.

The reason we choose Karatsuba's multiplication is that it outperforms Toom-Cook's multiplication for low to medium degree polynomials. This suggests that we should use Karatsuba's multiplication up to certain degrees and then switch to using Toom-Cook's multiplication. In other words, Toom-Cook should be used in combination with Karatsuba, but we may not need to switch to using Toom-Cook. To keep our implementations simple and flexible, we decided to ignore Toom-Cook and use only Karatsuba's multiplication.

Table 1 compares estimated multiplication costs of our instantiations, where we use Karatsuba's multiplication, with (extrapolations of) previous work, where we assume using NTT for polynomial multiplication. In this cost estimation for our Karatsuba's multiplication, we decompose polynomial degree n down to 16 then we switch to the schoolbook method for the actual multiplication.

1.2   Optimized Implementations

We analyzed the parameters of the (module-)LWR problem together with the expansion rate ω. We derived parameters achieving at least 128-bit security in the quantum core model [3]. We provide optimized implementations[1] of our PRF construction in which we also use vector instructions to obtain better performance. The timing results (see Sect. 5 for more details) show that evaluating PRF in a counter mode using our construction requires, on average, only 39.4 cycles per output byte.

Table 1. Extrapolated cost estimation of lattice-based PRFs with different underlying hardness assumptions for 128-bit security

schemes	assumptions	mod	key	pp.	mul
SPRING-BCH [6]	R ⌊sub prod⌉	257	16396	129	115
SPRING-CRT [6]	R ⌊sub prod⌉	514	18444	145	115
Our scheme, M	MLWR, GGM	2^{16}	192	24576	1991
Our scheme	LWR, GGM	2^{16}	200	2944000	2944
[7] + AKPW13, R [5]	RLWR, GGM	$> 2^{40}$	655360	5120	5243*
BPR12, syn, R [7]	RLWR, syn	$>2^{128}$	163840	–	10486*
BPR12, direct, R [7]	R ⌊sub prod⌉	$>2^{128}$	2097152	16384	10486*
[7] + AKPW13 [5]	LWR, GGM	$> 2^{40}$	313600000	3500	250880*
BPR12, direct [7]	⌊sub prod⌉	$>2^{128}$	1003520000	11200	501760*
BPR12, GGM [7]	LWR, GGM	$>2^{128}$	11200	31360000	1003520*
BPR12, GGM, R [7]	RLWR, GGM	$>2^{128}$	16384	67108864	42949673*
BPR12, syn [7]	LWR, syn	$>2^{128}$	74097496	–	351232000*

In the first two columns, abbreviations 'syn', 'R', 'M', '⌊sub prod⌉', 'MLWR' mean 'synthesizer', 'ring', 'module', 'rounded subset product' and 'module-LWR' respectively. Key and public parameter (pp.) are of size in bytes. Multiplication (mul) in the last column considers only the main matrix-matrix or matrix-vector product; the cost is shown in terms of thousand 16-bit-by-16-bit multiplication; asterisk ($*$) means extrapolated cost. Since we focus on constructions which provide security level at least 2^{128}, we extrapolate the cost of BPR-based schemes using dimension $n = 1024$ for RLWR (to allow NTT) and $n = 700$ for LWR. Note that in this comparison table we provide BPR-based schemes two advantages: (1) we consider modulus $q = 2^{128}$ (resp. 2^{40}) while it should be much more than these values for the proofs to be applicable; (2) for the synthesizer variant, we consider that all moduli are the same and take the smallest one. We do not include [12] in the comparison because it is a PRG not a PRF.

2   Preliminaries

We write vectors in bold lowercase letters and matrices in bold uppercase letters. We write log for $\log_2$ unless specified otherwise. In the context of distributions, we denote U a uniform distribution. We define the rounding function $\lfloor \cdot \rceil_p :$ $\mathbb{Z}_q \longrightarrow \mathbb{Z}_p$ as $\lfloor x \rceil_p = \lfloor x \cdot (p/q) \rfloor$ where $q > p \in \mathbb{Z}$. When applied to vectors, it means applied componentwise.

---

[1] Available at https://github.com/BeJade/mlwr-prf

2.1 GGM Construction

Goldreich, Goldwasser and Micali [22] proposed a method to construct a PRF from any length-doubling pseudorandom generator, i.e., expansion rate 2. To describe their construction, let G be a length-doubling pseudorandom generator where G_0 and G_1 denote the first half and the second half of G's output respectively, i.e, $G(k) = G_0(k)||G_1(k)$ where $|G_0(k)| = |G_1(k)| = \ell$. PRF with a key k and ℓ-bit input x, $F_k : \{0,1\}^\ell \to \{0,1\}^\ell$ is defined as:

$$F_k(x_1 x_2 \cdots x_\ell) = G_{x_\ell}(\cdots (G_{x_2}(G_{x_1}(k))) \cdots).$$

This construction can be depicted as a binary tree whose depth corresponds to the input length ℓ. The root of the tree gets the input key k as an input for the PRG evaluation whereas each left-child node gets G_0 from its parent to use as an input and each right-child node gets G_1. This process continues as many times as the input length. Evaluating PRF with an input x is done by looking at each bit of x and traversing the tree from the root to one of the leaves by going down to the left subtree if the bit is 0 and going down to the right subtree if the bit is 1. Note that we do not have to compute and store the entire binary tree; we only need to compute PRG along the path from the root to the corresponding leaf. Figure 1 depicts the above construction for $\ell = 3$. Solid lines show the path to compute $F_k(010)$.

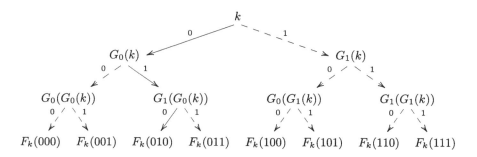

Fig. 1. GGM construction

Theorem 1 (GGM construction, adapted from [22,25]). *If G is a length-doubling ϵ-indistinguishable pseudorandom generator, then the construction outlined above is a $qd\epsilon$-indistinguishable pseudorandom function where q denotes the number of queries and d denotes the tree's depth.*

2.2 Hardness Assumptions

The security of cryptographic primitives usually relates to hardness assumptions that certain mathematical problems are difficult to solves. In this subsection, we recall definitions of hardness assumptions that we use in our constructions.

Definition 1 (Learning-with-errors (LWE)). *Let $q \geq 2$ be a modulus, m and n be dimensions such that $m \geq n \geq 1$, and χ be a distribution over $\mathbb{Z}$. The* learning-with-errors *problem is to distinguish, with non-negligible probability, between the following two distributions: $(\mathbf{A}, \mathbf{As} + \mathbf{e})$ and $U(\mathbb{Z}_q^{m \times n} \times \mathbb{Z}_q^m)$, where $\mathbf{A} \sim U(\mathbb{Z}_q^{m \times n})$, $\mathbf{s} \sim U(\mathbb{Z}_q^n)$ and $\mathbf{e} \sim \chi^m$.*

The LWE assumption states that the LWE problem for certain choices of parameters (q, m, n, χ) is hard for all probabilistic polynomial time algorithms. The LWE problem has been extended to ring-LWE by Lyubashevsky, Peikert and Regev [34] where the integer ring $\mathbb{Z}$ has been replaced by a polynomial ring $\mathcal{R}$. Since LWE and ring-LWE are very similar except for using different rings and vector dimensions, these problems were later on generalized by Brakerski, Gentry and Vaikuntanathan [13] to what they called a *general learning with errors problem*. Langlois and Stehlé [32] analyzed the hardness and explained the usefulness of this variant where they called it module-LWE. In this paper, we also use the term *module*.

Definition 2 (Module-LWE, adapted from [13]). *Let m and k be integer dimensions, let modulus $q \geq 2$ be a prime integer, let $\mathcal{R} = \mathbb{Z}[x]/(x^d + 1)$ where d is a power of two, let $\mathcal{R}_q = \mathcal{R}/q\mathcal{R}$, and let χ be a distribution over $\mathcal{R}$. The* module-LWE *problem is to distinguish, with non-negligible probability, between the following two distributions: $(\mathbf{A}, \mathbf{As} + \mathbf{e})$ and $U(\mathcal{R}_q^{m \times k} \times \mathcal{R}_q^m)$, where $\mathbf{A} \sim U(\mathcal{R}_q^{m \times k})$, $\mathbf{s} \sim U(\mathcal{R}_q^k)$ and $\mathbf{e} \sim \chi^m$.*

Banerjee, Peikert and Rosen [7] introduce the learning-with-rounding (LWR) problem whose error terms in the LWE problem are replaced by a deterministic rounding process. With some conditions on the modulus and the dimensions, they also proved that the LWR problem is as hard as the LWE problem. There also exist ring and module versions of LWR where the problems are defined analogously.

Definition 3 (Module-LWR, adapted from [7,13,32]). *Let m and k be integer dimensions, let moduli $q \geq p \geq 2$ be integers, let $\mathcal{R} = \mathbb{Z}[x]/(x^d + 1)$ where d is a power of two, and let $\mathcal{R}_q = \mathcal{R}/q\mathcal{R}$. The* module-LWR *problem is to distinguish, with non-negligible probability, between the following two distributions: $(\mathbf{A}, \lfloor \mathbf{As} \rceil_p)$ and $U(\mathcal{R}_q^{m \times k}) \times \lfloor U(\mathcal{R}_q^m) \rceil_p$, where $\mathbf{A} \sim U(\mathcal{R}_q^{m \times k})$ and $\mathbf{s} \sim U(\mathcal{R}_q^k)$.*

Note that the distribution $\lfloor U(\mathcal{R}_q^m) \rceil_p$ may seem inconvenient. However, by taking $p|q$, this distribution becomes identical to $U(\mathcal{R}_p^m)$ which is easier to work with.

We would like to make a remark that there also exist different (module-)LWR variants depending on the distributions of the secret $\mathbf{s}$ and the round-off bits. The variant that we use is the one with small secret where the distribution of the secret $\mathbf{s}$ is consistent with the round-off bits.

3 Our Construction

We aim at constructing an efficient and secure lattice-based PRF. Our construction is based on two main building blocks, namely, the GGM construction and the (module-)learning-with-rounding problem [7]. The former is used for constructing pseudorandom functions while the latter is used for the underlying hardness assumption of pseudorandom generators.

This section explains how we combine the aforementioned two building blocks to achieve a competitive performance PRF. We first start by explaining how we cope with the sequential nature of the GGM construction. Then we explain choices for the PRG and give justifications why we decided to work with the (module-)LWR. Finally, we give the outline of our construction.

3.1 Lower-Depth GGM-based PRF

Recall that the GGM-based pseudorandom function construction requires a length-doubling pseudorandom generator, and the construction can be depicted using a binary tree. Each node (except for the leaves) of the tree corresponds to an evaluation of a PRG whose input is from half of its parent's PRG output, i.e., front half for a left-child node, and back half for a right-child node. For the root of the tree, its input is the key k of the PRF.

Evaluating the GGM-based PRF is done by looking at each bit of the input x and traversing the tree from the root to one of the leaves by, say, if the current bit is 0 then go to the left subtree, if the current bit is 1 then go to the right subtree. One thing to be noticed is that the depth of the tree corresponds to the length of the PRF input, i.e., an ℓ-bit-input PRF implies a binary tree of depth ℓ.

Observe that the performance of the GGM construction heavily relies on the number of calls to the PRG which corresponds to the input length ℓ and, thus, the depth of the *binary* tree. The ℓ-sequential call is a major drawback of this construction, and it is unavoidable due to the nature of the construction, namely, one needs to traverse the tree level by level since the output from the previous level is used as the input to the next level. Our goal is to address this drawback.

Our approach is to generalize to using an ω-*ary tree* instead of a binary tree. This affects the original construction in three ways. First, we do not merely look at a single bit when we traverse the tree; instead, we examine $\log \omega$ bits at a time. Second, the tree's depth decreases to $\ell / \log \omega$ levels, meaning that the number of invocations to the underlying PRG also decreases to $\ell / \log \omega$ calls. By reducing the depth of the tree, this also reduces the security loss in the security reduction of the security proof of the GGM construction. Third, the construction now requires the output of the PRG to be ω times longer than the input length (not just length-doubling as in the original construction). Note however that this should not be viewed as a severe penalty because it is achievable in practice; we give a list of possible parameters, explain a concrete implementation and show timing results in Sect. 5.

In general, we may set ω to be any positive integer greater than 1, and if we set $\omega = 2$ then we obtain the original GGM construction. The construction works best when ω is a power of two, i.e., when $\log \omega$ is an integer. Note that we do not impose on a condition that ℓ is divisible by $\log \omega$. If ℓ is divisible by $\log \omega$, then it results in a complete ω-ary tree and every call to PRG has a full

ω choices of which part of the output to be used as the next input. Otherwise, the tree is not complete where nodes at the level before the leaves have about $2^{\ell}/\omega^{\lceil \ell/\log \omega \rceil - 1}$ child nodes.

Even though our construction does not remove the nature of the sequential invocations to the underlying PRG, we significantly decrease the number of calls (the tree's depth). That is, instead of requiring ℓ sequential calls for length ℓ input, our construction requires only $\ell/\log \omega$ calls. Notice that the asymptotic bound remains the same for the original GGM and our construction. However, our construction, indeed, helps improve the performance in practice (see Sect. 5 for more details on concrete implementations and timing results) since the number of calls to PRG decreases at least by a factor of 1.5.

3.2 (M)LWR-based PRG

Another component that we need in our construction is a secure PRG with the output length ω times larger than its input length. Since we target an efficient and post-quantum secure PRF construction, one natural candidate is the lattice-based cryptography. Therefore, we consider constructing PRG based on the learning-with-errors (LWE) [43] and the learning-with-rounding (LWR) [7] problems.

Recall that the LWE problem involves computing $(\mathbf{A}, \mathbf{b} = \langle \mathbf{A}, \mathbf{s} \rangle + \mathbf{e})$ where $\mathbf{A}$ is public, $\mathbf{s}$ is secret, and $\mathbf{e}$ is small error generated randomly. In case of the LWR problem, the process of adding small error $\mathbf{e}$ is replaced by deterministic rounding. The LWR problem was introduced in [7] where the authors also introduced a lattice-based PRF whose construction is based on a pseudorandom synthesizer [37–39] which requires a deterministic function. This requirement is opposite to the nature of LWE where errors are generated randomly. For this reason, LWR was used in [7]. In case of our construction, both LWE and LWR are possible. We use LWR for efficiency, i.e., to decrease the amount of randomness required (see below and Sect. 5). Therefore, we want to emphasize that the reason we use LWR slightly differs from that of [7].

To reduce the memory required for the secret vector $\mathbf{s} \in \mathbb{Z}_q^n$ and the public matrix $\mathbf{A} \in \mathbb{Z}_q^{m \times n}$, we consider using module-LWR [13,32] instead of LWR, i.e., using $\mathbf{s} \in \mathcal{R}_q^{n'}$ and $\mathbf{A} \in \mathcal{R}_q^{m' \times n'}$. We could have used ring-LWR [35], but we chose to work with modules because of the flexibility. As explained in [11] and [18]; there is only one ring to implement, and adjusting security is done by adjusting the dimension of the matrix. We explain our construction using LWR in Appendix A. In this section, we focus on our construction using module-LWR.

Until now, we have not yet mentioned how to obtain the length-ω-fold-output PRG from module-LWR. We recall our module-LWR-based construction then we explain how to satisfy the required length condition. In our construction, except for the initial input for the first call to the PRG, the subsequent calls use the output from previous calls. The output length condition requires that the number of bits of $\lfloor \mathbf{As} \rfloor_p$ must be at least ω times larger than $\mathbf{s}$ which is the input for the next call to the module-LWR-based PRG. We claim that this requirement is indeed achievable.

To see this, recall that the expansion rate r is the ratio between the output and the input length of the PRG (e.g., length-doubling PRG has $r = 2$) and we want $r \geq \omega$ for our construction. Let $q \geq p \geq 2$ be integers, let $\mathcal{R} = (\mathbb{Z}[x]/(x^d + 1))$, let $\mathbf{A} \in \mathcal{R}_q^{m \times n}$, and let $\mathbf{s} \in \mathcal{R}_{\log q - \log p}^n$ (i.e., $q' = \log q - \log p$). Note that each coefficient of $\mathbf{s}$ has the same magnitude as the round-off bits. The input $\mathbf{s}$ has size $nd(\log q - \log p)$, and the output $\lfloor \mathbf{As} \rfloor_p$ has size $md \log p$. Thus, we need to ensure that $\frac{md \log p}{nd(\log q - \log p)} \geq r$. One concrete example (which we also use in our implementation, see Sect. 5) to achieve $r \geq 16$ is to set parameters as follows: $q=2^{16}, d=256, n=3, m=16$ and $p=2^{12}$. This gives $\frac{16 \cdot 256 \cdot \log 2^{12}}{3 \cdot 256(\log 2^{16} - \log 2^{12})} \geq 16 = r$. We refer to Tables 2 and 4 for other possible parameters.

3.3   Construction Outline

In this subsection, we explain our efficient lattice-based PRF (see Appendix A for the LWR variant). Recall that the input to the PRF is a key k and a string x of length ℓ while the output is a pseudorandom string z. A public parameter in our construction is $\mathbf{A} \in \mathcal{R}_q^{m \times n}$.

Since our construction is more efficient when $\log \omega = \tilde{\omega}$ is an integer, we assume from now on that it is the case. Construction 1 outlines our PRF. We divide the construction into three parts, namely, pre-computation, main loop, and outputting. In the following, we explain each part in more details.

Construction 1. PRF from module-LWR

Input: PRF's key $k = \{0,1\}^*$ and a bit string $x = \{0,1\}^\ell$
Output: Pseudorandom string $z = \{0,1\}^{\ell'}$

1: $\mathbf{t} = \mathsf{Random}(k)$ $\left.\right\}$ Pre-computation
2: $\mathbf{s} = \mathsf{Reformat}(\mathbf{t})$
3: **for** $i = 0$ **to** $\ell - 1$ **step by** $\tilde{\omega}$ **do**
4:     $c = x[\tilde{\omega}i]\ x[\tilde{\omega}i+1]\ \ldots\ x[\tilde{\omega}i+\tilde{\omega}-1]$ ▷ View $\tilde{\omega}$ bits as number in $[0, \omega-1]$
5:     $\mathbf{t} = \mathbf{A}_c \cdot \mathbf{s}$ ▷ Multiply row c of $\mathbf{A}$ to $\mathbf{s}$
6:     $\mathbf{t} = \lfloor \mathbf{t} \rfloor$
7:     $\mathbf{s} = \mathsf{Reformat}(\mathbf{t})$ ▷ Reformat into $\mathbf{s}$
8: **end for**
9: **for** $i = 0$ **to** $m - 1$ **do**
10:     $\mathbf{t} = \mathbf{A}_i \cdot \mathbf{s}$
11:     $\mathbf{t} = \lfloor \mathbf{t} \rfloor$
12:     $z = z \| \mathbf{t}$ ▷ Concatenate output extracting from $\mathbf{t}$
13: **end for**
14: **return** z

Pre-computation. This part handles (1) generating randomness from the key k, i.e., $\mathsf{Random}(k)$, for example, using extendable output functions, and (2) reformatting into the vector $\mathbf{s}$, i.e., $\mathsf{Reformat}(\mathbf{t})$, for example, setting each 4 bits of $\mathbf{t}$ to each coefficient of $\mathbf{s}$. Note that these can be pre-computed per secret key k. For instance, evaluating the same function $F_k(\cdot)$ at different points, say, x and y, e.g., $F_k(x)$ and $F_k(y)$. Note that we could reformat k directly into $\mathbf{s}$ without feeding it as an input to generate random bits, i.e., calling Reformat($\mathbf{t}$) directly without calling Random(k). However, we have Random(k) for two reasons: first, in case the input k is not random, which would affect the security analysis of the underlying module-LWR problem; second, in case the input k does not have the preferred length, which would be problematic if it is too short. If the input k is already random and has long enough length, then Random(k) can be skipped. Nevertheless, we still perform Reformat($\mathbf{t}$) to convert random bits into a right format for the following steps.

Main Loop. This part handles the main loop which involves calling the underlying module-LWR-based PRG. The number of calls depends on the width of the tree (ω) which is one of several parameters to be optimized. In the construction outline, we present a general construction that is not specific to any particular width. In Sect. 5, we give a concrete example where we define all parameters including the tree's width ω.

One optimization in our construction is that each iteration involves a vector-vector multiplication and not a matrix-vector multiplication. We observed that we only need m/ω rows of the matrix $\mathbf{A}$ to multiply with the vector $\mathbf{s}$. This value m/ω can be as small as one, which is the case for our concrete implementation. Therefore, we assume that we select only one row of the matrix $\mathbf{A}$. Choosing which row is done by viewing $\tilde{\omega}$ bits of the input x as a number between 0 and $\omega - 1$ (line 4 in Construction 1) then selecting the corresponding row c (line 5 in Construction 1).

After having multiplied the selected row of the matrix $\mathbf{A}$ with the vector $\mathbf{s}$, before moving to the next $\tilde{\omega}$ bits of ℓ, we call Reformat($\mathbf{t}$) to extract bits from $\mathbf{t}$ and assign to $\mathbf{s}$ to be used in the following iteration. These steps are analogous to selecting front half ($G_0(\cdot)$) or back half ($G_1(\cdot)$) of the PRG for the next PRG's call in the original GGM construction.

Outputting. This part handles the output of the PRF. Before we reformat the output, we perform the final m iterations of vector-vector multiplications. In contrast to previous iterations where we multiply only m/ω rows of $\mathbf{A}$ with $\mathbf{s}$, for the output we multiply all m rows, i.e., the entire matrix $\mathbf{A}$. This has the advantage of significantly increasing the length of the PRF output. The final task of this part is to concatenate all the results and turn them into the desire format.

4   Security Analysis

The high-level structure of our PRF construction follows the GGM construction whose security relies on the security of the underlying PRG. Therefore, we mainly analyze the security of the (module-)LWR problem which we use as the expansion-rate-ω PRG in our lattice-based PRF construction. Note that in our generalized

GGM construction, it is possible that the tree's depth is lower than in the original one. For this reason, we also examine if this may incur any loss in the security reduction of the GGM construction.

4.1 GGM

Since our construction is essentially the generalization of the GGM construction, Theorem 1 also applies to our setting. Note that in the original GGM construction, the tree's depth corresponds to the bitlength ℓ of the input string to the PRF. In our generalized GGM construction, the tree's depth corresponds to $\ell/\tilde{\omega}$ where $2^{\tilde{\omega}}$ is the tree's width. If $\tilde{\omega} = 1$ then we recover the original GGM construction. This means that the tree's depth in the generalized GGM construction is no greater than in the original construction.

4.2 LWE and (M)LWR

Our construction relies on the hardness assumption of the (module-)LWR problem where each sample is a vector whose elements are from a polynomial ring (or an integer ring in case of the plain LWR variant). It can be seen that the module-LWR problem provides more structure than LWR. However, since there are no known attacks that exploit such additional structures (of either ring or module), we did not make use of the module structure in our security analysis.

In fact, we analyzed the hardness of the (module-)LWR problem as the LWE one where we consider the process of adding errors as being replaced by the process of rounding off bits. A reduction from the LWE to the LWR problem was first given by Banerjee, Peikert and Rosen [7], then further improved by Alwen, Krenn, Pietrzak and Wichs [5], Bogdanov, Guo, Masny, Richelson and Rosen [10], and Alperin-Sheriff and Apon [4]. We refer to those articles for more details.

To solve the LWE problem (see [3] for more details), the state-of-the-art algorithm is BKZ [16,44] and there are two variants, namely, the primal and the dual attacks. We estimate security for both variants and take the minimum between the two. The BKZ algorithm reduces a lattice basis by calling an SVP oracle with a smaller dimension b where there are two different approaches, namely, enumeration and sieving. We explore both approaches and take the minimum between the two. We estimate the complexity of solving SVP by using $2^{0.292b}$ as the classical and $2^{0.265b}$ as the quantum cost estimations [8,11,28–30,36,40]. We use Kyber's script [11] as a main tool to perform security analysis where our notion of bit security reflects security of the underlying LWE problem.

5   Implementation

To illustrate the practicality of our construction, we implemented two variants of our lower-depth GGM-based PRF, one with module-LWR and another one with LWR. In this section, we focus on the module-LWR variant and explain how we designed our implementation, derived parameters achieving at least 128-bit security, and optimized our implementation. (The script to estimate the security level and our implementation are publicly available at https://github.com/BeJade/mlwr-prf.) We also show the timing results of the two variants of our implementations and compared with previous work. Note that details on the LWR variant can be found in Appendix A.

5.1 Design

The goal of this subsection is to describe how we chose to implement each component in our construction. We give justifications of choices made and explain why we think they best suit our optimized implementation.

Polynomial Multiplication. In addition to the fundamental schoolbook multiplication, there exist other (polynomial) multiplication algorithms which achieve faster time complexity, for example, NTT, Toom-Cook, Karatsuba. The main reason that we cannot use NTT is that it requires modulus q to be of the form $q \equiv 1 \bmod 2n$ where n is the degree of the polynomial. With this condition, it rules out even moduli q.

We could have used Toom-Cook (to split degree-n polynomial into k degree-n/k polynomials) which can be considered as a generalization of Karatsuba ($k = 2$, i.e., splitting degree-n polynomial into 2 degree-$n/2$ polynomials). However, our analysis shows that Karatsuba's algorithm works better for low to medium degree polynomials where the switching point between Karatsuba and Toom-Cook is unclear. To keep our implementation simple and reusable in case of updating parameters, we decided to use Karatsuba's algorithm.

To multiply degree-n polynomials f and g, we start by splitting f into f_0 and f_1 each of degree $n/2$ (similarly for g). We repeat this splitting until we reach polynomials of degree 16, then we switch to using the schoolbook multiplication. We chose the cut-off at degree 16 because AVX2 instructions allow 16-way vectorization.

Karatsuba's algorithm is very well suited for vectorization. To see this, recall (refined) Karatsuba's identity [9]:

$$(f_0 + x^{n/2}f_1)(g_0 + x^{n/2}g_1) = (1 - x^{n/2})(f_0g_0 - x^{n/2}f_1g_1) + x^{n/2}(f_0 + f_1)(g_0 + g_1).$$

Computing $f_0 + f_1$ is done by loading the first, say 16, coefficients of f_0 into one 16-way vector and the first 16 coefficients of f_1 into another vector then adding them together. Next, we load the next 16 coefficients of f_0 and f_1 and add them together. We repeat these steps for all coefficients of f_0 and f_1 (also for $g_0 + g_1$). Multiplying by $x^{n/2}$ corresponds to working with coefficients at index $+n/2$. Note that when computing f_ig_j, the actual multiplication is performed once the degree of f_i and g_i reaches 16 and is computed using the schoolbook multiplication. We also vectorize this schoolbook multiplication by multiplying 16 pairs at once since there are enough independent multiplications to choose from. For example, for $d = 256, n = 3$, there are $3^4 = 81$ 16-by-16 multiplications.

Randomness Generation. Our construction requires randomness generation for deriving the initial vector $\mathbf{s}$. We decided to use hash functions with the extendable output function SHAKE-128 (standardized in FIPS 202 [41]). The reason why we chose SHAKE-128 is that it has received a lot of cryptanalysis at least in the SHA-3 competition. Another advantage in using SHAKE-128 is that we can adapt some parts of the publicly available optimized AVX2 implementation from Kyber [11].

Note that deriving the vector $\mathbf{s}$ can be pre-computed *per key k*. In many scenarios, the same key k is used for different evaluations of input string x. This means that once the key k is known, deriving $\mathbf{s}$ can be pre-computed for each key k and stored it even before knowing x.

Rounding Operation. To round numbers from $\log q$ bits to $\log p$ bits, we simply remove $(\log q - \log p)$ least significant bits. In the implementations, we use logical operation **and** with 1 for the bits that we want to keep and with 0 for the bits that we want to discard. Since q and p are fixed, the pattern of ones and zeros used for this logical operation is also fixed. Therefore, we keep this masking pattern as a constant.

Value Extraction. We need to extract from PRG output only the part to be used as an input for the next PRG call. We begin with masking the corresponding part of the vector $\mathbf{t}$, namely, to round from $\log q$ bits to $\log p$ bits. This is done by the masking technique similar to the rounding operation. Then we rearrange the rounded values into new vectors $\mathbf{s}_i$. That is, we extract each $\log q - \log p$ bits from $\mathbf{t}$ and assign to each $s_{i,j}$ for $0 \le i < n$ and $0 \le j < d$.

5.2   Parameters

We recall notations and parameters in our construction. Let q be a modulus and p be a rounding parameter such that $q > p$ and $\log q = \log p + \log B$ where q, p, and B are power of two. Let $\mathcal{R} = \mathbb{Z}_q[x]/(x^d + 1)$. Let $\mathbf{A} \in \mathcal{R}_q^{m \times n}$ be a random public matrix. Let $\mathbf{s} \in \mathcal{R}_{\log B}^n$ be a small secret vector. We want parameter sets satisfying the expansion-rate-ω output length requirement and achieving at least 128-bit security for the underlying module-LWR problem.

Consider the length condition for the module-LWR-based PRG, the input is the vector $\mathbf{s} \in \mathcal{R}_{\log B}^n$ and the output is the rounded vector $\lfloor \mathbf{As} \rceil_p \in \mathcal{R}_p^m$. This means that the output size is $m \cdot d \cdot \log p$ and the input size is $n \cdot d \cdot (\log B)$. Therefore, the equations that we consider is:

$$m \cdot d \cdot \log p \ge \omega \cdot (n \cdot d \cdot (\log B))$$
$$m \cdot d \cdot (\log q - (\log B)) \ge \omega \cdot (n \cdot d \cdot (\log B))$$
$$m \cdot (\log q - (\log B)) \ge \omega \cdot (n \cdot (\log B)).$$

Note that we want $\omega \ge 2$, and the larger ω is the shallower the tree becomes.

We modified Kyber's script [11] to suit our setting and use it to estimate the security of the underlying module-LWR problem. In this security analysis, the major modification is that we use a uniform distribution instead of a binomial one. The conditions in which we search for good parameter sets for the module-LWR variant are as follows:

- $q = 2^{16}$, fixed;
- $\log B \in \{1, 2, 3, 4\}$;
- $d \in \{128, 256\}$;
- $n \in \{5, 6\}$ for $d = 128$ and $n = 3$ for $d = 256$;
- $m \in \{4, 8, 16, 32\}$.

Good parameters that achieve at least 128-bit security and $\omega \geq 2$ are listed in Table 2.

Table 2. Good parameters achieving at least 128-bit module-LWR security and the expansion-rate-ω condition

d	m	n	$\log B$	security	ω	mul	mem	depth	cost
128	4	5	4	145	2	69120	5120	128	8294400
128	4	6	2	131	4	41472	6144	64	2654208
128	16	5	4	133	8	69120	20480	43	2972160
128	32	5	4	133	16	69120	40960	32	2211840
256	4	3	4	167	4	62208	6144	64	3981312
256	8	3	4	167	8	62208	12288	43	2674944
256	16	3	4	167	16	62208	24576	32	1990656
256	32	3	4	167	32	62208	49152	26	1617408

We fix the modulus $q = 2^{16}$. Abbreviations 'mem' denotes the size in bytes of the matrix $\mathbf{A}$; 'depth' denotes the tree's depth; 'mul' denotes the multiplication cost per depth; and 'cost' $=$ mul $\times$ depth denotes the total multiplication cost for the full input length ℓ.

From Table 2, we observe that the module-LWR variant with $d = 256$ provides higher security (with larger gap) than what we target, i.e., 128 vs. 167. Using $d = 128$ allows better adjustment in terms of security level, i.e., 131–145 is closer to 128, and less memory usage to store the matrix $\mathbf{A}$. However, it comes with a trade-off of increasing the multiplication cost.

According to the possible parameter sets, it is debatable which one should be selected for the implementation. Smaller m allows less memory usage at the price of increasing multiplication cost and higher tree's depth. On the other hand, larger m allows larger expansion rate ω. We decided that we prioritize the runtime (multiplication cost) and chose the parameter set with the tree's depth power of two to aid implementation. Concretely, we chose the second to last row of Table 2 with the following parameters: $q = 2^{16}$, $d = 256$, $m = 16$, $n = 3$ log $B = 4$, and $\omega = 16$. This gives the (M)LWR security estimation of 167. If we consider the security loss due to multiple PRF evaluations, this parameter set allows up to 2^{34} PRF queries to still preserve 128-bit PRF security.

As for comparison to the LWR variant, we state here the parameter set that we use in our implementation and refer to Appendix A for more details. Since we want to be able to compare to our module-LWR implementation, we decided to use similar parameters, namely, same q and ω. Concretely, we use the following parameters: $q = 2^{16}$, $\omega = 16$, $n = 800$, $m = 1840$, and $\log B = 2$. This gives the (M)LWR security estimation of 131.

5.3   Performance

To demonstrate the efficiency of our lattice-based PRF, we implemented Construction 1 and Construction 2 (see Appendix A) with the parameters mentioned in the previous subsection. We measured the run time of our implementations in cycle counts which are the medians of 10000 executions obtained from an Intel Core i7-6600U (Skylake) with TurboBoost turned off running at 2.6 GHz. Generating the public parameter $\mathbf{A}$ (setup phase) costs 78815 cycles. The pre-computation part (generating randomness, i.e., Random(k) and reformatting the vector, i.e., Reformat($\mathbf{t}$)) all together costs 4630 cycles. The main loop costs 711374 cycles. The outputting costs 236124 cycles. Note that these cycle counts are for 128-bit input and 6144-byte output.

We would like to emphasize that if we consider evaluating PRF with consecutive x in a counter mode, we do not need to compute the tree from its root to one of its leaves; we can reuse the computation from previous iterations. As a result, it takes only 242347 cycles for the main loop, and 236390 cycles for the outputting. Note that the cost of the main loop significantly decreases due to shorter paths to reach the leaves. However, the outputting costs stays the same because we always do one matrix-vector multiplication.

Table 3 below compares our timing results with SPRING [6] (in terms of numbers of cycles per output byte). Recall that SPRING has its security based

Table 3. Actual performance comparison of PRFs

Schemes	i7 Ivy Bridge	i5 Haswell	i7 Skylake
SPRING-BCH	46.0	19.5	–
SPRING-CRT	23.5	–	–
Ours, MLWR	–	–	39.4
Ours, LWR	–	–	64.2

Performance is measured in terms of the number of cycles per output byte. Cycle counts for our implementations are the total cost (include the pre-computation) on average to evaluate 100 inputs in a counter mode. Note that Haswell and Skylake have AVX2 instructions. Note also that the highest CPU frequency of Haswell is actually higher than that of Skylake. This suggests that if we were running on a machine with Haswell our implementations should not be slower than on a machine with Skylake.

on the rounded subset product hardness assumption while the security of our PRF relies on the more standard (module-)LWR hardness assumption.

A   LWR-based PRG

This Appendix explains our PRF construction based on the LWR hardness assumption. Note that, in general, this construction is very much similar to the one in the main article which is based on the module-LWR hardness assumption. In order not to repeat the same details, we only highlight the differences between the two constructions.

A.1   Construction

Construction 2 outlines our LWR-variant PRF. Recall that the PRF takes two inputs, namely, a key k and a string x of length ℓ, and outputs a pseudorandom string z. The matrix $\mathbf{A}$ is a public parameter. Similar to the module-LWR construction, the LWR construction is also divided into three parts: pre-computation, main loop, and outputting. Below, we emphasize the differences between the two constructions parts by parts.

Construction 2. PRF from LWR

Input: PRF's key $k = \{0,1\}^*$ and a bit string $x = \{0,1\}^\ell$
Output: Pseudorandom string $z = \{0,1\}^{\ell'}$

1: $\mathbf{t} = \mathsf{Random}(k)$ ⎫
2: $\mathbf{s} = \mathsf{Reformat}(\mathbf{t})$ ⎬ Pre-computation
3: **for** $i = 0$ **to** $\ell - 1$ **step by** $\tilde{\omega}$ **do**
4:     $c = x[\tilde{\omega}i]\ x[\tilde{\omega}i+1]\ \ldots\ x[\tilde{\omega}i+\tilde{\omega}-1]$ ▷ View $\tilde{\omega}$ bits as number in $[0, \omega-1]$
5:     **for** $j = c \cdot (m/\omega)$ **to** $(c+1) \cdot (m/\omega) - 1$ **do**
6:         $t_j = \mathbf{A}_{j} \cdot \mathbf{s}$ ▷ Multiply row j of $\mathbf{A}$ to $\mathbf{s}$
7:         $t_j = \lfloor t_j \rceil$
8:     **end for**
9:     $\mathbf{s} = \mathsf{Reformat}(\mathbf{t})$ ▷ Extract bits from $t_{c(m/\omega)}, t_{c(m/\omega)+1}, \ldots, t_{(c+1)(m/\omega)-1}$
10: **end for**
11: **for** $j = 0$ **to** $m - 1$ **do**
12:     $t_j = \mathbf{A}_j \cdot \mathbf{s}$
13:     $t_j = \lfloor t_j \rceil$
14:     $z = z || t_j$
15: **end for**
16: **return** z

Pre-computation. There is no differences in the way we generate randomness, i.e., $\mathsf{Random}(k)$, and reformat, i.e., $\mathsf{Reformat}(\mathbf{t})$. Note however that $\mathbf{s} \in \mathbb{Z}_{\log B}^n$ (instead of $\mathcal{R}_{\log B}^{n'}$).

The reasons for having Random(k) are also the same, namely, in case the input k is not random or does not have the preferred length. If this is not the case, then Random(k) can be skipped and directly proceed to Reformat($\mathbf{t}$).

Main Loop. Since the underlying PRG is now constructed from LWR, we need to change polynomial multiplications to integer multiplications. Nevertheless, a similar optimization for computing $\mathbf{As}$ is still applied, i.e., each iteration we compute vector-vector multiplications instead of a matrix-vector multiplication. For the LWR case, we need to multiply only m/ω rows of the matrix $\mathbf{A}$ to the vector $\mathbf{s}$. This time, m/ω is certainly more than one. We added an inner loop (line 5–8 in Construction 2) to iterate multiplying those rows. Once we multiply all those m/ω rows and before moving the next iteration of the outer loop, we call Reformat($\mathbf{t}$) to extract bits from $\mathbf{t}$ and assign to $\mathbf{s}$. Note that $\mathbf{t}$ contains m/ω elements.

Outputting. This part remains the same, namely, we perform the entire matrix-vector multiplication to increase the output length. Then we change the result into the desire format and output it.

A.2   Implementation

Two major differences between the module-LWR and the LWR implementations are multiplication algorithm and parameter set. In what follows, we explain how we handle multiplications when we cannot use fast polynomial multiplication algorithms, and then we state possible LWR parameter sets.

Multiplication. Since we use the plain LWR, i.e., having neither ring nor module additional structure, our multiplications are simply integer vector multiplications which can be implemented efficiently. Another advantage of using integers instead of polynomials is that we do not need to perform polynomial reductions.

Assume that we can perform w pairs of integer vector multiplications. To multiply row i of matrix $\mathbf{A}$ with vector $\mathbf{s}$, we load the first w elements of $\mathbf{A}_i$ and the first w elements of $\mathbf{s}$, then we perform integer vector-vector multiplication. After that, we load the next w element of $\mathbf{A}_i$ and the next w elements of $\mathbf{s}$, and again we perform another integer vector-vector multiplication. We repeat these steps until we multiply the entire row of $\mathbf{A}$ with $\mathbf{s}$. Since we always multiply $A_{i,j}$ with s_j, i.e, index j of $\mathbf{A}_i$ with index j of $\mathbf{s}$, this means that data are aligned in correct slots and no permutation needed. Therefore, this multiplication step works very well with vectorization.

Next step is to sum all the results of the integer vector-vector multiplications into a single integer. Unlike the multiplication step, this addition step requires permutations because we want to add data which contain in the same vector. To do so, we make use of the instruction `vphaddd` to perform horizontally additions and the instruction `vperm2i128` to perform permutations.

Parameters. We recall parameters in our construction. Let q be a modulus and p be a rounding parameter such that $q > p$ and $\log q = \log p + \log B$ where q, p, and B are power of two. Let $\mathbf{A} \in \mathbb{Z}_q^{m \times n}$ be a random public matrix.

Let $\mathbf{s} \in \mathbb{Z}_{\log B}^n$ be a small secret vector. Similar to the module-LWR variant, we want to set these parameters such that they satisfy the expansion-rate-ω output length requirement and achieve at least 128-bit security for the underlying LWR problem.

Recall the length condition. In our LWR-based PRG, the input is the vector $\mathbf{s}$ and the output is the rounded vector $\lfloor \mathbf{As} \rceil_p$. That is, we have the output size $m \cdot \log p$ and the input size $n \cdot (\log B)$. Therefore, the equation we consider is:

$$m \cdot \log p \geq \omega \cdot (n \cdot (\log B))$$
$$m \cdot (\log q - (\log B)) \geq \omega \cdot (n \cdot (\log B)).$$

Similar remarks of requiring $\omega \geq 2$ and larger the ω shallower the tree also apply to the LWR variant.

Now, we consider the security of the underlying LWR problem. We modified Kyber's script [11] to suit for our security estimation. Two main modifications are: (1) setting the ring dimension to 1 (because we use the plain LWR); and (2) using a uniform distribution instead of a binomial one. The conditions in which we search for good parameter sets are as follows:

- $q = 2^{16}$, fixed
- $\log B \in \{1, 2, 3, 4\}$
- n multiple of 32 in range $[640, 800]$
- m among 4, 8, 16 and 32 multiples of $\lceil n \cdot \log B / \log p \rceil$

Table 4 shows possible parameter sets for the LWR construction. To select which parameters to implement, we prioritize the runtime and choose the last row, namely, $m = 1840, n = 800, \log B = 2$ which gives $m/\omega = 115$, the tree's depth $= 32$, and the estimated security of 131.

Table 4. Good parameters achieving at least 128-bit LWR security and the expansion-rate-ω condition

m	n	$\log B$	security	ω	m/ω	mem	depth	mul
368	640	3	135	2	184	471040	128	15073280
384	672	3	143	2	192	516096	128	16515072
404	704	3	152	2	202	568832	128	18202624
424	736	2	131	4	106	624128	64	4993024
440	768	2	137	4	110	675840	64	5406720
460	800	1	129	8	115	736000	43	1995200
1840	800	2	131	16	115	2944000	32	2944000

We fix the modulus $q = 2^{16}$. Abbreviations 'mem' denotes size in bytes of matrix $\mathbf{A}$; 'depth' denotes tree's depth; and 'mul' $= m/\omega \times$ depth denotes the numbers of multiplications.

References

1. 25th Annual Symposium on Foundations of Computer Science, West Palm Beach, Florida, USA, 24–26 October 1984. IEEE Computer Society (1984)
2. 2018 IEEE European Symposium on Security and Privacy, EuroS&P 2018, London, United Kingdom, 24–26 April 2018. IEEE (2018)
3. Alkim, E., Ducas, L., Pöppelmann, T., Schwabe, P.: Post-quantum key exchange - a new hope. In: USENIX 2016 [24], pp. 327–343 (2016)
4. Alperin-Sheriff, J., Apon, D.: Dimension-preserving reductions from LWE to LWR. IACR Cryptology ePrint Archive 2016:589 (2016)
5. Alwen, J., Krenn, S., Pietrzak, K., Wichs, D.: Learning with rounding, revisited. In: CRYPTO 2013 [14], pp. 57–74 (2013)
6. Banerjee, A., Brenner, H., Leurent, G., Peikert, C., Rosen, A.: SPRING: fast pseudorandom functions from rounded ring products. In: FSE 2014 [17], pp. 38–57 (2014)
7. Banerjee, A., Peikert, C., Rosen, A.: Pseudorandom functions and lattices. In: EUROCRYPT 2012 [42], pp. 719–737 (2012)
8. Becker, A., Ducas, L., Gama, N., Laarhoven, T.: New directions in nearest neighbor searching with applications to lattice sieving. In: SODA 2016 [26], pp. 10–24 (2016)
9. Bernstein, D.J.: Batch binary edwards. In: CRYPTO [23], pp. 317–336 (2009)
10. Bogdanov, A., Guo, S., Masny, D., Richelson, S., Rosen, A.: On the hardness of learning with rounding over small modulus. In: TCC 2016 [27], pp. 209–224 (2016)
11. Bos, J.W.: CRYSTALS - Kyber: a CCA-secure module-lattice-based KEM. In: EuroS&P 2018 [2], pp. 353–367 (2018)
12. Bouillaguet, C., Delaplace, C., Fouque, P.-A., Kirchner, P.: Fast lattice-based encryption: stretching SPRING. In: PQCrypto 2017 [31], pp. 125–142 (2017)
13. Brakerski, Z., Gentry, C., Vaikuntanathan, V.: (Leveled)fully homomorphic encryption without bootstrapping. TOCT $6(3)$, 13:1–13:36 (2014)
14. Canetti, R., Garay, J.A. (eds.): CRYPTO 2013. LNCS, vol. 8042. Springer, Heidelberg (2013). https://doi.org/10.1007/978-3-642-40041-4
15. Charikar, M. (ed.): Proceedings of the Twenty-First Annual ACM-SIAM Symposium on Discrete Algorithms, SODA 2010, Austin, Texas, USA, 17–19 January 2010. SIAM (2010)
16. Chen, Y., Nguyen, P.Q.: BKZ 2.0: better lattice security estimates. In: ASIACRYPT 2011 [33], pp. 1–20 (2011)
17. Cid, C., Rechberger, C. (eds.): FSE 2014. LNCS, vol. 8540. Springer, Heidelberg (2015). https://doi.org/10.1007/978-3-662-46706-0
18. Ducas, L., Lepoint, T., Lyubashevsky, V., Schwabe, P., Seiler, G., Stehlé, D.: CRYSTALS - dilithium: digital signatures from module lattices. IACR Cryptology ePrint Archive 2017:633 (2017)
19. Gabow, H.N., Fagin, R. (eds.): Proceedings of the 37th Annual ACM Symposium on Theory of Computing, Baltimore, MD, USA, 22–24 May 2005. ACM (2005)
20. Gennaro, R., Robshaw, M. (eds.): CRYPTO 2015. LNCS, vol. 9215. Springer, Heidelberg (2015). https://doi.org/10.1007/978-3-662-47989-6
21. Gilbert, H. (ed.): EUROCRYPT 2010. LNCS, vol. 6110. Springer, Heidelberg (2010). https://doi.org/10.1007/978-3-642-13190-5
22. Goldreich, O., Goldwasser, S., Micali, S.: How to construct random functions (extended abstract). In: FOCS 1984 [1], pp. 464–479 (1984)
23. Halevi, S. (ed.): CRYPTO 2009. LNCS, vol. 5677. Springer, Heidelberg (2009). https://doi.org/10.1007/978-3-642-03356-8

24. Holz, T., Savage, S. (eds.): 25th USENIX Security Symposium, USENIX Security 2016, Austin, TX, USA, 10–12 August 2016. USENIX Association (2016)
25. Katz, J., Lindell, Y.: Introduction to Modern Cryptography. Chapman & Hall/CRC, Boca Raton (2007)
26. Krauthgamer, R. (ed.): Proceedings of the Twenty-Seventh Annual ACM-SIAM Symposium on Discrete Algorithms, SODA 2016, Arlington, VA, USA, 10–12 January 2016. SIAM (2016)
27. Kushilevitz, E., Malkin, T. (eds.): TCC 2016. LNCS, vol. 9563. Springer, Heidelberg (2016). https://doi.org/10.1007/978-3-662-49099-0
28. Laarhoven, T.: Search problems in cryptography. Ph.D. thesis, Eindhoven University of Technology, The Netherlands (2015)
29. Laarhoven, T.: Sieving for shortest vectors in lattices using angular locality-sensitive hashing. In: CRYPTO 2015 [20], pp. 3–22 (2015)
30. Laarhoven, T., Mosca, M., van de Pol, J.: Finding shortest lattice vectors faster using quantum search. Des. Codes Cryptogr. 77(2–3), 375–400 (2015)
31. Lange, T., Takagi, T. (eds.): PQCrypto 2017. LNCS, vol. 10346. Springer, Cham (2017). https://doi.org/10.1007/978-3-319-59879-6
32. Langlois, A., Stehlé, D.: Worst-case to average-case reductions for module lattices. Des. Codes Cryptogr. 75(3), 565–599 (2015)
33. Lee, D.H., Wang, X. (eds.): ASIACRYPT 2011. LNCS, vol. 7073. Springer, Heidelberg (2011). https://doi.org/10.1007/978-3-642-25385-0
34. Lyubashevsky, V., Peikert, C., Regev, O.: On ideal lattices and learning with errors over rings. In: EUROCRYPT 2010 [21], pp. 1–23 (2010)
35. Lyubashevsky, V., Peikert, C., Regev, O.: On ideal lattices and learning with errors over rings. J. ACM 60(6), 43:1–43:35 (2013). Preliminary version in Eurocrypt 2010 [21]
36. Micciancio, D., Voulgaris, P.: Faster exponential time algorithms for the shortest vector problem. In: SODA 2010 [15], pp. 1468–1480 (2010)
37. Naor, M., Reingold, O.: Synthesizers and their application to the parallel construction of pseudo-random functions. J. Comput. Syst. Sci. 58(2), 336–375 (1999). Preliminary version in FOCS 1995
38. Naor, M., Reingold, O.: Number-theoretic constructions of efficient pseudo-random functions. J. ACM 51(2), 231–262 (2004). Preliminary version in FOCS 1997
39. Naor, M., Reingold, O., Rosen, A.: Pseudorandom functions and factoring. SIAM J. Comput. 31(5), 1383–1404 (2002). Preliminary version in STOC 2000
40. Nguyen, P.Q., Vidick, T.: Sieve algorithms for the shortest vector problem are practical. J. Math. Cryptol. 2(2), 181–207 (2008)
41. National Institute of Standards and Technology. SHA-3 standard: Permutation-based hash and extendable-output functions. FIPS PUB 202 (2015). http://nvlpubs.nist.gov/nistpubs/FIPS/NIST.FIPS.202.pdf
42. Pointcheval, D., Johansson, T. (eds.): EUROCRYPT 2012. LNCS, vol. 7237. Springer, Heidelberg (2012). https://doi.org/10.1007/978-3-642-29011-4
43. Regev, O.: On lattices, learning with errors, random linear codes, and cryptography. In: STOC 2005 [19], pp. 84–93 (2005)
44. Schnorr, C.-P., Euchner, M.: Lattice basis reduction: improved practical algorithms and solving subset sum problems. Math. Program. 66(2), 181–199 (1994)

Author Index

Printed in the United States
By Bookmasters